THE
AMERICAN
BOOK
OF CHARTS

THE
AMERICAN
BOOK
OF CHARTS

By Lois M. Rodden

Published by
Astro Computing Services
P.O. Box 16430
San Diego, California 92116

Distributed by
Para Research
Rockport, Massachusetts 01966

Books by Lois M. Rodden
Mercury Method of Chart Comparison
Modern Transits
Profiles of Women
The American Book of Charts

International Standard Book Number 0-917086-23-6

Published by Astro Computing Services
P.O. Box 16430
San Diego, California 92116

Distributed by Para Research, Inc.
Whistlestop Mall
Rockport, Massachusetts 01966

Manufactured in the United States of America

First printing, July 1980

ACKNOWLEDGEMENTS

I am deeply indebted to my friends and colleagues in the astrological community who have generously contributed their recources of data, books, and magazines or their general assistance. This collection is respectfully dedicated to the following people:

Richard Adler
Terrell Adsit
Laurie Brady
Diane Clark
John Daniel
T. Patrick Davis
Cindy DeLee
Doris Chase Doane
Dr. Zipporah Dobyns
Ruth Elliot
Lynne Erricksson
Angela Gallo
Kim Griggs
Jim Haynes
Edward Helin
Richard Ideman
Robert Jansky

Judy Johns
Mark Johnson
Tony Joseph
Anna-Kria King
Terry Krall
Mary Lee Lewis
Gene Lockhart
Meil Marbell
Constance Mayer
Carole McDonald
Evelyn Michaels
Jan Moore
Paul Morgan
Ruth Hale Oliver
Marc Penfield
Marc Pottenger
Kelly Quinn

Jane Reynolds
Arlene Robertson
Amy Rodden
Lynn Rodden
Paul Rosner
Carl Scarsella, who quotes
the estate file of Frank
Hammer Baird
Philip Sedgwich
Victoria Shaw
Robert Skeetz
Karen Spahn
Phyllis Stanich
Gene Steele
Carol Tebbs
Barbara Watters
Christine Whittier

And to my international colleagues: Chryss Craswell and Daphne Jones of the Astrological Association of London, R.C. Davison of England, Bruno Huber of Switzerland, Jacqueline Fagan of New Zealand, Luc de Marre of Belgium, Gwen Stoney of Australia, and Ciro Discepolo of Italy.

For endless phone calls, letters, and hours spent in double-checking sources, my special thanks to Ruth Dewey of Denver, Jim Eshelman and Dana Holliday of Los Angeles, Marion March of Van Nuys, Joan McEvers of Idaho, and the staff of the Church of Light in Los Angeles.

January 22, 1980

TABLE OF CONTENTS

INTRODUCTION

In the past, astrological data has been presented for the most part without any designation of source. Recorded birth times, hearsay evidence, speculative or rectified birth times, and casual guesswork are all mixed together in a standard presentation. As a result, we have a morass of astrological literature one must wade through with discrimination, if not suspicion. As publications multiply in which we share our data, the basis of our studies, contradictions multiply and skepticism increases. Thus we find a pressing need to classify the accuracy of our data.

The American Book of Charts is a result of four years of concentrated focus on data research, of hours and months searching biographies and magazines, of "data-swaps" with many astrologers, of numerous mailings to public figures, and of correspondence with colleagues in America and Europe. The result is AN ASTROLOGICAL DATA REFERENCE COLLECTION that records in classification the information that we have from our combined sources.

That classification is simple.

A = ACCURATE DATA. Birth certificate; recorded birth times; data from the person himself or herself, or from a family member or personal friend. "A" includes royalty (unless contradicted), since royal births are recorded by the state or historians.

B = BIOGRAPHIES and AUTOBIOGRAPHIES, (unless contradicted).

C = CAUTION: NO SOURCE OF ORIGIN. Any time of birth that is not documented is open to question. "C" data includes birth times quoted from astrological magazines and books that don't supply the source of origin; data presented ambiguously as from a "personal source," without stating the source of origin; unnamed biographies that cannot be checked; and approximate times from biographies.

Stated speculative or rectified times are included (unless contradicted), since these are valid presentations for reference considerations. Occasionally an astrologer quotes a colleague with "B.C." or "from the person." If the data cannot be validated by correspondence about whether this is original information or hearsay evidence, it falls into the "C" category. The statement, "This is right", does not qualify as a source, but as an opinion.

All "C" data is unvalidated, so be careful.

DD = DIRTY DATA. *All* data with two or more conflicting statements of date, time, or place indicate that at least one (possibly all) have been rectified or speculated without designation. Perhaps one is accurate; perhaps all are wrong: discrimination and personal judgement are advised. When a quoted biography does not substantiate the data given but has been speculated or rectified without designation, this is DIRTY DATA.

1

The American Book of Charts presents five hundred "A" and "B" data in horoscope form, in placidian-tropical charts computed by the Astro Computing Service, P.O. Box 16297, San Diego, CA 92116. In addition, seven hundred "C" and "DD" supplementary data are given as a reference source.

The five hundred data presented in *Profiles Of Women*, published by The American Federation of Astrologers, 1979, are not included.

Data is volatile. None of us is exempt from the possibility of human error. There are cases when PM and AM are interchanged on birth records or in the transfer of information, and the most careful editing is required whenever numbers are copied. Handwritten records may be difficult to read or become obscured with age.

A certain amount of the data we share comes from the person directly. When that person is a client, the chances are much better that the data is accurate; a social exchange is more apt to be casual or suspect. The one who relates his or her birth time speaks from family history, and we often hear such statements as, "Mother thinks it was about 8:00 AM."

However, our "A" and "B" data give the best possibility of accuracy that we have available. Birth times recorded on-the-hour may require some examination for precision of minutes. The "A" and "B" data presented in the Reference Collection are as recorded, except that all Old Style dates of the Julian calendar have been recalculated to the New Style Gregorian calendar. Explanations and alternate quotes are given in the footnotes.

A great deal of the "C" data appears valid. When possible, I've written to the astrologer or author who quoted the data and have been heartened by the number of quotes that have been validated and thus moved into the "A" category. But in some cases, the original source remains elusive or cannot be traced. Other quotes of the "C" data are frankly suspect. Rather than give you my own opinion, I leave you to form your own, considering the credibility of the source.

My research included a scan of more than a thousand American publications dating from the 30s, loaned by the courtesy of Robert Skeetz and Jim Eshelman, with a minor amount of data from Carole McDonald's outstanding international library that dates from 1890. Before the 60s, so little data was available about public figures that collection was indiscriminate. Although the fine work of Cyril Fagan, Edward Lyndoe, Ralph Kraum, and Garth Allen, all of whom were regular contributors to the astrology of the 30s to 60s, often stood out as brilliant examples of research, many of their charts, and those of other contributors, were solar or speculative charts. In later issues, that stated speculation was repeated as a matter of fact, perpetuating opinion rather than record.

Other writers of the early twentieth century, as well as today, rapidly gained a credibility gap. Blanca Holmes stated that she rectified the given birth time if she thought the hour unsuitable. Evangeline Adams, though a charismatic figure, was not a mathematician, and her *One Hundred Horoscopes* contains many disproven nativities, as well as a large number of "6:00 AM, 12:00 Noon, 6:00 PM, etc." charts that appear to be casual speculations. Although Marion Meyer Drew writes that her *Headline Horoscopes* (pictured horoscopes, very few with data) "include no 'estimate' or 'calculated' data", a good percentage of her data have been invalidated by contradictory reports. In the *Sabian Symbols* one-thousand collection, the data that give no birth time are particularly suspect, and the mathematics of the planetary positions is laced with computation error. Maurice Wemyss is highly reputable, and Alan Leo's *Notable Nativities* is a conscientious work, but, again, they mainly repeat what information was available in that period.

Of our current studies, the Gauquelin Collection is an outstanding contribution. The birth times are recorded on the quarter hour, so may require tightening by rectification; but they are recorded — a vital point. In America, *Contemporary Sidereal Horoscopes* is a model of excellence, with all data from birth records.

Other collections contain a staggering number of quotes from non-existent sources and questionable data.

The DIRTY DATA category is an accumulation of inaccuracies, contradictions, and misquotes that represents carelessness, presumption, or superficiality. Obviously much of the DIRTY DATA is of undesignated speculative or rectified charts. A speculative chart is one in which no birth time is known, and the hour is calculated by the astrologer from an examination of character and events. A rectified chart is one in which an approximate time of birth is known, and the time is calculated to the minute by the astrologer from an examination of character and events, plus precision calculations of progressed planets and transit motion of planets.

Most of the cases in DIRTY DATA are quoted by ethical astrologers. We have all collected data without a qualified source. In our intellectual hunger, we have collected whatever was available. The birth alone holds a certain amount of information for our studies, and an approximate chart can give us the picture of planetary patterns, aspect configurations, and sign placements that adds to our expertise. Therefore, the charts in the "C" and "DD" categories can yield knowledge to those who are interested in a specific case and can be stimulating to those researchers who use the information as a base from which to search for greater accuracy.

However we must be aware of the quality of our data. Data without a specific, accurate time cannot be studied for the Midheaven, Ascendant, Moon degree, or house interpretation and *cannot be used for statistical research* that would involve any of these points.

We all begin in naivete, but with experience and sophistication that gullible attitude is replaced by discrimination — at least in the intelligent and ethical professional counselor or researcher who relies on accurate data. The purpose of including DIRTY DATA in this collection is both to give a reference catalogue and to emphasize our need in the astrological community to document the validity of all our data. *Without a designation of source, any data is unvalidated and requires further research.*

BIBLIOGRAPHY OF SOURCES FOR BIOGRAPHICAL INFORMATION AND BIRTH DATE VALIDATIONS.

Astrological Index To The World's Famous People by M. Cooper and A. Weaver (1975).

A Biographical Dictionary Of Film by David Thomson (New York: William Morrow and Company, Inc, 1976)

Collier's Encyclopedia (London and New York: MacMillan Educational Corp. and P.F. Collier Inc, 1979)

The Catholic Encyclopedia (New York: Encyclopedia Press Inc, 1913.)

Contemporary Authors, ed. Christine Nasso (Detroit: Gale Research Co, Book Tower, 1977).

Dictionary Of American Biography (New York: Charles Scribner's Sons, 1937).

Current Biography, ed. Charles Moritz (New York: The W.H. Wilson Co, 1940-1979).

Celebrity Register (New York: Simon and Schuster, 1973).

Encyclopaedia Britannica (William Benton publisher, 1943-1973; Helen Hemingway Benton publisher, 1973-74).

Encyclopedia Americana, International Edition (Danbury, Conn.: Americana Corp, 1978).

Famous People, compiled and published by Louis F. Mlecka (Brooksville, Fla., 1973).

The Filmgoer's Companion by Leslie Halliwell (New York: Hill and Wong, 1977).

Illustrated Encyclopedia Of Rock (New York: Harmony Books, 1977).

Information Please Almanac (New York: Information Please Publications Inc).

The Lincoln Library Of Sports Champions, 14 vols. (Columbus, Ohio: Sports Resources Co, 1974).

Lives Of Saints (New York: John J. Crawley and Co, 1954).

Notable American Women 1607-1950, A Biographical Dictionary (Cambridge, Mass: Belknap Press of Harvard University Press, 1971).

Notables In The American Theater (Clifton, N.J.: James T. White and Co, 1976).

New Encyclopedia Of Sports by Ralph Hickok (McGraw-Hill Book Co. 1977).

SCAN, Southern California Answering Network, a research service of the Los Angeles Public Library.

Twentieth Century Writing, ed. Kenneth Richardson: assoc. ed R. Clive Willis (New York: Transatlantic Arts Inc, 1969).

Whatever Become Of . . .? by Richard Lamparski, 5 vols. (New York: Crown Publishers Inc.)

Who's Who In Holywood 1900-1976 by David Ragan (New York: Arlington House).

Who's Who In America (Chicago: Marquis Who's Who Inc.)

Who Was Who In America, with World Notables (Chicago: Marquis Who's Who Inc).

The World Book Encyclopedia (Chicago: Field Enterprises Educational Corp).

50,000 Birthdays by Paul Field (1964).

Biographies as noted, magazines, journals, periodicals, and newspaper clippings.

ABBREVIATIONS

The following abbreviations are given for the most frequently used astrological data sources:

AA *American Astrology* magazine, Paul G. Clancy, founder and editor, 1933-1956; Joane Clancy editor from 1956.

AFA *American Federation of Astrologers Bulletin,* published from 1942.

AJA *American Journal of Astrology,* edited by Paul Clancy, 1936-37.

AQ *Astrological Quarterly,* published by the Astrological Lodge of London, 1926-1973, edited successively by C.E.O. Carter and R.C. Davison.

AQR *Astrological Quarterly Review,* published in London, 1973, R.M. Harmer editor.

BJA *British Journal of Astrology,* published in England 1914-1940, E.H. Bailey editor.

Circle *Circle Book of Charts,* compiled by Stephen Erlewine, American publication, 1972.

CSH *Contemporary Sidereal Horoscopes,* Sidereal Research Publications 1976, compiled by Katherine Clark, Allen Gilchrist, Janice Mackey, and Charles Dorminy.

CL Church of Light Research and Data department, P.O. Box 16832, Stanford Sta., Los Angeles, Ca 90076.

Dell *Horoscope* magazine, Dell publications from 1940, edited successively by Edward and Julia Wagner.

Drew *101 Headline Horoscopes* by Marion Meyer Drew, 1941, followed by a second volume, *101 Hard to Find Horoscopes,* 1962.

F/N *Famous Nativities* by Maurice Wemyss, published in London, 1938.

F/M *Astrology and the Feminist Movement* by Robert Jansky, 1977.

Gauquelin A series of six volumes of birth and planetary data, gathered by Michel and Francoise Gauquelin from 1949, published from 1970.

H/N *Horoscopes — Here and Now* by Robert Jansky, 1975.

M.A. *Modern Astrology,* published in London, Alan Leo editor and publisher, 1895-1917; Bessie Leo with Vivian Robson, 1917-1928.

M.H. *Mercury Hour,* American publications from 1974, Edith Custer editor and publisher.

NAJ *National Astrological Journal,* published in Hollywood, Edward A. Wagner editor, copyright 1933.

NN *1001 Notable Nativities* by Alan Leo, 1917.

Old-File A collection of 720 data, contributed by two astrologers who prefer to remain anonymous, as the data was gathered indiscriminately from whatever source was available, but without record of source.

Old Moore *Old Moore's Monthly Messenger,* published in London 1907-1914, Sepharial editor.

P.A. *Practical Astrology,* American publication, 1929.

PC *2001: The Penfield Collection* by Marc penfield, 1979.

SS *Sabian Symbols in Astrology* by Marc Edmund Jones, 1953.

Other magazines, periodicals and books as noted, with the author's apology for not always noting the full name of the contributor.

TIME ZONE DESIGNATIONS

Zero degrees E/W = GMT Greenwich Mean Time
or WET Western European Time
or U.T. Universal Time

West of Greenwich:
  60°W. = AST Atlantic Standard Time
  75°W. = EST Eastern Standard Time
  90°W. = CST Central Standard Time
105°W. = MST Mountain Standard Time
120°W. = PST Pacific Standard Time
135°W. = YST Yukon Standard Time
150°W. = CAT Central Alaska Standard Time
165°W. = NT Nome Standard Time

East of Greenwich:
  15°E. = MET Middle European Time/ or CET Central European Time
  30°E. = EET Eastern European Time

There is one time zone meridian for each fifteen degrees; however, many Eastern countries do not use the standard meridian as their time zone. Russia, for example, uses eleven time zones beginning with Standard Meridian 30 E00, India uses Zone 5.5 and Zone 6.5, etc.

It is strongly recommended that *Time Changes in the World* and *Time Changes in Canada-Mexico* by Doris Chase Doane be used to double-check data that may have been given as LMT. *The American Atlas,* published by *Astro Computing Service* (1978), is the finest reference work available on American longitudes and latitudes, and time changes.

For data given as Paris time, Amsterdam time, Dunsink time, etc, the chart must be erected on that time zone as used, since, these are not standard meridian zones. For LMT, no meridian correction is made.

War time or Daylight Savings time is designated by W (War) or D (Daylight) in place of the S (Standard). For these data, one hour is subtracted from the given time to find Standard time. Daylight time in Great Britain is designated by BST (British Summer Time); Daylight time in other GMT areas is designated GDT (Greenwich Daylight time). D-BST is Double British Summer time, a difference of two hours.

The Time Change books are a necessary requisite in the computation of accurate charts.

TIME CONVERSION TABLE
FROM OLD STYLE (JULIAN) TO NEW STYLE (GREGORIAN)

Note: On the Gregorian proleptic calendar, the year 0 is counted as one. For example, Augustus Caesar, at September 23, 63 B.C. OS converts to September 21, 62 B.C. NS.

March 5, 500 BC, to March 3, 300 BC ....minus 5 days
March 4, 300 BC, to March 2, 200 BC ....minus 4 days
March 3, 200 BC, to March 1, 100 BC ....minus 3 days
March 2, 100 BC, to February 29, 100 AD ....minus 2 days
March 1, 100 AD, to February 29, 200 AD ....minus 1 day
March 1, 200 AD, to February 29, 300 AD ....-0 + 0
March 1, 300, to February 29, 500 ....plus 1 day
March 1, 500, to February 29, 600 ....plus 2 days
March 1, 600, to February 29, 700 ....plus 3 days
March 1, 700, to February 29, 900 ....plus 4 days
March 1, 900, to February 29, 1000 ....plus 5 days
March 1, 1000, to February 29, 1100 ....plus 6 days
March 1, 1100, to February 29, 1300 ....plus 7 days
March 1, 1300, to February 29, 1400 ....plus 8 days
March 1, 1400, to February 29, 1500 ....plus 9 days
March 1, 1500, to February 29, 1700 ....plus 10 days
March 1, 1700, to February 29, 1800 ....plus 11 days
March 1, 1800, to February 29, 1900 ....plus 12 days
March 1, 1900, to February 29, 2100 ....plus 13 days
Taken from *The Explanatory Supplement to the Astronomical Ephemeris*, (London, 1961)

'A' and 'B' DATA CHARTS

ADENAUER, KONRAD
Chancellor

January 5, 1876
10:30 AM LMT
Cologne, Germany
6 E 53 50 N 59

Mayor of Cologne, 1917-1933. Imprisoned by the Nazis during World War II. Chancellor of the West German Republic after its formation in 1949 to 1963, leading his country through reconstruction to prosperity. (1876-1967)

A: Gauquelin #1846 Vol 5.[1]

SVP=✶ 6°59'28"
JULIAN DAY=2406258.91838

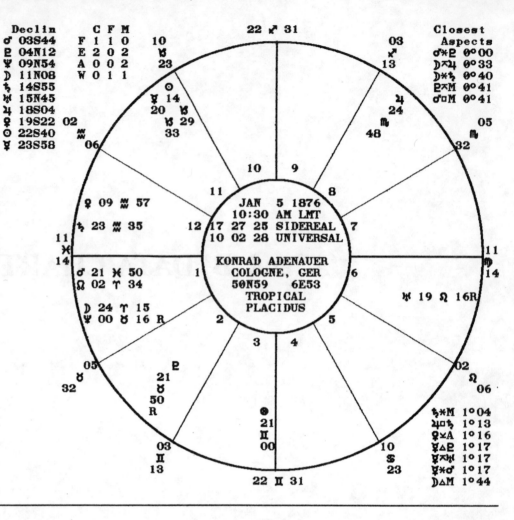

AGNEW, SPIRO
Politician

November 9, 1918
9:00 AM EST
Forest Hill, Md
76 W 23 39 N.35

Lawyer; governor of Maryland, 1967-1969; thirty-ninth vice-president, under Richard Nixon in 1969. Forced to resign in October 1973 for income tax evasion and allegedly accepting bribes. Controversial figure because of changes in mid-stream.

A: Barbara Watters in AFA, May 1972, from B.C.

SVP=✶ 6°23'19"
JULIAN DAY=2421907.08333

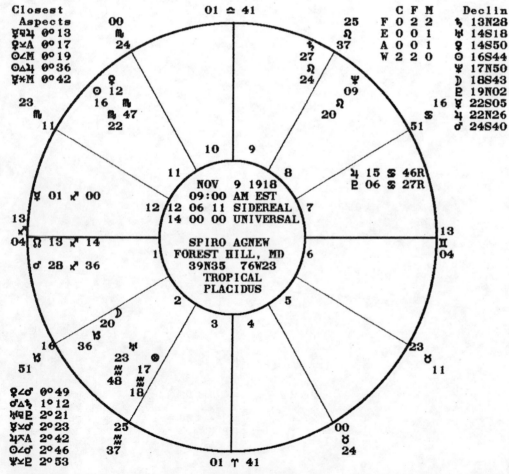

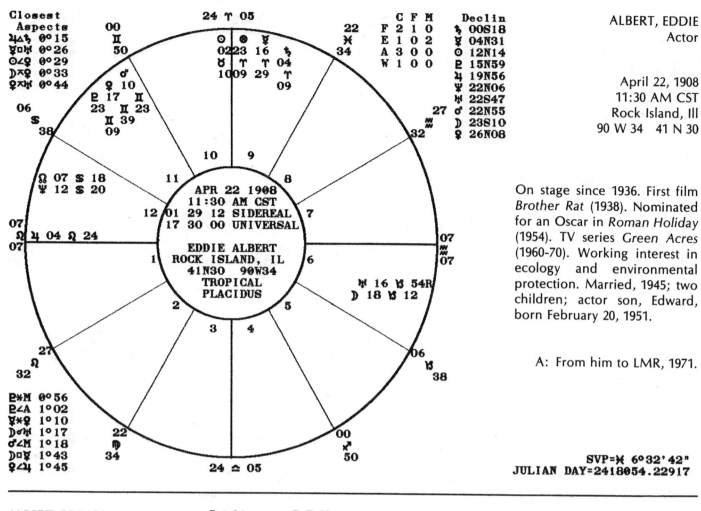

ALBERT, EDDIE
Actor

April 22, 1908
11:30 AM CST
Rock Island, Ill
90 W 34   41 N 30

On stage since 1936. First film *Brother Rat* (1938). Nominated for an Oscar in *Roman Holiday* (1954). TV series *Green Acres* (1960-70). Working interest in ecology and environmental protection. Married, 1945; two children; actor son, Edward, born February 20, 1951.

A: From him to LMR, 1971.

Center:
APR 22 1908
11:30 AM CST
01 29 12 SIDEREAL
17 30 00 UNIVERSAL

EDDIE ALBERT
ROCK ISLAND, IL
41N30   90W34
TROPICAL
PLACIDUS

SVP=✠ 6°32'42"
JULIAN DAY=2418054.22917

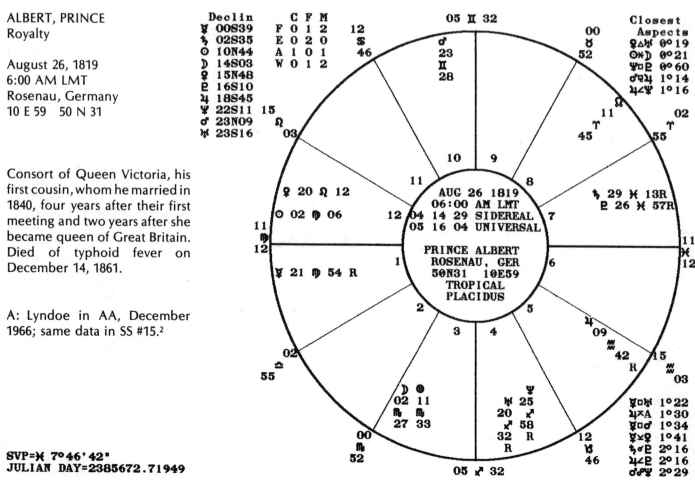

ALBERT, PRINCE
Royalty

August 26, 1819
6:00 AM LMT
Rosenau, Germany
10 E 59   50 N 31

Consort of Queen Victoria, his first cousin, whom he married in 1840, four years after their first meeting and two years after she became queen of Great Britain. Died of typhoid fever on December 14, 1861.

A: Lyndoe in AA, December 1966; same data in SS #15.²

SVP=✠ 7°46'42"
JULIAN DAY=2385672.71949

Center:
AUG 26 1819
06:00 AM LMT
04 14 29 SIDEREAL
05 16 04 UNIVERSAL

PRINCE ALBERT
ROSENAU, GER
50N31   10E59
TROPICAL
PLACIDUS

ALBERT VICTOR, PRINCE
Duke of Clarence

January 8, 1864
8:50 PM LMT
Windsor, England
0 W 37   51 N 29

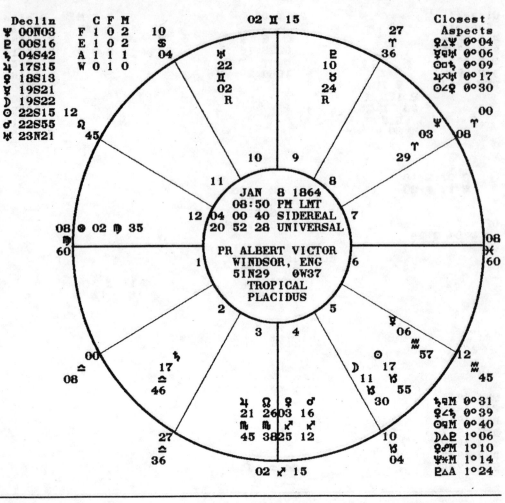

Declin		C F M	
♆ 00N03		F 1 0 2	10
♇ 00S16		E 1 0 2	♋
♄ 04S42		A 1 1 1	
♃ 17S15		W 0 1 0	
♀ 18S13			
☿ 19S21			
☽ 19S22			
☉ 22S15	12		
♂ 22S55			
⛢ 23N21			

Closest Aspects
♀△♆	0°04
☿⚹⛢	0°06
☉□♄	0°09
♃⚹⛢	0°17
♂∠♀	0°30
♄□M	0°31
♀∠♄	0°39
☉□M	0°40
☽△♇	1°06
♀⚹M	1°10
♆⚹M	1°14
♇△A	1°24

Apparently feeble-minded, dissipated, and unstable. Made a World Tour at 16 during which he contracted syphilis. Rumored to be Jack the Ripper, who murdered and mutilated five London trollops in 1888. Died in January 1892, reportedly of pneumonia.

A: Garth Allen in AA, July 1971, "according to royal records."[3]

SVP=♓ 7° 9' 15"
JULIAN DAY=2401879.36977

Closest Aspects
♃⚹A	0°04
☽⚺♂	0°08
☉⚹A	0°11
☉⚺♃	0°15
☿△M	0°31
☿△♄	0°59
♀□⛢	1°26
♄♂M	1°30
♄∠⛢	1°44
♂△A	1°49
♃∠♀	1°54
☽⚺♄	1°57

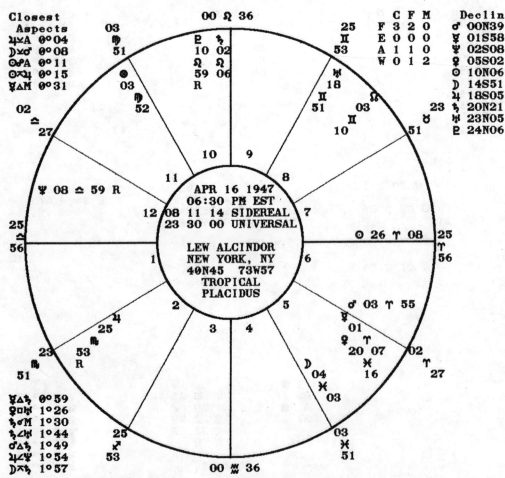

	C F M	Declin	
	F 3 2 0	♂ 00N39	
	E 0 0 0	☿ 01S58	
	A 1 1 0	♆ 02S08	
	W 0 1 2	♀ 05S02	
		☉ 10N06	
		☽ 14S51	
		♃ 18S05	
		♄ 20N21	
		⛢ 23N05	
		♇ 24N06	

ALCINDOR, LEW
KAREEM ABDUL-JABBAR
Basketball star

April 16, 1947
6:30 PM EST
New York, N.Y.
73 W 57   40 N 45

UCLA collegiate champion, history major. Professional start with the Milwaukee Braves in 1969. Voted most outstanding player of the 1970-71 season. Likes jazz; values his privacy. Stands at 7'2", the son of parents both over 6' tall.

A: Holliday quotes Helen Allen in Dell, July 1968, "data from him."

SVP=♓ 6° 0' 1"
JULIAN DAY=2432292.47917

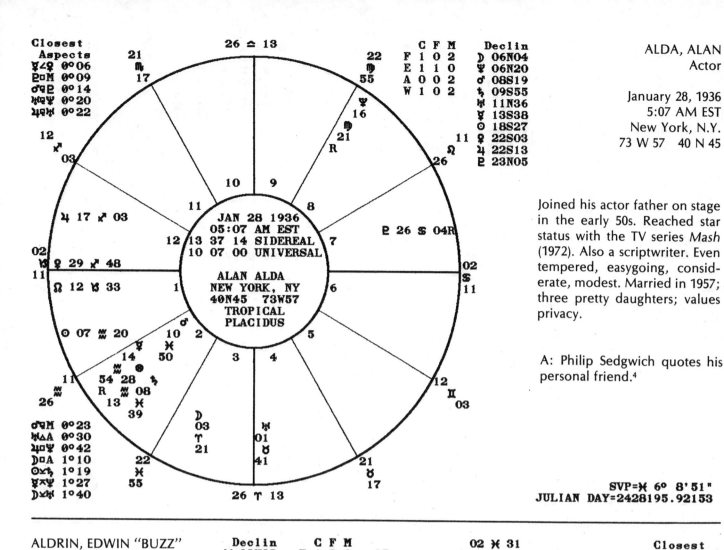

ALDA, ALAN
Actor

January 28, 1936
5:07 AM EST
New York, N.Y.
73 W 57   40 N 45

Joined his actor father on stage in the early 50s. Reached star status with the TV series *Mash* (1972). Also a scriptwriter. Even tempered, easygoing, considerate, modest. Married in 1957; three pretty daughters; values privacy.

A: Philip Sedgwich quotes his personal friend.[4]

SVP=⌖ 6° 8'51"
JULIAN DAY=2428195.92153

ALDRIN, EDWIN "BUZZ"
Astronaut

January 20, 1930
2:17 PM EST
Glen Ridge, N.J.
74 W 12   40 N 48

Selected as an astronaut in 1963. On July 20, 1969, with Armstrong, landed the lunar module Eagle on the moon while Collins remained in orbit in the spacecraft Columbia: an historic first. Author of an autobiography, *Return to Earth*.

A: CSH.

SVP=⌖ 6°14'21"
JULIAN DAY=2425997.30347

ALEXIS, CZAREVITCH
Prince

August 12, 1904 NS
1:15 PM LMT
St. Petersburg, Russia
30 E.15   59 N 55

Son of Nicholas and Alexandra; heir to the Russian monarchy. A hemopheliac whose condition was alleviated by the monk Rasputin. Shot to death with his parents and four sisters by a Bolshevik execution on July 16, 1918.

A: Kraum in M.A., September 1936 states, "according to his father's diary."[5]

SVP=✶ 6°35'32"
JULIAN DAY=2416704.96806

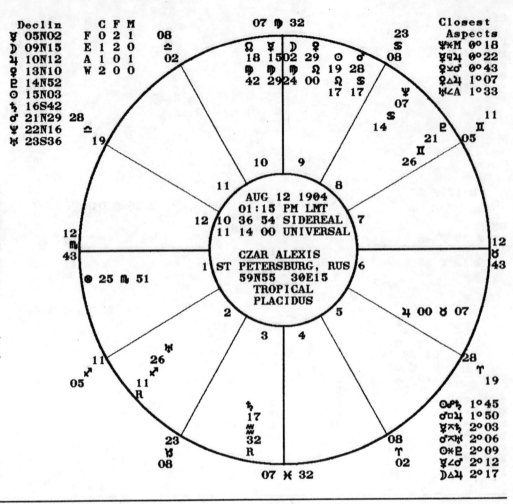

	Declin		C	F	M		
☿	05N02	F	0	2	1		
☽	09N15	E	1	2	0		
♃	10N12	A	1	0	1		
♀	13N10	W	2	0	0		
♇	14N52						
☉	15N03						
♄	16S42						
♂	21N29						
♆	22N16						
♅	23S36						

Closest Aspects
♆✶M	0°18
☿□♃	0°22
♀✶♂	0°43
♀△A	1°07
♃∠A	1°33

☉□♄	1°45
♂□♃	1°50
☿⊼♄	2°03
♂⊼♃	2°06
☉✶♇	2°09
☿∠♂	2°12
☽△♃	2°17

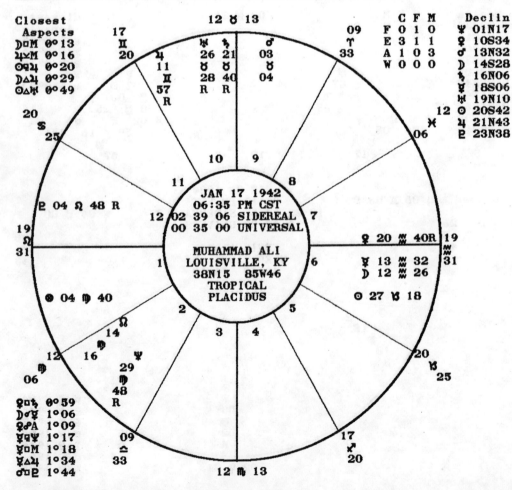

Closest Aspects
☽□M	0°13
♃✶M	0°16
☉♃⊼	0°20
☽△♃	0°29
☉△♅	0°49

♀□♄	0°59
☽♂☿	1°06
♀⊗A	1°09
☿⊼♆	1°17
☿□M	1°18
♅△♃	1°34
♂□♇	1°44

				Declin	
C	F	M		♆	01N17
F	0	1	0	♀	10S34
E	3	1	1	♂	13N32
A	1	0	3	☽	14S28
W	0	0	0	♄	16N06
				☿	18S06
				♅	19N10
				♀	20S42
				♃	21N43
				♇	23N38

ALI, MUHAMMAD
Boxing champion

January 17, 1942
6:35 PM CST
Louisville, Ky
85 W 46   38 N.15

World heavyweight boxing champion in 1964 by knocking out Sonny Listen. In 1967 his title declared vacant after he refused the military obligation. Later changed his name (from Cassius Clay) and reentered boxing in 1970. Biography *Sting Like a Bee* by Jose Torres.

A: Edwin Steinbrecker states B.C. in M.H., July 1979.

SVP=✶ 6° 4'11"
JULIAN DAY=2430377.52431

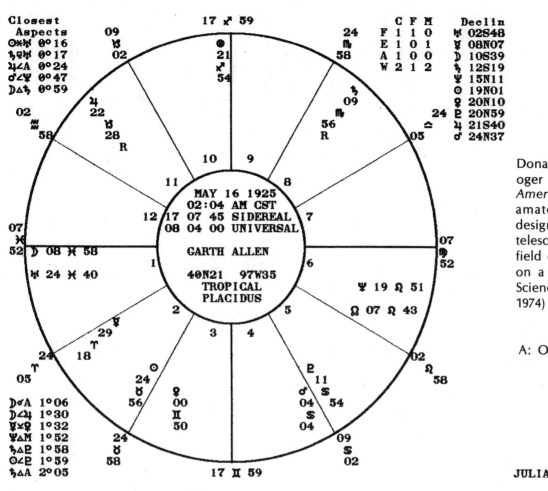

ALLEN, GARTH — Astrologer

May 16, 1925
2:04 AM CST
97 W 35   40 N 21

Closest Aspects

☉✶♅	0°16
♄⚹♅	0°17
♃∠♄	0°24
♂∠♆	0°47
☽△♄	0°59

	C	F	M	Declin
F	1	1	0	♅ 02S48
E	1	0	1	☿ 08N07
A	1	0	0	☽ 10S39
W	2	1	2	♄ 12S19
				♆ 15N11
				☉ 19N01
				♀ 20N10
				♇ 20N59
				♃ 21S40
				♂ 24N37

MAY 16 1925
02:04 AM CST
17 07 45 SIDEREAL
08 04 00 UNIVERSAL

GARTH ALLEN

40N21   97W35
TROPICAL
PLACIDUS

Donald Bradley, sidereal astrologer and senior editor of *American Astrology*. Lifelong amateur astronomer, who designed more than a dozen telescopes. Researcher in the field of meteorology at N.Y.U. on a grant from the National Science Foundation. (1925-1974)

A: Obituary in AA, August 1974.

☽♂A	1°06
☽∠♃	1°30
☿⚹♀	1°32
♆△M	1°52
♄△♇	1°58
☉∠♇	1°59
♄△A	2°05

SVP=♓ 6°18'21"
JULIAN DAY=2424286.83611

ALLEN, STEVE — Entertainer

December 26, 1921
7:00 AM EST
New York, N.Y.
73 W 57   40 N.45

Actor in films and TV; comic; singer; MC; writer of fiction (seventeen books), poetry, humor and scripts; songwriter (more than four thousand songs.) Talented, prolific, creative commentator and espouser of charitable and humanitarian causes.

A: Holliday quotes CL, "time given by him."

Declin					
♄ 00S44			C	F	M
♃ 05S22		F	0	1	2
♅ 09S52		E	0	0	2
♂ 10S15		A	0	2	0
♆ 16N16		W	1	1	1
☽ 16S59					
♇ 19N55					
♀ 23S06					
☉ 23S23					
☿ 24S59					

DEC 26 1921
07:00 AM EST
13 21 58 SIDEREAL
12 00 00 UNIVERSAL

STEVE ALLEN
NEW YORK, NY
40N45   73W57
TROPICAL
PLACIDUS

Closest Aspects

☽∠♃	0°30
☉∠☿	0°40
♅□M	0°45
♄⚹♅	0°46
♃✶♆	1°04

♀⚹M	1°19
♂⚹A	1°20
☽⚹☿	1°23
♆△A	1°55
♄⚹♇	1°55
☉∠☽	2°03
☽♂♂	2°09

SVP=♓ 6°20'52"
JULIAN DAY=2423050.00000

ALLMAN, GREGG
Musician

December 8, 1947
3:03 AM CST
Nashville, Tenn
86 W 47   36 N 10

Declin		C F M
♆ 03S35	F 0 2 3
☽ 08S16	E 0 1 1
♂ 13N02	A 1 2 0
♄ 14N57	W 0 0 0
☿ 19S38	
♃ 21S23	
☉ 22S39	
♇ 23N17	
♅ 23N29	
♀ 24S28	

Closest Aspects
| ♀⚹♃ 0°20 |
| ☉△♇ 0°35 |
| ♂☌M 0°39 |
| ☿☌♂ 1°00 |
| ☉∠A 1°24 |

Member of the drug-rock culture. The Allman Brothers Band
once among the super-stars
until dissolved in 1976 with hard
feelings. Third marriage was to
Cher in 1975 for several stormy
years. By 1979 off heroin, but
still hard-drinking.

A: From him to Kelly Quinn,
February 1977, B.C.[6]

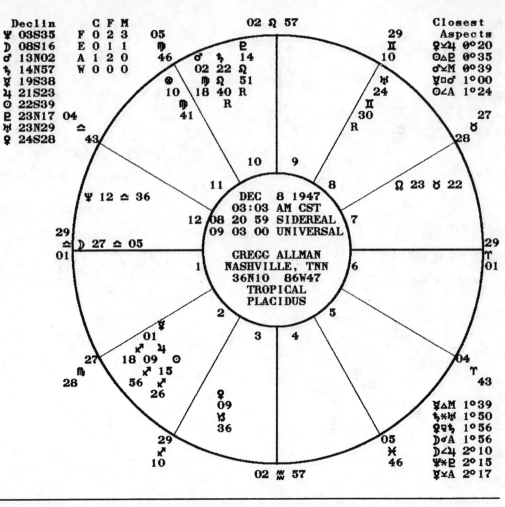

DEC 8 1947
03:03 AM CST
08 20 59 SIDEREAL
09 03 00 UNIVERSAL

GREGG ALLMAN
NASHVILLE, TNN
36N10 86W47
TROPICAL
PLACIDUS

SVP=♓ 5°59'27"
JULIAN DAY=2432527.87708

| ☿△M 1°39 |
| ♄⚹♅ 1°50 |
| ♀⚼♄ 1°56 |
| ☽♂A 1°56 |
| ☽△♃ 2°10 |
| ♆⚼♇ 2°15 |
| ☿⚺A 2°17 |

Closest Aspects
| ♇⚹M 0°09 |
| ☽♂♄ 0°40 |
| ☿☌♂ 0°45 |
| ♀△♆ 0°56 |
| ☉∠♀ 1°16 |

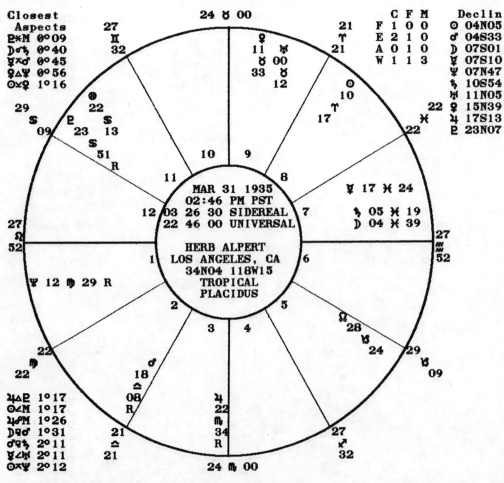

MAR 31 1935
02:46 PM PST
03 26 30 SIDEREAL
22 46 00 UNIVERSAL

HERB ALPERT
LOS ANGELES, CA
34N04 118W15
TROPICAL
PLACIDUS

C F M	Declin
F 1 0 0	☉ 04N05
E 2 1 0	♂ 04S33
A 0 1 0	☽ 07S01
W 1 1 3	☿ 07S10
	♆ 07N47
	♄ 10S54
	♅ 11N05
	♀ 15N39
	♃ 17S13
	♇ 23N07

ALPERT, HERB
Musician

March 31, 1935
2:46 PM PST
Los Angeles, Ca
118 W 15   34 N.04

Trumpet playing bandleader of
the seven-man Tijuana Brass,
started in 1962 and gaining in
popularity with South American
rhythms in the 60s at a time
when rock was becoming big.
First took trumpet lessons at age
8 as a duty, a habit, and then a
lifestyle.

A: CSH

| ♃△♇ 1°17 |
| ☉∠M 1°17 |
| ♃♂M 1°26 |
| ☽♂♂ 1°31 |
| ♂⚼♀ 2°11 |
| ☿∠♅ 2°11 |
| ☉♆♀ 2°12 |

SVP=♓ 6° 9'35"
JULIAN DAY=2427893.44861

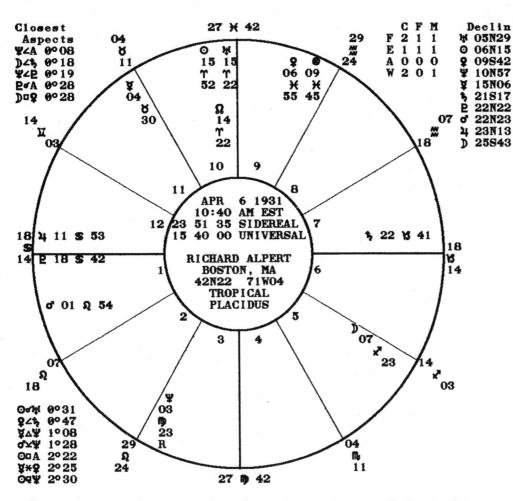

Closest Aspects

Ψ∠A 0°08
☽∠♄ 0°18
Ψ∠♄ 0°19
♇♂A 0°28
☽□♀ 0°28

27 ♓ 42

04
♉
11

⊙ ♅
15 15
♈ ♈
06 09
52 22
♂ ♓
55 45

04
♉
30

☊
14
♈
22

14
♊
03

10 9

12 | 23

APR 6 1931
10:40 AM EST
23 51 35 SIDEREAL
15 40 00 UNIVERSAL

RICHARD ALPERT
BOSTON, MA
42N22 71W04
TROPICAL
PLACIDUS

7

8

18 ♃ 11 ♋ 53
S
14 ♇ 18 ♋ 42

♄ 22 ♑ 41

18
♑
14

♂ 01 ♌ 54

1

2 3 4 5 6

07
♌
18

☽
07
♐
23

14
♐
03

⊙♂♅ 0°31
♀∠♃ 0°47
☿△Ψ 1°08
♂⊻Ψ 1°28
⊙□A 2°22
☿⚹♀ 2°25
⊙□Ψ 2°30

Ψ
03
♍
23
R

29
♌
24

04
♏
11

27 ♍ 42

C F M | **Declin**

F 2 1 1
E 1 1 1
A 0 0 0
W 2 0 1

♅ 05N29
⊙ 06N15
♀ 09S42
Ψ 10N57
☿ 15N06
♄ 21S17
♇ 22N22
♂ 22N23
♃ 23N13
☽ 25S43

29
♒
24

07

18

14

ALPERT, RICHARD
RAM DASS
Modern Guru

April 6, 1931
10:40 AM EST
Boston, Mass
71 W 04   42 N 22

Harvard professor until fired, along with Timothy Leary, for early experiments in LSD and other hallucinogens. Took the path of eastern philosophy. Published a collection of his writings and insights, *The Only Dance There Is.*

B: Dewey quotes data in his publication on p. 1.[7]

SVP=♓ 6°13'15"
JULIAN DAY=2426438.15278

ALY KHAN
Heir

June 13, 1911
2:00 PM MET
Turin, Italy
7 E.42   45 N 05

Pakistani representative to the United Nations. Son of Aga Khan III, called the richest man in the world. Noted playboy, sportsman, and horse breeder. Second marriage to Rita Hayworth in 1949, for four years. Died in a car crash, May 12, 1960.

B: Holliday quotes biography *Aly* by Leonard Slater, copy of B.C.

SVP=♓ 6°29'57"
JULIAN DAY=2419201.04167

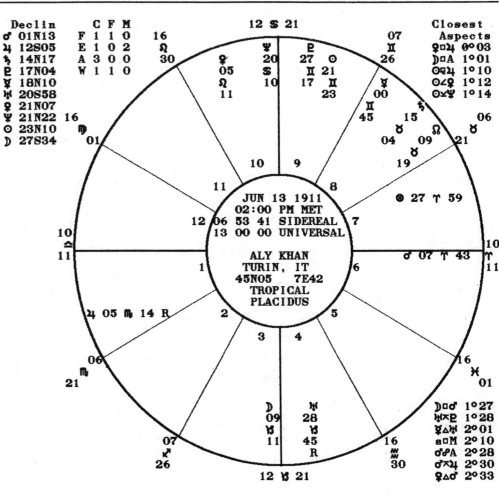

Declin | **C F M**

♂ 01N13
♃ 12S05
♄ 14N17
♇ 17N04
☿ 18N10
♅ 20S58
♀ 21N07
Ψ 21N22
⊙ 23N10
☽ 27S34

F 1 1 0
E 1 0 2
A 3 0 0
W 1 1 0

12 ♋ 21

16
♌
30

Ψ
20
♋
05
♌
11

♇
27
⊙
17 ♊
23

♊
26

07

♃ 05 ♏ 14 R

06
♏
21

JUN 13 1911
02:00 PM MET
06 53 41 SIDEREAL
13 00 00 UNIVERSAL

ALY KHAN
TURIN, IT
45N05   7E42
TROPICAL
PLACIDUS

♂ 07 ♈ 43

☿
00
♊
45
♂ 15

04 09

♊
19

⊕ 27 ♈ 59

21
♉
06

16
♓
01

☽
09
♑
11
R

♅
28
♑
45

Closest Aspects

♀∠♃ 0°03
☽□A 1°01
⊙□♃ 1°10
⊙∠♀ 1°12
⊙⚹Ψ 1°14

☽□♂ 1°27
♅⚹♇ 1°28
☿△♅ 2°01
a□M 2°10
♂♇A 2°28
♂△♃ 2°30
♀△♂ 2°33

07
♐
26

12 ♑ 21

16
♒
30

ANDERSON, HANS CHRISTIAN
Danish writer

April 2, 1805
1:00 AM LMT
Odense, Denmark
10 E 22   55 N.23

His fairy tale stories translated into more languages than any other book except the Bible. Also wrote plays, novels, poems, and travel books. Chiefly remembered for "The Ugly Duckling," "The Emperor's New Clothes," and "The Red Shoes." (1805-1875)

A: CL from official records quoted in a Danish magazine.

SVP=♓ 7°58'27"
JULIAN DAY=2380413.51287

Declin		C	F	M
♀	02S27	F	2	1	1
♄	02S34	E	1	0	0
☿	04N27	A	0	2	0
☉	04N41	W	0	1	2
♅	06S55				
♆	17S60				
☽	19N08				
♇	20S08				
♃	20S24				
♂	22N25				

Closest Aspects
♄∠♆ 0°03
♀□♇ 0°19
♅♀♆ 0°22
♀⊼M 0°24
♀△♆ 0°37

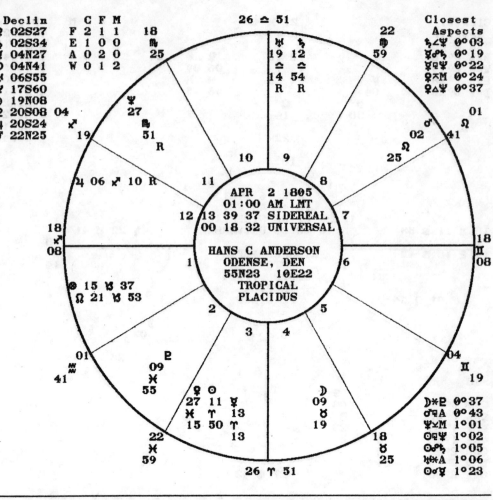

Closest Aspects	
☽⚹♇	0°37
♂□A	0°43
♆⊼M	1°01
☉□♆	1°02
☉⚹♄	1°05
♅⚹A	1°06
☉♂☿	1°23

Closest Aspects
♆⊼A 0°38
☉□♅ 1°01
♀△M 1°02
☽□♂ 1°03
☽∠♀ 1°06

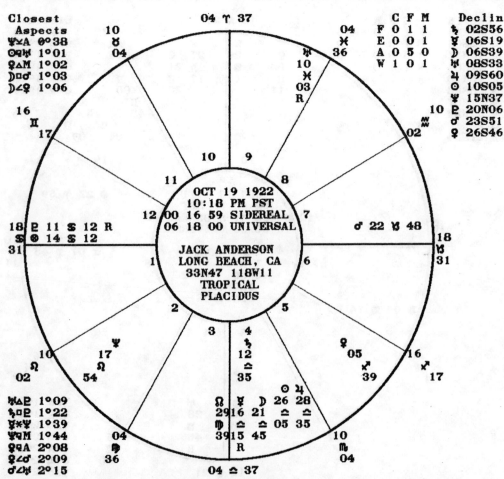

	C	F	M	Declin	
	F	0	1	1	♄	02S56
	E	0	0	1	☿	06S19
	A	0	5	0	☽	06S39
	W	1	0	1	♅	08S33
					♃	09S60
					☉	10S05
					♆	15N37
					♇	20N06
					♂	23S51
					♀	26S46

ANDERSON, JACK
Reporter

October 19, 1922
10:18 PM PST
Long Beach, Ca
118 W 11   33 N 47

Newspaper columnist and political reporter since 1947, with hard-hitting exposes of scandal and corruption in high places. *Washington Merry-go-round*, syndicated in 746 papers, with millions of readers. Also has radio and TV broadcasts.

A: CSH.

♅△♇ 1°09
♄□♇ 1°22
☿⚹♆ 1°39
♆⊼M 1°44
♀♀A 2°08
♀△♂ 2°09
♂∠♅ 2°15

SVP=♓ 6°20'18"
JULIAN DAY=2423347.76250

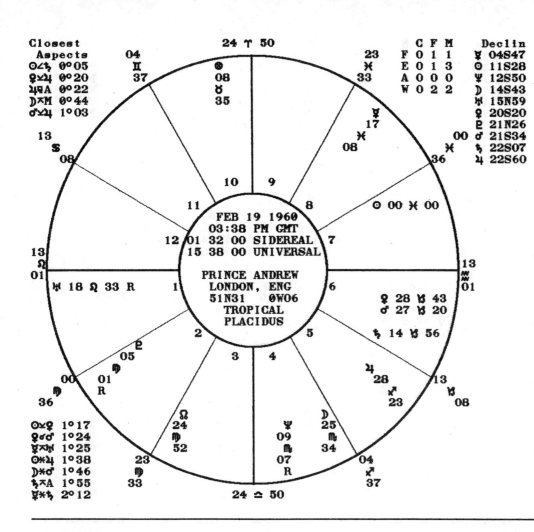

Closest
Aspects
⊙⊔♄ 0°05
♀⊼♃ 0°20
♃♀A 0°22
☽⊼M 0°44
♂⊼♃ 1°03

ANDREW, PRINCE
British royalty

February 19, 1960
3:38 PM GMT
London, England
0 W 06   51 N 31

Third child and second son of Queen Elizabeth II and Prince Philip. Second in the line of succession to the throne of Great Britain, after Prince Charles. Handsome and poised at 19.

A: Katherine Spencer in Dell, August 1960, "announced by royal physician."[8]

FEB 19 1960
03:38 PM GMT
01 32 00 SIDEREAL
15 38 00 UNIVERSAL

PRINCE ANDREW
LONDON, ENG
51N31   0W06
TROPICAL
PLACIDUS

⊙⊼♀ 1°17
♀♂♂ 1°24
☿⊼♅ 1°25
⊙⊼♃ 1°38
☽⊼♂ 1°46
♄⊼A 1°55
☿⊼♄ 2°12

SVP=♓ 5°48'59"
JULIAN DAY=2436984.15139

ANOREXIA NERVOSA
Female

October 2, 1950
5:09 AM EST
New York, N.Y.
73 W 57   40 N.45

A young woman of 18 afflicted with the "starvation illness," in which the victim cannot or will not eat, to the point of emaciation. Assaulted and raped under threat of a knife at approximately 10 p.m. on November 4, 1974.

A: Elizabeth Schattner in M.H., April 1979, B.C.

OCT 2 1950
05:09 AM EST
05 55 26 SIDEREAL
10 09 00 UNIVERSAL

ANOREXIA NERVOSA
NEW YORK, NY
40N45 73W57
TROPICAL
PLACIDUS

Closest
Aspects
a⊔M 0°08
♃△M 0°34
♀⊼♃ 0°38
♃⊼A 0°43
⊙⊔♅ 0°46

☽△♆ 0°52
♀⊔M 1°13
♀♂A 1°21
☿⊼♇ 1°31
☽⊼♇ 1°38
♆⊼♇ 2°30
♂⊼♆ 2°51

SVP=♓ 5°56'51"
JULIAN DAY=2433556.92292

ANOUILH, JEAN
Playwright

June 23, 1910
1:00 AM Paris time
Bordeaux, France
0 W 35   44 N 50

One of the leading dramatists after World War II. His heroes rejected society and conventional happiness, choosing to remain alone. Works include *The Lark* (1955) and *The Waltz of the Toreadors* (1956).

A: Gauquelin #28 Vol 6.

SVP:♓ 6°30'50"
JULIAN DAY=2418845.53519

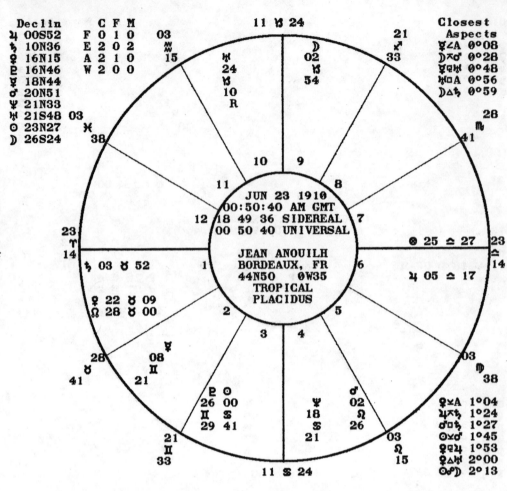

Declin
♃ 00S52
♄ 10N36
♀ 16N15
♇ 16N46
☿ 18N44
♂ 20N51
♆ 21N33
♅ 21S48
☉ 23N27
☽ 26S24

	C	F	M
F	0	1	0
E	2	0	2
A	2	1	0
W	2	0	0

Closest Aspects
☿∠A 0°08
☽♂ 0°28
♀⚹☿ 0°48
♅□A 0°56
☽△♄ 0°59

JUN 23 1910
00:50:40 AM GMT
18 49 36 SIDEREAL
00 50 40 UNIVERSAL

JEAN ANOUILH
BORDEAUX, FR
44N50 0W35
TROPICAL
PLACIDUS

♀⚹A 1°04
♃⚹♄ 1°24
♂□♄ 1°27
☉⚹♂ 1°45
♀⚹♃ 1°53
♀△♅ 2°00
☉☍☽ 2°13

ARCARO, EDDIE
Jockey

February 19, 1916
3:30 PM CST
Cincinnati, Ohio
84 W.31   39 N.06

Called "the greatest jockey of all time." Worked as a stablehand in 1929. First race, 1931. First win, January 14, 1932. From 1940-50 led the field ten times; 1950-55, a leader every year. Continual trouble and suspensions. Fighting spirit, pushed to lead.

A: Jim Haynes from B.C.

SVP:♓ 6°25'36"
JULIAN DAY=2420913.39583

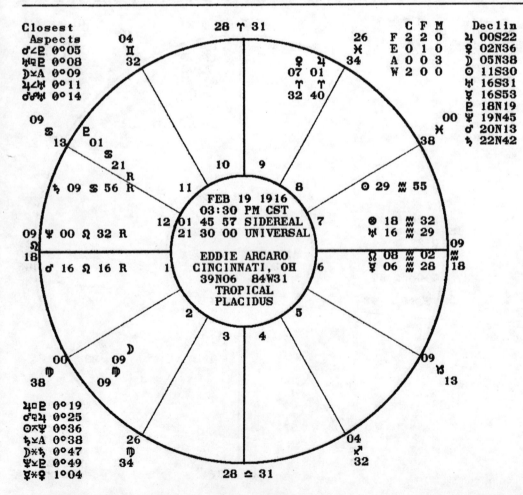

Closest Aspects
♂∠♇ 0°05
♅□♇ 0°08
☽⚹A 0°09
♃∠♅ 0°11
♂⚹♅ 0°14

	C	F	M
F	2	2	0
E	0	1	0
A	0	0	3
W	2	0	0

Declin
♃ 00S22
♀ 02N36
☽ 05N38
☉ 11S30
♅ 16S31
☿ 16S53
♇ 18N19
♆ 19N45
♂ 20N13
♄ 22N42

FEB 19 1916
03:30 PM CST
01 45 57 SIDEREAL
21 30 00 UNIVERSAL

EDDIE ARCARO
CINCINNATI, OH
39N06 84W31
TROPICAL
PLACIDUS

♃♇ 0°19
♂□♃ 0°25
☉⚹♆ 0°36
☽⚹A 0°38
☽⚹♄ 0°47
♆⚹♇ 0°49
☿⚹♀ 1°04

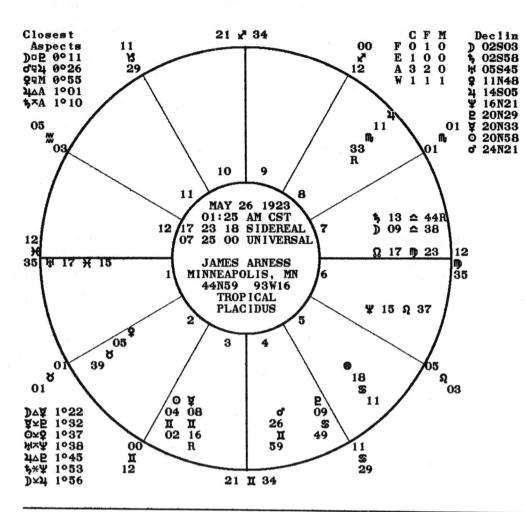

Closest Aspects
☽□♇ 0°11
♂□♃ 0°26
♀□M 0°55
♃△A 1°01
♄⚹A 1°10

☽△♅ 1°22
♀⚹♇ 1°32
☉⚹♀ 1°37
♅⚹♄ 1°38
♃△♇ 1°45
♄⚹♅ 1°53
☽⚹♃ 1°56

	C	F	M
F	0	1	0
E	1	0	0
A	3	2	0
W	1	1	1

Declin
☽ 02S03
♄ 02S58
♅ 05S45
☿ 11N48
♃ 14S05
♆ 16N21
♇ 20N29
♀ 20N33
☉ 20N58
♂ 24N21

Chart center:
MAY 26 1923
01:25 AM CST
17 23 18 SIDEREAL
07 25 00 UNIVERSAL

JAMES ARNESS
MINNEAPOLIS, MN
44N59 93W16
TROPICAL
PLACIDUS

ARNESS, JAMES
Actor

May 26, 1923
1:25 AM CST
Minneapolis, Minn
93 W.16   44 N.59

Theater since 1946. Cast in *Gunsmoke* (1955), an instant hit that played for the next twenty years on TV. Army war-time service, 1942-43, receiving a leg wound. Married 1948-63; three children. Married December 16, 1978, to 32-year old Janet Surtees.

A: McEvers quotes Kiyo, who knew Arness personally.

SVP=♓ 6°19'51"
JULIAN DAY=2423565.80903

ASHE, ARTHUR
Tennis champion

July 10, 1943
1:55 PM EWT
Ricmond, Va
77 W.27   37 N.33

Declin
♆ 01N26
☽ 02S54
♂ 10N24
♀ 10N55
♃ 20N09
♅ 21N24
♄ 21N46
☉ 22N17
♇ 23N38
☿ 23N46

	C	F	M
F	0	2	0
E	1	2	0
A	2	1	0
W	2	0	0

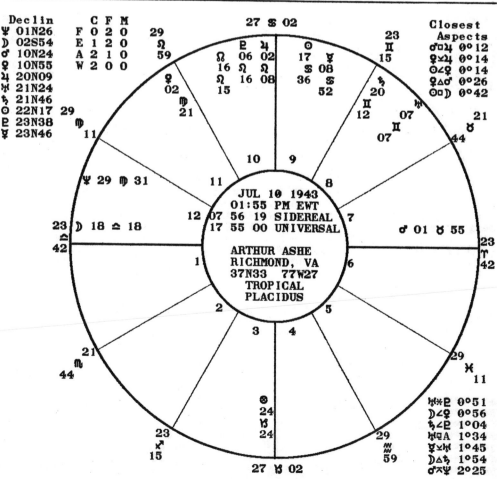

Chart center:
JUL 10 1943
01:55 PM EWT
07 56 19 SIDEREAL
17 55 00 UNIVERSAL

ARTHUR ASHE
RICHMOND, VA
37N33 77W27
TROPICAL
PLACIDUS

Closest Aspects
♂□♃ 0°12
♀⚹♃ 0°14
☉∠♀ 0°14
♀△♂ 0°26
☉□☽ 0°42

♅⚹♇ 0°51
☽∠♀ 0°56
♄∠♇ 1°04
♅□A 1°34
☿⚹♅ 1°45
☽△♄ 1°54
♂⚹♆ 2°25

First Black to win a major tennis championship — in the U.S. National Men's Singles in 1968. Won Wimbledon, 1975. Delayed a year by foot surgery in February 1977. Back into competition in 1978 to earn $260,000 in prize money. Married in March 1977.

A: AA, November 1975, quotes Ashe on *Today* show, July 10, 1975: "I;m going to be 32 today at 1:55 PM."

SVP=♓ 6° 3' 6"
JULIAN DAY=2430916.24653

ASTAIRE, FRED
Dancer, actor

May 10, 1899
9:16 PM CST
Omaha, Neb
96 W 01   41 N 17

Long-term beloved entertainment star. He and his sister a famous dance team for sixteen years from their first hit in 1916. Married in 1933; three children; widowed. Films include *Daddy Long Legs* (1955), *Funny Face* (1957), and *The Notorious Landlady* (1965).

A: Ed Helin from B.C.[9]

SVP=♓ 6°39'38"
JULIAN DAY=2414785.63611

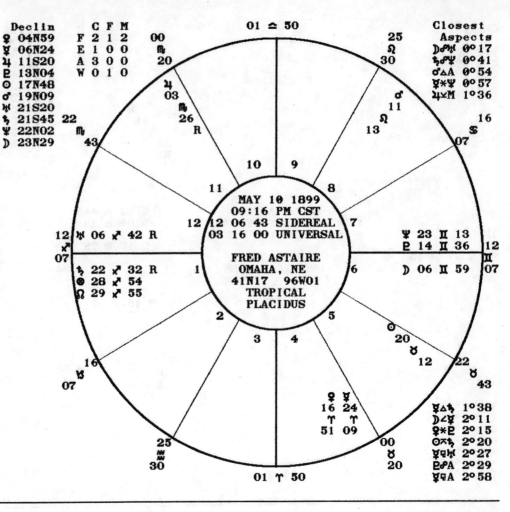

MAY 10 1899
09:16 PM CST
06 43 SIDEREAL
03 16 00 UNIVERSAL

FRED ASTAIRE
OMAHA, NE
41N17 96W01
TROPICAL
PLACIDUS

	Declin		C	F	M
♀	04N59	F	2	1	2
☿	06N24	E	1	0	0
♃	11S20	A	3	0	0
♇	13N04	W	0	1	0
☉	17N48				
♂	19N09				
♅	21S20				
♄	21S45				
♆	22N02				
☽	23N29				

Closest Aspects
☽♂♅ 0°17
♄♀♆ 0°41
♂△A 0°54
☿✳♆ 0°57
♃∠M 1°36

☿△♄ 1°38
☽∠♀ 2°11
♀✳♇ 2°15
☉□♄ 2°20
☿□♅ 2°27
♇♂A 2°29
☿□A 2°58

AUGUSTUS CAESAR
Roman Emperor

September 21, 62 B.C. NS
5:35 AM LMT
Rome, Italy
12 E.15   41 N.45

Grandson of Julius Caesar. A cold, calculating statesman who knew how to win popular affection. Became Emperor in 27 B.C. During his lifetime Rome reached its greatest glory, a golden age of literature and architecture. (62 B.C.-14 A.D.)

B: Fagan in AA, September 1969, quotes the historian Seutonius, *Lives of a Dozen Caesars*.[10]

SVP=♈ 3°55' 8"
JULIAN DAY=1698677.69861

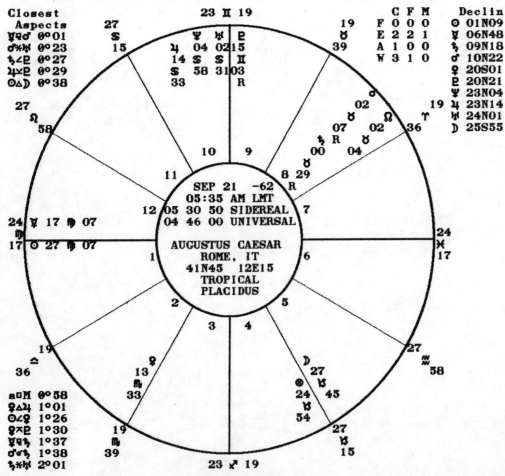

SEP 21 -62
05:35 AM LMT
05 30 50 SIDEREAL
04 46 00 UNIVERSAL

AUGUSTUS CAESAR
ROME, IT
41N45 12E15
TROPICAL
PLACIDUS

	C	F	M		Declin
F	0	0	0	☉	01N09
E	2	2	1	☿	06N48
A	1	0	0	♄	09N18
W	3	1	0	♂	10N22
				♀	20S01
				♇	20N21
				♆	23N04
				♃	23N14
				♅	24N01
				☽	25S55

Closest Aspects
☿♂♂ 0°01
♂✳♅ 0°23
♄∠♇ 0°27
♃∠♇ 0°29
☉△☽ 0°38

♂□M 0°58
♀△♃ 1°01
☉∠♀ 1°26
☿✳♇ 1°30
☿♂♄ 1°37
♂♂♄ 1°38
♄✳♅ 2°01

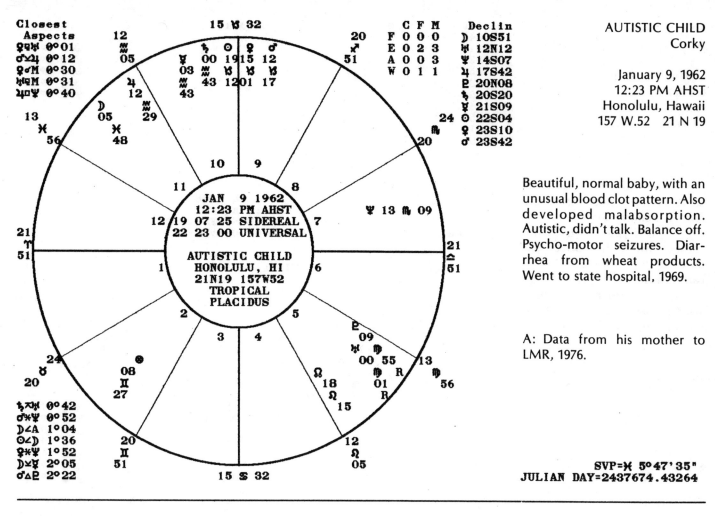

Closest Aspects

♀⊼♇	0°01	
♂⊼♃	0°12	
♀♂M	0°30	
♅♂M	0°31	
♃♂Ψ	0°40	

15 ♑ 32

AUTISTIC CHILD
Corky

January 9, 1962
12:23 PM AHST
Honolulu, Hawaii
157 W.52   21 N 19

	C	F	M		Declin
F	0	0	0	☽	10S51
E	0	2	3	♅	12N12
A	0	0	3	Ψ	14S07
W	0	1	1	♃	17S42
				♇	20N08
				♄	20S20
				☿	21S09
				☉	22S04
				♀	23S10
				♂	23S42

JAN 9 1962
12:23 PM AHST
19 07 25 SIDEREAL
22 23 00 UNIVERSAL

AUTISTIC CHILD
HONOLULU, HI
21N19 157W52
TROPICAL
PLACIDUS

Beautiful, normal baby, with an
unusual blood clot pattern. Also
developed malabsorption.
Autistic, didn't talk. Balance off.
Psycho-motor seizures. Diar-
rhea from wheat products.
Went to state hospital, 1969.

A: Data from his mother to
LMR, 1976.

♄⊼♅	0°42
♂⚹Ψ	0°52
☽∠A	1°04
☉∠☽	1°36
♀⚹Ψ	1°52
☽⚹☿	2°05
♂△♇	2°22

SVP=♓ 5°47'35"
JULIAN DAY=2437674.43264

AUTISTIC CHILD
Male

July 1, 1966
7:02 PM EDT
New York, N.Y.
73 W 57   40 N 45

Declin		C	F	M
♄	02S11	F	0	1	1
♅	06N09	E	0	2	0
Ψ	15S56	A	2	0	0
♇	18N46	W	2	1	1
☿	18N54				
♀	19N48				
♃	22N56				
☉	23N06				
♂	23N46				
☽	26S23				

Closest Aspects

♅♂♇	0°02	
☿⚷A	0°03	
☽⚷♄	0°03	
♃♂M	0°13	
Ψ⚹A	0°44	

JUL 1 1966
07:02 PM EDT
12 44 22 SIDEREAL
23 02 00 UNIVERSAL

AUTISTIC CHILD
NEW YORK, NY
40N45 73W57
TROPICAL
PLACIDUS

Noah-Jiro Greenfeld. Motor
development slow from
infancy. Hypertonic. Classified
as organic retardation by age 2.
Diagnosed as autistic at age 4.

A: Data given in *Life* magazine
in an article written by his
father, October 1970; time
given as "a few minutes after
7:00 this evening."

☿⚹♀	1°09
☉♂M	2°26
☉♂♃	2°38
☉⚹♀	3°10
♂♂A	3°24
☿∠☽	3°27
♅⚹Ψ	3°29

SVP=♓ 5°43'52"
JULIAN DAY=2439308.45972

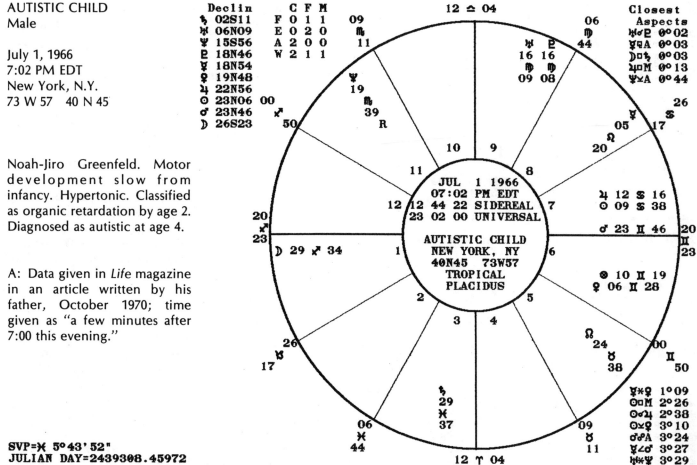

AYRES, LEW
Actor

December 28, 1908
00:15 AM CST
Minneapolis, Minn
93 W 16   44 N.59

Films from 1929 include *All Quiet on the Western Front* and *Johnny Belinda*. Retired in 1953 for a ten-year worldwide spiritual quest. Made documentaries of the world's religions. Later resumed career in films and TV. Third marriage to much younger Diana Hall, 1964; first child born December 27, 1968.

A: From him to D.C. Doane. (December 26 misprint in *Progressions in Action*.)

SVP=⌘ 6°32' 7"
JULIAN DAY=2418303.76042

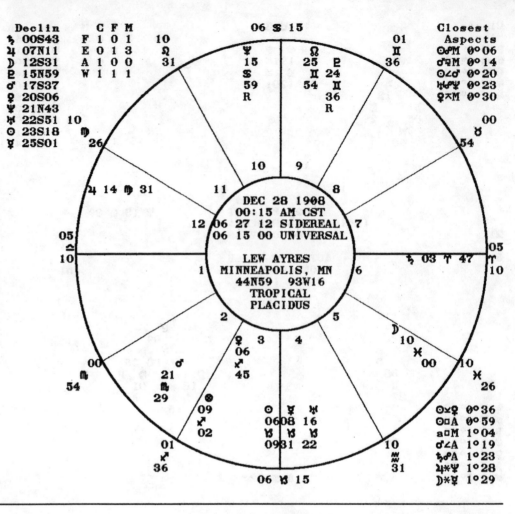

Declin		C	F	M		Closest Aspects
♄ 00S43	F	1	0	1		☉♂M 0°06
♃ 07N11	E	0	1	3		♂♃M 0°14
☽ 12S31	A	1	0	0		☉♂ 0°20
⚷ 15N59	W	1	1	1		♅Ψ 0°23
♂ 17S37						♀♃M 0°30
☿ 20S06						
Ψ 21N43						
♅ 22S51						
☉ 23S18						
⚷ 25S01						

☉⚹♀ 0°36
☉□A 0°59
a□M 1°04
♂♂A 1°19
♄♂A 1°23
♃⚹Ψ 1°28
☽⚹⚷ 1°29

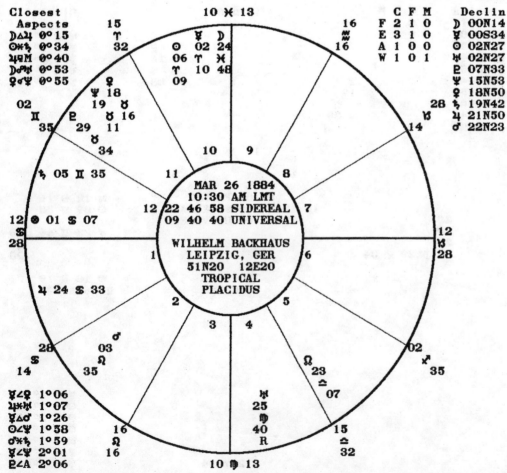

Closest Aspects

☽△♃ 0°15
☉⚹♄ 0°34
♃♂M 0°40
☽♂♅ 0°53
♀♂Ψ 0°55

	C	F	M	Declin
	F	2	1	0	☽ 00N14
	E	3	1	0	☿ 00S34
	A	1	0	0	☉ 02N27
	W	1	0	1	♅ 02N27
					♇ 07N33
					Ψ 15N53
					♀ 18N50
					♄ 19N42
					♃ 21N50
					♂ 22N23

BACKHAUS, WILHELM
Musician

March 26, 1884
10:30 AM LMT
Leipzig, Germany
12 E.20   51 N 20

Concert pianist in the classical German tradition. Guest performer with some of the world's outstanding orchestras. Throughout his career considered the foremost interpreter of Beethovan. (1884-1969)

A: Lockhart quotes *Modern Astrology*, September 1909, "from him, authenticized."

☿∠♀ 1°06
♃★♅ 1°07
♀△♂ 1°26
☉∠Ψ 1°58
♂★♄ 1°59
☿∠Ψ 2°01
♇∠A 2°06

SVP=⌘ 6°52'27"
JULIAN DAY=2409261.90324

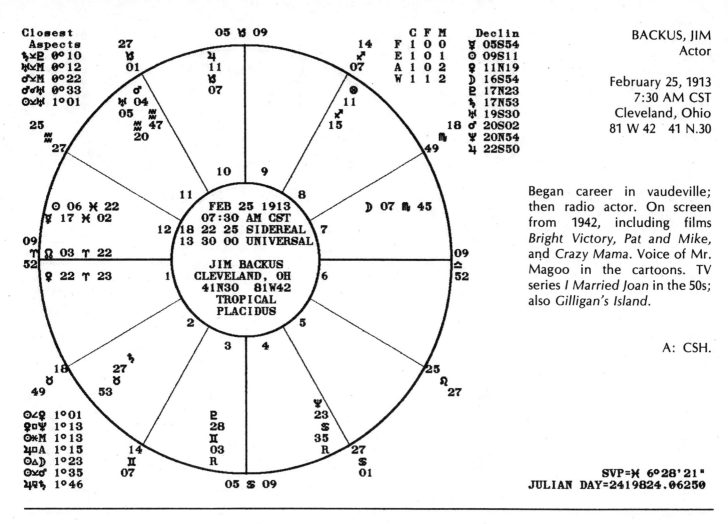

BACKUS, JIM
Actor

February 25, 1913
7:30 AM CST
Cleveland, Ohio
81 W 42   41 N.30

Began career in vaudeville; then radio actor. On screen from 1942, including films *Bright Victory*, *Pat and Mike*, and *Crazy Mama*. Voice of Mr. Magoo in the cartoons. TV series *I Married Joan* in the 50s; also *Gilligan's Island*.

A: CSH.

Closest Aspects

♄⚹♇	0°	10
♅⚼M	0°	12
♂⚼M	0°	22
♂♂♅	0°	33
☉⚼♅	1°	01

☉∠♀	1°	01
♀♂♆	1°	13
☉⚹M	1°	13
♃□A	1°	15
☉△☽	1°	23
☉⚼♂	1°	35
♃⚼♄	1°	46

Declin

☿	05S54
☉	09S11
♀	11N19
☽	16S54
♇	17N23
♄	17N53
♅	19S30
♂	20S02
♆	20N54
♃	22S50

C F M
F 1 0 0
E 1 0 1
A 1 0 2
W 1 1 2

FEB 25 1913
07:30 AM CST
18 22 25 SIDEREAL
13 30 00 UNIVERSAL

JIM BACKUS
CLEVELAND, OH
41N30 81W42
TROPICAL
PLACIDUS

SVP=♓ 6°28'21"
JULIAN DAY=2419824.06250

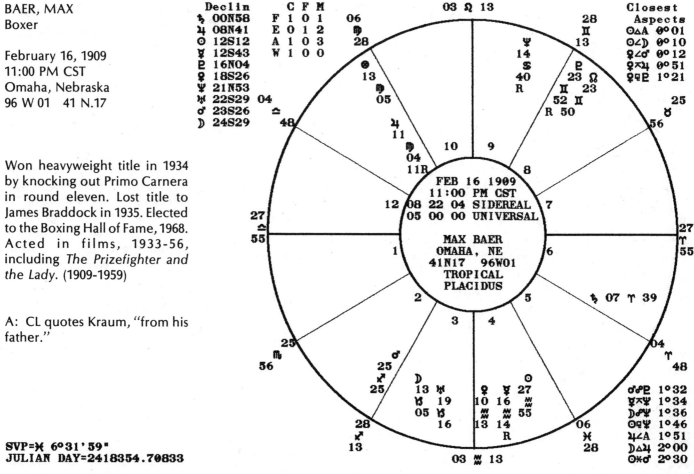

BAER, MAX
Boxer

February 16, 1909
11:00 PM CST
Omaha, Nebraska
96 W 01   41 N.17

Won heavyweight title in 1934 by knocking out Primo Carnera in round eleven. Lost title to James Braddock in 1935. Elected to the Boxing Hall of Fame, 1968. Acted in films, 1933-56, including *The Prizefighter and the Lady*. (1909-1959)

A: CL quotes Kraum, "from his father."

Declin

♄	00N58
♃	08N41
☉	12S12
☿	12S43
♇	16N04
♀	18S26
♆	21N53
♅	22S29
♂	23S26
☽	24S29

C F M
F 1 0 1
E 0 1 2
A 1 0 3
W 1 0 0

Closest Aspects

☉△A	0°	01
☉∠☽	0°	10
♀♂♂	0°	12
♀⚼♃	0°	51
♀⚼♇	1°	21

♂♂♇	1°	32
☿⚼♆	1°	34
☽⚼♅	1°	36
☉□♆	1°	46
♃∠A	1°	51
☽△♃	2°	00
☉⚹♂	2°	30

FEB 16 1909
11:00 PM CST
08 22 04 SIDEREAL
05 00 00 UNIVERSAL

MAX BAER
OMAHA, NE
41N17 96W01
TROPICAL
PLACIDUS

SVP=♓ 6°31'59"
JULIAN DAY=2418354.70833

BAILEY, JIM
Entertainer

January 10, 1938
11:30 PM EST
Philadelphia, Pa
75 W 10   39 N 57

Illusionist. Remarkable female impersonator of singing stars. With clothing, make-up, and style recreates the image of Judy Garland, Barbra Streisand, and Peggy Lee, among others.

A: Jansky H/N states, "from him."

SVP=♓ 6° 7'14"
JULIAN DAY=2428909.68750

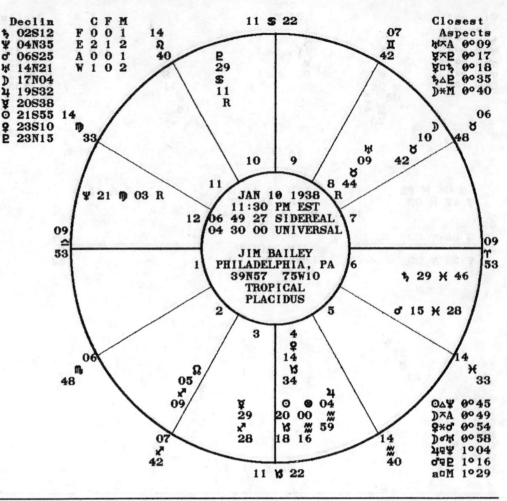

BAIRD, JOHN LOGIE
Scientist

August 13, 1888
8:00 AM LMT
Helensburgh, Scotland
4 W 40   56 N 00

Television developer in the 20s in England. Experimented with picture transmission by combining photography, optics, and radio, using the scanning disk with vacuum tube and photo-electric cells.

A: WEMYSS F/N #160, "recorded."

SVP=♓ 6°49' 8"
JULIAN DAY=2410862.84630

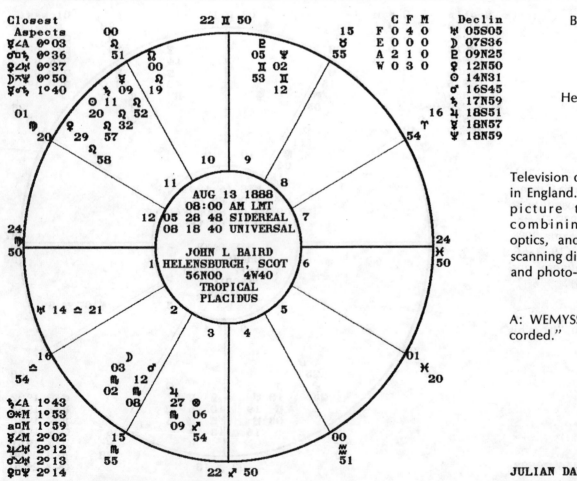

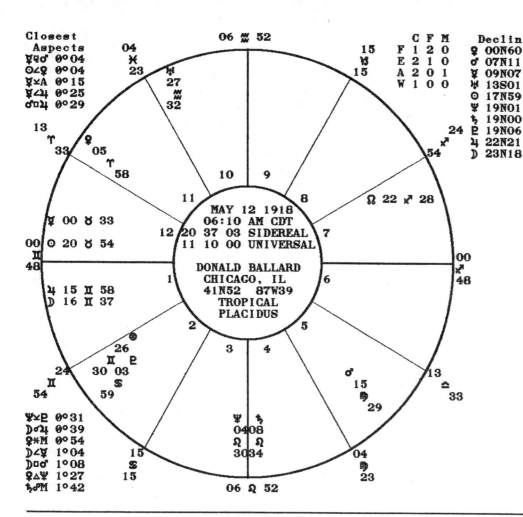

BALLARD, DONALD
Administrator

May 12, 1918
6:10 AM CDT
Chicago, Ill
87 W 39   41 N 52

Son of the founders of the Mighty I Am religious cult. Business administrator. With his mother charged on twenty-two counts of mail fraud, conspiracy, and plagiarism in 1940; convicted of two counts; reversal of conviction in 1946. The movement remained mighty through the 60s.

A: CL quotes Phyllis Stanick, "from the Ballards to Lucy Thompson."

Closest Aspects

♅ ☌ ♂	0°04	
☉ ∠ ♀	0°04	
☿ ⚹ A	0°15	
☿ ∠ ♃	0°25	
♂ ☌ ♃	0°29	

Declin

☿	00N60
♂	07N11
☿	09N07
♅	13S01
☉	17N59
♆	19N01
♄	19N00
♇	19N06
♃	22N21
☽	23N18

	C	F	M
F	1	2	0
E	2	1	0
A	2	0	1
W	1	0	0

MAY 12 1918
06:10 AM CDT
20 37 03 SIDEREAL
11 10 00 UNIVERSAL

DONALD BALLARD
CHICAGO, IL
41N52   87W39
TROPICAL
PLACIDUS

♆ ⚹ ♇	0°31	
☽ ☌ ♃	0°39	
♀ ⚹ M	0°54	
☽ ∠ ☿	1°04	
☽ ☌ ♂	1°08	
♀ △ ♆	1°27	
♄ ⚹ M	1°42	

SVP=♓ 6°23'43"
JULIAN DAY=2421725.96528

BALLARD, GUY
Religious founder

July 28, 1878
2:30 PM LMT
Newton, Ks
97 W 21   38 N 03

Co-founder of the Mighty I Am religious movement. Also known as "King of the Ancient Sahara" and "Beloved Daddy." Stated that he heard messages from the Ascended Masters, saw seventy thousand years of reincarnations, and healed five thousand people a year. (1878-1939)

A: CL quotes Phyllis Stanick, "from the Ballards to Lucy Thompson."[11]

SVP=♓ 6°57' 5"
JULIAN DAY=2407194.37458

Declin

♄	01S07
♇	05N53
♅	12N45
☿	12N50
♆	13N04
♂	15N06
☉	18N53
♃	20S24
♀	22N27
☽	23N35

	C	F	M
F	1	4	0
E	2	0	0
A	0	0	1
W	2	0	0

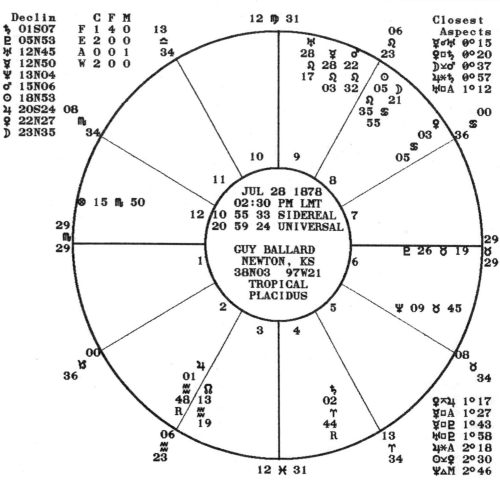

JUL 28 1878
02:30 PM LMT
10 55 33 SIDEREAL
20 59 24 UNIVERSAL

GUY BALLARD
NEWTON, KS
38N03   97W21
TROPICAL
PLACIDUS

Closest Aspects

☿ ☐ ♅	0°15	
♀ ☌ ♄	0°20	
☽ ☌ ♂	0°37	
♃ ⚹ ♄	0°57	
♅ ☐ A	1°12	
♀ ⚹ ♃	1°17	
☿ ☐ A	1°27	
☿ ☐ ♇	1°43	
♅ ☌ ♇	1°58	
♃ ⚹ A	2°18	
☉ ⚹ ♀	2°30	
♆ △ M	2°46	

BALZAC, HONORE DE
Writer

May 20, 1799
11:00 AM LMT
Tours, France
0 E.40   47 N 20

Novelist and playwright whose fame began in 1829. A dynamo of activity. Began his vast enterprise by writing a series, *The Human Comedy*, with two thousand characters. Impractical in mundane affairs; spent a lifetime in debt. (1799-1850)

A: Gauquelin #53 Vol 6.

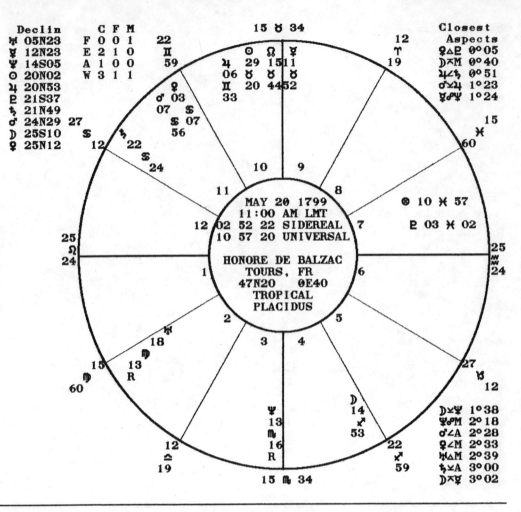

Declin		C F M
♅	05N23	F 0 0 1
☿	12N23	E 2 1 0
♆	14S05	A 1 0 0
☉	20N02	W 3 1 1
♃	20N53	
♇	21S37	
♄	21N49	
♂	24N29	
☽	25S10	
♀	25N12	

Closest Aspects
♀△♇ 0°05
☽⊼M 0°40
♃∠♄ 0°51
♂♃ 1°23
☿♆ 1°24

⊗ 10 ♓ 57
♇ 03 ♓ 02

☽⊼♆ 1°38
♆∠M 2°18
♂∠A 2°28
♀∠M 2°33
♅△M 2°39
♄⊼A 3°00
☽⊼♀ 3°02

SVP=♓ 8° 3'50"
JULIAN DAY=2378270.95648

Closest Aspects
♅♂♆ 0°04
☉∠M 0°04
♃⊼A 0°29
☿♇ 1°18
♅⊼M 1°22

	C F M	Declin	
	F 5 0 0	♂	00S48
	E 0 0 2	☿	01S32
	A 0 0 0	♀	01N50
	W 1 0 2	♃	02N46
		♄	04N34
		☉	07N37
		♇	15S03
		♆	22S18
		♅	23S39
		☽	25N39

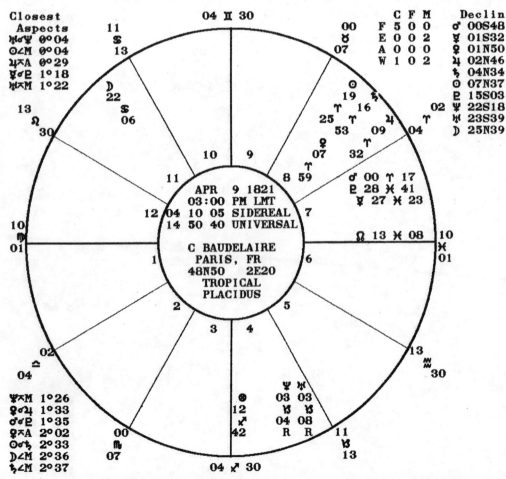

♆⊼M 1°26
♀♂♃ 1°33
♂♃ 1°35
♀⊼A 2°02
☉♂♄ 2°33
☽∠M 2°36
♄∠M 2°37

BAUDELAIRE, CHARLES
Writer

April 9, 1821
3:00 PM LMT
Paris, France
2 E 20   48 N.50

Poet, tormented by religion and the struggle between good and evil in man. His *Flowers of Evil* condemned as immoral in 1857. Sexually morbid, a sadist, dyed his hair green and moved frequently. Died from syphilis in 1867.

A: Gauquelin #63 Vol 6.

SVP=♓ 7°45'13"
JULIAN DAY=2386265.11852

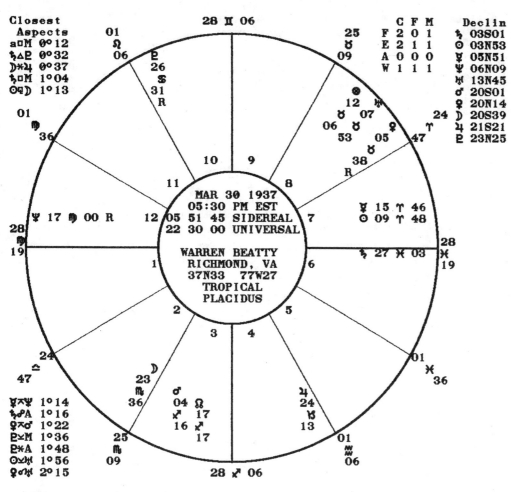

BEATTY, WARREN
Actor

March 30, 1937
5:30 PM EST
Richmond, Va
77 W 27   37 N 33

Closest Aspects

a□M	0°12
♄△♇	0°32
☽✶♃	0°37
♄□M	1°04
☉□☽	1°13

	C	F	M
F	2	0	1
E	2	1	1
A	0	0	0
W	1	1	1

Declin

♄	03S01
☉	03N53
☿	05N51
♆	06N09
♅	13N45
♂	20S01
♀	20N14
☽	20S39
♃	21S21
♇	23N25

MAR 30 1937
05:30 PM EST
05 51 45 SIDEREAL
22 30 00 UNIVERSAL

WARREN BEATTY
RICHMOND, VA
37N33 77W27
TROPICAL
PLACIDUS

♀✕♆	1°14
♄☌A	1°16
♀☌♂	1°22
♇✶M	1°36
♇✶A	1°48
☉□♅	1°56
♀☌♅	2°15

Nominated for Oscar as best actor in *Bonnie and Clyde* (1967). Other films include *Splendor in the Grass* (1961), and *Heaven Can Wait* (1978). High school football star, class president. Plays piano well. Shirley MacLaine's younger brother.

A: Holliday from B.C.

SVP=♓ 6° 7'53"
JULIAN DAY=2428623.43750

BELAFONTE, HARRY
Entertainer

March 1, 1927
10:30 AM EST
New York, N.Y.
73 W 57   40 N 45

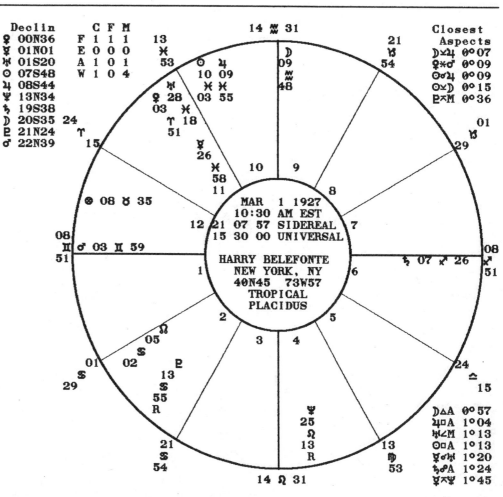

Declin

♀	00N36
☿	01N01
♅	01S20
☉	07S48
♃	08S44
♆	13N34
♄	19S38
☽	20S35
♇	21N24
♂	22N39

	C	F	M
F	1	1	1
E	0	0	0
A	1	0	1
W	1	0	4

MAR 1 1927
10:30 AM EST
21 07 57 SIDEREAL
15 30 00 UNIVERSAL

HARRY BELEFONTE
NEW YORK, NY
40N45 73W57
TROPICAL
PLACIDUS

Closest Aspects

☽✶♃	0°07
♀☌♂	0°09
☉☌♃	0°09
☉⊻☽	0°15
♇✕M	0°36

Singer, actor, worldwide show business star since 1950, with a repertoire of folk and ethnic ballads. Sellout performer with universal appeal. Won the TV Emmy for top musical performance in 1960. Married in 1948 for eight years.

A: Beatrice Redding in AA, November 1957, "personal interview, B.C."

☽□A	0°57
♃□A	1°04
♅∠M	1°13
☉□A	1°13
☿☌♅	1°20
♄☌A	1°24
☿✕♆	1°45

SVP=♓ 6°16'53"
JULIAN DAY=2424941.14583

BELL, ALEXANDER GRAHAM
Scientist

March 3, 1847
7:00 AM LMT
Edinburgh, Scotland
3 W 10   55 N.55

Educator; inventor. Taught music and speech in Scotland and in Boston, 1871, for deaf children. Married Mable Hubbard (who was deaf) in 1877. Patented the telephone in 1876, among other inventions. Elected to the Hall of Fame for Great Americans in 1950. (1847-1922)

A: Craswell quotes B.C. Same data in SS #81.

SVP=ℋ 7°23'29"
JULIAN DAY=2395723.80046

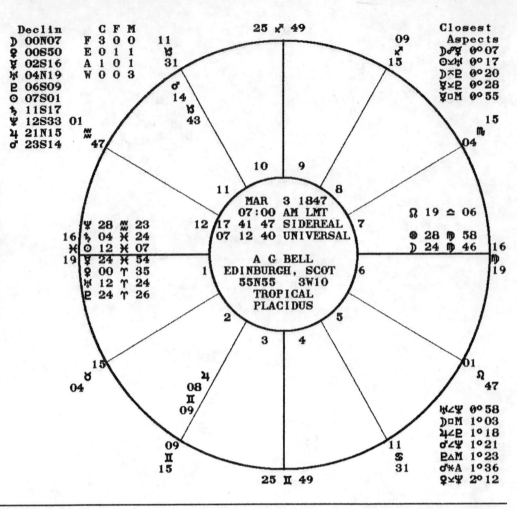

BELLAMY, RALPH
Actor

June 17, 1904
10:30 AM CST
Chicago, Ill
87 W 39   41 N.52

Player on radio and TV; more than four-hundred stage roles and eighty movies. Debut in N.Y. stage play *Town Boy* (1929); sixteen successful years on Broadway. TV series *Man Against Crime* in the 50s. Films include *Sunrise at Campobello* and *Rosemary's Baby* (1968).

A: CL, "from him to D.C. Doane," 1959.

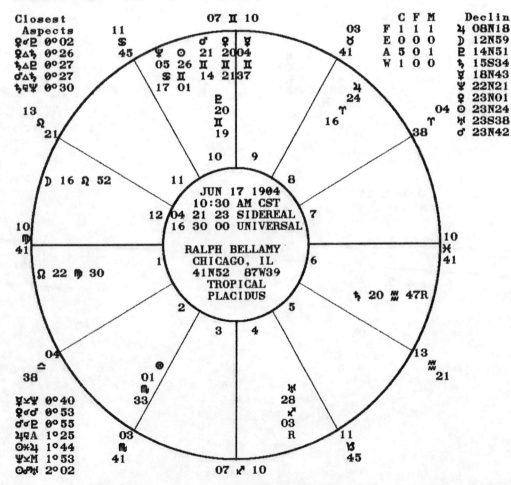

SVP=ℋ 6°35'40"
JULIAN DAY=2416649.18750

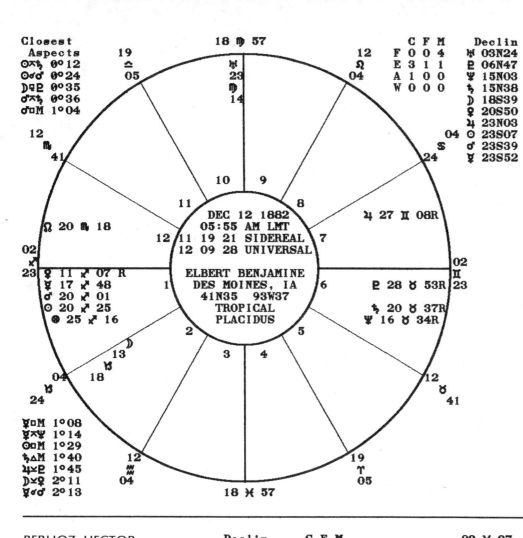

Chart 1 — Elbert Benjamine

Closest Aspects
- ☉☐♄ 0°12
- ♂☌☉ 0°24
- ☽☐♇ 0°35
- ♂☐♄ 0°36
- ♂☐M 1°04

⚷☐M 1°08
☿☍♆ 1°14
☉☐M 1°29
♄△M 1°40
♃☐♇ 1°45
☽⚹♀ 2°11
☿☌♂ 2°13

18 ♍ 57

	C	F	M
F	0	0	4
E	3	1	1
A	1	0	0
W	0	0	0

Declin
- ♅ 03N24
- ♇ 06N47
- ♆ 15N03
- ♄ 15N38
- ☽ 18S39
- ♀ 20S50
- ♃ 23N03
- ☉ 23S07
- ♂ 23S39
- ☿ 23S52

DEC 12 1882
05:55 AM LMT
11 19 21 SIDEREAL
12 09 28 UNIVERSAL

ELBERT BENJAMINE
DES MOINES, IA
41N35 93W37
TROPICAL
PLACIDUS

♃ 27 ♊ 08R

♇ 28 ♉ 53R
♄ 20 ♉ 37R
♆ 16 ♉ 34R

☿ 11 ♐ 07 R
♀ 17 ♐ 48
♂ 20 ♐ 01
☉ 20 ♐ 25
⊕ 25 ♐ 16

☊ 20 ♏ 18

18 ♓ 57

BENJAMINE, ELBERT
Astrologer

December 12, 1882
5:55 AM LMT
Des Moines, Iowa
93 W 37   41 N.35

C.C. Zain, founder of the *Church of Light* in Los Angeles. Author of the *Brotherhood of Light* series of philosophical and astrological textbooks. Studied to be a naturalist until 1900 when contacted the Brothers of Light during a mystical experience. (1882-1951)

A: CL, "from him."

SVP=♓ 6°53'26"
JULIAN DAY=2408792.00657

Chart 2 — Hector Berlioz

BERLIOZ, HECTOR
Composer

December 11, 1803
5:00 PM LMT
Grenoble, France
5 E 44   45 N 11

Known for orchestrating genius with program music. His work includes symphonies, voice and choral numbers, oratorios, and operas. Admired as a conductor, critic, and writer of books on music. Also wrote two volumes of *Memoirs*, published 1870. (1803-1869)

A: Gauquelin #1556 Vol 4.[12]

Declin
- ♄ 00N59
- ♅ 05S29
- ♃ 10S00
- ♆ 17S16
- ♇ 21S29
- ☽ 22S44
- ☉ 22S59
- ☿ 23S21
- ♂ 23S27
- ♀ 24S21

	C	F	M
F	0	0	3
E	0	0	1
A	0	3	0
W	0	2	1

02 ♓ 27

♇ 06 ♒ 26
♅ 10 ♒ 49
☊ 15 ♒

Closest Aspects
- ♄⚹M 0°10
- ♀☌♄ 0°31
- ♀⚹M 0°41
- ☿∠♃ 0°45
- ♀⚹♅ 0°48

DEC 11 1803
05:00 PM LMT
22 17 44 SIDEREAL
16 37 04 UNIVERSAL

HECTOR BERLIOZ
GRENOBLE, FR
45N11 5E44
TROPICAL
PLACIDUS

⊕ 01 ♊ 59

♀ 03 ♑ 08

☉ 18 ♐ 45
♂ 17 ♐ 49
☿ 14 ♐ 39
♆ 24 ♏ 25
☽ 20 ♏ 26

♃ 28 ♎

♅ 15 ♎
♄ 02 ♎ 27

☉☌♂ 0°56
♃△A 1°25
☉⚹☽ 1°41
♅☐M 2°00
a△M 2°09
☽∠♀ 2°18
♄☐A 2°19

02 ♍ 27

SVP=♓ 7°59'37"
JULIAN DAY=2379936.19241

BERMAN, DR. LOUIS
Endrocrinologist

March 15, 1893
00:51 AM EST
New York, N.Y.
73 W 57 40 N 45

Pioneer in the field; first to isolate the parathyroid hormone. Poor Jewish background, deep inferiority complex, avid for success; a self-made man. Books include *Glands Regulating Personality* (1921) and *Behind the Universe.* Died of a heart attack, May 16, 1946.

A: Rudhyar in AA, February 1949, "data from him in 1933."

SVP=♓ 6°45'11"
JULIAN DAY=2412537.74375

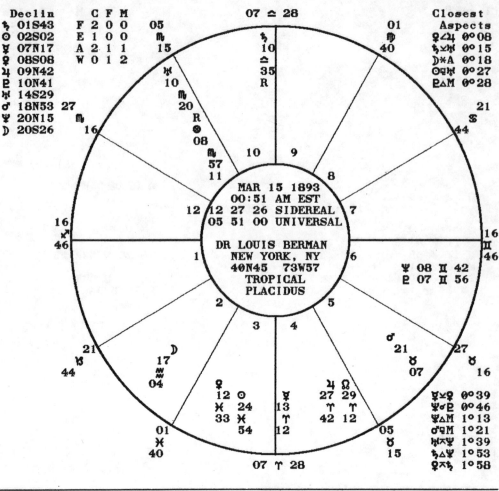

BERNANOS, GEORGES
Writer

February 20, 1888
9:00 AM LMT
Paris, France
2 E 20   48 N 50

Worked in an insurance company to support his wife and children. Began writing in the 20s; but 1936 before his novels and essays brought financial independence. Noted for powerful and violent works, including *Un Crime* (1935) and *Diary of a Country Priest* (1937). (1888-1948)

A: Gauquelin #89 Vol 6.

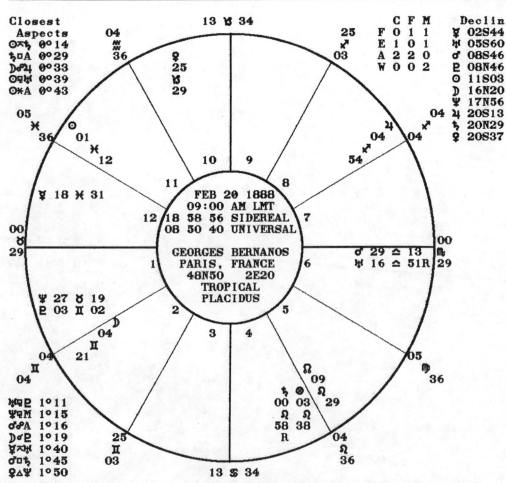

SVP=♓ 6°49'31"
JULIAN DAY=2410687.86852

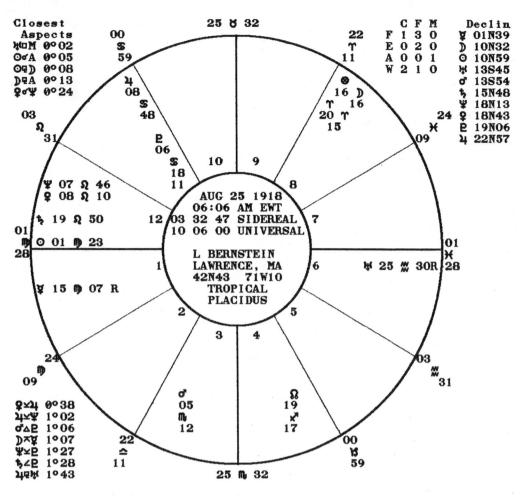

Closest Aspects

♅□M	0° 02
☉♂A	0° 05
☉♀☽	0° 08
☽♀A	0° 13
♀☌♆	0° 24

♀✶♃	0° 38
♃✶♆	1° 02
♂△♇	1° 06
☽✶♀	1° 07
♆✶♇	1° 27
♄∠♇	1° 28
♃♀♅	1° 43

AUG 25 1918
06:06 AM EWT
03 32 47 SIDEREAL
10 06 00 UNIVERSAL

L BERNSTEIN
LAWRENCE, MA
42N43 71W10
TROPICAL
PLACIDUS

	C	F	M	Declin
	F	1	3	0	☿ 01N39
	E	0	2	0	☽ 10N32
	A	0	0	1	☉ 10N59
	W	2	1	0	♅ 13S45
					♂ 13S54
					♄ 15N48
					♆ 18N13
					♀ 18N43
					♇ 19N06
					♃ 22N57

BERNSTEIN, LEONARD
Musician

August 25, 1918
6:06 AM EWT
Lawrence, Mass
71 W 10   42 N 43

Pianist, conductor, and composer of symphonies, ballets, musical comedies, chamber music, and film scores. After ten years and 943 concerts, retired from the N.Y. Philharmonic in May 1969 to devote his time to composition.

A: Dewey, "from him to Charles Cook" in Leek's *Astrology*, June 1972.

SVP=♓ 6°23'27"
JULIAN DAY=2421830.92083

BERRIGAN, DANIEL
Pacifist

May 9, 1921
6:30 PM CST
Virginia, Minn
92 W 32   47 N 31

Roman Catholic priest; antiwar activist. Wrote *The Trial of the Contonsville Nine* (1971), a documentary of the trial in which he, his brother Philip and seven others were found guilty of destroying draft cards. Also author of *No Bars to Manhood*.

A: CSH.

SVP=♓ 6°21'22"
JULIAN DAY=2422819.52083

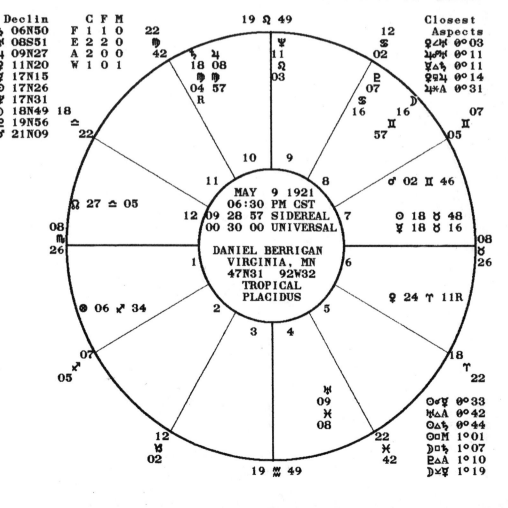

Declin

♄	06N50
♅	08S51
♃	09N27
♀	11N20
☿	17N15
☉	17N26
♆	17N31
☽	18N49
♇	19N56
♂	21N09

	C	F	M
F	1	1	0
E	2	2	0
A	2	0	0
W	1	0	1

MAY 9 1921
06:30 PM CST
09 28 57 SIDEREAL
00 30 00 UNIVERSAL

DANIEL BERRIGAN
VIRGINIA, MN
47N31 92W32
TROPICAL
PLACIDUS

Closest Aspects

♀∠♅	0° 03
♃☌♅	0° 11
☿△♄	0° 11
♀☌♃	0° 14
♃✶A	0° 31

☉♂☿	0° 33
♅△A	0° 42
☉□♂	0° 44
☉□M	1° 01
☽□♄	1° 07
♇♀A	1° 10
☽∠☿	1° 19

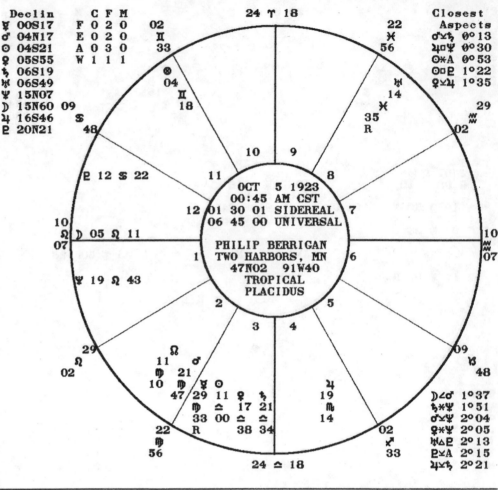

BERRIGAN, PHILIP
Pacifist

October 5, 1923
00:45 AM CST
Two Harbors, Minn
91 W 40   47 N 02

Declin		C F M		
☿ 00S17		F 0 2 0		02
♂ 04N17		E 0 2 0		♊
☉ 04S21		A 0 3 0		33
♀ 05S55		W 1 1 1		
♄ 06S19				
♅ 06S49				
♆ 15N07				
☽ 15N60	09			
♃ 16S46	♋			
♇ 20N21				

Closest Aspects

♂⊼♄	0°13
♃⊼♆	0°30
☉⊼A	0°53
☉□♇	1°22
♀⊼♃	1°35

Roman Catholic priest; antiwar activist. Charged with his brother Daniel and others of a plot to kidnap Kissinger and blow up the Washington D.C. tunnels in 1971; mis-trial declared in April 1972. Left the church. Married; two children born in 1974 and 1975.

A: CSH.

SVP=♓ 6°19'34"
JULIAN DAY=2423697.78125

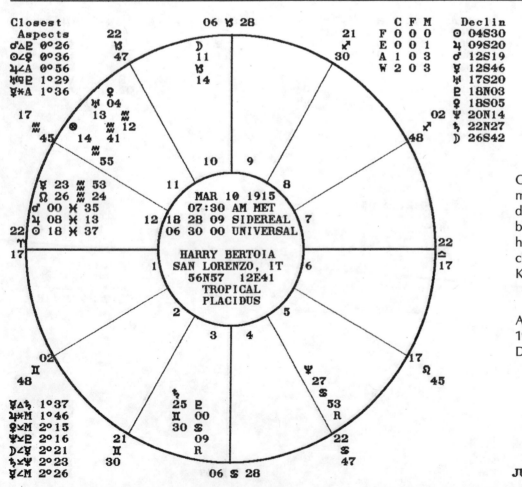

Closest Aspects

♂△♇	0°26
☉∠♀	0°36
♃∠A	0°56
♅□♇	1°29
☿⋆A	1°36

	C F M		Declin	
	F 0 0 0		☉ 04S30	
	E 0 0 1		♃ 09S20	
	A 1 0 3		♂ 12S19	
	W 2 0 3		☿ 12S46	
			♅ 17S20	
			♇ 18N03	
			♀ 18S05	
			♆ 20N14	
			♄ 22N27	
			☽ 26S42	

☿△♄	1°37
♃⋆M	1°46
♀⊼M	2°15
♆⊼♇	2°16
☽∠♅	2°21
♄⋆♆	2°23
☿∠M	2°26

BERTOIA, HARRY
Artisan

March 10, 1915
7:30 AM MET
San Lorenzo, Italy
12 E.41   56 N.57

Construction artist; creator of metal, wire, and blowtorch decorator screens used in office buildings, churches, airports, hotels. Also designed wire-shell chairs for home and patio for Knoll Associates, Inc.

A: Helen Wilson in AA, July 1961, "from his wife to D.C. Doane."

SVP=♓ 6°26'28"
JULIAN DAY=2420566.77083

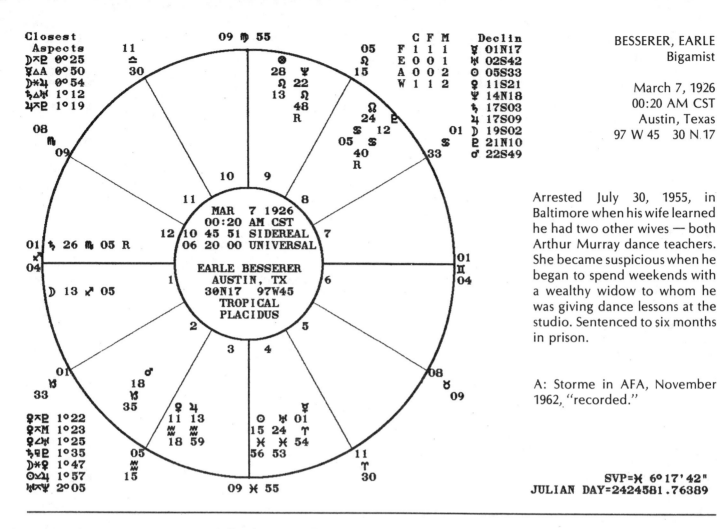

BESSERER, EARLE
Bigamist

March 7, 1926
00:20 AM CST
Austin, Texas
97 W 45   30 N 17

Arrested July 30, 1955, in Baltimore when his wife learned he had two other wives — both Arthur Murray dance teachers. She became suspicious when he began to spend weekends with a wealthy widow to whom he was giving dance lessons at the studio. Sentenced to six months in prison.

A: Storme in AFA, November 1962, "recorded."

SVP=✶ 6°17'42"
JULIAN DAY=2424581.76389

BING, RUDOLPH
Executive

January 9, 1902
8:00 AM MET
Vienna, Austria
16 E 23   48 N 12

General manager of the Metropolitan Opera Association in New York from 1950 to 1972. Formerly an opera and concert manager in Germany, England, and Scotland; helped found the Edinburgh Festival in 1947. Knighted by Queen Elizabeth in 1970.

A: CL quotes AFA, August 1963, "data from him."

SVP=✶ 6°37'28"
JULIAN DAY=2415758.79167

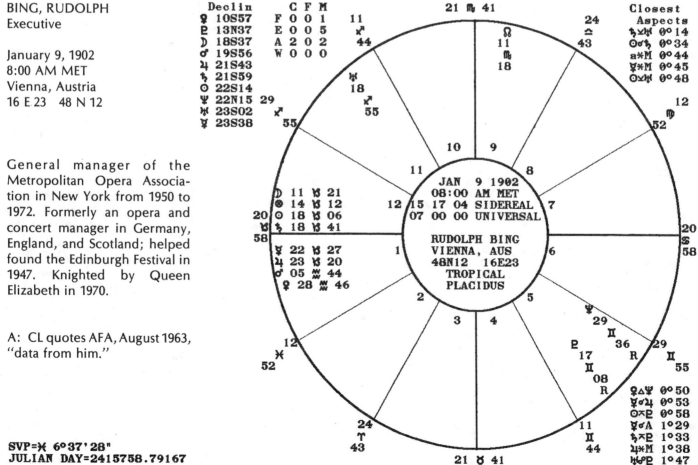

BIRTH DEFECTS
Peter Pell

January 14, 1970
8:21 AM EST
Breadlow Falls, Mass
71 W 04   42 N 22

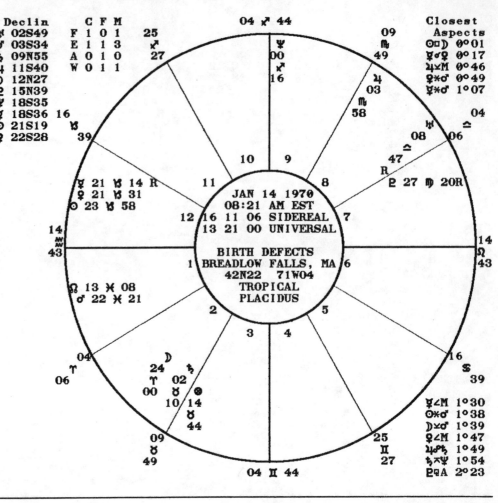

Born with spinal cord and nerves malformed; part of spinal cord exposed with no bone, muscle, or skin to protect it. Taken to a hospital in Boston where diagnosis was that surgery might save his life but would leave him crippled and retarded. Surgery not attempted. Lived twenty-three days.

A: Holliday from newspaper on date.

SVP=♓ 5°40'36"
JULIAN DAY=2440601.05625

Declin		C F M	
♅	02S49	F 1 0 1	25
♂	03S34	E 1 1 3	♐
♄	09N55	A 0 1 0	27
♃	11S40	W 0 1 1	
☽	12N27		
♇	15N39		
♆	18S35		
☿	18S36		16
☉	21S19		
♀	22S28		

Closest Aspects

☉□☽	0°01
☿♀♀	0°17
♃⚹M	0°46
♀♂♂	0°49
☿⚹♂	1°07
☿∠M	1°30
☉⚹♂	1°38
☽⚹♂	1°39
♀∠M	1°47
♃♂♄	1°49
♄⚹♆	1°54
♇☌A	2°23

Closest Aspects

♂⚹♃	0°08
♀♀M	0°24
♂♂♆	0°44
♃⚹♆	0°52
☉∠A	0°59
☽△A	1°00
♆⚹♇	1°14
♃⚹♄	1°42
♂♂♇	1°50
♂⚹♇	1°59
♃∠♇	2°07
☽∠♅	2°29

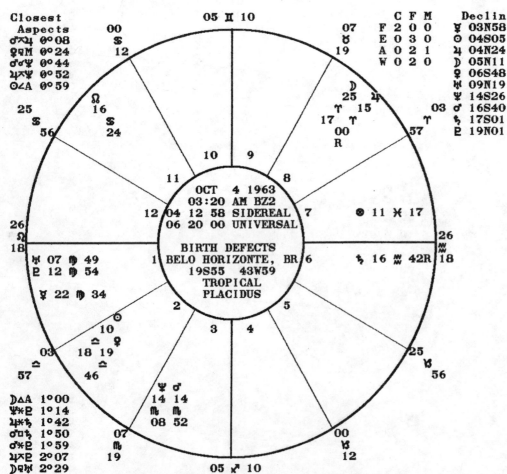

	C F M	Declin	
	F 2 0 0	☿	03N58
	E 0 3 0	☉	04S05
	A 0 2 1	♃	04N24
	W 0 2 0	☽	05N11
		♀	06S48
		♅	09N19
		♆	14S26
		♂	16S40
		♄	17S01
		♇	19N01

BIRTH DEFECTS
Male, Silvidera

October 4, 1963
3:20 AM BZ2 Zone 2.5
Belo Horizonte, Brazil
43 W 59   19 S 55

Born with two heads, four arms, two sets of lungs, and two stomachs. Heads breathe and eat separately. First child of a twenty year old mother who had taken two medical drugs when pregnant. Normal birth. Last report at age two months, survival medically uncertain.

A: CL from newspaper accounts

SVP=♓ 5°46'15"
JULIAN DAY=2438306.76389

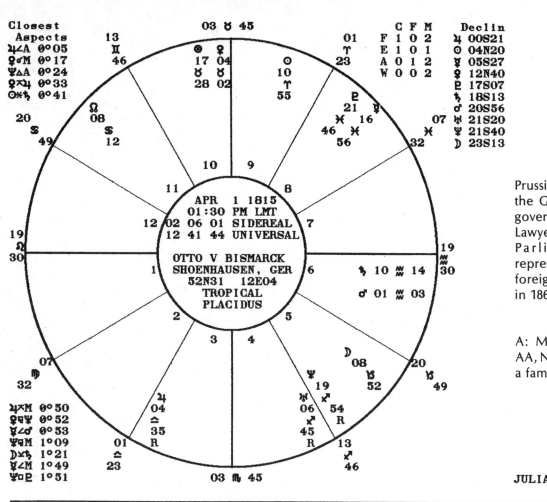

BISMARK, OTTO VON
Prime Minister

April 1, 1815
1:30 PM LMT
Shoenhausen, Germany
12 E 04 52 N 31

Prussian statesman who united the German people under the government of one empire. Lawyer from 1835; elected to Parliament, 1847; court representative; secretary of foreign affairs; prime minister in 1862. (1815-1898)

A: McEvers quotes Lyndoe in AA, November 1967, "drawn for a family member."[13]

SVP=♓ 7°50'38"
JULIAN DAY=2384065.02898

BLACK, HUGO
Jurist

February 27, 1886
11:57 PM CST
Harlan, Ala
85 W 50 33 N 17

Associate justice of the United States Supreme Court from 1937 until his death in 1971; one of the most distinguished jurists in the court's history. Called a militant humanist, often referred to himself as a "Clay County hillbilly."

A: Holliday from Vena Naughton, B.C.

SVP=♓ 6°51' 0"
JULIAN DAY=2409965.74792

BLAKE, WILLIAM
Artist and Writer

November 28, 1757
6:45 PM LMT
London, England
0 W 06   51 N.31

Engraver, painter, and poet; a master in each field. His works marked by genius, mysticism, and compassion: his *Prophetic Books* so complex and obscure that few profess to understand them. (1757-1827)

A: Craswell quotes Varley, a personal friend of Blake.[14]

SVP=♓ 8°38'35"
JULIAN DAY=2363123.28153

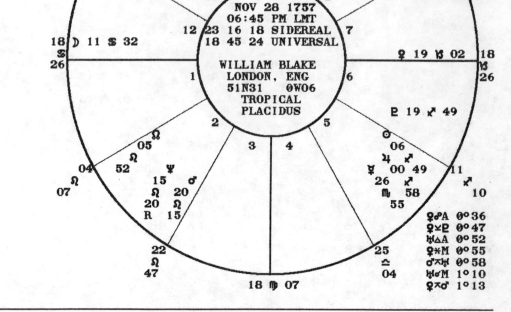

Declin		C F M		Closest Aspects
♅ 04S57	F 0 2 3			♀⚹♅ 0°16
♇ 15S25	E 0 0 1			a△M 0°19
♆ 16N24	A 0 0 1			☽⚼♆ 0°22
♄ 16S60	W 1 1 1			♂△♇ 0°26
♂ 17N03				♅✷♇ 0°32
☿ 19S04				
♃ 19S43				
☽ 20N52				
☉ 21S29				
♀ 24S27				

NOV 28 1757
06:45 PM LMT
12 23 16 18 SIDEREAL
18 45 24 UNIVERSAL
WILLIAM BLAKE
LONDON, ENG
51N31 0W06
TROPICAL
PLACIDUS

♀♊A 0°36
♀⚹♇ 0°47
♅△A 0°52
♀✷M 0°55
♂⚼♅ 0°58
♅♂M 1°10
♀♂♂ 1°13

BLUE, VIDA
Athlete

July 28, 1949
2:10 PM CST
Mansfield, La
93 W 43   32 N 02

Baseball pitcher. MVP, AL, in 1971, Oakland. Won twenty-four games in 1971. Pitched a no-hit game on September 21, 1971, for Oakland against Minn. Won the Cy Young Memorial award in 1971. Led AL with lowest ERA (1.82), 1971.

A: CSH.

SVP=♓ 5°57'55"
JULIAN DAY=2433126.34028

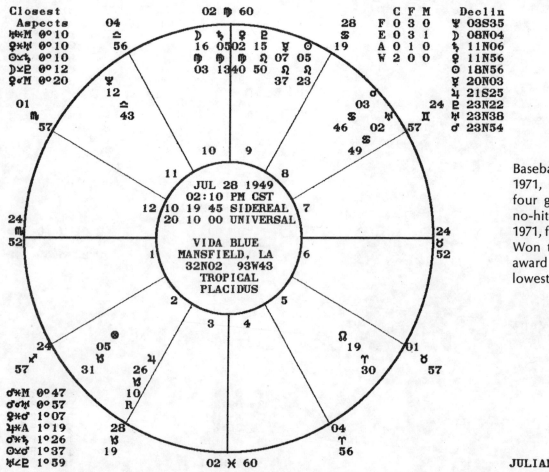

Closest Aspects		C F M		Declin
♅✷M 0°10		F 0 3 0		♆ 03S35
♀⚹♅ 0°10		E 0 3 1		☽ 08N04
☉⚹♄ 0°10		A 0 1 0		♄ 11N06
☽⚹♇ 0°12		W 2 0 0		♀ 11N56
♀♂M 0°20				☉ 18N56
				☿ 20N03
				♃ 21S25
				♇ 23N22
				♅ 23N38
				♂ 23N54

JUL 28 1949
02:10 PM CST
10 19 45 SIDEREAL
20 10 00 UNIVERSAL
VIDA BLUE
MANSFIELD, LA
32N02 93W43
TROPICAL
PLACIDUS

♂✷M 0°47
♂♂♅ 0°57
♀✷♇ 1°07
♃⚼A 1°19
♂✷♄ 1°26
☉⚼♂ 1°37
♅⚼♇ 1°59

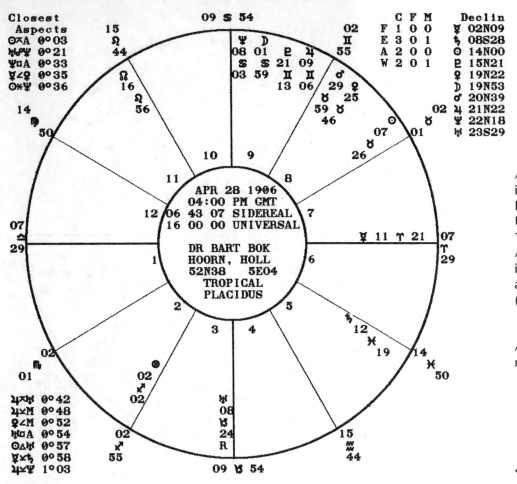

BOK, DR. BART
Educator

April 28, 1906
4:00 PM GMT
Hoorn, Holland
5 E 04   52 N 38

09 ♋ 54

Closest
Aspects
⊙∠A 0°03
⽊⚹♆ 0°21
♆□A 0°33
☿∠♀ 0°35
⊙⚹♆ 0°36

	C	F	M	Declin
F	1	0	0	☿ 02N09
E	3	0	1	♄ 08S28
A	2	0	0	⊙ 14N00
W	2	0	1	♇ 15N21
				♀ 19N22
				☽ 19N53
				♂ 20N39
				♃ 21N22
				♆ 22N18
				⽊ 23S29

APR 28 1906
04:00 PM GMT
06 43 07 SIDEREAL
16 00 00 UNIVERSAL

DR BART BOK
HOORN, HOLL
52N38   5E04
TROPICAL
PLACIDUS

♃⚹⽊ 0°42
♃⚹M 0°48
♀∠M 0°52
⽊□A 0°54
⊙△⽊ 0°57
☿⚹♄ 0°58
♃⚹♆ 1°03

09 ♑ 54

Astronomer. Came to the U.S. in 1929; naturalized, 1938. Professor of astronomy, University of Arizona emeritus, 1974. President of The American Astronomical Society. Books include *The Milky Way* (1941) and *The Astronomer's Universe* (1958).

A: Stated by him in *People* magazine, 1977.[15]

SVP=♓ 6°34'17"
JULIAN DAY=2417329.16667

BOWIE, DAVID
Rock star, actor

January 8, 1947
11:50 PM GMT
Brixton, England
0 W.06   51 N 28

Declin		C	F	M
♆ 02S53		F	0	3	1
♀ 16S39		E	0	0	3
♃ 17S14		A	1	1	0
♄ 19N07		W	0	1	0
☽ 21N17				
⊙ 22S15				
⽊ 23N03				
♂ 23S15				
♇ 23N36				
☿ 24S23				

13 ♋ 53

Closest
Aspects
♆♂A 0°10
⊙∠♀ 0°12
☽♂♇ 0°19
♀∠♂ 0°27
⊙♂♂ 0°39

Studied art in 1963, moving into the music scene with shows that staged glitter and flash with weird, sensational effects. First film, *The Image*. Later played an extraterrestial in *The Man Who Fell to Earth*. Took a male/female stance at 19; maintains an air of mystery.

B: Holliday quotes *David Bowie* by David Douglas, 1975, p. 3; states, "just before midnight."

JAN 8 1947
11:50 PM GMT
07 00 19 SIDEREAL
23 50 00 UNIVERSAL

DAVID BOWIE
BRIXTON, ENG
51N28   0W06
TROPICAL
PLACIDUS

⊙∠⽊ 0°47
☽⚹M 0°50
♇⚹M 1°09
♂∠M 1°26
☿□A 1°28
☿□♆ 1°38
♆⚹♇ 1°56

13 ♑ 53

SVP=♓ 6° 0'13"
JULIAN DAY=2432194.49306

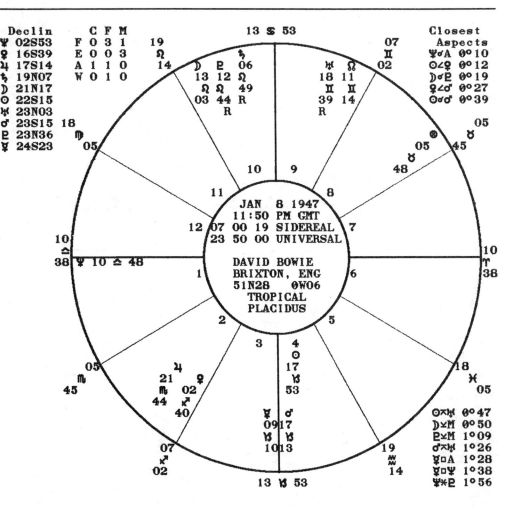

BRADY, IAN
Murdered

January 2, 1938
00:40 AM GMT
Glasgow, Scotland
4 W.16   55 N.51

He and his girl friend Myra Hindley (born July 23, 1942) sentenced to life imprisonment for the sadistic murder of a youth of 17, and two children aged 10 and 12. A biography by E. Williams published in 1969, titled *Beyond Belief*.

B: Holliday quotes the biography, p. 58, "40 minutes after midnight."[16]

SVP=✶ 6° 7' 15"
JULIAN DAY=2428900.52778

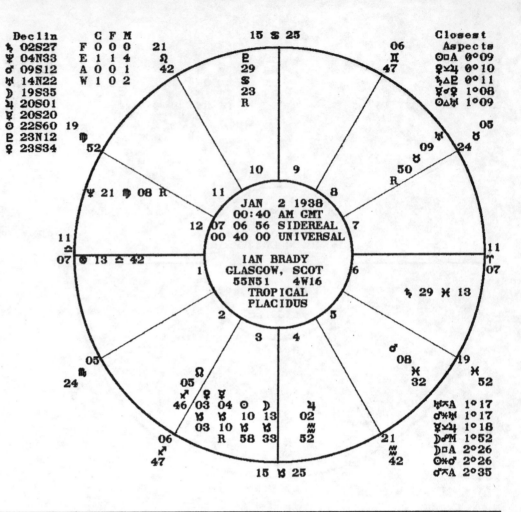

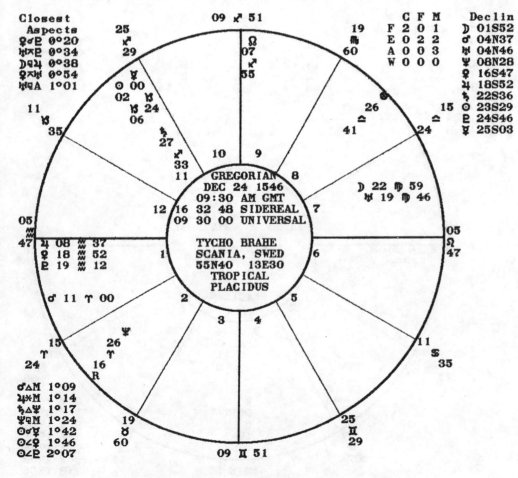

BRAHE, TYCHO
Scientist

December 24, 1546 NS
9:30 AM LAT
Scania, Sweden
13 E 30   55 N 40

Danish astronomer who contributed the technique of systematic observations and disproved the concept that no change could occur in the heavens. In a youthful duel, lost part of his nose and wore a replacement made of gold and silver. (1546-1601)

B: *Tycho Brahe* by J.L.E. Dreyer (Adams and Charles Black, 1890).[17]

SVP=✶11°34'33"
JULIAN DAY=2286081.89583

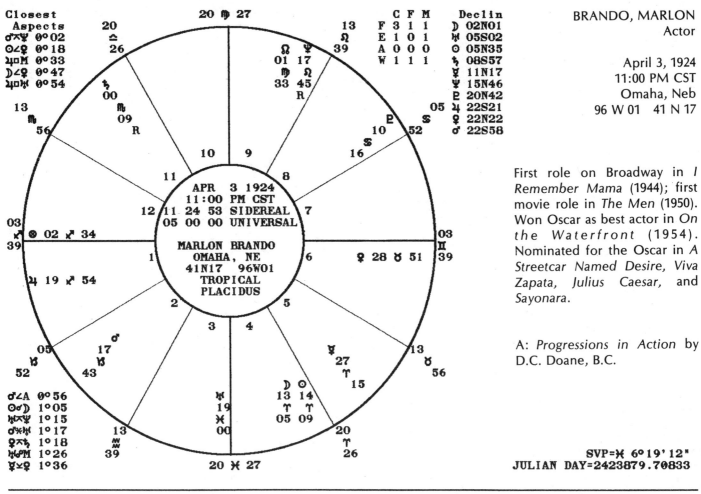

BRANDO, MARLON
Actor

April 3, 1924
11:00 PM CST
Omaha, Neb
96 W 01   41 N 17

First role on Broadway in *I Remember Mama* (1944); first movie role in *The Men* (1950). Won Oscar as best actor in *On the Waterfront* (1954). Nominated for the Oscar in *A Streetcar Named Desire, Viva Zapata, Julius Caesar,* and *Sayonara.*

A: *Progressions in Action* by D.C. Doane, B.C.

SVP=⊬ 6°19'12"
JULIAN DAY=2423879.70833

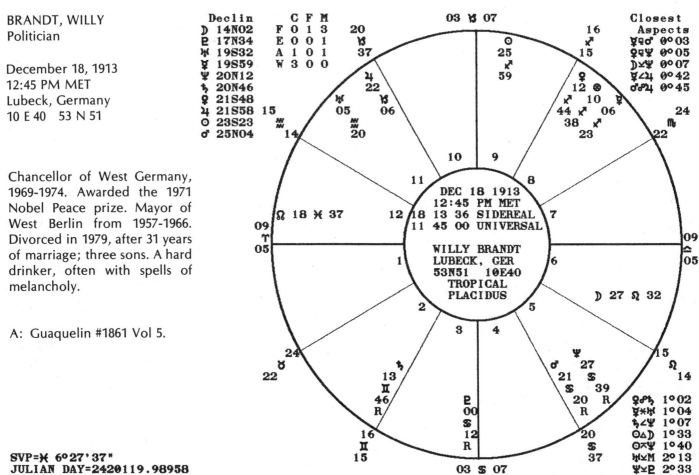

BRANDT, WILLY
Politician

December 18, 1913
12:45 PM MET
Lubeck, Germany
10 E 40   53 N 51

Chancellor of West Germany, 1969-1974. Awarded the 1971 Nobel Peace prize. Mayor of West Berlin from 1957-1966. Divorced in 1979, after 31 years of marriage; three sons. A hard drinker, often with spells of melancholy.

A: Guaquelin #1861 Vol 5.

SVP=⊬ 6°27'37"
JULIAN DAY=2420119.98958

BRAZZI, ROSSANO
Actor

September 18, 1916
6:15 AM MWT
Bologna, Italy
11 E.21   44 N 30

Handsome Italian romantic lead who was a national star from the 40s. Became internationally known after 1949 with successful films that include *A Certain Smile*, *Little Women*, *The Barefoot Contessa*, and *South Pacific*.

A; Guaquelin #820 Vol 5.

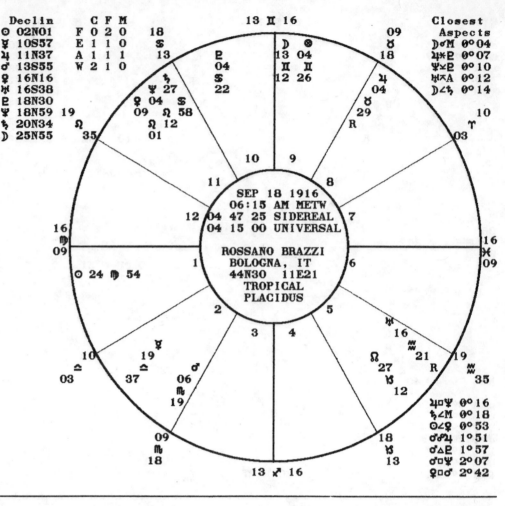

Declin		C	F	M
☉	02N01	F	0	2	0
☿	10S57	E	1	1	0
♃	11N37	A	1	1	1
♂	13S55	W	2	1	0
♀	16N16				
♅	16S38				
♇	18N30				
♆	18N59				
♄	20N34				
☽	25N55				

Closest Aspects
☽♂M 0°04
♃∗♇ 0°07
♆⊼♇ 0°10
♅△A 0°12
☽∠♄ 0°14

SEP 18 1916
06:15 AM METW
04 47 25 SIDEREAL
04 15 00 UNIVERSAL

ROSSANO BRAZZI
BOLOGNA , IT
44N30   11E21
TROPICAL
PLACIDUS

♃□♆ 0°16
♄∠M 0°18
☉∠♀ 0°53
♂∗♃ 1°51
♂△♇ 1°57
♂□♆ 2°07
♀□♂ 2°42

SVP=♓ 6°25' 6"
JULIAN DAY=2421124.67708

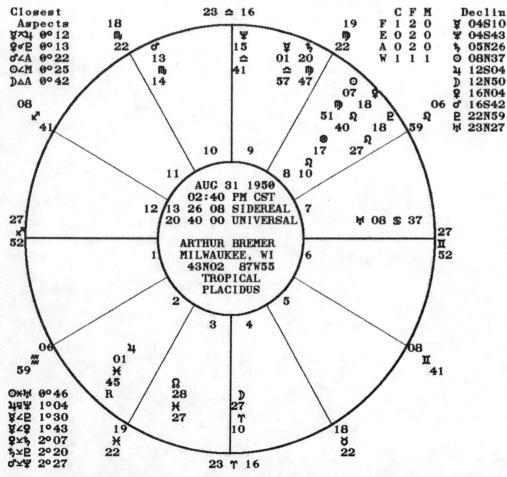

Closest Aspects
☿⊼♃ 0°12
♀♂♇ 0°13
♂∠A 0°22
☉∠M 0°25
☽△A 0°42

☉∗♅ 0°46
♃♂♆ 1°04
♀∠♂ 1°30
☿∠♂ 1°43
♀⊼♄ 2°07
♄∗♇ 2°20
♂♂♆ 2°27

AUG 31 1950
02:40 PM CST
13 26 08 SIDEREAL
20 40 00 UNIVERSAL

ARTHUR BREMER
MILWAUKEE, WI
43N02   87W55
TROPICAL
PLACIDUS

		C	F	M	Declin	
		F	1	2	0	☿	04S10
		E	0	2	0	♆	04S43
		A	0	2	0	♄	05N26
		W	1	1	1	☉	08N37
						♃	12S04
						☽	12N50
						♀	16N04
						♂	16S42
						♇	22N59
						♅	23N27

BREMER, ARTHUR
Psychotic

August 31, 1950
2:40 PM CST
Milwaukee, Wis
87 W 55   43 N 02

Attempted assassin who shot and paralyzed presidential candidate George Wallace on May 15, 1972, at a Laurel, Md. shopping center. His diary stresses his sexual frustration and preoccupation, obsessive and masochistic impotence.

B: Holliday from autobiography *Assassin's Diary* (Harper Press, 1973).[18]

SVP=♓ 5°56'54"
JULIAN DAY=2433525.36111

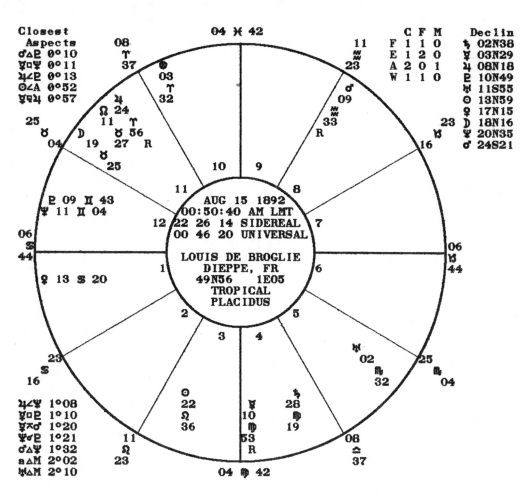

BROGLIE, LOUIS DE
Prince

August 15, 1892
1:00 AM Paris time
Dieppe, France
1 E 05   49 N 56

French theoretical physicist, famous for his wave theory. Received the Nobel Prize in physics in 1929 for his discovery of the wave nature of the electron. Professor of physics at the Faculté des Sciences, Paris, 1932. Author of more than twenty scientific works.

A: Gauquelin #2604 Vol 2.

Closest
Aspects
♂△♇ 0°10
☿□Ψ 0°11
♃□♇ 0°13
☉□A 0°52
☿□♃ 0°57

	C	F	M		Declin	
F	1	1	0	♄	02N38
E	1	2	0	☿	03N29
A	2	0	1	♃	08N18
W	1	1	0	♇	10N49
				♅	11S55
				☉	13N59
				♀	17N15
				☽	18N16
				Ψ	20N35
				♂	24S21

♃∠Ψ 1°08
☿□♇ 1°10
☿✶♂ 1°20
Ψ□♇ 1°21
♂△Ψ 1°32
a△M 2°02
♅△M 2°10

SVP=♓ 6°45'43"
JULIAN DAY=2412325.53218

BROWN, EDMUND G.
Politician

April 7, 1938
12:34 PM PST
San Francisco, Ca
122 W.26   37 N.47

Son of Governor Pat Brown. Four years Jesuit training in youth. Berkeley and Yale Law Schools. A Los Angeles law firm; into politics. Known as a workaholic. Elected governor of California, 1974. African safari with rock-star Linda Ronstadt, April 1979.

A: John Daniel from B.C.[19]

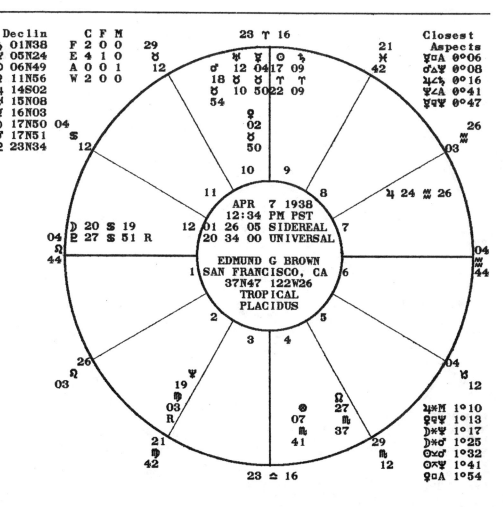

Declin			C	F	M
♄	01N38	F	2	0	0
Ψ	05N24	E	4	1	0
☉	06N49	A	0	0	1
♀	11N56	W	2	0	0
♃	14S02				
♅	15N08				
☿	16N03				
☽	17N50				
♂	17N51				
♇	23N34				

Closest
Aspects
☿□A 0°06
♂△Ψ 0°08
♃∠♄ 0°16
Ψ∠A 0°41
☿□Ψ 0°47

♃✶M 1°10
♀□Ψ 1°13
☽✶Ψ 1°17
☽✶♂ 1°25
☉□♃ 1°32
☉✶Ψ 1°41
♀□A 1°54

SVP=♓ 6° 7' 4"
JULIAN DAY=2428996.35694

BROWN, STEVE
Private pilot

August 13, 1938
7:15 AM CST
Des Moines, Iowa
93 W 37   41 N 35

Fell when hang gliding; broke entire body; never regained consciousness but lived for six weeks and died Christmas Eve, 1977. Lived his life to the hilt with zest. Had a violent car accident in 1967; companion killed. Was buried next to that companion exactly ten years later.

A: From him to Paul Morgan.

SVP=♓ 6° 6'46"
JULIAN DAY=2429124.05208

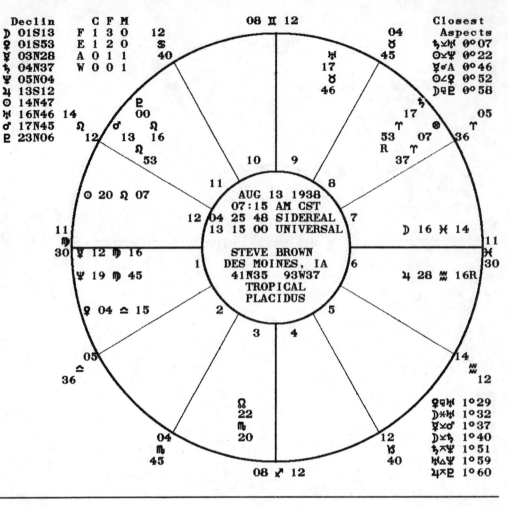

	Declin		C	F	M
☽	01S13	F	1	3	0
♀	01S53	E	1	2	0
☿	03N28	A	0	1	1
♄	04N37	W	0	0	1
♆	05N04				
♃	13S12				
☉	14N47				
♅	16N46				
♂	17N45				
♇	23N06				

Closest Aspects

♄⚹♅	0°07
☉⚹♆	0°22
☿♂A	0°46
☉∠♀	0°52
☽⚼♇	0°58

AUG 13 1938
07:15 AM CST
04 25 48 SIDEREAL
13 15 00 UNIVERSAL
STEVE BROWN
DES MOINES, IA
41N35 93W37
TROPICAL
PLACIDUS

♀⚼♅	1°29
☽⚹♅	1°32
☿∠♂	1°37
☽⚹♄	1°40
♄⚻♆	1°51
♅△♆	1°59
♃⚻♇	1°60

BRUCE, LENNY
Comedian

October 13, 1925
11:24 AM EST
Mineola, N.Y.
73 W 38   40 N 45

Satirist with biting social comment and controversial subject matter. One marriage to a stripper/drug user; one daughter; divorce. Wrote a largely fictionalized autobiography *How to Talk Dirty and Influence People* (1963). Died of heroin overdose, August 3, 1966.

A: CSH.

SVP=♓ 6°18' 2"
JULIAN DAY=2424437.18333

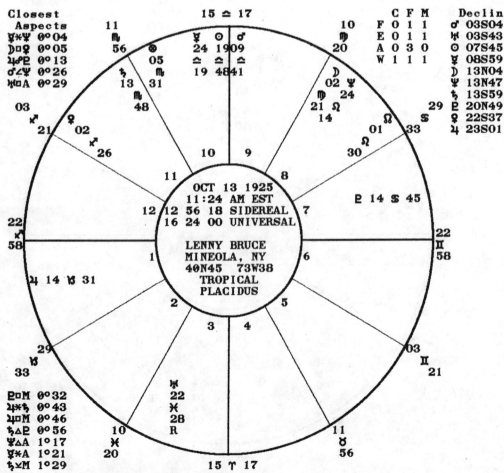

Closest Aspects

☿⚹♆	0°04
☽⚼♀	0°05
♃⚼♇	0°13
♂∠♆	0°26
♅□A	0°29

C	F	M		Declin
F	0	1	1	♂ 03S04
E	0	1	1	♅ 03S43
A	0	3	0	☉ 07S45
W	1	1	1	☿ 08S59
				☽ 13N04
				♆ 13N47
				♄ 13S59
				♇ 20N49
				♀ 22S37
				♃ 23S01

OCT 13 1925
11:24 AM EST
12 56 18 SIDEREAL
16 24 00 UNIVERSAL
LENNY BRUCE
MINEOLA, NY
40N45 73W38
TROPICAL
PLACIDUS

♇□M	0°32
♃⚹♄	0°43
♃□M	0°46
♄△♇	0°56
♆△A	1°17
☿⚹A	1°21
♄⚻M	1°29

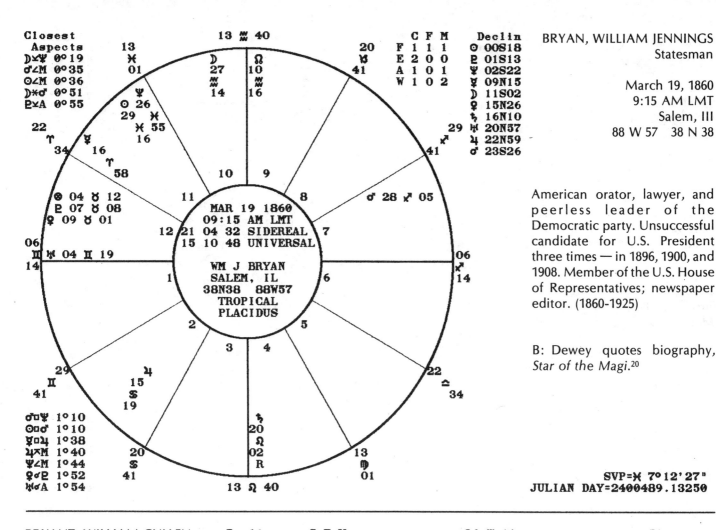

Closest Aspects

☽⚹♆ 0°19
♂∠M 0°35
☉∠M 0°36
☽⚹♂ 0°51
♇⚹A 0°55

♂□♆ 1°10
☉□♂ 1°10
☿□♃ 1°38
♃⚹M 1°40
♆∠M 1°44
♀⚹♇ 1°52
♅♂A 1°54

Declin

☉ 00S18
♇ 01S13
♆ 02S22
☿ 09N15
☽ 11S02
♀ 15N26
♄ 16N10
♅ 20N57
♃ 22N59
♂ 23S26

	C	F	M
F	1	1	1
E	2	0	0
A	1	0	1
W	1	0	2

MAR 19 1860
09:15 AM LMT
21 04 32 SIDEREAL
15 10 48 UNIVERSAL

WM J BRYAN
SALEM, IL
38N38 88W57
TROPICAL
PLACIDUS

BRYAN, WILLIAM JENNINGS
Statesman

March 19, 1860
9:15 AM LMT
Salem, Ill
88 W 57   38 N 38

American orator, lawyer, and peerless leader of the Democratic party. Unsuccessful candidate for U.S. President three times — in 1896, 1900, and 1908. Member of the U.S. House of Representatives; newspaper editor. (1860-1925)

B: Dewey quotes biography, *Star of the Magi.*[20]

SVP=♓ 7°12'27"
JULIAN DAY=2400489.13250

BRYANT, WILLIAM CULLEN
Writer

November 3, 1794
7:00 PM LMT
Cummington, Mass
72 W.55   42 N.28

Poet, editor, biographer, naturalist, traveler, and civic leader. An influence in his time who wrote his masterpiece, *Thanatopsis*, at age 17. Spent nearly half a century as co-owner and co-editor of the *Evening Post*. (1794-1874)

B: PC quotes *William Cullen Bryant* by Charles Brown, 1941; p. 4 states data from mother's diary.

Declin

☽ 05S25
♅ 11N13
♆ 11S19
☉ 15S24
♄ 17N19
☿ 23S19
♃ 23S29
♇ 23S41
♂ 24S20
♀ 27S25

	C	F	M
F	0	0	2
E	1	1	2
A	0	0	1
W	0	2	1

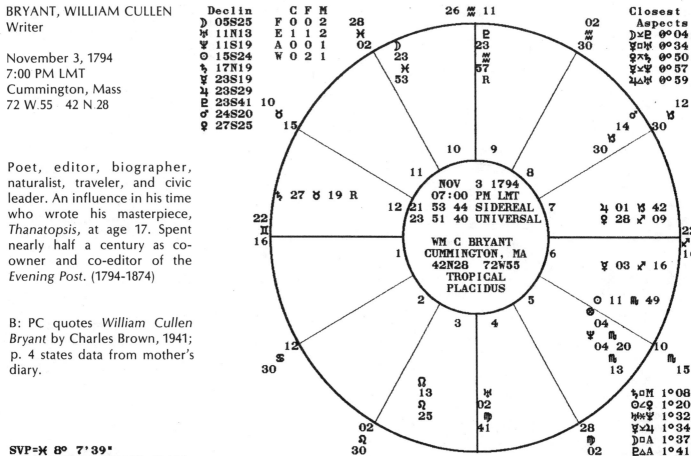

NOV 3 1794
07:00 PM LMT
21 53 44 SIDEREAL
23 51 40 UNIVERSAL

WM C BRYANT
CUMMINGTON, MA
42N28 72W55
TROPICAL
PLACIDUS

Closest Aspects

☽⚹♇ 0°04
☿□♅ 0°34
♀⚹♄ 0°50
☿⚹♆ 0°57
♃△M 0°59

♄□M 1°08
☉∠♀ 1°20
♅⚹♆ 1°32
☿∠♃ 1°34
☽□A 1°37
♇△A 1°41
♀⚹M 1°58

SVP=♓ 8° 7'39"
JULIAN DAY=2376612.49421

BUCKLEY, WILLIAM F.
Writer

November 24, 1925
5:45 PM EST
New York, N.Y.
73 W 57   40 N 45

Editor, publisher, and syndicated newspaper columnist. Though contentious and erudite, his magazine *National Review* is of conservative opinion. Narrator of the TV discussion show, *Firing Line*. First published book *God and Man at Yale*.

A: Dewey states, "time confirmed by his niece, from mother."

SVP=♓ 6°17'57"
JULIAN DAY=2424479.44792

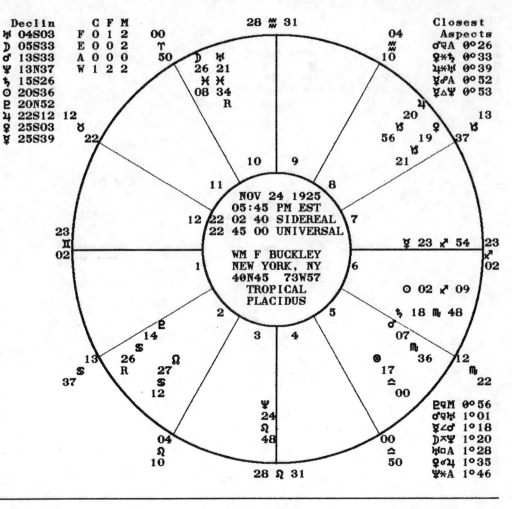

Declin		C F M				Closest Aspects
♅ 04S03	F 0 1 2					♂☌A 0°26
☽ 05S33	E 0 0 2					♀✶♄ 0°33
♂ 13S33	A 0 0 0					♃✶♅ 0°39
♆ 13N37	W 1 2 2					☿☍A 0°52
♄ 15S26						☿△♆ 0°53
☉ 20S36						
♇ 20N52						
♃ 22S12	12					
♀ 25S03						
☿ 25S39						

NOV 24 1925
05:45 PM EST
22 02 40 SIDEREAL
22 45 00 UNIVERSAL

WM F BUCKLEY
NEW YORK, NY
40N45 73W57
TROPICAL
PLACIDUS

♇☌M 0°56
♂☐♅ 1°01
☿☌♂ 1°18
☽⊼♆ 1°20
♅☐A 1°28
♀☌♃ 1°35
♆✶A 1°46

BURNELL, JOANNE
Fetal hibernation

September 30, 1977
5:25 AM BST
Brownhills, England
1 W 55   52 N 39

When her mother was two months pregnant, the fetus suspended growth for eleven weeks, a medically possible but rare occurrence. Healthy and normal birth after being in uterus for eleven months, (334 days.)

A: LMR, full data stated in the *National Enquirer*, January 1978.

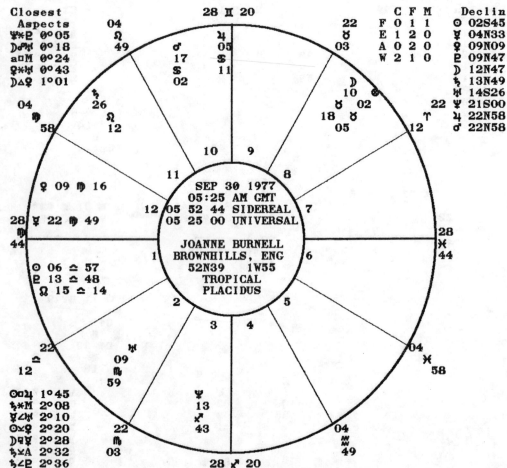

Closest Aspects		C F M			Declin
♆✶♇ 0°05		F 0 1 1			☉ 02S45
☽☐♅ 0°18		E 1 2 0			☿ 04N33
a☐M 0°24		A 0 2 0			♀ 09N09
♀✶♅ 0°43		W 2 1 0			♇ 09N47
☽△♀ 1°01					☽ 12N47
					♄ 13N49
					♅ 14S26
					♆ 21S00
					♃ 22N58
					♂ 22N58

SEP 30 1977
05:25 AM GMT
05 52 44 SIDEREAL
05 25 00 UNIVERSAL

JOANNE BURNELL
BROWNHILLS, ENG
52N39 1W55
TROPICAL
PLACIDUS

☉☐♃ 1°45
♄✶M 2°08
☿⊼♇ 2°10
☉✶♀ 2°20
☽☐☿ 2°28
♄✶A 2°32
♄⊼♇ 2°36

SVP=♓ 5°34'10"
JULIAN DAY=2443416.72569

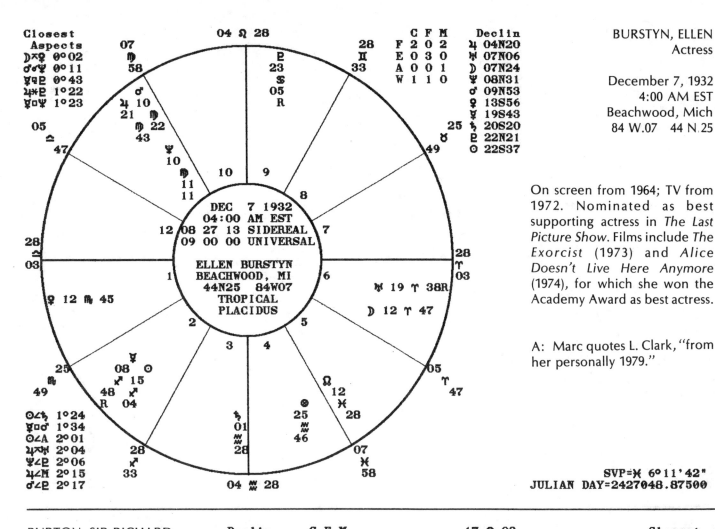

BURSTYN, ELLEN
Actress

December 7, 1932
4:00 AM EST
Beachwood, Mich
84 W.07   44 N.25

Closest
Aspects
☽⚹☿ 0°02
♂☌♆ 0°11
☿⚹♇ 0°43
♃⚹♇ 1°22
☿□♆ 1°23

DEC 7 1932
04:00 AM EST
08 27 13 SIDEREAL
09 00 00 UNIVERSAL

ELLEN BURSTYN
BEACHWOOD, MI
44N25 84W07
TROPICAL
PLACIDUS

☉⚹♄ 1°24
☿☌♂ 1°34
☉⚹A 2°01
♃⚹♅ 2°04
♆⚹♇ 2°06
♃⚹M 2°15
♂⚹♇ 2°17

On screen from 1964; TV from 1972. Nominated as best supporting actress in *The Last Picture Show*. Films include *The Exorcist* (1973) and *Alice Doesn't Live Here Anymore* (1974), for which she won the Academy Award as best actress.

A: Marc quotes L. Clark, "from her personally 1979."

SVP=♓ 6°11'42"
JULIAN DAY=2427048.87500

BURTON, SIR RICHARD
Adventurer

March 19, 1821
9:30 PM LMT
Hertford, England
0 W 04   51 N 48

British explorer, writer, and scholar of Islamic writings and languages. Traveled in Arabia, Ethiopia, and Africa, exploring the source of the Nile and writing books of his adventures. His famous translation of *The Arabian Nights* a classic. (1821-1890)

B: Pagan in *Pioneer to Poet*, "from him in the well-known biography by his wife."[21]

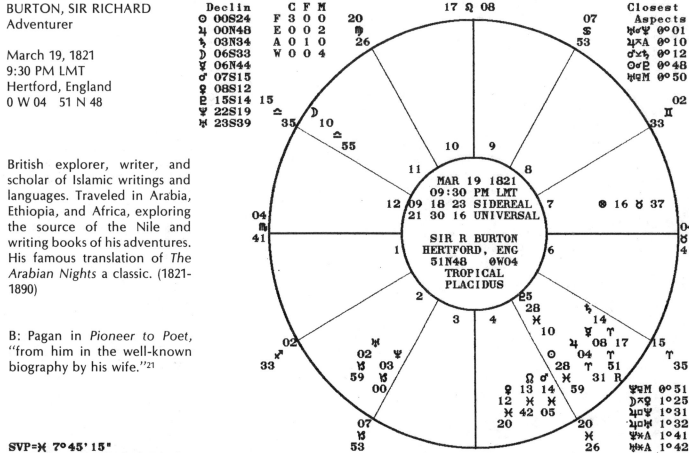

MAR 19 1821
09:30 PM LMT
09 18 23 SIDEREAL
21 30 16 UNIVERSAL

SIR R BURTON
HERTFORD, ENG
51N48 0W04
TROPICAL
PLACIDUS

Closest
Aspects
♅☌♆ 0°01
♃⚹A 0°10
♂⚹♄ 0°12
☉☌♇ 0°48
♅□M 0°50

♆□M 0°51
☽⚹☿ 1°25
♃□♅ 1°31
♃□M 1°32
♆⚹A 1°41
♅⚹A 1°42
♀☌♂ 1°45

SVP=♓ 7°45'15"
JULIAN DAY=2386244.39602

BURTON, ROBERT
Writer

February 18, 1577 NS
8:55 AM LMT
Lindley, England
1 W 00   52 N 30

Declin		C F M
♀	00S08	F 2 0 0
♃	09N15	E 0 1 1
☉	11S37	A 0 0 3
♂	11N48	W 1 1 1
☿	13S56	
♇	16S01	
☽	17S20	
♅	20S23	
♆	22N28	
♄	22S33	

Closest Aspects

☉☌♂	0°04
♀✳♅	0°12
☿✳A	0°13
♃△♄	0°25
☽✳♇	0°30

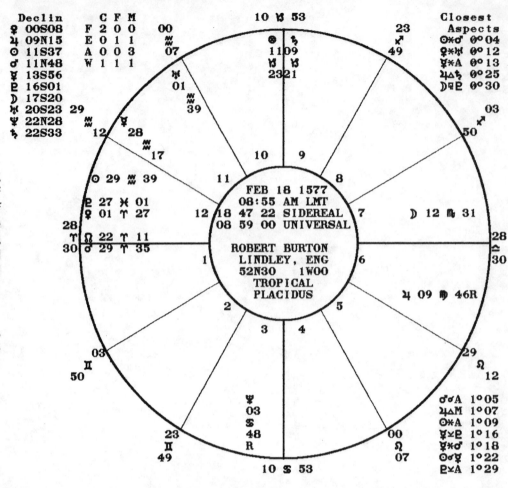

Astrologer, mathematician, scholar, reverend rector of Seagrave. Wrote *Anatomy of Melancholy* under the pseudonym *Democritus* (1621), apparently from deep personal awareness, since he was found hanging in his room in 1639.

A: BJA quotes his chart as recorded in his own file. Same data from Kraum in AFA, March 1962.[22]

SVP=♓11° 9'42"
JULIAN DAY=2297095.87431

Closest Aspects

♂⊼♆	0°01
☉✳A	0°11
☽⊼♇	0°26
♄✳♅	0°35
☿☌♂	0°39

C F M	Declin	
F 0 1 2	♅	06S44
E 0 0 1	♇	09N08
A 2 1 0	☉	12S25
W 1 2 0	♄	15N53
	♆	18N49
	☿	18S51
	♀	20S58
	♃	21S07
	☽	21N41
	♂	25S01

BYRD, RICHARD E.
Adventurer

October 25, 1888
11:30 AM EST
Winchester, Va
78 W 10   39 N 11

American rear admiral, aviator, and navigator who did more than any other man to direct the exploration of Antarctica between 1928-57. On May 6, 1926, with Floyd Bennett, became the first man to fly to the North Pole. His arctic base described in his book *Alone* 1938. (1888-1957)

A: CL quotes NAJ, April 1933, "data given by his mother."[23]

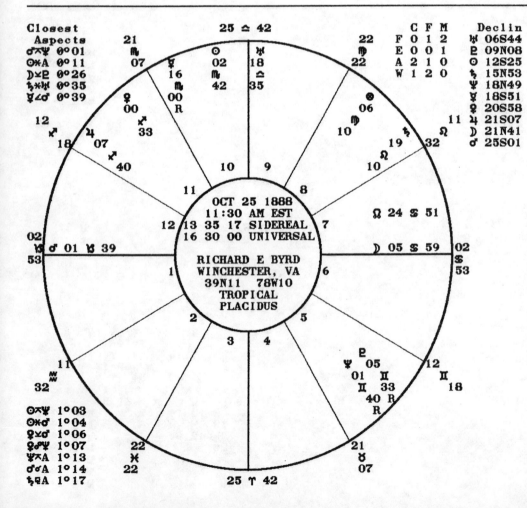

☉⊼♆	1°03
☉✳♂	1°04
♀⊼♆	1°06
☉✳♇	1°07
♆✳A	1°13
♂☌A	1°14
♄⊼A	1°17

SVP=♓ 6°49' 1"
JULIAN DAY=2410936.18750

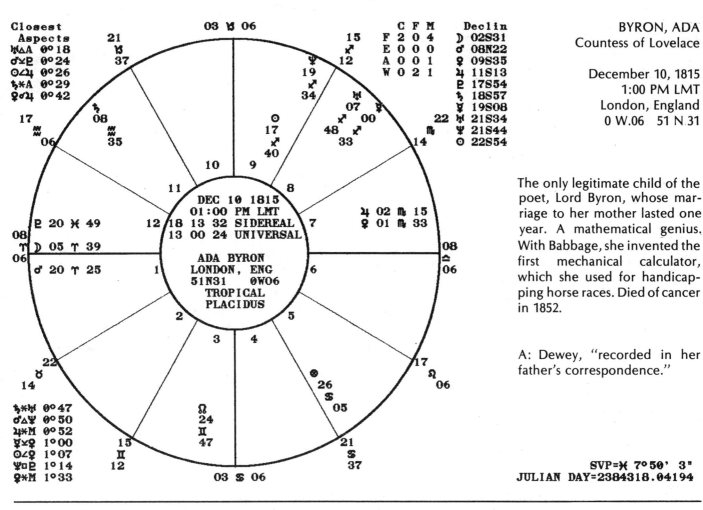

Closest Aspects

♅△A	0°18	
♂✶♇	0°24	
☉□♃	0°26	
♄✶A	0°29	
♀♂♃	0°42	

C	F	M	Declin	
F	2	0	4	☽ 02S31
E	0	0	0	♂ 08N22
A	0	0	1	♀ 09S35
W	0	2	1	♃ 11S13
				♇ 17S54
				♄ 18S57
				☿ 19S08
				♅ 21S34
				♆ 21S44
				☉ 22S54

BYRON, ADA
Countess of Lovelace

December 10, 1815
1:00 PM LMT
London, England
0 W.06   51 N.31

DEC 10 1815
01:00 PM LMT
18 13 32 SIDEREAL
13 00 24 UNIVERSAL

ADA BYRON
LONDON, ENG
51N31   0W06
TROPICAL
PLACIDUS

The only legitimate child of the poet, Lord Byron, whose marriage to her mother lasted one year. A mathematical genius. With Babbage, she invented the first mechanical calculator, which she used for handicapping horse races. Died of cancer in 1852.

A: Dewey, "recorded in her father's correspondence."

♄✶♅	0°47	
♂△♆	0°50	
♃□M	0°52	
☿✶♀	1°00	
☉∠♀	1°07	
♆□♇	1°14	
♀✶M	1°33	

SVP=♓ 7°50' 3"
JULIAN DAY=2384318.04194

BYRON, LORD
Poet

January 22, 1788
2:00 PM LMT
London, England
0 W 06   51 N 31

Born with a clubfoot; raised by an erratic mother after his father's death when he was age 3. Poor student but an avid reader. First poems published in 1806. Praised after 1812 as one of the great English Romantic poets. (1788-1824)

A: Dewey quotes NN #752, "family records in British museum."[24]

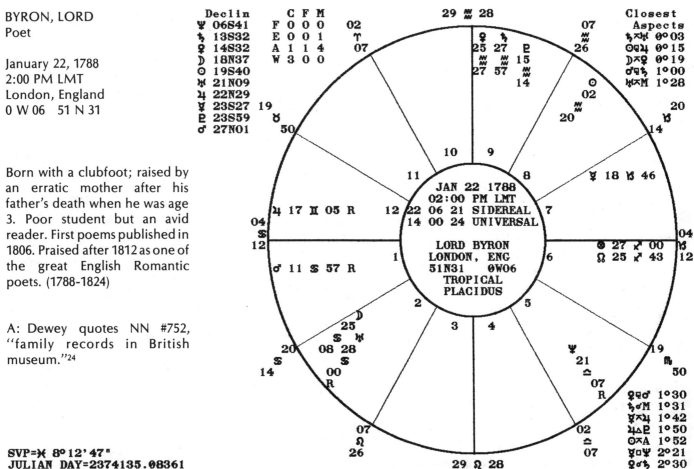

Declin	C	F	M
♆ 06S41	F	0	0	0
♄ 13S32	E	0	0	1
♀ 14S32	A	1	1	4
☽ 18N37	W	3	0	0
☉ 19S40			
♅ 21N09			
♃ 22N29			
♇ 23S27			
♂ 27N01			

JAN 22 1788
02:00 PM LMT
22 06 21 SIDEREAL
14 00 24 UNIVERSAL

LORD BYRON
LONDON, ENG
51N31   0W06
TROPICAL
PLACIDUS

Closest Aspects

♄✶♅	0°03	
☉□♃	0°15	
☽✶♀	0°19	
♂✶♄	1°00	
♅✶M	1°28	
♀□♂	1°30	
♄♂M	1°31	
☿✶♃	1°42	
♃△♇	1°50	
☉✶A	1°52	
☿□♆	2°21	
♀♂♄	2°30	

SVP=♓ 8°12'47"
JULIAN DAY=2374135.08361

CAGE, JOHN
Musician

September 5, 1912
5:00 AM PST
Los Angeles, Ca
118 W.15   34 N.04

Eclectically talented composer; avant-garde musician and music teacher; writer of essays and reviews, scores, and sketches. Photographer, reporter, and critic. Married, 1935. Biography written by R. Kostelanetz in 1970, *John Cage*.

A: CSH.

SVP=✕ 6°28'48"
JULIAN DAY=2419651.04167

Declin		C	F	M			Closest Aspects	
♂	00S06	F	0	1	1	06	♅⚹♇	0°01
♀	01N20	E	0	2	1		☽⚹♆	0°01
☉	06N51	A	3	1	0	07	♀⚹☿	0°13
☿	12N45	W	1	0	0		☽⚹☿	0°13
♇	17N21						♀⚹♇	0°33
♄	18N54							
♆	20N36							
♅	20S45							
♃	21S04							
☽	28N20							

♀△♅	0°35
♄☌M	0°57
♂△M	1°13
♃□A	1°35
♄□A	1°40
♂△♅	1°52
♂☍♇	1°53

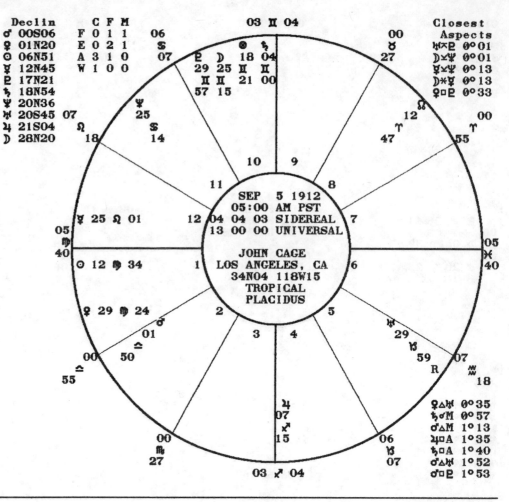

SEP 5 1912
05:00 AM PST
04 04 03 SIDEREAL
13 00 00 UNIVERSAL
JOHN CAGE
LOS ANGELES, CA
34N04 118W15
TROPICAL
PLACIDUS

CAMPBELL, GLEN
Singer, guitarist

April 22, 1936
8:14 PM CST
Delight, Ark
93 W.34   34 N.02

His country western and popular music includes "*Gentle on my Mind*" and "*By the Time I Get to Phoenix*." Started career as a guitarist in Hollywood for other vocalists. His own TV show, 1960-71. Films include *True Grit* and *Norwood*.

A: CL from *TV Guide*, May 2, 1970, p. 26.

Closest Aspects	
☽⚹♇	0°21
♀⚹♆	0°34
☽⚹♃	0°39
♀☌♂	0°41
☉∠♄	0°52

	C	F	M		Declin	
	F	1	0	1	♀	04N26
	E	5	1	0	♄	06S10
	A	0	0	0	♆	07N09
	W	1	0	1	☉	12N26
					♅	12N52
					♂	16N35
					☿	18N05
					☽	22N11
					♃	22S42
					♇	23N16

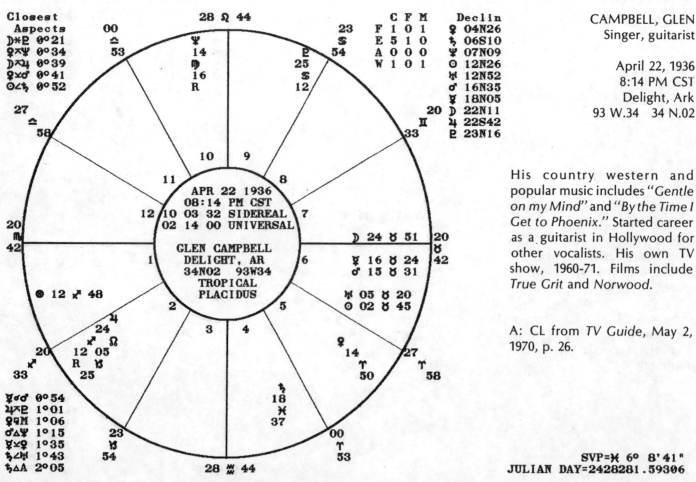

APR 22 1936
08:14 PM CST
10 03 32 SIDEREAL
02 14 00 UNIVERSAL
GLEN CAMPBELL
DELIGHT, AR
34N02 93W34
TROPICAL
PLACIDUS

☿☌♂	0°54
♃□♇	1°01
♀□M	1°06
♂△♆	1°15
☿⚹♀	1°35
♄∠♅	1°43
♄△A	2°05

SVP=✕ 6° 8'41"
JULIAN DAY=2428281.59306

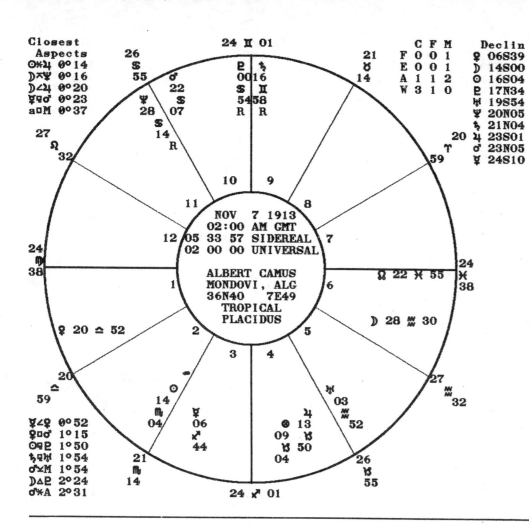

CAMUS, ALBERT
Writer

November 7, 1913
2:00 AM GMT
Mondovi, Algeria
7 E 49   36 N 40

Closest Aspects

☉✶♃	0°14
☽✶♇	0°16
☽△♃	0°20
☿♂♂	0°23
a□M	0°37

☿△♀	0°52
♀△♂	1°15
☉♂♇	1°50
♄♉♅	1°54
♂✶M	1°54
☽△♇	2°24
♂✶A	2°31

	C	F	M	Declin
F	0	0	1	♀ 06S39
E	0	0	1	☽ 14S00
A	1	1	2	☉ 16S04
W	3	1	0	♇ 17N34
				♅ 19S54
				♆ 20N05
				♄ 21N04
				♃ 23S01
				♂ 23N05
				☿ 24S10

NOV 7 1913
02:00 AM GMT
05 33 57 SIDEREAL
02 00 00 UNIVERSAL

ALBERT CAMUS
MONDOVI, ALG
36N40   7E49
TROPICAL
PLACIDUS

French essayist, novelist, and dramatist. Won the 1957 Nobel prize for literature. Technically skilled. Stressed humankind's need to carry out responsibilities in the fight against social evil. Books include *The Stranger* (1942) and *The Fall* (1957).

A: Gauquelin #168 Vol 6.

SVP=♓ 6°27'44"
JULIAN DAY=2420078.58333

CARPENTER, SCOTT
Astronaut

May 1, 1925
6:45 AM MST
Boulder, Colo
105 W 17   40 N 01

Declin		C	F	M
♅ 03S02	F	1	2	0
☿ 07N02	E	2	0	1
♄ 12S38	A	1	0	0
♀ 14N57	W	1	1	1
☉ 15N02				
♆ 15N12				
☽ 16N46				
♇ 20N59				
♃ 21S38				
♂ 24N33				

Made three orbits around the earth aboard the U.S. Mercury-Atlas 7. On May 1962 thought to be lost for forty-five minutes as he overshot the landing spot by about 250 miles. Later resigned from NASA to return to the Navy and pursue his interest in deep sea exploration.

A: CSH. (*Pioneers of Tomorrow* gives 2:00 PM, "from him.")

MAY 1 1925
06:45 AM MST
21 19 44 SIDEREAL
13 45 00 UNIVERSAL

SCOTT CARPENTER
BOULDER, CO
40N01 105W17
TROPICAL
PLACIDUS

Closest Aspects

♇✶A	0°11
☿□♃	0°21
☉♀♄	0°23
♄⊼A	0°26
♂□♅	0°36

♄△♇	0°38
☉✶A	0°49
☉△♂	0°58
♀✶♇	0°59
☉✶♇	1°01
♀✶A	1°10
♂△♄	1°21

SVP=♓ 6°18'23"
JULIAN DAY=2424272.07292

CARRADINE, DAVID
Actor

December 8, 1936
12:00 Noon PST
Hollywood, Ca
118 W 21   34 N 06

Stage, film, and star of TV series *Kung Fu*. Tempestuous private life included five hundred acid trips, naked neighborhood junkets, and a lawsuit for assault. By 1977 settled for shoes, marriage to his third lady, and deeper theatrical ambitions

A: CL from LA *Times*, September 22, 1968, "article by him."

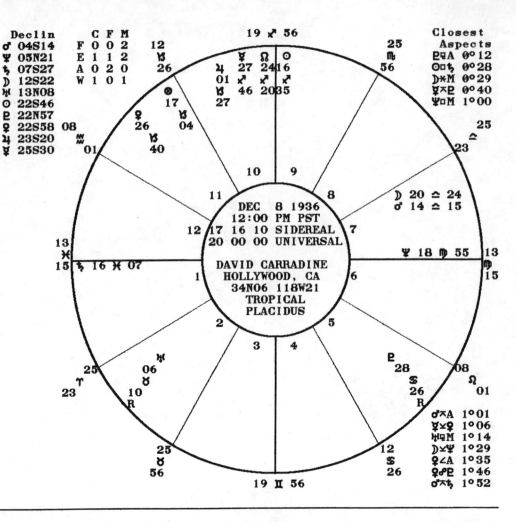

Declin		C	F	M
♂	04S14	F	0	0	2
♆	05N21	E	1	1	2
♄	07S27	A	0	2	0
☽	12S22	W	1	0	1
♅	13N08				
☉	22S46				
♇	22N57				
♀	22S58	08			
♃	23S20				
☿	25S30				

Closest Aspects
♇⊼A	0°12
☉⊼♄	0°28
☽✳M	0°29
☿⊼♇	0°40
♆□M	1°00
♂⊼A	1°01
☿⊼♀	1°06
♅□M	1°14
☽⊻♆	1°29
♀∠A	1°35
♀⊼♇	1°46
♂⊼♄	1°52

SVP=♓ 6° 8' 9"
JULIAN DAY=2428511.33333

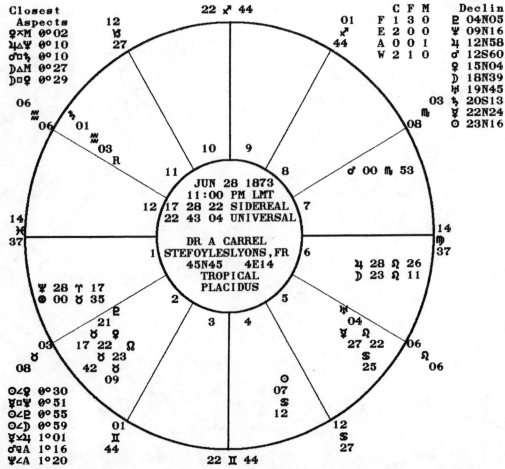

Closest Aspects
♀⊼M	0°02
♃△♆	0°10
♂∠♄	0°10
☽△M	0°27
☽□♀	0°29

	C	F	M	Declin	
	F	1	3	0	♇	04N05
	E	2	0	0	♆	09N16
	A	0	0	1	♃	12N58
	W	2	1	0	♂	12S60
					♀	15N04
					☽	18N39
					♅	19N45
					♄	20S13
					☿	22N24
					☉	23N16

☉∠♃	0°30
☿△♅	0°51
☉∠♇	0°55
☉⊼♆	0°59
☿⊼♃	1°01
♂∠A	1°16
♆∠A	1°20

CARREL, DR. ALEXIS
Scientist

June 28, 1873
11:00 PM LMT
Ste Foy Les Lyons, France
4 E 14   45 N 45

French surgeon and biologist who proved that tissues could survive apart from their organs if properly nourished. Won the 1912 Nobel prize in medicine for his work in blood vessel surgery and in transplanting organs and tissue. Books included *Man the Unknown* (1935). (1873-1944)

A: Gauquelin #130 Vol 2.²⁵

SVP=♓ 7° 1'47"
JULIAN DAY=2405338.44657

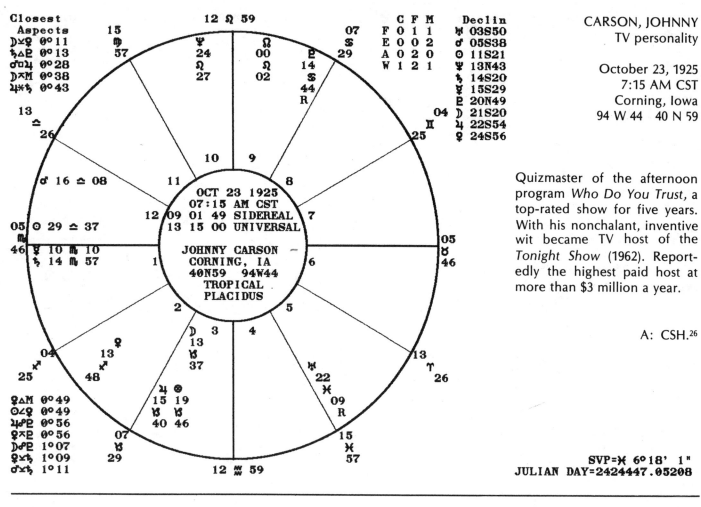

CARSON, JOHNNY
TV personality

October 23, 1925
7:15 AM CST
Corning, Iowa
94 W 44   40 N 59

Closest Aspects
D⚹⚥ 0°11
♄△♇ 0°13
♂□M 0°28
D✶M 0°38
♃✶♄ 0°43

	C F M	Declin
F	0 1 1	♅ 03S50
E	0 0 2	♂ 05S38
A	0 2 0	☉ 11S21
W	1 2 1	♆ 13N43
		♄ 14S20
		⚥ 15S29
		♇ 20N49
		D 21S20
		♃ 22S54
		♀ 24S56

12 ♌ 59
07 ♋ 29
♇ 14 ♋ 44 R
04 ♊ 25

15 ♍ 57
♆ 24 ♍ 27
00 ♌ 02

13 ♎ 26

♂ 16 ♎ 08

05 ♏ 46
☉ 29 ♎ 37
⚥ 10 ♏ 10
♄ 14 ♏ 57

05 ♉ 46

04 ♐ 25
♀ 13 ♐ 48

13 ♈ 26

D 13 ♑ 37
♃ 15 ♑ 40 ⊕ 19 ♑ 46

♅ 22 ♓ 09 R

07 ♑ 29

15 ♓ 57

12 ♒ 59

OCT 23 1925
07:15 AM CST
09 01 49 SIDEREAL
13 15 00 UNIVERSAL

JOHNNY CARSON —
CORNING, IA
40N59 94W44
TROPICAL
PLACIDUS

Quizmaster of the afternoon program *Who Do You Trust*, a top-rated show for five years. With his nonchalant, inventive wit became TV host of the *Tonight Show* (1962). Reportedly the highest paid host at more than $3 million a year.

A: CSH.[26]

SVP=♓ 6°18' 1"
JULIAN DAY=2424447.05208

♀△M 0°49
☉✶♀ 0°49
♃☌♇ 0°56
♀✶♇ 0°56
D☍♇ 1°07
♀✶♄ 1°09
♂✶♄ 1°11

CARTER, BILLY
First family

March 29, 1937
00:30 AM CST
Americus, Ga
84 W 13   32 N 03

Brother of President James Carter. Manager of the family $2.8 million peanut business. Married 1955; six children. Noted for beer-guzzling and for his availability to publicity hunters. In March 1979, entered Naval hospital for treatment for alcoholism.

A: Maxine Taylor in M.H., April 1979, states B.C.

Declin	C F M	
♄ 03S06	F	2 0 1
☉ 03N14	E	2 1 1
⚥ 04N16	A	0 0 0
♆ 06N08	W	1 1 1
♅ 13N43		
D 16S04		
♂ 19S56		
♀ 20N11		
♃ 21S24		
♇ 23N25		

21 ♎ 08
D 03 ♏ 49
18 ♏ 15
♆ 17 ♍ 02 R
17 ♍ 29

17 ♌ 18

09 ♌

♂ 03 ♐ 59
♃ 24 ♑ 00

☊ 17 ♐ 28

03 ♑ 30

MAR 29 1937
00:30 AM CST
13 18 07 SIDEREAL
06 30 00 UNIVERSAL

BILLY CARTER
AMERICUS, GA
32N03 84W13
TROPICAL
PLACIDUS

⊕ 29 ♋ 09
♇ 26 ♋ 31 R

03 ♋ 30

11 ♊ 15

♄ 26 ♈ 08 ☉ 08 ⚥ 12
♓ 51 ♈ 10 ♈ 21

♅ 05 ♉ 07
♀ 05 ♉ 48 R

18 ♉ 15

09 ♒ 18
17 ♒ 29

21 ♈ 08

Closest Aspects
D✶♂ 0°10
♄△♇ 0°19
D✶A 0°19
☉✶♅ 0°22
♂✶A 0°29

D∠♆ 1°47
♀✶♂ 1°48
D△♇ 1°58
♀☌♅ 2°00
♂∠M 2°09
♀△A 2°18
☉✶♀ 2°22

SVP=♓ 6° 7'53"
JULIAN DAY=2428621.77083

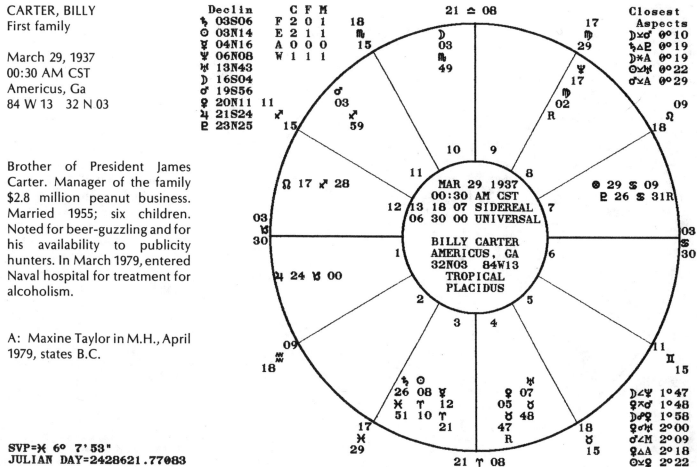

CARVALHO, CLARENCE
Homicide

July 4, 1925
3:18 AM AHST
Honolulu, Hawaii
157 W 52   21 N 19

Declin		C	F	M
⛢	02S31	F	0	3	1
♄	11S45	E	0	0	1
♆	14N52	A	0	0	0
☽	19S14	W	3	1	1
♂	20N09				
♇	20N57				
♀	21N19				
♃	22S24				
☿	22N25				
☉	22N54				

Closest Aspects
☉⚹A 0°10
☽⚹♃ 0°36
☉⚹♇ 1°00
♇⚼M 1°01
☿∠A 1°01

Homosexual assault and murder on September 11, 1949, and on October 2, 1949. The third victim on October 16, 1949, survived and identified him. Sentenced to thirty years in prison on December 5, 1952. Learned auto mechanics. Paroled in December 1968.

A: CL states B.C.

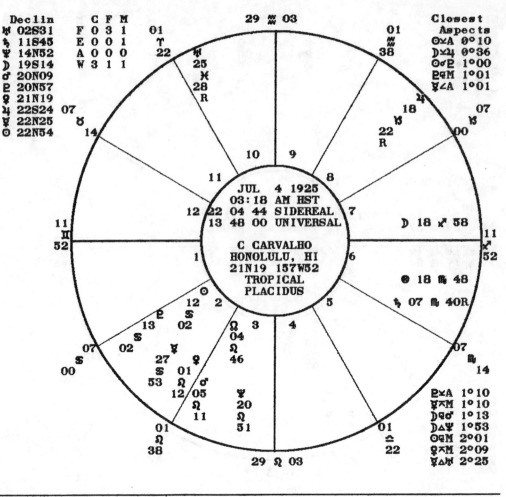

Closest Aspects
♇⚹A 1°10
☿⚼M 1°10
☽⚼♂ 1°13
☽△♆ 1°53
☉⚼M 2°01
♀⚹M 2°09
☿△⛢ 2°25

SVP=♓ 6°18'14"
JULIAN DAY=2424336.07500

Closest Aspects
♆⚹♇ 0°00
☽⚼♃ 0°08
⛢∠♇ 0°37
☽♇♆ 1°12
♃♆ 1°20

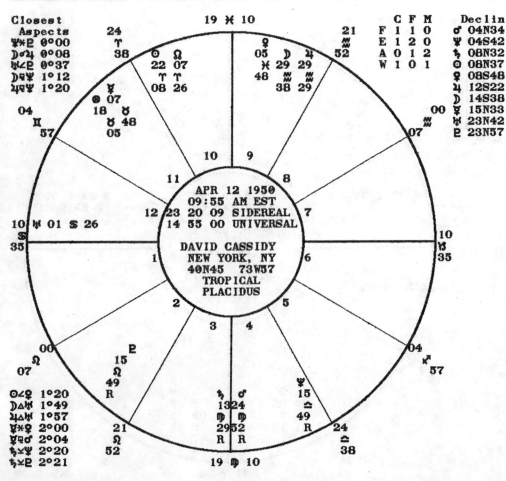

	Declin	C	F	M
♂	04N34	F	1	1	0
♆	04S42	E	1	2	0
♄	08N32	A	0	1	2
☉	08N37	W	1	0	1
♀	08S48				
♃	12S22				
☽	14S38				
☿	15N33				
⛢	23N42				
♇	23N57				

CASSIDY, DAVID
Singer, actor

April 12, 1950
9:55 AM EST
New York, N.Y.
73 W 57   40 N 45

Moved to Los Angeles in 1960 with his father, Jack Cassidy, and stepmother Shirley Jones. Became a young teeny-bopper hero as the TV star in series *The Partridge Family*. Recording artist. Retired at 25. Married Kay Lenz April 1977. Returned to TV in 1978 with *Police Story*.

A: Jansky, "from him to a colleague at work."

☉♂♀ 1°20
☽△♃ 1°49
♃△♆ 1°57
☿⚹♆ 2°00
☿⚹♇ 2°04
♄⚹♆ 2°20
♄⚹♇ 2°21

SVP=♓ 5°57'17"
JULIAN DAY=2433384.12153

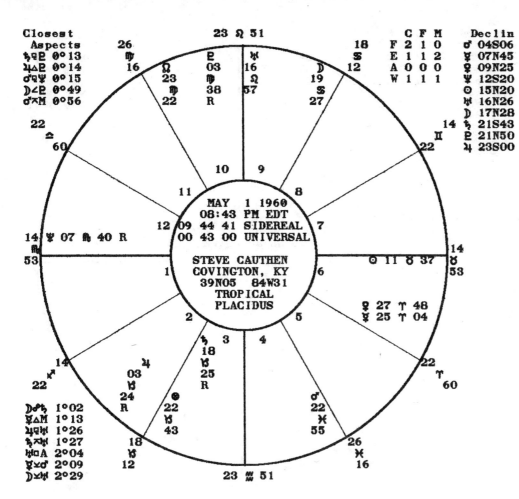

CAUTHEN, STEVE
Jockey

May 1, 1960
8:43 PM EDT
Covington, Ky
84 W.31   39 N 05

The "boy wonder" jockey from 1976, who once won twenty-three of fifty-four races in a single week. In two years won more than nine hundred races, including the Triple Crown in the spring of 1978. Rode two winners on New Year's day 1979, followed by a 110 losing streak, broken on February 1, 1979.

A: Jim Haynes states B.C.

SVP=♓ 5°48'53"
JULIAN DAY=2437056.52986

CELLINI, BENVENUTO
Artisan

November 12, 1500 NS
8:53 PM LMT
Florence, Italy
11 E.16   43 N.46

World renowned Renaissance artist and goldsmith; greatest designer of metal of the medieval period, if not of all time; also a fine sculptor. Fled to Rome after a duel, then to France. Author of a spirited, self-centered autobiography. (1500-1575)

A: Skeetz quotes Fagan in AA, August 1964, "taken from birth records."

SVP=♓12°13'39"
JULIAN DAY=2269239.33884

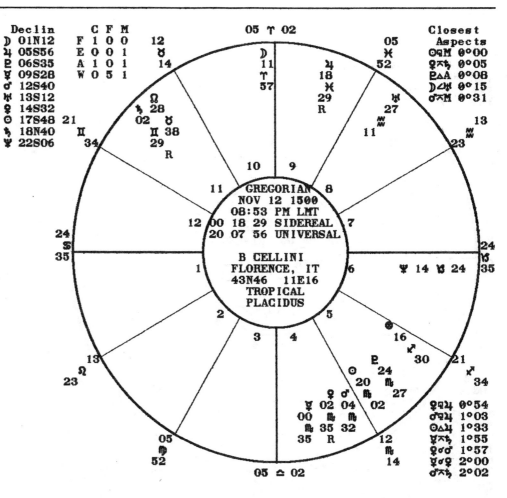

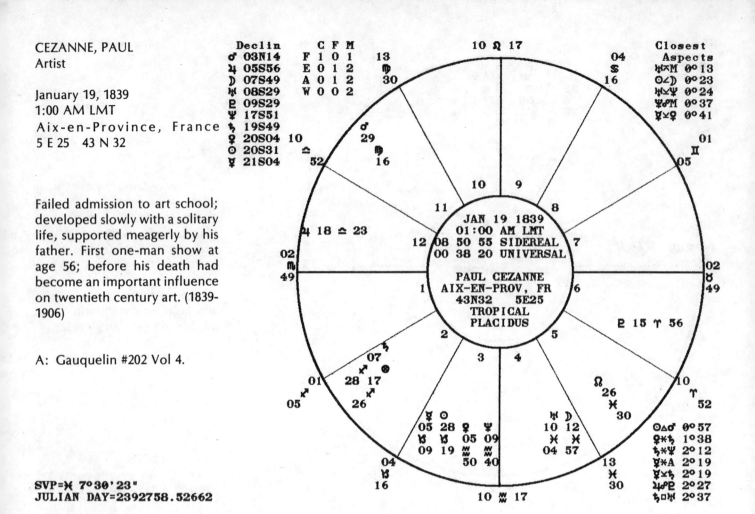

CEZANNE, PAUL
Artist

January 19, 1839
1:00 AM LMT
Aix-en-Province, France
5 E 25   43 N 32

Failed admission to art school; developed slowly with a solitary life, supported meagerly by his father. First one-man show at age 56; before his death had become an important influence on twentieth century art. (1839-1906)

A: Gauquelin #202 Vol 4.

SVP=✶ 7°30'23"
JULIAN DAY=2392758.52662

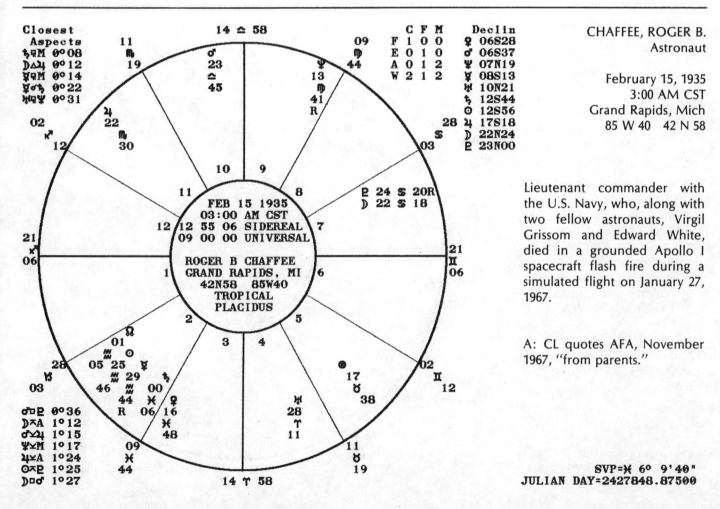

CHAFFEE, ROGER B.
Astronaut

February 15, 1935
3:00 AM CST
Grand Rapids, Mich
85 W 40   42 N 58

Lieutenant commander with the U.S. Navy, who, along with two fellow astronauts, Virgil Grissom and Edward White, died in a grounded Apollo I spacecraft flash fire during a simulated flight on January 27, 1967.

A: CL quotes AFA, November 1967, "from parents."

SVP=✶ 6° 9'40"
JULIAN DAY=2427848.87500

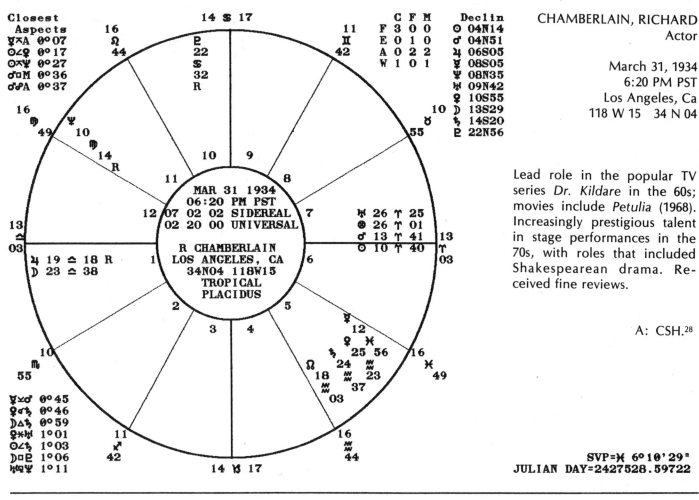

CHAMBERLAIN, RICHARD
Actor

March 31, 1934
6:20 PM PST
Los Angeles, Ca
118 W 15   34 N 04

Closest
Aspects
☿⚹A 0°07
☉∠♀ 0°17
☉⚹♇ 0°27
♂□M 0°36
♂☍A 0°37

14 ♋ 17

	C	F	M	Declin
F	3	0	0	☉ 04N14
E	0	1	0	♂ 04N51
A	0	2	2	♃ 06S05
W	1	0	1	☿ 08S05
				♆ 08N35
				♅ 09N42
				♀ 10S55
				☽ 13S29
				♄ 14S20
				♇ 22N56

MAR 31 1934
06:20 PM PST
07 02 02 SIDEREAL
02 20 00 UNIVERSAL

R CHAMBERLAIN
LOS ANGELES, CA
34N04 118W15
TROPICAL
PLACIDUS

Lead role in the popular TV series *Dr. Kildare* in the 60s; movies include *Petulia* (1968). Increasingly prestigious talent in stage performances in the 70s, with roles that included Shakespearean drama. Received fine reviews.

A: CSH.[28]

☿⚹♂ 0°45
♀☌♄ 0°46
☽△♄ 0°59
♀⚹♅ 1°01
☉∠♄ 1°03
☽□♇ 1°06
♅□♆ 1°11

SVP=♓ 6°10'29"
JULIAN DAY=2427528.59722

CHAMBERLAIN, WILT
Basketball star

August 21, 1936
11:27 PM EST
Philadelphia, Pa
75 W 10   39 N 57

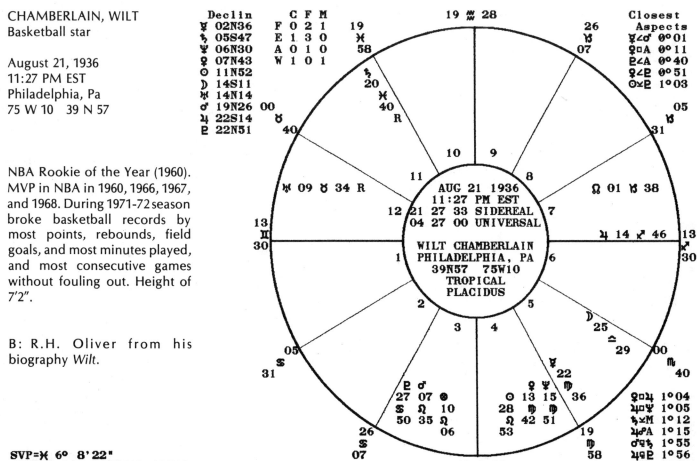

Declin		C	F	M
☿ 02N36	F	0	2	1
♄ 05S47	E	1	3	0
♆ 06N30	A	0	1	0
♀ 07N43	W	1	0	1
☉ 11N52				
☽ 14S11				
♅ 14N14				
♂ 19N26				
♃ 22S14				
♇ 22N51				

Closest
Aspects
☿∠♂ 0°01
♀□A 0°11
♇∠A 0°40
♀∠♇ 0°51
☉⚹♇ 1°03

AUG 21 1936
11:27 PM EST
21 27 33 SIDEREAL
04 27 00 UNIVERSAL

WILT CHAMBERLAIN
PHILADELPHIA, PA
39N57 75W10
TROPICAL
PLACIDUS

NBA Rookie of the Year (1960). MVP in NBA in 1960, 1966, 1967, and 1968. During 1971-72 season broke basketball records by most points, rebounds, field goals, and most minutes played, and most consecutive games without fouling out. Height of 7'2".

B: R.H. Oliver from his biography *Wilt*.

♀□♃ 1°04
♃□♆ 1°05
♄⚹M 1°12
♃♀A 1°15
♂♀♄ 1°55
♃♀♇ 1°56
☿♀♄ 1°56

SVP=♓ 6° 8'22"
JULIAN DAY=2428402.68542

CHAMBERS, JOE
Musician

August 22, 1942
1:00 PM CWT
Forest, Miss
89 W 29   32 N 22

One of thirteen farm children; four of the brothers formed a rock group, vocal and instrumental, that moved from gospel to soul to international rock-stardom. Albums include *The Chamber Brothers Greatest Hits* (1978).

A: From him (family Bible) to Amy Rodden, January 1979.

SVP=♓ 6° 3'45"
JULIAN DAY=2430594.25000

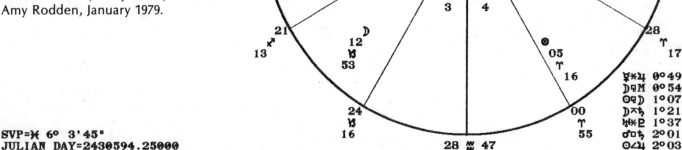

Declin		C F M		
Ψ 01N47		F 0 3 0		00
☿ 05N46		E 0 3 1		♎
♂ 07N23		A 2 0 0		55
☉ 11N49		W 1 0 0		
☽ 18S43				
♀ 19N03				
♄ 20N23				
♅ 20N53	28			
♃ 22N27	♎			
♇ 23N20	17			

Closest Aspects

☉♂M 0°13
Ψ☍M 0°18
☉⚹Ψ 0°31
☽△♂ 0°40
♀⚹♇ 0°48

♄ 11 ♊ 32
♅ 04 ♊ 26

☿⚹♃ 0°49
☽⚼M 0°54
☉⚼☽ 1°07
☽⚹♄ 1°21
♅⚹♇ 1°37
♂☌♄ 2°01
☉∠♃ 2°03

CHARLES, PRINCE
Royalty

November 14, 1948
9:14 PM GMT
London, England
0 W 06   51 N 31

First born son of Queen Elizabeth II and Prince Philip. Heir to the throne of England. Learned to be a sailor, airman, and soldier. Mastered the Welsh language and government studies at Cambridge. Speculation rife about whom he'll choose as his consort.

A: AFA, April 1973, from Judith Gee of England.

SVP=♓ 5°58'36"
JULIAN DAY=2432870.38472

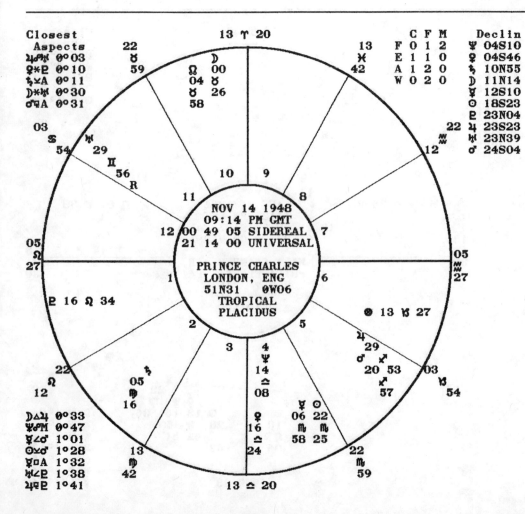

Closest Aspects

♃⚹♅ 0°03
♀⚹♇ 0°10
♄⚼A 0°11
☽⚹♅ 0°30
♂△A 0°31

	C F M	Declin	
	F 0 1 2	Ψ 04S10	
	E 1 1 0	♀ 04S46	
	A 1 2 0	♄ 10N55	
	W 0 2 0	☽ 11N14	
		☿ 12S10	
		☉ 18S23	
		♇ 23N04	
		♃ 23S23	
		♅ 23N39	
		♂ 24S04	

☽△♃ 0°33
Ψ⚼M 0°47
☿♂M 1°01
☉☌♂ 1°28
☿□A 1°32
♅∠♇ 1°38
♃⚼♇ 1°41

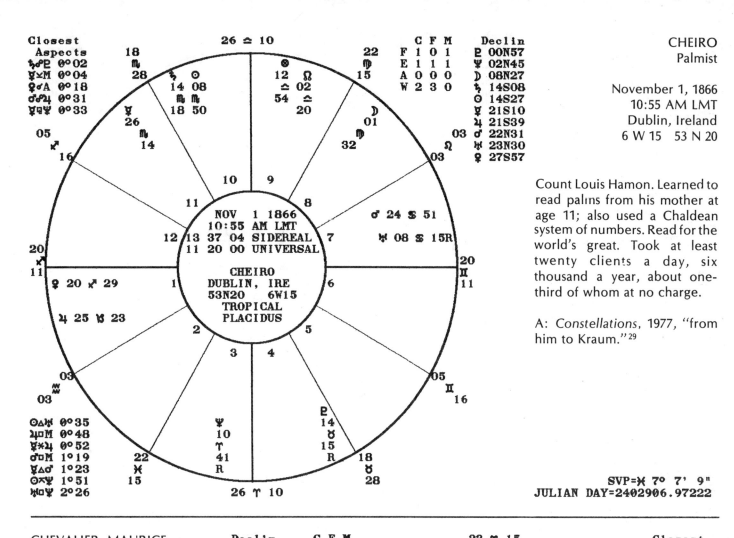

CHEIRO
Palmist

November 1, 1866
10:55 AM LMT
Dublin, Ireland
6 W 15   53 N 20

Closest Aspects

♄♂♇	0°02
☿⚹M	0°04
♀♂A	0°18
♂♃	0°31
☿∠♅Ψ	0°33

Declin

♇	00N57
Ψ	02N45
☽	08N27
♄	14S08
☉	14S27
☿	21S10
♃	21S39
♂	22N31
♅	23N30
♀	27S57

	C	F	M
F	1	0	1
E	1	1	1
A	0	0	0
W	2	3	0

NOV 1 1866
10:55 AM LMT
13 37 04 SIDEREAL
11 20 00 UNIVERSAL

CHEIRO
DUBLIN, IRE
53N20   6W15
TROPICAL
PLACIDUS

Count Louis Hamon. Learned to read palms from his mother at age 11; also used a Chaldean system of numbers. Read for the world's great. Took at least twenty clients a day, six thousand a year, about one-third of whom at no charge.

A: *Constellations*, 1977, "from him to Kraum."[29]

☉△♅	0°35
♃□M	0°48
☿⚹♃	0°52
♂□M	1°19
☿△♂	1°23
☉⚹Ψ	1°51
♅□Ψ	2°26

SVP=♓ 7° 7' 9"
JULIAN DAY=2402906.97222

CHEVALIER, MAURICE
Actor, singer

September 12, 1888
2:00 AM LMT
Paris, France
2 E.20   48 N.50

Born in the slums. Show career in Folies-Bergere, 1910. Hollywood films after the 30s. Nominated for Oscar as best actor in *The Love Parade* and *The Big Pond*. Delightful in *Gigi* (1958). Elegant and insouciant. Worth $4 to $6 million in property. (1888-1972)

A: Gauquelin #171 Vol 5.

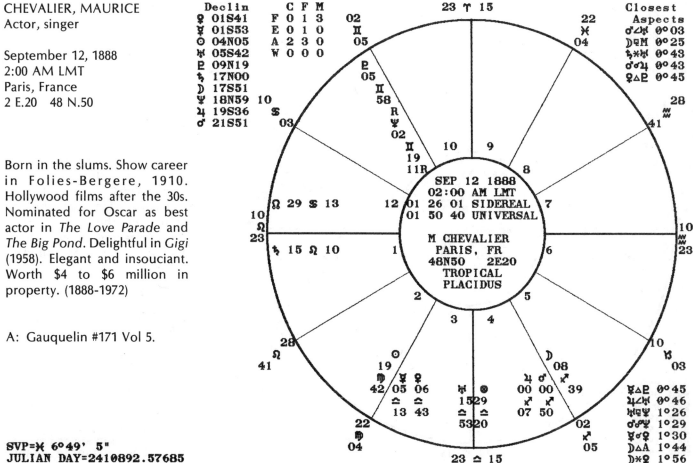

Declin

♀	01S41
☿	01S53
☉	04N05
♅	05S42
♇	09N19
♄	17N00
☽	17S51
Ψ	18N59
♃	19S36
♂	21S51

	C	F	M
F	0	1	3
E	0	1	0
A	2	3	0
W	0	0	0

SEP 12 1888
02:00 AM LMT
01 26 01 SIDEREAL
01 50 40 UNIVERSAL

M CHEVALIER
PARIS, FR
48N50   2E20
TROPICAL
PLACIDUS

Closest Aspects

♂∠♅	0°03
☽♇M	0°25
♄⚹♅	0°43
♂♂♃	0°43
♀△♇	0°45

☿△♇	0°45
♃∠♅	0°46
♅□Ψ	1°26
♂⚹Ψ	1°29
☿♂♀	1°30
☽△A	1°44
☽⚹♀	1°56

SVP=♓ 6°49' 5"
JULIAN DAY=2410892.57685

CHUBBUCK, CHRIS
News Commentator

August 24, 1944
5:15 AM EWT
Cleveland, Ohio
81 W 42   41 N 52

After promotion to public affairs director of a TV station in Florida, announced on July 15, 1974, "In keeping with our policy of bringing you the latest in blood and guts in living color, you are going to see another first - an attempted suicide." She shot herself with a .38 and died fourteen hours later.

A: Emmylu Landers in Dell, August 1975, from B.C.

SVP=ℋ 6° 2'13"
JULIAN DAY=2431326.88542

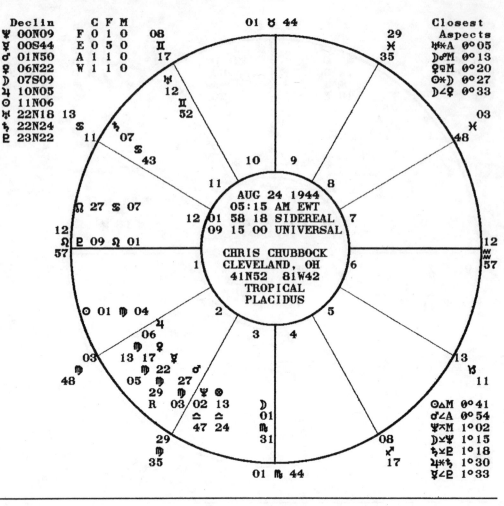

CHULALONGHORN, KING
Royalty

September 20, 1853
6:51 PM LMT
Bangkok, Thailand
100 E 31   13 N 45

Son of King Mongkut. Tutored by an Englishwoman, Anna Leonowens, (November 5, 1834). Made famous by the story *Anna and the King of Siam*. Became regent at age 15 upon his father's death. Ascended the throne in 1873.

A: CL from Dorothy Hughes in AFA, February 1971.

SVP=ℋ 7° 18'24"
JULIAN DAY=2398117.00620

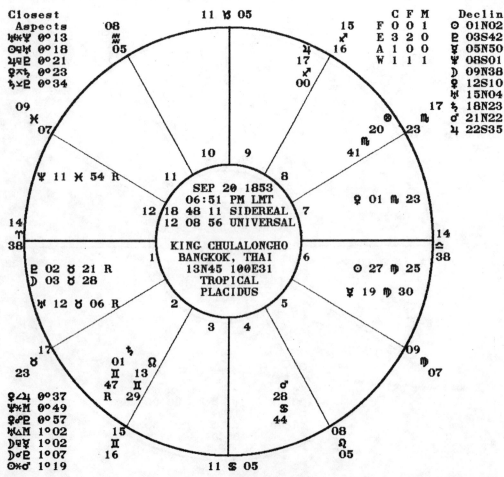

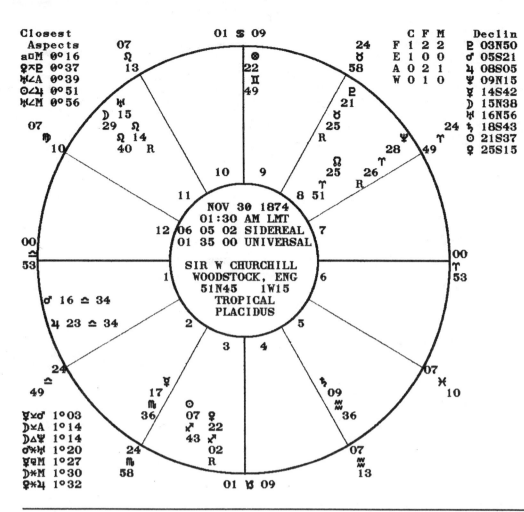

CHURCHILL, SIR WINSTON
Statesman

November 30, 1874
1:30 AM LMT
Woodstock, England
1 W 15   51 N 45

Prime minister of Great Britain (1940-45 and 1951-55). One of the great statesmen of world history and a legend in his own time. In 1953 knighted by the young Queen Elizabeth II. Awarded the Nobel prize in literature. (1874-1965)

B: T. Pat Davis quotes *Jennie* by R. G. Martin.[30]

Closest Aspects
a□M 0°16
♀✶♇ 0°37
♅∠A 0°39
☉∠♃ 0°51
♅∠M 0°56

♀✶♂ 1°03
☽✶A 1°14
☽△♇ 1°14
♂✶♅ 1°20
☿□M 1°27
☽✶M 1°30
♀✶♃ 1°32

	C	F	M
F	1	2	2
E	1	0	0
A	0	2	1
W	0	1	0

Declin
♇ 03N50
♂ 05S21
♃ 08S05
♆ 09N15
☿ 14S42
☽ 15N38
♅ 16N56
♄ 18S43
☉ 21S37
♀ 25S15

NOV 30 1874
01:30 AM LMT
06 05 02 SIDEREAL
01 35 00 UNIVERSAL

SIR W CHURCHILL
WOODSTOCK, ENG
51N45   1W15
TROPICAL
PLACIDUS

SVP=♓ 7° 0'30"
JULIAN DAY=2405857.56597

CLEMENCEAU, GEORGES
Statesman

September 28, 1841
9:30 PM LMT
Mouilleron, France
0 W 51   46 N 41

French patriot and statesman who led his country triumphantly through the last and most difficult period of World War I. Trained as a doctor; traveled and taught. Was mayor of Montmartre; served as deputy (1876); as premier (1906-09 and 1917). (1841-1929)

A: Gauquelin #162 Vol 2.

Declin
☉ 02S13
☽ 03S04
♅ 03S59
☿ 08S01
♇ 08S19
♀ 12N30
♆ 16S41
♃ 22S12
♄ 22S36
♂ 24S19

	C	F	M
F	1	1	3
E	0	0	0
A	0	2	1
W	0	0	2

Closest Aspects
☽□♂ 0°03
a△M 0°13
☿✶♇ 0°18
♄✶A 0°26
♃✶♆ 0°26

♂✶♆ 0°27
☽✶♆ 0°30
♄✶M 0°40
♂△♃ 0°52
♀☍M 0°52
☽□♃ 0°56
♀✶A 1°05

SEP 28 1841
09:30 PM LMT
21 59 56 SIDEREAL
21 33 24 UNIVERSAL

G CLEMENCEAU
MOUILLERON, FR
46N41   0W51
TROPICAL
PLACIDUS

SVP=♓ 7°27'56"
JULIAN DAY=2393742.39819

CLIBURN, VAN
Pianist

July 12, 1934
11:45 AM CST
Shreveport, La
93 W 45   32 N 31

Gained world fame in 1958 by winning the International Tchaikovsky Competition in Moscow against pianists from ninety countries. Began piano study at age 3 with his mother, a former concert pianist; later studied at Julliard.

A: Lockhart from B.C.[31]

SVP=♓ 6°10'13"
JULIAN DAY=2427631.23958

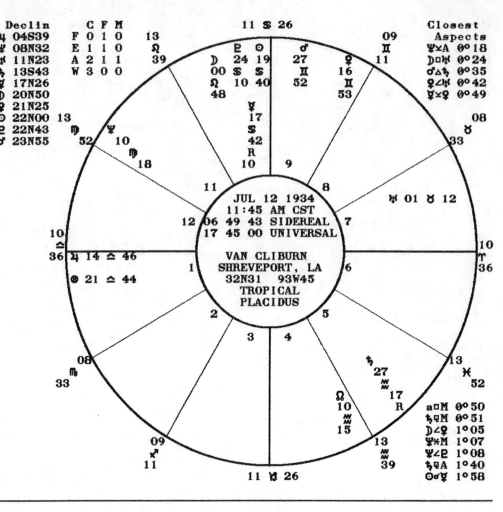

JUL 12 1934
11:45 AM CST
06 49 43 SIDEREAL
17 45 00 UNIVERSAL

VAN CLIBURN
SHREVEPORT, LA
32N31 93W45
TROPICAL
PLACIDUS

	Declin	C	F	M
♃	04S39	F 0	1	0
♆	08N32	E 1	1	0
♅	11N23	A 2	1	1
♄	13S43	W 3	0	0
☿	17N26			
☽	20N50			
♀	21N25			
☉	22N00			
♇	22N43			
♂	23N55			

Closest Aspects
♆☌A	0°18
☽□♅	0°24
♂△♄	0°35
♀∠♅	0°42
♀☌♀	0°49
a□M	0°50
♄□M	0°51
☽∠♀	1°05
♆*M	1°07
♆∠♇	1°08
♄□A	1°40
☉☌☿	1°58

CLIFT, MONTGOMERY
Actor

October 17, 1920
2:30 AM CST
Omaha, Neb
96 W 01   41 N 17

First film *Red River* made him an instant star. Nominated for an Oscar in *The Search*, *A Place in the Sun*, and *From Here to Eternity*. Brilliant first of the "method" actors, with deep emotional problems; homosexual, a drinker, and drug user. Died of a heart attack on July 23, 1966.

A: CL from B.C.

SVP=♓ 6°21'47"
JULIAN DAY=2422614.85417

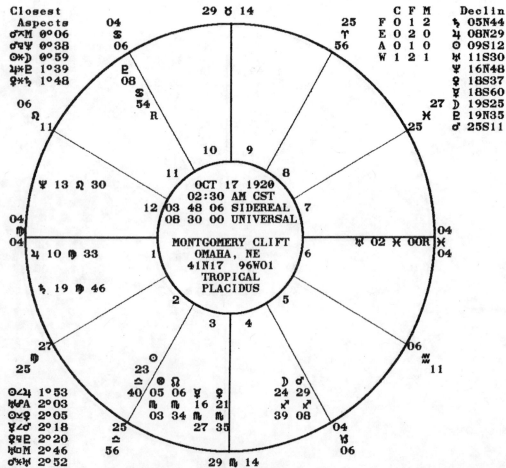

OCT 17 1920
02:30 AM CST
03 48 06 SIDEREAL
08 30 00 UNIVERSAL

MONTGOMERY CLIFT
OMAHA, NE
41N17 96W01
TROPICAL
PLACIDUS

Closest Aspects
♂*M	0°06
♂☌♆	0°38
☉*☽	0°59
♃*♇	1°39
♀*♄	1°48
☉∠♃	1°53
♅☌A	2°03
☉*♀	2°05
☿∠♂	2°18
♀□♇	2°20
♅□M	2°46
♂*♅	2°52

C	F	M		Declin
F 0	1	2	♄	05N44
E 0	2	0	♃	08N29
A 0	1	0	☉	09S12
W 1	2	1	♅	11S30
			♆	16N48
			♀	18S37
			☿	18S60
			☽	19S25
			♇	19N35
			♂	25S11

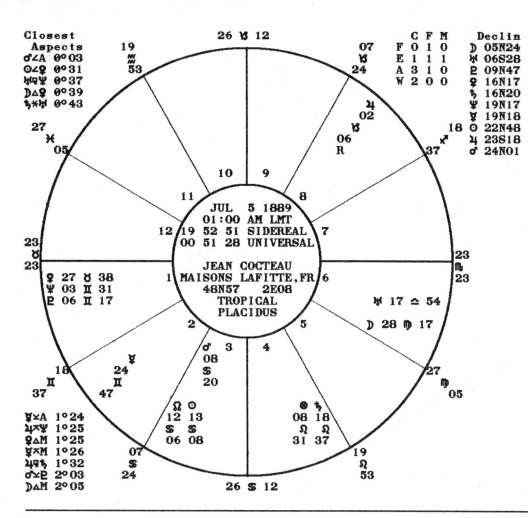

COCTEAU, JEAN
Artiste

July 5, 1889
1:00 AM LMT
Maisons Lafitte, France
2 E 08   48 N 57

French poet, novelist, critic, playwright, painter, and illustrator; also a stage and screen designer, and producer. Experimenter in many arts; constantly changing his style of work. Author of autobiography, *Professional Secrets* (1970). (1889-1963)

A: Gauquelin #237 Vol 4.[32]

SVP=⊬ 6°48'25"
JULIAN DAY=2411188.53574

Closest Aspects

♂∠♈	0°03
♂∠♀	0°31
♅♉	0°37
☽∆♈	0°39
♄⚹♅	0°43

☿⚹♈	1°24
♃⚹♆	1°25
♀∆♍	1°25
☿⚻♍	1°26
♃⚼♄	1°32
♂⚻♇	2°03
☽∆♍	2°05

Declin

☽	05N24
♅	06S28
♇	09N47
♀	16N17
♄	16N20
♆	19N17
☿	19N18
☉	22N48
♃	23S18
♂	24N01

CONNERY, SEAN
Actor

August 25, 1930
6:05 PM GDT
Edinburgh, Scotland
3 W 11   55 N 57

A 6'2" adonis who once competed for the Mr. Universe title. Joined an acting repertory company at 19; later was selected to play agent .007 in the *James Bond* series of films, which he grew to hate. Married; one child; divorced in 1971.

A: Craswell from B.C.

SVP=⊬ 6°13'48"
JULIAN DAY=2426214.21181

Declin

☿	01S33
☽	04N52
♅	05N14
♀	07S45
☉	10N51
♆	10N55
♇	21N54
♃	22N44
♄	22S45
♂	23N29

Closest Aspects

☉∠♀	0°19
♄♂♈	0°42
☿□♂	0°45
♀∠♆	1°11
♇∆♍	1°29

☉♂♆	1°30
♄∠♍	1°41
♀⚹♍	1°41
☉□♅	1°51
♆⚻♇	1°59
♄∆♈	2°11
♃□♅	2°11

COOGAN, JACKIE
Actor

October 26, 1914
2:51 AM PST
Los Angeles, Ca
118 W 15   34 N 04

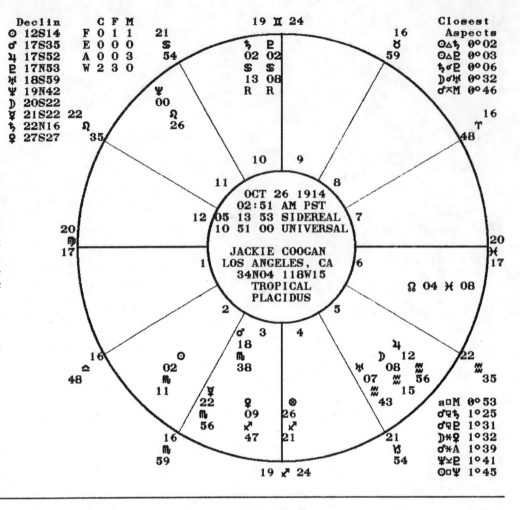

Declin		C F M
☉ 12S14	F 0 1 1
♂ 17S35	E 0 0 0
♃ 17S52	A 0 0 3
♇ 17N53	W 2 3 0
♅ 18S59	
♆ 19N42	
☽ 20S22	
☿ 21S22	
♄ 22N16	
♀ 27S27	

Closest Aspects
☉△♄ 0°02
☉△♇ 0°03
♄♂♇ 0°06
☽♂♅ 0°32
♂⊼M 0°46

a□M 0°53
♂♀♄ 1°25
♂♀♇ 1°31
☽⚹♀ 1°32
♂⚹A 1°39
♆⚹♇ 1°41
☉□♆ 1°45

OCT 26 1914
02:51 AM PST
05 13 53 SIDEREAL
10 51 00 UNIVERSAL

JACKIE COOGAN
LOS ANGELES, CA
34N04 118W15
TROPICAL
PLACIDUS

One of the greatest and most appealing of the American child actors. At the height of his earning power, his income dissipated by mismanagement and parental spending, a situation that resulted in labor laws to protect the income of working children.

A: CL from D.C. Doane, B.C.[33]

SVP=♓ 6°26'50"
JULIAN DAY=2420431.95208

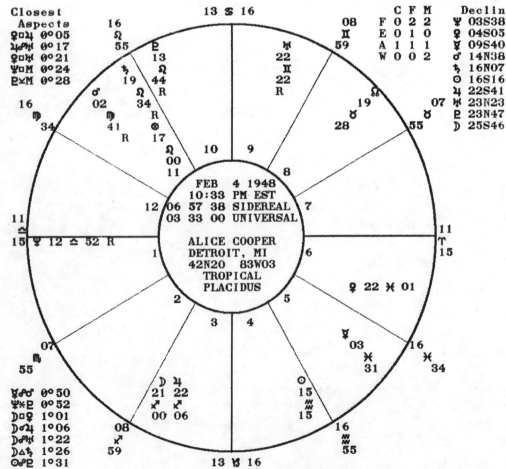

Closest Aspects
♀□♃ 0°05
♃♂♅ 0°17
♀□♅ 0°21
♆□M 0°24
♇⚹M 0°28

C F M	Declin
F 0 2 2	♆ 03S38
E 0 1 0	♀ 04S05
A 1 1 1	☿ 09S40
W 0 0 2	♂ 14N38
	♄ 16N07
	☉ 16S16
	♃ 22S41
	♅ 23N23
	♇ 23N47
	☽ 25S46

FEB 4 1948
10:33 PM EST
06 57 38 SIDEREAL
03 33 00 UNIVERSAL

ALICE COOPER
DETROIT, MI
42N20 83W03
TROPICAL
PLACIDUS

☿♂♂ 0°50
♆⚹♇ 0°52
☽□♀ 1°01
☽♂♃ 1°06
☽♂♅ 1°22
☽△♄ 1°26
☉♂♇ 1°31

COOPER, ALICE
Musician

February 4, 1948
10:33 PM EST
Detroit, Mich
83 W 03   42 N 20

American rock-star, flamboyant in makeup and weird stage effects in entertainment productions. Heavily into alcohol until his wife Sheryl (from March 1976) committed him to New York State Hospital to dry out in December 1977.

A: CSH.

SVP=♓ 5°59'16"
JULIAN DAY=2432586.64792

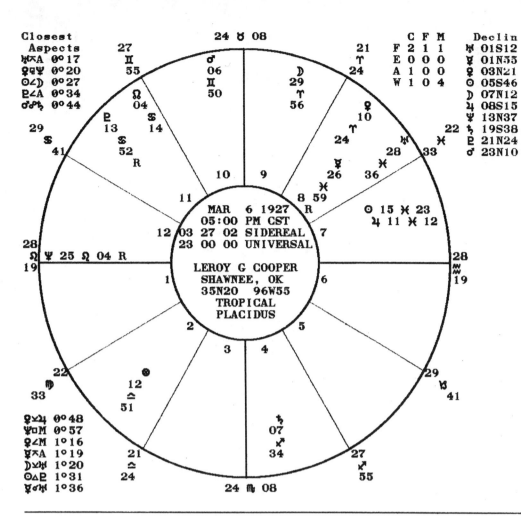

COOPER, LEROY GORDON
Astronaut

March 6, 1927
5:00 PM CST
Shawnee, Okla
96 W 55   35 N 20

Major USAF. Youngest of the seven original astronauts. Manned the fourth spacecraft Faith 7 on May 15, 1963, for twenty two orbits in thirty four hours, twenty minutes; conclusion of Project Mercury. Made the sixth manned space flight with Conrad on August 21, 1965, an eight-day journey.

A: From him to a private source, verified by LMR.

SVP=)(6° 16' 52"
JULIAN DAY=2424946.45833

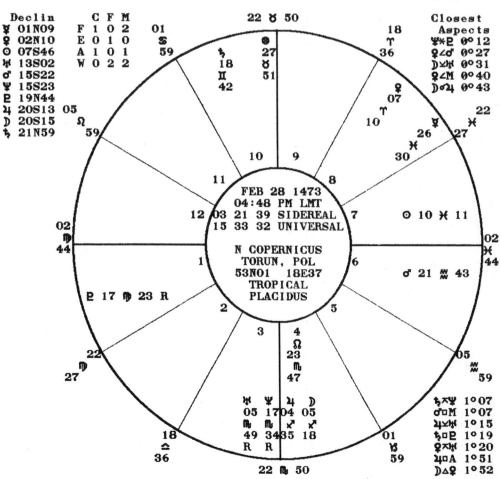

COPERNICUS, NICOLAUS
Astronomer

February 28, 1473 NS
4:48 PM LAT
Torun, Poland
18 E 37   53 N 01

Founder of modern astronomy; established the theory that the earth rotates daily on its axis and that planets revolve in orbits around the sun. Author of *Concerning the Revolutions of the Celestial Spheres* (1543). (1473-1543)

A: *Constellations*, 1977, from *Nicolaus Copernicus* by J. Szperkowicz; "data from astrologers present at his birth."

SVP=)(12° 36' 17"
JULIAN DAY=2259121.14829

COROT, JEAN-BATISSE
Artist

July 16, 1796
1:30 AM LMT
Paris, France
2 E.20   48 N 50

Landscape and figure painter; his portraits considered his best work. Studied art against his parents wishes in Italy (1825-28). Traveled a great deal on his small pension. Went through three major changes of style in his painting. (1796-1875)

A: Gauquelin #250 Vol 4.

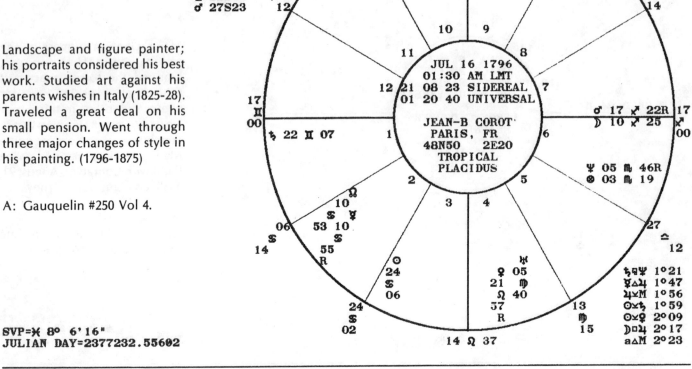

SVP=⅗ 8° 6'16"
JULIAN DAY=2377232.55602

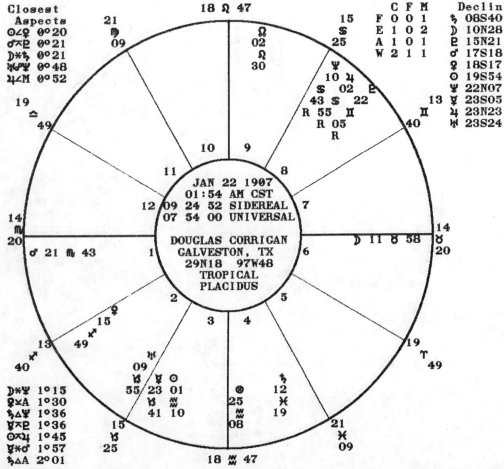

CORRIGAN, DOUGLAS
Pilot

January 22, 1907
1:54 AM CST
Galveston, Texas
97 W 48   29 N 18

Aviator who gained the nickname of "Wrong Way Corrigan" by flying in the wrong direction, arriving in Ireland on July 17, 1938, when he was headed for California. Earned about $35,000 from lectures, articles, and a movie about his misadventure.

A: CL from *Rising Star* magazine, September 1939, "data from him."

SVP=⅗ 6°33'41"
JULIAN DAY=2417597.82917

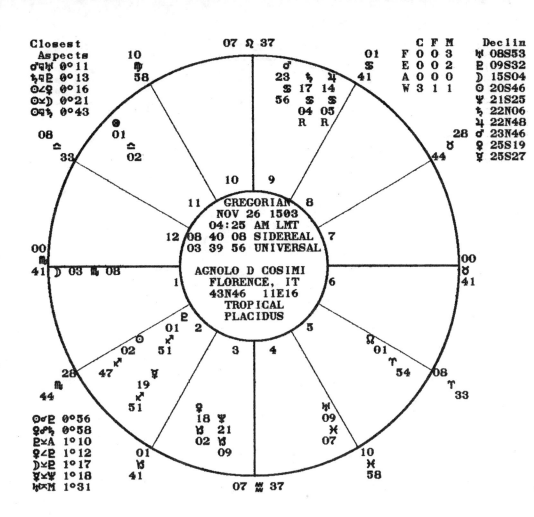

COSIMI, AGNOLO DI
Artist

November 26, 1503 NS
4:25 AM LMT
Florence, Italy
11 E.16   43 N 46

Il Brozino, one of the greatest portrait painters of the Medici court in the mid-16th century; greatest exponent of the style known as "mannerism". Adopted child and pupil of Pontormo. Most celebrated work now hangs in the National Gallery in London. (1503-1572)

B: Fagan in AA, March 1965, from *La Vita E Le Rime Di Angiolo Brozino* by Albertina Furno. [34]

SVP=⊬12°10'52"
JULIAN DAY=2270347.65273

COUBERT, GUSTAVE
Artist

June 10, 1819
3:00 AM LMT
Ornans, France
6 E 09   47 N.08

One of the developers of realism, whose works caused a scandal when first exhibited. When he was refused display in 1855, organized his own exhibits. Became involved in the Commune of Paris in 1871; imprisoned for his activities. (1819-1877)

A: Gauquelin #253 Vol 4.

SVP=⊬ 7°46'55"
JULIAN DAY=2385595.60792

COUSTEAU, JACQUES YVES
Oceanographer

June 11, 1910
1:15 PM Paris time
Ste Andre de Dubzac, France
0 W 27   44 N 59

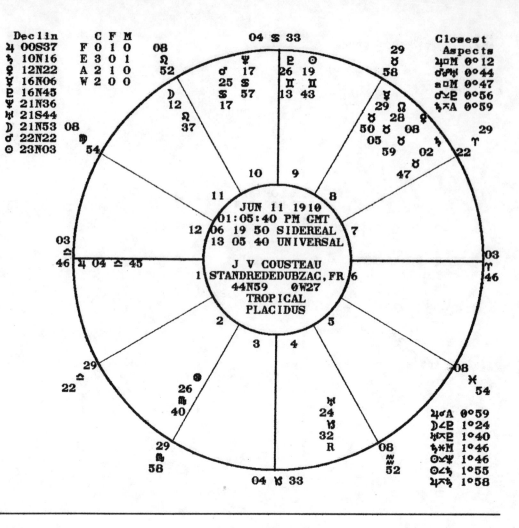

Declin		C	F	M
♃	00S37	F	0	1	0
♄	10N16	E	3	0	1
♀	12N22	A	2	1	0
☿	16N06	W	2	0	0
♇	16N45				
♆	21N36				
♅	21S44				
☽	21N53				
♂	22N22				
☉	23N03				

Closest Aspects
♃□M 0°12
♂♀♅ 0°44
☽□M 0°47
♂⚹♇ 0°56
♄⊼A 0°59

French underseas explorer who helped invent the Aqua-lung. With his crew, explored and photographed the ocean depths, salvaged sunken cargo, and aided scientific investigations. Author of *The Silent World.*

A: Gauquelin #444 Vol 3.

SVP=♓ 6°30'51"
JULIAN DAY=2418834.04560

♃♂A 0°59
☽∠♇ 1°24
♅⊼♇ 1°40
♄⚹M 1°46
☉⚹♆ 1°46
☉∠♄ 1°55
♃⊼♄ 1°58

Closest Aspects
☽△M 0°16
☉∠☽ 0°28
☉∠♀ 0°31
☽△♇ 0°40
♀△M 0°42

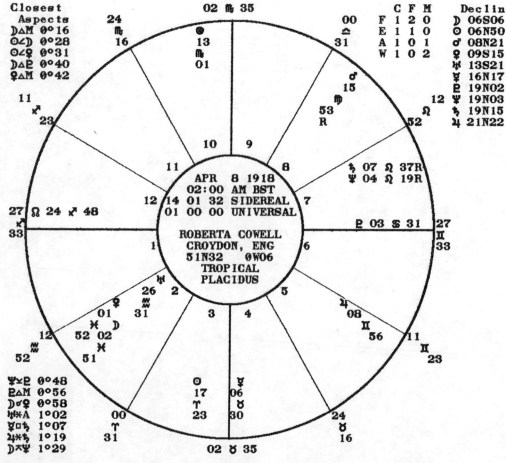

	C	F	M	Declin	
	F	1	2	0	☽	06S06
	E	1	1	0	☉	06N50
	A	1	0	1	♂	08N21
	W	1	0	2	♀	09S15
					♅	13S21
					☿	16N17
					♇	19N02
					♆	19N03
					♄	19N15
					♃	21N22

COWELL, ROBERTA
Transexual

April 8, 1918
2:00 AM BST
Croydon, Surrey, England
0 W.06   51 N 32

Father, a surgeon; mother, a fine pianist and singer. As Robert, was a racing motorist, a wartime fighter pilot; but stated that from the age of 10 felt to be a female soul. Made a sexual transition from age 30, with the final operation on May 17, 1971. Divorced the following year. Still loves sports, speed, and racing.

A: AQ, Winter 1954, "from her."

♆⚹♇ 0°48
♇△M 0°56
☽⚹♀ 0°58
♅⚹A 1°02
☿♂♄ 1°07
♃⚹♄ 1°19
☽⚹♆ 1°29

SVP=♓ 6°23'47"
JULIAN DAY=2421691.54167

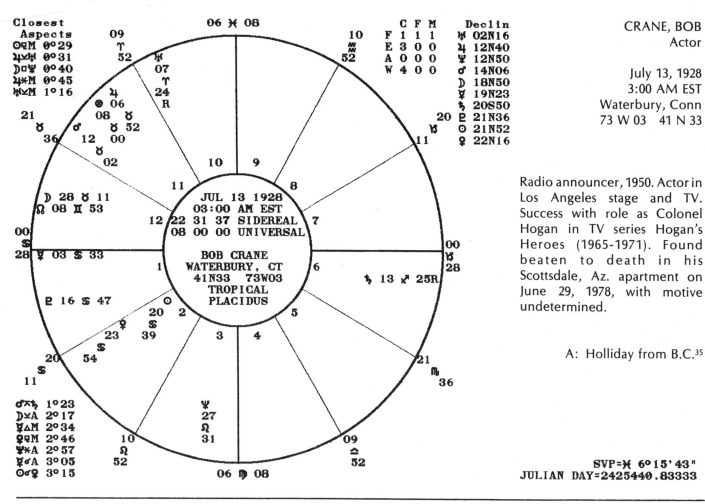

CRANE, BOB
Actor

July 13, 1928
3:00 AM EST
Waterbury, Conn
73 W 03   41 N 33

Radio announcer, 1950. Actor in Los Angeles stage and TV. Success with role as Colonel Hogan in TV series Hogan's Heroes (1965-1971). Found beaten to death in his Scottsdale, Az. apartment on June 29, 1978, with motive undetermined.

A: Holliday from B.C.[35]

SVP=✠ 6°15'43"
JULIAN DAY=2425440.83333

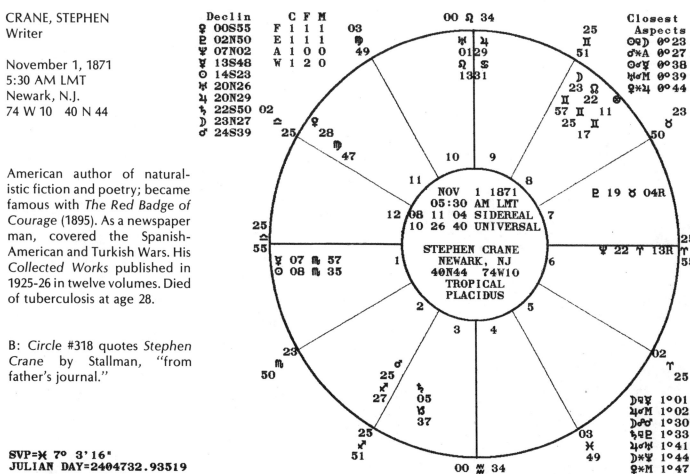

CRANE, STEPHEN
Writer

November 1, 1871
5:30 AM LMT
Newark, N.J.
74 W 10   40 N 44

American author of naturalistic fiction and poetry; became famous with *The Red Badge of Courage* (1895). As a newspaper man, covered the Spanish-American and Turkish Wars. His *Collected Works* published in 1925-26 in twelve volumes. Died of tuberculosis at age 28.

B: *Circle* #318 quotes *Stephen Crane* by Stallman, "from father's journal."

SVP=✠ 7° 3'16"
JULIAN DAY=2404732.93519

CRANE, STEPHEN
Restauranteur

February 7, 1917
11:00 PM CST
Crawfordsville, Ind
86 W 54   40 N 02

Once married to Lana Turner; came to their daughter Cheryl's defense when she stabbed her mother's lover to death on April 4, 1958; later put Cheryl in managerial position in one of his chain of restaurants.

A: CL quotes Reta Del Mar in Dell, July 1958, "data from him."

SVP=✶ 6°24'44"
JULIAN DAY=2421267.70833

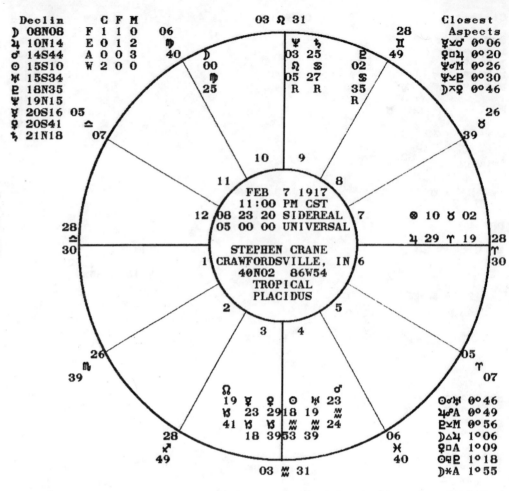

CROOKES, SIR WILLIAM
Scientist

June 17, 1832
5:30 PM LMT
London, England
0 W.06   51 N 31

English chemist and physicist who made many contributions; the foremost authority of his time on the industrial uses of chemistry. Invented the Crookes Tube, a radiometer and a spinthariscope. The founder and editor of The Chemical News. (1832-1919)

A: CL from WEMYSS Vol 11, "recorded in his diary."

SVP=✶ 7°36'10"
JULIAN DAY=2390352.22944

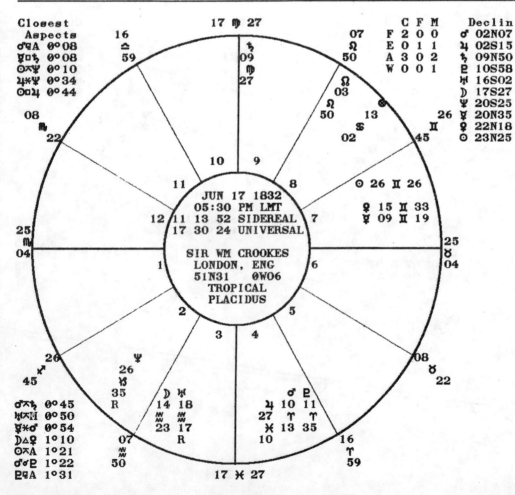

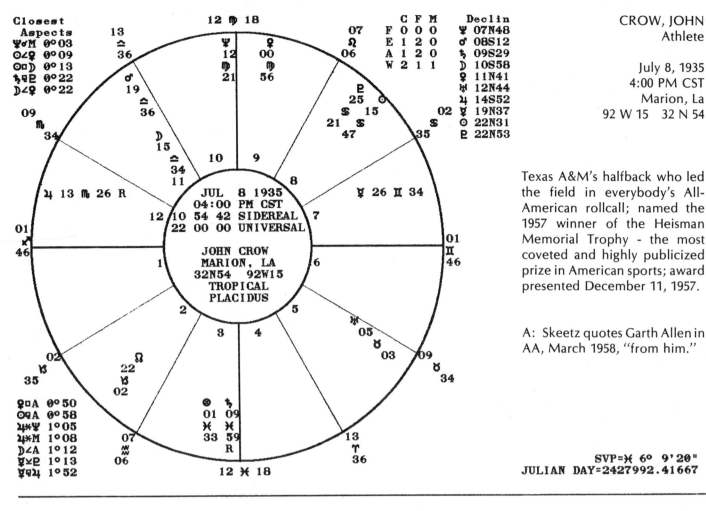

CROW, JOHN
Athlete

July 8, 1935
4:00 PM CST
Marion, La
92 W 15   32 N 54

Texas A&M's halfback who led the field in everybody's All-American rollcall; named the 1957 winner of the Heisman Memorial Trophy - the most coveted and highly publicized prize in American sports; award presented December 11, 1957.

A: Skeetz quotes Garth Allen in AA, March 1958, "from him."

SVP=♓ 6° 9'20"
JULIAN DAY=2427992.41667

CSONKA, LARRY
Football star

December 25, 1946
5:53 AM EST
Akron, Ohio
81 W 31   41 N 05

Big, brawny, 6'2", 237-pound fullback who played with the Dolphins from 1968-74; joined the Giants in 1976. Eclipsed records since he left college at Syracuse in 1968, but many injuries. Married; two sons.

A: CSH.

SVP=♓ 6° 0'16"
JULIAN DAY=2432179.95347

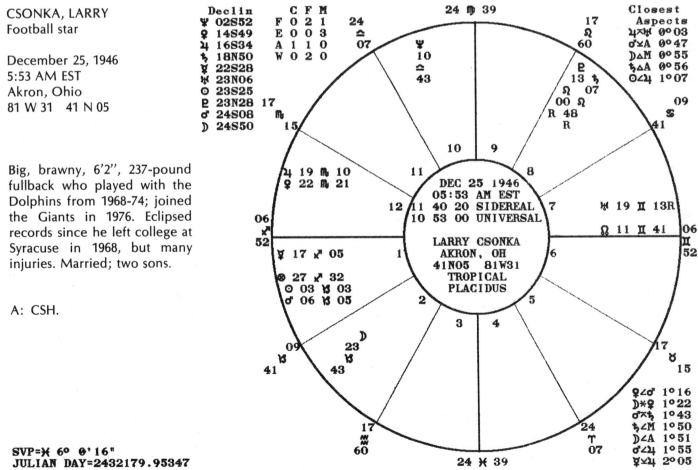

CUMMINGS, ROBERT
Actor

June 9, 1910
7:30 PM CST
Joplin, Miss
94 W 31   37 N 06

Hollywood's eternal juvenile, still youthful at 60. Broadway debut, 1931; films from 1935 include *Dial M for Murder* and *How to Be Very Popular*. TV series *My Hero* (1954) and *The Bob Cummings Show* (1955-59). Fourth marriage in 1971 to Regina Fong.

A: Circle #729 from *Righter's Guidebook*, 1957.[36]

SVP=✠ 6°30'52"
JULIAN DAY=2418832.56250

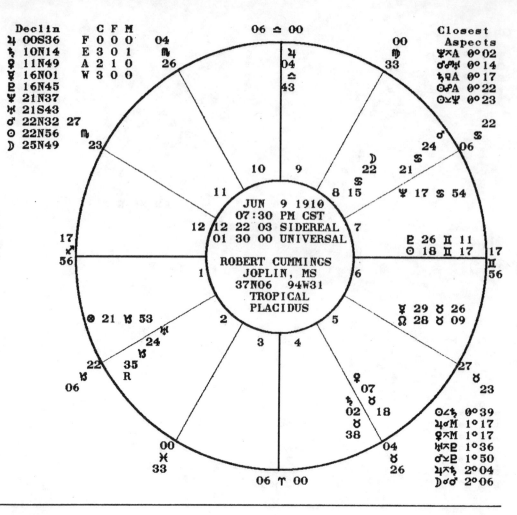

Declin		C	F	M
♃	00S36	F	0 0 0	04
♄	10N14	E	3 0 1	♏
♀	11N49	A	2 1 0	26
♇	16N01	W	3 0 0	
⛢	16N45			
♆	21N37			
♅	21S43			
♂	22N32	27		
☉	22N56	♏		
☽	25N49			

Closest Aspects
♆♈A 0°02
♂♐♅ 0°14
♄♈A 0°17
☉♐A 0°22
☉⚹♆ 0°23

☉♐♄ 0°39
♃♍M 1°17
♀♓M 1°17
♅♓♇ 1°36
♂⚹♇ 1°50
♃♐♈ 2°04
☽♂♂ 2°06

Closest Aspects
☿⚹♃ 0°09
☉⚹♀ 0°53
☿♐A 0°56
♃♐A 1°05
♂♐A 1°07

♆∠A 1°11
☽∠♇ 1°18
♅△♆ 2°01
☿♂♂ 2°03
☽⚹♄ 2°08
♂♃ 2°12
♀∠♄ 2°18

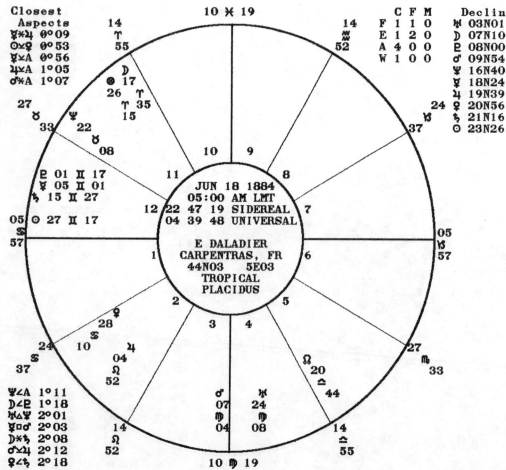

	C	F	M	Declin	
	F	1 1 0	♅	03N01
	E	1 2 0	☽	07N10
	A	4 0 0	♇	08N00
	W	1 0 0	♂	09N54
			♆	16N40
			☿	18N24
			♃	19N39
			♀	20N56
			♄	21N16
			☉	23N26

DALADIER, EDOUARD
Statesman

June 18, 1884
5:00 AM LMT
Carpentras, France
5 E.03   44 N 03

French radical socialist deputy from 1919-40; premier, 1933-34 and 1938-40. Agreed at Munich in 1938 to let Hitler partition Czechoslovakia. After France fell to Germany, imprisoned from 1941-45.

A: Gauquelin #1437 Vol 5.[37]

SVP=✠ 6°52'17"
JULIAN DAY=2409345.69431

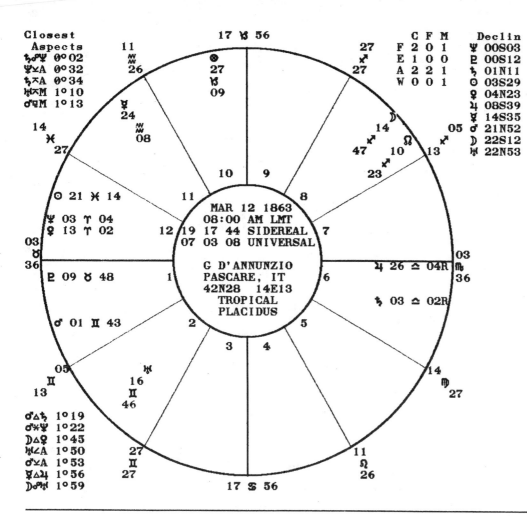

D'ANNUNZIO, GABRIELE
Prince

March 12, 1863
8:00 AM LMT
Pascare, Italy
14 E 13   42 N 28

Italian novelist, dramatist, and poet, who created a scandal by writing of his grand affair with Eleanor Duse in *The Flame of Love* (1900). Also an aviator and political leader who promoted patriotism and influenced Italy to enter World War I on the side of the Allies. (1863-1938)

A: Gauquelin #864 Vol 6.[38]

Closest Aspects
ħ♀Ψ 0°02
Ψ⊼A 0°32
ħ⊼A 0°34
�♅⊼M 1°10
♂⊻M 1°13

♂△ħ 1°19
♂✶Ψ 1°22
☽△♀ 1°45
♅∠A 1°50
♂⊻A 1°53
☿△♃ 1°56
☽♂♅ 1°59

C	F	M
F	2	0	1
E	1	0	0
A	2	2	1
W	0	0	1

Declin
Ψ 00S03
♇ 00S12
ħ 01N11
☉ 03S29
♀ 04N23
♃ 08S39
☿ 14S35
♂ 21N52
☽ 22S12
♅ 22N53

MAR 12 1863
08:00 AM LMT
19 17 44 SIDEREAL
07 03 08 UNIVERSAL

G D'ANNUNZIO
PASCARE, IT
42N28 14E13
TROPICAL
PLACIDUS

SVP=✶ 7° 9'54"
JULIAN DAY=2401576.79384

DAUMIER, HONORE
Artist

February 26, 1808
3:00 PM LMT
Marseille, France
5 E 23   43 N 19

French lithographer, caricaturist, and painter. Fame for biting satire; imprisoned once for six months in 1832 for a cartoon of King Louis Philippe. Produced about four thousand lithographs and some two hundred paintings; major recognition after his death. (1808-1879)

A: Gauquelin #269 Vol 4.

Declin
☿ 03S17
☽ 03S31
♂ 05S08
☉ 08S60
♅ 12S40
♃ 13S05
ħ 16S05
Ψ 19S28
♇ 19S35
♀ 20S02

C	F	M
F	0	0	1
E	0	0	1
A	0	0	1
W	0	2	5

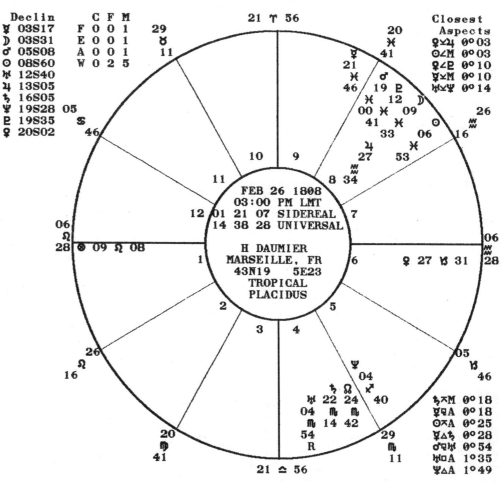

FEB 26 1808
03:00 PM LMT
01 21 07 SIDEREAL
14 38 28 UNIVERSAL

H DAUMIER
MARSEILLE, FR
43N19 5E23
TROPICAL
PLACIDUS

Closest Aspects
♀⊻♃ 0°03
☉∠M 0°03
♀∠♇ 0°10
☿⊻M 0°10
♅⊻Ψ 0°14

ħ⊼M 0°18
☿□A 0°18
☉⊼A 0°25
☿△♃ 0°28
♂□♅ 0°54
♅□A 1°35
Ψ△A 1°49

SVP=✶ 7°56' 1"
JULIAN DAY=2381474.11005

DA VINCI, LEONARDO
Universal genius

April 23, 1452 NS
9:40 PM LMT
Vinci, Italy
10 E 56 43 N 45

Inventor of engines of war; builder of moveable bridges and chariots; engineer skilled in science of artillery and sieges; sculptor and painter of brilliance. Experiments included oft-repeated attempt to build an airplane. (1452-1519)

B: Circle quotes *Leonardo Da Vinci*, published by Reynal and Co.[39]

Declin
☿ 01N31
♆ 01N33
♄ 02S54
☽ 06S29
♃ 11S49
☉ 12N46
♂ 17S39
♀ 19N15
♅ 22N06
♇ 26N02

	C	F	M
F	1	1	0
E	2	1	0
A	0	1	1
W	1	0	2

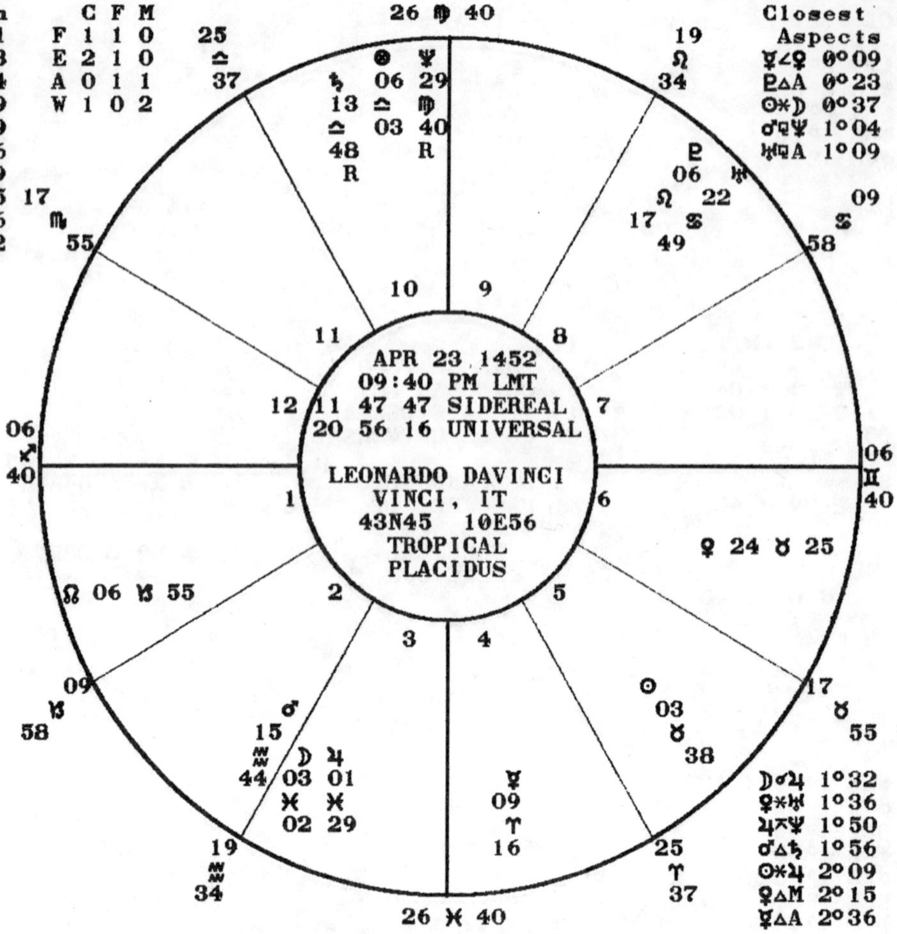
26 ♍ 40
APR 23 1452
09:40 PM LMT
11 47 47 SIDEREAL
20 56 16 UNIVERSAL
LEONARDO DAVINCI
VINCI, IT
43N45 10E56
TROPICAL
PLACIDUS
♀ 24 ♉ 25
☊ 06 ♑ 55
26 ♓ 40

Closest Aspects
☿∠♀ 0°09
♇△A 0°23
☉✶☽ 0°37
♂□♆ 1°04
♅□A 1°09

☽☌♃ 1°32
♀✶♅ 1°36
♃⊼♆ 1°50
♂△♄ 1°56
☉✶♃ 2°09
♀△M 2°15
☿△A 2°36

SVP=♓12°53'42"
JULIAN DAY=2251505.37241

Closest Aspects
♅△♆ 0°09
♄□♆ 0°13
☿⊻♂ 0°28
☉⊻♃ 0°35
♃□♇ 0°40

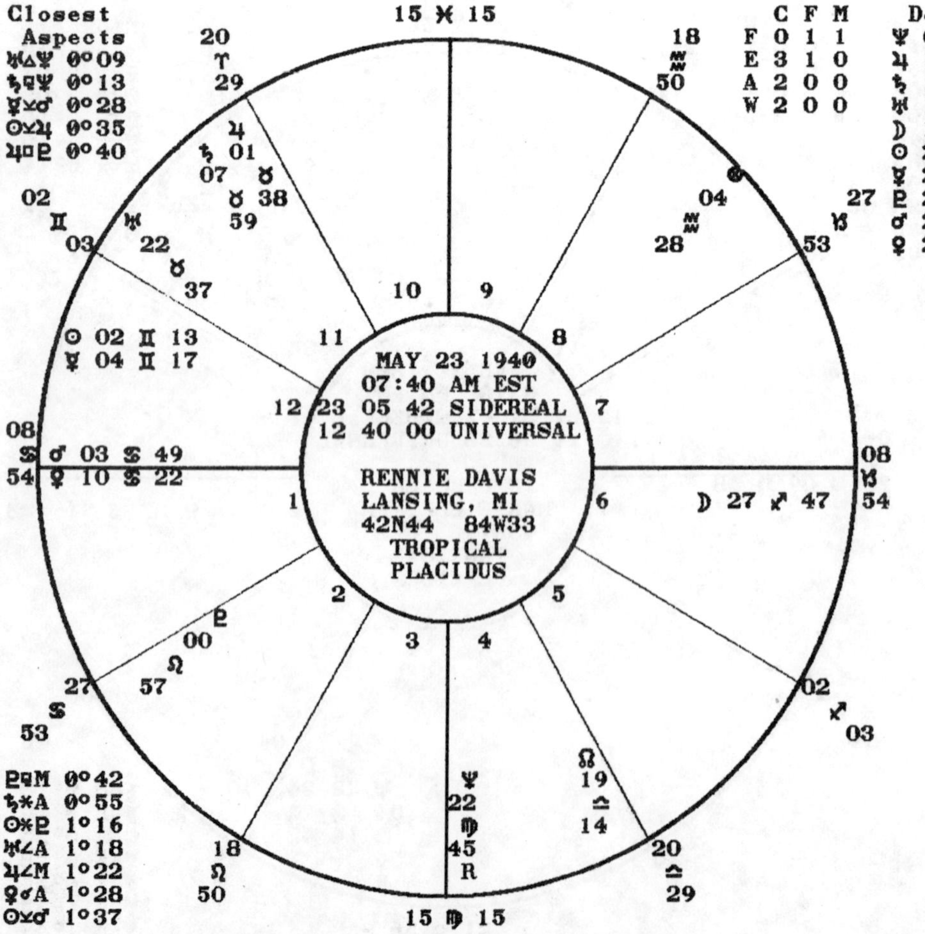
15 ♓ 15
MAY 23 1940
07:40 AM EST
23 05 42 SIDEREAL
12 40 00 UNIVERSAL
RENNIE DAVIS
LANSING, MI
42N44 84W33
TROPICAL
PLACIDUS
☉ 02 ♊ 13
☿ 04 ♊ 17
♂ 03 ♋ 49
♀ 10 ♋ 22
☽ 27 ♐ 47
15 ♍ 15

♇□M 0°42
♄✶A 0°55
☉✶♇ 1°16
♅∠A 1°18
♃∠M 1°22
♀☌A 1°28
☉⊻♂ 1°37

	C	F	M
F	0	1	1
E	3	1	0
A	2	0	0
W	2	0	0

Declin
♆ 04N01
♃ 11N02
♄ 12N05
♅ 18N10
☽ 18S38
☉ 20N37
☿ 21N39
♇ 23N42
♂ 24N31
♀ 26N20

DAVIS, RENNIE
Activist

May 23, 1940
7:40 AM EST
Lansing, Mich
84 W 33 42 N 44

Political activist with the Chicago Seven in the turbulent 60s. Spent three years in a Divine Light Ashram with guru Mahara Ji. Went into a third major life-phase in 1977, when he became a Hancock insurance broker with a wife and daughter.

A: CSH.

SVP=♓ 6° 5'27"
JULIAN DAY=2429773.02778

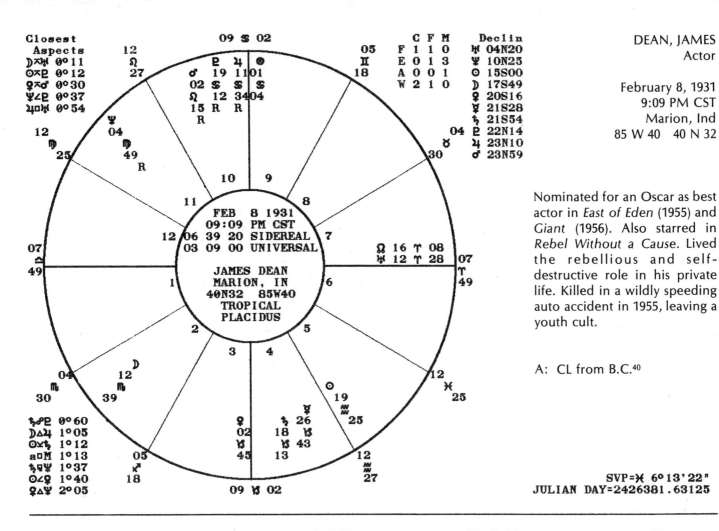

DEAN, JAMES
Actor

February 8, 1931
9:09 PM CST
Marion, Ind
85 W 40   40 N 32

Nominated for an Oscar as best actor in *East of Eden* (1955) and *Giant* (1956). Also starred in *Rebel Without a Cause*. Lived the rebellious and self-destructive role in his private life. Killed in a wildly speeding auto accident in 1955, leaving a youth cult.

A: CL from B.C.[40]

SVP=♓ 6°13'22"
JULIAN DAY=2426381.63125

DEAN, JOHN
Government official

October 14, 1938
2:55 PM EST
Akron, Ohio
81 W 31   41 N 05

In his autobiography, *Blind Ambition*, wrote his memoirs of the five years that began with his pre-Watergate introduction to President Richard Nixon and ended with the president's resignation in disgrace and Dean's own jail term.

A: Eshelman from B.C.

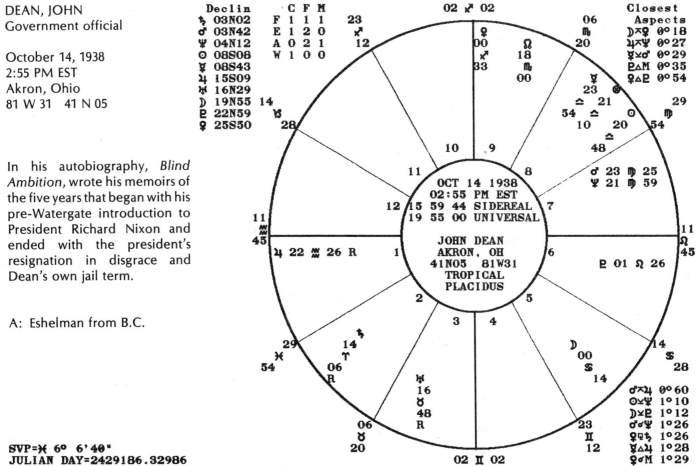

SVP=♓ 6° 6'40"
JULIAN DAY=2429186.32986

DEBUSSY, CLAUDE
Composer

August 22, 1862
4:30 AM LMT
St. Germain, France
2 E 06   48 N 53

Musical genius of the late 1800s, with his deft orchestration of works that include *The Prodigahfon*, *The Afternoon of a Faun*, and *The Sea*; also songs and piano music. Studied piano from age 7; later at the Paris Conservatory. Founded the impressionistic school. (1862-1918)

A: Gauquelin #1760 Vol 4.

SVP=♓ 7°10'21"
JULIAN DAY=2401374.68167

Declin		C	F	M
♆	00N00	F	2	2	0
♇	00S06	E	1	3	0
♃	01N17	A	1	0	0
♂	02N54	W	1	0	0
♄	04N50				
☉	11N54				
☿	12N31				
☽	19N27				
♀	20N05				
♅	23N09				

Closest Aspects
♄⚹A 0°21
☿⚹♀ 0°36
☉∠♃ 0°36
☽⚹♅ 0°53
☽⚹A 1°05

♇☌M 1°13
☽⚹♄ 1°26
♀⚹♃ 1°35
☿⚹♆ 1°46
☿☌♂ 1°47
♂⚹♅ 1°48
♅⚹A 1°58

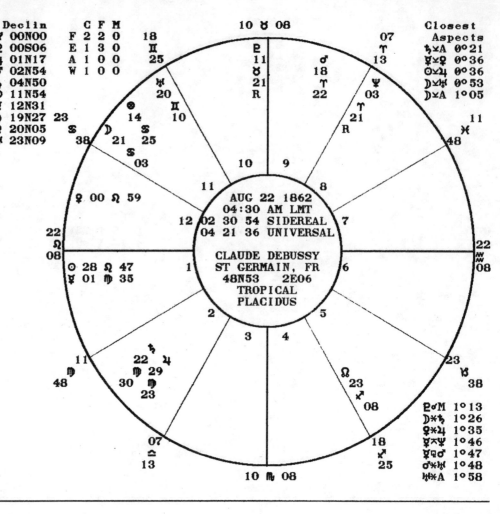

AUG 22 1862
04:30 AM LMT
02 30 54 SIDEREAL
04 21 36 UNIVERSAL
CLAUDE DEBUSSY
ST GERMAIN, FR
48N53 2E06
TROPICAL
PLACIDUS

Closest Aspects
♀⚹♆ 0°19
☽∠♀ 0°37
☉⚹♅ 0°55
♄⚹M 1°01
☽□♇ 1°15

JUL 19 1834
08:30 PM LMT
16 18 35 SIDEREAL
20 20 40 UNIVERSAL
EDGAR DEGAS
PARIS, FR
48N50 2E20
TROPICAL
PLACIDUS

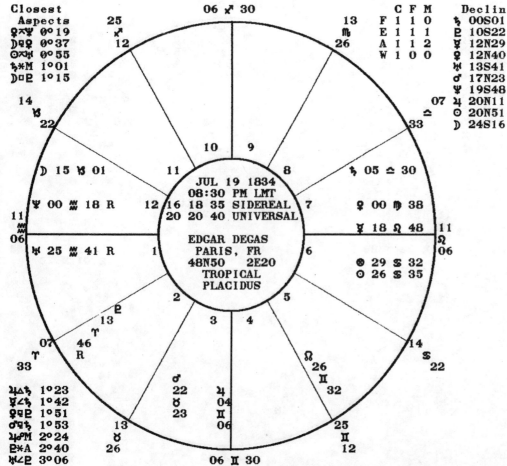

♃△♄ 1°23
☿∠♄ 1°42
♀□♇ 1°51
♂□♄ 1°53
♃□M 2°24
♇⚹A 2°40
♅∠♇ 3°06

	C	F	M	Declin	
	F	1	1	0	♄	00S01
	E	1	1	1	♇	10S22
	A	1	1	2	☿	12N29
	W	1	0	0	♀	12N40
					♅	13S41
					♂	17N23
					♆	19S48
					♃	20N11
					☉	20N51
					☽	24S16

DEGAS, EDGAR
Artist

July 19, 1834
8:30 PM LMT
Paris, France
2 E.20   48 N 50

French painter, pastelist, and sculptor. From a wealthy family; developed his style without the need to please the critics or public. A difficult person in friendships; broke with impressionistic painters in 1886 and became a virtual recluse. (1834-1917)

A: Gauquelin #281 Vol 4.

SVP=♓ 7°34'27"
JULIAN DAY=2391114.34769

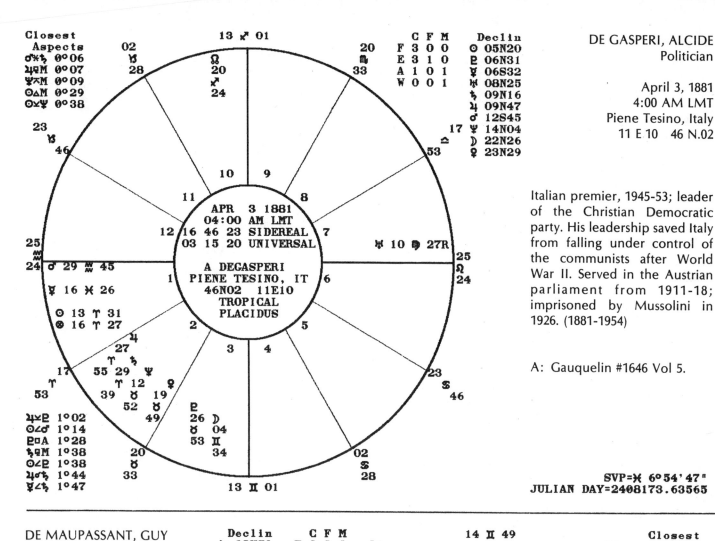

DE GASPERI, ALCIDE
Politician

April 3, 1881
4:00 AM LMT
Piene Tesino, Italy
11 E 10   46 N.02

Italian premier, 1945-53; leader of the Christian Democratic party. His leadership saved Italy from falling under control of the communists after World War II. Served in the Austrian parliament from 1911-18; imprisoned by Mussolini in 1926. (1881-1954)

A: Gauquelin #1646 Vol 5.

SVP=⌗ 6°54'47"
JULIAN DAY=2408173.63565

DE MAUPASSANT, GUY
Writer

August 5, 1850
8:00 AM LMT
Dieppe, France
1 E 05   49 N 56

Author of vivid, brutal stories that made him popular to readers; a master of short stories. A terse, biting, and impersonal style, dramatic and rich in effect. His novels include *A Life*, *Pierre and Jean* and *Bel Ami*. Died in an insane asylum in 1893.

A: Gauquelin #558 Vol 6.

SVP=⌗ 7°20'56"
JULIAN DAY=2396974.83032

DE MONT, RICHARD
Athlete

April 21, 1956
6:57 AM PST
San Francisco, Ca
122 W 26   37 N 47

Champion swimmer who won the Olympics meet. By suspicion he was medically tested, and drugs were found in his system. Disqualified from his championship - the first time in the history of the Olympics that this had happened.

A: CSH.

SVP=ℋ 5°51'56"
JULIAN DAY=2435585.12292

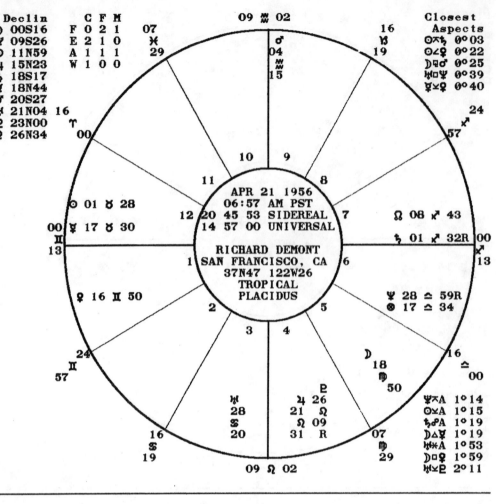

	Declin	C F M	
☽	00S16	F 0 2 1	07
♆	09S26	E 2 1 0	♓
☉	11N59	A 1 1 1	29
♃	15N23	W 1 0 0	
♄	18S17		
☿	18N44		
♂	20S27		
♅	21N04 16		
♇	23N00	♈	
♀	26N34		

Closest Aspects
☉⚹♄ 0°03
☉⚼♀ 0°22
☽⚼♄ 0°25
♅☌♆ 0°39
☿⚹♀ 0°40

APR 21 1956
06:57 AM PST
20 45 53 SIDEREAL
14 57 00 UNIVERSAL
RICHARD DEMONT
SAN FRANCISCO, CA
37N47 122W26
TROPICAL
PLACIDUS

☊ 08 ♐ 43
♄ 01 ♐ 32R 00

♆ 28 ♎ 59R
⊗ 17 ♎ 34

♅ 28 ♋ 20
♃ 26 ♌ 21 ♇ 09 R

♆⚹A 1°14
☉⚼A 1°15
♄⚼A 1°19
☽△☿ 1°19
♅⚹A 1°53
☽☌♀ 1°59
♅⚼♇ 2°11

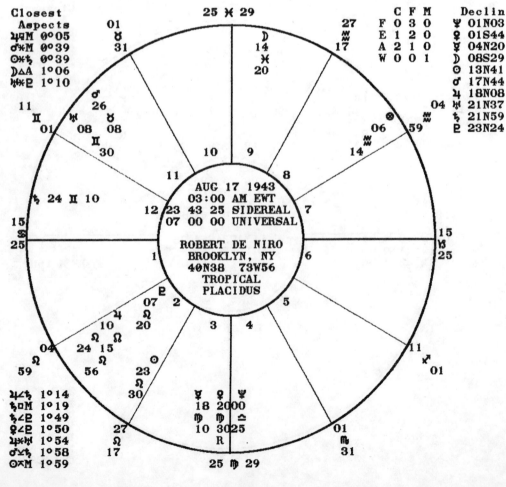

Closest
Aspects
♃⚼M 0°05
♂⚹M 0°39
☉⚹♄ 0°39
☽△A 1°06
♅⚹♇ 1°10

C F M	Declin	
F 0 3 0	♆	01N03
E 1 2 0	♀	01S44
A 2 1 0	☿	04N20
W 0 0 1	☽	08S29
	☉	13N41
	♂	17N44
	♃	18N08
	♅	21N37
	♄	21N59
	♇	23N24

AUG 17 1943
03:00 AM EWT
23 43 25 SIDEREAL
07 00 00 UNIVERSAL
ROBERT DE NIRO
BROOKLYN, NY
40N38 73W56
TROPICAL
PLACIDUS

♃⚼♄ 1°14
♄□M 1°19
♄⚼♇ 1°49
♀⚼♇ 1°50
♃⚹♅ 1°54
♂⚼♄ 1°58
☉⚹M 1°59

DE NIRO, ROBERT
Actor

August 17, 1943
3:00 AM EWT
Brooklyn, N.Y.
73 W.56   40 N.38

Debut in 1968 in an underground picture, *Greetings*. Critical and popular success from 1973 with dynamic portrayals in films that include *The Godfather, Part Two* (1974) and *Taxi Driver* (1976). School dropout at 16 to study acting; married 1976; an intensely private man.

A: Neil Marbell quotes a colleague, "from him."

SVP=ℋ 6° 3' 0"
JULIAN DAY=2430953.79167

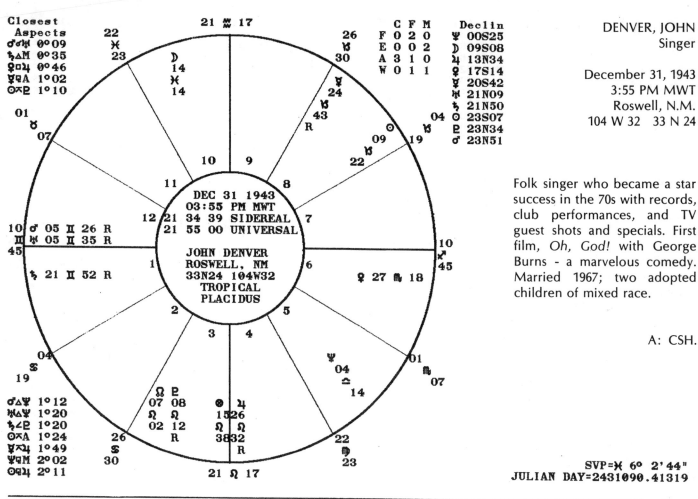

Closest Aspects

♂♂♅ 0°09
♄△M 0°35
♀□♃ 0°46
☿♇A 1°02
☉⚹♇ 1°10

21 ♒ 17

22 ♓ 23
14 ♓ 14
01 ♉ 07

10 ♂ 05 ♊ 26 R
45 ♅ 05 ♊ 35 R
♄ 21 ♊ 52 R

04 ♋ 19

♂△♅ 1°12
♅△♅ 1°20
♄⚼♇ 1°20
☉⚼A 1°24
☿⚼♃ 1°49
♅□M 2°02
☉□♃ 2°11

26 ♋ 30

DEC 31 1943
03:55 PM MWT
21 34 39 SIDEREAL
21 55 00 UNIVERSAL

JOHN DENVER
ROSWELL, NM
33N24 104W32
TROPICAL
PLACIDUS

21 ♌ 17

♎ ♇
07 08
♌ ♌
02 12
R

⊗ ♃
15 26
♌ ♌
38 32
R

♏
♀ 27 18

♍
22 23

♈
04 14

	C	F	M	Declin	
F	0	2	0	♅	00S25
E	0	0	2	☽	09S08
A	3	1	0	♃	13N34
W	0	1	1	♀	17S14
				☿	20S42
				♅	21N09
				♄	21N50
				☉	23S07
				♇	23N34
				♂	23N51

26 ♉ 30

♅ 24 43 R
♂ 22 09 ⊙ 19
04 ♑ 19
10 ♐ 45
01 ♏ 07

DENVER, JOHN
Singer

December 31, 1943
3:55 PM MWT
Roswell, N.M.
104 W 32   33 N 24

Folk singer who became a star success in the 70s with records, club performances, and TV guest shots and specials. First film, *Oh, God!* with George Burns - a marvelous comedy. Married 1967; two adopted children of mixed race.

A: CSH.

SVP=♓ 6° 2'44"
JULIAN DAY=2431090.41319

DEREK, JOHN
Actor

August 12, 1926
1:20 PM PST
Hollywood, Ca
118 W 21   34 N 06

Both parents acted in films. Coached at 17; drafted at 18 after one picture, *Since You Went Away*. Postwar contract with Columbia; named "most popular find" of 1949. Films include *All The King's Men* and *Rogues of Sherwood Forest*. Married 1948; two children; divorced.

A: CL from B.C.

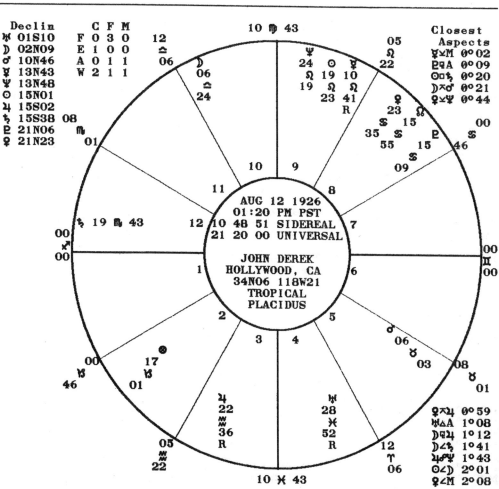

Declin		C	F	M
♅	01S10	F	0	3	0
☽	02N09	E	1	0	0
♂	10N46	A	0	1	1
☿	13N43	W	2	1	1
♆	13N48				
☉	15N01				
♃	15S02				
♄	15S38				
♇	21N06				
♀	21N23				

10 ♍ 43

12 ♎ 06
♆ ☉ ☿
24 19 10
♌ ♌ ♌
19 23 41
R

♀
23 ♌ 15
♋ 15 ♇
35 ♋ 55 ♋ 15
09 ♋

05 ♌
♎ 22

Closest Aspects

☿⚹M 0°02
♇♀A 0°09
⊙□♄ 0°20
☽⚼♂ 0°21
♀⚹♆ 0°44

00 ♊ 00

♂ 06 ♉ 03
08 ♉ 01

♀⚼♃ 0°59
♅△A 1°08
☽♀♃ 1°12
☽⚼♄ 1°41
♃⚼☽ 1°43
⊙□☽ 2°01
♀⚼M 2°08

♄ 19 ♏ 43

AUG 12 1926
01:20 PM PST
10 48 51 SIDEREAL
21 20 00 UNIVERSAL

JOHN DEREK
HOLLYWOOD, CA
34N06 118W21
TROPICAL
PLACIDUS

00 ♐ 00

00 ♑ 46

⊗
17 01

♈ 06

♃
22 ♒ 36 R

♅
28 ♓ 52 R

12 ♈ 06

10 ♓ 43

SVP=♓ 6°17'20"
JULIAN DAY=2424740.38889

DE SICA, VITTORIO
Director

July 7, 1901
11:00 AM MET
Sora, Italy
13 E 37   41 N 43

A bank accountant who began acting with a stage company in Rome in 1923; discovered by the ladies in 1930. Nominated for an Oscar in *A Farewell to Arms* (1954). Thirty films before he began directing. World-known with two Oscars for *Shoe Shine* and *Bicycle Thief*. (1901-1974)

A: Gauquelin #868 Vol 5.

SVP=♓ 6°37'52"
JULIAN DAY=2415572.91667

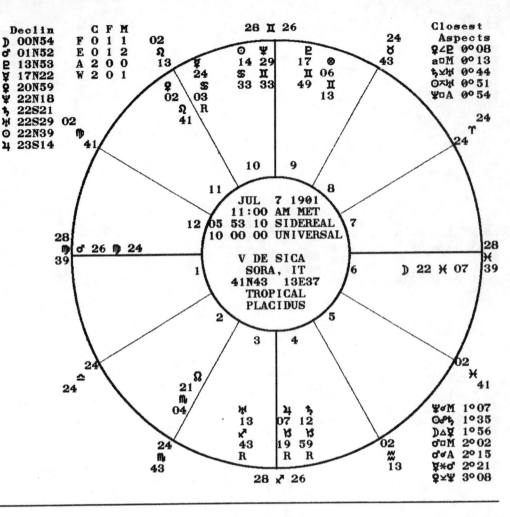

DILLINGER, JOHN
Gangster

June 22, 1903
7:05 AM CST
Mooresville, Ind
86 W 09   39 N 46

Public Enemy #1; supposedly gunned down in a dramatic shoot-out with FBI agents as he left a Chicago theater on July 22, 1934, having been betrayed by "the lady in red". His biography presents evidence that he escaped, and the man with 70 bullets in his body was a "ringer".

A: Garth Allen in AA, December 1970, quotes Llewelyn George.[41]

SVP=♓ 6°36'24"
JULIAN DAY=2416288.04514

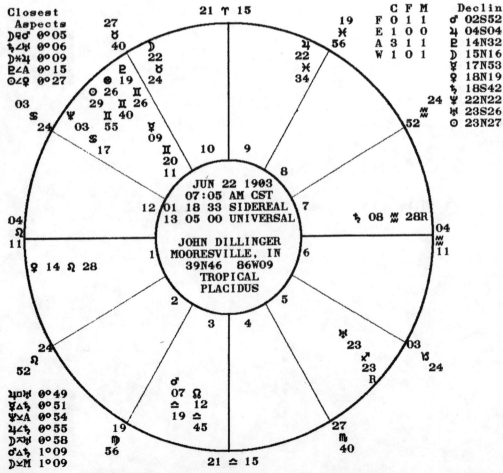

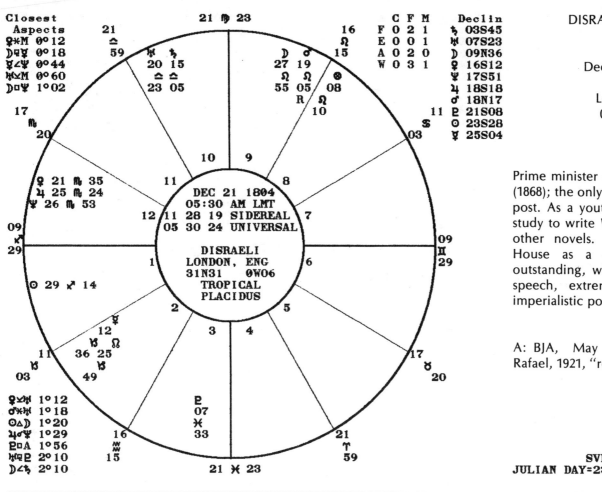

DISRAELI, BENJAMIN
Statesman

December 21, 1804
5:30 AM LMT
London, England
0 W 06   31 N 31

Closest Aspects

♀✱M	0°12
☽□♆	0°18
☿✱♆	0°44
♅☌M	0°60
☽□♆	1°02

♀✱♅	1°12
♂✱♅	1°18
☉△☽	1°20
♃☌♆	1°29
♇□A	1°56
♅□♇	2°10
☽∠♄	2°10

Declin

♄	03S45
♅	07S23
☽	09N36
♀	16S12
♆	17S51
♃	18S18
♂	18N17
♇	21S08
☉	23S28
☿	25S04

C	F	M
F	0	2	1
E	0	0	1
A	0	2	0
W	0	3	1

DEC 21 1804
05:30 AM LMT
11 28 19 SIDEREAL
05 30 24 UNIVERSAL

DISRAELI
LONDON, ENG
31N31   0W06
TROPICAL
PLACIDUS

Prime minister of Great Britain (1868); the only Jew to gain that post. As a youth, gave up law study to write *Vivian Grey* and other novels. Elected to the House as a Tory in 1837; outstanding, with exaggerated speech, extreme dress, and imperialistic policy. (1804-1881)

A: BJA, May 1922, quotes Rafael, 1921, "recorded time."

SVP=♓ 7°58'41"
JULIAN DAY=2380311.72944

DOOLEY, DR. TOM
Humanitarian

January 17, 1927
2:20 AM CST
St. Louis, Mo
90 W 12   38 N 37

Declin

♅	02S09
♃	12S26
♆	13N09
♂	17N28
♀	19S10
♄	19S16
☉	20S55
♇	21N16
☽	23N09
☿	23S43

C	F	M
F	0	1	1
E	1	0	2
A	0	0	2
W	2	0	1

JAN 17 1927
02:20 AM CST
10 02 15 SIDEREAL
08 20 00 UNIVERSAL

DR TOM DOOLEY
ST LOUIS, MO
38N37   90W12
TROPICAL
PLACIDUS

Closest Aspects

☉✱♅	0°03
♅✱♆	0°05
♃☌♇	0°07
☉⊼♆	0°09
☽✱♀	0°21

☽□♄	0°25
♆✱A	0°31
☿∠♃	0°46
☽△A	0°51
♂✱♇	1°00
♇∠M	1°14
♃☌M	1°21

Prosperous family; good education; enlisted in the Navy as a M.D. Became dedicated to the relief of suffering; established a "30-mat" hospital in Laos, September 1956; with Medico organization, 1958. Author of *The Night They Burned the Mountain*. Cancer operation, 1959; died two years later.

A: D.C. Doane from B.C.[42]

SVP=♓ 6°16'59"
JULIAN DAY=2424897.84722

DORE, GUSTAVE PAUL
Artist

January 6, 1832
6:00 AM LMT
Strasborg, France
7 E 50   48 N 35

French painter and sculptor, who illustrated literary masterpieces including the Bible, the works of Rabelais, Balzac, Dante, Tennyson, Cervantes, and others. His work in demand while he was still young; now hangs in French museums. (1832-1883)

A: Gauquelin #326 Vol 4.

SVP=ℋ 7°36'30"
JULIAN DAY=2390188.72824

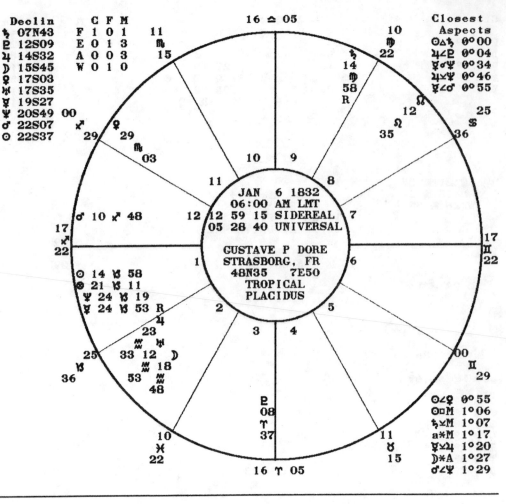

	Declin		C	F	M
♄	07N43	F	1	0	1
♇	12S09	E	0	1	3
♃	14S32	A	0	0	3
☽	15S45	W	0	1	0
♀	17S03				
♅	17S35				
☿	19S27				
♆	20S49				
♂	22S07				
☉	22S37				

Closest Aspects

☉△♄	0°00
♃♂♇	0°04
☿⚹♇	0°34
♃⚹♆	0°46
♃♂♂	0°55

☉♂⚷♇	0°55
☉□M	1°06
♄⚹M	1°07
a⚹M	1°17
☿⚹♃	1°20
☽⚹A	1°27
♂∠♆	1°29

DOUGLAS, LORD ALFRED
Homosexual

October 22, 1870
7:42 PM GMT
Worcester, England
2 W 14   52 N 11

Partner in a notorious love affair with Oscar Wilde in 1891, when he was 21 and Wilde, 37. His father, with whom he had bitter enmity, started legal action; Wilde was convicted and sent to prison, became a broken man.

A: Fagan in AA, February 1967, states data from Douglas to Hove; "Mother says 7:30 to 8:00 PM, closer to 8:00."[43]

SVP=ℋ 7° 4' 7"
JULIAN DAY=2404358.32083

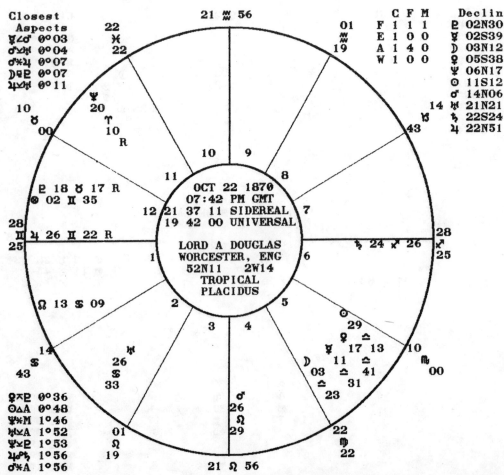

Closest Aspects

☿♂♂	0°03
♅♂♅	0°04
♂⚹♃	0°07
☽⚹♇	0°07
♃♂♅	0°11

	C	F	M
F	1	1	1
E	1	0	0
A	1	4	0
W	1	0	0

	Declin	
♇	02N30
☿	02S39
☽	03N12
♀	05S38
♆	06N17
☉	11S12
♂	14N06
♅	21N21
♄	22S24
♃	22N51

♀⚹♇	0°36
☉△A	0°48
♆⚹M	1°46
♅∠A	1°52
♀⚹♇	1°53
♃⚹♄	1°56
♂⚹A	1°56

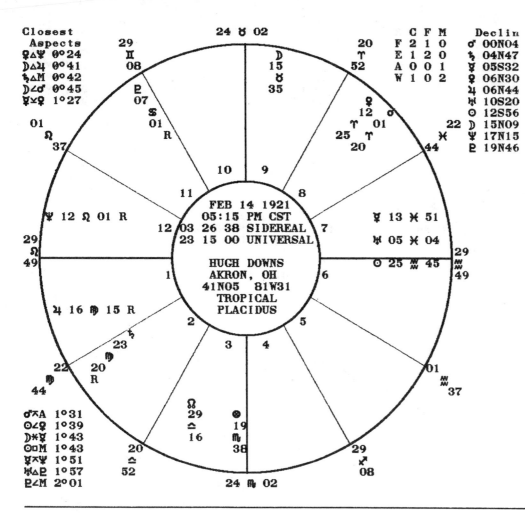

DOWNS, HUGH
TV personality

February 14, 1921
5:15 PM CST
Akron, Ohio
81 W 31   41 N 05

Hugh Downs chart data:

Closest Aspects
- ☿△♆ 0°24
- ☽△♃ 0°41
- ♄△M 0°42
- ☽∠♂ 0°45
- ☿⚹♀ 1°27
- ♂⚹A 1°31
- ☉∠♀ 1°39
- ☽⚹☿ 1°43
- ☉□M 1°43
- ☿△♆ 1°51
- ♅△♇ 1°57
- ♇∠M 2°01

Declin
- ♂ 00N04
- ♄ 04N47
- ☿ 05S32
- ♀ 06N30
- ♃ 06N44
- ♅ 10S20
- ☉ 12S56
- ☽ 15N09
- ♆ 17N15
- ♇ 19N46

	C	F	M
F	2	1	0
E	1	2	0
A	0	0	1
W	1	0	2

FEB 14 1921
05:15 PM CST
03 26 38 SIDEREAL
23 15 00 UNIVERSAL

HUGH DOWNS
AKRON, OH
41N05 81W31
TROPICAL
PLACIDUS

Began broadcasting in 1943; became an announcer in 1957. Host of quiz-show *Concentration* in the 50s, and for ten years NBC's morning show, *Today* (from 1962). Calls himself the world's champion dilettante with multiple eclectic interests and talents.

A: March states that he gave the data on a talk show.

SVP=♓ 6°21'30"
JULIAN DAY=2422735.46875

DUMAS, ALEXANDRE
Writer

July 24, 1802
5:30 AM LMT
Villers-Cotterets, France
3 E 07   49 N 15

One of the great French novelists and dramatists. Son of a general; grandson of a Black. Traveled widely, wrote prolifically, lived extravagantly, and died poor. Books include *The Count of Monte Cristo* and *The Three Musketeers*. (1802-1870)

A: Gauquelin #281 Vol 6.

Declin
- ♅ 00S42
- ♃ 10N10
- ♄ 10N58
- ♀ 11N35
- ♆ 15S44
- ♂ 16N53
- ☿ 16N52
- ☉ 20N04
- ♇ 21S19
- ☽ 24N46

	C	F	M
F	0	1	0
E	2	3	0
A	0	1	0
W	1	1	1

JUL 24 1802
05:30 AM LMT
01 34 51 SIDEREAL
05 17 32 UNIVERSAL

ALEX DUMAS
VILLERS-COTTEREIS
49N15 3E07
TROPICAL
PLACIDUS

Closest Aspects
- ♀⚹♅ 0°07
- ♃□♇ 0°17
- ♅∠♆ 0°28
- ♃♂ 0°31
- ♄□♇ 0°48
- ☿□♇ 1°19
- ☿△♃ 1°35
- ☉⚹☽ 1°52
- ☿⚹♂ 1°54
- ☿∠♀ 2°06
- ♂♂ 2°11
- ♀♂♄ 2°19

SVP=♓ 8° 0'52"
JULIAN DAY=2379430.72051

DYER, ALBERT
Murderer

October 20, 1904
7:15 AM EST
Indian Lake, N.Y.
74 W 16   43 N.47

Employed as a crossing guard on a school street; on July 26, 1937, lured three little girls into the hills, attacked, and strangled them. Adopted as a child; noted to have an insistent sexual drive. Sentenced to hang on August 27, 1937.

A: CL, "from a relative in Inglewood."

SVP=ⅹ 6°35'26"
JULIAN DAY=2416774.01042

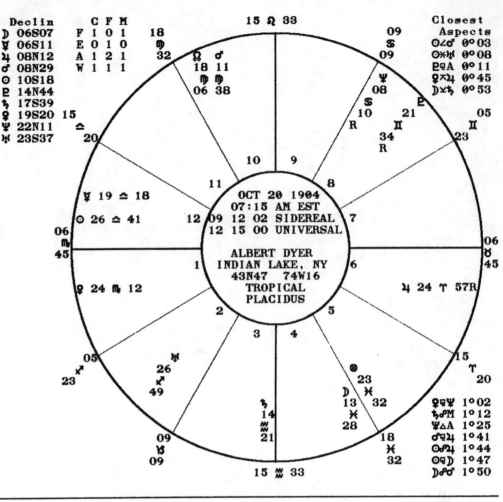

Declin		C	F	M
☽	06S07	F	1	0	1
☿	06S11	E	0	1	0
♃	08N12	A	1	2	1
♂	08N29	W	1	1	1
☉	10S18				
♇	14N44				
♄	17S39				
♀	19S20				
♆	22N11				
♅	23S37				

Closest Aspects
☉☌♂ 0°03
☉✳♅ 0°08
♇□A 0°11
♀☌♃ 0°45
☽□♄ 0°53

♀♆ 1°02
♄☍M 1°12
♆△A 1°25
♂□♃ 1°41
☉☌♃ 1°44
☉□☽ 1°47
☽☌♂ 1°50

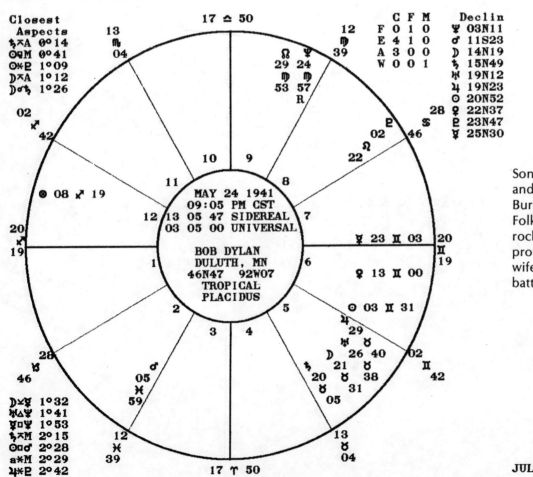

Closest Aspects
♄△A 0°14
☉☍M 0°41
☉✳♇ 1°09
☽✳A 1°12
☽☌♄ 1°26

☽✳♇ 1°32
♅△♆ 1°41
☿□♆ 1°53
☿☍M 2°15
☉□♂ 2°28
a✳M 2°29
♃✳♇ 2°42

	C	F	M	Declin	
	F	0	1	0	♆	03N11
	E	4	1	0	♂	11S23
	A	3	0	0	☽	14N19
	W	0	0	1	♄	15N49
					♅	19N12
					♃	19N23
					☉	20S52
					♀	22N37
					♇	23N47
					☿	25N30

DYLAN, BOB
Musician

May 24, 1941
9:05 PM CST
Duluth, Minn
92 W 07   46 N 47

Songwriter with a gravel voice and long hair; called the Robert Burns of the pop revolution. Folk artist who moved into folk-rock with songs of poetry and protest. Divorce in 1977 from his wife of eleven years; custody battle for their five children.

A: CSH.

SVP=ⅹ 6° 4'43"
JULIAN DAY=2430139.62847

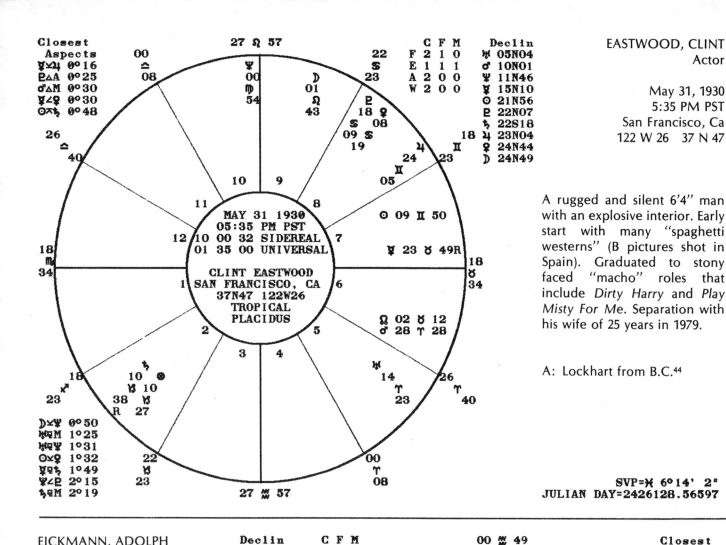

EASTWOOD, CLINT
Actor

May 31, 1930
5:35 PM PST
San Francisco, Ca
122 W 26   37 N 47

A rugged and silent 6'4" man with an explosive interior. Early start with many "spaghetti westerns" (B pictures shot in Spain). Graduated to stony faced "macho" roles that include *Dirty Harry* and *Play Misty For Me*. Separation with his wife of 25 years in 1979.

A: Lockhart from B.C.[44]

SVP=♓ 6°14' 2"
JULIAN DAY=2426128.56597

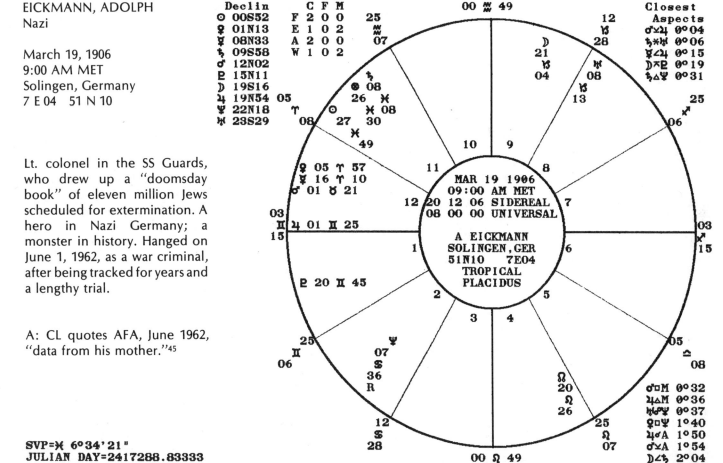

EICKMANN, ADOLPH
Nazi

March 19, 1906
9:00 AM MET
Solingen, Germany
7 E 04   51 N 10

Lt. colonel in the SS Guards, who drew up a "doomsday book" of eleven million Jews scheduled for extermination. A hero in Nazi Germany; a monster in history. Hanged on June 1, 1962, as a war criminal, after being tracked for years and a lengthy trial.

A: CL quotes AFA, June 1962, "data from his mother."[45]

SVP=♓ 6°34' 21"
JULIAN DAY=2417288.83333

EINSTEIN, ALBERT
Scientist

March 14, 1879
11:30 AM LMT
Ulm, Germany
10 E 00   48 N.30

Mathematician, physicist, who founded theory of relativity (1905) and general theory (1916). Awarded the 1921 Nobel prize for contributions to theoretical physics, especially for the discovery of photoelectric-effect law. (1879-1955)

A: Ebertin from a copy of the birth registration.

SVP=♓ 6°56'32"
JULIAN DAY=2407422.95139

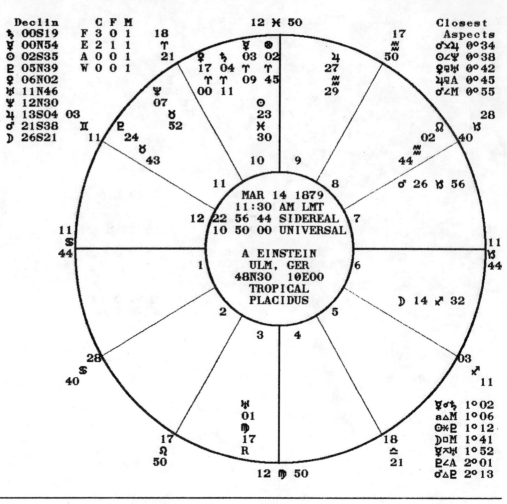

EISELE, DON
Astronaut

June 23, 1930
2:52 PM EST
Columbus, Ohio
83 W.00   39 N.58

Navigator of the eleven-day mission of Apollo 7, launched October 11, 1968, with a three man crew that included Schirra and Cunningham. Became the technical assistant for Manned Flight and Space Systems Research Division, Langley Research Center, 1970.

A: CSH. (*Pioneers of Tomorrow* gives 3:15 PM, "from him.")

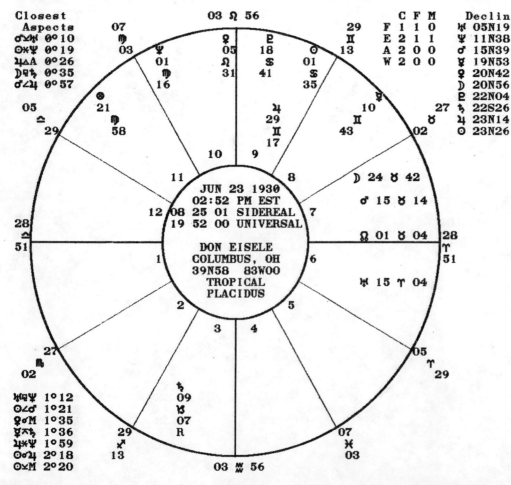

SVP=♓ 6°13'59"
JULIAN DAY=2426151.32778

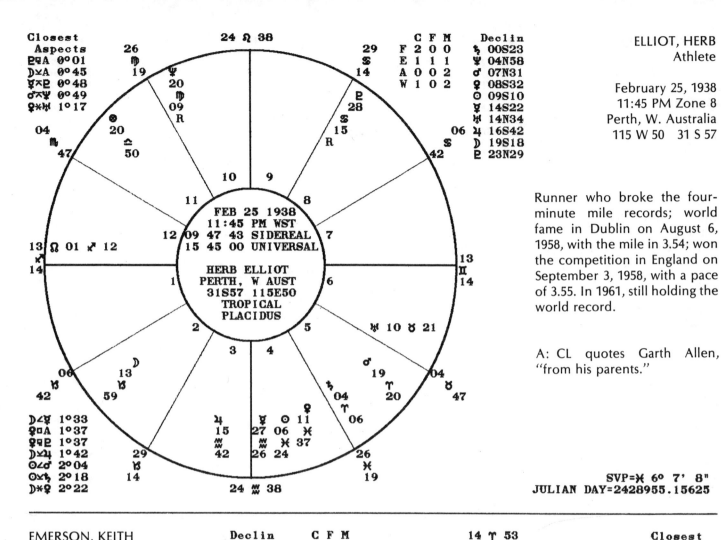

ELLIOT, HERB
Athlete

February 25, 1938
11:45 PM Zone 8
Perth, W. Australia
115 W 50   31 S 57

Runner who broke the four-minute mile records; world fame in Dublin on August 6, 1958, with the mile in 3.54; won the competition in England on September 3, 1958, with a pace of 3.55. In 1961, still holding the world record.

A: CL quotes Garth Allen, "from his parents."

SVP=♓ 6° 7' 8"
JULIAN DAY=2428955.15625

EMERSON, KEITH
Musician

November 2, 1944
10:15 PM GMT
Todmordine, England
2 W 06   53 N.43

Too much energy for one person to contain. Plays two electric guitars at once, plus Moog, piano, and other sound devices. Emerson, Lake and Palmer made their first appearance in New York in May 1971; greeted with nothing but superlatives for super top-rock.

A: From him to Amy Rodden, 1977.

SVP=♓ 6° 2' 6"
JULIAN DAY=2431397.42708

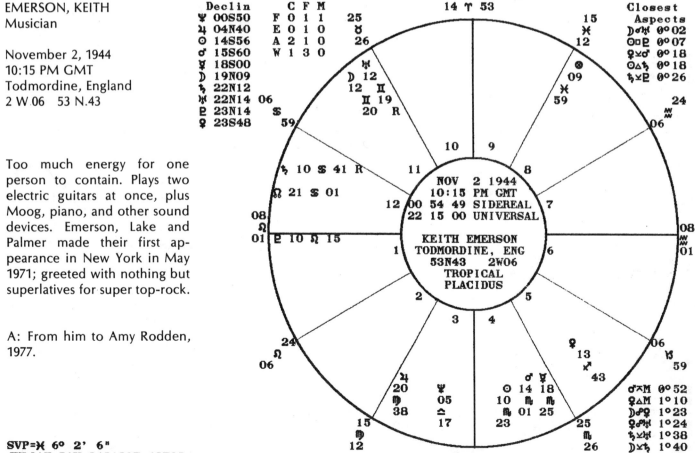

FALLA, MANUEL DE
Musician

November 23, 1876
6:00 AM LMT
Cadiz, Spain
6 W 17   36 N 32

Spanish composer who did much to develop interest in the music of his homeland. Won the first prize in a contest for the best national opera with *La Vida Breve* (1905). Gained world fame for his ballet *The Three Cornered Hat* in 1919. (1876-1946)

A: *Constellations*, 1977, Lockhart quotes data "from the birth record."

SVP=⊬ 6°58'40"
JULIAN DAY=2406581.76745

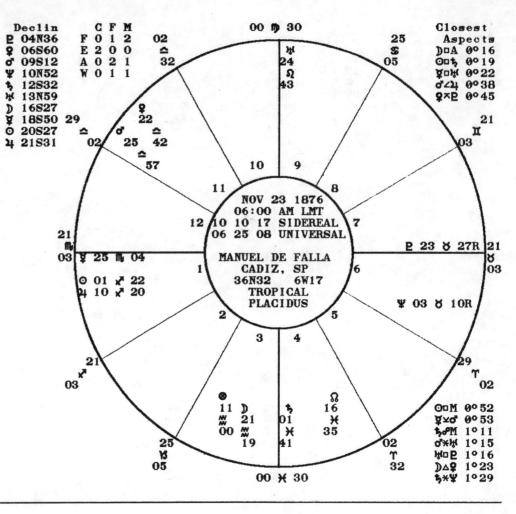

Declin			C F M		Closest Aspects
♇	04N36	F 0 1 2	02		☽□A 0°16
♀	06S60	E 2 0 0	≏		☉□♄ 0°19
♂	09S12	A 0 2 1	32		☿□♅ 0°22
♆	10N52	W 0 1 1			♂∠♃ 0°38
♄	12S32				♀✶♇ 0°45
♅	13N59				
☽	16S27				
☿	18S50				
☉	20S27				
♃	21S31				

NOV 23 1876
06:00 AM LMT
10 10 17 SIDEREAL
06 25 08 UNIVERSAL

MANUEL DE FALLA
CADIZ, SP
36N32 6W17
TROPICAL
PLACIDUS

☉□M 0°52
☿✶♂ 0°53
♄♂M 1°11
♂✶♅ 1°15
♅□♇ 1°16
☽△♀ 1°23
♄✶♆ 1°29

FELICIANO, JOSE
Musician

September 10, 1945
10:00 AM AST
Lares, P.R.
66 W 53   18 N 18

Blind from birth; Puerto Rican; moved to N.Y. at age 5. First guitar at 9; first professional appearance at 17. Learns the lyrics by braille. Two Grammys in 1969, for best new male artist and for best male vocal performance of "Light My Fire". Married.

A: CSH.

SVP=⊬ 6° 1'22"
JULIAN DAY=2431709.08333

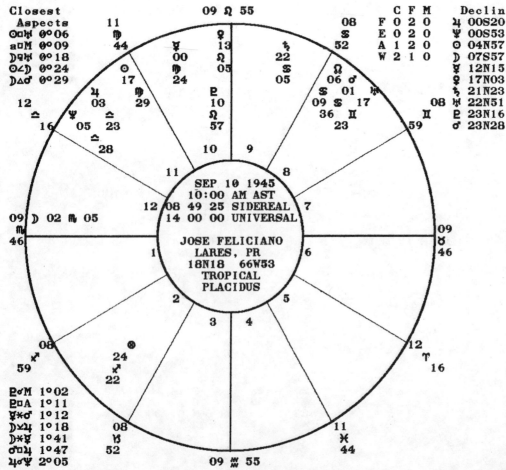

Closest Aspects		C F M		Declin
☉□♅ 0°06		F 0 2 0	♃	00S20
a□M 0°09		E 0 2 0	♆	00S53
☽□♅ 0°18		A 1 2 0	☉	04N57
☉∠☽ 0°24		W 2 1 0	☽	07S57
☽△♂ 0°29			☿	12N15
			♀	17N03
			♄	21N23
			♅	22N51
			♇	23N16
			♂	23N28

SEP 10 1945
10:00 AM AST
08 49 25 SIDEREAL
14 00 00 UNIVERSAL

JOSE FELICIANO
LARES, PR
18N18 66W53
TROPICAL
PLACIDUS

♇♂M 1°02
♇□A 1°11
☿✶♂ 1°12
☽∠♃ 1°18
☽✶☿ 1°41
♂□♃ 1°47
♃♂♆ 2°05

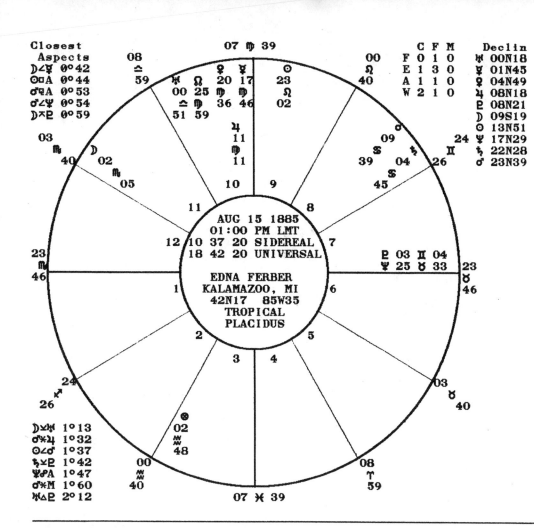

FERBER, EDNA
Writer

August 15, 1885
1:00 PM LMT
Kalamazoo, Mich
85 W.35   42 N 17

Novelist, playwright, winner of the Pulitzer prize for *So Big* (1925). Wrote many stories of early Americana, a number of which were made into movies, including *Show Boat* and *Cimarron*. Though an avid health enthusiast, died of cancer in 1965.

B: PC quotes "her mother's diary" in *Edna Ferber* by Julia Gilbert, p. 432.[46]

Closest Aspects
☽∠☿ 0°42
☉□A 0°44
♂□A 0°53
♂∠♆ 0°54
☽⊼♇ 0°59

☽⊼♅ 1°13
♂⚹♃ 1°32
☉∠♂ 1°37
♄⊼♇ 1°42
♆⚹A 1°47
♂⚹M 1°60
♅△♇ 2°12

Declin
♅ 00N18
☿ 01N45
♀ 04N49
♃ 08N18
♇ 08N21
☽ 09S19
☉ 13N51
♆ 17N29
♄ 22N28
♂ 23N39

C	F	M
F	0	1	0
E	1	3	0
A	1	1	0
W	2	1	0

AUG 15 1885
01:00 PM LMT
10 37 20 SIDEREAL
18 42 20 UNIVERSAL

EDNA FERBER
KALAMAZOO, MI
42N17   85W35
TROPICAL
PLACIDUS

SVP=♓ 6°51'24"
JULIAN DAY=2409769.27940

FERMI, ENRICO
Atomic scientist

September 29, 1901
7:00 PM MET
Rome, Italy
12 E 29   41 N 54

With Leo Szilard, discovered uranium fission and invented the atomic reactor (1942). Designed the first atomic piles and produced the first nuclear chain reaction in 1942; later worked on the Atomic Project in Los Alamos. (1901-1954)

A: Gauquelin #3027 Vol 2.[47]

Declin
☉ 02S20
☽ 11N51
☿ 12S16
♇ 13N47
♀ 17S12
♂ 18S16
♆ 22N16
♅ 22S28
♄ 22S46
♃ 23S31

C	F	M
F	1	0	1
E	0	0	2
A	1	2	0
W	1	2	0

SEP 29 1901
07:00 PM MET
19 21 07 SIDEREAL
18 00 00 UNIVERSAL

ENRICO FERMI
ROME, IT
41N54   12E29
TROPICAL
PLACIDUS

Closest Aspects
♂∠♃ 0°01
♇⚹M 0°03
♃△A 0°03
☿∠♃ 0°25
♂⚹M 0°51

♇∠A 0°53
♂∠♇ 0°54
☽⚹☿ 1°03
♀⊼♅ 1°07
☉∠♃ 1°17
☉∠♂ 1°18
☉⊼A 1°20

SVP=♓ 6°37'42"
JULIAN DAY=2415657.25000

FERNANDEL
Actor

May 8, 1903
7:00 AM Paris time
Marseilles, France
5 E 20   43 N 20

Mime and motion picture comedian with a long, sorrowful, equine face and a radiant toothy smile. One of France's leading box-office actors with a four-decade career from 1930. His films include four great *Con Camillo* political comedies. (1903-1971)

A: Gauquelin #320 Vol 5.

SVP=♓ 6°36'30"
JULIAN DAY=2416242.77037

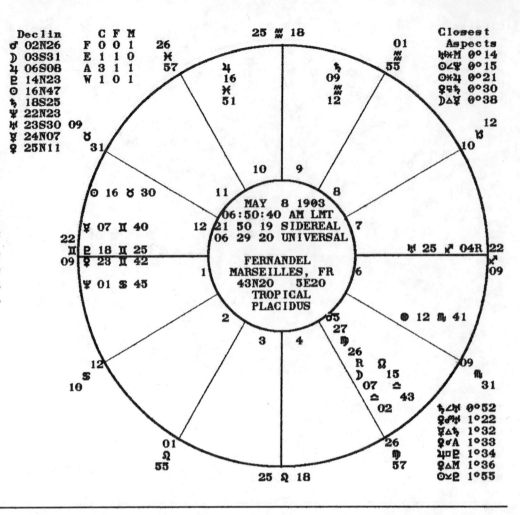

FISCHER, BOBBY
Chess grandmaster

March 9, 1943
2:39 PM CWT
Chicago, Ill
87 W 39   41 N 52

First won the U.S. championship at age 14; defeated in 1962 by Larry Evans; won again in 1963; lost to Evans in 1968; won in 1971. Became the World Chess Champion by defeating Russia's Boris Spassky in a contest that ended August 13, 1972.

B: D. Ames quotes *Profile of a Prodigy* by F. Brady, p. 2, in AA, May 1974.[48]

SVP=♓ 6° 3'21"
JULIAN DAY=2430793.31875

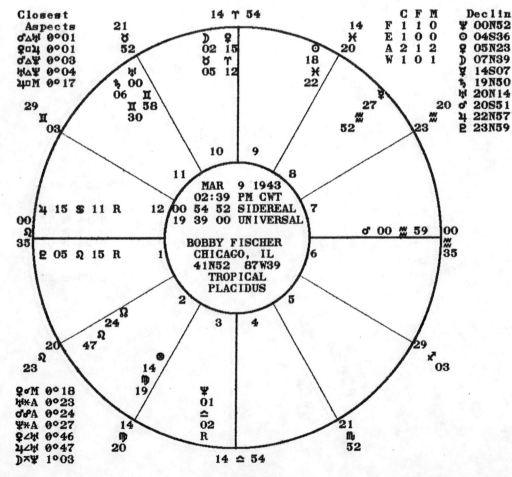

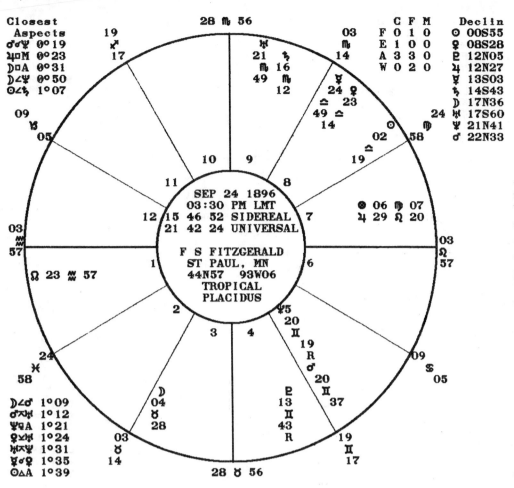

FITZGERALD, F. SCOTT
Writer

September 24, 1896
3:30 PM LMT
St. Paul, Minn
93 W 06   44 N 57

American novelist and short story writer of the Roaring Twenties. Sold everything he wrote after *This Side of Paradise* (1920), including *The Great Gatsby* and *Tender Is The Night*, plus 160 short stories. During his last years, a Hollywood script writer. (1896-1940)

B: R.H. Oliver quotes *Exiles From Paradise* by Sara Mayfield, 1971.[49]

SVP=♓ 6°41'56"
JULIAN DAY=2413827.40444

FLAMMARION, CAMILLE
Scientist

February 26, 1842
1:00 AM LMT
Haute Marne, France
2 E 20   48 N 20

French astronomer, writer, and scientist; in charge of an observatory near Paris (1882). Author of *The Wonder of Heaven* and *Dreams of an Astronomer*. Later in life, turned to controversial work on psychical research. (1842-1925)

A: Gauquelin #317 Vol 6.

SVP=♓ 7°27'32"
JULIAN DAY=2393892.53519

FLAUBERT, GUSTAVE
Writer

December 13, 1821
4:00 AM LMT
Rouen, France
1 E 08   49 N 26

French novelist best known for *Madame Bovary*, which ranks as one of the world's great novels. A cheerless pessimist; worked tirelessly to create an exact, realistic style, taking years to perfect a novel. In youth a law student (from 1840-43). (1821-1880)

A: *Constellations*, 1977, from Paul Choisnard; B.C. from France.[50]

SVP=♓ 7°44'35"
JULIAN DAY=2386512.66352

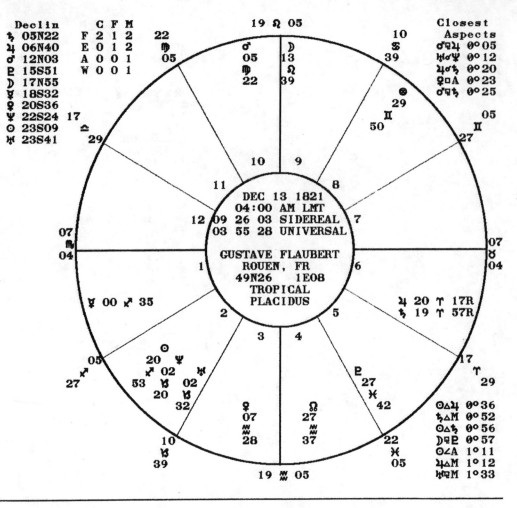

Declin		C F M
♄ 05N22	F 2 1 2
♃ 06N40	E 0 1 2
♂ 12N03	A 0 0 1
♇ 15S51	W 0 0 1
☽ 17N55	
☿ 18S32	
♀ 20S36	
♆ 22S24	
☉ 23S09	
♅ 23S41	

Closest Aspects
♂♇♃ 0°05
♅♂♆ 0°12
♃♇♄ 0°20
♀♇△ 0°23
♂♇♄ 0°25

☉△♃ 0°36
♄△M 0°52
☉△♄ 0°56
☽♇♇ 0°57
☉△△ 1°11
♃△M 1°12
♅♇M 1°33

DEC 13 1821
04:00 AM LMT
09 26 03 SIDEREAL
03 55 28 UNIVERSAL

GUSTAVE FLAUBERT
ROUEN, FR
49N26   1E08
TROPICAL
PLACIDUS

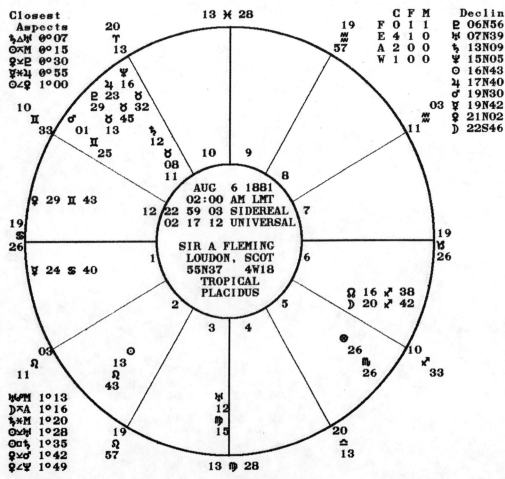

Closest Aspects
♄△♅ 0°07
☉♇M 0°15
♀♇♇ 0°30
♀♇♃ 0°55
☉△♀ 1°00

♅♇M 1°13
☽♇A 1°16
♄♇M 1°20
☉♇♅ 1°28
☉♇♄ 1°35
♀♇♂ 1°42
♀△♇ 1°49

	C F M	Declin
	F 0 1 1	♇ 06N56
	E 4 1 0	♅ 07N39
	A 2 0 0	♄ 13N09
	W 1 0 0	♆ 15N05
		☉ 16N43
		♃ 17N40
		♂ 19N30
		☿ 19N42
		♀ 21N02
		☽ 22S46

AUG 6 1881
02:00 AM LMT
22 59 03 SIDEREAL
02 17 12 UNIVERSAL

SIR A FLEMING
LOUDON, SCOT
55N37   4W18
TROPICAL
PLACIDUS

FLEMING, SIR ALEXANDER
Scientist

August 6, 1881
2:00 AM LMT
Loudon, Scotland
4 W 18   55 N 37

British bacteriologist at the University of London, who discovered the mold from which penicillin was derived (1929). Along with Sir Howard Florey and Ernst Chain, received the 1945 Nobel prize in medicine for the development of the drug. (1881-1955)

A: *Constellations*, 1977; B.C. from Astrological Journal, Fall 1967.

SVP=♓ 6°54'29"
JULIAN DAY=2408298.59528

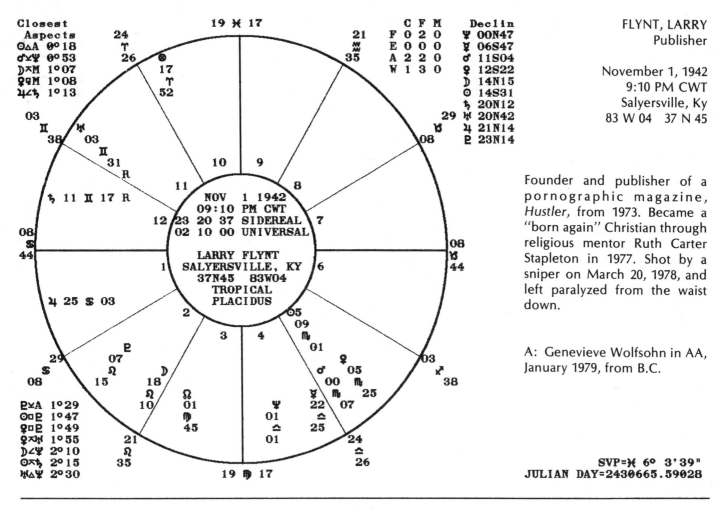

FLYNT, LARRY
Publisher

November 1, 1942
9:10 PM CWT
Salyersville, Ky
83 W 04   37 N 45

Founder and publisher of a pornographic magazine, *Hustler*, from 1973. Became a "born again" Christian through religious mentor Ruth Carter Stapleton in 1977. Shot by a sniper on March 20, 1978, and left paralyzed from the waist down.

A: Genevieve Wolfsohn in AA, January 1979, from B.C.

SVP=✶ 6° 3'39"
JULIAN DAY=2430665.59028

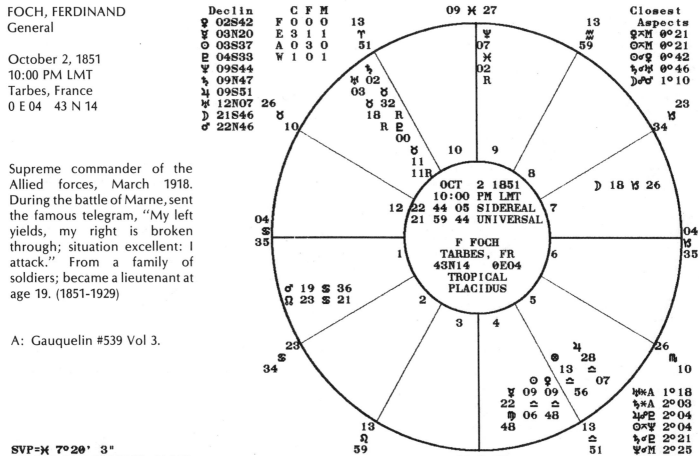

FOCH, FERDINAND
General

October 2, 1851
10:00 PM LMT
Tarbes, France
0 E 04   43 N 14

Supreme commander of the Allied forces, March 1918. During the battle of Marne, sent the famous telegram, "My left yields, my right is broken through; situation excellent: I attack." From a family of soldiers; became a lieutenant at age 19. (1851-1929)

A: Gauquelin #539 Vol 3.

SVP=✶ 7°20' 3"
JULIAN DAY=2397398.41648

FONDA, PETER
Actor

February 23, 1940
11:33 AM EST
New York, N.Y.
73 W 57 40 N 45

Broadway from 1961 with good reviews. Films include *The Wild Angels* and *Easy Rider*. At age 10, when his mother committed suicide, shot himself in the stomach; started psychiatric counseling at 11. Arrested for drug possession in 1966. Married 1961-72; two children.

A: Carol Tebbs, "from his wife Becky" to a mutual acquaintance.[51]

SVP=♓ 6° 5'36"
JULIAN DAY=2429683.18958

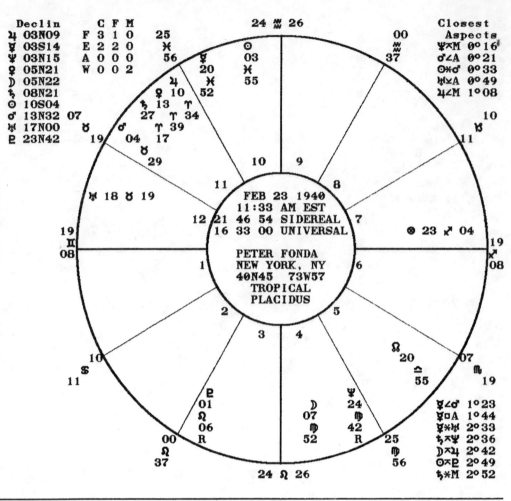

Declin

		C	F	M
♃	03N09	F	3 1 0
☿	03S14	E	2 2 0
♆	03N15	A	0 0 0
♀	05N21	W	0 0 2
☽	05N22		
♄	08N21		
☉	10S04		
♂	13N32		
♅	17N00		
♇	23N42		

Closest Aspects

♆⊼M	0°16'
♂∠A	0°21'
☉⚹♂	0°33'
♅⊼A	0°49'
♃∠M	1°08'
☿∠♂	1°23'
☿□A	1°44'
☿⚹♆	2°33'
♄⊼♃	2°36'
☽⊼♃	2°42'
☉⚹♇	2°49'
♄⚹M	2°52'

FOSTER, STEPHEN
Songwriter

July 4, 1826
12:30 PM LMT
Pittsburgh, Pa
80 W 01 40 N 26

Composer of more than two hundred sincere, sentimental folk songs, including "Swannee River" and "Beautiful Dreamer". Little musical training; could pick out any tune by ear; first published at age 16. A poor businessman; died of illness, poverty, and alcoholism in 1864.

A: *Brotherhood of Light*, Book XI, p. 194, "recorded in the family Bible."[52]

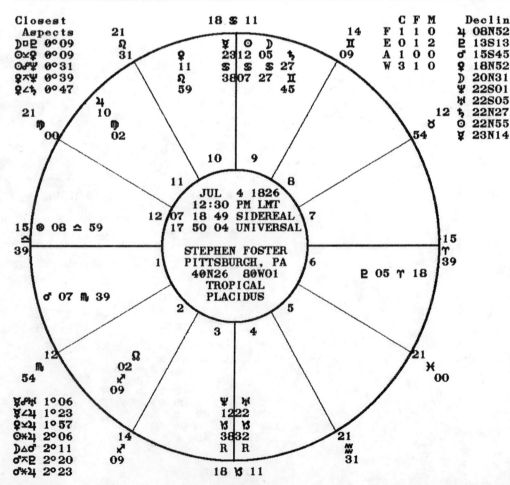

Closest Aspects

☽□♇	0°09'
☉⚹♀	0°09'
☉⊼♆	0°31'
♀⊼♆	0°39'
♀∠♄	0°47'
☿∠♅	1°06'
☿∠♃	1°23'
♀∠♃	1°57'
☉⚹♃	2°06'
☽△♂	2°11'
♂⊼♇	2°20'
♂⚹♃	2°23'

		C	F	M
		F	1 1 0
		E	0 1 2
		A	1 0 0
		W	3 1 0

Declin

♃	08N52
♇	13S13
♂	15S45
♀	18N52
☽	20N31
♆	22S01
♅	22S05
♄	22N27
☉	22N55
☿	23N14

SVP=♓ 7°40'39"
JULIAN DAY=2388177.24310

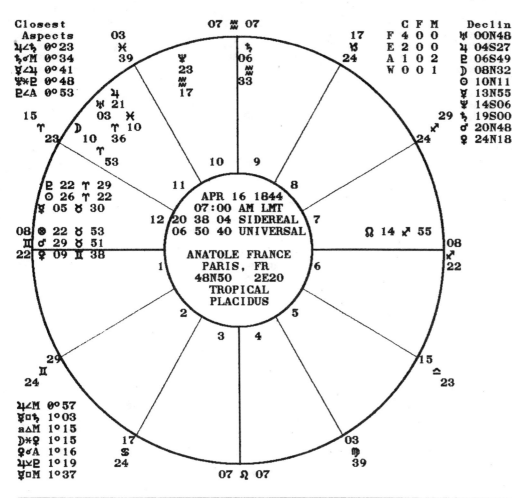

April 16, 1844
7:00 AM LMT
Paris, France
2 E 20   48 N 50

French novelist and critic; won the Nobel prize for literature in 1921. Fame in his lifetime that has since declined; author of fifty volumes in a wide variety of subjects, at least six of which will probably survive the changing tastes of time. (1844-1924)

A: Gauquelin #334 Vol 6.

Closest Aspects

2/3 0°23
3ₒM 0°34
☿⚹4 0°41
Ψ⚹P 0°48
P∠A 0°53

2∠M 0°57
☿□3 1°03
a∆M 1°15
)⚹♀ 1°15
♀ₒA 1°16
4∠P 1°19
☿□M 1°37

Declin

♅ 00N48
4 04S27
P 06S49
) 08N32
☉ 10N11
☿ 13N55
Ψ 14S06
3 19S00
♂ 20N48
♀ 24N18

	C	F	M
F	4	0	0
E	2	0	0
A	1	0	2
W	0	0	1

Chart center:
APR 16 1844
07:00 AM LMT
20 38 04 SIDEREAL
06 50 40 UNIVERSAL

ANATOLE FRANCE
PARIS, FR
48N50   2E20
TROPICAL
PLACIDUS

SVP=H 7°25'45"
JULIAN DAY=2394672.78519

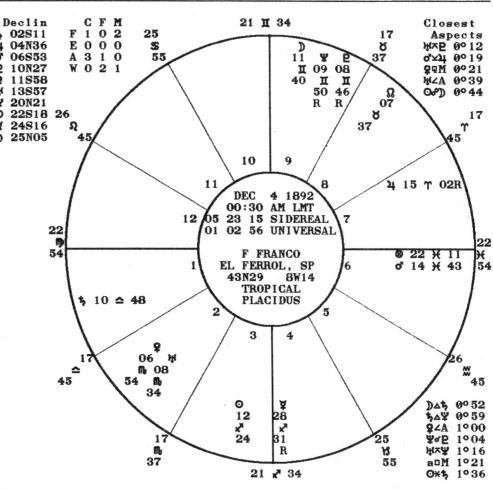

December 4, 1892
00:30 AM LMT
El Ferrol, Spain
8 W 14   43 N 29

A general from age 32, who became dictator of Spain on September 29, 1936. Commanded the rebel forces during the Spanish Civil War (1936-39); became chief of state. Maintained a strong anti-communist policy, though many disapproved of his methods. (1892-1975)

A: Fagan in AA, October 1958, "registered at the parish church."[53]

SVP=H 6°45'28"
JULIAN DAY=2412436.54370

Declin

3 02S11
4 04N36
♂ 06S53
P 10N27
♀ 11S58
♅ 13S57
Ψ 20N21
☉ 22S18
☿ 24S16
) 25N05

	C	F	M
F	1	0	2
E	0	0	0
A	3	1	0
W	0	2	1

Chart center:
DEC 4 1892
00:30 AM LMT
05 23 15 SIDEREAL
01 02 56 UNIVERSAL

F FRANCO
EL FERROL, SP
43N29   8W14
TROPICAL
PLACIDUS

Closest Aspects

♅⚹P 0°12
♂∠4 0°19
♀□M 0°21
♅∠A 0°39
☉⚹) 0°44

)∆A 0°52
3∆Ψ 0°59
♀∠A 1°00
♀ₒP 1°04
♅□Ψ 1°16
aₒM 1°21
☉⚹3 1°36

FRAZIER, JOE
Boxer

January 17, 1944
9:30 PM EWT
Beaufort, S.C.
80 W 40   32 N 26

Winner of the vacant heavyweight championship title in 1970, by knocking out Jimmy Ellis in round five. Also 1964 Olympic Games heavyweight champion. Fought an exciting exhibition with Muhammad Ali on March 8, 1971; lost the crown to George Foreman January 22, 1973.

A: Lockhart quotes *Current Biography*, 1971, for date and time.[54]

SVP=♓ 6° 2'41"
JULIAN DAY=2431107.56250

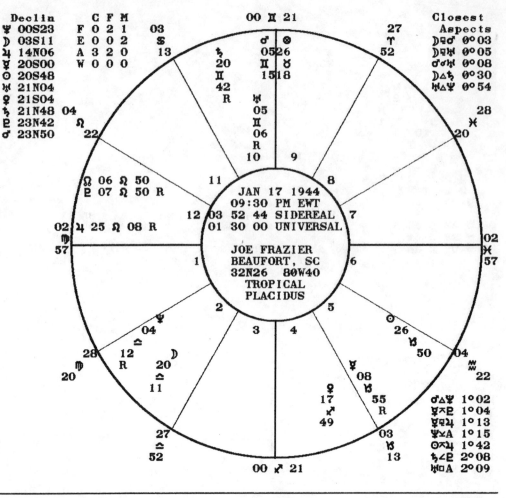

FREMONT, JOHN CHARLES
The Pathfinder

January 21, 1813
11:00 PM LMT
Savannah, Ga
81 W 06   32 N 05

U.S. General and explorer who mapped the Oregon trail beginning in 1842, reaching California in December 1845. Elected one of the first two U.S. Senators from California, 1850-51. It was said, "From the ashes of his campfires have sprung cities." (1813-1890)

A: *Constellations*, 1977, quotes AFA data exchange, "data from him."

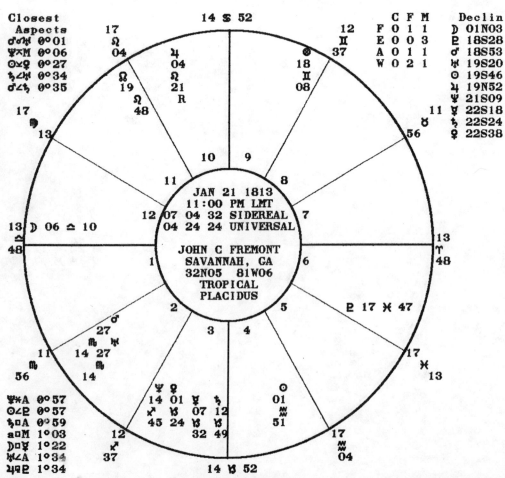

SVP=♓ 7°52'20"
JULIAN DAY=2383265.68361

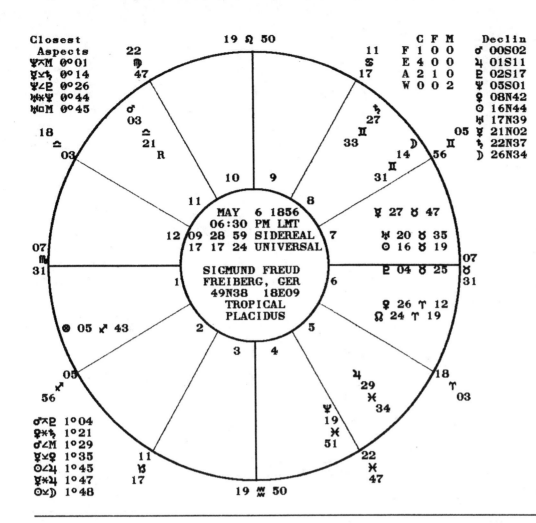

FREUD, SIGMUND
Psychologist

May 6, 1856
6:30 PM LMT
Frieberg (Pribor) Germany
18 E 09   49 N 38

Austrian physician who developed psychoanalysis; a pioneer in the field of subconscious exploration and mapping. Vienna professor, writer, and counselor until fleeing the Nazis to London in 1938. Died from cancer in 1939.

A: Phillip Lucas in M.H., October 1979, ''from a photograph of father's diary, in which the data was written in Hebrew and German.''[55]

SVP=ℋ 7°16' 3"
JULIAN DAY=2399076.22042

FROST, DAVID
Television host

April 7, 1939
10:30 AM GMT
Teterden, England
0 E 42   51 N 05

Actor, producer, with his own TV show in England in the 60s and in U.S. in the 70s. Host of *That Was the Week That Was* and of *The David Frost Revue*. A smooth, shrewd, and amiable interviewer of illustrious guests; rocketed himself to the top at an early age.

A: Paul Rosner quotes Diahann Carrol, from Frost.

SVP=ℋ 6° 6'18"
JULIAN DAY=2429360.93750

GABOR, ZSA ZSA
Actress

February 6, 1915
8:08 PM MET
Budapest, Hungary
19 E 05   47 N 30

Best known of the three glamorous Gabor sisters. Career in theater and movies; magazine cover girl; night clubs. Known for a half dozen marriages. Piercing wit, humor, and sophistication. Author of *How to Catch a Man - Keep a Man - Get Rid of a Man*.

B: Her autobiography, *My Story*, states the time; March states as a known fact that the year is 1915.[56]

SVP=✶ 6°26'33"
JULIAN DAY=2420535.29722

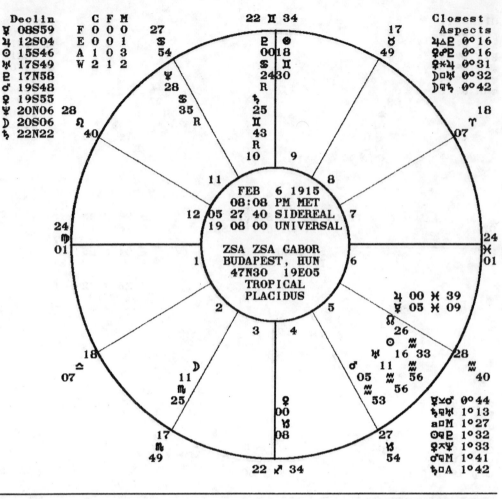

Declin		C F M
☿ 08S59	F 0 0 0
♃ 12S04	E 0 0 1
☉ 15S46	A 1 0 3
♅ 17S49	W 2 1 2
♇ 17N58	
♂ 19S48	
♀ 19S55	
♆ 20N06	
☽ 20S06	
♄ 22N22	

Closest Aspects
♃△♇ 0°16
♀♂♇ 0°16
♀✶♃ 0°31
☽□♅ 0°32
☽□♄ 0°42

♃ 00 ✶ 39
☿ 05 ✶ 09

☉ 16 ♒ 33
♅ 11
♂ 05 ♒ 56

♀ 53

♀✶☉ 0°44
♄□♅ 1°13
a□M 1°27
☉✶♇ 1°32
♀⊼♆ 1°33
♂□M 1°41
♄□A 1°42

GACEY, JOHN WAYNE
Murderer

March 17, 1942
00:20 AM CWT
Chicago, Ill
87 W 39   41 N 52

Twice married and divorced; an "upstanding" citizen. Second wife divorced him because of sexual impotency. Indicted January 13, 1979, for the sadistic sexual assault and murder of thirty-two young men and boys, most of whom were buried in the cellar.

A: Edith Custer in M.H., April 1979, "hospital birth record."[57]

SVP=✶ 6° 4' 5"
JULIAN DAY=2430435.72222

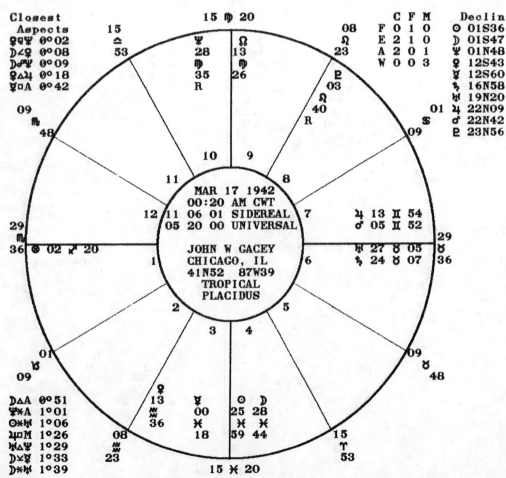

C F M	Declin
F 0 1 0	☉ 01S36
E 2 1 0	☽ 01S47
A 2 0 1	♆ 01N48
W 0 0 3	♀ 12S43
	☿ 12S60
	♄ 16N58
	♅ 19N20
	♃ 22N09
	♂ 22N42
	♇ 23N56

Closest Aspects
♀✶♆ 0°02
☽∠♀ 0°08
☽✶♆ 0°09
♀△♃ 0°18
☿□A 0°42

♃ 13 ♊ 54
♂ 05 ♊ 52

♅ 27 ♉ 05
♄ 24 ♉ 07

♀ 13 ♒ 00
☿ ♒ 36

☉ 25 ✶ 59
☽ 28 ✶ 44

☽△A 0°51
♆✶A 1°01
☉✶♅ 1°06
♃□M 1°26
♅△♀ 1°29
☽⊼♀ 1°33
☽✶♅ 1°39

GALILEO, GALILEI
Astronomer, physicist

February 25, 1564 NS
3:00 PM Sundial
Pisa, Italy
10 E 24 43 N 43

Closest Aspects
☽⚺♀ 0°03
☉⚻A 0°03
☉∠M 0°04
♄⚼♇ 0°07
☿☌♇ 0°24

	C	F	M
F	1	0	1
E	1	0	0
A	1	0	0
W	2	0	4

Declin
♀ 04S58
☿ 07S52
☉ 09S19
☽ 12N34
♆ 19N33
♇ 20S12
♃ 21N05
♄ 21N17
♂ 21N34
♅ 21S44

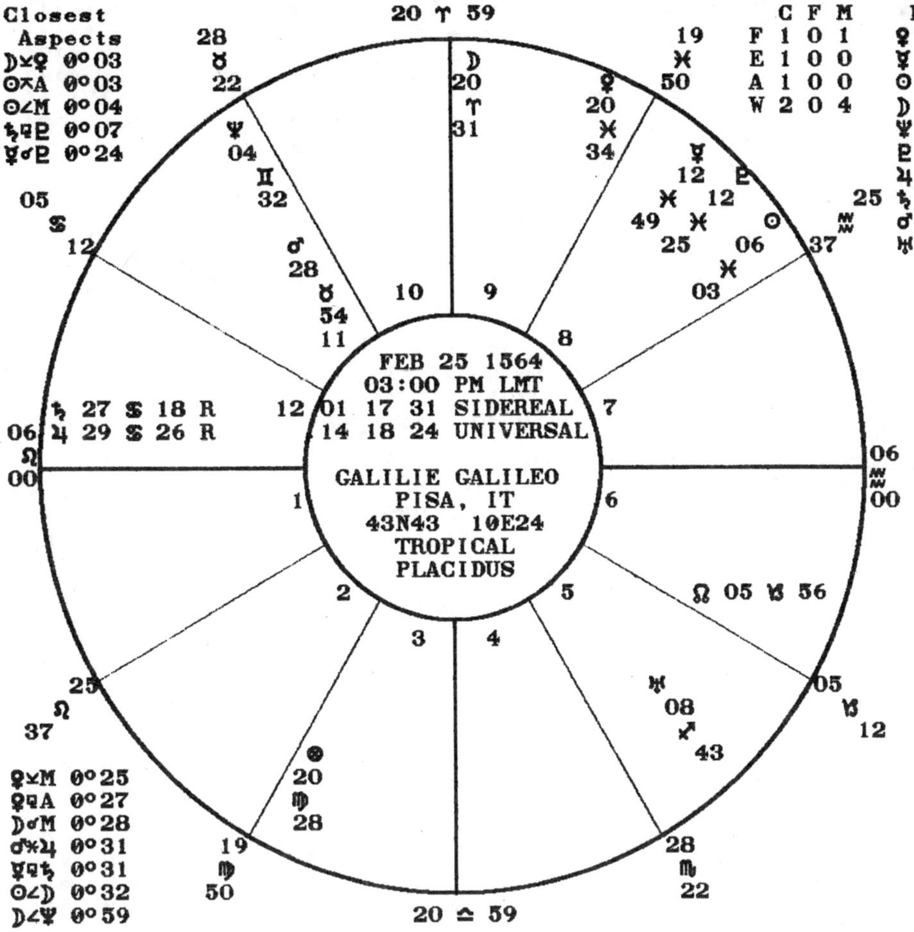

FEB 25 1564
03:00 PM LMT
01 17 31 SIDEREAL
14 18 24 UNIVERSAL
GALILIE GALILEO
PISA, IT
43N43 10E24
TROPICAL
PLACIDUS

♀⚺M 0°25
♀⚼A 0°27
☽☍M 0°28
♂⚹♃ 0°31
☿⚼♄ 0°31
☉∠☽ 0°32
☽∠♆ 0°59

Italian founder of modern experimental science; a great inventor and contributing genius in mathematics, which he taught for eighteen years, in physics, and in astronomy. Forced to recant by the Inquisition in 1632. Spent his last years writing. (1564-1642)

B: Blackwell in AA, June 1970, "from his own statement" in *Le Opere Di Gallilei,* Vol. 19, edited by Barbera.

SVP=♓11°20' 9"
JULIAN DAY=2292354.09611

GALSWORTHY, JOHN
Writer

August 14, 1867
2:30 PM LMT
Kinston, Surrey, England
0 W 15 51 N 25

Declin
♂ 00S26
♇ 01N48
♆ 04N23
♃ 11S14
☉ 14N25
☽ 14S32
♄ 15S08
☿ 16N22
♀ 18N38
♅ 23N19

	C	F	M
F	1	3	0
E	1	0	0
A	0	1	1
W	1	1	1

Closest Aspects
♃□A 0°34
♂∠♄ 0°40
☽⚻♅ 0°45
♇⚼M 1°03
♂⚼♇ 1°08

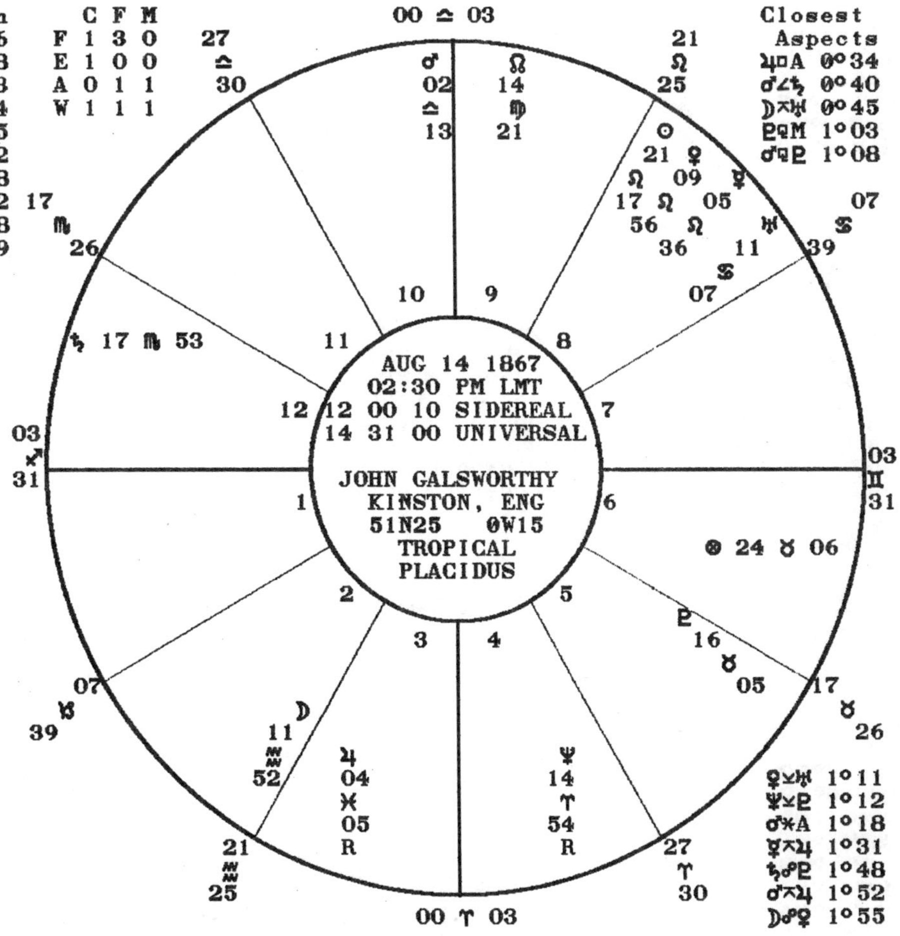

AUG 14 1867
02:30 PM LMT
12 00 10 SIDEREAL
14 31 00 UNIVERSAL
JOHN GALSWORTHY
KINSTON, ENG
51N25 0W15
TROPICAL
PLACIDUS

♀⚺♅ 1°11
♆⚺♇ 1°12
♂⚹A 1°18
☿⚻♃ 1°31
♄☍♇ 1°48
♂⚻♃ 1°52
☽☍♀ 1°55

British novelist, dramatist, and playwright; one of the most important writers of his time. Received the 1932 Nobel prize for literature; most noted for his series of novels about the Forsythe family from 1906 to 1928. (1867-1933)

B: PC quotes *The Life and Letters of John Galsworthy* by Marrot, 1936, p. 28.

SVP=♓ 7° 6'32"
JULIAN DAY=2403193.10486

GAUGUIN, PAUL
Artist

June 8, 1848
10:00 AM LMT
Paris, France
2 E 20   48 N 50

French painter, wood carver, and ceramicist; one of the pioneers of post-impressionism. In 1884 gave up a successful business and left his wife and five children to paint. Moved to Tahiti in 1891, where he produced his most famous and vivid work. (1848-1903)

A: Gauquelin #439 Vol 4. [58]

SVP=)(7°22'34"
JULIAN DAY=2396186.91019

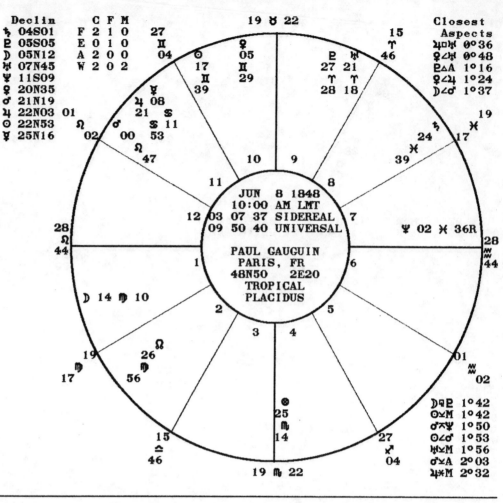

	Declin	C	F	M
♄	04S01	F	2 1 0
♇	05S05	E	0 1 0
☽	05N12	A	2 0 0
♅	07N45	W	2 0 2
♆	11S09		
♀	20N35		
♂	21N19		
♃	22N03		
☉	22N53		
☿	25N16		

Closest Aspects
♃□♅ 0°36
♀∠♅ 0°48
♇△A 1°16
♀∠♃ 1°24
☽∠♂ 1°37

☽♂♇ 1°42
☉⊻M 1°42
♂⊼♆ 1°50
☉∠♂ 1°53
♅⊻M 1°56
♂⊻A 2°03
♃✳M 2°32

GAUQUELIN, FRANCOISE
Scientist

June 19, 1929
4:00 AM MET
Neuchatel, Switzerland
7 E 54   45 N 49

Degrees in statistics and psychology. Though skeptical of astrology, began collaboration with Michel Gauquelin before their marriage in 1954. One son, born April 22, 1967. Author of books on memory and on communication, as well as papers on psychology in scientific publications.

A: From her to LMR, April 1979.

Closest Aspects
♇⊼M 0°03
♀♃♄ 0°06
☉♂♄ 0°07
☉∠♃ 0°14
a⊼M 0°48

♇⊻A 0°52
♃⊻♇ 0°52
♀✳♅ 1°03
☉✳♆ 1°41
♄△♆ 1°48
♀⊻♅ 1°57
☽♇♅ 2°04

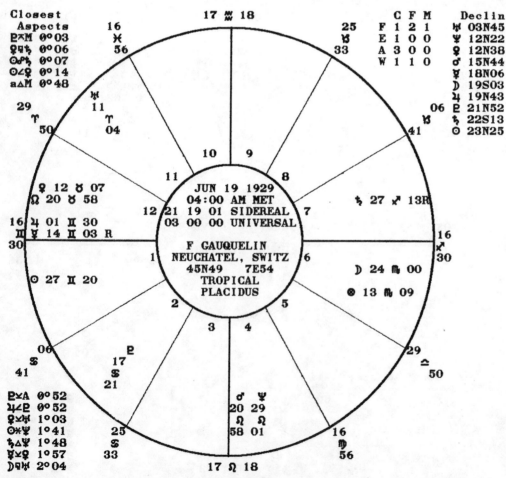

	C	F	M		Declin
F	1 2 1			♅	03N45
E	1 0 0			♆	12N22
A	3 0 0			♀	12N38
W	1 1 0			♂	15N44
				☿	18N06
				☽	19S03
				♃	19N43
				♇	21N52
				♄	22S13
				☉	23N25

SVP=)(6°14'54"
JULIAN DAY=2425781.62500

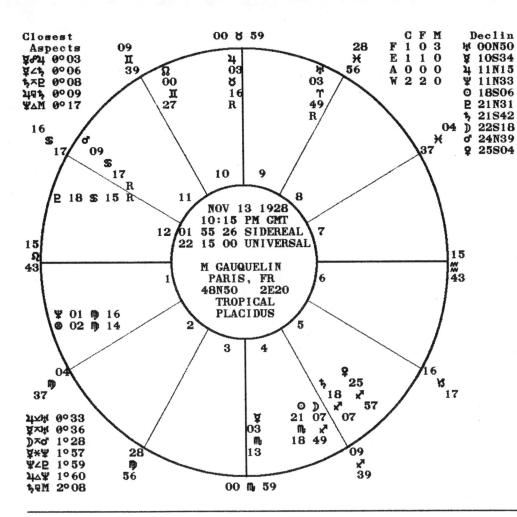

GAUQUELIN, MICHEL
Scientist

November 13, 1928
10:15 PM GMT
Paris, France
2 E 20   48 N 50

Degrees in statistics and psychology from the Sorbonne. Examined astrological data from 1950 to determine the degree of statistical evidence. A respected researcher who has compiled six massive volumes of data. Books include *Cosmic Clocks* (1967).

A: From him to LMR, 1979, "10:15 to 10:20 PM."

Closest Aspects
☿□♃ 0°03
☿∠♄ 0°06
♄☌♇ 0°08
♃□♄ 0°09
♆△M 0°17

NOV 13 1928
10:15 PM GMT
01 55 26 SIDEREAL
22 15 00 UNIVERSAL

M GAUQUELIN
PARIS, FR
48N50 2E20
TROPICAL
PLACIDUS

	C	F	M	Declin	
F	1	0	3	♅	00N50
E	1	1	0	☿	10S34
A	0	0	0	♃	11N15
W	2	2	0	♆	11N33
				☉	18S06
				♇	21N31
				♄	21S42
				☽	22S18
				♂	24N39
				♀	25S04

♃△♅ 0°33
☿△♅ 0°36
☽☌♂ 1°28
☿✱♆ 1°57
♆∠♇ 1°59
♃△♆ 1°60
♄□M 2°08

SVP=⅜ 6°15'27"
JULIAN DAY=2425564.42708

GELLER, URI
Telekenic

December 20, 1946
2:00 AM EET
Tel Aviv, Palestine
34 E 49   32 N 02

First paranormal experience on December 25, 1949. International reputation as a phenomenon by 1971, when he began to demonstrate his abilities professionally. Tested by Stanford Research Institute in 1972; odds pronounced to be trillion to one against chance.

A: Richard Nolle in Dell, February 1976; "data through Puharich, who wrote of Geller after testing."[59]

SVP=⅜ 6° 0'18"
JULIAN DAY=2432174.50000

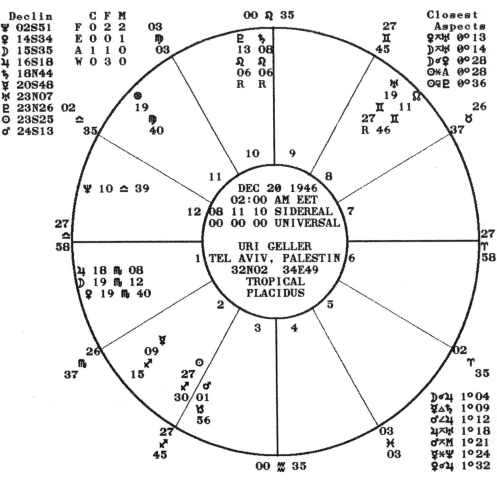

Declin		C	F	M
♆	02S51	F	0	2	2
♀	14S34	E	0	0	1
☽	15S35	A	1	1	0
♃	16S18	W	0	3	0
♄	18N44				
☿	20S48				
♅	23N07				
♇	23N26				
☉	23S25				
♂	24S13				

Closest Aspects
☿☌♅ 0°13
☽☌♅ 0°14
☽☌♀ 0°28
☉✱A 0°28
☉□♇ 0°36

DEC 20 1946
02:00 AM EET
08 11 10 SIDEREAL
00 00 00 UNIVERSAL

URI GELLER
TEL AVIV, PALESTIN
32N02 34E49
TROPICAL
PLACIDUS

☽☌♃ 1°04
☿△♄ 1°09
♂∠♃ 1°12
♃□M 1°18
♂□M 1°21
☿✱M 1°24
♀☌♃ 1°32

GIDE, ANDRE
Writer

November 22, 1869
3:00 AM LMT
Paris, France
2 E.20   48 N.50

French novelist, essayist, critic, and playwright; won the 1947 Nobel prize for literature. Drew on his own experience and concern with the search for new ethics to replace prejudice. In 1909 founded a monthly magazine that influenced the youth of France. (1869-1951)

A: Gauquelin #364 Vol 6.

SVP=♓ 7° 4'51"
JULIAN DAY=2404023.61852

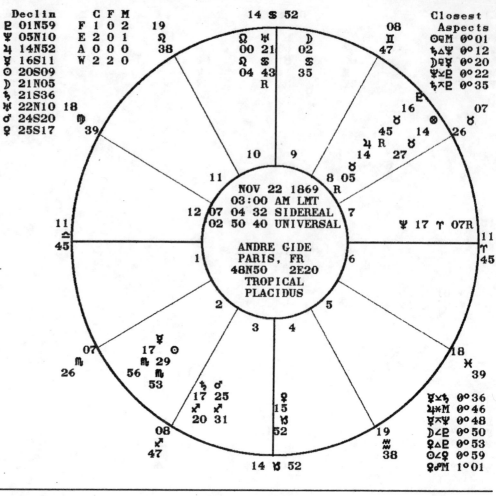

GLENN, JOHN H. JR.
Astronaut

July 18, 1921
4:00 PM CDT
Cambridge, Ohio
81 W.35   40 N.02

First American to orbit the earth, when his spacecraft, the U.S. Mercury-Atlas 6, circled the planet three times on February 20, 1962. Became an executive with the Royal Crown Cola Co. In 1974 ran for Congress to become a U.S. Senator.

A: CSH.60

SVP=♓ 6°21'11"
JULIAN DAY=2422889.37500

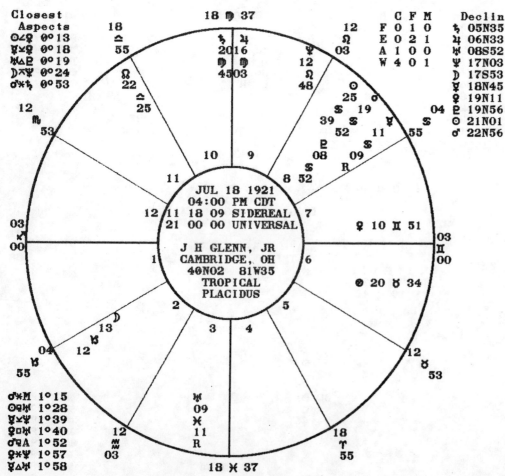

GODFREY, ARTHUR
Entertainer

August 31, 1903
8:00 AM EST
New York, N.Y.
73 W 57   40 N 45

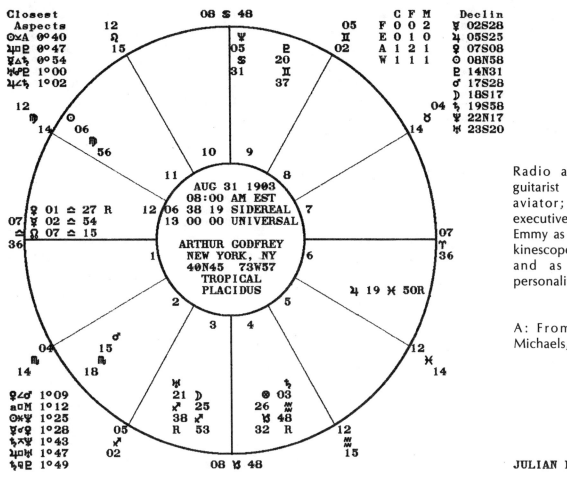

Closest
Aspects
⊙⚹A 0°40
♃□♇ 0°47
☿△♂ 0°54
♅⚹♇ 1°00
♃∠♄ 1°02

08 ♋ 48

	C F M	Declin
05 ♊	F 0 0 2	☿ 02S28
02	E 0 1 0	♃ 05S25
	A 1 2 1	♀ 07S08
	W 1 1 1	⊙ 08N58
		♇ 14N31
		♂ 17S28
		☽ 18S17
04		♄ 19S58
		♆ 22N17
		♅ 23S20

AUG 31 1903
08:00 AM EST
06 38 19 SIDEREAL
13 00 00 UNIVERSAL

ARTHUR GODFREY
NEW YORK, NY
40N45 73W57
TROPICAL
PLACIDUS

♀ 01 ♎ 27 R
☿ 02 ♎ 54
☊ 07 ♎ 15

♀∠♂ 1°09
a□M 1°12
⊙⚹♆ 1°25
☿⚹♀ 1°28
♄⚹♆ 1°43
♃□♅ 1°47
♄□♇ 1°49

Radio announcer; singer;
guitarist and ukelele player;
aviator; farmer; business
executive. Nominated for a TV
Emmy as the most outstanding
kinescoped personality of 1949,
and as most outstanding
personality in 1962 and 1963.

A: From him to Evelyn
Michaels, 1979.[61]

SVP=♓ 6°36'14"
JULIAN DAY=2416358.04167

GODZIK, GREGORY
Murder victim

March 23, 1959
3:54 PM CST
Chicago, Ill
87 W 39   41 N 52

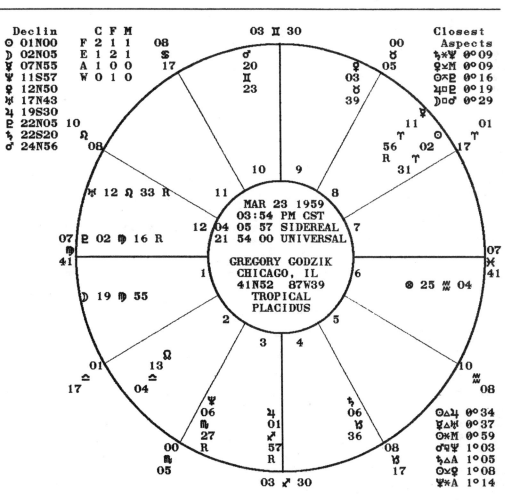

Declin	C F M
⊙ 01N00	F 2 1 1
☽ 02N05	E 1 2 1
☿ 07N55	A 1 0 0
♆ 11S57	W 0 1 0
♀ 12N50	
♅ 17N43	
♃ 19S30	
♇ 22N05	
♄ 22S20	
♂ 24N56	

03 ♊ 30

Closest
Aspects
♄⚹♆ 0°09
♀⚹M 0°09
⊙⚹♇ 0°16
♃□♇ 0°19
☽□♂ 0°29

MAR 23 1959
03:54 PM CST
04 05 57 SIDEREAL
21 54 00 UNIVERSAL

GREGORY GODZIK
CHICAGO, IL
41N52 87W39
TROPICAL
PLACIDUS

A young employee of John
Gacey, who told his parents that
Gacey was a good boss and paid
well. Disappeared on December 11, 1976. After Gacey was
arrested on December 12, 1978,
Godzik's body was found
buried in the basement, along
with twenty-seven other young
men.

A: M.H., April 1979, "birth
record from his mother."

⊙△♃ 0°34
☿△♅ 0°37
⊙⚹M 0°59
♂⚹♆ 1°03
♄△♀ 1°05
⊙⚹♀ 1°08
♆⚹A 1°14

03 ♐ 30

SVP=♓ 5°49'41"
JULIAN DAY=2436651.41250

GOEBBELS, PAUL JOSEPH
Nazi

October 29, 1897
11:30 PM MET
Rheydt, Germany
6 E 27   51 N 10

Official propogandist of Nazi
Germany; in control of all
public communication media.
Helped Hitler bring the Nazis to
power in 1933. A fanatical Nazi,
with his entire family,
committed suicide when
Germany fell. (1897-1945)

A: Gauquelin #1903 Vol 3.62

SVP=♓ 6°40'58"
JULIAN DAY=2414227.43750

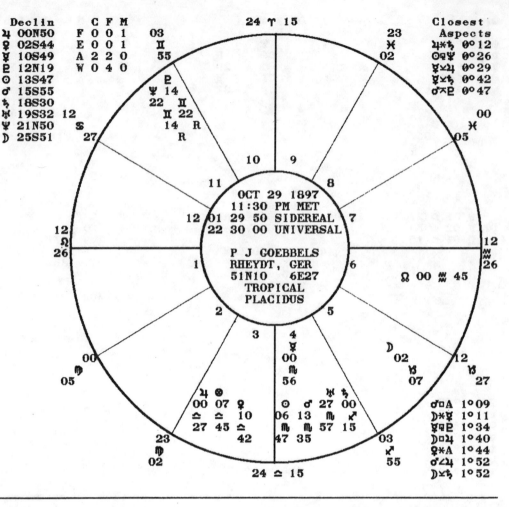

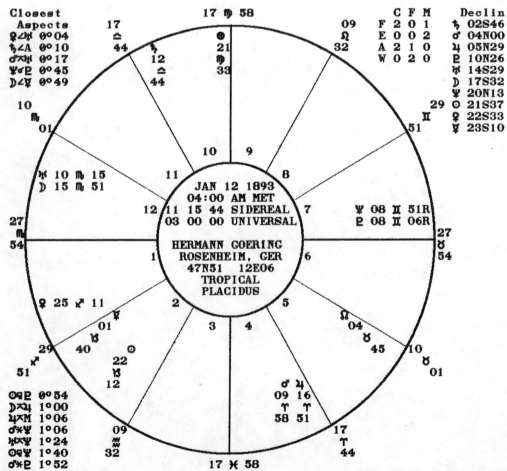

GOERING, HERMANN
Nazi

January 12, 1893
4:00 AM MET
Rosenheim, Germany
12 E 06   47 N 51

Second to Adolph Hitler as
leader of Nazi Germany. Reich
Marshall and Air Force
commander; head of the
German armament and war
industry. Loved extravagance
and show; jovial, ruthless.
Sentenced to hang for war
crimes; took poison in 1946.

A: Gauquelin #1881 Vol 3.63

SVP=♓ 6°45'21"
JULIAN DAY=2412475.62500

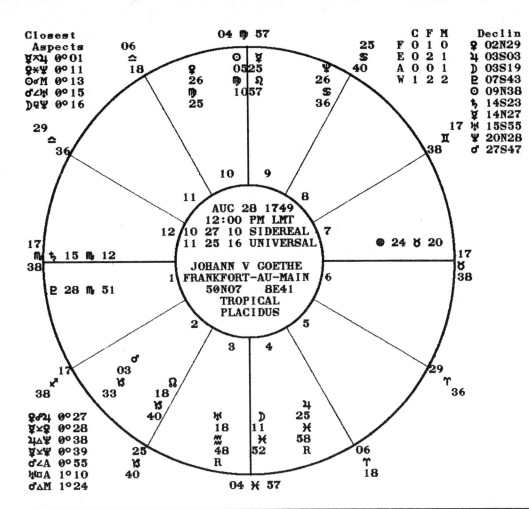

GOETHE, JOHANN VON
Writer

August 28, 1749 NS
12:00 Noon LMT
Frankfort-am-Main, Germany
8 E 41   50 N 07

Germany's most famous writer; a great literary genius of imagination and versatility, unsurpassed as a poet. Lawyer in 1771; first published in 1773; famous by age 25. Took sixty years to complete *Faust*. (1749-1832)

B: PC quotes his autobiography, in which he writes, "born mid-day when the clock struck 12:00." Ebertin, same data.

SVP=✶ 8°44'57"
JULIAN DAY=2360108.97588

GONAZLES, PANCHO
Tennis champion

May 9, 1928
4:45 AM PST
Los Angeles, Ca
118 W 15   34 N 04

Champion who won the professional tennis tour eight years in a row, from 1953 to 1960. After 1972, moved to Las Vegas with his third wife to become tennis director at the expensive hotel and entertainment complex, Caesars Palace.

A: CSH.

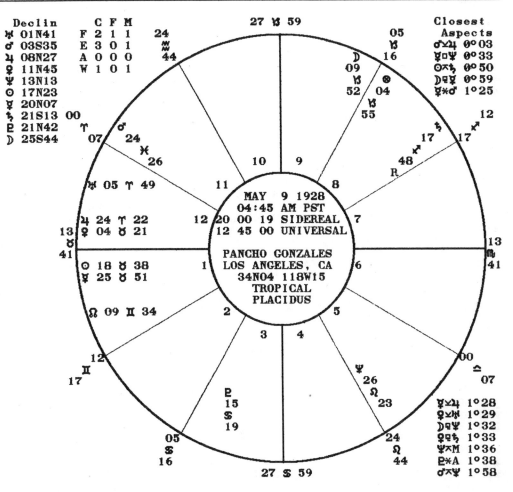

SVP=✶ 6°15'54"
JULIAN DAY=2425376.03125

GORDON, CHARLES
General

January 28, 1833
9:53 AM LMT
Woolwich, England
0 E 02   51 N 29

British soldier called "Chinese Gordon", who fought in the Crimean War and took part in an expedition to China in 1860. Helped capture Peking, serving as commander of the Chinese forces. Killed in a battle at Khartoum in 1885.

A: Pagan in *Pioneer to Poet* states, "hour recorded by his father in the family Bible."[64]

SVP=♓ 7°35'39"
JULIAN DAY=2390576.91171

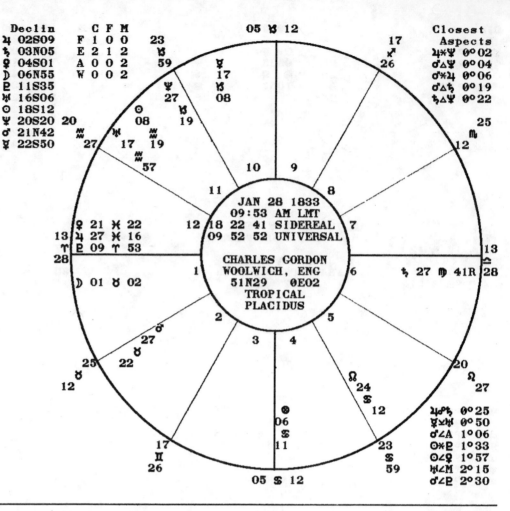

GORDON, RICHARD F.
Astronaut

October 5, 1929
12:45 PM PST
Seattle, Wash
122 W 20   47 N 36

U.S. Navy 1951; selected for NASA astronaut training, October 1963. Pilot of back-up crew for Gemini VIII flight; pilot Gemini XI mission, September 1966; Command Module pilot of Apollo X, November 1969; retired, 1972. Became executive vice-president of pro football team in 1972.

A: CSH.

SVP=♓ 6°14'38"
JULIAN DAY=2425890.36458

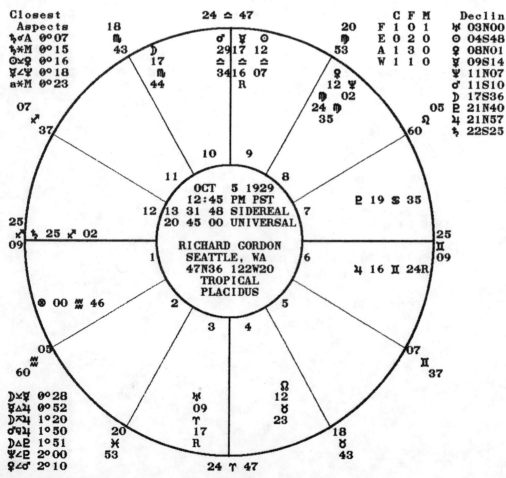

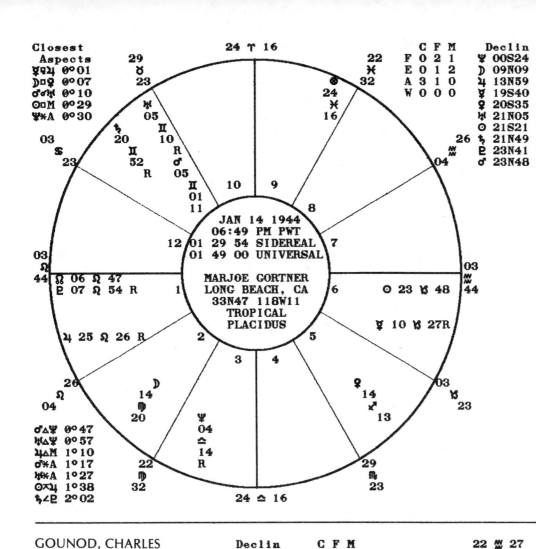

GORTNER, MARJOE
Boy evangelist

January 14, 1944
6:49 PM PWT
Long Beach, Ca
118 W 11   33 N 47

CFM   Declin
F 0 2 1   ♆ 00S24
E 0 1 2   ☽ 09N09
A 3 1 0   ♃ 13N59
W 0 0 0   ☿ 19S40
          ♀ 20S35
          ♅ 21N05
          ☉ 21S21
          ♄ 21N49
          ♇ 23N41
          ♂ 23N48

Closest
Aspects
☿⊼♃ 0°01
☽□♀ 0°07
♂☌♅ 0°10
☉□M 0°29
♆⚹A 0°30

JAN 14 1944
06:49 PM PWT
01 29 54 SIDEREAL
01 49 00 UNIVERSAL

MARJOE GORTNER
LONG BEACH, CA
33N47 118W11
TROPICAL
PLACIDUS

☉ 23 ♑ 48

☿ 10 ♑ 27R

♂△♆ 0°47
♅△♆ 0°57
♃⊼M 1°10
♂⚹A 1°17
♅⚹A 1°27
☉⊼♃ 1°38
♄∠♇ 2°02

From childhood, toured and preached to the Bible Belt for fifteen years. Became an actor in 1971, playing himself in *Marjoe*, followed by B films and TV. Producer of *When You Comin' Back, Red Ryder?* (1978). Married at 16; one daughter; married to Candy Clark, 1978, for a year.

A: CSH.

SVP=♓ 6° 2'41"
JULIAN DAY=2431104.57569

GOUNOD, CHARLES
Musician

June 17, 1818
4:00 AM LMT
Paris, France
2 E 20   48 N 50

Declin
♄ 06S30
♇ 15S58
☿ 17N16
♂ 17N27
♆ 22S04
♅ 22S59
♃ 23S03
☽ 23S14
☉ 23N23
♀ 23N29

CFM
F 0 1 3
E 0 0 1
A 2 0 0
W 1 0 2

Closest
Aspects
☉☌♆ 0°11
♄□♅ 0°14
♆⚹A 0°15
☉☌A 0°25
☽□♀ 1°02

JUN 17 1818
04:00 AM LMT
21 39 13 SIDEREAL
03 50 40 UNIVERSAL

CHARLES GOUNOD
PARIS, FR
48N50 2E20
TROPICAL
PLACIDUS

☿ 02 ♊ 42

☉ 25 ♊ 17

♃ 09 ♑ 46R

♆ 25 ♐ 07R
♅ 17 ♐ 52R
☽ 04 ♐ 06
⊗ 03 ♐ 41

French composer, whose first opera was performed in 1851. Wrote the opera *Faust* in 1859 and Ave Maria in 1859; other compositions include choral works and music for orchestra, piano and chamber groups. After 1860, composed for stage. (1818-1893)

A: Gauquelin #1929 Vol 4.65

♀

☉□♇ 1°05
♆□♇ 1°16
☽□☿ 1°25
♇△A 1°31
♀△♄ 2°02
☿□♅ 2°16
♃∠M 2°19

SVP=♓ 7°47'49"
JULIAN DAY=2385237.66019

GRIFFIN, MERV
Entertainer

July 6, 1925
4:45 AM PST
San Mateo, Ca
122 W 19   37 N 34

TV host of *The Merv Griffin Show*. Singer, pianist, and television personality. Nominated for Emmy as outstanding personality in variety program or series in 1962-63 season. Years as a singer with Freddie Martin's orchestra; radio and night club performer.

A: CSH.

SVP=℣ 6°18'13"
JULIAN DAY=2424338.03125

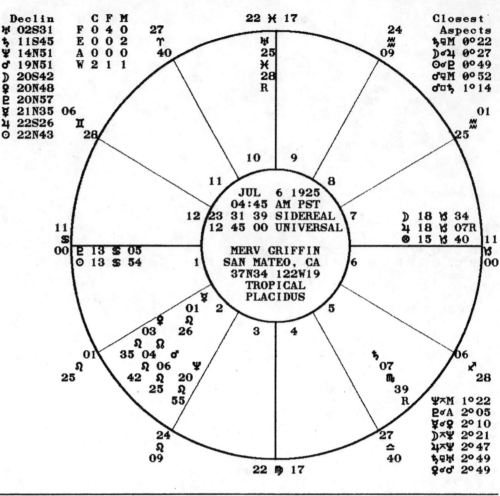

Declin		C F M
♅ 02S31		F 0 4 0
♄ 11S45		E 0 0 2
♆ 14N51		A 0 0 0
♂ 19N51		W 2 1 1
☽ 20S42		
☿ 20N48		
♇ 20N57		
♃ 21N35	06	
♃ 22S26		
☉ 22N43	28	

Closest Aspects
♄♇M 0°22
☽♃ 0°27
☉♇ 0°49
♂M 0°52
♂♄ 1°14

JUL 6 1925
04:45 AM PST
23 31 39 SIDEREAL
12 45 00 UNIVERSAL
MERV GRIFFIN
SAN MATEO, CA
37N34 122W19
TROPICAL
PLACIDUS

☽ 18 ♑ 34
♃ 18 ♑ 07R
⊗ 15 ♑ 40

♆♐M 1°22
♇♂A 2°05
☿♂♀ 2°10
☽⊼♆ 2°21
♃⊼♆ 2°47
♄♇♅ 2°49
♀♂♂ 2°49

GRISSOM, VIRGIL "GUS"
Astronaut

April 3, 1926
6:00 PM EST
Mitchell, Ind
86 W 28   38 N 22

One of the seven original astronauts (1959). Second American in space on Project Mercury (1961); first to maneuver a spacecraft manually from one orbital path to another; first to make two trips into outer space. Killed in flashfire on grounded spacecraft in 1967.

A: CL quotes AFA, November 1967, "from his mother."

SVP=℣ 6°17'39"
JULIAN DAY=2424609.45833

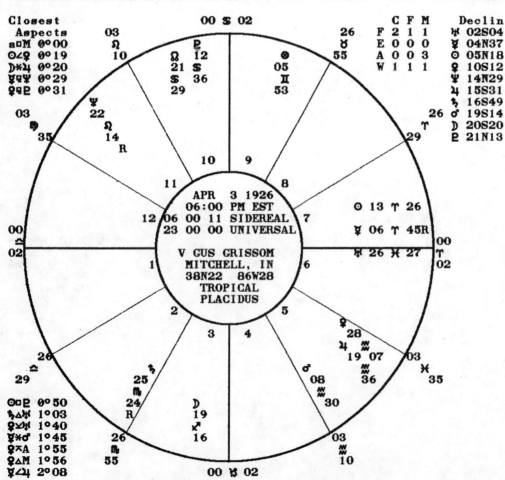

Closest Aspects
a□M 0°00
☉⊼♀ 0°19
☽⚹♃ 0°20
☿♀ 0°29
♀♇ 0°31

	C F M	Declin
	F 2 1 1	♅ 02S04
	E 0 0 0	☿ 04N37
	A 0 0 3	☉ 05N18
	W 1 1 1	♀ 10S12
		♆ 14N29
		♃ 15S31
		♄ 16S49
		♂ 19S14
		☽ 20S20
		♇ 21N13

APR 3 1926
06:00 PM EST
06 00 11 SIDEREAL
23 00 00 UNIVERSAL
V GUS GRISSOM
MITCHELL, IN
38N22 86W28
TROPICAL
PLACIDUS

☉ 13 ♈ 26
☿ 06 ♈ 45R

☉♇ 0°50
♄△♅ 1°03
♀⚹♅ 1°40
☿⚹♂ 1°45
♀⊼A 1°55
♀△M 1°56
♀⊼♃ 2°08

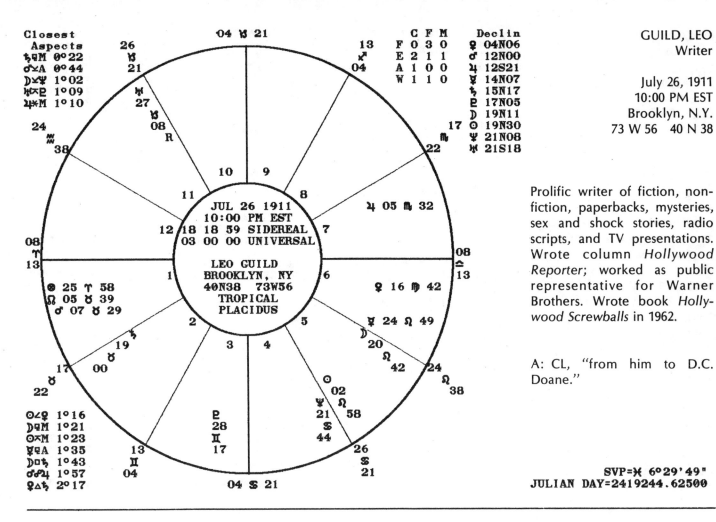

GUILD, LEO
Writer

July 26, 1911
10:00 PM EST
Brooklyn, N.Y.
73 W 56   40 N 38

Closest
Aspects
♄□M 0°22
♂⊼A 0°44
☽⊼Ψ 1°02
♅⊼♇ 1°09
♃⊼M 1°10

	C	F	M		Declin
F	0	3	0	♀	04N06
E	2	1	1	♂	12N00
A	1	0	0	♃	12S21
W	1	1	0	☿	14N07
				♄	15N17
				♇	17N05
				☽	19N11
				☉	19N30
				Ψ	21N08
				♅	21S18

JUL 26 1911
10:00 PM EST
18 18 59 SIDEREAL
03 00 00 UNIVERSAL

LEO GUILD
BROOKLYN, NY
40N38 73W56
TROPICAL
PLACIDUS

⊕ 25 ♈ 58
Ω 05 ♉ 39
♂ 07 ♉ 29

☉♂♀ 1°16
☽□M 1°21
☉⊼M 1°23
☿□A 1°35
☽□M 1°43
♂□♃ 1°57
♀△♄ 2°17

Prolific writer of fiction, non-fiction, paperbacks, mysteries, sex and shock stories, radio scripts, and TV presentations. Wrote column *Hollywood Reporter*; worked as public representative for Warner Brothers. Wrote book *Hollywood Screwballs* in 1962.

A: CL, "from him to D.C. Doane."

SVP=♓ 6°29'49"
JULIAN DAY=2419244.62500

GUTHRIE, ARLO
Musician

July 10, 1947
8:45 AM EST
Brooklyn, N.Y.
73 W 56   40 N 38

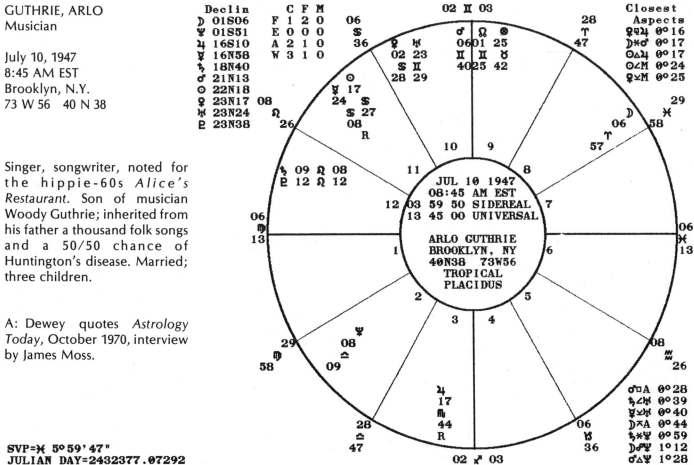

Declin		C	F	M
☽ 01S06	F	1	2	0
Ψ 01S51	E	0	0	0
♃ 16S10	A	2	1	0
☿ 16N58	W	3	1	0
♄ 18N40				
♂ 21N13				
☉ 22N18				
♀ 23N17				
♅ 23N24				
♇ 23N38				

02 ♊ 03

Closest
Aspects
♀□♃ 0°16
☽⚹♂ 0°17
☉△♃ 0°17
☉⊼M 0°24
♀⊼M 0°25

JUL 10 1947
08:45 AM EST
03 59 50 SIDEREAL
13 45 00 UNIVERSAL

ARLO GUTHRIE
BROOKLYN, NY
40N38 73W56
TROPICAL
PLACIDUS

Singer, songwriter, noted for the hippie-60s *Alice's Restaurant*. Son of musician Woody Guthrie; inherited from his father a thousand folk songs and a 50/50 chance of Huntington's disease. Married; three children.

A: Dewey quotes *Astrology Today*, October 1970, interview by James Moss.

♂□A 0°28
♄⊼♅ 0°39
☿⊼♅ 0°40
☽⊼A 0°44
♄⚹Ψ 0°59
☽♂Ψ 1°12
♂△Ψ 1°28

SVP=♓ 5°59'47"
JULIAN DAY=2432377.07292

02 ♐ 03

HAGGARD, MERLE
Musician

April 6, 1937
1:30 AM PST
Bakersfield, Ca
119 W 01   35 N 23

Songwriter and singer of rough-hewn, down-home country music. Had his first guitar at age 11; a renegade by 14; spent twenty-seven months in San Quentin. Paroled in February 1960. By 1962 was working in the music scene. With first record in 1963, on the way to the top of his field.

A: CSH.

SVP=✶ 6° 7' 52"
JULIAN DAY=2428629.89583

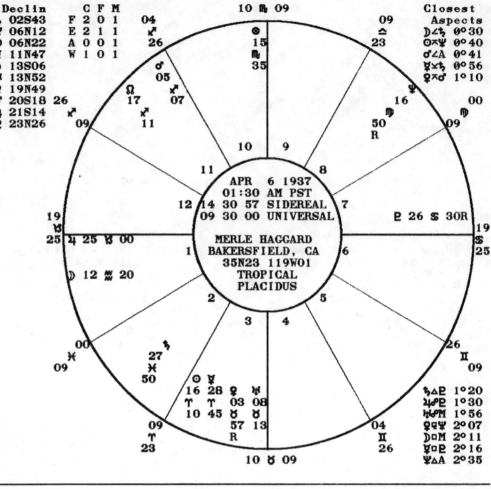

HALDEMAN, H.R.
Government official

October 27, 1926
3:30 AM PST
Los Angeles, Ca
118 W 15   34 N 04

Chief of staff to President Nixon. Convicted of conspiracy, obstruction of justice, and perjury in the Watergate scandals in 1976. Spent eighteen months in Lompoc prison; released on December 21, 1978. Author of *The Ends of Power* (1978).

A: CSH.

SVP=✶ 6°17'12"
JULIAN DAY=2424815.97917

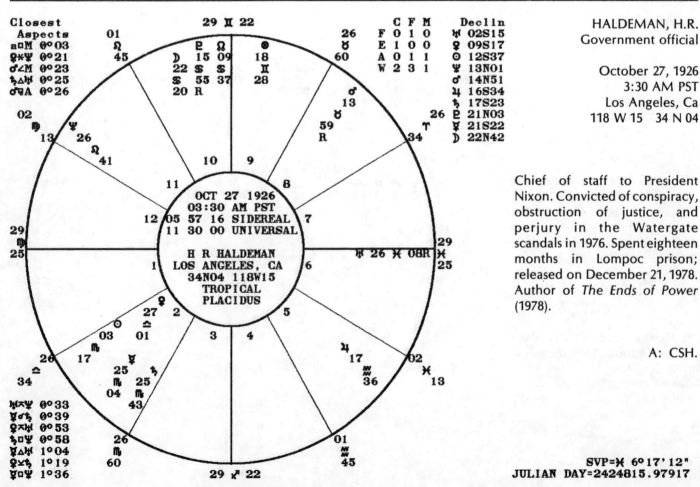

HAMILL, DOROTHY
Skating champion

July 26, 1956
10:00 PM CDT
Chicago, Ill
87 W 39 41 N 52

Closest Aspects
♆✶♇ 0°15
☉⚺♃ 0°20
♂□M 0°31
♀⚻♄ 0°37
♃⚺♅ 1°00

	C	F	M
F	0	4	0
E	0	1	0
A	1	1	0
W	0	1	2

Declin
☽ 00N53
♂ 07S56
♆ 09S03
♃ 11N03
♄ 17S19
♀ 18N04
☿ 18N53
☉ 19N15
♅ 20N06
♇ 22N15

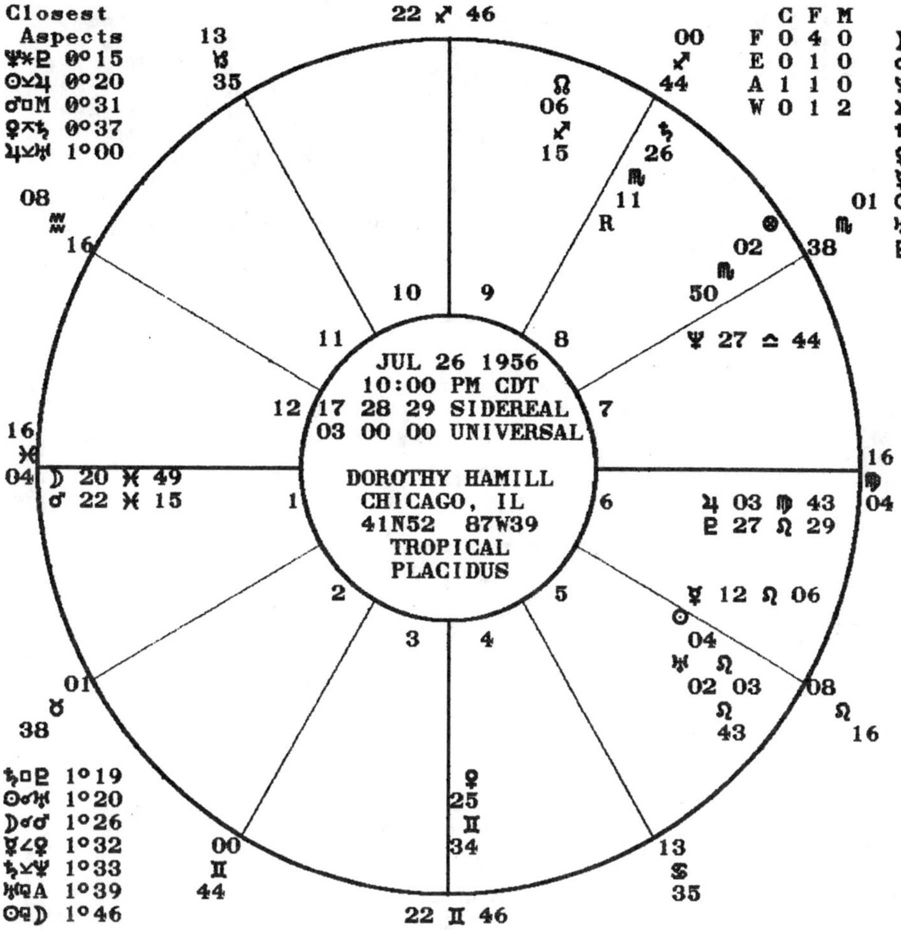

22 ♐ 46
00 ♐ 44
01 ♏ 38
16 ♍ 04
08 ♌ 16
13 ♋ 35
22 ♊ 46
00 ♊ 44
01 ♉ 38
16 ♓ 04
08 ♒ 16
13 ♑ 35
☊ 06 ♐ 15
♄ 26 ♏ 11 R
⊗ 02 ♏ 50
♆ 27 ♎ 44
♃ 03 ♍ 43
♇ 27 ♌ 29
☿ 12 ♌ 06
☉ 04
♅ ♌
02 03
♌
43
♀ 25 ♊ 34
☽ 20 ♓ 49
♂ 22 ♓ 15
JUL 26 1956
10:00 PM CDT
17 28 29 SIDEREAL
03 00 00 UNIVERSAL
DOROTHY HAMILL
CHICAGO, IL
41N52 87W39
TROPICAL
PLACIDUS

♄□♇ 1°19
☉☌♅ 1°20
☽☌♂ 1°26
☿∠♀ 1°32
♄⚺♆ 1°33
♅⚼A 1°39
☉⚼☽ 1°46

First pair of skates at age 8; dropped out of school at 14 (private tutor) to accelerate practice with perseverence and discipline. Won U.S. titles in 1974, '75, and '76; won the Olympics games gold medal in 1976, followed by the Women's World Title.

A: Mary Lee Lewis, "from her father."

SVP=♓ 5°51'42"
JULIAN DAY=2435681.62500

HARRISON, REX
Actor

March 5, 1908
5:00 AM GMT
Huyton, England
2 W 51 53 N 24

Declin
☽ 02N07
♄ 02S37
☉ 06S12
☿ 07S01
♀ 09N40
♂ 14N33
♇ 15N48
♃ 19N55
♆ 22N05
♅ 22S52

	C	F	M
F	2	1	0
E	1	0	1
A	1	0	0
W	1	0	3

Closest Aspects
♂∠♇ 0°08
♆⚼M 0°11
☿⚻♃ 0°22
☿∠A 1°00
♄△M 1°14

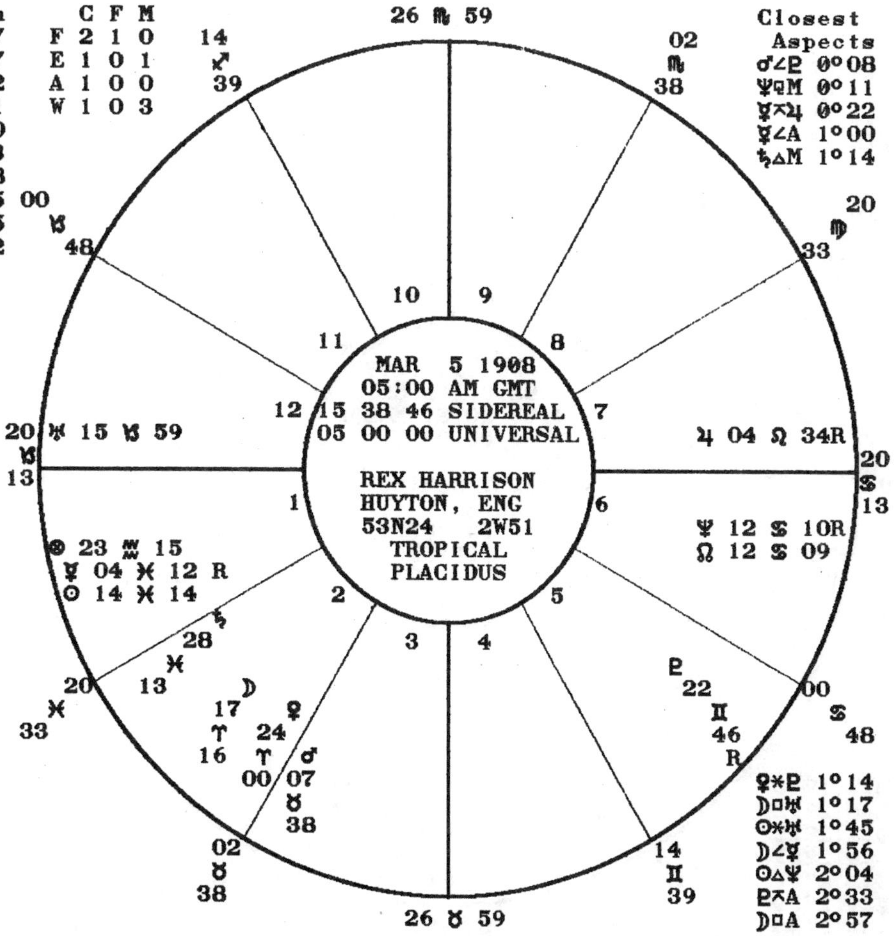

26 ♏ 59
14 ♐ 39
02 ♏ 38
20 ♍ 33
00 ♑ 48
20 ♑ 13
20 ♋ 13
20 ♓ 33
00 ♋ 48
02 ♉ 38
14 ♊ 39
26 ♉ 59
♅ 15 ♑ 59
♃ 04 ♌ 34R
♆ 12 ♋ 10R
☊ 12 ♋ 09
⊗ 23 ♒ 15
☿ 04 ♓ 12 R
☉ 14 ♓ 14
♄ 28 ♓ 13
☽ 17 ♈ 16
♀ 24 ♈ 00
♂ 07 ♉ 38
♇ 22 ♊ 46 R
MAR 5 1908
05:00 AM GMT
15 38 46 SIDEREAL
05 00 00 UNIVERSAL
REX HARRISON
HUYTON, ENG
53N24 2W51
TROPICAL
PLACIDUS

♀✶♇ 1°14
☽□♅ 1°17
☉✶♅ 1°45
☽∠☿ 1°56
☉△♆ 2°04
♇⚻A 2°33
☽□A 2°57

Won an Oscar as best actor in *My Fair Lady* (1964); nominated for the Oscar in *Cleopatra* (1963). Other films include *Anna and the King of Siam* (1948) and *Doctor Dolittle* (1967). Stage work includes *Bell, Book and Candle*. Sixth marriage in January 1979.

A: Skeetz quotes Holmes in AA, January 1957, "from his former wife, Lili Palmer."

SVP=♓ 6°32'47"
JULIAN DAY=2418005.70833

HAUPTMAN, BRUNO
Homicide

November 26, 1899
1:00 PM MET
Kamenz, Germany
14 E 06   51 N 16

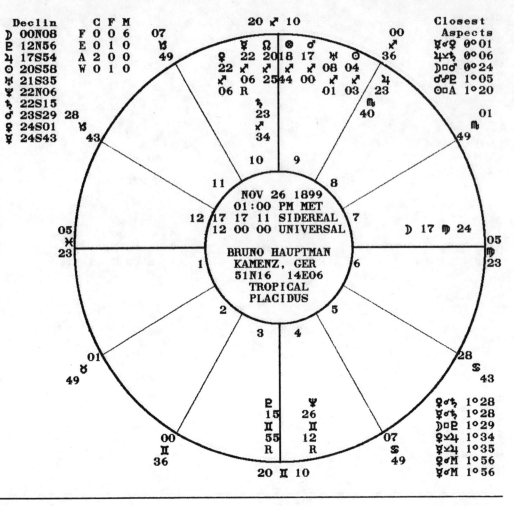

	Declin	C	F	M
☽	00N08	F	0	0	6
♇	12N56	E	0	1	0
♃	17S54	A	2	0	0
☉	20S58	W	0	1	0
♅	21S35				
♆	22N06				
♄	22S15				
♂	23S29	28			
♀	24S01				
☿	24S43				

Closest Aspects
☿☌♀ 0°01
♃☍♄ 0°06
♂☍♇ 1°05
☉☌A 1°20

Convicted of the March 1, 1932, kidnapping of the Lindburgh baby. Arrested September 19, 1934; trial, January 2, 1935; death sentence, February 13, 1935. First crime, 1919; sentenced to 5 years prison; paroled, 1923. Moved to U.S., 1923; married, 1925.

A: T.P. Davis quotes a radiogram "from his mother to Paul Clancy."[66]

SVP=♓ 6°39'11"
JULIAN DAY=2414985.00000

♀☌♄	1°28
☿☌♄	1°28
☽□♇	1°29
♀⚹♃	1°34
☿⚹♃	1°35
♀☌M	1°56
☿☌M	1°56

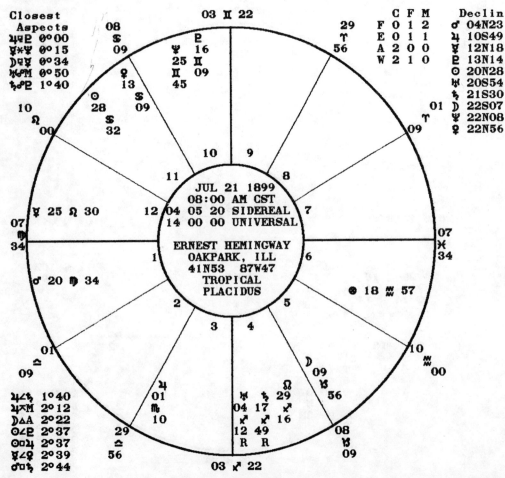

Closest Aspects
♃☌♇ 0°00
☿⚹♆ 0°15
☽□☿ 0°34
♅☌M 0°50
♄☍♇ 1°40

	C	F	M	Declin	
	F	0	1	2	♂	04N23
	E	0	1	1	♃	10S49
	A	2	0	0	☿	12N18
	W	2	1	0	♇	13N14
					☉	20N28
					♅	20S54
					♄	21S30
					☽	22S07
					♆	22N08
					♀	22N56

HEMINGWAY, ERNEST
Writer

July 21, 1899
8:00 AM CST
Oak Park, Ill
87 W 47   41 N 53

Novelist and adventurer. Awarded the 1953 Pulitzer prize for *The Old Man and the Sea*. Also received the 1954 Nobel prize in literature. Works include *The Sun Also Rises, A Farewell to Arms,* and *For Whom the Bell Tolls*. Suicide by gunshot on July 2, 1961.

A: R.H. Oliver, "from mother's unpublished papers."

♃∠♄	1°40
♃☌M	2°12
☽△A	2°22
☉∠♇	2°37
☉□♃	2°37
☿∠♀	2°39
♂☌♄	2°44

SVP=♓ 6°39'26"
JULIAN DAY=2414857.08333

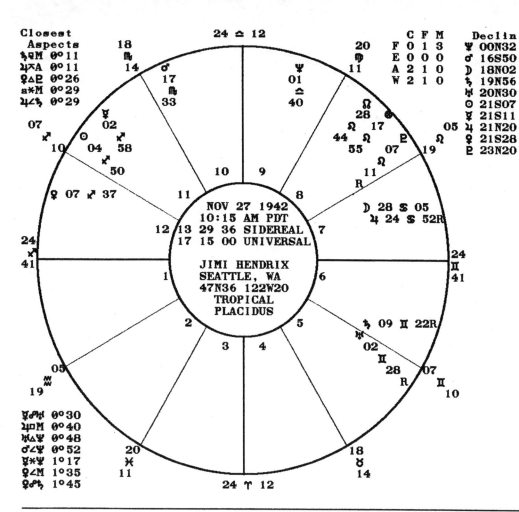

Closest Aspects

♄☌♍ 0°11
♃⊼A 0°11
♀△♇ 0°26
a✶♍ 0°29
♃∠♄ 0°29

NOV 27 1942
10:15 AM PDT
13 29 36 SIDEREAL
17 15 00 UNIVERSAL

JIMI HENDRIX
SEATTLE, WA
47N36 122W20
TROPICAL
PLACIDUS

	C	F	M
F	0	1	3
E	0	0	0
A	2	1	0
W	2	1	0

Declin

♇ 00N32
♂ 16S50
☽ 18N02
♄ 19N56
♅ 20N30
☉ 21S07
☿ 21S11
♃ 21N20
♀ 21S28
♇ 23N20

☿⚹♅ 0°30
♃□♍ 0°40
♅△♇ 0°48
♂∠♇ 0°52
☿⚹♇ 1°17
♀∠♍ 1°35
♀⚹♄ 1°45

HENDRIX, JIMI
Musician

November 27, 1942
10:15 AM PDT
Seattle, Wash
122 W 20   47 N 36

Singer-guitarist; rock super-star. Gained great popularity first in England, then with the American rock culture. Successful appearance at the Woodstock Festival. Choked to death on September 18, 1970, after drug and liquor over-indulgence.

A: CSH.

SVP=♓ 6° 3'35"
JULIAN DAY=2430691.21875

HESSE, HERMANN
Writer

July 2, 1877
6:30 PM LMT
Calw, Wuertenburg, Germany
8 E 03   48 N 00

Books include *The Glass Bead Game*, *Steppenwolf*, and *Siddhartha*. Winner of the Nobel prize in 1946. Guru to the youth from 1905 to his death in 1962. Afflicted with depression, hypochondria, thoughts of suicide, and bouts with alcoholism.

B: Holliday quotes *Portrait of Hesse* by Zeller; "time stated in mother's diary."

SVP=♓ 6°58' 5"
JULIAN DAY=2406803.24847

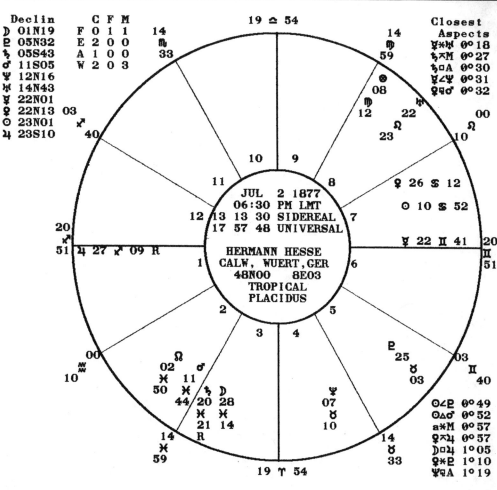

Declin

☽ 01N19
♇ 05N32
♄ 05S43
♂ 11S05
♆ 12N16
♅ 14N43
☿ 22N01
♀ 22N13
☉ 23N01
♃ 23S10

	C	F	M
F	0	1	1
E	2	0	0
A	1	0	0
W	2	0	3

JUL 2 1877
06:30 PM LMT
13 13 30 SIDEREAL
17 57 48 UNIVERSAL

HERMANN HESSE
CALW, WUERT, GER
48N00   8E03
TROPICAL
PLACIDUS

Closest Aspects

☿⚹♅ 0°18
♄⊼♍ 0°27
♄□A 0°30
☿∠♆ 0°31
♀☌♂ 0°32

☉∠♇ 0°49
☉△♂ 0°52
a✶♍ 0°57
♀⊼♃ 0°57
☽□♃ 1°05
♀⚹♇ 1°10
♆□A 1°19

HILTON, JAMES
Writer

September 9, 1900
2:10 AM GMT
Leigh, England
2 W 30   53 N 30

British novelist, widely known for *Goodbye, Mr. Chips, Lost Horizon* (1933), and *Random Harvest* (1941), all of which became motion pictures. Published his first novel, *Catherine Herself*, at age 20. Modest, retiring, a keen mountaineer; enjoyed music and travel. (1900-1954)

A: Carter states, "from him", in AQ, Spring 1955.[67]

SVP=♓ 6°38'31"
JULIAN DAY=2415271.59028

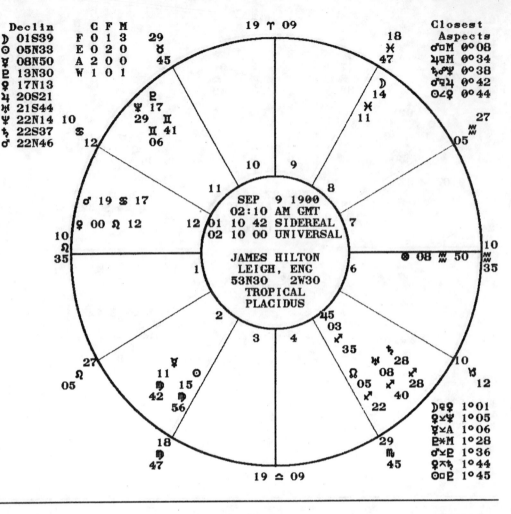

Declin		C	F	M
☽	01S39	F	0 1	3
☉	05N33	E	0 2	0
☿	08N50	A	2 0	0
♇	13N30	W	1 0	1
♀	17N13			
♃	20S21			
♅	21S44			
♆	22N14			
♄	22S37			
♂	22N46			

Closest Aspects
♂☌M 0°08
♃☍M 0°34
♄☍♀ 0°38
♂☌♃ 0°42
☉☍♇ 0°44

☽☌♀ 1°01
♀☌♆ 1°05
☿⊼A 1°06
♇⚹M 1°28
♂☌♄ 1°36
♀⊼♄ 1°44
☉☐♇ 1°45

HIMMLER, HEINRICH
Nazi

October 7, 1900
3:30 PM MET
Munich, Germany
11 E 35   48 N 08

One of the most sinister leaders of Nazi Germany; head of the police and Gestapo. Ordered the death of millions — starting with the "blood purge" of 1934 and ending with the systematic murder in the concentration camps. Died of cyanide capsule, May 23, 1945.

A: Gauquelin #1931 Vol 5.

SVP=♓ 6°38'28"
JULIAN DAY=2415300.10417

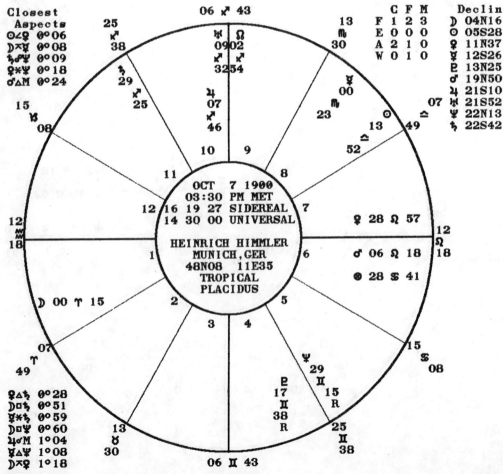

Closest Aspects
☉∠♇ 0°06
☽⊼♀ 0°08
♄☐♆ 0°09
♀⚹♆ 0°18
♂△M 0°24

♀△♄ 0°28
☽☐♄ 0°51
☿⚹♄ 0°59
☽☐♀ 0°60
♃☐M 1°04
♀△♆ 1°08
☽⊼♀ 1°18

	C	F	M	Declin	
	F	1 2	3	☽	04N16
	E	0 0	0	☉	05S28
	A	2 1	0	♀	11N37
	W	0 1	0	☿	12S26
				♇	13N25
				♂	19N50
				♃	21S10
				♅	21S52
				♆	22N13
				♄	22S42

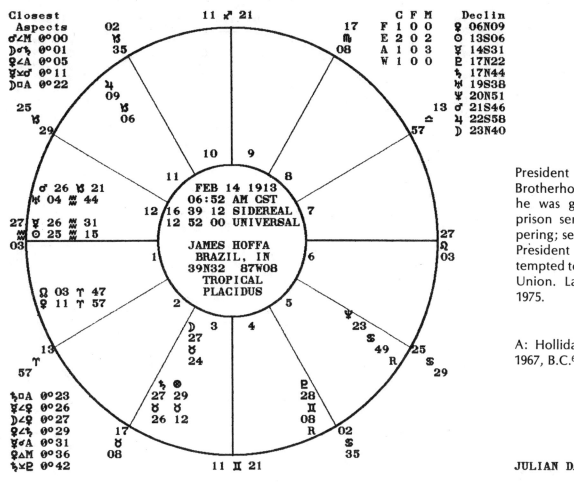

HOFFA, JAMES
Union leader

February 14, 1913
6:52 AM CST
Brazil, Ind
87 W 08   39 N 32

Chart 1 — James Hoffa

Closest Aspects
♂∠M	0°00
☽⚼♄	0°01
♀∠A	0°05
☿⚻♂	0°11
☽□A	0°22

Declin
♀	06N09
☉	13S06
☿	14S31
♇	17N22
♄	17N44
♅	19S38
♆	20S51
♂	21S46
♃	22S58
☽	23N40

C F M
F 1 0 0
E 2 0 2
A 1 0 3
W 1 0 0

FEB 14 1913
06:52 AM CST
16 39 12 SIDEREAL
12 52 00 UNIVERSAL

JAMES HOFFA
BRAZIL, IN
39N32   87W08
TROPICAL
PLACIDUS

President of the International Brotherhood of Teamsters until he was given a thirteen-year prison sentence for jury tampering; sentence commuted by President Nixon in 1971. Attempted to regain control of the Union. Last seen on July 30, 1975.

A: Holliday from AFA, October 1967, B.C.[68]

SVP=♓ 6°28'23"
JULIAN DAY=2419813.03611

HOFFMAN, DUSTIN
Actor

August 8, 1937
5:07 PM PST
Los Angeles, Ca
118 W 15   34 N 04

Chart 2 — Dustin Hoffman

Declin
☽	00N03
♄	00S24
♆	05N54
☿	06N48
♅	15N32
☉	16N02
♀	21N35
♃	22S26
♂	22S50
♇	23N01

C F M
F 1 1 1
E 1 3 1
A 0 0 0
W 2 0 0

AUG 8 1937
05:07 PM PST
14 22 28 SIDEREAL
01 07 00 UNIVERSAL

DUSTIN HOFFMAN
LOS ANGELES, CA
34N04   118W15
TROPICAL
PLACIDUS

Youthful acne and braces; studied music and planned to be a concert pianist. Tested and was cast in his first picture, *The Graduate*; instant stardom and the Academy Award as best actor. Other films include *Midnight Cowboy* in 1969, the year that he married.

A: Lockhart from B.C.[69]

Closest Aspects
♀∠♄	0°01
☽△A	0°02
♆△A	0°34
☽⚼♆	0°36
♂△♇	1°13
☽□♃	1°21
♃∠A	1°23
☉□♆	1°28
☿△♅	1°56
♃△♆	1°57
☉⚼A	2°02
☉⚼☽	2°05

SVP=♓ 6° 7'34"
JULIAN DAY=2428754.54653

HOLBROOK, HAL
Actor

February 17, 1925
3:16 AM EST
Cleveland, Ohio
81 W 42   41 N 30

Abandoned by his parents at age 2; raised by kin. First put his Twain show together in 1955, played it as a hit in 1959 — *Mark Twain Tonight!* With two thousand performances, the most successful one-man show in theater history. Other stage roles and films. Also the TV series, *The Bold Ones.*

A: CSH.

SVP=ℋ 6°18'30"
JULIAN DAY=2424198.84444

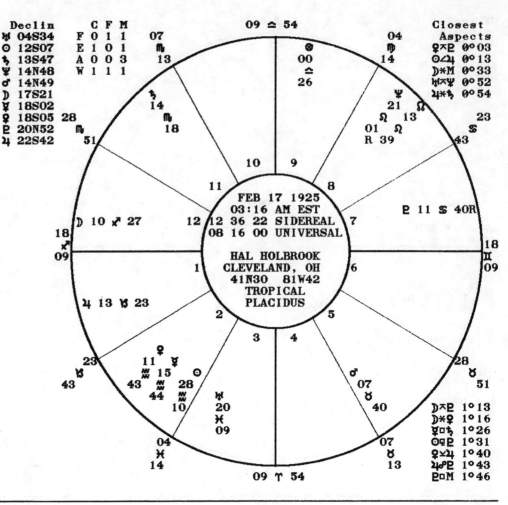

Declin		C F M
♅ 04S34	F	0 1 1
☉ 12S07	E	1 0 1
♄ 13S47	A	0 0 3
♆ 14N48	W	1 1 1
♂ 14N49		
☽ 17S21		
☿ 18S02		
♀ 18S05		
♇ 20N52		
♃ 22S42		

Closest Aspects
♀⊼♇ 0°03
☉∠♃ 0°13
☽⚹M 0°33
♅⊼♅ 0°52
♃⚹♆ 0°54
☽⊼♇ 1°13
☽⚹♀ 1°16
☿□♄ 1°26
☉⚹♃ 1°31
♀⚹♃ 1°40
♃⚹♇ 1°43
♇□M 1°46

HOLDEN, WILLIAM
Actor

April 17, 1918
5:00 PM CWT
O'Fallon, Ill
89 W 58   38 N 36

First starring in *Golden Boy* (1939). Won the Oscar as best actor in *Stalag 17* (1953); nominated for Oscar in *Sunset Boulevard* (1950). Business interests world-wide, including a part interest in a posh Safari Club in Africa.

A: CL from Ed Steinbrecker, from Illinois Dept. of Health.

SVP=ℋ 6°23'46"
JULIAN DAY=2421701.41667

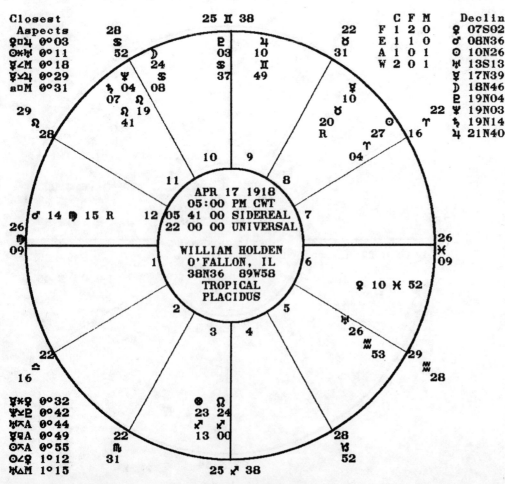

Closest Aspects
♀□♃ 0°03
☉⚹♅ 0°11
☿∠M 0°18
♀⚹♃ 0°29
a□M 0°31
♀⚹♀ 0°32
♆⚹♇ 0°42
♅⚹A 0°44
♅△A 0°49
☉⚹A 0°55
☉∠♀ 1°12
♅△M 1°15

	C F M	Declin
	F 1 2 0	♀ 07S02
	E 1 1 0	♂ 08N36
	A 1 0 1	☉ 10N26
	W 2 0 1	♅ 13S13
		☿ 17N39
		☽ 18N46
		♇ 19N04
		♆ 19N03
		♄ 19N14
		♃ 21N40

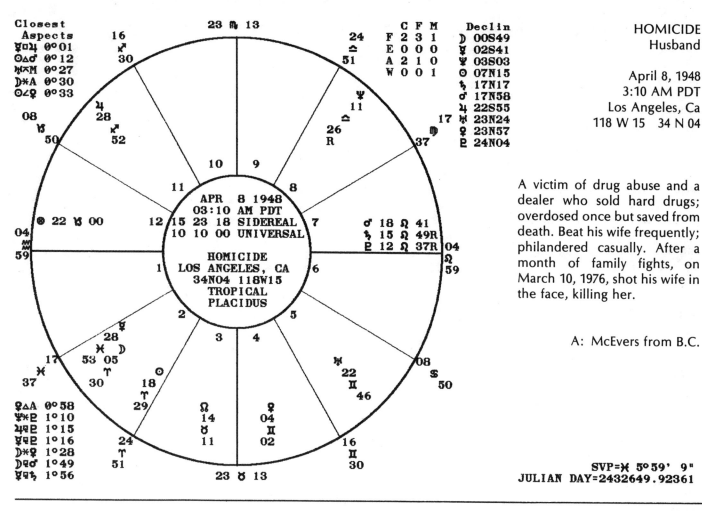

Closest Aspects

☿□♃ 0°01
☉△♂ 0°12
♅⚹M 0°27
☽⚹A 0°30
☉∠♀ 0°33

♀△A 0°58
♆⚹♇ 1°10
♃⚹♇ 1°15
☿☌♇ 1°16
☽⚹♀ 1°28
☽☌♂ 1°49
☿□♄ 1°56

	C	F	M	Declin	
F	2	3	1	☽	00S49
E	0	0	0	☿	02S41
A	2	1	0	♆	03S03
W	0	0	1	☉	07N15
				♄	17N17
				♂	17N58
				♃	22S55
				♅	23N24
				♀	23N57
				♇	24N04

HOMICIDE
Husband

April 8, 1948
3:10 AM PDT
Los Angeles, Ca
118 W 15   34 N 04

A victim of drug abuse and a dealer who sold hard drugs; overdosed once but saved from death. Beat his wife frequently; philandered casually. After a month of family fights, on March 10, 1976, shot his wife in the face, killing her.

A: McEvers from B.C.

APR 8 1948
03:10 AM PDT
15 23 18 SIDEREAL
10 10 00 UNIVERSAL

HOMICIDE
LOS ANGELES, CA
34N04 118W15
TROPICAL
PLACIDUS

SVP=♓ 5°59' 9"
JULIAN DAY=2432649.92361

HOMICIDE VICTIM
Wife

May 13, 1949
6:00 PM PST
Los Angeles, Ca
118 W 15   34 N 04

Married, mother of a son born in 1968. Her husband a drug user, dealer and philanderer. Caught him in bed with a girl friend in February, 1976, and beat up the girl. On March 10, 1976 Encino, Ca, at 7:39 PM her husband shot her in the face and killed her.

A: McEvers from B.C.

Declin		C	F	M
♆	03S34	F	0	2	1
♄	13N16	E	2	0	0
♂	14N38	A	3	1	1
☉	18N31	W	0	0	0
♃	19S59				
♀	20N02				
♅	23N39				
♇	23N56				
☿	24N44				
☽	26S20				

Closest Aspects

♇□A 0°11
☽⚹♃ 0°13
☿⚹♇ 0°15
☿⊼A 0°26
☽△♇ 0°27

♀□♄ 0°38
☽△A 0°38
♅∠♇ 0°44
♅□A 0°54
☽⚹♆ 0°57
♄⚹♅ 0°58
☿△♆ 1°09

MAY 13 1949
06:00 PM PST
09 32 57 SIDEREAL
02 00 00 UNIVERSAL

HOMICIDE VICTIM
LOS ANGELES, CA
34N04 118W15
TROPICAL
PLACIDUS

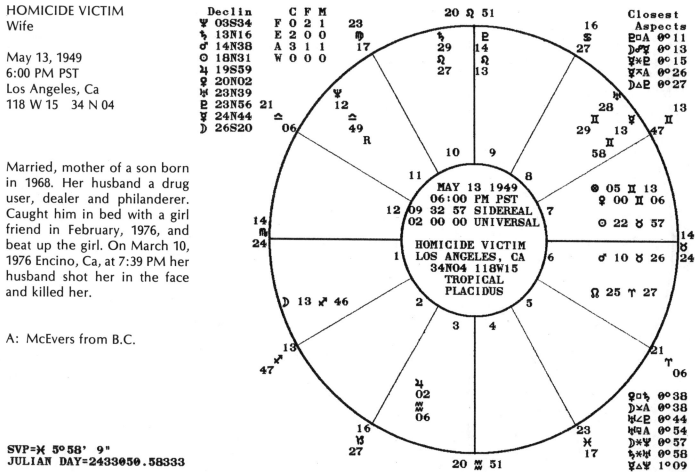

SVP=♓ 5°58' 9"
JULIAN DAY=2433050.58333

HOOVER, JOHN EDGAR
FBI Chief

January 1, 1895
7:00 AM EST
Washington, D.C.
77 W 02   38 N 54

Director of the FBI from 1942; developed the Bureau into one of the world's most efficient law-enforcement agencies. Famous for dramatic campaigns against public enemies and organized crime. A lawyer, who joined the Department of Justice in 1917. (1895-1972)

A: CL, "data from him in a letter."

Declin		C	F	M		Closest Aspects
☽	09S11	F	0	0	0	☿✶⛢ 0°11
☱	11N09	E	1	0	3	☿✶♄ 0°11
♄	11S09	A	3	0	0	♂✶♃ 0°27
♂	12N38	W	0	2	1	☱□M 0°29
⛢	17S05					⛢∠A 0°36
♆	20N57					
☉	23S00					
♀	23S10					
♃	23N15					
☿	24S43					

☽□☱	0°37
☉✶☱	0°38
☽□M	1°07
☉✶☽	1°16
♂∠☱	1°45
☿∠☱	2°03
♄✶A	2°28

SVP=♓ 6°43'31"
JULIAN DAY=2413195.00000

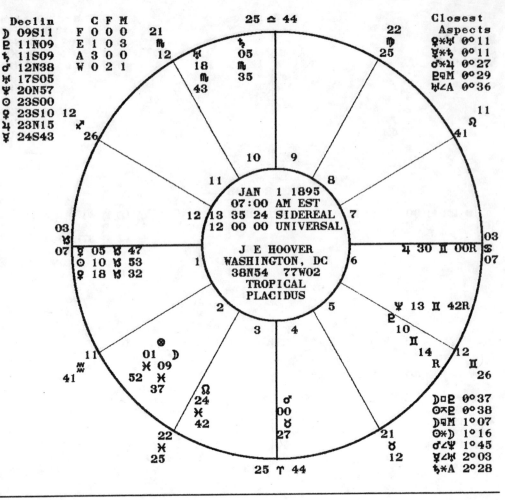

HORTON, ROBERT
Actor

July 29, 1924
12:07 PM PST
Los Angeles, Ca
118 W 15   34 N 04

Victim of a series of serious illnesses up to age 14; twice run over by an automobile; five times broke his arm. Studied drama at UCLA; then the Strasberg school in 1950; TV parts. Slow career start until *Wagon Train* (1957), a five-year TV series.

A: CL from AFA, stating B.C.

Closest Aspects			C	F	M	Declin	
☽∠☿	0°17		F	0	3	1	⛢ 04S16
☉□⛢	0°18		E	0	0	0	♄ 07S56
♂∆A	1°04		A	0	1	0	☿ 12N37
☿∠☱	1°10		W	3	0	2	♆ 15N12
♃∠♄	1°14						♂ 15S26
							♀ 17N36
							☉ 18N41
							☽ 19N25
							☱ 20N40
							♃ 21S28

☉∠♂	1°15
☽♂☱	1°28
⛢□♆	1°30
♃∆M	1°53
☉♂M	1°54
⛢□A	2°02
♀∆A	2°10

SVP=♓ 6°18'56"
JULIAN DAY=2423996.33819

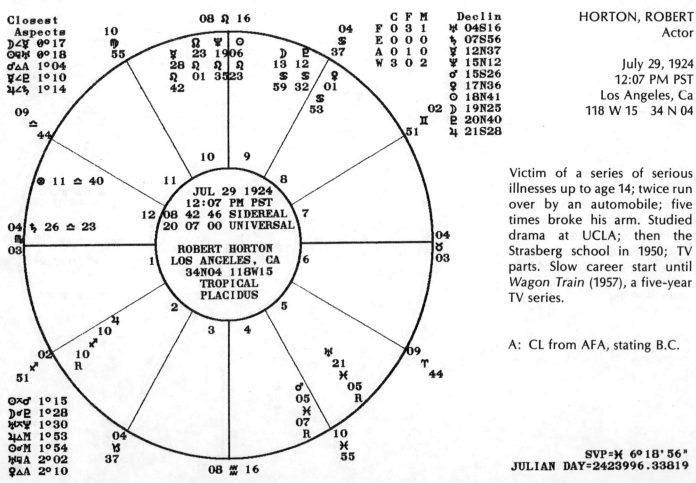

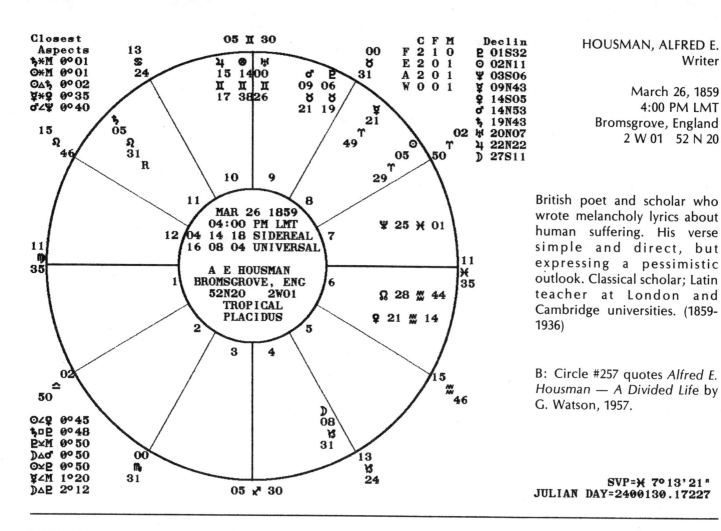

HOUSMAN, ALFRED E.
Writer

March 26, 1859
4:00 PM LMT
Bromsgrove, England
2 W 01   52 N 20

Closest Aspects

♄✳M	0°01
☉✳M	0°01
☉△♄	0°02
☿✳♀	0°35
♂∠♆	0°40

☉∠♀	0°45
♄□♇	0°48
♇✳M	0°50
☽△♂	0°50
☉✳♇	0°50
☿∠M	1°20
☽△♇	2°12

Declin

♇	01S32
☉	02N11
♆	03S06
☿	09N43
♀	14S05
♂	14N53
♄	19N43
♅	20N07
♃	22N22
☽	27S11

	C	F	M
F	2	1	0
E	2	0	1
A	2	0	1
W	0	0	1

Center of chart:
MAR 26 1859
04:00 PM LMT
04 14 18 SIDEREAL
16 08 04 UNIVERSAL
A E HOUSMAN
BROMSGROVE, ENG
52N20   2W01
TROPICAL
PLACIDUS

British poet and scholar who wrote melancholy lyrics about human suffering. His verse simple and direct, but expressing a pessimistic outlook. Classical scholar; Latin teacher at London and Cambridge universities. (1859-1936)

B: Circle #257 quotes *Alfred E. Housman — A Divided Life* by G. Watson, 1957.

SVP=♓ 7°13'21"
JULIAN DAY=2400130.17227

HOUSTON, JEAN
Psychologist

May 10, 1939
2:15 PM EDT
Brooklyn, N.Y.
73 W 56   40 N 38

Declin

♃	01S05
♆	04N48
♀	05N31
☿	06N44
♄	07N26
☽	12S13
♅	16N52
☉	17N32
♂	22S49
♇	23N38

	C	F	M
F	3	0	0
E	2	1	1
A	0	0	1
W	1	0	1

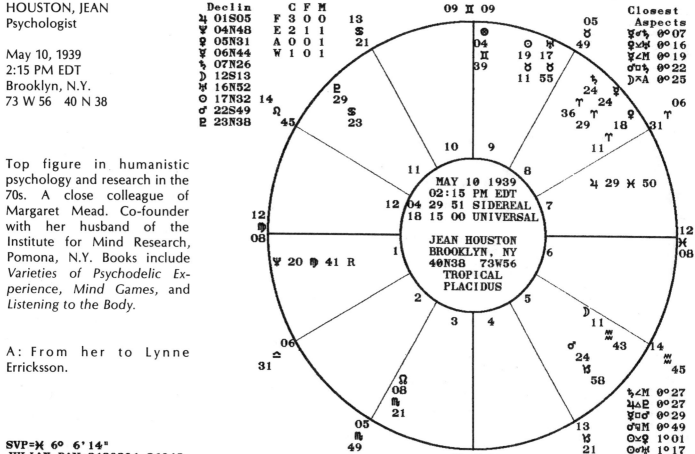

Center of chart:
MAY 10 1939
02:15 PM EDT
04 29 51 SIDEREAL
18 15 00 UNIVERSAL
JEAN HOUSTON
BROOKLYN, NY
40N38   73W56
TROPICAL
PLACIDUS

Closest Aspects

☿♂	0°07
♀∠♅	0°16
☿∠M	0°19
♂♄	0°22
☽✶A	0°25

♄∠M	0°27
♃△♇	0°27
☿♂	0°29
♂□M	0°49
☉✳♀	1°01
☉♅	1°17
☉△♆	1°29

Top figure in humanistic psychology and research in the 70s. A close colleague of Margaret Mead. Co-founder with her husband of the Institute for Mind Research, Pomona, N.Y. Books include *Varieties of Psychodelic Experience*, *Mind Games*, and *Listening to the Body*.

A: From her to Lynne Erricksson.

SVP=♓ 6° 6'14"
JULIAN DAY=2429394.26042

HUBBARD, ELBERT
Writer

June 19, 1856
7:00 AM LMT
Bloomington, Ill
89 W 00   40 N 29

American lecturer, publisher, editor and essayist; author of *Message to Garcia* (1899). Founded the Roycroft Shop (1895), specializing in book binding and crafts; published two magazines. Died in the sinking of the Lusitania in May 1915.

A: *Constellations*, 1977, quotes Kraum in NAJ, October 1934, "from his wife."[70]

SVP=H 7°15'55"
JULIAN DAY=2399120.03889

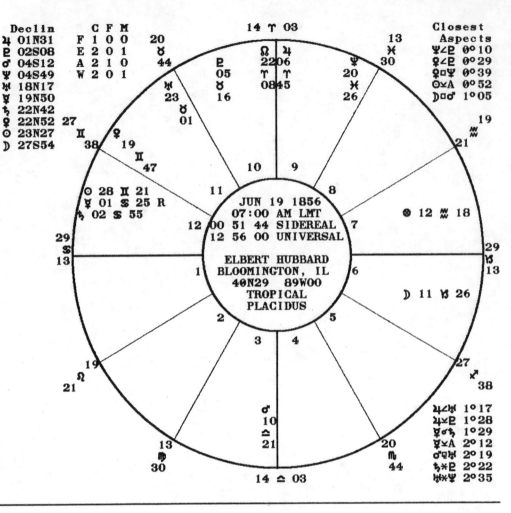

HUGO, VICTOR
Writer

February 26, 1802
10:30 PM LMT
Besancon, France
6 E 01   47 N 15

French poet, dramatist, novelist, essayist, and critic; a many sided genius. Hard working, politically active, and humanitarian. His work includes the play *Lucrezia Borgia* (1833), and the novels *The Hunchback of Notre Dame* (1831) and *Les Miserables* (1862). (1802-1885)

A: Gauquelin #423 Vol 6.[71]

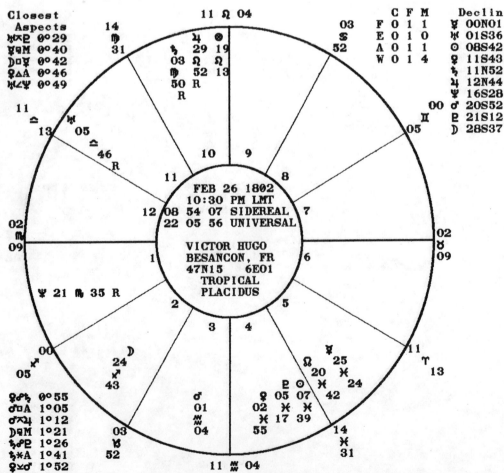

SVP=H 8° 1'14"
JULIAN DAY=2379283.42079

HUNTER, BEN
Disc Jockey

June 6, 1920
11:55 PM PST
Los Angeles, Ca
118 W 15   34 N 04

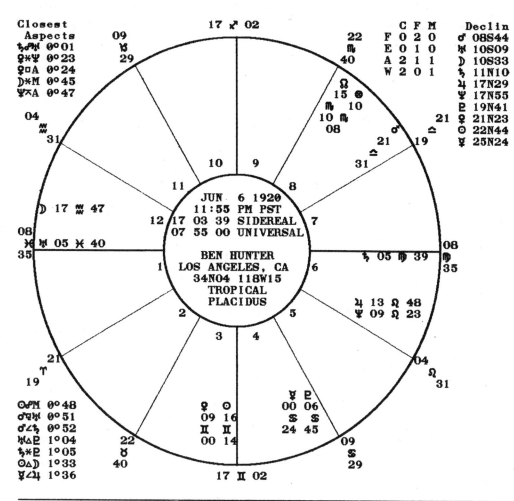

Closest Aspects		
♄♂♅	0°01	
♀✶♆	0°23	
♀□A	0°24	
☽✶M	0°45	
♆⊼A	0°47	

	C F M	Declin
F	0 2 0	♂ 08S44
E	0 1 0	♅ 10S09
A	2 1 1	☽ 10S33
W	2 0 1	♄ 11N10
		♃ 17N29
		♆ 17N55
		♇ 19N41
		♀ 21N23
		☉ 22N44
		☿ 25N24

☉♂M	0°48	
♂⊼♅	0°51	
♂∠♄	0°52	
♅△♇	1°04	
♄✶♇	1°05	
☉△☽	1°33	
☿∠♃	1°36	

Radio and TV personality; voted Mr. Disc Jockey of 1956. Stanford graduate in psychology and criminology. First worked as an announcer in the Air Force. Career established since 1944. *Night Owl* program played for years on radio. Married; three children.

A: Sydney Omarr in Dell, August 1958, "from him."[72]

SVP=♓ 6°22' 3"
JULIAN DAY=2422482.82986

HUXLEY, THOMAS HENRY
Scientist

May 4, 1825
9:30 AM LMT
Ealing, England
3 W 08   51 N 31

Declin		C F M
♇ 13S31	F	1 1 1
☉ 15N56	E	3 0 2
♂ 17N40	A	2 0 0
♃ 19N42	W	0 0 0
♄ 20N07		
♅ 21N21		
♆ 22S03		
♅ 22S25		
☽ 22S50		
♀ 26N15		

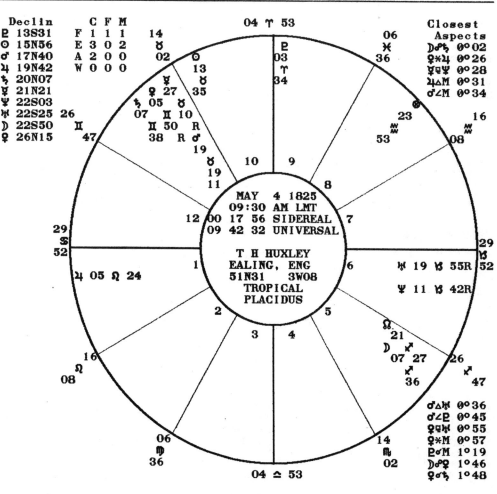

Closest Aspects		
☽♂♄	0°02	
♀✶♃	0°26	
♀♂♆	0°28	
♃△M	0°31	
♂∠M	0°34	

♂△♅	0°36	
♂∠♇	0°45	
♀♂♅	0°55	
♀✶M	0°57	
♇♂M	1°19	
☽♂♀	1°46	
♀♂♄	1°48	

Famous zoologist, lecturer, and writer, who helped advance scientific thought of his time. Surgeon in the British Navy with four years in the East Indies. Taught natural history from 1854 to 1885. President of the Royal Society, 1881-85. (1825-1895)

A: Lyndoe in AA, December 1968: "Though he put 8:00 AM in his autobiography, 9:30 is recorded in the family Bible."

SVP=♓ 7°41'37"
JULIAN DAY=2387750.90454

IRVING, WASHINGTON
Writer

April 3, 1783
8:30 PM LMT
New York, N.Y.
73 W 57   40 N 45

American essayist and historian. His essays "The Legend of Sleepy Hollow", "Rip Van Winkle", and others appeared serially in 1819-20. Wrote *A Tour on the Prairies* in 1835. Elected to the Hall of Fame for Great Americans in 1900.(1783-1859)

A: *Constellations*, 1977, quotes AFA data exchange, "from family Bible."

SVP=)(8° 17' 7"
JULIAN DAY=2372380.55958

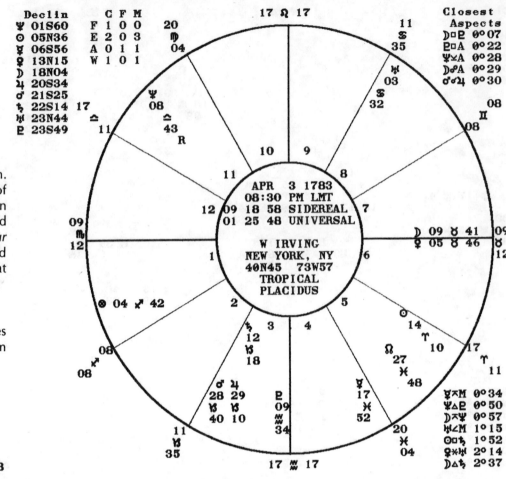

Declin		C	F	M
Ψ	01S60	F	1	0	0
☉	05N36	E	2	0	3
☿	06S56	A	0	1	1
♀	13N15	W	1	0	1
☽	18N04				
♃	20S34				
♂	21S25				
♄	22S14				
♅	23N44				
♇	23S49				

Closest Aspects
☽□♇ 0°07
♇□A 0°22
Ψ⚹A 0°28
☽☌A 0°29
♂☌♃ 0°30

☿⚹M 0°34
Ψ△♇ 0°50
☽⚹Ψ 0°57
♅∠M 1°15
☉□♄ 1°52
♀⚹♅ 2°14
☽△♄ 2°37

ISHERWOOD, CHRISTOPHER
Writer

August 26, 1904
11:45 PM GMT
Disley, England
2 W 02   53 N 22

Attended Oxford University. Moved to U.S. and became a citizen in 1946. A bachelor loner, whose principal concerns are Hindu philosophy, pacifism, and a search for meaning in life. His work includes *Lions and Shadows* (1938) and *Down There on a Visit* (1962).

B: PC quotes *Kathleen and Frank* by Isherwood, p. 272.

SVP=)(6° 35' 30"
JULIAN DAY=2416719.48958

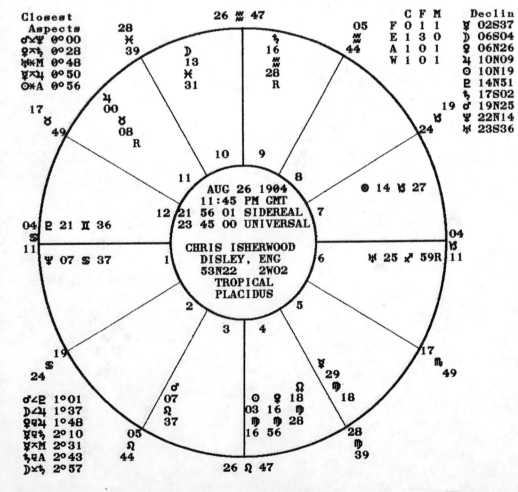

Closest Aspects
♂⚹Ψ 0°00
♀⚹♄ 0°28
♅⚹M 0°48
☿⚹♃ 0°50
☉⚹A 0°56

C	F	M		Declin
F	0	1	1	☿	02S37
E	1	3	0	☽	06S04
A	1	0	1	♀	06N26
W	1	0	1	♃	10N09
				☉	10N19
				♇	14N51
				♄	17S02
				♂	19N25
				Ψ	22N14
				♅	23S36

♂△♇ 1°01
☽△♃ 1°37
♀□♃ 1°48
☿⚹♇ 2°10
☿⚹M 2°31
♄☌A 2°43
☽⚹♄ 2°57

IVES, BURL
Singer, actor

June 14, 1909
6:00 AM CST
Hunt, Ill
88 W.01   39 N.00

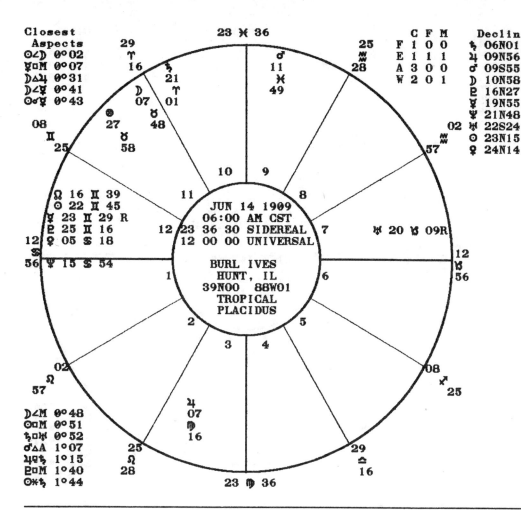

Closest
Aspects
O☌☽ 0°02
☿□☽ 0°07
☽△♃ 0°31
☽∠♄ 0°41
O☌☿ 0°43

	C	F	M
F	1	0	0
E	1	1	1
A	3	0	0
W	2	0	1

Declin
♄ 06N01
♃ 09N56
♂ 09S55
☽ 10N58
♇ 16N27
♅ 19N55
♆ 21N48
♅ 22S24
O 23N15
♀ 24N14

JUN 14 1909
06:00 AM CST
23 36 30 SIDEREAL
12 00 00 UNIVERSAL

BURL IVES
HUNT, IL
39N00 88W01
TROPICAL
PLACIDUS

☊ 16 Ⅱ 39
O 22 Ⅱ 45
☿ 23 Ⅱ 29 R
♇ 25 Ⅱ 16
♀ 05 ♋ 18
♆ 15 ♋ 54

♅ 20 ♑ 09R

♃ 07
♍ 16

☽∠M 0°48
O□M 0°51
♄□♅ 0°52
♂△A 1°07
♃∠♄ 1°15
♇□M 1°40
O✶♄ 1°44

Folk singer of early Americana ballads; actor in movies and TV. Won an Oscar as best supporting actor in *The Big Country* (1958). Known as the mightiest ballad singer of the century with songs that include "Jimmy Crack Corn" and "Blue Tail Fly".

B: PC quotes his autobiography *Wayfaring Stranger*, 1948, p. 2.

SVP=♓ 6°31'44"
JULIAN DAY=2418472.00000

JACOBI, DEREK
Actor

October 22, 1938
4:00 AM GMT
London, England
0 W 06   51 N 31

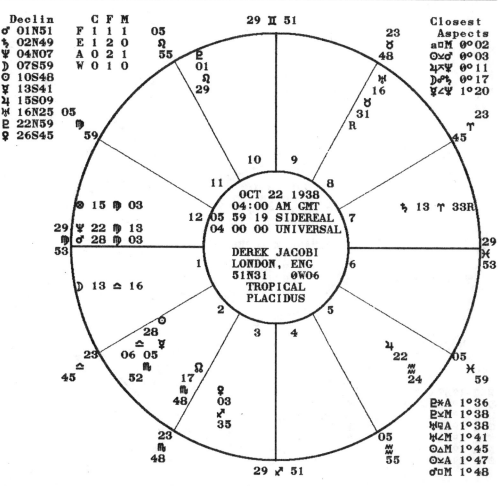

Declin
♂ 01N51
♄ 02N49
♆ 04N07
☽ 07S59
O 10S48
☿ 13S41
♃ 15S09
♅ 16N25
♇ 22N59
♀ 26S45

	C	F	M
F	1	1	1
E	1	2	0
A	0	2	1
W	0	1	0

OCT 22 1938
04:00 AM GMT
05 59 19 SIDEREAL
04 00 00 UNIVERSAL

DEREK JACOBI
LONDON, ENG
51N31 0W06
TROPICAL
PLACIDUS

⊕ 15 ♍ 03
♆ 22 ♍ 13
♂ 28 ♍ 03

☽ 13 ♎ 16

♄ 13 ♈ 33R

♃ 22

☿ 06 05

♀ 03

One of the finest actors of the English speaking theater. Played lead as Richard II in the PBS presentation of the Shakespearean plays (1979), after already demonstrating his talent in the virtuoso performance as lead in *I, Claudius* (1978).

A: Joan Abel in *Mercury Hour*, January 1979; "data from him by letter."

Closest
Aspects
a□M 0°02
O✶♂ 0°03
♃⊼♆ 0°11
☽♂♄ 0°17
☿∠♆ 1°20

♇✶A 1°36
♇✶M 1°38
♅□A 1°38
♅□M 1°41
O△M 1°45
O✶A 1°47
♂□M 1°48

SVP=♓ 6° 6'39"
JULIAN DAY=2429193.66667

JAGGER, MICK
Musician

July 26, 1943
6:30 AM D-BST
Dartford, England
0 E 12   51 N 27

Lead singer, rock-star with the Rolling Stones. Made an estimated $25 million from 1971-78. The 1969 movie *Gimme Shelter* documenting their American tour showed rock-culture at its worst, ending in an orgy of violence with four dead and hundreds injured.

B: *Circle* #1278 gives the date from *Mick Jagger* by J. Marks. Holliday quotes the time "stated in an interview with him" in *Scavullo on Men*.[73]

SVP=♓ 6° 3' 3"
JULIAN DAY=2430931.68750

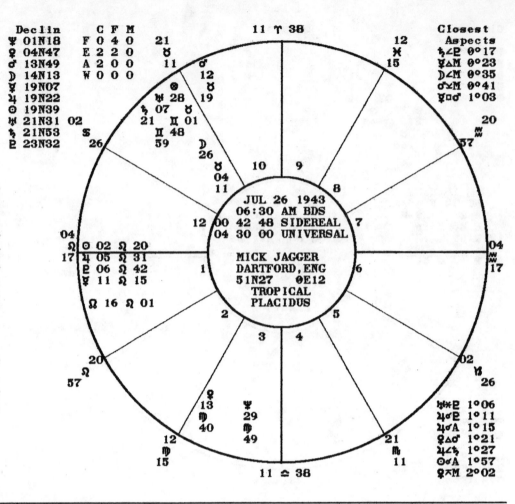

JAPANESE EMPEROR
Mutsohito Meiji Tenno

November 3, 1852
1:00 PM LMT
Kyoto, Japan
135 E 45   34 N 58

Emperor from age 15; reigned for forty five years as his country became a great power. The first Emperor ever looked upon by foreigners, who were admitted in 1853. More in contact with his people than any prior ruler. Of his fourteen children, nine died in youth.

A: CL from AFA, October 1938, time given as "half past the hour of the horse." Correct time given in the third edition of NN.[74]

SVP=♓ 7° 19' 10"
JULIAN DAY=2397795.66458

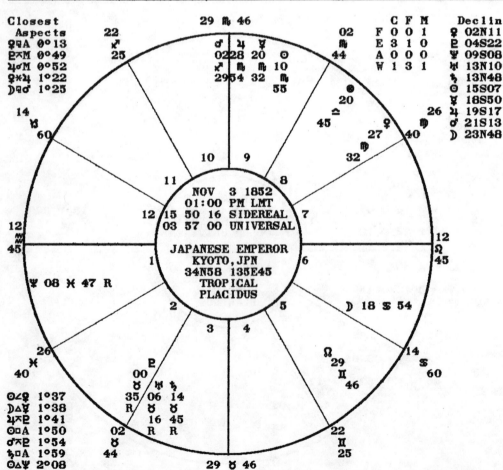

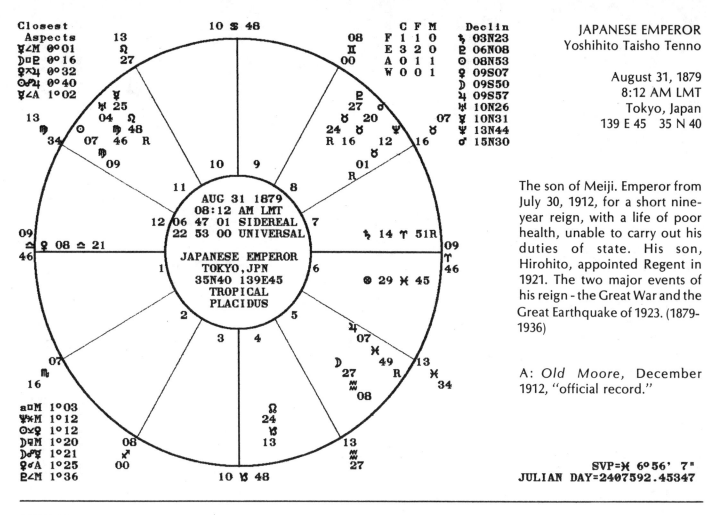

Closest Aspects

☿⊾M	0°01	
☽□♇	0°16	
♀⚹♃	0°32	
☉♂♃	0°40	
☿⊾A	1°02	

AUG 31 1879
08:12 AM LMT
06 47 01 SIDEREAL
22 53 00 UNIVERSAL

JAPANESE EMPEROR
TOKYO, JPN
35N40 139E45
TROPICAL
PLACIDUS

	C	F	M		Declin	
	F	1	1	0	♄	03N23
	E	3	2	0	♇	06N08
	A	0	1	1	☉	08N53
	W	0	0	1	♀	09S07
					☽	09S50
					♃	09S57
					♅	10N26
					☿	10N31
					♆	13N44
					♂	15N30

a□M	1°03	
♆⚹M	1°12	
☉⚹♀	1°12	
☽□M	1°20	
☽♂♀	1°21	
♀♂A	1°25	
♇⊾M	1°36	

JAPANESE EMPEROR
Yoshihito Taisho Tenno

August 31, 1879
8:12 AM LMT
Tokyo, Japan
139 E 45   35 N 40

The son of Meiji. Emperor from July 30, 1912, for a short nine-year reign, with a life of poor health, unable to carry out his duties of state. His son, Hirohito, appointed Regent in 1921. The two major events of his reign - the Great War and the Great Earthquake of 1923. (1879-1936)

A: *Old Moore*, December 1912, "official record."

SVP=♓ 6°56' 7"
JULIAN DAY=2407592.45347

JAPANESE EMPEROR
Emperor Hirohito

April 29, 1901
10:10 PM JST
Tokyo, Japan
139 E 45   35 N 40

Became the 124th ruler of Japan in December 1926, after a regency of five years. Though personally opposed to the militarism of the 30s, approved the decisions which led to World War II. After defeat, on January 1, 1946, renounced traditional claims of divinity and became a "symbol of the state."

A: Aries Osawa in *Astrology Now*, June 1976.

SVP=♓ 6°38' 2"
JULIAN DAY=2415504.04861

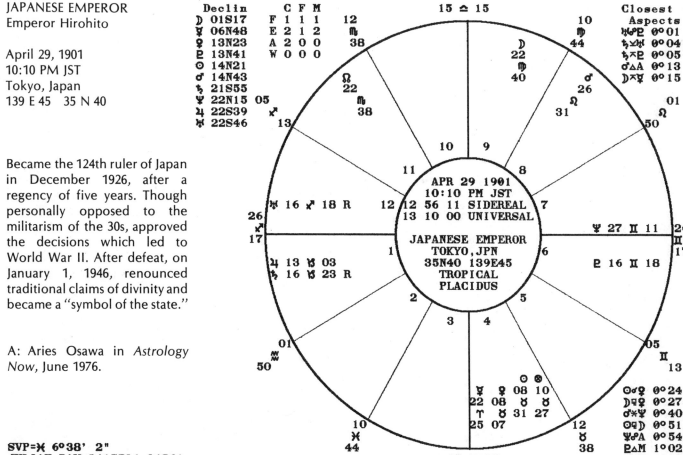

	Declin		C	F	M
☽	01S17		F	1	1	1
☿	06N48		E	2	1	2
♀	13N23		A	2	0	0
♇	13N41		W	0	0	0
☉	14N21					
♂	14N43					
♄	21S55					
♆	22N15					
♃	22S39					
♅	22S46					

APR 29 1901
10:10 PM JST
12 56 11 SIDEREAL
13 10 00 UNIVERSAL

JAPANESE EMPEROR
TOKYO, JPN
35N40 139E45
TROPICAL
PLACIDUS

Closest Aspects

♅⚹♇	0°01	
♄∠♅	0°04	
♄⚹♇	0°05	
♂△A	0°13	
☽⊼☿	0°15	

☉♂♀	0°24	
☽□♀	0°27	
♂⚹♆	0°40	
☉□☽	0°51	
♆♂A	0°54	
♇△M	1°02	
♅⚹M	1°03	

JAPANESE ROYALTY
Prince Akihito

December 23, 1933
6:39 AM JST
Tokyo, Japan
139 E 45 35 N 40

The son of Hirohito. Studied political science and economics at Gashushuin University to prepare as the 125th ruler of the world's oldest dynasty. Married a commoner, Michiko Shoda, on March 10, 1959; three children. Not a popular figure with the people.

A: Aries Osawa in *Astrology Now*, June 1976.

Declin
☽ 02S02
♃ 06S40
♆ 07N44
♅ 08N35
♀ 17S36
♄ 17S42
♂ 22S07
☿ 22S15
♇ 22N35
☉ 23S27

	C	F	M
F	1	0	1
E	0	1	2
A	0	1	2
W	1	0	1

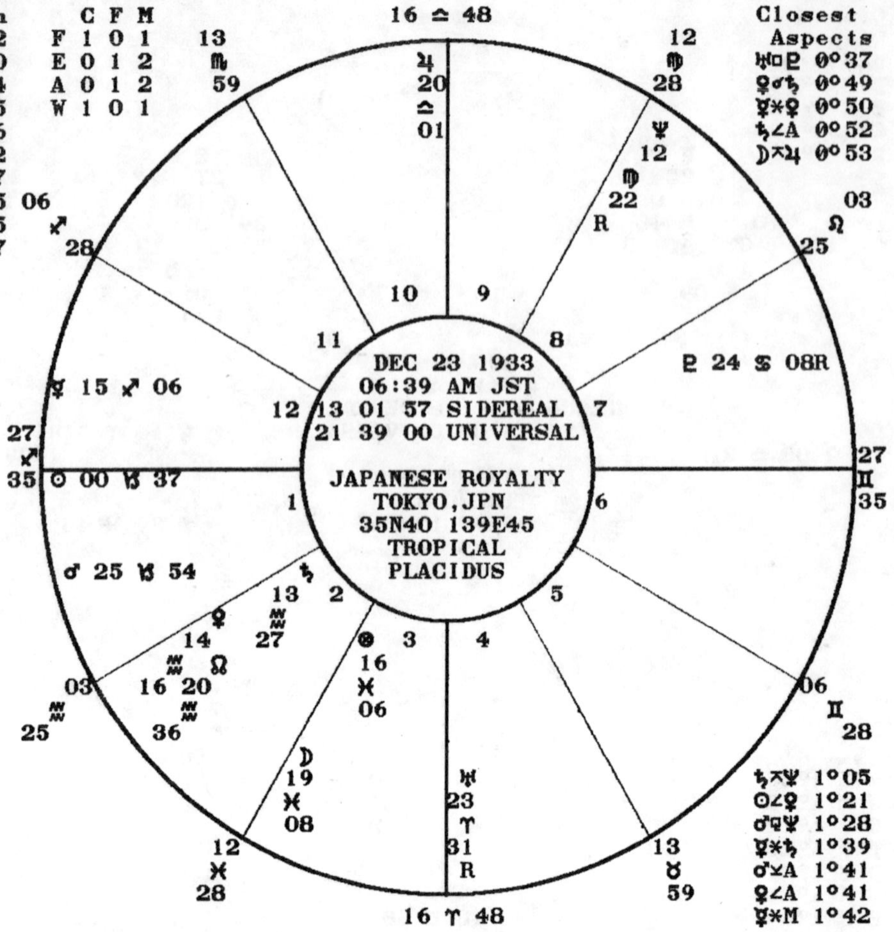

DEC 23 1933
06:39 AM JST
13 01 57 SIDEREAL
21 39 00 UNIVERSAL
JAPANESE ROYALTY
TOKYO,JPN
35N40 139E45
TROPICAL
PLACIDUS

Closest Aspects
♅□♇ 0°37
♀☌♄ 0°49
☿✶♀ 0°50
♄∠A 0°52
☽⚻♃ 0°53
♄⚻♆ 1°05
☉∠♀ 1°21
♂⚼♆ 1°28
☿✶♄ 1°39
♂⚺A 1°41
♀∠A 1°41
☿✶M 1°42

SVP=♓ 6°10'44"
JULIAN DAY=2427429.40208

JAPANESE ROYALTY
Prince Naruhito

February 23, 1960
4:15 PM JST
Tokyo, Japan
139 E 45 35 N 40

First son of Crown Princess Michiko and Crown Prince Akihito. Born four days after Prince Andrew of Great Britain. The child of a new-style love marriage; his mother a commoner who said that she'd raise her son herself and that he would go to public schools.

A: CL from Dell, August 1970; Dewey, same data from Dobyns.

Closest Aspects
☉⚺♀ 0°29
☽⚻♅ 0°36
♃⚼M 0°48
☉∠☽ 0°53
♅☌A 0°58

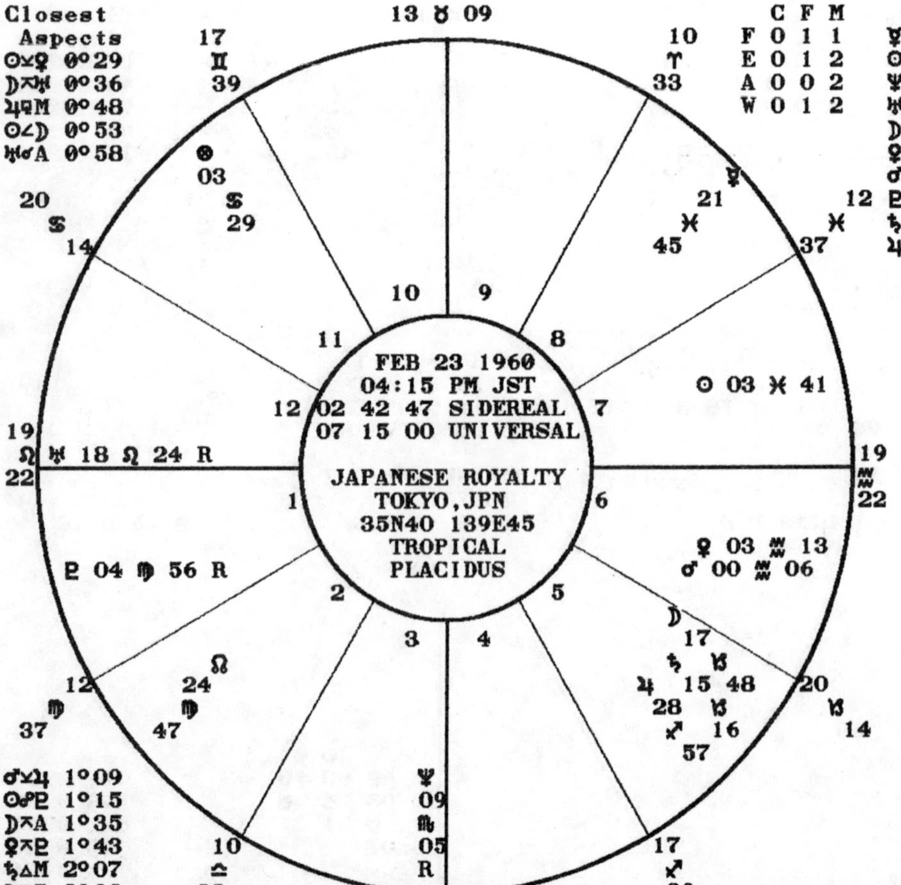

FEB 23 1960
04:15 PM JST
02 42 47 SIDEREAL
07 15 00 UNIVERSAL
JAPANESE ROYALTY
TOKYO,JPN
35N40 139E45
TROPICAL
PLACIDUS

	C	F	M
F	0	1	1
E	0	1	2
A	0	0	2
W	0	1	2

Declin
☿ 02S11
☉ 10S09
♆ 12S50
♅ 16N01
☽ 17S29
♀ 19S32
♂ 21S02
♇ 21N29
♄ 22S05
♃ 23S00

♂⚺♃ 1°09
☉☍♇ 1°15
☽⚻A 1°35
♀⚻♇ 1°43
♄△M 2°07
☽⚼♇ 2°08
☿⚼♆ 2°20

SVP=♓ 5°48'59"
JULIAN DAY=2436987.80208

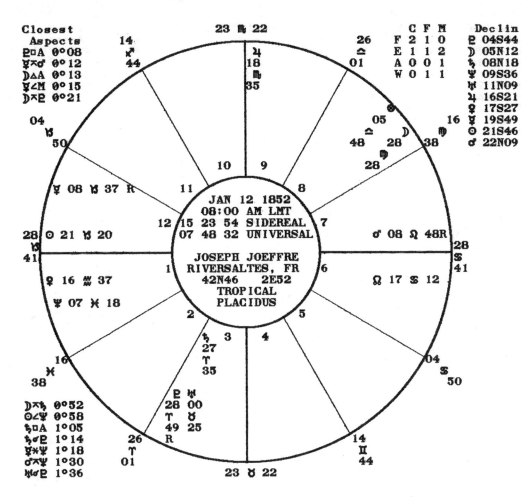

Closest Aspects

♇□A	0°08
☿☌♂	0°12
☽△A	0°13
☿∠M	0°15
☽⚹♇	0°21

23 ♏ 22

14 ♐ 44

18 ♏ 35

04 ♑ 50

☿ 08 ♑ 37 R

28 ♒ 41
⊙ 21 ♑ 20

♀ 16 ♒ 37

♆ 07 ♓ 18

16 ♓ 38

☽⚹♇ 0°52
⊙∠♆ 0°58
♄□A 1°05
♄⚹♇ 1°14
☿⚹♆ 1°18
♂⚹♇ 1°30
♅⚹♇ 1°36

26 ♈ 01

♇ ♅ 28 00 ♈ ♉ 49 25 R

23 ♉ 22

10 9 8 11 12 7 1 6 2 5 3 4

JAN 12 1852
08:00 AM LMT
15 23 54 SIDEREAL
07 48 32 UNIVERSAL

JOSEPH JOEFFRE
RIVERSALTES, FR
42N46 2E52
TROPICAL
PLACIDUS

♄ 27 ♈ 35

05 ♎ 48 28 ☽ 38
28 ♎ 28

16 ♍

♂ 08 ♌ 48R

28 ♋ 41
♌ 17 ♋ 12

04 ♋ 50

14 ♊ 44

	C	F	M		Declin
	F	2	1	0	♇ 04S44
26 ♎ 01	E	1	1	2	☽ 05N12
	A	0	0	1	♄ 08N18
	W	0	1	1	♆ 09S36
					♅ 11N09
					♃ 16S21
					♀ 17S27
					☿ 19S49
					⊙ 21S46
					♂ 22N09

JOEFFRE, JOSEPH
General

January 12, 1852
8:00 AM LMT
Riversaltes, France
2 E 52   42 N 46

Marshall of France who commanded the armies during the first two years of World War I; stopped the German onslaught in 1914. In 1916 replaced because he was considered too cautious. First trained as an engineer and worked in Indo China and Africa. (1852-1931)

A: *Constellations*, 1977, Lockhart quotes Gauquelin.

SVP=♓ 7°19'48"
JULIAN DAY=2397499.82537

JOHN, ELTON
Musician

March 25, 1947
4:00 PM D-BST
Pinner, Middlesex, England
0 W 23   51 N 36

Piano at age 3; scholarship at 12; rock music at 18. Frenetic, bisexual, with bizarre costuming and aura of excitement in performance. "Overnight" status as a rock megastar began in August 1970; led to annual $7 million in record sales.

A: Dewey states "confirmed by him."[75]

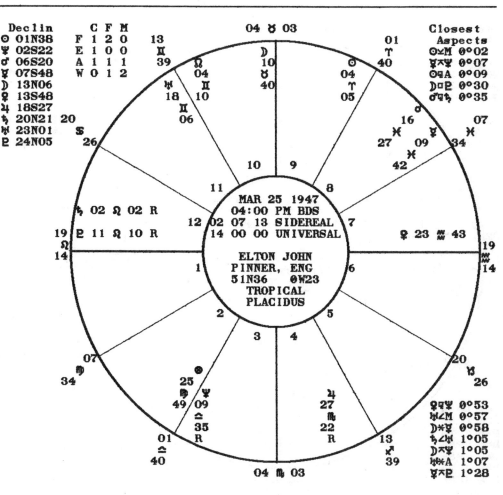

Declin		C	F	M
⊙ 01N38		F	1	2	0
♆ 02S22		E	1	0	0
♂ 06S20		A	1	1	1
☿ 07S48		W	0	1	2
☽ 13N06					
♀ 13S48					
♃ 18S27					
♄ 20N21					
♅ 23N01					
♇ 24N05					

04 ♉ 03

13 ♊ 39

04 ♊ 40

♄ 02 ♌ 02 R

19 ♌ 14
♇ 11 ♌ 10 R

07 ♍ 34

25 ♍ 49 ♆ 09 ♎ 35 01 ♎ 40 R

11 12 1 2 10 9 8 7 6 5 3 4

MAR 25 1947
04:00 PM BDS
02 07 13 SIDEREAL
14 00 00 UNIVERSAL

ELTON JOHN
PINNER, ENG
51N36 0W23
TROPICAL
PLACIDUS

☽ 01 ♈ 40
☿ 07 ♈
⊙ 04 ♈ 05
♂ 16 ♓ 42

27 ♓ 09 ♅ 34 ♓

♀ 23 ♍ 43

19 ♒ 14

20 ♑ 26

♃ 27 ♉ 22 R

13 ♐ 39

04 ♏ 03

Closest Aspects

⊙⚹M	0°02
☿⚹♆	0°07
⊙☌A	0°09
☽□♇	0°30
♂⚹♄	0°35
♀☌♆	0°53
♅∠M	0°57
☽⚹☿	0°58
♄∠♅	1°05
☽⚹♆	1°05
♅⚹A	1°07
☿⚹♇	1°28

SVP=♓ 6° 0' 4"
JULIAN DAY=2432270.08333

JOHN PAUL I
Pope

October 17, 1912
11:30 AM MET
Canole D'Agordo, Italy
12 E 06   46 N 15

Short reign as head of the Roman Catholic Church: selected as pope on August 26, 1978, and died 34 days later. Had a history of weak health, with tuberculosis in youth. After serving as bishop in 1958, named Patriarch of Venice by Pope Paul VI.

A: Tyl in *Astrology Now*, February 1979, "from colleague in Italy."

SVP=♓ 6°28'43"
JULIAN DAY=2419692.93750

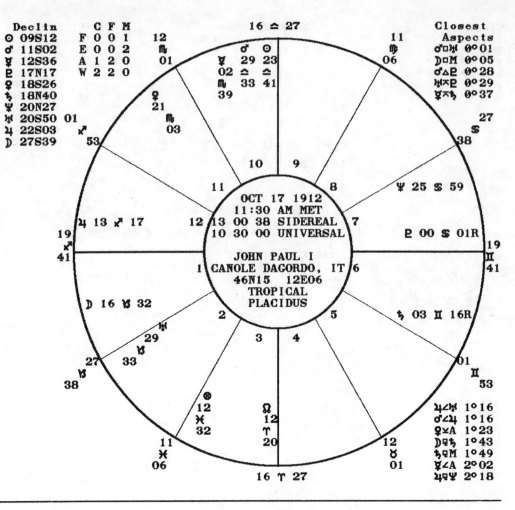

JONES, ANTHONY ARMSTRONG
Photographer

March 7, 1930
6:15 AM GMT
London, England
0 W 06   51 N 31

Titled Lord Snowdon with his marriage to Princess Margaret of England (1960-75). Continued working as a photographer. On a BBC documentary assignment in 1974, met Lucy Lindsay-Hogg, age 33: they married in December 1978.

A: Gleadow in AA, August 1960, "from his mother."

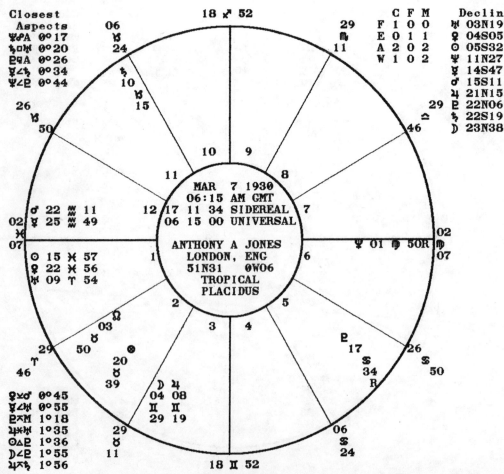

SVP=♓ 6°14'14"
JULIAN DAY=2426042.76042

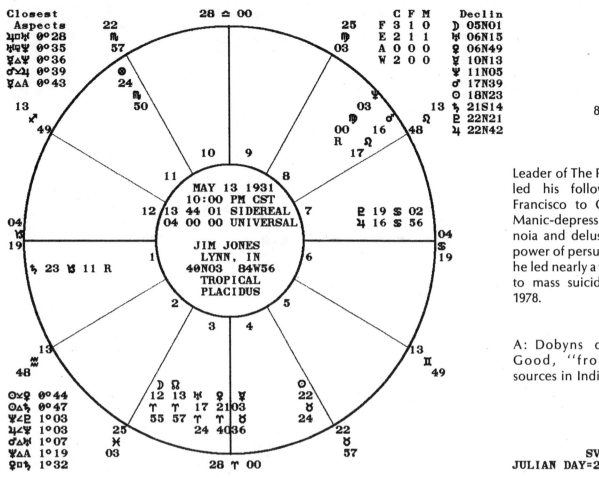

Closest Aspects

♃□♅	0°28
♅□♀	0°35
☿△♀	0°36
♂♂♃	0°39
☿△A	0°43

28 ♎ 00

22 ♏ 57

24 ♏ 50

13 ♐ 49

04 ♑ 19

13 ♒ 48

25 ♓ 03

C F M

F	3	1	0
E	2	1	1
A	0	0	0
W	2	0	0

25 ♍ 03

03 ♍

03 ♌

00 ♌ 17 R

13 ♌ 48

16 ♋

Declin

☽	05N01
♅	06N15
♀	06N49
☿	10N13
♇	11N05
♂	17N39
☉	18N23
♄	21S14
♇	22N21
♃	22N42

MAY 13 1931
10:00 PM CST
13 44 01 SIDEREAL
04 00 00 UNIVERSAL

JIM JONES
LYNN, IN
40N03 84W56
TROPICAL
PLACIDUS

♇ 19 ♋ 02
♃ 16 ♋ 56

04 ♋ 19

♄ 23 ♑ 11 R

13 ♊ 49

22 ♉ 57

☽ ♌ 12 13 ♈ 55
♅ ♀ 17 21 ♈ 57 24
☿ 03 ♉ 40 36

☉ 22 ♉ 24

☉♀	0°44
☉□♄	0°47
♆□♇	1°03
♃∠♆	1°03
♂△♅	1°07
♆△A	1°19
♀□♄	1°32

28 ♈ 00

JONES, JIM
Cult figure

May 13, 1931
10:00 PM CST
Lynn, Ind.
84 W 56   40 N 03

Leader of The People's Temple; led his followers from San Francisco to Guyana in 1977. Manic-depressive with paranoia and delusions; incredible power of persuasion with which he led nearly a thousand people to mass suicide in November 1978.

A: Dobyns quotes Beverly Good, "from newspaper sources in Indiana."

SVP=♓ 6°13'10"
JULIAN DAY=2426475.66667

JONES, MARC EDMUND
Writer, astrologer

October 1, 1888
8:37 AM CST
St. Louis, Mo
90 W 12   38 N 37

In youth a Hollywood script writer; became a full time astrologer. Books include *Guide to Horoscope Interpretations* (1972). Given a respectful and affectionate 90th birthday party by two hundred colleagues in 1978 while planning his next book. (1888-1980)

A: Data in his book *Sabian Symbols*.

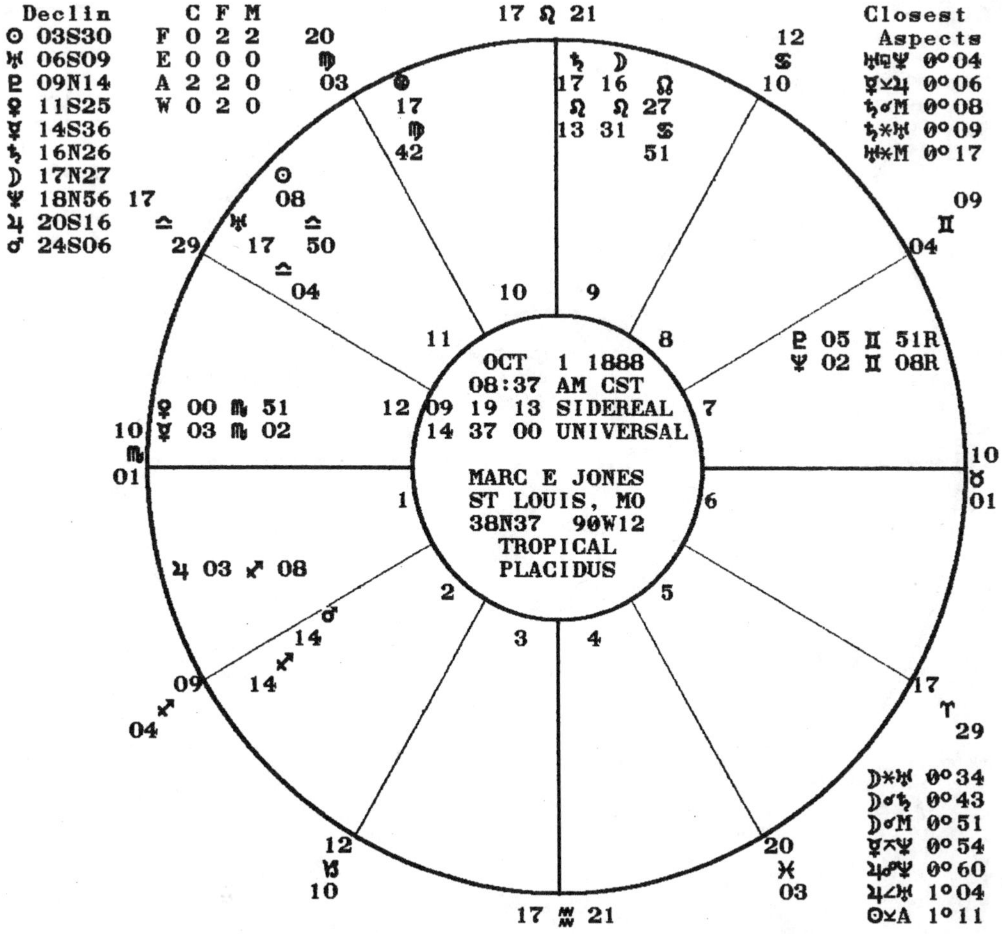

Declin

☉	03S30
♅	06S09
♇	09N14
♀	11S25
☿	14S36
♄	16N26
☽	17N27
♆	18N56
♃	20S16
♂	24S06

C F M

F	0	2	2
E	0	0	0
A	2	2	0
W	0	2	0

17 ♌ 21

20 ♍ 03

17 ♍ 42

29 ♎ 17

17 ♎ 50

04 ♎

Closest Aspects

♅□♆	0°04
☿♃	0°06
♄♂	0°08
♄*♅	0°09
♅*M	0°17

♄ ☽ 17 16 ♌
♌ ♌ 27
13 31 ♋
51

12 ♋

10 ♋

09 ♊ 04

♇ 05 ♊ 51R
♆ 02 ♊ 08R

OCT 1 1888
08:37 AM CST
09 19 13 SIDEREAL
14 37 00 UNIVERSAL

MARC E JONES
ST LOUIS, MO
38N37 90W12
TROPICAL
PLACIDUS

♀ 00 ♏ 51
☿ 03 ♏ 02

01 ♏

10 ♏

10 ♉ 01

♃ 03 ♐ 08

♂ 14 ♐
14 ♐

09 ♐
14 ♐

04 ♐

17 ♈ 29

12 ♓
20 ♓
03 ♓

♑
10

17 ♒ 21

☽*♅	0°34
☽♂♄	0°43
☽♂M	0°51
☿*♅	0°54
♃∠♆	0°60
♃∠M	1°04
☉*A	1°11

SVP=♓ 6°49' 3"
JULIAN DAY=2410912.10903

JORDAN, HAMILTON
Government official

September 21, 1944
6:07 PM EWT
Charlotte, N.C.
80 W 51   35 N 14

Right-hand man to Jimmy Carter since he first worked in the gubernatorial campaign in 1966. Appointed presidential assistant in January 1977; believed to be the most powerful senior aide.

A: Arlene Robertson, October 20, 1978, letter from Ms. Conners, Jordan's assistant, quoting his mother at "6:00 to 6:15 PM."

SVP=♓ 6° 2'10"
JULIAN DAY=2431355.42153

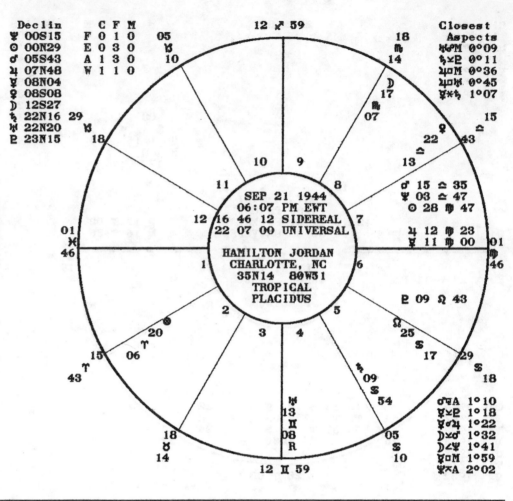

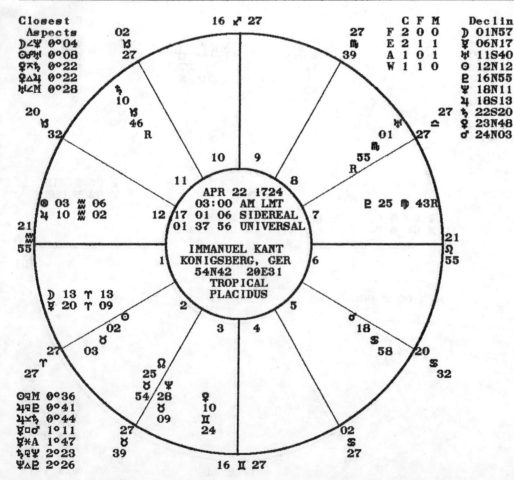

KANT, IMMANUEL
Writer

April 22, 1724
3:00 AM LMT
Konigsberg, Germany
20 E 31   54 N 42

German philosopher who wrote on aesthetics and ethics. Works include *Critique of Pure Reason* (1781) and *Critique of Practical Reason* (1788). Taught from 1746; lived his entire life in Konigsberg. (1724-1804)

A: *Constellations*, 1977, quotes M.A., May 1912; "birth time stated in *Fragmente Aus Kant's Leben* by Dr. Mortzfield, 1802, (not 5:00 AM.)"[76]

SVP=♓ 9° 6'43"
JULIAN DAY=2350849.56801

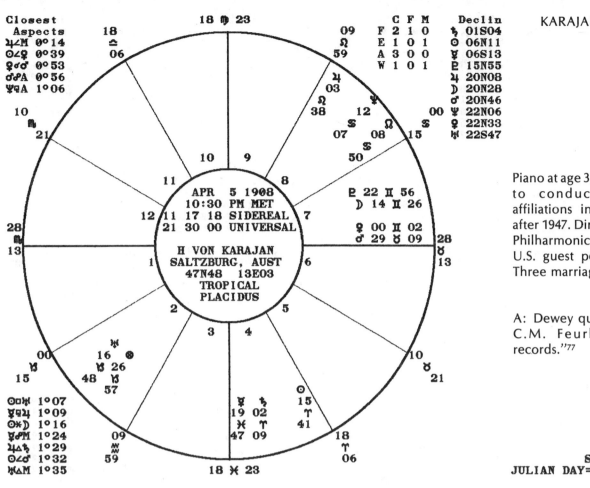

KARAJAN, HERBERT VON
Conductor

April 5, 1908
10:30 PM MET
Salzburg, Austria
13 E 03   47 N 48

Closest Aspects

♃∠M	0°14
☉□♀	0°39
♀♂♂	0°53
♂⚹A	0°56
♆⚹A	1°06

	C	F	M		Declin
F	2	1	0	♄	01S04
E	1	0	1	☉	06N11
A	3	0	0	☿	06S13
W	1	0	1	♇	15N55
				♃	20N08
				☽	20N28
				♂	20N46
				♆	22N06
				♀	22N33
				♅	22S47

☉□♅	1°07
☿□♃	1°09
☉⚹☽	1°16
☿⚹M	1°24
♃△♄	1°29
☉∠♂	1°32
♅△M	1°35

Piano at age 3; debut at 8; began to conduct at 20. Nazi affiliations in war-time. Tours after 1947. Director of the Berlin Philharmonic since 1954. First U.S. guest performance, 1955. Three marriages.

A: Dewey quotes Ebertin from C.M. Feurback, "rectory records."[77]

SVP=♓ 6°32'44"
JULIAN DAY=2418037.39583

KEATON, DIANA
Actress

January 5, 1946
2:53 AM PST
Los Angeles, Ca
118 W 15   34 N 04

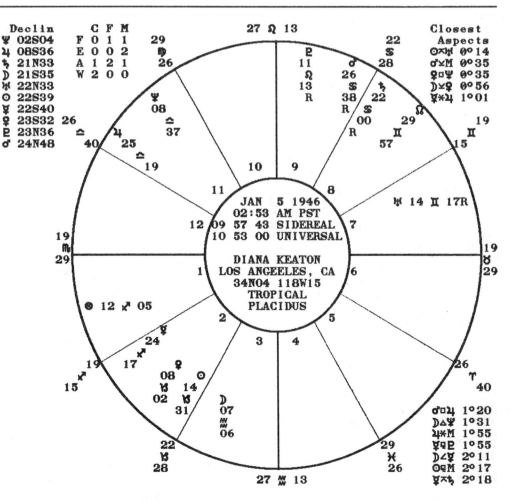

	Declin		C	F	M
♆	02S04	F	0	1	1
♃	08S36	E	0	0	2
♄	21N33	A	1	2	1
☽	21N35	W	2	0	0
♅	22N33				
☉	22S39				
☿	22S40				
♀	23S32				
♇	23N36				
♂	24N48				

Closest Aspects

☉⚹♅	0°14
♂⚹M	0°35
♀□♆	0°35
☽□♀	0°56
☿⚹♃	1°01

♂□♃	1°20
☽△♆	1°31
♃⚹M	1°55
☿□♇	1°55
☽∠♀	2°11
☉□M	2°17
☿⚺♄	2°18

Professional debut in *Hair* (1968). Met Woody Allen when they co-starred in a stage comedy, *Play It Again Sam*. First film, *Lovers and Other Strangers* (1971); followed by *The Godfather I* and *II*, *Looking for Mr. Goodbar*, *Interiors*, and *Annie Hall*, for which she won the Oscar in 1978.

A: Penfield states B.C. in M.H., October 1979.

SVP=♓ 6° 1' 6"
JULIAN DAY=2431825.95347

KENT, ROCKWELL
Artist

June 21, 1882
4:00 AM LMT
Terrytown Heights, N.Y.
73 W 54   41 N 05

American artist with oil paintings, watercolors, lithographs, and woodcuts in vigorous, romantic-realistic style. The author of several books, including his autobiography *It's Me O Lord* in 1955. (1882-1971)

A: Lockhart quotes article on Rockwell in NAJ, September 1934, "from Mr. Kent himself."

SVP=✶ 6°53'48"
JULIAN DAY=2408617.87194

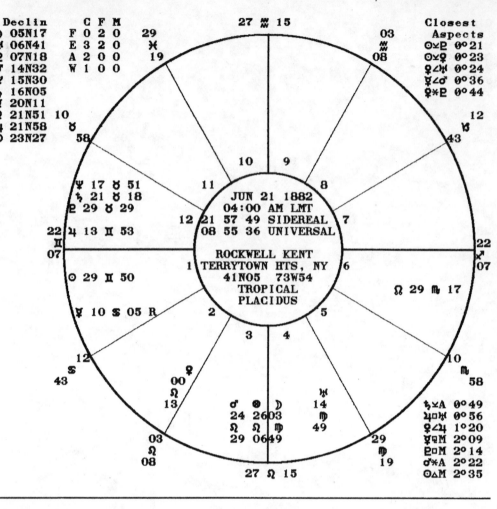

Declin	C	F	M	
☽ 05N17	F	0	2	0
♅ 06N41	E	3	2	0
♇ 07N18	A	2	0	0
♂ 14N32	W	1	0	0
♆ 15N30				
♄ 16N05				
☿ 20N11				
♀ 21N51				
♃ 21N58				
☉ 23N27				

Closest Aspects
☉✶♇ 0°21
☉✶♀ 0°23
♀∠♅ 0°24
☿∠♂ 0°36
♀✶♇ 0°44

JUN 21 1882
04:00 AM LMT
21 57 49 SIDEREAL
08 55 36 UNIVERSAL
ROCKWELL KENT
TERRYTOWN HTS, NY
41N05 73W54
TROPICAL
PLACIDUS

♄∠A 0°49
♃□♅ 0°56
♀∠♃ 1°20
☿□M 2°09
♇□M 2°14
♂∠A 2°22
☉△M 2°35

KEPLER, JOHANNES
Scientist

January 7, 1572 NS
2:30 PM LAT
Weil Der Stadt, Germany
7 E 39   47 N 36

German astronomer and mathematician who discovered three laws of planetary motion. Assistant, then successor to Tycho Brahe; upholder of Copernicus' theories. Also wrote astrological texts of the planetary influences. (1571-1630)

A: *Constellations*, 1977, Lockhart quotes *Kepler* by Max Caspar (1959), p. 29.

SVP=✶11°14' 7"
JULIAN DAY=2295227.08292

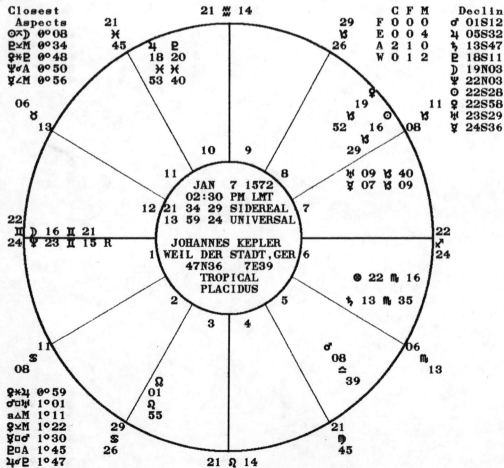

Closest Aspects
☉⚼☽ 0°08
♇∠M 0°34
♀✶♇ 0°48
♆☌A 0°50
☿∠M 0°56

	C	F	M	Declin
	F	0	0	0	♂ 01S12
	E	0	0	4	♃ 05S32
	A	2	1	0	♄ 13S47
	W	0	1	2	♇ 18S11
					☽ 19N03
					♆ 22N03
					☉ 22S28
					♀ 22S58
					♅ 23S29
					☿ 24S36

JAN 7 1572
02:30 PM LMT
21 34 29 SIDEREAL
13 59 24 UNIVERSAL
JOHANNES KEPLER
WEIL DER STADT, GER
47N36 7E39
TROPICAL
PLACIDUS

♀✶♃ 0°59
♂□♅ 1°01
a△M 1°11
♀∠M 1°22
☿☌♂ 1°30
♇□A 1°45
♃∠♇ 1°47

KEROUAC, JACK
Writer

March 12, 1922
5:00 PM EST
Lowell, Mass
71 W 19   42 N 38

Closest Aspects
☽⊻♆ 0°04
♅□M 0°12
♂□♅ 0°18
♆⊻A 0°25
☽☌A 0°29

	C	F	M
F	0	1	1
E	0	1	0
A	0	2	1
W	1	0	3

Declin	
♄	00N19
♀	01S29
☉	03S21
☽	04N21
♃	05S08
♅	08S24
☿	14S15
♆	16N51
♇	20N07
♂	21S17

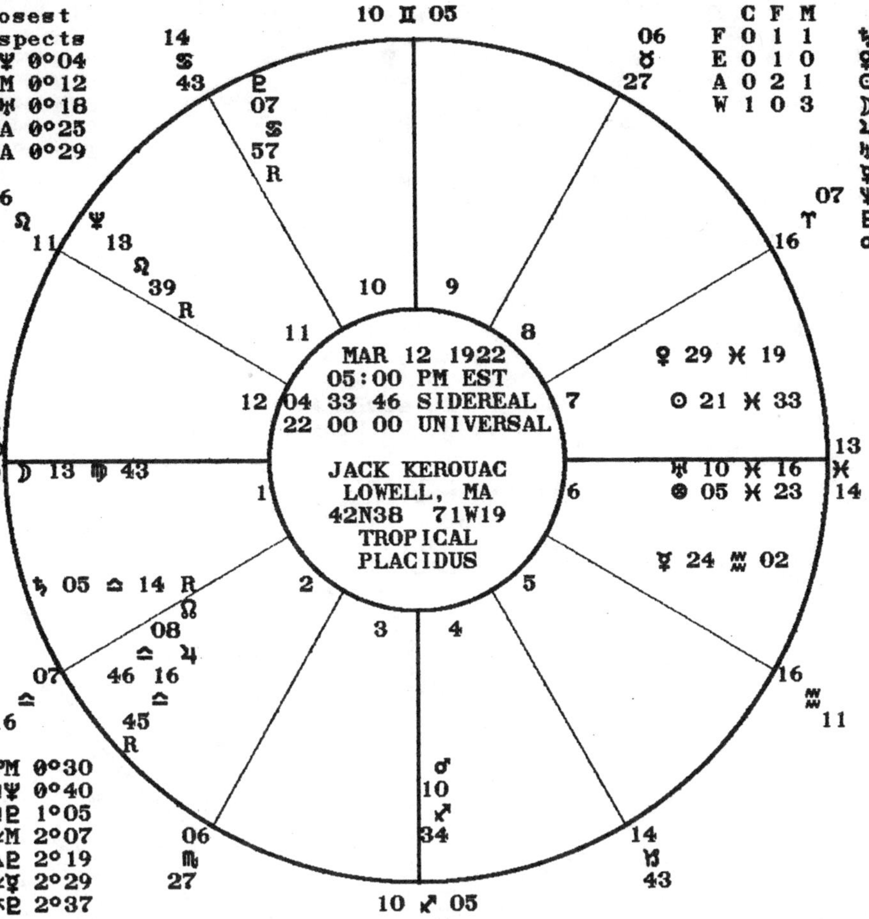

MAR 12 1922
05:00 PM EST
04 33 46 SIDEREAL
22 00 00 UNIVERSAL
JACK KEROUAC
LOWELL, MA
42N38 71W19
TROPICAL
PLACIDUS
10 ♊ 05
10 ♐ 05
♀ 29 ♓ 19
☉ 21 ♓ 33
♅ 10 ♓ 16
⊗ 05 ♓ 23
☿ 24 ♒ 02
☽ 13 ♍ 43
♄ 05 ♎ 14 R

☌☍M 0°30
♀□♆ 0°40
☿□♇ 1°05
♇⊻M 2°07
♅△♇ 2°19
☉⊻☿ 2°29
♂⊼♇ 2°37

American author, who originated the term "beat generation", and who repudiated middle-class values in his controversial novels. His Bohemian concepts pre-dated the alternate life-sytles of the 60s. Books include *On the Road* (1957) and *The Dharma Bums* (1958). (1922-1969)

B: Holliday quotes *Kerouac* by A. Charters (1973).[78]

SVP=♓ 6°20'43"
JULIAN DAY=2423126.41667

KILLY, JEAN CLAUDE
Skiier

August 30, 1943
5:10 AM DGWT
St. Cloud, France
2 E 12   48 N 51

Declin	
♆	00N53
♀	02S15
☿	03S26
☉	09N21
☽	13N09
♃	17N23
♂	19N26
♅	21N40
♄	22N01
♇	23N20

	C	F	M
F	0	3	0
E	0	2	0
A	3	2	0
W	0	0	0

Closest Aspects
☿△♂ 0°19
☽△M 0°59
♅✱♇ 1°03
♃☌A 1°19
♆∠A 1°21

Winner of the triple crown in the 1968 Olympics, the second man in history to do so. First came to the U.S. in the early 60s, where he won the World Pro Skiing title in 1973. Representative of ski equipment and sportswear by 1978.

A: Dewey quotes Gauquelin in M.H., October 1976.

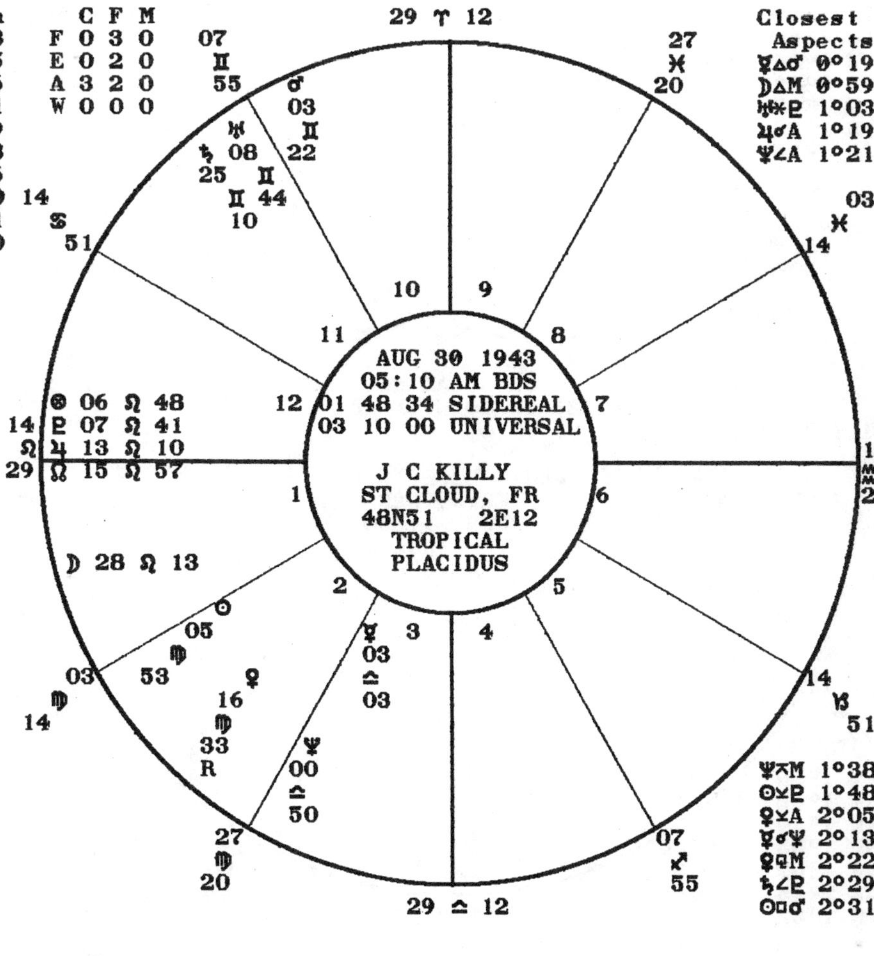

AUG 30 1943
05:10 AM BDS
01 48 34 SIDEREAL
03 10 00 UNIVERSAL
J C KILLY
ST CLOUD, FR
48N51 2E12
TROPICAL
PLACIDUS
29 ♈ 12
29 ♎ 12
⊗ 06 ♌ 48
♇ 07 ♌ 41
♃ 13 ♌ 10
☊ 15 ♌ 57
☽ 28 ♌ 13

♆⊼M 1°38
☉⊻♇ 1°48
♀⊻A 2°05
☿☌♆ 2°13
♀□M 2°22
♄∠♇ 2°29
☉□♂ 2°31

SVP=♓ 6° 2'59"
JULIAN DAY=2430966.63194

KING, MORGANA
Singer, actress

June 4, 1930
11:00 AM EST
Pleasantville, N.Y.
73 W 47   41 N 08

Recording artist from 1955; traveled the night club circuit for twenty five years. Her hit songs include "A Taste of Honey" (1963). Married Willie Dennis, trumpeter; widowed, 1965. Film debut as Mama Corleone in *The Godfather* (1971).

A: John Hanson in Dell, November 1972, "from her."

SVP=♓ 6°14' 2"
JULIAN DAY=2426132.16667

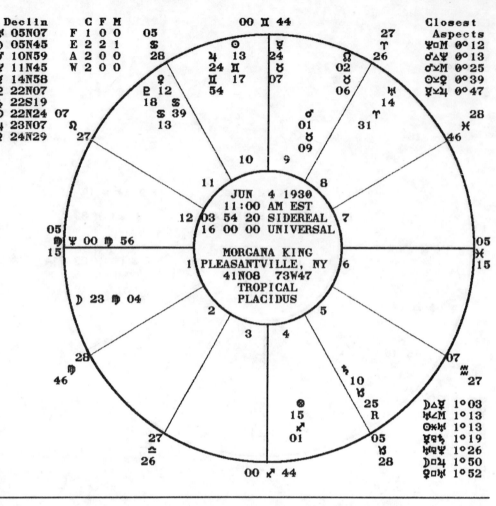

Declin		C F M				Closest Aspects
♅ 05N07	F 1 0 0					ΨM 0°12
☽ 05N45	E 2 2 1					♂△Ψ 0°13
♂ 10N59	A 2 0 0					♂∠M 0°25
Ψ 11N45	W 2 0 0					☉∗♀ 0°39
☿ 14N58						☿♃ 0°47
♇ 22N07						
♄ 22S19						
☉ 22N24						
♃ 23N07						
♀ 24N29						

☽△☿ 1°03	
♅∠M 1°13	
☉∗♅ 1°13	
☿♄ 1°19	
♅∗Ψ 1°26	
☽□♃ 1°50	
♀∠♅ 1°52	

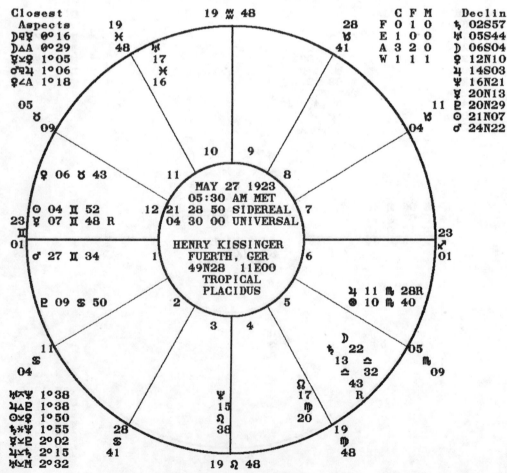

Closest Aspects	
☽♀ 0°16	
☽△A 0°29	
☿∗♀ 1°05	
♂♃ 1°06	
♀∠A 1°18	

	C F M	Declin
	F 0 1 0	♄ 02S57
	E 1 0 0	♅ 05S44
	A 3 2 0	☽ 06S04
	W 1 1 1	♀ 12N10
		♃ 14S03
		Ψ 16N21
		☿ 20N13
		♇ 20N29
		☉ 21N07
		♂ 24N22

♅∠♅ 1°38	
♃△♇ 1°38	
☉∗♀ 1°50	
♄∗Ψ 1°55	
☿∠♇ 2°02	
♃♄ 2°15	
♅∠M 2°32	

KISSINGER, HENRY
Secretary of State

May 27, 1923
5:30 AM MET
Fuerth, Bayern, Germany
11 E 00   49 N 28

Harvard professor until 1973, when he became Nixon's intimate political advisor and negotiator. Came to U.S. at 15 after Nazi persecution. Urbane, multilingual, brilliant. Married, 1949-64; two children. Married Nancy Maginnes on March 30, 1974.

A: Holliday quotes Troinski of the Astrological Association of London, from B.C.[79]

SVP=♓ 6°19'51"
JULIAN DAY=2423566.68750

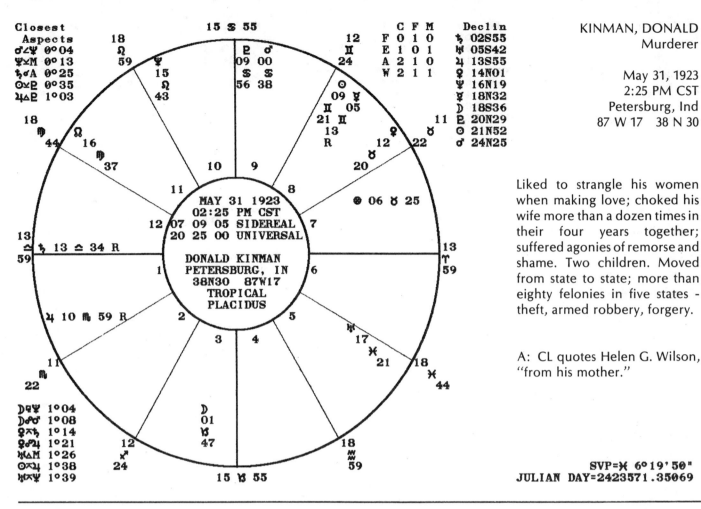

KINMAN, DONALD
Murderer

May 31, 1923
2:25 PM CST
Petersburg, Ind
87 W 17   38 N 30

Closest
Aspects
♂∠♆ 0°04
♆⚼M 0°13
♄☌A 0°25
☉✶♇ 0°35
♃△♇ 1°03

15 ♋ 55

MAY 31 1923
02:25 PM CST
07 09 05 SIDEREAL
20 25 00 UNIVERSAL

DONALD KINMAN
PETERSBURG, IN
38N30 87W17
TROPICAL
PLACIDUS

	C	F	M	Declin
F	0	1	0	♄ 02S55
E	1	0	1	♅ 05S42
A	2	1	0	♃ 13S55
W	2	1	1	♀ 14N01
				♆ 16N19
				☿ 18N32
				☽ 18S36
				♇ 20N29
				☉ 21N52
				♂ 24N25

♃✶♇ 1°03

♀✶♄ 1°14
♀✶♃ 1°21
♅☌M 1°26
☉☌♃ 1°38
♅△♆ 1°39

☽∠♆ 1°04
☽☍♂ 1°08

Liked to strangle his women when making love; choked his wife more than a dozen times in their four years together; suffered agonies of remorse and shame. Two children. Moved from state to state; more than eighty felonies in five states - theft, armed robbery, forgery.

A: CL quotes Helen G. Wilson, "from his mother."

SVP=♓ 6°19'50"
JULIAN DAY=2423571.35069

KINMAN'S VICTIM
The blonde

April 19, 1915
3:15 PM EST
Detroit, Mich
83 W 03   42 N 20

A pretty saleswoman; married and divorced; an alcoholic. Met Kinman on April 6, 1958; during sex relations he strangled her to death. After murdering a second girl in the same way on November 19, 1959, he gave himself up to authorities.

A: CL quotes Helen G. Wilson, "from research of the case."

SVP=♓ 6°26'24"
JULIAN DAY=2420607.34375

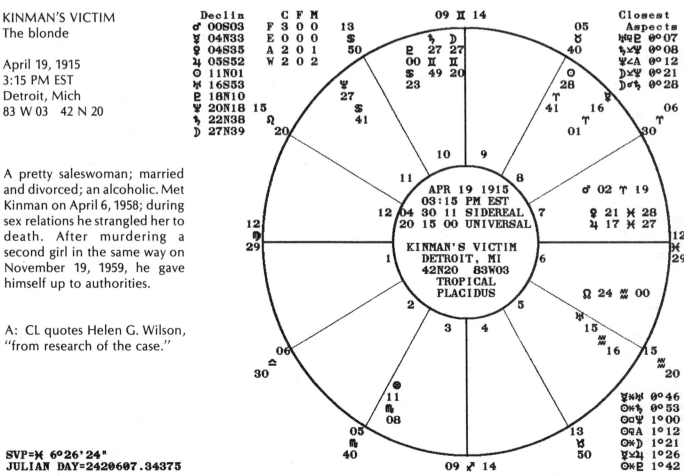

Declin		C	F	M
♂ 00S03		F	3	0	0
☿ 04N33		E	0	0	0
♀ 04S35		A	2	0	1
♃ 05S52		W	2	0	2
☉ 11N01				
♅ 16S53				
♇ 18N10				
♆ 20N18				
♄ 22N38				
☽ 27N39				

APR 19 1915
03:15 PM EST
04 30 11 SIDEREAL
20 15 00 UNIVERSAL

KINMAN'S VICTIM
DETROIT, MI
42N20 83W03
TROPICAL
PLACIDUS

Closest
Aspects
♅⚼♇ 0°07
♄∠♆ 0°08
♆∠A 0°12
☽⚼♅ 0°21
☽☌♄ 0°28

♂ 02 ♈ 19
♀ 21 ♓ 28
♃ 17 ♓ 27

� 24 ♒ 00

☿⚼♅ 0°46
☉✶♄ 0°53
☉□♆ 1°00
☉⚼A 1°12
☉✶☽ 1°21
☿✶♃ 1°26
☉✶♇ 1°42

KNIEVEL, EVEL
Daredevil

October 17, 1938
2:40 PM MST
Butte, Mont
112 W 32   46 N 00

Modern day gladiator with daring motorcycle stunts; almost killed a dozen times. High school dropout and hell-raiser; still spoiling for trouble in 1979. A movie was filmed of his life, *Evel Knievel*, in 1972. Married; three children.

A: CSH.[80]

SVP=♓ 6° 6'40"
JULIAN DAY=2429189.40278

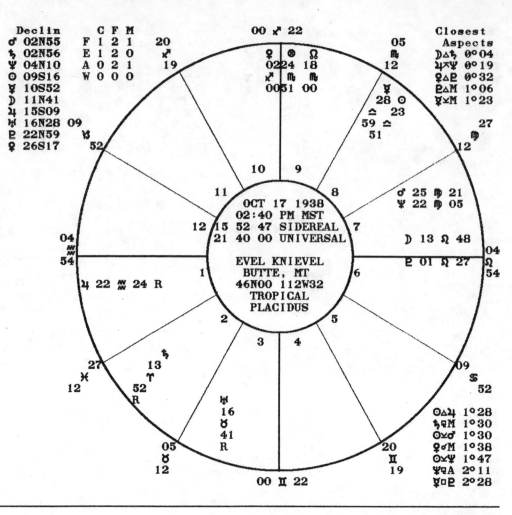

Declin		C F M	
♂ 02N55		F 1 2 1	20
♄ 02N56		E 1 2 0	19
♆ 04N10		A 0 2 1	
☉ 09S16		W 0 0 0	
☿ 10S52			
☽ 11N41			
♃ 15S09			
♅ 16N28	09		
♇ 22N59	♑		
♀ 26S17	52		

Closest Aspects
☽△♅ 0°04
♃♆ 0°19
♀△♇ 0°32
♇AM 1°06
☿⚹M 1°23

OCT 17 1938
02:40 PM MST
15 52 47 SIDEREAL
21 40 00 UNIVERSAL

EVEL KNIEVEL
BUTTE, MT
46N00 112W32
TROPICAL
PLACIDUS

♂ 25 ♍ 21
♆ 22 ♍ 05
☽ 13 ♌ 48
♇ 01 ♌ 27

☉△♃ 1°28
♄□M 1°30
☉⚹♂ 1°30
♀♂M 1°38
☉⚹♆ 1°47
♆A 2°11
☿□♇ 2°28

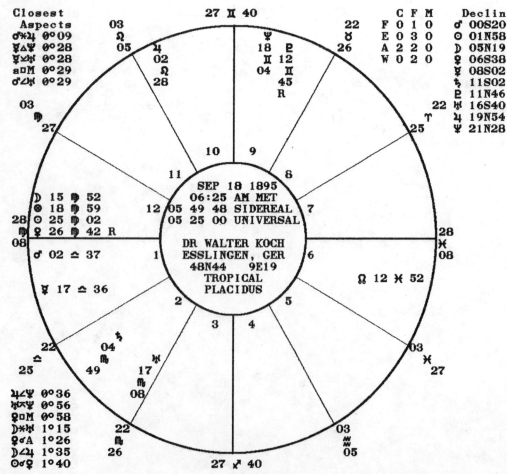

KOCH, DR. WALTER
Mathematician

September 18, 1895
6:25 AM MET
Esslingen, Germany
9 E 19   48 N 44

Researcher, intellectually eclectic with exceptional memory. Developed an astrological Table of Houses. Published hundreds of articles and scores of brochures and books on astrology after 1924. Injured in World War I: his right leg had a dozen surgeries.

A: *Constellations*, 1977, Lockhart quotes SPICA, January 1964, "data from him to Brig. Firebrace."

Closest Aspects
♂⚹♃ 0°09
☿△♆ 0°28
♀⚹♅ 0°28
a□M 0°29
♂∠♅ 0°29

	C F M	Declin
	F 0 1 0	♂ 00S20
	E 0 3 0	☉ 01N58
	A 2 2 0	☽ 05N19
	W 0 2 0	♀ 06S38
		♃ 08S02
		♄ 11S02
		♇ 11N46
		♅ 16S40
		♃ 19N54
		♆ 21N28

SEP 18 1895
06:25 AM MET
05 49 48 SIDEREAL
05 25 00 UNIVERSAL

DR WALTER KOCH
ESSLINGEN, GER
48N44 9E19
TROPICAL
PLACIDUS

♃∠♆ 0°36
♅⚹♆ 0°56
♀□M 0°58
☽⚹♅ 1°15
♀♂A 1°26
☽∠♃ 1°35
☉♂♀ 1°40

SVP=♓ 6°42'52"
JULIAN DAY=2413454.72569

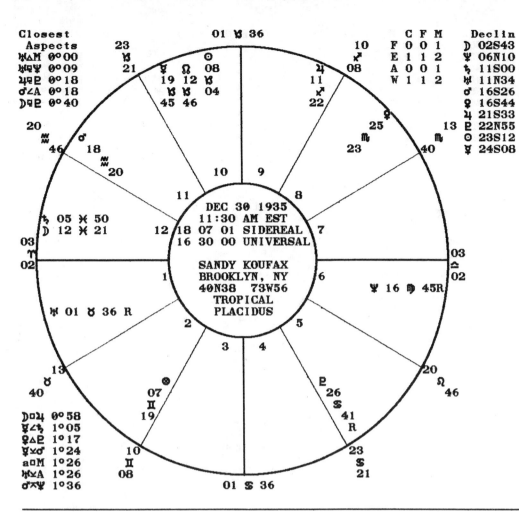

Closest Aspects

⛢△M	0°00
⛢□⛢	0°09
♃⚹♇	0°18
♂□A	0°18
☽□♇	0°40

☽□♃	0°58
☿∠♄	1°05
♀△♇	1°17
☿♂♂	1°24
a□M	1°26
⛢⚹A	1°26
♂⚹♆	1°36

Declin

☽	02S43
♆	06N10
♄	11S00
⛢	11N34
♂	16S26
♀	16S44
♃	21S33
♇	22N55
☉	23S12
☿	24S08

	C	F	M
F	0	0	1
E	1	1	2
A	0	0	1
W	1	1	2

KOUFAX, SANDY
Baseball star

December 30, 1935
11:30 AM EST
Brooklyn, N.Y.
73 W 56   40 N 38

DEC 30 1935
11:30 AM EST
18 07 01 SIDEREAL
16 30 00 UNIVERSAL

SANDY KOUFAX
BROOKLYN, NY
40N38 73W56
TROPICAL
PLACIDUS

Won the Cy Young award in 1963, '65, and '66. Pitched no-hitters from 1962 to 1965. Won twenty five games in 1963, twenty six games in 1965, and twenty seven games in 1966. Elected to National Baseball Hall of Fame in 1972. After retirement, became a baseball sportscaster.

A: From him to R.H. Oliver.

SVP=♓ 6° 8' 56"
JULIAN DAY=2428167.18750

KRAFFT, KARL ERNST
Astrologer

May 10, 1900
12:45 PM MET
Commugny, Switzerland
6 E 30   46 N 32

Declin

☽	05S23
♂	08N55
☿	08N55
♇	13N24
☉	17N34
♃	20S46
⛢	22S06
♆	22N10
♄	22S21
♀	26N55

	C	F	M
F	2	0	2
E	1	0	1
A	2	1	0
W	1	0	0

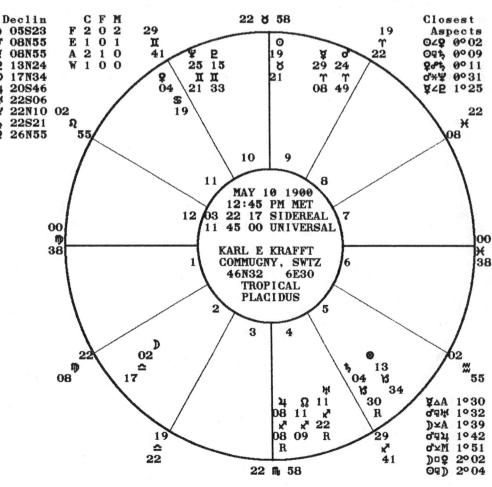

MAY 10 1900
12:45 PM MET
03 22 17 SIDEREAL
11 45 00 UNIVERSAL

KARL E KRAFFT
COMMUGNY, SWTZ
46N32 6E30
TROPICAL
PLACIDUS

Statistician and researcher, said to have cast and studied more than sixty thousand birth charts; one of the originators of *Cosmobiology*. Nazi advisor to Hess whom he told that Hitler had astrologically made a wrong decision: was sentenced to Buchenwalde and killed on January 8, 1945.

A: Ernest Grant in AA, July 1946, "data from him."[81]

Closest Aspects

☉♀♀	0°02
☉♀♄	0°09
♀♂♀	0°11
♂⚹♆	0°31
☿∠♇	1°25

☿△A	1°30
♂♂⛢	1°32
☽⚹A	1°39
♂♀♃	1°42
♂⚹M	1°51
☽♂♀	2°02
☉♀☽	2°04

SVP=♓ 6°38'49"
JULIAN DAY=2415149.98958

KREUGAR, IVAR
The Match King

March 2, 1880
5:30 AM Stockholm
Kalmar, Sweden
16 E 20   56 N 39

Business promoter, inter-
national financier. During and
after World War I, gained 65% of
world control of the production
of matches, using dishonest and
unscrupulous methods. The
stock market crash of 1929
undermined his business.
Committed suicide three years
later.

A: Skeetz quotes Lyndoe in AA,
November 1971, "data obtained
in Sweden."

SVP=✠ 6°55'41"
JULIAN DAY=2407776.68380

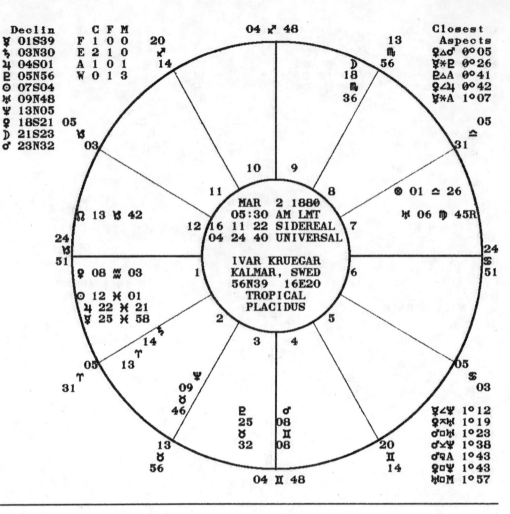

Declin		C	F	M
☿	01S39	F	1	0	0
♄	03N30	E	2	1	0
♃	04S01	A	1	0	1
♇	05N56	W	0	1	3
☉	07S04				
♅	09N48				
♆	13N05				
♀	18S21				
☽	21S23				
♂	23N32				

Closest
Aspects

♀△♂	0°05
☿✱♇	0°26
♇△A	0°41
♀∠♃	0°42
☿✱A	1°07

MAR   2 1880
05:30 AM LMT
16 11 22 SIDEREAL
04 24 40 UNIVERSAL

IVAR KRUEGAR
KALMAR, SWED
56N39 16E20
TROPICAL
PLACIDUS

☿∠♆	1°12
♀✱♅	1°19
♂□♅	1°23
♂∠♃	1°38
♂□A	1°43
♀□♆	1°43
♅□M	1°57

Closest
Aspects

☉∠♆	0°07
♂□♇	0°39
♃∠A	0°48
☉□☽	0°57
☽∠♅	1°03

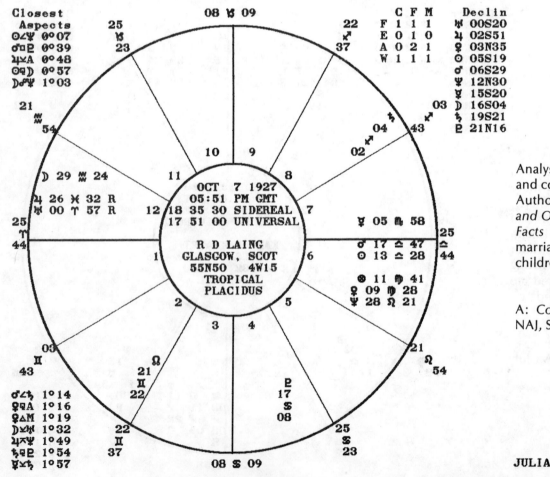

	C	F	M	Declin	
	F	1	1	1	♅	00S20
	E	0	1	0	♃	02S51
	A	0	2	1	♀	03N35
	W	1	1	1	☉	05S19
					♂	06S29
					♆	12N30
					☿	15S20
					☽	16S04
					♄	19S21
					♇	21N16

OCT   7 1927
05:51 PM GMT
18 35 30 SIDEREAL
17 51 00 UNIVERSAL

R D LAING
GLASGOW, SCOT
55N50 4W15
TROPICAL
PLACIDUS

♂∠♄	1°14
♀□A	1°16
♀△M	1°19
☽□♅	1°32
♃✱♆	1°49
♄□♇	1°54
☿∠♄	1°57

LAING, R.D.
Psychiatrist

October 7, 1927
5:51 PM GMT
Galscow, Scotland
4 W 15   55 N 50

Analyst, philosopher, writer,
and counter-culture cult figure.
Author of *The Politics of Family
and Other Essays* (1971) and *The
Facts of Life* (1976). Two
marriages and divorces; eight
children.

A: *Constellations*, 1977, from
NAJ, Spring 1976, "from him."[82]

SVP=✠ 6°16'24"
JULIAN DAY=2425161.24375

Closest Aspects

♂☌♄ 0°03
☿✶♇ 0°04
♆☍M 0°44
♃⊼♆ 1°08
☽∠♇ 1°08

	C	F	M
F	2	0	0
E	1	0	0
A	0	1	4
W	1	0	1

Declin

☉ 00S21
☽ 05N08
♆ 05S31
☿ 07N03
♄ 14S35
♂ 14S37
♀ 15S21
♃ 16N49
♅ 22N16
♇ 23S41

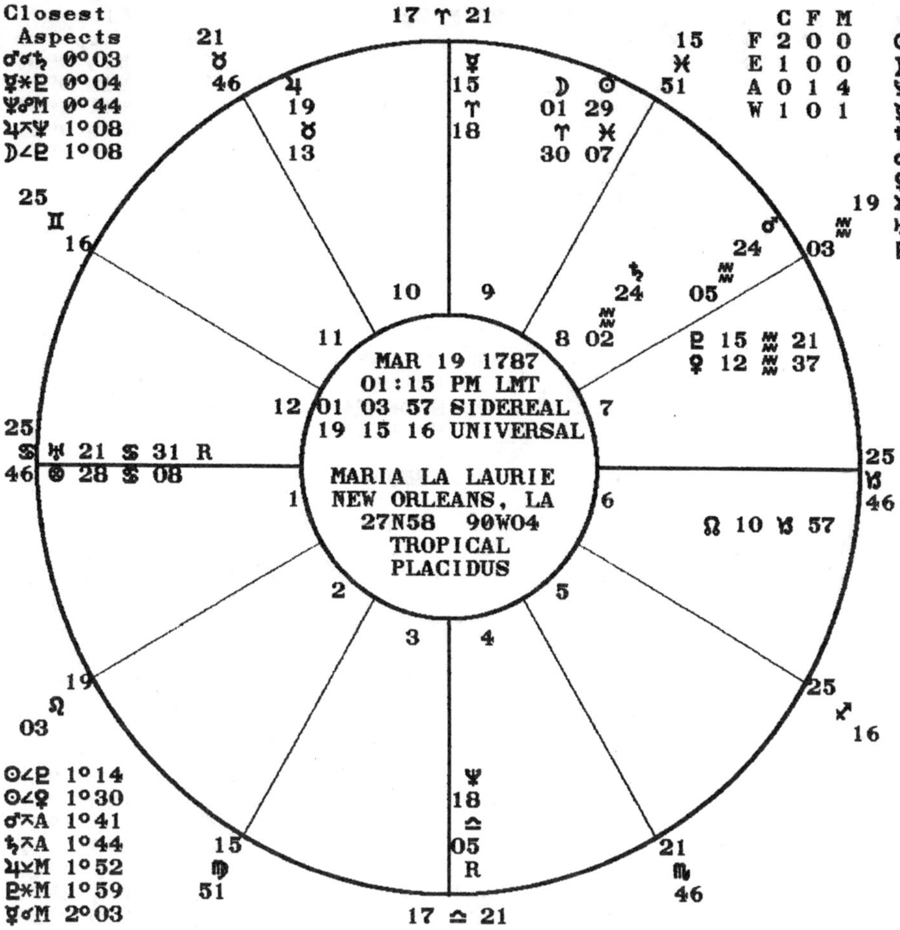
MAR 19 1787
01:15 PM LMT
01 03 57 SIDEREAL
19 15 16 UNIVERSAL
MARIA LA LAURIE
NEW ORLEANS, LA
27N58 90W04
TROPICAL
PLACIDUS

☉∠♇ 1°14
☉∠♀ 1°30
♂⊼A 1°41
♄⊼A 1°44
♃⚺M 1°52
♇✶M 1°59
☿☌M 2°03

LA LAURIE, MARIA

Suspected sadist

March 19, 1787
1:15 PM LMT
New Orleans, La
90 W 04 27 N 58

Married, 1800; widowed in four years; one daughter. Married, 1804; four children; widowed, 1816. Both deaths suspicious. Married, 1825. When her house burned down April 1834, instruments of torture were found; neighbors spoke of strange events in the house.

A: Lyndoe in AA, June 1978, "data given by her grandson, as her actual chart was among estate papers."

SVP=♓ 8°13'31"
JULIAN DAY=2373826.30227

LALO, EDOUARD

Musician

January 27, 1823
3:00 PM LMT
Lille, France
3 E 04 50 N 39

Declin

♄ 10N32
☽ 14N02
☿ 14S51
♇ 15S07
♂ 16S03
♀ 17S36
☉ 18S33
♃ 18N41
♆ 22S20
♅ 23S27

	C	F	M
F	0	1	0
E	2	0	2
A	0	0	4
W	0	0	1

French composer who gained fame for his violin concerto, *Symphonie Espagnole* (1873). His music considered characteristic of French culture at its best. Studied at the Paris Conservatory in 1839. Works include opera and the ballet *Namouna* (1882). (1823-1892)

A: Gauquelin #2022 Vol 4.

SVP=♓ 7°43'32"
JULIAN DAY=2386923.11648

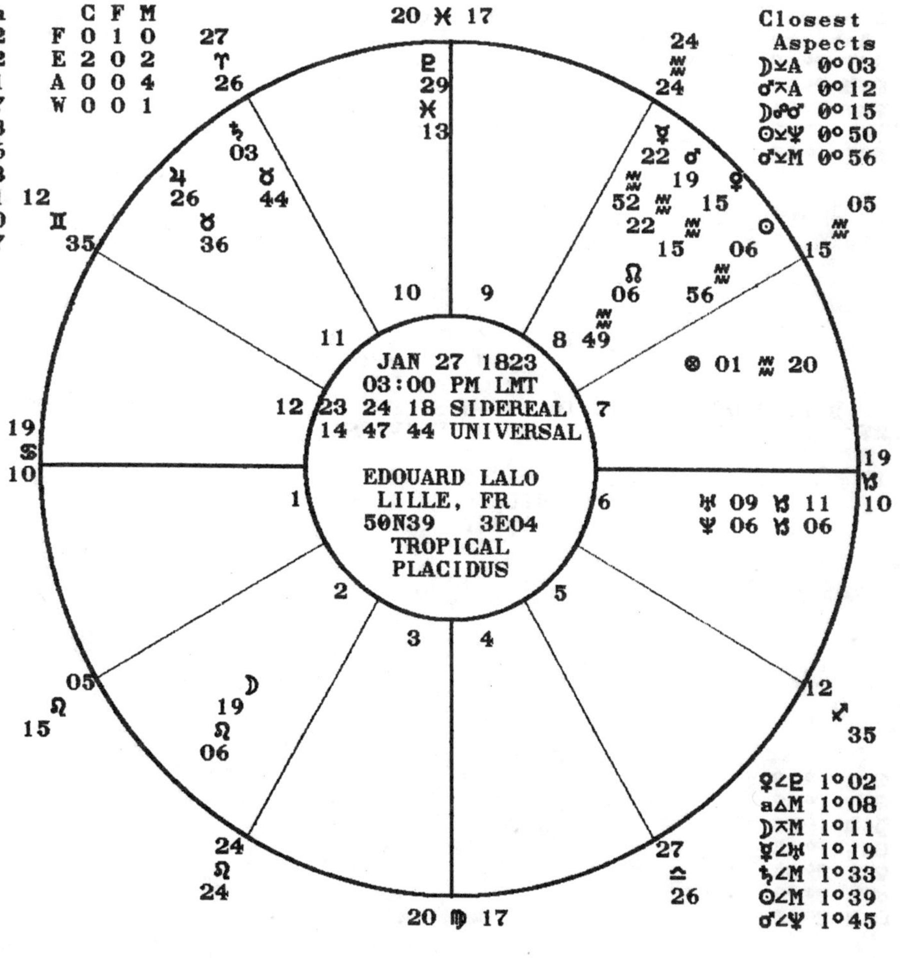
JAN 27 1823
03:00 PM LMT
23 24 18 SIDEREAL
14 47 44 UNIVERSAL
EDOUARD LALO
LILLE, FR
50N39 3E04
TROPICAL
PLACIDUS

Closest Aspects

☽⚺A 0°03
♂⊼A 0°12
☽☍♂ 0°15
☉⚺♆ 0°50
♂⚺M 0°56

♀∠♇ 1°02
a△M 1°08
☽⊼M 1°11
☿∠♅ 1°19
♄∠M 1°33
☉∠M 1°39
♂∠♆ 1°45

LANEHART, EDWIN
Body-builder

April 19, 1935
9:55 AM EST
Baltimore, Md
76 W 37   39 N 19

A professional physical culturist who won the dual titles of Mr. Maryland and Mr. Baltimore in 1956; won title of Mr. Free-State on October 7, 1961. Taught physical education for four years.

A: CL from AFA, June 1962, "data from him."

SVP=✠ 6° 9'34"
JULIAN DAY=2427912.12153

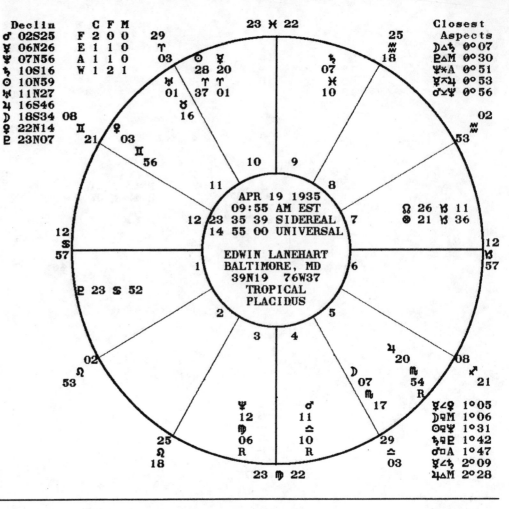

	Declin	C	F	M
♂	02S25	F	2	0	0
☿	06N26	E	1	1	0
♆	07N56	A	1	1	0
♄	10S16	W	1	2	1
☉	10N59				
♅	11N27				
♃	16S46				
☽	18S34				
♀	22N14				
♇	23N07				

Closest Aspects
☽△♄ 0°07
♇☌M 0°30
♆⚹A 0°51
☿⚹♃ 0°53
♂∠♆ 0°56

APR 19 1935
09:55 AM EST
23 35 39 SIDEREAL
14 55 00 UNIVERSAL

EDWIN LANEHART
BALTIMORE, MD
39N19 76W37
TROPICAL
PLACIDUS

☿∠♀ 1°05
☽⚼M 1°06
☉⚼♆ 1°31
♄⚼♇ 1°42
♂□A 1°47
☿∠♄ 2°09
♃△M 2°28

LANZA, MARIO
Singer

January 31, 1921
2:00 AM EST
Philadelphia, Pa
75 W 10   39 N 57

First recording artist to sell more than two million albums. Remembered for song "Be My Love". Movie debut in *That Midnight Kiss* (1949); also played the role of Caruso. Weight problems required crash diets: died after an eating binge October 7, 1959.

A: CL from B.C.

SVP=✠ 6°21'32"
JULIAN DAY=2422720.79167

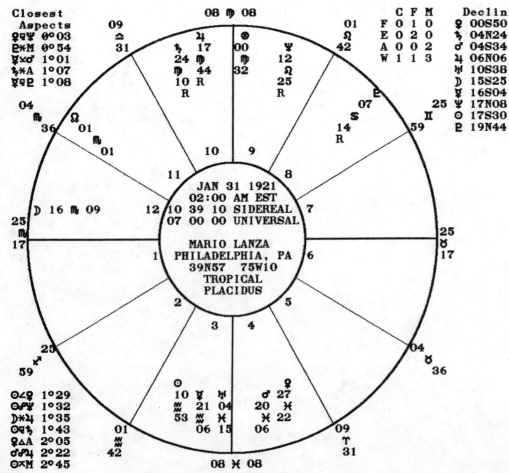

Closest Aspects
♀⚼♀ 0°03
♇⚹M 0°54
☿⚼♂ 1°01
♄⚹A 1°07
☿⚼♇ 1°08

	Declin	C	F	M
♀	00S50	F	0	1	0
♄	04N24	E	0	2	0
♂	04S34	A	0	0	2
♃	06N06	W	1	1	3
♅	10S38				
☽	15S25				
☿	16S04				
♆	17N08				
☉	17S30				
♇	19N44				

JAN 31 1921
02:00 AM EST
39 10 SIDEREAL
07 00 00 UNIVERSAL

MARIO LANZA
PHILADELPHIA, PA
39N57 75W10
TROPICAL
PLACIDUS

☉□♀ 1°29
♀⚼♆ 1°32
☽⚹♃ 1°35
☉□♄ 1°43
♀△A 2°05
♂□♃ 2°22
☉⚹M 2°45

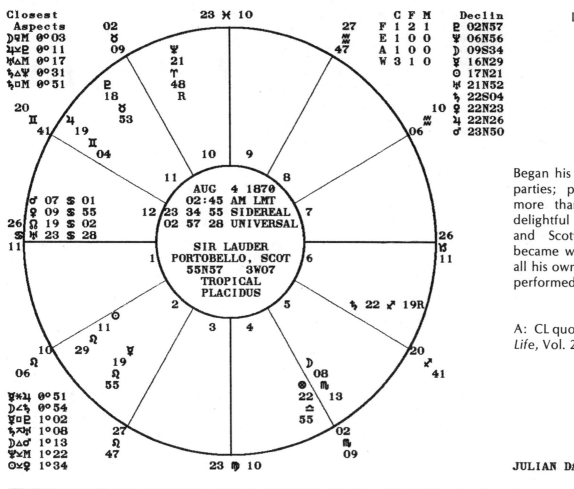

Closest Aspects

☽♀M	0°03
♃⚹♇	0°11
♅△M	0°17
♄△♆	0°31
♄□M	0°51

C	F	M	Declin		
F	1	2	1	♇	02N57
E	1	0	0	♆	06N56
A	1	0	0	☽	09S34
W	3	1	0	☿	16N29
				☉	17N21
				♅	21N52
				♄	22S04
				♀	22N23
				♃	22N26
				♂	23N50

LAUDER, SIR HARRY
Entertainer

August 4, 1870
2:45 AM LMT
Portobello, Scotland
3 W 07   55 N 57

AUG 4 1870
02:45 AM LMT
23 34 55 SIDEREAL
02 57 28 UNIVERSAL

SIR LAUDER
PORTOBELLO, SCOT
55N57 3W07
TROPICAL
PLACIDUS

Began his career by singing at parties; played on stage for more than forty years, with delightful character-sketches and Scottish dialect songs; became world beloved. Wrote all his own material and always performed solo. (1870-1950)

A: CL quotes Wemyss *Wheel of Life*, Vol. 2, "as recorded."[83]

☿⚹♃	0°51
☽∠♄	0°54
☿□♇	1°02
♄⚹♅	1°08
☽△♂	1°13
♆□M	1°22
☉⚹♀	1°34

SVP=♓ 7° 4' 15"
JULIAN DAY=2404278.62324

LEE, BRUCE
Actor

November 27, 1940
7:12 AM PST
San Francisco, Ca
122 W 26   37 N 47

Chinese-American actor, who portrayed heroism and grace in movies featuring karate, kung-fu, and other martial arts. His first imported Kung-fu movie from China wildly popular, leading to American films, which were largely responsible for the martial arts craze. (1940-1973)

A: *Constellations*, 1977, B.C. obtained by Robert Paige.

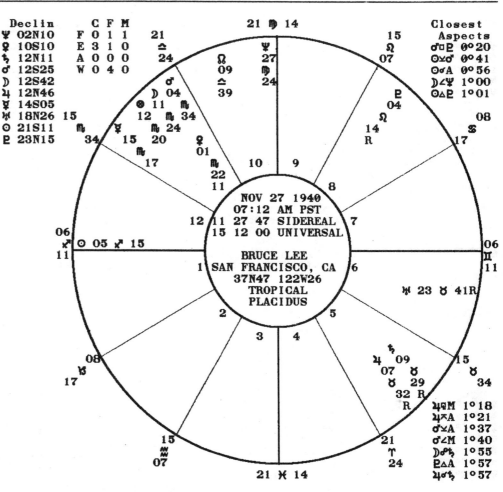

Declin		C	F	M
♆	02N10	F	0	1	1
♀	10S10	E	3	1	0
♄	12N11	A	0	0	0
♂	12S25	W	0	4	0
☽	12S42				
♃	12N46				
☿	14S05				
♅	18N26				
☉	21S11				
♇	23N15				

Closest Aspects

♂□♇	0°20
☉⚹♂	0°41
☉♂A	0°56
☽∠♆	1°00
☉△♇	1°01
♃♀M	1°18
♃⚹A	1°21
♂⚹A	1°37
♂∠M	1°40
☽⚹♄	1°55
♇△A	1°57
♃♂♄	1°57

NOV 27 1940
07:12 AM PST
11 27 47 SIDEREAL
15 12 00 UNIVERSAL

BRUCE LEE
SAN FRANCISCO, CA
37N47 122W26
TROPICAL
PLACIDUS

SVP=♓ 6° 5' 5"
JULIAN DAY=2429961.13333

LEGER, FERNAND
Artist

February 4, 1881
1:00 PM LMT
Argentan, France
0 W 01   48 N 45

French painter, one of the important artists of the 1900s and a member of the cubist movement. His highly individual style features bright, clear colors, accented by strong black, mainly abstract in design. His work includes *Man in the City*. (1881-1955)

A: Gauquelin #637 Vol 4.

SVP=♓ 6°54'53"
JULIAN DAY=2408116.04171

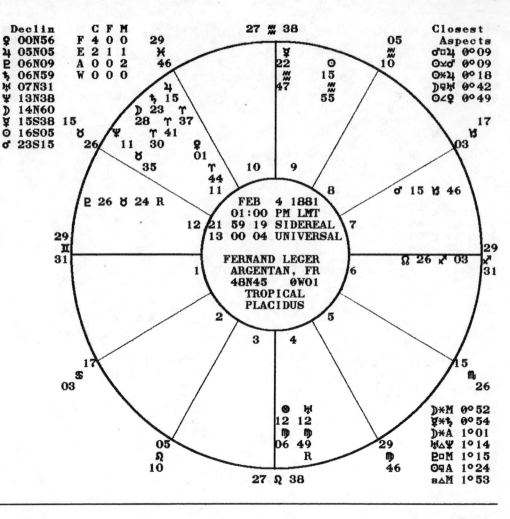

Declin		C F M		Closest Aspects	
♀	00N56	F 4 0 0		♂□♃	0°09
♃	05N05	E 2 1 1		⊙✶♂	0°09
♇	06N09	A 0 0 2		⊙✶♃	0°18
♄	06N59	W 0 0 0		☽□♅	0°42
♅	07N31			⊙∠♀	0°49
♆	13N38				
☽	14N60				
☿	15S38				
⊙	16S05				
♂	23S15				

FEB 4 1881
01:00 PM LMT
12 21 59 19 SIDEREAL
13 00 04 UNIVERSAL

FERNAND LEGER
ARGENTAN, FR
48N45   0W01
TROPICAL
PLACIDUS

☽✶M	0°52
☿✶♄	0°54
☽✶A	1°01
♅△♆	1°14
♇□M	1°15
⊙□A	1°24
a△M	1°53

LEIGH, VIVIEN
Actress

November 5, 1913
5:16 PM Zone 5.5
Darjeeling, India
88 E 29   26 N 58

Won the Oscar as best actress in *Gone With The Wind* (1939) and *A Streetcar Named Desire* (1951). Married to Sir Lawrence Olivier for twenty three turbulent years. Last film *Ship of Fools* (1965), two years before she died of TB. Later years nearly catatonic from shock-treatments as a manic depressive.

B: Holliday from *Lawrence Olivier* by Cottrell, 1975, "sunset."[84]

SVP=♓ 6°27'44"
JULIAN DAY=2420076.99028

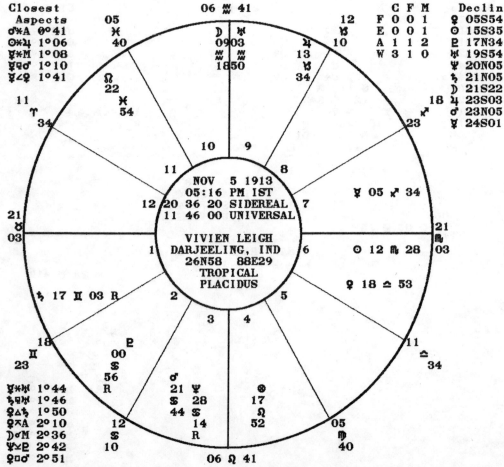

Closest Aspects		C F M		Declin	
♂✶A	0°41	F 0 0 1		♀	05S54
⊙✶♃	1°06	E 0 0 1		⊙	15S35
☿✶M	1°08	A 1 1 2		♇	17N34
☿♂♂	1°10	W 3 1 0		♅	19S54
☿∠♀	1°41			♆	20N05
				♄	21N05
				☽	21S22
				♃	23S03
				♂	23N05
				☿	24S01

NOV 5 1913
05:16 PM IST
12 20 36 20 SIDEREAL
11 46 00 UNIVERSAL

VIVIEN LEIGH
DARJEELING, IND
26N58   88E29
TROPICAL
PLACIDUS

☿✶♅	1°44
♄♇♅	1°46
♀△♄	1°50
♀✶A	2°10
☽♂M	2°36
♆✶♇	2°42
♀♂♂	2°51

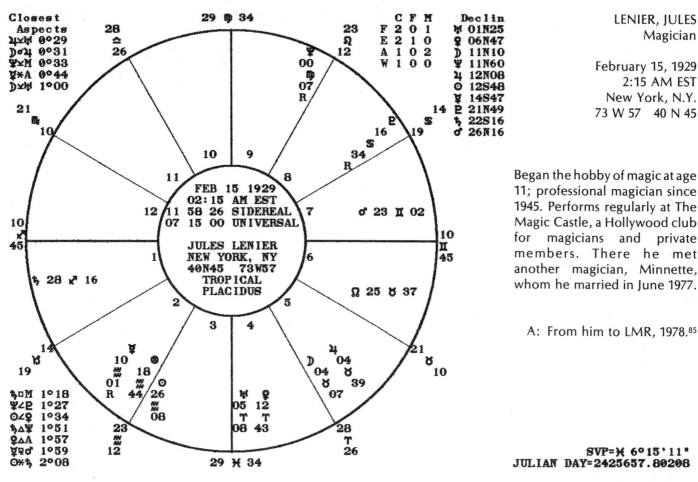

LENIER, JULES
Magician

February 15, 1929
2:15 AM EST
New York, N.Y.
73 W 57   40 N 45

Began the hobby of magic at age 11; professional magician since 1945. Performs regularly at The Magic Castle, a Hollywood club for magicians and private members. There he met another magician, Minnette, whom he married in June 1977.

A: From him to LMR, 1978.[85]

SVP=℉ 6°15'11"
JULIAN DAY=2425657.80208

LENNON, JOHN
Musician

October 9, 1940
8:30 AM BST
Liverpool, England
2 W 58   53 N 25

Megastar of The Beatles. First formed a music group 1956. The four Beatles together in 1961. Setting world records in record sales, by the end of 1977 the Beatles had sold an estimated 100 million singles and 100 million albums. Lennon wrote two books, *A Spaniard in the Works* and *In His Own Write*.

A: Sybil Leek's *Astrology*, January 1972, "from him recently by telephone."[86]

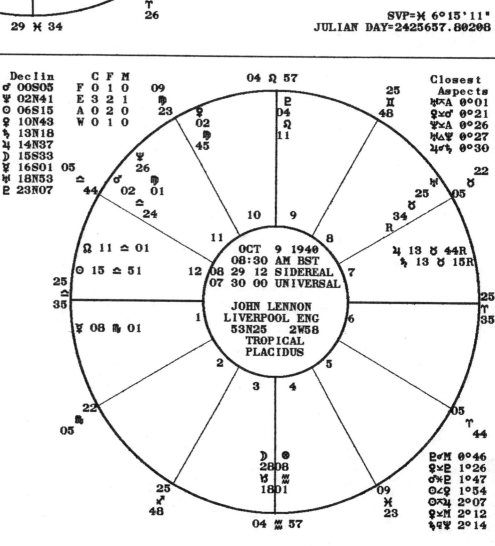

SVP=℉ 6° 5'10"
JULIAN DAY=2429911.81250

LEO, ALAN
Astrologer

August 7, 1860
5:49 AM LMT
Westminster, England
0 W 09   51 N 30

Began his study in reincarnation and karma in 1877. Met H.P. Blavatsky in 1890; became one of the founders of a Theosophical Lodge. Wrote a series of volumes of astrological text books. Married Bessie in 1896, a platonic agreement. (1860-1917)

B: Data in his book *Esoteric Astrology*.

SVP=⌘ 7°12' 6"
JULIAN DAY=2400629.74278

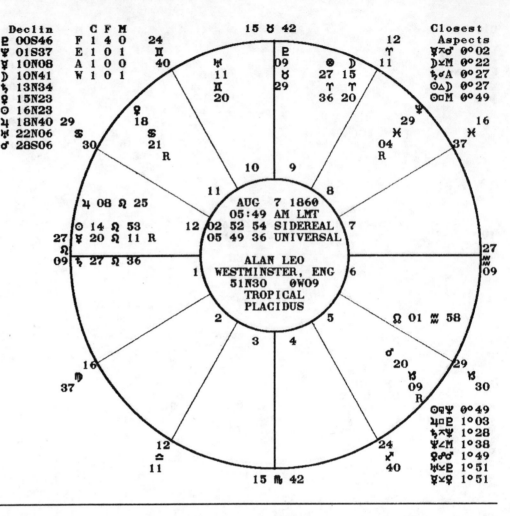

Declin	C	F	M
♇ 00S46	F	1	4	0
♆ 01S37	E	1	0	1
☿ 10N08	A	1	0	0
☽ 10N41	W	1	0	1
♄ 13N34			
♀ 15N23			
☉ 16N23			
♃ 18N40			
♅ 22N06			
♂ 28S06			

AUG 7 1860
05:49 AM LMT
02 52 54 SIDEREAL
05 49 36 UNIVERSAL

ALAN LEO
WESTMINSTER, ENG
51N30   0W09
TROPICAL
PLACIDUS

Closest Aspects

☿⚼♂	0°02
☽⚹M	0°22
☉△A	0°27
☉△☽	0°27
☉□M	0°49
☉□♆	0°49
♃□♇	1°03
♄⚹♆	1°28
♆∠M	1°38
♀⚼♂	1°49
♅⚹♇	1°51
☿⚹♀	1°51

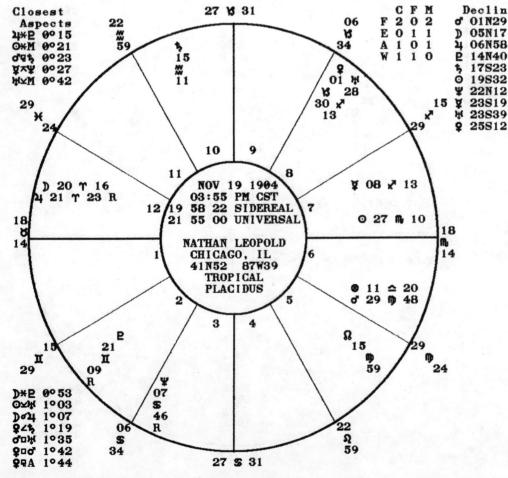

Closest Aspects

♃⚹♇	0°15
☉⚹M	0°21
♂⚼♃	0°23
☿⚼♆	0°27
♅⚹M	0°42

C	F	M	Declin
F	2	0	2	♂ 01N29
E	0	1	1	☽ 05N17
A	1	0	1	♃ 06N58
W	1	1	0	♇ 14N40
			♄ 17S23
			☉ 19S32
			♆ 22N12
			☿ 23S19
			♅ 23S39
			♀ 25S12

NOV 19 1904
03:55 PM CST
19 58 22 SIDEREAL
21 55 00 UNIVERSAL

NATHAN LEOPOLD
CHICAGO, IL
41N52   87W39
TROPICAL
PLACIDUS

☽⚹♇	0°53
☉⚼M	1°03
☽♂♃	1°07
☿⚼♃	1°19
♂⚼♅	1°35
♀♂♂	1°42
♀⚼A	1°44

LEOPOLD, NATHAN
Murderer

November 19, 1904
3:55 PM CST
Chicago, Ill
87 W 39   41 N 52

He and Richard Leob, both sons of wealthy and influential families, regarded as brilliant students, planned a "perfect crime" as a thrill. On May 21, 1924, they sadistically killed a young boy. Caught and given a life sentence; Leopold paroled in 1960. (1904-1971)

A: T.P. Davis, "data from his mother in a letter."

SVP=⌘ 6°35'22"
JULIAN DAY=2416804.41319

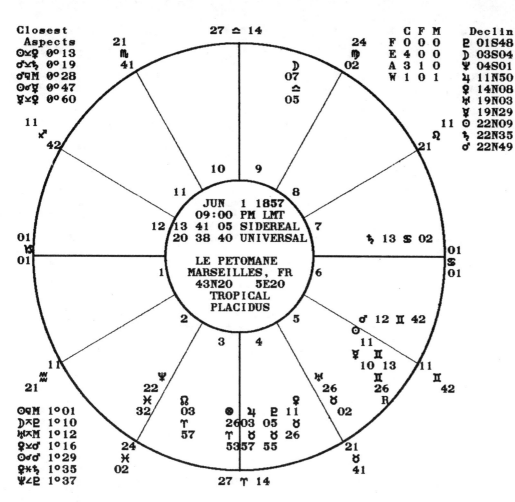

Closest
Aspects
☉⚹☿ 0°13
♂⚼♄ 0°19
♂⊓M 0°28
☉♂☿ 0°47
☿⚹☉ 0°60

27 ♎ 14

C F M   Declin
F 0 0 0   ♇ 01S48
E 4 0 0   ☽ 03S04
A 3 1 0   ♆ 04S01
W 1 0 1   ♃ 11N50
          ♀ 14N08
          ♅ 19N03
          ☿ 19N29
          ☉ 22N09
          ♄ 22N35
          ♂ 22N49

JUN 1 1857
09:00 PM LMT
13 41 05 SIDEREAL
20 38 40 UNIVERSAL

LE PETOMANE
MARSEILLES, FR
43N20 5E20
TROPICAL
PLACIDUS

♄ 13 ♋ 02

☉⊓M 1°01
☽⚹♇ 1°10
♅⚼M 1°12
♀⚼♂ 1°16
☉♂♂ 1°29
♀⚹♄ 1°35
♆⚼♇ 1°37

27 ♈ 14

LE PETOMANE
Novel entertainer

June 1, 1857
9:00 PM LMT
Marseilles, France
5 E 20   43 N 20

The rage of royalty and of
Europe; able to simulate
musical tones, machine-gun
fire, and other amusing sounds
by farting. His performance
outsold any stage performer of
the time. Discovered his unique
talent in youth. (1857-1945)

B: LMR from his biography *Le
Petomane*, written by his son,
1967, p. 18.

SVP=♓ 7°15' 3"
JULIAN DAY=2399467.36019

LEVANT, OSCAR
Entertainer

December 27, 1906
11:45 PM EST
Pittsburgh, Pa
80 W 01   40 N 26

Pianist, film actor, radio and TV
personality, author, and
composer. Known for caustic
wit and neurotic behavior; fame
from 1938. Composed two
string quartets, a piano
concerto, a nocturne, and a
number of songs. Author of *A
Smattering of Ignorance* (1940).
(1906-1972)

A: *Constellations*, 1977, from
Lockhart.

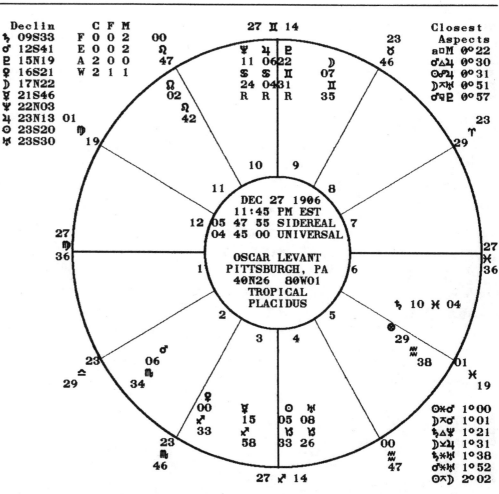

Declin   C F M
♄ 09S33   F 0 0 2
♂ 12S41   E 0 0 2
♇ 15N19   A 2 0 0
♀ 16S21   W 2 1 1
☽ 17N22
☿ 21S46
♆ 22N03
♃ 23N13
☉ 23S20
♅ 23S30

27 ♊ 14

DEC 27 1906
11:45 PM EST
05 47 55 SIDEREAL
04 45 00 UNIVERSAL

OSCAR LEVANT
PITTSBURGH, PA
40N26 80W01
TROPICAL
PLACIDUS

♄ 10 ♓ 04

27 ♐ 14

Closest
Aspects
a⊓M 0°22
♂△♃ 0°30
☉⚼♃ 0°31
☽⚼♅ 0°51
♂⚼♇ 0°57

☉⚹♂ 1°00
☽⚼♂ 1°01
♄△♆ 1°21
☽⚹♃ 1°31
♄⚹♅ 1°38
♂⚹♅ 1°52
☉⚼☽ 2°02

SVP=♓ 6°33'45"
JULIAN DAY=2417572.69792

LIBERACE
Entertainer

May 16, 1919
11:15 PM CDT
West Allis, Wis
88 W 00   43 N 01

World's highest paid pianist,
earning more than $2 million for
each twenty six week season:
once made $138,000 for a single
night's performance in 1954.
Played piano by ear at age 4;
lessons at 7; scholarship at 17.
Began professional career in
1940.

A: CSH.[87]

SVP=♓ 6°22'54"
JULIAN DAY=2422095.67708

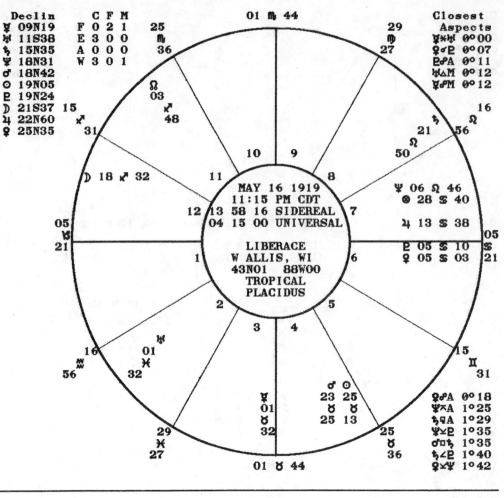

LINCOLN, ABRAHAM
U.S. President

February 12, 1809
6:54 AM LMT
Hodgenville, Ky
85 W 45   37 N 33

Worked as a rail splitter,
flatboatman, storekeeper,
postmaster, surveryor, and
lawyer in 1836. Member of the
legislature, 1834-41; U.S.
Representative, 1847-49;
president, 1861-65. Issued the
Emmancipation Proclamation,
January 1, 1863. Shot on April 14,
1865.

B: AA, April 1942, quotes a
personal account from *Women
Lincoln Loved* by Wm. E. Barton,
1927, pp. 81-85, "sun-up."[88]

SVP=♓ 7°55'16"
JULIAN DAY=2381826.02569

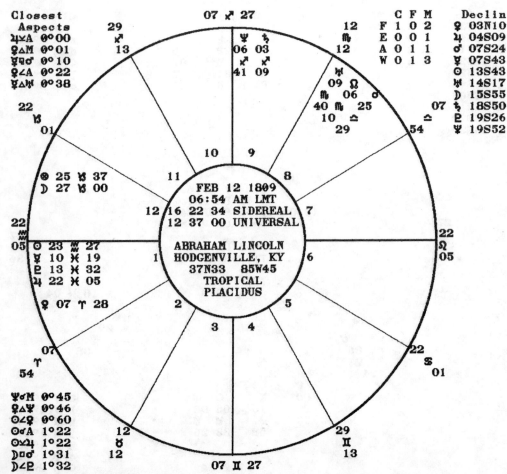

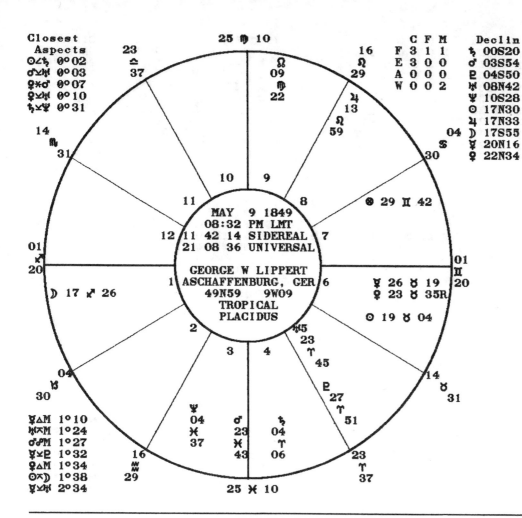

SVP=♓ 7°21'54"
JULIAN DAY=2396522.38097

LIPPERT, GEORGE W.
Three legged man

May 9, 1849
8:32 PM LMT
Aschaffenburg, Germany
9 W 09   49 N 59

MAY 9 1849
08:32 PM LMT
11 42 14 SIDEREAL
21 08 36 UNIVERSAL

GEORGE W LIPPERT
ASCHAFFENBURG, GER
49N59   9W09
TROPICAL
PLACIDUS

Closest
Aspects
☉⚷♄ 0°02
♂⚹♅ 0°03
♀⚷♂ 0°07
☿⚹♆ 0°10
♄⚹♆ 0°31

☿△M 1°10
♅⚹M 1°24
♂⚹♇ 1°27
☿⚹♇ 1°32
♀△M 1°34
☉⚹☽ 1°38
☿⚹♅ 2°34

	C F M	Declin
	F 3 1 1	♄ 00S20
	E 3 0 0	♂ 03S54
	A 0 0 0	♇ 04S50
	W 0 0 2	♅ 08N42
		♆ 10S28
		☉ 17N30
		♃ 17N33
		☽ 17S55
		☿ 20N16
		♀ 22N34

Left leg perfect with six toes on the foot. Two legs below right knee, with separate knee joints. Walked with all three legs until age 16; then strapped the far right leg up until it atrophyed. One of seven children, all normal. Carpenter and wood carver by trade.

A: AFA Bulletin excerpt, reprinted from *Signs of the Times*, February 1885, data from personal interview.

LODGE, HENRY CABOT
Statesman

July 5, 1902
4:20 AM EST
Nagant, Mass
70 W 55   42 N 25

Family background of six U.S. senators; became senator of Massachusetts, 1937-44; U.S. representative to the U.N. and Security Council, 1953-60. Ran for vice president with Nixon in 1960. Ambassador to S. Vietnam, 1963-67; ambassador to West Germany, 1968-69.

A: *Constellations*, 1977, quotes AFA data exchange, "from him."[89]

SVP=♓ 6°37' 6"
JULIAN DAY=2415935.88889

Declin	C F M
♇ 14N13	F 0 0 1
♃ 16S50	E 0 0 1
☽ 18N23	A 4 0 1
☿ 18N57	W 3 0 0
♀ 19N30	
♄ 21S08	
♆ 22N21	
☉ 22N52	
♅ 23S01	
♂ 23N21	

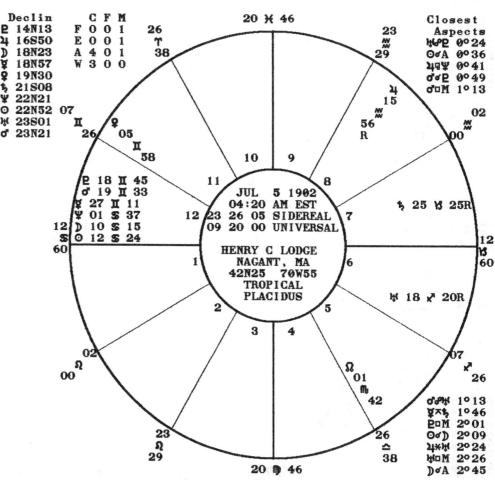

JUL 5 1902
04:20 AM EST
23 26 05 SIDEREAL
09 20 00 UNIVERSAL

HENRY C LODGE
NAGANT, MA
42N25   70W55
TROPICAL
PLACIDUS

Closest
Aspects
♅⚹♇ 0°24
☉♂ 0°36
♃♆ 0°41
♂⚹♇ 0°49
♂□M 1°13

♂⚹♅ 1°13
☿⚹♄ 1°46
♇□M 2°01
☉♂☽ 2°09
♃⚹♅ 2°24
♅□M 2°26
☽♂A 2°45

LONDON, JACK
Writer

January 12, 1876
2:00 PM LMT
San Francisco, Ca
122 W 26   36 N 47

American adventure writer and
story teller, who produced forty
three books in sixteen years,
including *The Son of the Wolf*
(1900), *The Sea Wolf* (1904), and
White Fang. With a childhood
background of poverty, had
financial difficulties all of his
life. (1876-1916)

B: *Constellations*, 1977,
Lockhart quotes *Jack London*,
by his wife.

SVP=♓ 6°59'26"
JULIAN DAY=2406266.42343

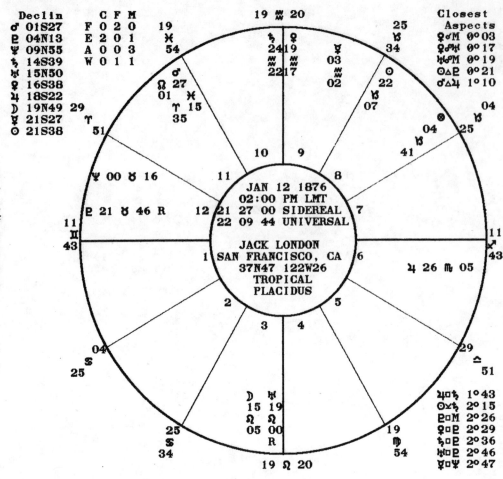

LOPER, DON
Designer

August 29, 1907
00:01 AM CST
Toledo, Ohio
83 W 33   41 N 39

Producer, director, choreographer, performer, costume
designer, and set designer.
Professional dancer for many
years, with three Broadway
musicals. A fashion wizard;
opened a Beverly Hills house of
haute couture in 1946. Three
marriages and divorces.

A: CL, "from him to D.C.
Doane."

SVP=♓ 6°33'12"
JULIAN DAY=2417816.75069

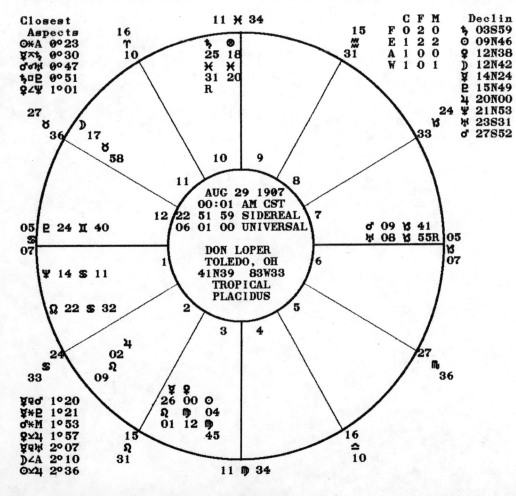

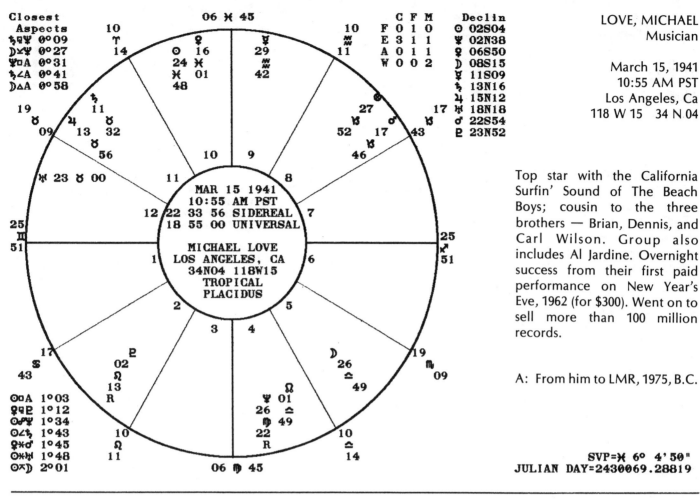

LOVE, MICHAEL
Musician

March 15, 1941
10:55 AM PST
Los Angeles, Ca
118 W 15   34 N 04

Top star with the California Surfin' Sound of The Beach Boys; cousin to the three brothers — Brian, Dennis, and Carl Wilson. Group also includes Al Jardine. Overnight success from their first paid performance on New Year's Eve, 1962 (for $300). Went on to sell more than 100 million records.

A: From him to LMR, 1975, B.C.

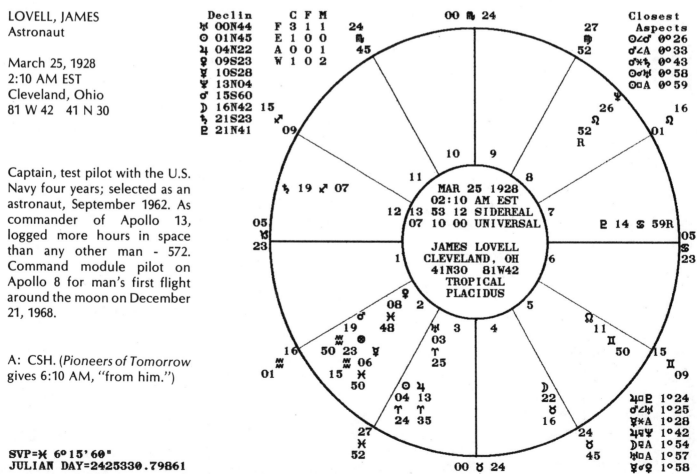

LOVELL, JAMES
Astronaut

March 25, 1928
2:10 AM EST
Cleveland, Ohio
81 W 42   41 N 30

Captain, test pilot with the U.S. Navy four years; selected as an astronaut, September 1962. As commander of Apollo 13, logged more hours in space than any other man - 572. Command module pilot on Apollo 8 for man's first flight around the moon on December 21, 1968.

A: CSH. (*Pioneers of Tomorrow* gives 6:10 AM, "from him.")

LUCKY FEMALE
Florence Hubbard

April 24, 1879
3:00 PM LMT
Muncie, Indiana
85 W 23   40 N 12

She answered a random phone call from the studio of *Truth or Consequences* game show on March 7, 1948. By correctly naming the mystery figure, she won one of the richest arrays of prizes and cash in radio history.

A: Skeetz quotes Garth Allen in Dell, March 1955, "from her."

SVP=♓ 6°56'28"
JULIAN DAY=2407464.36218

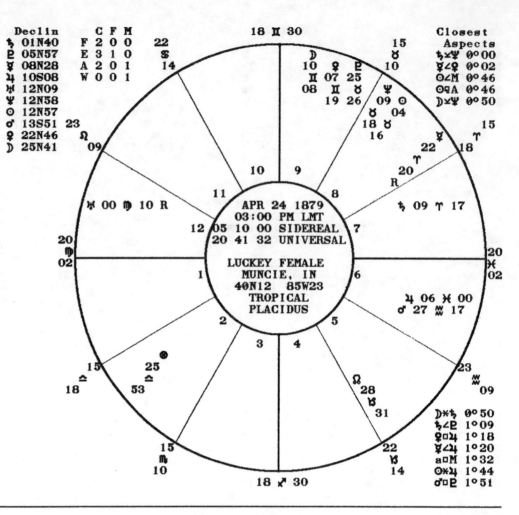

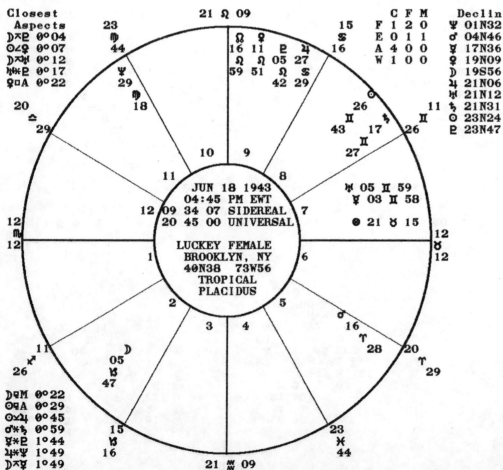

LUCKY FEMALE
Game show winner

June 18, 1943
4:45 PM EWT
Brooklyn, N.Y.
73 W 56   40 N 38

Television game show contestant who won prizes valued at $6000, including a new automobile, on August 4, 1972, in Los Angeles. The show went on the air at 8:00 PM PDT.

A: *Constellations*, Spring 1977, "from her to Farrel Pyle."

SVP=♓ 6° 3' 9"
JULIAN DAY=2430894.36458

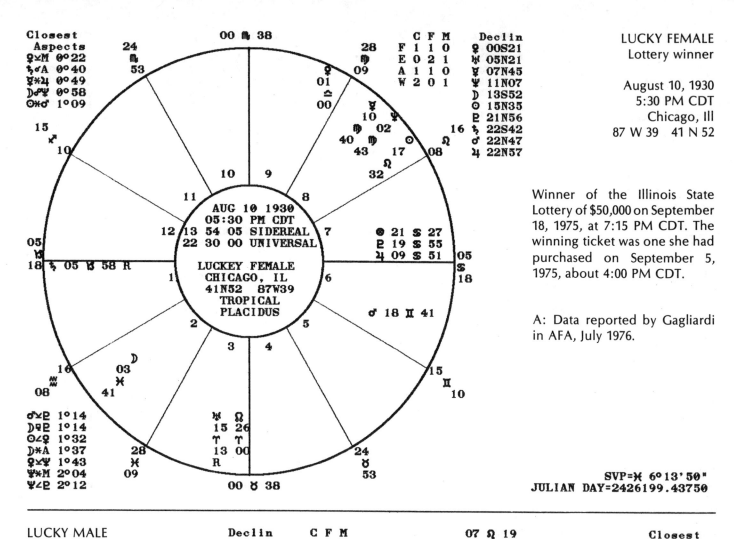

Closest Aspects

♀⊼M	0°22
♄♂A	0°40
☿⚹♃	0°49
☽⚹♆	0°58
☉⚹♂	1°09

	C	F	M	Declin
F	1	1	0	♀ 00S21
E	0	2	1	♅ 05N21
A	1	1	0	☿ 07N45
W	2	0	1	♆ 11N07
				☽ 13S52
				☉ 15N35
				♇ 21N56
				♄ 22S42
				♂ 22N47
				♃ 22N57

LUCKY FEMALE
Lottery winner

August 10, 1930
5:30 PM CDT
Chicago, Ill
87 W 39   41 N 52

AUG 10 1930
05:30 PM CDT
13 54 05 SIDEREAL
22 30 00 UNIVERSAL

LUCKEY FEMALE
CHICAGO, IL
41N52 87W39
TROPICAL
PLACIDUS

Winner of the Illinois State Lottery of $50,000 on September 18, 1975, at 7:15 PM CDT. The winning ticket was one she had purchased on September 5, 1975, about 4:00 PM CDT.

A: Data reported by Gagliardi in AFA, July 1976.

♂⚹♇	1°14
☽□♇	1°14
☉⚼♀	1°32
☽⚹A	1°37
♀⊼♆	1°43
♆⚹M	2°04
♆⊾♇	2°12

SVP=♓ 6°13'50"
JULIAN DAY=2426199.43750

LUCKY MALE
Las Vegas winner

February 6, 1926
00:01 AM CST
Washington, Texas
96 W 09   30 N 20

Won a total of $56,000 by playing Keno continuously from January 5th through the 7th, 1973. His biggest single win was $25,000 on January 7th at approximately 10:30 AM PST.

A: *Constellations*, Spring 1977, "from him to Farrel Pyle."

Declin		C	F	M
♅ 03S19		F	0	1	1
♀ 07S44		E	0	0	0
☽ 13S08		A	0	0	4
♆ 14N02		W	1	2	1
☉ 15S50					
♄ 16S59					
♃ 18S54					
☿ 19S48					
♇ 21N05					
♂ 23S41					

Closest Aspects

♃♂M	0°02
♅⊼♆	0°16
♃⊾♄	0°59
♅□M	1°01
☽□♀	1°04

FEB 6 1926
00:01 AM CST
08 38 52 SIDEREAL
06 01 00 UNIVERSAL

LUCKY MALE
WASHINGTON, TX
30N20 96W09
TROPICAL
PLACIDUS

☿⊾♅	1°15
♄□♆	1°49
♄△M	2°05
♀⊾♃	2°14
☿♂M	2°16
☉⚼♀	2°16
♂⚼♄	2°33

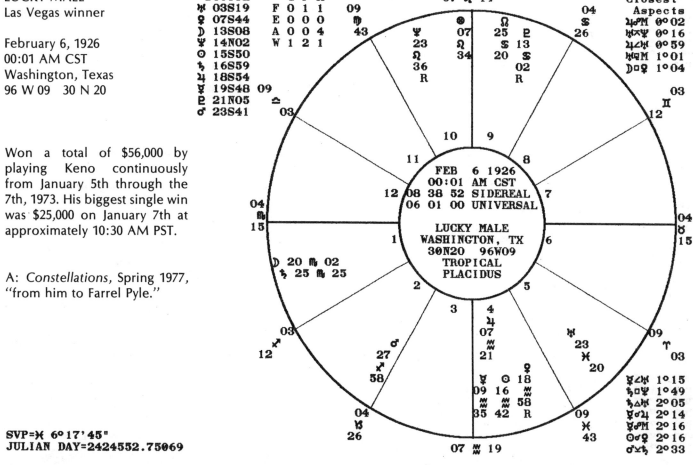

SVP=♓ 6°17'45"
JULIAN DAY=2424552.75069

LUCKY MALE
Sweepstakes winner

June 12, 1952
1:23 PM PDT
Santa Monica, Ca
118 W 29   34 N 01

Winner of the Irish Sweepstakes of $120,000 on October 3, 1970. The race held at Newmarket, England; the lucky winner was at his residence in Santa Monica at the time.

A: *Constellations*, Spring 1977, "from him to Farrel Pyle."

SVP=♓ 5°55′16″
JULIAN DAY=2434176.34931

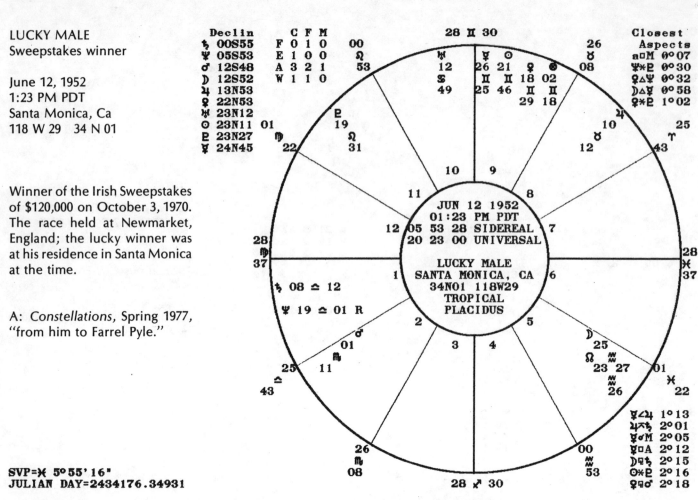

LUGOSI, BELA
Actor

October 20, 1882 NS
3:30 PM LMT
Lugos, Hungary
21 E 54   45 N 41

Twenty years on stage before a film career; best remembered for his horror roles in films *Count Dracula* (1931), *The Raven* (1935), *The Night Monster* (1942), and *Frankenstein Meets the Wolf Man* (1943). Allegedly a heroin addict; interested in occult study.

A: *Wynn's Astrology*, April 1939, "from him."[90]

SVP=♓ 6°53′33″
JULIAN DAY=2408739.08500

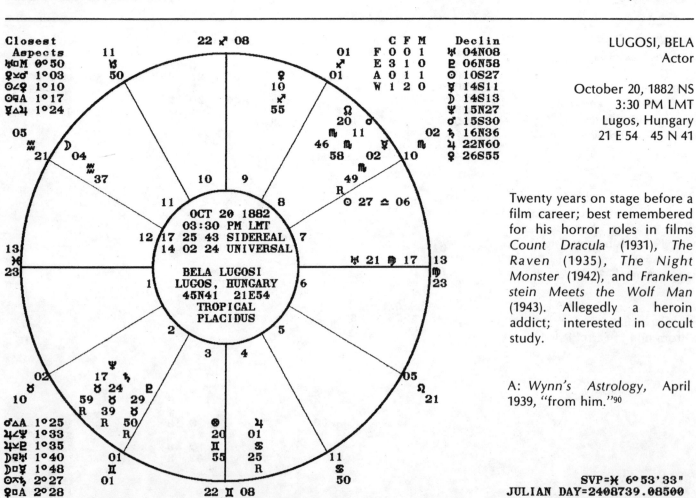

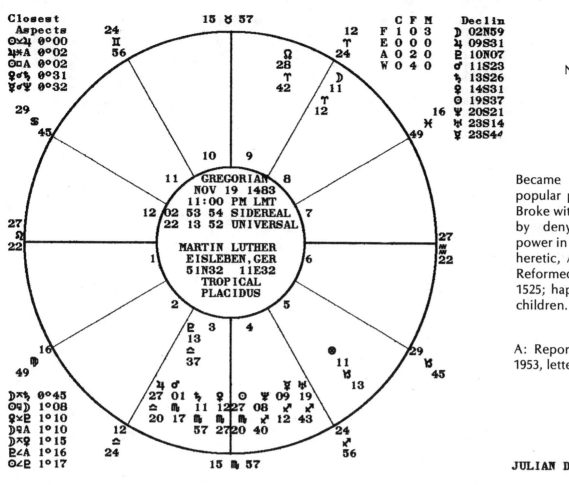

Martin Luther Chart

Closest Aspects

☉☌♃ 0°00
♃∗A 0°02
☉□A 0°02
♀☍♂ 0°31
☿☌♆ 0°32

C	F	M	Declin
F	1	0	3	☽ 02N59
E	0	0	0	♃ 09S31
A	0	2	0	♇ 10N07
W	0	4	0	♂ 11S23
			♄ 13S26
			♀ 14S31
			☉ 19S37
			♆ 20S21
			♅ 23S14
			☿ 23S44

LUTHER, MARTIN
Reformationist

November 19, 1483 NS
11:00 PM LMT
Eisleben, Germany
11 E 32   51 N 32

GREGORIAN
NOV 19 1483
11:00 PM LMT
02 53 54 SIDEREAL
22 13 52 UNIVERSAL

MARTIN LUTHER
EISLEBEN, GER
51N32 11E32
TROPICAL
PLACIDUS

Became a priest in 1507; a popular professor of theology. Broke with the Catholic Church by denying Papal supreme power in 1519. Condemned as a heretic, April 1525; began the Reformed Church. Married, 1525; happy home life with six children. (1483-1546)

A: Reported in AA, November 1953, letter from R.A.L.[91]

♌∗♄ 0°45
☉□☽ 1°08
♀∗♇ 1°10
☽⚼A 1°10
☽∗♀ 1°15
♇∠A 1°16
☉∠♇ 1°17

SVP=♓12°27'43"
JULIAN DAY=2263037.42630

LYNDE, PAUL
Actor

June 13, 1926
8:00 AM EST
Mt. Vernon, Ohio
82 W 29   40 N 23

Skill with self-deprecating wit and the improvised quip. Broadway debut in 1952; then movies. Guest on more than two hundred TV shows; a celebrity regular on *Hollywood Squares* game show since 1967. Number five of six children; never married.

A: From him to Angela Gallo.[92]

Declin

♅ 00S59
♂ 02S34
♃ 13S17
♀ 13N25
♆ 14N25
♄ 15S40
♇ 21N13
☽ 21N38
☉ 23N12
☿ 25N13

C	F	M
F	0	1	0
E	1	0	0
A	1	0	1
W	3	1	2

Closest Aspects

♂☌♅ 0°16
♅△A 0°26
☽∗♃ 0°35
♂△A 0°42
☉∗♆ 0°42

JUN 13 1926
08:00 AM EST
00 54 23 SIDEREAL
13 00 00 UNIVERSAL

PAUL LYNDE
MT VERNON, OH
40N23 82W29
TROPICAL
PLACIDUS

☉□♄ 1°04
♇□M 1°06
☽△♂ 1°15
♀∗♇ 1°26
♃⚼♇ 1°31
☽△♅ 1°31
♄□♆ 1°45

SVP=♓ 6°17'29"
JULIAN DAY=2424680.04167

MACHIAVELLI, NICOLO
Politician

May 11, 1469 NS
11:07 PM LMT
Florence, Italy
11 E 15   43 N 47

Italian statesman and student of politics, who advocated in his book, *The Prince*, that the end justifies the means. His name associated with treachery; his life demonstrated intrigue in political conflicts with the infamous Borgias. (1469-1527)

B: *Constellations*, from AA, November 1967.[93]

SVP=✶12°39'31"
JULIAN DAY=2257732.43194

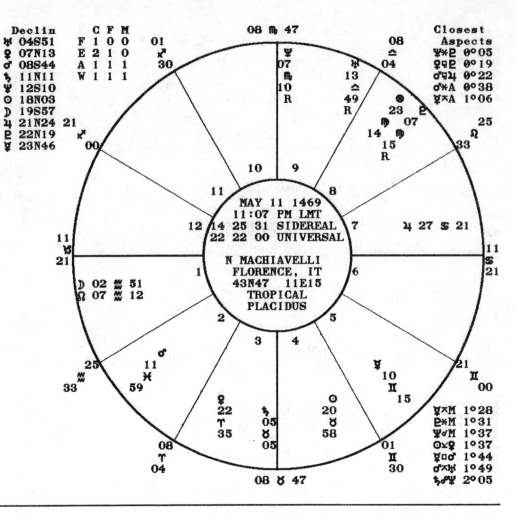

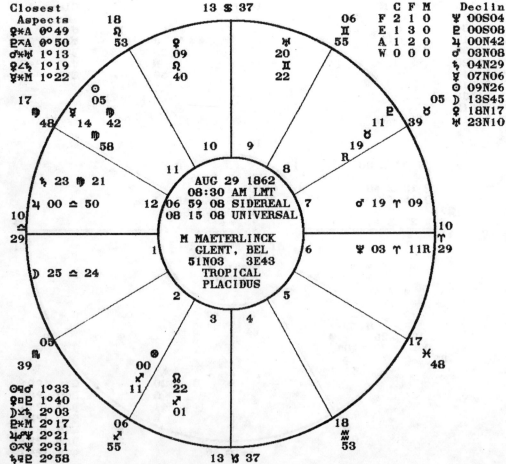

MAETERLINCK, MAURICE
Writer

August 29, 1862
8:30 AM LMT
Glent, Belgium
3 E 43   51 N 03

Belgium dramatist, essayist, philosopher, and naturalist; won the 1911 Nobel prize for literature. A lawyer, who inherited enough property to devote his time to writing. Books include nature studies, as well as *The Blind* (1891), and *The Interior* (1892). (1862-1949)

A: Gauquelin #1147 Vol 6.[94]

SVP=✶ 7°10'20"
JULIAN DAY=2401381.84384

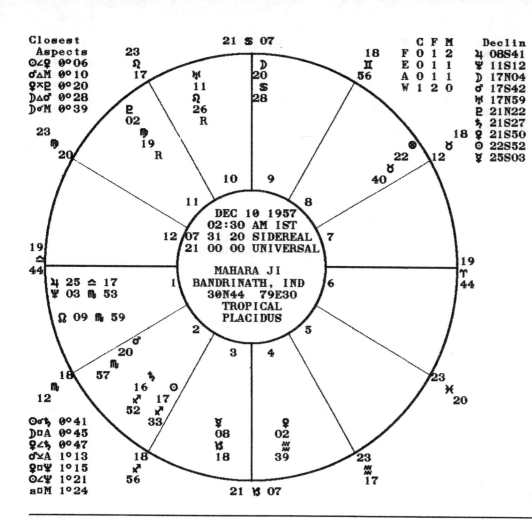

MAHARA JI
Youthful Guru

December 10, 1957
2:30 AM Zone 5.5
Bandrinath, India
79 E 30   30 N 44

Closest Aspects

☉∠♃	0°06
♂△M	0°10
♀⚹♇	0°20
☽△♂	0°28
☽♂M	0°39

☉♂♄	0°41
☽□A	0°45
♀∠♄	0°47
♂⚹A	1°13
♀∠♅	1°15
☉∠♆	1°21
a□M	1°24

Declin

♃	08S41
♆	11S12
☽	17N04
♂	17S42
♅	17N59
♇	21N22
♄	21S27
♀	21S50
☉	22S52
☿	25S03

Came to the U.S. from India in 1972 as a 14-year-old messiah with "the knowledge". His mission gained momentum; he gained a Mercedes Benz, a Lotus sports car, a half-million dollar home in Malibu. A wife and two children

A: Dewey, "from his mother" to two colleagues.

SVP=♓ 5°50'39"
JULIAN DAY=2436182.37500

MAILER, NORMAN
Writer

January 31, 1923
9:05 AM EST
Long Beach, N.J.
74 W 00   40 N 18

Declin

♂	02N46
♄	05S29
♅	07S51
☿	15S27
♃	15S53
♆	15N56
☽	16N42
☉	17S34
♀	19S32
♇	20N17

Novelist, journalist, poet, playwright, film maker, philosopher, lover, and pugilist: a prodigious talent. Won the Pulitzer prize in 1969 for *Armies of the Night*; also wrote *The Naked and the Dead* (1948). Acted in the film *Beyond the Law* (1968). A number of marriages.

A: CSH.

Closest Aspects

☽□♅	0°11
♃□♆	0°18
☽⚹M	0°42
☉∠A	0°50
♀∠A	0°55

☉⚹♅	1°03
☉⚹♇	1°07
☉∠M	1°34
☽△A	1°42
☉∠♃	1°44
♂□♇	2°09
♅△♇	2°11

SVP=♓ 6°20' 2"
JULIAN DAY=2423451.08681

MAIMON, MOSES BEN
Writer

April 6, 1135 NS
1:00 PM LMT
Cordoba, Spain
4 W 46   37 N 54

Jewish philosopher, physician, linguist, and master of Rabbinic literature; one of the great intellects of history. Appointed court physician to the great Saladin; wrote the fourteen Hebrew volumes, *Mishneh Torah*, the rabbinic teachings in their entirety.

B: Fagan in AA, February 1968, from *Trial and Triumph* by Macrison and Hubler.

SVP=✴17°18'34"
JULIAN DAY=2135705.05491

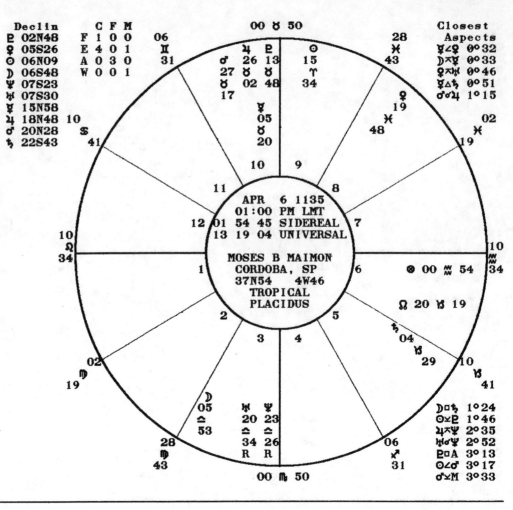

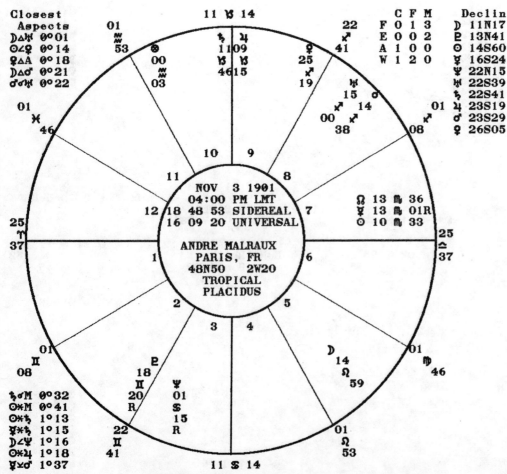

MALRAUX, ANDRE
Writer

November 3, 1901
4:00 PM Paris time
Paris, France
2 W 20   48 N 50

French author whose books are difficult to read because of complex structure. Two of his finest novels - *Man's Fate* (1934) and *Man's Hope* (1938). Fought in the 1927 Chinese revolution, in the Spanish Civil War, and in the French underground. (1901-1976)

A: Gauquelin #534 Vol 6.

SVP=✴ 6°37'38"
JULIAN DAY=2415692.17315

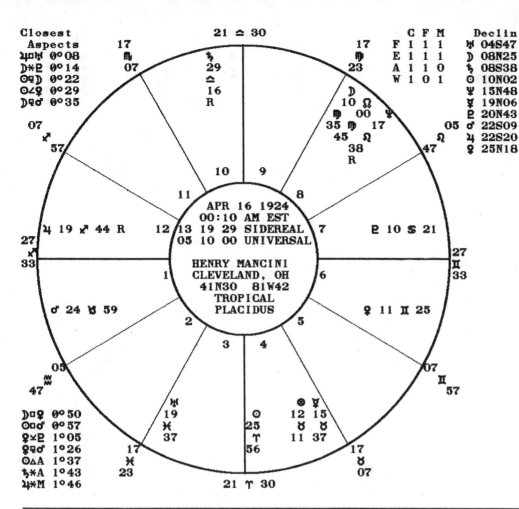

Closest Aspects
♃□♅ 0°08
☽✳♇ 0°14
☉⚼☽ 0°22
☉⚼♃ 0°29
☽♂♂ 0°35

21 ♎ 30

17 ♏
07
29 ♎
16
R

C F M
F 1 1 1
E 1 1 1
A 1 1 0
W 1 0 1

17 ♍
23

Declin
♅ 04S47
☽ 08N25
♄ 08S38
☉ 10N02
♆ 15N48
☿ 19N06
♇ 20N43
♂ 22S09
♃ 22S20
♀ 25N18

☽ 10 ♍
00
35 ♍ 17
45 ♌
38
R

05
♌
47

MANCINI, HENRY
Musician

April 16, 1924
00:10 AM EST
Cleveland, Ohio
81 W 42   41 N 30

APR 16 1924
00:10 AM EST
13 19 29 SIDEREAL
05 10 00 UNIVERSAL

HENRY MANCINI
CLEVELAND, OH
41N30 81W42
TROPICAL
PLACIDUS

♇ 10 ♋ 21

♀ 11 ♊ 25

Conductor-composer-arranger whose many awards include the Oscar for "Moon River", composed for the film *Breakfast at Tiffany's* (1961), and for the score of *Days of Wine and Roses*. Took lessons in piccolo at age 8; piano at 12; disliked practice until he discovered jazz.

A: From him to Jansky.

07 ♐
57

♃ 19 ♐ 44 R

27 ♐
33

27 ♊
33

♂ 24 ♑ 59

05 ♒
47

07 ♊
57

☽□♀ 0°50
☉□♂ 0°57
♀✳♇ 1°05
♀□♂ 1°26
☉△A 1°37
♄✳A 1°43
♃✳M 1°46

♅
19
♓
37

☉ 25 ♈ 56

⊗ ☿
12 15
♉ ♉
11 37

17 ♓
23

17 ♉
07

21 ♈ 30

SVP=♓ 6°19'11"
JULIAN DAY=2423891.71528

MANET, EDOUARD
Artist

January 23, 1832
7:00 PM LMT
Paris, France
2 E 20   48 N 50

Declin
☽ 04S00
♄ 08N02
♇ 11S59
♃ 13S12
♅ 17S18
☉ 19S32
☿ 20S25
♀ 20S37
♆ 20S42
♂ 23S32

C F M
F 1 0 2
E 0 1 2
A 0 1 3
W 0 0 0

27
♊
16

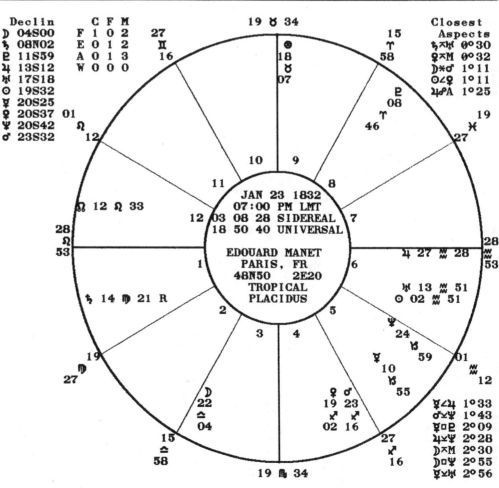

19 ♉ 34

⊗
18
07

15
♈
58

Closest Aspects
♄⚼♅ 0°30
♀⚼M 0°32
☽✳♂ 1°11
☉⚼♀ 1°11
♃♂A 1°25

01
♌

♌ 12 ♌ 33

12 ♌
♌

♇
08
♈
46

19
♒
27

JAN 23 1832
07:00 PM LMT
03 08 28 SIDEREAL
18 50 40 UNIVERSAL

EDOUARD MANET
PARIS, FR
48N50 2E20
TROPICAL
PLACIDUS

28
♌
53

28 ♒
53

♃ 27 ♍ 28

Sometimes called "the first modern painter". First received criticism for his new style; then scandal in 1865 for including a nude in his setting. The Impressionist movement grew from his milieu. Received the Legion of Honor in 1881. (1832-1883)

A: *Circle* #189 quotes Gauquelin.

♄ 14 ♍ 21 R

♅ 13 ♏ 51
☉ 02 ♒ 51

19
♍
27

♆ 24 ♑
59

01
♒

♍
12

☿
10
♑
55

☽
22
♎
04

♀ ♂
19 23
♐ ♐
02 16

27
♐
16

♍⚼♃ 1°33
♂♂♆ 1°43
☿♇ 2°09
♃⚼M 2°28
☽⚼M 2°30
☽□♀ 2°55
♀✳♅ 2°56

15
♎
58

19 ♏ 34

SVP=♓ 7°36'27"
JULIAN DAY=2390206.28519

MANN, THOMAS
Writer

June 6, 1875
12:15 PM LMT
Lubeck, Germany
10 E 41   53 N 52

Author of novels, plays, and essays, including *The Magic Mountain* (1924) and *Joseph In Egypt* (1938); awarded the 1929 Nobel prize for literature. Married in 1905; six children. Came to the U.S. in 1938. Respected and popular; personally hated discipline. (1875-1955)

A: March states, "from his daughter."[95]

SVP=♓ 7° 0' 1"
JULIAN DAY=2406045.98074

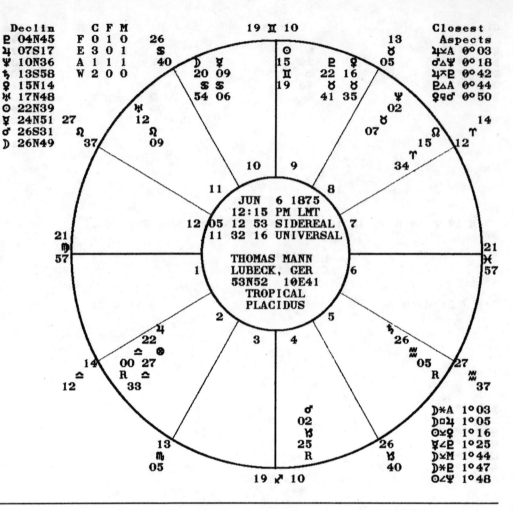

MARCONI, GUGLIELMO
Scientist

April 25, 1874
9:15 AM LMT
Bologna, Italy
11 E 21   44 N 30

Inventor of wireless telegraph and radio signals (1895) and radio magnetic detector (1902). With Carl Braun, awarded the 1909 Nobel prize for physics for their separate but parallel development of the wireless telegraph. (1874-1937)

A: Gauquelin #3071 Vol 2.[96]

SVP=♓ 7° 1' 3"
JULIAN DAY=2405638.85389

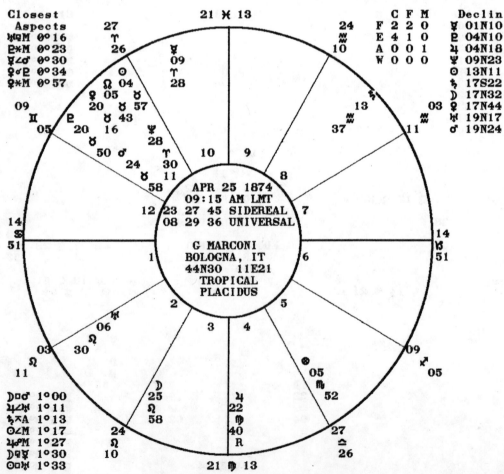

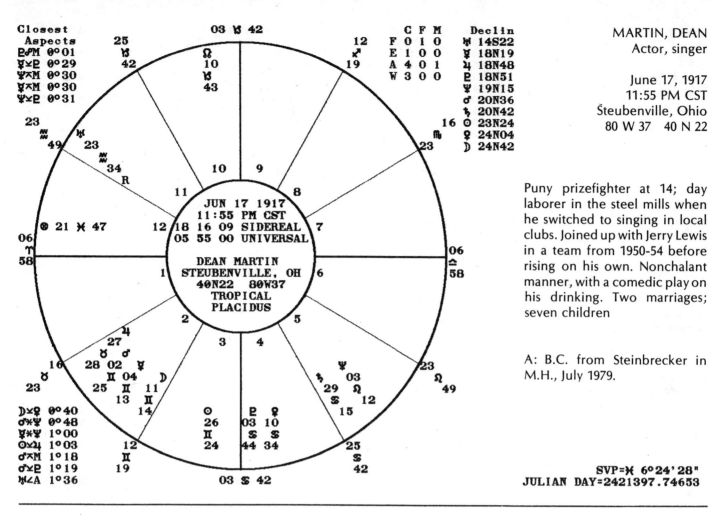

MARTIN, DEAN
Actor, singer

June 17, 1917
11:55 PM CST
Šteubenville, Ohio
80 W 37   40 N 22

Closest Aspects

♇⚷M	0°01	
☿⚹♇	0°29	
♆□M	0°30	
☿□M	0°30	
♆⚹♇	0°31	

Declin

♅	14S22
☿	18N19
♃	18N48
♇	18N51
♆	19N15
♂	20N36
♄	20N42
☉	23N24
♀	24N04
☽	24N42

C F M

F	0	1	0
E	1	0	0
A	4	0	1
W	3	0	0

JUN 17 1917
11:55 PM CST
18 16 09 SIDEREAL
05 55 00 UNIVERSAL

DEAN MARTIN
STEUBENVILLE, OH
40N22   80W37
TROPICAL
PLACIDUS

Puny prizefighter at 14; day laborer in the steel mills when he switched to singing in local clubs. Joined up with Jerry Lewis in a team from 1950-54 before rising on his own. Nonchalant manner, with a comedic play on his drinking. Two marriages; seven children

A: B.C. from Steinbrecker in M.H., July 1979.

☽⚹☿	0°40
♂⚹♆	0°48
☿⚹♆	1°00
☉⚹♃	1°03
♂□M	1°18
♂⚹♇	1°19
♅∠A	1°36

SVP=♓ 6°24'28"
JULIAN DAY=2421397.74653

MARTIN, DICK
Comedian

January 30, 1922
11:00 PM CST
Battle Creek, Mich
85 W 11   42 N 19

Declin

♄	00S40
☽	03S45
♃	06S05
♅	09S16
☿	11S23
♆	16N33
♂	16S41
☉	17S36
♀	19S14
♇	20N01

C F M

F	0	1	0
E	0	0	0
A	0	2	3
W	1	1	2

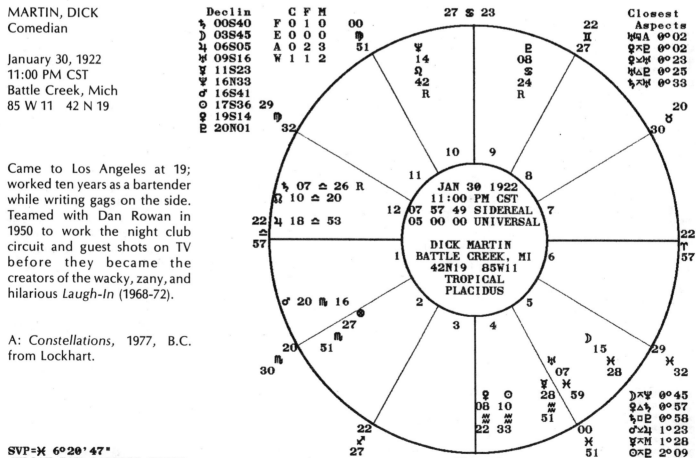

JAN 30 1922
11:00 PM CST
07 57 49 SIDEREAL
05 00 00 UNIVERSAL

DICK MARTIN
BATTLE CREEK, MI
42N19   85W11
TROPICAL
PLACIDUS

Came to Los Angeles at 19; worked ten years as a bartender while writing gags on the side. Teamed with Dan Rowan in 1950 to work the night club circuit and guest shots on TV before they became the creators of the wacky, zany, and hilarious *Laugh-In* (1968-72).

A: *Constellations*, 1977, B.C. from Lockhart.

Closest Aspects

♅□A	0°02
♀⚹♇	0°02
♀⚼♅	0°23
♅△♇	0°25
♄⚼♅	0°33

☽⚼♆	0°45
♀△♄	0°57
♄□♇	0°58
♂□♃	1°23
☿□M	1°28
☉□♃	2°09
♂∠♄	2°10

SVP=♓ 6°20'47"
JULIAN DAY=2423085.70833

MARX, KARL
Communist

May 5, 1818
2:00 AM LMT
Trier, Germany
6 E 06   49 N 45

German philosopher and developer of the theory of socialism. Studied law; became a newspaper editor. With Engels, presented *The Communist Manifesto* (1847), *Das Capital* (1848). A dialectical materialist; helped found the Social Democratic Labor Party in 1869. (1818-1883)

A: WEMYSS F/N #157, "as recorded."[98]

SVP=)(7°47'57"
JULIAN DAY=2385194.56639

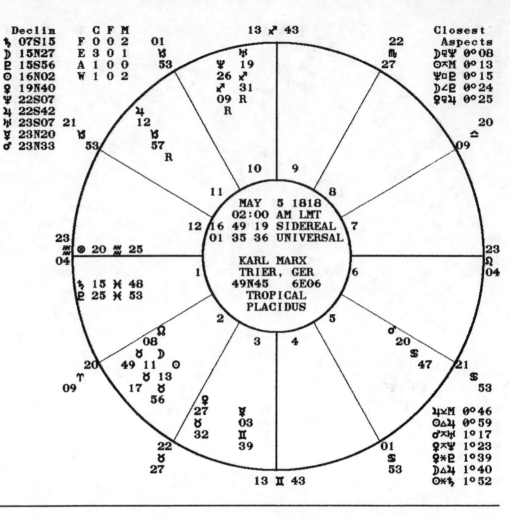

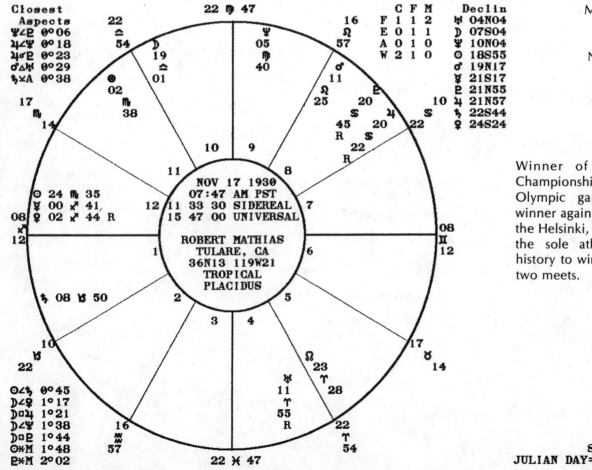

MATHIAS, ROBERT
Athlete

November 17, 1930
7:47 AM PST
Tulare, Ca
119 W 21   36 N 13

Winner of the Decathlon Championship in 1948 at the Olympic games in London; winner again four years later at the Helsinki, Finland Olympics; the sole athlete in modern history to win the decathlon at two meets.

A: CSH.

SVP=)(6°13'38"
JULIAN DAY=2426298.15764

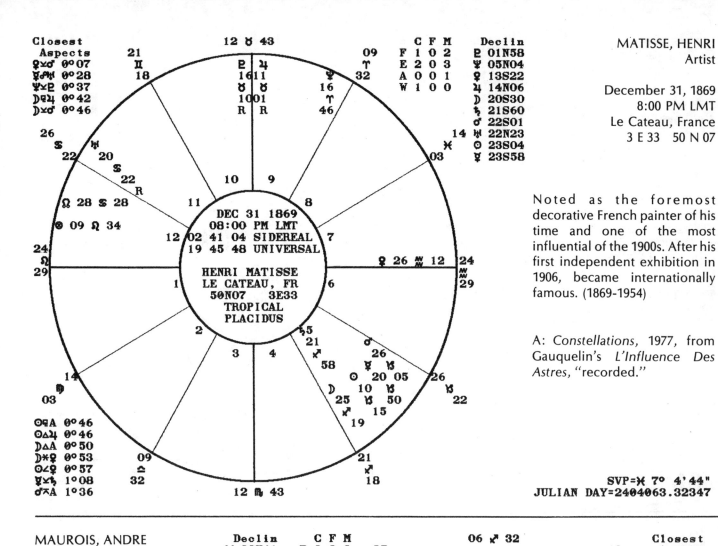

MATISSE, HENRI
Artist

December 31, 1869
8:00 PM LMT
Le Cateau, France
3 E 33   50 N 07

Noted as the foremost decorative French painter of his time and one of the most influential of the 1900s. After his first independent exhibition in 1906, became internationally famous. (1869-1954)

A: *Constellations*, 1977, from Gauquelin's *L'Influence Des Astres*, "recorded."

SVP=♓ 7° 4'44"
JULIAN DAY=2404063.32347

Closest Aspects
♀✭♂ 0°07
☿∠♅ 0°28
♆☌♇ 0°37
☽∠♃ 0°42
☽∠♂ 0°46

C F M   Declin
F 1 0 2   ♇ 01N58
E 2 0 3   ♆ 05N04
A 0 0 1   ♀ 13S22
W 1 0 0   ♃ 14N06
           ☽ 20S30
           ♄ 21S60
           ♂ 22S01
           ♅ 22N23
           ☉ 23S04
           ☿ 23S58

DEC 31 1869
08:00 PM LMT
02 41 04 SIDEREAL
19 45 48 UNIVERSAL

HENRI MATISSE
LE CATEAU, FR
50N07   3E33
TROPICAL
PLACIDUS

⊙¬A 0°46
⊙△♃ 0°46
☽△A 0°50
☽✱♀ 0°53
⊙∠♄ 0°57
☿∠♄ 1°08
♂∠A 1°36

MAUROIS, ANDRE
Writer

July 26, 1885
8:00 PM LMT
Elbeuf, France
1 E 01   49 N 17

Emile Herzog, a French writer of essays and novels, best known as a biographer. His works include *Ariel: The Life of Shelley* (1924), *Disraeli* (1927), *Byron* (1930), and *Dickens* (1934). Lectured widely in European and U.S. tours. (1885-1967)

A: Gauquelin #534 Vol 6.

SVP=♓ 6°51'26"
JULIAN DAY=2409749.33051

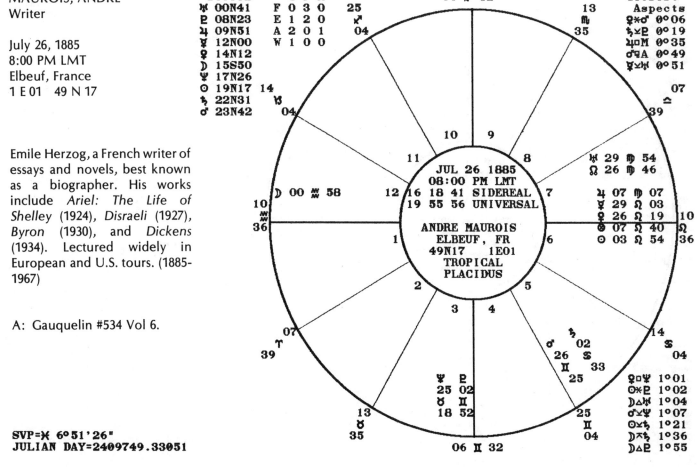

Declin
♅ 00N41
♇ 08N23
♃ 09N51
☿ 12N00
♀ 14N12
☽ 15S50
♆ 17N26
☉ 19N17
♄ 22N31
♂ 23N42

C F M
F 0 3 0
E 1 2 0
A 2 0 1
W 1 0 0

JUL 26 1885
08:00 PM LMT
16 18 41 SIDEREAL
19 55 56 UNIVERSAL

ANDRE MAUROIS
ELBEUF, FR
49N17   1E01
TROPICAL
PLACIDUS

Closest Aspects
♀✱♂ 0°06
♄⊻♇ 0°19
♃□M 0°35
♂¬A 0°49
☿⊻♅ 0°51

♀□♆ 1°01
⊙✱♇ 1°02
☽△♅ 1°04
♂⊻♆ 1°07
⊙⊻♄ 1°21
☽⊼♄ 1°36
☽△♇ 1°55

MAY, ROLLO
Psychologist

April 21, 1909
2:20 AM CST
Ada, Ohio
83 W 49   40 N 46

Psychoanalyst, lecturer, successful and popular pioneer of existential psychology. Author of a dozen books, including *Love and Will*, *The Meaning of Anxiety*, and *Power and Innocence*. Two marriages and divorces.

A: CSH.

SVP=♓ 6°31'52"
JULIAN DAY=2418417.84722

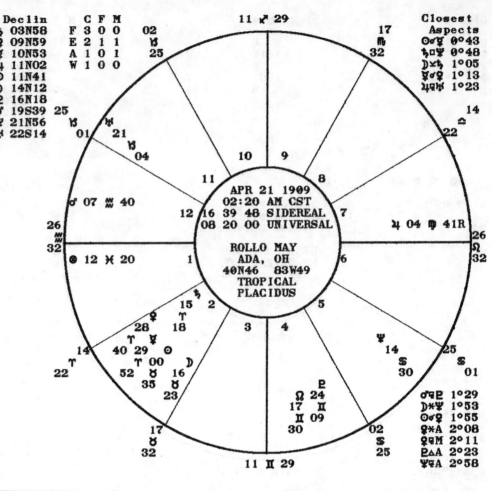

MAYFAIR BOY
Jewel thief

September 13, 1916
4:15 AM BST
St. Johns Woods, England
0 W 11   51 N 31

As a lark, with two other young men, robbed Cartiers of London in December 1937 of rings valued at 16,824 pounds; caught and sentenced to three years in prison. Wrote an autobiography, *Mayfair Boy*.

A: AQ, Autumn 1972, quotes data in the biography.

SVP=♓ 6°25' 7"
JULIAN DAY=2421119.63542

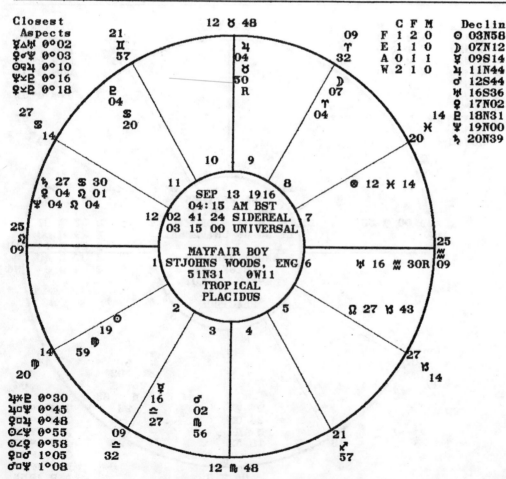

May 6, 1931
10:30 PM CST
Westfield, Ala
86 W 58   33 N 22

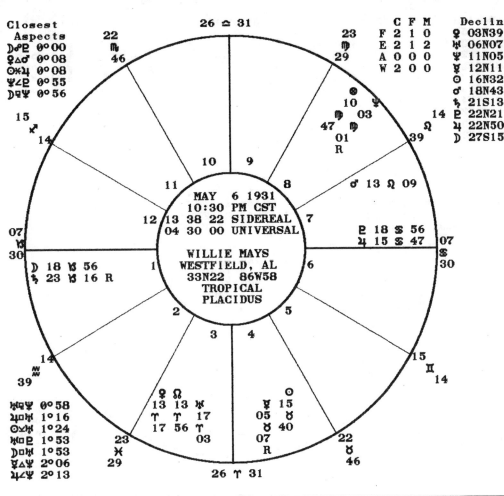

Closest
Aspects

☽⚺♇	0°00	
♀△♂	0°08	
☉⚹♃	0°08	
♆∠♃	0°55	
☽⚻♆	0°56	

	C	F	M		Declin	
F	2	1	0	♀	03N39
E	2	1	2	♅	06N07
A	0	0	0	♆	11N05
W	2	0	0	☿	12N11
				☉	16N32
				♂	18N43
				♄	21S13
				♇	22N21
				♃	22N50
				☽	27S15

♅⚹♆	0°58	
♃□♅	1°16	
☉⚹♅	1°24	
♅□♇	1°53	
☽□♅	1°53	
☿△♆	2°06	
♃∠♆	2°13	

MAY 6 1931
10:30 PM CST
13 38 22 SIDEREAL
04 30 00 UNIVERSAL

WILLIE MAYS
WESTFIELD, AL
33N22 86W58
TROPICAL
PLACIDUS

Played twenty-two years with the New York and San Francisco Giants, and the New York Mets. Fabled for basket catches and boundless enthusiasm in the 50s. Impressive hitting statistics - .302 average, 660 homers, 2,062 runs scored. A rifle arm and quicksilver moves.

A: CSH.

SVP=♓ 6°13'11"
JULIAN DAY=2426468.68750

July 19, 1950
1:09 AM PDT
Los Angeles, Ca
118 W 15   34 N 04

Declin		C	F	M
♆	04S19	F	0	2	0
☽	06N35	E	0	2	0
♂	07S06	A	1	2	0
♄	07N22	W	2	0	1
♃	10S10				
☿	20N42				
☉	20N56				
♀	22N22				
♇	23N22				
♅	23N33				

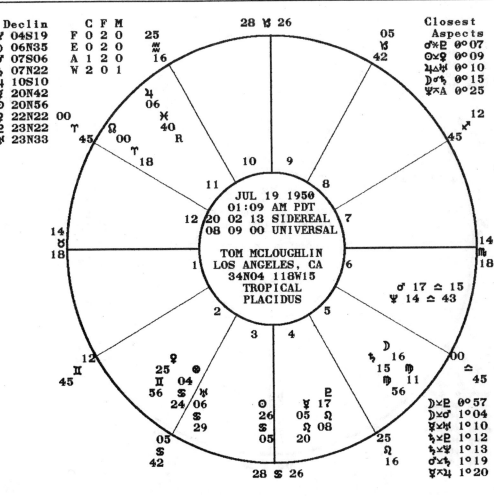

Singer with a rock-band at 16; went to Paris in 1970 to study mime with Marcel Marceau. Local gigs and a 30-city tour of U.S., 1971. Formed the L.A. Mime Troup in 1973, which played the *Dick Van Dyke Show* in 1976. Films include *Sleeper*, *The Black Hole*, and *Prophesy*.

A: From him to LMR, 1967, B.C.

JUL 19 1950
01:09 AM PDT
20 02 13 SIDEREAL
08 09 00 UNIVERSAL

TOM McLOUGHLIN
LOS ANGELES, CA
34N04 118W15
TROPICAL
PLACIDUS

Closest
Aspects

♂⚹♇	0°07	
☉⚹♀	0°09	
♃△♅	0°10	
☽♂♄	0°15	
♆⚻△	0°25	

☽⚹♇	0°57	
☽⚹♂	1°04	
☿⚹♅	1°10	
♄⚹♇	1°12	
☽⚹♆	1°13	
♂⚹♄	1°19	
☿⚻♃	1°20	

SVP=♓ 5°57' 1"
JULIAN DAY=2433481.83958

McNAMERA, ROBERT S.
Government cabinet

June 9, 1916
5:45 AM PST
San Francisco, Ca
122 W 26   37 N 47

Phi Beta Kappa at U.C. Financial analyst, comptroller, and president of Ford Motor Co.; the first Ford president outside of the family. Secretary of defense of U.S. in President Johnson's cabinet; "hawk" member. Later headed the World Bank.

B: *Constellations*, 1977, Blackwell quotes *McNamara: His Ordeal in the Pentagon* by Trewhitt (1971).

SVP=ℋ 6°25'22"
JULIAN DAY=2421024.07292

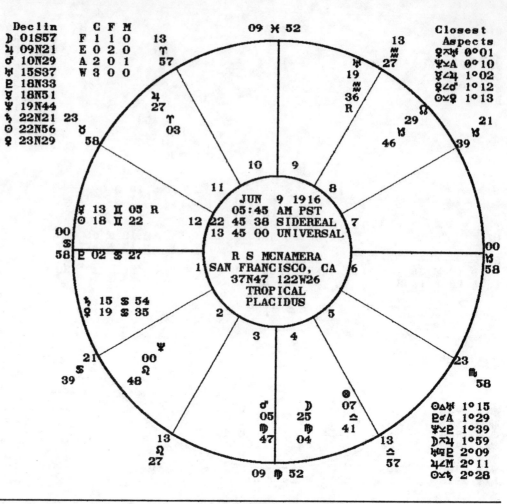

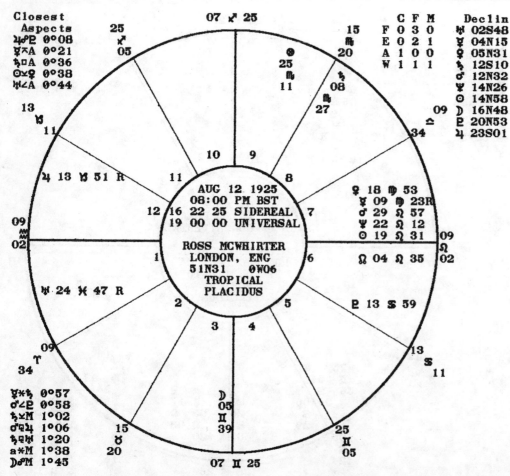

McWHIRTER, ROSS
Journalist

August 12, 1925
8:00 PM BST
London, England
0 W 06   51 N 31

Wrote *The Guinness Book of Records* with his twin brother, Norris, who was born twenty minutes earlier. After posting a reward for the capture of the bombers of London, shot by the IRA at his front door on November 27, 1975.

B: Holliday quotes *The Guinness Book of Records*.

SVP=ℋ 6°18' 8"
JULIAN DAY=2424375.29167

MEHTA, ZUBIN
Conductor

April 29, 1936
2:50 AM IST
Bombay, India
72 E 48 19 N 00

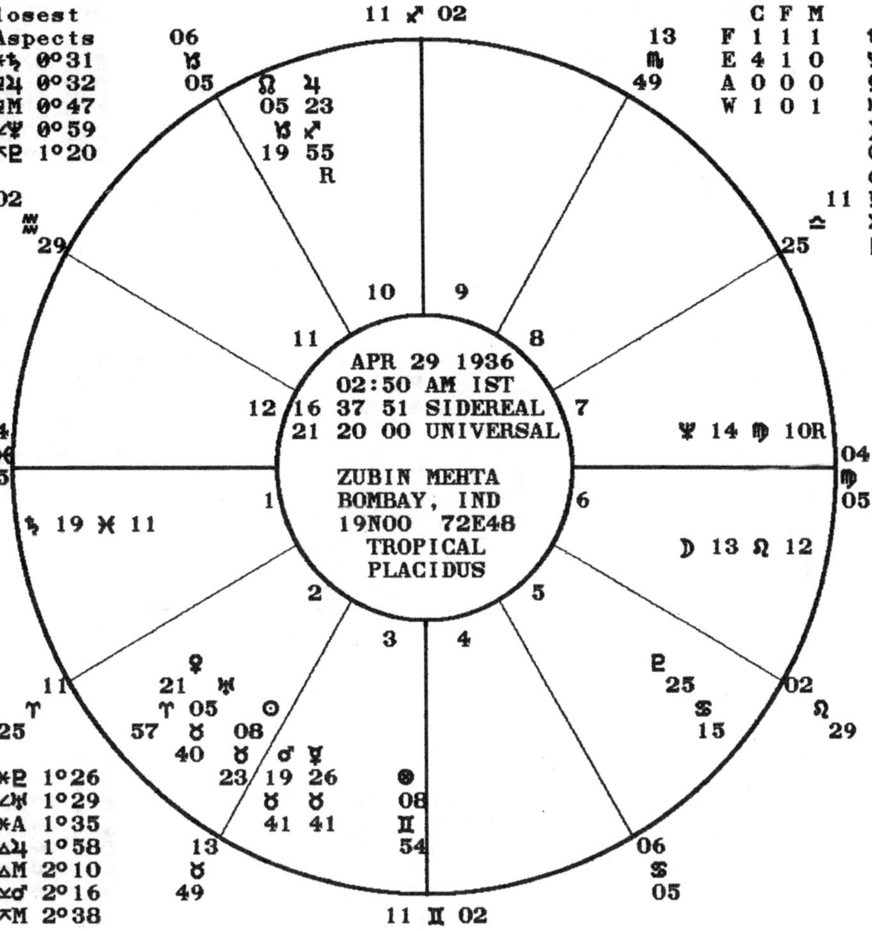

APR 29 1936
02:50 AM IST
16 37 51 SIDEREAL
21 20 00 UNIVERSAL
ZUBIN MEHTA
BOMBAY, IND
19N00 72E48
TROPICAL
PLACIDUS

Closest Aspects
♂✶♄ 0°31
☉⚼♃ 0°32
♇□M 0°47
☽⚺♆ 0°59
♃⚻♇ 1°20

♀✶♇ 1°26
♄∠♅ 1°29
♅⚼A 1°35
♀△♃ 1°58
☽△M 2°10
♀⚺♂ 2°16
☉⚻M 2°38

	C	F	M
F	1	1	1
E	4	1	0
A	0	0	0
W	1	0	1

Declin
♄ 05S58
♆ 07N11
♀ 07N11
♅ 12N59
☽ 13N51
☉ 14N18
♂ 17N49
☿ 21N33
♃ 22S42
♇ 23N16

Started on piano and violin at age 7 by his conductor father, Mehili; gained a conductor diploma in 1957. World guest conductor at 24, when he was named the resident conductor of the Montreal Symphony; held the same post with the L.A. Philharmonic the following year.

B: Penfield quotes *The Zubin Mehta Story* by Brookspan and Yockey, p. 5.

SVP=♓ 6° 8'40"
JULIAN DAY=2428287.38889

MELVILLE, HERMAN
Writer

August 1, 1819
11:30 PM LMT
New York, N.Y.
73 W 57 40 N 45

Declin
♄ 02S02
☿ 09N30
♇ 15S56
♃ 17S53
☉ 18N02
♂ 21N08
♀ 22N07
♆ 22S11
♅ 23S17
☽ 27S15

	C	F	M
F	1	1	3
E	0	1	0
A	1	0	1
W	1	0	1

One of America's greatest writers of novels, as well as some poetry based on his experience and powerful imagination. Worked as a seaman from 1839-45; books include *Typee* (1846), *Omoo* (1847), and the classic *Moby Dick (1851). (1819-1891)*

B: *Constellations*, 1977, as recorded in the family Bible, reproduced in *The Melville Log* by J. Keyda (1951).

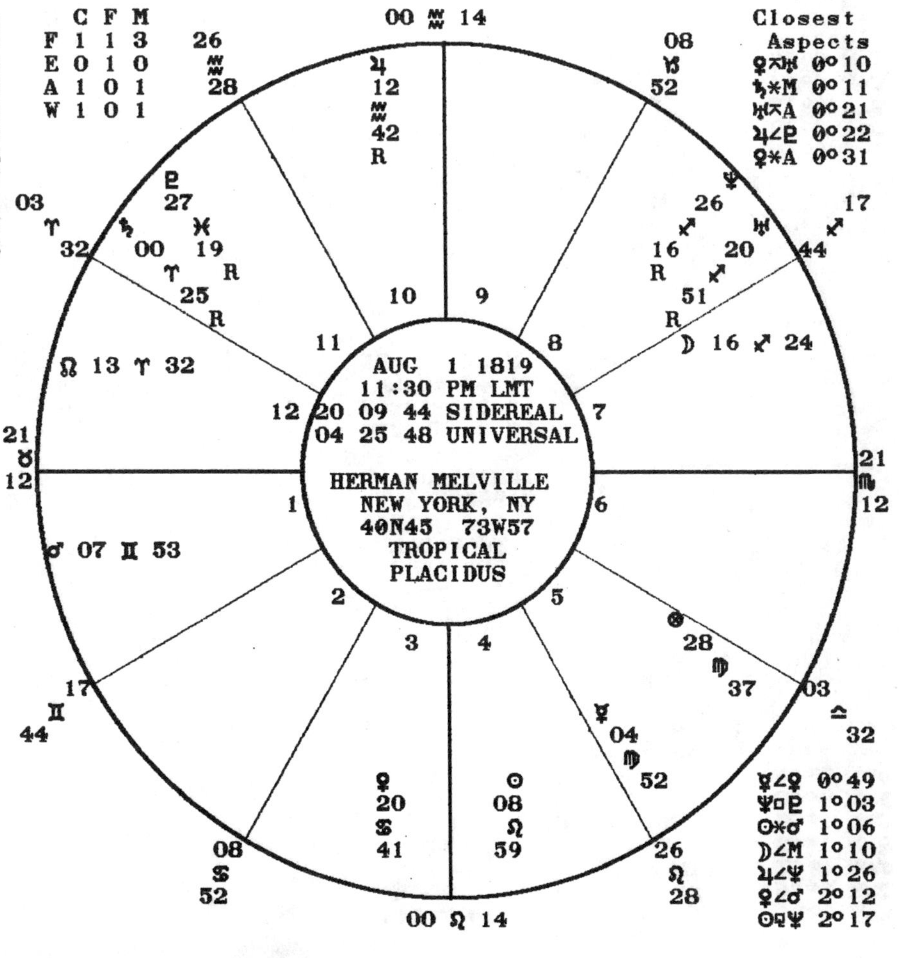

AUG 1 1819
11:30 PM LMT
20 09 44 SIDEREAL
04 25 48 UNIVERSAL
HERMAN MELVILLE
NEW YORK, NY
40N45 73W57
TROPICAL
PLACIDUS

Closest Aspects
♀⚻♅ 0°10
♄✶M 0°11
♅⚻A 0°21
♃∠♇ 0°22
♀✶A 0°31

♅∠♀ 0°49
♆□♇ 1°03
☉✶♂ 1°06
☽∠M 1°10
♃∠♆ 1°26
♀∠♂ 2°12
☉⚼♆ 2°17

SVP=♓ 7°46'46"
JULIAN DAY=2385648.68458

MENUHIN, YEHUDI
Violinist

April 22, 1917
11:30 PM EST
New York, N.Y.
73 W 57   40 N 45

Child prodigy who began to play the violin at age 3; first public performance at age 7, playing Beethoven in San Francisco; a recital at 8 in Manhattan Opera House, N.Y. A musical genius and a profound artist who has played with all the great world symphonies.

A: Dewey quotes C.C. Zain, "given to Herndon by his parents."[99]

SVP=♓ 6°24'36"
JULIAN DAY=2421341.68750

Declin		C F M	
♂ 07N39		F 1 1 0	21
♀ 11N05		E 5 0 0	
☉ 12N20		A 0 0 1	11
♅ 14S27		W 2 0 0	
♃ 15N20			
♇ 18N47			
♆ 19N30			
☿ 20N59	11		
♄ 21N35	♐		
☽ 22N17	57		

Closest Aspects:
♆△A	0°02
☉⚹♇	0°09
☽□♅	0°13
☉□♆	0°20
☉△A	0°22
☽♂♆	0°27
♆⚹♇	0°28
♀△A	0°28
♇♂A	0°30
♀□♆	0°30
☿□♅	0°40
☉♂♀	0°50

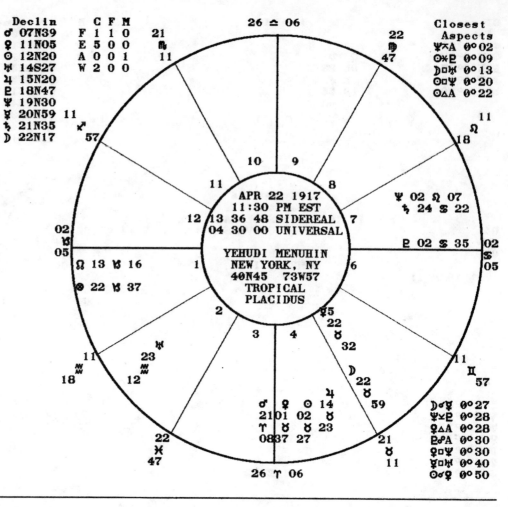

MICHAELANGELO
Universal genius

March 15, 1475 NS
1:45 AM LMT
Caprese, Italy
11 E 59   43 N 45

Italian renaissance artist and inventor; one of the great minds of all time. Chiefly interested in sculpture of the human body. Noted for his frescoes on the ceiling of the Sistine Chapel in Rome. An apprentice painter at 12; full creative force after 1502. (1475-1564)

B: *Circle* quotes *The Life of Michaelangelo* by J.A. Symonds.[100]

SVP=♓12°34'45"
JULIAN DAY=2259865.53963

Closest Aspects:
♂△♃	0°13
♆⚹♇	0°14
♀△A	0°17
☉□A	0°23
☉⚹♀	0°40
☽♂♄	0°46
☽⚹♃	0°48
♂⚹M	1°09
☽⚹M	1°42
♂△♄	1°47
♆⚹M	1°56
♄△♅	2°01

C F M		Declin	
F 1 0 0		☉ 02S23	
E 0 1 0		♂ 05S20	
A 0 0 2		☽ 07S18	
W 1 2 3		☿ 13S45	
		♅ 16S00	
		♀ 16N00	
		♆ 16S33	
		♇ 18N32	
		♃ 19S49	
		♄ 22N36	

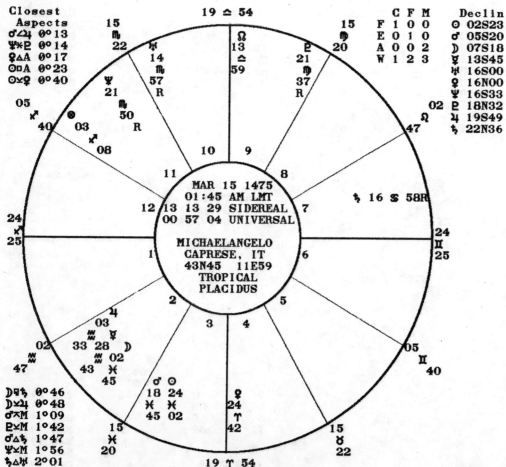

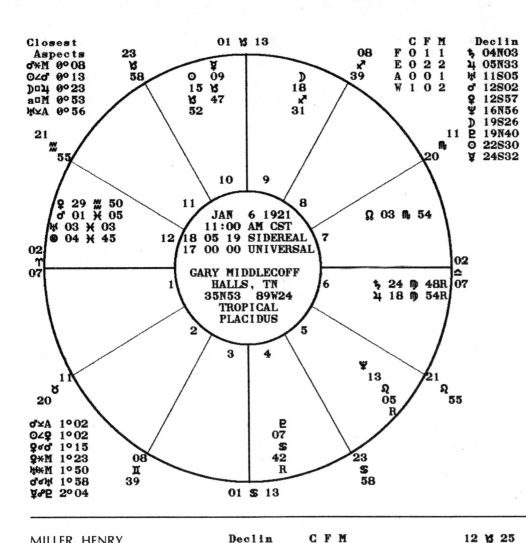

MIDDLECOFF, GARY
Golfer

January 6, 1921
11:00 AM CST
Halls, Tenn
89 W 24   35 N 53

Dentist and amateur golfer; holder of Memphis and Tennessee amateur championships. The first amateur to win both North and South Open (1945). Turned professional in 1947; won U.S. Open in 1949 and 1956. Won Masters in 1955; Vardon Trophy in 1956.

A: CSH.

Gary Middlecoff chart

Closest Aspects
♂✶M 0°08
☉☌♂ 0°13
☽□♃ 0°23
a□M 0°53
♅✶A 0°56

♂✶A 1°02
☉∠♀ 1°02
♀∠♂ 1°15
♀✶M 1°23
♅✶M 1°50
♂♂♅ 1°58
☿♂♇ 2°04

01 ♑ 13
☉ 09 ♑ 15 47 52
☽ 18 ♐ 31
08 ♐ 39

Declin
♄ 04N03
♃ 05N33
♅ 11S05
♂ 12S02
♀ 12S57
♇ 16N56
☽ 19S26
♇ 19N40
☉ 22S30
☿ 24S32

C F M
F 0 1 1
E 0 2 2
A 0 0 1
W 1 0 2

♀ 29 ♏ 50
♂ 01 ♓ 05
♅ 03 ♓ 03
⊕ 04 ♓ 45

02 ♈ 07

♃ 18 ♍ 54R
♄ 24 ♍ 48R
02 ♎ 07

☊ 03 ♏ 54
11 ♏ 20

♇ 07 ♋ 42 R
♆ 13 ♌ 05 R
23 ♋ 58
21 ♌ 55

08 ♊ 39
01 ♋ 13
11 ♉ 20

JAN 6 1921
11:00 AM CST
18 05 19 SIDEREAL
17 00 00 UNIVERSAL

GARY MIDDLECOFF
HALLS, TN
35N53   89W24
TROPICAL
PLACIDUS

SVP=♓ 6°21'35"
JULIAN DAY=2422696.20833

MILLER, HENRY
Writer

December 26, 1891
12:30 PM EST
Brooklyn, N.Y.
73 W 56   40 N 38

Books banned as obscene in the U.S. for many years, including *Tropic of Cancer* and *Tropic of Capricorn*. Works mostly drawn from personal experience and observation; stories of the women he loved and the friends he cherished: richly lusty and earthy. (1891-1980)

B: CL quotes *My Friend Henry Miller*, "midi-30."

Henry Miller chart

Declin
♄ 02N02
♃ 07S56
♇ 10N04
♅ 12S48
♂ 14S31
☽ 14S35
♆ 19N52
☿ 21S14
♀ 21S55
☉ 23S22

C F M
F 0 0 0
E 0 1 3
A 2 0 0
W 0 3 1

Closest Aspects
☽△A 0°11
♃✶M 0°12
☽✶M 0°23
♆♂♇ 0°27
☉✶♅ 0°28

♇∠A 0°35
♂✶M 0°43
♀△♄ 0°48
♂∠♃ 0°55
♆∠A 1°02
☽♂♂ 1°06
♀♃ 1°34

12 ♑ 25
21 ♐ 26
☿ 09 ♑ 04 ☉ 50 ♑ 42 R
05 ♒ 25
♀ 29 ♒ 11
27 ♏

♃ 12 ♓ 37
22 ♈ 58
⊕ 01 ♓ 03
26 ♓

☽ 12 ♏ 47
♂ 11 ♏ 41
♅ 05 ♏ 10
22 ♎ 58

♄ 29 ♍ 59
06 ♍ 26

☊ 25 ♉ 41
♆ 06 ♊ 56 R
♇ 07 ♊ 22 R
27 ♉ 39

05 ♌ 25
21 ♊ 26
12 ♋ 25

DEC 26 1891
12:30 PM EST
18 53 58 SIDEREAL
17 30 00 UNIVERSAL

HENRY MILLER
BROOKLYN, NY
40N38   73W56
TROPICAL
PLACIDUS

SVP=♓ 6°46'18"
JULIAN DAY=2412093.22917

MILLER, KIMI KAI
Unusual birth

June 6, 1965
6:15 PM PDT
San Bernardino, Ca
117 W 19   34 N 07

Daughter of Lucille Miller, convicted of first degree murder of her husband in a flaming automobile on October 8, 1964, and serving life sentence. Mother taken from prison to bear Kimi, her fourth child; returned to prison after the birth.

A: CL from *Herald Examiner* on date.

SVP=ℋ 5°44'50"
JULIAN DAY=2438918.55208

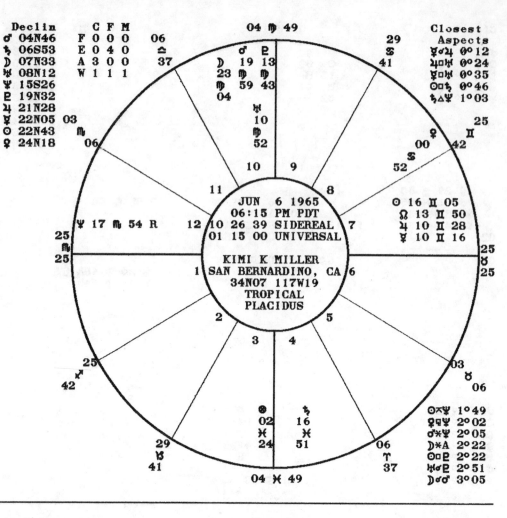

MILLET, JEAN FRANCOIS
Artist

October 4, 1814
8:00 PM LMT
Gruchy, France
1 W 30   49 N 40

Remembered for *The Angelus, The Gleaners,* and *The Man with the Hoe.* Worked largely in dark, muddy colors; a sentimental traditionalist. A temperamental man, who was self-taught. Finally admitted to the French Academy in 1847. Lived a life of modest poverty. (1814-1875)

A: Gauquelin #772 Vol 4.

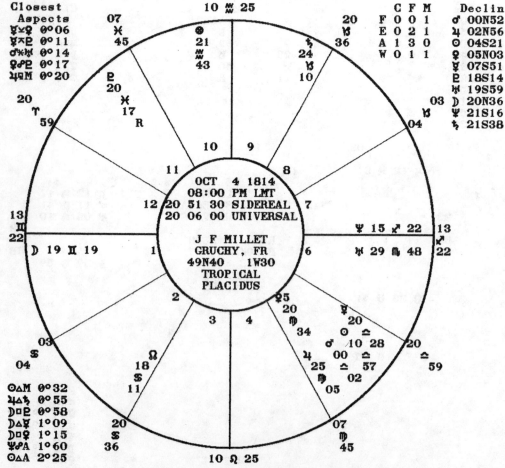

SVP=ℋ 7°51' 2"
JULIAN DAY=2383886.33750

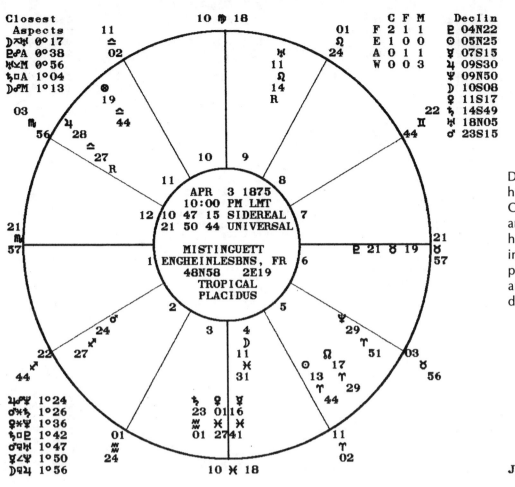

Closest
Aspects
☽⊼♅ 0°17
♇⚹♈ 0°38
♅☌♏ 0°56
♄☌A 1°04
☽⚹♏ 1°13

10 ♍ 18

11   ⚊
02

♅
11

24

Ω
14
R

01 C F M
F 2 1 1
E 1 0 0
A 0 1 1
W 0 0 3

Declin
♇ 04N22
⊙ 05N25
☿ 07S15
♃ 09S30
♆ 09N50
☽ 10S08
♀ 11S17
♄ 14S49
♅ 18N05
♂ 23S15

MISTINGUETTE
Entertainer

April 3, 1875
10:00 PM LMT
Enghein-les-Baines, France
2 E 19   48 N 58

Ⓐ
19

⚊
44

22   Ⅱ
44

03
♏
56   ♃
28

⚊
27
R

10

9

8

21
♏
57

APR 3 1875
10:00 PM LMT
10 47 15 SIDEREAL
21 50 44 UNIVERSAL

MISTINGUETT
ENGHEINLESBNS, FR
48N58 2E19
TROPICAL
PLACIDUS

7

♇ 21 ♉ 19

21
♉
57

Dazzling queen of French music halls who took Maurice Chevalier to her heart as lover and protege when he was still in his teens. They danced together in Folies Bergere until her possessiveness drove him away and into marriage with another dancer.

A: Gauquelin #552 Vol 5.

♂
24

27 ♐
22
44

♐
27

2

♆
29

⚊
♈
51   03

5

3   4
☽
11
♓
31

⊙ Ω
13 ♈ 17
♈
44   29

♉

56

11
♈
02

♃⚹♆ 1°24
♂⚹♄ 1°26
♀⚹♆ 1°36
♄□♇ 1°42
♂♁♅ 1°47
☿∠♆ 1°50
☽♁♃ 1°56

♄ ♀ ☿
23 01 16
♒ ♓ ♓
01 27 41

01
♒
24

10 ♓ 18

SVP=♓ 7° 0'11"
JULIAN DAY=2405982.41023

MITCHELL, JOHN
Government official

September 5, 1913
3:30 AM CST
Detroit, Mich.
83 W 03   42 N 20

Successful Wall Street lawyer and law-partner of Richard Nixon before he took over as manager of the presidential campaign in 1968. Named attorney general in President Nixon's cabinet. Sentenced to prison in June 1977 to serve term on Watergate conviction.

A: CSH.

Declin
⊙ 06N59
☿ 12N25
♇ 17N39
♀ 18N46
♅ 19S50
♆ 20N15
☽ 20S15
♄ 21N14
♂ 23N03
♃ 23S25

C F M
F 0 1 0
E 0 2 1
A 2 0 1
W 2 1 0

15 ♉ 48

21
Ⅱ
43

25

♄
17
Ⅱ

07

♂ 24
♇ 01 Ⅱ
35
♋
01 07

12
♈
49

♓
24
10

Closest
Aspects
⊙∠♆ 0°11
♇∠♏ 0°13
♂⚹A 0°22
♀⚹♅ 0°30
♃□A 0°45

15

♓
39

Ω

♆ 27 ♋ 23
♀ 04 Ω 42

23
Ω
45

10   9

11

12   8

SEP 5 1913
03:30 AM CST
02 53 20 SIDEREAL
09 30 00 UNIVERSAL

JOHN MITCHELL
DETROIT, MI
42N20 83W03
TROPICAL
PLACIDUS

7

23
♒
45

☿ 01 ♍ 47

⊙ 12 ♍ 12

1

6

♅ 04 ♒ 12R

2

5

15
♍
39

Ⓐ
26
⚊
32

3   4

☽
14
♏
59

♃
08
♑
00

25
♑
07

SVP=♓ 6°27'52"
JULIAN DAY=2420015.89583

12
⚊
49

21

♐
43

☿⚹♇ 0°46
☽♁♏ 0°49
☽♁♇ 1°02
♄♁♅ 1°37
♄⚹♏ 1°47
♀∠♈ 2°07
☿⊼♃ 2°25

15 ♏ 48

MODIGLIANI, AMADEO
Artist

July 12, 1884
9:00 AM LMT
Livorno, Italy
10 E 20   43 N 33

Italian portrait painter of artists,
poets, musicians, and models,
usually with long bodies and
oval heads. Moved to Paris in
1906 and supported himself for
a while by sketching cafe
portraits; later also did
sculpture. (1884-1920)

A: Gauquelin #1212 Vol 4.

SVP=♓ 6°52'13"
JULIAN DAY=2409369.84630

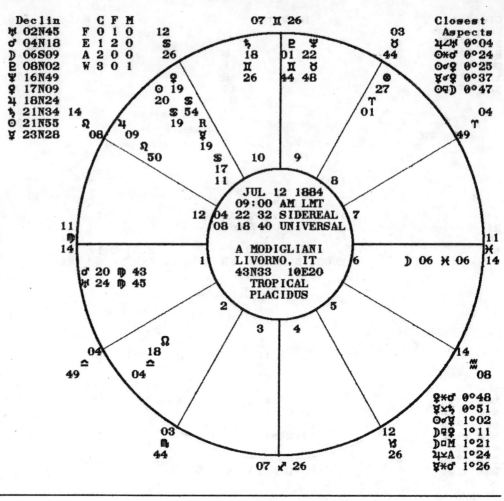

Declin		C F M			Closest Aspects
♅ 02N45	F 0 1 0				♃✶⚷ 0°04
♂ 04N18	E 1 2 0				⊙✶♂ 0°24
☽ 06S09	A 2 0 0				♀✶♂ 0°25
♇ 08N02	W 3 0 1				☿✶♀ 0°37
♆ 16N49					⊙□☽ 0°47
♀ 17N09					
♃ 18N24					
♄ 21N34					
⊙ 21N55					
☿ 23N28					

JUL 12 1884
09:00 AM LMT
04 22 32 SIDEREAL
08 18 40 UNIVERSAL

A MODIGLIANI
LIVORNO, IT
43N33 10E20
TROPICAL
PLACIDUS

♀✶♂ 0°48
☿✶♄ 0°51
⊙♂♀ 1°02
☽♂♀ 1°11
☽□M 1°21
♃△A 1°24
☿✶♂ 1°26

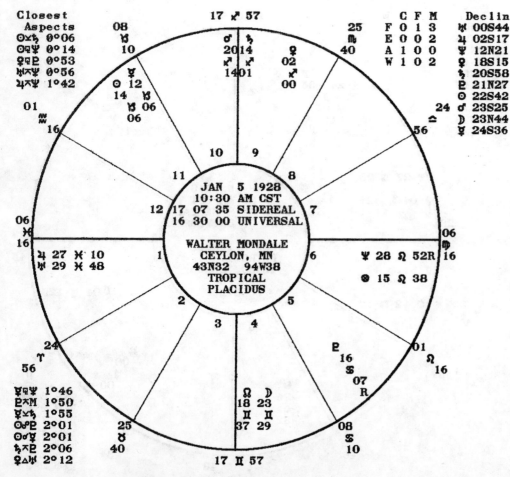

Closest Aspects		C F M	Declin
⊙✶♄ 0°06		F 0 1 3	♅ 00S44
⊙♂♆ 0°14		E 0 0 2	♃ 02S17
♀⚹♇ 0°53		A 1 0 0	♆ 12N21
♅✶♄ 0°56		W 1 0 2	♀ 18S15
♃✶♅ 1°42			♄ 20S58
			♇ 21N27
			⊙ 22S42
			♂ 23S25
			☽ 23N44
			☿ 24S36

JAN 5 1928
10:30 AM CST
17 07 35 SIDEREAL
16 30 00 UNIVERSAL

WALTER MONDALE
CEYLON, MN
43N32 94W38
TROPICAL
PLACIDUS

♀♂♆ 1°46
♇✶M 1°50
☿✶♄ 1°55
⊙♂♇ 2°01
⊙♂♇ 2°01
♄✶♇ 2°06
♀△♅ 2°12

MONDALE, WALTER
U.S. Vice President

January 5, 1928
10:30 AM CST
Ceylon, Minn
94 W 38   43 N 32

Minnesota attorney general in
1960; senator in 1964; became
the U.S. vice president under
Jimmy Carter in 1976 - a close
working relationship. Known as
ambitious, industrious, and
tactful. Married to Joan; three
children born in 1958, 1960, and
1963.

A: CSH.

SVP=♓ 6°16'10"
JULIAN DAY=2425251.18750

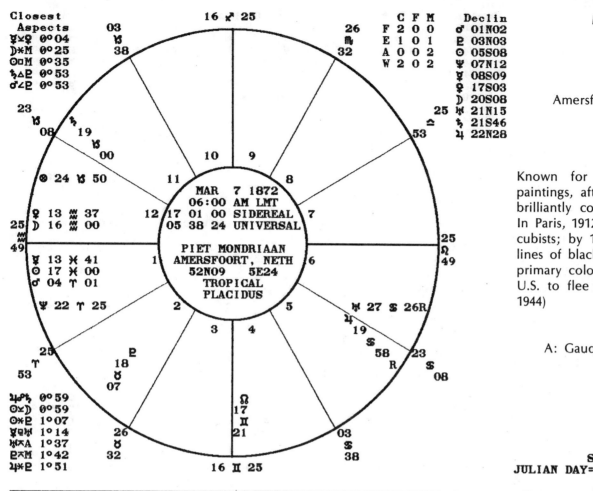

Closest Aspects

☿☍♀ 0°04
☽✳M 0°25
☉□M 0°35
♄△♇ 0°53
♂∠♇ 0°53

� 16 ♐ 25

	C	F	M
F	2	0	0
E	1	0	1
A	0	0	2
W	2	0	2

Declin

♂	01N02
♇	03N03
☉	05S08
♆	07N12
☿	08S09
☽	20S08
♅	21N15
♄	21S46
♃	22N28

MONDRIAN, PIET
Artist

March 7, 1872
6:00 AM LMT
Amersfoort, Netherlands
5 E 24   52 N 09

MAR 7 1872
06:00 AM LMT
17 01 00 SIDEREAL
05 38 24 UNIVERSAL

PIET MONDRIAAN
AMERSFOORT, NETH
52N09   5E24
TROPICAL
PLACIDUS

Known for pure geometric paintings, after early work of brilliantly colored landscapes. In Paris, 1912, inspired by the cubists; by 1919 used straight lines of black and white, with primary colors. Moved to the U.S. to flee the Nazis. (1872-1944)

A: Gauquelin #1456 Vol 4.

♃∠♄ 0°59
☉∠☽ 0°59
☉✳♇ 1°07
☿□♅ 1°14
♅✳A 1°37
♇△M 1°42
♃✳♇ 1°51

SVP=♓ 7° 2'55"
JULIAN DAY=2404859.73500

MONGKUT, KING
Rama IV

October 19, 1804
3:00 AM LMT
Bangkok, Thailand
100 E 31   13 N 45

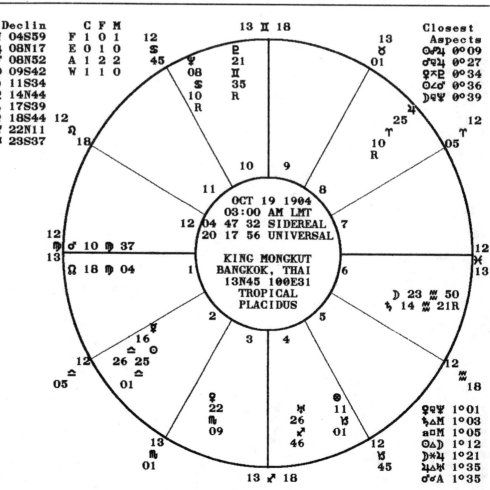

Declin

☿	04S59
♃	08N17
♂	08N52
☉	09S42
☽	11S34
♇	14N44
♄	17S39
♀	18S44
♆	22N11
♅	23S37

	C	F	M
F	1	0	1
E	0	1	0
A	1	2	2
W	1	1	0

OCT 19 1804
03:00 AM LMT
04 47 32 SIDEREAL
20 17 56 UNIVERSAL

KING MONGKUT
BANGKOK, THAI
13N45 100E31
TROPICAL
PLACIDUS

Closest Aspects

☉♂♃ 0°09
♂♃♃ 0°27
♀☍♇ 0°34
☉♂♂ 0°36
☽♂♆ 0°39

Lived as a celibate monk for twenty seven years before assuming the throne. Small in stature; progressive, unpretentious, devout, just. Allowed his many wives to "withdraw" from palace life to marry if they chose; said to have sixty-seven children. Glamorized in *Anna and the King of Siam*.

A: Hughes in AFA, February 1971.

♀♂♆ 1°01
♄△M 1°03
a□M 1°05
☉△☽ 1°12
☽✳♃ 1°21
♃△♅ 1°35
♂♂A 1°35

SVP=♓ 6°35'26"
JULIAN DAY=2416772.34579

MOORE, ROBIN
Writer

October 31, 1925
7:30 PM EST
Cambridge, Mass
71 W 06   42 N 22

Author of *The Green Berets*, which sold more than three million copies. Co-author of approximately twenty books between 1975-1979, including *The French Connection*, which was made into a motion picture. Has a paperback publication company, Condor.

A: From his sister Marcia Moore, in AA, November 1967.

SVP=✳ 6°18' 0"
JULIAN DAY=2424455.52083

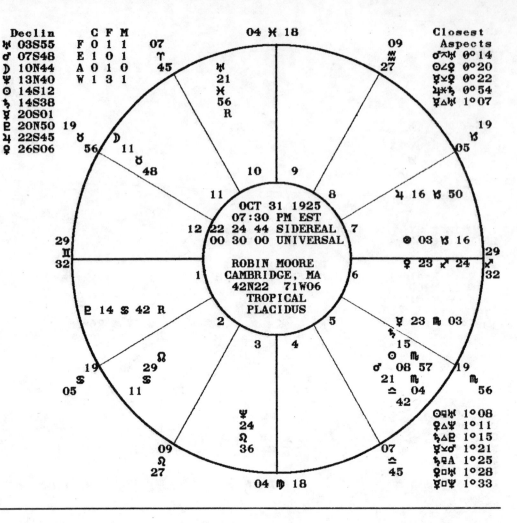

	Declin	C F M
♅	03S55	F 0 1 1
♂	07S48	E 1 0 1
☽	10N44	A 0 1 0
♆	13N40	W 1 3 1
☉	14S12	
♄	14S38	
☿	20S01	
♇	20N50	19
♃	22S45	
♀	26S06	

Closest Aspects
♂☍♅	0°14
☉☌♀	0°20
♃☌♄	0°54
☿△♅	1°07

OCT 31 1925
07:30 PM EST
12 22 24 44 SIDEREAL
00 30 00 UNIVERSAL

ROBIN MOORE
CAMBRIDGE, MA
42N22 71W06
TROPICAL
PLACIDUS

☉□♅	1°08
♀△♆	1°11
♄△♇	1°15
☿☌♂	1°21
♄□A	1°25
♀□♅	1°28
☿□♆	1°33

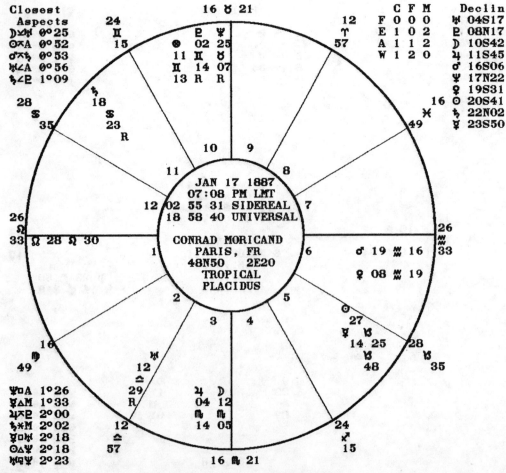

Closest Aspects
☽☌♅	0°25
☉⚹A	0°52
♂☍♄	0°53
♅∠A	0°56
♄∠♇	1°09

C F M		Declin
F 0 0 0	♅	04S17
E 1 0 2	♇	08N17
A 1 1 2	☽	10S42
W 1 2 0	♃	11S45
	♂	16S06
	♆	17N22
	♀	19S31
	☉	20S41
	♄	22N02
	☿	23S50

JAN 17 1887
07:08 PM LMT
02 55 31 SIDEREAL
18 58 40 UNIVERSAL

CONRAD MORICAND
PARIS, FR
48N50 2E20
TROPICAL
PLACIDUS

♆□A	1°26
☿△M	1°33
♃□♇	2°00
♄⚹M	2°02
☿□♅	2°18
☉△♆	2°18
♅□♀	2°23

MORICAND, CONRAD
Opportunist

January 17, 1887
7:08 PM LMT
Paris, France
2 E 20   48 N 50

Astrologer friend of Aleister Crowley. Became acquainted with Henry Miller in Paris, 1936. A scholar, pornographer, occultist, who "had an answer for everything." A wretch and a scoundrel according to Miller, who wrote his story in *A Devil in Paradise*. (1887-1954)

B: Holliday from the Miller biography.

SVP=✳ 6°50'21"
JULIAN DAY=2410289.29074

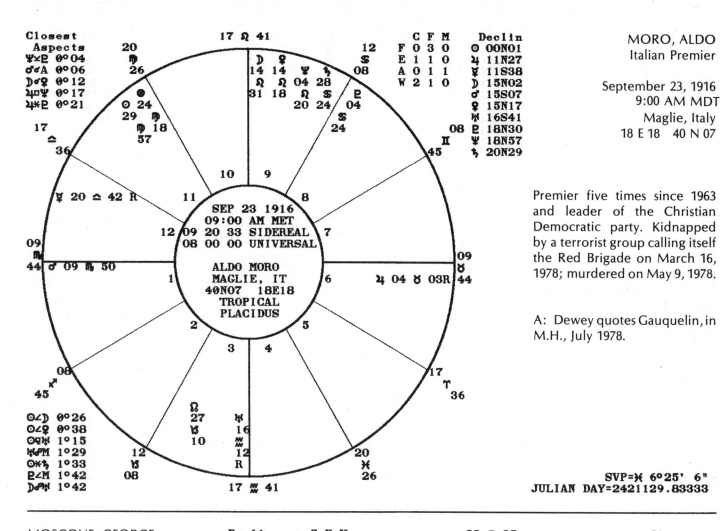

MORO, ALDO
Italian Premier

September 23, 1916
9:00 AM MDT
Maglie, Italy
18 E 18 40 N 07

Premier five times since 1963 and leader of the Christian Democratic party. Kidnapped by a terrorist group calling itself the Red Brigade on March 16, 1978; murdered on May 9, 1978.

A: Dewey quotes Gauquelin, in M.H., July 1978.

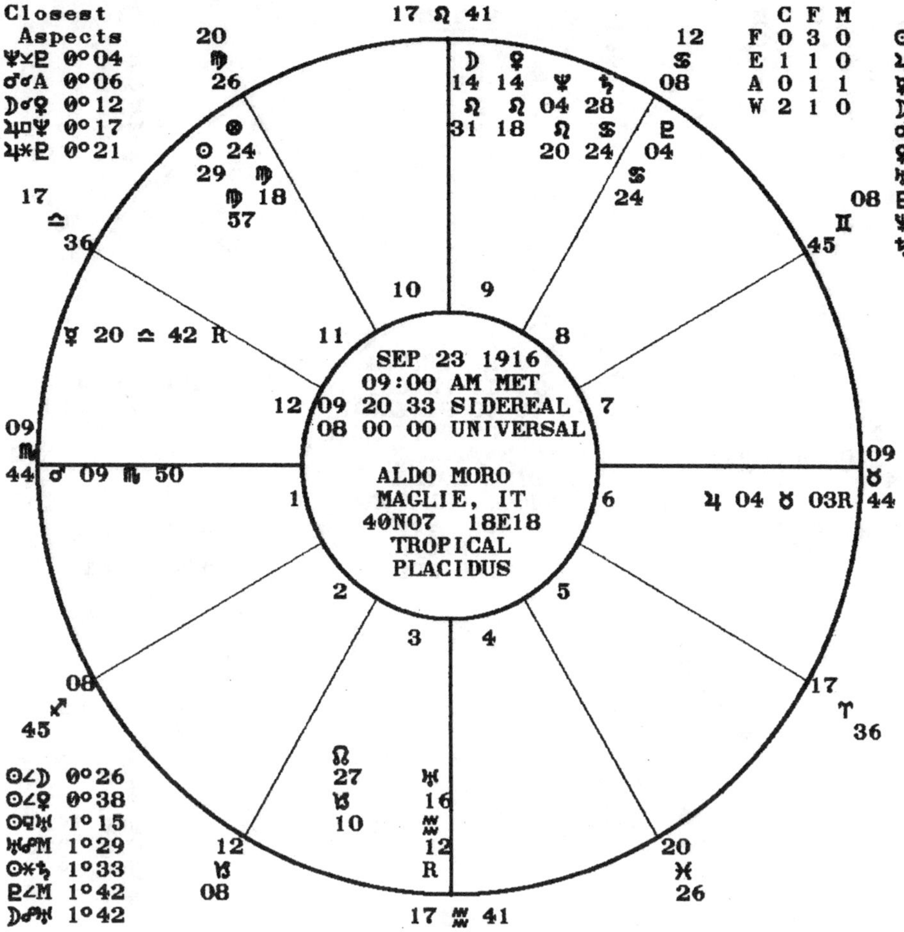
SEP 23 1916
09:00 AM MET
09 20 33 SIDEREAL
08 00 00 UNIVERSAL
ALDO MORO
MAGLIE, IT
40N07 18E18
TROPICAL
PLACIDUS

Closest Aspects
♆⊻♇ 0°04
♂☌A 0°06
☽☌♀ 0°12
♃□♆ 0°17
♃✶♇ 0°21

☉∠☽ 0°26
☉∠♀ 0°38
☉⚻♅ 1°15
♅☍M 1°29
☉✶♄ 1°33
♇∠M 1°42
☽☍♅ 1°42

	C	F	M
F	0	3	0
E	1	1	0
A	0	1	1
W	2	1	0

Declin
☉ 00N01
♃ 11N27
☿ 11S38
☽ 15N02
♂ 15S07
♀ 15N17
♅ 16S41
♇ 18N30
♆ 18N57
♄ 20N29

SVP=♓ 6°25' 6"
JULIAN DAY=2421129.83333

MOSCONE, GEORGE
Politician

November 24, 1929
4:00 AM PST
San Francisco, Ca
122 W 26 37 N 47

Mayor of San Francisco from 1975; known for his humanitarian approach to public office. Along with Supervisor Harvey Milk, shot and assassinated by a former city supervisor, Dan White, at City Hall on November 27, 1978.

A: D.C. Doane from B.C.

Declin
♅ 02N23
♆ 10N48
☽ 11N07
♀ 14S48
☿ 20S30
☉ 20S31
♂ 21S20
♃ 21N32
♇ 21N45
♄ 22S37

	C	F	M
F	1	0	4
E	0	2	0
A	1	0	0
W	1	1	0

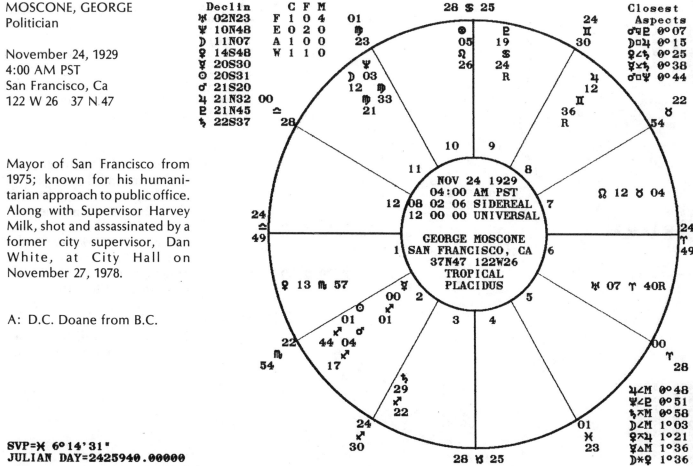

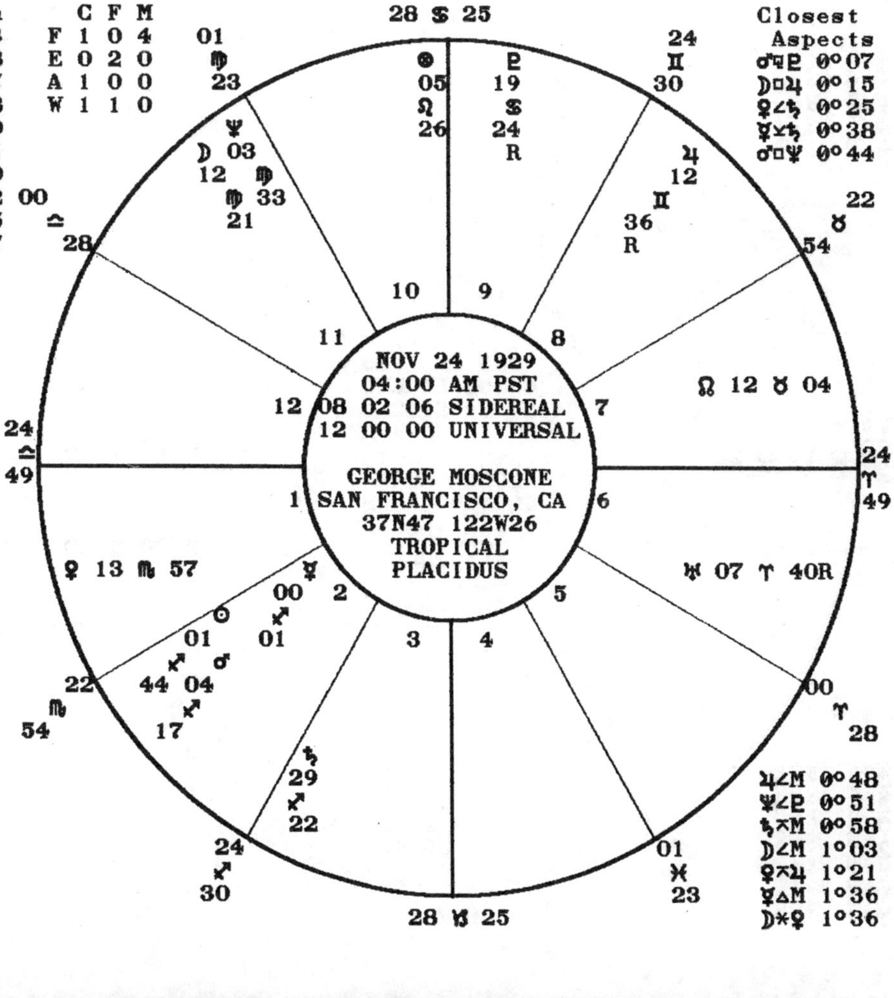
NOV 24 1929
04:00 AM PST
08 02 06 SIDEREAL
12 00 00 UNIVERSAL
GEORGE MOSCONE
SAN FRANCISCO, CA
37N47 122W26
TROPICAL
PLACIDUS

Closest Aspects
♂☌♇ 0°07
☽□♃ 0°15
♀∠♄ 0°25
☿⊻♄ 0°38
♂□♆ 0°44

♃∠M 0°48
♆∠♇ 0°51
♄⊼M 0°58
☽∠M 1°03
♀⊼♃ 1°21
☿△M 1°36
☽✶♀ 1°36

SVP=♓ 6°14'31"
JULIAN DAY=2425940.00000

MOYERS, BILL
Journalist

June 5, 1934
11:15 PM CST
Hugo, Olka
95 W 31   34 N 01

Reporter and sports editor, 1949-56; went into political service from 1959-67. Published *Newsday*, 1967-70; Editor-in-chief of *Bill Moyer's Journal* from 1970. Three Emmy awards for outstanding broadcasting; author of *Listening to America: A Traveler Rediscovers His Country* (1971).

A: CSH.

SVP=♓ 6°10'20"
JULIAN DAY=2427594.71875

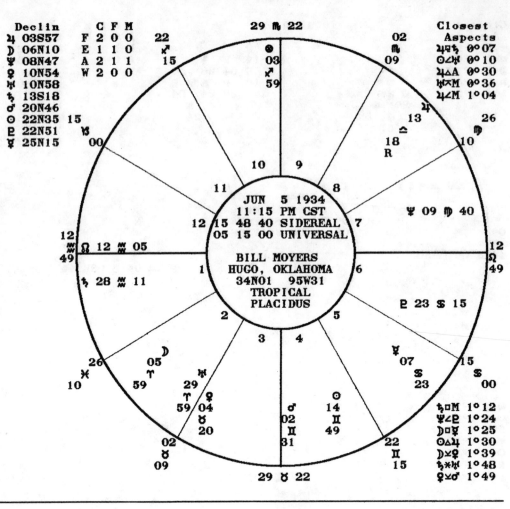

MOZART, WOLFGANG
Musician

January 27, 1756
8:00 PM LMT
Salzburg, Austria
13 E 01   47 N 48

Composer who learned to play the harpsichord at age 3; composed music at age 5. Wrote more than 50 symphonies and many other works; operas include *The Marriage of Figaro* and *Don Giovanni*. Wrote *The Magic Flute* when ill and depressed. (1756-1791)

A: Lyndoe in AA, September 1966; "authentic data recorded by his father."[101]

SVP=♓ 8°39'56"
JULIAN DAY=2362452.29718

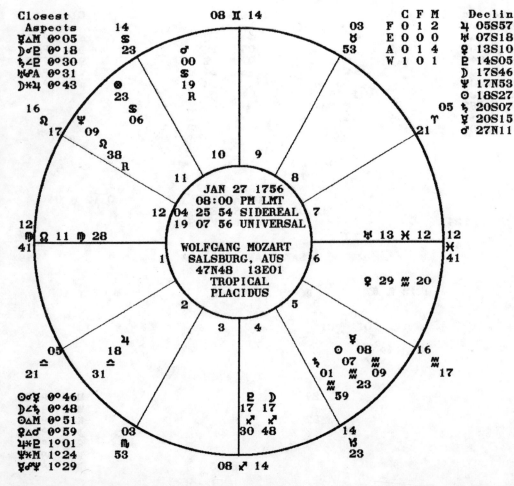

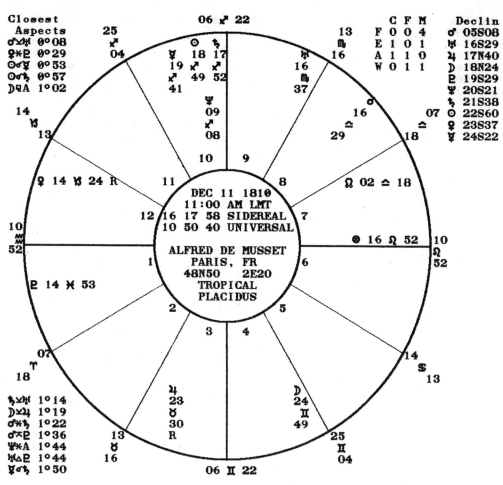

Chart 1: MUSSET, ALFRED DE

MUSSET, ALFRED DE
Writer

December 11, 1810
11:00 AM LMT
Paris, France
2 E 20   48 N 50

Closest Aspects

♂⊼♅	0°08
♀✶♇	0°29
☉♂☿	0°53
☉♂♂	0°57
☽⊼A	1°02

		C F M	Declin
	F	0 0 4	♂ 05S08
	E	1 0 1	♅ 16S29
	A	1 1 0	♃ 17N40
	W	0 1 1	☽ 18N24
			♇ 19S29
			♆ 20S21
			♄ 21S38
			☉ 22S60
			♀ 23S37
			☿ 24S22

Inner chart data:

DEC 11 1810
11:00 AM LMT
16 17 58 SIDEREAL
10 50 40 UNIVERSAL

ALFRED DE MUSSET
PARIS, FR
48N50 2E20
TROPICAL
PLACIDUS

French poet, dramatist, and novelist; remembered chiefly for his plays. Wrote his best poems in memory of his love for George Sand. Raised in an intellectual environment; wrote in a witty, poetic style, with deep character understanding. (1810-1857)

A: Gauquelin #593 Vol 6.

♄⊼♅	1°14
☽⊼♃	1°19
♂✶♄	1°22
♂⊼♇	1°36
♆✶A	1°44
♅△♇	1°44
☿♂♄	1°50

SVP=♓ 7°53'56"
JULIAN DAY=2382492.95185

Chart 2: MUSSOLINI, BENITO

MUSSOLINI, BENITO
Dictator

July 29, 1883
2:00 PM LMT
Dovia il Predappio, Italy
12 E 02   44 N 13

Declin		C F M
♅ 04N18	F	0 2 0
♇ 07N40	E	1 1 0
♆ 16N18	A	4 0 0
☉ 18N47	W	2 0 0
☽ 19N12		
♄ 19N47		
☿ 20N30		
♀ 22N07		
♂ 22N09		
♃ 22N17		

Ruler of Italy from 1922 to 1943. Led Italy to war on the side of the Germans after France fell in May 1940. Imprisoned after the Allies invaded Italy, July 1943; rescued by the Germans in September 1943, but assasinated by Italian partisans, April 28, 1945.

A: Gauquelin #1745 Vol 5.

Inner chart data:

JUL 29 1883
02:00 PM LMT
10 27 23 SIDEREAL
13 11 52 UNIVERSAL

BENITO MUSSOLINI
DOVIAIL PREDAPP, IT
44N13 12E02
TROPICAL
PLACIDUS

Closest Aspects

♅✶A	0°00
♆♂A	0°02
♅△♇	0°02
☉♂♅	0°09
☿⊼♅	0°19

☉♂☿	0°29
☿⊼M	0°32
♀✶♆	0°39
♀△A	0°41
♀✶M	0°41
♀⊾♄	1°00
☉⊼M	1°01

SVP=♓ 6°52'56"
JULIAN DAY=2409021.04991

NARCOLEPTIC FAMILY
Female

November 28, 1913
7:30 AM CST

93 W 46   38 N 22

Married woman with a family, who would become drowsy and fall asleep in any situation - the victim of a rare, hereditary disease of unknown cause. For twenty-five years, took mild "pep" pills throughout the day in order to stay awake.

A: Data submitted by Sue Stanzione to AA, May 1967.

SVP=♓ 6°27'41"
JULIAN DAY=2420100.06250

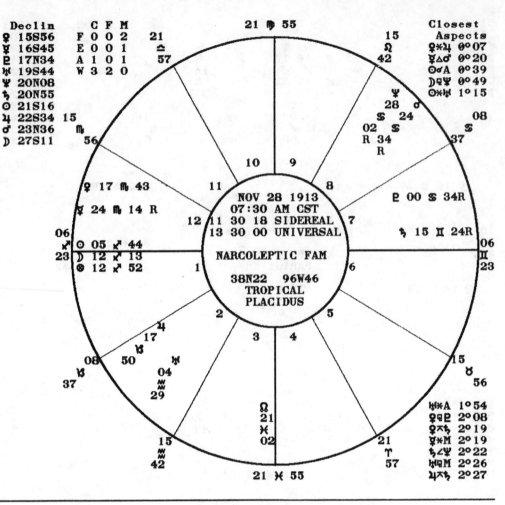

NARCOLEPTIC FAMILY
Female

August 20, 1933
4:30 AM PST
Los Angeles, Ca
118 W 15   34 N 04

Daughter of the prior woman; a more acute case than her mother. Took two "pep" pills every morning with her coffee, and perhaps another during the day. The pills prescribed by her physician; taken every day from 1951.

A: Data submitted by Sue Stanzione to AA, May 1967.

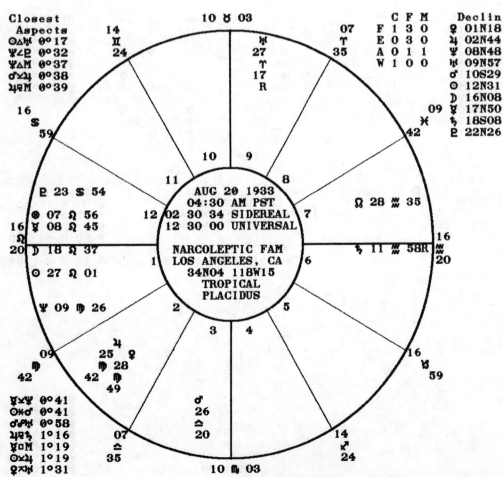

SVP=♓ 6°11' 1"
JULIAN DAY=2427305.02083

NARCOLEPTIC FAMILY
Male

January 29, 1952
3:30 PM PST

118 W 30   34 N 01

Grandson and son of the two prior women. By age 15 an obvious inheritor of the family narcolepsia. Dozes a lot during the day, not doing well in school work though he shows mechanical aptitude. Lethargic compared to his brothers and sisters.

A: Data submitted by Sue Stanzione to AA, May 1967.

Closest Aspects
♀□M 0°28
☽⚻♇ 0°31
☽⚻♆ 0°34
♃□♅ 0°51
☉✶♃ 0°60

	C	F	M
F	1	1	0
E	0	0	2
A	0	2	1
W	1	1	1

Declin
☽ 01S50
♃ 02N53
♄ 03S33
♆ 06S55
♂ 11S12
☉ 18S00
♀ 22S12
☿ 22S39
♇ 23N18
♅ 23N23

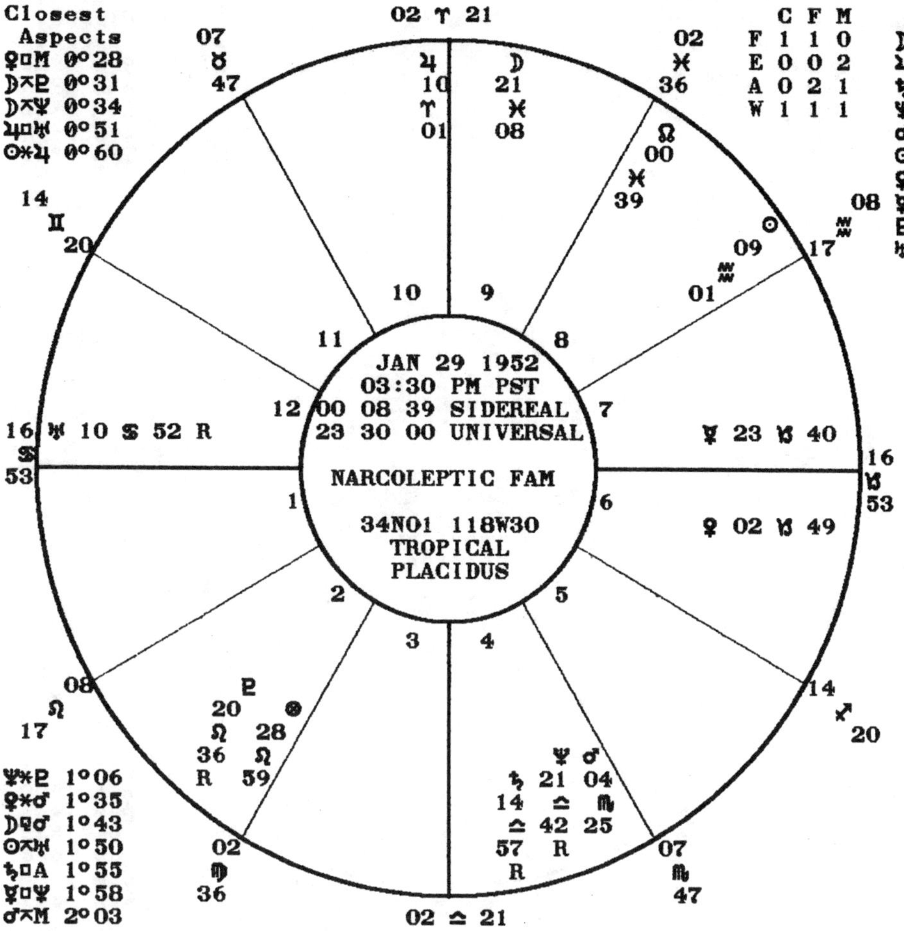

JAN 29 1952
03:30 PM PST
00 08 39 SIDEREAL
23 30 00 UNIVERSAL
NARCOLEPTIC FAM
34N01 118W30
TROPICAL
PLACIDUS
♅ 10 ♋ 52 R
☿ 23 ♑ 40
♀ 02 ♑ 49
02 ♈ 21
02 ♎ 21

♆✶♇ 1°06
♀✶♂ 1°35
☽⚼♂ 1°43
☉⚻♅ 1°50
♄□A 1°55
☿□♆ 1°58
♂⚻M 2°03

SVP=♓ 5°55'35"
JULIAN DAY=2434041.47917

NARCOLEPTIC
Tillie Shawn

May 27, 1901
9:28 PM LMT

97 W 10   49 N 47

Narcolepsia first appeared at age 30, when she would inadvertently fall asleep, regardless of place or situation. Uninjured, but totally wrecked her car on November 11, 1940. While serving as a W.A.C. during World War II, took benzedrine to stay awake.

A: D.C. Doane in AA, May 1966, recorded.

Declin
☽ 06S50
♂ 10N22
♇ 13N48
☉ 21N20
♄ 22S02
♆ 22N17
♀ 22N36
♅ 22S39
♃ 22S48
☿ 25N09

	C	F	M
F	0	0	1
E	0	1	2
A	5	1	0
W	0	0	0

Closest Aspects
♄⚺♅ 0°19
☉□♂ 0°21
♀⚼M 0°42
♆△M 0°58
♅∠M 1°14

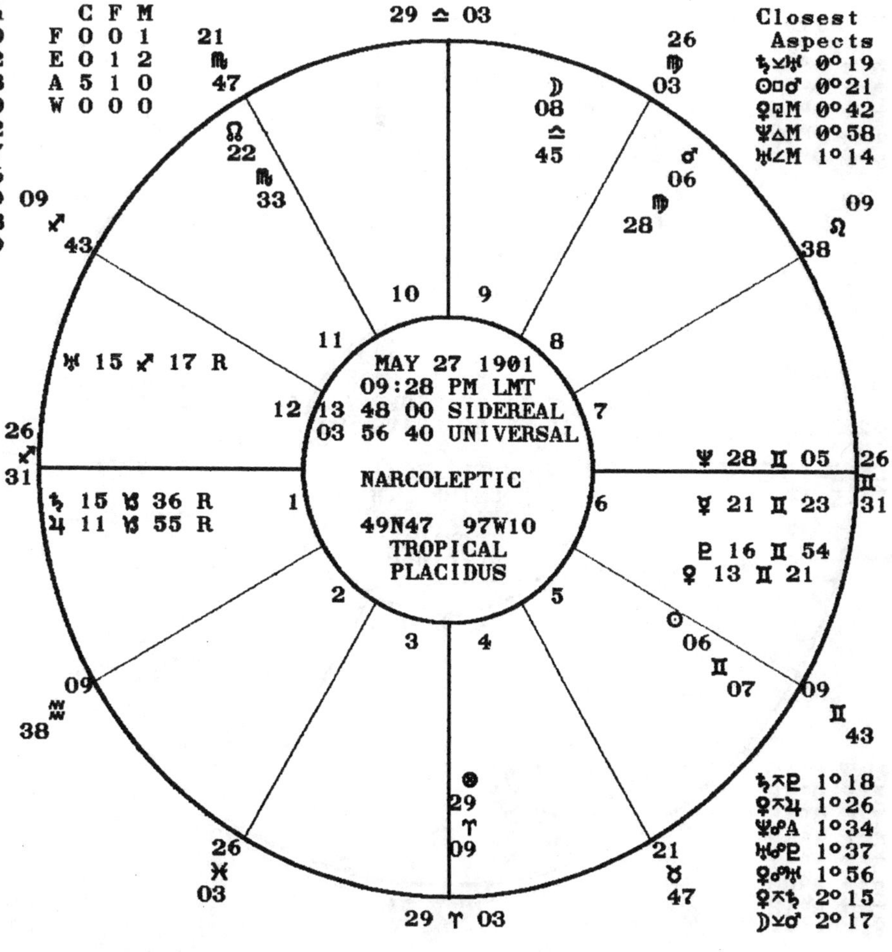

MAY 27 1901
09:28 PM LMT
13 48 00 SIDEREAL
03 56 40 UNIVERSAL
NARCOLEPTIC
49N47 97W10
TROPICAL
PLACIDUS
♅ 15 ♐ 17 R
♄ 15 ♑ 36 R
♃ 11 ♑ 55 R
♆ 28 ♊ 05
☿ 21 ♊ 23
♇ 16 ♊ 54
♀ 13 ♊ 21
29 ♎ 03
29 ♈ 03

♄⚻♇ 1°18
♀⚻♃ 1°26
♆☍A 1°34
♅☍♇ 1°37
♀☍♅ 1°56
♀⚻♄ 2°15
☽⚺♂ 2°17

SVP=♓ 6°37'58"
JULIAN DAY=2415532.66435

NASH, GRAHAM
Musician

February 2, 1942
1:50 AM DBST
Blackpool, England
3 W 00   53 N 50

British rocker imported by Mama Cass Elliott, who met and teamed up with David Crosby and Stephen Stills to form the West Coast sound of Crosby, Stills and Nash. They signed a seven-million-dollar, seven-album studio contract in 1977, reunited after a two-year separation, recording all their own music.

A: From him to Linda Clark.

SVP=Ж 6° 5'39"
JULIAN DAY=2429661.49306

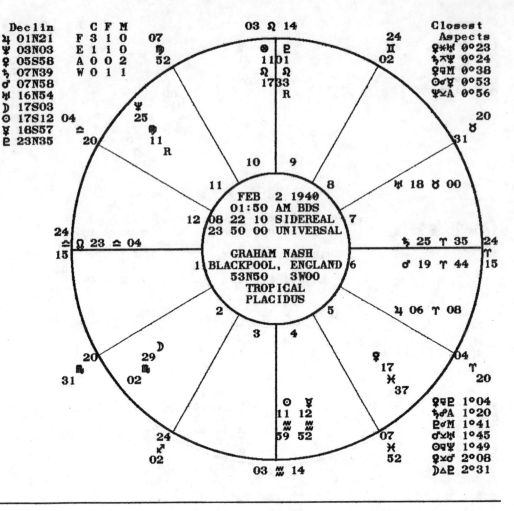

NESMITH, MICHAEL
Musician

December 30, 1942
11:59 AM CWT
Houston, Texas
95 W 22   29 N 46

Member of a rock-group called *The Monkees* who had their own TV series for a while, patterned on the irreverent humor and style of The Beatles. Later formed his own group called Mike Nesmith And The Second National Band; had a hit song, "Joann".

A: CSH.

SVP=Ж 6° 3'30"
JULIAN DAY=2430724.20764

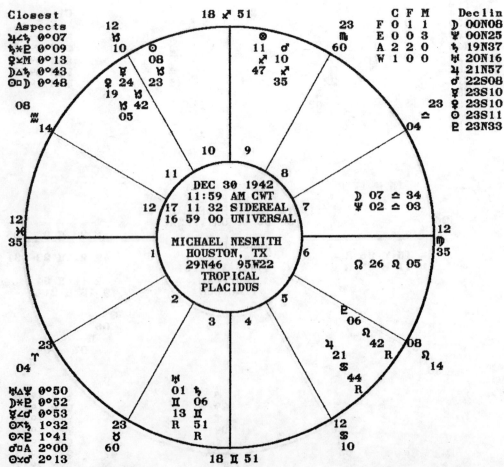

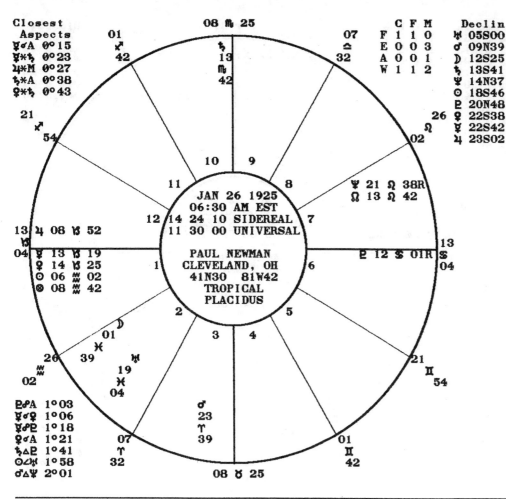

NEWMAN, PAUL
Actor

January 26, 1925
6:30 AM EST
Cleveland, Ohio
81 W 42   41 N 30

Paul Newman Chart

Closest Aspects:
☿♂A 0°15
☿✳♄ 0°23
♃✳M 0°27
♄✳A 0°38
♀✳♄ 0°43

♇♂A 1°03
☿♂♀ 1°06
☿♂♇ 1°18
♀♂A 1°21
♄△♇ 1°41
☉∠♅ 1°58
♂△♆ 2°01

	C	F	M
F	1	1	0
E	0	0	3
A	0	0	1
W	1	1	2

Declin
♅ 05S00
♂ 09N39
☽ 12S25
♄ 13S41
♆ 14N37
☉ 18S46
♇ 20N48
♀ 22S38
☿ 22S42
♃ 23S02

Center:
JAN 26 1925
06:30 AM EST
14 24 10 SIDEREAL
11 30 00 UNIVERSAL

PAUL NEWMAN
CLEVELAND, OH
41N30 81W42
TROPICAL
PLACIDUS

His first picture, *The Silver Chalice*, was dreadful; but talent developed with *Long Hot Summer*, *The Hustler*, *Hud*, and more; reached the $1 million a picture class. Began to produce and direct in the late 60s. Politically involved. Two marriages; three children each.

A: CSH.[102]

SVP=♓ 6°18'33"
JULIAN DAY=2424176.97917

NICHOLS, BEVERLY
Writer

September 9, 1899
6:30 PM GMT
Bristol, England
2 W 40   51 N 25

Beverly Nichols Chart

Declin
☉ 05N12
♀ 07N12
♂ 08S37
☿ 12N28
♃ 13S08
♇ 13N10
☽ 17S57
♅ 20S56
♄ 21S37
♆ 22N09

	C	F	M
F	0	1	2
E	0	2	0
A	2	1	0
W	0	2	0

Center:
SEP 9 1899
06:30 PM GMT
17 33 40 SIDEREAL
18 30 00 UNIVERSAL

BEVERLY NICHOLS
BRISTOL, ENG
51N25 2W40
TROPICAL
PLACIDUS

Closest Aspects:
☽∠M 0°02
☉□♇ 0°08
☉□♄ 0°32
♀♂A 0°35
♄♂♇ 0°40

♃∠M 1°26
☽♂♃ 1°28
♂✳M 1°36
♀□♇ 1°38
☉♂♀ 1°46
♇□A 2°14
♀□♄ 2°19

Wrote a horror tale of the brutal nightmare of his early life and his hatred of his father, a sadistic alcoholic, in *Father Figure* - a far cry from his gardening books, stories about cats, and tales of quiet life for which he's well known.

B: Holliday from *Father Figure*, 1972.

SVP=♓ 6°39'20"
JULIAN DAY=2414907.27083

NICHOLSON, JACK
Actor

April 22, 1937
11:00 AM EST
Neptune, N.J.
74 W 01   40 N 13

Arrived in Hollywood in 1954; worked at MGM before going on-camera. Oscar nominee for *Easy Rider*, after which he gave up LSD when he woke up one morning in a tree. Other films include *Five Easy Pieces, Carnal Knowledge*, and the award winning *One Flew Over the Cuckoo's Nest.''*

A: From him to Mark Johnson.

SVP=✶ 6° 7'51"
JULIAN DAY=2428646.16667

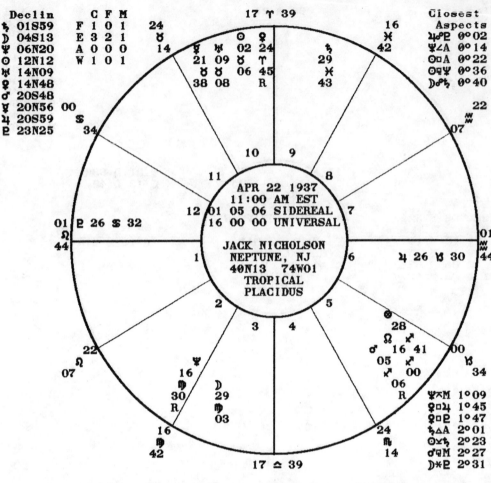

Declin					Closest Aspects		
♄ 01S59	F 1 0 1				♃☌♇	0°02
☽ 04S13	E 3 2 1				♆∠A	0°14
♆ 06N20	A 0 0 0				☉□♆	0°22
☉ 12N12	W 1 0 1				☽□♄	0°40
♅ 14N09						
♀ 14N48						
♂ 20S48						
☿ 20N56						
♃ 20S59						
♇ 23N25						

♆⊼M	1°09
♀□♃	1°45
♀□♇	1°47
♄△A	2°01
☉⊼♃	2°23
♂□M	2°27
☽✶♇	2°31

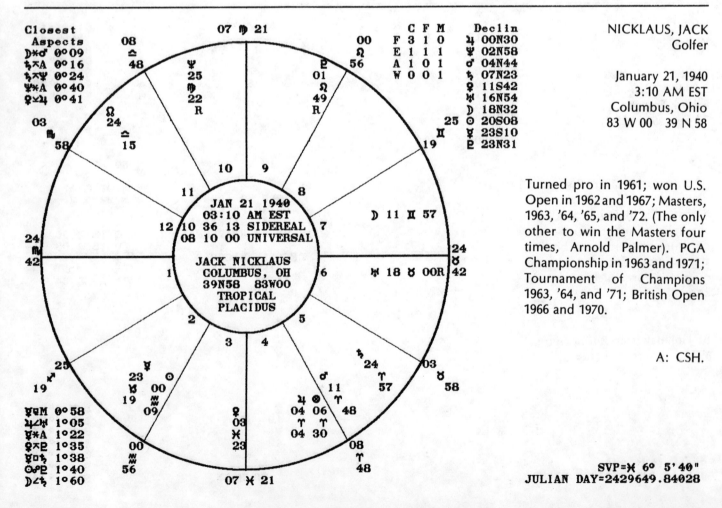

Closest Aspects	
☽✶♂	0°09
♄⊼A	0°16
♄⊼♆	0°24
♆✶A	0°40
♀∠♃	0°41

C F M	Declin	
F 3 1 0	♃ 00N30	
E 1 1 1	♆ 02N58	
A 1 0 1	♂ 04N44	
W 0 0 1	♄ 07N23	
	♀ 11S42	
	♅ 16N54	
	☽ 18N32	
	☉ 20S08	
	☿ 23S10	
	♇ 23N31	

☿⊼M	0°58
♃□♅	1°05
☿✶A	1°22
♀□♃	1°35
♀□♄	1°38
☉✶♇	1°40
☽∠♄	1°60

NICKLAUS, JACK
Golfer

January 21, 1940
3:10 AM EST
Columbus, Ohio
83 W 00   39 N 58

Turned pro in 1961; won U.S. Open in 1962 and 1967; Masters, 1963, '64, '65, and '72. (The only other to win the Masters four times, Arnold Palmer). PGA Championship in 1963 and 1971; Tournament of Champions 1963, '64, and '71; British Open 1966 and 1970.

A: CSH.

SVP=✶ 6° 5'40"
JULIAN DAY=2429649.84028

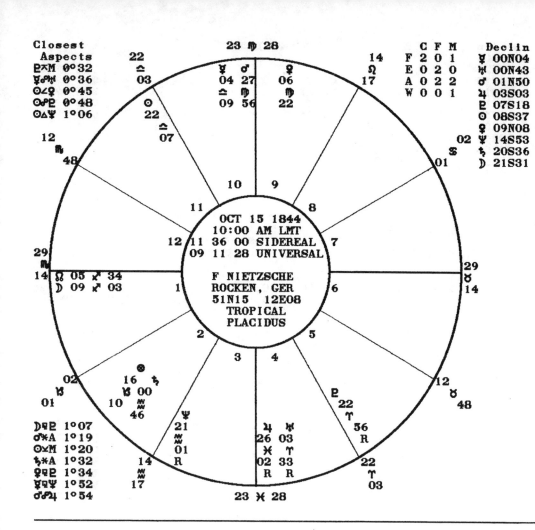

NIETZSCHE, FRIEDRICH
Philosopher

October 15, 1844
10:00 AM LMT
Rocken, Germany
12 E 08   51 N 15

The most influential German philosopher since Kant and Hegel. Taught classes until 1879; spent the next ten years in loneliness, writing his major works, including *Thus Spake Zarathustra*, and *Twilight of the Gods*. Became insane in 1889; died the following year.

B: *Constellations*, 1977, stated in *The Young Nietzsche*, according to M.A., November 1914, p. 522, quoted by Lockhart.[103]

SVP=♓ 7°25'21"
JULIAN DAY=2394854.88296

Closest Aspects
♇⚹M	0°32
☿⚹♅	0°36
☉∠♀	0°45
☉⚹♇	0°48
☉△♆	1°06
☽⚹♇	1°07
♂⚹A	1°19
☉⚹M	1°20
♄⚹A	1°32
♀⚹♇	1°34
☿⚹♆	1°52
♂☍♃	1°54

Chart center:
OCT 15 1844
10:00 AM LMT
11 36 00 SIDEREAL
09 11 28 UNIVERSAL
F NIETZSCHE
ROCKEN, GER
51N15 12E08
TROPICAL
PLACIDUS

Declin
♅	00N04
♆	00N43
♂	01N50
♃	03S03
♇	07S18
☉	08S37
♀	09N08
♆	14S53
♄	20S36
☽	21S31

C F M
F 2 0 1
E 0 2 0
A 0 2 2
W 0 0 1

NOBILE, UMBERTO
Explorer

January 21, 1885
3:15 PM LMT
Lauro, Italy
14 E 37   40 N 52

General in the Italian Air Force and Arctic explorer. First expedition in 1926. Crashed in his polar dirigible *The Italia* in 1928; was held responsible and forced to resign. In 1945 Italy restored his rank. In 1946 elected to parliament.

A: Gauquelin #3089 Vol 3.

SVP=♓ 6°51'49"
JULIAN DAY=2409563.09481

Declin
♅	00S26
☽	01N03
♇	07N34
♃	11N02
♆	16N12
♂	19S42
☉	19S46
☿	21S21
♄	21N32
♀	22S52

C F M
F 1 0 0
E 1 1 2
A 2 1 2
W 0 0 0

Chart center:
JAN 21 1885
03:15 PM LMT
23 19 26 SIDEREAL
14 16 32 UNIVERSAL
UMBERTO NOBILE
LAURO, IT
40N52 14E37
TROPICAL
PLACIDUS

Closest Aspects
♀⚹♂	0°10
☉⚹☽	0°13
♀⚹♆	0°47
♄□M	1°03
☉△♅	1°03
☿⚹♂	1°08
☉⚹♄	1°08
☽⚹♅	1°16
☿⚹♀	1°18
☽⚹♇	1°18
♃⚹♅	1°28
☉△♇	1°31

NORTH, JAY WAVERLY
Child actor

August 3, 1951
9:36 AM PDT
Los Angeles, Ca
118 W 15   34 N 04

TV commercials from age 6. Cast in the lead role of the character based on the comic strip, *Dennis the Menace*, a TV series which ran for five years during which he aged from 7 to 12. Starred in a film *Maya* (1965), which later became a TV series.

A: CL from B.C.

SVP=✶ 5°56' 2"
JULIAN DAY=2433862.19167

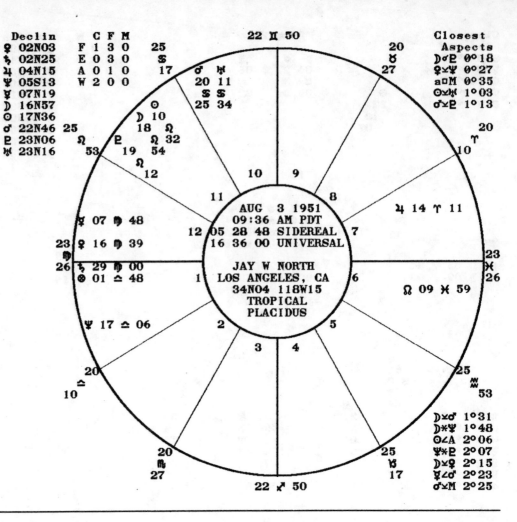

Declin		C	F	M	
♀ 02N03		F	1	3	0	25
♀ 02N25		E	0	3	0	
♃ 04N15		A	0	1	0	17
♆ 05S13		W	2	0	0	
☿ 07N19						
☽ 16N57						
☉ 17N36						
♂ 22N46	25					
♇ 23N06						
♅ 23N16						

Closest Aspects

☽☌♇ 0°18
♀☌♆ 0°27
a□M 0°35
☉✶♅ 1°03
♂✶♇ 1°13

☽✶♂ 1°31
☽✶♆ 1°48
☉∠A 2°06
♆✶♇ 2°07
☽∠♀ 2°15
☿∠♂ 2°23
♂✶M 2°25

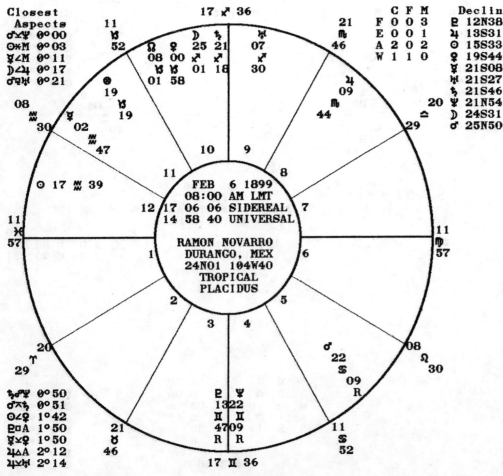

Closest Aspects

♂✶♆ 0°00
☉✶M 0°03
☿∠M 0°11
☽∠♃ 0°17
♂☌♅ 0°21

♄∠♆ 0°50
♂✶♄ 0°51
☉∠♀ 1°42
♇☌A 1°50
☿✶♀ 1°50
♃△A 2°12
♃✶♅ 2°14

	C	F	M	Declin
	F	0	0	3	♇ 12N38
	E	0	0	1	♃ 13S31
	A	2	0	2	☉ 15S33
	W	1	1	0	♀ 19S44
					☿ 21S08
					♅ 21S27
					♄ 21S46
					♆ 21N54
					☽ 24S31
					♂ 25N50

NOVARRO, RAMON
Actor

February 6, 1899
8:00 AM LMT
Durango, Mexico
104 W 40   24 N 01

Mexican-born star of silent films who won wide acclaim in dashing roles in *The Prisoner of Zenda* and *Ben Hur*. Co-starred with Garbo in *Mata Hari* (1932); made several other films in the early days of sound. Murdered by a homosexual lover, October 30, 1968.

A: McEvers quotes AFA, September 1968, "data from him."[104]

SVP=✶ 6°39'48"
JULIAN DAY=2414692.12407

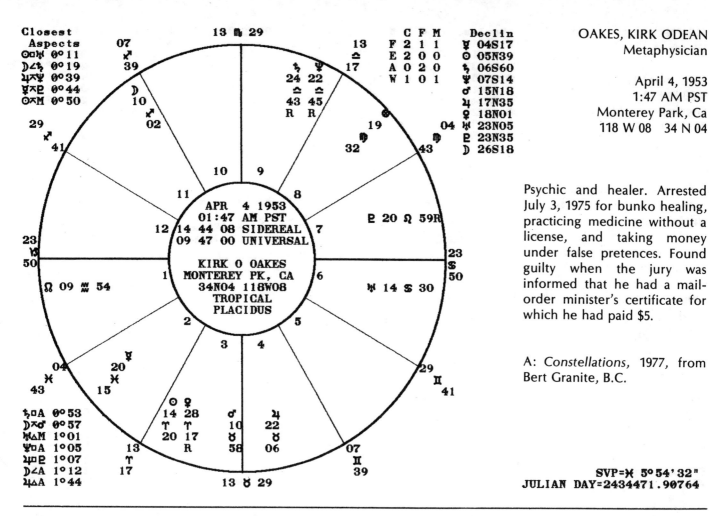

OAKES, KIRK ODEAN
Metaphysician

April 4, 1953
1:47 AM PST
Monterey Park, Ca
118 W 08   34 N 04

Psychic and healer. Arrested July 3, 1975 for bunko healing, practicing medicine without a license, and taking money under false pretences. Found guilty when the jury was informed that he had a mail-order minister's certificate for which he had paid $5.

A: *Constellations*, 1977, from Bert Granite, B.C.

SVP=♓ 5° 54' 32"
JULIAN DAY=2434471.90764

ODETS, CLIFFORD
Writer

July 18, 1906
1:00 PM EST
Philadelphia, Pa
75 W 10   39 N 57

Playwright whose Broadway productions include *Awake and Sing* (1935), *Golden Boy* (1937), (which ran for 250 performances), and *Clash by Night* (1942). Films include *None But The Lonely Heart* (1944). Described as sincere; a hard worker, with nice manners. (1906-1963)

A: McEvers quotes Holmes in AA, July 1957, "a client of mine in 1942."[105]

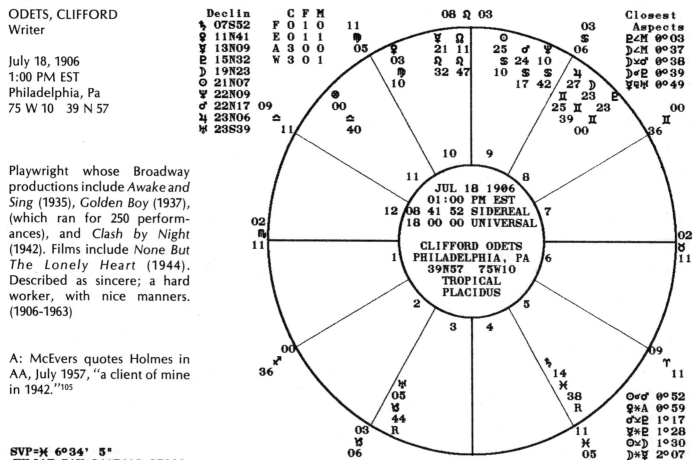

SVP=♓ 6° 34' 5"
JULIAN DAY=2417410.25000

O'HENRY
Writer

September 11, 1862
9:00 PM LMT
Greensboro, N.C.
79 W 48   36 N 04

William Sydney Porter, one of America's favorite short story writers. Indicted for embezzlement of bank funds; entered penitentiary at Columbus, Ohio, where he spent three years writing to earn money to support his daughter. (1862-1910)

A: Craswell states, "recorded in the family Bible."

SVP=✕ 7°10'19"
JULIAN DAY=2401395.59667

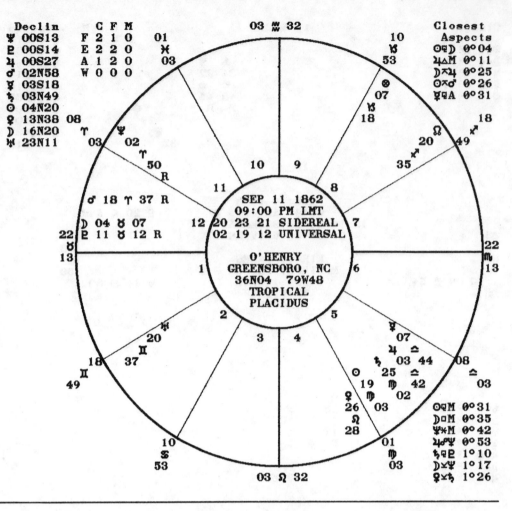

Declin	C F M	Closest Aspects
♆ 00S13	F 2 1 0	⊙⚹☽ 0°04
♇ 00S14	E 2 2 0	♃△♃ 0°11
♃ 00S27	A 1 2 0	☽⚺♃ 0°25
♂ 02N58	W 0 0 0	⊙☌♂ 0°26
☿ 03S18		♀♇A 0°31
♄ 03N49		
♅ 04N20		
♀ 13N38		
☽ 16N20		
♅ 23N11		

⊙⚹M 0°31
☽⚺M 0°35
♆⚹M 0°42
♃⚼♆ 0°53
♄⚼♇ 1°10
☽⚹♆ 1°17
♀⚹♄ 1°26

SEP 11 1862
09:00 PM LMT
20 23 21 SIDEREAL
02 19 12 UNIVERSAL
O'HENRY
GREENSBORO, NC
36N04 79W48
TROPICAL
PLACIDUS

OLIVIER, SIR LAWRENCE
Actor

May 22, 1907
5:00 AM GMT
Dorking, England
0 W 20   51 N 14

Won Oscar as best actor in *Hamlet* (1948), which he also produced and directed. Scored an impressive eleven award nominations for outstanding films, as well as a TV Emmy for *The Moon and Sixpence* (1970). Broadway debut, 1929. Knighted by King George V in 1947.

B: Holliday from *Lawrence Olivier* by John Cottrel, 1975.

SVP=✕ 6°33'27"
JULIAN DAY=2417717.70833

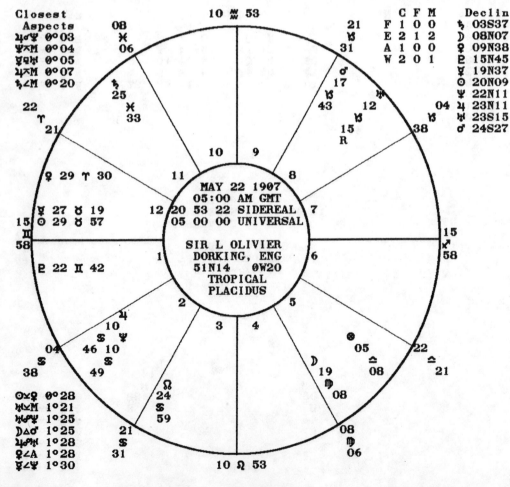

Closest Aspects		C F M	Declin
♃☌♆ 0°03		F 1 0 0	♄ 03S37
♆⚺M 0°04		E 2 1 2	☽ 08N07
☿⚼♅ 0°05		A 1 0 0	♀ 09N38
♃⚼M 0°07		W 2 0 1	♇ 15N45
♄∠M 0°20			☿ 19N37
			⊙ 20N09
			♆ 22N11
			♃ 23N11
			♅ 23S15
			♂ 24S27

⊙⚺♀ 0°28
♅⚼M 1°21
♅⚼♆ 1°25
☽△♂ 1°25
♃⚼♅ 1°28
♀∠A 1°28
☿∠♆ 1°30

MAY 22 1907
05:00 AM GMT
20 53 22 SIDEREAL
05 00 00 UNIVERSAL
SIR L OLIVIER
DORKING, ENG
51N14 0W20
TROPICAL
PLACIDUS

O'NEAL, RYAN
Actor

April 20, 1941
9:34 AM PST
Los Angeles, Ca
118 W 15   34 N 04

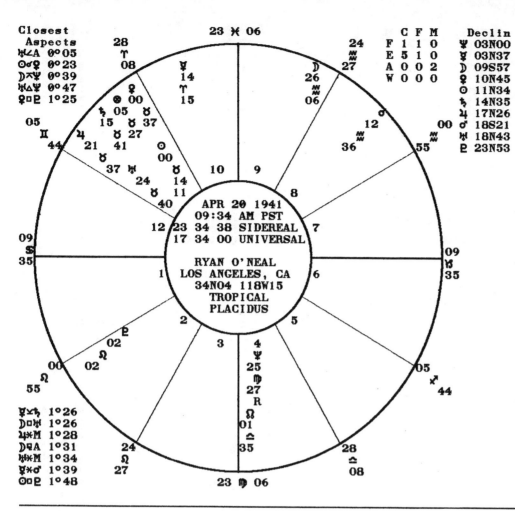

Closest Aspects

♅∠A	0°05	
☉♂♀	0°23	
☽⚹♆	0°39	
♅△♆	0°47	
♀⚼♇	1°25	

☿⚹♄	1°26	
☽□♅	1°26	
♃⚹M	1°28	
☽⚼A	1°31	
♅⚹M	1°34	
☿⚹♂	1°39	
☉□♇	1°48	

Declin

♆	03N00
☿	03N37
☽	09S57
♀	10N45
☉	11N34
♄	14N35
♃	17N26
♂	18S21
♅	18N43
♇	23N53

	C	F	M
F	1	1	0
E	5	1	0
A	0	0	2
W	0	0	0

APR 20 1941
09:34 AM PST
23 34 38 SIDEREAL
17 34 00 UNIVERSAL

RYAN O'NEAL
LOS ANGELES, CA
34N04 118W15
TROPICAL
PLACIDUS

First job in films as a stunt man. Cast in TV series *Peyton Place*; married co-player Leigh Taylor-Young; one son; two children from his former marriage to Joanna Moore. Appeared in many TV series; nominated for Oscar as best actor in the film *Love Story* (1970).

A: Holliday from B.C.

SVP=♓ 6° 4'47"
JULIAN DAY=2430105.23194

O'NEILL, JOHN J.
Writer

June 21, 1889
8:15 AM EST
New York, N.Y.
73 W 57   40 N 45

Reporter from 1907; science editor of the New York *Tribune* from 1934 until his death in 1953. Winner of the Pulitzer prize for journalism in 1937. His books include *Enter Atomic Energy* (1940) and *Prodigal Genius: The Life of Nikola Tesla* (1944).

A: Tobey in Dell, March 1960, "from him."

Declin

☽	01N01
♅	06S26
♇	09N46
♀	13N37
♄	16N46
♆	19N13
☿	19N12
♃	23S13
☉	23N27
♂	24N10

	C	F	M
F	1	1	0
E	1	0	1
A	4	1	0
W	1	0	0

JUN 21 1889
08:15 AM EST
02 18 54 SIDEREAL
13 15 00 UNIVERSAL

JOHN J O'NEILL
NEW YORK, NY
40N45 73W57
TROPICAL
PLACIDUS

Closest Aspects

♅□♆	0°12	
♀□A	0°15	
♄⚹♅	0°41	
♄♂A	0°42	
♃⚼♆	0°43	

☉♂♂	0°57	
☉⚼☿	0°57	
♀□♄	0°58	
♇⚹M	1°04	
☉∠A	1°12	
☽⚹♀	1°18	
♅⚹A	1°24	

SVP=♓ 6°48'28"
JULIAN DAY=2411175.05208

PAAR, JACK
TV Host

May 1, 1917
11:55 PM CST
Canton, Ohio
81 W 23   40 N 48

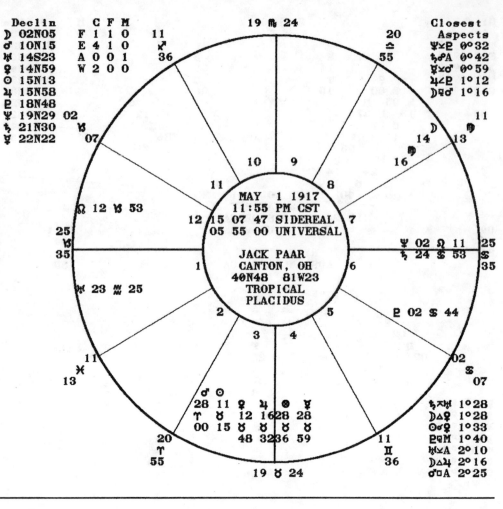

Declin
☽ 02N05
♂ 10N15
♅ 14S23
♀ 14N59
☉ 15N13
♃ 15N58
♇ 18N48
♆ 19N29
♄ 21N30
☿ 22N22

C F M
F 1 1 0
E 4 1 0
A 0 0 1
W 2 0 0

Closest
Aspects
♆⊻♇ 0°32
♄♂A 0°42
☿♂♂ 0°59
♃∠♇ 1°12
☽♂♂ 1°16

Comedian; singer; TV interviewer on his own series, *The
Tonight Show,* 1957, for which
he was nominated for the TV
Emmy. Host of *The Jack Paar
Show,* 1958-59. First broadcast
with a man-on-the-street
program. Married, 1943; one
daughter.

A: CSH.

SVP=♓ 6°24'35"
JULIAN DAY=2421350.74653

PACKARD, VANCE
Writer

May 22, 1914
5:30 AM EST
Granville, Pa
77 W 38   40 N 33

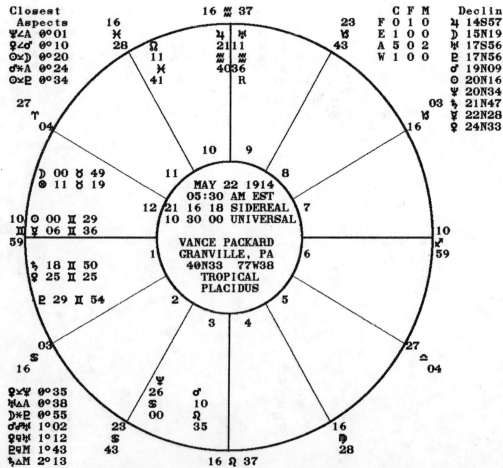

Closest
Aspects
♆∠A 0°01
♀∠♂ 0°10
☉⊻☽ 0°20
♂✶A 0°24
☉⊻♇ 0°34

C F M
F 0 1 0
E 1 0 0
A 5 0 2
W 1 0 0

Declin
♃ 14S57
☽ 15N19
♅ 17S56
♇ 17N56
♂ 19N09
☉ 20N16
♆ 20N34
♄ 21N47
☿ 22N28
♀ 24N33

Peripatetic career as writer-
journalist, magazine staff
member. First smash book *The
Hidden Persuaders* (1957),
followed by *Status Seekers* and
The Sexual Wilderness, and
more. Often ahead of the
scientists in diagnosis. Married
1938; three children.

A: CSH.

SVP=♓ 6°27'14"
JULIAN DAY=2420274.93750

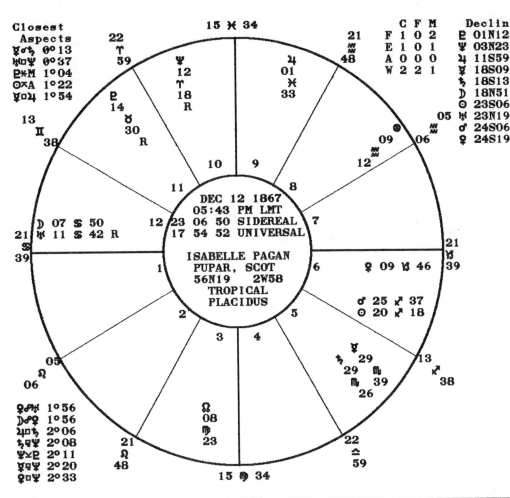

PAGAN, ISABELLE
Writer, astrologer

December 12, 1867
5:43 PM LMT
Pupar, Fife, Scotland
2 W 58   56 N 19

Closest
Aspects
☿σ♂ 0°13
♅□♇ 0°37
♇⚹M 1°04
☉⚹A 1°22
☿□♃ 1°54

	C	F	M		Declin
F	1	0	2	♇	01N12
E	1	0	1	♆	03N23
A	0	0	0	♃	11S59
W	2	2	1	♅	18S09
				♄	18S13
				☽	18N51
				☉	23S06
				♅	23N19
				♂	24S06
				♀	24S19

DEC 12 1867
05:43 PM LMT
23 06 50 SIDEREAL
17 54 52 UNIVERSAL

ISABELLE PAGAN
PUPAR, SCOT
56N19   2W58
TROPICAL
PLACIDUS

♀σ♅ 1°56
☽σ♀ 1°56
♃□♄ 2°06
♄σ♆ 2°08
♆⚹♇ 2°11
☿σ♆ 2°20
♀σ♆ 2°33

Astrological books include
From Pioneer to Poet (1911);
lectured on the subject in
different countries under the
auspices of the Theosophical
Society. Member of the
Edinburgh branch of the
Scottish Society for the
Speaking of Verse. (1867-1960)

A: Eshelman, data given in AA,
October 1964.

SVP=♓ 7° 6'19"
JULIAN DAY=2403313.24644

PASTEUR, LOUIS
Scientist

December 27, 1822
2:00 AM LMT
Dole, Jura, France
5 E 30   47 N 08

	Declin		C	F	M
♄	10N16	F	0	0	0
♇	15S25	E	2	0	6
♃	18N47	A	1	0	0
♂	22S20	W	0	0	1
♆	22S23				
☉	23S22				
♅	23S34				
♀	23S52				
☿	24S47				
☽	26N50				

DEC 27 1822
02:00 AM LMT
08 19 55 SIDEREAL
01 38 00 UNIVERSAL

LOUIS PASTEUR
DOLE, FR
47N08   5E30
TROPICAL
PLACIDUS

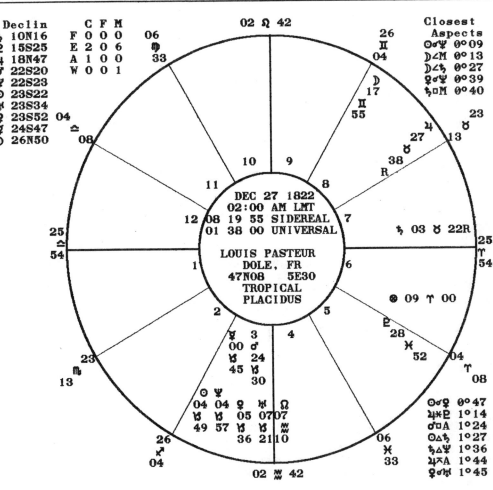

French biochemist and
bacteriologist. Founder of
preventative medicine: proved
germ theory of disease.
Professor of geology, physics,
and chemistry. Discovered the
bacteria causing anthrax;
developed a method of
innoculation ; developed the
process of pasteurization. (1822-
1895)

A: Gauquelin #555 Vol 2.

Closest
Aspects
☉σ♆ 0°09
☽∠M 0°13
☽∠♄ 0°27
♀σ♆ 0°39
♄□M 0°40

☉σ♀ 0°47
♃⚹♇ 1°14
♂□A 1°24
☉△♄ 1°27
♄△♆ 1°36
♃⚹A 1°44
♀σ♅ 1°45

SVP=♓ 7°43'38"
JULIAN DAY=2386891.56806

PATTON, GEORGE
General

November 11, 1885
6:38 PM PST
San Marino, Ca
118 W 06   34 N 07

Army officer in command of U.S. forces in Morocco, 1942, under General Eisenhower. Tactician and practioner of mobile tank warfare in World War II. A loved and hated man; outspoken, blunt, profane, colorful, and dramatic. (1885-1945)

A: Dewey quotes data, "from family Bible."[106]

SVP=⌖ 6°51'16"
JULIAN DAY=2409857.60972

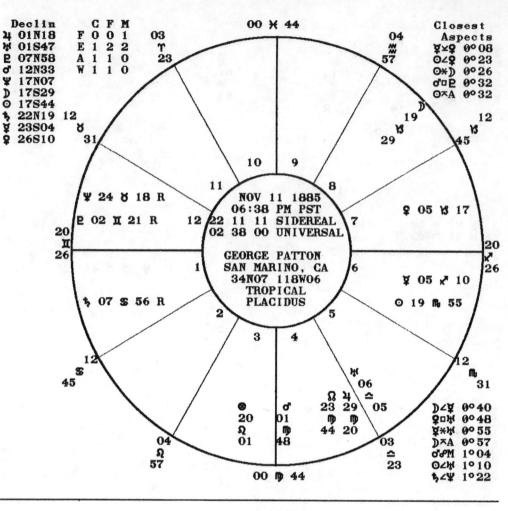

PECK, GREGORY
Actor

April 5, 1916
8:00 AM PST
La Jolla, Ca
117 W 16   32 N 51

Stage and film star. Won an Oscar as best actor in *To Kill a Mockingbird* (1962). Nominated for the Oscar in *The Keys of the Kingdom* (1945), *The Yearling* (1946), *Gentleman's Agreement* (1947), and *Twelve O'Clock High* (1949).

A: AFA from B.C.

SVP=⌖ 6°25'31"
JULIAN DAY=2420959.16667

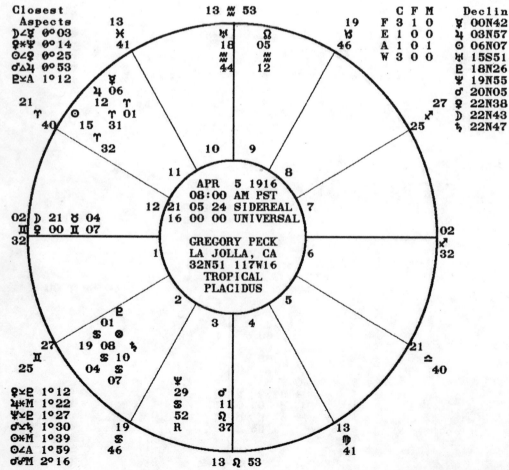

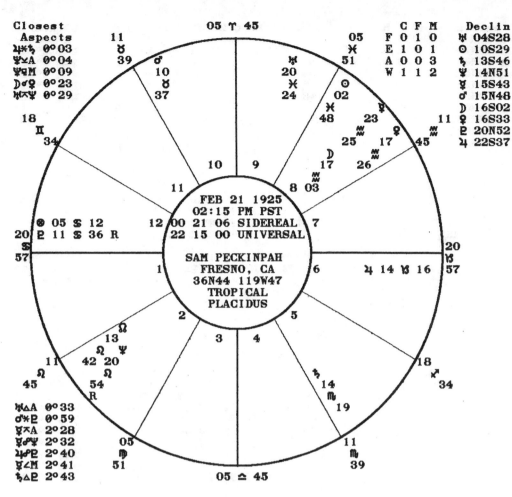

Closest Aspects

♃⚹♅	0°03	
♆⚺A	0°04	
♆⚼M	0°09	
☽♂♀	0°23	
♅⚹♆	0°29	

FEB 21 1925
02:15 PM PST
00 21 06 SIDEREAL
22 15 00 UNIVERSAL

SAM PECKINPAH
FRESNO, CA
36N44 119W47
TROPICAL
PLACIDUS

♅△A	0°33	
♂⚹♇	0°59	
☿⚺A	2°28	
♀⚹♆	2°32	
♃⚼♇	2°40	
☿∠M	2°41	
♄△♇	2°43	

	Declin	
♅	04S28	
☉	10S29	
♄	13S46	
♆	14N51	
☿	15S43	
♂	15N48	
☽	16S02	
♀	16S33	
♇	20N52	
♃	22S37	

C	F	M
F	0	1	0
E	1	0	1
A	0	0	3
W	1	1	2

PECKINPAH, SAM
Movie director

February 21, 1925
2:15 PM PST
Fresno, Ca
119 W 47   36 N 44

Grew up with strict discipline and military school. Became a screenwriter, whose work included *Invasion of the Body Snatchers* and the creation of *The Rifleman*. As a movie director, became the darling of the violence freaks with *The Wild Bunch* and *Straw Dogs*.

A: CSH.

SVP=♓ 6°18'30"
JULIAN DAY=2424203.42708

PEPPARD, GEORGE
Actor

October 1, 1928
8:29 PM EST
Detroit, Mich
83 W 03   42 N 20

Star of TV series *Banacek* (1972). Films include *Breakfast at Tiffany's* (1961) and *How the West Was Won* (1962). When not acting, lives on a ranch in northern California. Third marriage in 1975 for four years; three children. Gave up alcohol in early 1979.

A: Julia Mahdak in M.H., October 1976, "from him by telephone."

SVP=♓ 6°15'33"
JULIAN DAY=2425521.56181

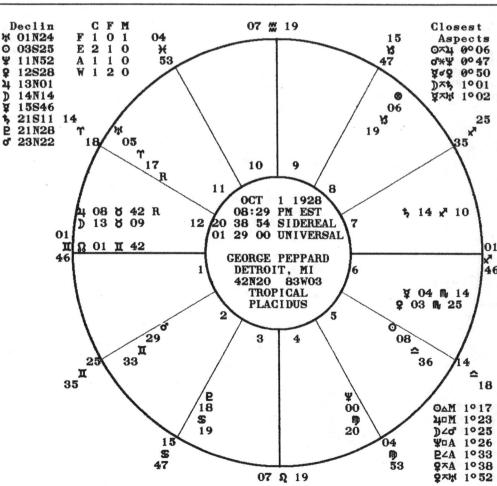

	Declin	
♅	01N24	
☉	03S25	
♆	11N52	
♀	12S28	
♃	13N01	
☽	14N14	
☿	15S46	
♄	21S11	
♇	21N28	
♂	23N22	

C	F	M
F	1	0	1
E	2	1	0
A	1	1	0
W	1	2	0

OCT 1 1928
08:29 PM EST
20 38 54 SIDEREAL
01 29 00 UNIVERSAL

GEORGE PEPPARD
DETROIT, MI
42N20 83W03
TROPICAL
PLACIDUS

Closest Aspects

☉⚹♃	0°06	
♂⚹♆	0°47	
☿♂♀	0°50	
☽⚺♄	1°01	
☿⚺♅	1°02	
☉△M	1°17	
♃⚼M	1°23	
☽♂♂	1°25	
♆⚼A	1°26	
♇∠A	1°33	
♀⚺A	1°38	
☿⚺♅	1°52	

PERRY, TROY
Minister

July 27, 1940
11:30 PM EST
Tallahassee, Fla
84 W 17   39 N 27

Pastor of a primarily homosexual congregation of the Los Angeles Metropolitan Church: conducted his first service on October 6, 1968. His autobiography published in 1972 — *The Lord Is My Shepherd And He Knows I'm Gay.*

A: From him to Kim Griggs, 1974.

SVP=ℋ 6° 5'17"
JULIAN DAY=2429838.68750

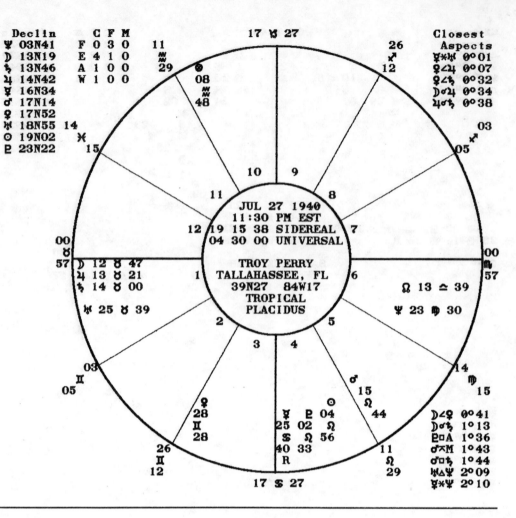

Declin		C	F	M
♆	03N41	F	0	3	0
☽	13N19	E	4	1	0
♄	13N46	A	1	0	0
♃	14N42	W	1	0	0
☿	16N34			
♂	17N14			
♀	17N52			
♅	18N55			
☉	19N02			
♇	23N22			

Closest Aspects
♀✶♅	0°01
♀∠♃	0°07
♀∠♂	0°32
☽∠♃	0°34
♃∠♂	0°38

☽∠♀	0°41
☽♂♄	1°13
♇∠A	1°36
♂✶M	1°43
♂∠♄	1°44
♅△♆	2°09
☿✶♆	2°10

Closest Aspects
☽□♃	0°01
♀△A	0°05
♀♂M	0°14
a✶M	0°20
☉∠♆	0°21

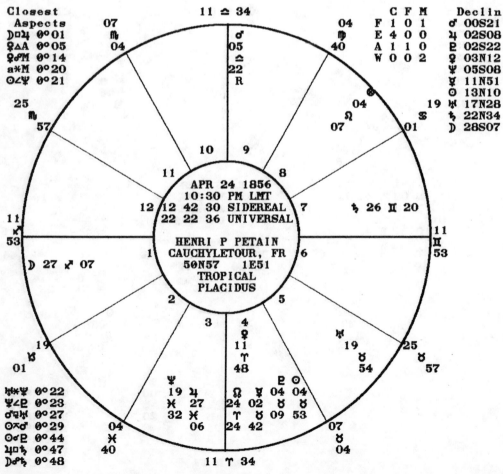

		C	F	M
		F	1	0	1
		E	4	0	0
		A	1	1	0
		W	0	0	2

Declin
♂	00S21
♃	02S08
♇	02S22
♀	03N12
♆	05S08
☿	11N51
☉	13N10
♅	17N28
♄	22N34
☽	28S07

♅✶♆	0°22
♀∠♇	0°23
♂△♅	0°27
☉♂♂	0°29
☉∠♇	0°44
♃♂♄	0°47
☽♂♄	0°48

PETAIN, HENRI PHILIPPE
Premier

April 24, 1856
10:30 PM LMT
Cauchy-le-Tour, France
1 E 51   50 N 57

National hero of France with military leadership in World War I. Premier on June 6, 1940. In the German armistice, collaborated with the Nazis; tried for treason in 1945 and sentenced to death. DeGaulle reduced the sentence to life in prison, where he died in 1951.

A: Gauquelin #866 Vol 3.

SVP=ℋ 7°16' 5"
JULIAN DAY=2399064.43236

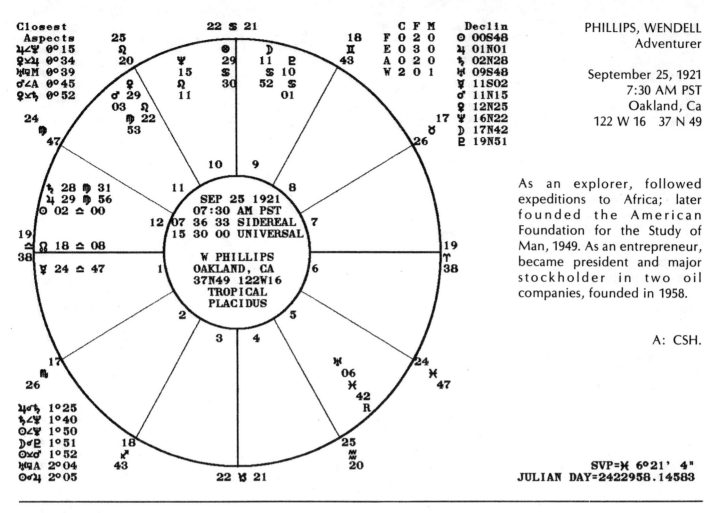

PHILLIPS, WENDELL
Adventurer

September 25, 1921
7:30 AM PST
Oakland, Ca
122 W 16   37 N 49

As an explorer, followed expeditions to Africa; later founded the American Foundation for the Study of Man, 1949. As an entrepreneur, became president and major stockholder in two oil companies, founded in 1958.

A: CSH.

SVP=♓ 6°21' 4"
JULIAN DAY=2422958.14583

PICCARD, AUGUSTE
Physicist

January 28, 1884
11:00 PM LMT
Basel, Switzerland
7 E 35   47 N 33

Inventor of an airtight gondola he attached to a huge balloon, in which he ascended about 53,000 feet in 1932. In 1953, descended some 10,330 feet into the sea in a bathyscope. His twin brother Jean was an aeronautical engineer and chemist. (1884-1962)

A: WEMYSS F/N #143, "recorded."

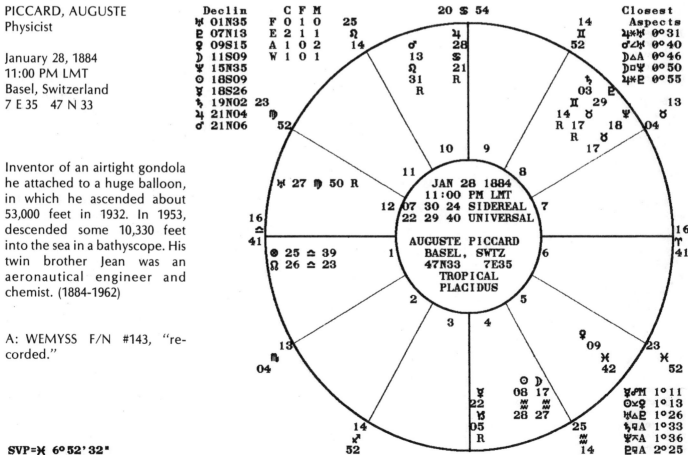

SVP=♓ 6°52'32"
JULIAN DAY=2409204.43727

POITIER, SIDNEY
Actor

February 20, 1927
9:00 PM EST
Miami, Fla
80 W 11   25 N 47

Won the Oscar as best actor in *Lilies of the Field* (1963). Nominated for an Oscar in *The Defiant Ones* (1958). Screen debut in *No Way Out* (1949). First born of eight children; lived in Nassau to age 15. First played on Broadway 1946. Father of four daughters.

A: *Circle* #1078 states, "from him on the *Dick Cavett Show*."

SVP=✠ 6°16'54"
JULIAN DAY=2424932.58333

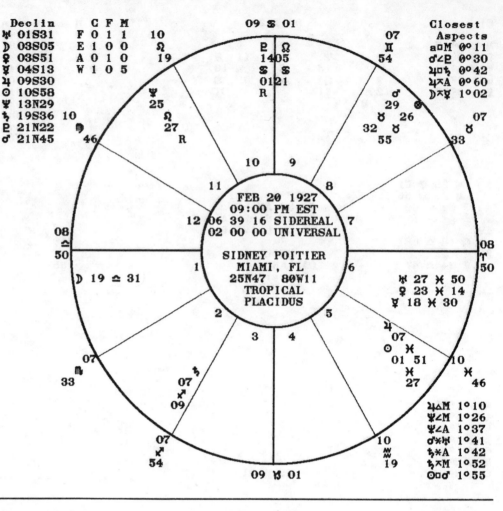

PRESLEY, ELVIS
Entertainer

January 8, 1935
4:35 AM CST
Tupelo, Miss
88 W 43   34 N 16

Singer and superstar who made forty-five gold records and twenty consecutive movie hits. Religious fundamentalist background, but lived and traveled like a potentate with an entourage. Married, May 1, 1967; one daughter. Died of heart failure, August 16, 1977.

A: CSH.[107]

SVP=✠ 6° 9'46"
JULIAN DAY=2427810.94097

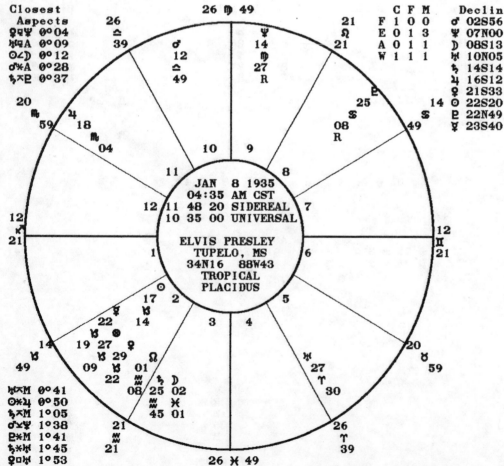

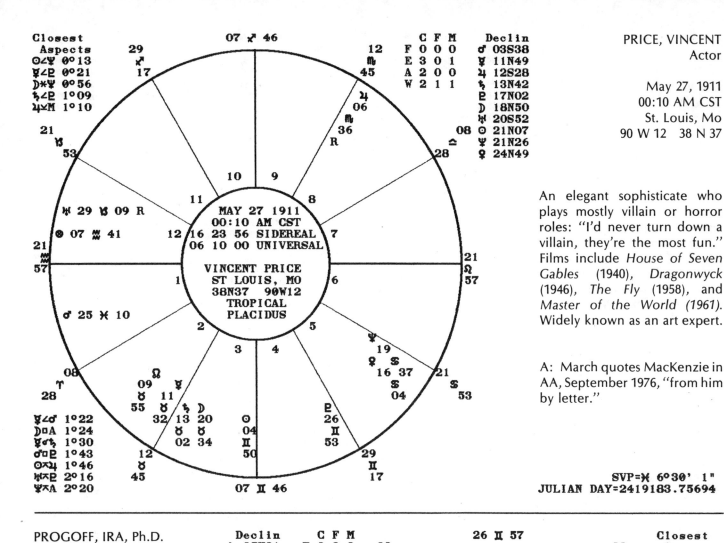

PRICE, VINCENT
Actor

May 27, 1911
00:10 AM CST
St. Louis, Mo
90 W 12   38 N 37

Closest
Aspects
☉∠Ψ 0°13
☿∠♇ 0°21
☽⚹Ψ 0°56
♄∠♇ 1°09
♃⚹M 1°10

07 ♐ 46

MAY 27 1911
00:10 AM CST
16 23 56 SIDEREAL
06 10 00 UNIVERSAL

VINCENT PRICE
ST LOUIS, MO
38N37 90W12
TROPICAL
PLACIDUS

	C	F	M	Declin
F	0	0	0	♂ 03S38
E	3	0	1	☿ 11N49
A	2	0	0	♃ 12S28
W	2	1	1	♄ 13N42
				♇ 17N02
				☽ 18N50
				♅ 20S52
				☉ 21N07
				Ψ 21N26
				♀ 24N49

07 ♊ 46

♀∠♂ 1°22
☽□A 1°24
☿∠♄ 1°30
♂∠♇ 1°43
☉∠♃ 1°46
♅∠♇ 2°16
Ψ∠A 2°20

An elegant sophisticate who plays mostly villain or horror roles: "I'd never turn down a villain, they're the most fun." Films include *House of Seven Gables* (1940), *Dragonwyck* (1946), *The Fly* (1958), and *Master of the World* (1961). Widely known as an art expert.

A: March quotes MacKenzie in AA, September 1976, "from him by letter."

SVP=♓ 6°30' 1"
JULIAN DAY=2419183.75694

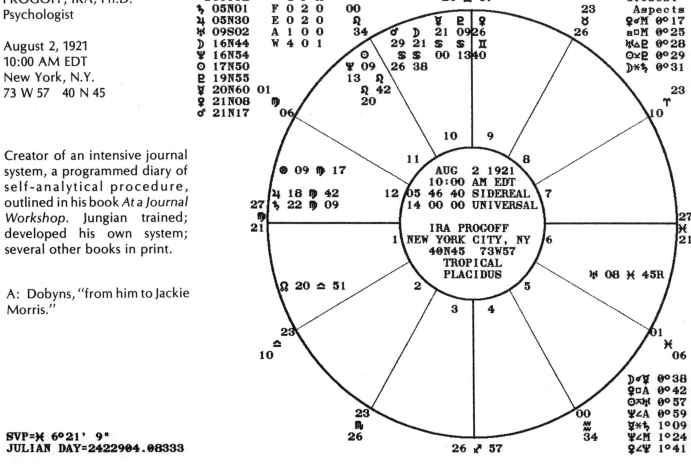

PROGOFF, IRA, Ph.D.
Psychologist

August 2, 1921
10:00 AM EDT
New York, N.Y.
73 W 57   40 N 45

Declin		C	F	M
♄	05N01	F	0	2	0
♃	05N30	E	0	2	0
♅	09S02	A	1	0	0
☽	16N44	W	4	0	1
Ψ	16N54				
☉	17N50				
♇	19N55				
☿	20N60				
♀	21N08				
♂	21N17				

AUG 2 1921
10:00 AM EDT
05 46 40 SIDEREAL
14 00 00 UNIVERSAL

IRA PROGOFF
NEW YORK CITY, NY
40N45 73W57
TROPICAL
PLACIDUS

Closest
Aspects
♀♂M 0°17
a□M 0°25
♅△♇ 0°28
☉⚹♇ 0°29
☽⚹♄ 0°31

Creator of an intensive journal system, a programmed diary of self-analytical procedure, outlined in his book *At a Journal Workshop*. Jungian trained; developed his own system; several other books in print.

A: Dobyns, "from him to Jackie Morris."

☽♂☿ 0°38
♀□A 0°42
☉∠♅ 0°57
Ψ∠A 0°59
☿⚹♄ 1°09
Ψ∠M 1°24
♀∠Ψ 1°41

SVP=♓ 6°21' 9"
JULIAN DAY=2422904.08333

PROUST, MARCEL
Writer

July 10, 1871
11:30 PM LMT
Paris, France
2 E 20   48 N 50

	Declin		C	F	M
♇	03N22	F	1	0	0
♂	04S41	E	2	1	1
♆	07N45	A	0	1	0
☽	08N49	W	4	0	0
♀	11N01				
♅	21N24				
☉	22N13				
♄	22S35				
♃	23N02				
☿	23N42				

Closest Aspects
☉∠☿ 0°24
☉♂ 0°37
♃⚼♍ 0°39
☽∆♀ 0°43
♂□♃ 0°47

One of the greatest French novelists of the 1900s, with a complex literary style. Work called immoral and decadent for several decades before he was recognized. His greatest work — *Remembrance of Things Past*. (1871-1922)

A: Gauquelin #658 Vol 6.

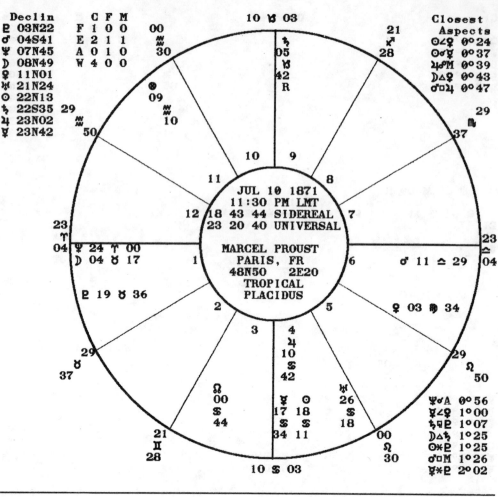

SVP=♓ 7° 3'29"
JULIAN DAY=2404619.47269

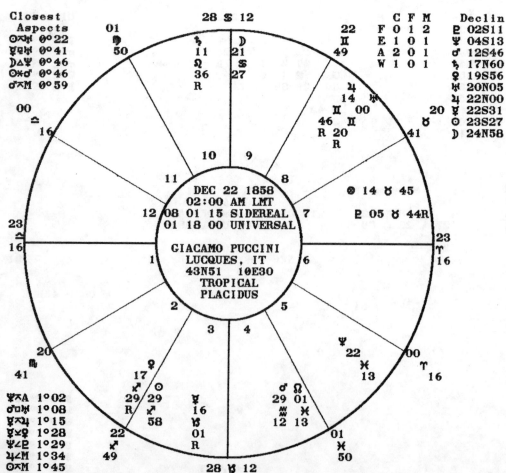

Closest Aspects
☉⚼♅ 0°22
☿⚼♅ 0°41
☽∆♆ 0°46
☉⚹♂ 0°46
♂⚼♍ 0°59

	C	F	M		Declin
	F	0	1	2	♇	02S11
	E	1	0	1	♆	04S13
	A	2	0	1	♂	12S46
	W	1	0	1	♄	17N60
					♀	19S56
					♅	20N05
					♃	22N00
					☿	22S31
					☉	23S27
					☽	24N58

PUCCINI, GIACAMO
Musician

December 22, 1858
2:00 AM LMT
Lucques, Italy
10 E 30   43 N 51

Born into a musical family, an Italian operatic composer famous for his melodic writing and bold dramatic harmonics. Recognized for his first opera *Le Villi* (1884); successful with *Manon Lescaut* (1893); beloved for *Tosca* (1900) and *Madame Butterfly* (1904). (1858-1924)

A: *Constellations*, 1977, Lockhart quotes, "birth record."

♆⚼A 1°02
♂□♅ 1°08
☿⚼♃ 1°15
☿⚹♀ 1°28
♆∠♇ 1°29
♃⚼♍ 1°34
☉⚼♍ 1°45

SVP=♓ 7°13'35"
JULIAN DAY=2400035.55417

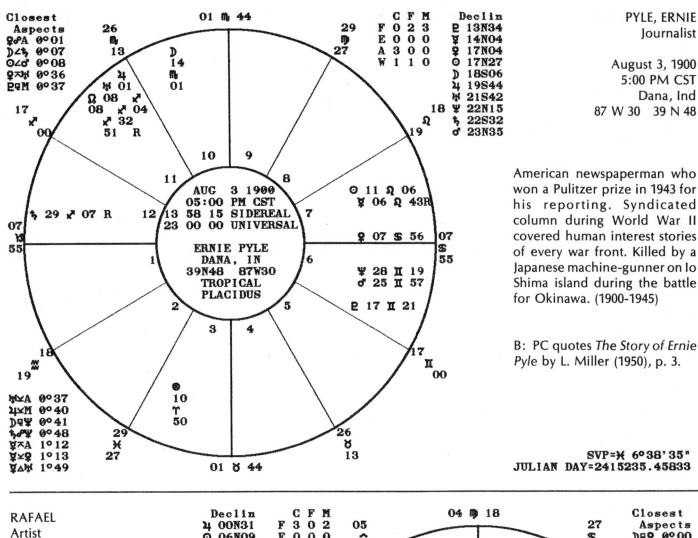

PYLE, ERNIE
Journalist

August 3, 1900
5:00 PM CST
Dana, Ind
87 W 30   39 N 48

American newspaperman who won a Pulitzer prize in 1943 for his reporting. Syndicated column during World War II covered human interest stories of every war front. Killed by a Japanese machine-gunner on Io Shima island during the battle for Okinawa. (1900-1945)

B: PC quotes *The Story of Ernie Pyle* by L. Miller (1950), p. 3.

SVP=ℋ 6°38'35"
JULIAN DAY=2415235.45833

RAFAEL
Artist

April 5, 1483 NS
9:30 PM LMT
Urbino, Italy
12 E 38   43 N 44

One of the greatest painters of the Italian Renaissance; admired for his tranquil Madonnas. His whole view of nature ideally beautiful and peaceful. Studied and painted in England, 1504-1508; in Rome for the last twelve years of his life. (1483-1520)

A: Fagan in AA, March 1965, quotes Vasari, circa 1511.[108]

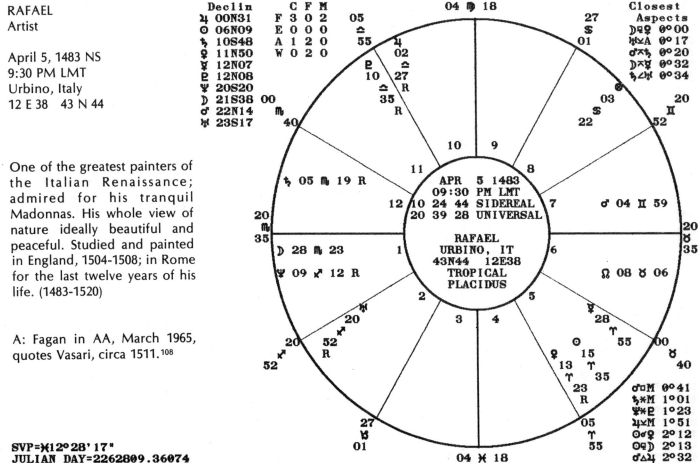

SVP=ℋ12°28'17"
JULIAN DAY=2262809.36074

RAVEL, MAURICE
Musician

March 7, 1875
10:00 PM LMT
Clibourne, France
1 W 41   43 N 23

Composer; achieved world renown for *Bolero,* as well as ballet *Daphnis et Chloe,* performed in 1912. His works for orchestra, including *Mother Goose Suite,* widely recognized. An auto accident in 1932 brought a nervous breakdown from which he never recovered. (1875-1937)

A: Gauquelin #2218 Vol 4.

Declin		C F M	
♇ 04N09	F 1 1 1	15
☉ 05S09	E 1 0 0	♍
☿ 06S56	A 0 0 2	51
☽ 07S09	W 0 1 3	
♆ 09N31		
♃ 10S27		
♄ 15S40		
♅ 17N55	13	
♀ 18S14	♎	
♂ 21S39	00	

Closest Aspects	
♀☐♃ 0°04
♀△♈ 0°22
♂△M 0°23
♂△♈ 0°29
♄☐♇ 0°39

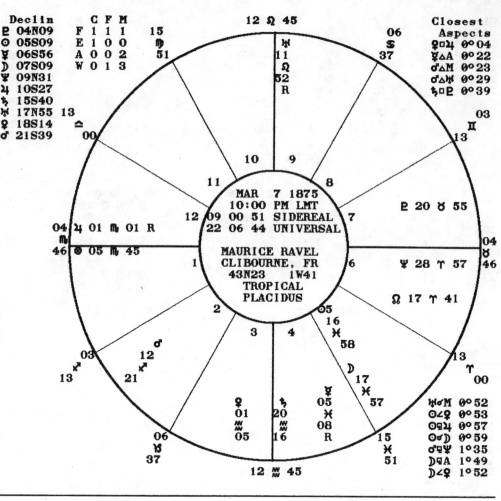

MAR 7 1875
10:00 PM LMT
09 00 51 SIDEREAL
22 06 44 UNIVERSAL
MAURICE RAVEL
CLIBOURNE, FR
43N23   1W41
TROPICAL
PLACIDUS

SVP=♓ 7° 0'14"
JULIAN DAY=2405955.42134

Closest Aspects	
☽♂ 0°19
☉∠M 0°21
♇⚹A 0°35
☿♂♆ 0°54
☽☐♃ 0°60

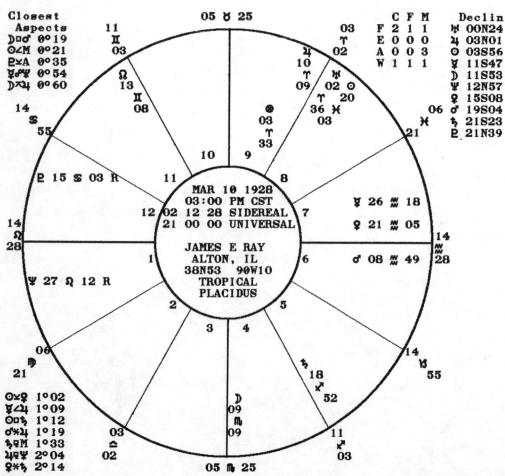

MAR 10 1928
03:00 PM CST
02 12 28 SIDEREAL
21 00 00 UNIVERSAL
JAMES E RAY
ALTON, IL
38N53   90W10
TROPICAL
PLACIDUS

	C F M	Declin	
	F 2 1 1	♅ 00N24
	E 0 0 0	♃ 03N01
	A 0 0 3	☉ 03S56
	W 1 1 1	☿ 11S47
		☽ 11S53
		♆ 12N57
		♀ 15S08
		♂ 19S04
		♄ 21S23
		♇ 21N39

RAY, JAMES EARL
Assassin

March 10, 1928
3:00 PM CST
Alton, Ill
90 W 10   38 N 53

Long criminal record; attempted robbery May 6, 1952, shot in arm, two years prison; again March 1955, got forty-five months Leavenworth; again April 21, 1959, sentenced to twenty years in State Penitentiary. Escaped April 23, 1967; shot Dr. Martin Luther King, April 14, 1968.

A: Bertucelli in M.H., July 1978, from B.C.

Closest Aspects	
☉⚹♀ 1°02
☿△♃ 1°09
☉☐♀ 1°12
♂⚹♃ 1°19
♄♈M 1°33
♃♂♆ 2°04
♀⚹♄ 2°14

SVP=♓ 6°16' 1"
JULIAN DAY=2425316.37500

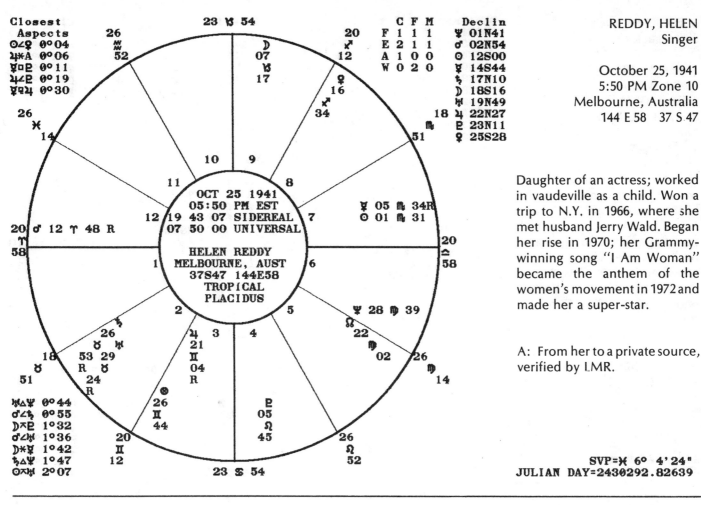

REDDY, HELEN
Singer

October 25, 1941
5:50 PM Zone 10
Melbourne, Australia
144 E 58   37 S 47

Closest
Aspects
☉∠♀ 0°04
♃✱A 0°06
☿□♇ 0°11
♃∠♇ 0°19
☿∠♃ 0°30

OCT 25 1941
05:50 PM EST
19 43 07 SIDEREAL
07 50 00 UNIVERSAL

HELEN REDDY
MELBOURNE, AUST
37S47 144E58
TROPICAL
PLACIDUS

	C	F	M	Declin
F	1	1	1	♆ 01N41
E	2	1	1	♂ 02N54
A	1	0	0	☉ 12S00
W	0	2	0	☿ 14S44
				♄ 17N10
				☽ 18S16
				♅ 19N49
				♃ 22N27
				♇ 23N11
				♀ 25S28

☿ 05 ♏ 34R
☉ 01 ♏ 31

♆ 28 ♍ 39

Daughter of an actress; worked
in vaudeville as a child. Won a
trip to N.Y. in 1966, where she
met husband Jerry Wald. Began
her rise in 1970; her Grammy-
winning song "I Am Woman"
became the anthem of the
women's movement in 1972 and
made her a super-star.

A: From her to a private source,
verified by LMR.

♅△♆ 0°44
♂∠♄ 0°55
☽✶♇ 1°32
♂∠♅ 1°36
☽✶☿ 1°42
♄△♆ 1°47
☉∠♅ 2°07

SVP=♓ 6° 4'24"
JULIAN DAY=2430292.82639

REDFORD, ROBERT
Actor

August 18, 1936
8:02 PM PST
Santa Monica, Ca
118 W 29   34 N 01

Selective in his choice of films,
that include *Butch Cassidy and
the Sundance Kid*, *Downhill
Racer*, and *The Great Gatsby*.
University of Colorado on a
baseball scholarship. Likes
sports, with a passion for skiing.
Claustrophobic; values his
privacy. Married twenty years.

A: Lockhart from B.C.

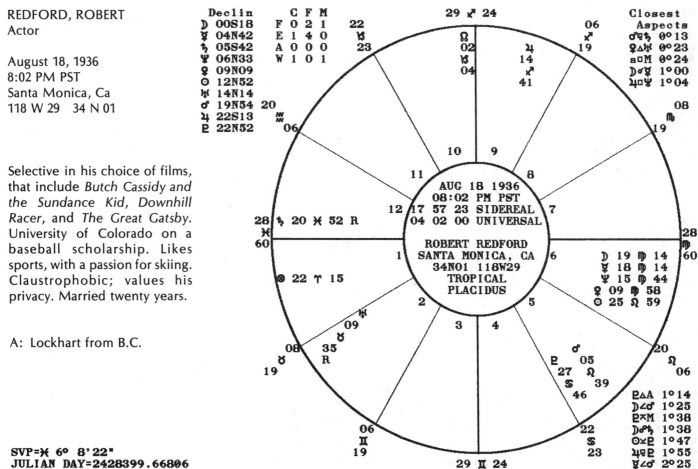

Declin		C	F	M
☽ 00S18	F	0	2	1
☿ 04N42	E	1	4	0
♄ 05S42	A	0	0	0
♆ 06N33	W	1	0	1
♀ 09N09				
☉ 12N52				
♅ 14N14				
♂ 19N54				
♃ 22S13				
♇ 22N52				

AUG 18 1936
08:02 PM PST
17 57 23 SIDEREAL
04 02 00 UNIVERSAL

ROBERT REDFORD
SANTA MONICA, CA
34N01 118W29
TROPICAL
PLACIDUS

Closest
Aspects
♂♃ 0°13
♀△♅ 0°23
a□M 0°24
☽♂ 1°00
♃□♆ 1°04

☽ 19 ♍ 14
☿ 18 ♍ 14
♆ 15 ♍ 44
♀ 09 ♍ 58
☉ 25 ♌ 59

♇△A 1°14
☽∠♂ 1°25
♇✶M 1°38
☽✶♄ 1°38
☉✶♇ 1°47
♃♇ 1°55
☿∠♂ 2°25

SVP=♓ 6° 8'22"
JULIAN DAY=2428399.66806

REED, JERRY
Singer, actor

March 20, 1937
4:56 AM CST
Atlanta, Ga
84 W 23   33 N 45

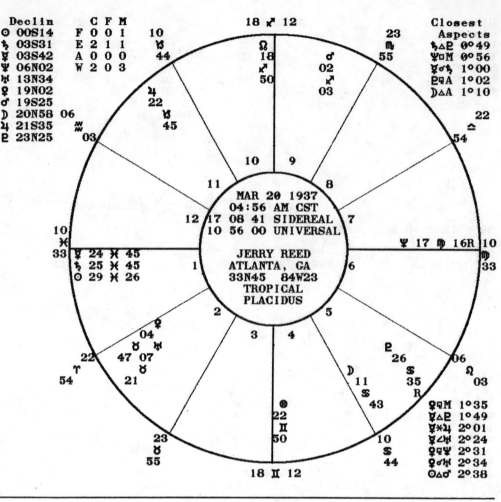

Declin

		C F M	
☉	00S14	F 0 0 1	
♄	03S31	E 2 1 1	
♅	03S42	A 0 0 0	
♆	06N02	W 2 0 3	
♀	19N02		
♂	19S25		
☽	20N58		
♃	21S35		
♇	23N25		

Closest
Aspects

♄△♇	0°49
♆M	0°56
☿♂♄	1°00
♇⊓A	1°02
☽△A	1°10

MAR 20 1937
04:56 AM CST
17 08 41 SIDEREAL
10 56 00 UNIVERSAL

JERRY REED
ATLANTA, GA
33N45 84W23
TROPICAL
PLACIDUS

♀⊓M	1°35
☿△♇	1°49
☿✶♃	2°01
☿∠♅	2°24
♀♂♆	2°31
♀♂♅	2°34
☉△♂	2°38

Country western singer, song-writer, and recording artist. Songs include the hit "Amos Moses". Whippet thin, with sparkling charm. First appeared on TV on the *Glenn Campbell Show*, April 1970. Films include *Smokey and the Bear*. TV series pilot, June 7, 1979, *Good Ol' Boys*.

A: From him to LMR, April 1970, B.C.

SVP=♓ 6° 7'54"
JULIAN DAY=2428612.95556

REEVES, CHRISTOPHER
Actor

September 25, 1952
3:30 AM EDT
New York, N.Y.
73 W 57   40 N 45

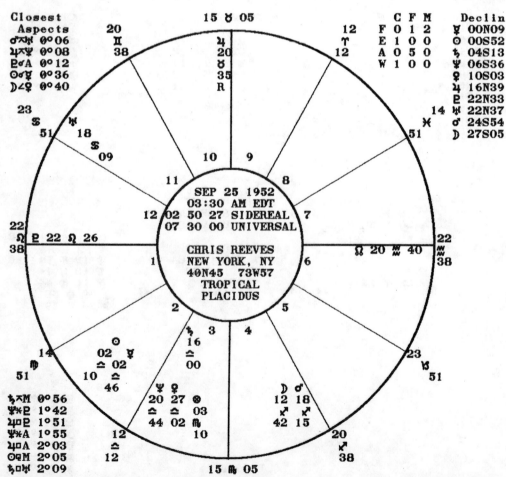

Closest
Aspects

♂⊼♅	0°06
♃✶♆	0°08
♇♂A	0°12
☉♂♀	0°36
☽∠♀	0°40

		C F M		Declin	
		F 0 1 2	☿	00N09	
		E 1 0 0	☉	00S52	
		A 0 5 0	♄	04S13	
		W 1 0 0	♆	06S36	
			♀	10S03	
			♃	16N39	
			♇	22N33	
			♅	22N37	
			♂	24S54	
			☽	27S05	

SEP 25 1952
03:30 AM EDT
02 50 27 SIDEREAL
07 30 00 UNIVERSAL

CHRIS REEVES
NEW YORK, NY
40N45 73W57
TROPICAL
PLACIDUS

Well cast as the lead in *Superman*, for $250,000. Prior experience in a TV soap opera *Love of Life*; appeared in the movie *Gray Lady Down*; played Broadway with Katherine Hepburn in *A Matter of Gravity*. Studies classical piano; is a sailor.

A: Terry Krall quotes Robert St. Germaine, "from him."

♄⊼M	0°56
♆✶♇	1°42
♃⊼♇	1°51
♆✶A	1°55
♃⊓A	2°03
☉⊓M	2°05
♄⊓♅	2°09

SVP=♓ 5°55' 1"
JULIAN DAY=2434280.81250

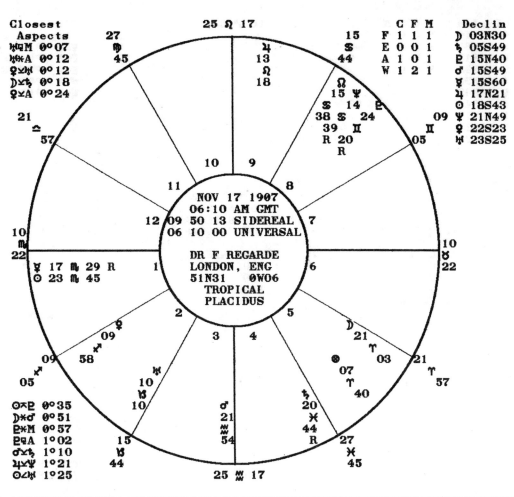

REGARDE, DR. FRANCIS
Occultist

November 17, 1907
6:10 AM GMT
London, England
0 W 06   51 N 31

Closest Aspects

⛢□M	0°07
⛢⚹A	0°12
♀□⛢	0°12
☽⚼♄	0°18
♀⚹A	0°24

	C	F	M		Declin
F	1	1	1	☽	03N30
E	0	0	1	♄	05S49
A	1	0	1	♇	15N40
W	1	2	1	♂	15S49
				☿	15S60
				♃	17N21
				☉	18S43
				♆	21N49
				♀	22S23
				⛢	23S25

NOV 17 1907
06:10 AM GMT
09 50 13 SIDEREAL
06 10 00 UNIVERSAL

DR F REGARDE
LONDON, ENG
51N31   0W06
TROPICAL
PLACIDUS

☉□♇	0°35
☽⚹♂	0°51
♇⚹M	0°57
♇⚼A	1°02
♂⚼♄	1°10
♃⚹♆	1°21
☉⚼⛢	1°25

Prolific spokesman for the Hermetic Order of the Golden Dawn; works on balance and accuracy. Began study with Crowley in 1928; worked as his secretary; joined the Golden Dawn in 1934. Books include *The Tree Of Life* and *The Middle Pillar*.

A: From him to Eshelman by phone, March 1979.

SVP=♓ 6°33' 4"
JULIAN DAY=2417896.75694

REMARQUE, ERICK MARIA
Writer

June 22, 1898
8:15 PM MET
Osnabruck, Germany
8 E 03   52 N 17

	Declin
♃	00N41
♇	12N52
♂	14N21
☽	15N34
♄	19S42
⛢	20S04
♀	21N14
♆	21N58
☿	23N21
☉	23N27

	C	F	M
F	0	2	2
E	1	0	0
A	3	1	0
W	1	0	0

Closest Aspects

☉□♃	0°02
♇⚼M	0°16
☿⚼♆	0°20
⛢⚹M	0°28
☽⚼♂	0°37

JUN 22 1898
08:15 PM MET
13 51 09 SIDEREAL
19 15 00 UNIVERSAL

ERICK M REMARQUE
OSNABRUCK, GER
52N17   8E03
TROPICAL
PLACIDUS

Author of the famous World War I novel *All Quiet on the Western Front* (1929). Served as a German soldier in the war. Moved to U.S. in 1939 to become a citizen in 1947. Novels include *Arch of Triumph* (1946) and *A Time to Love and a Time to Die* (1954). (1898-1970)

A: March, "from his sister."[109]

☉⚼⛢	0°59
♃⚹⛢	1°01
☽⚼A	1°19
☉△M	1°27
♃⚼M	1°29
♆⚼A	1°47
♀⚹♃	1°47

SVP=♓ 6°40'22"
JULIAN DAY=2414463.30208

RENAN, ERNEST
Writer

February 28, 1823
6:00 AM LMT
Treguier, France
3 W 15   48 N 50

French historian and religious scholar. Became famous for his *Life of Jesus* (1863), the first of a series of books on the early history of Christianity. Studied for the priesthood, but lost his belief in the Church. Became an expert in ancient languages. (1823-1892)

A: Gauquelin #679 Vol 6.

SVP=♓ 7°43'28"
JULIAN DAY=2386954.75903

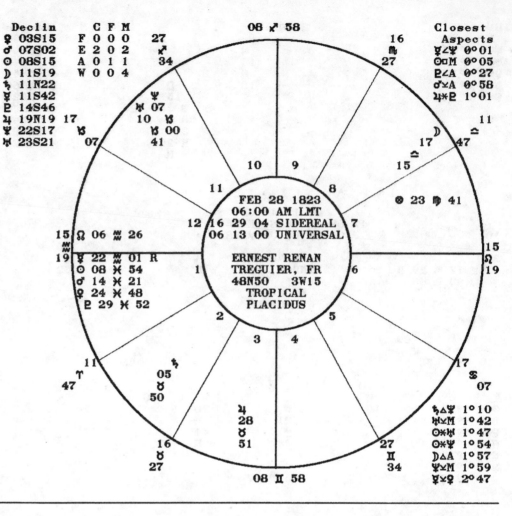

Declin		C	F	M
♀ 03S15		F	0	0	0	27
♂ 07S02		E	2	0	2	
☉ 08S15		A	0	1	1	34
☽ 11S19		W	0	0	4	
♄ 11N22	
☿ 11S42	
♇ 14S46	
♃ 19N19	
♆ 22S17	
♅ 23S21	

Closest Aspects
☿∠♆ 0°01
☉□M 0°05
♇∠A 0°27
♂⊼A 0°58
♃✶♇ 1°01

♄△♆ 1°10
♅⊼M 1°42
☉✶♅ 1°47
☉✶♆ 1°54
☽△A 1°57
♆⊼M 1°59
☿⊼♀ 2°47

FEB 28 1823
06:00 AM LMT
16 29 04 SIDEREAL
06 13 00 UNIVERSAL
ERNEST RENAN
TREGUIER, FR
48N50   3W15
TROPICAL
PLACIDUS

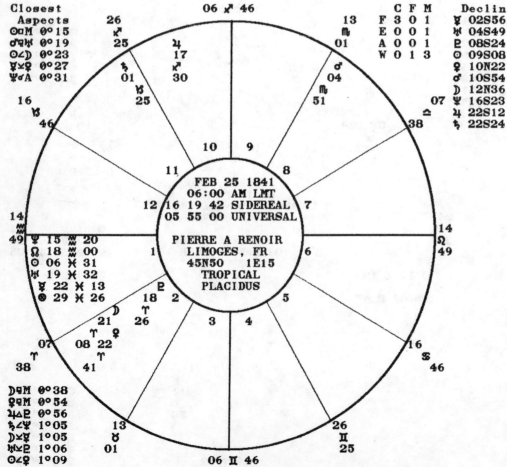

Closest Aspects
☉□M 0°15
♂□♅ 0°19
☉∠☽ 0°23
☿⊼♀ 0°27
♆∠A 0°31

☽□M 0°38
♀□M 0°54
♃△♇ 0°56
♄∠♆ 1°05
☽✶☿ 1°05
♅∠♇ 1°06
☉∠♀ 1°09

C	F	M	Declin
F	3	0	1	☿ 02S56
E	0	0	1	♅ 04S49
A	0	0	1	♇ 08S24
W	0	1	3	☉ 09S08
				♀ 10N22
				♂ 10S54
				☽ 12N36
				♆ 16S23
				♃ 22S12
				♄ 22S24

FEB 25 1841
06:00 AM LMT
16 19 42 SIDEREAL
05 55 00 UNIVERSAL
PIERRE A RENOIR
LIMOGES, FR
45N50   1E15
TROPICAL
PLACIDUS

RENOIR, PIERRE AUGUSTE
Artist

February 25, 1841
6:00 AM LMT
Limoges, France
1 E 15   45 N 50

French impressionist painter, famous for his pictures of young girls and children, and intimate portraits of French middle-class life. When crippled with arthritis, had brushes tied to his hands to continue his work. (1841-1919)

A: Gauquelin #946 Vol 4.

SVP=♓ 7°28'26"
JULIAN DAY=2393526.74653

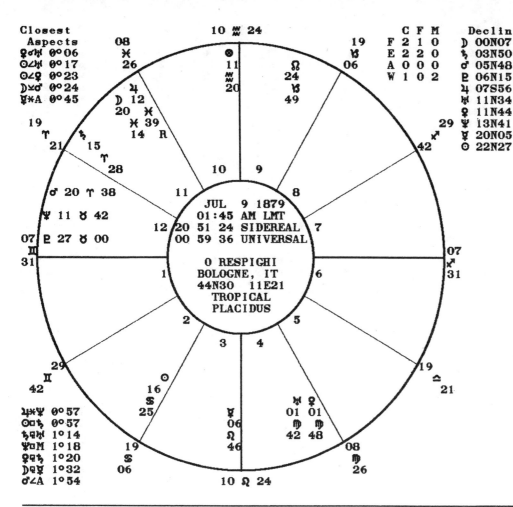

Closest Aspects

☿♂♅ 0°06
☉⊥♄☉ 0°17
☉⊥♀ 0°23
☽♂♂ 0°24
☿⚹A 0°45

JUL 9 1879
01:45 AM LMT
20 51 24 SIDEREAL
00 59 36 UNIVERSAL

O RESPIGHI
BOLOGNE, IT
44N30 11E21
TROPICAL
PLACIDUS

	C	F	M
F	2	1	0
E	2	2	0
A	0	0	0
W	1	0	2

Declin

☽ 00N07
♄ 03N50
♂ 05N48
♇ 06N15
♃ 07S56
♅ 11N34
♀ 11N44
♆ 13N41
☿ 20N05
☉ 22N27

♃⚹♆ 0°57
☉□♄ 0°57
♄♅ 1°14
♆□M 1°18
♀♄ 1°20
☽□☿ 1°32
♂⊥A 1°54

RESPIGHI, OTTORINO
Musician

July 9, 1879
1:45 AM LMT
Bologne, Italy
11 E 21   44 N 30

One of the best-known Italian composers of the early 1900s; helped revive interest in older music, as evidenced by his *Gregorian Concerto* (1922). His tone poems, *The Fountains of Rome* (1917) and *The Pines of Rome* (1924) are well appreciated. (1879-1936)

A: *Constellations*, 1977, Lockhart quotes birth records.

SVP=♓ 6°56'15"
JULIAN DAY=2407539.54139

REVENTLOW, LANCE
Heir

February 24, 1936
10:30 AM GMT
London, England
0 W 06   51 N 31

As the only son of Barbara Hutton, heir to the Woolworth fortune. Sportscar designer and racer; financial backer of the car with American V-8 engines in Lotus bodies that dominated the races. Killed in a plane crash, 1972.

B: Holliday from *Barbara Hutton* by Dean Jennings (1968).[110]

SVP=♓ 6° 8'47"
JULIAN DAY=2428222.93750

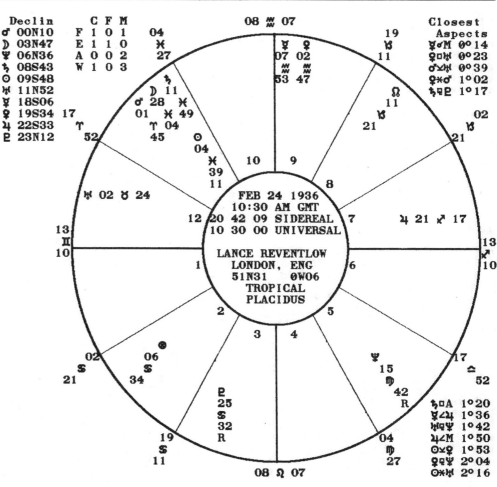

Declin

♂ 00N10
☽ 03N47
♆ 06N36
♄ 08S43
☉ 09S48
♅ 11N52
☿ 18S06
♀ 19S34
♃ 22S33
♇ 23N12

	C	F	M
F	1	0	1
E	1	1	0
A	0	0	2
W	1	0	3

FEB 24 1936
10:30 AM GMT
20 42 09 SIDEREAL
10 30 00 UNIVERSAL

LANCE REVENTLOW
LONDON, ENG
51N31 0W06
TROPICAL
PLACIDUS

Closest Aspects

☿♂M 0°14
♀♂♅ 0°23
♂⊥♅ 0°39
♀⚹♂ 1°02
♄⊥♇ 1°17

♄□A 1°20
☿♃ 1°36
♅♆♀ 1°42
♃⊥M 1°50
☉⊥♀ 1°53
♀♂♀ 2°04
☉⚹♅ 2°16

REYNOLDS, BURT
Actor

February 11, 1936
12:10 PM EST
Lansing, Mich
84 W 33   42 N 44

Signed with the Baltimore Colts until an auto accident took him off the tackle line into acting. First impressive role in *Deliverance* (1972). Three-year marriage to Judy Carne; noted romances with Dinah Shore and, from 1976, Sally Field.

A: From him to Angela Gallo.[111]

SVP=)(6° 8'49"
JULIAN DAY=2428210.21528

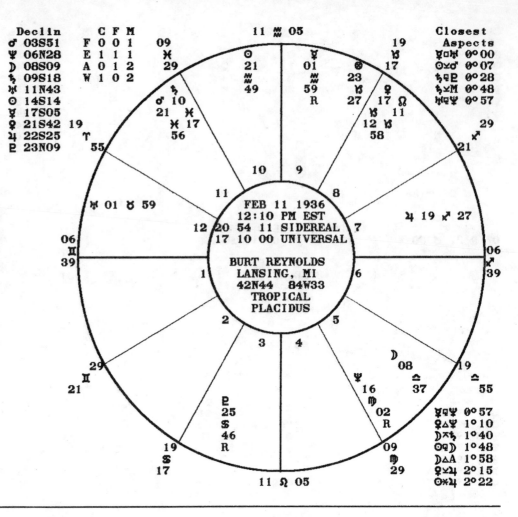

REZA, ZOOROSH ALI
Crown Prince

October 31, 1960
11:55 AM Zone 3.5
Teheran, Iran
51 E 26   35 N 40

The first-born son of Farah Diba and Mohammed Reza Pahlavi; heir to the Peacock kingdom. Trained with discipline to become Shah at age 28. Moved to Texas in July 1978 to train as a jet-pilot at Reese AFB while insurrection raged in Iran.

A: G. Allen in AA, February 1961. Same data from AQ, Winter 1960, "official sources."[112]

SVP=)(5°48'31"
JULIAN DAY=2437238.85069

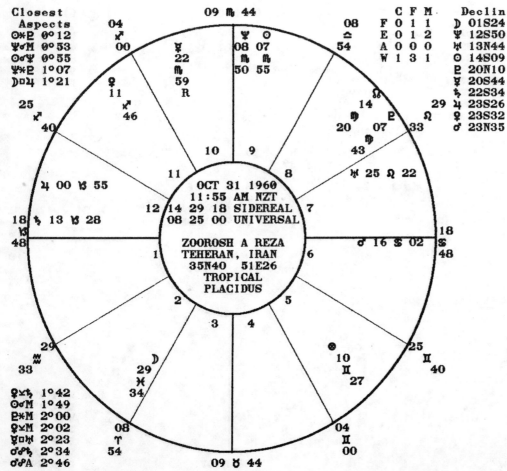

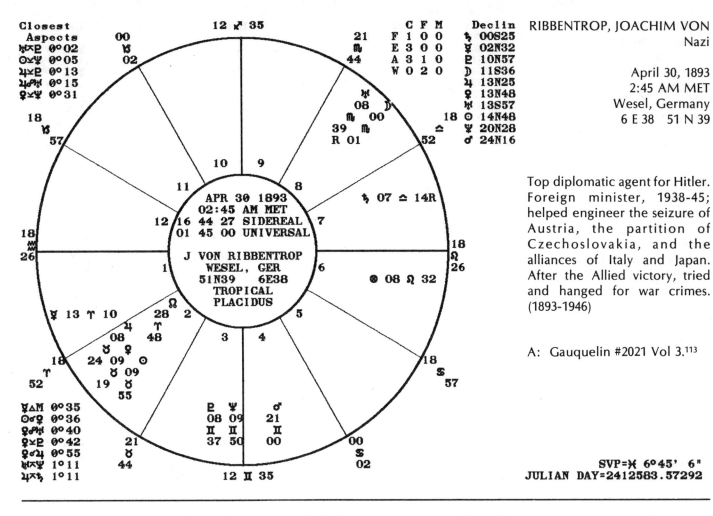

RIBBENTROP, JOACHIM VON
Nazi

April 30, 1893
2:45 AM MET
Wesel, Germany
6 E 38   51 N 39

Closest Aspects
♅☌♇ 0°02
☉⚹♆ 0°05
♃⚹♇ 0°13
♃♂♅ 0°15
♀⚹♆ 0°31

	C	F	M
F	1	0	0
E	3	0	0
A	3	1	0
W	0	2	0

Declin
♄ 00S25
☿ 02N32
♇ 10N57
☽ 11S36
♃ 13N25
♀ 13N48
♅ 13S57
☉ 14N48
♆ 20N28
♂ 24N16

APR 30 1893
02:45 AM MET
16 44 27 SIDEREAL
01 45 00 UNIVERSAL

J VON RIBBENTROP
WESEL, GER
51N39   6E38
TROPICAL
PLACIDUS

♄ 07 ♎ 14R

⊗ 08 ♌ 32

♇ ♆ ♂
08 09 21
♊ ♊ ♊
37 50 00

☿△M 0°35
☉☌♀ 0°36
♀♀M 0°40
♀⚹♇ 0°42
♀☌♃ 0°55
♅⚹♆ 1°11
♃⚹♄ 1°11

Top diplomatic agent for Hitler. Foreign minister, 1938-45; helped engineer the seizure of Austria, the partition of Czechoslovakia, and the alliances of Italy and Japan. After the Allied victory, tried and hanged for war crimes. (1893-1946)

A: Gauquelin #2021 Vol 3.[113]

SVP=♓ 6°45' 6"
JULIAN DAY=2412583.57292

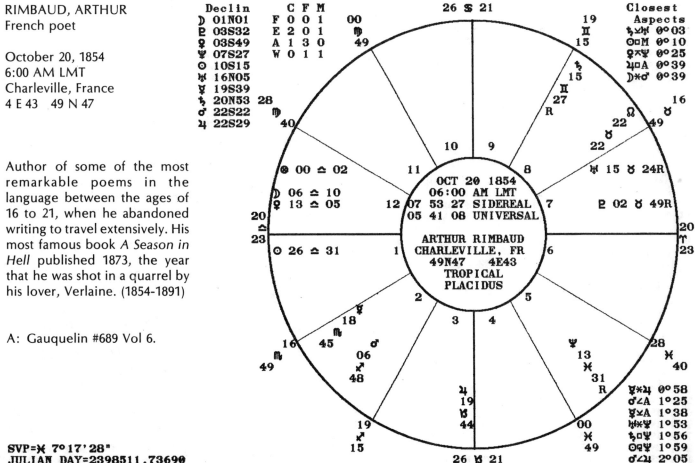

RIMBAUD, ARTHUR
French poet

October 20, 1854
6:00 AM LMT
Charleville, France
4 E 43   49 N 47

Declin
☽ 01N01
♇ 03S32
♀ 03S49
♆ 07S27
☉ 10S15
♅ 16N05
☿ 19S39
♄ 20N53
♂ 22S22
♃ 22S29

	C	F	M
F	0	0	1
E	2	0	1
A	1	3	0
W	0	1	1

Closest Aspects
♄⚹♅ 0°03
☉☌M 0°10
♀⚹♆ 0°25
♃□A 0°39
☽⚹♂ 0°39

OCT 20 1854
06:00 AM LMT
07 53 27 SIDEREAL
05 41 08 UNIVERSAL

ARTHUR RIMBAUD
CHARLEVILLE, FR
49N47   4E43
TROPICAL
PLACIDUS

⊗ 00 ♎ 02

☽ 06 ♎ 10
♀ 13 ♎ 05

☉ 26 ♎ 31

♅ 15 ♉ 24R

♇ 02 ♉ 49R

☿
♏
06
♐
48

♆
13
♓
31
R

♓
40

♓
49

Author of some of the most remarkable poems in the language between the ages of 16 to 21, when he abandoned writing to travel extensively. His most famous book *A Season in Hell* published 1873, the year that he was shot in a quarrel by his lover, Verlaine. (1854-1891)

A: Gauquelin #689 Vol 6.

☿⚹♃ 0°58
♂△A 1°25
☿△A 1°38
♅⚹♃ 1°53
♄□M 1°56
☉☌♆ 1°59
♂☌♃ 2°05

SVP=♓ 7°17'28"
JULIAN DAY=2398511.73690

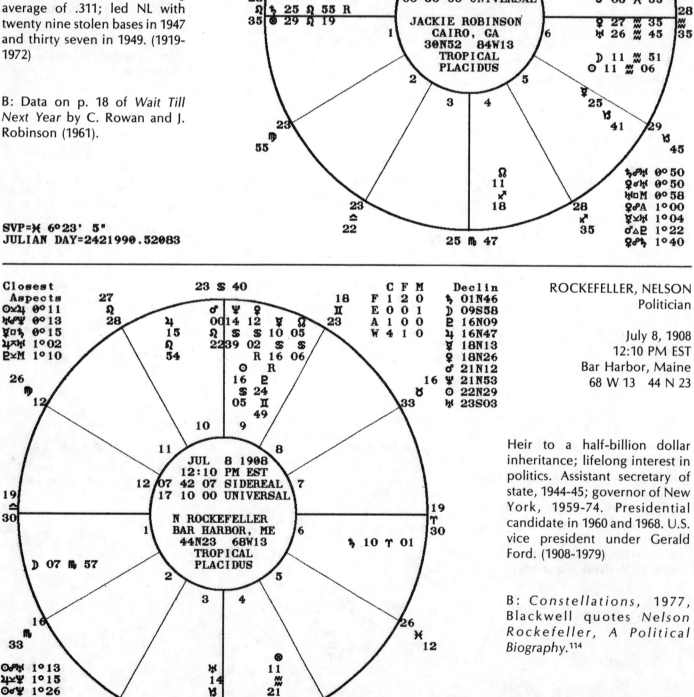

ROBINSON, JACKIE
Baseball player

January 31, 1919
6:30 PM CST
Cairo, Ga
84 W 13   30 N 52

First Black to play in major leagues, with Brooklyn in 1947. Elected to National Baseball Hall of Fame, 1962. Lifetime batting average of .311; led NL with twenty nine stolen bases in 1947 and thirty seven in 1949. (1919-1972)

B: Data on p. 18 of *Wait Till Next Year* by C. Rowan and J. Robinson (1961).

SVP=✶ 6°23' 5"
JULIAN DAY=2421990.52083

ROCKEFELLER, NELSON
Politician

July 8, 1908
12:10 PM EST
Bar Harbor, Maine
68 W 13   44 N 23

Heir to a half-billion dollar inheritance; lifelong interest in politics. Assistant secretary of state, 1944-45; governor of New York, 1959-74. Presidential candidate in 1960 and 1968. U.S. vice president under Gerald Ford. (1908-1979)

B: *Constellations*, 1977, Blackwell quotes *Nelson Rockefeller, A Political Biography*.[114]

SVP=✶ 6°32'31"
JULIAN DAY=2418131.21528

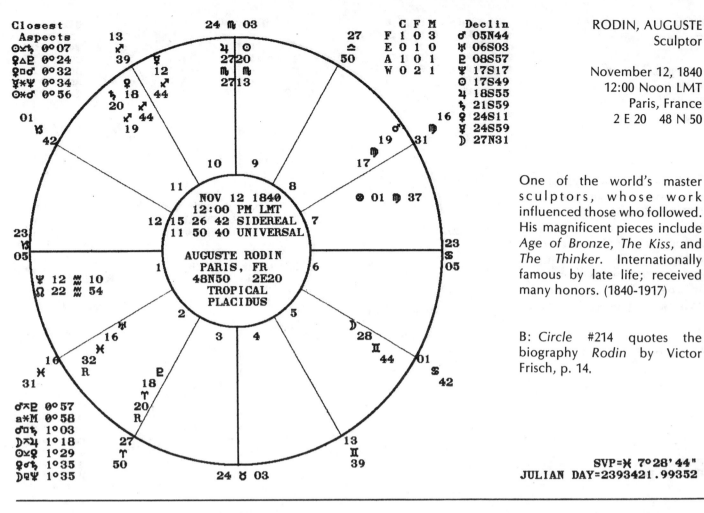

Closest Aspects

☉⊼♄	0°07
♀△♇	0°24
♀□♂	0°32
☿⚹♆	0°34
☉⚹♂	0°56

♂⊼♇	0°57
a⚹M	0°58
♂□♄	1°03
☽⊼♃	1°18
☉⚹♀	1°29
♀♂♄	1°35
☽□♆	1°35

Declin

♂	05N44
♅	06S03
♇	08S57
♆	17S17
☉	17S49
♃	18S55
♄	21S59
♀	24S11
☿	24S59
☽	27N31

	C	F	M
F	1	0	3
E	0	1	0
A	1	0	1
W	0	2	1

RODIN, AUGUSTE
Sculptor

November 12, 1840
12:00 Noon LMT
Paris, France
2 E 20   48 N 50

NOV 12 1840
12:00 PM LMT
15 26 42 SIDEREAL
11 50 40 UNIVERSAL

AUGUSTE RODIN
PARIS, FR
48N50   2E20
TROPICAL
PLACIDUS

One of the world's master sculptors, whose work influenced those who followed. His magnificent pieces include *Age of Bronze*, *The Kiss*, and *The Thinker*. Internationally famous by late life; received many honors. (1840-1917)

B: *Circle* #214 quotes the biography *Rodin* by Victor Frisch, p. 14.

SVP=♓ 7°28'44"
JULIAN DAY=2393421.99352

ROGERS, ROY
Entertainer

November 5, 1911
12:15 PM CST
Cincinnati, Ohio
84 W 31   39 N 06

Leading cowboy motion picture star of the 30s; acted in more than ninety films with his horse, Trigger. Also known for his traveling rodeo, radio and TV shows, and many recordings. Widowed in 1946; second marriage to Dale Evans.

A: CSH.

Declin

♀	00N54
☽	11N29
♄	14N30
☉	15S31
♇	16N58
♃	17S36
☿	18S31
♆	20N47
♅	21S31
♂	21N57

	C	F	M
F	0	0	0
E	2	1	1
A	2	0	0
W	1	3	0

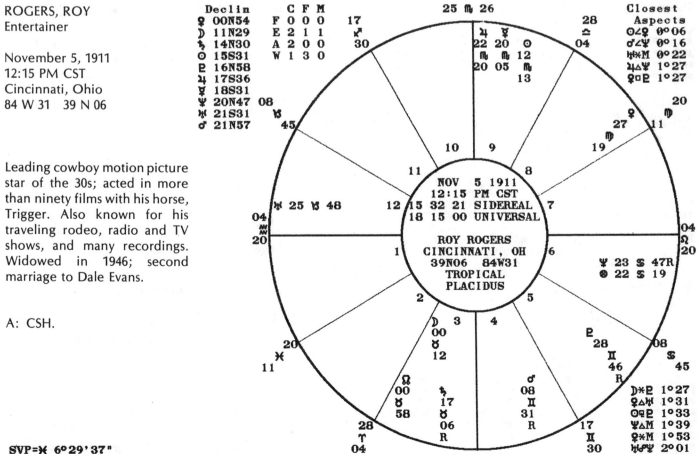

NOV 5 1911
12:15 PM CST
15 32 21 SIDEREAL
18 15 00 UNIVERSAL

ROY ROGERS
CINCINNATI, OH
39N06   84W31
TROPICAL
PLACIDUS

Closest Aspects

☉♂♀	0°06
♂∠♆	0°16
♅⚹M	0°22
♃△♆	1°27
♀□♇	1°27

☽⚹♇	1°27
♀△♅	1°31
☉□♇	1°33
♆△M	1°39
♀⚹M	1°53
♅♂♀	2°01
☿♂♃	2°15

SVP=♓ 6°29'37"
JULIAN DAY=2419346.26042

ROMMEL, ERWIN
General

November 15, 1891
12:00 Noon MET
Heidenheim, Germany
10 E 09   48 N 42

Declin		C F M
♄	02N51	F 0 0 2
♂	05S08	E 1 1 0
♃	09S40	A 2 1 0
♇	10N08	W 0 2 1
♅	12S05	
☽	15N28	
☉	18S29	
♆	20N03	29
♀	21S55	
☿	22S18	

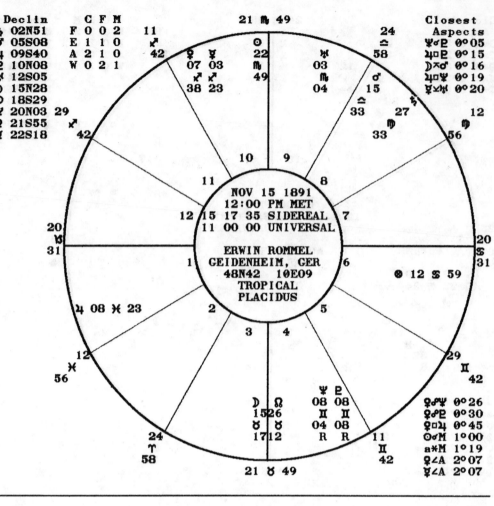

Field marshal in charge of the Nazi North African campaign, 1941-43. Called "The Desert Fox." Favored by Hitler; unpopular with his own officers and men. Forced to kill himself with poison after his conspiracy in the 1944 attempt to assassinate Hitler. (1891-1944)

A: Gauquelin #2098 Vol 3.

SVP=♓ 6°46'26"
JULIAN DAY=2412051.95833

Closest Aspects
♆♂♇	0°05
♃□♇	0°15
☽∠♂	0°16
♃□♆	0°19
☿✶♅	0°20
♀♂♆	0°26
♀♂♇	0°30
♀□♃	0°45
☉♂M	1°00
a✶M	1°19
♀∠A	2°07
☿∠A	2°07

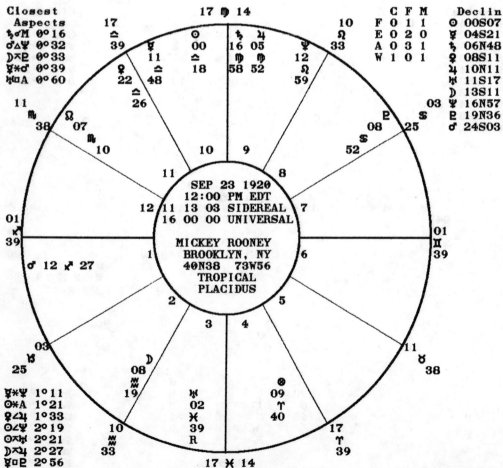

ROONEY, MICKEY
Actor

September 23, 1920
12:00 Noon EDT
Brooklyn, N.Y.
73 W 56   40 N 38

	C F M	Declin	
☉	F 0 1 1	00S07	
☿	E 0 2 0	04S21	
♄	A 0 3 1	06N48	
♀	W 1 0 1	08S11	
♃		10N11	
♅		11S17	
☽		13S11	
♆		16N57	
♇		19N36	
♂		24S03	

Closest Aspects
♄♂M	0°16
♂△♆	0°32
☽✶♇	0°33
☿✶♆	0°39
♅♂A	0°60
☿✶♆	1°11
☉✶A	1°21
♀□♃	1°33
☉∠♃	2°19
☉□♅	2°21
☽∠♃	2°27
☿♂♇	2°56

Talented from youth; nominated for Oscars in *Babes in Arms* (1939), *The Human Comedy* (1943), and *The Bold and the Brave* (1956). Life marked by big debts, bankruptcy, and marriages - number eight to 39-year-old Jan Chamberlain in 1978.

A: CL quotes Lynne Palmer, "from him."[115]

SVP=♓ 6°21'49"
JULIAN DAY=2422591.16667

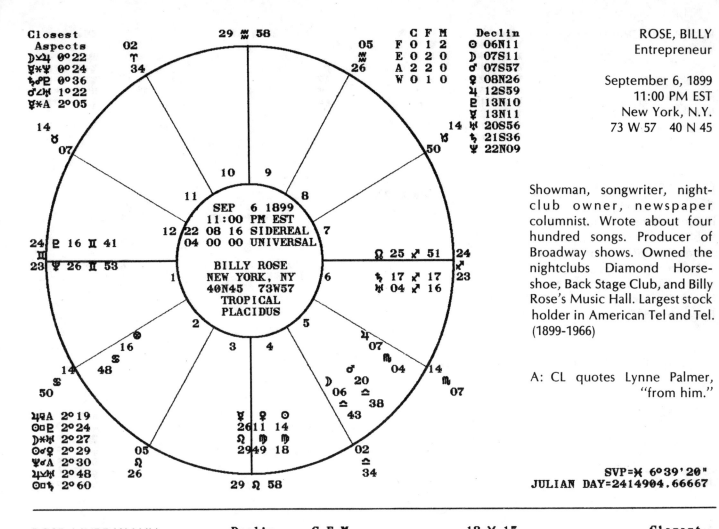

ROSE, BILLY
Entrepreneur

September 6, 1899
11:00 PM EST
New York, N.Y.
73 W 57   40 N 45

Closest
Aspects

☽⚼♃	0°22
☿✱♆	0°24
♄∠♇	0°36
♂♂♅	1°22
☿✱A	2°05

SEP 6 1899
11:00 PM EST
22 08 16 SIDEREAL
04 00 00 UNIVERSAL

BILLY ROSE
NEW YORK, NY
40N45 73W57
TROPICAL
PLACIDUS

C F M

F	0 1 2
E	0 2 0
A	2 2 0
W	0 1 0

Declin

☉	06N11
☽	07S11
♂	07S57
♀	08N26
♃	12S59
♇	13N10
☿	13N11
♅	20S56
♄	21S36
♆	22N09

♃♂A	2°19
☉□♇	2°24
☽✱♅	2°27
☉♂♀	2°29
♆♂A	2°30
♃∠♅	2°48
☉□♄	2°60

Showman, songwriter, night-club owner, newspaper columnist. Wrote about four hundred songs. Producer of Broadway shows. Owned the nightclubs Diamond Horse-shoe, Back Stage Club, and Billy Rose's Music Hall. Largest stock holder in American Tel and Tel. (1899-1966)

A: CL quotes Lynne Palmer, "from him."

SVP=♓ 6°39'20"
JULIAN DAY=2414904.66667

ROSE, MURRAY IAIN
Athlete

January 6, 1939
4:23 PM GMT
Birmingham, England
1 W 54   53 N 28

Australian swimmer and youngest triple gold medal winner in history at the Olympic Games. Won at 1956 games in Melbourne at age 17; won three gold medals at Rome Olympics, 1960. March 1964, made a movie *Ride the Wild Surf* as a stuntman; later became a TV commentator.

A: Garth Allen in AA, June 1958, "from the family to Arthur de Dion."

SVP=♓ 6° 6'28"
JULIAN DAY=2429270.18264

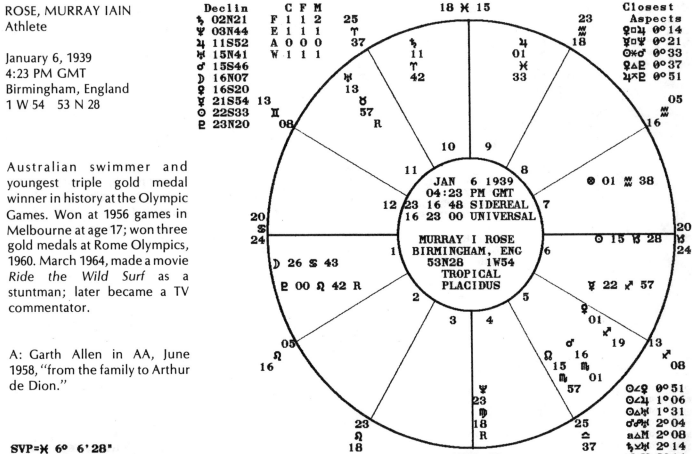

Declin

♄	02N21
♆	03N44
♃	11S52
♅	15N41
♂	15S46
☽	16N07
♀	16S20
☿	21S54
☉	22S33
♇	23N20

C F M

F	1 1 2
E	1 1 1
A	0 0 0
W	1 1 1

JAN 6 1939
04:23 PM GMT
23 16 48 SIDEREAL
16 23 00 UNIVERSAL

MURRAY I ROSE
BIRMINGHAM, ENG
53N28 1W54
TROPICAL
PLACIDUS

Closest
Aspects

♀∠♃	0°14
☿□♆	0°21
☉✱♂	0°33
♀△♇	0°37
♃⚼♇	0°51

☉♂♀	0°51
☉♂♃	1°06
☉△♅	1°31
♂♂♅	2°04
a△M	2°08
♄⚼♅	2°14
♂△M	2°14

ROSTAND, EDMOND
Writer

April 1, 1868
5:00 PM LMT
Marseilles, France
5 E 23   43 N 19

French playwright and poet. Became a lawyer, but his interest turned to journalism. Published his first volume of poems in 1890. His poetic play *The Romancers* produced in Paris four years later. Most famous work, *Cyrano De Bergerac* (1897). (1868-1918)

A: Gauquelin #701 Vol 6.

SVP=♓ 7° 6' 5"
JULIAN DAY=2403424.19338

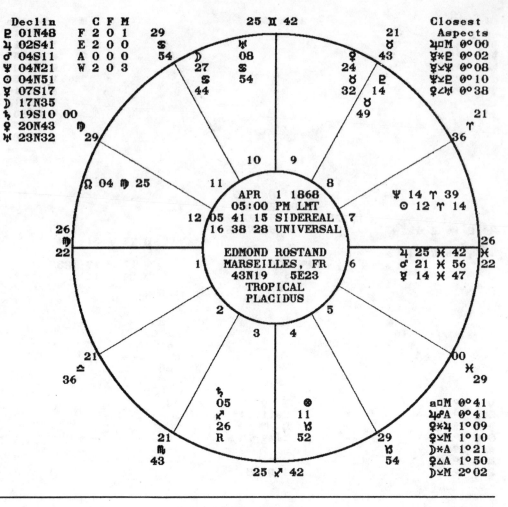

	Declin	C F M
♇	01N48	F 2 0 1
♃	02S41	E 2 0 0
♂	04S11	A 0 0 0
♆	04N21	W 2 0 3
☉	04N51	
☿	07S17	
☽	17N35	
♄	19S10	
♀	20N43	
♅	23N32	

Closest Aspects
♃□M 0°00
☿⚹♇ 0°02
☿⚹♇ 0°08
♆⚹♇ 0°10
♀∠♅ 0°38

a□M 0°41
♃⚹A 0°41
♀⚹♃ 1°09
♀∠M 1°10
☽⚹A 1°21
♀△A 1°50
☽∠M 2°02

RUBIN, JERRY
Activist

July 14, 1938
10:34 AM EST
Cincinnati, Ohio
84 W 31   39 N 06

A political activist in the turbulent 60s; a long-haired, bearded, vegetarian Yippie leader. After spending six years in pop psychology, est, yoga, bioenergetics, and Zen, joined the capitalist world with books and lectures in the 70s.

A: CSH.

SVP=♓ 6° 6'50"
JULIAN DAY=2429094.14861

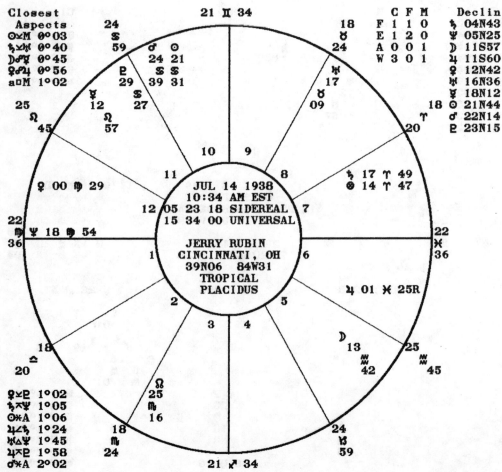

Closest Aspects
☉∠M 0°03
♄∠♅ 0°40
☽⚹♀ 0°45
♀⚹♃ 0°56
a□M 1°02

♀⚹♇ 1°02
♄⚹♆ 1°05
☉⚹A 1°06
♃⚹♅ 1°24
♅△♆ 1°45
♃⚹♇ 1°58
♂⚹A 2°02

C F M		Declin
F 1 1 0	♄	04N43
E 1 2 0	♆	05N25
A 0 0 1	☽	11S57
W 3 0 1	♃	11S60
	♀	12N42
	♅	16N36
	☿	18N12
	☉	21N44
	♂	22N14
	♇	23N15

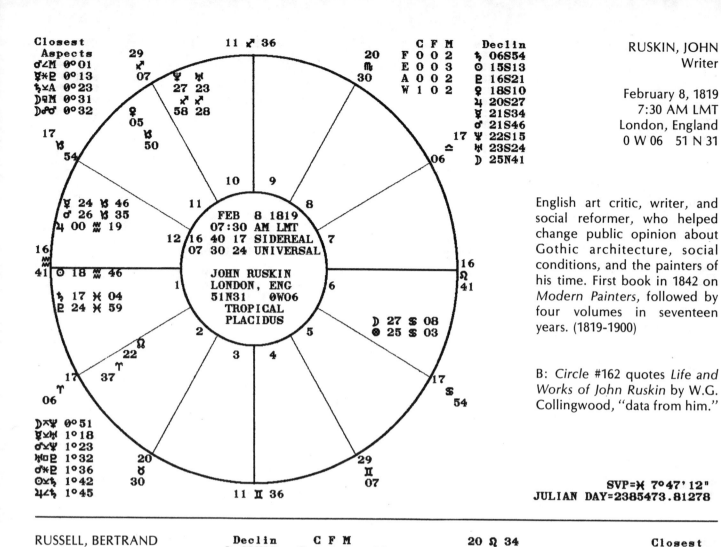

RUSKIN, JOHN
Writer

February 8, 1819
7:30 AM LMT
London, England
0 W 06   51 N 31

English art critic, writer, and social reformer, who helped change public opinion about Gothic architecture, social conditions, and the painters of his time. First book in 1842 on *Modern Painters*, followed by four volumes in seventeen years. (1819-1900)

B: *Circle #162* quotes *Life and Works of John Ruskin* by W.G. Collingwood, "data from him."

SVP=⊹ 7°47'12"
JULIAN DAY=2385473.81278

RUSSELL, BERTRAND
Writer

May 18, 1872
5:45 PM LMT
Trelleck, Wales
2 W 43   51 N 45

British mathematician and philosopher. Received the 1950 Nobel prize for literature for his writings as a defender of humanity and freedom of thought. Author of more than forty books on philosophy, education, politics, and sex; outspoken and controversial. (1872-1970)

B: CL from *Passionate Skeptic* by Alan Wood (1957), p. 15.[116]

SVP=⊹ 7° 2'47"
JULIAN DAY=2404932.24713

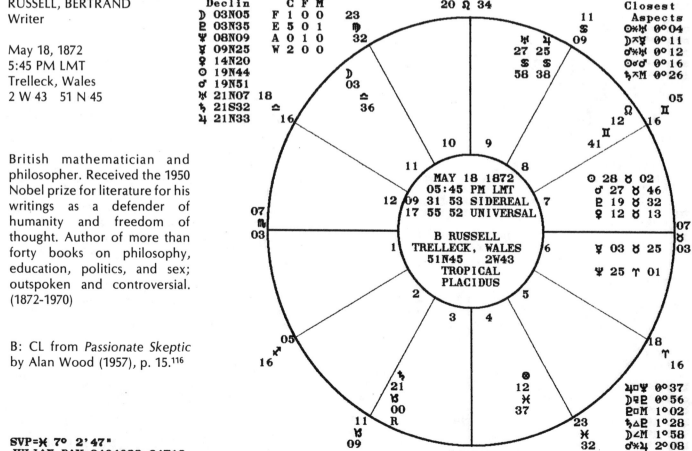

ST. CLAIR, DAVID
Writer

October 21, 1932
3:30 AM EST
Newton Falls, Ohio
80 W 59   41 N 11

A journalist who lived in and wrote about Brazil and South America after 1960, contributing many articles to the various publications of Time Inc. Books include *Safari, The Mighty Amazon,* and *Drum and Candle* (1971), a story of Voodoo and spiritism.

A: From him to LMR, 1971.

SVP=✕ 6°11'50"
JULIAN DAY=2427001.85417

Declin		C F M
♀ 06N21	F 1 1 0
♃ 06N52	E 0 3 1
♅ 07N39	A 0 1 0
♆ 08N46	W 2 1 0
☉ 10S40	
☿ 16S26	
♂ 16N54	
♄ 20S58	
♇ 22N13	
☽ 27N31	

Closest Aspects
☽△♅ 0°13
♂⚹M 0°32
☉⚼♄ 0°40
♆∠♇ 0°59
♀□M 1°05

♀♂♃ 1°15
♂⚹A 1°17
♃♀♄ 1°28
♀⚹♂ 1°37
a□M 1°49
♅⚹A 2°07
☉∠♃ 2°08

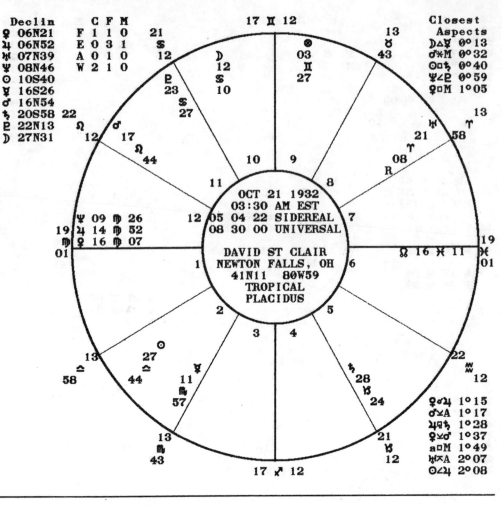

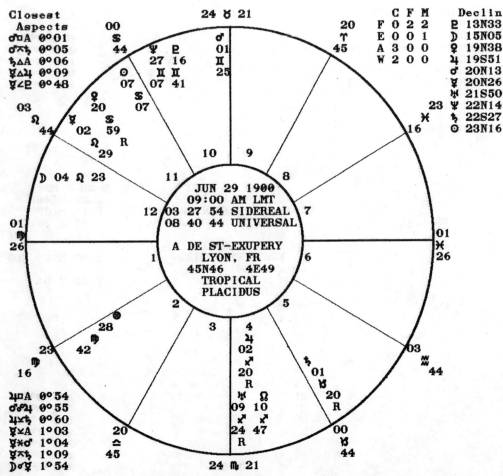

SAINT-EXUPERY, ANTOINE DE
Pilot: writer

June 29, 1900
9:00 AM Paris time
Lyon, France
4 E 49   45 N 46

Chief influence in the creation of the literature of aviation. Author of *Night Flight* (1932), *Wind, Sand and Stars* (1939), and *The Little Prince* (1943). An air pioneer; opened commercial routes and disappeared over the Alps while on an Allied mission. (1900-1944)

A: Gauquelin #1030 Vol 4.

Closest Aspects
♂□A 0°01
♄⚹♅ 0°05
♄△A 0°06
☿△♃ 0°09
☿∠♇ 0°48

♃♀A 0°54
♂□♃ 0°55
♃⚹♅ 0°60
☿⚹A 1°03
☿⚹♂ 1°04
☿⚹♄ 1°09
☽♂☿ 1°54

C F M	Declin
F 0 2 2	♇ 13N33
E 0 0 1	☽ 15N05
A 3 0 0	♀ 19N38
W 2 0 0	♃ 19S51
	♂ 20N13
	☿ 20N26
	♅ 21S50
	♆ 22N14
	♄ 22S27
	☉ 23N16

SVP=✕ 6°38'40"
JULIAN DAY=2415199.86162

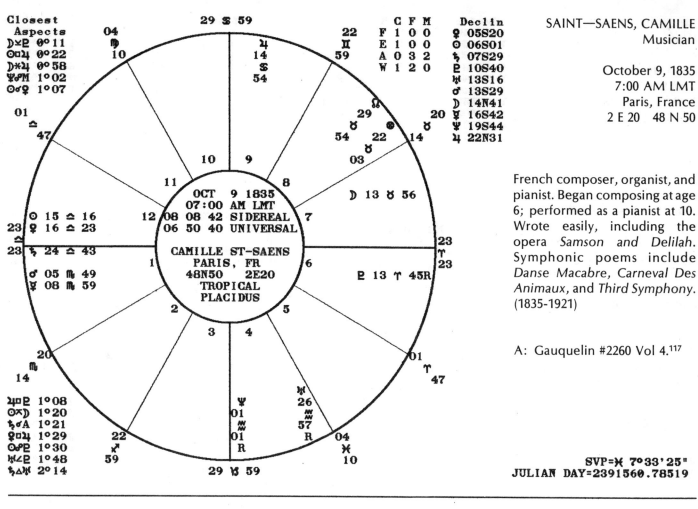

SAINT—SAENS, CAMILLE
Musician

October 9, 1835
7:00 AM LMT
Paris, France
2 E 20   48 N 50

French composer, organist, and pianist. Began composing at age 6; performed as a pianist at 10. Wrote easily, including the opera *Samson and Delilah*. Symphonic poems include *Danse Macabre*, *Carneval Des Animaux*, and *Third Symphony*. (1835-1921)

A: Gauquelin #2260 Vol 4.[117]

SVP=⅞ 7°33'25"
JULIAN DAY=2391560.78519

SANDBURG, CARL
Writer

January 6, 1878
00:05 AM LMT
Galesburg, Ill
90 W 23   40 N 57

American poet and author. Biographer of Lincoln in *Abraham Lincoln: The War Years* (1939). In 1940 won the Pulitzer prize for history. Awarded the 1941 Pulitzer prize for poetry. Wrote children's books and many poems; numerous awards for his accomplishments.

A: CL from his mother, "a little after midnight."[118]

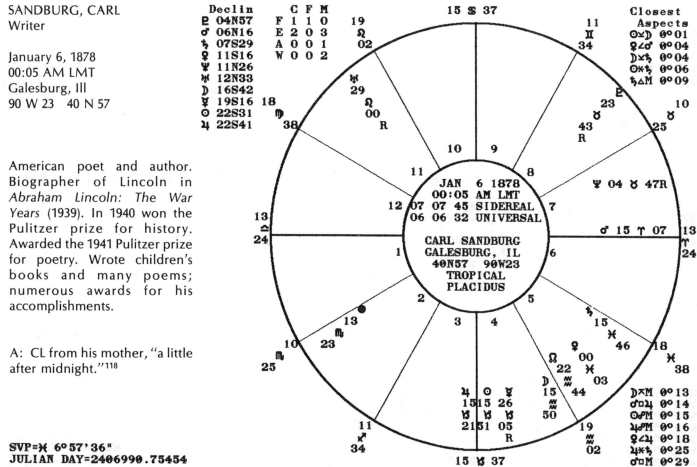

SVP=⅞ 6°57'36"
JULIAN DAY=2406990.75454

SANDERS, GEORGE
Actor

July 3, 1906 NS
6:00 AM LMT
St. Petersburg, Russia
30 E 15   59 N 55

His ninety movies from 1936 included *The Ghost and Mrs. Muir.* Suicide on April 25, 1972, with a note: "Dear World. I am leaving you because I'm bored. I feel I have lived long enough. I am leaving you with your worries in this sweet cesspool and good luck."

B: *Circle* #668 quotes *Memoirs of a Professional Cad*, states "assumed New Style."

SVP=✕ 6°34' 7"
JULIAN DAY=2417394.66597

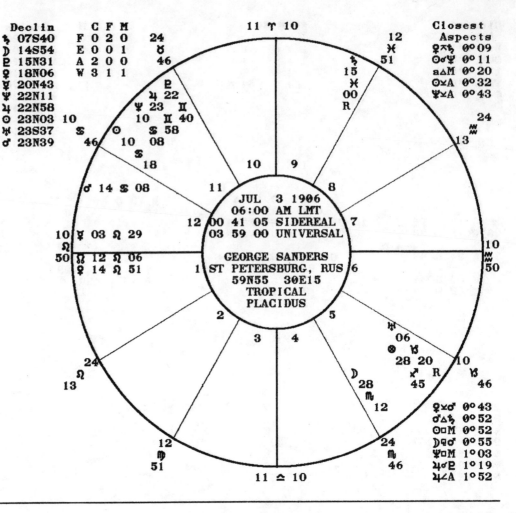

SANDERS, GEORGE chart:
JUL 3 1906
06:00 AM LMT
00 41 05 SIDEREAL
03 59 00 UNIVERSAL
GEORGE SANDERS
ST PETERSBURG, RUS
59N55 30E15
TROPICAL
PLACIDUS

Declin
♄ 07S40
☽ 14S54
♇ 15N31
♀ 18N06
☿ 20N43
♆ 22N11
♃ 22N58
☉ 23N03
♅ 23S37
♂ 23N39

C F M
F 0 2 0
E 0 0 1
A 2 0 0
W 3 1 1

Closest Aspects
♀⊼♄ 0°09
☉♂♆ 0°11
a△M 0°20
☉∠A 0°32
♆∠A 0°43
♀⚹♂ 0°43
♂△♄ 0°52
☉□M 0°52
☽♋♂ 0°55
♆□M 1°03
♃♋♇ 1°19
♃∠A 1°52

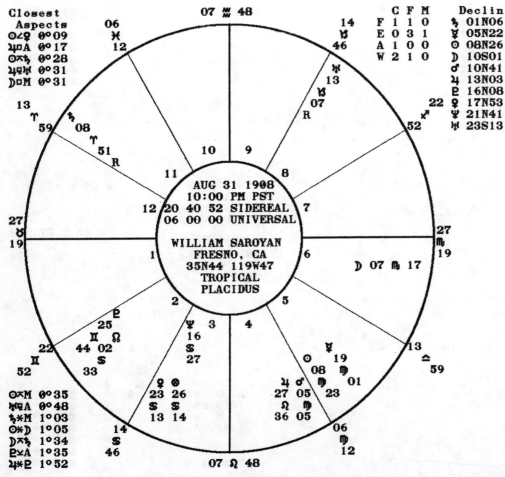

WILLIAM SAROYAN chart:
AUG 31 1908
10:00 PM PST
20 40 52 SIDEREAL
06 00 00 UNIVERSAL
WILLIAM SAROYAN
FRESNO, CA
35N44 119W47
TROPICAL
PLACIDUS

Closest Aspects
☉∠♀ 0°09
♃∠A 0°17
☉⊼♄ 0°28
♃♋♅ 0°31
☽□M 0°31

C F M
F 1 1 0
E 0 3 1
A 1 0 0
W 2 1 0

Declin
♄ 01N06
☿ 05N22
☉ 08N26
☽ 10S01
♂ 10N41
♃ 13N03
♀ 16N08
♇ 17N53
♆ 21N41
♅ 23S13

☉⊼M 0°35
♅♋A 0°48
♄⚹M 1°03
☉⚹☽ 1°05
☽⊼A 1°34
♇∠A 1°35
♃⚹♇ 1°52

SAROYAN, WILLIAM
Writer

August 31, 1908
10:00 PM PST
Fresno, Ca
119 W 47   35 N 44

American writer of short stories, novels, and plays. Little formal education. Immediate fame in 1934 with a short story. Wrote a book of short stories, *Love, Here Is My Hat* (1938); the play, *The Time of Your Life* (1940); novels include *The Human Comedy* (1942).

A: Dewey, "data verified by him" in AA, November 1939.

SVP=✕ 6°32'23"
JULIAN DAY=2418185.75000

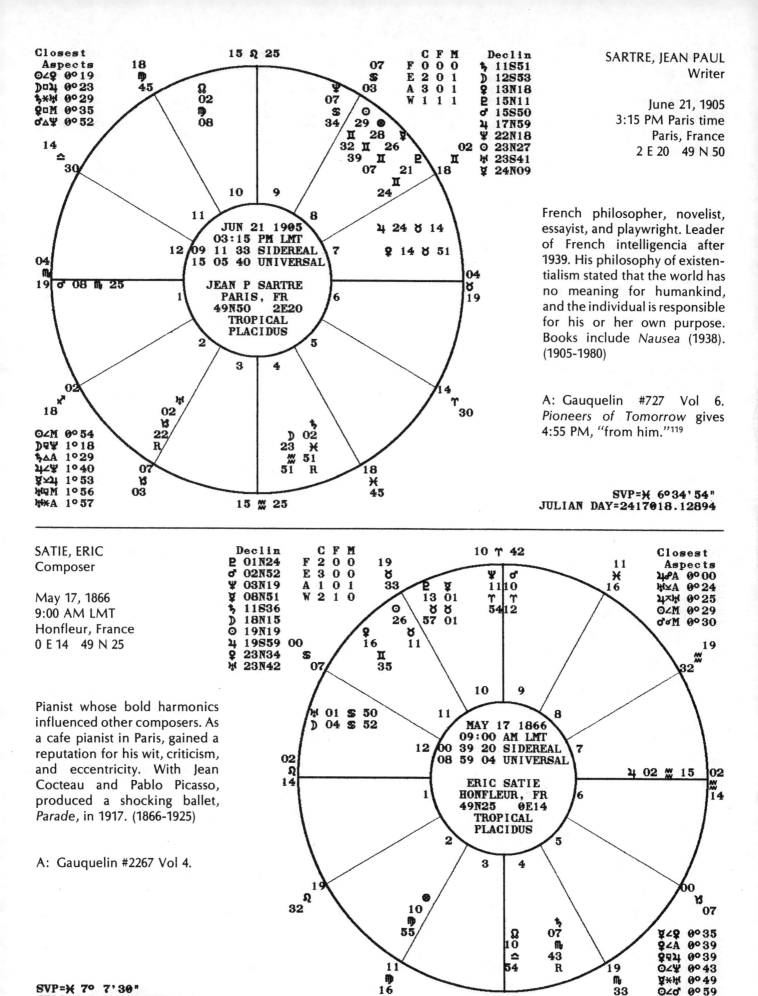

Closest Aspects

☉∠♀	0°19
☽□♃	0°23
♄✳♅	0°29
♀□M	0°35
♂△♆	0°52

15 ♌ 25

18 ♍ 45

☊ 02 ♍ 08

14 ♎ 30

04 ♏
19 ♂ 08 ♏ 25

02 ♐
18

C F M

F	0 0 0
E	2 0 1
A	3 0 1
W	1 1 1

07
♋ 03
07 ♋
34 ☉ 29 ⊕
Ⅱ 28 ☿
32 Ⅱ 26
39 Ⅱ
07 ♇ 21
24 Ⅱ

02 Ⅱ 18

♃ 24 ♉ 14
♀ 14 ♉ 51

04 ♉ 19

14 ♈ 30

JUN 21 1905
03:15 PM LMT
09 11 33 SIDEREAL
15 05 40 UNIVERSAL

JEAN P SARTRE
PARIS, FR
49N50 2E20
TROPICAL
PLACIDUS

♅ 02
22 ♑
R

07 ♑
03

15 ♒ 25

☽ 02
23 ♓
♒ 51
51 R

18 ♓
45

Declin

♄	11S51
☽	12S53
♀	13N18
♇	15N11
♂	15S50
♃	17N59
♆	22N18
☉	23N27
♅	23S41
☿	24N09

Closest Aspects

☉∠M	0°54
☽✳♆	1°18
♄△A	1°29
♃∠♆	1°40
☿✶♃	1°53
♅□M	1°56
♅✳A	1°57

SARTRE, JEAN PAUL
Writer

June 21, 1905
3:15 PM Paris time
Paris, France
2 E 20   49 N 50

French philosopher, novelist, essayist, and playwright. Leader of French intelligencia after 1939. His philosophy of existentialism stated that the world has no meaning for humankind, and the individual is responsible for his or her own purpose. Books include *Nausea* (1938). (1905-1980)

A: Gauquelin #727 Vol 6. *Pioneers of Tomorrow* gives 4:55 PM, "from him."[119]

SVP=♓ 6°34'54"
JULIAN DAY=2417018.12894

SATIE, ERIC
Composer

May 17, 1866
9:00 AM LMT
Honfleur, France
0 E 14   49 N 25

Pianist whose bold harmonics influenced other composers. As a cafe pianist in Paris, gained a reputation for his wit, criticism, and eccentricity. With Jean Cocteau and Pablo Picasso, produced a shocking ballet, *Parade*, in 1917. (1866-1925)

A: Gauquelin #2267 Vol 4.

SVP=♓ 7° 7'30"
JULIAN DAY=2402738.87435

Declin

♇	01N24
♂	02S52
♆	03N19
☿	08N51
♄	11S36
☽	18N15
☉	19N19
♃	19N59
♀	23N34
♅	23N42

C F M

F	2 0 0
E	3 0 0
A	1 0 1
W	2 1 0

10 ♈ 42

19 ♉
33

11 ♇ 10
13 01 ♈
☉ ♉ 54 12
26 57 01

♀ 16
11
Ⅱ 35

♆ ♂
♅ ☿
♈ ♈

11 ♒
16

11 ♓
16

♅ 01 ♋ 50
☽ 04 ♋ 52

02 ♌
14 ☊

19 ♌
32 ☊

MAY 17 1866
09:00 AM LMT
00 39 20 SIDEREAL
08 59 04 UNIVERSAL

ERIC SATIE
HONFLEUR, FR
49N25 0E14
TROPICAL
PLACIDUS

⊕
10 ♍
55

♄
10 07 ♏
♎ 43
54 R

11 ♍
16

♃ 02 ♒ 15

02 ♒
14

00 ♑
07

Closest Aspects

♃♂A	0°00
♅∠A	0°24
♃✶♅	0°25
☉∠M	0°29
♂♂M	0°30
☿∠♀	0°35
♀∠A	0°39
♀□♃	0°39
☉∠♆	0°43
☿✶♅	0°49
☉∠♂	0°59
♆♂M	1°12

10 ♎ 42

SCHIRRA, WALTER
Astronaut

March 12, 1923
11:55 PM EST
Hackensack, N.Y.
74 W 03   40 N 53

After active service of flying ninety combat missions in Korea, selected for astronaut training in April 1959. Pilot of Gemini VI in the first outer space rendezvous between two manned space vehicles, December 15, 1965.

A: CSH. (*Pioneers of Tomorrow* gives 4:55 PM "from him.")

SVP=✠ 6°19'58"
JULIAN DAY=2423491.70486

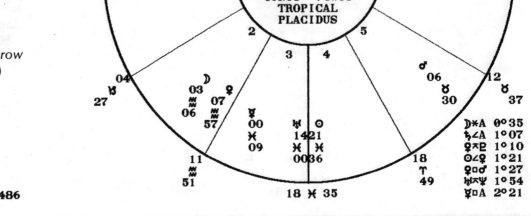

Declin		C	F	M
☉ 03S20	F	0	1	0
♄ 04S47	E	1	0	0
♅ 06S58	A	0	1	2
☿ 13S20	W	1	1	3
♂ 14N02				
☽ 15S40				
♃ 16S13				
♆ 16N16				
♀ 17S28				
♇ 20N23				

Closest Aspects
♄⚹M 0°03
☉☌♂ 0°06
♃⚹♄ 0°13
♃⚹M 0°16
☽☐M 0°29

MAR 12 1923
11:55 PM EST
11 18 01 SIDEREAL
04 55 00 UNIVERSAL

WATER SCHIRRA
HACKENSACK, NJ
40N53 74W03
TROPICAL
PLACIDUS

☽⚹A 0°35
♄⚿A 1°07
♀⚹♇ 1°10
☉⚿A 1°21
♀☌♂ 1°27
♅⚹♆ 1°54
☿☐A 2°21

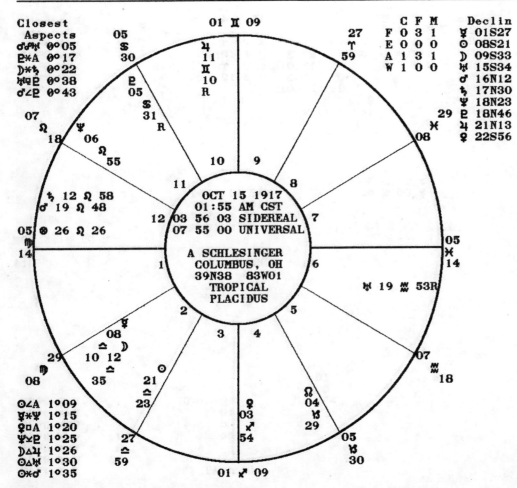

Closest Aspects
♂♅ 0°05
♇⚹A 0°17
☽⚹♄ 0°22
♅♇ 0°38
♂⚿♇ 0°43

OCT 15 1917
01:55 AM CST
03 56 03 SIDEREAL
07 55 00 UNIVERSAL

A SCHLESINGER
COLUMBUS, OH
39N38 83W01
TROPICAL
PLACIDUS

☉☐A 1°09
☿⚹♆ 1°15
♀☌A 1°20
♀⚹♇ 1°25
☽△♃ 1°26
☉△♅ 1°30
☉⚹♂ 1°35

	C	F	M	Declin
F	0	3	1	☿ 01S27
E	0	0	0	☉ 08S21
A	1	3	1	☽ 09S33
W	1	0	0	♅ 15S34
				♂ 16N12
				♄ 17N30
				♆ 18N23
				♇ 18N46
				♃ 21N13
				♀ 22S56

SCHLESINGER, ARTHUR JR.
Writer

October 15, 1917
1:55 AM CST
Columbus, Ohio
83 W 01   39 N 38

Author and historian. Awarded two Pulitzer prizes, for *The Age of Jackson* (1945) and *A Thousand Days: J.F. Kennedy in the White House* (1966). The son of a man known as the dean of American historians; became a professor of history at Harvard in 1946.

A: CSH.

SVP=✠ 6°24'12"
JULIAN DAY=2421516.82986

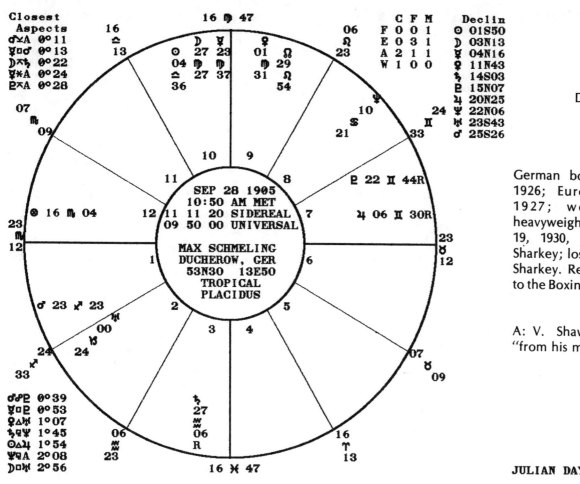

Closest
Aspects
♂⊼A 0°11
☿⊽♂ 0°13
☽⊼♄ 0°22
☿⚹A 0°24
♇⊼A 0°28

	C	F	M		Declin
F	0	0	1	⊙	01S50
E	0	3	1	☽	03N13
A	2	1	1	☿	04N16
W	1	0	0	♄	14S03
				♇	15N07
				♃	20N25
				♆	22N06
				♅	23S43
				♂	25S26

SEP 28 1905
10:50 AM MET
11 11 20 SIDEREAL
09 50 00 UNIVERSAL

MAX SCHMELING
DUCHEROW, GER
53N30 13E50
TROPICAL
PLACIDUS

♂⊽♇ 0°39
☿⊽♇ 0°53
♀△♅ 1°07
♄⊽♆ 1°45
⊙△♃ 1°54
♆A 2°08
☽□♅ 2°56

SCHMELING, MAX
Boxer

September 28, 1905
10:50 AM MET
Ducherow, Germany
13 E 50   53 N 30

German boxing champion in
1926; European champion,
1927; won the vacant
heavyweight boxing title, June
19, 1930, by defeating Jack
Sharkey; lost the title in 1932 to
Sharkey. Retired, 1948. Elected
to the Boxing Hall of Fame, 1970.

A: V. Shaw quotes Ebertin,
"from his mother."

SVP=♓ 6°34'43"
JULIAN DAY=2417116.90972

SCHUBERT, FRANZ PETER
Musician

January 31, 1797
1:30 PM LMT
Vienna, Austria
16 E 20   48 N 14

Austrian composer of six
hundred songs, including
"Death and the Maiden", "The
Erlking", and "Do You Know
the Land"; also many sym-
phonies and chamber music.
Recognized as one of the
greatest masters of song.
Eccentric in his private life;
sickly. (1797-1828)

A: CL from AFA, July 1962,
"recorded time by his father."

SVP=♓ 8° 5'48"
JULIAN DAY=2377432.01713

Declin		C	F	M
♂	03N59	F	1	0	0
♃	06S39	E	0	1	1
♅	07N51	A	1	0	3
☽	08S24	W	0	1	2
☿	10S27				
♆	13S21				
⊙	17S09				
♄	22N01				
♀	22S25				
♇	22S35				

JAN 31 1797
01:30 PM LMT
22 14 46 SIDEREAL
12 24 40 UNIVERSAL

FRANZ P SCHUBERT
VIENNA, AUS
48N14 16E20
TROPICAL
PLACIDUS

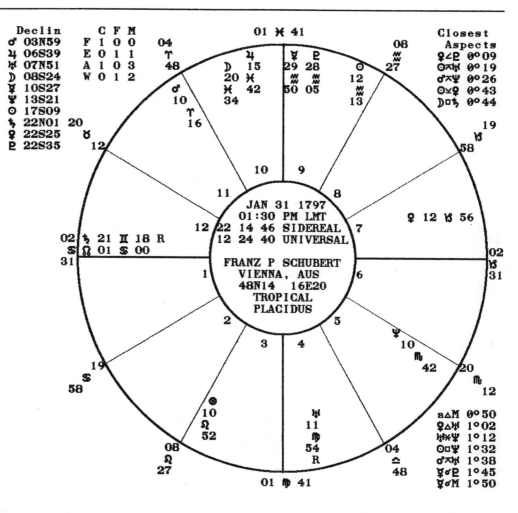

Closest
Aspects
♀∠♇ 0°09
⊙⊼♅ 0°19
♂⊼♆ 0°26
⊙⚹♀ 0°43
☽□♄ 0°44

a△M 0°50
♀△♅ 1°02
♅⚹♆ 1°12
⊙□♆ 1°32
♂⊼♅ 1°38
☿⊽♇ 1°45
☿⊽M 1°50

SCHWARZENEGGER, ARNOLD
Body-builder

July 30, 1947
4:10 AM MDT
Graz, Austria
15 E 26   47 N 05

Declin		C	F	M	
♆	01S59	F	0	3	0	01
♃	16S19	E	0	0	1	♉
♄	18N01	A	2	1	0	21
☉	18N45	W	2	1	0	
☿	19N19					
♀	21N31					
♂	23N07					
♅	23N27					13
♇	23N29					
☽	26S09					

Closest Aspects
☿∠♃ 0°04
♅□M 0°09
☽∠♃ 0°32
☉♂♂ 0°58
♂✶A 1°01

Prize-winning physical culturist, entrepreneur, showman, and movie strong man. Won titles of Mr. World, Mr. Universe (five times), and Mr. Olympia (six times). Appeared in movie *Pumping Iron*. Biography published, 1977 - *Arnold: The Education of a Body Builder*.

A: D.C. Doane, "from him to a colleague", 1979.

SVP=H 5°59'44"
JULIAN DAY=2432396.59028

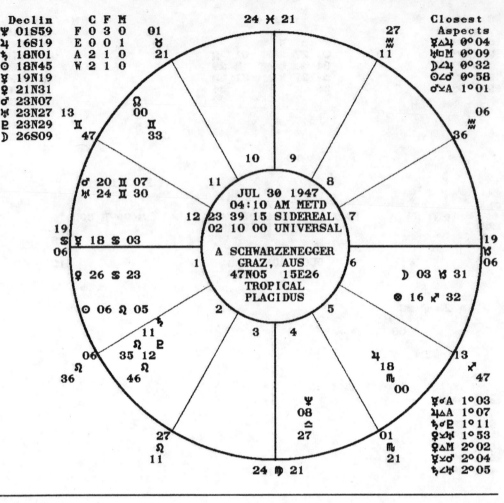

JUL 30 1947
04:10 AM METD
23 39 15 SIDEREAL
02 10 00 UNIVERSAL

A SCHWARZENEGGER
GRAZ, AUS
47N05 15E26
TROPICAL
PLACIDUS

♅♂A 1°03
♃△A 1°07
♄♀♇ 1°11
♀∠♅ 1°53
♀△M 2°02
☿♂♂ 2°04
♄∠♅ 2°05

Closest Aspects
♂♂♅ 0°00
♀✶♄ 0°04
♂♂♄ 0°07
♄♂♅ 0°08
♀△♅ 0°11

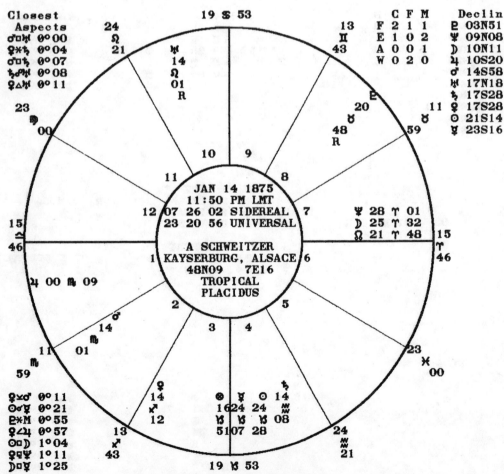

JAN 14 1875
11:50 PM LMT
07 26 02 SIDEREAL
23 20 56 UNIVERSAL

A SCHWEITZER
KAYSERBURG, ALSACE
48N09 7E16
TROPICAL
PLACIDUS

	C	F	M	Declin	
13	F	2	1	1	♇	03N51
♊	E	1	0	2	♆	09N08
43	A	0	0	1	☽	10N11
	W	0	2	0	♃	10S20
					♂	14S58
					♅	17N18
					♄	17S28
					♀	17S28
					☉	21S14
					☿	23S16

SCHWEITZER, ALBERT
Humanitarian

January 14, 1875
11:50 PM LMT
Kayserburg, Alsace
7 E 16   48 N 09

German philosopher, physician, musician, clergyman, missionary, and writer on theology: brilliantly accomplished in each area. Called the true Christian of his time, with a creed based on reverence for life. Winner of the 1952 Nobel Peace prize. (1875-1965)

A: Huber states B.C.[120]

♀♂☿ 0°11
☉♂♂ 0°21
♇✶M 0°55
♀∠♃ 0°57
☉□☽ 1°04
♀♂♅ 1°11
☽□☿ 1°25

SVP=H 7° 0'22"
JULIAN DAY=2405903.47287

SCOTT, DAVID R.
Astronaut

June 6, 1932
4:04 AM CST
Fort Sam Houston, Tex
98 W 27   29 N 27

Flew the Gemini 8 with Armstrong, March 16, 1966; docked with Agena. On the Apollo 9, March 3, 1969, performed rendezvous and docking. Mission commander of Apollo 15, June 26, 1971; spent sixty-six hours on the moon exploring in a lunar dune buggy.

A: CSH.

Closest Aspects
☉⚺♀ 0°04
☿∠♅ 0°10
♆∠♇ 0°26
♄☌M 0°27
♆⚻M 0°30

	C	F	M
F	1	1	0
E	1	1	0
A	2	0	1
W	3	0	0

Declin
♅ 08N07
♆ 10N17
♃ 16N28
♂ 16N58
♄ 19S29
☿ 21N16
♇ 22N30
☉ 22N39
♀ 24N19
☽ 27N57

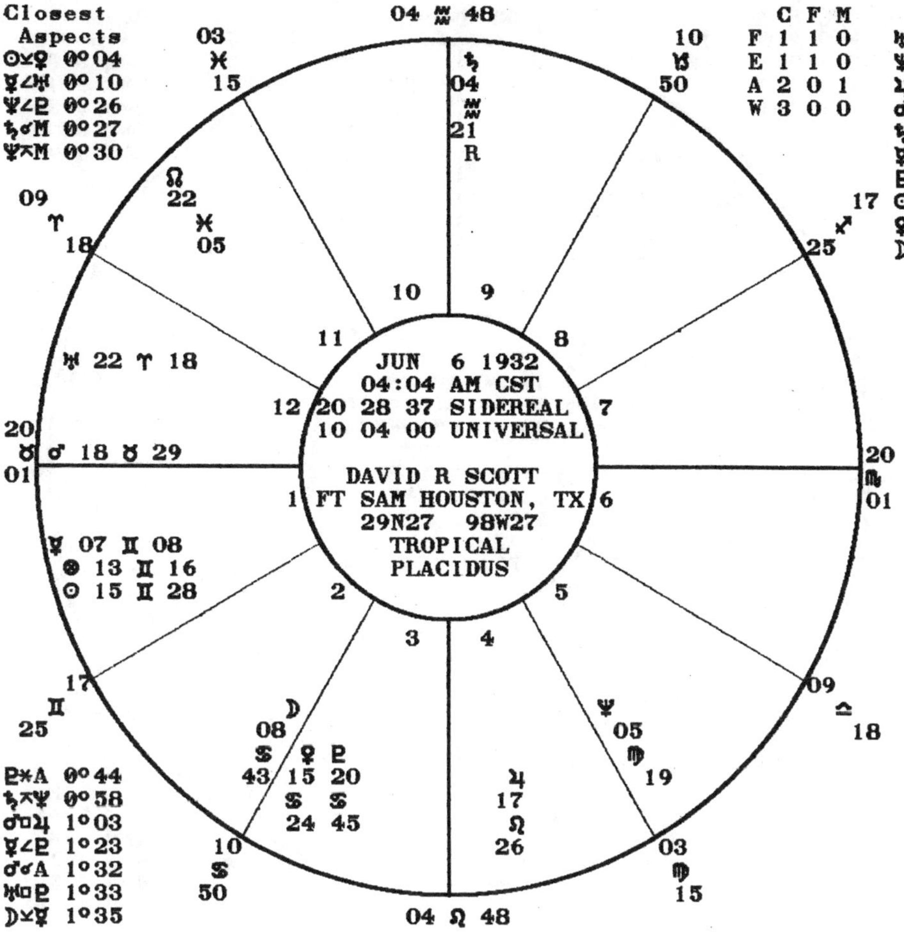
JUN 6 1932
04:04 AM CST
20 28 37 SIDEREAL
10 04 00 UNIVERSAL
DAVID R SCOTT
FT SAM HOUSTON, TX
29N27 98W27
TROPICAL
PLACIDUS

♇✶A 0°44
♄⚻♆ 0°58
♂□♃ 1°03
☿∠♇ 1°23
♂☌A 1°32
♅□♇ 1°33
☽⚺☿ 1°35

SVP=♓ 6°12'10"
JULIAN DAY=2426864.91944

SEBRING, JAY
Beautician

October 10, 1933
1:05 AM CST
Fairfield, Ala
86 W 55   33 N 29

Hairdresser who established his own expensive Hollywood salon. Murdered in the Manson ritual killings with four other people on August 9, 1969, by Atkins, Watson, Krenwinkel, and Kasabian, carrying guns and knives.

A: From him to LMR, 1967.[121]

Declin
♃ 01S34
☉ 06S30
♆ 08N08
♅ 09N24
☿ 14S35
♄ 18S45
♂ 21S08
♀ 21S47
♇ 22N22
☽ 27N42

	C	F	M
F	1	0	1
E	0	1	0
A	0	2	1
W	2	2	0

Closest Aspects
☽∠A 0°03
☉✶A 0°18
♄□M 0°27
♅□♆ 0°28
☽⚻♂ 0°42

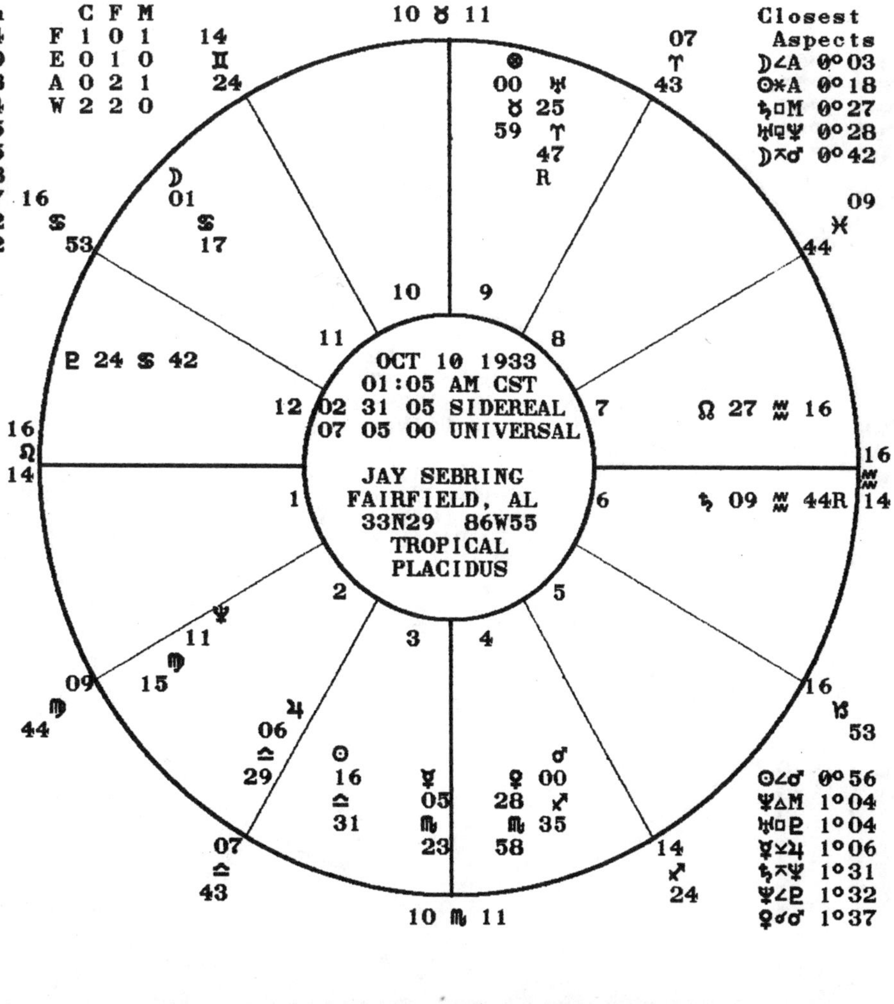
OCT 10 1933
01:05 AM CST
02 31 05 SIDEREAL
07 05 00 UNIVERSAL
JAY SEBRING
FAIRFIELD, AL
33N29 86W55
TROPICAL
PLACIDUS

☉∠♂ 0°56
♆△M 1°04
♅□♇ 1°04
☿⚺♃ 1°06
♄⚻♆ 1°31
♆∠♇ 1°32
♀☌♂ 1°37

SVP=♓ 6°10'56"
JULIAN DAY=2427355.79514

SELLERS, PETER
Actor

September 8, 1925
6:00 AM BST
London, England
0 W.06   51 N.31

Comedy-character star, called "the man with a thousand voices." Theatrical family background; films from 1950 that include *The Mouse That Roared* and the delightful *Pink Pussycat* series. Married 1951, 1964, and August 24, 1970.

A: Dewey quotes Frank Freeman in AA, June 1971, "from him."[122]

SVP=)(6°18' 5"
JULIAN DAY=2424401.70833

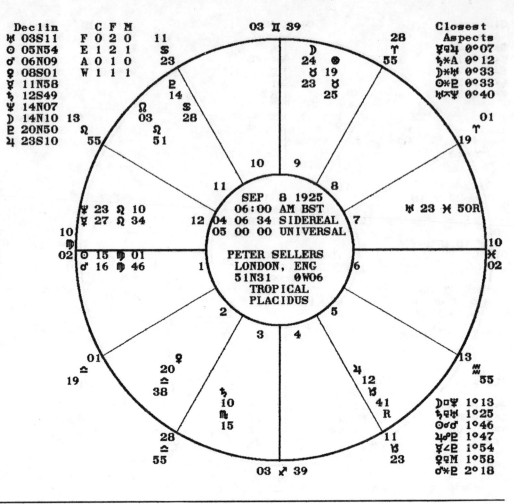

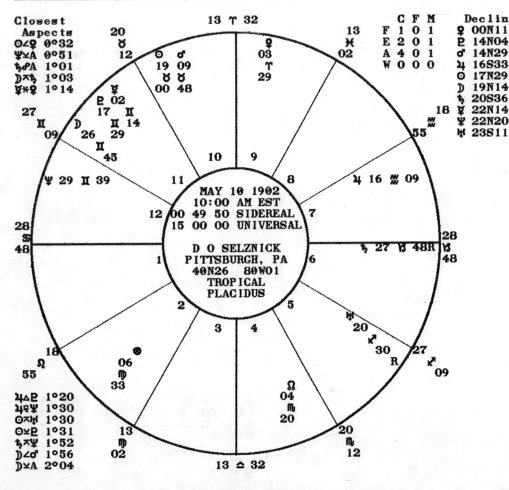

SELZNICK, DAVID O.
Film producer

May 10, 1902
10:00 AM EST
Pittsburgh, Pa
80 W.01   40 N.26

Among the top five "champion of champions" producers for twenty-two consecutive years, 1936-1958. Received the Irving Thalberg Memorial Award, 1939. Films include Oscar winners *Gone With The Wind* (1939) and *Rebecca* (1940). (1902-1965)

A: CL quotes letter "from him to Tobey, April 1932."

SVP=)(6°37' 15"
JULIAN DAY=2415880.12500

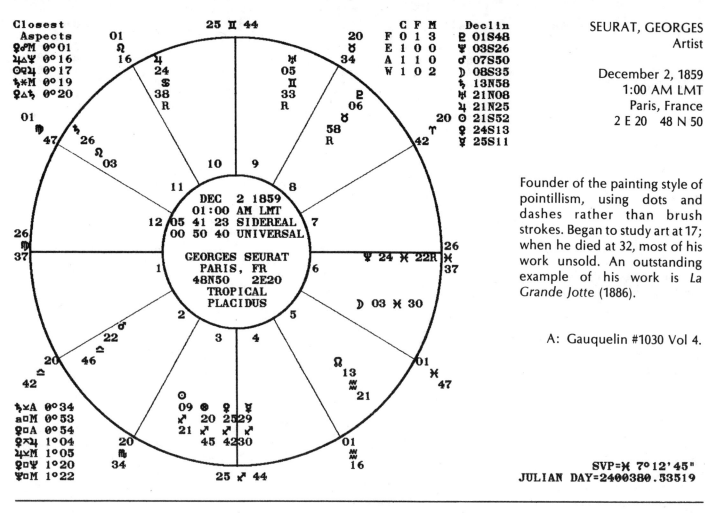

SEURAT, GEORGES
Artist

December 2, 1859
1:00 AM LMT
Paris, France
2 E 20   48 N 50

Closest Aspects

♀♂M	0°01
♃△♆	0°16
☉□♃	0°17
♄✳M	0°19
♀△♄	0°20

	C	F	M		Declin
F	0	1	3	♇	01S48
E	1	0	0	♆	03S26
A	1	1	0	♂	07S50
W	1	0	2	☽	08S35
				♄	13N58
				♅	21N08
				♃	21N25
				☉	21S52
				♀	24S13
				☿	25S11

DEC 2 1859
01:00 AM LMT
05 41 23 SIDEREAL
00 50 40 UNIVERSAL

GEORGES SEURAT
PARIS, FR
48N50 2E20
TROPICAL
PLACIDUS

Founder of the painting style of pointillism, using dots and dashes rather than brush strokes. Began to study art at 17; when he died at 32, most of his work unsold. An outstanding example of his work is *La Grande Jotte* (1886).

A: Gauquelin #1030 Vol 4.

♄✳A	0°34
a□M	0°53
♀□A	0°54
♀⊼♃	1°04
♃✳M	1°05
♀□♆	1°20
♆□M	1°22

SVP=♓ 7°12'45"
JULIAN DAY=2400380.53519

SHARIF, OMAR
Actor

April 10, 1932
5:30 PM EET
Alexandria, Egypt
29 E 54   31 N 11

Declin				C	F	M
♂	01N27			F	4	1	0
♅	07N03			E	0	1	0
☉	08N02			A	2	0	1
☿	09N59			W	1	0	0
♆	10N14
♃	17N58
♄	19S31
♇	22N34
♀	24N14
☽	27N02

APR 10 1932
05:30 PM EET
06 44 11 SIDEREAL
15 30 00 UNIVERSAL

OMAR SHARIF
ALEXANDRIA, EGYPT
31N11 29E54
TROPICAL
PLACIDUS

An Egyptian who usually portrays an Oriental or Balkan-born leading man, and great screen lover. Films include *Dr. Zhivago* and *Funny Girl*. A noted bridge player, who attends tournaments to build master points. Divorced; one son.

A: Dewey quotes him in an interview, April 29, 1975, in *National Enquirer*.[123]

Closest Aspects

☉□♆	0°01
♂⊼♅	0°11
♀✳♂	0°12
☿□♇	0°14
☿⊼♅	0°20
☉♂♅	0°21
☽✳M	0°22
☉△♀	0°22
♀□♆	0°23
♆∠♇	0°34
♅□♇	0°34
☉□♇	0°35

SVP=♓ 6°12'19"
JULIAN DAY=2426808.14583

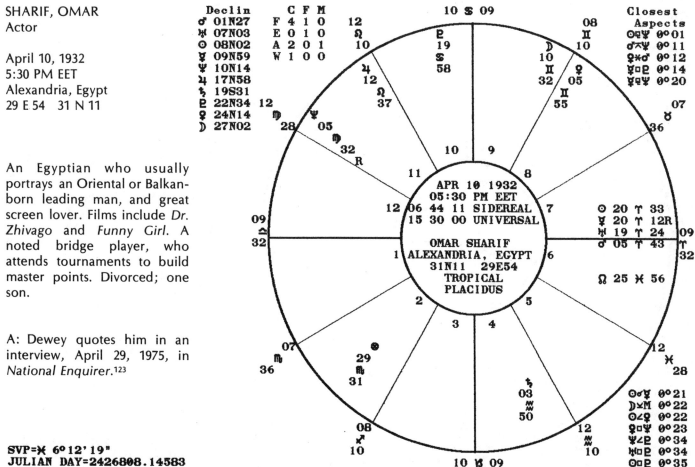

SHAW, GEORGE BERNARD
Writer

July 26, 1856
00:40 AM Dunsink
Dublin, Ireland
6 W 15   53 N 20

British critic, novelist, and dramatist; awarded the 1925 Nobel prize for literature. Advocator of socialistic views. Works include the play *Man and Superman*, novels *Love Among the Artists* and *An Unsocial Socialist*. (1856-1950)

A: *Constellations*, 1977, Lockhart quotes Wemyss, "as stated by his older sister."[124]

SVP=)(7°15'49"
JULIAN DAY=2399156.54514

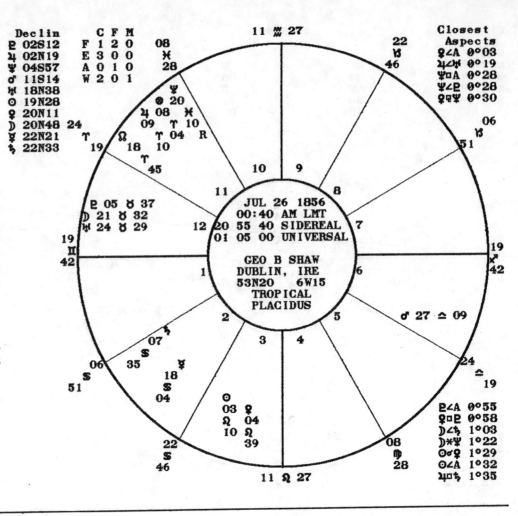

Declin

♇	02S12
♃	02N19
♆	04S57
♂	11S14
♅	18N38
☉	19N28
♀	20N11
☽	20N48 24
☿	22N21
♄	22N33

C F M
F 1 2 0
E 3 0 0
A 0 1 0
W 2 0 1

Closest Aspects

♀∠A	0°03
♃∠⋇	0°19
♆∠A	0°28
♀∠♇	0°28
♀⋇♆	0°30

♇∠A	0°55
♀⊐♇	0°58
☽∠⋇	1°03
☽⋇♆	1°22
☉♂♀	1°29
☉∠A	1°32
♃⊓♄	1°35

JUL 26 1856
00:40 AM LMT
20 55 40 SIDEREAL
01 05 00 UNIVERSAL

GEO B SHAW
DUBLIN, IRE
53N20   6W15
TROPICAL
PLACIDUS

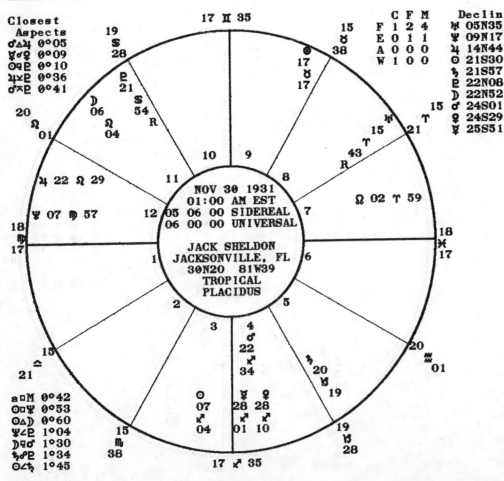

Closest Aspects

♂△♃	0°05
☿♂♀	0°09
☉♇♇	0°10
♃♇♇	0°36
♂⋇♇	0°41

a⊐M	0°42
☉⋇♆	0°53
☉△☽	0°60
♀⋇♇	1°04
☽∠♂	1°30
♄♂♇	1°34
☉∠♃	1°45

C F M
F 1 2 4
E 0 1 1
A 0 0 0
W 1 0 0

Declin

♅	05N35
♆	09N17
♃	14N44
☉	21S30
♄	21S57
♇	22N08
☽	22N52
♂	24S01
♀	24S29
☿	25S51

NOV 30 1931
01:00 AM EST
05 06 00 SIDEREAL
06 00 00 UNIVERSAL

JACK SHELDON
JACKSONVILLE, FL
30N20   81W39
TROPICAL
PLACIDUS

SHELDON, JACK
Musician

November 30, 1931
1:00 AM EST
Jacksonville, Fla
81 W 39   30 N 20

Trumpet player with the Mort Lindsey Orchestra in the TV *Merv Griffin Show*. Recording artist, singer, and professional musician from 1956. Comic actor in films and TV; had his own TV show, *Run Buddy Run*. First moved to L.A. in 1947 as a swimming instructor.

A: MacKenzie in AA, November 1977, "from his fiancee."

SVP=)(6°12'39"
JULIAN DAY=2426675.75000

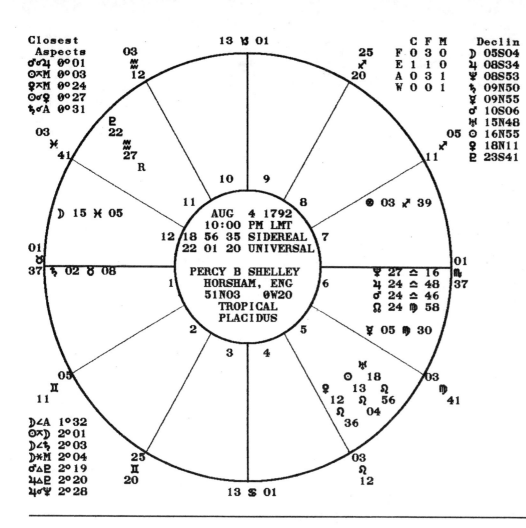

SHELLEY, PERCY BYSSHE
English poet

August 4, 1792
10:00 PM LMT
Horsham, England
0 W 20   51 N 03

Recognized as one of the greatest of lyric poets. His first wife committed suicide in 1816; he was denied custody of the children because of his atheism. Married Mary Godwin, with whom he had eloped in 1814. Drowned in a lake storm in 1822.

A: *Circle* #110, from "father's and grandfather's statements in his biography."[125]

SVP=✶ 8° 9' 18"
JULIAN DAY=2375791.41759

Closest Aspects
♂♃ 0°01
☉✶M 0°03
♀✶M 0°24
☉♂♀ 0°27
♄♂A 0°31

♃ 15 ♓ 05

♄ 02 ♉ 08

☽∠A 1°32
☉✶☽ 2°01
☽∠♄ 2°03
☽✶M 2°04
♂△♇ 2°19
♃♇ 2°20
♃♂♆ 2°28

Declin		
☽	05S04	
♃	08S34	
♆	08S53	
♄	09N50	
☿	09N55	
♂	10S06	
♅	15N48	
☉	16N55	
♀	18N11	
♇	23S41	

C	F	M
F	0	3	0
E	1	1	0
A	0	3	1
W	0	0	1

AUG 4 1792
10:00 PM LMT
18 56 35 SIDEREAL
22 01 20 UNIVERSAL

PERCY B SHELLEY
HORSHAM, ENG
51N03   0W20
TROPICAL
PLACIDUS

SHEPPARD, DR. SAM
Physician

December 29, 1923
5:30 AM EST
Cleveland, Ohio
81 W 42   41 N 30

Accused of murdering his wife, who was beaten to death in her own bed on July 4, 1954. Indicted six weeks later; served twelve years in prison before exonerated. Tried to return to medicine; failed; became a pro wrestler; died of drugs and alcohol, April 6, 1970.

A: Dewey quotes R.H. Oliver, from B.C.[126]

SVP=✶ 6° 19' 23"
JULIAN DAY=2423782.93750

Declin		
☽	05N44	
♅	06S56	
♄	09S29	
♆	15N03	
♂	16S00	
♇	20N27	
♃	20S54	
♀	20S57	
☿	21S56	
☉	23S17	

C	F	M
F	0	1	1
E	0	1	2
A	0	0	1
W	1	2	1

DEC 29 1923
05:30 AM EST
11 30 37 SIDEREAL
10 30 00 UNIVERSAL

DR SAM SHEPPARD
CLEVELAND, OH
41N30   81W42
TROPICAL
PLACIDUS

Closest Aspects
☽♂♀ 0°20
♀✶A 0°48
☉✶♃ 0°53
☽∠♆ 1°30
♄∠♅ 1°33

☉♂♆ 1°39
♆∠M 1°58
☉✶A 2°01
♂△♅ 2°07
☽✶♂ 2°15
♅△♇ 2°45
☽∠♄ 2°49

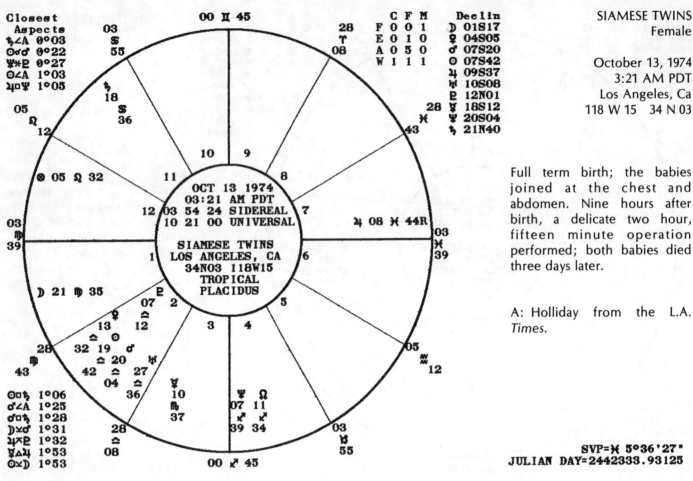

SIAMESE TWINS
Female

October 13, 1974
3:21 AM PDT
Los Angeles, Ca
118 W 15   34 N 03

Full term birth; the babies joined at the chest and abdomen. Nine hours after birth, a delicate two hour, fifteen minute operation performed; both babies died three days later.

A: Holliday from the L.A. *Times.*

SVP=♓ 5°36'27"
JULIAN DAY=2442333.93125

SIAMESE TWINS
Caesarian

April 6, 1962
10:15 AM EST

83 W 00   41 N 01

Birth weight 10½ lbs. Joined face to face from midchest to lower abdomen; perfectly formed and normal otherwise. On June 28, at 7:00 AM surgery performed; went well until the membrane surrounding the two hearts was separated. One baby died in surgery; the other, later. Parents have two other sons.

A: Data reported by CL.

SVP=♓ 5°47'25"
JULIAN DAY=2437761.13542

SIAMESE TWINS
Angirio and Fotani

June 24, 1961
3:38 PM EST

81 W 40   41 N 29

Caesarian, weight 6 lb. 4 oz. Joined from chest to abdomen; two hearts, one liver. Three-hour operation performed at 6:00 PM of the same day; Angirio died a few hours later. Father a 44-year old machinist; mother has three daughters by a prior marriage.

A: Data reported by CL.

SVP=♓ 5°48' 0"
JULIAN DAY=2437475.35972

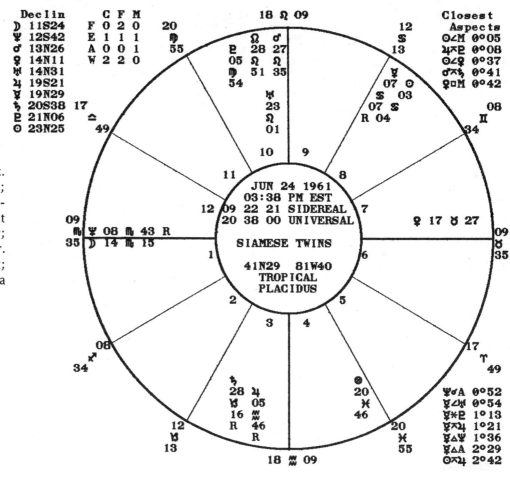

SIAMESE TWINS
David Bartley

August 10, 1963
11:27 AM PDT
Glendale, Ca
118 W 15   34 N 09

At birth, joined at breastbone; sharing a common liver. Surgery performed to separate the two babies; the brother died four days later of blood infection, and David survived.

A: Data reported by CL from newspaper account.

SVP=♓ 5°46'20"
JULIAN DAY=2438252.26875

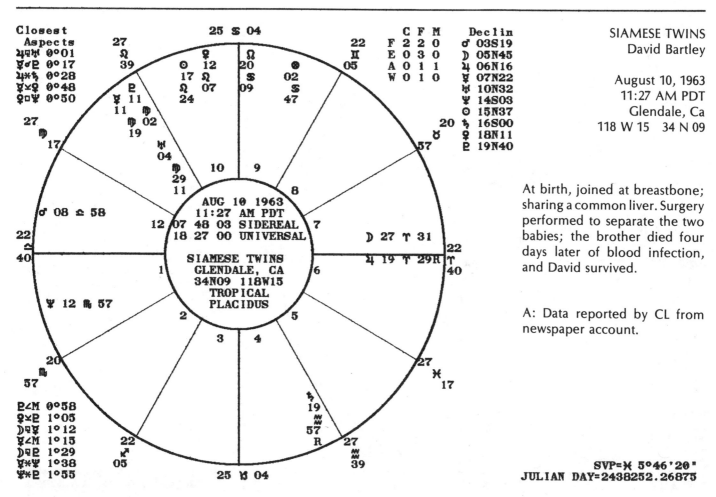

SHIELDS, BROOKE
Actress

May 31, 1965
1:45 PM EDT
New York, N.Y.
73 W 57 40 N 45

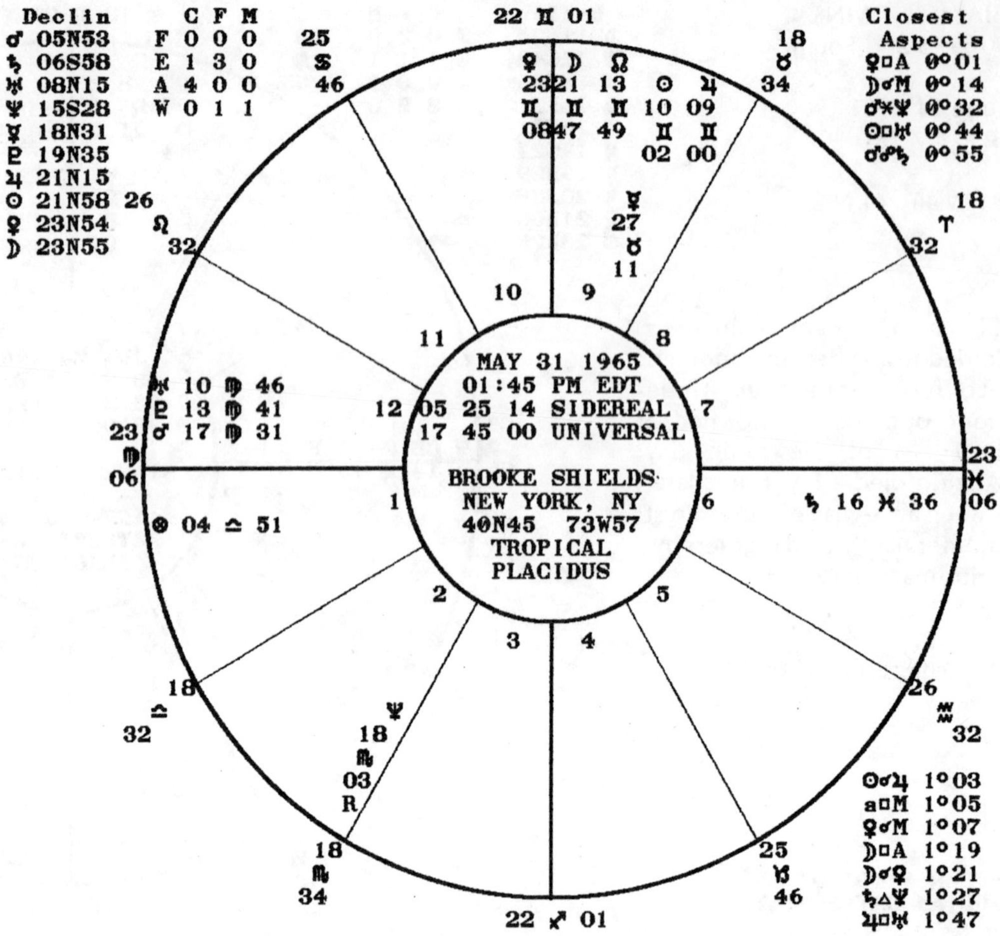

Declin
♂ 05N53
♄ 06S58
♅ 08N15
♆ 15S28
☿ 18N31
♇ 19N35
♃ 21N15
☉ 21N58
♀ 23N54
☽ 23N55
C F M
F 0 0 0
E 1 3 0
A 4 0 0
W 0 1 1
Closest Aspects
♀□A 0°01
☽☌M 0°14
♂✶♆ 0°32
☉□♅ 0°44
♂☍♄ 0°55
☉☌♃ 1°03
a□M 1°05
♀☌M 1°07
☽□A 1°19
☽☌♀ 1°21
♄△♆ 1°27
♃□♅ 1°47
22 ♊ 01
22 ♐ 01
MAY 31 1965
01:45 PM EDT
05 25 14 SIDEREAL
17 45 00 UNIVERSAL
BROOKE SHIELDS
NEW YORK, NY
40N45 73W57
TROPICAL
PLACIDUS
♅ 10 ♍ 46
♇ 13 ♍ 41
♂ 17 ♍ 31
⊗ 04 ♎ 51
♄ 16 ♓ 36

Professional photographic model from age 11 months. In her controversial first film, *Pretty Baby*, played a child prostitute at the age of 12. Teenage millionaire within two years and five more movies.

B: Tracy Marks in M.H., October 1978, quotes *The Brooke Book*.

SVP=♓ 5°44'51"
JULIAN DAY=2438912.23958

SIMPSON, O.J.
Athlete

July 9, 1947
8:08 AM PST
San Francisco, Ca
122 W 26 37 N 47

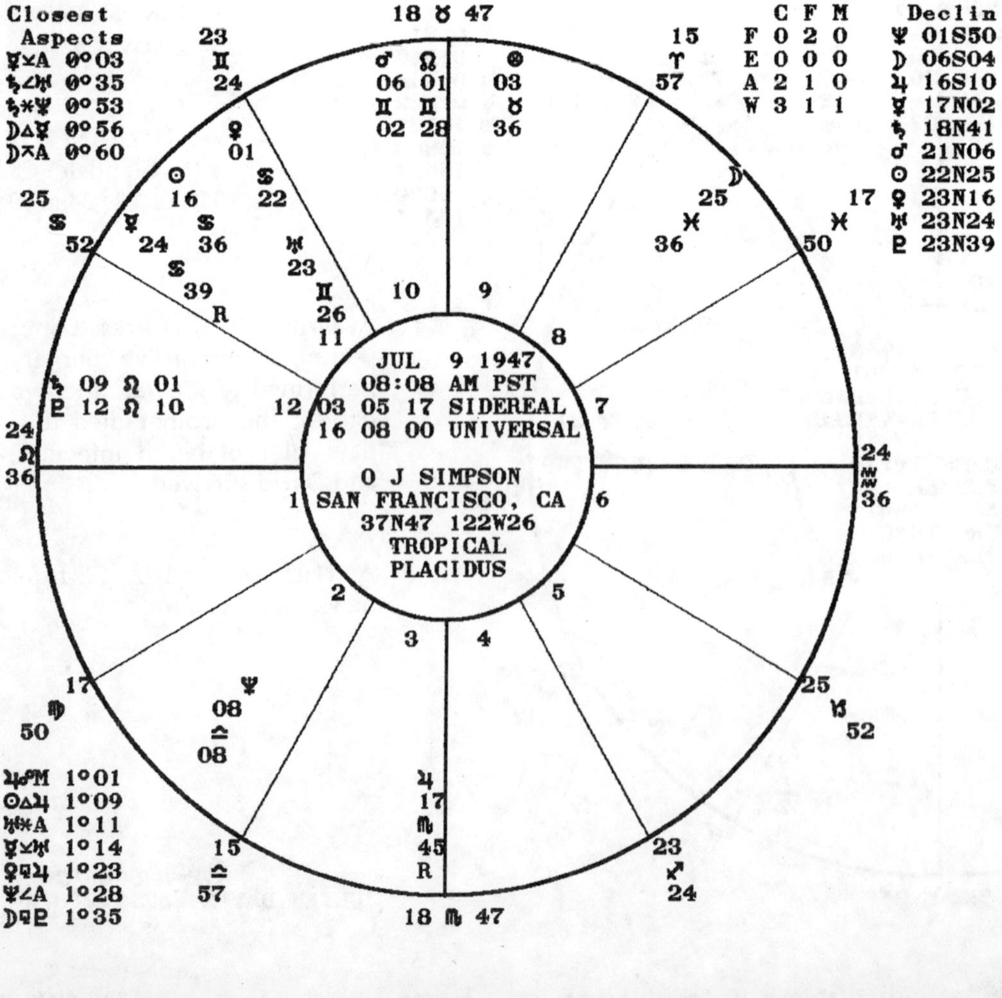

Closest Aspects
☿⚺A 0°03
♄∠♅ 0°35
♄✶♆ 0°53
☽△☿ 0°56
☽⚻A 0°60
♃☍M 1°01
☉△♃ 1°09
♅✶A 1°11
☿⚺♅ 1°14
♀⚼♃ 1°23
♆∠A 1°28
☽⚼♇ 1°35
C F M
F 0 2 0
E 0 0 0
A 2 1 0
W 3 1 1
Declin
♆ 01S50
☽ 06S04
♃ 16S10
☿ 17N02
♄ 18N41
♂ 21N06
☉ 22N25
♀ 23N16
♅ 23N24
♇ 23N39
18 ♉ 47
18 ♏ 47
JUL 9 1947
08:08 AM PST
03 05 17 SIDEREAL
16 08 00 UNIVERSAL
O J SIMPSON
SAN FRANCISCO, CA
37N47 122W26
TROPICAL
PLACIDUS
♄ 09 ♌ 01
♇ 12 ♌ 10

Football player who set ten NFL records in nine years with the Buffalo Bills. Winner of the 1968 Heisman Trophy. Millionaire with the sponsorship of commercial products in magazines and on TV. Motion pictures. Married in 1968 for eleven years; three children.

A: CSH.

SVP=♓ 5°59'48"
JULIAN DAY=2432376.17222

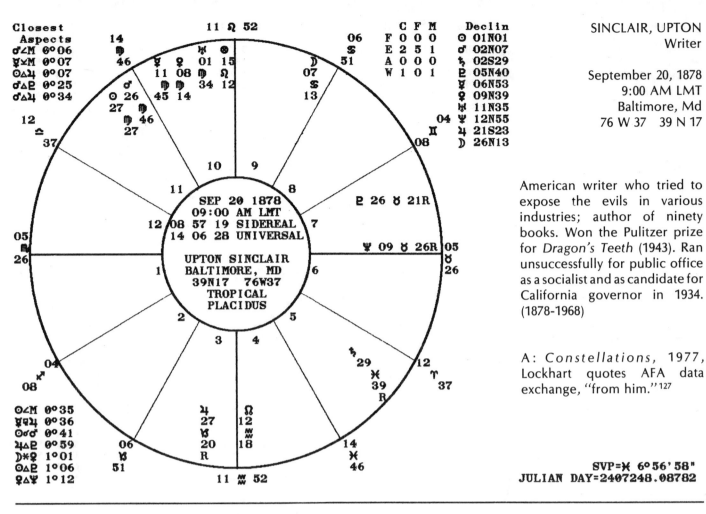

SINCLAIR, UPTON
Writer

September 20, 1878
9:00 AM LMT
Baltimore, Md
76 W 37   39 N 17

American writer who tried to expose the evils in various industries; author of ninety books. Won the Pulitzer prize for *Dragon's Teeth* (1943). Ran unsuccessfully for public office as a socialist and as candidate for California governor in 1934. (1878-1968)

A: *Constellations*, 1977, Lockhart quotes AFA data exchange, "from him."[127]

SLEZAK, WALTER
Actor

May 3, 1902
1:41 AM MET
Vienna, Austria
16 E 20   48 N 14

Came to the U.S. in 1930; many Broadway hits from the 30s to 50s. Films include *Lifeboat* (1944) and *Call Me Madam* (1953). Tony award for *Fanny* (1954). Married; three children. Tried every diet possible in his weight ups and downs.

B: McEvers quotes auto-biography, *What Time's The Next Swan?* (1962), p. 1.[128]

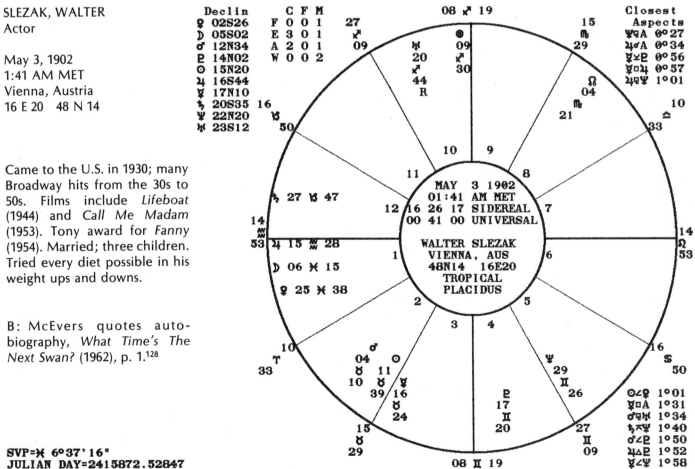

SMOTHERS, TOM
Comedian

February 2, 1937
5:44 PM EST
New York, N.Y.
73 W 57   40 N 45

Played with his brother Dick on the popular and controversial TV *Smothers Brothers Comedy Hour* from 1965-69; censorship problems with their humor. Recorded on thirteen LPs, three of which were gold. Twice divorced; one son in 1965.

A: From him to Angela Gallo.[129]

SVP=♓ 6° 7'59"
JULIAN DAY=2428567.44722

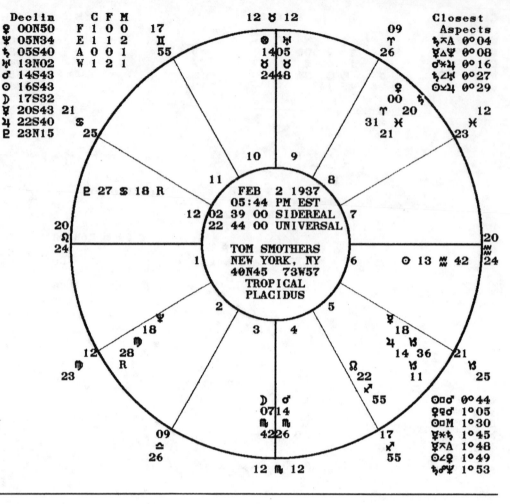

SNOW, PHOEBE
Singer, songwriter

July 17, 1950
6:00 AM EDT
New York, N.Y.
73 W 57   40 N 45

Recording artist; a hit with her first album in 1975. Tour scheduled but cancelled for the birth of her first daughter on December 12, 1975, a child with hydrocephalus. Became a mystic and optimist through the lessons of turmoil and grief.

A: From her to Ruth Elliot.

SVP=♓ 5°57' 1"
JULIAN DAY=2433479.91667

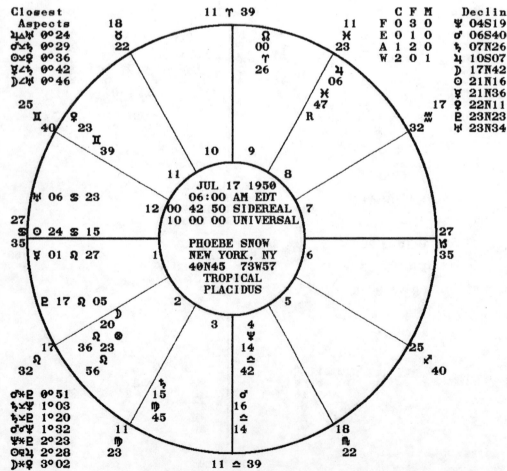

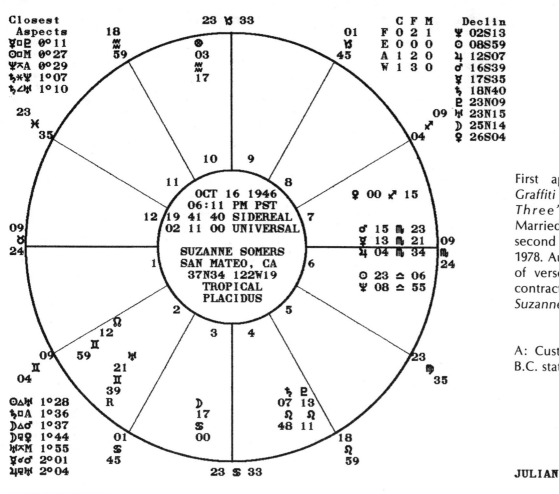

SOMERS, SUZANNE
Actress

October 16, 1946
6:11 PM PST
San Mateo, Ca
122 W 19   37 N 34

First appeared in *American Graffiti* before the hit TV series *Three's Company* (1977). Married and a mother at 17; second marriage to Alan Hamel, 1978. Author of two collections of verse. Signed a $3 million contract with CBS in 1979 for a *Suzanne Somers Show*.

A: Custer from Eugene Moore, B.C. stated in M.H.

Closest Aspects

☿□♇ 0°11
☉□M 0°27
♆△A 0°29
♄✶♆ 1°07
♄∠♅ 1°10

☉△♅ 1°28
♄□A 1°36
☽△♂ 1°37
☽□♀ 1°44
♅✶M 1°55
☿♂♂ 2°01
♃♇♅ 2°04

Declin
♆ 02S13
☉ 08S59
♃ 12S07
♂ 16S39
☿ 17S35
♄ 18N40
♇ 23N09
♅ 23N15
☽ 25N14
♀ 26S04

SVP=♓ 6° 0'27"
JULIAN DAY=2432110.59097

OCT 16 1946
06:11 PM PST
19 41 40 SIDEREAL
02 11 00 UNIVERSAL

SUZANNE SOMERS
SAN MATEO, CA
37N34 122W19
TROPICAL
PLACIDUS

SORRENTINO, JOE
Jurist

May 16, 1937
7:00 AM EDT
Brooklyn, N.Y.
73 W 56   40 N 38

Teen-age gang hoodlum; jail first at age 14; discharged from the Marines for fighting at 18. About-face to Harvard Law School, 1966; became a juvenile and municipal court judge and crusader for juvenile rights. Books include autobiography, *Up From Never*.

A: From him to LMR by letter March 1979, "family records."

SVP=♓ 6° 7'47"
JULIAN DAY=2428669.95833

Declin
♄ 01S05
♆ 06N26
♀ 08N18
☽ 11N59
♅ 14N35
☿ 15N24
☉ 19N04
♂ 20S44
♃ 20S54
♇ 23N22

MAY 16 1937
07:00 AM EDT
21 39 14 SIDEREAL
11 00 00 UNIVERSAL

JOE SORRENTINO
BROOKLYN, NY
40N38 73W56
TROPICAL
PLACIDUS

Closest Aspects

☿∠♄ 0°15
☿✶A 0°18
♃♇♇ 0°32
♆□A 0°53
☽✶♆ 1°10

☿△♆ 1°11
☉✶♇ 1°38
♀✶M 2°03
☽✶A 2°03
☽□♃ 2°05
♂△♃ 2°09
☉△♃ 2°10

SPAHN, WARREN
Athlete

April 23, 1921
3:55 PM EST
Buffalo, N.Y.
87 W 53 42 N 53

Baseball pitcher who won the Cy Young Memorial award, 1957. Led NL with strikeouts in 1949, '50, '51, and '52 with Boston. Won twenty or more games in 1947, '49, to '61, and '63. Pitched no hit games in 1960 and '61 for Milwaukee; eighteen seasons with Milwaukee Braves.

A: CL quotes Drew, "from him."[130]

SVP=✶ 6°21'24"
JULIAN DAY=2422803.37153

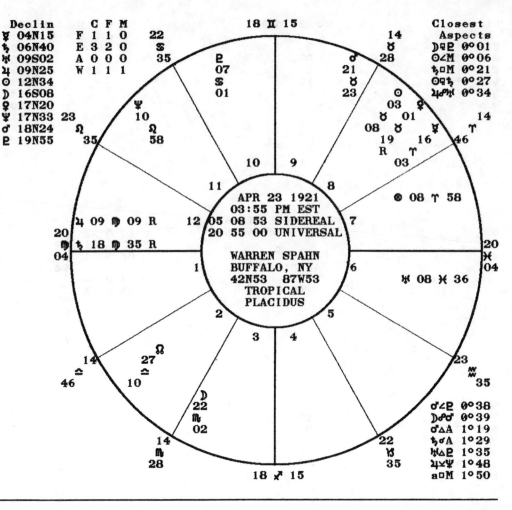

Declin		C	F	M
☿ 04N15	F	1	1	0
♄ 06N40	E	3	2	0
♅ 09S02	A	0	0	0
♃ 09N25	W	1	1	1
☉ 12N34				
☽ 16S08				
♀ 17N20				
♆ 17N33				
♂ 18N24				
♇ 19N55				

Closest Aspects
☽□♇ 0°01
☉□M 0°06
♄□M 0°21
☉□♃ 0°27
♃□♅ 0°34

⊕ 08 ♈ 58

♅ 08 ✶ 36

♂∠♇ 0°38
☽♂♂ 0°39
♂△A 1°19
♄∠A 1°29
♅△♇ 1°35
♃⋆♆ 1°48
a□M 1°50

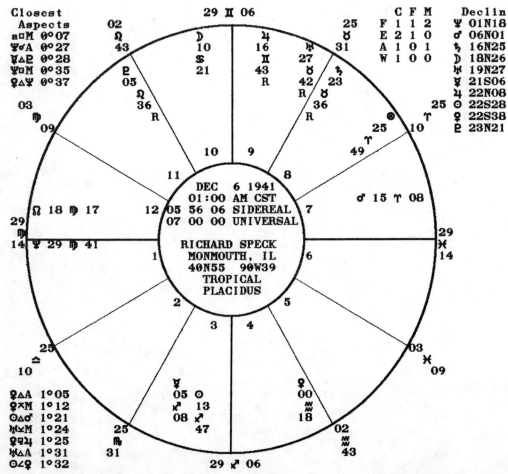

Closest Aspects
a□M 0°07
♆♂A 0°27
☿△♇ 0°28
♆□M 0°35
♀△♆ 0°37

♀△A 1°05
♀⋆M 1°12
☉♂♂ 1°21
♅⋆M 1°24
♀♂♃ 1°25
♅△A 1°31
☉∠♀ 1°32

	C	F	M	Declin
F	1	1	2	♆ 01N18
E	2	1	0	♂ 06N01
A	1	0	1	♄ 16N25
W	1	0	0	☽ 18N26
				♅ 19N27
				☿ 21S06
				♃ 22N08
				☉ 22S28
				♀ 22S38
				♇ 23N21

♂ 15 ♈ 08

SPECK, RICHARD
Murderer

December 6, 1941
1:00 M CST
Monmouth, Ill
90 W 39 40 N 55

Had been married and divorced; claimed to hate his ex-wife. On June 13, 1966, after drinking and taking drugs, gained entry to a dormitory for student nurses; knifed and strangled eight women, one of whom he raped.

A: *Constellations*, 1977, Lockhart quotes AA, January 1967, B.C.

SVP=✶ 6° 4'19"
JULIAN DAY=2430334.79167

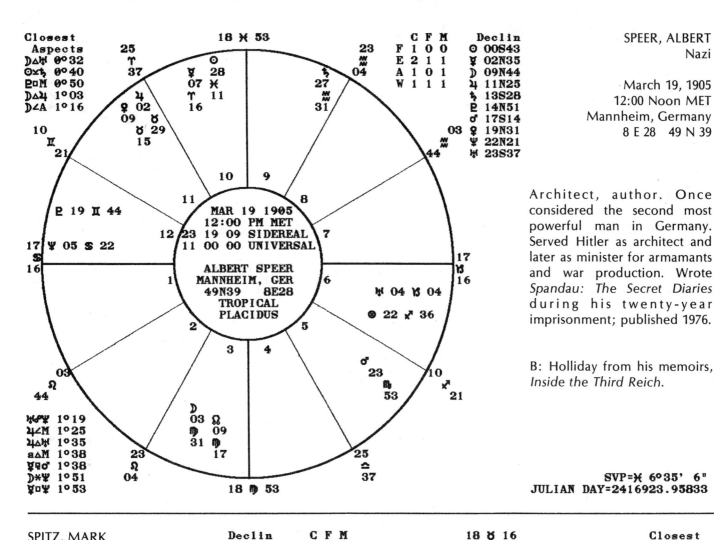

SPEER, ALBERT
Nazi

March 19, 1905
12:00 Noon MET
Mannheim, Germany
8 E 28   49 N 39

Closest
Aspects

☽△♅	0°32
☉✶♄	0°40
♀□M	0°50
☽△♃	1°03
☽∠A	1°16

	C	F	M		Declin
F	1	0	0	☉	00S43
E	2	1	1	☿	02N35
A	1	0	1	☽	09N44
W	1	1	1	♃	11N25
				♄	13S28
				♇	14S51
				♂	17S14
				♀	19N31
				♆	22N21
				♅	23S37

Architect, author. Once considered the second most powerful man in Germany. Served Hitler as architect and later as minister for armamants and war production. Wrote *Spandau: The Secret Diaries* during his twenty-year imprisonment; published 1976.

B: Holliday from his memoirs, *Inside the Third Reich.*

♅✶♆	1°19
♃∠M	1°25
♃△♅	1°35
a△M	1°38
☿♂♂	1°38
☽✶♆	1°51
☿□♆	1°53

SVP=♓ 6°35' 6"
JULIAN DAY=2416923.95833

SPITZ, MARK
Swimming champion

February 10, 1950
5:45 PM PST
Modesto, Ca
121 W 00   37 N 39

	Declin		C	F	M
♂	01S19	F	0	1	1
♆	05S15	E	0	1	1
♄	06N47	A	0	2	3
♀	11S12	W	1	0	0
☉	14S15				
♃	16S36				
☿	20S32				
♇	23N40				
♅	23N43				
☽	26S10				

Moved to Hawaii at age 2, where he learned to walk and swim. Back to California at 14; worked out every morning to become known as the world's best swimmer by age 17, breaking five world marks in international competitions. In the 1972 Olympics won a record seven gold medals.

A: Lockhart from B.C.

Closest
Aspects

♃□♅	0°06
♆✶♇	0°19
♄△M	0°24
♅∠♇	0°38
♄✶♆	0°40

♃□♇	0°44
♄✶♇	0°59
♃△♆	1°03
♆∠M	1°04
♇□M	1°23
♃✶♄	1°43
☿✶A	1°45

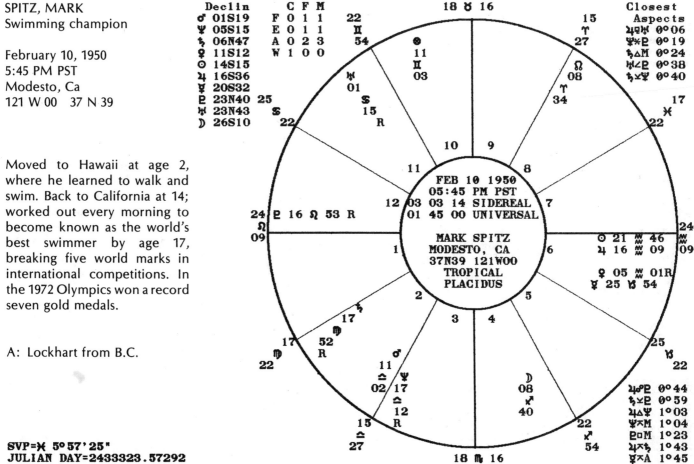

SVP=♓ 5°57'25"
JULIAN DAY=2433323.57292

STACK, ROBERT
Actor

January 13, 1919
4:40 PM PST
Los Angeles, Ca
118 W 15   34 N 04

Son of a millionaire father, who "majored in polo" before acting. Mediocre roles for twenty years in thirty movies before his nomination for an Oscar in the film *Written on the Wind* (1956). Won Emmys for his TV series *The Untouchables* in the 1950 and 1960 seasons.

A: CSH.

SVP=✶ 6°23' 8"
JULIAN DAY=2421972.52778

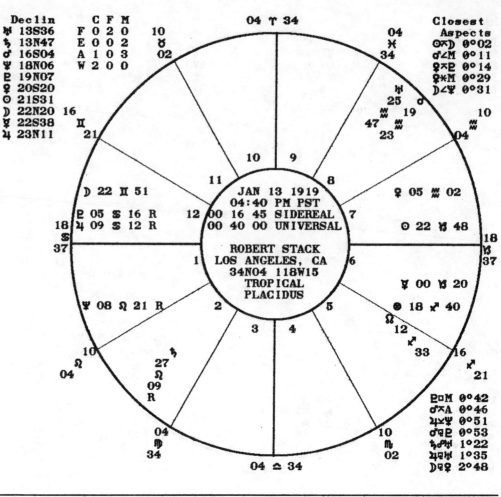

STARR, RINGO
Drummer

July 7, 1940
00:05 AM BST
Liverpool, England
2 W 58   53 N 25

Superstar with The Beatles. Poor childhood; quit school to work at 14. Became part of an all-time phenomena of success in the 60s. The Beatles went their separate ways in 1971. Ringo acted solo in three movies, including *Candy* and *The Magic Christian*.

B: *Circle* #1251 quotes *The Beatles* by H. Davies, "just after midnight."

SVP=✶ 6° 5'20"
JULIAN DAY=2429817.46181

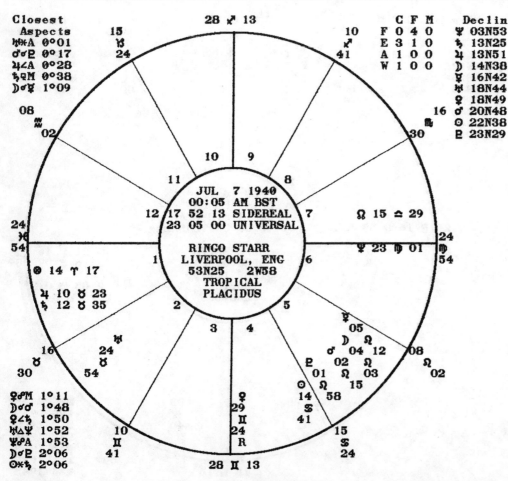

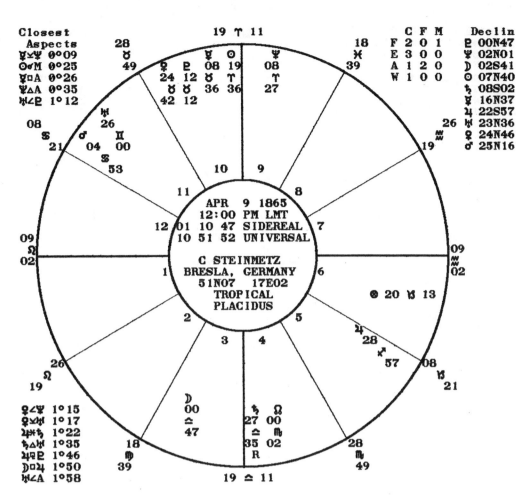

Closest Aspects

☿⊼Ψ 0°09
☉♂M 0°25
☿□A 0°26
Ψ△A 0°35
♅⊼♇ 1°12

♀⊼A 1°15
♀⊼♅ 1°17
♃⊼♄ 1°22
♄△♅ 1°35
♃⊼♇ 1°46
☽□♃ 1°50
♅⊼A 1°58

	C	F	M
F	2	0	1
E	3	0	0
A	1	2	0
W	1	0	0

Declin

♇ 00N47
Ψ 02N01
☽ 02S41
☉ 07N40
♄ 08S02
☿ 16N37
♃ 22S57
♅ 23N36
♀ 24N46
♂ 25N16

STEINMETZ, CHARLES P.
Scientist

April 9, 1865
12:00 Noon LMT
Bresla, Germany
17 E 02   51 N 07

APR 9 1865
12:00 PM LMT
01 10 47 SIDEREAL
10 51 52 UNIVERSAL

C STEINMETZ
BRESLA, GERMANY
51N07   17E02
TROPICAL
PLACIDUS

German mathematician and electrical engineer; a scientific genius with many experimental discoveries and inventions; ranked with Edison and Tesla. Taught electricity and wrote books on the theory of alternating current. Background of poverty and physical deformity of a hunchback. (1865-1923)

A: Holliday quotes Kraum in *Best of the NAJ*, "given by him."

SVP=♓ 7° 8'19"
JULIAN DAY=2402335.95269

STEVENS, CAT
Musician

July 21, 1948
12:00 Noon BST
London, England
0 W 06   51 N 31

Declin

♂ 00S41
Ψ 02S44
♄ 15N08
♀ 17N50
☉ 20N27
☿ 21N44
♃ 22S44
♇ 23N30
♅ 23N36
☽ 24S25

	C	F	M
F	0	2	1
E	0	0	0
A	2	2	1
W	2	0	0

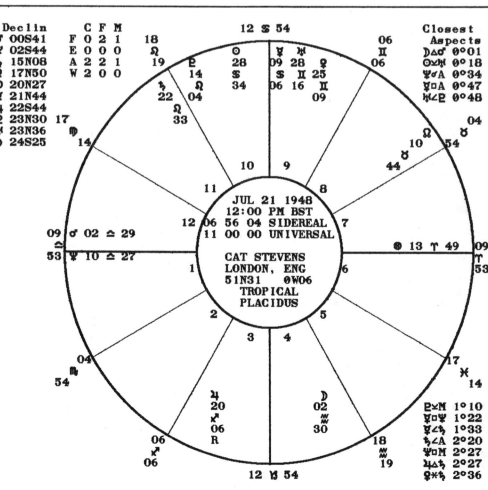

JUL 21 1948
12:00 PM BST
06 56 04 SIDEREAL
11 00 00 UNIVERSAL

CAT STEVENS
LONDON, ENG
51N31   0W06
TROPICAL
PLACIDUS

Closest Aspects

☽△♂ 0°01
☉⊼♅ 0°18
Ψ♂A 0°34
☿□A 0°47
♅⊼♇ 0°48

♇⊼M 1°10
☿⊼Ψ 1°22
☿⊼A 1°33
♄⊼A 2°20
Ψ□M 2°27
♃△♄ 2°27
♀⊼♄ 2°36

Singer, pianist, guitarist, songwriter. First appeared as a cleancut teen-age idol, after a pause of illness and depression; returned as a shaggy singer and writer of songs with considerable depth and meaning; began turning out gold albums by 1971.

A: Dewey quotes Richard West, "from him."

SVP=♓ 5°58'51"
JULIAN DAY=2432753.95833

STEVENSON, ADLAI
Statesman

February 5, 1900
11:55 AM PST
Los Angeles, Ca
118 W 15   34 N 04

Declin		C	F	M
☿	04S45	F	0	0	2
♇	12N59	E	1	0	1
☉	15S52	A	2	0	3
☽	16N45	W	0	0	1
♂	18S17				
☿	18S44				
♃	20S42				
♆	22N03				
♅	22S09				
♄	22S27				

Intellectual and moral giant.
Assistant secretary of the navy,
1941-44; assistant secretary of
state, 1945; governor of Illinois,
1949-53; U.S. representative for
the U.N., 1961-65. Candidate for
the presidency in 1952 and 1956.
(1900-1965)

A: CL quotes Mabel Smith, the
black housegirl who helped
with the birth, who said "three
to five minutes before
Noon."[131]

SVP=⧓ 6°38'59"
JULIAN DAY=2415056.32986

Closest
Aspects
♂✳♅ 0°01
☉∠♃ 0°02
☿✳M 0°05
☽∠♀ 0°19
☿△♇ 1°09

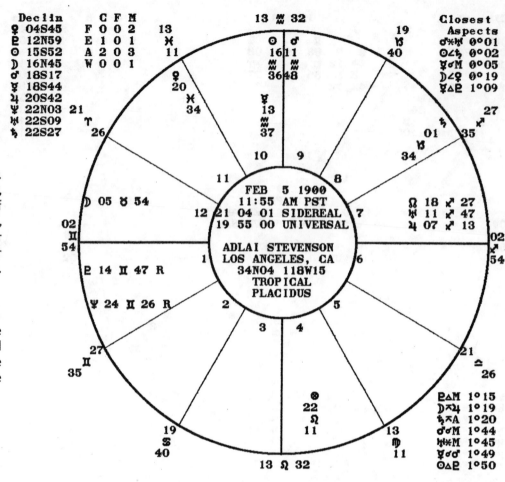

FEB 5 1900
11:55 AM PST
21 04 01 SIDEREAL
19 55 00 UNIVERSAL
ADLAI STEVENSON
LOS ANGELES, CA
34N04 118W15
TROPICAL
PLACIDUS

♇△M 1°15
☽⊼♃ 1°19
♄⊼A 1°20
♂♂M 1°44
♅✳M 1°45
☿♂♂ 1°49
☉△♇ 1°50

Closest
Aspects
☿✳♄ 0°03
☉✳♇ 0°05
☿∠♇ 0°12
♀□M 0°37
♅△♆ 0°39

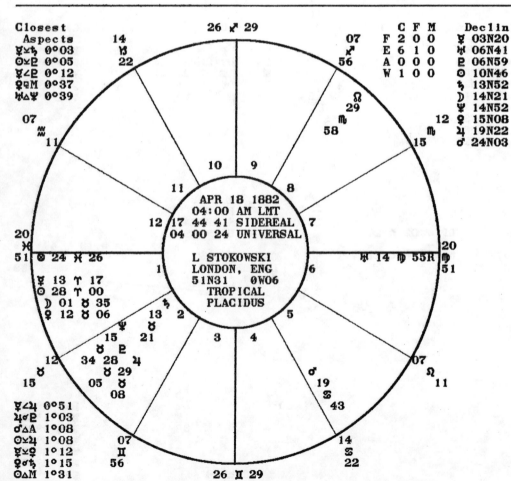

APR 18 1882
04:00 AM LMT
17 44 41 SIDEREAL
04 00 24 UNIVERSAL
L STOKOWSKI
LONDON, ENG
51N31 0W06
TROPICAL
PLACIDUS

	C	F	M	Declin	
	F	2	0	0	☿	03N20
	E	6	1	0	♅	06N41
	A	0	0	0	♇	06N59
	W	1	0	0	☉	10N46
					♄	13N52
					☽	14N21
					♆	14N52
					♀	15N08
					♃	19N22
					♂	24N03

STOKOWSKI, LEOPOLD
Musician

April 18, 1882
4:00 AM LMT
London, England
0 W 06   51 N 31

Student of violin and organ at
16; came to U.S. in 1905 with a
job as organist. Began to
conduct in 1908; was Cincinnati
Symphony Orchestra con-
ductor, 1909-12; Philadelphia
Orchestra, 1914-36; and New
York Symphony, 1944-45. (1882-
1977)

A: CL "from him personally."
[134]

☿∠♃ 0°51
♃✳♇ 1°03
♂△A 1°08
☉⊼♃ 1°08
☿✳♀ 1°12
♀♂ 1°15
☉△M 1°31

SVP=⧓ 6°53'57"
JULIAN DAY=2408553.66694

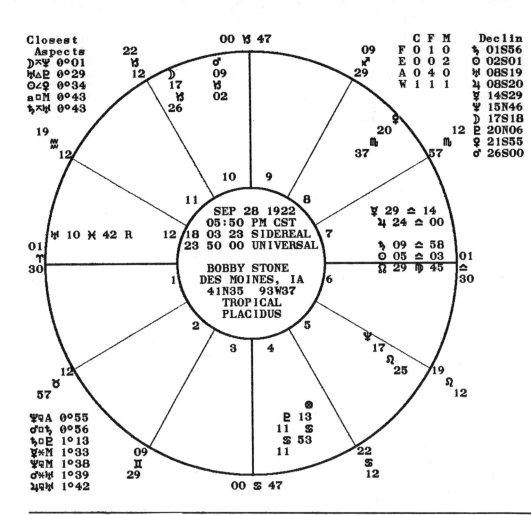

SVP=✶ 6°20'19"
JULIAN DAY=2423326.49306

STONE, BOBBY
Actor

September 28, 1922
5:50 PM CST
Des Moines, Iowa
93 W 37   41 N 35

One of the movies youthful *Dead-End Kids*, a gang of hoodlums who got into comedic and human interest problems in which virtue always prevailed. As an adult, an assistant director of motion pictures. Died in 1977 of stomach cancer.

A: From him to Gene Steele, B.C.

STRAHL, LOTTE VON
Psychic
December 30, 1895
9:00 AM MET
Oldenberg, Germany
8 E 12   53 N 07

Tall, with imposing dignity. Titled as baroness through marriage. A world-known Dutch psychic who worked with the European governments during World War II; abilities tested by parapsychology groups. Lectured and gave readings in the U.S. after the 50s.

A: From her to Diane Clarke.

SVP=✶ 6°42'36"
JULIAN DAY=2413557.83333

STRAUSS, RICHARD
Musician

June 11, 1864
6:00 AM LMT
Munich, Germany
11 E 35   48 N 08

German composer of *Schneider-polka* for the piano when he was age 6. Won success without a struggle; conducted widely; composed incessantly; wrote more than one hundred songs. Married Pauline de Ahna, prima donna of his first opera, *Grentram*. (1864-1949)

B: Dewey quotes data from father's diary in *Richard Strauss: The Man and His Work* by Ernst Krause.

SVP=♓ 7° 8' 56"
JULIAN DAY=2402033.71782

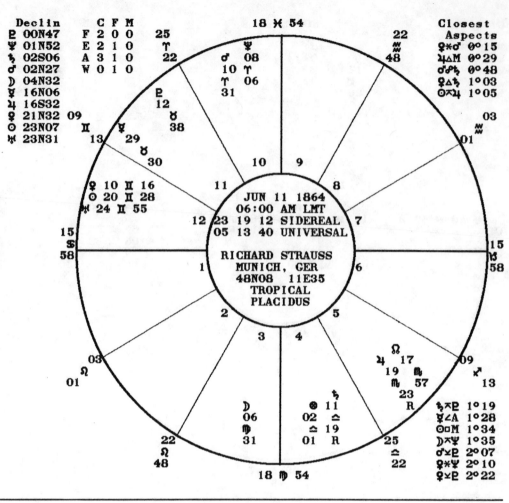

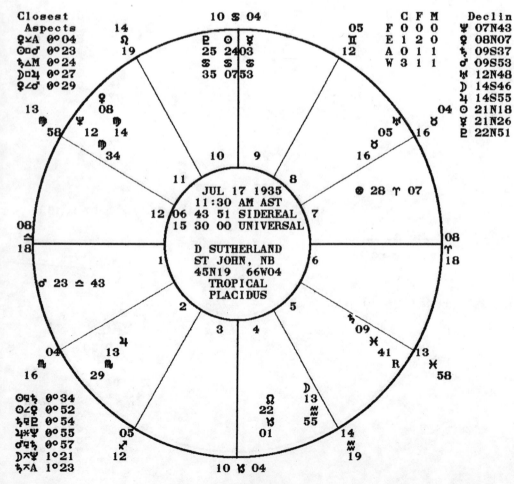

SUTHERLAND, DONALD
Actor

July 17, 1935
11:30 AM AST
St. John, N.B. Canada
66 W 04   45 N 19

At first an obscure repertory actor who played in such gems as *Die, Die, My Darling* and other horror and B pictures. Tall, apparently casual; low-key profile but markedly different in each role, from M.A.S.H. to the award-winning *Klute*.

A: From him to Mark Johnson.

SVP=♓ 6° 9' 19"
JULIAN DAY=2428001.14583

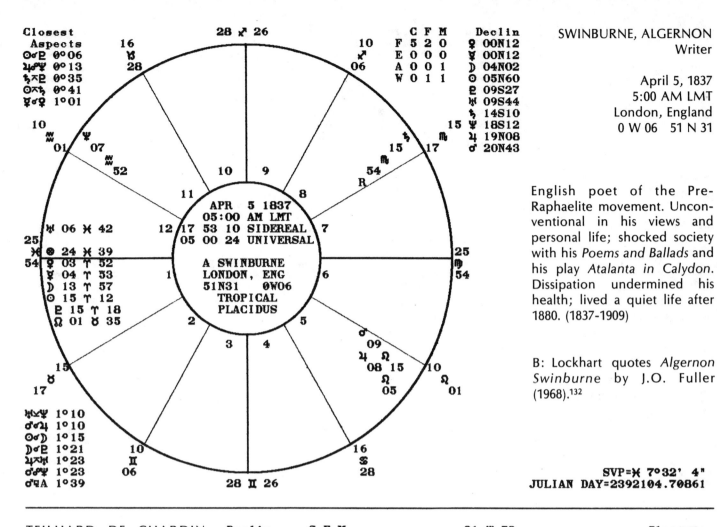

Closest Aspects

☉✶♇	0°06	
♃✶♅	0°13	
♄⚻♇	0°35	
☉□♄	0°41	
☿♂♀	1°01	

28 ♐ 26

16
♅
28

10 ♏
01

♈ 07
♅
52

10   9

11   8

APR 5 1837
05:00 AM LMT
17 53 10 SIDEREAL
05 00 24 UNIVERSAL

A SWINBURNE
LONDON, ENG
51N31 0W06
TROPICAL
PLACIDUS

12   7

1   6

2   5

3   4

C F M
F 5 2 0
E 0 0 0
A 0 0 1
W 0 1 1

Declin

♀	00N12
☿	00N12
☽	04N02
☉	05N60
♀	09S27
♅	09S44
♄	14S10
♆	18S12
♃	19N08
♂	20N43

06 ♐
54
R

15 ♏
15 17
54

♅ 06 ♓ 42
25 ⊕ 24 ♓ 39
54 ♀ 03 ♈ 52
♀ 04 ♈ 53
☽ 13 ♈ 57
☉ 15 ♈ 12
♇ 15 ♈ 18
☊ 01 ♉ 35

25
♍
54

01 ♍
♍ 01
10
10

♂ 09
♃ ♈
08 15
♈
05

16
♋
28

♅⚹♆ 1°10
♂♃ 1°10
☉♂☽ 1°15
☽♂♇ 1°21
♃⚻♅ 1°23
♂⚹♆ 1°23
♂⚻A 1°39

♉
17
15

10
♊
06

28 ♊ 26

SWINBURNE, ALGERNON
Writer

April 5, 1837
5:00 AM LMT
London, England
0 W 06   51 N 31

English poet of the Pre-Raphaelite movement. Unconventional in his views and personal life; shocked society with his *Poems and Ballads* and his play *Atalanta in Calydon*. Dissipation undermined his health; lived a quiet life after 1880. (1837-1909)

B: Lockhart quotes *Algernon Swinburne* by J.O. Fuller (1968).[132]

SVP=♓ 7°32' 4"
JULIAN DAY=2392104.70861

TEILHARD DE CHARDIN, PIERRE
Jesuit priest

May 1, 1881
7:00 AM LMT
Orcines, France
3 E 05   45 N 47

Declin

♂	04S43
♇	06N43
☿	07N06
♅	08N40
♄	10N31
♃	12N09
♆	14N23
☉	15N08
♀	20N58
☽	22N55

C F M
F 1 0 0
E 6 1 0
A 1 0 0
W 0 0 1

Monk who achieved distinction in paleontology and geology; many years in China with archaeological expeditions inland and in Asia and South Africa, with visits to U.S. and France. Acclaimed for scientific and genetic research.

A: Gauquelin #763 Vol 6.

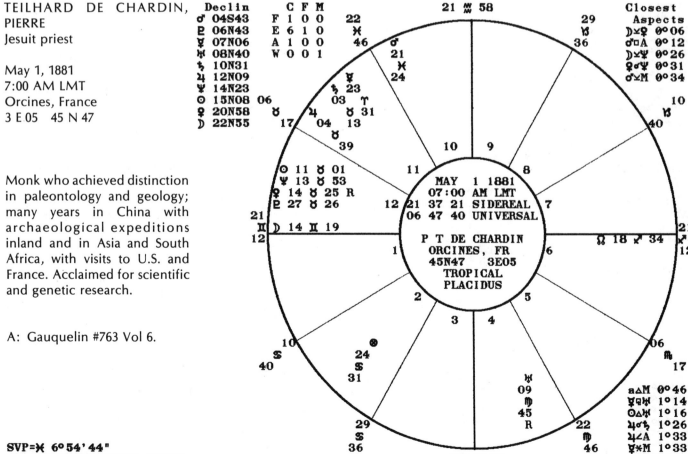

21 ♒ 58

22 ♒
♂
21 ♓
24 ♓

♄ ♒ 23
03 ♈
♃ ♉ 31
♉ 04 13
39

Closest Aspects

☽⚻♀	0°06	
♂□A	0°12	
☽⚹♆	0°26	
♀♂♆	0°31	
♂∠M	0°34	

29
♑
36

10
♑
40

10   9

11   8

☉ 11 ♉ 01
♆ 13 ♉ 53
♀ 14 ♉ 25 R
♇ 27 ♉ 26
21
12 ☽ 14 ♊ 19

MAY 1 1881
07:00 AM LMT
21 37 21 SIDEREAL
06 47 40 UNIVERSAL

P T DE CHARDIN
ORCINES, FR
45N47 3E05
TROPICAL
PLACIDUS

12   7

☊ 18 ♐ 34
21
♐
12

1   6

2   5

3   4

♍
06
♍
17

⊕
24
♋
31

☿
09
♍
45
R

♅
09
♍
45

22
♍
46

21 ♌ 58

SVP=♓ 6°54'44"
JULIAN DAY=2408201.78310

a△M	0°46
☿□♅	1°14
☉△♃	1°16
♃♂♂	1°26
♃∠A	1°33
☿✶M	1°33
♂∠♃	1°45

TENNYSON, ALFRED LORD
Writer
August 6, 1809
00:05 AM LMT
Somersby, England
0 W 01   53 N 16

Victorian English poet whose career began when he published *Poems, Chiefly Lyrical* (1830). His work includes ''Ode on the Death of Wellington'' (1852) and "Charge of the Light Brigade" (1854). The beauty of his poetry entitles him to rank among the greatest. (1809-1892)

A: *Constellations*, 1977, Lockhart quotes *Astrology*, October 1892, "from him, a few minutes after midnight."

SVP=♓ 7° 54' 55"
JULIAN DAY=2382000.50352

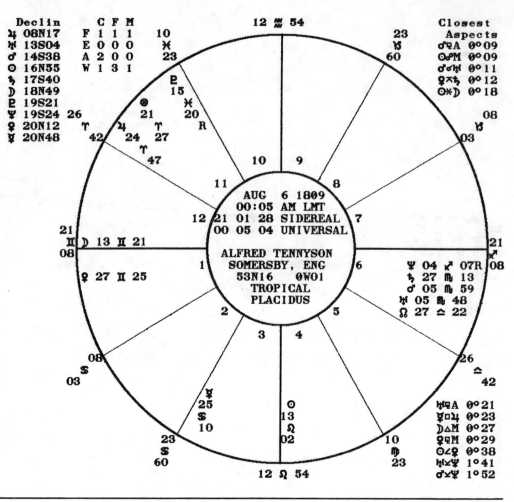

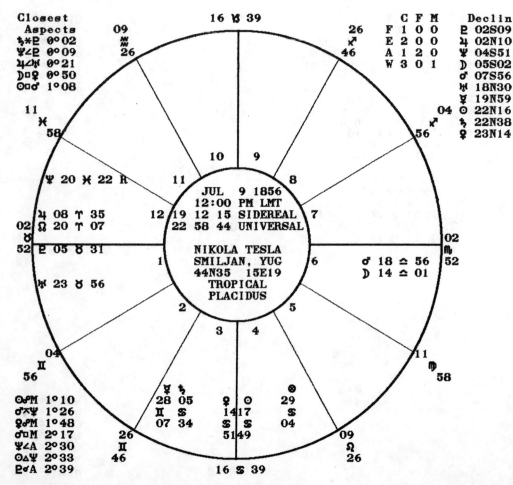

TESLA, NIKOLA
Genius

July 9/10, 1856
12:00 Midnight LMT
Smiljan, Yugoslavia
15 E 19   44 N 35

Scientist, inventor, who came to U.S. in 1884. First to conceive an effective method of utilizing the alternating current; in 1888 patented the induction motor; many inventions. His biography, *The Prodigal Genius* by J.J. O'Neill, published in 1944. (1856-1943)

B: Data in the biography, "the stroke of midnight."

SVP=♓ 7° 15' 52"
JULIAN DAY=2399140.45745

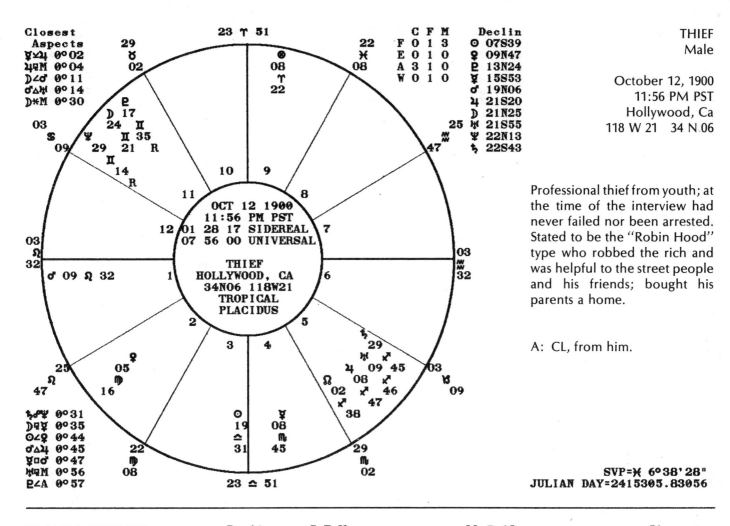

Closest
Aspects
☿⚹♃ 0°02
♃☌M 0°04
☽☌♂ 0°11
♂△♅ 0°14
☽⚹M 0°30

23 ♈ 51

29 ♉
02

⊗ 08
♈ 22

22 ♓ 08

	C	F	M
F	0	1	3
E	0	1	0
A	3	1	0
W	0	1	0

Declin
☉ 07S39
♀ 09N47
♇ 13N24
☿ 15S53
♂ 19N06
♃ 21S20
☽ 21N25
♅ 21N55
♆ 22N13
♄ 22S43

THIEF
Male

October 12, 1900
11:56 PM PST
Hollywood, Ca
118 W 21   34 N 06

♇ 17
☽ 24 ♊ 35
♆ 21 R
29 R
♊ 14
R

03 ♋
09

25 ♒
47

10   9

11   8

OCT 12 1900
11:56 PM PST
01 28 17 SIDEREAL
07 56 00 UNIVERSAL

12   7

THIEF
HOLLYWOOD, CA
34N06 118W21
TROPICAL
PLACIDUS

03 ♌
32

03 ♒
32

♂ 09 ♌ 32   1

2   5   6

3   4

25 ♌
47

05 ♀
♍ 16

22
♍ 08

☉ 19 ♎ 31

☿ 08 ♏ 45

♄ 29
♅ 09 ♐ 45
♃ 09 45
☊ 08 ♐ 02 46
♐ 47
38

03 ♑
09

29 ♏
02

Professional thief from youth; at
the time of the interview had
never failed nor been arrested.
Stated to be the "Robin Hood"
type who robbed the rich and
was helpful to the street people
and his friends; bought his
parents a home.

A: CL, from him.

♄⚹♆ 0°31
☽□☿ 0°35
☉∠♀ 0°44
♂△♃ 0°45
☿☌♂ 0°47
♅□M 0°56
♇∠A 0°57

23 ♎ 51

SVP=♓ 6°38'28"
JULIAN DAY=2415305.83056

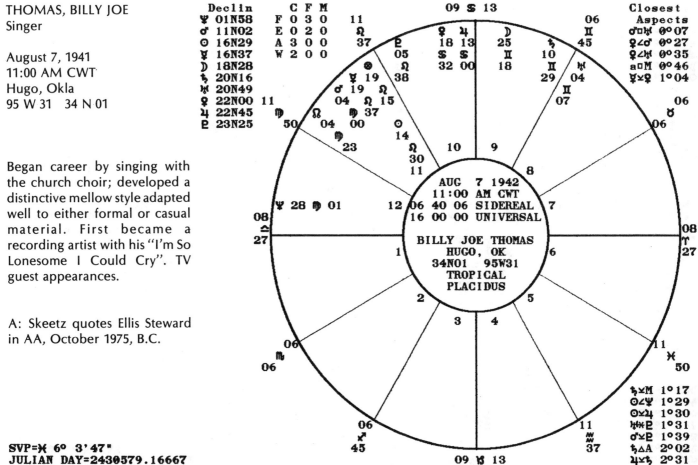

THOMAS, BILLY JOE
Singer

August 7, 1941
11:00 AM CWT
Hugo, Okla
95 W 31   34 N 01

Declin
♆ 01N58
♂ 11N02
☉ 16N29
☿ 16N37
☽ 18N28
♄ 20N16
♅ 20N49
♀ 22N00
♃ 22N45
♇ 23N25

	C	F	M
F	0	3	0
E	0	2	0
A	3	0	0
W	2	0	0

09 ♋ 13

Closest
Aspects
♂☌♅ 0°07
♀∠♂ 0°27
♀∠♅ 0°35
a□M 0°46
☿⚹♀ 1°04

11 ♌
37

♀ ♃
18 13
♇
25
☽
♄ 06
10

06 ♊
45

Began career by singing with
the church choir; developed a
distinctive mellow style adapted
well to either formal or casual
material. First became a
recording artist with his "I'm So
Lonesome I Could Cry". TV
guest appearances.

A: Skeetz quotes Ellis Steward
in AA, October 1975, B.C.

⊗ ♊
05
♊
32 00

♄ ♊
18

♊
29 ♅ 04
♊
07

06
♉

♆ 28 ♍ 01

08 ♎
27

☿ 19 ♌
♂ 19 ♌
04 ♌ 15
♍ 37
♍ 04 00
♍
50
♍ 23

10   9   8

11   12

☉ ♌
14
♌
30
11

AUG 7 1942
11:00 AM CWT
06 40 06 SIDEREAL
16 00 00 UNIVERSAL

BILLY JOE THOMAS
HUGO, OK
34N01 95W31
TROPICAL
PLACIDUS

08 ♈
27

1   6

2   5

3   4

11 ♓
50

06
♍

06
♐ 45

11
♒
37

09 ♑ 13

♄⚹M 1°17
☉∠♆ 1°29
☉⚹♃ 1°30
♅⚹♇ 1°31
♂∠♇ 1°39
♄△A 2°02
♃⚹♄ 2°31

SVP=♓ 6° 3'47"
JULIAN DAY=2430579.16667

THOMAS, MICHAEL TILSON
Conductor

December 21, 1944
9:44 AM PDT
Los Angeles, Ca
118 W 14   34 N 04

Played piano by ear at age 5; lessons at 10; decided on music as a career in 1962; pianist with the greats for six years. Assistant conductor of Boston Symphony at 25. When the director took sick and he was called in at intermission, became full director at age 26.

A: Lockhart from B.C.

SVP=✶ 6° 1'58"
JULIAN DAY=2431446.19722

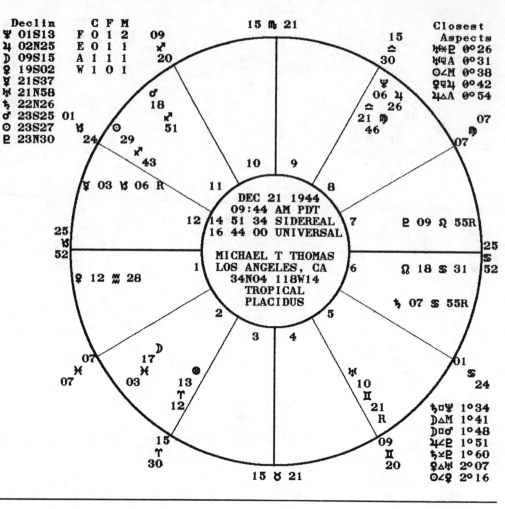

Declin		C F M		Closest Aspects
♆ 01S13		F 0 1 2		♅✶♇ 0°26
♃ 02N25		E 0 1 1		♅△♈ 0°31
☽ 09S15		A 1 1 1		☉∠M 0°38
♀ 19S02		W 1 0 1		♀♇♃ 0°42
☿ 21S37				♃△♈ 0°54
♅ 21N58				
♄ 22N26				♄□♆ 1°34
♂ 23S25				☽△M 1°41
☉ 23S27				☽♂ 1°48
♇ 23N30				♃∠♇ 1°51
				♄✶♇ 1°60
				♀△♅ 2°07
				☉∠♀ 2°16

TORN, RIP
Actor

February 6, 1931
1:05 AM CST
Austin, Texas
97 W 45   30 N 17

A qualified architectural draftsman before a New York theatrical debut in 1955. Film debut the following year in *Baby Doll*; other films include *Sweet Bird of Youth* (1962) and *Tropic of Cancer* (1970); many TV shows. Second marriage to Geraldyne Page.

A: CL from B.C.

SVP=✶ 6°13'22"
JULIAN DAY=2426378.79514

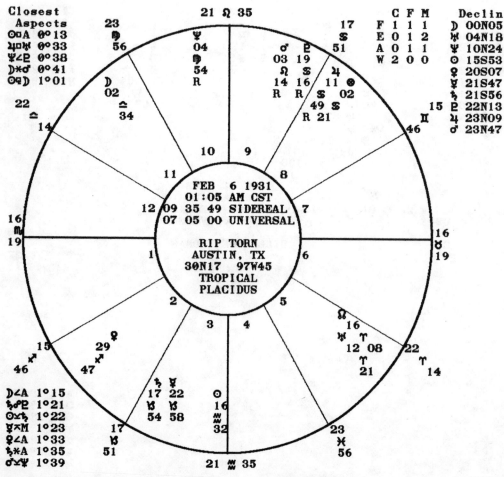

Closest Aspects			Declin
☉□A 0°13			☽ 00N05
♃□♅ 0°33			♅ 04N18
♆∠♇ 0°38			♆ 10N24
☽✶♂ 0°41			☉ 15S53
☉□☽ 1°01			♀ 20S07
			☿ 21S47
			♄ 21S56
			♇ 22N13
			♃ 23N09
			♂ 23N47

C F M
F 1 1 1
E 0 1 2
A 0 1 1
W 2 0 0

☽∠A 1°15	
♄✶♄ 1°21	
☉✶♄ 1°22	
☿✶M 1°23	
♀△A 1°33	
♄✶A 1°35	
♂∠♆ 1°39	

TOSCANINI, ARTURO
Conductor

March 25, 1867
2:00 AM LMT
Parma, Italy
10 E 10   44 N 48

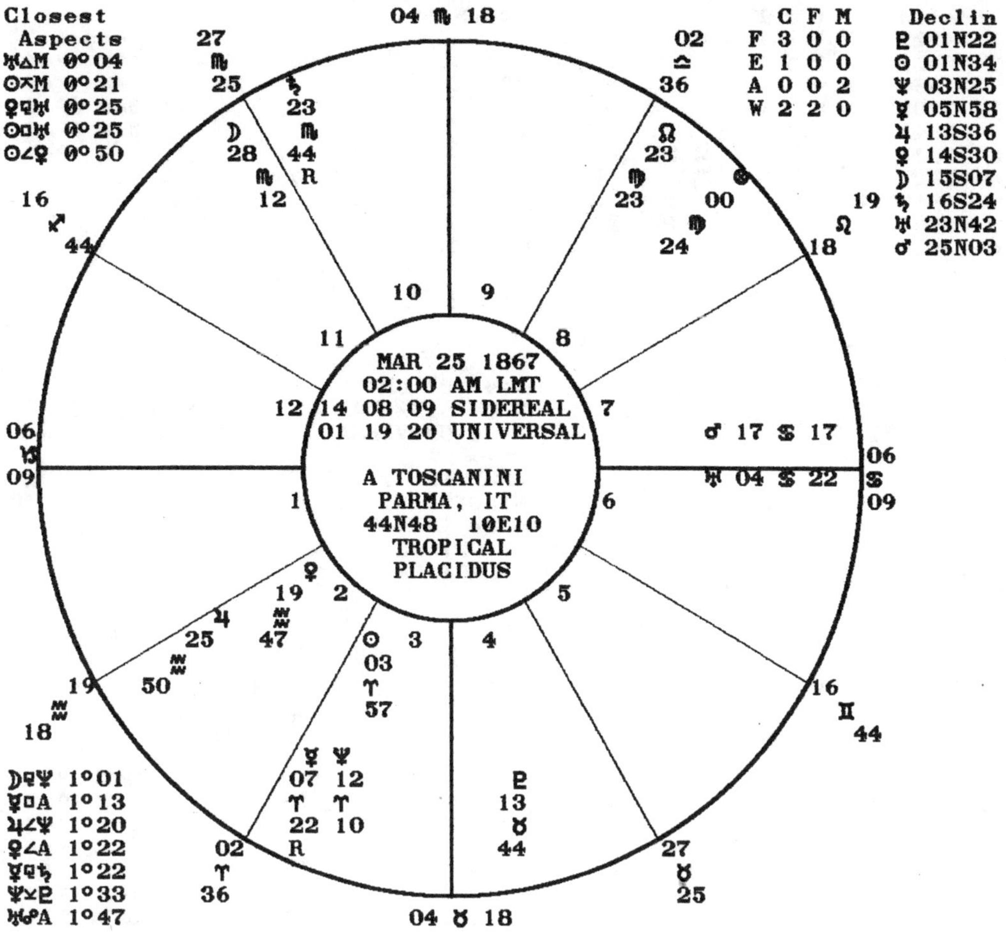
Closest Aspects
♅△M 0°04
☉⊼M 0°21
♀⚻♅ 0°25
☉□♅ 0°25
☉∠♀ 0°50
C F M
F 3 0 0
E 1 0 0
A 0 0 2
W 2 2 0
Declin
♇ 01N22
☉ 01N34
♆ 03N25
☿ 05N58
♃ 13S36
♀ 14S30
☽ 15S07
♄ 16S24
♅ 23N42
♂ 25N03
MAR 25 1867
02:00 AM LMT
14 08 09 SIDEREAL
01 19 20 UNIVERSAL
A TOSCANINI
PARMA, IT
44N48 10E10
TROPICAL
PLACIDUS
☽⚻♆ 1°01
☿□A 1°13
♃∠♆ 1°20
♀∠A 1°22
☿⚻♄ 1°22
♆⚺♇ 1°33
♅☍A 1°47

SVP=♓ 7° 6'51"
JULIAN DAY=2403050.55509

Considered by many to be the greatest conductor of his time; leader of some of the world's foremost orchestras and opera companies. Cellist from age 9. At age 19, on last minute notice led a performance of *Aida*; memorized all the major works.

A: CL, "data from him personally."[136]

TOULOUSE-LAUTREC, HENRI
Artist

November 24, 1864
6:00 AM LMT
Albi, France
2 E 09   43 N 56

French painter, lithographer, and designer of posters. Known for vivid portrayals of the Parisian music and dance hall performers. Physically deformed as a result of breaking both thighs in youthful riding accidents. Alcohol sanitarium, 1899; died of a stroke at 37.

A: Gauquelin #1078 Vol 4.

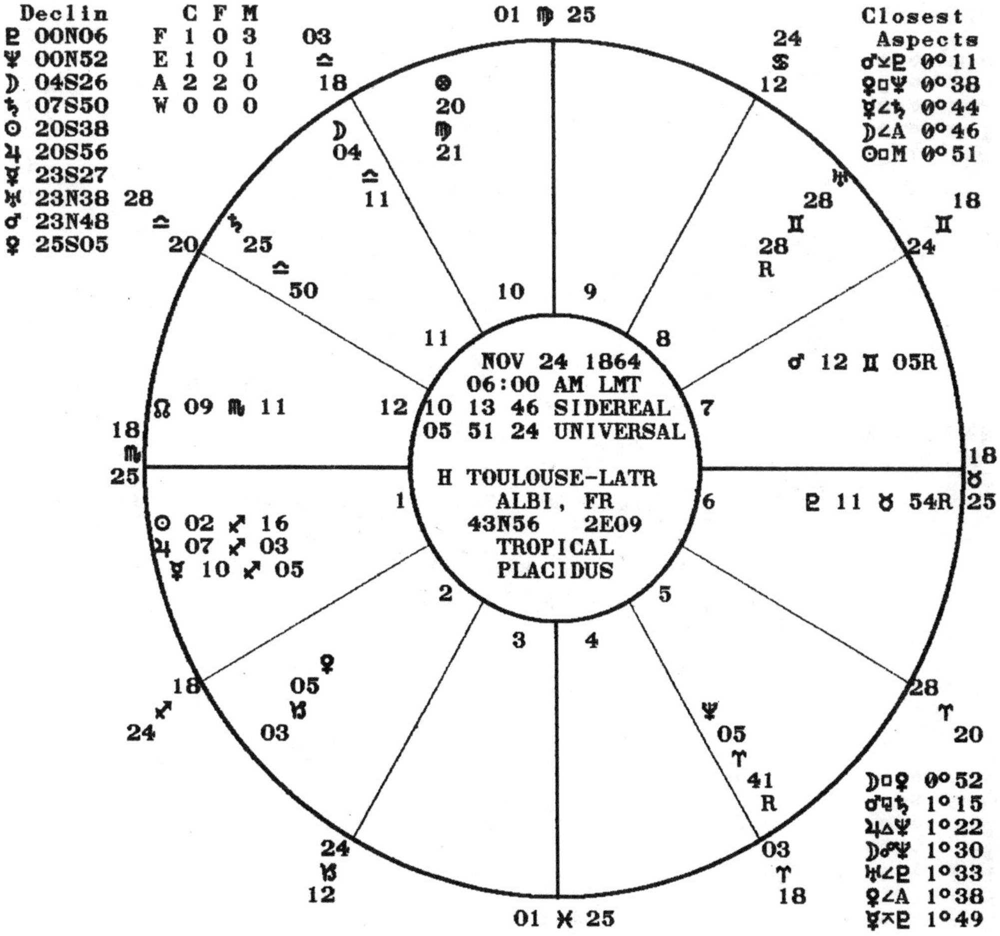
Declin
♇ 00N06
♆ 00N52
☽ 04S26
♄ 07S50
☉ 20S38
♃ 20S56
☿ 23S27
♅ 23N38
♂ 23N48
♀ 25S05
C F M
F 1 0 3
E 1 0 1
A 2 2 0
W 0 0 0
Closest Aspects
♂⚺♇ 0°11
♀□♆ 0°38
☿∠♄ 0°44
☽∠A 0°46
☉□M 0°51
NOV 24 1864
06:00 AM LMT
10 13 46 SIDEREAL
05 51 24 UNIVERSAL
H TOULOUSE-LATR
ALBI, FR
43N56 2E09
TROPICAL
PLACIDUS
☽□♀ 0°52
♂⚻♄ 1°15
♃△♆ 1°22
☽☍♆ 1°30
♅∠♇ 1°33
♀∠A 1°38
☿⊼♇ 1°49

SVP=♓ 7° 8'36"
JULIAN DAY=2402199.74403

TRACY, HARRY
Murderer

October 23, 1875
9:45 PM LMT
Minong, Wis
91 W 49   46 N 06

Killed a sheriff in 1893; history of burglaries, hold-ups, and cattle rustling. Sentenced to twenty years prison in 1901. Killed four guards to escape on June 9, 1902; shot his partner. Cornered on August 5, 1902; shot himself in the head rather than be captured.

A: CL quotes AFA, December 1938, "from his mother."

SVP=♓ 6°59'40"
JULIAN DAY=2406185.66130

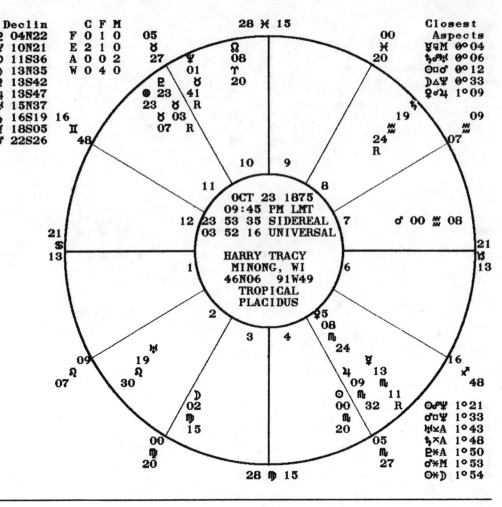

Declin		C F M		Closest Aspects
♇ 04N22	F 0 1 0		☿□M 0°04
♆ 10N21	E 2 1 0		♄□♂ 0°06
☉ 11S36	A 0 0 2		☉□♂ 0°12
☽ 13N35	W 0 4 0		☽△♆ 0°33
♃ 13S42			♀△♃ 1°09
♃ 13S47			
♅ 15N37			
♄ 16S19			
☿ 18S05			
♂ 22S26			

OCT 23 1875
09:45 PM LMT
23 53 35 SIDEREAL
03 52 16 UNIVERSAL

HARRY TRACY
MINONG, WI
46N06 91W49
TROPICAL
PLACIDUS

☉♂♆ 1°21
♂□♆ 1°33
♅⚹A 1°43
♄⚹A 1°48
♇⚹A 1°50
♂⚹M 1°53
☉⚹☽ 1°54

TRAVOLTA, JOHN
Actor

February 18, 1954
2:53 PM EST
Englewood, N.J.
73 W 59   40 N 54

Popular in TV series *Welcome Back, Kotter*. Became a superstar in films *Saturday Night Fever* and *Grease* (1978). At 22, a May-December romance with Diana Hyland, 41, that ended with her tragic death. Poor reviews for film *Moment By Moment* (1979).

A: Eugene A. Moore in M.H., January 1979, B.C.

SVP=♓ 5°53'44"
JULIAN DAY=2434792.32847

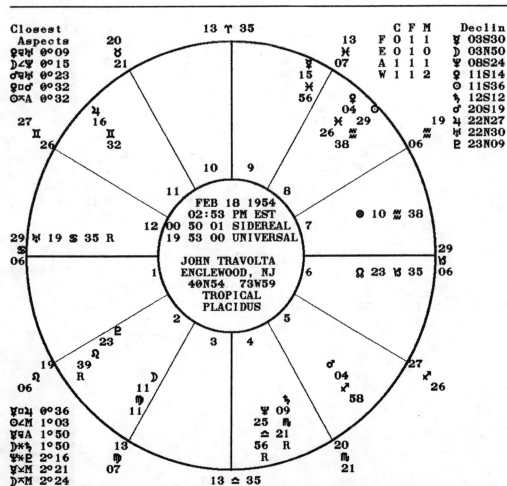

Closest Aspects		C F M	Declin
♀□♅ 0°09		F 0 1 1	☿ 03S30
☽∠♆ 0°15		E 0 1 0	☽ 03N50
♂□♅ 0°23		A 1 1 1	♆ 08S24
♀□♂ 0°32		W 1 1 2	♀ 11S14
☉⚹A 0°32			☉ 11S36
			♄ 12S12
			♂ 20S19
			♃ 22N27
			♅ 22N30
			♇ 23N09

FEB 18 1954
02:53 PM EST
00 50 01 SIDEREAL
19 53 00 UNIVERSAL

JOHN TRAVOLTA
ENGLEWOOD, NJ
40N54 73W59
TROPICAL
PLACIDUS

☿□♄ 0°36
☉∠M 1°03
♅□A 1°50
♆⚹♇ 2°16
☿∠M 2°21
☽⚹M 2°24

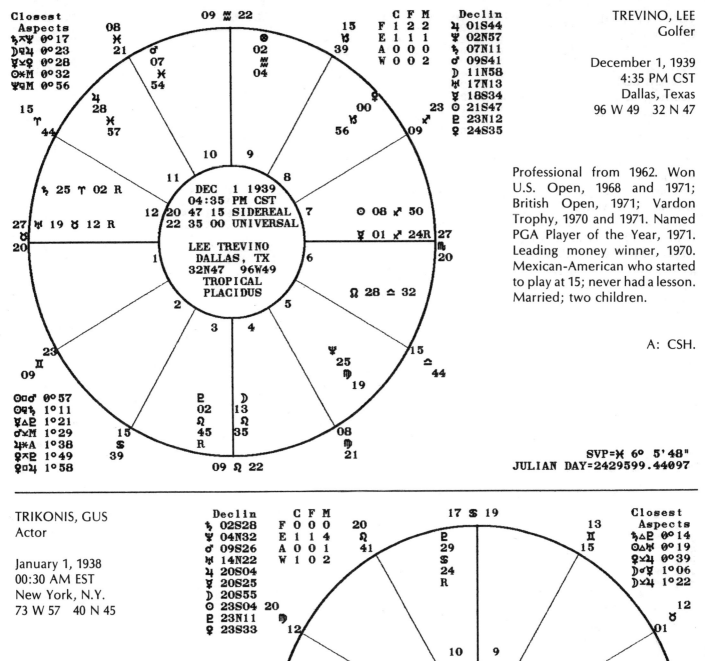

TREVINO, LEE
Golfer

December 1, 1939
4:35 PM CST
Dallas, Texas
96 W 49   32 N 47

Professional from 1962. Won U.S. Open, 1968 and 1971; British Open, 1971; Vardon Trophy, 1970 and 1971. Named PGA Player of the Year, 1971. Leading money winner, 1970. Mexican-American who started to play at 15; never had a lesson. Married; two children.

A: CSH.

SVP=♓ 6° 5'48"
JULIAN DAY=2429599.44097

Closest Aspects
♄⚹♆ 0°17
☽⚼♃ 0°23
☿⚼♀ 0°28
☉⚹M 0°32
♆⚼M 0°56

☉□♂ 0°57
☉⚹♄ 1°11
☿△♇ 1°21
♂⚹M 1°29
♃⚹A 1°38
♀⚹♇ 1°49
♀□♃ 1°58

	C	F	M	Declin	
F	1	2	2	♃	01S44
E	1	1	1	♆	02N57
A	0	0	0	♄	07N11
W	0	0	2	♂	09S41
				☽	11N58
				♅	17N13
				☿	18S34
				☉	21S47
				♇	23N12
				♀	24S35

DEC 1 1939
04:35 PM CST
20 47 15 SIDEREAL
22 35 00 UNIVERSAL

LEE TREVINO
DALLAS, TX
32N47   96W49
TROPICAL
PLACIDUS

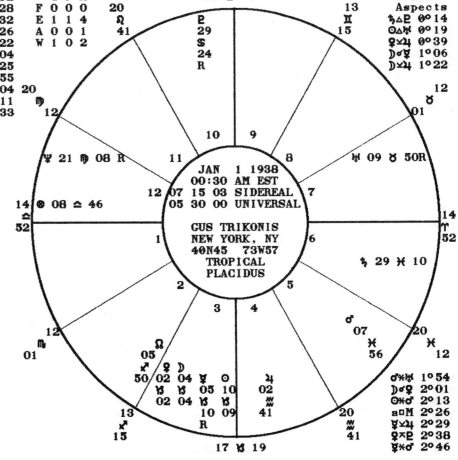

TRIKONIS, GUS
Actor

January 1, 1938
00:30 AM EST
New York, N.Y.
73 W 57   40 N 45

Dancer; singer; in such films as *West Side Story* and *The Unsinkable Molly Brown*; on screen in the 60s. When separated from his wife, Goldie Hawn, in 1973 claimed community property of $75,000 from her. A director by 1975.

A: CL, Christine Whittier, "from him."[134]

SVP=♓ 6° 7'16"
JULIAN DAY=2428899.72917

Declin	
♄	02S28
♆	04N32
♂	09S26
♅	14N22
♃	20S04
☿	20S25
☽	20S55
☉	23S04
♇	23N11
♀	23S33

	C	F	M
F	0	0	0
E	1	1	4
A	0	0	1
W	1	0	2

JAN 1 1938
00:30 AM EST
07 15 03 SIDEREAL
05 30 00 UNIVERSAL

GUS TRIKONIS
NEW YORK, NY
40N45   73W57
TROPICAL
PLACIDUS

Closest Aspects
♄△♇ 0°14
☉△♅ 0°19
♀⚼♃ 0°39
☽♂♀ 1°06
☽⚹♃ 1°22

♂⚹♅ 1°54
☽♂♀ 2°01
☉♂♂ 2°13
a□M 2°26
☿⚼♃ 2°29
♀⚹♇ 2°38
☿⚹♂ 2°46

TUNA, CHARLIE
Disc Jockey

April 18, 1944
3:42 AM CDT
Kearney, Neb
99 W 05   40 N 42

First job announcing at age 14; first big station at 21. Heard daily around the world through Armed Forces radio. Moved to L.A., 1967; married; three children. Interest in UFOs and psychic phenomena; coaches little league teams. Embarrased by fan-club publicity.

A: From him to Lynn Rodden, B.C.

SVP=♓ 6° 2'31"
JULIAN DAY=2431198.86250

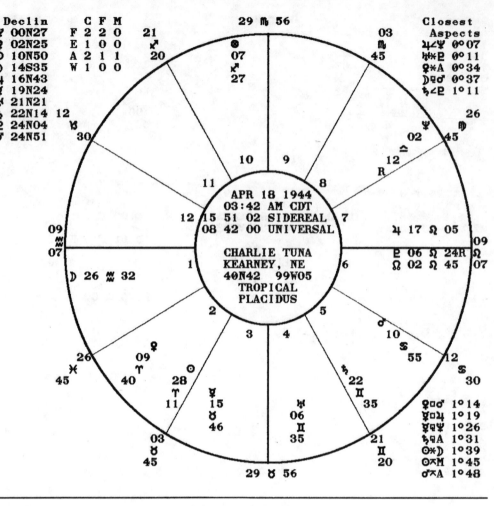

TYL, NOEL
Multi-talented

December 31, 1936
3:57 PM EST
West Chester, Pa
75 W 36   39 N 58

Wagnerian opera singer. Astrologer, writer, managing editor of *Astrology Now* from March 1975. Degrees in psychology and business management. Books include *The Horoscope As Identity* and a twelve-volume series of textbooks (1974).

A: From him to LMR, 1974.

SVP=♓ 6° 8' 4"
JULIAN DAY=2428534.37292

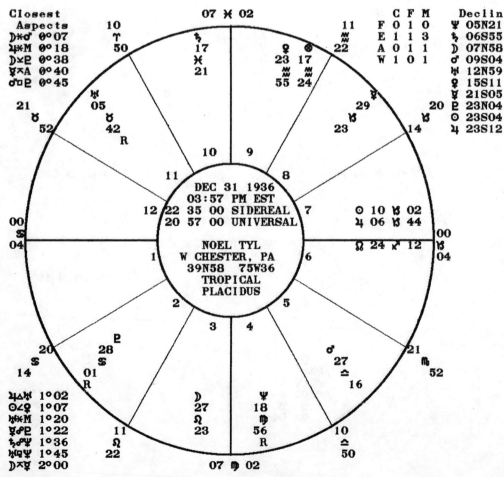

USTINOV, PETER
Actor

April 16, 1921
11:00 AM BST
London, England
0 W 06 51 N 31

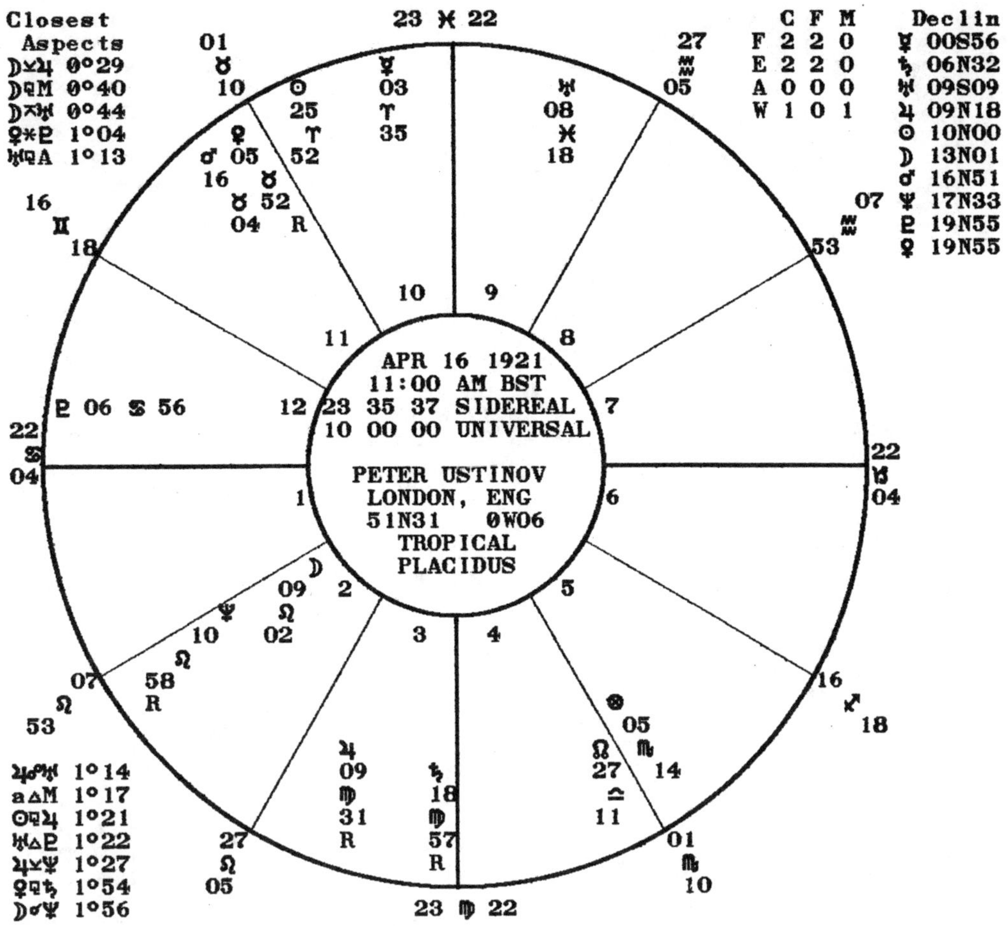
Closest Aspects
☽⊻♃ 0°29
☽⚼M 0°40
☽⚻♅ 0°44
♀✶♇ 1°04
♅⚼A 1°13
C F M
F 2 2 0
E 2 2 0
A 0 0 0
W 1 0 1
Declin
☿ 00S56
♄ 06N32
♅ 09S09
♃ 09N18
☉ 10N00
☽ 13N01
♂ 16N51
♆ 17N33
♇ 19N55
♀ 19N55
APR 16 1921
11:00 AM BST
23 35 37 SIDEREAL
10 00 00 UNIVERSAL
PETER USTINOV
LONDON, ENG
51N31 0W06
TROPICAL
PLACIDUS
♃☍♅ 1°14
a△M 1°17
☉⚼♃ 1°21
♅△♇ 1°22
♃⊻♆ 1°27
♀⚼♄ 1°54
☽☌♆ 1°56

Cultured and talented, a published writer of fiction, plays, and cartoons. Acting debut, 1938. Won Oscar as best supporting actor in *Spartacus* (1960) and *Topkapi* (1964); nominated for Oscar in *Quo Vadis* (1951). Won TV Emmy for *The Life of Samuel Johnson* (1957).

B: Holliday quotes autobiography *Dear Me*, at "11 o'clock", quotes Davies for AM.[135]

SVP=♓ 6°21'24"
JULIAN DAY=2422795.91667

USTON, KEN
Gambler

January 12, 1935
3:00 AM EST
New York, N.Y.
73 W 57 40 N 45

Executive in a stock-broker firm. By 1978 not admitted to any casinos after five years of winning $3.3 million with black jack system. Biography *The Big Player* (1977) written with Roger Rapaport. TV video-tape, March 1979, *Beat The Game*.

A: From him to LMR, March 1979.

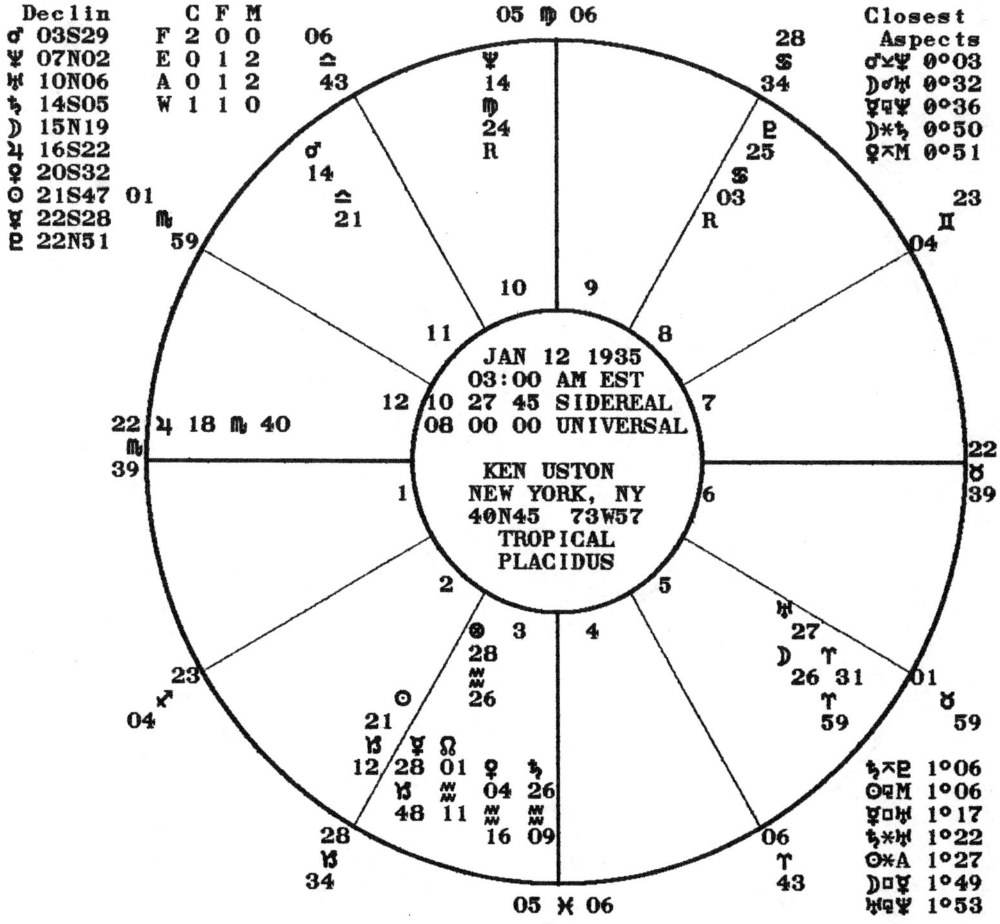
Declin
♂ 03S29
♆ 07N02
♅ 10N06
♄ 14S05
☽ 15N19
♃ 16S22
♀ 20S32
☉ 21S47
☿ 22S28
♇ 22N51
C F M
F 2 0 0
E 0 1 2
A 0 1 2
W 1 1 0
Closest Aspects
♂⊻♆ 0°03
☽☍♅ 0°32
☿⚼♆ 0°36
☽✶♄ 0°50
♀⚻M 0°51
JAN 12 1935
03:00 AM EST
10 27 45 SIDEREAL
08 00 00 UNIVERSAL
KEN USTON
NEW YORK, NY
40N45 73W57
TROPICAL
PLACIDUS
♄⚻♇ 1°06
☉⚼M 1°06
☿□♅ 1°17
♄✶♅ 1°22
☉✶A 1°27
☽□☿ 1°49
♅⚼♆ 1°53

SVP=♓ 6° 9'46"
JULIAN DAY=2427814.83333

VAILLANT, AUGUSTE
Anarchist

December 27, 1861
3:00 AM LMT
Mezieres, France
4 E 13   49 N 45

Political activist who threw a bomb into the Chamber of Deputies in Paris on December 9, 1893. After trial and sentence, sent to the guillotine on February 5, 1894, 7:12 AM LMT, Paris.

A: CL quotes Fagan, "from official sources."

SVP=♓ 7°10'55"
JULIAN DAY=2401136.61329

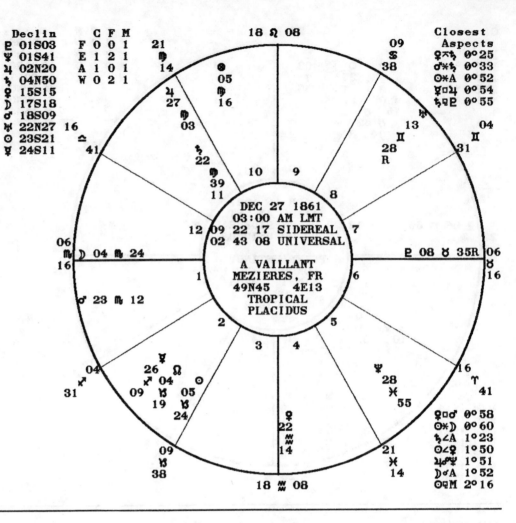

	Declin	C F M
♇	01S03	F 0 0 1
♆	01S41	E 1 2 1
♃	02N20	A 1 0 1
♄	04N50	W 0 2 1
♀	15S15	
☽	17S18	
♂	18S09	
♅	22N27	
☉	23S21	
☿	24S11	

Closest Aspects
☿☌♄ 0°25
♂□♄ 0°33
☉⚹A 0°52
☿□♃ 0°54
♄□♇ 0°55
♀□♂ 0°58
☉⚹☽ 0°60
♄∠A 1°23
☉□♀ 1°50
♃⚹♆ 1°51
☽☌A 1°52
☉□M 2°16

Closest Aspects
♆⚻A 0°03
☉⚻☽ 0°23
♀☌♂ 0°28
♅□A 0°51
♅△♆ 0°53
♃☌♅ 0°57
♂☌♃ 1°11
☿⚹♇ 1°28
♀☌♃ 1°39
♃□A 1°48
♃△♆ 1°51
♂□♅ 2°08

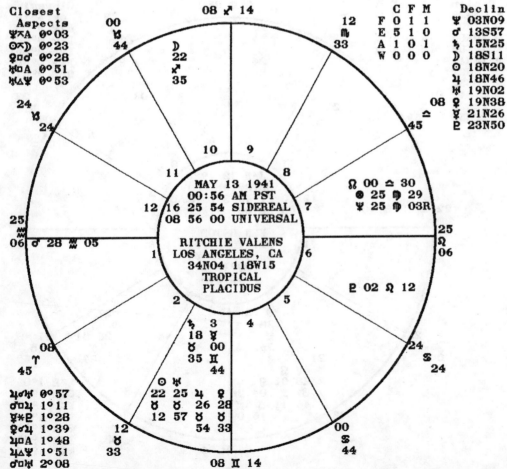

	C F M	Declin
	F 0 1 1	♆ 03N09
	E 5 1 0	♂ 13S57
	A 1 0 1	♄ 15N25
	W 0 0 0	☽ 18S11
		☉ 18N20
		♃ 18N46
		♅ 19N02
		♀ 19N38
		☿ 21N26
		♇ 23N50

VALENS, RITCHIE
Singer

May 13, 1941
00:56 AM PST
Los Angeles, Ca
118 W 15   34 N 04

Background of poverty; rented a hall for a music-gig to pay the home rent. "Discovered" by a talent scout; overnight success as a rock-star. First record broke the charts; made $75,000 in 1958. Killed in a plane crash along with Buddy Holly on February 3, 1959.

A: CL from B.C.

SVP=♓ 6° 4'44"
JULIAN DAY=2430127.87222

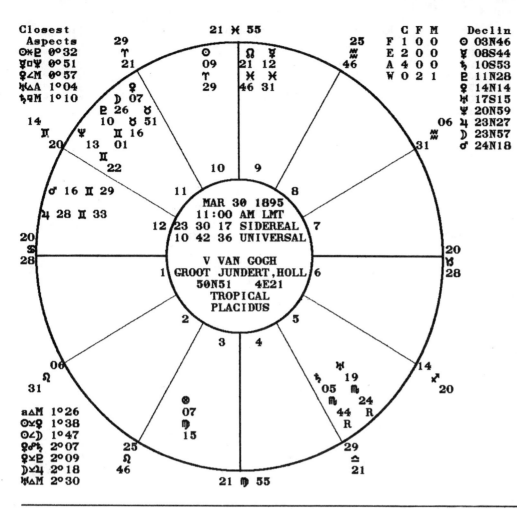

Closest Aspects

⊙✶♇ 0°32
☿□♆ 0°51
♀□M 0°57
♅△A 1°04
♄□M 1°10

a△M 1°26
⊙✶♀ 1°38
⊙∠☽ 1°47
♀⚹♄ 2°07
♀⚹♇ 2°09
☽✶♃ 2°18
♅△M 2°30

21 ♓ 55

29 ♈ 21
⊙ 09 ♈ 29

♀ 07
♇ 26 ♉
10 ♉ 51
☽ 16
♆ 13 ♊ 01
22

♂ 16 ♊ 29
♃ 28 ♊ 33

20 ♋ 28

06 ♌ 31

⊛ 07 ♍ 15

☊ 21 ♍ 12 ♓ 31 ♄ 05 ♏ 19 24 R 44 R

☋ 25 ♌ 46

21 ♍ 55

29 ♎ 21

14 ♐ 20

20 ♑ 28

	C	F	M
F	1	0	0
E	2	0	0
A	4	0	0
W	0	2	1

Declin

⊙ 03N46
☿ 08S44
♄ 10S53
♇ 11N28
♀ 14N14
♅ 17S15
♆ 20N59
♃ 23N27
☽ 23N57
♂ 24N18

MAR 30 1895
11:00 AM LMT
23 30 17 SIDEREAL
10 42 36 UNIVERSAL

V VAN GOGH
GROOT JUNDERT, HOLL
50N51 4E21
TROPICAL
PLACIDUS

VAN GOGH, VINCENT
Artist

March 30, 1895
11:00 AM LMT
Groot Jundert, Holland
4 E 21   50 N 51

A legend, from his tragic life and brilliant canvases. Intense, difficult, and unhappy. Disappointed in love and religion; turned to art. Supported by his older, devoted brother. Increasing mental disturbance; placed under care in 1890, too late; suicide in July.

A: Gauquelin #1444 Vol 4.

SVP=♓ 6°43'19"
JULIAN DAY=2413282.94625

VERDI, GIUSEPPE
Musician

October 10, 1813
8:00 PM LMT
Roncole, Italy
10 E 04   45 N 01

Composer known as the Grand Old Man of Italian Opera. First opera, *Oberto*, written at age 20; followed by thirty more, including *Falstaff* and *Aida*. His work came to a tragic stop when he lost his wife and two children between 1838 and 1842 but revived several years later. (1813-1901)

B: *Constellations*, 1977, Lockhart quotes the biography *Gerick and Pougin* (1886).

SVP=♓ 7°51'49"
JULIAN DAY=2383527.30537

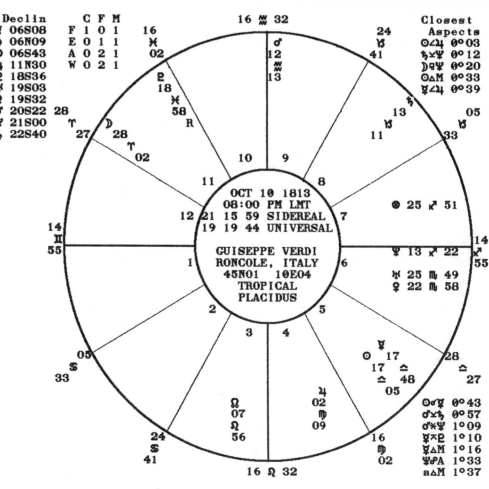

Declin

☿ 06S08
☽ 06N09
⊙ 06S43
♃ 11N30
♇ 18S36
♅ 19S03
♀ 19S32
♂ 20S22
♆ 21S00
♄ 22S40

	C	F	M
F	1	0	1
E	0	1	1
A	0	2	1
W	0	2	1

16 ♒ 32

♂ 16 ♒ 12
02 ♒ 13

♇ 18 ♓ 58 R

☽ 28 ♈ 27
♈ 02

24 ♑ 41
♄ 13 ♑ 11

♆ 13 ♐ 22
14 ♐ 55

⊛ 25 ♐ 51

♅ 25 ♏ 49
♀ 22 ♏ 58

⊙ 17 ♎ 17
☿ 17 ♎ 48
05

♃ 02 ♍ 09

♌ 07
☋ 02 ♌ 56

16 ♌ 32

OCT 10 1813
08:00 PM LMT
21 15 59 SIDEREAL
19 19 44 UNIVERSAL

GUISEPPE VERDI
RONCOLE, ITALY
45N01 10E04
TROPICAL
PLACIDUS

Closest Aspects

⊙∠♃ 0°03
♄⚹♆ 0°12
☽□♆ 0°20
⊙△M 0°33
☿∠♃ 0°39

⊙♂♀ 0°43
♂⚹♄ 0°57
♂✶♆ 1°09
☿△♇ 1°10
☿△M 1°16
♆⚹A 1°33
a△M 1°37

14 ♊ 55

05 ♋ 33

VERLAINE, PAUL
Poet

March 30, 1844
9:00 PM LMT
Metz, France
6 E 10   49 N 09

Famous for symbolism, subtle tenderness, and delicate quality. Many of his poems set to music by Faure and Debussy. Personal life unhappy and disorganized; imprisoned for two years for shooting his lover, Rimbaud, after a quarrel in 1873.

A: R.H. Oliver in *Astro-psychiatry*, "recorded."[136]

SVP=♓ 7°25'47"
JULIAN DAY=2394656.35787

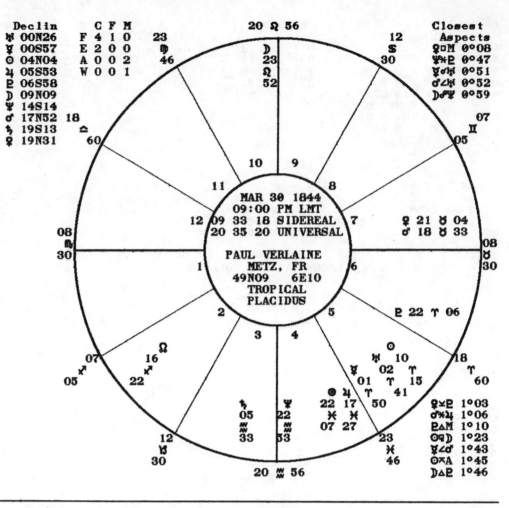

Declin		C F M	
♅	00N26	F 4 1 0	23
☿	00S57	E 2 0 0	♍
☉	04N04	A 0 0 2	46
♃	05S53	W 0 0 1	
♇	06S58		
☽	09N09		
♆	14S14		
♂	17N52	18	
♄	19S13	♎	
♀	19N31	60	

Closest Aspects
♀□M 0°08
♆⚹♇ 0°47
♀♂♅ 0°51
♂∠♃ 0°52
☽⚹♆ 0°59

MAR 30 1844
09:00 PM LMT
09 33 18 SIDEREAL
20 35 20 UNIVERSAL
PAUL VERLAINE
METZ, FR
49N09 6E10
TROPICAL
PLACIDUS

♀⚹♇ 1°03
♂□♃ 1°06
♇∆M 1°10
☉□☽ 1°23
☿∠♂ 1°43
☉∆A 1°45
☽∆♇ 1°46

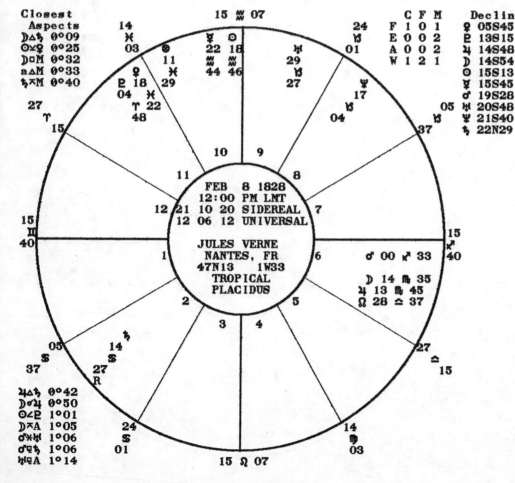

Closest Aspects
☽∆♄ 0°09
☉⚹♀ 0°25
☽□M 0°32
a∆M 0°33
♄⚹M 0°40

	C F M	Declin	
	F 1 0 1	♀	05S45
	E 0 0 2	♇	13S15
	A 0 0 2	♃	14S48
	W 1 2 1	☽	14S54
		☉	15S13
		☿	15S45
		♂	19S28
		♅	20S48
		♆	21S40
		♄	22N29

FEB 8 1828
12:00 PM LMT
10 20 SIDEREAL
12 06 12 UNIVERSAL
JULES VERNE
NANTES, FR
47N13 1W33
TROPICAL
PLACIDUS

♃∆♇ 0°42
☽♂♃ 0°50
☉□♇ 1°01
☽⚹A 1°05
♂□♅ 1°06
♂□♅ 1°06
♅□A 1°14

VERNE, JULES
Writer

February 8, 1828
12:00 Noon LMT
Nantes, France
1 W 33   47 N 13

Widely popular in science fiction, with amazing anticipation of future discoveries. Books include *From the Earth to the Moon* (1865), *20,000 Leagues Under The Sea* (1870), and *Around the World in Eighty Days* (1872). Studied law in Paris; personal life uneventful. (1828-1905)

A: Gauquelin #794 Vol 6.

SVP=♓ 7°39'24"
JULIAN DAY=2388761.00431

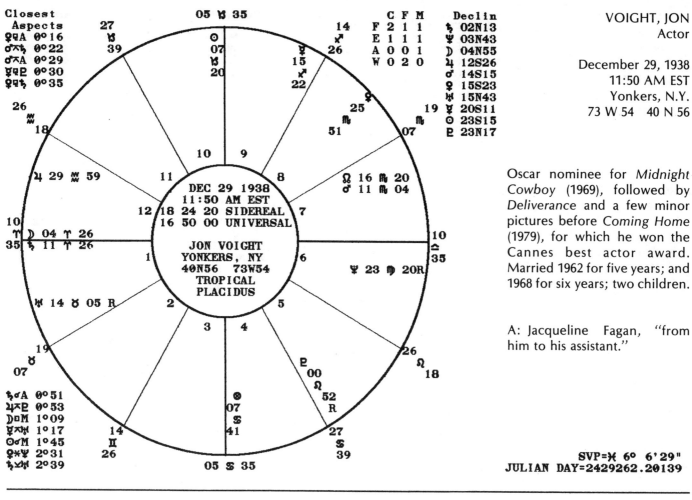

VOIGHT, JON
Actor

December 29, 1938
11:50 AM EST
Yonkers, N.Y.
73 W 54   40 N 56

Oscar nominee for *Midnight Cowboy* (1969), followed by *Deliverance* and a few minor pictures before *Coming Home* (1979), for which he won the Cannes best actor award. Married 1962 for five years; and 1968 for six years; two children.

A: Jacqueline Fagan, "from him to his assistant."

SVP=X 6° 6'29"
JULIAN DAY=2429262.20139

WALLACE, GEORGE
Politician

August 25, 1919
3:30 AM CWT
Clio, Ala
85 W 37   31 N 43

Governor of Alabama in 1963 for three terms. Segregationist. Presidential candidate in 1968 and in 1972, when he was shot and paralyzed by 21-year old Arthur Bremer on May 15, at a Laurel, Mississippi, shopping center while campaigning.

A: March quotes Elizabeth Mayo, "from his mother."[137]

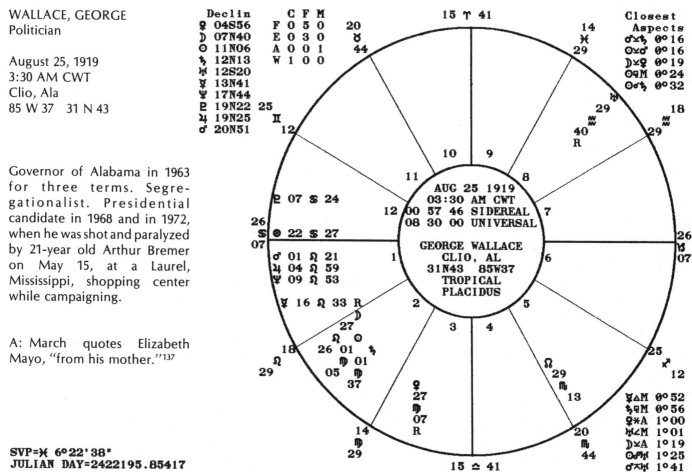

SVP=X 6°22'38"
JULIAN DAY=2422195.85417

WARREN, EARL
Chief Justice

March 19, 1891
2:00 AM PST
Los Angeles, Ca
118 W 15   34 N 04

Law degree; served in World War I; then California district attorney. Three-times governor of California from 1942. Unsuccessful bid for the presidential nomination in 1948 and 1952. Chief justice of the U.S. from 1953, a liberal and influential officer.

A: CL, "from his father."

SVP=♓ 6°46'59"
JULIAN DAY=2411810.91667

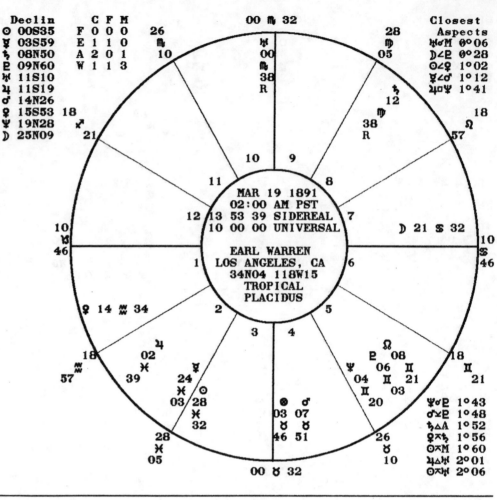

Declin		C F M		Closest Aspects
☉ 00S35	F 0 0 0	26		⛢☌M 0°06
☿ 03S59	E 1 1 0	♏		☽⊾♇ 0°28
♄ 08N50	A 2 0 1	10		☉☌♀ 1°02
♇ 09N60	W 1 1 3			☿☌♂ 1°12
⛢ 11S10				♃☌♆ 1°41
♃ 11S19				
♂ 14N26				
♀ 15S53				
♆ 19N28				
☽ 25N09				

MAR 19 1891
02:00 AM PST
13 53 39 SIDEREAL
10 00 00 UNIVERSAL

EARL WARREN
LOS ANGELES, CA
34N04 118W15
TROPICAL
PLACIDUS

♆☌♇ 1°43	
♂☌♇ 1°48	
♄△A 1°52	
♀⊼♄ 1°56	
☉☌M 1°60	
♃△⛢ 2°01	
☉⊼⛢ 2°06	

WATSON, CHARLES "TEX"
Murderer

December 2, 1945
9:15 PM CST
Dallas, Texas
96 W 49   32 N 47

Following orders of Charles Manson, on August 9, 1969, stabbed eight-month pregnant Sharon Tate to death as Atkins held her. Also involved in the La Bianca killings. Sentenced to life; claims to have found Jesus; preaches one sermon a month in prison.

A: *Constellations*, 1977, Lockhart from B.C.

SVP=♓ 6° 1'12"
JULIAN DAY=2431792.63542

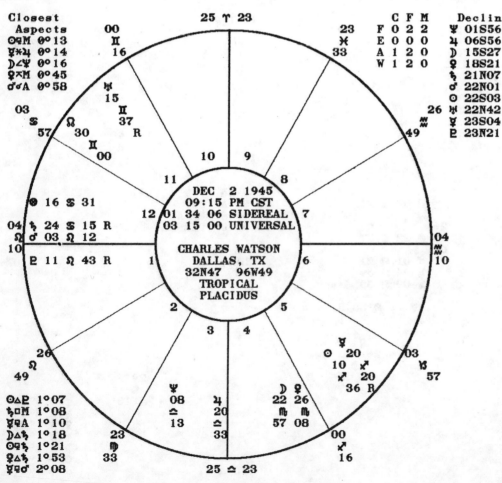

Closest Aspects		C F M		Declin
☉☌M 0°13		F 0 2 2		♆ 01S56
☿⚹♃ 0°14		E 0 0 0		♃ 06S56
☽⊾♆ 0°16		A 1 2 0		☽ 15S27
♀⊼M 0°45		W 1 2 0		♀ 18S21
♂☌A 0°58				♄ 21N07
				♂ 22N01
				☉ 22S03
				⛢ 22N42
				☿ 23S04
				♇ 23N21

DEC 2 1945
09:15 PM CST
01 34 06 SIDEREAL
03 15 00 UNIVERSAL

CHARLES WATSON
DALLAS, TX
32N47 96W49
TROPICAL
PLACIDUS

☉△♇ 1°07	
♄□M 1°08	
☿♀A 1°10	
☽△♄ 1°18	
☉⚹♄ 1°21	
♀△♄ 1°53	
☿☌A 2°08	

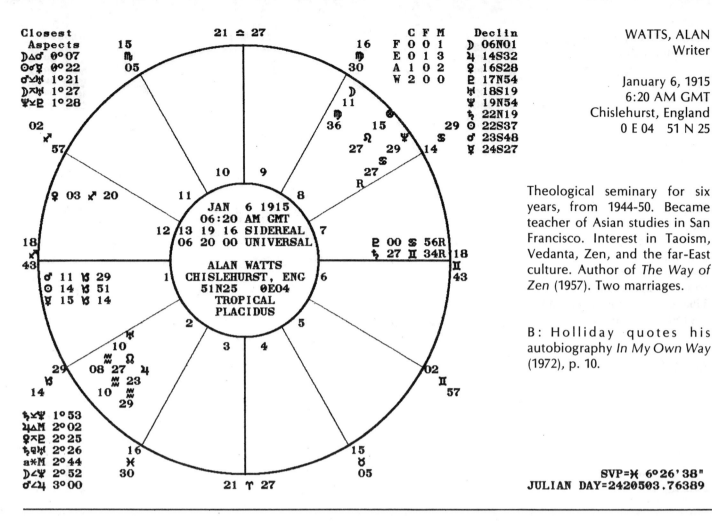

WATTS, ALAN
Writer

January 6, 1915
6:20 AM GMT
Chislehurst, England
0 E 04   51 N 25

Closest
Aspects
☽△♂ 0°07
☉♂☿ 0°22
♂⊼♅ 1°21
☽⊼♅ 1°27
♆⊼♇ 1°28

C F M   Declin
F 0 0 1   ☽ 06N01
E 0 1 3   ♃ 14S32
A 1 0 2   ♀ 16S28
W 2 0 0   ♇ 17N54
          ♅ 18S19
          ♆ 19N54
          ♄ 22N19
          ☉ 22S37
          ♂ 23S48
          ☿ 24S27

JAN 6 1915
06:20 AM GMT
13 19 16 SIDEREAL
06 20 00 UNIVERSAL

ALAN WATTS
CHISLEHURST, ENG
51N25   0E04
TROPICAL
PLACIDUS

♇ 00 ♋ 56R
♄ 27 ♊ 34R

Theological seminary for six years, from 1944-50. Became teacher of Asian studies in San Francisco. Interest in Taoism, Vedanta, Zen, and the far-East culture. Author of *The Way of Zen* (1957). Two marriages.

B: Holliday quotes his autobiography *In My Own Way* (1972), p. 10.

♂ 11 ♑ 29
☉ 14 ♑ 51
☿ 15 ♑ 14

♄⊼♆ 1°53
♃△M 2°02
♀⊼♇ 2°25
♄⊓♅ 2°26
a✱M 2°44
☽∠♆ 2°52
♂∠♃ 3°00

SVP=♓ 6°26'38"
JULIAN DAY=2420503.76389

WEAVER, DENNIS
Actor

June 4, 1925
4:00 PM CST
Joplin, Mo
94 W 31   37 N 06

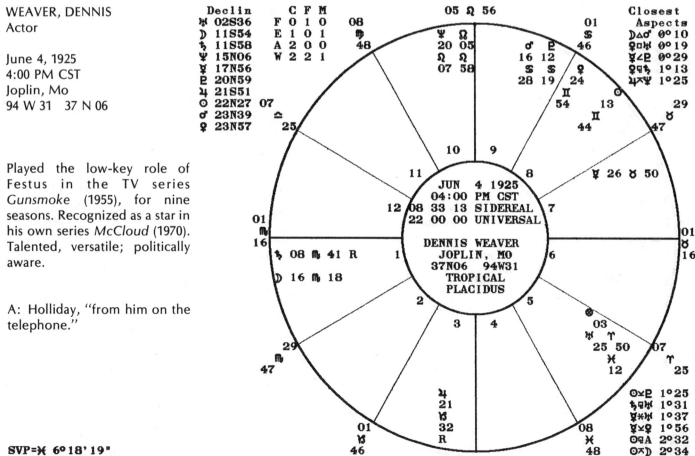

Declin
♅ 02S36
☽ 11S54
♄ 11S58
♆ 15N06
☿ 17N56
♇ 20N59
♃ 21S51
☉ 22N27
♂ 23N39
♀ 23N57

C F M
F 0 1 0
E 1 0 1
A 2 0 0
W 2 2 1

Closest
Aspects
☽△♂ 0°10
♀△♅ 0°19
☿⊼♇ 0°29
♀△♄ 1°13
♃⊼♆ 1°25

JUN 4 1925
04:00 PM CST
08 33 13 SIDEREAL
22 00 00 UNIVERSAL

DENNIS WEAVER
JOPLIN, MO
37N06   94W31
TROPICAL
PLACIDUS

♄ 08 ♏ 41 R
☽ 16 ♏ 18

☿ 26 ♉ 50

Played the low-key role of Festus in the TV series *Gunsmoke* (1955), for nine seasons. Recognized as a star in his own series *McCloud* (1970). Talented, versatile; politically aware.

A: Holliday, "from him on the telephone."

♃
21
♑
32
R

☉⊼♇ 1°25
♄□♅ 1°31
☿✱♅ 1°37
☿⊼♀ 1°56
☉△A 2°32
☉□☽ 2°34
☉⊼♂ 2°44

SVP=♓ 6°18'19"
JULIAN DAY=2424306.41667

WEISMULLER, JOHNNY
Swimmer, actor

June 2, 1904
6:30 PM EST
Windber, Pa
78 W 50   40 N 14

Winner of five Olympic gold medals, establishing a new record with each. First film *Tarzan, The Ape Man* (1932); continued in a film series to 1948. *Jungle Jim* pictures in 1949 and 1952 became a TV series in 1958. Debilitating strokes in the 70s left brain damage.

A: CL, "from his mother."

SVP=Ⅹ 6°35'42"
JULIAN DAY=2416634.47917

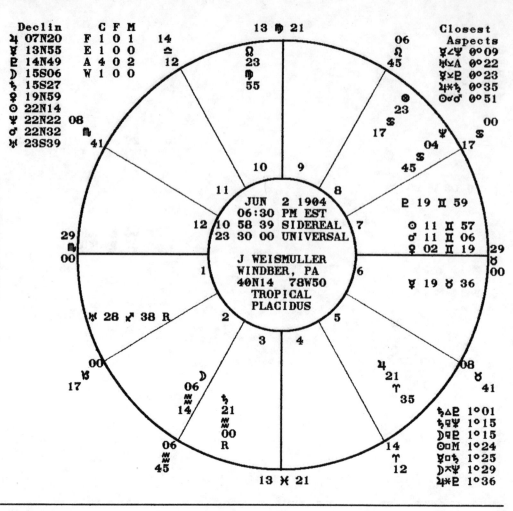

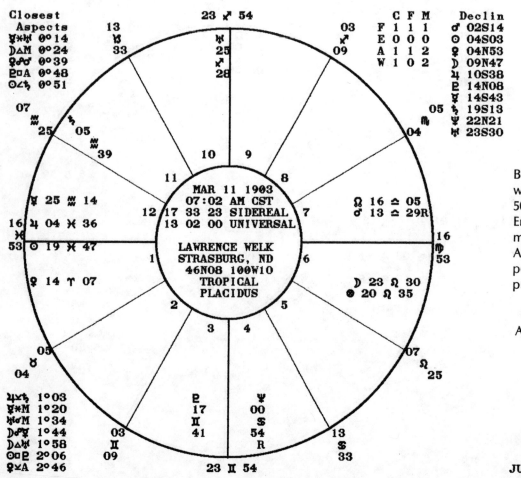

WELK, LAWRENCE
Musician

March 11, 1903
7:02 AM CST
Strasburg, N.D.
100 W 10   46 N 08

Bandleader, accordian player with his own TV show from the 50s to the 70s. Nominated for TV Emmy as the most outstanding male performer in 1953. Although he has young performers, his show appeals primarily to the over-30 group.

A: CL, "from him personally."

SVP=Ⅹ 6°36'35"
JULIAN DAY=2416185.04306

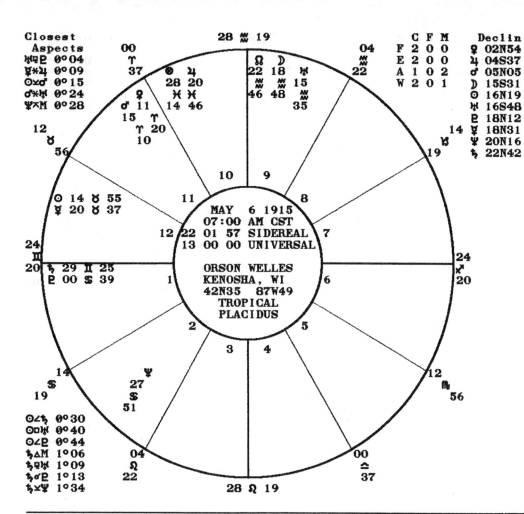

WELLES, ORSON
Actor

May 6, 1915
7:00 AM CST
Kenosha, Wis
87 W 49   42 N 35

Director, producer, writer, and actor; a brilliant talent. Nominated for Oscar as best actor in *Citizen Kane* (1941). Other films include *Long Hot Summer* (1958) and *The Trial* (1963). Guest shots in many TV dramas. Presented his sensational *War of the Worlds* radio show in 1938.

A: CL quotes Ed Steinbrecker, "from office of Register of Deeds."

SVP=ℋ 6°26'21"
JULIAN DAY=2420624.04167

WELLINGTON, DUKE OF
General

May 1, 1769
11:58 PM LMT
Dublin, Ireland
6 W 15   53 N 20

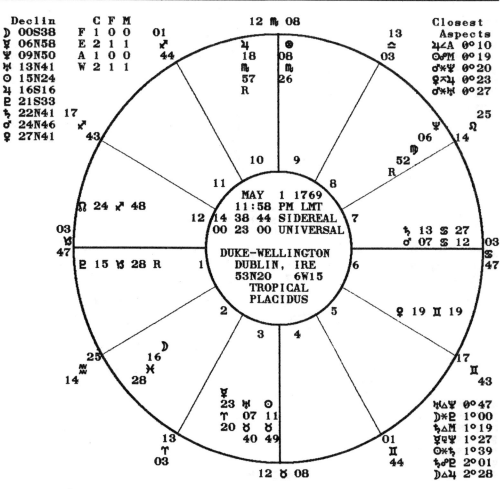

Arthur Wellesley, British soldier and statesman who was known as "The Iron Duke". Famous as the general who defeated Napolean at the Battle of Waterloo, 1815; later served as prime minister. Entered the army at 18; rose rapidly; commander in 1809. (1769-1852)

A: *Constellations*, 1977, Lockhart quotes Raphael's *Manual of Astrology*, "from a close relative, midnight ending the day."

SVP=ℋ 8°28'30"
JULIAN DAY=2367295.51597

WELLS, H.G.
Writer

September 21, 1866
4:30 PM LMT
Bromley, England
0 E 01   51 N 25

Historian, prognosticator, economist, novelist; known for science fiction predictions of the future. First novel was (1895); other work includes *The Outline of History* (1920) and *The Shape of Things to Come* (1933), which was made into a motion picture. (1866-1946)

B: *H.G. Wells* by MacKenzie (1973), data on p. 3.[138]

SVP=♓ 7° 7'13"
JULIAN DAY=2402866.18745

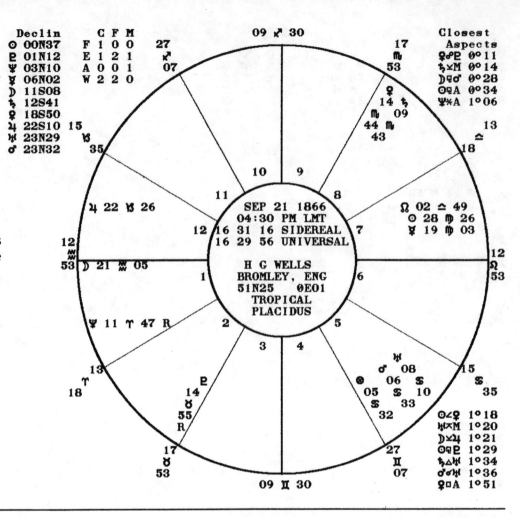

Declin		C F M		Closest Aspects
☉ 00N37		F 1 0 0		♀☌♇ 0°11
♇ 01N12		E 1 2 1		♄⚹M 0°14
♆ 03N10		A 0 0 1		☽☍♂ 0°28
☿ 06N02		W 2 2 0		☉☍A 0°34
☽ 11S08				♆⚹A 1°06
♄ 12S41				
♀ 18S50				
♃ 22S10				
♅ 23N29				
♂ 23N32				

SEP 21 1866
04:30 PM LMT
16 31 16 SIDEREAL
16 29 56 UNIVERSAL

H G WELLS
BROMLEY, ENG
51N25 0E01
TROPICAL
PLACIDUS

☊ 02 ♎ 49
☉ 28 ♍ 26
☿ 19 ♍ 03

☉☍♇ 1°18	
♅⚹M 1°20	
☽⚹♃ 1°21	
☉☍♇ 1°29	
♄△♃ 1°34	
♂☌♅ 1°36	
♀□A 1°51	

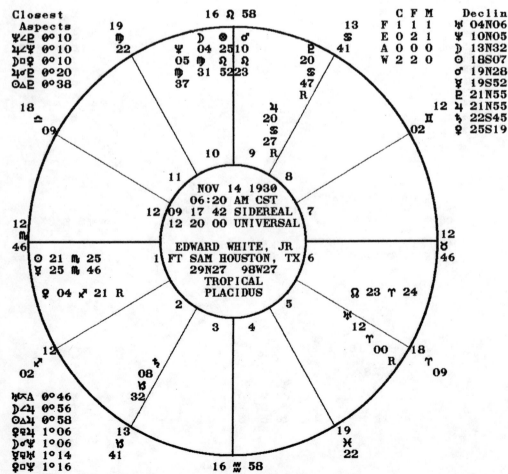

WHITE, EDWARD JR.
Astronaut

November 14, 1930
6:20 AM CST
Fort Sam Houston, Tex
98 W 27   29 N 27

First American astronaut to emerge from an orbiting spacecraft; first man to control his movements while floating in space, 1965. Killed in a flash fire aboard grounded spacecraft simulation of Project Apollo flight, January 27, 1967.

A: Holliday quotes AFA, May 1967, B.C.

Closest Aspects	
♆∠♇ 0°10	
♃∠♆ 0°10	
☽☌♀ 0°10	
♃☌♇ 0°20	
☉△♇ 0°38	

NOV 14 1930
06:20 AM CST
09 17 42 SIDEREAL
12 20 00 UNIVERSAL

EDWARD WHITE, JR
FT SAM HOUSTON, TX
29N27 98W27
TROPICAL
PLACIDUS

C F M		Declin
F 1 1 1		♅ 04N06
E 0 2 1		♆ 10N05
A 0 0 0		☽ 13N32
W 2 2 0		☉ 18S07
		♂ 19N28
		☿ 19S52
		♇ 21N55
		♃ 21N55
		♄ 22S45
		♀ 25S19

♅⚹A 0°46	
☽∠♃ 0°56	
☉△♃ 0°58	
♀⚹♃ 1°06	
☽☌♆ 1°06	
♀☌♅ 1°14	
♀□♆ 1°16	

SVP=♓ 6°13'38"
JULIAN DAY=2426295.01389

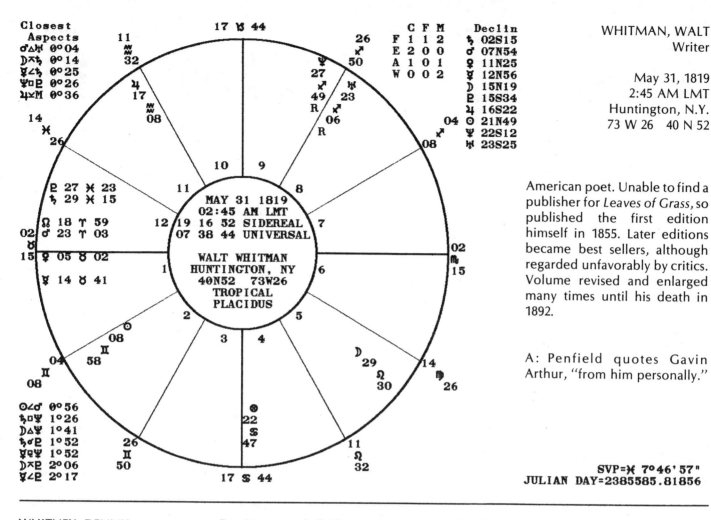

WHITMAN, WALT
Writer

May 31, 1819
2:45 AM LMT
Huntington, N.Y.
73 W 26   40 N 52

American poet. Unable to find a publisher for *Leaves of Grass*, so published the first edition himself in 1855. Later editions became best sellers, although regarded unfavorably by critics. Volume revised and enlarged many times until his death in 1892.

A: Penfield quotes Gavin Arthur, "from him personally."

SVP=✶ 7° 46' 57"
JULIAN DAY=2385585.81856

WHITNEY, DENNIS
Murderer

August 15, 1942
11:00 PM PWT
Riverside, Ca
117 W 22   33 N 59

Shot and killed a victim after each of five hold-ups on February 12, 20, 21, 28, and 29, 1960. A victim on March 5 lived to identify him; captured after he'd beaten and shot a woman to death on March 6. Trial on May 4, 1960; life imprisonment.

A: CL, "from his father."

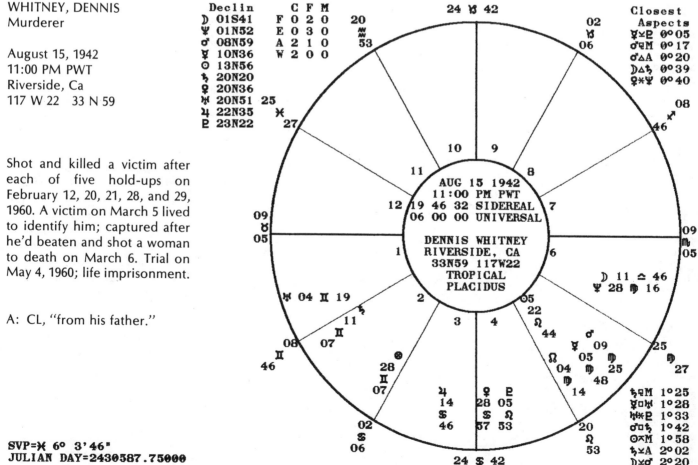

SVP=✶ 6° 3' 46"
JULIAN DAY=2430587.75000

WIESENTHAL, SIMON
Nazi hunter

December 31, 1908
11:30 PM MET
Bucazca, Poland
21 E 00   49 N 50

Made a career of tracking down war criminals in 1945, after being in a concentration camp where his mother and kin were exterminated. Eichmann and numerous other notorious Nazis apprehended because of his dogged sleuthing.

B: Holliday quotes data from his autobiography, *The Murderers Among Us* (1967), p. 23.

SVP=♓ 6°32' 6"
JULIAN DAY=2418307.43750

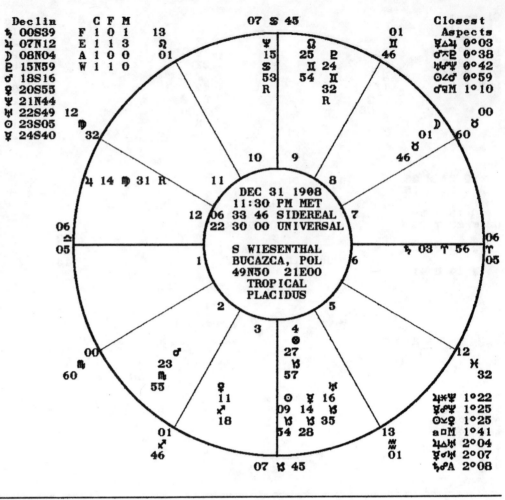

WILDE, OSCAR
Writer

October 16, 1854
3:00 AM Dunsink
Dublin, Ireland
6 W 15   53 N 20

Irish poet and dramatist. Married May 29, 1884; two sons. At the peak of success, disaster when he was accused of a homosexual affair and brought suit for libel. Lost the case; imprisoned for two years in 1895; spent last years a broken man. (1854-1900)

A: Fagan in AA, September 1963, "baptismal certificate."[139]

SVP=♓ 7°17'28"
JULIAN DAY=2398507.64236

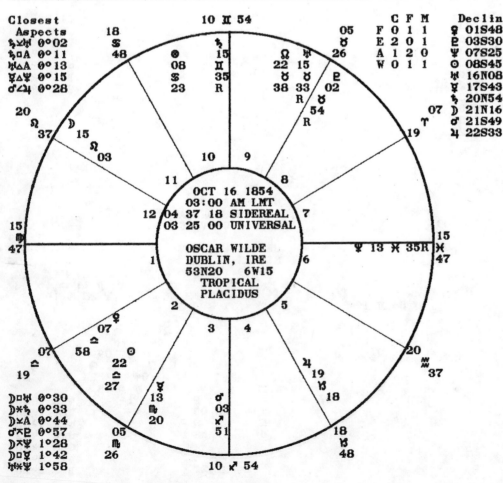

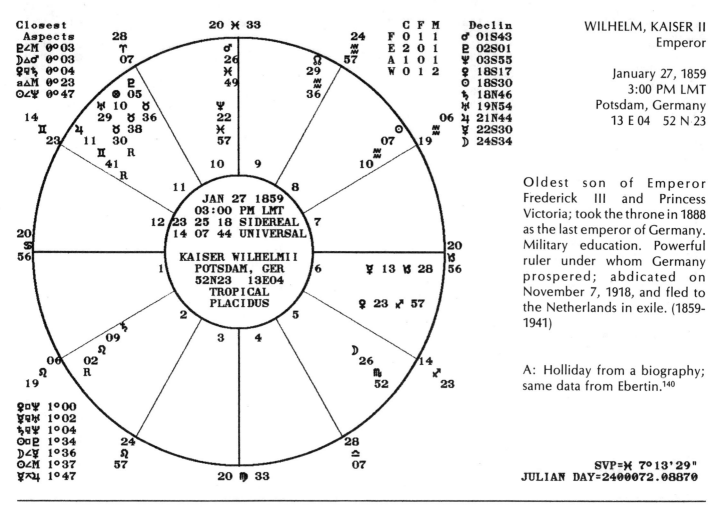

WILHELM, KAISER II
Emperor

January 27, 1859
3:00 PM LMT
Potsdam, Germany
13 E 04   52 N 23

Oldest son of Emperor Frederick III and Princess Victoria; took the throne in 1888 as the last emperor of Germany. Military education. Powerful ruler under whom Germany prospered; abdicated on November 7, 1918, and fled to the Netherlands in exile. (1859-1941)

A: Holliday from a biography; same data from Ebertin.[140]

SVP=♓ 7°13'29"
JULIAN DAY=2400072.08870

WILLKIE, WENDELL
Politician

February 18, 1892
5:00 AM CST
Elwood, Ind
85 W 50   40 N 17

Lawyer who became a business executive before entering politics. An unusual political career because he rose to prominance without the party machine. Republican presidential candidate, 1940. Author of *One World* (1943). (1892-1944)

A: CL, "from his older sister", and from Fagan, "quoting him."

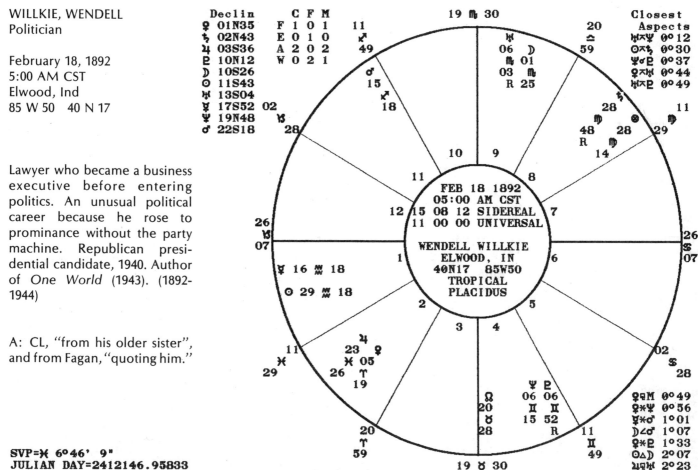

SVP=♓ 6°46' 9"
JULIAN DAY=2412146.95833

WINDSOR, DUKE OF
Royalty

June 23, 1894
9:55 PM GMT
Richmond, Surray, England
0 W 18   51 N 27

Prince Edward, oldest son of King George V. Reigned as King Edward VIII for less than a year, 1936, when he gave up the throne "to marry the woman I love", Wallis Simpson. Governor of the Bahama Islands, 1940-45. (1894-1972)

A: Fagan in AA, November 1976, "official news release."[141]

SVP=♓ 6°44' 1"
JULIAN DAY=2413003.41319

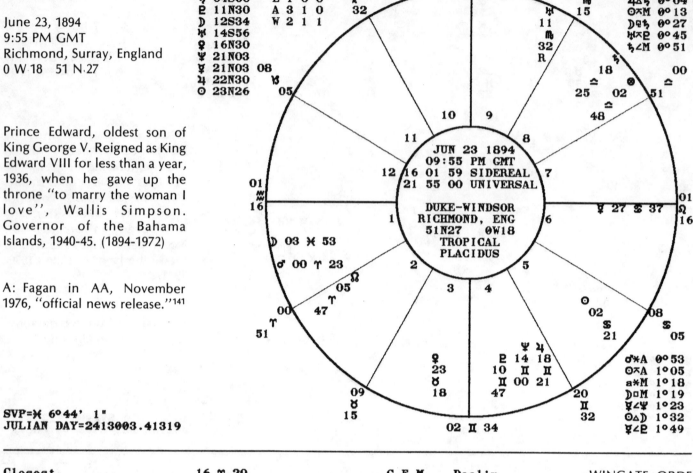

	Declin	C	F	M
♂	02S25	F	1 0 0
♄	04S50	E	1 0 0
♇	11N30	A	3 1 0
☽	12S34	W	2 1 1
♅	14S56		
♀	16N30		
♆	21N03		
☿	21N03		
♃	22N30		
☉	23N26		

Closest Aspects
♃△♄ 0°04
☉□M 0°13
☽□♄ 0°27
♅⚹♇ 0°45
♄∠M 0°51

♂⚹A 0°53
☉⚹A 1°05
a⚹M 1°18
☽□M 1°19
☿∠♆ 1°23
☉△☽ 1°32
☿∠♇ 1°49

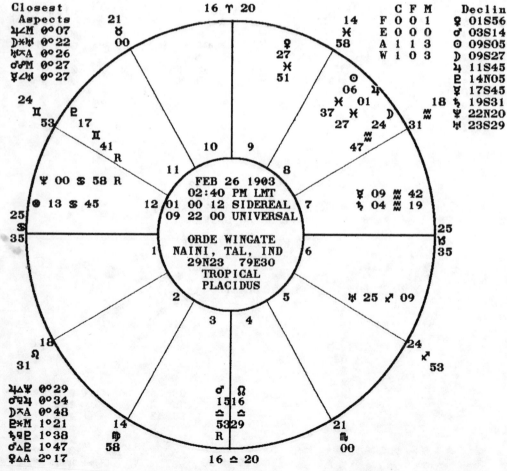

Closest Aspects
♃∠M 0°07
☽⚹♅ 0°22
♅⚹A 0°26
♂⚹♆ 0°27
☿∠♅ 0°27

♃△♆ 0°29
♂⚹♃ 0°34
☽⚹A 0°48
♇⚹M 1°21
♄⚹♇ 1°38
♂△♇ 1°47
♀△A 2°17

C	F	M		Declin
F	0 0 1		♀	01S56
E	0 0 0		♂	03S14
A	1 1 3		☉	09S05
W	1 0 3		☽	09S27
			♃	11S45
			♇	14N05
			☿	17S45
			♄	19S31
			♆	22N20
			♅	23S29

WINGATE, ORDE
Military leader

February 26, 1903
2:40 PM LMT
Naini, Tal, India
79 E 30   29 N 23

One of seven children. Known for genius. A soldier all of his life. Became a major general; organized a daring and effective commando force in 1941 to slice behind Japanese lines; cut off the Burma railroad in 1944. Died in an airplane crash, April 1944.

B: PC quotes *Orde Wingate* by C. Sykes (1959); p. 19 quotes a letter from his father.[142]

SVP=♓ 6°36'37"
JULIAN DAY=2416171.89028

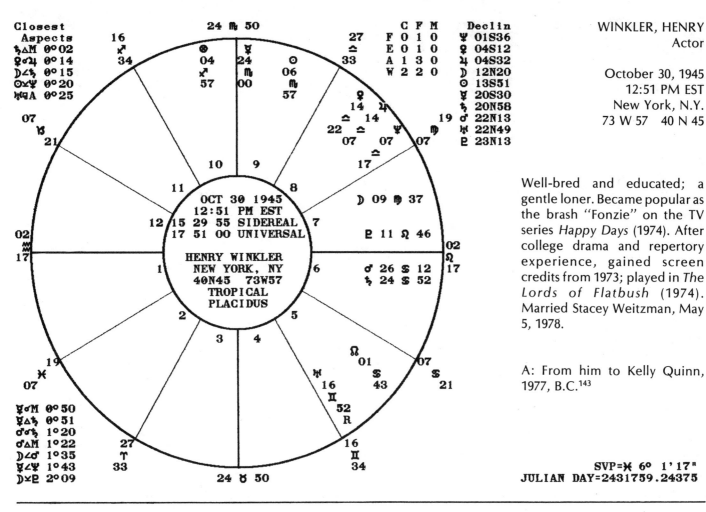

WINKLER, HENRY
Actor

October 30, 1945
12:51 PM EST
New York, N.Y.
73 W 57   40 N 45

Well-bred and educated; a gentle loner. Became popular as the brash "Fonzie" on the TV series *Happy Days* (1974). After college drama and repertory experience, gained screen credits from 1973; played in *The Lords of Flatbush* (1974). Married Stacey Weitzman, May 5, 1978.

A: From him to Kelly Quinn, 1977, B.C.[143]

Closest Aspects
ħ△M 0°02
♀♂♃ 0°14
☽∠♃ 0°15
☉✶Ψ 0°20
♅□A 0°25

Declin
Ψ 01S36
♀ 04S12
♃ 04S32
☽ 12N20
☉ 13S51
☿ 20S30
ħ 20N58
♂ 22N13
♅ 22N49
♇ 23N13

C	F	M
F 0	1	0
E 0	1	0
A 1	3	0
W 2	2	0

Chart center:
OCT 30 1945
12:51 PM EST
15 29 55 SIDEREAL
17 51 00 UNIVERSAL
HENRY WINKLER
NEW YORK, NY
40N45 73W57
TROPICAL
PLACIDUS

☿♂M 0°50
☿△ħ 0°51
♂♂ħ 1°20
♂△M 1°22
☽∠♂ 1°35
☿∠Ψ 1°43
☽✶♇ 2°09

SVP=♓ 6° 1'17"
JULIAN DAY=2431759.24375

WINTERS, JONATHAN
Comedian

November 11, 1925
8:23 PM CST
Dayton, Ohio
84 W 12   39 N 45

Master of mimicry who appeared on the *Jack Paar Show* regularly and on many TV specials; had his own TV series, 1956-70. Hosted entertainment special *Holiday On Ice* in the 60s. Breakdown, May 1959; period in private sanitorium. Married; two children.

A: Jansky, "from him, verified by correspondence."

SVP=♓ 6°17'59"
JULIAN DAY=2424466.59931

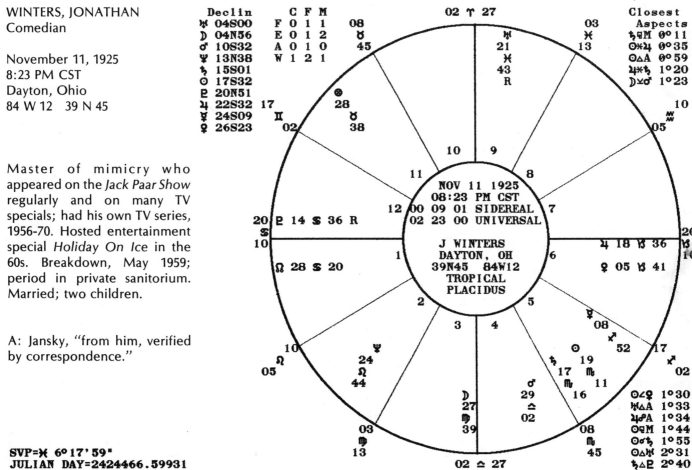

Declin
♅ 04S00
☽ 04N56
♂ 10S32
Ψ 13N38
ħ 15S01
☉ 17S32
♇ 20N51
♃ 22S32
☿ 24S09
♀ 26S23

C	F	M
F 0	1	1
E 0	1	2
A 0	1	0
W 1	2	1

Chart center:
NOV 11 1925
08:23 PM CST
00 09 01 SIDEREAL
02 23 00 UNIVERSAL
J WINTERS
DAYTON, OH
39N45 84W12
TROPICAL
PLACIDUS

Closest Aspects
ħ□M 0°11
☉✶♃ 0°35
☉△A 0°59
♃✶ħ 1°20
☽∠♂ 1°23

☉∠♀ 1°30
♅△A 1°33
♃∠A 1°34
☉□M 1°44
☉♂ħ 1°55
☉△♅ 2°31
ħ△♇ 2°40

YEATS, WILLIAM BUTLER
Writer

June 13, 1865
10:40 PM Dunsink
Dublin, Ireland
6 W 15   53 N 20

Irish poet and dramatist; awarded the 1923 Nobel prize for literature. First published in 1887. Works include *The Wind Among the Reeds* (1899), *Responsibilities* (1912) and *The Tower* (1927). Active interest in mysticism. (1865-1939)

A: *Constellations*, 1977, quotes Fagan in AA, January 1964.[144]

SVP=ℋ 7° 8'10"
JULIAN DAY=2402401.46181

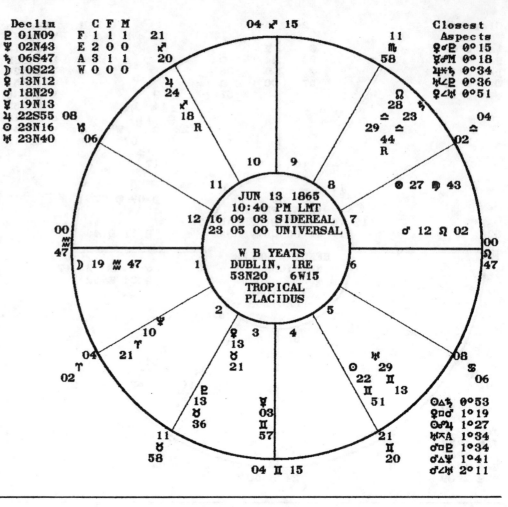

Declin		C	F	M
♇ 01N09	F	1	1	1
♆ 02N43	E	2	0	0
♄ 06S47	A	3	1	1
☽ 10S22	W	0	0	0
♀ 13N12				
♂ 18N29				
☿ 19N13				
♃ 22S55				
☉ 23N16				
♅ 23N40				

Closest Aspects
♀♂♇ 0°15
☿♂M 0°18
♃⚹♄ 0°34
♃∠♇ 0°36
♀∠♃ 0°51

JUN 13 1865
10:40 PM LMT
16 09 03 SIDEREAL
23 05 00 UNIVERSAL

W B YEATS
DUBLIN, IRE
53N20 6W15
TROPICAL
PLACIDUS

♃ 24 ♐ 18 R
04 ♐ 15
11 ♏ 58
28 ♎ 23 ♄
29 ♎ 44 R
⊕ 27 ♍ 43
♂ 12 ♌ 02
☉ 29 ♅
22 ♊ 13
♊ 51
08 ♋ 06
♇ 13 ♉ 36
♀ 13 ♉ 21
♆ 10 ♈ 21
04 ♈
02 ♈
00 ♈ 47
☽ 19 ♒ 47
00 ♒ 47
☿ 03 ♊ 57
04 ♊ 15
21 ♊ 20
21 ♋

☉△♄ 0°53
♀♐♂ 1°19
☉♂♃ 1°27
♅⚹♃ 1°34
♂♐♇ 1°34
♂△♆ 1°41
♂∠♅ 2°11

Closest Aspects
♄♐M 0°22
☉♐♃ 0°39
♆♐♇ 0°48
♀△♃ 0°54
♅⚹♆ 1°03

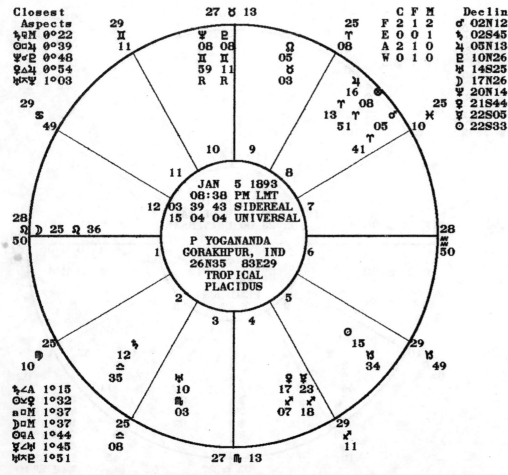

JAN 5 1893
08:38 PM LMT
03 39 43 SIDEREAL
15 04 04 UNIVERSAL

P YOGANANDA
GORAKHPUR, IND
26N35 83E29
TROPICAL
PLACIDUS

27 ♉ 13
♆ ♇ 08 08
♊ ♊ 59 11 R R
05 ♌ 03 ♉
♃ 16 ⊕
08 ♈ ♂ 25 ♓
13 ♈ 05 10
51 ♈
41 ♈
25 ♐
28 ♒ 50
29 ♒ 49
28 ♒ 50
☽ 25 ♌ 36
29 ♋
♍ 10
♄ 12 ♎ 35
25 ♎ 08
♅ 10 ♏ 03
♀ 17 ♐ ☿ 23
07 ♐ 18
☉ 15 ♑ 34
29 ♑ 49
29 ♐ 11
27 ♏ 13

	C	F	M	Declin
F	2	1	2	♂ 02N12
E	0	0	1	♄ 02S45
A	2	1	0	♃ 05N13
W	0	1	0	♇ 10N26
				♅ 14S25
				☽ 17N26
				♆ 20N14
				♀ 21S44
				☿ 22S05
				☉ 22S33

YOGANANDA, PARAMHANSA
Mystic

January 5, 1893
8:38 PM LMT
Gorakhpur, India
83 E 29   26 N 35

Founder of the Self-Realization Movement. World-traveled from an early age on his spiritual quest; later taught, lectured, and carried Eastern philosophy to the West. A lifelong celibate and mystic. Wrote *Autobiography of a Yogi*. (1893-1952)

A: M.H., July 1976, "according to the SRI."

♄∠A 1°15
☉□♀ 1°32
a □M 1°37
☽□M 1°37
☉□A 1°44
☿∠N 1°45
♅⚹♇ 1°51

SVP=ℋ 6°45'21"
JULIAN DAY=2412469.12782

'C' and 'DD' DATA

AARON, HANK February 5, 1934 Mobil, Ala
Baseball player 7:45 PM CST 88W08 30N41

| ☉ 16-♒-35 | ☿ 28-♒-52 | ♂ 01-♓-31 | ♄ 18-♒-33 | ♆ 11-♍-40R | A 15-♍-54 |
| ☽ 00-♏-08 | ♀ 15-♒-08R | ♃ 23-♎-12 | ♅ 23-♈-59 | ♇ 23-♋-11R | M 15-♊-00 |

One of the first of baseball's Black super-stars; played with the Braves from 1954. A great batting champion: when he retired in 1976, had scored a lifetime total of 755 homers.

C: Holliday quotes Kissinger in Dell, May 1974.

ADLER, ALFRED February 7, 1870 Vienna, Austria
Psychiatrist 00:15 AM LMT 16E20 48N13

| ☉ 18-♒-02 | ☿ 09-♒-41R | ♂ 25-♒-22 | ♄ 25-♐-47 | ♆ 17-♈-15 | A 06-♏-58 |
| ☽ 28-♈-24 | ♀ 12-♓-35R | ♃ 12-♉-46 | ♅ 18-♋-49R | ♇ 16-♉-02 | M 18-♌-11 |

Known for studies on the inferiority complex, child guidance, delinquency, and social interest. Director of the first child psychology clinic in 1920 in Vienna. Moved to New York in 1934. (1870-1937)

DD: M.H., July 1976, Dewey quotes Ebertin. Rudhyar in *World Astrology*, December 1945, states, "probably around 2:00 PM." AQ, Summer 1948, Ward gives February 8, 1870, 2:00 PM. *Americana* has February 7, 1870.

ADRIAN, GILBERT March 3, 1903 Naugatuck, Conn
Designer 11:05 AM EST 73W03 41N21

| ☉ 11-♓-55 | ☿ 15-♒-14 | ♂ 15-♎-11R | ♄ 04-♒-52 | ♆ 00-♋-56R | A 21-♊-28 |
| ☽ 02-♉-15 | ♀ 04-♈-24 | ♃ 02-♓-43 | ♅ 25-♐-18 | ♇ 17-♊-40 | M 26-♒-13 |

Top American designer who created fashions for MGM motion picture wardrobes, as well as custom made clothing. Awarded the Circle of New York Fashion Critic's "Winnie" award, 1945. (1903-1959)

C: SS #11.

AGA KHAN III November 2, 1877 Karachi, Pakistan
Moslem potentate 6:00 PM LMT 67E02 24N52

| ☉ 10-♏-15 | ☿ 03-♏-23 | ♂ 13-♓-18 | ♄ 13-♓-47R | ♆ 06-♉-02R | A 23-♉-18 |
| ☽ 02-♎-53 | ♀ 23-♐-59 | ♃ 01-♑-21 | ♅ 29-♌-00 | ♇ 24-♉-48R | M 09-♒-29 |

Founder of the All-India League; headed the Indian delegation to the League of Nations. Called the richest man in the world: estate estimated at $34 billion.

C: CL from AFA, October 1954. *Raphael's Almanac*, 1937, states, "in the evening."

AGA KHAN, SULTANA August 15, 1898 Chambery (La Savoie) France
Josephine Andree Carron 11:15 PM Paris time 5E55 45N35

| ☉ 23-♌-04 | ☿ 19-♍-12 | ♂ 18-♊-42 | ♄ 05-♐-41 | ♆ 24-♊-18 | A 08-♊-55 |
| ☽ 06-♌-24 | ♀ 06-♎-07 | ♃ 08-♎-34 | ♅ 29-♏-32 | ♇ 15-♊-33 | M 10-♒-39 |

Daughter of a hotel keeper; modest and charming; Roman Catholic. Became engaged in December 1929 to Sultan Mahomet Shah, the Aga Khan, spiritual head of 50 million followers of Islam. After marriage, her home became a half dozen gorgeous palaces.

C: AQ, September 1932, "from French newspapers."

ALEXANDER THE GREAT July 17, 355 B.C. NS Pella, Macedonia
World conqueror 10:00 AM to 12:00 Noon 22E30 40N40

| ☉ 23-♋-23 | ☿ 18-♋-01 | ♂ 03-♎-04 | ♄ 02-♊-34 | ♆ 18-♍-33 | A 19-♎-42 |
| ☽ 26-♒-28 | ♀ 07-♊-59 | ♃ 22-♎-34 | ♅ 10-♑-28R | ♇ 22-♈-16 | M 23-♋-02 |

Great general and king. A pupil of Aristotle at age 14; military commander at 18; king of Macedonia at 20; victor of Asia Minor by 22. Married a Persian princess. Died of malaria, June 13, 332 B.C. OS; left one infant son.

DD: M.A., July 1930, quotes *Die Astrologie*, June 1927, "On the 6th Hekatombaeon when equivalent to 6th Loos — July 22, 356 B.C. OS." AFA Bulletin gives the same data according to Wemyss, specified OS. NN #437 quotes Lyndholt for July 1, 357 B.C. NS.

ALEXANDER III — March 10, 1845 NS — Leningrad, Russia
Czar of Russia — 2:30 PM LMT — 30E15 59N55

☉ 19-♓-50	☿ 08-♓-49	♂ 01-♑-05	♄ 14-♒-16	♆ 24-♒-23	A 20-♌-12
☽ 17-♈-34	♀ 02-♓-41	♃ 10-♈-26	♅ 05-♈-16	♇ 22-♈-38	M 27-♈-31

A strict authoritarian; under his rule from 1881 to 1894 education suffered. Strengthened the police system and persecuted revolutionaries and Jews. However, Russia continued great industrial strides; science, music, and literature flourished. (1845-1894)

DD: PC quotes SS #21 (no time given.) The Old-file has 1:10 PM.

ALEXANDRA, CZARINA — June 6, 1872 — Darmstadt, Germany
Russian royalty — 6:00 AM LMT — 8E39 49N53

☉ 15-♊-45	☿ 26-♉-12	♂ 10-♊-46	♄ 20-♑-13R	♆ 25-♈-35	A 13-♋-37
☽ 16-♊-42	♀ 04-♊-50	♃ 28-♋-53	♅ 28-♋-46	♇ 19-♉-56	M 13-♓-39

German princess who married Prince Nicholas on November 26, 1894; bore four daughters and a son. Shot to death with her entire family by a Bolshevik execution on July 16, 1918.

DD: Mary Frances Wood in M.H., July 1977, quotes M.A., July 1922, with speculative data. PC quotes SS #23 (no time given) of 4:00 AM LMT. M.A., June 1930, Hesse gives "early in the day."

ALGER, HORATIO — January 13, 1832 — Revere, Mass
Writer — 9:00 AM LMT — 71W01 42N25

☉ 22-♑-27	☿ 16-♑-00R	♂ 16-♐-00	♄ 14-♍-46R	♆ 24-♑-36	A 20-♒-58
☽ 25-♉-17	♀ 07-♐-18	♃ 25-♒-09	♅ 13-♒-17	♇ 08-♈-40	M 08-♐-46

American author who wrote a famous series of more than a hundred books for boys, with prominant theme of "rags to riches and respectability." Minister of the Unitarian Church in 1864 for two years; resigned to write full time.

DD: PC states, "family records." The Old-file has 6:50 AM.

ALIOTO, JOSEPH — February 12, 1916 — San Francisco, Ca
Politician — 7:46 AM PST — 122W26 37N47

☉ 22-♒-37	☿ 07-♒-46R	♂ 19-♌-02R	♄ 10-♋-15R	♆ 00-♌-42R	A 06-♓-34
☽ 11-♊-33	♀ 28-♓-49	♃ 00-♈-05	♅ 16-♒-05	♇ 01-♋-26R	M 16-♐-37

Multimillionaire lawyer; mayor of San Francisco, re-elected to a second term in 1971 despite a federal grand jury indictment charging him with nine counts of bribery, conspiracy, and mail fraud.

DD: AFA, February 1970, "rectified from the time given by his mother of 7:30 to 8:00 AM." PC gives 7:30 AM, "personal."

ALLIGATOR MAN — December 18, 1904 — Savanah, Ga
Circus act — 4:30 PM EST — 81W06 32N05

☉ 26-♐-34	☿ 16-♑-06	♂ 16-♎-18	♄ 17-♒-17	♆ 07-♋-04R	A 14-♊-52
☽ 10-♉-14	♀ 06-♒-39	♃ 20-♈-15	♅ 29-♐-54	♇ 20-♊-36R	M 26-♒-13

With skin like an alligator over his entire body, worked as a circus sideshow freak. Normal otherwise, with a pleasant personality. Reports state that his mother was frightened by an alligator when she was pregnant with him.

C: CL from AFA, November 1954.

ANASTASIA June 17, 1901 NS Peterhof, Russia
Grand Duchess 11:00 PM LMT 29E54 59N53

☉ 25-♊-56	☿ 20-♋-29	♂ 16-♍-06	♄ 14-♑-23R	♆ 28-♊-50	A 28-♑-00
☽ 13-♋-30	♀ 08-♋-46	♃ 09-♑-47R	♅ 14-♐-26R	♇ 17-♊-23	M 11-♐-55

The youngest of the four daughters of Alexandra and Nicholas II, the last Czar of Russia; rumored to have escaped the family execution in 1918.

DD: Mary Frances Wood in M.H., July 1977, quotes M.A., June 1922, with speculative data. SS #37 gives this date, no time. March has the date with a time of 11:55 PM from a biography. The date is in *Nicholas and Alexandra* by Massie. AA, November 1958, states "According to Wemyss' compilation of data, Anastasia was born June 17, 1901, rather late at night." Vignali in A.J., Autumn 1969, states that the Official Russian Gazette gave June 18, 1901, 6:00 AM, St. Petersburgh.

Wood writes in M.H., January 1978: "I wrote to Dr. John Manahan, whom I had met to ask him for his wife's birth data. Mrs. Manahan is the woman who says she is the real Anatasia, and has been trying for years to prove her claim. Since I had met and dined with the Manahans, Dr. Manahan graciously sent me the data — he says that Anastasia was born June 5, 1901 OS = June 18, 1901 NS, 3:00 AM local time (1:00 AM GMT) in Peterhof." PC gives Mrs. Manahan's data; adds that a 1910 magazine gives the time of 11:00 PM, "reportedly from royal archives."

ANDERSON, PAUL October 17, 1932 Toccoa, Ga
Weight lifter 5:30 AM EST 83W19 34N35

☉ 23-♎-51	☿ 05-♏-57	♂ 15-♌-33	♄ 28-♑-18	♆ 09-♍-20	A 08-♎-18
☽ 25-♉-17	♀ 11-♍-35	♃ 14-♍-08	♅ 21-♈-18R	♇ 23-♋-27	M 09-♋-06

Known as the world's strongest man; in 1955 lifted more weight in one single attempt than anyone in history — 6,270 pounds in the back lift. Won championship gold medals for U.S.A. at Melbourne Olympics on November 26, 1956.

C: CL from Garth Allen, in AA, August 1957.

ANTHONY, EARL C. December 18, 1880 Washington, D.C.
Entrepreneur 5:30 AM LMT 89W05 40N42

☉ 26-♐-58	☿ 06-♐-57	♂ 10-♐-20	♄ 22-♈-09R	♆ 11-♉-50R	A 03-♐-56
☽ 16-♋-18	♀ 05-♒-42	♃ 09-♈-57	♅ 13-♍-47	♇ 26-♉-51R	M 19-♍-02

Millionaire radio show owner; also an automotive dealer. (1880-1961)

C: CL quotes Mrs. Young, who worked for the family (not stated so, but presumed to be from him).

ANTHONY, JOHN J. September 1, 1902 New York, N.Y.
Radio personality 2:00 PM EST 73W57 40N45

☉ 08-♍-23	☿ 26-♍-24	♂ 28-♋-13	♄ 21-♑-40R	♆ 03-♋-22	A 20-♐-20
☽ 02-♍-48	♀ 15-♌-52	♃ 09-♒-06R	♅ 17-♐-17	♇ 19-♊-38	M 12-♎-01

The "question and answer" broadcaster who offered advice on marital problems to millions of listeners from the early 30s to 1953 on *The Good Will Hour*. Founded the Marital Relations Institute in 1927.

DD: CL from Carol Peele 1968. *Current Biography* Obit gives 1898-1970.

ARBUCKLE, ROSCOE "FATTY" March 24, 1887 Smith Center, Ks
Comedian 12:00 Noon LMT 98W47 39N47

☉ 03-♈-49	☿ 28-♓-49R	♂ 10-♈-54	♄ 15-♋-37	♆ 25-♉-40	A 19-♋-55
☽ 04-♈-55	♀ 00-♉-18	♃ 04-♏-14R	♅ 10-♎-45R	♇ 02-♊-20	M 02-♈-05

One of the great comics of the silent screen, whose career was destroyed by a wild party on Labor Day weekend, 1921. An actress, Virginia Rappe, died, allegedly while having sexual relations with Arbuckle. The autopsy showed she'd died of cystitis. Arbuckle found not guilty in his three sensational trials, but was never again acceptable to the public. Died at age 46 of a heart attack.

DD: CL from Ellen Wood. SS #42 gives no time, computes to 7:16 AM LMT; but planet positions do not conform. PC quotes SS at 8:00 AM. The Old-file has 7:50 AM.

ARLISS, GEORGE April 10, 1868 London, England
English actor 00:30 AM LMT 0W06 51N31

☉ 20-♈-25   ☿ 23-♓-17   ♂ 28-♓-25   ♄ 05-♐-09R   ♆ 14-♈-58   A 23-♐-46
☽ 24-♏-32   ♀ 03-♊-52   ♃ 27-♓-39   ♅ 09-♋-03   ♇ 14-♉-59   M 28-♎-01

Stage actor who became an international screen star at age 53; remade some of his early films later as talkies before he retired in 1937. Films include *The Man Who Played God* and the Oscar winning *Disraeli*.

DD: CL, old data file. SS #44 gives 00:06 AM LMT. *Who's Who in Hollywood* gives 1869, but *Current Biography* Obit has 1868-1946.

ARMSTRONG, LOUIS July 4, 1900 New Orleans, La
Musician 00:01 AM CST 90W04 29N58

☉ 11-♋-47   ☿ 07-♌-49   ♂ 04-♊-52   ♄ 00-♑-59R   ♆ 27-♊-18   A 17-♈-16
☽ 03-♎-29   ♀ 18-♋-22R   ♃ 01-♐-56R   ♅ 09-♐-14R   ♇ 16-♊-47   M 11-♑-01

Career began in 1922 as a jazz trumpeter. Also raspy-voiced singer and band-leader: memorable for "Mack the Knife", "Hello Dolly", and "When the Saints Go Marchin' In." (1900-1971)

DD: CL quotes Andre Barbault of Paris, "data from him." R.H. Oliver rectifies the time to 11:05 PM from his biography that states, "Mother said late — fireworks still exploding; brother said close to midnight." Jansky gives 00:20 AM CST.

ASTOR, JOHN JACOB July 17, 1763 Waldorf, Germany
Entrepreneur 5:00 PM LMT 8E42 49N30

☉ 24-♋-41   ☿ 13-♋-01R   ♂ 17-♋-16   ♄ 07-♉-04   ♆ 24-♌-57   A 12-♐-51
☽ 24-♎-07   ♀ 28-♊-33   ♃ 07-♊-47   ♅ 17-♈-08   ♇ 01-♑-41R   M 11-♎-06

Fur trader and financier; founded the Astor fortune. Came to New York at 20; entered the fur trade in 1787; eventually won a monopoly of the U.S. trade. Invested his money in Manhattan farm land, which later became New York City. Estate valued at $20 million. (1763-1848)

DD: PC speculative. Old-file has 00:30 AM LMT.

ASTOR, JOHN JACOB IV July 13, 1864 Rhinebeck, N.Y.
Heir 12:30 PM LMT 73W54 41N56

☉ 21-♋-29   ☿ 17-♋-02   ♂ 03-♉-23   ♄ 12-♎-04   ♆ 08-♈-21R   A 22-♎-57
☽ 09-♏-29   ♀ 20-♋-10   ♃ 17-♏-44R   ♅ 26-♊-49   ♇ 13-♉-07   M 27-♋-17

Great-grandson of the family founder. Managed real estate; wrote science-fiction; invented various devices, including a marine turbine and a bicycle brake. Died in the sinking of the Titanic, April 14, 1912.

C: CL from Mrs. Wiemmer.

ATLAS, CHARLES October 30, 1893 Acri, Italy
Body-builder 1:19 PM LMT 16E20 39N30

☉ 07-♏-19   ☿ 29-♏-31   ♂ 18-♎-17   ♄ 18-♎-25   ♆ 13-♊-03R   A 11-♒-22
☽ 18-♋-31   ♀ 21-♐-18   ♃ 28-♉-51R   ♅ 10-♏-49   ♇ 10-♊-22R   M 00-♐-56

Physical culturist, titled the "World's most perfectly developed man." As a puny youth, began physical culture development and devised a system called Dynamic Tension. Publicized his system in 1942 by pulling six cars chained together, for a mile.

DD: Ben Allen Fields in AA, November 1946, speculative time. PC quotes SS at 2:00 PM; not in SS. Drew gives 1:00 PM "near Chicago."

ATTLEE, CLEMENT R. January 3, 1883 London, England
Politician 8:10 AM LMT 0W06 51N31

☉ 12-♑-40	☿ 22-♑-47	♂ 06-♑-25	♄ 19-♉-33R	♆ 16-♉-11R	A 11-♑-56
☽ 02-♏-19	♀ 07-♐-54	♃ 24-♊-15R	♅ 23-♍-21R	♇ 28-♉-33R	M 17-♏-35

British Labor Party leader, 1935-55; Prime Minister of Great Britain, 1945-51. From 1904, four years of law practice; social service work; lecturer in London School of Economics; Mayor of Stepney. (1883-1967)

C: Davison in AA, February 1951, speculative time.

AURIOL, VINCENT August 27, 1884 Revel, France
Statesman 6:00 PM LMT 2E00 43N27

☉ 04-♍-48	☿ 01-♎-40	♂ 19-♎-25	♄ 22-♊-52	♆ 23-♉-21R	A 19-♒-08
☽ 24-♏-54	♀ 21-♋-37	♃ 19-♌-56	♅ 27-♍-02	♇ 02-♊-09	M 08-♐-08

French writer, lawyer, and statesman. Leader of the Socialist party; first president of the Fourth Republic 1947-54. Backed DeGaulle's return to power in 1958 but later charged him with violating the consitution. (1884-1966)

DD: R. Gleadow in AA, July 1951. *Current Biography* Obit gives August 25, 1884.

BACH, JOHANN SEBASTIAN March 31, 1685 NS Eisenach, Germany
Musician 5:45 AM LMT 10E18 50N59

☉ 11-♈-06	☿ 19-♓-08	♂ 11-♐-00	♄ 11-♍-47R	♆ 03-♓-06	A 12-♈-38
☽ 28-♒-17	♀ 17-♓-39	♃ 18-♎-30R	♅ 04-♉-51	♇ 17-♋-26	M 04-♑-58

Composer of the Brandenburg concertos and suites, and preludes. His magnificant chorale, *Komm, Susser Tod,* was accepted after he died of a stroke on July 22, 1750. Two marriages; more than twenty children.

DD: Dewey quotes *450 Themes De Musicians.* Kraum speculates 9:38 AM LMT in AA, February 1963; Eshelman speculates 10:58 AM LMT; PC speculates 12:14 PM LMT. AQ, Winter 1964, Genuit gives 2:00 PM from *Astrology Aukunftsbogen.*

BACHARACH, BURT May 12, 1929 Kansas City, Mo
Musician 1:40 AM CST 94W35 39N06

☉ 21-♉-05	☿ 12-♊-30	♂ 29-♋-35	♄ 29-♐-41R	♆ 28-♌-35	A 27-♒-36
☽ 03-♋-39	♀ 21-♈-40	♃ 22-♉-42	♅ 09-♈-44	♇ 16-♋-34	M 11-♐-33

American composer of popular music. Studied piano, played as an accompanist before increasing popularity. Lush, melodic, and soft rhythms based on Latin beats and soft-rock. His music includes "Raindrops Keep Fallin' on My Head", which won the Oscar for 1970.

DD: PC speculative. Old-file has 1:30 AM CST.

BACON, SIR FRANCIS February 1, 1561 NS London, England
Writer 7:38 AM Sundial 0W06 51N31

☉ 12-♒-19	☿ 06-♒-02R	♂ 06-♐-30	♄ 14-♊-06R	♆ 27-♉-45R	A 09-♒-02
☽ 29-♈-18	♀ 09-♓-14	♃ 19-♈-24	♅ 25-♏-05	♇ 08-♓-13	M 07-♐-28

Philosopher, statesman, and jurist, whose essays rank among the greatest ever written. Became a lawyer in 1582; held office under Queen Elizabeth I; became a member of parliament. In 1621, accused of taking bribes and fined 40,000 pounds. (1561-1626)

C: Eshelman quotes William Lilly. (January 22, 1961 OS)

BADEN-POWELL, SIR ROBERT February 22, 1857 Oxford, England
Military man 6:20 AM LMT 1W15 51N45

☉ 03-♓-38	☿ 06-♒-58	♂ 29-♓-58	♄ 07-♋-29R	♆ 19-♓-30	A 11-♒-10
☽ 04-♒-22	♀ 19-♈-57	♃ 10-♈-48	♅ 21-♉-17	♇ 03-♉-54	M 08-♐-50

Founder of the Boy Scouts in England 1907, as a result of his army experiences. With his sister Agnes, organized the Girl Guides two years later. Author of several books on scouting and military campaigns. (1857-1941)

DD: CL from Fagan in AA, August 1964. PC quotes SS #54 (no time given) at 6:00 AM LMT. Old-file has 6:15 AM LMT.

BAILEY, F. LEE	June 10, 1933	Waltham, Mass
Attorney	2:00 AM EST	71W14 42N23

☉ 18-♊-56	☿ 03-♋-21	♂ 16-♍-44	♄ 16-♒-13R	♆ 07-♍-32	A 07-♉-28
☽ 18-♑-31	♀ 02-♋-09	♃ 14-♍-41	♅ 26-♈-18	♇ 22-♋-05	M 20-♑-18

Harvard drop-out who joined the Marines to be a jet pilot. At Boston U. scored one of the highest academic averages in the law school history to commence his flamboyant practice. Three marriages; three children. Author of a mystery novel, *Secrets* (1979).

C: Though daylight-time was in effect, R.H. Oliver says his mother stated specifically 2:00 AM EST. PC states 3:00 AM EDT as B.C.

BANCROFT, ANNE	September 7, 1931	Bronx, N.Y.
Actress	11:50 AM EDT	73W54 40N51

☉ 14-♍-03	☿ 09-♍-03R	♂ 23-♎-34	♄ 16-♑-49R	♆ 05-♍-51	A 16-♏-40
☽ 12-♋-38	♀ 13-♍-55	♃ 11-♌-21	♅ 18-♈-39R	♇ 21-♋-44	M 27-♌-09

On screen from 1952; won the Oscar as best actress in *The Miracle Worker;* nominated as best actress in *The Pumpkin Eater* and *The Graduate*. Married to Mel Brooks.

DD: PC "personal." Old-file has 12:45 PM EDT.

BANDARANAIKE, R.D.	January 8, 1899	Colombo, Ceylon
Politician	9:00 AM Zone 5.5	79E53 6N57

☉ 17-♑-41	☿ 24-♐-33	♂ 02-♌-55R	♄ 18-♐-28	♆ 22-♊-44R	A 26-♒-01
☽ 25-♏-08	♀ 07-♐-06	♃ 06-♏-58	♅ 06-♐-18	♇ 14-♊-07R	M 01-♐-57

Prime Minister of Ceylon 1956-59; assassinated by a fanatic Buddhist monk on September 25, 1959, for advocating Western sytle medicine instead of herbal remedies.

C: CL from AFA, February 1965. The profile and chart of his wife, Sirimavo Bandaranaike, who succeeded him as Prime Minister, are given in *Profiles of Women*.

BANG-JENSEN, POVL	April 6, 1909	Copenhagen, Denmark
Politician	9:20 AM MET	12E34 55N40

☉ 15-♈-54	☿ 00-♈-32	♂ 27-♑-41	♄ 13-♈-25	♆ 14-♋-21	A 09-♋-24
☽ 21-♎-21	♀ 10-♈-06	♃ 05-♍-30R	♅ 20-♑-55	♇ 23-♊-57	M 29-♒-26

Lawyer in 1937; emissary to Washington in 1939. Political advisor to the U.N. Security Council, 1949. Refused to give the names of eighty-one witnesses of the Hungarian uprising of 1956; dismissed July 3, 1958. Body found November 26, 1959; listed as suicide but suspected to be a political murder.

C: Skeetz quotes Lyndoe in AA, March 1962, data from Danish journal *Kontakt Med Tiden*.

BANKHEAD, TALLULAH	January 31, 1903	Huntsville, Ala
Actress	9:00 PM CST	86W35 34N44

☉ 11-♒-05	☿ 14-♒-13R	♂ 14-♎-33	♄ 01-♒-27	♆ 01-♋-20R	A 28-♍-48
☽ 19-♓-36	♀ 26-♒-23	♃ 25-♒-24	♅ 24-♐-12	♇ 17-♊-50R	M 28-♊-41

Celebrated from the 20s for electric, throaty performances on stage and films, as well as a lusty life-style off-stage. Author of autobiography *Tallulah* (1952). (1903-1968)

DD: Dewey quotes an interview by Jensen in *World Astrology*, July 1951, in which Bankhead verifies the date; the article further states, "about 9:00 PM." D.C. Doane writes: "Tallulah had no authenticated birth data. Two weeks after her birth, her Aunt went to record it and inadvertently gave her own wedding date." SS #62 gives 1902.

BARA, THEDA   July 20, 1890   Cincinnati, Ohio
Actress   10:45 PM CST   84W31   39N06

☉ 28-♋-20   ☿ 26-♋-19   ♂ 29-♏-48   ♄ 02-♍-21   ♆ 06-♊-09   A 25-♈-42
☽ 13-♍-44   ♀ 06-♍-07   ♃ 08-♒-26R   ♅ 22-♎-47   ♇ 07-♊-30   M 14-♑-24

Called "the Vamp", as the embodiment of the silent screen image of sexuality run amok; a product of publicity hype. Made all of her films in only four years, 1915-19, including *Salome* and *Cleopatra*. (1890-1955)

DD: PC speculative. Old-file has 11:00 PM CST.

BARNARD, CHRISTIAAN   November 8, 1922   Beaufort West, S.A.
Heart surgeon   8:00 PM EET   22E35   32S15

☉ 15-♏-36   ☿ 29-♎-47   ♂ 06-♒-20   ♄ 14-♎-52   ♆ 18-♌-08   A 11-♊-25
☽ 01-♋-57   ♀ 09-♐-29R   ♃ 02-♏-49   ♅ 09-♓-44R   ♇ 11-♋-05R   M 24-♓-17

Performed the first renowned human heart transplant in 1967; retired from surgery in 1980 because of arthritis. Writer of a biography, several novels, and a political appraisal of South Africa. Producer of TV documentaries.

DD: PC states, "personal from his autobiography." *One Life* by Barnard has no data.

BARRIE, JAMES   May 9, 1860   Kirriemuir, Scotland
Writer   6:30 AM LMT   3W01   56N40

☉ 18-♉-49   ☿ 23-♈-49   ♂ 22-♑-17   ♄ 19-♌-29   ♆ 28-♓-39   A 05-♋-21
☽ 09-♑-05   ♀ 04-♋-13   ♃ 20-♋-15   ♅ 06-♊-40   ♇ 08-♉-14   M 22-♒-27

Of his fiction and plays, most famous for *Peter Pan*, first presented on stage in 1904. Worked as a journalist before his sketches and stories became popular; knighted in 1913. (1860-1937)

C: CL from Kraum, 1934; same data in SS #65.

BARRYMORE, JOHN   February 15, 1882   Philadelphia, Pa
Actor   00:10 AM EST   75W10   39N57

☉ 26-♒-28   ☿ 09-♓-26R   ♂ 27-♊-53   ♄ 06-♉-57   ♆ 13-♉-55   A 15-♏-40
☽ 15-♑-31   ♀ 25-♒-03   ♃ 18-♉-19   ♅ 17-♍-22R   ♇ 27-♉-21   M 25-♌-20

Known as "the Great Profile". Broadway debut, 1903. Fame in silent films, later in talkies, including *Grand Hotel* (1932) and *Romeo and Juliet* (1936). Biography *Good Night, Sweet Prince* by Gene Fowler (1944); autobiography *Confessions of an Actor* (1926). (1882-1942)

DD: Ben Allen Fields in AA, February 1949: "A friend obtained this data in a personally written statement the winter of 1939." This same date is in *Americana*, *Circle Book*, and *Great Times, Good Times*. Holliday quotes AA, "personally obtained," for the same date, 12:33 PM EST.

   Astrology and the Occult Sciences, Summer 1942, states, "Manly Hall has a letter from Warner Bros. on file, that gives February 15, 1882, 00:20 AM." However, AA, December 1973, states, "Birth records in Philadelphia are for February 14, 1882." This date is given by Buell Huggins in *The Astrology Magazine*, January 1970, 12:04 PM LMT; same date given in *Famous People* and SS #68.

BARRYMORE, LIONEL   April 28, 1878   Philadelphia, Pa
Actor   12:15 PM EST   75W10   39N57

☉ 08-♉-15   ☿ 19-♉-55R   ♂ 25-♊-15   ♄ 28-♓-26   ♆ 07-♉-17   A 20-♌-32
☽ 25-♓-52   ♀ 22-♓-11   ♃ 06-♒-02   ♅ 25-♌-20R   ♇ 24-♉-36   M 12-♉-44

Member of a famous acting family; on stage from 1893; films from 1909. *Rasputin and the Empress* (1932) was the only film in which Ethel, John, and Lionel appeared together. Author of autobiography, *We Barrymores*. (1878-1954)

DD: PC quotes *Great Times, Good Times* by James Kotsilibas-Davis, "which states in the afternoon." That biography gives no times, states on p. 119: "On the afternoon of April 12, 1878, the doctor was summoned; he left behind him that evening a grateful and replenished household." *Famous People* and *Circle* #354 give April 28, 1878.

The profile and chart of Ethel, sister of John and Lionel, are given in *Profiles of Women.*

BARTHOLDI, FREDERIC AUGUSTE August 2, 1834 Colmar, France
Sculptor 6:30 AM LMT 7E21 48N05

☉ 09-♌-24	☿ 14-♌-18R	♂ 01-♊-27	♄ 06-♎-31	♆ 29-♑-57R	A 29-♌-09
☽ 00-♋-36	♀ 16-♍-28	♃ 06-♊-26	♅ 25-♒-12R	♇ 13-♈-43R	M 20-♉-18

Studied architecture and painting before sculpture; made many monuments in France. Designed the Statue of Liberty, which stands in the New York Harbor; helped raise the funds to build it. (1834-1904)

DD: PC quotes Gauquelin (LMR cannot locate it in Gauquelin Vol 4). Old-file has 6:05 AM LMT.

BARTOK, BELA March 25, 1881 Nagyszentmiklos, Hungary
Musician 9:00 AM LMT 20E38 46N05

☉ 04-♈-48	☿ 12-♓-50	♂ 22-♒-58	♄ 28-♈-34	♆ 12-♉-35	A 14-♊-48
☽ 03-♒-29	♀ 15-♉-49	♃ 25-♈-50	♅ 10-♍-46R	♇ 26-♉-44	M 15-♒-26

Hungary's leading composer of recent times. Began to study music at 5 and composition at 9; became a skilled pianist in 1901. Later taught piano and toured professionally. Though ill in later years, composed until his death in 1945.

DD: PC states, "recorded." Old-file has 9:20 AM LMT.

BARUCH, BERNARD August 19, 1870 Camden, S.C.
Entrepreneur 1:50 PM LMT 80W36 34N12

☉ 26-♌-32	☿ 17-♍-08	♂ 17-♋-17	♄ 21-♐-58R	♆ 21-♈-40R	A 10-♐-57
☽ 01-♊-44	♀ 28-♋-44	♃ 21-♊-43	♅ 24-♋-21	♇ 18-♉-55R	M 25-♍-01

Financier and statesman, who served as an unpaid advisor to seven presidents of the U.S. From his first jobs at $3 a week, became a millionaire by age 30 as a member of a Wall Street firm, with a seat on the N.Y. stock exchange. (1870-1965)

DD: CL from AFA, July 1965; same data in SS #72. Old-file has 2:05 PM LMT.

BATISTA, FULGENCIO January 16, 1901 Banes, Oriente, Cuba
Dictator 5:48 AM EST 75W44 20N45

☉ 25-♑-39	☿ 22-♑-01	♂ 12-♍-28R	♄ 09-♑-31	♆ 27-♊-07R	A 11-♑-13
☽ 05-♐-12	♀ 29-♐-58	♃ 29-♐-23	♅ 15-♐-08	♇ 16-♊-01R	M 23-♎-11

Born in obscurity and poverty. Joined the army April 14, 1921. Overthrew the Machado regime, August 1933, in a coup; as General seized control of the government, March 10, 1952, to become ruler of Cuba's six million people.

DD: Skeetz quotes M.A. Smollin in AA, May 1959, speculative time. *Wynn's Astrology*, June 1945, quotes a letter from a subscriber for 7:45 PM.

BEAUTY QUEEN August 20, 1942 No place given
Miss America 11:40 AM EST 82W43 41N27

☉ 27-♌-01	☿ 13-♍-28	♂ 12-♍-15	♄ 11-♊-24	♆ 28-♍-25	A 05-♏-47
☽ 13-♐-06	♀ 04-♌-21	♃ 15-♋-39	♅ 04-♊-24	♇ 06-♌-00	M 13-♌-12

Jacquelyn Jeanne Mayer, who won the contest as Miss America of 1963 on September 8, 1962.

C: CL from AFA, March 1963.

BEAUTY QUEEN April 16, 1945 No place given
Mardi Gras Queen 1962 3:23 PM EST 79W42 41N38

☉ 26-♈-28 ☿ 20-♈-55R ♂ 17-♓-40 ♄ 05-♋-24 ♆ 04-♎-29R A 14-♍-48
☽ 26-♊-05 ♀ 24-♈-37R ♃ 18-♍-41R ♅ 10-♊-35 ♇ 07-♌-55R M 12-♊-09

C: CL from AFA.

BEEBE, LUCIUS December 2, 1902 Wakefield, Mass
Journalist 7:00 AM EST 71W04 42N30

☉ 09-♐-23 ☿ 03-♐-51 ♂ 21-♍-34 ♄ 24-♑-39 ♆ 02-♋-56R A 09-♐-25
☽ 05-♑-39 ♀ 10-♐-13 ♃ 12-♒-42 ♅ 20-♐-45 ♇ 18-♊-52R M 29-♍-16

Newspaper columnist known as a dandy for his elegant dress. Wrote books about the American West and the Railroads; owned and published a newspaper, 1952-60; author of twenty books. (1902-1966)

DD: CL quotes Blanca Holmes, "from him." In AA, February 1959, Holmes pictures a solar chart (no data) for December 9, 1902. This is the date (December 9, 1902) that is given in *The New Century Cyclopedia* and in *Current Biography* Obit. SS #79 gives December 3, 1902, 1:04 AM. PC gives December 3, 1902, 7:00 AM, "personal."

BEERY, WALLACE April 1, 1886 Kansas City, Mo
Actor 2:47 PM CST 94W35 39N06

☉ 12-♈-03 ☿ 23-♈-33R ♂ 07-♍-20R ♄ 02-♋-15 ♆ 23-♉-43 A 25-♌-47
☽ 11-♓-08 ♀ 29-♒-55 ♃ 29-♍-41R ♅ 05-♎-24R ♇ 01-♊-31 M 19-♉-45

Played villanous roles in early silent films; evolved into tough/tender image. Won the Oscar as best actor in *The Champ* (1931); nominated for the Oscar in *The Big House* (1929). Immortalized in film *Min and Bill* (1930). (1886-1949)

DD: Holliday from AFA, March 1956; same date in *Americana*. *Famous People* and *Celebrities* give 1889. *Who's Who in Hollywood* gives 1881.

BEETHOVAN, LUDWIG VON December 16, 1770 Bonn, Germany
Musician 3:40 AM LMT 7E06 50N45

☉ 24-♐-18 ☿ 21-♐-59 ♂ 22-♊-41R ♄ 15-♌-49R ♆ 13-♍-59R A 05-♏-16
☽ 13-♐-01 ♀ 26-♑-42 ♃ 03-♑-09 ♅ 12-♉-09R ♇ 16-♑-21 M 17-♌-20

Composer who became totally deaf about 1819. From 1800 to 1815, completed eight symphonies, five piano concertos, the opera *Fidelio*, and other masterpieces. The last work, The Ninth Symphony, represents the climax of his genius.

DD: Eshelman quotes Lyndoe in AA, May 1970. Kraum in AA, December 1970, corrects Lyndoe; says there was an error in quoting *Mensch Im Alle*, March 1935; states that the true time was 1:29 PM LMT. Jansky gives 4:11:40 AM LMT. March has a time of 1:00 PM LMT.

BEITZEL, RUSSEL December 17, 1900 York, Pa
Homicide 12:00 Noon EST 76W47 39N54

☉ 25-♐-21 ☿ 06-♐-43 ♂ 08-♍-37 ♄ 06-♑-01 ♆ 27-♊-55R A 19-♓-59
☽ 06-♏-12 ♀ 23-♏-04 ♃ 22-♐-43 ♅ 13-♐-28 ♇ 16-♊-31R M 24-♐-37

Charged with murder on August 30, 1928; pleaded not guilty. On January 1, 1930, killed his common-law wife; sent to prison.

C: CL old data file.

BELASCO, DAVID July 25, 1853 San Francisco, Ca
Producer 11:40 PM LMT 122W26 37N47

☉ 03-♌-10 ☿ 29-♌-26 ♂ 22-♊-39 ♄ 29-♉-44 ♆ 13-♓-19R A 14-♉-22
☽ 15-♈-17 ♀ 23-♌-05 ♃ 15-♐-02R ♅ 12-♉-20 ♇ 02-♉-44 M 26-♑-53

A leading American theatrical producer for nearly forty years, controlling every aspect of his productions from writing to directing. In 1904, built the Belasco theater in Washington, D.C. (1853-1931)
C: CL old data file; same data in SS #80. The same date (no time) is in *David Belasco* by Lise-Lone Marker (1975), p. 13.

268

BELLINI, VINCENZO　　　November 3, 1801　　　Milan, Italy
Musician　　　　　　　　　10:25 AM LMT　　　　9E12　45N28

⊙ 10-♏-32　☿ 03-♐-37　♂ 07-♏-06　♄ 05-♍-42　♆ 18-♏-49　A 23-♐-06
☽ 03-♎-48　♀ 08-♎-40　♃ 02-♍-12　♅ 04-♎-37　♇ 03-♓-31R　M 19-♎-57

Italian opera composer, representative of the Bel Canto School: wrote operas celebrated for their lyrical beauty and dazzling vocal embellishments. First opera performed in 1825.

DD: PC speculative time. Old-file has 4:00 AM LMT. Penfield in 1979 quotes *Bellini* by L. Orrey (1969), p. 5 for "the night of November 2/3, 1801." Verified by LMR.

BEN-GURION, DAVID　　　October 16, 1886　　　Plonsk, Poland
Statesman　　　　　　　　　12:24 PM LMT　　　　20E15　52N25

⊙ 23-♎-01　☿ 05-♏-18　♂ 07-♐-46　♄ 22-♋-13　♆ 27-♉-18R　A 26-♐-55
☽ 01-♊-33　♀ 11-♎-05　♃ 17-♎-48　♅ 09-♎-03　♇ 03-♊-45R　M 03-♏-06

First prime minister of the State of Israel; one of the founders: read the Declaration of Israel's Independence. Formed the General Federation of Jewish Labor. (1886-1973)

DD: CL from *Bulletin of Astro-Science*, May 1959; PC quotes the same data from Ebertin. Old-file has 5:40 AM LMT. Luc de Marre adds that 12:40 PM was published by H. Schwarz in *Sieben Tage*, October 1955, no source.

BENITES, MANUEL　　　May 4, 1936　　　Palma del Rio, Spain
El Cordobes　　　　　　　4:00 PM GMT　　　　5W18　37N42

⊙ 14-♉-00　☿ 04-♊-48　♂ 23-♉-49　♄ 19-♓-42　♆ 14-♍-06R　A 05-♎-46
☽ 22-♎-24　♀ 29-♈-02　♃ 23-♐-33R　♅ 06-♉-00　♇ 25-♋-18　M 06-♋-29

Bullfighter who captured the imagination of the Spanish people; became a legend for courage; none fight so close to the horns as he. As the highest paid bullfighter in history, received $1.8 million for 121 fights in 1970.

DD: PC quotes *Or I'll Dress You In Mourning,* "which states according to his sister that he was born in the middle of the afternoon." That biography, by L. Collins and D. Lapierre (1968), states on p. 13, "On this 20th day of May 1964, he had just turned 28 years old." On p. 27 it describes the children playing in the yard: " . . . a warm afternoon . . . heard the baby's cry."

　Current Biography, 1966, states, "May 4, 1936 is on his identify card; however, the date is disputed: suggested dates are December 16, 1935, and December 10, 1937. Church records state that he was baptised on March 19, 1938." PC adds that a French source gives 7:00 AM (same date).

BENNETT, HERBERT JOHN　　August 9, 1878　　　London, England
Murderer　　　　　　　　　6:00 PM LMT　　　　0W06　51N31

⊙ 16-♌-57　☿ 13-♍-57　♂ 00-♍-03　♄ 02-♈-21R　♆ 09-♉-49　A 15-♑-15
☽ 09-♑-13　♀ 17-♋-15　♃ 00-♒-18R　♅ 29-♌-00　♇ 26-♉-25　M 20-♏-32

Unhappily married at age 17. Met Miss Meadows, July 1, 1900; told her he was single and began an affair. Strangled his wife with a pair of shoelaces on Yarmouth Beach, September 22, 1900. Trial, February 25, 1901; convicted March 2, 1901.

DD: CL from Tucker in *Predicting From The Stars* (1960). Ellen Wood's file has 11:31 PM LMT. M.A., May 1901, Wallace gives August 9, 1879, speculative 5:57 PM, with a location of Stone, near Dartford.

BENNY, JACK　　　February 14, 1894　　　Waukegan, Ill
Comedian　　　　　　　4:04 AM CST　　　　87W50　42N22

⊙ 25-♒-45　☿ 08-♓-06　♂ 00-♑-31　♄ 25-♎-03R　♆ 10-♊-45R　A 03-♑-59
☽ 08-♊-25　♀ 28-♒-57R　♃ 22-♉-54　♅ 15-♏-20　♇ 08-♊-49R　M 29-♎-39

Film, stage, and TV entertainment super-star; many movies, 1930-45. Made a joke for years of his flop, *The Horn Blows at Midnight.* TV Emmy, 1957, for *The Jack Benny Show.* Married in 1927 to Mary Livingston. (1894-1974)

C: SS #89.

BERLIN, IRVING May 11, 1888 NS Temum, Russia
Composer 7:45 AM LMT 65E29 57N11
☉ 20-♉-50 ☿ 21-♉-01 ♂ 12-♎-44R ♄ 01-♌-04 ♆ 29-♉-25 A 21-♋-53
☽ 21-♉-44 ♀ 04-♉-14 ♃ 02-♐-53R ♅ 13-♎-47R ♇ 04-♊-10 M 14-♓-22

Came to U.S. as a child. Composed more than one thousand songs, with first big break, "Alexander's Ragtime Band" (1911). Others include "White Christmas," "No Business Like Show Business," and "Remember." Wrote the music for films *Top Hat* and *On The Avenue.*

DD: PC quotes Drew, "who gave neither the time nor location." LMR notes that Drew pictures a chart for MC 7 Aries, Ascendant 24 Cancer = 9:07 AM LMT, at a latitude of 40/41 N 00. Old-file has 7:00 AM, same date and place as PC. Penfield in 1979 quotes *Horoscopes of Composers* by Kassandra K. (1978), for 9:15 AM, "from Drew."

BERMAN, SHELLEY February 23, 1926 Chicago, Ill
Comedian 6:00 AM CST 87W39 41N52
☉ 04-♓-08 ☿ 10-♓-28 ♂ 10-♑-11 ♄ 25-♏-59 ♆ 23-♌-07R A 18-♒-17
☽ 18-♋-41 ♀ 10-♒-48R ♃ 11-♒-21 ♅ 24-♓-13 ♇ 12-♋-47R M 06-♐-49

American cabaret monologuist; nightclub work and TV. Films include *The Best Man* (1964), *The Wheeler Dealers* (1964), and *Every Home Should Have One* (1970).

C: CL quotes Drew.

BERNHARDT, SARAH October 23, 1844 Paris, France
Actress 00:10 AM LMT 2E20 48N50
☉ 29-♎-42 ☿ 14-♎-51 ♂ 02-♎-47 ♄ 00-♒-57 ♆ 20-♒-58R A 19-♌-26
☽ 23-♓-05 ♀ 14-♍-36 ♃ 25-♓-17R ♅ 03-♈-17R ♇ 22-♈-47R M 06-♉-20

Actress from 1862; world famous legend in her own time. Illegitimate daughter of a prostitute; mistress of a prince. One marriage in 1882 for a year. After a leg injury in 1905, suffered for nine years before amputation. Continued to perform, write, sculpt, and manage her own theater. (1844-1923)

DD: SCAN quotes *The Gilded State* for the date that Bernhardt herself observed. LMR speculates the time just past midnight. *Britannica* gives October 22/23, 1844.

Blanche Broderick in *Current Astrology,* Winter 1947, states: "A carefully documented biography written by a member of her family gives a copy of her baptismal certificate with the date October 23, 1844. She herself refers to this date in her *Memoirs.* Another biographer, a close friend of many years, places the hour of her birth at "about 8:00 PM." Rectified to 7:53 PM.

BJA, May 1923, Sepharial gives October 23, 1845, approximately 7:15 AM, "from the Times." CL and SS #93 give September 25, 1844. *Who Was Who* gives October 22, 1845; other sources give other dates. SS and CL give 8:00 PM.

BIERCE, AMBROSE June 24, 1842 Meigs Co, Ohio
Journalist 10:00 AM LMT 82W00 39N00
☉ 02-♋-36 ☿ 21-♋-41 ♂ 02-♋-57 ♄ 11-♑-47R ♆ 18-♒-59R A 02-♍-10
☽ 22-♑-34 ♀ 01-♌-03 ♃ 19-♑-45R ♅ 28-♓-16 ♇ 21-♈-47 M 27-♉-38

American short story writer and journalist. Became the Washington D.C. correspondent for the Hearst papers in 1897. His various works comedic, cynical, sarcastic, and macabre. *Collected Works* published from 1909 to 1912. Disappeared in Mexico in 1913, with no trace ever found.

DD: PC states speculative. Old-file has 9:35 AM LMT.

BIRTH DEFECTS October 1, 1926 New York, N.Y
Deformity 9:30 PM EST 73W57 40N45
☉ 08-♎-08 ☿ 17-♎-36 ♂ 19-♉-24R ♄ 23-♏-02 ♆ 26-♌-04 A 25-♊-51
☽ 15-♌-33 ♀ 25-♍-19 ♃ 17-♒-34R ♅ 27-♓-01R ♇ 15-♋-54 M 01-♓-35

(No sex given). Malformed skull, heart, and connecting veins, with arteries outside of body.

C: CL from Wemyss Vol IV.

BIRTH DEFECTS — June 17, 1939 — Seattle, Wash
Male — 3:41 PM PST — 122W20 47N36

| ☉ 25-♊-52 | ☿ 08-♋-17 | ♂ 04-♒-34 | ♄ 28-♈-37 | ♆ 20-♍-37 | A 05-♏-28 |
| ☽ 01-♋-34 | ♀ 04-♊-20 | ♃ 06-♈-05 | ♅ 20-♉-01 | ♇ 00-♌-05 | M 15-♌-47 |

Born with no testicles.

C: CL old data file.

BIRTH DEFECTS — September 12, 1950 — No place given
Male — 1:40 AM PDT — 122W30 48N00

| ☉ 19-♍-01 | ☿ 28-♍-46R | ♂ 20-♏-49 | ♄ 22-♍-13 | ♆ 16-♎-04 | A 22-♋-31 |
| ☽ 21-♍-51 | ♀ 02-♍-51 | ♃ 00-♓-19R | ♅ 09-♋-00 | ♇ 18-♌-47 | M 28-♓-08 |

Born without a rectum; died September 28, 1950, 6:15 PM PDT.

C: CL old date file.

BISSETT, ROY — December 27, 1900 — Washington, D.C.
Murder victim — 4:40 AM EST — 77W02 38N54

| ☉ 05-♑-13 | ☿ 20-♐-45 | ♂ 10-♍-52 | ♄ 07-♑-10 | ♆ 27-♊-39R | A 28-♏-40 |
| ☽ 13-♓-21 | ♀ 05-♐-03 | ♃ 24-♐-55 | ♅ 14-♐-03 | ♇ 16-♊-21R | M 11-♍-59 |

Killed in Griffith Park, Los Angeles, on October 1, 1939.

C: CL from Pherol Ergett, February 1962.

BJORNSON, BJORNSTERNE — December 8, 1832 — Kvikne, Norway
Writer — 00:05 AM LMT — 10E19 62N36

| ☉ 15-♐-57 | ☿ 06-♑-43 | ♂ 22-♉-51R | ♄ 27-♍-15 | ♆ 25-♑-27 | A 22-♍-52 |
| ☽ 17-♊-41 | ♀ 19-♑-30 | ♃ 19-♓-45 | ♅ 15-♒-26 | ♇ 09-♈-41R | M 18-♊-57 |

Great Norwegian novelist, lyric poet, and dramatist; won the Nobel prize for literature in 1903. Directed a theater; was an editor, lecturer, and political speaker. Optimistic and democratic in views. (1832-1910)

DD. PC quotes SS #100. Old-file has 00:30 AM LMT. Wemyss F/N #88 states, "when the big bear was shining brightest."

BOGART, HUMPHREY — January 23, 1899 — New York, N.Y.
Actor — 1:40 PM EST — 73W57 40N45

| ☉ 03-♒-36 | ☿ 12-♑-25 | ♂ 26-♋-48R | ♄ 20-♐-04 | ♆ 22-♊-23R | A 21-♊-20 |
| ☽ 00-♋-50 | ♀ 18-♐-16 | ♃ 08-♏-43 | ♅ 07-♐-01 | ♇ 13-♊-55R | M 26-♒-42 |

Won the Oscar as best actor in *The African Queen* (1951); nominated as best actor in *Casablanca* (1943) and *The Caine Mutiny* (1954). Died of cancer, January 14, 1957.

DD: PC states, "personal source." Kaye and DeJersey in Dell, September 1978, 6:37 AM EST, speculative. The date is from *Circle #565*, stated as B.C. (December 25 given out as studio hype). Richard Ideman quotes Bogart's widow, Lauren Bacall, "He was unsure of his birth date or time."

The profile and chart of Lauren Bacall are given in *Profiles of Women*.

BOK, EDWARD WILLIAM — October 9, 1863 — Helder, Netherlands
Writer — 2:00 PM LMT — 4E44 52N59

| ☉ 15-♎-46 | ☿ 19-♎-51R | ♂ 13-♎-35 | ♄ 09-♎-31 | ♆ 04-♈-23R | A 12-♑-35 |
| ☽ 08-♍-08 | ♀ 29-♍-22R | ♃ 02-♏-59 | ♅ 25-♊-03R | ♇ 11-♉-47R | M 20-♏-08 |

Moved to U.S. at age 6; first job at 10; an editor by 21. Editor-in-chief of *Ladies' Home Journal*, 1889-1919. Awarded the 1921 Pulitzer prize for his autobiography, *The Americanization of Edward Bok*. (1863-1930)

DD: CL old file. AFA, June 1961, Emmylu Landers rectified to 1:48 PM LMT.

BONNEY, WILLIAM   November 23, 1859   Brooklyn, N.Y.
Billy the Kid   10:00 AM LMT   73W56 40N38

| ☉ 00-♐-50 | ☿ 22-♐-15 | ♂ 17-♎-30 | ♄ 25-♌-53 | ♆ 24-♓-24R | A 09-♑-43 |
| ☽ 19-♏-07 | ♀ 15-♐-10 | ♃ 25-♋-04R | ♅ 05-♊-55R | ♇ 07-♉-06R | M 04-♏-19 |

Outlaw: said to have stabbed his first man to death at age 12. Became a cattle rustler and gunslinger. Captured 1881. Escaped, tracked down, and shot in July 1881.

DD: CL from Drew. Davison in AA, October 1948, says, "actual hour unknown"; speculates 3:00 AM. PC quotes SS for 9:30 AM: not in SS.

BOONE, PAT   June 1, 1934   Jacksonville, Fla
Singer   8:35 PM EST   81W39 30N20

| ☉ 10-♊-50 | ☿ 01-♋-10 | ♂ 29-♉-34 | ♄ 28-♒-09 | ♆ 09-♍-38 | A 27-♐-29 |
| ☽ 08-♒-17 | ♀ 29-♈-36 | ♃ 13-♎-23R | ♅ 29-♈-48 | ♇ 23-♋-10 | M 12-♎-59 |

As a singer sold 18 million records by age 24. As an actor, played in *April Love* (1957), *Mardi Gras* (1948), and *Journey to the Center of the Earth* (1960), among other films. Had his own TV show in the 50s. Wrote *Twixt Twelve and Twenty* in 1959. Still has the clean-cut American boy image in his 40s. The father of four daughters.

DD: Judy Johns from an astrology magazine. PC states 8:00 PM, "personal source."

BOOTH, BRAMWELL   March 8, 1856   Halifax, England
Salvation Army Chief   8:30 PM LMT   1W55 53N45

| ☉ 18-♓-30 | ☿ 21-♒-56 | ♂ 20-♎-28R | ♄ 23-♊-16 | ♆ 17-♓-54 | A 16-♎-34 |
| ☽ 16-♈-49 | ♀ 14-♒-25 | ♃ 16-♓-10 | ♅ 17-♉-39 | ♇ 03-♉-10 | M 22-♋-26 |

Second son of William Booth, who commanded the Salvation Army work in the U.S. from 1887 to 1896. When requested to resign leadership of the Army by the High Council, Bramwell founded an organization called the Volunteers of America. (1856-1940)

C: M.A., November 1912; same date in BJA, February 1929. (*World Book* gives 1857).

BOOTH, WILLIAM   April 10, 1829   Nottingham, England
Salvation Army General   12:00 Noon LMT   1W10 52N55

| ☉ 20-♈-21 | ☿ 26-♓-12 | ♂ 01-♊-15 | ♄ 27-♋-30 | ♆ 20-♑-33 | A 10-♌-44 |
| ☽ 13-♋-42 | ♀ 09-♈-45 | ♃ 15-♐-08R | ♅ 06-♒-01 | ♇ 07-♈-15 | M 19-♈-59 |

Methodist minister who withdrew from the church in 1861 to dedicate his life to work among the poor. With his wife, in 1865 began evangelical work in London; founded a mission band that became known as the Salvation Army in 1878. (1829-1912)

C: M.A., November 1912, speculative time.

BORGE, VICTOR   January 3, 1909   Copenhagen, Denmark
Pianist, humorist   9:19 PM MET   12E35 55N41

| ☉ 12-♑-52 | ☿ 19-♑-13 | ♂ 25-♏-50 | ♄ 04-♈-04 | ♆ 15-♋-48R | A 10-♍-09 |
| ☽ 10-♊-37 | ♀ 14-♐-55 | ♃ 14-♍-30R | ♅ 16-♑-45 | ♇ 24-♊-29R | M 02-♊-14 |

Actor, composer, pianist, writer, and director. Nominated for the TV Emmy for best specialty act, single or group, 1955. Broadway career hit in *Comedy in Music*.

C: Scarsella from Baird.

BORGLUM, GUTZON   March 25, 1867   Bear Lake, Idaho
Sculptor   8:00 PM LMT   111W15 42N00

| ☉ 05-♈-01 | ☿ 06-♈-29R | ♂ 17-♋-38 | ♄ 23-♏-42R | ♆ 12-♈-13 | A 25-♎-52 |
| ☽ 11-♐-14 | ♀ 21-♒-01 | ♃ 26-♒-04 | ♅ 04-♋-22 | ♇ 13-♉-45 | M 00-♌-53 |

Sculptor of the faces in the Black Hills at Mount Rushmore, S.C.; also statue of Sheridan in Washington D.C. and large head of Lincoln at the Capitol, Washington, D.C.

DD: PC speculative. Old-file has 11:00 AM LMT, same date. *Famous People* gives March 25, 1871.

BORODIN, ALEXANDER November 12, 1833 NS Leningrad, Russia
Chemist/Composer 3:00 AM LMT 30E15 59N55

☉ 19-♏-27 ☿ 09-♐-59 ♂ 16-♏-16 ♄ 06-♎-53 ♆ 26-♑-56 A 03-♎-41
☽ 23-♏-28 ♀ 21-♎-49 ♃ 28-♈-07R ♅ 18-♒-43 ♇ 11-♈-02R M 05-♋-26

Research chemist, teacher, and administrator of the St. Petersburg School of Medicine. Though he insisted on remaining a musical amateur, achieved a high standing in both music and science. (1833-1887)

DD: PC speculative. Old-file has November 11, 1833, 4:00 AM, the same date as given in *Americana.*

BRAGDEN, CLAUDE August 1, 1866 Orberlin, Ohio
Architect 4:39 AM LMT 82W13 41N18

☉ 08-♌-52 ☿ 04-♍-04 ♂ 05-♊-05 ♄ 06-♏-04 ♆ 12-♈-46R A 04-♌-52
☽ 07-♈-53 ♀ 17-♍-38 ♃ 25-♑-49R ♅ 06-♋-12 ♇ 15-♉-07 M 21-♈-09

Author of *The Beautiful Necessity,* as well as other books on the philosophy of art, on geometric ornamentation, on literature and mysticism, and on the theater.

C: Skeetz quotes Rudhyar in AA, February 1938. Same data in SS #123.

BRAHMS, JOHANNES May 7, 1833 Hamburg, Germany
Musician 3:30 AM LMT 10E00 50N33

☉ 16-♉-16 ☿ 21-♈-55 ♂ 16-♋-33 ♄ 21-♍-30R ♆ 29-♑-23R A 16-♈-25
☽ 24-♐-13 ♀ 01-♊-57R ♃ 20-♈-07 ♅ 22-♒-23 ♇ 11-♈-59 M 06-♑-37

German romantic composer of instrumental classical music of every variety except opera. As a child prodigy, performed a piano concert by age 15; wrote music by 20 that is still played. A gruff, humorous, and disorderly man. Never married. (1833-1897)

DD: CL from Kraum in *Astrologische Rundschau,* NAJ July 1935. Lyndoe in AA, January 1968, gives 3:40 AM LMT. SS #124 gives 3:41 AM LMT. Jansky gives 4:00 PM LMT.

BRASNO, GEORGE December 23, 1911 Old Bridge, N.J.
Midget 5:00 PM EST 74W22 40N25

☉ 00-♑-59 ☿ 05-♑-05R ♂ 24-♉-34R ♄ 13-♉-47R ♆ 22-♋-59R A 07-♋-42
☽ 06-♒-24 ♀ 16-♏-16 ♃ 02-♐-52 ♅ 27-♑-48 ♇ 27-♊-55R M 15-♓-50

Brother of Olive Brasno; their father (October 10, 1884) was small also; the other five members of the family were normal size. With Olive created a theatrical act that charmed the audience; played night clubs and acted in MGM's *The Great Barnum.*

C: Holliday quotes *Best of the NAJ* 1979.
The data for his sister Olive are given in *Profiles of Women.*

BRIDGES, HARRY STYLES September 9, 1898 Pembroke, Maine
Politican 10:30 AM EST 67 W11 44N57

☉ 16-♍-56 ☿ 09-♍-37R ♂ 04-♋-03 ♄ 06-♐-25 ♆ 24-♊-42 A 18-♏-22
☽ 05-♋-21 ♀ 02-♏-56 ♃ 13-♎-20 ♅ 29-♏-58 ♇ 15-♊-42 M 02-♍-01

Governor of New Hampshire 1935-37; U.S. senator from New Hampshire in 1937. (1898-1961)

DD: CL from AFA, May 1940. SS #130 gives 10:39 AM EST.

BRONSON, CHARLES November 3, 1922 Ehrenfeld, Pa
Actor 8:45 PM EST 78W47 40N22

☉ 10-♏-52 ☿ 23-♎-04 ♂ 03-♒-00 ♄ 14-♎-20 ♆ 18-♌-06 A 10-♋-18
☽ 03-♉-03 ♀ 09-♐-50 ♃ 01-♏-48 ♅ 09-♓-47R ♇ 11-♋-07R M 19-♓-07

Joined his father in the coal mines before his screen debut in 1951; films include *Miss Sadie Thompson, Battle of the Bulge, The Mechanic,* and *Death Wish,* as well as his early run of western and war movies. His 68th film was *Love and Bullets* (1979). Married to Jill Ireland; five children.

DD: Holliday quotes speculative chart in Dell. Old-file has 8:55 PM EST.

BROWN, EDMUND G. SR. April 21, 1905 San Francisco, Ca
Politician 2:21 PM PST 122W26 37N47

☉ 01-♉-07 ☿ 04-♉-20R ♂ 22-♏-47R ♄ 00-♓-43 ♆ 05-♋-44 A 07-♍-21
☽ 04-♐-12 ♀ 09-♉-49R ♃ 10-♉-10 ♅ 04-♑-10R ♇ 20-♊-06 M 04-♊-08

Lawyer from 1927. Became active in politics as San Francisco district attorney; state attorney general, 1950 and 1954; California governor, 1958 and 1962. Lost to Reagan in 1966. His son Jerry became California governor in 1974.

DD: CL from *Bulletin of Astro Science,* May 1959. Holliday has 12:48 PM PST from an unrecorded source, the same data as Scarsella, from Baird.

BROWN, JOHN May 9, 1800 Torrington, Ct
Radical 3:00 AM LMT 73W04 41N48

☉ 18-♉-24 ☿ 24-♈-06 ♂ 06-♓-43 ♄ 04-♌-24 ♆ 15-♏-48R A 03-♈-21
☽ 22-♏-37 ♀ 24-♈-51 ♃ 00-♋-49 ♅ 23-♍-12R ♇ 04-♓-15 M 01-♑-44

Abolitionist whose attempts to free the slaves cost a number of lives and led indirectly to the Civil War. For insurrection, was captured by General Lee on October 18, 1859, tried, and hanged on December 2. Two marriages; 20 children.

DD: PC speculative. Old-file has 6:45 PM LMT.

BRUCKNER, ANTON September 4, 1824 Ansfelden, Austria
Musician 4:00 AM LMT 13E49 47N53

☉ 11-♍-29 ☿ 08-♎-08 ♂ 17-♏-11 ♄ 07-♊-37 ♆ 06-♑-55R A 25-♌-41
☽ 24-♑-03 ♀ 21-♍-30 ♃ 03-♌-34 ♅ 11-♑-57R ♇ 02-♈-29R M 15-♉-39

Austrian composer and organist, best known for his spendidly constructed lengthy nine symphonies. Personal life uneventful; his personality, unassuming. (1824-1896)

DD: SS #145. Old-file has 5:10 PM LMT. M.A., September 1936, same data but for Ansfelden Bei Linz, 14 E.14/48 N.18, from *De Mystieke Wereld,* July 1936.

BRUMMELL, GEORGE BRYAN June 7, 1778 London, England
English dandy 2:30 AM LMT 0W06 51N31

☉ 16-♊-19 ☿ 09-♊-01R ♂ 15-♊-25 ♄ 09-♏-35R ♆ 26-♍-31 A 18-♉-48
☽ 13-♏-07 ♀ 05-♋-53 ♃ 21-♌-09 ♅ 15-♊-29 ♇ 01-♒-24R M 21-♑-20

Known as Beau Brummell; set the style for men's clothing and manners for twenty years. With a modest inheritance and the friendship of the Prince of Wales, lived a "gentleman's life" until ending up in debtor's prison in 1835. Died in France in a mental institution five years later.

DD: PC speculative. Old-file has 1:35 PM LMT.

BURBANK, LUTHER March 7, 1849 Lancaster, Mass
Horticulturist 11:57 PM LMT 71W41 47N28

☉ 17-♓-32 ☿ 26-♒-46R ♂ 05-♒-52 ♄ 26-♓-44 ♆ 02-♓-51 A 28-♏-06
☽ 07-♍-13 ♀ 03-♉-46 ♃ 14-♌-00R ♅ 20-♈-17 ♇ 26-♈-28 M 13-♍-45

American plant breeder, who developed new strains and improved existing agriculture by crossing and selection. As a youthful gardner, established a successful nursury which he sold in 1893 to begin an experimental farm. (1849-1926)

C: SS #150.

BURNHAM, DANIEL H. September 4, 1846 Henderson, N.Y.
Architect 3:00 AM LMT 76W10 43N51

☉ 11-♍-23 ☿ 26-♌-51R ♂ 13-♍-23 ♄ 26-♒-23R ♆ 26-♒-21R A 12-♌-41
☽ 24-♒-00 ♀ 15-♌-41 ♃ 15-♊-06 ♅ 13-♈-26R ♇ 25-♈-39R M 00-♉-10

A noted American architect and city planner. With his partner, helped to rebuild Chicago after the 1871 fire. His firm active in the early development of the skyscraper. (1846-1912)

DD: PC speculative. Old-file has 3:45 AM LMT.

BURNS, ROBERT   January 25, 1759   Alloway, Scotland
Writer   7:00 AM LMT   4W38 55N30

☉ 05-♒-08   ☿ 23-♑-34R   ♂ 10-♒-44   ♄ 02-♓-54   ♆ 16-♌-30R   A 10-♑-04
☽ 19-♐-30   ♀ 08-♒-11   ♃ 08-♑-35   ♅ 24-♓-26   ♇ 24-♐-01   M 21-♏-43

Poet, whose poems and songs made him the national poet of Scotland. Wrote more than two hundred songs, including "Comin' Thru' the Rye." (1759-1796)

DD: PC quotes Pagan. Pagan in *Pioneer to Poet* states, "hour unknown." PC also quotes AFA as "between midnight and sunrise; speculative at 2:37 AM." BJA, February 1936, editor rectifies to 2:56 AM.

BURROUGHS, EDGAR RICE September 1, 1875   Chicago, Ill
Writer   7:00 AM LMT   87W39 41N52

☉ 09-♍-20   ☿ 06-♍-07R   ♂ 08-♌-43   ♄ 14-♑-53R   ♆ 26-♈-02R   A 26-♍-51
☽ 22-♌-37   ♀ 22-♍-20   ♃ 17-♌-27   ♅ 03-♌-49   ♇ 20-♉-47R   M 26-♊-19

American author, whose first book, *Tarzan of the Apes* (1914), and its many sequels sold by the millions in many languages. Established his own publication company and founded Tarzana, Ca. (1875-1950)

DD: PC speculative. Old-file has 6:50 AM LMT.

BURTON, RICHARD   November 10, 1925   Pontrhydyfen, Wales
Actor   7:58 PM GMT   3W51 52N17

☉ 17-♏-55   ☿ 07-♐-08   ♂ 28-♎-11   ♄ 17-♏-07   ♆ 24-♌-43   A 16-♋-05
☽ 11-♍-59   ♀ 04-♑-18   ♃ 18-♑-23   ♅ 21-♓-44R   ♇ 14-♋-37R   M 13-♓-50

Number twelve of thirteen children. Became a brilliant Shakespearean actor, with the title role in *Hamlet* (1953). Nominated for the Oscar as best actor in a half dozen magnificent films.

DD: Davison in *Synastry*, who writes: "From an American source, rectified. I would not recommend accepting any stated time as correct to the minute unless proper rectification tests have been applied." *Celebrity Horoscopes* quotes Robert Prete for 5:55 AM GMT, the same time as given by G. Kissinger in Dell December 1975. PC gives 11:00 PM. "personal." Scarsella quotes Baird for 8:44 AM. AQ, Summer 1967, Beryl Sidney gives 8:26 PM.

BUSCH, FRITZ   March 13, 1890   Siegen, Germany
Musician   9:00 AM MET   8E01 50N53

☉ 22-♓-43   ☿ 00-♓-52   ♂ 04-♐-46   ♄ 28-♌-47R   ♆ 02-♊-01   A 27-♉-03
☽ 11-♐-59   ♀ 28-♓-22   ♃ 03-♒-40   ♅ 25-♎-58R   ♇ 05-♊-03   M 26-♑-53

One of eight sons, most of whom were musically gifted. Violinist, pianist, conductor; reorganized the Dresden State Opera. In disfavor with the Nazis, went to South America. Moved to U.S. in 1941.

C: Skeetz quotes AA, October 1948, data from *Sterne Und Mensch*.

BUSH, GEORGE   June 12, 1924   Milton, Mass
Politician   11:30 AM EDT   71W05 42N15

☉ 21-♊-21   ☿ 29-♉-24   ♂ 25-♒-28   ♄ 25-♎-50R   ♆ 18-♌-08   A 08-♍-14
☽ 17-♎-47   ♀ 17-♋-27R   ♃ 14-♐-12R   ♅ 21-♓-26   ♇ 11-♋-21   M 04-♊-05

Yale graduate 1948. Business executive and owner of Zapata Petroleum. First public office as GOP chairman, 1963; congressman in 1966 for two terms; a diplomatic year in China, 1974; director of the CIA, 1975-77. Married Barbara Pierce in January 1945.

C: Jansky, from him by letter, 11:00 AM to 12:00 PM, "from his mother's recollection."

BYWATERS, FREDERICK　　June 27, 1902　　　London, England
Murderer　　　　　　　　9:33 AM GMT　　　0W06　51N31

☉ 04-♋-47　　☿ 29-♊-24R　　♂ 14-♊-02　　♄ 25-♑-58R　　♆ 01-♋-19　　A 07-♍-17
☽ 16-♓-19　　♀ 26-♉-41　　♃ 16-♒-33R　　♅ 18-♐-38R　　♇ 18-♊-34　　M 29-♉-54

Merchant seaman who had a torrid love affair with Edith Jesse Thompson. On October 3, 1922, with her encouragement, stabbed her husband to death. Hanged on January 9, 1923.

C: CL from a Tucker article.

The profile and chart of Edith Jesse Thompson, who was indicted and hanged with Bywaters, are given in *Profiles of Women.*

CAAN, JAMES　　　　March 26, 1940　　　Bronx, N.Y.
Actor　　　　　　　　　12:45 PM EST　　　73W54　40N51

☉ 05-♈-55　　☿ 17-♓-06R　　♂ 26-♉-00　　♄ 00-♉-45　　♆ 23-♍-49R　　A 02-♌-08
☽ 16-♏-33　　♀ 20-♉-19　　♃ 17-♈-57　　♅ 19-♉-27　　♇ 00-♌-41R　　M 17-♈-45

Theater and TV before films; first stage role paid $37.50 a week. On screen from 1963; films include *Irma La Douce, Rollerball,* and *The Godfather.* Married at 21 for four years; one daughter.

DD: *Power of Pluto* quotes Arroyo in *Karma and Transformation.* PC speculates 1:00 PM.

CABELL, JAMES BRANCH　　April 14, 1879　　　Richmond, Va
Writer　　　　　　　　　6:30 AM LMT　　　77W27　37N33

☉ 24-♈-09　　☿ 29-♈-02R　　♂ 19-♒-39　　♄ 08-♈-03　　♆ 08-♉-54　　A 15-♉-22
☽ 04-♒-54　　♀ 24-♉-51　　♃ 04-♓-05　　♅ 00-♍-20R　　♇ 25-♉-13　　M 27-♑-41

American author with fame that rested largely on his attempts to suppress his book *Jurgin* (1919), one of a series of risque (for the time) novels written between 1904-29. After 1929, wrote as Branch Cabell. (1879-1958)

DD: SS #160. Old-file has 6:40 AM LMT

CAGLIOSTRO, ALLESANDRO DI　　June 2, 1743 NS　　　Palermo, Italy
Charlatan　　　　　　　　11:08 AM LMT　　　13E23　38N07

☉ 11-♊-22　　☿ 00-♋-35　　♂ 05-♍-52　　♄ 29-♌-42　　♆ 10-♋-39　　A 14-♍-28
☽ 18-♎-00　　♀ 14-♋-28　　♃ 05-♍-47　　♅ 26-♑-40R　　♇ 14-♏-07R　　M 12-♊-21

Played alternate roles of alchemist, forger of documents, dispenser of love philters and elixirs of youth, pretidigitator, healer, medium, soothsayer, and procurer. Imprisoned as a heretic in 1779, where he died in 1795.

DD: Kraum in AFA, Auguts 1961. PC quotes Kraum for 11:30 AM and AFA for 11:08 AM. Old-file has 11:20 AM LMT.

CAGNEY, JAMES　　　　July 17, 1899　　　New York, N.Y.
Actor　　　　　　　　　9:00 AM EST　　　73W57　40N45

☉ 24-♋-43　　☿ 21-♌-09　　♂ 18-♍-09　　♄ 18-♐-01R　　♆ 25-♊-37　　A 15-♍-07
☽ 13-♏-38　　♀ 08-♋-16　　♃ 00-♏-54　　♅ 04-♐-17R　　♇ 16-♊-05　　M 12-♊-41

Crag-faced tough-guy. Overnight star in *Public Enemy* (1931) when he squashed a grapefruit in Mae Clark's face. Shy millionaire who never so much as got a parking ticket. Married; two adopted children. Retired in 1963.

DD: J. Johns from an astrology magazine years ago. PC gives the same data as speculative. Same date in *Filmgoer's Companion.* However, 1904 is given in *Current Biography* (1942), *Americana, Famous People,* and *Biographical Dictionary of Film.*

CALDWELL, ERSKINE　　December 17, 1903　　　Coweta Co, Ga
Writer　　　　　　　　　8:55 PM CST　　　84W48　33N23

☉ 25-♐-01　　☿ 09-♑-28　　♂ 04-♒-28　　♄ 06-♒-33　　♆ 04-♋-49R　　A 21-♌-46
☽ 16-♐-10　　♀ 09-♏-22　　♃ 15-♓-50　　♅ 25-♐-46　　♇ 19-♊-35R　　M 16-♉-58

One of America's best-selling writers; his two most successful novels — *Tobacco Road* (1932) and *God's Little Acre* (1933). At various times, ran guns for a revolution, played pro football, acted as a bodyguard, worked as a cotton-picker and a mill hand.

DD: PC, "personal." Old-file has 8:30 PM CST.

CALHOUN, RORY	August 8, 1922	Los Angeles, Ca
Actor	1:30 AM PST	118W15 34N04

☉ 15-♌-02	☿ 16-♌-17	♂ 14-♐-24	♄ 04-♎-11	♆ 15-♌-40	A 27-♊-37
☽ 23-♒-03	♀ 27-♍-46	♃ 14-♎-19	♅ 12-♓-40R	♇ 10-♋-27	M 08-♓-44

On screen from 1944 in *River of No Return, Black Spurs,* and more. In the 70s one of TV's most suave villains. Reform school for thefts as a youth. When divorced after twenty-one years of marriage in 1970 on charges of adultery with seventy-nine women, said, "Hell, twice that." Remarried, 1971.

DD: PC, "personal." Old-file has 12:50 PM PST.

CALLEY, WILLIAM L.	June 8, 1943	Miami, Fla
Army lieutenant	6:12 PM EWT	80W11 25N47

☉ 17-♊-14	☿ 27-♉-35	♂ 09-♈-15	♄ 16-♊-10	♆ 29-♍-17R	A 22-♏-24
☽ 23-♌-10	♀ 01-♌-31	♃ 25-♋-29	♅ 05-♊-25	♇ 05-♌-29	M 27-♌-01

Convicted of the 1967 My Lai massacre of several hundred civilians; symbol of the American conscience in an untenable war. After three and a half years of house arrest and prison, released on November 9, 1974. Married in 1975; became an insurance salesman.

DD: Eugene Moore in AFA, February 1977; Dewey states that this is a speculative time. Judy Johns has 3:30 PM from Jansky.

CAMPANELLA, ROY	November 19, 1921	New York, N.Y.
Baseball catcher	6:15 AM EST	73W57 40N40

☉ 26-♏-36	☿ 07-♏-36	♂ 07-♎-50	♄ 04-♎-42	♆ 15-♌-58R	A 19-♏-21
☽ 16-♋-49	♀ 06-♏-59	♃ 11-♎-08	♅ 05-♓-43	♇ 09-♋-46R	M 00-♍-41

Led in the fielding average of catchers; elected to the National Baseball Hall of Fame, 1969. An auto accident, January 28, 1958, left him partially paralyzed. Became a baseball coach in a wheelchair.

C: CL from Drew.

CANDIES, JOHN	December 19, 1919	Des Allemands, La
Prodigy	2:30 AM CST	90W28 29N49

☉ 26-♐-24	☿ 04-♐-55	♂ 10-♎-08	♄ 11-♍-40	♆ 11-♌-13R	A 29-♎-26
☽ 22-♏-54	♀ 11-♏-26	♃ 17-♌-49R	♅ 28-♒-29	♇ 06-♋-56R	M 01-♌-41

Mathematical child wizard: under age 10, astounded observers by doing problems up to twenty figures. Would glance at the figures, gaze in space for a few seconds, and write the answer. Shy, talked with his grandmother and aunt, who at first opposed his further education.

C: Diana Herschel in P.A., July 1929.

CANTOR, EDDIE	January 31, 1892	New York, N.Y.
Entertainer	8:30 PM EST	73W57 40N45

☉ 11-♒-42	☿ 20-♑-01	♂ 04-♐-31	♄ 29-♍-42R	♆ 06-♊-19R	A 21-♍-30
☽ 13-♓-47	♀ 14-♓-08	♃ 19-♓-31	♅ 06-♏-03	♇ 06-♊-56R	M 20-♊-09

Stage, radio, TV, and movie star, known for tears-and-laughter comedy and popping eyeballs. After vaudeville and burlesque, starred in musical comedies in the 20s: had a fiscal loss in the crash of '29. Active in charity work; started the March of Dimes. (1892-1964)

DD: CL from BJA, April 1936. McEvers quotes Jansky at 8:05 PM EST. PC quotes SS #163 (time computed for 8:00 PM EST). Drew pictures a chart for 9:07 PM EST.

CAPONE, AL	January 18, 1899	Brooklyn, N.Y.
Gangster	9:30 AM EST	73W58 40N50

☉ 28-♑-20 ☿ 05-♑-37 ♂ 28-♋-51R ♄ 19-♐-34 ♆ 22-♊-29R A 15-♓-06
☽ 27-♈-18 ♀ 14-♐-07 ♃ 08-♏-13 ♅ 06-♐-48 ♇ 13-♊-58R M 22-♐-03

Public Enemy #1, a powerful Chicago gangster who boasted, "I own the police" at age 29. A tough gang-kid from his Brooklyn childhood; moved up into organized crime; had a personal "army" of one thousand guns.

DD: CL from Julie Baum in AFA, April 1975. PC gives January 17, 1899, 6:00 AM EST from Drew, quotes AFA at 12:17 PM. *Capone* by John Kobler (1971), on p. 18 gives January 17, 1899.

CAPOTE, TRUMAN	September 30, 1924	New Orleans, La
Writer	00:05 AM CST	90W04 29N58

☉ 06-♎-48 ☿ 19-♍-27 ♂ 25-♒-45 ♄ 01-♏-46 ♆ 21-♌-45 A 21-♋-27
☽ 25-♎-17 ♀ 21-♌-56 ♃ 14-♐-15 ♅ 18-♓-50R ♇ 13-♋-31 M 10-♈-46

First published at age 16; received the O'Henry Memorial Award at 18; has never had a rejection slip. Books include *In Other Voices, Other Rooms* (1948), *In Cold Blood* (1966), and *Answered Prayers* (1976).

DD: Prince in *Constellations,* December 1976. PC gives 00:15 AM, "personal." McEvers quotes Jansky at 00:08 AM CST.

CARLYLE, THOMAS	December 4, 1795	Ecclefechan, Scotland
Writer	5:00 PM LMT	3W17 55N06

☉ 12-♐-36 ☿ 22-♏-15 ♂ 18-♎-21 ♄ 10-♊-02R ♆ 07-♏-24 A 06-♋-06
☽ 28-♍-49 ♀ 24-♐-58 ♃ 05-♒-05 ♅ 07-♍-58 ♇ 25-♒-30 M 26-♒-14

Oldest of nine children. Well educated, entered university at 14; considered a genius. Too independent to remain a teacher; became a magazine writer. Married, 1826; widowed, 1866. First important publication, *The Life of Schiller* (1825). (1795-1881)

DD: PC quotes Pagan. Pagan in *Pioneer to Poet* states, "Hour uncertain, probably toward dusk."

CARNEGIE, ANDREW	November 25, 1835	Dunfermline, Scotland
Entrepreneur	6:00 AM LMT	3W25 56 N05

☉ 02-♐-18 ☿ 12-♏-30 ♂ 09-♐-10 ♄ 00-♏-17 ♆ 01-♒-31 A 11-♏-46
☽ 08-♒-38 ♀ 15-♐-13 ♃ 15-♋-09R ♅ 26-♒-46 ♇ 12-♈-58R M 01-♍-27

Consolidated his steel industries in 1899 as Carnegie Steel Co.; merged in 1901 into the greatest corporation the world had ever known — U.S. Steel Corp. A philanthropist whose gifts to civic organizations are estimated at $350 million. (1835-1919)

DD: *Circle* #200 quotes "data given to E. Adams by Carnegie or someone close to him." *Andrew Carnegie* by Joseph F. Wall (1970), describes his birth on p. 17: "Midwife hurried... to tell the man, waiting in near darkness by his loom that his son was born." As was customary, people brought gifts: "The mother was congratulated in the evening hours... the cottage lights continued to burn until late that night." The detailed description implies that the birth was at sunset, and LMR notes that sunset was 3:40 PM LMT. SS #170 gives 6:00 AM. PC quotes SS for 5:00 AM LMT.

CARROLL, LEWIS	January 27, 1832	Daresburg, England
Writer	3:48 AM LMT	2W38 53N21

☉ 06-♒-17 ☿ 12-♑-16 ♂ 25-♐-41 ♄ 14-♍-11R ♆ 25-♑-07 A 01-♐-43
☽ 03-♐-21 ♀ 22-♐-57 ♃ 28-♒-15 ♅ 14-♒-03 ♇ 08-♈-48 M 29-♍-47

Charles Ludwidge Dodgson, a logician and mathematician. Stammered badly and was deaf in one ear. A shy, fussy bachelor, regarded as a crank. Created the fantasy stories of *Alice in Wonderland* (1865) and *Through the Looking-Glass* (1872). (1832-1898)

DD: Daath in M.A., 1901; same data from Lyndoe in AA, November 1966, and SS #175. J. Johns quotes Jansky at 4:00 AM LMT. PC adds that 4:10 AM is given by Adams.

CARSON, KIT	December 24, 1809	Madison Co, Ky
Frontiersman	8:30 PM LMT	84W17 37N45

☉ 02-♑-57	☿ 29-♐-45	♂ 16-♒-12	♄ 09-♐-24	♆ 07-♐-32	A 20-♌-04
☽ 07-♌-31	♀ 13-♐-36	♃ 15-♈-19	♅ 12-♏-58	♇ 13-♓-47	M 13-♉-08

Archetype of the American pioneer: mountain man, trapper, Indian fighter, rancher, army general. Life of wanderlust from age 15, when he ran away to join a wagon train to Santa Fe and Taos. Said to have killed more men than Billy the Kid. (1809-1868)

DD: PC quotes *Kit Carson* by Stanley Vestal, "in the morning." That biography states on p. 3, "On Christmas Day in the morning, 1809." *Kit Carson's Own Story of His Life*, edited by Blanche Grant (1926), states on p. 9, "I was born on the 24 Decr. 1809 in Madison County, Ky." PC also quotes *Kit Carson* by Noel Gerson, "which states he was born late in the evening." LMR cannot locate that biography.

CARSON, RACHEL	May 27, 1907	Springdale, Pa
Scientist	1:00 PM EST	79W47 40N32

☉ 05-♊-17	☿ 09-♊-28	♂ 18-♑-27	♄ 25-♓-57	♆ 10-♋-59	A 17-♍-34
☽ 07-♐-27	♀ 06-♉-09	♃ 11-♋-52	♅ 12-♑-05R	♇ 22-♊-49	M 15-♊-35

Marine biologist and science writer, employed by the U.S. Fish and Wildlife Service. Author of *The Sea Around Us* (1951). (1907-1964)

DD: Jansky in F/M quotes Penfield. PC states speculative.

CARTEEK, JOHN	January 22, 1861	Rockland, Mich
Champion wrestler	1:45 AM LMT	89W11 46N44

☉ 02-♒-21	☿ 26-♑-15	♂ 11-♈-58	♄ 08-♍-33R	♆ 27-♓-11	A 12-♏-56
☽ 07-♊-44	♀ 05-♑-20	♃ 24-♌-30R	♅ 08-♊-14R	♇ 07-♉-30	M 25-♌-38

Started to wrestle when young, but went to college for a law degree. In 1899, went into professional wrestling; became an unqualified star success in music halls and exhibitions. In little more than a year, beat 250 men, including champions.

C: M.A., November 1902, quotes a correspondent.

CARVER, GEORGE WASHINGTON	May 24, 1864	Diamond Grove, Mo
Scientist	7:10 PM LMT	94W19 37N00

☉ 04-♊-03	☿ 01-♊-32R	♂ 27-♓-56	♄ 11-♎-38R	♆ 07-♈-46	A 05-♐-19
☽ 19-♑-39	♀ 19-♉-16	♃ 21-♏-16R	♅ 23-♊-55	♇ 12-♉-18	M 19-♍-32

Botanist, naturalist, chemist. B.S. degree, 1894; M.S. in Agriculture, 1896. Known for his remarkable research on the industrial uses of the peanut, from which he made more than three hundred products. (1864?-1943)

DD: CL from MacKenzie, 1961; same data in SS #179. *Famous People* gives January 5, 1864. *Americana* states, "Carver was born to slave parents and his date is unknown, but deduced to be on or near July 12, 1861."

CASALS, PABLO	December 29, 1876	Vendrell, Spain
Musician	11:00 PM LMT	1E33 41N10

☉ 08-♑-40	☿ 23-♑-05	♂ 19-♏-46	♄ 03-♓-55	♆ 02-♉-33R	A 25-♍-03
☽ 25-♊-01	♀ 07-♐-36	♃ 18-♐-33	♅ 24-♌-19R	♇ 22-♉-51R	M 24-♊-15

Renowned cellist and conductor, one of the most outstanding string players of the 20th century. Left his native Spain in 1930, after the Civil War, in protest against the rule of Franco. Lived in France and Puerto Rico and made concert tours. (1876-1973)

DD: CL quotes *Astrological Review*, "from him." Same date given in *Britannica*. PC same data, "personal"; adds that *Pablo Casals* by H. Kirk states, "late at night." McEvers quotes Jansky for the same date, 8:34 PM LT. Phillip Lucas in M.H., October 1979, gives December 30 1876, 8:00 PM LMT, "data from birth record according to F. Snethlage in *L'Astrologue* #19."

CASANOVA, GIOVANNI   April 2, 1725   Venice, Italy
Romantic   8:00 PM LMT   12E20   45N26

☉ 12-♈-58   ☿ 28-♓-42   ♂ 14-♓-13   ♄ 21-♑-27   ♆ 29-♉-43   A 00-♏-55
☽ 09-♐-24   ♀ 22-♓-51   ♃ 06-♓-05   ♅ 07-♏-33R   ♇ 28-♍-36R   M 08-♌-37

Considered the greatest of historic lovers. As a youth, left many jobs, from soldiering to playing the fiddle, because of entangling affairs with women. His *Memoirs*, published from 1826-38 in twelve volumes, relate his escapades. (1725-1798)

DD: PC speculative. AQ, Winter 1970, Gilman speculates 9:00 PM LMT.

CASE, MARY   October 3, 1910   Lancaster, Pa
Murder victim   8:05 AM EST   76W19   40N02

☉ 09-♎-26   ☿ 26-♍-31R   ♂ 07-♎-31   ♄ 04-♉-55R   ♆ 21-♋-26   A 02-♏-48
☽ 11-♎-34   ♀ 25-♍-45   ♃ 21-♎-32   ♅ 21-♑-16   ♇ 27-♊-57R   M 08-♌-51

On January 11, 1937, killed in her own home by a rapist who gained admittance by posing as a tradesman.

C: CL from Tucker in *Astro Diagnosis* (1959).

CASH, JOHNNY   February 26, 1932   Pine Bluff, Ark
Singer   7:30 AM CST   92W01   34N13

☉ 06-♓-45   ☿ 06-♓-29   ♂ 01-♓-09   ♄ 00-♒-15   ♆ 06-♍-37R   A 23-♓-20
☽ 07-♏-57   ♀ 16-♈-32   ♃ 15-♌-14R   ♅ 17-♈-02   ♇ 20-♋-13R   M 26-♐-02

Shot out of obscurity in cotton-patch Arkansas to become one of the charismatic figures of the mid-50s folk scene, with country western music that includes "Folsom Prison Blues" and "I Walk the Line." Had his own TV show briefly; by the late 60s was a best selling artist.

DD: M.H., October 1979, Colleen Gauthier quotes his mother. Jansky H/N states 8:09 AM CST, "from him to a colleague." Same data in PC.

CASTENEDA, CARLOS   December 25, 1925   Cajamarca, Peru
Anthropologist   2:00 PM EST   78W31   7S10

☉ 03-♑-30   ☿ 12-♐-09   ♂ 28-♏-29   ♄ 22-♏-12   ♆ 24-♌-34R   A 00-♉-53
☽ 14-♉-26   ♀ 17-♒-01   ♃ 27-♑-25   ♅ 21-♓-49   ♇ 13-♋-53R   M 28-♑-09

While a student, spent five years in Mexico as an apprentice to a Yaqui Indian sorcerer. Wrote *The Teachings of Don Juan* (1968), *The Separate Reality* (1971), *Tales of Power* (1974), and *Trilogy* (1974).

DD: Ideman from *Cosmic Seed* magazine. Jansky gives 1:45 PM EST from *Astrological Review*, 1973/74. PC quotes both sources for 1:59 PM EST.

CERF, BENNETT   May 25, 1898   New York, N.Y.
Writer   12:00 Noon EST   73W57   40N45

☉ 04-♊-27   ☿ 10-♉-12   ♂ 20-♈-31   ♄ 09-♐-20R   ♆ 21-♊-33   A 09-♍-42
☽ 00-♌-42   ♀ 29-♊-19   ♃ 00-♎-21R   ♅ 01-♐-25R   ♇ 13-♊-58   M 06-♊-13

American author and publisher; head of Random House from 1927 to 1970. Witty regular panelist on TV's *What's My Line?* for sixteen years. (1898-1971).

DD: CL quotes Drew. PC states same data, "personal." Judy Johns quotes Jansky for 12:10 PM EST. *Tucker Research Quarterly*, January 1961, gives 00:12 AM EST.

CERMAK, ANTON   May 9, 1873   Kadno, Bohemia
Politician   9:45 AM LMT   14E05   50N08

☉ 18-♉-46   ☿ 23-♈-01   ♂ 03-♏-08R   ♄ 02-♒-43   ♆ 26-♈-52   A 05-♌-23
☽ 12-♎-15   ♀ 13-♉-01R   ♃ 22-♌-12   ♅ 02-♌-10   ♇ 20-♉-14   M 14-♈-39

Mayor of Chicago, 1931-33. On February 15, 1933, shot by an assassin who aimed at President Roosevelt; died of the wounds on March 6, 1933.

C: CL old file. (PC quotes CL for May 7, 1873.) May 9, 1873 given in *Famous People*.

CHAGALL, MARC July 7, 1887 NS Vitebsk, Russia
Artist 3:00 PM LMT 30E12 55N12

| ☉ 15-♋-02 | ☿ 09-♌-49 | ♂ 26-♊-40 | ♄ 24-♋-37 | ♆ 29-♉-13 | A 10-♏-08 |
| ☽ 11-♒-11 | ♀ 00-♍-27 | ♃ 26-♎-17 | ♅ 08-♎-34 | ♇ 04-♊-27 | M 28-♌-00 |

Russian-French painter whose works are fantasies saturated with emotions, ideas, and images of Jewish folklore and religion, blended with the customs of Russian provincial life. Powerful and original work. From early poverty to recognition after World War I.

DD: PC speculative. Old-file has 2:45 PM LMT.

CHAMBERLAIN, NEVILLE March 18, 1869 Birmingham, England
Statesman 2:21 AM LMT 1W55 52N25

| ☉ 27-♓-33 | ☿ 29-♒-52 | ♂ 15-♌-43R | ♄ 17-♐-06 | ♆ 16-♈-16 | A 26-♐-58 |
| ☽ 20-♉-11 | ♀ 14-♓-06 | ♃ 20-♈-05 | ♅ 13-♋-19R | ♇ 15-♉-29 | M 03-♏-10 |

Minister of health, 1926-29; chancellor of the exchequer, 1932-37; prime minister of Great Britain, 1937-40. Closely associated with the policy of appeasement toward Nazi Germany, leading to the Munich agreement of 1938, by which he hoped for "peace in our time." Forced to resign by World War II. (1869-1940)

C: SS #187. BJA, March 1939, Bailey gives 2:20:37 AM LMT rectified.

CHANDLER, OTIS November 23, 1927 Los Angeles, Ca
Publisher 9:30 PM PST 118W15 34N04

| ☉ 00-♐-56 | ☿ 11-♏-26 | ♂ 20-♏-02 | ♄ 09-♐-06 | ♆ 29-♌-10 | A 07-♌-06 |
| ☽ 28-♏-48 | ♀ 14-♎-18 | ♃ 23-♓-39 | ♅ 29-♓-36R | ♇ 16-♋-54R | M 28-♈-27 |

Succeeded his father as publisher of the Los Angeles *Times* on April 1960; modernized it to gain the fourth largest circulation of any national paper. Married in 1951; five children. Rugged, handsome, ruthless, ambitious.

DD: PC, "personal." Old-file has 9:40 PM PST.

CHANEY, LON April 1, 1883 Colorado Springs, Colo
Actor 7:24 AM LMT 104W49 38N50

| ☉ 11-♈-31 | ☿ 27-♓-02 | ♂ 15-♓-02 | ♄ 23-♉-30 | ♆ 17-♉-10 | A 17-♉-20 |
| ☽ 20-♑-40 | ♀ 29-♒-14 | ♃ 24-♊-32 | ♅ 20-♍-27R | ♇ 28-♉-43 | M 28-♑-29 |

Called "The Man of a Thousand Faces"; best known for horror pictures. Played Quasimoto in *The Hunchback of Notre Dame*. Also starred in *The Phantom of the Opera* and many other films. (1883-1930)

DD: Holliday quotes Kraum in *Best of the NAJ*, 1979, "private source." Same data from CL quoting AFA, February 1956. SS #189 gives 7:19 AM.

CHAPLIN, CHARLES April 16, 1889 London, England
Actor 8:00 PM GMT 0W06 51N31

| ☉ 27-♈-00 | ☿ 17-♈-50 | ♂ 13-♉-35 | ♄ 13-♌-26 | ♆ 00-♊-43 | A 08-♏-37 |
| ☽ 09-♏-24 | ♀ 18-♉-07R | ♃ 08-♑-10 | ♅ 19-♎-39R | ♇ 04-♊-35 | M 22-♌-42 |

Internationally famous mime and all-star comedian with his character Charlie the Tramp. Won awards and acclaim for *The Kid*, *The Great Dictator*, *City Lights*, and *Modern Times*. Lived in the U.S. from 1910 to 1952. (1889-1977)

DD: Bruno Huber states B.C. PC gives the same data, "from his autobiography." Howard Hammitt in AA, December 1973, states "recorded birth time of 7:00 PM was given in an article by Tucker in 1955." SS #191 gives Noon. Drew, who states, "I have known and talked with Mr. Chaplin," pictures a chart for 1:07 PM GMT (MC 14 Taurus.)

CHEKHOV, ANTON January 29, 1860 NS Taganrog, Russia
Writer 2:00 AM LMT 38E57 47N14

| ☉ 08-♒-20 | ☿ 23-♑-49 | ♂ 28-♏-34 | ♄ 23-♌-47R | ♆ 25-♓-10 | A 19-♏-44 |
| ☽ 12-♈-59 | ♀ 07-♓-53 | ♃ 17-♋-56R | ♅ 03-♊-47R | ♇ 06-♉-34 | M 05-♍-39 |

Russian writer of short stories and plays, still pertinent and popular. Practiced medicine and wrote until 1886, when he devoted full time to literature. Work includes the plays *The Seagull* and *The Three Sisters*. Died of TB at age 44.

DD: PC speculative. Old-file has 5:10 AM LMT. Lyndoe in AA, March 1980, gives, "About daybreak generally accepted in Russia," and prints a chart for approximately 5:00 AM LMT, January 17, 1860 OS. Eshelman speculates 7:12 AM LMT.

CHESTERTON, G.K.	May 29, 1874	London, England
Writer	2:45 AM LMT	0W06 51N31

☉ 07-♊-31	☿ 12-♊-45	♂ 18-♊-17	♄ 14-♒-18R	♆ 29-♈-41	A 09-♉-11
☽ 12-♏-58	♀ 01-♋-31	♃ 21-♍-59	♅ 07-♌-19	♇ 21-♉-36	M 16-♑-20

Poet, essayist, and novelist; one of the most original and forceful British writers of his time. His novels include *The Man Who Was Thursday* (1908) and a series of detective-crime fiction. (1874-1936)

DD: PC speculative. Old-file has 3:10 AM LMT.

CHILD MOLESTER	March 3, 1933	No place given
Male	00:34 AM CST	90W31 14N38

☉ 12-♓-15	☿ 29-♓-46	♂ 10-♍-15R	♄ 11-♒-10	♆ 08-♍-43R	A 13-♐-45
☽ 29-♉-38	♀ 29-♒-45	♃ 19-♍-08R	♅ 21-♈-07	♇ 21-♋-27R	M 17-♍-34

Picked up by the police several times but never held. Would not admit to any sex deviation. Was reported by the family and sentenced to California State Hospital for sex offenders in 1964.

C: CL from AFA, November 1965.

CHRYSLER, WALTER P.	April 2, 1875	Wamego, Ks
Industrialist	12:02 PM LMT	98W18 39N12

☉ 12-♈-37	☿ 15-♓-19	♂ 24-♐-00	♄ 22-♒-55	♆ 29-♈-49	A 27-♋-08
☽ 25-♒-40	♀ 00-♓-09	♃ 28-♎-36R	♅ 11-♌-15R	♇ 21-♉-18	M 12-♈-10

American automobile manufacturer: founder of Chrysler Corp. and first president, 1925-35. Began work at Buick in 1912; became president four years later; was vice president of GM. Retired as a millionaire at 45. Four years later produced his first automobile. (1875-1940)

DD: SS #205. Old-file has 1:00 PM LMT.

CHURCHILL, LORD RANDOLPH	February 12/13, 1849	Blenheim Palace, England
Politician	Midnight LMT	1W18 51N50

☉ 24-♒-14	☿ 10-♓-59	♂ 18-♑-22	♄ 23-♓-58	♆ 01-♓-58	A 06-♏-58
☽ 00-♏-28	♀ 09-♈-48	♃ 16-♌-41R	♅ 19-♈-15	♇ 26-♈-06	M 20-♌-31

An English gentleman who entered parliament in 1874. Married Jennie Jerome in 1874; fathered Winston. Died of syphilis in 1895.

DD: Chart pictured in Leo's *Esoteric Astrology*. BJA, November 1936, Bailey rectifies to 11:54 PM of February 12. PC quotes Leo for February 13, 1849, 00:15 AM LMT. February 13 given in *Americana*.

The profile and speculative chart of Lady Churchill are given in *Profiles of Women*.

CLARK, GEORGE ROGERS	November 19, 1752	Charlottesville, Va
Military officer	10:30 AM LMT	78W30 38N02

☉ 27-♏-48	☿ 01-♐-26	♂ 07-♏-42	♄ 23-♐-55	♆ 04-♌-15R	A 16-♑-17
☽ 02-♉-42	♀ 21-♐-51	♃ 15-♋-18R	♅ 29-♒-32	♇ 08-♐-17	M 08-♏-56

American soldier and frontiersman who won important victories in the Northwest Territory during the Revolutionary War. When the peace treaty was signed in 1783, this territory came under U.S. possession. (1752-1818)

DD: PC speculative. Old-file has 10:50 AM LMT.

CLARK, JIM   March 4, 1936   Westerkilmany, Scotland
Race car driver   3:25 PM GMT   3W00   56N23

☉ 13-♓-54   ☿ 18-♒-06   ♂ 08-♈-47   ♄ 12-♓-57   ♆ 15-♍-27R   A 20-♌-59
☽ 04-♌-10   ♀ 14-♒-04   ♃ 22-♐-22   ♅ 02-♉-45   ♇ 25-♋-24R   M 02-♉-40

Nicknamed "The Flying Scot" by winning twenty-five Grand Prix races. First man in history to win both the Formula One world driving championship in 1963 and the Indianopolis 400 in 1965 (151 m.p.h.). Killed in the German Formula Two race on April 7, 1968.

C: Holliday from the *Astrological Association Journal*.

COBB, TYRUS R. "TY"   December 18, 1886   Banks Co, Ga
Baseball player   6:13 AM LMT   83W30   34N20

☉ 26-♐-32   ☿ 05-♐-16   ♂ 25-♑-25   ♄ 20-♋-48R   ♆ 25-♉-38R   A 15-♐-01
☽ 29-♍-20   ♀ 00-♑-15   ♃ 00-♏-15   ♅ 12-♎-05   ♇ 02-♊-39R   M 00-♎-17

Played mostly with Detroit and Philadelphia; regarded as the greatest hitter and base-runner in history. Set a top number of records; had twenty-four-year lifetime batting average of .367. (1886-1961)

C: CL from Ziegler, April 1965. PC quotes CL for 6:47 AM EST.

CODY, BUFFALO BILL   February 26, 1846   Le Claire, Iowa
Marksman   8:00 AM LMT   90W26   41N35

☉ 07-♓-38   ☿ 01-♓-17   ♂ 12-♉-28   ♄ 23-♒-21   ♆ 26-♒-04   A 10-♈-39
☽ 18-♓-23   ♀ 14-♓-36R   ♃ 06-♉-50   ♅ 08-♈-23   ♇ 23-♈-23   M 05-♑-32

Frontiersman, Indian scout, and showman. Rider for the Pony Express, 1860; scout for Kansas cavalry, 1863; Army service, 1863-65; scout for the 5th U.S. Cavalry, 1868-72. Organized and managed Buffalo Bill's Wild West Show, 1883. (1846-1917)

DD: Scarsella from Baird. PC speculates 2:35 PM LMT.

COHEN, MICKEY   September 4, 1913   New York, N.Y.
Mobster   6:44 AM EST   73W58   40N45

☉ 11-♍-19   ☿ 00-♍-04   ♂ 23-♊-35   ♄ 17-♊-32   ♆ 27-♋-21   A 26-♍-04
☽ 02-♏-03   ♀ 03-♌-38   ♃ 08-♑-00R   ♅ 04-♒-13R   ♇ 01-♋-00   M 25-♊-27

Elusive member of the rackets; finally convicted on income tax evasion, July 30, 1961; sentenced to fifteen years in prison and a $30,000 fine.

C: Scarsella from Baird.

COLEMAN, RONALD   February 9, 1891   Richmond, England
Actor   5:45 AM GMT   0W18   51N27

☉ 20-♒-14   ☿ 24-♑-45   ♂ 10-♈-18   ♄ 15-♍-34R   ♆ 04-♊-00R   A 11-♑-54
☽ 22-♒-21   ♀ 03-♑-33   ♃ 23-♒-36   ♅ 01-♏-24R   ♇ 05-♊-55R   M 17-♏-27

Gentlemanly romantic English star; won Oscar as best actor in *A Double Life* (1947); nominated for the Oscar in *Bulldog Drummond*, *Condemned*, and *Random Harvest* (1942). (1891-1958)

DD: CL from Miss Whitney. SS #214 gives 6:00 PM. PC quotes SS for 6:00 AM.

CONNERS, BRUCE   December 20, 1918   Montana
Athlete   00:30 AM MST   112W00   47N00

☉ 27-♐-37   ☿ 23-♐-40R   ♂ 29-♑-56   ♄ 28-♌-09R   ♆ 08-♌-56R   A 28-♍-56
☽ 00-♌-03   ♀ 03-♑-59   ♃ 12-♋-29R   ♅ 24-♒-41   ♇ 05-♋-46R   M 28-♊-42

Weight lifter who won a championship title.

C: CL from Gene Smith.

CONRAD, JOSEPH December 3, 1857 NS Berdichev, Russia
Writer 3:30 PM LMT 28E35 49N55

| ☉ 11-♐-24 | ☿ 19-♐-18 | ♂ 10-♎-05 | ♄ 27-♋-50R | ♆ 19-♓-53 | A 03-♊-53 |
| ☽ 11-♋-20 | ♀ 20-♏-36 | ♃ 07-♉-17R | ♅ 26-♉-38R | ♇ 04-♉-59R | M 02-♒-33 |

British novelist of Polish ancestry; famous for his romantic and tragic stories about life in Malaya, the Congo, and Europe. Works include *Tales of Unrest* (1898), his famous *Lord Jim* (1900), and *Personal Records* (1912). (1857-1924)

DD: PC speculative. Old-file gives Poland, 2:00 AM LMT. *Americana* states Berdichev, once part of Poland.

CONSTABLE, JOHN June 11, 1776 East Bergholt, England
Artist 1:00 AM LMT 1E27 52N20

| ☉ 20-♊-33 | ☿ 14-♋-57 | ♂ 04-♊-50 | ♄ 14-♎-33R | ♆ 22-♍-09 | A 12-♈-10 |
| ☽ 15-♈-03 | ♀ 03-♊-56 | ♃ 00-♋-31 | ♅ 07-♊-37 | ♇ 27-♑-51R | M 04-♑-31 |

Generally considered one of the greatest English landscape painters of spring and summer scenes, never winter: works natural and brilliant. Fame began in Paris 1824 with a prize for *The Hay-Wain*. Lived a life of ease, through inheritance. (1776-1837)

DD: PC speculative. Old-file has 1:35 PM LMT.

COOK, JAMES November 7, 1728 NS Marton, Yorkshire, England
British navigator 11:27 AM LMT 1W12 54N32

| ☉ 15-♏-20 | ☿ 06-♐-24 | ♂ 22-♐-11 | ♄ 20-♒-27 | ♆ 09-♊-58R | A 00-♑-58 |
| ☽ 01-♒-35 | ♀ 04-♐-44 | ♃ 05-♋-49R | ♅ 22-♏-10 | ♇ 08-♎-54 | M 11-♏-03 |

Famous explorer of the Pacific Ocean, with three voyages to the South Pacific region in 1768, 1772, and 1776. As a child, showed superior abilities. Joined the British Navy as a seaman; rose rapidly to positions of command. Murdered in Hawaii on February 14, 1779.

DD: Gwen Stoney quotes his logs as given in biography by J.C. Beaglehole, time speculative, (October 27, 1728 OS). PC gives October 27, 1728 as NS, 6:10 AM LMT speculative. C.M. and J.M. McCan in Dell, November 1979, give October 28, 1728 OS (the same date as given in *Britannica*) with 4:15 AM LMT.

COOPER, GARY May 7, 1901 Helena, Mont
Actor 5:45 AM MST 112W02 46N36

| ☉ 16-♉-15 | ☿ 07-♉-54 | ♂ 28-♌-47 | ♄ 16-♑-17R | ♆ 27-♊-24 | A 28-♉-34 |
| ☽ 27-♐-53 | ♀ 17-♉-58 | ♃ 12-♑-59R | ♅ 16-♐-03R | ♇ 16-♊-27 | M 01-♒-38 |

Won the Oscar as best actor in *Sargeant York* (1941) and *High Noon* (1952). Nominated for the Oscar in *Mr. Deeds Goes to Town, The Pride of the Yankees,* and *For Whom the Bell Tolls.* Last film, *The Naked Edge,* was in 1961. (1901-1961)

DD: CL from news clippings, 1961. J. Johns has 7:40 AM MST.

COOPER, JACKIE September 15, 1922 Los Angeles, Ca
Actor 12:05 PM PST 118W15 34N04

| ☉ 22-♍-11 | ☿ 18-♎-07 | ♂ 01-♑-17 | ♄ 08-♎-22 | ♆ 17-♌-02 | A 12-♐-23 |
| ☽ 09-♋-24 | ♀ 08-♏-31 | ♃ 21-♎-16 | ♅ 11-♓-11R | ♇ 11-♋-05 | M 26-♍-44 |

On screen from 1925; nominated for the Oscar as best actor in *Skippy* (1930). Played in the 1931 classic, *The Champ,* and in *Treasure Island* (1935). Nominated for a TV Emmy for outstanding performance in the series *Hennesey,* 1960/61.

DD: P.A. August 1933. Same date in SS #222. Drew gives "before noon."

COOPER, JAMES FENIMORE September 15, 1789 Burlington, N.J.
Writer 6:00 PM LMT 74W51 40N04

☉ 23-♍-27 ☿ 07-♎-47 ♂ 19-♋-23 ♄ 19-♓-34R ♆ 21-♎-57 A 21-♓-58
☽ 06-♌-24 ♀ 22-♎-15 ♃ 20-♌-18 ♅ 08-♌-02 ♇ 17-♒-08R M 25-♐-42

An important American novelist, with sea-romance and wilderness adventures. Expelled from Yale, went to sea. Retired and married in 1811. His first book published in 1820, followed by *The Spy, The Leather-Stocking Tales, The Last of the Mohicans,* and others. (1789-1851)

DD: PC speculative. Old-file has 3:00 AM LMT.

CORBETT, GENTLEMAN JIM September 1, 1866 San Francisco, Ca
Boxer 11:00 AM LMT 122 W26 37N47

☉ 09-♍-04 ☿ 22-♌-48 ♂ 25-♊-08 ♄ 07-♏-55 ♆ 12-♈-16R A 15-♏-02
☽ 06-♊-19 ♀ 23-♎-21 ♃ 22-♑-53R ♅ 07-♋-36 ♇ 15-♉-06R M 23-♌-23

Won the heavyweight title in 1892 by knocking out John J. Sullivan in round twenty-one; lost to Bob Fitzsimmons in 1897. After retiring from the ring, became the first prize fighter to act in movies. Died of cancer on February 18, 1933.

DD: PC speculative. Old-file has 11:25 AM LMT.

COUE, EMILE February 26, 1857 Troyes, France
Writer 4:00 AM LMT 4E05 48N18

☉ 07-♓-32 ☿ 10-♒-36 ♂ 02-♈-57 ♄ 07-♋-23R ♆ 19-♓-38 A 06-♑-28
☽ 00-♈-02 ♀ 23-♈-56 ♃ 11-♈-39 ♅ 21-♉-22 ♇ 03-♉-57 M 08-♏-19

French self-proclaimed psychotherapist, best known for his proverbial formula, "Every day in every way I am getting better and better." Apothecary, 1882-1910; studied hypnotism and suggestion; opened a clinic in Nancy. His many books include *Self Mastery Through Auto-Suggestion* (1922). (1857-1926)

DD: M.A., July 1922; same data in SS #225. PC quotes Gauquelin for same: LMR cannot locate data in Gauquelin Vol 6. Old-file has 3:45 AM; CL has 4:08 AM LMT.

COULTHARD, HELEN July 13, 1894 Penrith, England
Youthful minister 8:45 AM GMT 2W44 54N40

☉ 20-♋-54 ☿ 02-♌-47R ♂ 12-♈-17 ♄ 18-♎-49 ♆ 14-♊-39 A 09-♍-35
☽ 00-♐-46 ♀ 15-♊-55 ♃ 22-♊-41 ♅ 11-♏-16R ♇ 11-♊-11 M 01-♊-50

Born in the slums. Became a power in the neighborhood after preaching her first sermon at age 9. Became a revivalist, winning and holding her audience with gentle appeal. Delicate health, simple tastes; wrote poems and prose.

C: M.A., December 1919, from Higgs.

CRENSHAW, JAMES May 24, 1908 Richland, Ore
Journalist 12:36 PM PST 117W10 44N46

☉ 03-♊-14 ☿ 21-♊-32 ♂ 01-♋-29 ♄ 07-♈-27 ♆ 13-♋-05 A 17-♍-43
☽ 27-♓-25 ♀ 14-♋-45 ♃ 07-♌-55 ♅ 16-♑-28R ♇ 23-♊-47 M 15-♊-08

Newspaper reporter on the staff of California papers for twenty-five years. Began in 1935 to collect material on the after-life world. Wrote articles on psychic subjects, as well as the biography of Reverend Richard Zenor, a medium, in *Telephone Between Worlds*.

C: *Celebrity Horoscopes*, rectified time.
The data for his wife, the medium Brenda Crenshaw, are given in *Profiles of Women*.

CRISP, DONALD July 27, 1886 London, England
Actor 12:53 PM GMT 0W06 51N31

☉ 04-♌-21 ☿ 29-♌-22 ♂ 14-♎-17 ♄ 15-♋-00 ♆ 27-♉-31 A 03-♏-53
☽ 13-♊-53 ♀ 02-♋-05 ♃ 01-♎-43 ♅ 04-♎-31 ♇ 03-♊-49 M 15-♌-49

Durable career from 1911: played silent leads; assistant director of *Birth of a Nation;* director of *Son of Zorro* and *Svengali;* supporting actor in more than seventy films, including *Mutiny on the Bounty, Wuthering Heights,* and *How Green Was My Valley.* (1886?-1974)

DD: CL old file. *Who's Who in Hollywood* gives 1881. *Filmgoer's Companion* and *Biographical Dictionary of Film* both give 1880.

CROCKETT, DAVY   August 17, 1786   Limestone, Tenn
American legend   1:30 PM LMT   82W38   36N14

⊙ 24-♌-54   ☿ 21-♍-14   ♂ 20-♍-59   ♄ 12-♒-49R   ♆ 14-♎-44   A 04-♐-24
☽ 09-♊-01   ♀ 02-♎-41   ♃ 20-♉-25   ♅ 23-♋-19   ♇ 13-♒-06R   M 17-♍-49

Frontiersman, hunter, scout, soldier, and congressman; a legend in his own time. Also a humorist who wrote and told tall tales about himself. Died in the famous battle of the Alamo on March 6, 1836.

DD: Kraum in AFA, October 1962, speculative. PC speculates 7:30 AM LMT. Old-file has 9:15 PM LMT. G. Allen in AA, October 1955, quotes Crockett's own journal for the date, "whether by day or night I know not."

CROMWELL, OLIVER   May 5, 1599 NS   Huntingdon, England
Politician   3:00 AM LMT   0W12   51N15

⊙ 13-♉-58   ☿ 16-♉-27   ♂ 10-♈-31   ♄ 10-♎-46R   ♆ 22-♌-28   A 23-♓-55
☽ 15-♍-37   ♀ 29-♉-56   ♃ 15-♋-04   ♅ 28-♈-58   ♇ 21-♈-27   M 27-♐-39

Prominent family; a land owner; a man of iron will and high moral purpose. Married at 21; four sons, four daughters. Became parliamentary general in the English Civil War; later was named Lord Protector. (1599-1658)

DD: *Life of Cromwell* by John Buchan. M.A., Janury 1937, states that his authority was John Booker's *Astrological Practice Book.* AQ, Spring 1952, Harvey quotes Lilly (c. 1600) for 3:00 AM. M.A., September 1896, quotes a nativity by Partridge, physician to Queen Elizabeth, for 1:05 AM. M.A., May 1907, states that Sibly quoted Partridge for 3:46 PM rectified.

    M.A., January 1937, notes that both Sibly and Gadbury give 3:46 PM; however, NN #613 quotes Gadbury for 3:45 AM LMT, and NN #068 quotes Partridge for 1:00 AM LMT. Adams, *One Hundred Horoscopes,* pictures a chart for 6:00 AM LMT. All the above data is for April 25, 1599 OS, the date that is given in *Americana. Wynn's Astrology,* May 1946, gives April 24, 1599 OS, 3:47 AM.

CROMWELL, RICHARD   October 14, 1626 NS   Huntingdon, England
Politician   1:50 AM LMT   0W12   51N15

⊙ 20-♎-38   ☿ 17-♎-18R   ♂ 13-♎-51   ♄ 22-♍-41   ♆ 23-♎-56   A 01-♍-49
☽ 12-♌-22   ♀ 00-♐-58   ♃ 06-♏-53   ♅ 00-♍-27   ♇ 18-♉-12R   M 22-♉-26

Son of Oliver Cromwell. After his father's death, tried to continue the same policy but lacked his father's power. In May 1659 had to resign in favor of the restoration of Charles II. (1626-1712)

C: NN #645 quotes Gadbury.

CRONIN, A.J.   July 19, 1896   Cardross, Scotland
Writer   3:45 AM GMT   4W34   55N27

⊙ 26-♋-55   ☿ 13-♋-06   ♂ 12-♉-02   ♄ 12-♏-26   ♆ 19-♊-12   A 22-♋-24
☽ 16-♏-30   ♀ 29-♋-35   ♃ 14-♌-49   ♅ 20-♏-29R   ♇ 13-♊-13   M 18-♓-10

British novelist who gave up a medical practice to write. Had served as a surgeon in World War I. During an illness wrote his first novel in 1931 — an immediate success. Books include *The Citadel* (1937), *Keys of the Kingdon* (1941), and *The Northern Light* (1958).

C: Craswell from AQR Vol 5 #4.

CROSBY, BING	May 2, 1903	Tacoma, Wash
Singer, actor	4:00 PM PST	122W26 47N14

☉ 11-♉-23	☿ 00-♊-40	♂ 27-♍-42R	♄ 09-♒-04	♆ 01-♋-36	A 05-♎-24
☽ 24-♋-01	♀ 17-♊-30	♃ 15-♓-54	♅ 25-♐-13R	♇ 18-♊-19	M 06-♋-41

A mellow baritone, with a career including fifty-eight movies from 1932-66, hundreds of radio and TV programs, and records that eventually sold more than 300 million copies. Two marriages; seven children. Multimillionaire. (1903-1977)

C: *Bing* by Bob Thomas (1977) states: "Some said 1901, the studio said 1904, Bing just shrugged and went along with it. After his death a parish priest said records state May 2, 1903." Prior date given as May 2, 1904, time of 4:00 PM PST in SS #232. *World Book* Obit gives May 2, 1903. PC gives May 3, 1903, "parish records."

The profile and chart for his widow, Kathryn Grant Crosby, and the data for his daughter Mary Frances Crosby, are given in *Profiles of Women*.

CROSBY, PERCY LEO	December 8, 1891	Brooklyn, N.Y.
Cartoonist	4:00 AM EST	73W56 40N38

☉ 16-♐-01	☿ 06-♑-17	♂ 00-♏-05	♄ 29-♍-13	♆ 07-♊-25R	A 07-♏-48
☽ 11-♓-33	♀ 06-♑-17	♃ 10-♓-08	♅ 04-♏-21	♇ 07-♊-42R	M 15-♌-26

Originator of the cartoon character "Skippy." Five years of art school. Sold his first cartoons in 1923; introduced Skippy into a newspaper strip in 1925. By age 39, was making $120,000 a year and living on a 2,100-acre Virginia farm. Two marriages; three children.

C: Redding in AA, November 1936, gives the approximate time.

CROWLEY, ALEISTER	October 12, 1875	Leamington Spa, England
Mystic	11:42 PM LMT	1W40 52N15

☉ 19-♎-14	☿ 13-♏-22	♂ 22-♑-54	♄ 19-♒-31R	♆ 02-♉-00R	A 09-♌-02
☽ 22-♓-52	♀ 24-♎-26	♃ 07-♏-08	♅ 19-♌-08	♇ 23-♉-14R	M 18-♈-03

Inherited 30,000 pounds; traveled; exiled from many countries for infamous exploits in black magic, hypnotism, and lechery. Published *Equinox of the Gods* in more than a dozen volumes; wrote poetry and pornography. Insane, nearly penniless, and alone, died of cocaine and heroin on December 1, 1947.

DD: Eshelman quotes *Confessions of Aleister Crowley*, in which he gives a time of 11:00 PM to midnight; however he published a chart in *Equinox* that is set for pre-11:00 PM. Eshelman gives a speculative/rectified time of 11:42 PM from careful research. Dewey quotes the *Equinox* chart of 10:50 PM LMT. McEvers quotes LeGros in AA at 10:58 PM LMT. Alice Reichard gives 12:00 Midnight. Penfield states in M.H. Extra, January 1980, that *Equinox of the Gods* gives 10:32 PM.

CULBERTSON, ELY	August 4, 1891 NS	Ploesti, Rumania
Bridge expert	4:07 AM LMT	26E02 44N57

☉ 11-♌-23	☿ 05-♍-34	♂ 09-♌-53	♄ 15-♍-35	♆ 08-♊-39	A 02-♌-38
☽ 04-♌-25	♀ 29-♋-02	♃ 16-♓-50R	♅ 27-♎-40	♇ 08-♊-38	M 15-♈-20

Moved to U.S. after the Russian revolution of 1917 wiped out the family fortune. Began to play contract bridge professionally; won national recognition in a contest of 1931. Became a writer and editor, as well as champion. Devoted much of his later life to world peace. As well as bridge books, wrote *Total Peace* (1943).

C: CL from Dell, September 1952. (July 22, 1891 OS)

CUMMINGS, E.E.	October 14, 1894	Cambridge, Mass
Writer	5:15 AM EST	71W06 42N22

☉ 21-♎-04	☿ 14-♏-57	♂ 29-♈-41R	♄ 27-♎-11	♆ 15-♊-38R	A 12-♎-10
☽ 16-♈-49	♀ 09-♎-13	♃ 06-♋-10	♅ 14-♏-09	♇ 11-♊-35R	M 14-♋-22

American poet, famous for his use of split words, a lack of capital letters, and creative punctuation. Fiercely independent and eccentric; a happy, unashamed, one-man romantic movement. His collection, *Poems: 1923-1954,* won a special citation.

DD: PC speculative. Old-file has 12:40 PM EST.

CURIE, PIERRE May 15, 1859 Paris, France
Chemist 2:00 AM LMT 2E20 48N50

☉ 23-♉-41	☿ 29-♈-12	♂ 13-♊-40	♄ 06-♌-40	♆ 26-♓-36	A 13-♓-29
☽ 01-♏-55	♀ 18-♈-39	♃ 24-♊-17	♅ 02-♊-56	♇ 07-♉-25	M 22-♐-54

Professor of physics at the Sorbonne. Co-discoverer of radium with his wife, Marie.They shared the Nobel prize of 1903 with Henri Becquerel. Run over by a dray and killed instantly in Paris on April 19, 1906.

C: March quotes an article by G. Allen that presents a chart with MC 22 Sagittarius, Ascendant 11 Pisces 30.

The profile and speculative chart of Madame Marie Curie are given in *Profiles of Women.*

CVETIC, MATT March 4, 1909 Pittsburgh, Pa
Spy 8:09 AM EST 80W01 40N26

☉ 13-♓-20	☿ 16-♒-36	♂ 05-♑-42	♄ 09-♈-23	♆ 14-♋-26R	A 15-♈-14
☽ 15-♌-16	♀ 29-♒-20	♃ 09-♍-05R	♅ 19-♑-57	♇ 23-♊-48R	M 08-♑-10

As an FBI agent, entered the Communist Party, February 1943; worked seven years as an undercover agent, until ordered to testify at the Capitol. Under the name of Mr. Stanton, lived a double life, unknown even to his wife, who left him with their two sons.

C: McDonald quotes M.E. Knotts in an AFA bulletin.

DAGUERRE, LOUIS November 18, 1789 Cormeilles, France
Inventor 1:00 PM LMT 0E23 49N15

☉ 26-♏-42	☿ 07-♏-35	♂ 22-♌-06	♄ 16-♓-30R	♆ 24-♎-14	A 24-♒-49
☽ 15-♐-02	♀ 08-♑-51	♃ 00-♍-01	♅ 09-♌-34R	♇ 16-♒-49	M 14-♐-19

French painter who perfected the daguerreotype process of making permanent pictures. First worked with Piepce, a French physicist, and perfected the process after Piepce's death in 1833. (1789-1851)

DD: PC speculative. Old-file has 9:10 PM LMT.

DALAI-LAMA December 18, 1933 Sining, Chinghai, China
Lord of Tibet 00:41 AM Zone #3 91E41 29N43

☉ 25-♐-22	☿ 07-♐-37	♂ 21-♑-52	♄ 12-♒-58	♆ 12-♍-23R	A 23-♍-44
☽ 04-♑-11	♀ 10-♒-24	♃ 19-♎-19	♅ 23-♈-34R	♇ 24-♋-14R	M 23-♊-25

Supreme ruler until the Chinese Communists invaded his country in 1950. Tibetans believe him to be the reborn soul of his predecessor, and the Holy Men searched through the nation's children to find him in this, his 14th incarnation.

DD: AQ, Fall, 1959, from Abayakoon. AQ, Summer 1962, states the same data, adds that the "overshadowing" took place June 6, 1935, 10:10 AM, Amdo, Chinghai. *Bulletin of Astro Science,* May 1959, gives birth data of June 6, 1935, 7:10 PM IST, Chinghai Province, Kohonor Dist. *Seven Years In Tibet* by H. Harrer gives June 6, 1935.

DALEY, RICHARD J. May 15, 1902 Chicago, Ill.
Politician 4:30 AM CST 87W39 41N52

☉ 23-♉-39	☿ 11-♊-12	♂ 13-♉-21	♄ 27-♑-46R	♆ 29-♊-48	A 21-♉-36
☽ 04-♍-20	♀ 08-♈-34	♃ 16-♒-31	♅ 20-♐-20R	♇ 17-♊-35	M 29-♑-53

Democratic mayor of Chicago from 1955. One of the most powerful political leaders in the U.S., called "the last of the big-city bosses." Died December 1976, of a heart attack in his doctor's office.

DD: PC, "personal." Old-file has 4:00 AM CST.

DAMIEN, FATHER JOSEPH January 3, 1840 Tremelo, Belgium
Missionary 12:30 PM LMT 4E42 50N59

☉ 12-♑-16 ☿ 19-♐-51 ♂ 10-♒-13 ♄ 16-♐-09 ♆ 11-♒-13 A 12-♉-09
☽ 26-♐-41 ♀ 26-♏-20 ♃ 13-♏-30 ♅ 13-♓-14 ♇ 16-♈-53 M 18-♑-11

A Roman Catholic priest who gave his life to the care of lepers in a colony at Molokai, Hawaii. First sent to Hawaii as resident priest, but because of the difficulty in getting doctors, began to help. Stricken with leprosy in 1885 and died three years later.

DD: PC speculative. Old-file has 10:25 AM LMT.

DANA, RICHARD HENRY August 1, 1815 Cambridge, Mass
Writer 3:10 PM LMT 71W06 42N22

☉ 08-♌-36 ☿ 24-♋-14R ♂ 19-♈-52 ♄ 09-♒-01R ♆ 17-♐-22R A 07-♐-40
☽ 20-♊-36 ♀ 24-♍-22 ♃ 05-♎-58 ♅ 02-♐-56R ♇ 22-♓-40R M 26-♍-47

Maritime lawyer and author who wrote *Two Years before the Mast* in 1840. Also wrote *A Seaman's Friend* in 1841 to help seamen know their rights and secure justice. (1815-1882)

DD: PC speculative. Old-file has 2:50 PM LMT.

DANIELSON, THEODORE February 6, 1922 Chicago, Ill
Matricide 11:45 PM CST 87W39 41N52

☉ 17-♒-41 ☿ 00-♓-57R ♂ 24-♏-03 ♄ 07-♎-13R ♆ 14-♌-30R A 05-♏-15
☽ 12-♊-14 ♀ 17-♒-12 ♃ 18-♎-52R ♅ 08-♓-22 ♇ 08-♋-17R M 12-♌-42

Stabbed his mother to death on March 2, 1938, with a kitchen knife. His motive was noted as apparently being resentment.

C: CL from Tucker in *Astromedical Diagnosis* (1959). T.P. Davis writes, "I have Danielson's B.C., no time recorded: don't know Tucker's source."

DARIN, BOBBY May 14, 1936 New York, N.Y.
Actor, singer 5:00 AM EDT 73W57 40N45

☉ 23-♉-22 ☿ 12-♊-52 ♂ 00-♊-42 ♄ 20-♓-30 ♆ 14-♍-01R A 07-♉-53
☽ 24-♒-52 ♀ 10-♉-57 ♃ 22-♐-44R ♅ 06-♉-33 ♇ 25-♋-26 M 21-♑-15

Pop-singer with greatest hit of "Mack the Knife." Oscar nomineee in *Captain Newman, M.D. That Funny Feeling* was one of three comedies he played with his wife of the time, Sandra Dee. (1936-1937)

C: CL quotes Drew for an approximate time.

DARROW, CLARENCE April 18, 1857 Farmdale, Ohio
Lawyer 7:50 PM LMT 80W37 41N26

☉ 28-♈-55 ☿ 08-♉-06 ♂ 11-♉-42 ♄ 08-♋-47 ♆ 21-♓-32 A 12-♏-44
☽ 17-♒-48 ♀ 27-♉-53 ♃ 23-♈-52 ♅ 23-♉-31 ♇ 04-♉-57 M 22-♌-14

Famous because of cases that were the topics of daily conversation, such as the Scopes trial in which he defended a schoolteacher accused of illegally teaching the Darwinian theory of evolution, 1925. Published *The Story of my Life* (1932). (1857-1938)

DD: CL from *Astrological Review,* Autumn 1959. Old-file has 9:30 PM LMT. PC quotes SS #245 (no time given) at 8:00 PM LMT.

DARWIN, CHARLES February 12, 1908 Shrewsbury, England
Naturalist 3:00 AM LMT 2W45 52N42

☉ 22-♒-01 ☿ 10-♓-03 ♂ 22-♈-22 ♄ 25-♓-38 ♆ 12-♋-31R A 06-♐-38
☽ 25-♊-14 ♀ 27-♓-36 ♃ 06-♌-52R ♅ 15-♑-00 ♇ 22-♊-53R M 06-♎-18

Scientist whose theories of evolution through natural selection caused a revolution in biological science. A storm of debate followed the publication of *The Origin of Species* (1859); the furor increased in 1871 with *The Descent of Man.* Married in 1839; five sons. (1809-1882)

DD: Dell, April 1949. PC speculates 6:00 AM LMT, "possibly from AA, April 1949." AQ, Summer 1964, Rodgers speculates a Virgo ascendent.

DAVIS, JEFF   August 22, 1883   No place given
Hobo king   10:24 PM LMT   84W31   39N06

☉ 29-♌-39   ☿ 20-♍-25   ♂ 29-♊-23   ♄ 09-♊-19   ♆ 21-♉-06   A 25-♉-55
☽ 02-♉-25   ♀ 21-♌-52   ♃ 23-♋-46   ♅ 22-♍-13   ♇ 01-♊-12   M 04-♒-46

Wandering nomad who rode the rails, chose the free and untrammeled life as satisfactory for his tranquility and peace of mind.

C: Skeetz quotes Pryor in AA, May 1963.

DAVIS, SAMMY JR.   December 8, 1925   New York, N.Y.
Entertainer   1:20 PM EST   73W57   40N45

☉ 16-♐-10   ☿ 22-♐-58R   ♂ 16-♏-54   ♄ 20-♏-24   ♆ 24-♌-45R   A 13-♈-53
☽ 19-♍-00   ♀ 02-♒-58   ♃ 23-♑-42   ♅ 21-♓-35   ♇ 14-♋-13R   M 07-♑-23

A small package of big talent as an actor, dancer, singer, comedian, TV and night-club performer. Nominated for an Emmy as best speciality act in 1955. Versatile and talented, with wit and humor. Lost an eye in an automobile accident on November 19, 1954.

DD: LeGros in AA, October 1957. Old-file has 1:11 PM EST.

DELINGER, JACK   June 22, 1926   Oakland, Ca
Body-builder   11:22 PM PST   122W16   37N49

☉ 01-♋-04   ☿ 20-♋-41   ♂ 05-♈-39   ♄ 20-♏-10R   ♆ 22-♌-40   A 12-♓-02
☽ 27-♏-38   ♀ 23-♉-31   ♃ 27-♒-05R   ♅ 29-♓-23   ♇ 13-♋-54   M 19-♐-50

On May 21, 1949, won the contest to gain the title of Mr. America; later won Mr. Universe title.

C: CL from AFA, June 1962.

DELIUS, FREDERICK   January 29, 1862   Bradford, England
Musician   9:00 AM LMT   1W35   53N58

☉ 09-♒-16   ☿ 21-♒-12   ♂ 15-♐-36   ♄ 22-♍-01R   ♆ 29-♓-32   A 12-♓-23
☽ 29-♑-46   ♀ 14-♓-25   ♃ 26-♍-59R   ♅ 12-♊-29R   ♇ 08-♉-28   M 23-♐-54

English composer whose works reflect the influence and color of the places in which he lived — England, the American mountains and forests, and the Atlantic ocean. Subtitled an orchestral nocturne *Paris, The Song of a Great City* (1899). (1862-1934)

C: Dewey quotes Leslie Russell in *Brief Biographies*.

DEMARA, ESTERNADO WALDO   December 12, 1921   Lawrence, Mass
The Great Imposter   7:30 AM EST   71W10   42N43

☉ 19-♐-58   ☿ 11-♐-36   ♂ 21-♎-44   ♄ 06-♎-29   ♆ 15-♌-49R   A 24-♐-04
☽ 16-♉-42   ♀ 05-♐-55   ♃ 14-♎-53   ♅ 06-♓-01   ♇ 09-♋-23R   M 18-♎-26

Capable, even brilliant impersonator of other people from 1941 to 1963: a doctor, a prison warden, a Latin teacher, and more. From 1963, has been a dedicated non-denominational preacher under his own name. Biography, *The Great Imposter*, written by R. Crichton.

C: CL from Drew. PC quotes Drew for Boston.

DE MILLE, CECIL B.   August 12, 1881   Ashfield, Mass
Movie producer   5:14 AM LMT   72W48   42N31

☉ 19-♌-47   ☿ 02-♌-25   ♂ 05-♊-29   ♄ 12-♉-18   ♆ 16-♉-34   A 20-♌-52
☽ 25-♓-33   ♀ 06-♋-36   ♃ 24-♉-27   ♅ 12-♍-37   ♇ 29-♉-15   M 11-♉-56

Specialized in spectacular films with giant settings and casts of thousands. In 1949, received a special award for thirty-five years of motion picture pioneering. *The Greatest Show on Earth* won the Academny Award in 1952; others include *The Ten Commandments* and *The Sign of the Cross*. (1881-1953)

C: CL.

DEMPSEY, JACK June 24, 1895 Manassa, Colo
Boxer 11:00 PM MST 105W56 37N11

☉ 03-♋-23	☿ 12-♋-59R	♂ 08-♌-58	♄ 00-♏-36R	♆ 16-♊-12	A 09-♓-30
☽ 05-♌-17	♀ 18-♌-05	♃ 14-♋-33	♅ 16-♏-14R	♇ 11-♊-46	M 18-♐-13

Won the heavyweight boxing title in 1919 by knocking out Jess Willard in round three; lost the title to Gene Tunney, 1926. Retired to referee boxing and wrestling, 1940. Elected to the Boxing Hall of Fame, 1954. Biography *Dempsey* published in 1960.

DD: CL old data box. SS #264 gives 5:30 AM

DEPEW, CHANCEY April 23, 1834 Peekskill, N.Y.
Statesman 6:04 AM LMT 73W55 41N17

☉ 02-♉-47	☿ 05-♈-57	♂ 17-♓-48	♄ 05-♎-31R	♆ 01-♒-34	A 21-♉-04
☽ 00-♏-40	♀ 14-♉-36	♃ 14-♉-38	♅ 25-♒-58	♇ 12-♈-42	M 29-♑-50

Renowned as a corporation lawyer; president of the N.Y. Central Railroad, 1885-99; Republican U.S. senator from N.Y., 1899-1911. Well known for witty after dinner speeches. (1834-1928)

C: CL. PC quotes CL for 6:00 AM LMT.

DE SADE, MARQUIS June 2, 1740 Paris, France
Notorious sadist 9:13 PM LMT 2E20 48N50

☉ 12-♊-28	☿ 18-♉-45	♂ 24-♈-45	♄ 22-♋-06	♆ 04-♋-12	A 00-♑-04
☽ 15-♍-49	♀ 27-♋-27	♃ 17-♊-17	♅ 13-♑-51R	♇ 06-♏-06R	M 02-♏-02

From an aristocratic family; became a spoiled roue, a sexual sadist. Wrote luridly brilliant pornographic works, electrifying tales of depravity, translated into a dozen languages. Spent most of his life in prison for crimes of sado-masochistic violence.

DD: AQ, Summer 1971, Kraum speculative. Goodrich in AA, July 1967, speculates 7:15 AM LMT. PC speculates 2:00 AM LMT.

DESAI, MORARJEE February 29, 1896 No place given
Statesman 1:38 PM IST 72E00 21N00

☉ 10-♓-17	☿ 13-♒-41	♂ 27-♑-40	♄ 19-♏-06R	♆ 15-♊-15	A 02-♋-02
☽ 17-♍-32	♀ 06-♒-59	♃ 00-♌-04R	♅ 24-♏-30R	♇ 10-♊-46	M 21-♓-59

An associate and disciple of Mohandes Gandhi in India's struggle for independence. As an ardent nationalist in youth, imprisoned five times — once for seven years. Became prime minister of India on March 24, 1977, succeeding Indira Gandhi.

D: M.H., July 1977, Prem H. Joshi of India

DESCARTES, RENE March 31, 1596 Le Haye, France
Scientist 2:00 AM LMT 0W43 46N58

☉ 10-♈-32	☿ 29-♈-28	♂ 22-♊-01	♄ 02-♍-12R	♆ 16-♌-02R	A 10-♑-32
☽ 05-♉-13	♀ 05-♉-46	♃ 15-♈-18	♅ 15-♈-37	♇ 17-♈-41	M 11-♏-03

Mathematician who invented analytic geometry; philosopher who founded a concept based on masterful logic, with the beginning point of all perception based on a certainty of one's own existance. (1596-1650)

DD: PC quotes Barbault, "who believes he had Capricorn rising." Old-file has 2:15 AM LMT.

DESTINN, EMMA February 26, 1878 Prague, Czechoslovakia
Singer 3:58 PM LMT 14E26 50N05

☉ 07-♓-55	☿ 20-♒-12	♂ 16-♉-43	♄ 21-♓-11	♆ 05-♉-16	A 21-♌-19
☽ 07-♑-21	♀ 29-♒-15R	♃ 26-♑-49	♅ 26-♌-59R	♇ 23-♉-38	M 08-♉-12

Bohemian operatic soprano, noted for range and voice control as well as acting skill. Debut, 1898, in Berlin, where she sang for ten years. New York debut in 1908; eight years with the Metropolitan Opera Co; retired, 1921. (1878-1930)

DD: SS #266. Same date in *Americana*. Jansky gives 1877, 3:00 PM.

DEWEY, JOHN   October 20, 1859   Burlington, Vt
Educator   9:52 AM LMT   73W12   42N29

| ☉ 26-♎-41 | ☿ 03-♏-04 | ♂ 26-♍-07 | ♄ 24-♌-02 | ♆ 24-♓-56R | A 05-♐-54 |
| ☽ 14-♌-45 | ♀ 02-♏-36 | ♃ 24-♋-25 | ♅ 07-♊-10R | ♇ 07-♉-44R | M 26-♍-13 |

American philosopher, the most influential thinker of his day. Professor of philosophy; lecturer; author of *Democracy and Education* (1916) and *Experience and Education* (1938), among other books. (1859-1952)

C: M.E. Jones in an AFA bulletin, as "the chart I use . . ." Same data in SS #270. PC quotes SS at 9:45 AM LMT.

DIAMOND, LEGGS   July 10, 1897   Philadelphia, Pa
Gangster   2:00 AM EST   75W10   39N57

| ☉ 18-♋-13 | ☿ 11-♋-30 | ♂ 01-♍-01 | ♄ 24-♏-23R | ♆ 21-♊-04 | A 09-♊-39 |
| ☽ 24-♏-45 | ♀ 02-♊-37 | ♃ 07-♍-34 | ♅ 25-♏-13R | ♇ 14-♊-01 | M 15-♒-50 |

New York hoodlum, thief, and mobster; shot to death by rival gangsters while in bed with his show-girl lover in a hotel in Albany.

DD: SS #273. Van Norstrand in AA, February 1962, gives the same data and time, but New York City.

DICKENS, CHARLES   February 7, 1812   Portsmouth, England
Writer   7:50 PM LMT   1W05   40N48

| ☉ 17-♒-58 | ☿ 22-♑-10 | ♂ 07-♈-33 | ♄ 04-♑-22 | ♆ 13-♐-01 | A 17-♍-33 |
| ☽ 12-♐-36 | ♀ 16-♓-17 | ♃ 26-♊-29R | ♅ 23-♏-15 | ♇ 16-♓-58 | M 15-♊-32 |

Most popular and perhaps the greatest of the English novelists. His work include *Pickwick Papers* (1837), *Oliver Twist* (1839), *A Christmas Carol* (1843), and *A Tale of Two Cities* (1859). (1812-1870)

DD: Holliday quotes *The Elements of Astrology* by Dr. Broughton 1906, "data from him to Professor Wilson, an astrologer in London." Lyndoe in AA, February 1970, gives 11:59 PM LMT, "from his own statement, about midnight." *Constellations*, 1977, Lockhart quotes data in *Childhood and Youth of Charles Dickens* by Langton (1883), "about midnight." PC quotes SS #274 and computes time for 00:30 AM LMT.

DIESEL, RUDOLF   March 18, 1858   Paris, France
Engineer   3:43 PM LMT   2E20   48N50

| ☉ 27-♓-46 | ☿ 21-♓-02 | ♂ 29-♏-12 | ♄ 21-♋-26R | ♆ 22-♓-34 | A 03-♍-51 |
| ☽ 08-♉-57 | ♀ 02-♈-17 | ♃ 14-♉-44 | ♅ 26-♉-04 | ♇ 05-♉-14 | M 26-♉-19 |

German mechanical engineer who founded a factory after he developed an internal combustion machine that uses oil as fuel, successfully operative by 1897. In 1913, mysteriously disappeared from a German ship bound for London.

C: CL from *Bulletin of Astro Science*, March 1958. PC quotes CL for 3:30 PM LMT.

DIX, DOROTHY   November 18, 1861   Woodstock, Tenn
Writer   3:45 PM LMT   89W53   35N20

| ☉ 26-♏-35 | ☿ 13-♏-09R | ♂ 27-♎-53 | ♄ 20-♍-58 | ♆ 28-♓-58R | A 06-♉-25 |
| ☽ 11-♊-23 | ♀ 11-♑-55 | ♃ 23-♍-11 | ♅ 15-♊-03R | ♇ 09-♉-07R | M 22-♑-22 |

Advice columnist who pioneered the *advice to the lovelorn* columns. To support herself and her incurably ill husband, became a writer for women's pages in 1896; eventually appeared in three hundred papers with practical down-to-earth advice.

DD: Jansky quotes Penfield, states that *Dorothy Dix, Her Book* confirms the data. That book is an advice-book; gives no dates of any kind. PC gives the same date, 4:00 PM speculative. *Index To Women* gives 1879-1951. November 18, 1870, given in *Current Biography* (1940) and Obit (1952)

DIXON, JEANE   January 4, 1904   Medford, Wis
Psychic   4:45 AM CST   90W20   45N09

| ☉ 12-♑-40 | ☿ 01-♒-39 | ♂ 18-♒-03 | ♄ 08-♒-23 | ♆ 04-♋-19R | A 03-♐-08 |
| ☽ 29-♋-39 | ♀ 29-♏-11 | ♃ 18-♓-18 | ♅ 26-♐-48 | ♇ 19-♊-16R | M 22-♍-58 |

"The Seeress of Washington", writer, realtor. Psychic through dreams, visions, and the crystal ball. Gained national attention in late 1963 with her prediction of JFK's assassination.

DD: M.H., April 1977, Dorothy Moore quotes *The Witnesses* by Denis Bryan 1976, quoting the date from one of her brothers. Jan Moore writes, "We met in 1966, she was a little coy at first, then told me January 5, 1918, 4:45 AM." *A Gift of Prophesy* states "shortly before the World War Armistice." An extensive article in *National Enquirer* on October 27, 1973, has various affidavits and documents for 1904, 1910, and 1918. Apparently the lady is more concerned with the future than the past.

DOOLITTLE, JAMES   December 14, 1896   Alameda, Ca
General   4:25 PM PST   122W15   37N46

| ☉ 23-♐-36 | ☿ 02-♑-37 | ♂ 18-♊-16R | ♄ 25-♏-24 | ♆ 18-♊-46R | A 18-♊-19 |
| ☽ 26-♈-13 | ♀ 02-♒-39 | ♃ 10-♍-03 | ♅ 26-♏-30 | ♇ 12-♊-32R | M 25-♒-55 |

Air Force General, aeronautical engineer, scientist, boxer, stunt pilot, and vice president of Shell Oil Co. Awarded the congressional Medal of Honor for leading the carrier based attack on Tokyo in 1942.

C: SS #285.

DORS, DIANA   October 23, 1931   Slough, Middlesex, Eng
Actress   6:00 AM GMT   0W35   51N30

| ☉ 28-♎-52 | ☿ 01-♏-55 | ♂ 24-♏-49 | ♄ 17-♑-27 | ♆ 07-♍-20 | A 21-♎-12 |
| ☽ 22-♓-57 | ♀ 10-♏-45 | ♃ 19-♌-14 | ♅ 16-♈-55R | ♇ 22-♋-10 | M 28-♋-01 |

Blond bombshell with an ample bosom who's been playing a good-time girl since the mid-40s.

DD: Craswell quotes *Astrology* Vol 29 #4. AQR, Winter 1956, states "around sunrise at Swindon, Wilts, 'not Slough as reported.'"

DOSTEOVSKI, FYODOR   November 11, 1821 NS   Moscow, Russia
Writer   9:47 AM LMT   37E36   55N45

| ☉ 18-♏-37 | ☿ 06-♐-41R | ♂ 23-♌-08 | ♄ 21-♈-21R | ♆ 01-♑-15 | A 11-♐-35 |
| ☽ 10-♊-56 | ♀ 01-♑-02 | ♃ 22-♈-15R | ♅ 00-♑-48 | ♇ 27-♓-53R | M 18-♎-17 |

In youth, arrested and sentenced to death for political conspiracy; reprieved and sent to a Siberian labor camp for four years. Financially improvident life, but became one of Russia's great novelists. His works include *Crime and Punishment* (1866) and *The Brothers Karamazov* (1880). (1821-1881).

DD: Craswell quotes *Astrology* Vol 34, from *Le Zodique*. Same date in *Americana*. PC gives November 11, 1830, NS, 6:30 PM speculative.

DOUGLAS, DONALD WILLS JR.   April 6, 1892   Brooklyn, N.Y.
Entrepreneur   6:00 AM EST   73W56   40N38

| ☉ 17-♈-06 | ☿ 04-♉-03 | ♂ 13-♑-51 | ♄ 25-♍-13R | ♆ 06-♊-57 | A 27-♈-27 |
| ☽ 12-♌-58 | ♀ 01-♊-03 | ♃ 04-♈-57 | ♅ 04-♏-47R | ♇ 07-♊-15 | M 14-♑-59 |

American aircraft manufacturer who organized the Douglas Co. in 1920, which became the Douglas Aircraft Corp. in 1928. Designed the army planes that first flew around the world in 1924. His firm made commercial planes such as the DC-3.

D: SS #287, same data in *Illustrated Astrology*, October 1940.

DOUGLAS, MIKE August 11, 1925 Chicago, Ill
Entertainer 5:00 PM CST 87W39 41N52

☉ 18-♌-43 ☿ 09-♍-27R ♂ 29-♌-25 ♄ 08-♏-24 ♆ 22-♌-11 A 14-♑-00
☽ 25-♉-23 ♀ 17-♍-52 ♃ 13-♑-56R ♅ 24-♓-48R ♇ 13-♋-58 M 09-♏-38

Sang with the Kay Kayser band; became an emcee in clubs and theaters. TV host of his own show in the 60s and 70s; won the TV Emmy in 1967 for the best individual achievement in daytime programming.

DD: PC states "personal," adds that 1920 is also given. Same date in *Celebrity Register*. Joy Rank in AA, July 1977, gives August 11, 1920, 5:30 PM CDT.

DOUGLAS, STEPHEN A. April 23, 1813 Brandon, Vt
Politician 11:50 AM LMT 73W08 43N48

☉ 03-♉-06 ☿ 29-♈-13R ♂ 20-♑-53 ♄ 19-♑-20 ♆ 15-♐-13R A 13-♌-15
☽ 01-♒-18 ♀ 24-♈-41 ♃ 00-♌-18 ♅ 26-♏-54R ♇ 19-♓-59 M 00-♉-58

U.S. representative, 1843-47; U.S. senator, 1847-61; drafter Kansas-Nebraska Bill, 1854, which left slavery decision to the territories. Presidential nominee in 1856 and 1860; debating opponent of Abraham Lincoln, who defeated him for the presidency. (1813-1861)

C: *The Astrol Review*, October 1937, quotes Dr. Broughton's files.

DOYLE, ARTHUR CONAN May 22, 1859 Edinburgh, Scotland
Writer 4:55 AM LMT 3W10 55N55

☉ 00-♊-33 ☿ 05-♉-25 ♂ 18-♊-29 ♄ 07-♌-10 ♆ 26-♓-45 A 23-♊-09
☽ 00-♒-46 ♀ 27-♈-08 ♃ 25-♊-49 ♅ 03-♊-21 ♇ 07-♉-34 M 10-♒-36

Physician who practiced medicine until 1891. Author. Works include *History of Spiritualism*; however, best known as the creator of the modern detective story, and of the characters Sherlock Holmes and his colleague Watson. (1859-1930)

C: CL from Wemyss, *Wheel of Life* Vol 3; same data in SS #291.

DREISER, THEODORE August 27, 1871 Terre Haute, Ind
Writer 8:30 AM LMT 87W25 39N28

☉ 03-♍-50 ☿ 00-♎-15 ♂ 09-♏-24 ♄ 03-♑-22R ♆ 23-♈-50R A 10-♎-20
☽ 28-♑-33 ♀ 09-♎-24 ♃ 20-♋-51 ♅ 29-♋-07 ♇ 19-♉-52R M 11-♋-51

American realistic novelist who interpreted life frankly. Subject to early criticism, *An American Tragedy* was banned in Boston in 1925. Raised in poverty, worked in newspapers and as an editor, 1907-10. Books include *A Place in the Sun* and several autobiographical works. (1871-1945)

C: CL from AFA, March 1959. SS #294 has 8:27 AM.

DRESSLER, MARIE November 9, 1869 Cobourg, Ont. Canada
Actress 7:57 PM LMT 78W09 43N56

☉ 17-♏-43 ☿ 29-♎-51 ♂ 16-♐-29 ♄ 15-♐-58 ♆ 17-♈-23R A 11-♋-33
☽ 05-♒-32 ♀ 02-♑-12 ♃ 15-♉-41R ♅ 21-♋-55R ♇ 16-♉-58R M 17-♓-29

Debut in Mack Sennett's first feature length movie, *Tillie's Nightmare*. Won the Oscar as best actress in *Min and Bill* (1931). Nominated for the Oscar in *A Ship Comes In* (1928) and *Emma* (1932). (1869-1934)

DD: SS #295. Same date from *Astrological Reference, Famous People* and *Celebrities*. Her autobiography (1934) says, "I admit to age 63." CL quotes Kraum in NAJ, August 1934, with 1871, 7:18 PM LMT. *Astrological Index* gives 1871.

DUFF, HOWARD November 24, 1917 Bremerton, Wash
Actor 11:00 AM PST 122W38 47N34

☉ 01-♐-57 ☿ 13-♐-42 ♂ 11-♍-36 ♄ 14-♌-32 ♆ 07-♌-03R A 17-♑-23
☽ 09-♈-48 ♀ 19-♑-05 ♃ 07-♊-02R ♅ 20-♒-04 ♇ 05-♋-06R M 17-♏-59

On screen from 1947; co-starring roles in films that include *All My Sons, Lady From Texas*, and *Panic in the City*. TV guest roles; radio series, *Sam Spade*. Married Ida Lupino.

C: Holliday quotes CL.

DUHEM, JOE   August 14, 1931   Beloit, Wis
Athlete   9:30 AM CST   89W02   42N31

| ☉ 20-♌-52 | ☿ 17-♍-11 | ♂ 08-♎-04 | ♄ 17-♑-46R | ♆ 04-♍-58 | A 12-♎-07 |
| ☽ 01-♍-55 | ♀ 14-♌-11 | ♃ 06-♌-16 | ♅ 19-♈-14R | ♇ 21-♋-14 | M 14-♋-20 |

High school baseball star awarded a bonus for signing a major league contract on June 17, 1950. His selection by scouts the result of steady, hard plugging away on the field.

C: Skeetz quotes G. Allen in Dell, March 1955.

DUKE, JAMES BUCHANAN   December 23, 1856   Durham, N.C.
Industrialist   11:00 PM LMT   78W54   36N00

| ☉ 02-♑-37 | ☿ 10-♑-36 | ♂ 13-♒-07 | ♄ 11-♋-25R | ♆ 17-♓-50 | A 19-♍-58 |
| ☽ 25-♏-48 | ♀ 10-♒-59 | ♃ 00-♈-47 | ♅ 21-♉-33R | ♇ 03-♉-46R | M 18-♊-51 |

American businessman and philanthropist who organized the American Tobacco Company in 1890. Duke University was named after him, and he established endowments and donated large funds. (1856-1925)

DD: PC speculative. Old-file has 5:15 AM LMT.

DULLES, JOHN FOSTER   February 25, 1888   Washington, D.C.
Statesman   6:58 AM EST   77W02   38N54

| ☉ 06-♓-22 | ☿ 19-♓-06R | ♂ 29-♎-50 | ♄ 00-♌-39R | ♆ 27-♉-22 | A 08-♓-58 |
| ☽ 10-♌-04 | ♀ 01-♒-44 | ♃ 05-♐-20 | ♅ 16-♎-43R | ♇ 03-♊-03 | M 18-♐-17 |

Secretary of state, 1953-59, under President Eisenhower. Held diplomatic positions under Presidents Wilson, Roosevelt, and Truman. His grandfather, John W. Foster, and an uncle, Robert Lansing, both served as secretary of state. (1888-1959)

DD: CL from *Bulletin of Astro Science*, January 1958. PC adds that Dell, February 1960, shows a chart with 12 Scorpio Ascendant = 11:11 PM EST.

DU MAURIER, GEORGE   March 6, 1834   Paris, France
Artist, writer   5:50 AM LMT   2E20   48N50

| ☉ 15-♓-12 | ☿ 01-♈-59 | ♂ 10-♒-33 | ♄ 09-♎-05R | ♆ 00-♒-41 | A 21-♒-37 |
| ☽ 28-♑-40 | ♀ 14-♓-46 | ♃ 04-♉-01 | ♅ 23-♒-50 | ♇ 11-♈-34 | M 12-♐-27 |

English artist who was a regular contributor of drawings to *Punch*; also illustrated many books. Writer, whose most famous novels were *Peter Ibbetson* and *Tribly*. Early loss of his left eye led to failing sight. (1834-1896)

DD: Chart pictured in Adams' *One Hundred Horoscopes*. SS #300 has 5:47 AM. Old-file has 5:20 AM LMT. BJA, December 1925, Bailey gives 5:45 AM LMT.

DURER, ALBRECHT   May 30, 1471 NS   Nuremberg, Germany
Artist   10:25 AM LMT   11E05   49N27

| ☉ 08-♊-28 | ☿ 02-♋-12 | ♂ 26-♌-13 | ♄ 08-♋-48 | ♆ 17-♏-52R | A 26-♌-48 |
| ☽ 08-♌-31 | ♀ 03-♊-18 | ♃ 05-♑-39R | ♅ 07-♏-23R | ♇ 18-♍-03 | M 16-♉-21 |

Painter, engraver, and designer; one of the foremost German artists of the Renaissance, who combined a love of the ancient world with a deep Christian spirit. Became the favorite painter of Emperor Maximilian I. (1471-1528)

C: Fagan in AA, December 1964, states that the horoscope was calculated by Bishop Lucas Gauricus and included in his *Tractatus Astrologicus*. Same chart pictured by Adams, *One Hundred Horoscopes*. (May 21, 1471 OS)

DUVALIER, FRANCOIS April 14, 1907 Port au Prince, Haiti
"Papa Doc" 7:40 AM LMT 72W20 18N33

☉ 23-♈-25 ☿ 25-♓-54 ♂ 05-♑-50 ♄ 21-♓-58 ♆ 10-♋-00 A 25-♉-34
☽ 13-♉-37 ♀ 14-♓-38 ♃ 04-♋-26 ♅ 12-♑-43 ♇ 22-♊-00 M 14-♒-04

Haitian dictator who practiced medicine for ten years before going into politics. Became president in 1957; by 1964 declared it to be a lifetime post. His regime was corruption-ridden, terroristic, authoritarian. Died in 1971; succeeded by his 19-year-old son.

DD: PC speculative. Old-file has 7:30 AM LMT.

DVORAK, ANTONIN September 8, 1841 Nelahozeves, Czech
Musician 11:00 AM LMT 14E30 50N25

☉ 15-♍-32 ☿ 14-♍-31 ♂ 01-♐-05 ♄ 26-♐-32 ♆ 14-♒-52R A 14-♏-17
☽ 13-♊-18 ♀ 04-♌-43 ♃ 11-♐-36 ♅ 22-♓-38R ♇ 20-♈-32R M 00-♍-13

Composer, teacher, and violinist, who introduced the concerto form into Czech music. Wrote nine symphonies. His Slavonic Dances and Rhapsodies highly popular, as well as *The New World Symphony*. (1841-1904)

DD: PC states, "recorded." Old-file has 8:30 PM LMT.

DWARF January 8, 1909 Huntington Park, Ca
Male 2:00 AM PST 118W14 33N58

☉ 17-♑-31 ☿ 26-♑-46 ♂ 28-♏-52 ♄ 04-♈-19 ♆ 15-♋-40R A 11-♏-00
☽ 08-♌-09 ♀ 20-♐-36 ♃ 14-♍-24R ♅ 17-♑-02 ♇ 24-♊-24R M 16-♌-37

Two feet tall; head and body normal; short arms and legs.

C: CL old file.

EAGLETON, THOMAS September 4, 1929 St. Louis, Mo
Politician 3:00 AM CST 90W12 38N37

☉ 11-♍-20 ☿ 06-♎-48 ♂ 08-♎-41 ♄ 23-♐-56 ♆ 01-♍-30 A 10-♌-08
☽ 23-♍-05 ♀ 04-♌-35 ♃ 14-♊-51 ♅ 10-♈-29R ♇ 19-♋-12 M 29-♈-53

Senator from Missouri; vice-presidential running mate of George McGovern, 1972. Had been hospitalized and received shock treatment for depression, a fact that came out disastrously when he was running for public office.

DD: Eshelman in AA, December 1972: "Three different sources give times that span an hour, 3:00 AM is the middle time given."

ECKNER, DR. HUGO August 10, 1868 Flensburg, Germany
Aeronautical engineer 10:30 AM LMT 9E25 54N44

☉ 17-♌-59 ☿ 01-♌-00 ♂ 27-♊-22 ♄ 29-♏-06 ♆ 17-♈-13R A 17-♎-58
☽ 04-♉-43 ♀ 16-♋-15 ♃ 14-♈-09R ♅ 15-♋-13 ♇ 17-♉-02 M 24-♋-43

Airship pioneer, who helped Count Von Zeppelin's firm to develop the rigid airships. Piloted the Graf Zeppelin flight around the world, 1929. Commanded the Hindenberg, which burned May 6, 1937, and virtually ended rigid airship travel. (1868-1954)

DD: WEMYSS F/N #121, "according to *Astrosophie* December 1932." Hill in *Student Astrologer*, August 1936, gives 10:22 AM LMT.

EDDY, NELSON June 29, 1901 Providence, R.I.
Singer 9:55 PM EST 71W24 41N49

☉ 07-♋-36 ☿ 26-♋-00 ♂ 22-♍-26 ♄ 13-♑-31R ♆ 29-♊-17 A 25-♒-41
☽ 16-♐-14 ♀ 23-♋-46 ♃ 08-♑-15R ♅ 13-♐-58R ♇ 17-♊-40 M 11-♐-23

A baritone, who appeared with soprano Jeannette MacDonald in musical films of the 30s and 40s, including *Rose Marie* (1936) and *New Moon* (1940). Successful radio career after starring in sixteen films; became a night club entertainer. (1901-1967)

DD: CL from SS #309 (no time given.) Old-file has 10:20 PM EST. Scarsella has 9:28 PM EST, from Baird quoting Roberta Wilson.

EISENHOWER, DWIGHT D.   October 14, 1890   Denison, Texas
Statesman   5:19 PM LMT   96W33   33N45

☉ 21-♎-35	☿ 03-♎-31	♂ 14-♑-05	♄ 12-♍-44	♆ 06-♊-29R	A 20-♈-02
☽ 03-♏-42	♀ 06-♐-07	♃ 02-♒-46	♅ 26-♎-44	♇ 07-♊-39R	M 12-♑-09

One of the most popular and influential statesmen in history. As an Army general, commander in chief of the Allied Forces in N. Africa; led the invasion of Sicily and Italy. U.S. president from 1953-61 — the first Republican in the White House in twenty years. (1890-1969)

DD: *Horoscopes of U.S. Presidents* by D.C. Doane. AA, July 1952, Gleadow states, "Said to have been born after a thunderstorm in the late afternoon or early evening, rectified to 6:00 PM." AQ, Winter 1952, gives "5:54 PM rectified." AQ, Spring 1953, Gleadow states, "Given time of late afternoon, rectified to 5:11 PM." PC quotes DCD for 5:45 PM CST, and Dell, June 1948 and February 1953, for 6:30 PM.

EISENHOWER, MAMIE   November 14, 1896   Boone, Iowa
First Lady   1:00 PM CST   93W53   42N04

☉ 22-♏-57	☿ 14-♏-54	♂ 28-♊-15R	♄ 21-♏-53	♆ 19-♊-36R	A 18-♒-54
☽ 21-♓-27	♀ 25-♐-52	♃ 07-♍-42	♅ 24-♏-41	♇ 13-♊-06R	M 07-♐-18

Daughter of a well-to-do meat packer. Met Dwight Eisenhower in 1915; married on July 1, 1916. Of their two sons, the first died at age 3; the second, John, went to West Point and served in World War II. (1896-1979)

DD: PC quotes AA, 1956. Old-file has 12:45 PM CST.

ELGAR, SIR EDWARD   June 2, 1857   Worcester, England
Musician   2:30 PM LMT   2W13   52N11

☉ 11-♊-56	☿ 10-♊-01R	♂ 13-♊-13	♄ 13-♋-07	♆ 22-♓-33	A 12-♎-56
☽ 15-♎-59	♀ 11-♉-29	♃ 04-♉-07	♅ 26-♉-04	♇ 05-♉-56	M 17-♋-04

British composer best known for *Pomp and Circumstance*, a set of five marches. Largely self-taught; brought new life to the choral form. Also wrote two symphonies, a violin concerto, and a cello concerto. (1857-1934)
DD: PC speculative. Old-file has 2:00 AM LMT.

ELIOT, T.S.   September 26, 1888   St. Louis, Mo.
Writer   7:45 AM CST   90W12   38N37

☉ 03-♎-53	☿ 26-♎-34	♂ 10-♐-43	♄ 16-♌-44	♆ 02-♊-12R	A 25-♎-41
☽ 14-♊-22	♀ 24-♎-38	♃ 02-♐-17	♅ 16-♎-45	♇ 05-♊-53R	M 29-♋-40

An American influential poet of his time; an essayist and a playwright; awarded the Nobel prize for literature in 1948 for his work in modern poetry. Became an Anglo-Catholic in religion, a classicist in literature, and a royalist in politics.

DD: Watts in AQ, Winter 1955. PC speculates 4:00 AM CST. Old-file has 1:45 AM CST.

ELLIS, HAVELOCK   February 2, 1859   Croydon, Surray, England
Writer   8:30 AM LMT   0W06   51N22

☉ 13-♒-02	☿ 20-♑-58	♂ 01-♈-08	♄ 08-♌-33R	♆ 23-♓-08	A 05-♓-44
☽ 05-♒-31	♀ 28-♐-19	♃ 11-♊-33R	♅ 29-♉-27R	♇ 05-♉-37	M 20-♐-21

Qualified as a physician but devoted his life to psychology. Wrote a seven-volume *Studies in the Psychology of Sex* (1897-1928), also *The Psychology of Conflict* (1919), and *The Dance of Life* (1923). (1859-1939)

DD: AQ, Winter 1934; same data from A. Rondell in AA, April 1943. Adams pictures a chart for 8:15 AM LMT; same data in SS #319.

ELLIS, RUTH October 9, 1926 Rhyl, N. Wales
Murderess 6:41 PM GMT 3W20 53N19

| ☉ 15-♎-43 | ☿ 29-♎-48 | ♂ 18-♉-38R | ♄ 23-♏-48 | ♆ 26-♌-17 | A 24-♉-07 |
| ☽ 17-♏-52 | ♀ 04-♎-53 | ♃ 17-♒-21R | ♅ 26-♓-44R | ♇ 15-♋-56 | M 22-♑-43 |

Unwed mother at 17; short marriage, 1950. Second child. Affair with racing driver, David Blakely, who took her money and beat her up, causing miscarriages in 1954 and 1955. Jealous of his affairs, she shot four bullets into him on April 10, 1955. Executed, July 13, 1955.

C: Skeetz quotes Tucker in AA, August 1963.

ENGELS, FRIEDRICH November 28, 1820 Barmen, Germany
Communist founder 00:48 AM LMT 7E13 51N17

| ☉ 05-♐-45 | ☿ 22-♐-25R | ♂ 17-♐-16 | ♄ 06-♈-53R | ♆ 29-♐-41 | A 22-♍-06 |
| ☽ 09-♍-52 | ♀ 24-♎-43 | ♃ 14-♓-02 | ♅ 27-♐-39 | ♇ 26-♓-36R | M 19-♊-43 |

Met Marx in the early 1840s; collaborated in the research and writing of *Das Capital*, the fundamental textbook of modern communism. A newspaper writer at 18, became a liberal activist; wrote the *Communist Manifesto* (1848). (1820-1895)

DD: Rudhyar in AA, May 1938. PC speculates 10:30 PM LMT.

ERHARD, WERNER September 5, 1935 Philadelphia, Pa
Founder of est 11:25 PM EST 75W10 30N57

| ☉ 12-♍-37 | ☿ 04-♎-06 | ♂ 23-♏-06 | ♄ 06-♓-23R | ♆ 14-♍-15 | A 11-♊-54 |
| ☽ 13-♐-06 | ♀ 16-♍-08R | ♃ 17-♏-50 | ♅ 05-♉-15R | ♇ 26-♋-50 | M 17-♒-56 |

Consciousness movement leader, entrepreneur-guru, head and founder of est, multi-million dollar merchandiser of enlightenment. Studied the disciplines of east and west; inaugerated est on October 4, 1971, in San Francisco.

DD: Terry Krall quotes *Werner Erhardt* by W.W. Bartley (1978), p. 4, "from his mother." M.H.,July 1976, Perkins states "data from his wife" of 12:00 Noon EST.

EUGENIE, QUEEN May 5, 1826 Granada, Spain
Royalty 11:55 AM LMT 3W35 37N10

| ☉ 14-♉-25 | ☿ 28-♈-20R | ♂ 14-♏-08R | ♄ 20-♊-09 | ♆ 13-♑-54R | A 20-♌-36 |
| ☽ 27-♈-15 | ♀ 28-♉-45 | ♃ 04-♍-30 | ♅ 24-♑-05R | ♇ 04-♈-39 | M 14-♉-03 |

Empress of France as the wife of Napoleon III, whom she married in 1853. Noted for beauty, charm, and great extravagance. After 1870, forced to live in exile. (1826-1920)

DD: SS #322. Old-file has 12:35 PM LMT.

EVANS, CHRIS February 19, 1847 No place given
Outlaw 11:20 AM LMT 73W15 42N59

| ☉ 00-♓-27 | ☿ 03-♓-01 | ♂ 06-♑-28 | ♄ 03-♓-00 | ♆ 27-♒-56 | A 12-♊-59 |
| ☽ 28-♈-49 | ♀ 16-♓-07 | ♃ 07-♊-13 | ♅ 11-♈-51 | ♇ 24-♈-15 | M 16-♒-32 |

Notorious desperado of his period, as a California bandit, train robber, and highwayman.

C: M.A., February 1896.

EYTHE, WILLIAM April 7, 1918 Mars, Pa
Actor 2:00 AM EWT 80W01 40N42

| ☉ 16-♈-37 | ☿ 05-♉-44 | ♂ 16-♍-04R | ♄ 07-♌-37R | ♆ 04-♌-20R | A 02-♑-34 |
| ☽ 21-♒-16 | ♀ 01-♓-12 | ♃ 08-♊-47 | ♅ 26-♒-29 | ♇ 03-♋-31 | M 26-♎-37 |

In youth acted in Canada, New York, and on Broadway in *The Moon Is Down*, which led to a movie test. Played in *The Ox-Bow Incident* (1942), *Song of Bernadette* (1943), and *Centennial Summer* (1945), among other films.

C: Skeetz quotes Blanca Holmes in AA, May 1946.

FALCONER, WILLIAM   February 21, 1732 NS   Edinburgh, Scotland
Naval poet   10:39 PM LMT   3W10   55N55
☉ 02-♓-38   ☿ 06-♒-01   ♂ 22-♏-56   ♄ 02-♈-37   ♆ 14-♊-40R   A 27-♎-01
☽ 07-♑-25   ♀ 28-♓-35   ♃ 08-♎-41R   ♅ 10-♐-03   ♇ 17-♎-22R   M 08-♌-25

Went to sea as a boy; survived a shipwreck of the Britannia off the coast of Greece, 1750; wrote a long poem *The Shipwreck* (1762) that was widely praised. Also compiled *Universal Marine Dictionary* (1769). Died in 1769 on the Aurora, that was lost off the coast of Mozambique. (Born on the same day as George Washington).

C: WEMYSS F/N #10, "time unknown, speculative."

FALLON, WILLIAM F.   January 23, 1886   New York, N.Y.
Lawyer   11:50 PM EST   73W57   40N45
☉ 04-♒-11   ☿ 14-♑-33   ♂ 25-♍-13   ♄ 02-♋-44R   ♆ 22-♉-48R   A 25-♎-18
☽ 28-♍-09   ♀ 07-♓-42   ♃ 05-♎-59R   ♅ 07-♎-39R   ♇ 01-♊-13R   M 29-♋-49

Famous New York criminal lawyer, who had three motion pictures based on his flamboyant career. Died in 1927 from a heart attack; a heavy drinker.

C: CL.

FARRELL, CHARLES   August 9, 1905   Walpole, Mass
Actor   9:05 AM EST   71W15   42N09
☉ 16-♌-17   ☿ 12-♍-08   ♂ 23-♏-32   ♄ 00-♓-33R   ♆ 09-♋-18   A 05-♎-47
☽ 07-♐-56   ♀ 03-♋-35   ♃ 03-♊-04   ♅ 00-♑-38R   ♇ 22-♊-23   M 06-♋-47

Long and durable Hollywood career in films. Started the Tennis Club with Ralph Bellamy in Palm Springs in 1931; built it into the Raquet Club; sold on January 9, 1958 for $1 million. In February 1959, with his wife joined Alcoholics Anonymous.

C: CL old file.

FAULKNER, WILLIAM   September 25, 1897   New Albany, Miss
Writer   11:00 PM CST   89W00   34N29
☉ 03-♎-22   ☿ 26-♍-01R   ♂ 20-♎-37   ♄ 26-♏-51   ♆ 22-♊-33R   A 07-♋-43
☽ 28-♍-28   ♀ 29-♌-28   ♃ 23-♍-29   ♅ 26-♏-12   ♇ 14-♊-42R   M 20-♓-29

American novelist; awarded the 1949 Nobel prize in literature, and the Pulitzer prize for his novel *The Fable* (1954). First published in 1926. Films made from his books include *Today We Live* (1933), *The Long Hot Summer* (1958), and *The Sound and the Fury* (1959). (1897-1962)

C: PC quotes *Faulkner* by Joseph Blotner, "which states very late at night." That biography states on p. 62, "The doctor emerged from Maud Faulkner's room at 11:00 PM to tell her husband he was the father of a boy." LMR suggests that the time be rectified to an earlier time than 11:00 PM.

FAYE, ALICE   May 4/5, 1912   New York, N.Y.
Actress   Midnight EST   73W57   40N45
☉ 14-♉-19   ☿ 20-♈-22   ♂ 16-♋-35   ♄ 22-♉-18   ♆ 21-♋-18   A 21-♑-59
☽ 28-♐-08   ♀ 27-♈-43   ♃ 13-♐-42R   ♅ 03-♒-27   ♇ 27-♊-29   M 16-♏-13

Film queen of the 30s and 40s, called "America's Singing Sweetheart." Named a correspondent in Rudy Valley's divorce suit. Later married Tony Martin, and then Phil Harris; two children.

DD: Pryor in AFA, October 1971. Same data printed by Sidney Skolsky in Hollywood *Citizen News*, February 13, 1940; same data in SS #333. *Astrological Reference* gives May 5, 1912; *Astrological Index* gives May 5, 1915.

FELLINI, FEDERICO   January 20, 1920   Remini, Italy
Director   9:00 PM MET   12E35   44N03
☉ 29-♑-29   ☿ 19-♑-09   ♂ 25-♎-35   ♄ 10-♍-57R   ♆ 10-♌-27R   A 15-♍-48
☽ 25-♑-01   ♀ 19-♐-34   ♃ 14-♌-54R   ♅ 29-♒-54   ♇ 06-♋-17R   M 12-♊-55

Began as a gagman and scenarist; met Rossellini, 1944; collaborated for eight years. Scripted the Oscar winning *Open City* (1947); directed *La Strada* (1954), *La Dolce Vita* (1961), and *Satyricon* (1970). Thrives on chaos and confusion.

A: Lockhart quotes Pauline Messina in Dell, August 1965. 9:00 PM MET confirmed from birth record by Ciro Discepolo.

FIELD, MARSHALL	August 18, 1834	Conway, Mass
Entrepreneur	10:00 PM LMT	72W42 42N31

☉ 25-♌-36	☿ 08-♌-10	♂ 12-♊-21	♄ 08-♎-05	♆ 29-♑-31R	A 15-♉-05
☽ 23-♒-03	♀ 06-♎-08	♃ 08-♊-52	♅ 24-♒-32R	♇ 13-♈-33R	M 25-♑-02

Founder of a family fortune as a department-store owner and through investments in real estate. The family continued to be prominent in merchandising, publishing, and philanthropy. (1834-1906)

DD: PC speculative. Old-file has 6:00 PM LMT.

FINCH, DR. BERNARD	January 7, 1918	Covina, Ca
Murderer	4:41 AM PST	117W52 34N05

☉ 16-♑-26	☿ 07-♑-01R	♂ 29-♍-01	♄ 12-♌-59R	♆ 06-♌-15R	A 13-♐-47
☽ 09-♏-11	♀ 25-♒-26	♃ 02-♊-05R	♅ 21-♒-41	♇ 04-♋-15R	M 28-♍-32

Physician. Hired Carole Tregoff at his clinic December 1955; began an affair. On July 18, 1959, shot his wife in the back; left her on the lawn. Two trials with hung juries; April 6, 1961, both Finch and Tregoff sentenced to life imprisonment.

C: CL from news clippings, 1959-61.

FLANAGAN, EDWARD	July 13, 1886	Roscommon, Ireland
Catholic priest	6:00 PM LMT	8W15 53N30

☉ 21-♋-13	☿ 17-♌-21	♂ 06-♎-27	♄ 13-♋-15	♆ 27-♉-13	A 17-♐-49
☽ 24-♐-29	♀ 15-♊-50	♃ 29-♍-43	♅ 04-♎-03	♇ 03-♊-37	M 23-♎-18

Came to the U.S. in 1904; went to University and became a priest in Nebraska. Became interested in juveniles who were homeless, troubled, or deprived; in 1917, founded Boy's Town. (1886-1948)

DD: PC speculative. Old-file has 6:15 PM LMT.

FLEMING, IAN	May 28, 1908	London, England
Writer	00:10 AM GMT	0W06 51 N31

☉ 06-♊-15	☿ 26-♊-43	♂ 03-♋-32	♄ 07-♈-43	♆ 13-♋-11	A 12-♒-16
☽ 10-♉-27	♀ 16-♋-35	♃ 08-♌-23	♅ 16-♑-23R	♇ 23-♊-51	M 09-♐-14

British writer of adventure fiction, whose tongue-in-cheek novels about the fantastic exploits of James Bond won him international fame and a series of successful movies. His other books include the children's story *Chitty-Chitty-Bang-Bang*. (1908-1964)

DD: PC speculative. Old-file has 3:50 AM GMT.

FLICK, FREDERICK	July 10, 1883	Ernsdorf-Kreuztal, Germany
Entrepreneur	11:00 PM LMT approx	8E00 50N57

☉ 18-♋-15	☿ 29-♊-22	♂ 00-♊-17	♄ 05-♊-45	♆ 20-♉-33	A 08-♈-10
☽ 03-♎-05	♀ 28-♊-50	♃ 14-♋-24	♅ 20-♍-04	♇ 00-♊-46	M 03-♑-13

German industrialist, who had a spectacular career at an early age. Recouped 75% of his World War II losses to become one of the most important industrialists on a grand scale in West Germany.

C: Luc de Marre quotes Ebertin, 1960; reference time from Muller-Schilback, Kredenbach, no source.

FOKKER, ANTHONY	April 6, 1890	Kediri, Java
Engineer	7:00 AM LMT	106E45 6S30

☉ 16-♈-08	☿ 12-♈-35	♂ 11-♐-29	♄ 27-♌-28R	♆ 02-♊-33	A 30-♈-00
☽ 23-♎-30	♀ 27-♈-45	♃ 07-♒-44	♅ 25-♎-03R	♇ 05-♊-20	M 27-♑-10

Pilot and aircraft manufacturer. Moved to Germany at 20; established his first manufacturing plant near Berlin within two years. Designed monoplanes, bi-planes, and tri-planes; supplied aircraft for Germany in World War I. (1890-1939)

C: *World Astrology*, April 1940, Benjamine states, "It is said that his biography gives this data." Same data in SS #345. CL states same data from UP News Obit, December 31, 1941.

FONDA, HENRY	May 16, 1905	Grand Island, Neb
Actor	2:00 AM CST	98W21 40N55

☉ 24-♉-46	☿ 00-♉-19	♂ 14-♏-47R	♄ 02-♓-15	♆ 06-♋-20	A 04-♓-28
☽ 18-♎-55	♀ 28-♈-23R	♃ 15-♉-59	♅ 03-♑-41R	♇ 20-♊-34	M 16-♐-12

Top talented stage and screen star for many years. Nominated for an Oscar for *The Grapes of Wrath* (1940). Star of TV series *The Smith Family*. Hasn't seen two-thirds of his films; said he'd "be embarrassed." Married five times; his second wife, Frances Brokaw, the mother of Jane and Peter, was a suicide in 1950.

DD: Holliday from AFA, September 1956. Kraum in *Best of NAJ*, 1979, gives May 19, 1905, 2:00 AM, "private source." *Americana* has May 16, 1905.

FORD, HENRY	July 30, 1863	Greenfield, Mich
Entrepreneur	2:22 PM LMT	85W15 43N11

☉ 07-♌-05	☿ 03-♌-11	♂ 28-♌-07	♄ 01-♎-33	♆ 06-♈-00R	A 26-♏-58
☽ 10-♒-53	♀ 22-♍-18	♃ 20-♎-26	♅ 23-♊-30	♇ 12-♉-18	M 12-♍-03

Automobile manufacturer who developed the mass-produced Model T car and sold it at a price the average person could afford. Sold more than 15 million cars from 1908 to 1927. Began as a machinist; built a gasoline engine, 1893; organized Ford Motor Co., 1903. (1863-1947)

DD: CL from Benjamine; same data in SS #347. *Circle* #281 states, "Shortly after 2:00 PM from *Henry Ford's Own Story* by R.W. Lane." That biography, on p. 3 states, " . . . the rain stopped about 2 o'clock in the afternoon . . . later William Ford came out of the house, grinning a little . . . it's a boy."

Lyndoe in AA, October 1960, gives "approximately 1:45 PM", adds, "Some reference books give just after 2:00 PM but this is not the timing Mr. Ford gave me personally." PC quotes *Young Henry Ford* by Sidney Olson at 7:00 AM LMT: LMR has been unable to locate that biography.

FORD, HENRY II	September 4, 1917	Detroit, Mich
Heir	7:15 AM EST	83W03 42N20

☉ 11-♍-22	☿ 04-♎-00	♂ 25-♋-01	♄ 09-♌-01	♆ 05-♌-57	A 25-♍-07
☽ 23-♈-28	♀ 15-♎-38	♃ 10-♊-25	♅ 20-♒-57R	♇ 05-♋-20	M 24-♊-15

Grandson of the founder of Ford Motor Co.; eldest son of Edsel Bryant Ford. When his father died in 1943, became vice-president of the corporation; took over the presidency from his grandfather in September 1945.

DD: PC speculative. Old-file has 7:10 AM EST.

FORRESTAL, JAMES	February 15, 1892	Beacon, N.Y.
Statesman	2:30 PM EST	73W58 41N30

☉ 26-♒-38	☿ 12-♒-01	♂ 13-♐-40	♄ 28-♍-58R	♆ 06-♊-15	A 22-♋-29
☽ 00-♎-06	♀ 02-♈-07	♃ 22-♓-49	♅ 06-♏-04R	♇ 06-♊-52R	M 04-♈-09

Undersecretary of the Navy, 1940-44; secretary of the Navy, 1944-47; U.S. secretary of defense, July 1947 to March 1949. Resigned in 1949 from overwork and exhaustion; suicide on May 22, 1949.

C: G. Allen in AA, May 1964. Dewey has February 14, 1892; February 15 check in *Americana* and in *New Century Cyclopedia*.

FORTE, FABIAN February 6, 1943 Philadelphia, Pa
Singer, actor 6:56 AM LMT 75W10 39N57
☉ 16-♒-50 ☿ 24-♑-58 ♂ 07-♑-49 ♄ 05-♊-35 ♆ 01-♎-45R A 12-♒-21
☽ 07-♓-52 ♀ 06-♓-24 ♃ 16-♋-58R ♅ 00-♊-34R ♇ 05-♌-52R M 01-♐-51

Idolized pop singer with the young crowd; first film, 1959. Movies include *Hound-Dog Man*, *Ride the Wild Surf*, *Pretty Boy Floyd*, more.

C: CL quotes Drew who says sunrise.

FRIML, RUDOLF December 7, 1879 Prague, Czech
Musician 2:30 AM LMT 14E26 50N05
☉ 14-♐-37 ☿ 22-♐-30R ♂ 13-♉-37R ♄ 08-♈-59R ♆ 09-♉-47R A 16-♎-27
☽ 17-♍-37 ♀ 27-♎-51 ♃ 05-♓-17 ♅ 08-♍-59 ♇ 26-♉-05R M 21-♋-14

Composer of such highly successful operettas as *The Firefly, Rose Marie,* and *The Vagabond King.* Wrote much light, pleasing music. Studied piano and composition in youth and came to the U.S. in 1901 as an accompanist and concert pianist.

DD: PC, "personal." Old-file has 2:00 AM LMT.

FROHMAN, DANIEL August 22, 1851 Sandusky, Ohio
Entrepreneur 2:00 AM LMT 82W42 41N27
☉ 28-♌-34 ☿ 25-♍-26 ♂ 25-♊-00 ♄ 04-♉-18R ♆ 08-♓-07R A 19-♋-23
☽ 26-♊-04 ♀ 18-♌-05 ♃ 20-♎-02 ♅ 04-♉-19R ♇ 00-♉-44R M 00-♈-01

As a showman, one of America's greatest theatrical managers for sixty years, mostly in New York City. (1851-1940)

C: SS #360.

FROST, ROBERT March 26, 1874 San Francisco, Ca
Writer 7:00 AM LMT 122W26 37N47
☉ 05-♈-48 ☿ 22-♓-17R ♂ 03-♉-43 ♄ 11-♒-38 ♆ 27-♈-24 A 00-♉-04
☽ 25-♋-47 ♀ 13-♈-33 ♃ 25-♍-43R ♅ 06-♌-35R ♇ 20-♉-15 M 17-♑-26

Often ranked as the leading American poet of his generation. Won the Pulitzer prize four times — in 1924, '31, '37, and '43. His first book published when he was 32. Supported himself by teaching and farming. (1874-1963)

DD: PC speculative. Old-file has 4:20 AM LMT. Date verified in *Amy* by Jean Gould, 1975.

FULBRIGHT, JAMES W. April 9, 1905 Summit, Mo
Politician 4:56 AM CST 90W43 37N57
☉ 18-♈-55 ☿ 06-♉-35 ♂ 24-♏-48R ♄ 29-♒-39 ♆ 05-♋-31 A 00-♈-30
☽ 08-♊-21 ♀ 14-♉-29R ♃ 07-♉-14 ♅ 04-♑-14R ♇ 19-♊-55 M 00-♑-16

Rhodes scholar; president of the University of Arkansas, 1939-41. U.S. senator from Arkansas; sponsored the Fulbright Act, adopted in 1946, which provides funds for an exchange of students from the U.S. and other countries.

C: Holliday from CL.

FURTWANGLER, WILHELM January 25, 1886 Berlin, Germany
Musician 9:00 PM MET 13E25 52N30
☉ 05-♒-50 ☿ 16-♑-54 ♂ 25-♍-14 ♄ 02-♋-37R ♆ 22-♉-48R A 21-♍-58
☽ 20-♎-47 ♀ 07-♓-58 ♃ 05-♎-57R ♅ 07-♎-38R ♇ 01-♊-12R M 19-♊-24

Noted German conductor, who directed orchestras in European cities from 1911 to 1922. Then became permanent conductor of the Berlin Philharmonic and the Leipzig Orchestra. (1886-1954)

DD: Edward Strater in AFA, May 1954, from *L'Astrologie Moderne*. T. Joseph quotes Wangemann for 8:10 PM Heidelberg.

GABLE, CLARK February 1, 1901 Cadiz, Ohio
Actor 5:30 AM CST 81W00 40N16

☉ 11-♒-57	☿ 19-♒-25	♂ 10-♍-07R	♄ 11-♑-18	♆ 26-♊-46R	A 20-♑-57
☽ 15-♋-56	♀ 19-♑-57	♃ 02-♑-44	♅ 15-♐-52	♇ 15-♊-49R	M 14-♏-57

Top Hollywood star, called "The King." Stock company at 19. Broadway in *What Price Glory* (1924); first film *The Painted Desert* (1930). Served in the U.S. Air Corp in World War II. Later films include *Mutiny on the Bounty, It Happened One Night,* and *Gone with the Wind.* (1901-1960)

DD: PC quotes *Gable* by Jean Garceau. *Dear Mr. Gable* by Jean Garceau (1961) states on p. 18, " . . . made his entry into the world at 5:30 that morning." *Gable* by Chester Williams (1968) gives the date, "as a blizzard raged outside," no time. Dewey quotes "doctor's data," given in *The King* by Samuels, of 9:15 PM CST: LMR has been unable to locate that biography. McEvers quotes Jan Moore, "from doctor's records, 3:30 AM CST." CL gives 8:50 PM LMT. SS #361 gives 9:00 PM. Kraum's personal notebook has 4:40 AM.

The profile and chart of his second wife, Carole Lombard, are given in *Profiles of Women*.

GAGARIN, YURI March 9, 1934 Smolensk, Russia
Cosmonaut 6:30 AM EET 32E03 54N46

☉ 17-♓-55	☿ 11-♓-33R	♂ 25-♓-58	♄ 22-♒-13	♆ 10-♍-49R	A 18-♓-02
☽ 23-♐-36	♀ 10-♒-22	♃ 21-♎-49R	♅ 25-♈-13	♇ 22-♋-41R	M 26-♐-05

First man in space when he orbited the earth in Vostok spaceship on April 12, 1961. Killed in a test plane flight March 27, 1968.

DD: AQ, December 1968, Davison, speculative. PC speculates 8:20 PM EET. Old-file has 8:00 PM EET.

GALLAGHER, THOMAS February 23, 1918 New York, N.Y.
Writer 4:00 PM EST 73W57 40N45

☉ 04-♓-27	☿ 20-♒-47	♂ 00-♎-31R	♄ 09-♌-18R	♆ 04-♌-58R	A 15-♌-54
☽ 12-♌-12	♀ 13-♒-40R	♃ 02-♊-48	♅ 24-♒-19	♇ 03-♋-32R	M 06-♉-19

First book, *The Gathering Darkness,* was one of ten books nominated for the coveted National Book Award in 1952. *The Monogamist* published in 1955, followed by the nonfiction *Fire at Sea* (1959).

C: Skeetz quotes Garth Allen in AA, September 1974.

GALLI—CURCI, AMELITA November 18, 1889 Milan, Italy
Singer 4:45 AM LMT 9E24 43N27

☉ 26-♏-03	☿ 14-♏-54	♂ 04-♎-22	♄ 03-♍-17	♆ 03-♊-21R	A 29-♎-44
☽ 22-♍-38	♀ 03-♏-58	♃ 08-♑-10	♅ 24-♎-24	♇ 06-♊-07R	M 06-♌-16

Italian coloratura soprano. Had her debut before she ever had a voice lesson, as Gilda in *Rigoletto* (1909). Chicago Opera Co, 1916-20; N.Y. Metropolitan from 1920 to her retirement in 1937. (1889-1963)

DD: Dewey quotes Romiser from "The World of Song" in *World Astrology*, May 1946. PC quotes the same source for 6:00 AM LMT.

GAMONET, YVES May 15, 1933 Sarreguemines, France
Murderer 8:00 PM GDT 7E08 49N05

☉ 24-♉-28	☿ 09-♉-55	♂ 06-♍-46	♄ 16-♒-16	♆ 07-♍-24R	A 24-♏-20
☽ 15-♒-10	♀ 00-♊-51	♃ 13-♍-20	♅ 25-♈-07	♇ 21-♋-35	M 13-♍-55

Psychopathic killer; attempted to rape a dancehall girl; when she resisted, shot her dead.

C: CL quotes Tucker in *Astrology and the Abnormal Mind* (1960).

GANDHI, MOHANDES   October 2, 1869   Porbandar, India
Mahatma   7:11:48 AM LMT   69E37 21N38

| ☉ 08-♎-56 | ☿ 03-♏-47 | ♂ 18-♏-24 | ♄ 12-♐-22 | ♆ 18-♈-25R | A 26-♎-37 |
| ☽ 19-♌-58 | ♀ 16-♏-27 | ♃ 20-♉-10R | ♅ 21-♋-41 | ♇ 17-♉-39R | M 26-♋-46 |

Spiritual and political leader of India. Lawyer, civil rights champion. Began the freedom movement in 1919 with nonviolent disobedience. India broke from England in August 1947. During Hindu-Moslem riots, shot to death on January 30, 1948.

DD: Fagan in AFA, March 1948, "Shake 1791, Bhadrapad Vadya 12th, three Ghatis and 12 Palas after sunrise, (7:11:48 AM LMT) from Yeshawant K. Pradhan in *Voice of India*, February 1924, confirmed by Ramon, who gives, however, 7:56 AM IST." Fagan himself gives 2:29:48 AM GMT in AA, October 1976.

   WEMYSS F/N #63 gives "one hour, 16' 48" after sunrise." NN #242 gives 7:09 AM LMT. Huggins in the *Astrology Magazine*, January 1970, gives 7:45 AM LMT. SS #367 gives 7:33 AM LMT. Thiruvenkatacharya in *The Astrology Magazine*, December 1966, gives 11:00 PM rectified.

GARCIA, MANUEL   January 18, 1866   Seville, Spain
Bullfighter   1:15 AM LMT   6W00 37N23

| ☉ 27-♑-48 | ☿ 04-♑-25 | ♂ 08-♑-21 | ♄ 11-♏-24 | ♆ 08-♈-02 | A 07-♏-23 |
| ☽ 12-♒-52 | ♀ 18-♑-23 | ♃ 14-♑-24 | ♅ 00-♋-50R | ♇ 12-♉-15R | M 13-♌-31 |

Fearless and popular matador; wounded thirty times in the ring. Gored in the chest, died from the wounds on May 27, 1894.

C: Eshelman quotes Fagan in AA, June 1963. CL gives same data from WEMYSS VOL V.

GARDNER, ERLE STANLEY   July 17, 1887   Malden, Mass
Writer   8:14 AM LMT   71W04 42N26

| ☉ 24-♋-34 | ☿ 12-♌-03R | ♂ 03-♋-25 | ♄ 25-♋-54 | ♆ 29-♉-29 | A 05-♍-31 |
| ☽ 12-♊-53 | ♀ 10-♍-04 | ♃ 26-♎-51 | ♅ 08-♎-47 | ♇ 04-♊-37 | M 00-♊-41 |

Famous mystery-novelist who wrote more than one hundred forty books. Based on his own experiences as a lawyer, created lawyer-detective Perry Mason — later the basis of a TV series. (1887?-1970)

DD: Scarsella from Baird. *Current Biography* Obit, *Famous People* and *Americana* give July 17, 1889.

GARFIELD, JOHN   March 4, 1913   New York, N.Y.
Actor   7:30 PM EST   73W57 40N45

| ☉ 13-♓-51 | ☿ 00-♈-08 | ♂ 10-♒-31 | ♄ 28-♉-19 | ♆ 23-♋-27R | A 04-♎-32 |
| ☽ 11-♒-27 | ♀ 28-♈-41 | ♃ 12-♑-23 | ♅ 05-♒-43 | ♇ 28-♊-01R | M 05-♋-14 |

Played in thirty-one films from 1938-51, including *Golden Boy*, *Body and Soul*, and *Force of Evil*. Weak heart since 1947; died at the height of his career, 1952.

DD: PC states, "his biography gave the time as in the evening." The only biography LMR could locate was *John Garfield* by George Morris (1977): p. 16 gives date but no time.

GARFUNKEL, ART   November 5, 1941   New York, N.Y.
Musician, actor   11:00 PM EST   73W57 40N45

| ☉ 13-♏-21 | ☿ 26-♎-28 | ♂ 11-♈-13R | ♄ 26-♉-00R | ♆ 29-♍-01 | A 13-♌-36 |
| ☽ 06-♊-00 | ♀ 29-♐-43 | ♃ 20-♊-15R | ♅ 28-♉-57R | ♇ 05-♌-47 | M 03-♉-15 |

Teamed with Paul Simon to write many hit songs that were cogent and poetic, with social comment; they separated in 1971. Films include *Catch 22* and *Carnal Knowledge* (1971).

DD: Dewey quotes Houldson in Dell, October 1970; same data from Holliday. PC states the same data as B.C. Old-file has 11:25 PM EST.

GENET, JEAN December 19, 1910 Paris, France
Writer 8:30 AM Paris time 2E20 48N50

☉ 26-♐-34	☿ 15-♑-24	♂ 29-♏-12	♄ 29-♈-52R	♆ 20-♋-49R	A 04-♑-32
☽ 06-♌-18	♀ 02-♑-06	♃ 07-♏-25	♅ 23-♑-40	♇ 26-♊-56R	M 06-♏-54

French novelist, playwright, and poet. Accused of stealing at age 10; five years in the reformatory; escaped to join the French Foreign Legion. Various prisons from 1930, for crimes including prostitution and homosexuality. Began to write seriously in 1939; impressive acknowledgement by 1947. Autobiography *A Thief's Journal* (1949).

DD: PC speculative. Old-file gives the same date, 8:40 AM LMT. *Americana* gives December 10, 1910.

GEORGE, HENRY September 2, 1839 Philadelphia, Pa
Social reformer 12:00 Noon LMT 75W10 39N57

☉ 09-♍-30	☿ 09-♍-10R	♂ 09-♏-31	♄ 04-♐-14	♆ 10-♒-28R	A 26-♏-22
☽ 06-♋-29	♀ 17-♎-15	♃ 18-♎-34	♅ 14-♓-38R	♇ 18-♈-34R	M 09-♍-36

Self supporting from age 14; sailed to Australia; hunted gold in British Columbia; later became a printer, reporter, and newspaper editor. In 1886, almost became mayor of N.Y. As a political economist, originated the single tax. (1839-1897)

C: CL from NN #790.

GERSHWIN, GEORGE September 26, 1898 New York, N.Y.
Musician 11:09 AM EST 73W57 40N45

☉ 03-♎-35	☿ 17-♍-04	♂ 13-♋-45	♄ 07-♐-27	♆ 24-♊-48	A 06-♐-01
☽ 20-♒-37	♀ 19-♏-56	♃ 16-♎-54	♅ 00-♐-32	♇ 15-♊-41R	M 23-♍-14

American composer, famous for *Rhapsody in Blue*; also wrote "I Got Rhythm," "Lady Be Good," "The Man I Love," and more. Wrote many musical comedies. Just before he died with a brain tumor, produced the hit black opera, *Porgy and Bess*. (1898-1937)

DD: CL, rectified. Same data in SS #384. March remembers the time from a biography as 11:00 AM. Huggins in *The Astrology Magazine*, January 1970, gives 11:15 AM LMT.

GETTY, J. PAUL December 15, 1892 Minneapolis, Minn
Entrepreneur 8:43 AM LMT 93W16 44N59

☉ 24-♐-10	☿ 16-♐-15R	♂ 22-♓-02	♄ 11-♎-38	♆ 09-♊-30R	A 09-♑-23
☽ 13-♏-31	♀ 21-♏-07	♃ 15-♈-03	♅ 09-♏-10	♇ 08-♊-32R	M 07-♏-50

Financial tycoon and America's richest man. Joined his father in the oil business in 1914; inherited $15 million that he parlayed into an oil and real estate empire valued at $2 to $4 billion. (1892-1976)

DD: CL from Helen Allen in AFA, July 1963. CL notes that three various times are given. Mark Johnson quotes Garth Allen in AA, January 1964, for 10:43 AM. PC quotes *J.P. Getty* by Ralph Hewins as 8:30 AM CST. *The Richest American: J. Paul Getty* by Ralph Hewins (1960), states the data on p. 38, "Ten days before Christmas, 1892, father knew at 9:00 AM that Sarah was safely delivered of their son."

GIANNINI, AMADEO P. May 6, 1870 San Jose, Ca
Financier 5:00 AM LMT 121W53 37N20

☉ 15-♉-46	☿ 06-♊-28	♂ 03-♉-57	♄ 27-♐-52R	♆ 20-♈-15	A 14-♉-26
☽ 20-♋-25	♀ 29-♓-42	♃ 29-♉-18	♅ 18-♋-38	♇ 17-♉-24	M 27-♑-08

American businessman who founded the Bank of America, the world's largest commercial bank. In 1904, founded the Bank of Italy in San Francisco; gradually formed a huge banking system. (1870-1949)

DD: PC, "recorded." Old-file has 5:35 AM LMT.

GIBBONS, CARDINAL JAMES	July 23, 1834	Baltimore, Md
Cardinal	6:00 AM LMT	76W37 39N17

☉ 00-♌-02	☿ 18-♌-58R	♂ 24-♉-51	♄ 05-♎-45	♆ 00-♒-13R	A 12-♌-44
☽ 01-♓-08	♀ 04-♍-55	♃ 04-♊-46	♅ 25-♒-33R	♇ 13-♈-46R	M 02-♉-55

Second American to be named a cardinal of the Roman Catholic Church, 1886. Ordained in 1861. A parish priest, bishop, vicar apostolic; Bishop of Richmond and Archbishop of Baltimore, 1877. Author of religious books, including *Faith of Our Fathers* (1834-1921).

C: Chart pictured in Adams' *One Hundred Horoscopes*. PC quotes same data from SS #386 (no time given).

GILBERT, CLARENCE H.	December 13, 1874	No place given
Jurist	12:00 Noon LMT	89W00 38N00

☉ 21-♐-37	☿ 04-♐-14	♂ 24-♎-52	♄ 10-♒-45	♆ 28-♈-12R	A 17-♓-17
☽ 17-♒-04	♀ 14-♐-18R	♃ 25-♎-56	♅ 15-♌-02R	♇ 21-♉-11R	M 22-♐-53

Portland, Oregon, juvenile judge; active for many years in matters relating to corrective institutions. Appointed to the Advisory Committee of the National Probation Association, 1936.

C: Benjamine in *International Astrology*, February 1937.

GILBERT, JOHN	July 10, 1892	Logan, Utah
Actor	10:00 PM MST	111W50 41N44

☉ 19-♋-18	☿ 09-♌-54	♂ 17-♒-01R	♄ 25-♍-06	♆ 10-♊-15	A 00-♓-20
☽ 03-♒-20	♀ 17-♋-02R	♃ 23-♈-08	♅ 01-♏-59	♇ 09-♊-14	M 14-♐-05

Handsome matinee idol of the 20s who rose from a screen extra to superstar. Made fifteen talkies, which ruined his career. Lost money in the crash of '29. Four marriages. Also loved Garbo, with whom he played in *Flesh and the Devil*. (1892-1936)

DD: CL from Tucker in *Predicting from the Stars* (1960). *Americana* and *Biographical Dictionary of Film* give 1897. *Filmgoer's Companion* gives 1895.

GINSBURG, ALLEN	June 3, 1926	Paterson, N.J.
Publisher, poet	1:00 AM EDT	74W11 40N55

☉ 11-♊-54	☿ 10-♊-08	♂ 21-♓-49	♄ 21-♏-20R	♆ 22-♌-15	A 24-♓-20
☽ 10-♓-43	♀ 00-♉-29	♃ 26-♒-54	♅ 29-♓-02	♇ 13-♋-26	M 27-♐-01

A bearded bard of scatological colloquialisms. Held a B.A. in the straight life as a market consultant before dropping out to become a symbol of the anger under flower-power. After a series of mystical visions in 1948, spent eight months in a mental institution.

DD: PC, "from his father." Old-file has 1:15 AM. *American Atlas* gives EST. E. Rivers in Leek's *Astrology*, May 1970, gives 7:00 AM.

GISCARD D'ESTAING, VALERY	February 2, 1926	Koblenz, Germany
Statesman	9:28 PM MET	7E35 50N22

☉ 13-♒-16	☿ 03-♒-57	♂ 25-♐-35	♄ 25-♏-15	♆ 23-♌-42R	A 27-♍-45
☽ 07-♎-13	♀ 21-♒-01R	♃ 06-♒-33	♅ 23-♓-10	♇ 13-♋-06R	M 27-♊-07

President of France, May 19, 1974, succeeding Georges Pompidous. Served with the French resistance during Nazi occupation in World War II. Began his government career specializing in finance, 1952. Wealthy, aristocratic, intellectual; skis, hunts, plays football, flies his own plane. Married; four children.

DD: DeForge in AA, September 1976. PC gives February 6, 1926, 10:04 AM MET, "recorded", says "another source gives 7:45 AM." Old-file has February 6, 1926, 7:50 AM MET. *World Book Supplement* (1975) gives February 2, 1926.

GISH, LILLIAN	October 14, 1896	Springfield, Ohio
Actress	3:30 AM CST	83W49 39N55

☉ 21-♎-33	☿ 10-♎-37R	♂ 27-♊-02	♄ 18-♏-14	♆ 20-♊-11R	A 23-♍-41
☽ 00-♒-50	♀ 17-♏-16	♃ 03-♍-01	♅ 22-♏-48	♇ 13-♊-34R	M 22-♊-45

Silent film star, along with her sister Dorothy, two years younger. Featured in many pictures after 1912, including *The Birth of a Nation* (1915). A "natural" as an actress; not as good in talkies as on the stage, where she was luminous.

DD: PC speculative. Old-file gives the same date, 3:15 AM. CL gives 1894, 5:40 AM CST; however, five reference sources give 1896. *Current Biography*, 1944, states that Lillian was born October 14, 1896; Dorothy, March 11, 1898. (*World Book* Obit gives 1901-1968 for Dorothy).

GLADSTONE, WILLIAM	December 29, 1809	Liverpool, England
Statesman	8:15 AM LMT	3W00 53N25

☉ 07-♑-18	☿ 06-♑-32	♂ 19-♒-32	♄ 09-♐-52	♆ 07-♐-41	A 05-♑-04
☽ 00-♎-08	♀ 18-♐-56	♃ 15-♈-34	♅ 13-♏-09	♇ 13-♓-50	M 13-♏-35

Prime minister of Great Britain, 1868-74, under Queen Victoria. Wealthy family. Wanted to be a priest but entered public office to please his father; found his place in finance to become one of the most famous British political leaders. Died of cancer in 1898.

DD: Chart pictured in Adams' *One Hundred Horoscopes*. Leo's *Esoteric Astrology* pictures a chart for 8:00 AM. Pagan in *Pioneer to Poet* says, "about 8:00 AM (breakfast time.)" SS #389 gives 9:00 AM.

GOGOL, NIKOLAI	March 31, 1809 NS	Sorochinsk, Russia
Writer	6:00 PM LMT	53E15 52N30

☉ 10-♈-28	☿ 12-♓-44	♂ 21-♎-50R	♄ 03-♐-35R	♆ 06-♐-44R	A 05-♎-57
☽ 09-♎-54	♀ 25-♉-17	♃ 03-♈-19	♅ 08-♏-46R	♇ 14-♓-45	M 07-♋-51

Major Russian novelist and dramatist. Failed in early efforts to be an actor; was a civil service clerk and a history teacher. His first collection of stories in 1831 brought him attention. (1809-1852)

DD: PC quotes Barbault, "who believed he had Libra rising," adds, "I have seen another chart which placed the birth around midnight." Old-file has the same date, 11:40 PM LMT. *Britannica* gives the same date, specified New Style; however, *Americana* has April 1, 1809, specified New Style.

GOLDBERG, ARTHUR	August 8, 1908	Chicago, Ill
Politician	3:30 AM CST	87W39 41N52

☉ 15-♌-24	☿ 02-♌-39	♂ 19-♌-55	♄ 09-♈-57R	♆ 15-♋-45	A 28-♋-43
☽ 22-♐-39	♀ 07-♋-44	♃ 22-♌-25	♅ 13-♑-43R	♇ 25-♊-26	M 12-♈-20

Attorney and counsellor to labor groups. Became U.S. secretary of labor, 1961; associate justice of the U.S. Supreme Court, 1962; resigned in 1965 to become ambassador to the U.N. for three years.

C: Pryor in AFA, April 1970.

GOLDMAN, EMMA	June 27, 1869	Kaunas, Lithuania
Anarchist	3:00 PM LMT	23E55 54N54

☉ 05-♋-51	☿ 01-♋-49R	♂ 17-♍-47	♄ 12-♐-14R	♆ 19-♈-24	A 03-♏-59
☽ 16-♒-43	♀ 19-♋-11	♃ 13-♉-09	♅ 16-♋-54	♇ 17-♉-33	M 18-♌-15

Advocated and practiced personal and political freedom that would be audacious even in the 70s. Ran a N.Y. periodical, *Mother Earth*; preached and practiced free love; lectured on atheism, patriotism, and birth control. (1869-1940)

DD: PC speculative. Old-file has 2:15 PM LMT.

GOLDWATER, BARRY	January 1, 1909	Phoenix, Az
Politician	1:00 AM MST	112W04 33N27

☉ 10-♑-18	☿ 15-♑-07	♂ 24-♏-10	♄ 03-♈-57	♆ 15-♋-52R	A 15-♎-27
☽ 07-♉-10	♀ 11-♐-48	♃ 14-♍-31R	♅ 16-♑-36	♇ 24-♊-32R	M 16-♋-51

Became a colonel in the U.S. Air Force; went into politics. Elected U.S. senator from Arizona in 1952; candidate for president against L.B. Johnson, 1964.

DD: AA, May 1965, prints a letter from him to Nadine Bullard in which he gives this time, "from his aged mother's recollection." However, Jansky quotes a letter from him, 1979, in which he states the time of his birth is unknown. CL quotes Drew at 6:25 AM MST, "approximate time given by a student, considered right." Jansky quotes a speculative chart in AA, July 1964, of 1:02 AM MST. King Keyes says at the First Temple of Astrology they quote Mrs. Goldwater at 00:01 AM MST.

GOLDWYN, SAMUEL   August 27, 1882 NS   Warsaw, Poland
Movie producer   4:29 AM LMT   21E00   52N12

☉ 03-♍-43	☿ 15-♍-01	♂ 05-♎-31	♄ 26-♉-03	♆ 18-♉-50R	A 26-♌-57
☽ 08-♒-45	♀ 17-♎-48	♃ 27-♊-05	♅ 17-♍-59	♇ 00-♊-15	M 14-♉-58

Came to the U.S. in 1896. Became one of the pioneering Hollywood entrepreneurs. Originated Goldwyn Pictures in 1919; later merged with Louis Mayer to form MGM. Personally produced the Oscar winning *The Best Years of Our Lives* (1946). (1882-1974)

DD: CL from Ziegler. Same data in *Famous People; World Book Obit* gives 1882. *Circle #387* and *50,000 Birthdays* give August 14, 1882. McEvers quotes *Goldwyn* by Arthur Marx for the date August 27, 1881, (no time).

GOREN, CHARLES   March 4, 1901   Philadelphia, Pa
Bridge expert   1:00 AM EST   75W10   39N57

☉ 12-♓-59	☿ 19-♓-38R	♂ 29-♌-05R	♄ 14-♑-12	♆ 26-♊-27R	A 08-♐-24
☽ 00-♍-43	♀ 28-♒-18	♃ 08-♑-16	♅ 16-♐-45	♇ 15-♊-41	M 25-♍-48

Held a law degree, 1922; practiced until the mid-30s when he gave up law for full-time professional contract bridge. Wrote more than fifty books, translated into nine languages; was syndicated in daily newspaper columns. Never married.

C: CL quotes Drew for "approximate time."

GORKY, MAXIM   March 28, 1868 NS   Nizhni Novgorod, Russia
Writer   3:00 AM LMT   44E00   56N20

☉ 07-♈-36	☿ 11-♓-36	♂ 18-♓-16	♄ 05-♐-33R	♆ 14-♈-28	A 10-♑-03
☽ 22-♉-31	♀ 19-♉-11	♃ 24-♓-35	♅ 08-♋-51	♇ 14-♉-44	M 23-♏-05

Grew up in poverty and harshness; had little schooling; but preached an heroic and optimistic view of life that was new to Russian literature at that time. Gained fame when his first stories were published in 1898. (1868-1936)

DD: PC speculative, states "Barbault believed he had Pisces rising." Old-file has 2:35 AM LMT. Date in *Americana* specified New Style.

GOULD, JAY   May 27, 1836   Roxbury, N.Y.
Entrepreneur   5:35 AM LMT   74W34   42N17

☉ 06-♊-06	☿ 28-♊-59	♂ 00-♉-49	♄ 29-♎-33R	♆ 05-♒-54R	A 21-♊-09
☽ 21-♎-41	♀ 21-♋-01	♃ 15-♋-51	♅ 04-♓-28	♇ 15-♈-25	M 26-♒-32

Began his career in 1860 by buying a small railroad, selling for profit, repeating the process. Made millions by manipulating Erie stock; said to have owned one-tenth of every mile of railroads in the U.S. Estate valued at $72 million. *Gould's Millions* written by O'Conner (1962).

DD: *Wynn's Astrology*, March 1943, same data in SS #400. Old-file has 6:00 AM LMT.

GOULET, ROBERT   November 26, 1931   Lawrence, Mass
Singer, actor   11:50 AM EST   71W10   42N43

☉ 03-♐-28	☿ 23-♐-36	♂ 19-♐-55	♄ 19-♑-59	♆ 07-♍-56	A 19-♒-09
☽ 19-♊-42	♀ 23-♐-45	♃ 22-♌-22	♅ 15-♈-47R	♇ 21-♋-56R	M 07-♐-46

Canadian singer and leading man; won a Tony in Broadway musical *The Happy Time*. Films include *I'd Rather Be Rich* (1954) and *Honeymoon Hotel* (1964). TV series *The Blue Light* (1964).

DD: CL from Ziegler, April 1965. Jansky gives 8:35 AM EST. PC gives 1933, 8:15 AM EST, "personal." Four reference sources give 1933.

GRAHAM, BILLY   November 7, 1918   Charlotte, N.C.
Evangelist   4:28 AM EST   80W51 35N13

☉ 14-♏-10	☿ 27-♏-44	♂ 26-♐-58	♄ 27-♌-17	♆ 09-♌-19	A 14-♎-06
☽ 23-♐-07	♀ 10-♏-02	♃ 15-♋-48R	♅ 23-♒-48	♇ 06-♋-29R	M 15-♋-36

Southern Baptist preacher who was "born again" in 1934. After 1947, spread his word by way of nine hundred radio stations and TV crusades. Publishes a magazine *Decision*, with more than four million circulation. Married, 1943; five children and fourteen grandchildren by 1979.

DD: Dewey quotes Dobyns, from Ken Gilman. CL gives 4:30 AM EST. PC gives November 17 (corrected on erata sheet), 9:30 AM EST from Drew. Scarsella has 8:15 AM TLT from Baird.

GRANT, CARY   January 18, 1904   Bristol, England
Actor   1:07 AM GMT   2W36 51N27

☉ 26-♑-32	☿ 25-♑-14R	♂ 28-♒-44	♄ 09-♒-57	♆ 03-♋-57R	A 28-♎-16
☽ 00-♒-47	♀ 15-♐-13	♃ 20-♓-42	♅ 27-♐-35	♇ 19-♊-03R	M 07-♌-46

Hollywood debut, 1932; first breakthrough in *Sylvia Scarlett* (1936). More than sixty films — tragedy, comedy and drama; at his best as the epitome of charm, sophistication, and humor. Four marriages; one child with his third wife, Dyan Cannon.

DD: CL from *Today's Astrology*, May 1941. SS #404 gives January 14, 1904. PC quotes SS for January 18, 1904. LMR quotes *Cary Grant* by Albert Cavoni (1971), p. 16, "During the first morning hour of Monday, January 18, 1904 . . ."

GRAVES, ROBERT   July 24, 1895   Wimbledon, England
Writer   5:00 PM GMT   0W13 51N25

☉ 01-♌-29	☿ 11-♋-41	♂ 27-♌-16	♄ 00-♏-53	♆ 17-♊-10	A 16-♐-24
☽ 06-♍-13	♀ 16-♍-16	♃ 21-♋-09	♅ 15-♏-51R	♇ 12-♊-20	M 18-♎-22

English novelist, poet, and critic. Earned his living with historical novels, but his first love was always poetry. Author of *I, Claudius* (1934) and the nonfiction *A Survey of Modernistic Poetry* (1927).

C: CL from AFA, July 1967. PC gives the same data as "personal."

GREY, JOEL   April 11, 1932   Cleveland, Ohio
Entertainer   4:00 AM EST   81W42 41N30

☉ 21-♈-16	☿ 19-♈-38R	♂ 06-♈-17	♄ 03-♒-52	♆ 05-♍-31R	A 00-♓-22
☽ 19-♊-22	♀ 06-♊-40	♃ 12-♌-37	♅ 19-♈-27	♇ 19-♋-58	M 14-♐-01

Actor and dancer; on stage from age 10. A player for twenty-four years before winning an Oscar for *Cabaret* (1972), and stardom. Stage lead in *The Grand Tour* (1979). Married 1958; two children.

DD: Holliday, unrecorded source. Ideman states that "he said he had Pisces rising."

GRIFFITH, DAVID WARK   January 22, 1878   La Grange, Ky
Movie producer   10:30 AM LMT   85W23 38N25

☉ 02-♒-35	☿ 11-♑-47	♂ 25-♈-00	♄ 17-♓-15	♆ 04-♉-46	A 15-♈-27
☽ 23-♍-15	♀ 09-♓-06	♃ 19-♑-09	♅ 28-♌-28R	♇ 23-♉-36R	M 08-♑-37

Before entering the movie field, acted in and managed road companies that presented stage plays. Became a pioneer director and producer in Hollywood; produced the first full-length feature picture in 1915, *Birth of a Nation*. (1878-1948)

DD: NAJ, November 1935, "private source." CL gives 10:33 AM LMT, "from *Photoplay* magazine, February 1918." PC gives 1875, says "an old biography gives the time of around 5:00 PM." Old-file has 1875, 5:35 PM. *Americana* and *Famous People* give 1875; *World Book* gives 1880.

GROFE, FERDE		March 27, 1892		New York, N.Y.	
Musician		4:00 AM EST		73W57 40N45	
☉ 07-♈-10	☿ 25-♈-13	♂ 08-♑-04	♄ 25-♍-58R	♆ 06-♊-43	A 21-♒-03
☽ 20-♓-26	♀ 19-♉-49	♃ 02-♈-31	♅ 05-♏-10R	♇ 07-♊-06	M 08-♐-04

American composer, conductor, violinist with the Los Angeles Symphony Orchestra, pianist, and arranger with Paul Whiteman band, 1919-1933. Style of symphonic jazz; work includes *Grand Canyon Suite* (1931). (1892-1972)

C: Jasond in *Astrological Review,* December 1937; same data in SS #412 (no time given).

GROPPI, JAMES E.		November 16, 1930		Milwaukee, Wis	
Catholic priest		1:00 PM CST		87W55 43N02	
☉ 23-♏-42	☿ 29-♏-20	♂ 11-♌-09	♄ 08-♑-45	♆ 05-♍-39	A 28-♒-40
☽ 06-♎-49	♀ 03-♐-12R	♃ 20-♋-23R	♅ 11-♈-56R	♇ 20-♋-46R	M 13-♐-36

Social activist priest who was arrested and jailed on several ocassions for lecturing and leading demonstrators against injustice in the turbulent 60s.

C: Louise Ivey in AFA, June 1970.

GUEVARRA, CHE		June 6, 1928		Rosario, Argentina	
Revolutionary		10:00 PM AST		60W45 33S00	
☉ 16-♊-04	☿ 09-♋-04	♂ 15-♈-54	♄ 15-♐-49R	♆ 26-♌-39	A 21-♒-38
☽ 26-♑-01	♀ 09-♊-22	♃ 00-♉-35	♅ 06-♈-53	♇ 15-♋-53	M 16-♏-56

Latin American guerilla leader revolutionary who attempted to spread Castroite communism in South America. First joined the Castro force as a doctor; entered the militia in 1956. Captured by a Bolivian Army unit and shot October 6, 1967. Author of *Geurrilla Warfare* (1961).

DD: March quotes a French astrology magazine, 1977, "from father." PC gives June 14, 1928, 9:30 PM AST, "recorded." Old-file has June 14, 9:40 PM AST. *Americana* gives June 14, 1928.

GUINNESS, SIR ALEC		April 2, 1914		London, England	
Actor		5:45 AM GMT		0W06 51N31	
☉ 11-♈-39	☿ 14-♓-34	♂ 16-♋-46	♄ 13-♊-23	♆ 25-♋-26R	A 13-♈-58
☽ 23-♊-04	♀ 23-♈-53	♃ 15-♒-20	♅ 10-♒-48	♇ 29-♊-09	M 05-♑-24

World famous British star. Debut in the early 30s; first film success in *Great Expectations* (1947); won the Oscar as best actor in *Bridge on the River Kwai* (1958). Other films include *Kind Hearts and Coronets* and *The Lavender Hill Mob*. Knighted in 1959.

DD: Craswell quotes AQR Vol 5 #4. AQR, Winter 1958, gives 5:54 AM GMT.

HALE, ALAN SR.		February 10, 1892		Washington, D.C.	
Actor		3:00 PM EST		77W03 38N53	
☉ 21-♒-36	☿ 04-♒-14	♂ 10-♐-35	♄ 29-♍-15R	♆ 06-♊-15R	A 20-♋-34
☽ 28-♋-31	♀ 26-♓-04	♃ 21-♓-41	♅ 06-♏-05R	♇ 06-♊-53R	M 03-♈-38

Handsome young lead in his teens; star or co-star in silent films, including *Four Horsemen of the Apocolypse*. Garrulous and gregarious character actor in one hundred fifty later films, including *Robin Hood, Dodge City,* and *Destination Tokyo.* (1892-1950)

C: CL from AFA, April 1955; same data in SS #422.

HALE, NATHAN   June 6, 1755   Coventry, Ct
Patriot   5:00 AM LMT   72W21   41N47

☉ 15-♊-14   ☿ 19-♊-57   ♂ 20-♈-11   ♄ 28-♑-17R   ♆ 06-♌-37   A 22-♊-43
☽ 06-♉-01   ♀ 08-♉-52   ♃ 10-♍-08   ♅ 15-♓-13   ♇ 14-♐-34R   M 27-♒-15

During the Revolutionary War, infiltrated British lines to gain information of position. Captured and hanged by the British as a spy on September 22, 1776, saying "I regret that I have but one life to give for my country."

DD: PC speculative. Old-file has 4:20 AM LMT.

HALLIBURTON, RICHARD   January 9, 1900   Brownsville, Tenn
Adventurer   2:30 PM CST   89W16   35N36

☉ 19-♑-11   ☿ 01-♑-06   ♂ 20-♑-43   ♄ 28-♐-44   ♆ 24-♊-59R   A 15-♊-47
☽ 09-♉-36   ♀ 17-♒-23   ♃ 02-♐-49   ♅ 10-♐-37   ♇ 15-♊-06R   M 24-♒-52

American adventurer, author, lecturer, and explorer. Visited many parts of the world and wrote excitedly about what he saw. His daring got him into dangerous situations that gave suspense to his writing. (1900-1939)

DD: PC speculative. Old-file has 2:00 PM CST.

HAMMARSKJOLD, DAG   July 29, 1905   Jonkoping, Sweden
Statesman   11:30 AM MET   14E10   57N47

☉ 05-♌-36   ☿ 02-♍-32   ♂ 18-♏-22   ♄ 01-♓-18R   ♆ 08-♋-56   A 18-♎-05
☽ 01-♋-21   ♀ 21-♊-26   ♃ 01-♊-25   ♅ 00-♑-57R   ♇ 22-♊-12   M 26-♋-04

Swedish economist; secretary-general of the U.N., 1953-61. Awarded posthumously the 1961 Nobel Peace prize, particularly for establishing and keeping a peace force in the Middle East after the 1956 Suez crisis. Killed in a plane crash, September 18, 1961.

DD: CL quotes Drew for "an approximate time." Judy Johns has 5:25 AM MET, from Jansky.

HART, WILLIAM S.   December 6, 1870   Newberry, N.Y.
Cowboy actor   8:33 AM LMT   74W01   41N30

☉ 14-♐-17   ☿ 21-♐-55   ♂ 19-♍-57   ♄ 29-♐-01   ♆ 19-♈-11R   A 00-♑-44
☽ 27-♉-26   ♀ 13-♐-52   ♃ 22-♊-20R   ♅ 26-♋-04R   ♇ 17-♉-28R   M 25-♎-14

First became a hero in a play, *The Squaw Man* (1905), followed by many movies to become a beloved Western star. Also wrote several novels. When he died in 1946, left a 225-acre ranch to the county as a park for the children, with no charge to enter.

C: CL old file. Date check in *Americana*.

HARTE, BRETT   August 25, 1839   Albany, N.Y.
Writer   4:12 AM LMT   73W45   42N39

☉ 01-♍-26   ☿ 16-♍-03R   ♂ 04-♏-06   ♄ 03-♐-57   ♆ 10-♒-40R   A 18-♌-12
☽ 07-♓-45   ♀ 12-♎-57   ♃ 17-♎-02   ♅ 14-♓-58R   ♇ 18-♈-41R   M 08-♉-20

Great and influential American story teller, chiefly about life in the early California mining camps. With little education, drifted into journalism in 1854; became the first editor of the *Overland Monthly* in 1868. His writings fill twenty volumes. (1839-1902)

DD: PC quotes SS #435 (no time given). Old-file has the same date, 4:00 PM LMT. *World Book* and *Americana* both give August 25, 1836.

HARTFORD, HUNTINGTON April 18, 1911   New York, N.Y.
Millionaire   8:00 AM EST   73W57   40N45

☉ 27-♈-22   ☿ 16-♉-19   ♂ 26-♒-26   ♄ 08-♉-07   ♆ 18-♋-52   A 18-♊-59
☽ 21-♐-50   ♀ 00-♊-55   ♃ 11-♏-16R   ♅ 29-♑-14   ♇ 26-♊-10   M 24-♒-16

Heir to the A&P fortune; varied career in a number of enterprises; philanthropist. Three marriages. Says of himself, "a little emotionally unstable, analytical, a perfectionist, a crusader, with a creative side."

C: Holliday from CL, "time unknown, speculative."

HARVEY, LEN July 11, 1907 Galburton, Cornwall, England
Boxer 4:25 PM GMT 4W40 50N33

☉ 18-♋-12	☿ 07-♌-15R	♂ 11-♑-53R	♄ 27-♓-27R	♆ 12-♋-35	A 26-♏-52
☽ 29-♋-34	♀ 00-♋-30	♃ 21-♋-34	♅ 10-♑-25R	♇ 23-♊-51	M 19-♍-08

British boxing champion who first won the title on February 8, 1934. By July 1939, held five boxing titles.

C: CL from Tucker, 1960.

HAWKING, STEPHEN 1/8/42

HAYAKAWA, SESSUE June 10, 1889 Tokyo, Japan
Actor 00:11 AM JST 139E45 35N40

☉ 18-♊-54	☿ 02-♋-41R	♂ 21-♊-16	♄ 16-♌-04	♆ 02-♊-40	A 23-♓-10
☽ 24-♎-02	♀ 08-♉-14	♃ 05-♑-17R	♅ 17-♎-59R	♇ 05-♊-45	M 26-♐-02

Played in more than one hundred forty films in Japan, England, France, and the U.S. from 1914, including *Bridge on the River Kwai* (1957). An ordained Zen Buddhist priest; wrote an autobiography, *Zen Showed Me the Way* (1960).

DD: Scarsella from Baird. *Current Biography* and *Famous People* both give 1890.

HEADRICK, RICHARD April 29, 1917 Los Angeles, Ca
"Little Minister" 9:05 PM PST 118W15 34N04

☉ 09-♉-17	☿ 28-♉-11	♂ 26-♈-28	♄ 24-♋-45	♆ 02-♌-10	A 11-♐-10
☽ 20-♌-00	♀ 10-♉-17	♃ 16-♉-03	♅ 23-♒-23	♇ 02-♋-42	M 25-♍-11

Preached by age 12 in churches of different denominations in California and elsewhere. Tall, lithe, and compact. Swam at 6 weeks; played in movies at age 2; took violin at 3; began to preach at age 4.

C: D. Herschel in *Practical Astrology*, May 1929.

HEATH, NEVILLE June 6, 1917 London, England
Murderer 9:30 AM BST 0W06 51N31

☉ 15-♊-05	☿ 22-♉-54	♂ 23-♉-56	♄ 27-♋-56	♆ 02-♌-52	A 22-♌-33
☽ 26-♐-17	♀ 26-♊-02	♃ 24-♉-48	♅ 23-♒-41R	♇ 03-♋-27	M 09-♉-01

Sadist noted for "crimes too horrible to describe," the gruesome killings of girls and women. On June 21, 1946, committed an appalling and prolonged murder of a masochist. Arrested, tried, and hanged. Noted as being handsome, charming.

C: CL, rectified by Fagan in AA, September 1954; time noted as 9:00 to 10:00 AM BST.

HEDIN, SVEN February 19, 1865 Stockholm, Sweden
Adventurer 4:02 AM LMT 18E00 59N20

☉ 00-♓-32	☿ 10-♒-35	♂ 11-♊-35	♄ 00-♏-13R	♆ 06-♈-40	A 15-♐-54
☽ 03-♐-01	♀ 16-♈-52	♃ 24-♐-36	♅ 25-♊-29R	♇ 11-♉-25	M 01-♏-44

Swedish explorer who provided the first maps and information about areas in Central Asia; led expeditions in Persia, Turkestan, Tibet, China, and Mongolia. Author of more than thirty books, including *Through Asia* (1898), *Overland to India* (1910), and *The Silk Road* (1936). (1865-1952)

DD: SS #445. Old-file has 3:30 AM.

HEIFETZ, JASCHA February 2, 1901 Vilna, Lithuania
Musician 3:00 AM EET 25E17 54N41

☉ 12-♒-34	☿ 20-♒-30	♂ 09-♍-57R	♄ 11-♑-22	♆ 26-♊-46R	A 05-♐-31
☽ 23-♋-54	♀ 20-♑-42	♃ 02-♑-51	♅ 15-♐-54	♇ 15-♊-49R	M 07-♎-28

Violinist who began training with his father at age 3; entered the Imperial School of Music at 5; public debut at 6; international fame by 13. Soloist with virtually all the world's great orchestras; famous for international tours as well as recordings.

DD: CL from SS #447 (no time given). Old-file has 3:20 AM.

HEINDEL, MAX July 23, 1865 Copenhagen, Denmark
Metaphysician 4:32 AM LMT 12E34 55N40

☉ 00-♌-14	☿ 20-♌-58	♂ 05-♍-49	♄ 24-♎-11	♆ 10-♈-34R	A 06-♌-16
☽ 04-♌-50	♀ 14-♊-44	♃ 20-♐-03R	♅ 01-♋-30	♇ 14-♉-08	M 09-♈-41

Founder of the Rosicrucian Fellowship of U.S. in Seattle in the early 1900s; later transferred headquarters to Oceanside, Ca. A Christian disciple, who had been a Theosophist for three years prior to forming his own non-profit corporation.

DD: AA, September 1949, *Many Things* column. CL has the same date and time but a place of 10E00/54N00. SS #449 gives 4:45 AM. PC quotes SS for July 22, 1865. Old-file has 4:50 AM.

HEIRENS, WILLIAM November 15, 1928 Chicago, Ill
Murderer 8:30 PM CST 87W39 41N52

☉ 23-♏-30	☿ 06-♏-13	♂ 09-♋-12R	♄ 18-♐-21	♆ 01-♍-18	A 23-♋-29
☽ 03-♑-29	♀ 28-♐-37	♃ 03-♉-00R	♅ 03-♈-46R	♇ 18-♋-14R	M 05-♈-12

Sadist, thief, killer, and dual personality who paralyzed Chicago with fear as he left notes after dismembering victims. Biography *Before I Kill More* by Lucy Freeman (1956).

DD: Dewey quotes Bradley in AA, February 1975. Victoria Shaw speculates 8:40 PM, the same time that Eshelman gives from Bradley's *Solar Lunar Returns*. PC states 8:40 PM CST as B.C.

HEISENBERG, WERNER December 5, 1901 Wurtzburg, Germany
Physicist 4:45 AM MET 9E57 49N48

☉ 12-♐-20	☿ 27-♏-16	♂ 08-♑-22	♄ 14-♑-40	♆ 00-♋-34R	A 05-♏-27
☽ 07-♎-45	♀ 29-♑-35	♃ 15-♑-22	♅ 16-♐-49	♇ 17-♊-47R	M 17-♌-00

Taught physics at Copenhagen, 1926; Leipzig, 1927; University of Berlin, 1942. Famous for studies in theoretical atomic physics; developed the Principle of Uncertainty. Won the 1932 Nobel prize for founding quantum mechanics.

C: Dewey quotes Ebertin.

HENRY VIII, KING July 7, 1491 NS Greenwich, England
British royalty 10:40 AM LAT 00W00 51N29

☉ 14-♋-39	☿ 06-♌-46	♂ 26-♍-17	♄ 06-♒-50R	♆ 24-♐-55R	A 26-♍-29
☽ 11-♈-46	♀ 00-♊-50	♃ 24-♊-29	♅ 23-♑-04R	♇ 29-♎-27R	M 25-♊-25

Second son of Henry VII; after his brother died, assumed the throne in April 1509. Formidable appetites and influence; responsible for the break of the English church with Rome and the establishment of the Church of England. Six wives; father of Elizabeth I. (1491-1547)

DD: M.A., May 1907, from Sibly (June 28, 1491 OS). M.A., March 1932, gives June 27, 1491 OS, 10:40 PM, "from Ashmole Ms #243 in the Bodlien Library," states same data from Gadbury.

Lyndoe in AA, March 1970, quotes two sources, Gauricus and Cardan for June 28, 1491 OS, 7:00 AM LMT, and Gadbury for 10:30 AM LMT. Harvey in AA, September 1964, says, "according to my findings," June 28, 1491 OS, 8:45 AM Sundial. Adams pictures a chart for June 28, 1491 OS, 11:00 AM LMT. Scarsella has 12:30 PM LMT, from Baird.

HERRLIGKOFFER, KARL June 13, 1916 Schweinfurt, Germany
Adventurer 8:35 AM MET 10E13 50N03

☉ 21-♊-56	☿ 11-♊-31R	♂ 07-♍-42	♄ 16-♋-21	♆ 00-♌-55	A 13-♌-46
☽ 15-♏-55	♀ 19-♋-42R	♃ 27-♈-46	♅ 19-♒-33R	♇ 02-♋-32	M 27-♈-12

Physician and natural scientist; mountain climber. As head of the expedition, conquered Nanga Parbat with Herman Buhl.

C: CL Reynolds quotes Ebertin.

HEYERDAHL, THOR October 6, 1914 Larvik, Norway
Adventurer 4:40 PM MET 10E02 59N05

☉ 12-♎-32	☿ 05-♏-50	♂ 04-♏-55	♄ 02-♋-16	♆ 00-♌-14	A 22-♒-28
☽ 08-♉-45	♀ 27-♏-21	♃ 12-♒-28R	♅ 07-♒-45R	♇ 02-♋-14R	M 20-♐-20

Norwegian sailor and a descendant of the Vikings. In 1947, sailed a balsa raft, Kon Tiki, across the Pacific. In 1969, sailed the Atlantic in Ra; failed 600 miles short of land. Second attempt on the Ra II succeeded, March 17 to July 12, 1970.

DD: Ebertin in *Cosmobiology International*, July 1972. J. Johns has 3:45 PM MET, from Jansky.

HICHMAN, WILLIAM February 1, 1908 Hartford, Ark
Murderer 8:45 AM CST 94W23 35N01

☉ 11-♒-22	☿ 24-♒-00	♂ 15-♈-01	♄ 24-♓-31	♆ 12-♋-45R	A 10-♓-20
☽ 00-♒-46	♀ 14-♓-48	♃ 08-♌-14R	♅ 14-♑-27	♇ 22-♊-59R	M 18-♐-18

Kidnapper and murderer of 12-year-old Marian Parker on February 17, 1937.

DD: Holliday quotes Robert Hand. SS #457 gives 4:45 AM CST. Mary Bell in *Astrological Bulletin*, April 1928, gives the same date, 4:30 AM: "The data was telegraphed for by the San Francisco Call." V. Shaw quotes *In Defense of the Fox: The Trail of William E. Hichman*, by his attorney, Richart Kantillon: "he was just over 18 at the time" in December 1927. The L.A. *Record* and L.A. *Times* both state, "age 20 today" on February 1, 1928.

T.P Davis writes: "I've seen several dates and years. The State of Arkansas has no record of his birth, as a result of the laws effective at the time. It cannot be validated officially."

HILTON, CONRAD December 25, 1887 San Antonio, Texas
Entrepreneur 5:20 AM MST 106W52 33N55

☉ 03-♑-27	☿ 19-♐-47	♂ 09-♎-38	♄ 05-♌-17R	♆ 27-♉-46R	A 17-♐-31
☽ 08-♉-27	♀ 18-♏-08	♃ 26-♏-16	♅ 16-♎-54	♇ 03-♊-30R	M 00-♎-13

Hotel magnate who parlayed a $5000 investment in 1919 into a hotel chain worth more than a half billion dollars. Had a hotel collection by 1949; by 1964, sixty-one hotels in nineteen countries; by 1978, one hundred eighty-five hotels, seventy-five in foreign cities. Autobiography *Be My Guest*. (1887-1979)

DD: Reynolds quotes Ebertin. CL quotes Ziegler, January 1958, at 5:18 AM LMT. PC quotes SS for 5:18 AM MST; not in SS. Old-file gives Waco, Texas, 6:25 AM MST. *Americana* gives San Antonio.

HILTON, NICKY July 6, 1926 Dallas, Texas
Heir 8:00 AM CST 96W49 32N47

☉ 13-♋-43	☿ 09-♌-41	♂ 14-♈-25	♄ 19-♏-40R	♆ 23-♌-02	A 15-♌-20
☽ 04-♊-22	♀ 09-♊-03	♃ 26-♒-31R	♅ 29-♓-26R	♇ 14-♋-15	M 09-♉-22

Oldest son of Conrad Hilton and heir to the hotel fortune. Youthful marriage to Elizabeth Taylor; the first for them both. Died of a heart attack, 1969.

C: CL from Nell Botterill, 1958.

HINDENBURG, PAUL VON October 2, 1847 Posnan, Poland
Statesman 2:59 PM MET 16E53 52N25

☉ 08-♎-45	☿ 18-♎-04	♂ 15-♉-06R	♄ 07-♓-25R	♆ 27-♒-59R	A 25-♑-14
☽ 23-♋-46	♀ 10-♎-31R	♃ 18-♋-30	♅ 16-♈-33R	♇ 26-♈-13R	M 29-♏-30

German military leader of World War II. A national hero in 1916; became the first president of the German Republic by popular vote in 1925. In the 1930 election, appointed Hitler as chancellor. Conservative, loyal, narrow — a better military than civic leader. (1847-1934)

DD: WEMYSS F/N #129, same data in SS #459. BJA, May 1918, Sepharial gives 8:08 AM Berlin time.

HODIAK, JOHN   April 16, 1914   Pittsburgh, Pa
Actor   4:30 PM EST   80W01   40N26

☉ 26-♈-02	☿ 00-♈-19	♂ 22-♋-57	♄ 14-♊-44	♆ 25-♋-28	A 27-♍-20
☽ 20-♑-53	♀ 11-♉-58	♃ 17-♒-46	♅ 11-♒-15	♇ 29-♊-17	M 26-♊-56

First worked as a radio actor in Chicago before a contract with MGM. Big break in *Lifeboat* (1943); also played in *Marriage Is A Private Affair* (1944) and *A Bell for Adono* (1945).

C: CL from AFA, February 1956; same data in SS #463.

HIRSCHBACH, HEDE M.   March 13, 1890   Siegen, Germany
Musician   9:00 AM MET   8E01   50N53

☉ 22-♓-43	☿ 00-♓-52	♂ 04-♐-46	♄ 28-♌-47R	♆ 02-♊-01	A 27-♉-03
☽ 11-♐-59	♀ 28-♓-22	♃ 03-♒-40	♅ 25-♎-58R	♇ 05-♊-03	M 26-♑-53

One of eight sons, most of them highly gifted musicians. After a quarrel with Goering, with his family, left Germany; won fame in South America as a conductor. Moved to U.S. in 1941; for years an outstanding figure in American music.

C: Busch in AA, October 1948.

HOLM, CELESTE   April 29, 1917   New York, N.Y.
Actress   6:00 AM EST   73W57   40N45

☉ 08-♉-33	☿ 27-♉-47	♂ 25-♈-54	♄ 24-♋-43	♆ 02-♌-10	A 28-♉-10
☽ 11-♌-06	♀ 09-♉-22	♃ 15-♉-52	♅ 23-♒-22	♇ 02-♋-41	M 05-♒-31

Singer, pianist, entertainer, actress. Won the Oscar as best supporting actress in *Gentleman's Agreement* (1947), *Come to the Stable* (1949), and in *All About Eve* (1950). Appeared on stage in *Oklahoma!*; versatile in night clubs and supper shows.

DD: SS #468. Five reference sources give 1919.

HOLMES, OLIVER WENDELL   March 8, 1841   Boston, Mass
Jurist   8:43 PM LMT   71W04   42N22

☉ 18-♓-21	☿ 04-♈-56	♂ 06-♏-00	♄ 02-♑-09	♆ 15-♒-45	A 21-♎-17
☽ 07-♎-43	♀ 04-♉-35	♃ 18-♐-40	♅ 20-♓-12	♇ 18-♈-40	M 25-♋-21

Appointed justice of the U.S. Supreme Court in 1902 by President T. Roosevelt; known as "the great dissenter." Elected to the Hall of Fame for Great Americans in 1965. (1841-1935)

DD: CL old file quotes Kraum, "rectified from 8:00 to 9:00 PM." PC quotes *Justice Oliver Wendell Holmes* by Silus Bent at 9:00 PM LMT. That biography (1932) states on p. 24 that Holmes' father wrote to his sister that the boy was born "between 8:00 and 9:00 last night."

HOLST, GUSTAVE   September 21, 1874   Cheltenham, England
Musician   00:30 AM LMT   2W05   51N55

☉ 27-♍-51	☿ 08-♎-25	♂ 03-♍-02	♄ 08-♒-02R	♆ 00-♉-14R	A 02-♌-09
☽ 22-♑-24	♀ 14-♏-12	♃ 09-♎-00	♅ 13-♌-40	♇ 22-♉-33R	M 07-♈-52

British composer, remembered for orchestral suite *The Planets* and operas, including *The Perfect Fool*. Born to a musical family; studied piano, trombone, and composition; served as musical director at a girl's school from 1905-34. (1874-1934)

C: SS #473.

HOMICIDE #I   October 5, 1883   No place given
Family A   5:15 AM LMT   10E54   48N00

☉ 11-♎-36	☿ 15-♎-36R	♂ 25-♋-03	♄ 09-♊-59R	♆ 20-♉-39R	A 01-♎-40
☽ 24-♏-17	♀ 15-♎-22	♃ 01-♌-10	♅ 24-♍-53	♇ 01-♊-00R	M 02-♋-05

Homicide, suicide; father who shot his two sons and then himself on November 2, 1925.

C: CL from AFA, May 1939.

HOMICIDE #2	October 11, 1919	No place given
Family A	10:45 AM MET	10E54 48N00

☉ 17-♎-02	☿ 26-♎-59	♂ 00-♍-46	♄ 07-♍-17	♆ 11-♌-13	A 03-♐-10
☽ 12-♉-33	♀ 12-♍-02	♃ 13-♌-40	♅ 28-♒-05R	♇ 07-♋-47R	M 25-♍-44

Male victim; shot by his father on November 2, 1925.

C: CL from AFA, August 1939.

HOMICIDE #3	December 13, 1910	No place given
Family A	9:45 PM MET	10E54 48N00

☉ 20-♐-59	☿ 07-♑-39	♂ 25-♏-24	♄ 00-♉-02R	♆ 20-♋-57R	A 26-♌-10
☽ 14-♉-26	♀ 25-♐-12	♃ 06-♏-26	♅ 23-♑-23	♇ 27-♊-02R	M 16-♉-16

Male victim; shot by his father on November 2, 1925.

C: CL from AFA, August 1939.

HOMICIDE #4	June 21, 1901	No place given
Family B	2:00 AM MET	12E29 51N00

☉ 28-♊-57	☿ 22-♋-54	♂ 17-♍-42	♄ 14-♑-10R	♆ 28-♊-57	A 22-♉-48
☽ 26-♌-25	♀ 12-♋-39	♃ 09-♑-24R	♅ 14-♐-19R	♇ 17-♊-27	M 24-♑-07

Killed her three children and herself with gas on December 7, 1927.

C: CL from AFA, August 1939, from *Handbook of Horoscopic Data*: same source for the following three children.

HOMICIDE #5	March 23, 1923	No place given
Family B	9:30 PM MET	12E29 51N00

☉ 02-♈-12	☿ 17-♓-29	♂ 13-♉-57	♄ 17-♎-54R	♆ 15-♌-42R	A 05-♏-31
☽ 11-♊-05	♀ 20-♒-15	♃ 18-♏-26R	♅ 14-♓-36	♇ 09-♋-05R	M 17-♌-50

Male victim; killed by his mother with gas, December 7, 1927.

HOMICIDE #6	January 30, 1925	No place given
Family B	3:30 AM MET	12E29 51N00

☉ 09-♒-43	☿ 18-♑-10	♂ 25-♈-58	♄ 13-♏-51	♆ 21-♌-32R	A 02-♐-57
☽ 21-♈-14	♀ 18-♑-57	♃ 09-♑-39	♅ 19-♓-14	♇ 11-♋-57R	M 28-♍-41

Female victim; killed by her mother with gas, December 7, 1927.

HOMICIDE #7	March 4, 1926	No place given
Family B	12:30 PM MET	12E29 51N00

☉ 13-♓-09	☿ 27-♓-10	♂ 16-♑-35	♄ 26-♏-04	♆ 22-♌-53R	A 15-♋-53
☽ 06-♏-51	♀ 10-♒-42	♃ 13-♒-22	♅ 24-♓-43	♇ 12-♋-41R	M 15-♓-17

Male victim; killed by his mother with gas, December 7, 1927.

HOMICIDE #8	February 21, 1925	No place given
Family C	5:15 PM MET	14E31 51N00

☉ 02-♓-33	☿ 23-♒-00	♂ 10-♉-28	♄ 14-♏-19	♆ 20-♌-54R	A 01-♍-14
☽ 13-♒-23	♀ 17-♒-07	♃ 14-♑-13	♅ 20-♓-24	♇ 11-♋-36R	M 21-♉-45

Male victim; murdered by mother who then hanged herself on March 19, 1929.

C: CL from AFA, August 1939.

HOMICIDE #9	June 18, 1922	No place given
Family C	8:00 PM MET	14E31 51N00

☉ 26-♊-43	☿ 26-♊-04R	♂ 16-♐-13R	♄ 01-♎-01	♆ 13-♌-58	A 24-♐-07
☽ 10-♈-47	♀ 28-♋-56	♃ 09-♎-12	♅ 13-♓-36R	♇ 09-♋-14	M 27-♎-44

Male victim; murdered by mother who then hanged herself on March 19, 1929.

C: CL from AFA, August 1939.

HOMICIDE #10 April 14, 1920 No place given
Family C 9:00 PM MET 14E31 51N00

☉ 24-♈-33 ☿ 27-♓-16 ♂ 03-♏-20R ♄ 05-♍-14R ♆ 08-♌-45R A 17-♏-26
☽ 02-♓-15 ♀ 03-♈-23 ♃ 08-♌-17 ♅ 04-♓-26 ♇ 05-♋-48 M 05-♍-23

Female victim; murdered by mother who then hanged herself on March 19, 1929.

HOMICIDE #11 August 2, 1932 Miami, Fla
Male victim 10:36 AM EST 80W11 25N47

☉ 10-♌-06 ☿ 01-♍-51 ♂ 28-♊-33 ♄ 00-♒-46R ♆ 06-♍-41 A 13-♎-21
☽ 13-♌-10 ♀ 01-♋-48 ♃ 28-♌-09 ♅ 23-♈-23R ♇ 22-♋-13 M 13-♋-39

Kidnapped and killed by suffocation on May 28, 1938, by McCall, who was caught and sentenced to the death penalty.

C: CL from Carl Anderson of Miami, 1938.

HOMICIDE #12 April 2, 1943 No place given
Male juvenile 8:02 AM EWT 77W01 38N53

☉ 11-♈-52 ☿ 09-♈-56 ♂ 18-♒-45 ♄ 08-♊-16 ♆ 00-♎-23R A 07-♉-23
☽ 10-♓-26 ♀ 14-♉-02 ♃ 15-♋-54 ♅ 01-♊-46 ♇ 04-♌-59R M 21-♑-42

Ran away from home and a strict Leo father on October 16, 1962. Reached California broke; took a cab; had the cabby drive to a side road and shot him in the back of the head. Caught; trial, January 1963; entered a plea of guilty.

C: CL from AFA, November 1965.

HOMICIDE #13 September 27, 1955 No place given
Male victim 2:00 PM CST 90W00 30N00

☉ 03-♎-56 ☿ 27-♎-53 ♂ 20-♍-01 ♄ 18-♏-13 ♆ 27-♎-05 A 20-♑-46
☽ 14-♒-56 ♀ 11-♎-05 ♃ 22-♌-34 ♅ 01-♌-34 ♇ 27-♌-39 M 08-♏-12

Uneducated slovenly mother gave birth at home alone; took the baby and left it by the sewer. When found two hours later it was badly eaten by ants; lived two days. The parents were foster siblings; a 4-year-old child at home had cerebral palsy.

C: CL.

HOPE, BOB May 29, 1903 London, England
Comedian 3:36 PM GMT 0W06 51N31

☉ 07-♊-05 ☿ 14-♊-27R ♂ 29-♍-45 ♄ 09-♒-15R ♆ 02-♋-25 A 21-♎-02
☽ 14-♋-33 ♀ 18-♋-19 ♃ 20-♓-09 ♅ 24-♐-20R ♇ 18-♊-53 M 27-♋-48

Entertainer, superstar, noted for quick-witted one-liners on current events and world tours for service men. Radio debut, 1935; first movie, 1938; sixty-one film roles by 1979; TV from 1950. Recipient of forty-two honorary awards. Married, 1933; four adopted children.

DD: CL from *Bulletin of Astro Science*, May 1959. *Americana* gives the same date but Eltham, England.

HOUDINI, HARRY April 6, 1874 Budapest, Hungary
Magician 2:24 AM LMT 19E05 47N30

☉ 16-♈-04 ☿ 21-♓-23 ♂ 11-♉-14 ♄ 12-♒-27 ♆ 27-♈-47 A 22-♑-51
☽ 00-♐-41 ♀ 26-♈-28 ♃ 24-♍-28R ♅ 06-♌-28R ♇ 20-♉-27 M 22-♏-34

One of the world's greatest magicians with sensational and dangerous feats as an escape artist. Joined the circus as a young trapeze performer; took up magic and appeared with his wife at theaters and dime museums; waged a lifelong contest against spiritualism. Died of peritonitis in 1926.

DD: SS #480 (which gave Appleton, Wis: he was one year old when his parents immigrated to the U.S.). M.A., October 1904, Alan Leo writes, "He sent us his time of birth," April 6, 1873, 4:00 AM, Appleton, Wis. The CL old file has 1873; 4:00 AM from AFA, December 1955.

M.H., April 1979, Jeane Wolfe Hitt quotes *Houdini, a Magician Among the Spirits*, p. 277 for the date April 5, 1874. CL quotes Dan F. Hill, "A book on magicians gave March 24, 1874, Budapest, by official certificate." This converts to April 5, 1874 NS.

HOWARD, LESLIE   April 3, 1893   London, England
Actor   10:27 AM GMT   0W06   51N31

☉ 13-♈-53	☿ 09-♈-40R	♂ 03-♊-42	♄ 09-♎-06R	♆ 09-♊-04	A 18-♋-04
☽ 07-♏-41	♀ 06-♈-23	♃ 02-♉-04	♅ 09-♏-44R	♇ 08-♊-09	M 17-♓-38

British actor whose films include *Major Barbara, The Scarlet Pumpernil,* and *Gone with the Wind*. Lost in an aircraft in 1943; believed to have been shot down.

C: CL from Kraum article in NAJ, August 1934. PC quotes CL for 10:30 AM GMT.

HUGHES, HOWARD   December 24, 1905   Houston, Texas
Entrepreneur   10:15 PM CST   95W22   29N46

☉ 02-♑-44	☿ 15-♐-03R	♂ 28-♒-10	♄ 28-♒-40	♆ 09-♋-11R	A 05-♍-08
☽ 19-♐-14	♀ 20-♐-28	♃ 27-♉-43R	♅ 04-♑-17	♇ 21-♊-31R	M 03-♊-25

Industrialist, film producer, and aviator. Set world speed record in 1935 of 352 MPH. Had control of TWA for years; head of Hughes Tool Corp; invested in Las Vegas land and property. Reclusive in later years. Estate valued at $2.5 billion. (1905-1976)

DD: CL from Benjamine's papers. AFA, August 1957, gives 10:23 AM CST. Mark Johnson quotes Elaine Monago for 10:34 PM, "confirmed by Norwell." PC gives 11:00 PM, "personal to his astrologer." Bob Paige quotes a cousin of Hughes, that he liked to celebrate his birthday on Christmas day, but was born on December 24th, "shortly before midnight."

Dewey states that noon is given in two different biographies that stated that his father would pop in and out of the home from his office to check on the forthcoming birth, and as the clock was striking twelve noon, the doctor came down and told him he had a son. Dewey rectifies to 11:52 AM CST.

HUMPHREY, HUBERT H.   May 27, 1911   Wallace, S.D.
Politician   4:43 AM LMT   97W29   45N05

☉ 05-♊-02	☿ 11-♉-40	♂ 25-♓-19	♄ 13-♉-03	♆ 19-♋-38	A 10-♊-09
☽ 23-♉-43	♀ 16-♋-18	♃ 06-♏-35R	♅ 29-♑-09R	♇ 26-♊-53	M 12-♒-11

Vice-president of the U.S. from 1965-69 under President L.B. Johnson. U.S. senator from Minn., 1949-64; elected three times; unsuccessful bid for president in 1968. (1911-1978)

DD: D.C. Doane writes, "The data came from his father." Joylyn Hill in M.H., August 1976, gives 5:13 AM CST, AFA Data Exchange, "from his father." March quotes Elizabeth Mayo in AFA for 8:40 PM, "from his father."

HURKOS, PETER   May 21, 1911   Rotterdam, Holland
Psychic   6:00 AM Amsterdam   4E29   51N55

☉ 29-♉-03	☿ 09-♉-05	♂ 20-♓-44	♄ 12-♉-17	♆ 19-♋-28	A 00-♋-53
☽ 27-♒-15	♀ 09-♋-13	♃ 07-♏-14R	♅ 29-♑-15R	♇ 26-♊-45	M 25-♒-04

Unconscious for three days after a fall; awakened to find that he had ESP. Upon testing, was declared psychometric. Claims 87% accuracy; does professional work and TV guest appearances. Subject of a biography *Psychic* (1961). Married 1956-61; one daughter.

DD: CL from AA, August 1965; Dewey quotes same data from AA quoting L. Ivey, "from his wife." *Constellations*, 1977, quotes Peter Stapleton, "from Hurkos himself," for 5:00 AM, Dord, Holland.

HUXLEY, ALDOUS   July 26, 1894   Godalming, England
Writer   1:20 AM GMT   0W36   51N12

| ☉ 03-♌-00 | ☿ 24-♋-58R | ♂ 19-♈-17 | ♄ 19-♎-24 | ♆ 15-♊-01 | A 26-♊-02 |
| ☽ 05-♉-10 | ♀ 00-♋-55 | ♃ 25-♊-22 | ♅ 11-♏-16 | ♇ 11-♊-24 | M 20-♒-44 |

Grandson of Thomas and brother of Julian Huxley. An English novelist, who became famous for sophisticated and witty novels, including *Point Counter Point* (1928) and *Brave New World* (1932). (1894-1963)

DD: PC speculative; "based on a report that he was born very early in the morning." Old-file has 00:10 AM GMT.

IBSEN, HENRIK   March 20, 1828   Skien, Norway
Writer   2:45 PM LMT   9E38   59N13

| ☉ 29-♓-58 | ☿ 24-♓-47R | ♂ 22-♐-46 | ♄ 13-♋-21 | ♆ 18-♑-08 | A 28-♌-15 |
| ☽ 28-♉-11 | ♀ 08-♉-03 | ♃ 13-♏-46R | ♅ 01-♒-25 | ♇ 05-♈-42 | M 11-♉-46 |

Norwegian dramatist; considered the father of modern drama, since he presented realism in the theater. World-wide attention for *The Doll's House* (1879) and *Ghosts* (1881). Noted for depth portrayals, as in *Hedda Gabler* (1890). (1828-1906)

DD: Eshelman quotes Lyndoe in AA, April 1967, speculative chart. PC speculates 2:00 PM LMT.

INGEMAR, JOHANSSON   September 22, 1932   Taleborg, Sweden
Boxer   8:20 AM MET   11E58   57N41

| ☉ 29-♍-04 | ☿ 23-♍-07 | ♂ 00-♌-54 | ♄ 28-♑-12R | ♆ 08-♍-31 | A 21-♎-13 |
| ☽ 20-♊-57 | ♀ 13-♌-44 | ♃ 09-♍-04 | ♅ 22-♈-17R | ♇ 23-♋-14 | M 00-♌-42 |

Heavyweight champion of the world, June 1959. Excellent business judgement; ladies man. Married at 17; later divorced.

C: Scarsella from Baird.

JAMES, HENRY   April 15, 1843   New York, N.Y.
Writer   2:00 PM LMT   73W57   40N45

| ☉ 25-♈-09 | ☿ 15-♈-09 | ♂ 19-♐-40 | ♄ 25-♑-29 | ♆ 21-♒-05 | A 01-♍-00 |
| ☽ 11-♏-58 | ♀ 13-♓-19 | ♃ 21-♒-57 | ♅ 29-♓-46 | ♇ 21-♈-29 | M 25-♉-37 |

One of the great American novelists, who also wrote many fine short stories. Educated in Europe; later chose to live in England; never married. His work includes *The Bostonians*, *The Ambassadors*, and *The Golden Bowl*. (1843-1916)

DD: PC speculative. Old-file has 9:40 AM LMT.

JAMES, JESSE   September 4/5, 1847   Centerville, Mo
Outlaw   Midnight LMT   90W58   37N26

| ☉ 12-♍-02 | ☿ 28-♌-44 | ♂ 12-♉-40 | ♄ 09-♓-20R | ♆ 28-♒-37R | A 02-♋-51 |
| ☽ 22-♋-39 | ♀ 16-♎-40 | ♃ 14-♋-40 | ♅ 17-♈-33R | ♇ 26-♈-39R | M 12-♓-21 |

Distinguished as an unerring pistol shot and man of courage. With his brother Frank, led a gang. When a $10,000 reward was offered for him dead or alive, he was shot in the back by a member of his gang on April 3, 1882, and died immediately.

DD: SS #500. PC gives Kearney, Mo. *Americana* gives September 5, 1847, Western Missouri.

JAMES, WILLIAM   January 11, 1842   New York, N.Y.
Philosopher   4:30 AM LMT   73W57   40N45

| ☉ 20-♑-50 | ☿ 16-♑-58 | ♂ 03-♓-47 | ♄ 07-♑-14 | ♆ 15-♒-48 | A 09-♐-25 |
| ☽ 17-♑-44 | ♀ 07-♑-59 | ♃ 05-♑-36 | ♅ 21-♓-10 | ♇ 18-♈-55 | M 27-♍-48 |

Brother of novelist Henry James. A philosopher and psychologist widely known as the father of American pragmatic philosophy. His work includes *Varieties of Religious Experience* and *Principles of Psychology*, which made him known internationally. (1842-1910)

DD: PC speculative. Old-file has 5:25 AM LMT.

JEFFERS, ROBINSON January 10, 1887 Allegheny, Pa
Writer 10:00 AM EST 80W01 40N28

☉ 20-♑-07   ☿ 03-♑-58   ♂ 13-♒-36   ♄ 18-♋-58R   ♆ 25-♉-12R   A 04-♓-20
☽ 29-♋-22   ♀ 29-♑-20   ♃ 03-♏-28   ♅ 12-♎-28   ♇ 02-♊-18R   M 16-♐-00

American poet, who wrote story and lyric poems dark with pessimism about the value of human individuality. After world travel, settled in Carmel, Ca in 1914. His *Medea* was adapted from the ancient Greek. (1887-1962)

DD: PC quotes *Stonemason of Torhouse* by M. Bennet (1966), p. 15. CL states 1:00 AM EST, "from him personally." *Student Astrology*, July 1938, Storme gives 12:58 AM EST.

JOHNSON, CLAUDIA December 22, 1912 Marshall, Texas
First Lady 4:00 AM CST 94W23 32N33

☉ 00-♑-13   ☿ 09-♐-19   ♂ 15-♐-55   ♄ 28-♉-25R   ♆ 25-♋-17R   A 17-♏-24
☽ 06-♊-30   ♀ 11-♒-22   ♃ 27-♐-24   ♅ 01-♒-39   ♇ 29-♊-01R   M 23-♌-53

"Lady Bird", wife of U.S. President Lyndon B. Johnson from 1934. Their fortunes turned upward thanks to her management of their ranching and broadcasting properties. Their two daughters both married during their father's presidential adminsitration.

DD: PC, "personal." Old-file has 3:45 AM CST.

JOHNSON, RAFER August 18, 1935 Kingsburg, Ca
Athlete 6:10 AM PST 119W38 36N31

☉ 24-♌-42   ☿ 03-♍-17   ♂ 11-♏-25   ♄ 07-♓-47R   ♆ 13-♍-35   A 04-♍-30
☽ 21-♈-39   ♀ 22-♍-45R   ♃ 15-♏-30   ♅ 05-♉-30R   ♇ 26-♋-25   M 01-♊-06

Decathlon champion who won the Gold Medal at the 1955 Pan Am games, the silver medal at the 1956 Australian Olympics, and the gold medal at the 1960 Olympics. Called "the gentle giant" at 6'4". Played in more than a dozen films, with as many TV appearances. By 1979 the traveling vice president of community relations for Continental Telephone.

C: CL from Drew.

JOLLIET, LOUIS September 21, 1645 NS Quebec City, Que, Canada
Explorer 6:00 AM LMT 71W13 46N48

☉ 28-♍-41   ☿ 22-♎-40   ♂ 19-♎-25   ♄ 03-♉-20R   ♆ 03-♐-16   A 00-♎-27
☽ 15-♎-36   ♀ 18-♎-40   ♃ 04-♋-19   ♅ 23-♏-34   ♇ 07-♊-05R   M 00-♋-33

Educated for the priesthood; took minor orders in 1663 but left in 1667. Went to France to study geography. Returned to Canada, 1668. Became a fur trader and explored the area around the Great Lakes. (1645-1700)

DD: PC speculative. Old-file has the same date, 5:15 AM. *Americana* states, "born at or near Quebec, baptised September 21, 1645."

JOLSON, AL June 7, 1886 NS Sreknik, Lithuania
Actor 12:00 Noon LMT 23E30 55N02

☉ 16-♊-33   ☿ 10-♊-49   ♂ 18-♍-32   ♄ 08-♋-35   ♆ 26-♉-05   A 20-♍-25
☽ 21-♌-46   ♀ 04-♉-07   ♃ 26-♍-24   ♅ 03-♎-35R   ♇ 02-♊-54   M 16-♊-53

Singer and actor, who starred in the first full-length talking picture, *The Jazz Singer* (1927); also starred in *Sonny Boy* (1929). His life story was made into the film *The Jolson Story* (1947). (1886?-1950)

DD: PC, "from his biography which states close to noon." *Jolson* by Michael Freedland (1972) states on p. 22: "When the birth actually occured, no one now knows. It could have been any time between 1880-88. It could have been January or July. In the Russian Pale of Settlement in the 1880's, no one thought of birth certificates. Years later he was to decide that the year was 1886 and the day May 26. He like the idea of a spring birthday."

JONSON, BEN June 21, 1573 NS London, England
Playwright 1:30 AM LMT 0W06 51N31

☉ 29-♊-13 ☿ 03-♋-08R ♂ 24-♊-42 ♄ 21-♏-14R ♆ 27-♊-17 A 16-♉-09
☽ 08-♏-25 ♀ 18-♊-36 ♃ 24-♉-02 ♅ 16-♑-13R ♇ 24-♓-50 M 19-♑-51

English playwright and poet. Trained as a minister; disliked it. Joined the Army. Then entered the theater as an actor and playwright. His literary career began in 1597. Married in 1595; none of his three children survived him.

DD: PC speculative. Old-file gives Westminster, England, 2:00 AM. AA, January 1971 quotes *Britannica*, "born two months after his father's death, in or near London, probably on June 11, 1573, and most certainly not before October 1572."

Kraum in AA, March 1971, gives June 11, 1572 OS, speculative 3:16 PM LMT. LMR finds that a recent edition of the *Britannica* gives "in or near London, probably June 11, 1572", a year earlier than the prior *Britannica* quote.

JOYCE, JAMES February 2, 1882 Dublin, Ireland
Writer 6:00 AM Dunsink 6W15 53N20

☉ 13-♒-21 ☿ 00-♓-28 ♂ 26-♊-58R ♄ 06-♉-11 ♆ 13-♉-48 A 00-♑-24
☽ 02-♌-27 ♀ 08-♒-48 ♃ 17-♉-06 ♅ 17-♍-51R ♇ 27-♉-21R M 08-♏-28

Original and controversial writer, who revolutionized plot, character, and style of fiction. First novel, *A Portrait of the Artist as a Young Man* (1916); other works include *Ulysses* (1922) and *Finnegan's Wake* (1939). (1882-1941)

C: Lockhart quotes Ron Storme in AQR. PC gives the same data from MMD, but as LMT.

JUDGE, WILLIAM QUAN April 13, 1851 Dublin, Ireland
Theosophist 5:07 AM LMT 6W15 53N20

☉ 22-♈-42 ☿ 04-♉-51 ♂ 20-♓-12 ♄ 23-♈-50 ♆ 08-♓-20 A 19-♈-21
☽ 15-♍-17 ♀ 10-♓-50 ♃ 17-♎-31R ♅ 29-♈-51 ♇ 29-♈-08 M 06-♑-57

Associated with the Theosophical Society from its inception; actively engaged in its advancement in America, one of the pioneers and vice-president. Edited *The Path* for years; author of a number of books.

C: M.A., January 1895, rectified by Alan Leo from 4:00 to 6:00 AM, "stated by him."

JUNG, CARL GUSTAV July 26, 1875 Kesswil, Switzerland
Psychiatrist 7:26 PM GMT 9E19 47N36

☉ 03-♌-20 ☿ 13-♋-48 ♂ 21-♐-23 ♄ 24-♒-12R ♆ 03-♉-03 A 12-♒-56
☽ 15-♉-49 ♀ 17-♋-32 ♃ 23-♎-48 ♅ 14-♌-48 ♇ 23-♉-30 M 06-♐-44

Outstanding influence on the development of his field, with his theory and practice of analytical psychology. Broke with Freud to place greater emphasis on growth of mankind by archetypal vital forces in the individual. Professor at the University of Basel, 1943. (1875-1961)

DD: AJA, September 1962, "He told a member of the association that he was born when the last rays of the setting sun lit the room." AQ, June 1964, Delphia gives 7:37 PM, Thurgen, Switz., "data supplied by Dr. Jung." AQ, Sumer 1951, gives 8:45 PM, Kesswil, "from him." AQ, Fall 1954, Dr. Unger gives 7:24 PM, near Zurich. AQ, Fall 1961, gives 7:30 PM, Bale, Switz. R.H. Oliver quotes M. Morrell of the AA staff for 7:20 PM Berne time, Zurich, Switz., "from New York Jungian analysts, quoting his daughter." Same data in SS #512.

Kesswil, Switz., is given in *Britannica;* Thurgen is the region. The problem seems to be in the definition of sunset time. Eshelman gives sunset, calculated for the moment that the upper limb of the sun crossed the astronomical horizon, corrected for refraction but neglecting parallax, as 7:41 PM LMT. (Twilight at that date and latitude ended at 9:38 PM LMT).

KAISER, HENRY	May 9, 1882	Canajorharie, N.Y.
Industrialist	10:36 AM LMT	74W35 42N54

☉ 18-♉-52	☿ 27-♉-36	♂ 00-♌-38	♄ 16-♉-05	♆ 16-♉-22	A 10-♌-56
☽ 07-♒-21	♀ 08-♊-28	♃ 03-♊-58	♅ 14-♍-29R	♇ 28-♉-33	M 28-♈-22

From 1931 to 1945, worked on more than seventy major construction projects and developed assembly line methods in ship-building in World War II. Automotive manufacturer from 1946; extended interest to aviation, aluminum, steel, magnesium, and housing; companies all merged into Kaiser Industries in 1956.

DD: CL from *Today's Astrology,* June 1958. PC gives 10:00 AM, "personal."

KEFAUVER, ESTES	July 26, 1903	Madisonville, Tenn
Politician	8:00 AM LMT	84W22 35N31

☉ 02-♌-23	☿ 02-♌-15	♂ 23-♎-42	♄ 06-♒-16R	♆ 04-♋-31	A 07-♍-40
☽ 01-♍-18	♀ 16-♍-40	♃ 23-♓-03R	♅ 22-♐-10R	♇ 20-♊-09	M 05-♊-01

Democratic U.S. senator from Tennessee, 1948; headed the Senate committee investigating crime, 1950-51; candidate for vice president on the Adlai Stevenson ticket in 1956. (1903-1963)

DD: D.C. Doane from AFA, March 1952, which gives the time as "around 8:00 AM" and includes a rectified time of 7:47 AM. Dewey quotes Dobyns at 8:23 AM CST.

KELLERMAN, SALLY	June 2, 1937	Long Beach, Ca
Actress	7:37 AM PST	118W11 33N47

☉ 11-♊-40	☿ 18-♉-32	♂ 23-♏-35R	♄ 03-♈-31	♆ 16-♍-11	A 20-♋-38
☽ 16-♓-59	♀ 28-♈-52	♃ 26-♑-48R	♅ 11-♉-26	♇ 27-♋-05	M 07-♈-21

On screen from 1957 in co-starring roles in films that include *The Boston Strangler, Last of the Red Hot Lovers, Lost Horizon,* and *Welcome to L.A.* Nominated as best supporting actress in *M.A.S.H.*

C: Laurie Brady, 1978.

KENNEDY, JOSEPH SR.	September 6, 1888	Boston, Mass
Entrepreneur	7:06 AM EST	71W04 42N22

☉ 14-♍-17	☿ 26-♍-00	♂ 27-♏-10	♄ 14-♌-31	♆ 02-♊-20R	A 05-♎-02
☽ 18-♍-13	♀ 29-♍-49	♃ 29-♏-24	♅ 15-♎-34	♇ 05-♊-58R	M 05-♋-55

Financier; U.S. ambassador to the Court of St. James, 1937-40; early film maker. Father of President John J. Kennedy and senators Robert and Edward Kennedy. (1888-1969)

DD: Scarsella from Baird. PC speculates 2:15 AM EST, quotes Marcia Moore for 8:00 PM.

KENNEDY, ROSE	July 22, 1890	Boston, Mass
First family	10:00 AM EST	71W04 42N22

☉ 29-♋-41	☿ 29-♋-20	♂ 00-♐-07	♄ 02-♍-31	♆ 06-♊-11	A 03-♎-19
☽ 00-♎-58	♀ 07-♍-47	♃ 08-♒-16R	♅ 22-♎-48	♇ 07-♊-31	M 03-♋-54

Wife of Joseph Kennedy; mother of nine children, including two U.S. senators and one American president; known for her strength in the face of multiple tragedies that have struck five of her children.

DD: PC, "personal." Judy Johns file has 11:00 AM EST.

KETTERING, CHARLES	August 29, 1876	Laudenville, Ohio
Engineer	6:22 AM LMT	82W06 40N36

☉ 06-♍-26	☿ 26-♍-46	♂ 01-♍-02	♄ 04-♓-34R	♆ 05-♉-12R	A 16-♍-55
☽ 06-♑-28	♀ 23-♋-23	♃ 24-♏-35	♅ 21-♌-22	♇ 24-♉-34R	M 14-♊-49

Inventor of an automobile self-starter in 1911 and the ignition system later known as Delco. Directed GM research lab for more than twenty-five years. Worked on inventions of the electric cash register, ethyl gasoline, a high combustion auto engine, and more. (1876-1958)

C: CL from *Bulletin of Astro Science,* January 1959.

KEY, FRANCIS SCOTT August 1, 1779 Baltimore, Md
Lawyer 7:00 PM LMT 76W37 39N17

☉ 09-♌-27	☿ 01-♍-21	♂ 22-♏-54	♄ 20-♏-23	♆ 29-♍-26	A 07-♒-08
☽ 00-♈-05	♀ 18-♋-24	♃ 25-♍-23	♅ 22-♊-38	♇ 01-♒-57R	M 27-♏-42

Well-known Washington lawyer and amateur verse writer. Became famous for writing the words of *"The Star Spangled Banner,"* the national anthem. Wrote the poem during the War of 1812. (1779-1843)

DD: PC quotes Matthews, "born at sunset." Old-file has 6:45 PM LMT. (LMR computes sunset at 5:04 PM LMT). Scarsella from Baird has 1780, 10:56 AM LMT, Friedrichs Co, Md. *World Book* gives 1779, Friedrichs Co. (now Carroll) Md.

KHRUSHCHEV, NIKITA April 29, 1894 NS Kursk, Russia
Statesman 12:30 PM LMT 36E58 40N57

☉ 09-♉-03	☿ 18-♈-06	♂ 22-♒-35	♄ 20-♎-31R	♆ 11-♊-59	A 24-♌-27
☽ 23-♒-14	♀ 22-♓-54	♃ 05-♊-37	♅ 13-♏-31R	♇ 09-♊-34	M 17-♉-19

First secretary of the Communist Party of the Soviet Union, 1953-64. Premier of Russia, 1958-64. (1894-1971)

DD: CL from *Das Neue Zeitalter,* a German newspaper, December 26, 1959. *Americana* gives April 16, 1894, which converts to April 28, 1894 NS. AQR, Spring 1961, states April 17, 1894, given as NS, 12:30 PM LMT, but adds that when he visited the U.S. he said he didn't know the year.

Eshelman quotes Garth Allen: "A 1959 series of articles by journalists John Lewis and Eckert Goodman which ran in the New York Daily News stated that Khrushchev was born March 17, 1893 or April 17, 1894 in the village of Kalinovka, N.E. border of Ukrania, Kursk. The records disappeared when the village was destroyed during the war, and Khrushchev settled on the latter date as 'it makes me feel younger.' "

KING, DR. MARTIN LUTHER January 15, 1929 Atlanta, Ga
Minister 11:00 AM CST 84W23 33N45

☉ 25-♑-06	☿ 11-♒-42	♂ 21-♊-55R	♄ 25-♐-21	♆ 00-♍-54R	A 23-♈-03
☽ 19-♓-03	♀ 10-♓-31	♃ 01-♉-10	♅ 03-♈-57	♇ 17-♋-08R	M 14-♑-04

Preacher and leader of the civil rights movement; founder and president of Southern Christian Leadership Conference. Awarded the 1964 Nobel Peace prize. Assassinated by James Earl Ray on April 4, 1968 in Memphis, Tenn.

DD: Ebertin. Dewey quotes Dell, September 1970, for "high noon, as stated by his mother." March has 8:42 PM from Kiyo. Huggins in *The Astrology Magazine,* January 1970, gives 1:00 PM LMT. Jim Lewis in M.H., April 1979, from the base of "around noon" presents a highly rational rectification with the Astro-Carto-Graphy map of 11:21 AM CST.

KIPLING, RUDYARD December 30, 1865 Bombay, India
Writer 4:53 PM LMT 72E50 19N11

☉ 08-♑-53	☿ 24-♐-06R	♂ 24-♐-28	♄ 10-♏-08	♆ 07-♈-49	A 00-♋-48
☽ 15-♊-09	♀ 25-♐-03	♃ 10-♑-07	♅ 01-♋-35R	♇ 12-♉-22R	M 21-♓-30

British poet and novelist; awarded the Nobel prize for literature in 1907. Works include *The Jungle Book* (1894), *Captains Courageous* (1897), and the autobiography, *Something of Myself* (1937). First worked as a journalist on the Allahabad Pioneer in India. (1865-1936)

C: CL from RISING STAR July 1938, same data in SS #525.

KITCHENER, LORD GEORGE June 24, 1850 Ballylongford, Ireland
General 10:50 PM LMT 9W28 52N33

☉ 03-♋-00	☿ 15-♊-05	♂ 23-♌-22	♄ 19-♈-44	♆ 06-♓-59R	A 25-♒-17
☽ 07-♑-16	♀ 02-♌-05	♃ 16-♍-04	♅ 29-♈-37	♇ 29-♈-37	M 16-♐-26

Served in Palestine, Cyprus, and Egypt, then South Africa in 1899 as second in command. British secretary of state for war in 1914. Ambitious and dictatorial; popular with the people. Killed in the explosion of a ship headed for Russia on June 5, 1916.

DD: Lyndoe in AA, March 1960, "from a witness present at his birth." SS #527 gives 00:37 AM LMT. Old-file has 1:00 AM. M.A., January 1917, gives "half-hour after midnight," stated by Hazelrigg "from Lord Kitchener himself." M.A., February 1917, Shirley states, "He personally told a friend he didn't know his time of birth." The publication printed a letter from his sister, that their mother gave his birthday as June 24, and as her birthday was two days away, they always celebrated together; that his time was not known." BJA, January 1917, printed a copy of his baptism certificate that gave his birth date as June 15, 1850.

KLEE, PAUL
Artist

December 18, 1879
10:45 AM LMT

Munchenbuschee, Switzerland
7E28   47N02

☉ 26-♐-10   ☿ 10-♐-13R   ♂ 13-♉-04   ♄ 09-♈-00   ♆ 09-♉-33R   A 18-♒-20
☽ 02-♓-04   ♀ 09-♏-57   ♃ 06-♓-50   ♅ 09-♍-00R   ♇ 25-♉-54R   M 09-♐-35

A master of contemporary art; one of the most original artists of his time, with thousands of paintings, drawings, and prints that express his highly imaginative vision. Taught in a famous German school of design. Lived in Bern from 1933 until his death in 1940.

DD: PC speculative. Old-file has 11:00 PM LMT. T. Joseph quotes Wangemann for 4:00 AM LMT.

KNOX, RONNIE
Athlete

February 14, 1935
7:00 PM CST

Chicago, Ill
87W39   41N52

☉ 25-♒-25   ☿ 00-♓-05R   ♂ 23-♎-42   ♄ 00-♓-03   ♆ 13-♍-42R   A 15-♍-28
☽ 18-♋-20   ♀ 16-♓-23   ♃ 22-♏-28   ♅ 28-♈-10   ♇ 24-♋-21R   M 12-♊-54

Track star of UCLA; popular with a large public following; called "the pinup boy" by *Time* magazine. Movie contract with MGM in 1956.

C: CL from Drew; same data in the Powwow Corner of AA, September 1956.

KOCH, ROBERT
Scientist

December 11, 1843
8:33 PM MET

Hanover, Germany
9E20   52N29

☉ 19-♐-10   ☿ 21-♐-28   ♂ 29-♒-03   ♄ 23-♑-49   ♆ 19-♒-11   A 13-♌-14
☽ 15-♌-06   ♀ 06-♑-37   ♃ 22-♒-54   ♅ 28-♓-21   ♇ 21-♈-02R   M 24-♈-15

Isolated bacillus tuberculosis at age 39. In 1877, demonstrated the techniques for fixing and staining bacteria; his work on wounds, septicema, and splenic fever gained him a seat on the Imperial Board of Health, 1880. Awarded the Nobel prize in 1905. (1843-1910)

C: Lyndoe in AA, November 1969, date from home archives, time speculative.

KORNING, ROBERT
Murderer

January 1, 1901
6:30 PM MET

Meissen, Germany
13E29   51N10

☉ 10-♑-39   ☿ 28-♐-48   ♂ 11-♍-44   ♄ 07-♑-47   ♆ 27-♊-30R   A 08-♌-19
☽ 28-♉-36   ♀ 11-♐-40   ♃ 26-♐-07   ♅ 14-♐-21   ♇ 16-♊-15R   M 18-♈-03

Married in 1929; friends thought him a jolly good fellow; double life. Bodies found on November 8, 1929, June 6, 1930, June 11, 1935, July 9, 1936, and May 23, 1937; arrested, October 4, 1937; convicted of rape and murder. Executed, June 1938.

C: CL from AFA, March 1941, translation of article by Julius Sauer in *Sterne Und Mensch*, November 1938.

KOPECHNE, MARY JO
Drowning victim

July 26, 1940
1:00 PM PST

Forty Fort, Pa
75W52   41N17

☉ 03-♌-34   ☿ 26-♋-21R   ♂ 14-♌-49   ♄ 13-♉-55   ♆ 23-♍-28   A 07-♏-58
☽ 25-♈-35   ♀ 28-♊-01   ♃ 13-♉-11   ♅ 25-♉-36   ♇ 02-♌-31   M 15-♌-57

Government employee of Senator Robert F. Kennedy, 1968. Drowned while a passenger in a car driven by Senator Edward Kennedy when it plunged off a brige into a tidal pool at Chappaquiddick. The investigation cleared Kennedy of manslaughter suspicion.

C: Eshelman speculative.

KRUPP, ALFRED VON August 13, 1907 Essen, Germany
Entrepreneur 2:45 PM MET 7E00 51N28

☉ 19-♌-39 ☿ 00-♌-51 ♂ 07-♑-06 ♄ 26-♓-29R ♆ 13-♋-44 A 29-♏-09
☽ 08-♎-51 ♀ 10-♌-49 ♃ 28-♋-51 ♅ 09-♑-15R ♇ 24-♊-28 M 23-♍-34

Fifth head of the great steel industrial empire in West Germany; chairman from 1942. Sentenced to twelve years in prison after World War II; commuted in 1951; re-built the concern but no longer manufacturing arms. Biography, *The Arms of Krupp*. (1907-1967)

DD: AQ Spring 1976 quotes Ebertin in DIREKTIONEN. PC states 2:00 PM, "recorded."

LA GUARDIA, FIORELLA December 11, 1882 New York, N.Y.
Politician 4:00 PM EST 73W57 40N45

☉ 19-♐-47 ☿ 16-♐-49 ♂ 19-♐-33 ♄ 20-♉-40R ♆ 16-♉-35R A 12-♊-39
☽ 04-♑-44 ♀ 11-♐-28R ♃ 27-♊-14R ♅ 23-♍-13 ♇ 28-♉-54R M 18-♒-01

At age 21, job in U.S. consulate; lawyer, 1910; into politics; entered Congress, 1915. Active service in the war; again into Congress in 1922 for four terms. Became the 99th Mayor of New York City, 1934-45. (1882-1947)

DD: *Constellations,* Spring 1977, Richard Adler quotes a 1950 issue of AFA. PC quotes Drew and SS #538 (no time given) for 2:30 PM EST. LMR computes Drew's chart for 2:17 PM EST (MC 24 Capricorn).

LANDOWSKA, WANDA July 5, 1879 Warsaw, Poland
Musician 4:00 PM LMT 21E00 52N14

☉ 13-♋-09 ☿ 00-♌-54 ♂ 18-♈-21 ♄ 15-♈-20 ♆ 11-♉-37 A 20-♏-53
☽ 05-♒-24 ♀ 28-♌-20 ♃ 12-♓-42R ♅ 01-♍-32 ♇ 26-♉-57 M 11-♍-48

Polish harpsichordist, pianist, and composer. From 1906, made concert tours throughout Europe and Africa on both instruments; gradually the harpsichord became her speciality. American debut, 1923; moved to U.S. in 1941. (1879-1959)

DD: PC speculative Old-file has 8:15 PM LMT.

LANGTRY, LILLIE October 13, 1853 Isle of Jersey
Actress 6:00 AM LMT 2W06 49N11

☉ 19-♎-49 ☿ 29-♎-03 ♂ 12-♌-02 ♄ 01-♊-03R ♆ 11-♓-22R A 15-♎-44
☽ 05-♓-18 ♀ 28-♏-40 ♃ 20-♐-11 ♅ 11-♉-22R ♇ 01-♉-58R M 20-♋-04

"Jersey Lillie." Became a stage favorite in England and the U.S. by sheer charm. Her life was dramatized in an excellent BBC TV series *Lillie* (1979), including her adventures and love affairs, and friendships with the great of her day. (1853-1929)

DD: PC quotes SS and NN. Not in SS; NN #174 gives a speculative horoscope by Kymry. Old-file has 5:30 AM LMT. Date check in *The Life and Loves of Lillie Langtry* by Noel B. Gerson (1971).

LASKY, JESSE L. September 13, 1880 San Francisco, Ca
Movie producer 3:15 AM LMT 122W26 37N47

☉ 21-♍-01 ☿ 17-♍-34 ♂ 04-♎-37 ♄ 27-♈-59R ♆ 14-♉-08R A 20-♌-48
☽ 13-♑-31 ♀ 07-♎-47 ♃ 17-♈-31R ♅ 10-♍-08 ♇ 28-♉-19R M 14-♉-02

After youthful adventures in vaudeville as a cornetist, and in Alaska as a fortune hunter, formed a play company in 1914; three years later merged with Adolph Zukor to form Paramount Pictures. (1880-1958)

DD: CL from SS #550 (no time given). PC quotes SS at 3:30 AM LMT.

LAUGHTON, CHARLES July 1, 1899 Scarborough, England
Actor 6:00 AM GMT 0W24 54N17

☉ 09-♋-09 ☿ 26-♋-53 ♂ 08-♍-32 ♄ 19-♐-00R ♆ 25-♊-03 A 04-♌-59
☽ 22-♈-26 ♀ 18-♊-23 ♃ 00-♏-20 ♅ 04-♐-43R ♇ 15-♊-45 M 09-♈-27

Famous for his magnificent voice and diction in character portrayals on stage and screen. Successful from the beginning of his career; films include *Mutiny on the Bounty, Ruggles of Red Gap,* and *The Private Life of Henry VIII.* (1899-1962)

DD: CL from *Rafael's Almanac,* 1936. Old-file has 10:40 PM GMT.

LAWRENCE, D.H.   September 11, 1885   Eastwood, England
Writer   6:45 PM LMT   1W49 52N57

| ☉ 19-♍-09 | ☿ 04-♍-50R | ♂ 26-♋-51 | ♄ 07-♋-03 | ♆ 25-♉-33R | A 05-♈-38 |
| ☽ 27-♎-03 | ♀ 23-♎-14 | ♃ 16-♍-59 | ♅ 02-♎-25 | ♇ 03-♊-06R | M 02-♑-01 |

English novelist and poet, who championed the concept that man should bring his instincts and emotions into balance with his intellect in such novels as *Sons and Lovers* (1913), *Women in Love* (1920), and *Lady Chatterley's Lover* (1928). (1885-1930)

DD: CL from *Predictions,* September 1960. Old-file has 5:20 AM LMT. Beecroft in AQ, June 1963, speculates 7:30 PM LMT.

LAWRENCE, GERTRUDE   July 4, 1898   London, England
Actress   10:30 AM GMT   0W06 51N31

| ☉ 12-♋-25 | ☿ 17-♋-21 | ♂ 19-♉-42 | ♄ 06-♐-39R | ♆ 23-♊-01 | A 22-♍-51 |
| ☽ 20-♑-17 | ♀ 16-♌-58 | ♃ 02-♎-23 | ♅ 29-♏-59R | ♇ 14-♊-52 | M 20-♊-41 |

Achieved stardom in both England and the U.S., admired for sparkling performances in plays that include *The King and I, Pygmalion,* and *Tonight at 8:30.* (1898?-1952)

DD: PC speculative. Old-file has 11:00 AM GMT., same date. *Famous People* gives 1900, *Astrological Index* gives 1901. *Americana* has July 4, 1898.

LAWRENCE, T.E.   August 16, 1888   Tremodoc, Wales
Adventurer   5:00 AM GMT   4W15 52N50

| ☉ 23-♌-42 | ☿ 15-♌-33 | ♂ 13-♏-50 | ♄ 11-♌-54 | ♆ 02-♊-14 | A 22-♌-36 |
| ☽ 13-♐-42 | ♀ 03-♍-30 | ♃ 27-♏-20 | ♅ 14-♎-29 | ♇ 05-♊-54 | M 08-♉-09 |

British soldier of fortune, writer, archaeologist, with military intelligence; organizer of the Arab revolt against Turkey with military and diplomatic genius. Author of *Seven Pillars of Wisdom* (1926). Killed in a motorcycle accident in England May 13, 1935.

DD: March quotes *The Secret Lives of Lawrence of Arabia* by Knightly and Simon for "early morning." LMR quotes *Lawrence of Arabia* by Aldington (1955) for a carefully researched report on p. 25, "Thomas Edward, according to his mother, was born in the small hours of the 16th of August, 1888, Tremodoc: he was registered as born on the 15th by his father."

  CL quotes Tucker for August 15, 1888, 7:27 AM GMT, Portmadoc, Carner, Wales. BJA, July 1935, Bailey gives August 15, 9:24 AM, rectified. SS #554 gives August 15, 11:00 PM GMT. PC quotes SS for 11:30 PM GMT, but adds that *T.E. Lawrence* by Desmond Steward states he was born in the early hours of the morning, August 15.

LAZARUS, MELL   May 3, 1927   New York, N.Y.
Cartoonist   9:00 AM EDT   73W57 40N45

| ☉ 12-♉-06 | ☿ 24-♈-39 | ♂ 09-♋-41 | ♄ 06-♐-01R | ♆ 24-♌-12R | A 03-♋-06 |
| ☽ 09-♊-42 | ♀ 19-♊-47 | ♃ 24-♓-13 | ♅ 01-♈-43 | ♇ 14-♋-02 | M 09-♓-56 |

Creator of the cartoon series *Momma,* syndicated in 110 U.S. Newspapers, and *Miss Peach,* first syndicated in 1957 and appearing in 155 U.S. and European papers. Author of three plays, a novel, *The Boss is Crazy Too,* and an anthology, *The Momma Treasury.*

C: From him to LMR, November 1978, "from mother's recall." LMR speculates the time to be later, to put Neptune in the second house trine Mercury in the tenth.

LEARY, TIMOTHY   October 22, 1920   Springfield, Mass
Psychodelicist   10:45 AM EDT   72W35 42N06

| ☉ 28-♎-54 | ☿ 22-♏-43 | ♂ 02-♑-58 | ♄ 20-♍-21 | ♆ 13-♌-35 | A 09-♐-44 |
| ☽ 27-♒-49 | ♀ 28-♏-03 | ♃ 11-♍-30 | ♅ 01-♓-55R | ♇ 08-♋-53R | M 29-♍-20 |

High priest of the 60s LSD movement. Harvard professor until fired for experiments with hallucinogenics. The first of twenty-nine arrests for posession was in 1965. Escape from prison in 1970 for two years. A third marriage in Europe. Parole in 1976.

DD: CL from *Handbook* by Michael Mayer. PC gives 10:40 AM EDT as "personal." Walter Breen in Leek's *Astrology*, September 1970, gives 9:43 AM EST, "rectified." Dewey states, "he told a friend of mine that he had Cancer rising." Old-file has 9:45 AM EDT.

LE CORBUSIER   October 6, 1887   La Chaux de Fonds, Switz.
Architect   9:00 PM LMT   6E50   47N06

☉ 13-♎-16   ☿ 01-♏-08   ♂ 25-♌-24   ♄ 04-♌-56   ♆ 29-♉-47R   A 28-♊-10
☽ 04-♊-42   ♀ 20-♍-58R   ♃ 09-♏-12   ♅ 12-♎-54   ♇ 04-♊-50R   M 28-♒-00

Swiss architect, who won international fame as a designer of buildings in the functional style. Also became known as a painter and writer. Designed houses as "machines for living," with creative style that was a forerunner for later design. (1887-1965)

DD: AQ, Summer 1959, Friedjung. PC, same data, "recorded." Old-file has 9:10 PM LMT.

LEE, GYPSY ROSE   February 9, 1914   Seattle, Wash
Entertainer   4:30 AM PST   122W26   37N47

☉ 19-♒-56   ☿ 01-♓-18   ♂ 05-♋-46R   ♄ 11-♊-13R   ♆ 26-♋-13R   A 26-♐-00
☽ 03-♌-36   ♀ 19-♒-23   ♃ 04-♒-26   ♅ 08-♒-17   ♇ 29-♊-16R   M 25-♎-48

World's most famous striptease artist; later appeared in films and TV. Author of mystery novels and her memoirs in *Gypsy* (1957).

DD: McEvers from a biography, speculative time. Same date given in *Current Biography*, 1943, and *50,000 Birthdays*. PC gives January 9, 1914, says "date verified," time of 4:35 AM PST computed from SS #559. Same date given in *Famous People, Information Please,* and *Current Biography* Obit, 1970. SS #559 gives January 10, 1910. Same date in *Celebrities.*

LEE, PEGGY   May 26, 1920   Jamestown, N.D.
Singer   4:00 AM CST   98W42   46N54

☉ 04-♊-50   ☿ 05-♊-16   ♂ 21-♎-28R   ♄ 05-♍-09   ♆ 09-♌-07   A 16-♉-05
☽ 23-♍-40   ♀ 24-♉-23   ♃ 12-♌-01   ♅ 05-♓-35   ♇ 06-♋-29   M 23-♑-08

Recording artist of more than five hundred records; songwriter and arranger; also plays supper clubs, TV, movies, with a 1956 Oscar nomination for *Pete Kelly's Blues.* Married, 1943-51; one daughter; three more marriages.

C: Laurie Brady, 1978. Date check *Celebrity Register.*

LEMMON, JACK   February 8, 1925   Waltham, Mass
Actor   2:00 PM EST   71W14   42N23

☉ 19-♒-32   ☿ 02-♒-12   ♂ 02-♉-10   ♄ 14-♏-09   ♆ 21-♌-16R   A 13-♋-29
☽ 18-♌-13   ♀ 01-♒-02   ♃ 11-♑-41   ♅ 19-♓-42   ♇ 11-♋-47R   M 21-♓-26

On screen from 1954; nominated as best supporting actor in *Mister Roberts.* Won the Oscar as best actor in *Save the Tiger.* Nominated as the best actor in *Some Like it Hot, The Apartment,* and *Days of Wine and Roses.*

DD: PC, "personal." Old-file gives Boston, 2:10 PM EST. *Current Biography*, 1961, gives Boston.

LENIN, NICOLAI   April 22, 1870 NS   Simbirsk, Russia
Communist   9:42 PM LMT   48E26   54N17

☉ 02-♉-24   ☿ 12-♉-40   ♂ 23-♈-37   ♄ 28-♐-21R   ♆ 19-♈-45   A 28-♏-19
☽ 03-♒-24   ♀ 16-♓-53   ♃ 26-♉-09   ♅ 18-♋-13   ♇ 17-♉-06   M 25-♍-45

Leader of the communist movement in Russia and the founder of the Soviet Union. A fanatical believer in the doctrine of Karl Marx; spread it throughout Russia and tried to put it into practice. (1870-1942)

DD: CL quotes Rudhyar in AA, June 1938, who writes, "I have not been able to find any records of his time of birth: speculative." SS #566 gives the same date (no time) but prints planet positions for April 10, 1870. AQ, Summer 1972, states that April 10, 1870 is New Style. M.A., April 1931, Wemyss quotes *Revue Belge*, 1927, #2, for April 10, 1870 NS (March 29, 1870 OS). AJ, Summer 1967, reports that the Russians celebrate Lenin's birthday in Russia on April 22. *Britannica* gives April 9 OS = April 21, 1870 NS.

LEWIS, JERRY	March 16, 1926	Newark, N.Y.
Comedian	12:15 PM EST	74W06 43N03

☉ 25-♓-22	☿ 13-♈-11	♂ 25-♑-22	♄ 25-♏-59R	♆ 22-♌-35R	A 16-♋-28
☽ 00-♉-41	♀ 15-♒-10	♃ 16-♒-00	♅ 25-♓-25	♇ 12-♋-36R	M 24-♓-45

Top star: a success in team with Dean Martin from 1950-54; TV variety shows, films, and Las Vegas and club circuit. Sponsor of the annual Muscular Dystrophy Association drive since 1966. One marriage; six sons.

DD: *Constellations*, 1977, Lockhart quotes B.C. March states 11:55 PM, "from him personally" to a friend. Holliday has 00:30 AM EST.

LEWIS, JOHN L.	February 12, 1880	Lucas, Iowa
Union leader	00:30 AM LMT	93W27 41N02

☉ 22-♒-59	☿ 21-♒-02	♂ 29-♉-00	♄ 12-♈-13	♆ 09-♉-25	A 16-♏-28
☽ 15-♓-48	♀ 15-♑-08	♃ 17-♓-52	♅ 07-♍-34R	♇ 25-♉-27	M 27-♌-00

President of the United Mine Workers Union, 1920-60. Started work in the mines at age 12. Elected legislature agent UMW, 1909; vice-president, 1917. Awarded the Presidential Medal of Freedom, 1964. (1880-1969)

DD: *Wynn's Astrology*, February 1942, "between Midnight and 1:00 AM, data from Kathryn Lewis, his secretary, as stated by his mother." SS #576 gives 00:40 AM.

LEWIS, MERIWETHER	August 18, 1774	Charlottesville, Va
Explorer	9:00 AM LMT	78W30 38N02

☉ 25-♌-35	☿ 25-♌-44R	♂ 07-♋-05	♄ 25-♍-08	♆ 19-♍-21	A 09-♎-45
☽ 14-♑-06	♀ 21-♋-13	♃ 15-♉-39	♅ 02-♊-15	♇ 22-♑-46R	M 11-♋-01

Commander of the expedition that first explored the Missouri and Columbia rivers and that area. Also served as governor of the Louisiana Territory. The Lewis and Clark Expedition began in 1804. (1774-1809)

DD: PC speculative. Old-file has 6:00 PM LMT.

LEWIS, SINCLAIR	February 7, 1885	Sauk Center, Minn
Writer	4:00 PM CST	94W57 34N44

☉ 19-♒-22	☿ 27-♑-05	♂ 20-♒-10	♄ 17-♊-22R	♆ 20-♉-33	A 06-♌-11
☽ 00-♐-14	♀ 27-♑-56	♃ 02-♍-22R	♅ 02-♎-28R	♇ 00-♊-11R	M 19-♈-43

First American novelist to win a Nobel prize for literature in 1930. Had been awarded a Pulitzer prize in 1926 but refused to accept it, saying he did not believe in prizes and felt that other writers were more worthy. (1885-1951)

DD: PC speculative. Old-file has 1:35 AM CST.

LEY, WILLIE	October 2, 1906	Berlin, Germany
Scientist, writer	5:00 AM MET	13W24 52N30

☉ 08-♎-03	☿ 14-♎-04	♂ 12-♍-25	♄ 09-♓-42R	♆ 12-♋-35	A 25-♍-22
☽ 03-♈-45	♀ 23-♏-53	♃ 09-♋-49	♅ 04-♑-38	♇ 23-♊-46R	M 23-♊-54

Science writer, lecturer, rocket engineer. Founded the Society for Space Travel in Germany 1927. Fled the Nazis to the U.S. in 1935. Prolific writer on space travel and rocketry. (1906-1969)

C: Penfield quotes Walter Breen, 1977.

LIE, TRYGVE H.   July 16, 1896   Oslo, Norway
Statesman   4:47 PM TLT   10E42   59N47

| ☉ 24-♋-32 | ☿ 08-♋-32 | ♂ 10-♉-21 | ♄ 12-♏-26 | ♆ 19-♊-07 | A 29-♏-54 |
| ☽ 11-♎-17 | ♀ 26-♋-31 | ♃ 14-♌-17 | ♅ 20-♏-30R | ♇ 13-♊-11 | M 07-♎-20 |

Lawyer in 1919; appointed secretary general of Norwegian Labor Party; minister of foreign affairs, 1941. Spoke fluent English, German, and some Russian. Became U.N. Secretary 1946. (1896-1968)

C: Submitted by Alfa Lindanger in AA, July 1946. Same data in SS #577.

LIELKE, ELMER ARTHUR   February 7, 1924   Minot, N.D.
Homicide, suicide   12:38 PM MST   101W18   48N14

| ☉ 17-♒-44 | ☿ 22-♑-21 | ♂ 12-♐-11 | ♄ 02-♏-20 | ♆ 19-♌-03R | A 13-♊-46 |
| ☽ 21-♓-00 | ♀ 23-♓-29 | ♃ 15-♐-02 | ♅ 15-♓-52 | ♇ 10-♋-38R | M 12-♒-21 |

Worked as a state reformatory guard. Visited his ex-wife on November 26, 1964. Pried open the door as she, her beau and daughter were watching TV; shot and killed Lorraine with two bullets from a .22 Ruger, wounded her beau, shot and killed her sleeping ten-year old son, shot and killed himself.

C: CL from George Storkk, November 1964.

LIELKE, LORRAINE   September 27, 1926   Warm Beach, Wash
Murder victim   1:00 AM PST   122W22   48N10

| ☉ 03-♎-30 | ☿ 09-♎-40 | ♂ 19-♉-26 | ♄ 22-♏-36 | ♆ 25-♌-55 | A 07-♌-27 |
| ☽ 17-♊-22 | ♀ 19-♍-26 | ♃ 17-♒-47R | ♅ 27-♓-13R | ♇ 15-♋-52 | M 19-♈-32 |

Third marriage to Elmer, 1950 or '51; two children by prior marriages. Separated, 1963, after being beaten by her husband. Made a settlement of $6000 from an auto accident (February 23, 1964) of which Elmer wanted one third, the night he killed her.

C: CL from George Storkk, November 1964.

LIEKLE, SANDRA VINCENT   June 9, 1946   Seattle, Wash
Victim's daughter   11:45 AM PST   122W20   47N36

| ☉ 18-♊-21 | ☿ 29-♊-29 | ♂ 24-♌-07 | ♄ 23-♋-16 | ♆ 05-♎-51R | A 16-♍-20 |
| ☽ 24-♎-21 | ♀ 20-♋-02 | ♃ 17-♎-29R | ♅ 17-♊-37 | ♇ 09-♌-57 | M 12-♊-55 |

First child of Lorraine Lielke from her first marriage. When her step-father broke into the house with a tire iron on November 26, 1964 (just after midnight of the 25th), fled outdoors to call for help and escaped the killings.

C: CL from George Storkk, November 1964.

LIND, JENNY   October 6, 1820   Stockholm, Sweden
Singer   6:00 PM LMT   18E00   49N20

| ☉ 13-♎-20 | ☿ 16-♎-59 | ♂ 09-♏-40 | ♄ 09-♈-52R | ♆ 28-♐-18 | A 01-♉-58 |
| ☽ 06-♎-52 | ♀ 27-♌-05 | ♃ 15-♓-09R | ♅ 25-♐-19 | ♇ 27-♓-18R | M 14-♑-03 |

Operatic soprano called "The Swedish Nightengale." Brilliant career in opera and on the concert stage, with a controlled, rich and warm coloratura voice. Debut in 1838. Gave up her opera career in 1849 and toured the U.S. with P.T. Barnum. (1820-1887)

DD: PC states, "recorded." Jansky gives 5:37:48 PM LMT.

LINDBURGH, CHAS. AUGUSTUS January 20, 1859   Stockholm, Sweden
Legal economist   1:36 PM LMT   18E03   42N20

| ☉ 29-♑-59 | ☿ 05-♑-36 | ♂ 21-♓-30 | ♄ 09-♌-36R | ♆ 22-♓-46 | A 17-♊-01 |
| ☽ 21-♌-30 | ♀ 19-♐-28 | ♃ 11-♊-58R | ♅ 29-♉-35R | ♇ 05-♉-35 | M 20-♒-58 |

Politician, writer, lecturer, lawyer. Raised, educated, and began a law practice in Minnesota. Elected to the U.S. House of Representatives, 1907-17. Books include *Banking and Currency* (1913) and *The Economic Pinch* (1923). (1859-1924)

C: CL from Helena Puxley.

LINDBERGH, CHARLES   February 4, 1902   Detroit, Mich
Pilot   2:30 AM CST   83W03 42N20

☉ 14-♒-37 ☿ 02-♓-51 ♂ 26-♒-20 ♄ 21-♑-43 ♆ 29-♊-00R A 08-♐-28
☽ 25-♐-54 ♀ 01-♓-11R ♃ 29-♑-26 ♅ 20-♐-11 ♇ 16-♊-48R M 27-♍-51

Most famous hero of his day for a solo, non-stop flight from New York to Paris, May 20-21, 1927; awarded the Congressional Medal of Honor. Won the Pulitzer prize in 1954 for his biography *The Spirit of St. Louis*. Also wrote *We* (1936) and *Of Flight and Life* (1948). (1902-1974)

DD: CL from news clippings. Same data in SS #581 and in WEMYSS F/N #29. AFA, August 1939, gives 3:02 AM LMT.
    The profile and chart of his wife, Anne Morrow Lindbergh, who was also a pilot and a writer, are given in *Profiles of Women*.

LINDSAY, JOHN V.   November 24, 1921   New York, N.Y.
Politician   7:00 AM EST   73W57 40N45

☉ 01-♐-41 ☿ 14-♏-17 ♂ 10-♎-53 ♄ 05-♎-09 ♆ 15-♌-58R A 02-♐-09
☽ 27-♍-57 ♀ 13-♏-17 ♃ 12-♎-01 ♅ 05-♓-45 ♇ 09-♋-42R M 17-♍-59

Won five battle stars in World War II action. Practiced law in N. Y., 1948-58; assistant to the attorney general, 1955-56. Elected Mayor of New York City, 1965. Regarded as one of the strong voices of liberalism.

DD: CL from Watters in AFA, April 1972, who writes, "From Al Morrison, allegedly B.C." Leek's *Astrology*, July 1970, gives 11:00 PM, speculative. Leeks *Astrology*, April 1972, Cook gives 3:30 AM. PC, same data as "personal."

LINKLETTER, ART   July 17, 1912   Moosejaw, Sask, Canada
Entertainer   4:38 AM MST   105W35 50N28

☉ 24-♋-29 ☿ 20-♌-07 ♂ 00-♍-14 ♄ 01-♊-01 ♆ 23-♋-33 A 28-♋-35
☽ 06-♍-03 ♀ 27-♋-39 ♃ 05-♐-57R ♅ 01-♒-46R ♇ 29-♊-08 M 04-♈-11

Emcee and ad-libber extraordinary; talked to some 30,000 people in sixteen years of radio and TV. His three shows, *People Are Funny*, *House Party*, and *Life With Linkletter*, highly popular. First became an announcer in 1933, with ability to talk extemporaneously and non-stop.

C: Scarsella quotes Baird, data from Ziegler.

LISTER, JOSEPH   April 5, 1827   Upton, England
Physician   5:30 AM LMT   0W00 51N40

☉ 14-♈-40 ☿ 15-♈-40R ♂ 12-♉-34 ♄ 00-♋-15 ♆ 16-♑-09 A 12-♈-35
☽ 21-♋-37 ♀ 00-♓-28 ♃ 08-♎-52R ♅ 27-♑-54 ♇ 05-♈-01 M 04-♑-49

Founder of antiseptic surgery. His application of antiseptics so revolutionized surgery that it became safe for the first time to open the body. The first medical man to be elevated to the peerage, in 1897. (1827-1912)

DD: PC speculative. Old-file has 5:55 AM LMT.

LLOYD GEORGE, DAVID   January 17, 1863   Manchester, England
Statesman   7:55 AM LMT   2W15 53N29

☉ 26-♑-47 ☿ 12-♒-20 ♂ 01-♉-01 ♄ 05-♎-31R ♆ 01-♈-26 A 20-♑-27
☽ 23-♐-59 ♀ 05-♒-44 ♃ 26-♎-24 ♅ 17-♊-14R ♇ 09-♉-25R M 27-♏-17

British politician: lawyer at age 21; member of parliament at 27; an eloquent orator. Became Prime Minister in World War I; proved himself to be a great war leader. Resigned in 1922 and never again regained his former power. (1863-1945)

DD: Lyndoe in AA, Augusts 1963, "from him in 1930." Same data in SS #584. Shirley says 8:55 AM, "from him to an astrologer," in M.A., August 1913. BJA, February 1937, Bailey says 8:55 AM is the authentic time, "not the later given times of 8:15 or 8:27 AM."

LOEB, RICHARD   June 11, 1905   Chicago, Ill
Murderer   8:51 AM CST   87W39   41N52

| ☉ 19-♊-59 | ☿ 05-♊-20 | ♂ 08-♏-31R | ♄ 02-♓-54 | ♆ 07-♋-12 | A 16-♌-40 |
| ☽ 04-♎-07 | ♀ 07-♉-22 | ♃ 22-♉-03 | ♅ 02-♑-46R | ♇ 21-♊-10 | M 06-♉-43 |

He and Nathan Leopold, both sons of wealthy and influential families, regarded as brilliant students, sadistically killed a young boy as a "thrill killing" and a perfect crime on May 21, 1924. Trial, July 21; life sentence, September 1924. Loeb died in prison after an attack by another prisoner.

DD: CL quotes Lyndoe article, which states, "time from mother." Lyndoe in AA, May 1960, says, "chart has wide acceptance as correct." T.P. Davis quotes Julie Baum at 4:59 AM CST, adds that the Chicago Vital Statistics Dept says they have no records: the accuracy of the data is open to question. Old-file has 11:15 AM CST. PC quotes SS #586 (no time given) for 9:00 AM CST, adds that "his mother gives 8:51 AM."

LOMBARDO, GUY   June 19, 1902   London, Ont, Canada
Musician   10:00 AM EST   81W15   42N59

| ☉ 27-♊-22 | ☿ 03-♋-45R | ♂ 08-♊-36 | ♄ 26-♑-27R | ♆ 01-♋-02 | A 29-♌-35 |
| ☽ 11-♐-21 | ♀ 17-♉-43 | ♃ 16-♒-58R | ♅ 18-♐-57R | ♇ 18-♊-23 | M 23-♉-03 |

Bandleader of "The Royal Canadians," a primarily family group. Steady popularity through the 30s and 40s; launched an American tradition by welcoming in the New Year with "the sweetest music this side of Heaven." (1902-1977)

DD: SS #588. Jansky gives 10:00 PM EST.

LOOS, ANITA   April 26, 1889   Etna, Ca
Writer   00:04 AM PST   122W25   41N29

| ☉ 06-♉-16 | ☿ 07-♉-31 | ♂ 20-♉-25 | ♄ 13-♌-33 | ♆ 01-♊-02 | A 09-♑-38 |
| ☽ 22-♓-45 | ♀ 13-♉-48R | ♃ 08-♑-16R | ♅ 19-♎-16R | ♇ 04-♊-46 | M 04-♏-54 |

Wrote first scenario at age 12; became an author of sophisticated film short features. The first of the Lorelei Lee stories appeared in 1925, with *Gentlemen Prefer Blondes* in 1925, and *Gentlemen Marry Brunettes* in 1928, both made into movies.

DD: CL from Ellen Wood, 1960. All other sources give Sissons, Ca. April 26, 1893 given in six reference sources. *People* magazine photographed Loos in March 1977, said "83-year old" = 1893. April 16, 1893 given in two reference sources. SS #591 gives May 6, 1910, 9:10 AM, San Diego, Ca.

LORRE, PETER   June 6, 1904   Near Budapest, Hungary
Actor   1:20 AM MET   19E05   47N30

| ☉ 14-♊-51 | ☿ 21-♉-37 | ♂ 13-♊-12 | ♄ 20-♒-59R | ♆ 04-♋-51 | A 16-♈-30 |
| ☽ 12-♓-21 | ♀ 06-♊-02 | ♃ 22-♈-10 | ♅ 28-♐-31R | ♇ 20-♊-03 | M 07-♑-25 |

Gentle voice, insidious and sinister manner in movies, whose girth in later years matched his talent. Films include *The Maltese Falcon, Casablanca* and the series of eight *Mr. Moto* films. Last film *Torn Curtain* for Hitchcock. (1904-1964)

DD: Craswell. *Famous People* and *Notables in the American Theatre* give June 26, 1904.

LOUIS, JOE   May 13, 1914   Lafayette, Ala
Boxer   8:00 AM CST   83W24   32N54

| ☉ 21-♉-57 | ☿ 17-♉-20 | ♂ 05-♌-56 | ♄ 17-♊-44 | ♆ 25-♋-48 | A 10-♋-10 |
| ☽ 11-♑-53 | ♀ 14-♊-39 | ♃ 21-♒-00 | ♅ 11-♒-37 | ♇ 29-♊-43 | M 24-♓-38 |

Won the heavyweight title in 1937 by knocking out James Braddock. Retired in 1949 as the undefeated champion after eighteen action-packed years in the ring, defending his title twenty-five times. Earned an estimated $8.7 million. Open-heart surgery in 1978 was followed by a crippling stroke.

DD: SS #597. Old-file has 8:50 AM. AQ, Fall 1950, Davison gives May 13, 1914, 4:12 PM GMT = 10:12 PM CST of the 12th. Drew pictures a chart for 8:25 AM CST.

LOWELL, AMY February 9, 1874 Brookline, Mass
Writer 1:30 AM LMT 71W07 42N20

☉ 20-♒-23 ☿ 24-♒-46 ♂ 30-♓-00 ♄ 06-♒-54 ♆ 26-♈-06 A 25-♏-33
☽ 15-♏-38 ♀ 16-♒-55 ♃ 00-♎-53R ♅ 08-♌-01R ♇ 19-♉-48 M 10-♍-09

Heavy-set, militant literary leader in the development of modern American poetry, who paid no attention to the Boston Brahmins who raised eyebrows at her lesbian life style. Her dozen volumes of verse began with *A Dome of Many Colored Glass.* (1874-1925)

C: PC from *Amy* by Jean Gould, "early in the morning." Biography published in 1975, states on p. 7, "the morning of February 9, 1874."

LOWELL, JAMES RUSSELL February 22, 1819 Cambridge, Mass
Writer 9:45 AM LMT 71W06 42N22

☉ 03-♓-11 ☿ 15-♒-12 ♂ 07-♒-38 ♄ 18-♓-44 ♆ 28-♐-18 A 16-♉-17
☽ 06-♒-57 ♀ 17-♑-16 ♃ 03-♒-32 ♅ 23-♐-58 ♇ 25-♓-19 M 25-♑-55

Outstanding American poet; equally well known as a literary critic, teacher and diplomat. Studied as a lawyer without much interest; first volume of poems published in 1841. Professor at Harvard, 1855; minister to Spain, 1877. Married and widowed twice. (1819-1891)

DD: Huggins in *The Astrology Magazine,* January 1970; same data in SS #599. Old-file has 9:25 AM LMT. *Amy* by Jean Gould (1975) gives his birthdate as February 10, 1819, making the point that the poet, Amy Lowell, his relative, celebrated her birthday one day before him.

LOWELL, PERCIVAL March 13, 1855 Boston, Mass
Scientist 7:45 AM LMT 71W04 42N22

☉ 22-♓-24 ☿ 09-♓-06R ♂ 28-♓-29 ♄ 09-♊-53 ♆ 15-♓-54 A 29-♈-20
☽ 17-♑-43 ♀ 13-♈-54 ♃ 19-♒-32 ♅ 13-♉-48 ♇ 02-♉-17 M 15-♑-30

American astronomer, known for his belief in possible life on Mars. Began a career in business before building the Lowell Observatory at Flagstaff, Az. In 1905 his studies led him to predict the discovery of the planet Pluto. Author of several books.

DD: SS #600. Judy Johns has 7:10 AM LMT, from Jansky.

LUBBE, MARINUS VAN DER January 13, 1909 Leiden, Netherlands
Radical 5:30 AM Amsterdam 4E30 52N10

☉ 12-♑-14 ☿ 18-♑-12 ♂ 25-♏-26 ♄ 04-♈-02 ♆ 15-♋-49R A 09-♐-40
☽ 02-♊-32 ♀ 14-♐-09 ♃ 14-♍-30R ♅ 16-♑-43 ♇ 24-♊-30R M 10-♎-01

Convicted of burning the Reichstag on February 27, 1933, a week before elections, supposedly as a protest. Appeared stupid at the trial, unaware of the implications; was condemned and executed with an axe on January 10, 1934.

DD: WEMYSS F/N #182, data according to *De Mystieke Wereld,* November 1933. Same data in SS #602. AQ, Fall 1935, gives 3:30 PM GMT.

LUCE, HENRY R. April 3, 1898 Tengchow, China
Publisher 1:30 PM LMT 117E14 35N08

☉ 13-♈-30 ☿ 00-♉-09 ♂ 10-♓-09 ♄ 12-♐-09R ♆ 20-♊-03 A 13-♌-48
☽ 27-♌-35 ♀ 25-♈-00 ♃ 04-♎-20R ♅ 03-♐-16R ♇ 12-♊-58 M 06-♉-24

One of the foremost publishers and editors of the U.S. Introduced *Time* magazine, 1923; *Life* magazine, 1936; *Fortune,* 1930, and a number of other publications. (1898-1967)

DD: PC speculative. Old-file has 8:25 AM LMT. (The profile and chart of his wife, Clare Booth Luce, are given in *Profiles of Women.*

LUCIANO, CHARLES "LUCKY" November 24, 1897 Lercara Friddi, Sicily
Gangster 11:00 PM MET 12E34 37N42

☉ 02-♐-56 ☿ 12-♐-18 ♂ 01-♐-57 ♄ 03-♐-16 ♆ 21-♊-38R A 24-♌-52
☽ 10-♐-30 ♀ 13-♏-04 ♃ 05-♎-03 ♅ 29-♏-32 ♇ 13-♊-56R M 19-♉-08

Moved to U.S. in 1906; began a teen-age career in crime; by 1931 director of a crime syndicate and leader of organized crime in the East. Rackets in narcotics, prostitution, slot machines, loan sharking, and "protection." Deported in 1946. (1897-1962)

DD: PC quotes *The Last Testament of Lucky Luciano* by Martin Gosch, date on p. 3, and the time from SS #603. SS gives November 11, 1897 (no time stated). *Americana* gives November *11, 1896, near Palermo. Daphne Jones quotes L'Astrologue,* 1970, for November 24, 1892, 12:00 Noon.

LUCKY #1	November 8, 1869	Chartres, France
Male	5:00 AM LMT	1E30 48N25

☉ 15-♏-51	☿ 27-♎-28	♂ 15-♐-07	♄ 15-♐-46	♆ 17-♈-25R	A 23-♎-40
☽ 11-♑-46	♀ 00-♑-04	♃ 15-♉-56R	♅ 21-♋-56R	♇ 17-♉-01R	M 00-♌-13

E. Chamberlin, a baker's helper who won a million francs in a French lottery on December 15, 1894.

C: Skeetz quotes Garth Allen in Dell, March 1955.

LUCKY #2	April 3, 1897	Essen, Germany
Male	8:43 AM GMT	7E00 51N28

☉ 13-♈-51	☿ 15-♈-11	♂ 05-♋-54	♄ 00-♐-16R	♆ 17-♊-52	A 02-♋-26
☽ 26-♈-52	♀ 16-♉-35	♃ 01-♍-02R	♅ 28-♏-38R	♇ 12-♊-00	M 27-♒-30

J.W.E. won $100,000 in lottery cash on August 4, 1936; residing in the U.S. at the time of his stroke of luck.

C: Skeetz quotes Garth Allen in Dell, 1955. (GMT given, though Germany is on MET).

LUCKY #3	April 11, 1893	Stamford, Conn
Male	9:30 AM EST	73W32 41N03

☉ 21-♈-55	☿ 04-♈-55R	♂ 09-♊-02	♄ 08-♎-29R	♆ 09-♊-17	A 05-♋-34
☽ 16-♒-37	♀ 16-♈-30	♃ 04-♉-00	♅ 09-♏-25R	♇ 08-♊-17	M 12-♓-38

Won an Irish Sweepstakes, which netted him more than $90,000 after taxes.

C: Skeetz quotes Garth Allen in Dell, March 1955.

LUCKY #4	January 5, 1915	New York, N.Y.
Female	8:55 AM EST	73W57 40N45

☉ 14-♑-10	☿ 14-♑-07	♂ 10-♑-58	♄ 27-♊-38R	♆ 29-♋-28R	A 10-♒-34
☽ 02-♍-28	♀ 02-♐-56	♃ 23-♒-20	♅ 10-♒-06	♇ 00-♋-56R	M 01-♐-01

Went halves on an Irish Sweepstakes ticket on July 16, 1936, with Female #5. In late October, they learned to their great delight that their ticket was worth $2,965, a tidy sum for two young ladies in moderate circumstances.

C: Skeetz quotes Garth Allen in Dell, March 1955.

LUCKY #5	September 11, 1909	Chicago, Ill
Female	10:25 PM CST	87W39 41N52

☉ 18-♍-45	☿ 14-♎-43	♂ 04-♈-10R	♄ 22-♈-03R	♆ 18-♋-53	A 22-♊-26
☽ 21-♌-40	♀ 24-♎-15	♃ 23-♍-36	♅ 17-♑-12R	♇ 26-♊-51	M 26-♒-55

Went halves on an Irish Sweepstakes ticket with Female #4; won $2,965 between them.

C: Skeetz quotes Garth Allen in Dell, March 1955.

LUCKY #6	July 12, 1931	Oklahoma City, Ok
Female	3:00 AM CST	97W30 35N30

☉ 19-♋-03	☿ 02-♌-58	♂ 17-♍-49	♄ 20-♑-02R	♆ 03-♍-52	A 15-♊-22
☽ 09-♊-03	♀ 03-♋-20	♃ 28-♋-54	♅ 19-♈-18	♇ 20-♋-23	M 24-♒-30

A young mother, chosen to be *Queen for a Day* on March 23, 1951, 11:30 AM, Hollywood. On the TV show, won $100 cash, a washing machine, deep freezer, vacuum cleaner, complete new wardrobe, and an exotic vacation.

C: Skeetz quotes Garth Allen in Dell, March 1955.

LUCKY #7 November 11, 1912 No place given
Male 9:07 AM CST 87W00 41N00

☉ 18-♏-53	☿ 09-♐-36	♂ 16-♏-51	♄ 01-♊-33R	♆ 25-♋-58R	A 19-♐-23
☽ 19-♐-39	♀ 21-♐-58	♃ 18-♐-17	♅ 29-♑-59	♇ 29-♊-45R	M 11-♎-02

Won $100,000 in the first Old Gold contest.

C: CL from *Student Astrology*, 1938.

LYON, SUE July 10, 1946 Davenport, Iowa
Actress 1:36 AM CST 90W35 41N32

☉ 17-♋-26	☿ 12-♌-56	♂ 11-♍-35	♄ 27-♋-00	♆ 05-♎-59	A 02-♊-39
☽ 02-♐-35	♀ 25-♌-58	♃ 18-♎-24	♅ 19-♊-22	♇ 10-♌-41	M 08-♒-37

On screen from 1962, including the title role in *Lolita*: other films include *The Night of the Iguana* and *Evel Knievel* (1972). Three sensational marriages — to an actor, to a Black sports figure, and on November 4, 1973, to a behind-bars killer for one inconsumate year.

C: Laurie Brady 1978.

MacARTHUR, DOUGLAS January 26, 1880 Little Rock, Ark
General 10:13 AM LMT 92W17 34N45

☉ 06-♒-09	☿ 23-♑-25	♂ 22-♉-02	♄ 10-♈-46	♆ 09-♉-17	A 13-♈-20
☽ 27-♋-33	♀ 25-♐-12	♃ 14-♓-09	♅ 08-♍-12R	♇ 25-♉-28R	M 07-♑-54

Graduated first in his class at West Point, 1903; participated in the Mexican War; commander of the 42nd Division in France in World War I; became supreme commander of the Allied Forces in the Pacific, 1942. (1880-1964)

DD: CL from Dell, September 1964, "rectified by Lt. Commdr. Williams." Same data in SS #614. Jansky H/N quotes Dell, January 1949, at 6:30 PM LMT. Rona de Thuge in AA, May 1952, gives 10:12:19 PM LMT, from "the mother's method of rectification." AQ, Fall 1950, Clancy rectifies to 10:37 PM. AFA Bulletin, Hey rectifies to 11:51 AM LMT. (Rectification an improper term for speculation).

MacLEAN, DONALD D. May 28, 1913 Bristol, England
Traitor 2:00 AM GMT 2W35 51N27

☉ 06-♊-08	☿ 00-♊-09	♂ 15-♈-10	♄ 07-♊-20	♆ 23-♋-59	A 05-♈-48
☽ 07-♓-00	♀ 28-♈-32	♃ 17-♑-04R	♅ 07-♒-27R	♇ 28-♊-59	M 02-♑-14

Diplomatic spy in England who defected to Russia on May 26, 1951, disappearing with his bosom buddy, Guy Burgess.

C: CL quotes Lyndoe in AA, September 1956.

MacMILLAN, HAROLD February 10, 1894 London, England
Statesman 11:20 PM GMT 0W06 51N31

☉ 22-♒-16	☿ 01-♓-53	♂ 28-♐-07	♄ 25-♎-06R	♆ 10-♊-46R	A 28-♎-45
☽ 21-♈-20	♀ 01-♓-00R	♃ 22-♉-35	♅ 15-♏-19	♇ 08-♊-50R	M 08-♌-29

Prime minister of Great Britain in 1957, upon the resignation of Anthony Eden. Served under Churchill from 1951-55, then under Eden. In World War II, wounded three times and received the Military Cross.

C: Holliday from BAJ Vol 4 #2, Ebertin "private source."

MALMGREN, FINN January 9, 1895 Falun, Sweden
Meteorologist 8:43 PM LMT 15E38 60N38

☉ 19-♑-21	☿ 19-♑-10	♂ 03-♉-53	♄ 06-♏-08	♆ 13-♊-30R	A 11-♍-29
☽ 28-♊-43	♀ 28-♑-59	♃ 28-♊-57R	♅ 19-♏-04	♇ 10-♊-07R	M 01-♊-56

Accompanied Nobile on the Italia derigible to a North Pole expedition in 1928. The ship crashed on May 25. With two other men, sent on May 31 to reach the supply ship; without food for forty-five days. When rescue arrived on July 12, missing; cannabalism suspected.

C: Lyndoe in AA, March 1978.

MALTHUS, THOMAS February 17, 1766 Guilford, England
Economist 4:00 PM LMT 0W34 51N14

☉ 29-♒-05	☿ 05-♒-46	♂ 16-♐-46	♄ 29-♉-08	♆ 01-♍-41R	A 16-♌-07
☽ 10-♊-37	♀ 09-♈-14	♃ 15-♌-58R	♅ 22-♈-17	♇ 08-♑-59	M 29-♈-42

English political economist who developed the theory that population would outstrip food supply. Ordained minister of the Church of England in 1797; continued to work as professor of history and economics. Wrote *Principals of Political Economy* (1820). (1766-1834)

DD: PC speculative. Old-file has the same date, 4:20 PM LMT. *Americana* and *Britannica* both give February 14, 1766.

MAO TSE TUNG December 26, 1893 Siangton, Hunau, China
Communist 7:30 AM Suntime 112E47 27N55

☉ 04-♑-30	☿ 15-♐-47	♂ 25-♏-53	♄ 23-♎-52	♆ 11-♊-33R	A 13-♑-12
☽ 14-♌-08	♀ 20-♒-11	♃ 22-♉-09R	♅ 14-♏-03	♇ 09-♊-21R	M 29-♎-16

Chinese political leader, author, poet. Chairman of the Central Committee of the Chinese Communist party, which he helped establish in 1921. (1893-1976)

DD: John Daniel. *Constellations*, 1977, states "Between 7:00 to 9:00 AM LAT" from AA, March 1951, letter from Henry T. Loo, according to a biography published in China. Dewey has Shaoshan, Honan, China, 113E30/25N00, from AFA, December 1952, quoting a biography published by the Chinese Communist party.

Dewey includes a delightful quote: "He was born on the 19th day of the 11th month of the 19th year Kwagshu at the dragon hour. The year Kuei-szu (black serpent), the month Chuastzu (green rat), the day Tingyu (red cock), the chuschen (green dragon) between 7:00 to 9:00 AM. AFA Suggests Ascendant 1 Capricorn 23. Do you know anyone who is expert in Chinese?"

MARCH, JUAN October 4, 1880 No place given
Entrepreneur 4:00 PM LMT 3E00 39N35

☉ 11-♎-47	☿ 24-♎-15	♂ 18-♎-34	♄ 26-♈-35R	♆ 13-♉-44R	A 03-♓-02
☽ 17-♎-44	♀ 03-♏-58	♃ 14-♈-53R	♅ 11-♍-24	♇ 28-♉-07R	M 14-♐-59

Son of a pig-dealer; became a smuggler; opened a tobacco firm in Morocco. In World War I, became a trader; called "the last pirate." Unable to read or write, made over $5 million; financially backed Franco. Died in his 80s.

C: Lyndoe in AA, October 1962.

MARCIANO, ROCKY September 1, 1924 Brockton, Mass
Boxer 5:20 PM EDT 71W01 42N05

☉ 09-♍-07	☿ 26-♍-12R	♂ 27-♒-55R	♄ 28-♎-50	♆ 20-♌-50	A 27-♑-48
☽ 10-♎-38	♀ 23-♋-30	♃ 11-♐-03	♅ 19-♓-57R	♇ 13-♋-13	M 22-♏-09

Won the heavyweight title in 1952 by defeating Joe Walcott. During his career, had a perfect record, winning all forty-nine of his professional fights. Retired April 27, 1956; elected to the Boxing Hall of Fame, 1967. Killed in a private plane crash August 31, 1969.

DD: CL from Drew. Same date given in *Astrological Index*. September 1, 1923 given in *Famous People, Americana, World Book* Obit and from the Sports Department of the L.A. Library.

MARCUS, MASTER September 19, 1955 San Francisco, Ca
Kidnapped 00:20 AM PST 122W26 37N47

☉ 25-♍-38	☿ 22-♎-02	♂ 14-♍-36	♄ 17-♏-26	♆ 26-♎-48	A 17-♋-11
☽ 02-♏-37	♀ 00-♎-31	♃ 20-♌-55	♅ 01-♌-15	♇ 27-♌-25	M 00-♈-03

Taken from the hospital when three days old; returned unharmed a week later. The son of a physician.

C: CL from AFA, February 1959.

MARKAY, GENE   December 11, 1895   Jackson, Mich
Writer   7:06 PM CST   84W24 42N15

☉ 19-♐-48   ☿ 14-♐-59   ♂ 29-♏-55   ♄ 14-♏-33   ♆ 16-♊-34R   A 29-♋-55
☽ 25-♎-43   ♀ 03-♏-30   ♃ 08-♌-43R   ♅ 22-♏-00   ♇ 11-♊-36R   M 13-♈-41

Naval officer. A journalist and novelist with a penchant for movie stars; married successively to Joan Bennet, Hedy Lamarr, and Myrna Loy.

C: CL.

MARKHAM, EDWIN   April 23, 1852   Oregon City, Ore
Writer   6:00 AM LMT   122W36 45N21

☉ 03-♉-33   ☿ 13-♉-27R   ♂ 06-♌-18   ♄ 06-♉-57   ♆ 10-♓-49   A 24-♉-24
☽ 19-♊-08   ♀ 17-♊-56   ♃ 20-♏-13R   ♅ 04-♉-18   ♇ 00-♉-21   M 29-♑-36

American poet and lecturer; won recognition with his poem "The Man with the Hoe" (1908); also wrote *Lincoln and Other Poems* (1901) and *New Poems* (1932). For several years, a California school teacher and superintendent; moved to N.Y. after 1899. (1852-1940)

C: Fleischer in *Astrological Review*, May 1936; same data in SS #648.

MARQUAND, JOHN P.   November 10, 1893   Wilmington, Del
Writer   6:00 AM EST   75W33 39N45

☉ 18-♏-18   ☿ 10-♐-43   ♂ 25-♎-29   ♄ 19-♎-41   ♆ 12-♊-48R   A 09-♏-11
☽ 09-♐-26   ♀ 03-♑-46   ♃ 27-♉-28R   ♅ 11-♏-30   ♇ 10-♊-12R   M 16-♌-49

American novelist who pictured the decay of aristocratic society in Boston with gentle but effective satire. Won the 1937 Pulitzer prize for *The Late George Apley*. Won first success with romantic novels and detective stories.

DD: PC speculative. Old-file has 11:35 PM EST.

MARX, GROUCHO   October 2, 1895   New York, N.Y.
Comedian   4:46 AM EST   73W57 40N45

☉ 10-♊-32   ☿ 16-♉-34   ♂ 16-♋-19   ♄ 01-♈-22   ♆ 08-♉-29   A 28-♊-29
☽ 12-♊-14   ♀ 26-♈-50   ♃ 07-♒-06R   ♅ 25-♌-42   ♇ 25-♉-21   M 22-♒-11

Mustached, cigar-smoking member of the madcap Marx Brothers team; master of the irreverent wisecrack, pun, and insult. Early career in vaudeville and stage; starred in insane Marx Brothers films. Height in the 50s with radio and TV show, *You Bet Your Life*. Wrote *Groucho and Me* (1959) and *Memoirs of a Mangy Lover* (1963). (1895?-1977)

DD: CL from AFA, April 1961. Same date in *Famous People* and *Celebrities*. PC states 1890, from B.C. Same date in *Current Biography*, 1977, and *Americana*.

MASEFIELD, JOHN   June 1, 1878   Ledbury, England
Writer   5:00 AM LMT   2W25 52N03

☉ 08-♎-57   ☿ 04-♏-31   ♂ 11-♎-53   ♄ 06-♏-20   ♆ 18-♊-02R   A 24-♍-46
☽ 22-♓-04   ♀ 19-♍-17R   ♃ 04-♌-45   ♅ 17-♏-48   ♇ 12-♊-41R   M 23-♊-57

English poet who became the twenty-second poet laureate of England in 1930. Wrote more than a hundred works, including an autobiography, *So Long to Learn*, in 1952.

DD: PC speculative. Old-file has 3:00 PM LMT.

MASTERS, EDGAR LEE   August 23, 1869   Garnett, Kansas
Writer   4:00 AM LMT   95W14 38N17

☉ 00-♍-16   ☿ 10-♍-59   ♂ 21-♎-46   ♄ 10-♐-36   ♆ 19-♈-19R   A 13-♌-08
☽ 13-♓-59   ♀ 28-♍-38   ♃ 20-♉-31   ♅ 20-♋-12   ♇ 17-♉-58R   M 04-♉-00

Poet, novelist, and biographer, who wrote with simplicity, insight, and drama; a shrewd portrayer of human motive. Worked as a lawyer from 1891 to 1920; then devoted full time to writing. (1869-1950)

DD: PC quotes "his autobiography *Across Spoon River*." *Spoon River Anthology* by Masters (1914) is a collection of his verse; it gives NO data.

MASTROIANNI, MARCELLO October 18, 1924 Rome, Italy
Actor 6:00 AM MET 12E29 48N54

☉ 24-♎-32	☿ 19-♎-04	♂ 29-♒-31	♄ 03-♏-52	♆ 22-♌-12	A 17-♎-22
☽ 24-♊-41	♀ 12-♍-01	♃ 17-♐-09	♅ 18-♓-14R	♇ 13-♋-33R	M 22-♋-07

On screen from 1947; an Italian star nominated as best actor in *Divorce Italian Style*. Films include *La Dolce Vita, Marriage Italian Style,* and *Casanova 70.*

DD: PC speculative. Old-file has the same date, 5:40 AM MET. *Current Biography,* 1963, gives September 28, 1924. *Americana* gives September 8, 1924. *Famous People* gives November 18, 1925. Ciro Discepolo gives September 28, 1924, 12:15 PM, Frosinone, Italy.

MATTHEWS, EDWARD October 13, 1931 Texarkana, Ark
Baseball player 4:00 PM CST 94W03 34N26

☉ 19-♎-36	☿ 16-♎-10	♂ 18-♏-13	♄ 17-♑-03	♆ 07-♍-04	A 11-♓-02
☽ 22-♏-48	♀ 29-♎-06	♃ 17-♌-54	♅ 17-♈-18R	♇ 22-♋-09	M 18-♐-27

Handsome, popular player with the Milwaukee Braves, said to have "the wrists that made Milwaukee famous."

C: Scarsella, Baird's file, "from Louise Ivey."

MAUGHAM, W. SOMERSET January 25, 1874 Paris, France
Writer 6:00 AM LMT 2E20 48N50

☉ 05-♒-09	☿ 28-♑-48	♂ 18-♓-33	♄ 05-♒-07	♆ 25-♈-52	A 04-♑-21
☽ 07-♉-54	♀ 28-♑-04	♃ 01-♎-40R	♅ 08-♌-40R	♇ 19-♉-48R	M 06-♏-42

Noted English novelist, playwright, and short story writer. Studied to be a doctor but never practiced medicine. His work includes *Of Human Bondage, The Moon and Sixpence,* and *The Razor's Edge.* (1874-1965)

DD: PC speculative. Old-file has 11:20 AM LMT.

MAULDIN, BILL October 29, 1921 Mountain Park, N.M.
Cartoonist 10:15 PM MST 105W54 32N58

☉ 06-♏-15	☿ 09-♏-03R	♂ 25-♍-25	♄ 02-♎-38	♆ 15-♌-52	A 24-♋-08
☽ 26-♎-19	♀ 11-♎-45	♃ 07-♎-14	♅ 05-♓-50R	♇ 10-♋-00R	M 11-♈-24

Outstanding soldier cartoonist during World War II, who won a 1945 Pulitzer prize for his cartoons. His best known work is *Up Front,* a collection of war cartoons and the stories behind them.

DD: PC, "personal." Old-file has 10:10 PM MST.

MAYO, CHARLES July 19, 1865 Rochester, Minn
Physician 2:00 AM LMT 92W28 40N01

☉ 26-♋-36	☿ 14-♌-36	♂ 03-♍-28	♄ 24-♎-02	♆ 10-♈-35R	A 22-♊-20
☽ 13-♊-59	♀ 10-♊-59	♃ 20-♐-20R	♅ 01-♋-17	♇ 14-♉-06	M 24-♒-51

The younger son of William Worrall Mayo, who started the Mayo Clinic in 1889 with his father and brother William. Famous for reducing the death rate in goiter surgery. Professor of surgery at the Clinic. (1865-1939)

DD: SS #665. Old-file has 2:12 AM LMT.

MAYO, WILLIAM June 29, 1861 Le Sueur, Minn
Physician 3:00 AM LMT 93W55 44N27

☉ 07-♋-32	☿ 02-♌-30	♂ 26-♋-29	♄ 05-♍-13	♆ 01-♈-38	A 18-♊-00
☽ 29-♓-31	♀ 20-♋-45	♃ 24-♌-52	♅ 13-♊-40	♇ 10-♉-08	M 20-♒-02

The older son of William Worrall Mayo, who started the Mayo Clinic in 1889 with his father and brother Charles. Won fame for his surgical skill in gallstones, cancer, and stomach operations. (1861-1939)

DD: PC from SS #666 (no time given). Old-file has 3:09 AM LMT.

McCARTNEY, PAUL June 18, 1942 Liverpool, England
Musician 2:30 AM DBST 2W58 53N25

☉ 26-♊-09 ☿ 18-♊-34R ♂ 02-♌-24 ♄ 05-♊-09 ♆ 27-♍-07 A 00-♈-24
☽ 11-♌-37 ♀ 18-♉-27 ♃ 01-♋-43 ♅ 01-♊-57 ♇ 04-♌-16 M 00-♑-09

Megastar of The Beatles from 1961, who set world records in record sales — by the end of 1977 an estimated 100 million singles and 100 million albums. After Bangladesh, world travel, and marriage, formed his own record label, Apple.

DD: PC, "recorded." Old-file has 1:25 AM DBST. Daphne Jones writes, "rectified from about midnight" in *Astro Review* to 2:05 AM DBST. Townley in *The Composite Chart* speculates midnight.

McINTYRE, O.O. February 18, 1884 Plattsburg, Mo
Writer 6:53 PM CST 94W27 39N34

☉ 29-♒-50 ☿ 04-♒-06 ♂ 05-♌-47R ♄ 03-♊-25 ♆ 18-♉-25 A 11-♍-44
☽ 28-♏-47 ♀ 05-♈-26 ♃ 25-♋-57R ♅ 27-♍-12R ♇ 29-♉-15 M 08-♊-54

American syndicated columnist and author. Died of a heart attack, February 14, 1938.

DD: *Student Astrology,* May 1937, M. Major. AA, June 1938, Sims states, "Midnight to 2:00 AM, from him."

McKUEN, ROD April 29, 1933 Oakland, Ca
Writer 10:30 AM PST 122W16 37N49

☉ 08-♉-58 ☿ 13-♈-41 ♂ 02-♍-37 ♄ 15-♒-46 ♆ 07-♍-30R A 27-♋-27
☽ 03-♋-43 ♀ 11-♉-06 ♃ 13-♍-28R ♅ 24-♈-16 ♇ 21-♋-22 M 13-♈-35

American writer of songs and verse, composer. Does not call himself a poet although his books of poems are best sellers. Boyhood drifter — the Army, odd jobs. Remained a bachelor. Work includes *Stanyon Street and Other Sorrows* and *Fields of Wonder* (1971).

DD: PC, Jansky, and Leek all agree on the time but get different years. McKuen's autobiography *Finding my Father* gives 1933.

MEHER BABA, SRI February 25, 1894 Bombay, India
The silent guru 4:35 AM LMT 72E48 19N00

☉ 06-♓-23 ☿ 24-♓-25 ♂ 07-♑-53 ♄ 24-♎-44R ♆ 10-♊-45 A 04-♒-22
☽ 07-♏-55 ♀ 22-♒-48R ♃ 24-♉-04 ♅ 15-♏-20R ♇ 08-♊-49 M 16-♏-03

A Parsi. In thirteen years of complete silence, spelled with quick fingers on the alphabet board words such as, "I am the Supreme Spirit." Called to the spiritual life in May, 1913, by the kiss of a mystic Tara. His biography, *The Perfect Master,* written by C.B. Purdom.

DD: SS #667. Same data from Rudhyar in AA, March 1938, "Official birth time, slightly rectified." Holliday quotes Kraum in *Best of the NAJ,* 1979, for 5:00 AM, "private source."

MELBA, DAME NELLIE May 19, 1860 Melbourne, Australia
Singer 7:40 AM LMT 144E58 37N47

☉ 28-♉-06 ☿ 08-♉-29 ♂ 25-♑-32 ♄ 19-♌-53 ♆ 28-♓-53 A 10-♋-11
☽ 05-♉-55 ♀ 13-♋-11 ♃ 21-♋-49 ♅ 07-♊-13 ♇ 08-♉-27 M 21-♓-05

Famous coloratura soprano, who first sang in public at the age of 6. Her operatic debut in 1887 as Gilda in *Rigoletto*. Sang in Italy, Russia, Denmark, and England, with an American debut in 1893. (1860-1931)

DD: Dewey quotes *World Astrology,* May 1946, from John Romiser. PC quotes the same source for 10:30 AM LMT. *Americana* and *Colliers* both give May 19, 1861. Gwen Stoney quotes *Melba* by John Hetherington, p. 1 for May 19, 1861: "Her mother lay with her baby on her arm as the sound of church bells floated through the window on the evening air" (say 6:45 - 7:00 PM).

MELCHIOR, LAURITZ March 20, 1890 Copenhagen, Denmark
Singer 12:51 PM LMT 12E35 55N41

☉ 29-♓-51	☿ 12-♓-13	♂ 07-♐-13	♄ 28-♌-19R	♆ 02-♊-09	A 07-♌-30
☽ 24-♓-50	♀ 07-♈-17	♃ 05-♒-00	♅ 25-♎-43R	♇ 05-♊-07	M 11-♈-40

Danish operatic tenor who sang with the Metropolitan Opera Co. from 1926-1950. (1890-1973)

C: SS #669.

MENCKEN, HENRY L. September 12, 1880 Baltimore, Md
Writer 8:45 PM LMT 76W37 39N17

☉ 20-♍-38	☿ 16-♍-49	♂ 04-♎-22	♄ 28-♈-00R	♆ 14-♉-08R	A 21-♉-43
☽ 07-♑-52	♀ 07-♎-17	♃ 17-♈-33R	♅ 10-♍-07	♇ 28-♉-19R	M 01-♒-27

American editor and satirist. Reporter from 1899; editor from 1905; editorial writer, columnist, and reporter till 1948. Magazine co-editor, 1924. Writer of essays and social commentary. Author of *American Language* in four volumes (1919-48). (1880-1956)

C: AFA, February 1959.

MANJOU, ADOLPH February 18, 1890 Pittsburgh, Pa
Actor 8:30 PM EST 80W01 40N26

☉ 00-♓-24	☿ 04-♒-11	♂ 25-♏-31	♄ 00-♍-31R	♆ 01-♊-47	A 01-♎-09
☽ 25-♒-11	♀ 00-♓-33	♃ 29-♑-06	♅ 26-♎-32R	♇ 04-♊-57	M 01-♋-19

One of Hollywood's most debonair of stars, who played in more than two hundred films. Nominated for the Oscar as best actor in *The Front Page* (1930). In the early 50s, had his own TV show, *My Favorite Story.* (1890-1963)

DD: CL from BJA, March 1936; same data in SS #672. PC states 8:45 PM EST as B.C.

MERMAN, ETHEL January 16, 1908 New York, N.Y.
Entertainer 2:00 AM EST 73W57 40N45

☉ 24-♑-46	☿ 25-♑-56	♂ 03-♈-34	♄ 23-♓-00	♆ 13-♋-10R	A 13-♏-36
☽ 00-♋-08	♀ 24-♒-44	♃ 10-♌-23R	♅ 13-♑-31	♇ 23-♊-13R	M 23-♌-02

Started on Broadway in *Girl Crazy* (1930) when she sang "I've Got Rhythm," setting the audience on fire. Displayed her big, brassy voice in films that included *There's No Business Like Show Business* (1954) and *Call Me Madam* (1959).

DD: PC speculative. Same date in *Astrological Reference* and *Astrological Index*. The year 1909 given in *Information Please, Famous People , and Celebrities.* The year 1901 given in *50,000 Birthdays.*

MESMER, FRANZ May 23, 1733 Constance, Germany
Physician 8:00 AM LMT 11E59 43N45

☉ 02-♊-03	☿ 16-♉-05R	♂ 20-♊-35	♄ 25-♈-11	♆ 18-♊-44	A 21-♋-35
☽ 02-♎-01	♀ 25-♉-36	♃ 01-♏-45R	♅ 13-♐-07R	♇ 17-♎-45R	M 00-♈-58

Pioneer in the practice of hypnotism. His "seances" in which he "magnetized" patients created a sensation, but the medical profession considered him a fraud.

DD: PC quotes F/N. F/N #110 is an untimed flat chart. *World Book* gives Iznang, Austria.

MIES VAN DER ROHE, LUDWIG March 27, 1886 Aachens, Germany
Architect 2:00 PM LMT 6E05 50N47

☉ 06-♈-49	☿ 23-♈-32	♂ 08-♍-32R	♄ 01-♋-59	♆ 23-♉-34	A 21-♌-00
☽ 08-♑-08	♀ 26-♒-50	♃ 00-♎-21R	♅ 05-♎-38R	♇ 01-♊-27	M 07-♉-15

German architect, who won fame for the sparce, clean, uncluttered design of his buildings of brick, steel, and glass. Built his first steel framed building in 1927. Known for his motto, "Less is more." (1886-1969)

DD: PC, "recorded." Old-file has 2:25 PM LMT.

MILLER, ARTHUR — October 17, 1915 — New York, N.Y.
Writer — 5:12 AM EST — 73W57 40N45

☉ 22-♎-58	☿ 03-♏-58R	♂ 05-♌-10	♄ 16-♋-22	♆ 02-♌-34	A 11-♎-00
☽ 16-♒-25	♀ 02-♏-07	♃ 19-♓-57R	♅ 11-♒-45R	♇ 03-♋-17R	M 12-♋-47

Noted American dramatist, who won awards for *All My sons* and the Pulitzer prize for *Death of a Salesman* in 1949. Began as a writer for radio before his first Broadway success. Lives with his third wife on a 350-acre estate in Connecticut.

C: CL quotes Drew.
The profile and chart of his second wife, Marilyn Monroe, are given in *Profiles of Women.*

MISHIMA, YUKIO — January 14, 1925 — Tokyo, Japan
Writer — 11:15 AM JST — 139E45 35N40

☉ 23-♑-25	☿ 29-♐-51	♂ 15-♈-48	♄ 13-♏-01	♆ 21-♌-56R	A 25-♈-36
☽ 07-♍-21	♀ 28-♐-58	♃ 06-♑-07	♅ 18-♓-33	♇ 12-♋-16R	M 15-♑-14

Japanese author, whose prolific output included novels, short stories, plays, and essays, including *The Sailor Who Fell From Grace with the Sea* (1963). On November 25, 1970, committed seppuku, or ritual suicide, as a protest against the loss of national tradition.

DD: PC speculative. Old-file has 8:00 AM JST.

MOLOTOV, YVACHESLAV — March 9, 1890 NS — Bialystok, Poland
Statesman — 4:45 AM LMT — 23E10 53N08

☉ 18-♓-32	☿ 24-♒-44	♂ 03-♐-12	♄ 29-♌-05R	♆ 01-♊-57	A 25-♑-02
☽ 16-♎-02	♀ 23-♓-08	♃ 02-♒-51	♅ 26-♎-06R	♇ 05-♊-01	M 00-♐-11

Became widely known during two terms as foreign minister of Russia. Demoted in 1957 for his opposition to Khrushchev; expelled from the party; sent into virtual exile as ambassador to Outer Mongolia.

DD: Drew, "information through a newspaper friend in N.Y. but cannot verify it otherwise." PC gives March 21, 1890 NS, from SS #689, which gives the date and planetary positions for March 9, 1890. Old-file has March 29, 1890, 3:35 AM LMT. *Americana* gives March 9, 1890 (not specified OS/NS).

MONTAND, YVES — October 31, 1921 — Monsummano, Italy
Actor — 5:30 AM MET — 10E45 43N50

☉ 07-♏-13	☿ 07-♏-48R	♂ 26-♍-01	♄ 02-♎-44	♆ 15-♌-53	A 20-♎-52
☽ 09-♏-49	♀ 12-♎-57	♃ 07-♎-26	♅ 05-♓-49R	♇ 09-♋-59R	M 25-♋-14

French actor-singer, an excellent mime and dancer, who had a one-man Broadway smash of twenty French chansons in the Henry Miller Theater in 1959. Films include *The Crucible* (1958), *Grand Prix* (1966), and *The Confession* (1970). Married to Simone Signoret, 1950.

C: Holliday quotes Drew. Date check in *Information Please.*
The data for his wife, Simone Signoret, are given in *Profiles of Women.*

MONTEVERDI, CLAUDIO — May 25, 1567 NS — Cremona, Italy
Composer — 9:30 AM LMT — 9E01 45N08

☉ 03-♊-11	☿ 23-♊-46	♂ 21-♈-57	♄ 07-♍-17	♆ 13-♊-20	A 10-♌-45
☽ 00-♍-41	♀ 22-♊-04	♃ 00-♏-56R	♅ 20-♐-43R	♇ 17-♓-47	M 26-♈-35

Italian composer and music reformer, who became the first great composer of opera and brought the madrigal form to its highest point of technical development in Italy. Published his first work at age 16; in 1616 was music director in Venice. (1567-1643)

DD: PC quotes Barbault, "who gives him Leo rising." Old-file has 7:15 AM LMT (May 15, 1567 OS).

MONTGOMERY, ROBERT May 21, 1904 Beacon, N.Y.
Actor 3:14 AM EST 73E58 41N30

☉ 29-♉-50	☿ 18-♉-14R	♂ 02-♊-16	♄ 20-♒-55	♆ 04-♋-19	A 00-♉-49
☽ 15-♌-31	♀ 16-♉-50	♃ 19-♈-02	♅ 29-♐-06R	♇ 19-♊-42	M 16-♑-40

Since age 21, stage and film; director and producer of movies and TV. Nominated for the Oscar as best actor in *Night Must Fall* (1937) and *Here Comes Mr. Jordan* (1941). Nominated for a TV Emmy in 1951. Saw action in World War II. Married April 14, 1928; two children.

C: Holliday from CL.

The profile and chart of his daughter, actress Elizabeth Montgomery, are given in *Profiles of Women.*

MOORE, ROGER October 14, 1927 London, England
Actor 1:00 AM GMT 0W06 51N31

☉ 19-♎-41	☿ 13-♏-49	♂ 21-♎-58	♄ 04-♐-36	♆ 28-♌-31	A 22-♌-27
☽ 04-♊-09	♀ 11-♍-27	♃ 25-♓-48R	♅ 00-♈-42R	♇ 17-♋-09	M 08-♉-52

Appeared in various TV series, including *The Saint, The Alaskans, Ivanhoe, Maverick,* and *The Persuaders.* Movies include *The Miracle* (1959) and *The Sins of Rachel Cade* (1961).

C: Skeetz quotes Mary Frances Woods. Some data in PC, "recorded."

MOORE, THOMAS May 28, 1779 Dublin, Ireland
Writer 7:00 PM LMT 6W15 53N20

☉ 07-♊-12	☿ 17-♉-32	♂ 15-♏-55R	♄ 22-♏-39R	♆ 28-♍-44R	A 25-♏-38
☽ 21-♏-28	♀ 00-♉-27	♃ 17-♍-35	♅ 19-♊-01	♇ 03-♒-13R	M 20-♍-23

Irish poet, who wrote the words of some of the best-loved songs in the English language, including "Believe Me If All Those Endearing Young Charms" and "The Last Rose of Summer." His work includes a biography of Bryan (1830). (1779-1852)

C: Chart pictured in Adams *One Hundred Horoscopes.*

MORE, KENNETH September 20, 1914 Gerrards Cross, Bucks, Eng
Actor 2:30 PM GMT 0W34 51N35

☉ 26-♍-47	☿ 12-♎-57	♂ 24-♎-04	♄ 01-♋-46	♆ 29-♋-56	A 02-♑-15
☽ 06-♎-37	♀ 13-♏-07	♃ 13-♒-02R	♅ 08-♒-00R	♇ 02-♋-12	M 07-♏-56

English star. On screen from 1948 in films that include *No Highway in the Sky, Doctor in the House,* and *The Sheriff of Fractured Jaw;* equally adept in comedy or drama.

C: BJA.

MORGAN, J. PIERPONT SR. April 17, 1837 Hartford, Ct
Entrepreneur 3:00 AM LMT 72W41 41N46

☉ 27-♈-05	☿ 29-♈-27	♂ 12-♌-09	♄ 15-♏-07R	♆ 08-♒-04	A 26-♒-20
☽ 15-♍-13	♀ 18-♈-51	♃ 08-♌-22	♅ 07-♓-15	♇ 15-♈-36	M 11-♐-45

The founder of F.P. Morgan and Co., 1895; his firm controlled many corporations. Had art collections valued from $50 to $100 million. (1837-1913)

DD: Lockhart quotes *J.P. Morgan Sr.* by H. Satterlee, p. 1. Same data in SS #696. The chart pictured in Adams' *One Hundred Horoscopes* is for 1:10 PM LMT: Since he was one of Adams' most famous clients, the time may be presumed to be from him.

MORGAN J. PIERPONT JR. September 7, 1867 Irvington, N.Y.
Son and heir 9:15 PM LMT 73W52 41N02

☉ 14-♍-56	☿ 08-♍-12	♂ 18-♎-02	♄ 19-♏-14	♆ 14-♈-26R	A 25-♉-19
☽ 08-♑-02	♀ 10-♍-14	♃ 00-♓-55R	♅ 12-♋-09	♇ 16-♉-00R	M 03-♒-08

The last family member to head the great banking House of Morgan; a financier-banker whose personal fortune at one time was estimated at five hundred million dollars. (1867-1943)

C: CL from Edward Doane; same data from Fleischer in *Astrological Review,* September 1936, and in SS #697.

MORRIS, WILLIAM March 24, 1834 Walthamstow, England
Artist, writer 1:00 AM LMT 0W01 51N34
☉ 02-♈-56 ☿ 11-♈-04R ♂ 24-♒-18 ♄ 07-♎-46R ♆ 01-♒-08 A 15-♐-31
☽ 15-♍-27 ♀ 06-♈-57 ♃ 07-♉-42 ♅ 24-♒-45 ♇ 11-♈-59 M 17-♎-23

Poet and artist, reformer — a man of many talents. In 1861, he helped found Morris and Co. to produce home furnishings; in 1891, founded the Kelmscott Press to make fine paper and produce books (1834-1896)

DD: PC quotes SS #701 (no time given). Old-file has 1:25 AM LMT.

MORSE, SAMUEL F.B. April 27, 1791 Charlestown, Mass
Artist, inventor 10:30 AM LMT 71W04 42N23
☉ 07-♉-15 ☿ 22-♉-04 ♂ 26-♈-25 ♄ 12-♈-21 ♆ 25-♎-59R A 00-♌-21
☽ 05-♓-04 ♀ 05-♊-09 ♃ 22-♍-14R ♅ 10-♌-11 ♇ 21-♒-50 M 14-♈-10

Developer of the first successful electric telegraph and inventor of the Morse code. On May 24, 1844, tapped out his first telegraph message. Was also an excellent portrait painter. (1791-1872)

DD: PC speculative. Old-file has 4:15 AM LMT.

MUIR, JOHN April 21, 1838 Dunbar, Scotland
Naturalist 3:00 AM LMT 2W31 55N58
☉ 00-♉-33 ☿ 20-♉-09 ♂ 18-♈-43 ♄ 27-♏-21R ♆ 10-♒-17 A 16-♒-08
☽ 17-♓-05 ♀ 17-♓-07 ♃ 09-♍-08R ♅ 11-♓-11 ♇ 16-♈-41 M 15-♐-02

Explorer and writer, who campaigned for forest conservation in the U.S. Supported himself by teaching and farm work; roamed through the U.S. Europe, Asia, and Arctic. (1838-1914)

DD: PC speculative. Old-file has 9:35 AM LMT.

MUNI, PAUL September 22, 1897 Lemberg, Austria
Actor 5:00 AM MET 24E00 49N50
☉ 29-♍-24 ☿ 00-♎-03R ♂ 17-♎-56 ♄ 26-♏-31 ♆ 22-♊-33 A 26-♍-36
☽ 03-♌-47 ♀ 24-♌-37 ♃ 22-♍-37 ♅ 26-♏-02 ♇ 14-♊-43R M 25-♊-40

Oscar winner as the best actor in 1936. Famous for biographical roles that include *The Story of Louis Pasteur, The Story of Emile Zola,* and *Juarez*. His Broadway successes include *Key Largo* and *Inherit the Wind*. (1897-1967)

DD: SS #705. The same year is given in *Photoplay Annual* and *50,000 Birthdays*. September 22, 1895, given in *Americana, Famous People,* and *World Book* Obit.

MURRAY, ARTHUR April 4, 1895 New York, N.Y.
Dance teacher 8:44 AM EST 73W57 40N45
☉ 14-♈-32 ☿ 19-♓-16 ♂ 19-♊-31 ♄ 05-♏-24R ♆ 13-♊-29 A 17-♊-03
☽ 06-♌-38 ♀ 14-♉-05 ♃ 29-♊-10 ♅ 19-♏-15R ♇ 10-♊-05 M 22-♒-19

Shy and diffident until he learned to dance. First taught in a dime-a-dance hall. Began a mailorder course by 1925 and established studios throughout the country in 47 cities, to become king of the ballroom dance instructors.

C: Scarsella, Baird from Ziegler.

MURRAY, KATHRYN September 15, 1906 Jersey City, N.J.
Dance teacher 8:30 AM EST 74W04 40N44
☉ 21-♍-47 ☿ 14-♍-04 ♂ 01-♍-56 ♄ 10-♓-51R ♆ 12-♋-23 A 25-♎-20
☽ 14-♌-47 ♀ 08-♏-07 ♃ 08-♋-01 ♅ 04-♑-30 ♇ 23-♊-45 M 29-♋-51

After marriage to Arthur Murray on April 24, 1925, worked in charge of all personnel of the studios. Married 35 years; twin daughters.

C: Scarsella, Baird from Ziegler.

MUSIAL, STAN November 21, 1920 Donora, Pa
Baseball player 7:28 AM EST 79W52 40N11

☉ 28-♏-55   ☿ 17-♏-36R   ♂ 25-♑-23   ♄ 23-♍-06   ♆ 13-♌-45R   A 01-♐-10
☽ 29-♓-51   ♀ 04-♑-38   ♃ 16-♍-05   ♅ 01-♓-48   ♇ 08-♋-35R   M 16-♍-14

Played for St. Louis; MVP, NL, 1943, '46, and '48. Leading hitter of NL, 1943, '46, '48, '50 to '52, and '57. Elected to the National Baseball Hall of Fame, 1969

C: CL from *Bulletin of Astro Science,* July 1958

MUSKIE, EDMUND March 28, 1914 Rumford, Maine
Politician 5:00 AM EST 70W33 44N33

☉ 06-♈-53   ☿ 11-♓-52   ♂ 14-♋-55   ♄ 13-♊-00   ♆ 25-♋-27R   A 19-♓-27
☽ 24-♈-51   ♀ 17-♈-54   ♃ 14-♒-27   ♅ 10-♒-38   ♇ 29-♊-07   M 24-♐-53

Served in the Maine House of Representatives, 1947-51; Democratic floor leader, 1949-51. Elected governor, 1953 and 1956. First Democratic U.S. senator ever elected by popular vote in Maine, 1958.

DD: CL from Watters in AFA, April 1972. Old-file has 4:40 AM EST.

MUSSORGSKY, MODEST March 21, 1839 NS Karevo, Russia
Musician 8:00 PM LMT 28E26 57N48

☉ 00-♈-28   ☿ 08-♈-40   ♂ 17-♍-21R   ♄ 10-♐-20R   ♆ 11-♒-50   A 18-♎-24
☽ 24-♊-30   ♀ 22-♈-44   ♃ 15-♎-32R   ♅ 13-♓-26   ♇ 16-♈-57   M 26-♋-33

Russian composer, most famous for his opera *Boris Godunov;* also wrote *A Night on Bald Mountain* and *Pictures from an Exhibition.* First piano recital at 9; little formal musical education. Heavy drinking took its toll; died at 42.

DD: PC speculative. Old-file has 10:00 AM LMT.

NADAR, GEORGE October 19, 1921 Los Angeles, Ca
Actor 6:20 PM PST 118W15 34N03

☉ 26-♎-09   ☿ 16-♏-18R   ♂ 19-♍-09   ♄ 01-♎-29   ♆ 15-♌-44   A 19-♉-38
☽ 03-♊-53   ♀ 29-♍-14   ♃ 05-♎-10   ♅ 06-♓-00R   ♇ 10-♋-03R   M 02-♒-29

On screen from 1950 as Universal's handsome leading man; made a decade of films abroad; returned to Hollywood still a bachelor, with character roles on TV. Films include *Rustlers on Horseback, Carnival Story,* and *Six Bridges to Cross.*

C: CL from Marc Brooks, 1958. PC states same data as B.C.

NAMATH, JOE May 31, 1943 Beaver Falls, Pa
Football star 6:20 AM EST 80W19 40N45

☉ 09-♊-08   ☿ 27-♉-46R   ♂ 03-♈-02   ♄ 15-♊-04   ♆ 29-♍-18R   A 29-♊-44
☽ 10-♉-15   ♀ 22-♋-24   ♃ 23-♋-52   ♅ 04-♊-56   ♇ 05-♌-19   M 05-♓-58

In football, had a history of injuries and operations on his left knee, as well as a nerve injury in 1971, a broken wrist, and shoulder. One of the richest and most celebrated athletes, with commercial endorsements. TV series in 1978, *The Waverly Wonders.*

DD: McEvers quotes Jansky for B.C. PC states "personally from his mother" of 00:30 AM EST.

NAPOLEON I August 15, 1769 Ajaccio, Corsica
Conqueror 11:30 AM LAT 8E44 41N55

☉ 22-♌-46   ☿ 06-♌-10   ♂ 12-♍-04   ♄ 25-♋-55   ♆ 08-♍-42   A 06-♏-21
☽ 28-♑-56   ♀ 07-♋-03   ♃ 15-♏-01   ♅ 11-♉-31   ♇ 13-♑-21R   M 14-♌-08

One of the great military commanders in history. Military school at age 10; commission at 16; experience from the French revolution; fame by age 26. Founded an empire until his downfall at Waterloo in 1814. Exiled; died of cancer, May 5, 1821.

DD: Roscoe Hope in AA, April 1980, "Recently, Alison in *History of Napoleon* stated the time 'from family sources.' " Barbault in *Traite Pratique de Astrologie* quotes the French translation of *Memoirs of T. Nasica,* magistrate of Ajaccio from 1821-29 for "about 11:00 AM." *Wynn's Astrol,* June 1944, gives 11:28 AM, "according to P.J. Swift, an English astrologer, published 1812."

Fagan in AA, September 1959, gives 9:45 AM LAT, "Data given by Napoleon himself to a Corsican astrologer, according to John Worsdale, a contemporary of the period, who rectified the time to 9:52 AM." Davison in AQ, Winter 1957, gives 1:13 PM.

NASH OGDEN	August 19, 1902	Rye, N.Y.
Writer	1:30 AM EST	73W41 40N59

☉ 25-♌-20	☿ 03-♍-01	♂ 19-♋-32	♄ 22-♑-19R	♆ 03-♋-04	A 11-♋-08
☽ 25-♒-33	♀ 29-♋-24	♃ 10-♒-36R	♅ 17-♐-18R	♇ 19-♊-31	M 19-♓-39

Gifted American writer of light, humorous verse, from his first book *Hard Lines* (1931) to *Versus* (1949) to *You Can't Get There from Here* (1957), and more. Taught school for one year; spent several years in the editing and publishing business; lectured and appeared as a TV guest panelist. (1902-1971)

DD: CL quotes Drew. Old-file has 11:35 PM EST.

NASSER, ABDAL GAMAL	January 15, 1918	Beni Mar, Egypt
Statesman	4:28 AM EET	31E11 27N11

☉ 24-♑-09	☿ 03-♑-31	♂ 00-♎-51	♄ 12-♌-26R	♆ 06-♌-02R	A 20-♐-09
☽ 23-♒-35	♀ 27-♒-58	♃ 01-♊-42R	♅ 22-♒-04	♇ 04-♋-06R	M 02-♎-05

On July 23, 1952, led the coup that forced King Farouk to abdicate; became a towering hero to the Egyptians. President, 1956; president of the United Arab Republic from 1958 until his death in 1970.

DD: Lyndoe in *Predictions,* February 1956; same data in AQ, Fall 1967. Smollin in AA, November 1958, speculates "sunrise." PC quotes Drew for 11:00 AM EET, states that "Sybil Leek gave 4:00 AM, while another chart placed his Ascendant in Taurus."

NATION, CARRY	November 25, 1846	Garrard Ct, Ky
Temperance agitator	7:30 PM LMT	84W35 37N47

☉ 03-♐-27	☿ 24-♐-56	♂ 07-♏-25	♄ 24-♒-48	♆ 25-♒-29	A 14-♋-42
☽ 04-♓-53	♀ 28-♏-36	♃ 12-♊-40R	♅ 10-♈-33R	♇ 24-♈-14R	M 26-♓-50

Became well known for her violent efforts to stop the sales of alcoholic beverages; arrested often for disturbing the peace. In 1867, married a drunkard who soon died; in 1877 married a lawyer-minister. Began to see visions and felt destined. (1846-1911)

DC: PC speculative. Old-file has 7:15 PM LMT.

NEGRI, POLA	January 3, 1897	Lipno, Poland
Actress	6:00 PM MET	19E12 52N49

☉ 13-♑-39	☿ 02-♒-24	♂ 12-♊-37R	♄ 27-♏-26	♆ 18-♊-14R	A 10-♌-12
☽ 19-♑-34	♀ 26-♒-09	♃ 10-♍-05R	♅ 27-♏-33	♇ 12-♊-11R	M 19-♈-16

One of the most famous stars of the early silent screen; wrote her autobiography *Memoirs of a Star* (1970), in which she begins, "I was born on the eve of the new century, December 31, 1899."

DD: CL old file. Same date in *Astrological Index* (OS/NS?) PC gives January 3, 1897 NS 6:00 PM, "personal."

NEWMAN, JOHN HENRY	February 21, 1801	London, England
Theologian	7:00 AM LMT	0W06 51N30

☉ 02-♓-14	☿ 07-♓-17	♂ 01-♊-39	♄ 19-♌-41R	♆ 19-♏-25R	A 27-♒-33
☽ 10-♊-22	♀ 16-♈-57	♃ 25-♋-38R	♅ 01-♎-00R	♇ 03-♓-52	M 16-♐-51

Precocious intellectually and spiritually; had a deep and lasting conversion in August 1816; trained for the ministry. In 1845, after being an Anglican priest for twenty years, converted to Catholicism and became a Cardinal in 1879. Author of many books.

DD: PC speculative. Old-file has 6:30 AM LMT.

NEWTON, WAYNE   April 3, 1942   Norfolk, Va
Entertainer   8:22 AM EWT   76W18 36N51

☉ 13-♈-07   ☿ 26-♓-53   ♂ 16-♊-13   ♄ 25-♉-48   ♆ 28-♍-06R   A 15-♉-46
☽ 10-♏-01   ♀ 27-♒-15   ♃ 16-♊-19   ♅ 27-♉-47   ♇ 03-♌-30R   M 28-♑-18

Highest paid cabaret singer, with a guaranteed $8 million per year for Las Vegas performances. Plays eleven instruments; has absolute pitch in a three octave range; never had musical training. Part Indian. Married Elaine Okamura, a Japanese-Hawaiian stewardess in 1969.

C: CL from Lily Ireland. PC quotes CL for the same data but EST. *American Atlas* gives EWT.

NIARCHOS, STAVROS S.   July 3, 1909   Athens, Greece
Entrepreneur   00:51 PM LMT   23E43 37N59

☉ 10-♋-51   ☿ 20-♊-52   ♂ 22-♓-05   ♄ 22-♈-19   ♆ 16-♋-36   A 19-♎-10
☽ 10-♑-19   ♀ 28-♋-32   ♃ 09-♍-52   ♅ 19-♑-26R ♇ 25-♊-43   M 21-♋-50

Greek shipping executive and art collector. Brother-in-law and business partner to Ari Onassis; owner of one of the largest privately owned tanker fleets in the world. Four marriages; first son born in 1942.

C: CL quotes Drew.

NIEMOLLER, MARTIN   January 14, 1892   Lippstadt, Germany
Theologian   11:45 PM MET   8W20 51N40

☉ 24-♑-18   ☿ 00-♑-46   ♂ 23-♏-48   ♄ 00-♎-08R   ♆ 06-♊-32R   A 09-♎-28
☽ 03-♌-57   ♀ 23-♒-03   ♃ 16-♓-00   ♅ 05-♏-47   ♇ 07-♊-06R   M 12-♋-22

Commanded a U-boat in the German Navy, 1917-19. Studied theology, 1920-23; ordained 1924. Books include *From U-Boat to Pulpit* (1934). Became president of the World Council of Churches. Preached against the Nazis and was imprisoned in Dachau 1937-45.

DD: Dewey from AFA, October 1952. *Current Biographies*, 1943, gives the same date, but *Americana* gives January 1, 1892.

NIGHTINGALE, FLORENCE   May 12, 1820   Florence, Italy
Nurse   2:00 PM LMT   11E15 43N47

☉ 21-♉-40   ☿ 25-♈-50   ♂ 10-♌-33   ♄ 09-♈-20   ♆ 00-♑-28R   A 22-♍-28
☽ 23-♉-54   ♀ 06-♋-44   ♃ 17-♓-44   ♅ 28-♐-13R   ♇ 28-♓-16   M 21-♊-01

Left her wealthy family to learn nursing at 33; became hospital superintendent. A selfless heroine in the Crimean War; became a world-known authority on the care of the sick; founded the nursing profession as we know it today. (1820-1910)

DD: Jansky F/M from *Astrological Index*, a book which gives the date only. PC same data, as speculative. Redding in AA, April 1937, speculates 8:45 AM.

NIJINSKI, VASLAV   March 12, 1890 NS   Kiev, Russia
Ballet dancer   10:30 PM LMT   30E22 50N27

☉ 22-♓-14   ☿ 00-♓-09   ♂ 04-♐-35   ♄ 28-♌-49R   ♆ 02-♊-01   A 11-♏-10
☽ 05-♐-25   ♀ 27-♓-46   ♃ 03-♒-35   ♅ 25-♎-59R   ♇ 05-♊-03   M 25-♌-40

The greatest male dancer of all time, especially noted for his high and soaring leaps. Entered ballet school at age 9; debut 1908. Married a dancer in 1913. Hospitalized with hopeless schizophrenia at the age of 28. (1890-1950)

DD: Dewey quotes a rectified chart given by both AFA and Michael Erlewine from the biography of his wife, Romola, in which she states, "Born in the evening after his mother danced at the theater." *Chronicle Nativities* makes the same quote, that "he was born an hour after his mother performed at the theater, approximately 10:30 PM LMT." SS #723 gives 2:45 PM LMT (February 28, 1890 OS).

NIMOY, LEONARD	March 26, 1931	Boston, Mass
Actor	4:15 AM EST	71W04 42N22

☉ 04-♈-45	☿ 15-♈-11	♂ 29-♋-13	♄ 22-♑-07	♆ 03-♍-37R	A 26-♒-26
☽ 24-♊-35	♀ 23-♒-40	♃ 11-♋-02	♅ 14-♈-43	♇ 18-♋-42R	M 12-♐-02

Lean years as an actor from 1951, before the role of Spock in the TV series *Star Trek*, 1965-67. Increasing status as a powerful dramatic talent; notable on stage in *Equus*. Photographer; author of three volumes of verse and his autobiography *I Am Not Spock*.

DD: Jansky from Penfield. PC states, "personal." March quotes Nimoy, who stated on a TV show that he was Aries with Scorpio rising.

NOBEL, ALFRED	October 31, 1833	Stockholm, Sweden
Inventor	6:40 AM LMT	18E03 59N20

☉ 07-♏-35	☿ 23-♏-26	♂ 08-♏-05	♄ 05-♎-37	♆ 26-♑-45	A 00-♏-50
☽ 07-♊-53	♀ 07-♎-13	♃ 29-♈-36R	♅ 18-♒-38	♇ 11-♈-13R	M 16-♌-49

Swedish chemist, who invented dynamite. After preparing a nitroglycerin explosive, was considered a public enemy. In later years, suffered guilt and became increasingly ill and nervous. Founded the Nobel prizes; in his will left a fund of $9 million for awards. (1833-1896)

DD: PC speculative. Old-file has 5:55 AM LMT.

NOSTRADAMUS, MICHEL DE	December 24, 1503 NS	St. Remy, France
Physician	12:00 Noon LMT	4E50 43N48

☉ 01-♑-37	☿ 04-♑-13R	♂ 18-♋-40R	♄ 15-♋-13R	♆ 22-♑-04	A 03-♈-12
☽ 15-♏-48	♀ 02-♒-23	♃ 11-♋-01R	♅ 09-♓-37	♇ 02-♐-54	M 01-♑-34

After losing his wife and two sons to the plague in 1533, retired for ten years; returned as an astrologer who gained fame for his prophesies in verse form in works such as *Centuries* (1555). (1503-1566)

DD: *Astrology and the Occult Sciences,* Summer 1942, Kraum quotes "data from his friend recorded as 'around noon'." Jeane Hitt gives 11:40 AM in M.H., April 1978 (December 14, 1503 OS).

NUREYEV, RUDOLPH	March 17, 1938	Irkutsk, Russia
Ballet dancer	1:00 PM LMT	104E20 52N16

☉ 26-♓-00	☿ 04-♈-28	♂ 03-♉-33	♄ 06-♈-28	♆ 19-♍-37R	A 03-♌-46
☽ 08-♎-54	♀ 06-♈-04	♃ 20-♒-04	♅ 11-♉-06	♇ 27-♋-59R	M 09-♈-58

With outstanding technique and compelling stage presence, one of the most famous dancers in the West, particularly brilliant partnership with Margot Fonteyn. Trained in Leningrad; a principal dancer in the Kiev company until he sought asylum in France 1962.

DD: PC quotes *The Complete Astrologer*. Dewey states he was born on a train near Lake Baikal. Marguerite Leisge at the CL quotes him personally, 1977, that he does not know his time of birth.

OAKLEY, ANNIE	August 13, 1860	Darke Co, Ohio
Markswoman	12:00 Noon LMT	84W35 40N07

☉ 21-♌-07	☿ 15-♌-07R	♂ 19-♑-27R	♄ 28-♌-25	♆ 28-♓-57R	A 11-♏-30
☽ 07-♋-46	♀ 18-♋-32	♃ 09-♌-51	♅ 11-♊-32	♇ 09-♉-28R	M 19-♌-58

Expert shot with a pistol, rifle, or shotgun; five-foot-tall star of Buffalo Bill's Wild West Show for seventeen years. Began shooting at the age of 9, supporting her family by bringing in game.

DD: PC speculative. Old-file has 9:10 PM LMT.

O'CASEY, SEAN
Writer

March 30, 1880			Dublin, Ireland		
9:00 AM LMT			6W15 53N20		

☉ 10-♈-04	☿ 07-♈-32R	♂ 23-♊-11	♄ 17-♈-37	♆ 10-♉-35	A 28-♊-53
☽ 02-♐-03	♀ 12-♓-29	♃ 29-♓-10	♅ 05-♍-37R	♇ 25-♉-53	M 20-♒-45

A playwright, who became one of the most important authors of the Irish literary revival. Almost no formal education; began as a common laborer. Fought for Irish independence but eventually moved to England. (1880-1964)

DD: PC speculative. Old-file has 6:00 PM LMT.

OFFENBACH, JACQUES
Musician

June 20, 1819			Cologne, Germany		
3:00 AM LMT			6E58 50N57		

☉ 27-♊-53	☿ 14-♊-30	♂ 07-♉-40	♄ 00-♈-18	♆ 27-♐-18R	A 14-♊-37
☽ 29-♉-35	♀ 28-♉-36	♃ 16-♒-52R	♅ 22-♐-18R	♇ 27-♓-32	M 10-♒-01

Franco-German composer, who won fame as a manager, director, and composer of ninety French operettas between 1855 and 1880. Began violincello at 14; was soon playing in the orchestra. Began conducting in 1850. (1819-1880)

DD: PC, "recorded." Old-file has 3:10 AM LMT.

OLCOTT, HENRY STEEL
Theosophist

August 2, 1832			Orange, N.J.		
11:15 AM LMT			74W14 40N46		

☉ 10-♌-17	☿ 05-♍-38	♂ 10-♉-39	♄ 13-♍-35	♆ 25-♑-24R	A 23-♎-44
☽ 01-♏-01	♀ 12-♌-01	♃ 28-♓-17R	♅ 16-♒-50R	♇ 11-♈-36R	M 27-♋-54

Lawyer, journalist, and investigator. A spiritualist in belief; met H.P. Blavatsky in Vermont. They co-founded the Theosophical Society on November 17, 1875. Noted for integrity, honesty, and moral courage. (1832-1907)

C: CL from SS #735 (no time given); same data pictured in Adams' *One Hundred Horoscopes*. Same data from Sepharial in M.A., May 1894.

The profile and chart of Madame Helena P. Blavatsky are given in *Profiles of Women*.

O'LOUGHLIN, HERBERT J.
Traveler

November 22, 1908			Oak Park, Ill		
11:00 AM CST			87W47 41N53		

☉ 00-♐-01	☿ 13-♏-17	♂ 28-♎-08	♄ 03-♈-33R	♆ 16-♋-49R	A 26-♑-29
☽ 15-♏-26	♀ 23-♎-02	♃ 12-♍-19	♅ 14-♑-27	♇ 25-♊-17R	M 20-♏-56

Passenger on the Hindenburg derigible for the trip from England to America. When it burst into flames upon landing May 6, 1937, saved himself by jumping through red hot girders fifteen feet to the ground.

C: CL from *Astrology*, October 1938.

OMAR KHAYYAM
Poet

July 25, 1050 NS			Khorassan, Persia		
5:40 AM LMT			58E00 35N00		

☉ 01-♌-06	☿ 28-♌-27	♂ 00-♋-04	♄ 08-♒-54R	♆ 18-♈-18R	A 08-♌-10
☽ 03-♋-06	♀ 09-♋-40	♃ 19-♈-34	♅ 13-♎-01	♇ 10-♒-23R	M 29-♈-17

Persian poet, astronomer, and mathematician. His one long poem, *The Rubiyat*, brought him lasting fame. Composed more than 750 four-line verses. As royal astronomer, he changed the Persian calendar; also wrote an Arabic book on algebra.

DD: AJA, Spring 1937, Van Norstrand states, "from the chart I have, the atrologer supposed he was born a few minutes after sunrise." AQ, Spring 1937, Fagan states July 25, 1050 as OS, corrected to July 31, 1050 NS: in AA, April 1940, he asks Van Norstrand for his historical source and validation. PC gives May 18, 1048 OS 4:18 AM LMT, Nishapur, Persia 58E45 36N13, "from an old book on Hindu astrology." Old-file has the same date, 4:48 AM. The *World Book* gives ?. *Americana* gives "about 11/32."

ONASSIS, ARISTOTLE September 21, 1906 Izmir, Turkey
Entrepreneur 5:58 AM LMT 27E08 38N26

☉ 27-♍-16	☿ 24-♍-35	♂ 05-♍-29	♄ 10-♓-26R	♆ 12-♋-28	A 28-♍-53
☽ 02-♏-35	♀ 13-♏-40	♃ 08-♋-42	♅ 04-♑-31	♇ 23-♊-46	M 28-♊-45

Greek shipping magnate and one of the world's richest men; a modern day potentate. Started his career at age 16 with $60 in his pocket; made his first million by age 25. Second marriage to the widowed Jacqueline Kennedy, 1968. (1906?-1975)

DD: CL quotes Drew. Penfield quotes Edith Custer, "Ari Onassis registered for the draft board in World War I and swore he was born in Salonika on September 21, 1900." (Information taken from a news clipping.) Dewey states, "His tombstone reads 1900." January 20, 1906 given by McEvers (10:50 AM), by PC, quoting Marcia Moore (10:00 AM), and in *Onassis; An Extravagant Life* by Frank Bardy (1977). *Famous People* gives January 15, 1906. *World Book* Obit gives March 15, 1906.

The data of his widow, Jacqueline Kennedy Onassis, are given in *Profiles of Women*, with several speculative times. The profile and chart of his daughter and heir, Christina Onassis, are also given in *Profiles of Women*.

O'NEILL, EUGENE October 16, 1888 New York, N.Y.
Writer 1:30 AM EST 73W57 40N45

☉ 23-♎-20	☿ 16-♏-42	♂ 24-♐-44	♄ 18-♌-30	♆ 01-♊-52R	A 27-♌-27
☽ 12-♓-18	♀ 18-♏-57	♃ 05-♐-48	♅ 18-♎-00	♇ 05-♊-41R	M 21-♉-11

American playwright, who won four Pulitzer prizes — for *Beyond the Horizon* (1920), *Anna Christie* (1922), *Strange Interlude* (1928) and *Long Day's Journey into Night* (1957). The son of an actor; worked as a sailor, actor, and reporter before 1914. (1888-1953)

DD: Fleischer in *Astrological Review*, October 1935. PC quotes *Eugene O'Neill* by A. Gelb, "in the middle of the afternoon," rectified to 2:40 PM EST. That biography states on p. 55, "On a Tuesday afternoon, October 16, 1888."

OPPENHEIMER, J. ROBERT April 22, 1904 New York, N.Y.
Nuclear physicist 8:15 AM EST 73W47 40N45

☉ 01-♉-58	☿ 21-♉-58	♂ 11-♉-38	♄ 19-♒-46	♆ 03-♋-33	A 27-♊-08
☽ 23-♋-28	♀ 11-♈-33	♃ 12-♈-34	♅ 29-♐-49R	♇ 19-♊-07	M 03-♓-01

Head of the U.S. Atomic Energy Commission General Advisory Committee, 1947-52; known as "the father of the Atom Bomb." Declared a security risk, 1953. Head of the Institute of Advanced Study at Princeton, 1953-66. Received the Fermi Award, 1963. (1908-1967)

DD: CL from Gilbert Ibarra, November 1964. Dewey quotes Ebertin in his *Pluto* book at 12:00 noon. PC quotes Ebertin at 8:00 PM EST. Old-file has 7:45 PM EST.

ORSINI, PRINCE RAIMONDO November 18, 1931 Rome, Italy
Royalty 3:14 AM MET 12E15 41N45

☉ 24-♏-47	☿ 11-♐-41	♂ 13-♐-32	♄ 19-♑-13	♆ 07-♍-50	A 09-♎-22
☽ 05-♓-52	♀ 13-♐-00	♃ 21-♌-53	♅ 16-♈-01R	♇ 22-♋-02R	M 10-♋-57

Member of a noble Italian family, prominent from the 11th century with popes and statesmen. Linked romantically with Princess Soraya after she divorced the Shah of Iran.

C: Skeetz quotes Tucker in Dell, October 1959.

ORWELL, GEORGE June 25, 1903 Motihari, India
Writer 11:30 AM LMT 84E55 26N40

☉ 02-♋-30 ☿ 11-♊-01 ♂ 08-♎-25 ♄ 08-♒-20R ♆ 03-♋-23 A 25-♍-15
☽ 02-♋-18 ♀ 17-♌-17 ♃ 22-♓-44 ♅ 23-♐-16R ♇ 19-♊-30 M 25-♊-08

Eric Blair, English novelist and essayist who won his greatest successes in 1946, with his amusing anticommunist satire *Animal Farm,* and in 1949 with *Nineteen Eighty-Four.* (1903-1950)

DD: PC speculative. Old-file has 2:40 PM LMT.

OVERELL, BUELAH LOUISE April 30, 1929 Los Angeles, Ca
Homicide suspect 3:34 PM PST 118W15 34N04

☉ 10-♉-07 ☿ 24-♉-43 ♂ 23-♋-32 ♄ 00-♑-09R ♆ 28-♌-37R A 03-♎-05
☽ 28-♑-08 ♀ 23-♈-54R ♃ 20-♉-01 ♅ 09-♈-11 ♇ 16-♋-24 M 03-♋-22

Parents killed in a yacht explosion in Santa Ana March 15, 1947. Brought to trial for suspected murder with her lover, George "Bud" Gollem (born March 1, 1926, Los Angeles). Both acquitted October 5, 1947. Married to a policeman, July 1949.

C: Scarsella from Baird.

OWEN, REVEREND G. VALE June 26, 1869 Birmingham, England
Medium 6:00 PM GMT 1W55 52N25

☉ 05-♋-05 ☿ 02-♋-16R ♂ 17-♍-21 ♄ 12-♐-18R ♆ 19-♈-23 A 04-♐-49
☽ 06-♒-46 ♀ 18-♋-11 ♃ 13-♉-00 ♅ 16-♋-51 ♇ 17-♉-32 M 03-♎-15

Received notice in 1920 because of his publication in the *Weekly Dispatch* of a series of communications on life in the world after death, messages by automatic writing from his dead mother and friends. Tall, thin, grave; began automatic writing in 1913.

C: M.A., May 1920.

PADEREWSKI, IGNACE JAN November 18, 1860 NS Kurylowka, Russia
Musician 3:00 AM LMT 26E34 48N40

☉ 25-♏-58 ☿ 14-♐-26R ♂ 27-♒-58 ♄ 08-♍-37 ♆ 26-♓-42R A 08-♎-59
☽ 29-♑-48 ♀ 15-♎-25 ♃ 26-♌-03 ♅ 10-♊-35R ♇ 08-♉-10R M 11-♋-19

Polish pianist and composer. Began piano lessons at 6; entered the Warsaw conservatory at 12; was appointed a professor at 18. Concert pianist from 1891. Became a statesman, working for Polish freedom during World War I; resumed concerts in 1922. (1860-1941)

DD: PC speculative. Old-file gives 1:36 AM LMT, Warsaw, Poland. *World Book* gives Podolia, the Ukraine. M.A., November 1939, Alan Leo gives November 6, 1860, "according to a biography by R. Landau which does not state OS/NS;" he speculates 2:30 AM LMT, assuming the date to be New Style.

PAHLAVI, MOHAMMED REZA October 26, 1919 Teheran, Iran
Shah of Iran 8:15 AM Zone 3.5 51E26 35N45

☉ 01-♏-43 ☿ 19-♏-27 ♂ 09-♍-40 ♄ 08-♍-46 ♆ 11-♌-26 A 24-♏-20
☽ 27-♏-10 ♀ 19-♍-02 ♃ 15-♌-39 ♅ 27-♒-51R ♇ 07-♋-44R M 04-♍-19

An absolute monarch from 1941; formally crowned in 1967. Built his kingdom into a modern super-power, supplying the world with 25% of its oil. With his country torn by strife and insurrection in 1978, driven out with his family in early 1979.

DD: CL quotes Drew. Dewey quotes Ebertin at 11:30 PM, says that Ebertin later stated the data was not from an infallible source. The autobiography *Mission for My Country* (1960) gives the date on p. 51 (no time given or inferred). Scarsella quotes Baird for 10:00 AM Iran time, from Ziegler.

The profiles and charts for Soraya, the former Empress, and Farah Diba, Empress of Iran, are given in *Profiles of Women.*

PARK, TOM | June 1, 1924 | Newcastle-upon Tyne, England
Swimmer | 4:00 AM BST | 3W52 54N58

☉ 10-♊-22 ☿ 16-♉-37 ♂ 20-♒-18 ♄ 26-♎-14R ♆ 17-♌-54 A 12-♊-50
☽ 24-♉-40 ♀ 16-♋-08 ♃ 15-♐-39R ♅ 21-♓-15 ♇ 11-♋-05 M 03-♒-12

C: CL from Garth Allen in AA, October 1956.

PARKMAN, FRANCIS | September 16, 1823 | Boston, Mass
Writer | 10:00 AM LMT | 71W04 42N22

☉ 22-♍-54 ☿ 17-♎-25 ♂ 06-♌-32 ♄ 23-♉-48R ♆ 04-♑-40R A 12-♏-27
☽ 10-♒-05 ♀ 24-♎-25 ♃ 08-♋-13 ♅ 07-♑-38R ♇ 01-♈-08R M 22-♌-23

One of America's greatest historians, who wrote vivid accounts of the role of the Indians with his famous *The Oregon Trail*. Poor health; wrote with great difficulty; almost blind. (1823-1893)

DD: PC speculative. Old-file has 9:15 AM LMT.

PARRISH, MAXFIELD | July 25, 1870 | Philadelphia, Pa
Artist | 6:00 PM LMT | 75W10 39N57

☉ 02-♌-43 ☿ 01-♌-17 ♂ 00-♋-54 ♄ 22-♐-42R ♆ 21-♈-50R A 11-♑-40
☽ 02-♋-30 ♀ 29-♊-02 ♃ 17-♊-20 ♅ 22-♋-55 ♇ 18-♉-49 M 05-♏-45

American painter and illustrator, who portrayed a world of rich color and poetic fancy. Created posters, magazine covers, murals, and other decorations with skillful craftsmanship and distinctively elegant style. (1870-1966)

DD: PC speculative. Old-file has 5:30 AM LMT.

PASCAL, BLAISE | June 19, 1623 | Clermont-Ferrand, France
Scientist | 6:00 AM LMT | 3E05 45N47

☉ 27-♊-23 ☿ 09-♋-45 ♂ 15-♑-39R ♄ 03-♌-14 ♆ 15-♎-02R A 19-♋-59
☽ 21-♓-54 ♀ 26-♋-41 ♃ 00-♌-48 ♅ 10-♌-23 ♇ 15-♉-18 M 26-♓-50

French religious philosopher, mathematician, and scientist, who remains known in history for his work in science. At the age of 12 taught himself geometry; wrote a treatise at 16. (1623-1662)

DD: PC from Matthews, "who believed he had Cancer rising; Barbault thought he had Leo rising." Old-file has 5:15 AM LMT.

PASTERNAK, BORIS | February 10, 1890 NS | Moscow, Russia
Writer | 4:00 PM LMT | 37E35 55N45

☉ 21-♒-49 ☿ 00-♒-49R ♂ 21-♏-29 ♄ 01-♍-11R ♆ 01-♊-45R A 14-♌-05
☽ 24-♎-36 ♀ 19-♒-54 ♃ 27-♑-13 ♅ 26-♎-39R ♇ 04-♊-57R M 22-♈-15

Russian novelist and poet, who won the 1958 Nobel prize for literature. Rejected the award because of pressure from the Russian government. His novel *Doctor Zhivago* not published in Russia. (1890-1960)

DD: PC speculative. Old-file has 3:45 PM LMT.

PATTI, ADELINA | February 10, 1843 | Madrid, Spain
Singer | 4:00 PM Madrid time | 3W42 40N26

☉ 21-♒-20 ☿ 29-♒-45R ♂ 24-♏-25 ♄ 20-♑-41 ♆ 19-♒-03 A 01-♌-56
☽ 26-♊-11 ♀ 06-♑-00 ♃ 08-♒-37 ♅ 26-♓-14 ♇ 20-♈-11 M 17-♈-46

Italian soprano, who was taken to New York by her parents, both opera singers, to sing in a concert at age 8, November 24, 1851. London debut, 1861; Milan debut, 1877. Not an outstanding actress but brilliantly gifted in music. Retired, 1895. (1843-1919)

DD: SS #754. Same data in *Urania*, published early 20th century. NN #798 gives the same date, "according to the *Book of Baptisms*." Same date in *New Century Cyclopedia*. Adams' *One Hundred Horoscopes* pictures a chart for February 19, 1843, 3:30 PM LMT, Madrid; same date given in *Americana*.

PAULING, LINUS February 28, 1901 Portland, Ore
Scientist 7:26 AM PST 122W37 45N32

| ☉ 09-♓-23 | ☿ 21-♓-44R | ♂ 00-♍-25R | ♄ 13-♑-54 | ♆ 26-♊-28R | A 23-♓-26 |
| ☽ 14-♋-52 | ♀ 23-♒-49 | ♃ 07-♑-42 | ♅ 16-♐-41 | ♇ 15-♊-41 | M 26-♐-55 |

Winner of the 1954 Nobel prize in chemistry for his studies in molecular structure, especially the nature of the bonding of atoms in molecules. Professor of chemistry at Stanford University.

C: CL.

PAVAROTTI, LUCIANO October 12, 1935 Modena, Italy
Singer 1:30 AM MET 10E54 44N37

| ☉ 17-♎-45 | ☿ 00-♏-36R | ♂ 17-♐-46 | ♄ 04-♓-07R | ♆ 15-♍-32 | A 20-♌-35 |
| ☽ 15-♈-18 | ♀ 09-♍-20 | ♃ 24-♏-05 | ♅ 04-♉-09R | ♇ 27-♋-21 | M 10-♉-29 |

A teacher for two years before becoming a professional singer; debut in 1961 in *La Boheme*. A golden, lyric operatic tenor, hailed as "greater than Caruso." Married; three daughters. By 1979 his worldwide bookings extended into 1994.

C: Charles Cook in Leek's *Astrology*, November 1972. PC same data, as "recorded."

PAVLOVA, ANNA January 31, 1882 NS Leningrad, Russia
Ballerina 9:00 AM LMT 30E15 59N55

| ☉ 11-♒-22 | ☿ 27-♒-33 | ♂ 27-♊-01R | ♄ 06-♉-06 | ♆ 13-♉-47 | A 10-♓-34 |
| ☽ 08-♋-56 | ♀ 06-♒-20 | ♃ 16-♉-57 | ♅ 17-♍-55R | ♇ 27-♉-21R | M 25-♐-47 |

The most famous ballerina of her generation: in 1907 became the first Russian ballet star to appear in other European countries. Made her debut in London and New York in 1910. (1882-1931)

DD: PC speculative. Old-file has 8:40 AM LMT. *Britannica* states, "The actual date has been variously quoted; the most authoritative is perhaps the one given in the Russian edition of her husband's biography of her, January 31, 1882."

PEALE, NORMAN VINCENT May 31, 1898 Bowersville, Ohio
Minister 6:11 AM CST 83W44 39N35

| ☉ 10-♊-01 | ☿ 15-♉-43 | ♂ 24-♈-52 | ♄ 08-♐-55R | ♆ 21-♊-46 | A 08-♋-04 |
| ☽ 14-♎-07 | ♀ 06-♋-20 | ♃ 00-♎-22 | ♅ 01-♐-11R | ♇ 14-♊-06 | M 16-♓-59 |

American clergyman, who won fame for his writings and his radio and TV programs to a weekly audience of several million people. Books include *The Power of Positive Thinking* (1952). Edited a magazine, *Guideposts*, and a newspaper column, *Confident Living*.

C: Holliday from CL.

PEARL, BILL October 31, 1930 Prineville, Ore
Body-builder 8:00 AM PST 120W51 44N18

| ☉ 07-♏-31 | ☿ 03-♏-27 | ♂ 05-♌-02 | ♄ 07-♑-21 | ♆ 05-♍-23 | A 22-♏-00 |
| ☽ 02-♓-17 | ♀ 07-♐-21 | ♃ 20-♋-25 | ♅ 12-♈-27R | ♇ 20-♋-52R | M 06-♍-38 |

Won the title of Mr. America in the contest held at Indianapolis, June 8, 1953.

C: Skeetz quotes Garth Allen in Dell, March 1955.

PEARY, ROBERT E. May 6, 1856 Cresson, Pa
Adventurer 12:04 PM LMT 78W36 40N28

| ☉ 16-♉-19 | ☿ 27-♉-47 | ♂ 03-♎-21R | ♄ 27-♊-33 | ♆ 19-♓-51 | A 25-♌-00 |
| ☽ 14-♊-32 | ♀ 26-♈-12 | ♃ 29-♓-34 | ♅ 20-♉-35 | ♇ 04-♉-25 | M 18-♉-13 |

Admiral, engineer, and scientist; with the Civil Engineer Corp of the U.S. Navy took part in a survey of Nicaragua Canal route, 1885-87. Proved Greenland to be an island and the North Pole to be in the center of a vast sea covered with ice; was the first man to reach the North Pole on April 6, 1909. (1856-1920)

C: SS #759.

PERLS, FRITZ   July 8, 1893   Berlin, Germany
Psychologist   5:30 AM MET   13E25   52N30

☉ 16-♋-11	☿ 12-♌-25	♂ 05-♌-05	♄ 06-♎-46	♆ 12-♊-19	A 02-♌-37
☽ 02-♉-31	♀ 04-♌-12	♃ 23-♉-41	♅ 06-♏-39R	♇ 10-♊-08	M 07-♈-55

Author and co-founder of the Gestalt school of psychotherapy. (1893-1970)

DD: Dewey quotes a time rectified from "dawn," given to Dobyns by a co-worker of Perls at Esalen. PC gives 5:00 AM MET, "personal."

PERON, EVA   May 7, 1908   Buenos Aires, Argentina
Political wife   5:10 AM Cordoba time   58W27   34S36

☉ 16-♉-24	☿ 15-♉-59	♂ 20-♊-04	♄ 05-♈-46	♆ 12-♋-37	A 01-♉-44
☽ 04-♌-40	♀ 01-♋-28	♃ 05-♌-42	♅ 16-♑-48R	♇ 23-♊-25	M 05-♒-41

Maria Evita Duarte de Peron, an actress in radio and movies before she married Juan Peron in 1945; helped him to rise to power; became one of the most influential women of her time.

DD: Craswell from *Astrology* Vol 26 #3. Blanca Matias in Dell, November 1957 writes: "She was one of four illigimate children born in lowly circumstances. Touchy about her age, she had the year changed from official records, implying that she was 23 years younger than her husband when there was actually 13 years between them. The year was definitely confirmed when her younger brother died as his date of birth, December 10, 1914, was printed in his obituary. Eva born on May 7, 1908. My speculative time is for 5 Scorpio Ascendant." May 7, 1908 is given in *50,000 Birthdays*.

PC states, "private sources in Buenos Aires" give May 17, 1919, Los Toledos, Argentina, 3:00 AM LMT. In M.H., January 1980, Penfield states, "In a new paperback, *Eva: Evita* by Paul Montgomery there's a statement which corraborates her date as May 7, 1919, Los Toledos, 5:00 AM." Holliday reports a Thames TV program, *Queen of Hearts*, June 1979, stated she was born May 17, 1917, early in the morning. Constance Mayer has a chart for May 17, 1908, 5:10 PM LMT, from an astrology magazine. *Astrological Index* gives May 7, 1919. *Current Biography* Obit gives May 7, 1919 to July 26, 1952.

PERON, JUAN   October 8, 1895   Lobos, Argentina
Statesman   6:30 AM LMT   59W06   35S11

☉ 24-♎-48	☿ 09-♏-56R	♂ 22-♎-30	♄ 08-♏-11	♆ 17-♊-52R	A 19-♏-34
☽ 27-♎-15	♀ 19-♍-08	♃ 06-♌-52	♅ 18-♏-41	♇ 12-♊-32R	M 01-♌-54

President of Argentina from 1946 to 1955. Opposition to his regime became intense; the army and navy forced his resignation after a three-day revolt. (1895-1974)

DD: PC, "recorded." Old file has 7:00 AM LMT. LMR notes that Argentina was on Local Time of Cordoba from 1894-1920.

PERSHING, JOHN J.   January 13, 1860   Laclede, Mo
Military officer   4:30 AM LMT   93W10   38N47

☉ 22-♑-32	☿ 01-♑-20	♂ 19-♏-06	♄ 24-♌-52R	♆ 24-♓-47	A 11-♐-22
☽ 28-♍-37	♀ 18-♒-39	♃ 19-♋-55R	♅ 04-♊-03R	♇ 06-♉-33R	M 29-♍-37

Commander of the American expeditionary forces in Europe during World War I — the first U.S. army ever sent to Europe. After the war, received the highest rank that had ever been given an American army officer, General of the Armies of the U.S. (1860-1948)

DD: Rectified by PC, who states: "Date from *Guerrilla Warrior* by Donald Smythe, which states he was born on a very cold night when snow was falling. SS gives the date of September 13, 1860, with Sagittarius rising. The time here is calculated to give him Sagittarius rising using the January date."

LMR notes that the data is not in SS. Old-file gives the same date, 4:50 AM. *World Book* and *Americana* give September 13, 1860. The biography quoted states on p. 3, "John Joseph was born probably on January 13, 1860." The Appendix devotes most of p. 283 to the question of his birth. He gave September 13; however, a witness gave January 13 and remembered it was cold that night, and snow was falling. Several other statements of early acquaintances confirm the January 13 date.

PETIOT, DR. January 14, 1897 Auxerre, France
Murderer 3:00 AM Paris time 3E34 47N48

☉ 24-♑-16	☿ 09-♒-47R	♂ 11-♊-35R	♄ 28-♏-21	♆ 18-♊-00R	A 21-♏-21
☽ 29-♉-18	♀ 08-♓-18	♃ 09-♍-36R	♅ 28-♏-00	♇ 12-♊-02R	M 08-♍-26

French mass murderer, convicted of the death of sixty-seven people. Arrested, October 31, 1944; death sentence given, April 4, 1946; executed, May 26, 1946.

C: CL from Tucker, March 1958.

PETTIT, PAUL November 29, 1931 Los Angeles, Ca
Baseball player 12:05 PM PST 118W15 34N04

☉ 06-♐-39	☿ 27-♐-32	♂ 22-♐-16	♄ 20-♑-17	♆ 07-♍-57	A 01-♓-05
☽ 00-♌-33	♀ 27-♐-39	♃ 22-♌-29	♅ 15-♈-43R	♇ 21-♋-54R	M 12-♐-14

Signed secretly with the Pittsburgh Pirates on October 17, 1949; final contract with the Buc representatives proper on January 31, 1950, for a bonus of $100,000; of headline interest over the nation.

C: Skeetz quotes Garth Allen in Dell, March 1955.

PETTY, SIR WILLIAM June 5, 1623 NS Romsey, Hants, England
Political economist 11:45 PM LMT 1W30 50N59

☉ 14-♊-45	☿ 11-♊-30	♂ 17-♑-11R	♄ 01-♌-49	♆ 15-♎-07R	A 17-♒-45
☽ 12-♍-42	♀ 10-♋-43	♃ 28-♋-13	♅ 09-♌-47	♇ 15-♉-03	M 11-♐-48

Went to sea as a boy; abandoned on the French coast at age 15; studied there with the Jesuits. Served in the English navy; became a medical student, 1644; a doctor of physics, 1647; a professor of anatomy, 1651. Conducted the first scientific survey, 1652; made a map of Ireland, 1673. Wrote a major work on taxes, 1662; became recognized as an economy expert. (1623-1687)

DD: WEMYSS #156, "according to the Ashmole Ms #192, May 26, 1623 OS." *Americana* gives May 16, 1623 (presumed OS).

PHILIPS, MARK September 22, 1948 Tewksbury, England
Royal family 1:45 AM BST 2W10 51N40

☉ 28-♍-55	☿ 24-♎-44	♂ 12-♏-23	♄ 00-♍-20	♆ 12-♎-13	A 03-♌-50
☽ 09-♉-12	♀ 14-♌-01	♃ 21-♐-09	♅ 00-♋-29	♇ 15-♌-51	M 10-♈-45

Married Princess Anne of Great Britain on November 14, 1973; they had met at the Mexico City Olympics 1968. Though a commoner, his blood line can be traced to Edward I.

DD: Craswell quotes Ebertin, "between 1:00 to 2:00 AM BST", rectified by PC. Old-file has 1:40 AM BST.
 The profile and chart of Princess Anne are given in *Profiles of Women*.

PICASSO, PABLO October 25, 1881 Malaga, Spain
Artist 11:15 PM LMT 4W25 36N43

☉ 02-♏-43	☿ 24-♏-14	♂ 12-♋-22	♄ 09-♉-27R	♆ 15-♉-31R	A 05-♌-38
☽ 08-♐-13	♀ 04-♎-32	♃ 23-♉-34R	♅ 17-♍-02	♇ 28-♉-47R	M 25-♈-05

Spanish artist, who ranks among the great masters. Lived most of his life in France, where in sixty years he created some five thousand paintings, drawings, etchings, lithographs, sculptures, and ceramics. (1881-1973)

DD: *Circle* #378, from AFA Yearbook, 1954; same data in *Picasso, His Life and Work* by Roland Penrose (1958) and in *Pablo Picasso* by Pierre Cabanne, quoted by PC. AQ, Summer 1957, Storme gives the same data, "from an article in the *New Yorker*, based on birth records."AQ, Winter 1965, Revill states 9:30 PM, "noted by him in a biography published 1946." CL quotes AFA, September 1960, at 9:30 PM.

R.H. Oliver gives 11:59 PM LMT in *Aspects,* Spring 1979. March has 12:03 PM and 11:35 AM from two different biographies. Steinbrecker has 7:30 AM and 7:30 PM from two different biographies. Leek's *Astrology* has 00:17 AM LMT.

PICKFORD, MARY	April 9, 1892	Toronto, Ont, Canada
Actress	3:00 AM EST	79W27 43N38

☉ 19-♈-56	☿ 04-♉-30	♂ 15-♑-28	♄ 25-♍-01R	♆ 07-♊-02	A 07-♒-50
☽ 17-♍-59	♀ 04-♊-11	♃ 05-♈-38	♅ 04-♏-40R	♇ 07-♊-18	M 00-♐-49

First stage appearance at age 5; became a great star in silent films. In *Coquette,* the first actress to win an Oscar in a talkie, 1928/29. In more than two hundred films; a co-founder of United Artists and of the Motion Picture Academy. (1892?-1979)

DD: SS #767. L.A. *Times* Obit, May 30, 1979 says, "age 86" = 1892. Dewey quotes the same date from Carnegie, *Five Minute Biographies,* in AA, November 1942. CL quotes Kraum in NAJ for April 9, 1893, 3:00 AM, the same date as given in *Astrological Index.* April 8, 1893 is given in *Celebrities, Famous People,* and *Information Please.*

PIKE, JAMES	February 14, 1913	Oklahoma City, Ok
Minister	4:00 AM CST	97W30 35N30

☉ 25-♒-08	☿ 26-♒-18	♂ 26-♑-15	♄ 27-♉-26	♆ 23-♋-50R	A 28-♐-26
☽ 25-♉-51	♀ 11-♈-50	♃ 09-♑-04	♅ 04-♒-44	♇ 28-♊-08R	M 17-♎-42

Joined the Episcopal Church, 1944; ordained a clergyman, 1946. Chaplain and Dean of the Department of Religion at Columbia U., 1949-52; Dean of the Cathedral, 1952-58; Bishop of California, 1958-66. Died in the Judean wilderness during a visit to Israel in 1969.

DD: Holliday from CL. PC quotes "his wife" at 3:30 PM CST. Scarsella has 11:07 AM from Baird.

PIO, PADRE	March 25, 1887	Italian village
Stigmatist	4:57 PM Rome time	14E08 41N07

☉ 04-♈-42	☿ 28-♓-03R	♂ 11-♈-35	♄ 15-♋-38	♆ 25-♉-42	A 21-♍-27
☽ 15-♈-34	♀ 01-♉-24	♃ 04-♏-09R	♅ 10-♎-43R	♇ 02-♊-21	M 20-♊-03

Capuchin monk, who lived in the monastery at San Giovanni Rotondo, Italy. The stigmata appeared on September 20, 1918, and remained visible for the rest of his life. Visited by multitudes of the sick and afflicted; donations helped him to build a hospital. (1887-1968)

C: Dobyns from Ebertin.

PLAYER, GARY	November 1, 1935	Johannesburg, B.S.A.
Golfer	5:12 AM EET	28E04 26S12

☉ 07-♏-49	☿ 19-♎-22	♂ 02-♑-32	♄ 03-♓-33R	♆ 16-♍-07	A 22-♏-25
☽ 03-♑-06	♀ 22-♍-29	♃ 28-♏-16	♅ 03-♉-20R	♇ 27-♋-25R	M 08-♌-10

Became professional in 1953. Won the Masters, 1961; the PGA Championships, 1962 and 1972; U.S. Open, 1965; Tournament of Champions, 1969; the British Open, 1959 and 1968. Married; four children; owns an 800-acre farm in South Africa.

C: CL from Drew.

POE, EDGAR ALLEN	January 19, 1809	Boston, Mass
Writer	1:00 AM LMT	71W04 42N22

☉ 28-♑-50	☿ 28-♑-37	♂ 18-♎-36	♄ 01-♐-33	♆ 06-♐-12	A 03-♏-34
☽ 09-♓-33	♀ 09-♓-06	♃ 16-♓-52	♅ 09-♏-24	♇ 12-♓-59	M 10-♌-45

First published in 1827, with poetry and short stories widely translated; work often macabre and mysterious. Addicted to alcohol, heroin, and opium, with periods of insanity. Married, 1836; widowed, 1847. Elected to the Hall of Fame for Great Americans, 1910. (1809-1849)

DD: Dewey, "supposedly from family records." McEvers quotes Margaret Latvala at 3:38 AM LMT. PC quotes Louis MacNiece in his book *Astrology* at 1:30 AM LMT and Barbault at 2:00 AM LMT. M.A., January 1932, Alan Leo speculates 7:57 AM LMT.

PORTER, COLE   June 9, 1891   Peru, Ind
Musician   4:00 AM CST   86W04 40N45

☉ 18-♊-15 ☿ 24-♉-50 ♂ 03-♋-47 ♄ 10-♍-59 ♆ 06-♊-57 A 13-♊-40
☽ 21-♋-11 ♀ 21-♉-21 ♃ 16-♓-45 ♅ 27-♎-35R ♇ 07-♊-37 M 18-♒-59

American composer of popular music and many successful musical comedies, as well as music for the motion pictures. First studied law; changed his subject to composition. Songs include "Begin the Beguine" and "Night and Day." (1891?-1964)

DD: PC speculative. Old-file has the same date, 4:15 AM CST. *Americana* and *Famous People* both give June 9, 1893. *World Book* gives 1892.

PORTER, PORTIA   June 10, 1916   San Antonio, Tex
Bullfighter   4:21 AM CST   98W30 29N25

☉ 19-♊-11 ☿ 12-♊-40R ♂ 06-♍-13 ♄ 16-♋-00 ♆ 00-♌-50 A 29-♉-15
☽ 06-♎-10 ♀ 19-♋-39 ♃ 27-♈-13 ♅ 19-♒-36R ♇ 02-♋-28 M 12-♒-43

World's only known woman bullfighter.

C: Jameson in *American Association of Scientific Astrology.*

POST, EMILY   October 27, 1872   Baltimore, Md
Writer   4:25 AM LMT   76W37 29N17

☉ 04-♏-18 ☿ 13-♏-16 ♂ 13-♍-11 ♄ 15-♑-52 ♆ 24-♈-39R A 09-♎-53
☽ 07-♍-25 ♀ 01-♐-23 ♃ 27-♌-40 ♅ 05-♌-47 ♇ 20-♉-06R M 11-♋-19

First published in 1922; became the authority on proper behavior. Her guidebook on manners a best-seller through thirty-nine printings and ten editions, selling over a million copies.

DD: Jansky F/M from *Astrological Index*, which gives the date only. PC speculates 4:45 AM LMT. *World Book* gives 1873? *Americana* gives October 3, 1873.

POUND, EZRA   October 30, 1885   Hailey, Idaho
Writer   12:20 PM PST   114W19 43N31

☉ 07-♏-36 ☿ 16-♏-34 ♂ 25-♌-25 ♄ 08-♋-18R ♆ 24-♉-38R A 26-♑-48
☽ 08-♌-54 ♀ 21-♐-16 ♃ 27-♍-08 ♅ 05-♎-26 ♇ 02-♊-34R M 22-♏-24

American poet, essayist, and critic, who founded many magazines and led literary movements. Spent most of his life in Europe; criticized materialism and capitalism; broadcast fascist propaganda during World War II. Went into a mental hospital from 1945-58.

DD: PC speculative. Old-file has 11:55 AM LMT.

POWELL, JOHN WESLEY   March 24, 1834   Mt. Morris, N.Y.
Geologist   1:00 PM LMT   77W52 42N44

☉ 03-♈-38 ☿ 10-♈-38R ♂ 24-♒-51 ♄ 07-♎-43R ♆ 01-♒-09 A 03-♌-25
☽ 26-♍-26 ♀ 07-♈-50 ♃ 07-♉-51 ♅ 24-♒-47 ♇ 12-♈-00 M 18-♈-09

American authority on irrigation; a student of the Indians. Became director of the Bureau of Ethnology in 1879 and of the Geological Survey in 1881. Was a major in the Union Army during the Civil War. (1834-1902)

DD: PC from SS #773 (no time given). Old-file has 1:25 PM LMT.

PROKOFIEV, SERGEI   April 23, 1891 NS   Sontsovka, Russia
Musician   5:00 PM LMT   35E01 48N30

☉ 03-♉-09 ☿ 21-♉-54 ♂ 02-♊-23 ♄ 10-♍-38R ♆ 05-♊-16 A 11-♎-57
☽ 26-♎-18 ♀ 25-♓-28 ♃ 10-♓-04 ♅ 29-♎-13R ♇ 06-♊-35 M 15-♋-04

Composer of marches, army songs, and a symphonic suite, as well as an opera, *War and Peace,* based on Tolstoi's novel. Also wrote cantata *Seven, They Are Seven* and a musical fairy tale of *Peter and the Wolf.* Died of a stroke, March 4, 1953.

DD: PC, "from his autobiography, published in Moscow." Old-file has 5:15 PM LMT.

PROSTITUTE #1 | February 9, 1919 | No place given
Call girl | 5:00 PM CST | 94W25 39N06

☉ 20-♒-10	☿ 09-♒-53	♂ 10-♓-37	♄ 25-♌-12R	♆ 07-♌-36R	A 11-♌-44
☽ 18-♊-10	♀ 08-♓-44	♃ 06-♋-28R	♅ 27-♒-16	♇ 04-♋-49R	M 01-♉-44

C: Blanca Holmes in AFA, May 1971.

PROSTITUTE #2 | December 11, 1935 | Phoenix, Az
Ginna | 9:42 PM MST | 112W04 33N27

☉ 19-♐-14	☿ 20-♐-17	♂ 03-♒-53	♄ 04-♓-31	♆ 16-♍-46	A 16-♌-44
☽ 14-♋-47	♀ 04-♏-02	♃ 07-♐-21	♅ 01-♉-55R	♇ 27-♋-02R	M 10-♉-49

Professional prostitute; constant selection of poor male relationships in personal life. Troubled, grieved, anxious. Four children born between 1954-1963.

C: LMR file, source unknown.

PROSTITUTE #3 | April 4, 1903 | Bay City, Mich
Rita | 11:00 PM CST | 83W53 43N36

☉ 14-♈-15	☿ 06-♈-04	♂ 04-♎-45R	♄ 07-♒-42	♆ 01-♋-03	A 12-♐-00
☽ 15-♋-59	♀ 14-♉-16	♃ 10-♓-15	♅ 25-♐-38R	♇ 17-♊-52	M 03-♎-44

Owns and operated a house of prostitution in Reno, where it's legal.

C: CL from Robert Karg, March 1962.

PROSTITUTE #4 | January 17, 1940 | Hugo, Ok
Mickey | 6:00 PM CST | 75W31 34N01

☉ 26-♑-45	☿ 17-♑-58	♂ 09-♈-31	♄ 24-♈-49	♆ 25-♍-24R	A 02-♌-24
☽ 29-♈-22	♀ 29-♒-17	♃ 03-♈-32	♅ 18-♉-01R	♇ 01-♌-53R	M 22-♈-26

C: CL from Robert Karg, March 1962.

PROSTITUTION | March 16, 1904 | Berlin, Germany
Male | 8:30 PM MET | 13E25 52N30

☉ 25-♓-48	☿ 16-♓-25	♂ 14-♈-18	♄ 16-♒-43	♆ 03-♋-08	A 20-♎-45
☽ 21-♓-09	♀ 26-♒-31	♃ 03-♈-45	♅ 29-♐-48	♇ 18-♊-43	M 27-♋-47

Ran a house of prostitution in Rome until Mussolini came into power.

C: Blanca Holmes in AFA, June 1971.

PULITZER, JOSEPH | April 10, 1847 | Mako, Hungary
Publisher | 5:00 AM LMT | 20E30 46N15

☉ 19-♈-39	☿ 04-♈-12R	♂ 11-♒-52	♄ 08-♓-42	♆ 29-♒-37	A 05-♈-29
☽ 09-♒-09	♀ 17-♉-07	♃ 13-♊-29	♅ 14-♈-30	♇ 25-♈-14	M 02-♑-32

A poor and uneducated Hungarian immigrant, who became one of the greatest American newspaper publishers. Established the Pulitzer prizes for achievements in journalism, music, literature, and art. (1847-1911)

DD: PC speculative. Old-file has 4:35 PM LMT.

QUINLAN, KAREN ANN | March 29, 1954 | Scranton, Pa
Coma victim | 11:43 PM EST | 75W40 41N25

☉ 08-♈-57	☿ 11-♓-14	♂ 24-♐-32	♄ 08-♏-00R	♆ 25-♎-08R	A 12-♐-24
☽ 09-♒-41	♀ 23-♈-27	♃ 19-♊-56	♅ 19-♋-00	♇ 22-♌-49R	M 02-♎-19

Went into a coma on April 15, 1975, after reportedly drinking a gin and tonic and taking tranquilizers; had mysterious bruises on body. Kept alive for years on mechanical respirator; parents won a landmark case to get the equipment removed and she slept on. By April 1979, weighed seventy pounds.

C: Doris Kaye in M.H., July 1978, speculative/rectified.

RABELAIS, FRANCOIS
Writer	February 12, 1494 NS		Chinon, France		
	00:40 AM LMT		0E14 47N12		

☉ 23-♒-24 ☿ 04-♓-51R ♂ 20-♓-44 ♄ 03-♓-36 ♆ 02-♑-40 A 15-♏-51
☽ 12-♑-51 ♀ 04-♈-11 ♃ 10-♍-07R ♅ 04-♒-07 ♇ 09-♏-50R M 00-♍-05

Famous French satirist, who made riotous fun of politics, the church, justice, and education — a master of the grotesque. Broad and coarse, humor often at the expense of women. A monk until the late 1520s, when he studied medicine and published books.

DD: PC, "data and time speculative (February 3, 1494 OS). Place according to most authorities." Old-file has the same date, 00:30 AM. *World Book* gives 1494? "near Chinon." *Americana* gives 1493, 1490, or 1495.

RACINE, JEAN
Writer	December 21, 1639		Soissons, France		
	3:00 AM LMT		3E19 49N23		

☉ 29-♐-11 ☿ 06-♑-35 ♂ 10-♏-23 ♄ 15-♒-13 ♆ 23-♏-37 A 02-♏-01
☽ 15-♏-01 ♀ 05-♐-13R ♃ 19-♐-43 ♅ 02-♏-29 ♇ 29-♉-44R M 11-♌-58

One of the foremost writers of French poetic drama. The production of *Andromaque* in 1667, the first of his seven masterpieces, is one of the most important events in the history of the French theater. (1639-1699)

DD: PC, "recorded." Old-file has 2:50 AM LMT.

RAMAKRISHNA
Mahatma	February 18, 1836		Karmarpukar, India		
	5:25 AM LMT		87W58 22N55		

☉ 28-♒-24 ☿ 06-♓-43R ♂ 13-♒-48 ♄ 05-♏-15R ♆ 04-♒-24 A 07-♒-45
☽ 13-♓-03 ♀ 00-♈-36 ♃ 06-♋-07R ♅ 00-♓-24 ♇ 13-♈-16 M 20-♏-40

Renowned as the founder of the Ramakrishna Mission (the Vedanta Society). Assistant in the temples of the goddess Kali; from 1885 devoted his life to his religious ideals. As a pantheist, believed that all religious paths lead to God-consciousness.

DD: *Circle* #194 from the Isherwood biography, "around dawn," time rectified by Rudhyar. Same date in *Americana*. CL quotes *Practical Astrology*, March 1927, for February 20, 1833, 7:30 AM LMT.

RASPUTIN, GRIGORI
Monk	June 17, 1872		Tobolsk, Russia		
	10:42 PM LMT		68E30 58N15		

☉ 26-♊-46 ☿ 18-♊-07 ♂ 18-♊-44 ♄ 19-♑-32R ♆ 25-♈-51 A 26-♑-54
☽ 08-♏-45 ♀ 18-♊-57 ♃ 01-♌-08 ♅ 29-♋-22 ♇ 20-♉-10 M 08-♐-32

Siberian peasant, who gained the reputation of a saint and healer, with great influence on the last Russian Czar. Introduced to Nicholas and Alexandra in 1907 to help their hemopheliac son; became involved in court politics and decisions; assassinated in December 1916. Stated to be greedy and dissolute.

DD: Manly Hall in *Astrological Review*, March 1935. AJA, Summer 1968, quotes *Kosmobiologie* for July 20, 1872, 2:31 AM, Prokovskoie. PC quotes Brunhubner in his book on *Pluto* for July 29, 1871, 9:45 PM. An L.A. *Times* article on September 25, 1978, gives the year as 1871, the place as Pokrovsko. *World Book* gives 1872-1916.

AA, May 1943, states the claim of a photostat of a letter from his daughter giving January 10, 1870 OS = January 22, 1870 NS, "no hour known." PC states the same date in *Rasputin*, by his daughter Maria, and adds "late at night." That biography states, "The night of January 23, 1871 . . . a meteor turned downward and before it hit the earth . . . he was born."

RATHBONE, BASIL — June 13, 1892 — Johannesburg, S.A.
Actor — 00:30 AM LMT — 28E04 26S12

☉ 22-♊-20	☿ 12-♊-59	♂ 14-♒-17	♄ 23-♍-37	♆ 09-♊-17	A 29-♓-17
☽ 20-♑-19	♀ 25-♋-37	♃ 19-♈-15	♅ 02-♏-17R	♇ 08-♊-39	M 29-♐-16

British actor of stage and films for more than forty years; best remembered for the *Sherlock Holmes* series on radio and film in the 40s and 50s. Nominated for the Oscar in *Romeo and Juliet* (1936) and for *If I Were King* (1938); last appearance on Broadway, 1959. (1892-1967)

DD: CL from SS #782 (no time given). Drew pictures a chart for 1:00 AM LMT.

REAGAN, RONALD — February 6, 1911 — Tampico, Ill
Actor, politician — 1:20 AM CST — 89W47 41N38

☉ 16-♒-24	☿ 21-♑-24	♂ 03-♑-55	♄ 00-♉-49	♆ 19-♋-29R	A 21-♏-07
☽ 12-♉-01	♀ 03-♓-31	♃ 13-♏-44	♅ 26-♑-30	♇ 26-♊-05R	M 03-♍-37

Sportscaster, 1932-37; movies from 1937; host of TV's *Death Valley Days* in the early 60s. Became Republican governor of California, November 8, 1966.

DD: AFA, April 1968, quotes "a close friend of the family." AA, March 1976, states that it has a questionnaire returned from Reagon stating "early moring." D.C. Doane in a Dell issue gives 2:00 AM CST. Joylyn Hill in M.H., December 1975, quotes Carrol Righter for 2:00 PM CST; same data from Pryor in AFA, October 1971, and Gallo in *Celebrity Horoscopes*. Mayo in AFA, March 1976, gives 1:53 PM CST. Angel Thompson quotes a letter from his office, May 1980, that "the Governor was born pre-dawn."

REUTHER, WALTER — September 1, 1907 — Wheeling, W. Va
Labor union official — 10:04 PM EST — 80W43 40N04

☉ 08-♍-30	☿ 03-♍-38	♂ 10-♑-46	♄ 25-♓-15R	♆ 14-♋-17	A 24-♉-31
☽ 04-♋-46	♀ 05-♍-00	♃ 02-♌-56	♅ 08-♑-51R	♇ 24-♊-42	M 03-♒-06

President of the United Auto Workers, 1946-70; considered one of the most socially and politically progressive of U.S. labor leaders. (1907-1970)

DD: CL from Drew; same data in SS #787. Old-file has 10:25 PM.

REYNOLDS, SIR JOSHUA — July 27, 1723 NS — Plympton, England
Artist — 9:30 AM LMT — 4W03 50N22

☉ 03-♌-39	☿ 22-♋-34R	♂ 22-♉-00	♄ 23-♐-39R	♆ 29-♉-07	A 27-♍-51
☽ 08-♊-00	♀ 07-♋-07	♃ 29-♐-45R	♅ 25-♎-24	♇ 23-♍-40	M 27-♊-14

English portrait painter, who became known as one of the greatest, with social and financial success. First president of the Royal Academy; knighted by King George III in 1768; "Painter to the King" in 1784. (1723-1792)

DD: Chart pictured in Adams' *One Hundred Horoscopes*; same data in NN #239. PC quotes NN at 9:40 AM LMT. Old-file has 12:00 noon (July 16, 1723 OS).

RHODES, CECIL JOHN — July 5, 1853 — Hertfordshire, England
Statesman — 7:00 PM LMT — 0W04 51N48

☉ 13-♋-34	☿ 05-♌-28	♂ 08-♊-32	♄ 27-♉-50	♆ 13-♓-38R	A 25-♐-43
☽ 06-♋-10	♀ 27-♋-56	♃ 16-♐-37R	♅ 11-♉-48	♇ 02-♉-37	M 00-♏-49

British diamond king, statesman, and empire builder. Went to South Africa in 1870; made a fortune in the next three years working the diamond fields. Elected to the Cape Colony assembly, 1881; premier, 1890; helped direct the Boer War, 1899. Left his fortune to public service. (1853-1902)

DD: SS #789, same data pictured in Adams' *One Hundred Horoscopes* and in Leo's *Esoteric Astrology*. AFA, March 1967, Musselwhite gives 7:08 PM, Bishop Stortford in Hertfordshire.

RICHTER, LES October 6, 1930 Fresno, Ca
Football player 1:00 AM PST 119W47 36N44

☉ 12-♎-23 ☿ 24-♍-32 ♂ 22-♋-47 ♄ 05-♑-49 ♆ 04-♍-43 A 10-♌-43
☽ 26-♓-32 ♀ 26-♏-06 ♃ 18-♋-49 ♅ 13-♈-25R ♇ 20-♋-50 M 01-♉-41

Twice voted the Ram's most valuable player; played seven times in Pro Bowl (twice in the Rose Bowl) in his nine-year career, 1954-62. Top pro in both football and rugby before becoming president of Riverside Raceway, Ca.

C: CL from AA, June 1956.

RICHTHOFEN, MANFRED VON May 2, 1892 NS Breslau, Poland
Pilot 9:30 PM MET 17E02 51N07

☉ 12-♉-51 ☿ 24-♈-03R ♂ 27-♑-59 ♄ 23-♍-45R ♆ 07-♊-46 A 08-♐-01
☽ 01-♌-39 ♀ 28-♊-19 ♃ 11-♈-05 ♅ 03-♏-41R ♇ 07-♊-44 M 06-♎-15

German flying ace of World War I, known as "the Red Baron"; personally credited with eighty allied planes shot down. Prosperous family with his father in the military; became a lieutenant in 1912; went into the flying service, 1915; combat, 1916. Shot down in his red Fokker on April 21, 1918.

DD: PC speculative. Old-file has 9:45 PM MET.

RICKENBACKER, EDDIE October 8, 1890 Columbus, Ohio
Pilot 8:00 AM LMT 83W00 39N58

☉ 15-♎-13 ☿ 00-♎-20R ♂ 09-♑-42 ♄ 12-♍-01 ♆ 06-♊-36R A 07-♏-26
☽ 14-♌-47 ♀ 00-♐-51 ♃ 02-♒-30 ♅ 26-♎-20 ♇ 07-♊-43R M 14-♌-40

American flying ace of World War I, who shot down twenty-six enemy planes. An early race car driver; owned the Indianapolis Speedway for eighteen years. In 1938, after a widely varied career, became president of Eastern Airlines. (1890-1973)

DD: Holliday from AA, June 1943, which published a letter from Eastern Airlines dated November 7, 1942, that states, "Our records show his time of birth to be about 8:00 AM." No date of birth was given in the letter. October 8, 1890 given in *Americana* and *Celebrity Register*, SS #792 (8:00 AM), Old-file (8:55 AM) and Drew (10:15 AM LMT).

AFA, January 1943, gives 1889, 4:58 PM LMT. CL quotes Colonel Frank Noyes who states, "data from his mother" of October 8, 1889, 4:30 PM, given in AA, April 1968.

RILEY, JAMES WHITCOMB October 7, 1849 Greenfield, Ind
Writer 9:00 AM LMT 85W45 39N47

☉ 14-♎-13 ☿ 08-♏-27 ♂ 29-♊-45 ♄ 03-♈-47R ♆ 02-♓-24R A 18-♏-31
☽ 25-♊-28 ♀ 09-♍-40 ♃ 12-♍-06 ♅ 24-♈-41R ♇ 28-♈-07R M 29-♌-00

Won fame as "The Hoosier Poet" by writing much verse in the dialect of his home state. A grammar school education; worked as a sign painter and actor; on the staff of the local paper; a talented mimic. (1849-1916)

DD: PC speculative. Old-file has 3:10 AM LMT. Ralph Kraum's personal notebook held October 7, 1849, "Sunday morning."

RILKE, RAINER MARIA December 4, 1875 Prague, Czechoslovakia
Writer 00:01 AM LMT 14E26 50N05

☉ 11-♐-26 ☿ 29-♏-13 ♂ 28-♒-27 ♄ 20-♒-47 ♆ 00-♉-39R A 17-♍-32
☽ 16-♒-52 ♀ 29-♐-27 ♃ 18-♏-25 ♅ 19-♌-58R ♇ 22-♉-18R M 13-♊-58

German lyric poet, preoccupied with the problems of God and death; work includes the posthumous publications *Journey of My Other Self* (1930) and *Poems from the Book of Hours* (1941). In 1901, married the sculptress Klara Westoff. Died of blood poisoning from the prick of a rose thorn, 1926.

DD: PC, "recorded." Old-file has 10:35 PM LMT. T. Joseph quotes Wangemann for 11:15 PM LMT.

RIMSKY-KORSAKOV, NICHOLAS March 18, 1844 NS Tikhvin, Russia
Musician 10:30 AM LMT 33E29 59N30

☉ 27-♓-52	☿ 09-♓-37	♂ 09-♉-50	♄ 04-♒-34	♆ 22-♒-30	A 16-♋-35
☽ 20-♓-15	♀ 06-♉-28	♃ 14-♓-31	♅ 01-♈-58	♇ 21-♈-49	M 01-♓-28

Russian composer, famous for his colorful and brilliant orchestration. Wrote fifteen operas, three symphonies, several choral works, and a book on instrumentation. (1844-1908)

C: CL from WEMYSS, *Wheel of Life*; same data in SS #793 (March 6, 1844 OS).

RIPLEY, ROBERT December 26, 1893 Santa Rosa, Ca
Cartoonist 1:15 AM PST 122W43 38N26

☉ 04-♑-53	☿ 16-♐-19	♂ 26-♏-09	♄ 23-♎-54	♆ 11-♊-32R	A 17-♎-06
☽ 19-♌-46	♀ 20-♒-31	♃ 22-♉-07R	♅ 14-♏-04	♇ 09-♊-21R	M 19-♋-31

American cartoonist, who became internationally famous by collecting odd and unusual facts. Started his feature *Believe It or Not* in December 1918; still appears in more than three hundred newspapers throughout the world, with a daily readership of seventy million. (1893-1949)

DD: CL, "rectified by several astrologers independently." PC states same date in *True* magazine. SS #794 gives December 25, 1893 (no time given); same date in *Americana*.

RIVERA, DIEGO December 8, 1886 Guanajuato, Mexico
Artist 11:00 PM LMT 101W17 21N00

☉ 17-♐-08	☿ 04-♐-43R	♂ 18-♑-13	♄ 21-♋-24R	♆ 25-♉-52R	A 04-♍-50
☽ 20-♉-27	♀ 18-♐-36	♃ 28-♎-41	♅ 11-♎-48	♇ 02-♊-49R	M 04-♊-51

A controversial Mexican painter; a communist whose favorite themes were revolution and labor. Also noted for his paintings of children. Led a successful campaign to permit Mexican artists to decorate the walls of government buildings. (1886-1957)

DD: PC quotes *Diego Rivera* by Bertram Wolfe for "late evening." That biography describes his mother's earlier three still births, then states that on this day her sister had run errands all day in preparation, since her labor had begun. Sister made a last trip to the apothecary; when his father came home, there were twin boys. No time is stated; the inference (since father came home from work) is for late day or early evening.

My Art, My Life by Diego Rivera (1960) states on p. 19, "A twin brother and I were born on the night of December 8, 1886 . . . I, the older . . . brother a few minutes later." (His brother died at age 2).

ROBERTS, ORAL January 24, 1918 Ada, Oklahoma
Minister 11:00 AM CST 96W41 34N46

☉ 03-♒-55	☿ 09-♑-17	♂ 02-♎-27	♄ 11-♌-41R	♆ 05-♌-46R	A 17-♈-47
☽ 06-♋-12	♀ 28-♒-06R	♃ 01-♊-29R	♅ 22-♒-35	♇ 03-♋-56R	M 10-♑-35

A preacher of the Pentecostal Holiness Church, who has become one of the best known evangelists in the world. Had his call to the ministry in 1935 and built up a following. By 1972 his annual cash flow was some $17 million. His books include *God's Formula for Success and Prosperity*.

DD: Carla Norton in M.H., July 1978, "from him in a newscast." Howard Hammitt in M.H., March 1976, gives 11:30 AM, "from Robert's publication *Abundant Life*." PC gives 11:30 AM, from his autobiography, *The Call*.

ROBERTS, ROBIN September 30, 1926 Springfield, Ill
Baseball pitcher 5:35 AM CST 89W39 39N48

☉ 06-♎-33	☿ 14-♎-55	♂ 19-♉-27R	♄ 22-♏-53	♆ 26-♌-01	A 02-♎-03
☽ 26-♋-12	♀ 23-♍-18	♃ 17-♒-38R	♅ 27-♓-05R	♇ 15-♋-53	M 02-♋-21

Outstanding player with the Philadelphia NL, who had twenty-eight victories to seven defeats in 1952; won his one hundredth game in the major leagues on June 6, 1953. At the season's end, had pitched twenty-two winning games.

C: CL from *Bulletin of Astro-Science*, July 1958.

ROBESPIERRE, MAXIMILIAN	May 6, 1758	Arras, France
Revolutionary	2:00 AM LMT	2E45 50N20

☉ 15-♉-24	☿ 05-♊-15	♂ 17-♌-00	♄ 02-♓-49	♆ 12-♌-37	A 25-♒-14
☽ 27-♈-51	♀ 04-♈-45	♃ 18-♐-18R	♅ 25-♓-55	♇ 22-♐-21R	M 15-♐-07

An orphan, small in stature, pale, and sincere. Became a lawyer; entered politics; as a fanatical idealist called "the Incorruptable," became the symbol of the French Revolution. (1758-1794)

C: Chart pictured in Adams' *One Hundred Horoscopes*. Same chart pictured in Leo's *Esoteric Astrology*.

ROBINSON, EDWARD G.	December 12, 1893 NS	Bucharest, Rumania
Actor	5:00 PM LMT	26E06 44N26

☉ 13-♉-04	☿ 05-♉-40	♂ 28-♉-36	♄ 18-♍-13R	♆ 11-♌-00	A 00-♐-48
☽ 26-♓-44	♀ 25-♈-50R	♃ 08-♍-56R	♅ 08-♓-57	♇ 07-♋-10	M 17-♍-21

Well known for movie gangster roles in films that include *All My Sons* (1948), *Seven Thieves* (1960), and *Old Man Who Cried Wolf* (1970). Died of cancer on January 26, 1973.

C: CL from *Today's Astrology*, January 1939; same data in SS #796.

ROBINSON, SUGAR RAY	May 3, 1921	Detroit, Mich
Boxer	9:00 PM EST	83W03 42N20

☉ 13-♉-04	☿ 05-♉-40	♂ 28-♉-36	♄ 18-♍-13R	♆ 11-♌-00	A 00-♐-48
☽ 26-♓-44	♀ 25-♈-50R	♃ 08-♍-56R	♅ 08-♓-57	♇ 07-♋-10	M 17-♍-21

Won the lightweight boxing title, 1940, and the middleweight boxing title, 1951. In a 25-year career, won 175 of his 202 bouts. Retired 1965; became a Hollywood actor, 1968; entered into the Boxing Hall of Fame, 1978.

DD: CL from Cedric Lemont in *Astrology*, January 1952. *Famous People* and *Americana* both give May 3, 1920.

ROCKEFELLER, JOHN D. SR.	July 8, 1839	Richford, N.Y.
Entrepreneur	11:55 PM LMT	76W12 42N23

☉ 16-♋-15	☿ 29-♋-27	♂ 06-♎-15	♄ 04-♐-25R	♆ 11-♒-54R	A 26-♈-41
☽ 23-♊-05	♀ 00-♍-51	♃ 10-♎-23	♅ 16-♓-17R	♇ 18-♈-53	M 14-♑-00

Industrialist and founder of the Standard Oil enterprise and of the first great American oil fortune. At the time of his retirement in 1902, his fortune estimated at more than a billion dollars. Established four great charitable corporations. (1839-1937)

DD: PC quotes *John D. Rockefeller Sr.* by Alan Nevinas as "just before midnight." That biography gives the date on p. 22 (no time). AFA Data Exchange quotes Troinski for July 8, 1839, "shortly before midnight." SS #799 gives July 8/9, 1839, Midnight. M.A., April 1930, Keene gives 3:47 PM LMT, N.Y.

ROCKNE, KNUTE	March 4, 1888	Voss, Norway
Athlete	2:07 PM LMT	6E25 60N40

☉ 14-♓-27	☿ 12-♓-52R	♂ 00-♏-12R	♄ 00-♌-13R	♆ 27-♉-28	A 14-♌-05
☽ 07-♐-01	♀ 11-♒-33	♃ 05-♐-52	♅ 16-♎-28R	♇ 03-♊-05	M 15-♈-44

Football coach and Notre Dame star end. In 1913, with Gus Dorais, practiced the then new forward pass; they were the first to take advantage of its offensive success. Had five undefeated seasons. Killed in a plane crash, March 31, 1931.

DD: *Astrological Bulletina*, October 1931, Lemont states, "Reliable source, believed to be accurate." PC states same data as "recorded." *Knute Kenneth Rockne* by Francis Wallace (1960) states the date on p. 20 (no time given). Same year given in *Famous People* and *World Book*. Pryor in AFA, October 1971, gives March 4, 1889, 2:09 AM GMT.

ROEHM, ERNST   November 28, 1887   Munich, Germany
Nazi military   1:00 AM LMT   11E33 48N09

| ☉ 05-♐-29 | ☿ 17-♏-39 | ♂ 25-♍-33 | ♄ 06-♌-26R | ♆ 28-♉-29R | A 23-♍-49 |
| ☽ 06-♉-13 | ♀ 18-♎-47 | ♃ 20-♏-32 | ♅ 15-♎-54 | ♇ 04-♊-00R | M 22-♊-16 |

Homosexual commander of the Nazi Storm Troopers. His discontent and ambition in 1933-34 began to be a worry to the top echelon, who closed ranks against him. Failed to gain powerful allies; on June 30, 1934, he and his followers were raided and shot to death.

C: Dewey quotes Ebertin.

ROGERS, WILL   November 4, 1879   Oologah, Ok
Actor   8:15 PM LMT   95W43 36N27

| ☉ 12-♏-20 | ☿ 29-♏-46 | ♂ 22-♉-55R | ♄ 10-♈-09R | ♆ 10-♉-36R | A 05-♋-46 |
| ☽ 17-♋-54 | ♀ 29-♍-56 | ♃ 02-♓-55 | ♅ 08-♍-17 | ♇ 26-♉-41R | M 16-♓-38 |

Played on stage and in films as a noted homespun philosopher and humorist. Started life as a cowhand and became a great roper. First stage appearance, 1905; reached fame in the Ziegfield Follies of 1916. Film debut, 1918; toured Europe, 1926. (1879-1935)

DD: CL from *Motion Picture Almanac*, 1931, states same data from Kraum in NAJ, December 1934. *Constellations*, 1977, quotes Kraum in NAJ, December 1934, for the same date, 9:51 PM, "from private sources." LMR records NAJ, December 1934, as 9:15 PM LMT. AFA, October 1954, gives 9:16 PM LMT. Scarsella quotes Baird for 9:16 PM LMT, Johndro. PC quotes SS #802 (no time given) for 8:30 PM LMT.

RONSARD, PIERRE DE   September 21, 1524 NS   Blois, France
Writer   6:00 AM LMT   1W20 47N35

| ☉ 27-♍-49 | ☿ 20-♍-36 | ♂ 13-♌-25 | ♄ 17-♓-37R | ♆ 07-♓-43R | A 29-♍-48 |
| ☽ 10-♓-40 | ♀ 06-♏-01 | ♃ 04-♈-46R | ♅ 08-♊-35R | ♇ 13-♑-22R | M 29-♊-45 |

Leader of the Pleiade, a group of Renaissance poets who established French poetry on classical models. From a nobel family; a page in court and a diplomat until he withdrew from public life in the 1540s with growing deafness; turned to poetry. (1524-1585)

DD: PC from Barbault. Old-file gives Loir et Cher, France, 7:00 AM LMT. *Americana* gives Vendome, France, September 11, 1524 OS.

ROSETTI, DANTE GABRIEL   May 12, 1828   London, England
Artist, writer   5:00 AM LMT   0W06 51N31

| ☉ 21-♉-24 | ☿ 08-♉-23 | ♂ 12-♑-47 | ♄ 16-♋-13 | ♆ 18-♑-16R | A 06-♊-12 |
| ☽ 01-♉-03 | ♀ 06-♋-35 | ♃ 08-♏-00R | ♅ 02-♒-19R | ♇ 06-♈-54 | M 02-♒-34 |

English painter and poet, who helped found the Pre-Raphaelite Brotherhood in 1848 — a movement in art to revive the simplicity, purity, and idealism of early artists. His best writing a group of love sonnets, *The House of Life*. (1828-1882)

DD: Chart pictured in Adams' *One Hundred Horoscopes*. PC quotes same data from NN. Old-file has 4:50 AM LMT.

ROTHSCHILD, BARON   February 23, 1743   Frankfurt, Germany
Entrepreneur   7:45 PM LMT   8E41 50N07

| ☉ 04-♓-51 | ☿ 22-♓-15 | ♂ 24-♌-19R | ♄ 02-♍-04R | ♆ 09-♋-27R | A 05-♎-52 |
| ☽ 27-♒-03 | ♀ 13-♓-48 | ♃ 09-♍-53R | ♅ 25-♑-18 | ♇ 16-♏-14R | M 07-♋-31 |

Financier, who established the family fortune by opening a money exchange and investment house. At his death left a famous banking house and huge fortune to his five sons. (1743-1812)

DD: PC speculative. Old-file has 3:10 PM LMT.

RUBINSTEIN, ANTON — November 28, 1829 NS — Vichvatinetz, Russia
Musician — 3:30 PM LMT — 29E01 47N10

☉ 06-♐-07	☿ 21-♏-48	♂ 01-♏-01	♄ 18-♌-10	♆ 18-♑-45	A 23-♉-25
☽ 00-♑-37	♀ 21-♑-27	♃ 21-♐-55	♅ 03-♒-23	♇ 06-♈-33R	M 27-♑-36

Russian pianist and composer, whose tours throughout Europe and America made him the most famous pianist of his time. Began to teach at age 16; in 1858 became court pianist and concert conductor. In 1863, founded the St. Petersburg Conservatory.

DD: PC rectifies the time from *Free Artist* by Catherine D. Bowen, "close to sunset." LMR speculates that the time would be later, since the biography states on p. 6, " . . . blustery winter night when, driving back to the farm after a visit with friend . . . mother takes shelter at an inn and there, on November 28, 1829, Anton was born." (The biography doesn't specify OS/NS).

RUBINSTEIN, ARTUR — January 28, 1886 NS — Lodz, Poland
Musician — 2:35 PM MET — 19E30 51N46

☉ 08-♒-37	☿ 20-♑-54	♂ 25-♍-11R	♄ 02-♋-28R	♆ 22-♉-47R	A 20-♋-06
☽ 26-♏-16	♀ 08-♓-09	♃ 05-♎-54R	♅ 07-♎-35R	♇ 01-♊-11R	M 20-♓-12

Brilliant pianist, who studied in Berlin and appeared at age 12 as a soloist with the Berlin Symphony. First American tour, 1906; began to tour widely in 1913. After World War II broke out, moved to California, became an American citizen in 1946.

DD: PC speculative. Old-file has 7:30 AM MET.

RUBINSTEIN, HELENA — December 25, 1870 NS — Krakow, Poland
Entrepreneur — 8:00 AM MET — 19E59 50N05

☉ 03-♑-21	☿ 20-♑-45	♂ 27-♍-59	♄ 01-♑-13	♆ 19-♈-02R	A 07-♑-01
☽ 10-♒-37	♀ 07-♑-26	♃ 19-♊-49R	♅ 25-♋-26R	♇ 17-♉-12R	M 11-♏-00

Began to tap her marketing genius by selling homemade face cream in 1890; then operated salons and went into mass production to build up a fortune of $100 million. Short, plump, and plain; a hard worker and shrewd executive; collected antiques as a hobby.

DD: Jansky F/M quotes *Astrological Index*, a book which gives the date only. PC speculates 8:35 AM LMT. *Current Biography* Obit gives 1871?-1965. *Woman's Almanac* gives 1872.

RUBINSTEIN, SERGE — June 24, 1908 NS — St. Petersburg, Russia
Mystery man — 1:56 AM RST — 30E20 59N55

☉ 02-♋-05	☿ 17-♋-31R	♂ 20-♋-58	♄ 09-♈-30	♆ 14-♋-06	A 04-♋-03
☽ 07-♉-38	♀ 20-♋-06R	♃ 13-♌-01	♅ 15-♑-28R	♇ 24-♊-29	M 13-♒-39

Financial juggler and "wizard of sorts." Lived dangerously; died violently by a murder which remains a mystery; shot to death, January 28, 1955, in New York.

C: Scarsella, Baird from Ziegler.

RUDOLPH, ARCHDUKE — August 21, 1858 — Vienna, Austria
Royalty — 10:15 PM LMT — 16E20 48N14

☉ 28-♌-27	☿ 25-♍-33	♂ 04-♐-28	♄ 05-♌-28	♆ 24-♓-12R	A 00-♊-09
☽ 27-♑-42	♀ 10-♎-42	♃ 17-♊-52	♅ 03-♊-19	♇ 07-♉-32R	M 01-♒-24

Son of Emperor Francis Joseph I and Empress Elizabeth. Committed suicide with Baroness Maria Vetsera (born March 19, 1871) at Mayerling on January 31, 1889. The scandal was excluded from official dossiers, and all persons connected were sworn to secrecy.

DD: Eshelman quotes Zadkiel; same data in SS #811. Old-file has 10:40 PM LMT.

RUNYAN, DAMON — October 8, 1880 — Manhattan, Ks
Writer — 6:18 AM LMT — 96W35 39N11

☉ 15-♎-37	☿ 00-♏-16	♂ 21-♎-08	♄ 26-♈-17R	♆ 13-♉-39R	A 17-♎-42
☽ 12-♐-44	♀ 08-♏-45	♃ 14-♈-21R	♅ 11-♍-37	♇ 28-♉-04R	M 20-♋-22

American journalist, author, and motion picture producer. Enlisted in the Spanish American War at 14; newspaper reporter by 1900 for ten years. Covered sports and wars from 1911; columnist after 1937 for the Hearst chain. Published from 1911; writer-producer, 1942.

DD: CL from *Damon Runyan Story* by Ed Weiner (1948). That biography gives October 3, 1880 (no time). *Current Biography* Obit gives October 4, 1884-1946.

RUTH, GEORGE HERMAN "BABE" February 6, 1895 Baltimore, Md
Baseball player 1:45 PM EST 76W37 39N17

☉ 17-♒-47	☿ 05-♓-29	♂ 17-♉-25	♄ 07-♏-12	♆ 13-♊-04R	A 01-♋-53
☽ 06-♋-15	♀ 04-♓-02	♃ 26-♊-34R	♅ 19-♏-49	♇ 09-♊-50R	M 09-♓-44

Baseball's most popular star and greatest slugger. Hit sixty home runs in 1927; a lifetime (twenty-two years) batting average of .342. Elected to the National Baseball Hall of Fame, 1936. (1895-1948)

DD: G. Kissinger in Dell, May 1974. PC states the same data as B.C. M. Wynne in AFA, September 1948, gives 12:53 PM EST. Huggins in *The Astrology Magazine*, January 1970, gives 11:30 AM LMT. Dewey says there is a B.C. time available with Moon in Cancer on the Ascendant.

RZESHEWSKI, SAMUEL May 26, 1912 Ozorkow, Poland
Prodigy 11:59 PM MET 19E20 51N58

☉ 05-♊-17	☿ 13-♉-47	♂ 29-♋-12	♄ 25-♉-06	♆ 21-♋-48	A 12-♒-46
☽ 17-♎-46	♀ 24-♉-23	♃ 11-♐-14R	♅ 03-♒-19R	♇ 27-♊-55	M 09-♐-52

Chess boy wonder, who at age 8 played the twelve world's best chess experts at once. Never hesitated in play; with total efficiency, won all the games in twenty-nine minutes.

C: CL from *Practical Astrology*, February 1927.

SACRAMENTO JOE July 14, 1874 Cincinnati, Ohio
Circus act 3:00 PM LMT 84W31 39N06

☉ 22-♋-09	☿ 08-♌-55R	♂ 19-♋-23	♄ 12-♒-24R	♆ 00-♉-43	A 23-♏-54
☽ 06-♌-34	♀ 27-♌-35	♃ 26-♍-15	♅ 09-♌-41	♇ 22-♉-26	M 05-♍-44

In the restaurant business until he had typhoid fever in 1898; after that grew so fat he couldn't get in the door; began to exhibit as a freak; stated to be the "fattest man in the world" at 601 pounds. Said to have elephatiasis, a "wasting" disease.

C: BJA, July 1925, Bailey quotes *Astrological Bulletina*, April 1920, rectifies to 2:39 PM LMT.

SADAT, ANWAR December 25, 1918 Mit abu el Kom, Egypt
Statesman 00:20 AM EET 31E00 30N48

☉ 02-♑-19	☿ 18-♐-51R	♂ 03-♒-34	♄ 28-♌-03R	♆ 08-♌-51R	A 07-♎-28
☽ 28-♍-35	♀ 09-♑-48	♃ 11-♋-53R	♅ 24-♒-52	♇ 05-♋-40R	M 07-♋-55

President of Egypt; head of the Arab Socialist Union party. After thirty technical years of war with Israel, began peace gestures with Israeli Prime Minister Menachem Begin in November 1977; reached a treaty agreement, September 17, 1978, for which the two men won the 1978 Nobel Peace prize.

DD: PC speculative, from "reports that he was born shortly after midnight." Terrell Adsit quotes the same data from Eugene Moore, but for Tala Ilu Nuliya, near Cairo (after midnight).

SALK, JONAS October 28, 1914 New York, N.Y.
Scientist 11:15 AM EST 73W57 40N45

☉ 04-♏-24	☿ 22-♏-52R	♂ 20-♏-12	♄ 02-♋-10R	♆ 00-♌-27	A 03-♑-44
☽ 06-♓-10	♀ 10-♐-37	♃ 13-♒-03	♅ 07-♒-44	♇ 02-♋-06R	M 27-♎-57

Using dead virus, developed a polio vaccine in 1953. Received many honors, including the Congressional Gold Medal for "great achievement in the field of medicine."

DD: CL quotes Drew; Dewey quotes Dobyns for the same data. J. Johns has 5:10 AM EST.

SANSOM, ODETTE April 28, 1912 Amiens, France
Spy 00:30 AM GMT 2E20 49N55

☉ 07-♉-21	☿ 18-♈-55R	♂ 12-♋-29	♄ 21-♉-23	♆ 21-♋-11	A 14-♑-28
☽ 25-♍-00	♀ 18-♈-54	♃ 14-♐-20R	♅ 03-♒-25	♇ 27-♊-21	M 17-♏-55

Infiltrated enemy-occupied France to work with great courage and distinction until arrested, April 1943. Refused to give information to the Gestapo, even when tortured with a red-hot iron and had her toenails pulled out. After two years in solitary confinement, liberated by the Allies: Awarded the George Cross.

C: Joan Rodgers in AA, March 1951; story told in *Odette* by J. Tickell.

SARNOFF, DAVID February 27, 1891 NS Uzlian, Russia
TV executive 4:20 PM LMT 27E30 53N50

☉ 08-♓-45	☿ 19-♒-45	♂ 23-♈-40	♄ 14-♍-12R	♆ 04-♊-04	A 27-♌-24
☽ 20-♎-19	♀ 22-♑-33	♃ 28-♒-00	♅ 01-♏-10R	♇ 05-♊-55	M 14-♉-36

Called "the father of modern television". Part of RCA from 1919; president and chairman of the board from 1930. Said he'd "hitched his wagon to the electron." One of his three sons, Robert, became President of NBC in 1955. (1891-1971)

DD: CL from SS #824 (no time given). Drew pictures a chart of 2:30 AM LMT. PC quotes SS and Drew for 3:00 PM. Old-file has 2:45 PM.

SCHACHT, HJALMAR January 22, 1877 Tingleff, Germany
Entrepreneur 10:15 PM LMT 9E15 54N56

☉ 03-♒-05	☿ 11-♒-41R	♂ 05-♐-25	♄ 06-♓-17	♆ 02-♉-32	A 10-♎-51
☽ 06-♉-19	♀ 07-♑-22	♃ 23-♐-35	♅ 23-♌-30R	♇ 22-♉-39R	M 14-♋-51

German financier, banker, former government official, financial administrator of occupied Belgium in World War I; guided German national financial policy during most of the Nazi regime. Imprisoned by the Nazis in 1944 on suspicion; acquitted of war crimes at Nuremberg. Recouped his fortune in the post-war years. (1877-1970)

DD: AFA, June 1945, World War II Charts. Same date in *Americana*. SS #827 gives January 30, 1876, 11:40 AM LMT; Drew states the same data "given in *Berliner Tageblatt*."

SCHIPA, TITO December 28, 1889 Lecce, Italy
Singer 1:30 AM LMT 18E00 40N15

☉ 06-♑-31	☿ 17-♑-58	♂ 27-♎-44	♄ 03-♍-45R	♆ 02-♊-18R	A 23-♎-11
☽ 21-♓-28	♀ 23-♐-57	♃ 16-♑-54	♅ 26-♎-11	♇ 05-♊-23R	M 27-♋-07

Italian operatic tenor, who joined the Chicago Opera Co. in 1919; a leading tenor there for thirteen years. Became a member of the Metropolitan Opera Co. in 1932.

DD: CL from AFA, May 1967. *World Book* Obit gives 1890-1965.

SCHMIDT, HELMUT December 23, 1918 Hamburg, Germany
Statesman 10:15 PM MET 10E00 53N33

☉ 01-♑-15	☿ 19-♐-39R	♂ 02-♒-44	♄ 28-♌-04R	♆ 08-♌-52R	A 09-♍-41
☽ 15-♍-54	♀ 08-♑-29	♃ 12-♋-01R	♅ 24-♒-50	♇ 05-♋-41R	M 02-♊-25

Chancellor of West Germany, who took over when Willy Brandt resigned because of a spy scandal in 1974. An economic conservative politician from 1931; put Germany on its feet with less inflation and unemployment than any European country; enormously popular.

C: Holliday quotes Troinski in *Transit*, from the *Astrological Association*.

SCHOPENHAUER, ARTHUR February 22, 1788 Danzig, Germany
Writer 12:00 Noon LMT 18E39 54N21

☉ 03-♓-33	☿ 12-♓-12	♂ 08-♋-32	♄ 01-♓-37	♆ 20-♎-51R	A 08-♋-02
☽ 15-♍-50	♀ 03-♈-36	♃ 16-♊-44	♅ 26-♋-48R	♇ 16-♒-09	M 29-♒-55

German philosopher, who became widely known for his fine prose style and his pessimism. His philosophy athiestic but influenced by Eastern thought. His main work, *The World As Will and Idea.* (1788-1860)

DD: AQ, Summer 1970, Data Dept. Old-file has 11:40 AM LMT.

SCHWAB, CHARLES M. February 18, 1862 Williamsberg, Pa
Steel king 3:15:40 AM LMT 79W53 40N27

☉ 29-♒-29 ☿ 13-♓-59R ♂ 29-♐-12 ♄ 20-♍-50R ♆ 00-♈-09 A 25-♐-42
☽ 16-♎-42 ♀ 11-♓-47R ♃ 25-♍-21R ♅ 12-♊-18R ♇ 08-♉-35 M 18-♎-24

Started as a stake driver at $1 a day; studied engineering at night. Became first president of U.S. Steel, 1901; assumed control of Bethlehem Steel Corp. and directed its growth into ship-building, munitions and allied fields. (1862-1939)

C: CL, no time known, speculative chart.

SCOTT, GEORGE C. October 18, 1927 Wise, Va
Actor 8:45 AM CST 92W35 36N59

☉ 24-♎-13 ☿ 18-♏-46 ♂ 25-♎-02 ♄ 05-♐-03 ♆ 28-♌-38 A 00-♐-44
☽ 06-♌-11 ♀ 13-♍-38 ♃ 25-♓-19R ♅ 00-♈-32R ♇ 17-♋-09 M 13-♍-27

First noticed in a Shakespeare Festival, 1957; films include Oscar nominees *Anatomy of a Murder, The Hustler, Dr. Strangelove* (1964), and *Patton* (1970). Five marriages; six children. Noted for hot-headed temper. Joined AA in 1967.

DD: PC, "personal." Old-file has 8:35 AM CST.

SCRIABIN, ALEXANDER January 6, 1872 NS Moscow, Russia
Musician 2:00 PM LMT 37E36 55N45

☉ 15-♑-31 ☿ 05-♑-48R ♂ 16-♒-29 ♄ 12-♑-38 ♆ 21-♈-16 A 25-♊-11
☽ 18-♏-01 ♀ 01-♐-03 ♃ 26-♋-07R ♅ 29-♋-45R ♇ 18-♉-01R M 12-♒-54

Russian composer, who crowded as many notes as possible into a single chord. *Poeme D'Estase* for orchestra has marked originality and freedom in many passages. Wrote ten sonatas, many preludes, and a piano concerto. (1872-1915)

DD: SS #838. Old-file has 2:15 PM LMT.

SEALE, BOBBY October 22, 1936 Dallas, Texas
Activist 10:30 PM CST 96W49 32N47

☉ 29-♎-36 ☿ 13-♎-30 ♂ 16-♍-25 ♄ 16-♓-25R ♆ 18-♍-02 A 16-♋-11
☽ 25-♑-26 ♀ 29-♏-59 ♃ 21-♐-48 ♅ 07-♉-55R ♇ 28-♋-45 M 02-♈-17

Co-founder of the Black Panthers in 1966, with Huey Newton — a "power to the people" program. Known for flaming rhetoric; often clashed with the police and behind bars in 1969 as one of the Chicago Eight. New tactics of working through politics by 1972.

DD: Dewey from *Handbook* by M. Meyer. Old-file has 10:00 PM CST.

SEARLE, RONALD March 3, 1920 Cambridge, England
Artist 1:45 PM GMT 0E07 52N12

☉ 12-♓-42 ☿ 00-♈-49 ♂ 08-♏-20 ♄ 07-♍-56R ♆ 09-♌-19R A 02-♌-28
☽ 26-♌-00 ♀ 11-♒-31 ♃ 09-♌-38R ♅ 02-♓-18 ♇ 05-♋-43R M 08-♈-03

First drawings published from 1935-39. Captured and a prisoner of war in Japanese camps, 1942-45. Contributed to magazines, national publications, *Punch, Life, New Yorker,* and more. One-man international exhibits from 1950. Two marriages.

C: Richard Adler from AQ, Winter 1953, Elwell.

SEGOVIA, ANDRES February 18, 1894 Linares, Spain
Musician 9:00 PM LMT 3W37 38N06

☉ 00-♓-15 ☿ 15-♓-46 ♂ 03-♑-37 ♄ 24-♎-56R ♆ 10-♊-45R A 11-♎-14
☽ 13-♌-45 ♀ 26-♒-10R ♃ 23-♉-21 ♅ 15-♏-21R ♇ 08-♊-49R M 12-♋-43

One of the world's foremost guitarists: his remarkable virtuosity and musicianship helped elevate the guitar to importance as a solo classical instrument.

DD: PC speculative. Old-file has the same date, 9:45 PM LMT. *World Book* and *Americana* give February 17, 1893.

SERLING, ROD December 25, 1924 Syracuse, N.Y.
Writer 3:15 PM EST 76W09 43N03
☉ 03-♑-48 ☿ 07-♑-27R ♂ 03-♈-52 ♄ 11-♏-32 ♆ 22-♌-20R A 15-♊-52
☽ 29-♐-20 ♀ 05-♐-00 ♃ 01-♑-44 ♅ 17-♓-57 ♇ 12-♋-40R M 19-♒-14
Paratrooper in World War II, who made sixty jumps. Became a fledgling radio writer in 1948; a regular contributor to TV by 1951. TV host of *Twilight Zone* for five years; writer-host of *Night Gallery*, 1970. Won a total of six Emmy awards. Married; two daughters. (1924-1975)

C: Leek's *Astrology*, January 1971, Dr. J. Hayes; same data CL; same data PC as "personal."

SEXTUPLETS September 16, 1973 Denver, Colo
Stanek family 10:45 to 11:34 PM CDT 104W59 39N44
☉ 24-♍-07 ☿ 05-♎-54 ♂ 09-♉-13 ♄ 03-♋-56 ♆ 04-♐-56 A 26-♉-31
☽ 21-♉-15 ♀ 04-♏-25 ♃ 02-♒-30R ♅ 21-♎-37 ♇ 03-♎-53 M 04-♒-52
A: Holliday from newspaper on date, with an accurate time for the first and last born of the six infants.

SHAW, ROBERT April 30, 1916 Red Bluff, Ca
Musician 5:45 AM PST 122W15 40N11
☉ 09-♉-52 ☿ 26-♉-25 ♂ 18-♌-15 ♄ 11-♋-44 ♆ 29-♋-59 A 20-♉-24
☽ 20-♈-18 ♀ 25-♊-16 ♃ 18-♈-27 ♅ 19-♒-28 ♇ 01-♋-37 M 29-♑-59
American conductor who founded *The Robert Shaw Chorale* in 1948 and directed it until 1953. Organized the *Collegiate Chorale*, 1941; directed the *RCA Victor Chorale*, 1944-48. Associate conductor of the Cleveland Orchestra, 1956.

C: CL, from Faith Harrington, 1958.

SHAWN, TED October 21, 1891 Kansas City, Mo
Dancer 10:39 AM CST 94W35 39N06
☉ 28-♎-00 ☿ 23-♎-41 ♂ 29-♍-51 ♄ 25-♍-03 ♆ 08-♊-39R A 16-♐-16
☽ 23-♊-26 ♀ 06-♏-40 ♃ 08-♓-25R ♅ 01-♏-31 ♇ 08-♊-32R M 05-♎-27
First studied dance as a therapy for paralyzed legs; became an outstanding dancer and choreographer; called "the father of modern dance." With his wife, Ruth St. Dennis, founded the school and troup *Denishawn*, which trained many dancers and performed worldwide. (1891-1972)

C: SS #843. The profile and chart of Ruth St. Dennis are given in *Profiles of Women*.

SHEARER, NORMA August 10, 1904 Montreal, Que, Canada
Actress 10:00 AM EST 73W35 45N33
☉ 17-♌-31 ☿ 13-♍-07 ♂ 27-♋-05 ♄ 17-♒-40R ♆ 07-♋-11 A 15-♎-10
☽ 04-♌-39 ♀ 26-♌-44 ♃ 00-♉-04 ♅ 26-♐-13R ♇ 21-♊-24 M 18-♋-33
Won the Oscar as best actress in *The Divorcee*. Nominated for an Oscar in *Their Own Desire, A Free Soul, The Barretts of Wimpole Street, Romeo and Juliet,* and *Marie Antoinette.* Married to Irving Thalburg, 1927; widowed, 1937. Retired in 1942 to marry Martin Arrouge.

DD: CL. Same date in *Famous People, 50,000 Birthdays,* and *Who's Who in Hollywood.* SS #844 gives 1903.

SHOEMAKER, WILLY　　　August 19, 1931　　　　Fabens, Texas
Jockey　　　　　　　　　　1:30 AM MST　　　　　106W10　31N30

⊙ 25-♌-24　　☿ 19-♍-17　　♂ 11-♎-03　　♄ 17-♑-31R　　♆ 05-♍-08　　A 03-♋-10
☽ 10-♏-49　　♀ 20-♌-00　　♃ 07-♌-18　　♅ 19-♈-09R　　♇ 21-♋-21　　M 17-♓-01

From his first race on March 19, 1949, rode 72,000 winners in thirty years, twice as many as any other jockey. His mounts have won more money than any in racing history. A premature baby, weighed in at 2½ pounds; is now 100 pounds at 4'11".

DD: CL. PC states 1:23 AM MST as B.C.

SHOSTAKOVICH, DIMITRI　September 25, 1906 NS　　Leningrad, Russia
Musician　　　　　　　　　　5:00 PM LMT　　　　　30E20　59N55

⊙ 01-♎-37　　☿ 02-♎-41　　♂ 08-♍-18　　♄ 10-♓-08R　　♆ 12-♋-32　　A 16-♒-48
☽ 06-♑-24　　♀ 17-♏-56　　♃ 09-♋-12　　♅ 04-♑-33　　♇ 23-♊-46R　　M 19-♐-27

Russian composer noted for daring and experimental style. Frequently in and out of government favor; winner of the Stalin prize in 1940; subject to disapproval in 1945; restored to popularity after 1953. (1906-1975)

DD: PC quotes *Dimitri Shastokovich* by D. Rabnovich. That biography (1959) states the date on p. 14, specified New Style (no time).

SHOLES, CHRISTOPHER　　February 14, 1819　　　Mooresville, Pa
Inventor　　　　　　　　　　5:45 AM LMT　　　　　75W24　40N45

⊙ 24-♒-58　　☿ 03-♒-04　　♂ 01-♒-19　　♄ 17-♓-46　　♆ 28-♐-07　　A 29-♑-30
☽ 12-♎-55　　♀ 10-♑-23　　♃ 01-♒-42　　♅ 23-♐-42　　♇ 25-♓-07　　M 22-♏-17

Inventor of the typewriter, patented in June 1868. Worked as newspaper apprentice at age 14; went on to the staff with the *News* in Milwaukee. Described as unselfish, kindhearted and companionable, just, and modest. Founded the Excelsior church for several years during his middle years.

C: Fairchild in AA, February 1948, speculative.

SIBELIUS, JAN　　　　　December 8, 1865　　　Tavestehus, Finland
Musician　　　　　　　　　　9:30 PM Helsinki　　　24E27　61N00

⊙ 16-♐-49　　☿ 07-♑-20　　♂ 08-♐-36　　♄ 08-♏-08　　♆ 07-♈-49R　　A 29-♌-41
☽ 03-♍-32　　♀ 27-♏-51　　♃ 05-♑-09　　♅ 02-♋-30R　　♇ 12-♉-38R　　M 12-♉-32

Finnish composer who became the best known of his nation's musicians; composed on a government grant after 1897. Significant compositions continued until 1925. (1865-1957)

DD: PC quotes *Jan Sibelius* by N. Ringbom in Swedish, gives LMT. That biography, English translation, states the date and place on p. 4 (no time reference). Penfield in 1979 quotes *Sibelius* by E. Tawaststjerna (1976), Vol 1, p. 10, December 8, 1865, "half-past twelve", no AM/PM specified.

SIEGAL, BUGSY　　　　　February 28, 1906　　　New York, N.Y.
Gangster　　　　　　　　　　11:22 PM EST　　　　73W57　40N45

⊙ 09-♓-41　　☿ 17-♓-00　　♂ 18-♈-04　　♄ 05-♓-57　　♆ 07-♋-42R　　A 16-♏-55
☽ 15-♉-35　　♀ 13-♓-19　　♃ 28-♉-52　　♅ 07-♑-42　　♇ 20-♊-43R　　M 27-♌-25

Mobster connected with narcotics, gambling, bookmaking, jewel and fur thefts, and opium dealing from Mexico to California. Competitor to Lucky Luciano. President of Nevada Projects Corp., which operated the Flamingo hotel and casino. Popular in early Hollywood movie society; shot in the back by machine-gun in a Hollywood home.

C: CL quotes Drew.

SIMMS, G.R.　　　　　　September, 2, 1847　　　London, England
Writer　　　　　　　　　　　6:00 PM LMT　　　　　0W06　51N31

⊙ 09-♍-36　　☿ 24-♌-23　　♂ 11-♉-58　　♄ 09-♓-31R　　♆ 28-♒-41R　　A 18-♒-53
☽ 20-♊-22　　♀ 15-♎-54　　♃ 14-♋-15　　♅ 17-♈-37R　　♇ 26-♈-40R　　M 12-♐-43

Journalist and columnist, who under a pen name Dagonet wrote innumerable melodramas, farces, comedies, and stage productions. Books include *Dagonet Ballads* and *Memoirs of a Landlady*.

DD: BJA, April 1927, Bailey. Daath in M.A., April 1901, gives 4:00 AM LMT.

SIMON, PAUL October 13, 1941 New York, N.Y.
Musician 00:30 AM EST 73W57 40N45

☉ 19-♎-29	☿ 11-♏-52	♂ 16-♈-01R	♄ 27-♉-38R	♆ 28-♍-15	A 12-♌-44
☽ 16-♋-00	♀ 02-♐-48	♃ 21-♊-26R	♅ 29-♉-47R	♇ 05-♌-39	M 02-♉-07

Songwriter, who teamed with Art Garfunkle in high school until they separated in 1971; traveled extensively on tours. They won the English record industry award for the best international single and album in twenty-five years with *Bridge over Troubled Waters* (1978).

C: Holliday quotes E. Houldson in Dell, October 1970.

SINNETT, A.P. January 18, 1840 London, England
Theosophist 11:30 PM LMT 0W06 51N31

☉ 27-♑-59	☿ 06-♑-33	♂ 22-♒-24	♄ 17-♐-46	♆ 11-♒-47	A 03-♎-28
☽ 26-♋-51	♀ 13-♐-50	♃ 15-♏-43	♅ 13-♓-50	♇ 16-♈-57	M 04-♋-30

Journalist; editor of the Hong-Kong *Daily Press* at age 25. Editor of *The Pioneer* in India, 1872. With his wife, joined Theosophy in 1879; active in the movement from 1881, when he published *The Occult World*, followed by *Esoteric Buddhism*. One son.

C: M.A., August 1921.

SKINNER, B.F. March 20, 1904 Sesquehanna, Pa
Psychologist Early morning 75W36 41N56

☉ 29-♓-26	☿ 23-♓-13	♂ 17-♈-04	♄ 17-♒-05	♆ 03-♋-09	A 28-♓-22
☽ 05-♉-43	♀ 00-♓-59	♃ 04-♈-38	♅ 29-♐-52	♇ 18-♊-44	M 29-♐-10

One of the most influential psychologists and controversial figures in the science of human behavior; adored as a messiah and abhored as a menace. Harvard psychology professor; he made behavioral modification studies with rats and pigeons. Books include *The Behavior of Organisms* (1938) and *Beyond Freedom and Dignity* (1971).

C: Holliday, from a biography.

SMETNA, BEDRICH March 2, 1824 Litomysl, Czechoslovakia
Musician 10:00 AM Prague 16E23 49N53

☉ 11-♓-47	☿ 14-♒-53	♂ 11-♎-45R	♄ 18-♉-40	♆ 09-♑-12	A 12-♊-02
☽ 27-♓-41	♀ 04-♒-18	♃ 01-♋-07	♅ 14-♑-49	♇ 01-♈-01	M 09-♒-03

Bohemian composer, who wrote many operas and symphonic poems; acknowedged founder of a Czech national music. Played first violin in a quartet at age 5. (1824-1884)

DD: PC, "recorded." Old-file has 9:45 AM LMT.

SMITH, CAPTAIN CHARLES February 9, 1897 Brisbane, Australia
Pilot 4:30 AM Zone #10 153E08 27S29

☉ 20-♒-19	☿ 25-♑-28	♂ 14-♊-40	♄ 00-♐-03	♆ 17-♊-35R	A 07-♒-20
☽ 09-♉-02	♀ 06-♈-47	♃ 07-♍-10R	♅ 28-♏-48	♇ 11-♊-47R	M 01-♏-55

Commander of the first America-to-Australia airplane flight on May 31, 1928; made the flight in three hops, via Honolulu and the Fiji Islands.

C: Keene in P.A., February 1929, "considered authentic."

SMITH, CAPTAIN JOHN January 19, 1580 NS Willoughby, England
American colonist 8:45 AM LMT 0W12 53N14

☉ 28-♑-33	☿ 14-♒-26	♂ 23-♐-00	♄ 06-♒-31	♆ 11-♋-17R	A 14-♒-48
☽ 20-♎-51	♀ 05-♒-21	♃ 07-♐-31	♅ 11-♒-23	♇ 29-♓-42	M 10-♐-39

English soldier and adventurer, who played a vital role in founding Virginia and New England. Arrived in Jamestown in 1607; accused of mutiny but later cleared; became president of the colony in 1608. (1580-1631)

DD: PC speculative. Old-file has 8:20 AM (January 9, 1580 OS). *Americana* states, "baptized January 9, 1580."

SMITH, JOSEPH December 23, 1805 Sharon, Vt
Mormon 6:00 PM LMT 72W26 43N47

☉ 01-♑-46	☿ 20-♑-50	♂ 12-♑-31	♄ 26-♎-45	♆ 29-♏-04	A 22-♋-30
☽ 03-♒-33	♀ 18-♒-43	♃ 20-♐-32	♅ 25-♎-02	♇ 08-♓-50	M 02-♈-12

Had a deep religious conversion at age 14 — a series of visions in September 1823. The angel Moroni instructed him to translate plates given on September 22, 1827, into the Book of Mormon. Married, January 18, 1827; said to have had fifty wives. With his brother, shot to death by a mob on June 27, 1844.

DD: Chart pictured in Adams' *One Hundred Horoscopes*. PC quotes Adams and NN (NN #231, speculative horoscope) for 6:15 PM LMT. Old-file has 5:30 PM LMT.

SMITH, DR. LENDON H. June 3, 1921 Portland, Ore
Writer 00:10 AM PST 122W37 45N32

☉ 12-♊-11	☿ 04-♋-36	♂ 19-♊-31	♄ 18-♍-07	♆ 11-♌-26	A 25-♒-02
☽ 03-♉-58	♀ 00-♉-41	♃ 10-♍-06	♅ 09-♓-35	♇ 07-♋-45	M 12-♐-35

Teacher, author, frequent entertaining guest on the *Tonight Show* and other TV programs speaking on hyperactivity, allergies, and illness in general, especially as related to diet. Star of a TV special, *My Mom's Having a Baby* (1978). Books include *The Children's Doctor* and *New Wive's Tales*.

C: From him to LMR, September 1978, "close to midnight or after."

SMITH, TOMMY April 12, 1918 Buffalo, N.Y.
Murderer 4:00 AM EWT 78W53 42N53

☉ 21-♈-36	☿ 09-♉-27	♂ 15-♍-01R	♄ 07-♌-37	♆ 04-♌-19R	A 11-♒-31
☽ 07-♉-42	♀ 05-♓-41	♃ 09-♊-44	♅ 26-♒-41	♇ 03-♋-33	M 02-♐-53

On February 5, 1937, killed Mary Ellen Babcock. On February 12, 1937, stabbed Frances Fitzgeralds. Also confessed to attempted sadistic torture of other young girls.

C: CL from AA, October 1937.

SMUTS, JAN CHRISTIAAN May 24, 1870 Reibeeck, West S.A.
Statesman 4:45 AM LMT 18E40 44N46

☉ 02-♊-43	☿ 18-♊-07R	♂ 16-♉-56	♄ 26-♐-54R	♆ 20-♈-49	A 07-♊-42
☽ 23-♓-55	♀ 17-♈-46	♃ 03-♊-25	♅ 19-♋-20	♇ 17-♉-48	M 10-♒-20

Lawyer; state attorney of the Transvaal Republic; general in the Boer War. After 1910, served as minister of the interior, defense, finance, and justice. Price minister of the Union of South Africa, 1919.

DD: SS #851. Old-file has 4:00 AM LMT. Morrison in *World Astrology*, December 1944, speculates noon.

SNEAD, SAM May 27, 1912 Hot Springs, Va
Golfer 3:00 AM EST 70W50 38N00

☉ 05-♊-39	☿ 14-♉-22	♂ 29-♋-25	♄ 25-♉-09	♆ 21-♋-49	A 23-♈-43
☽ 22-♎-42	♀ 24-♉-50	♃ 11-♐-11R	♅ 03-♒-19R	♇ 27-♊-56	M 13-♑-31

Winner of the PGA Championships, Masters, Vardon Trophy, Tournament of Champions, and British Open, all between 1942 and 1946. Named PGA Player of the Year, 1949. Elected to Golf's Hall of Fame, 1953.

C: CL quotes Drew.

SOLZHENITSYN, ALEKSANDR December 11, 1918 Kislovadsk, Russia
Writer 11:30 AM LMT 42E44 44N01

☉ 18-♐-31	☿ 03-♑-22R	♂ 22-♑-57	♄ 28-♌-15R	♆ 09-♌-06R	A 27-♒-15
☽ 21-♓-50	♀ 22-♐-44	♃ 13-♋-34R	♅ 24-♒-23	♇ 05-♋-56R	M 13-♐-10

Soviet novelist and historian, who brilliantly exposed the brutal and dehumanizing conditions of life in the Stalin era. Exiled in 1974 for actions allegedly incompatible with Soviet citizenship. Nobel prize for literature, 1970. Books include *One Day in the Life of Ivan Denisovich* (1962) taken from personal experience.

DD: Dewey quotes him for the date, as written to Joylynn Hill, (He did not know the time.) PC speculates 11:30 AM. Old-file has 11:00 AM.

SOUSA, JOHN PHILIP November 6, 1854 Washington, D.C.
Musician 8:00 PM LMT 77W02 38N54

☉ 14-♏-20	☿ 05-♐-02	♂ 19-♐-55	♄ 14-♊-30R	♆ 13-♓-15R	A 05-♋-46
☽ 09-♊-42	♀ 05-♏-24	♃ 22-♑-04	♅ 14-♉-41R	♇ 02-♉-29R	M 14-♓-42

Composer and bandmaster of the U.S. Marine Corp, 1880; organized Sousa's Band, 1892, which visited Europe and toured the world. His music includes "The Stars and Stripes Forever" and "The Washington Post." (1854-1932)

DD: PC speculative. Jansky gives 3:58:16 PM EST.

SPENCER, HERBERT April 27, 1820 Derby, England
Writer 11:59 PM LMT 1W30 52N55

☉ 07-♉-36	☿ 16-♈-43	♂ 03-♌-42	♄ 07-♈-45	♆ 00-♑-42R	A 00-♑-32
☽ 02-♏-49	♀ 21-♊-23	♃ 15-♓-08	♅ 28-♐-35R	♇ 28-♓-00	M 08-♏-00

English philosopher, who was the first to coin the phrase "survival of the fittest." Well educated; an intellectual friend of his father. First published with *Social Status* (1850). Two volume *Autobiography* published posthumously. Health deteriorated to chronic disorder of the brain in his old age.

C: Chart pictured in Adams' *One Hundred Horoscopes.*

SPENGLER, OSWALD May 29, 1880 Blakenburg, Germany
Writer 6:40 PM LMT 10E14 51N15

☉ 08-♊-40	☿ 04-♊-04	♂ 28-♋-09	♄ 24-♈-50	♆ 12-♉-46	A 24-♏-40
☽ 23-♒-38	♀ 26-♉-21	♃ 12-♈-20	♅ 05-♍-00	♇ 27-♉-09	M 16-♍-34

German philosopher of history. In *The Decline of the West* (1926-28), held that the key to history is the law of societies and civilizations, which rise and fall in cycles, and that Western civilization is in a period of decay. (1880-1936)

C: WEMYSS #113 from *Neue Sternblatter,* September 1932; same data in SS #857. T. Joseph quotes Wangemann for 5:46:12 PM MET.

SPOCK, DR. BENJAMIN May 2, 1903 New Haven, Conn
Physician 2:00 AM EST 72W55 41N18

☉ 10-♉-42	☿ 29-♉-35	♂ 27-♍-46R	♄ 09-♒-03	♆ 01-♋-35	A 28-♒-00
☽ 13-♋-50	♀ 16-♊-40	♃ 15-♓-46	♅ 25-♐-14R	♇ 18-♊-18	M 12-♐-34

Pediatrician and author; guru to millions of American parents. His book, *Baby and Child Care,* sold 28 million copies. Married in 1924 for 49 years; divorced in 1973 to marry 32-year-old Mary Councille. Two sons, born in 1934 and 1945.

C: *Progressions in Action,* by DCD, "data from Drew."

STAMPONATO, JOHNNY October 19, 1915 Woodstock, Ill
Homocide victim 4:11 AM CST 88W27 42N19

☉ 24-♎-57	☿ 01-♏-55R	♂ 06-♌-13	♄ 16-♋-24	♆ 02-♌-35	A 00-♎-52
☽ 12-♓-54	♀ 04-♏-37	♃ 19-♓-47R	♅ 11-♒-45R	♇ 03-♋-17R	M 01-♋-01

Mother died a few days after his birth; father died, 1953. Two marriages. Known as a small scale hoodlum. Lover of Lana Turner, until stabbed to death by her dauther Cheryl Crane, April 4, 1958.

C: Scarsella from Baird, speculative. The chart and profile of Cheryl Crane and the data of Lana Turner are given in *Profiles of Women*.

STALIN, JOSEPH January 2, 1880 NS Gori, Russia
Statesman 8:15 AM Zone #2 44E05 42N00

⊙ 11-♑-17 ☿ 19-♐-01 ♂ 14-♉-47 ♄ 09-♈-22 ♆ 09-♉-21R A 09-♒-52
☽ 03-♍-52 ♀ 26-♏-35 ♃ 09-♓-17 ♅ 08-♍-51R ♇ 25-♉-41R M 01-♐-14

Became a Marxist at age 15. Defeated Trotsky for leadership after the death of Lenin. Founded party paper PRAVDA, 1911. Became prime minister and leader of the Communist Party of the Soviet Union. Author of many books on socialism. (1880?-1953)

DD: Kraum in AA, June 1969, states the date is proven at December 21, 1879 OS = January 2, 1880 NS, time unknown, speculative. PC gives the same data as "recorded," adds that AFA, May 1953, gives 3:27 AM.

   Rudhyar in AA, July 1938, gives December 21, 1879 NS, speculative time 3:05 AM. Same date from C.W. Lemont in AA, October 1942, speculative 4:21 AM. Penfield in 1979 quotes *Stalin* by Ian Grey for December 9, 1879 OS = December 21, 1879 NS, says this date is on his tomb.

   The editor writes in AA, May 1969, "Our files contain no less than seven speculative charts for Stalin, based on five different dates, each one citing a biographical source or flat statement on a Russian embassy's letterhead as the authority."

STANFORD, LELAND March 9, 1824 Watervliet, N.Y.
Entrepreneur 10:30 PM LMT 73W42 42N44

⊙ 19-♓-33 ☿ 24-♒-34 ♂ 09-♎-48R ♄ 19-♉-18 ♆ 09-♑-21 A 12-♏-42
☽ 09-♋-31 ♀ 13-♒-39 ♃ 01-♋-21 ♅ 15-♑-06 ♇ 01-♈-12 M 22-♌-54

A lawyer in 1848; a railroad builder. Entered politics in 1861 to become governor of California and a U.S. senator. In 1885, with a gift of land and securities, founded Stanford Univesity in memory of his son. (1824-1893)

DD: PC speculative. Old-file has 10:20 PM LMT.

STEAD, WILLIAM T. July 5, 1849 Embleton, Durham, England
Writer 8:40 AM LMT 1W20 54N40

⊙ 13-♋-08 ☿ 05-♋-33R ♂ 05-♉-20 ♄ 07-♈-49 ♆ 04-♓-37R A 05-♍-13
☽ 10-♑-58 ♀ 28-♉-43 ♃ 22-♌-20 ♅ 25-♈-59 ♇ 28-♈-46 M 25-♉-34

British journalist, philanthropist and champion of justice. First edited a newspaper in 1871: introduced modern methods, undertook crusades. Wrote extensively on subjects that ranged from psychic phenomena to world peace. Died on the Titanic, April 5, 1912.

DD: Lyndoe in AA, February 1963, "from him." Leo in M.A., July 1912, states, "He gave his time as 'before breakfast'." rectified to 6:00 AM LMT, notes that "other maps have calculated 7:00 AM and 8:53 AM." PC quotes SS #863 (no time given) for 6:00 AM.

STEINBECK, JOHN February 27, 1902 Salinas, Ca
Writer 3:00 PM PST 121W39 36N40

⊙ 08-♓-26 ☿ 21-♒-19R ♂ 14-♓-58 ♄ 24-♑-11 ♆ 28-♊-42R A 03-♌-09
☽ 11-♏-30 ♀ 18-♒-42R ♃ 04-♒-44 ♅ 20-♐-58 ♇ 16-♊-41R M 21-♈-50

Books include the best sellers that were made into movies — *Of Mice and Men* (1937), *The Grapes of Wrath* (1939), and *The Moon is Down* (1942). Received the Nobel prize in literature 1962. (1902-1968)

C: PC speculates the time from *John Steinbeck* by Nelson Vanjean (1950), which states on p. 17 that "his sisters were sent to the circus at 2:00 PM: after the last show they went home to find a new baby brother."

STEINER, RUDOLPH | February 27, 1861 NS | Kraljevic, Yugoslavia
Writer | 11:00 PM LMT | 20E43 43N42

☉ 09-♓-20 ☿ 27-♓-26 ♂ 06-♉-56 ♄ 05-♍-53R ♆ 28-♓-20 A 10-♏-21
☽ 17-♎-17 ♀ 20-♒-49 ♃ 19-♌-52R ♅ 08-♊-04 ♇ 07-♉-46 M 20-♌-17

Founder of his own society of Anthroposophy and a school for liberal arts in 1913; lectured and wrote extensively, including his autobiographical *Mein Lebensgang* (1924). (1861-1925)

DD: CL from AFA, October 1952. SS #865 gives 11:15 PM; same data pictured in Adams' *One Hundred Horoscopes*. Old-file has 11:30 PM. Pownall gives 1:00 PM in AJ, Spring 1961. March quotes AJ, Spring 1980 for 11:15 PM LMT "from his wife" with 14E34/45N16.

STENDHAL | January 23, 1783 | Grenoble, France
Writer | 1:00 AM LMT | 5E44 45N11

☉ 03-♒-00 ☿ 09-♒-53 ♂ 10-♐-18 ♄ 06-♑-55 ♆ 10-♎-12R A 05-♏-39
☽ 24-♍-24 ♀ 07-♒-22 ♃ 15-♑-38 ♅ 04-♋-14R ♇ 07-♒-42 M 14-♌-45

Marie Henri Beyle, one of the great literary figures of the 19th century France. Best remembered for *The Red and the Black* and *The Charterhouse of Parma*. (1783-1842)

DD: PC, "recorded." Old-file has 00:25 AM LMT.

STERN, ISAAC | July 21, 1920 | Kreminiecz, Russia
Musician | 4:00 AM LMT | 25E44 40N06

☉ 28-♋-00 ☿ 08-♌-07R ♂ 04-♏-26 ♄ 09-♍-12 ♆ 10-♌-46 A 17-♋-20
☽ 07-♎-51 ♀ 02-♌-46 ♃ 22-♌-01 ♅ 05-♓-02R ♇ 07-♋-49 M 28-♓-25

American violinst known for fine artistry. Symphonic debut as an 11-year old virtuoso, followed by a concert series tour. N.Y. debut in 1937; Carnegie Hall, 1943. A gregarious dynamo of nervous energy. Three children with his second wife.

C: CL quotes Drew as "approximately sunrise," rectified.

STEVENSON, ROBERT LOUIS | November 13, 1850 | Edinburgh, Scotland
Writer | 1:30 PM LMT | 3W10 55N55

☉ 20-♏-52 ☿ 12-♏-16 ♂ 25-♏-35 ♄ 15-♈-09R ♆ 04-♓-15R A 18-♒-35
☽ 08-♓-16 ♀ 29-♐-12 ♃ 13-♎-25 ♅ 27-♈-26R ♇ 28-♈-25R M 16-♐-01

Scottish novelist and poet, whose works were full of life, originality, and humor. Books include *Treasure Island* (1883) and *The Strange Case of Dr. Jekyll and Mr. Hyde* (1886). (1850-1894).

C: SS #869, NN #243 and Adams all give the same data. PC states same data, "from his baby book."

STEWARD, JACKIE | June 11, 1939 | Dumbuck, Dumbarton
Racer | 2:50 PM BST | 4W32 55N56

☉ 19-♊-47 ☿ 25-♊-00 ♂ 03-♒-56 ♄ 28-♈-03 ♆ 20-♍-34 A 17-♎-54
☽ 05-♈-57 ♀ 26-♉-36 ♃ 05-♈-15 ♅ 19-♉-41 ♇ 29-♋-57 M 25-♋-04

Race car champion in the Formula One competition.

DD: Craswell states B.C. Holliday same data. Pat Geisler in M.H., October 1978, says that "her husband cornered Stewart at a party to get the birth data, and he gave his time as 10:45 PM."

STEWART, JAMES | May 20, 1908 | Indiana, Pa
Actor | 00:10 AM EST | 79W09 40N37

☉ 28-♉-46 ☿ 13-♊-01 ♂ 28-♊-28 ♄ 07-♈-01 ♆ 12-♋-57 A 06-♒-37
☽ 21-♑-38 ♀ 11-♋-41 ♃ 07-♌-16 ♅ 16-♑-34R ♇ 23-♊-41 M 28-♏-04

Won the Oscar as best actor in *The Philapelphia Story* (1940); nominated for an Oscar in *Mr. Smith Goes to Washington* (1939), *It's a Wonderful Life* (1946), *Harvey* (1950), and *Anatomy of a Murder* (1959). Outstanding record during World War II in the Air Force; retired as a brigadier general.

C: CL from *Today's Astrology*, 1940.

STOKES, CARL B.	June 21, 1927	Cleveland, Ohio
Politician	10:30 AM EST	81W42 41N30

☉ 29-♊-17	☿ 24-♋-22	♂ 09-♌-15	♄ 02-♐-33R	♆ 24-♌-46	A 17-♍-56
☽ 19-♓-22	♀ 14-♌-19	♃ 01-♈-49	♅ 03-♈-17	♇ 15-♋-02	M 15-♊-53

Great-grandson of a slave. Became the first Black mayor of a major U.S. city. Served in World War II before completing high school and college. Law degree, 1956. Politics by 1962; Cleveland mayor, 1967 and 1969; TV newscaster by 1972.

C: Herman Webb in AA, May 1968.

STOUT, REX	December 1, 1886	Novelsville, Ind
Writer	10:30 PM LMT	86W01 40N03

☉ 09-♐-57	☿ 13-♐-07R	♂ 12-♑-45	♄ 21-♋-48R	♆ 26-♉-03R	A 26-♌-59
☽ 24-♒-34	♀ 09-♐-43	♃ 27-♎-24	♅ 11-♎-32	♇ 02-♊-56R	M 20-♉-52

American novelist and writer of mystery stories, best known for his stories of *Nero Wolfe*, the detective who generally solves crimes without leaving home. Other books include *Triple Jeopardy* (1952) and *Three Witnesses* (1956). Forty-two books in forty-one years. (1886-1975)

DD: PC quotes *Rex Stout* by John McAleer (1977), "which states he was born very late at night." That biography states on p. 36, "Temperatures dropped from 24 degrees at 7:00 AM to zero at Midnight . . . He was born as the thermometer plummeted." The date is also given in *Nero Wolfe of West Thirty-Fifth St* by Baring-Gould (1969), but again, no time.

STOWE, HARRIET BEECHER	June 14, 1811	Litchfield, Ct
Writer	11:00 AM LMT	73W11 41N45

☉ 22-♊-37	☿ 05-♊-21	♂ 26-♏-20R	♄ 23-♐-26R	♆ 09-♐-29R	A 12-♍-00
☽ 04-♈-54	♀ 21-♉-29	♃ 15-♊-58	♅ 15-♏-26R	♇ 18-♓-13	M 08-♊-46

American novelist, with stories that deal with the New England past. Chiefly remembered for her overnight famous novel on antislavery, *Uncle Tom's Cabin* (1852). Married in 1836 and had seven children. (1811-1896)

DD: PC speculative. Old-file has 11:35 AM LMT.

STRACK, ROBERT LUDWIG	August 11, 1932	Bruhl, Germany
Murderer	12:30 PM MET	6E58 40N52

☉ 18-♌-33	☿ 29-♌-17R	♂ 04-♋-25	♄ 00-♒-08R	♆ 07-♍-00	A 08-♏-43
☽ 17-♐-04	♀ 06-♋-30	♃ 00-♍-02	♅ 23-♈-19R	♇ 22-♋-26	M 16-♌-44

On October 13, 1965, picked up two 11-year-old girls who were lost, bought them food, took them to his father's cottage, raped, murdered, and mutilated them. Called "The Beat of Cologne". Wrote *Diary of a Criminal*, which was withheld from the public.

C: CL from Fagan in AA, December 1966, "data taken from a German astrological magazine."

STRAVINSKY, IGOR	June 17, 1882 NS	Oranienbaum, Russia
Musician	10:30 AM LMT	29E43 59N53

☉ 26-♊-00	☿ 11-♋-13R	♂ 22-♌-09	♄ 20-♉-51	♆ 17-♉-44	A 13-♍-12
☽ 14-♋-45	♀ 25-♋-24	♃ 12-♊-58	♅ 14-♍-43	♇ 29-♉-24	M 04-♊-57

Russian born composer; the most significant muscial innovator of the 20th century. Decided on music as a career in 1903; became famous overnight in 1910 when his ballet *The Firebird* was performed. After 1914, left Russia for Switzerland, France, and U.S. in 1939. (1882-1971)

DD: PC quotes *L'Astrologie Moderne;* same date in *Americana, Famous People,* and *Current Biography* Obit. CL quotes AFA, October 1953, for June 18, 1882 NS, 10:30 AM LMT, "from the archives of Dr. Moufang."

SULLIVAN, SIR ARTHUR	May 13, 1842	London, England
Musician	4:47 PM LMT	0W06 51N31

☉ 22-♉-28	☿ 26-♉-00	♂ 04-♊-25	♄ 14-♑-07R	♆ 19-♒-15	A 23-♎-03
☽ 02-♋-50	♀ 10-♊-07	♃ 22-♑-39R	♅ 27-♓-17	♇ 21-♈-08	M 00-♌-34

British composer, who teamed with William S. Gilbert to write the operettas *H.M.S. Pinafore* (1878), *The Pirates of Penzance* (1879), *The Mikado* (1885), and more. A learned musician; taught and conducted as well; knighted by Queen Victoria in 1883. (1842-1900)

DD: BJA, March 29, rectified from a given statement of "early evening." Same data in SS #877. Old file has 5:20 PM LMT.

SULLIVAN, ED	September 28, 1902	New York, N.Y.
TV Host	3:30 AM EST	73W57 40N45

☉ 04-♎-16	☿ 00-♏-02	♂ 14-♌-46	♄ 21-♑-11	♆ 03-♋-42	A 06-♍-04
☽ 22-♌-15	♀ 18-♍-37	♃ 07-♒-29R	♅ 17-♐-42	♇ 19-♊-41R	M 01-♊-50

Host of his own TV variety show from 1950; in fourteen years had fourteen thousand performers on 724 shows. Former sportswriter, radio, and vaudeville performer; entered the TV field in 1948, compared to a cigar-store Indian stiff in motion, with a saturnine face. (1902-1974)

DD: CL from SS #878 (no time given). Scarsella quotes Baird for 7:01 AM EST, from Ziegler.

SUNDAY, BILLY	November 19, 1863	Amers, Iowa
Evangelist	6:00 AM LMT	93W37 42N02

☉ 26-♏-43	☿ 19-♏-38	♂ 11-♏-02	♄ 14-♎-12	♆ 03-♈-29R	A 15-♏-08
☽ 14-♓-41	♀ 11-♎-38	♃ 11-♏-54	♅ 24-♊-06R	♇ 11-♉-03R	M 25-♌-46

After childhood in an orphanage, entered a baseball career in 1883, until a conversion experience in 1886. Became an assistant evangelist; ordained, 1903, as a Presbyterian revivalist. Flamboyant acrobatics in the pulpit brought him wide popularity. (1863?-1935)

DD: M.A., March 1916, Alan Leo says, "We are informed . . ." SS #881 gives 6:05 AM. Old-file has the same date, 6:35 AM LMT. *Current Biography* Obit gives 1862.

SWEDENBORG, EMANUEL	February 8, 1688 NS	Stockholm, Sweden
Writer	5:30 AM LMT	18E03 59N20

☉ 19-♒-26	☿ 00-♒-33	♂ 28-♈-10	♄ 25-♎-01R	♆ 07-♓-39	A 24-♐-24
☽ 14-♉-34	♀ 02-♑-52	♃ 15-♑-14	♅ 14-♉-50	♇ 21-♋-55R	M 13-♏-07

Brilliant, eclectic educator from physics and astronomy to the Bible. Worked on the Board of Mines, 1716. In 1745 had a transcendent religious experience in which God commissioned him to present a new revelation, based on the premise that Heaven and Hell are not places but states of being.

DD: Leo in M.A., April 1892; same chart pictured in Adams *One Hundred Horoscopes.* PC quotes NN #023 for 6:00 AM LMT. Old-file has 5:25 AM LMT. *Britannica* gives January 29, 1688 OS. *World Book* gives 1688-1772.

TAFT, ROBERT	September 8, 1889	Cincinnati, Ohio
Politician	4:44 AM LMT	84W31 39N06

☉ 15-♍-55	☿ 09-♎-26	♂ 20-♌-39	♄ 26-♌-43	♆ 04-♊-34R	A 04-♍-51
☽ 00-♓-49	♀ 07-♌-48	♃ 28-♐-45	♅ 20-♎-08	♇ 06-♊-56R	M 00-♊-49

Harvard Law School; Ohio bar, 1913; into a law firm. First public office as assistant councilman, 1917-19; House of Representatives, 1921-26; Ohio senator, 1931-32; Republican U.S. senator from Ohio from 1938. Died of cancer, 1953.

DD: AQ, Winter 1952, rectified from a given "before 5:00 AM." AFA, February 1952, states, "shortly before 5:00 PM from a family member." Scarsella quotes Baird for 1:30 AM LMT, from AFA.

TAGORE, RANDINDRANATH May 7, 1861 Calcutta, India
Writer 4:02 AM LMT 88E20 22N35
☉ 16-♉-19 ☿ 29-♈-52 ♂ 22-♊-06 ♄ 02-♍-40 ♆ 00-♈-45 A 20-♈-04
☽ 13-♈-03 ♀ 15-♉-03 ♃ 17-♌-52 ♅ 10-♊-34 ♇ 09-♉-07 M 14-♑-02
Indian poet; awarded the 1913 Nobel prize in literature. Established a school in Bengal, which developed into an international university called Visva-Bharati. Author of about sixty poetic works, a number of stories and plays, and more than three thousand songs set to music. (1861-1941)

DD: B.V. Ramon in AA, June 1948; same data in SS #887. Old-file has 3:35 AM LMT.

TANEY, ROGER March 17, 1777 Calvert Co, Md
Jurist 4:00 AM LMT 76W35 38N32
☉ 27-♓-08 ☿ 29-♒-31 ♂ 14-♎-39R ♄ 02-♏-24R ♆ 25-♍-42R A 07-♒-27
☽ 10-♋-47 ♀ 13-♉-02 ♃ 15-♋-15 ♅ 07-♊-24 ♇ 29-♑-32 M 27-♏-32

One of the great chief justices of the U.S.; but the merit of his work clouded by his decision in the Dred Scott case, which helped bring on the Civil War. Law practice from 1799; political service for several years in the state Senate. (1777-1864)

DD: PC speculative. Old-file has 7:25 AM LMT.

TARKINGTON, BOOTH July 29, 1869 Indianapolis, Ind
Writer 10:00 AM LMT 86W19 39N46
☉ 06-♌-29 ☿ 22-♋-12 ♂ 06-♎-16 ♄ 10-♐-44R ♆ 19-♈-34R A 05-♎-52
☽ 13-♈-44 ♀ 28-♌-28 ♃ 18-♉-14 ♅ 18-♋-50 ♇ 17-♉-55 M 06-♋-44
American novelist and playwright; awarded the 1919 Pulitzer prize in fiction for *Magnificant Andersons* and the 1922 Pulitzer prize for *Alice Adams.* Works include *Monsieur Beaucaire* (1900) and *Penrod* (1914). (1869-1946)

DD: CL from AFA, February 1958; same data in SS #890. Old-file has 9:30 AM LMT.

TATIANA, DUCHESS June 10, 1897 NS Peterhof, Russia
Royalty 11:00 AM LMT 29E54 59N53
☉ 19-♊-41 ☿ 28-♉-01 ♂ 13-♌-10 ♄ 25-♏-49R ♆ 19-♊-59 A 13-♍-48
☽ 16-♎-49 ♀ 07-♉-52 ♃ 03-♍-07 ♅ 26-♏-05R ♇ 13-♊-22 M 05-♊-52
Second daughter of Czar Nicholas and Czarina Alexandra; executed with her entire family by the Bolsheviks on July 16, 1918.

C: Mary Frances Wood in M.H., July 1977, quotes speculative data from M.A., June 1922. PC states same data, "recorded." BJA, August 1915; same date from Bailey who says, "cannot ascertain time."

TAYLOR, DR. FLOYD June 5, 1923 Boston, Mass
Scientist 8:00 PM EDT 71W04 42N22
☉ 14-♊-16 ☿ 02-♊-59R ♂ 04-♋-01 ♄ 13-♎-27R ♆ 15-♌-49 A 11-♐-56
☽ 09-♓-55 ♀ 18-♉-32 ♃ 10-♏-30R ♅ 17-♓-26 ♇ 10-♋-03 M 02-♎-31
Research scientist with a Ph.D. in psychology; entered the field of atomics: designs chairs for space capsules. While an Army Air Force pilot in 1942, shot down three times.

C: CL from Lily Ireland, July 1964.

TETRAZZINI, LUISA June 29, 1871 Florence, Italy
Singer 4:04 AM LMT 11E15 43N47

☉ 06-♋-54 ☿ 22-♊-49 ♂ 05-♎-39 ♄ 06-♑-34R ♆ 23-♈-51 A 02-♋-08
☽ 18-♏-49 ♀ 21-♌-21 ♃ 08-♋-01 ♅ 25-♋-36 ♇ 19-♉-25 M 05-♓-59

One of Italy's greatest coloratura sopranos in pre-World War I history. Debut 1890, with 13 years in Italy and South America relatively unnoticed; first big success in Poland and Russia, 1903, and San Francisco, 1904, when she created a sensation. (1871-1940)

DD: Dewey quotes *World Astrology*, May 1946, from *The World of Song* by J.B. Romiser. PC quotes the same source for 3:30 AM LMT.

THACKERAY, WILLIAM M. July 18, 1811 Calcutta, India
Writer 2:00 PM LMT 88E20 22N35

☉ 24-♋-44 ☿ 17-♋-49 ♂ 26-♏-03 ♄ 21-♐-09R ♆ 08-♐-44R A 20-♏-02
☽ 00-♋-28 ♀ 01-♋-58 ♃ 23-♊-31 ♅ 14-♏-48R ♇ 18-♓-04R M 22-♌-53

One of the greatest British novelists of the Victorian age: he and Charles Dickens were the outstanding novelists of their time. Remembered for *Vanity Fair* and other works. (1811-1863)

DD: PC quotes SS; not in SS. Old-file has 4:15 PM LMT.

THAW, HARRY K. January 12, 1871 Pittsburgh, Pa
Homicide 8:00 AM LMT 80W01 40N26

☉ 21-♑-57 ☿ 03-♒-26R ♂ 04-♎-06 ♄ 03-♑-21 ♆ 19-♈-04 A 01-♒-26
☽ 29-♍-46 ♀ 00-♒-24 ♃ 17-♊-46R ♅ 24-♋-40R ♇ 17-♉-01R M 23-♏-58

A young Pittsburgh millionaire, who married Evelyn Nesbitt. Tormented with violent jealousy because of her former lover. On June 25, 1906, shot and killed Stanford White. The verdict, "not guilty by reason of insanity"; spent some years in and out of asylums.

DD: CL from Tucker. Dewey quotes NN for the same data, stated speculative. Ellen Wood file gives 12:15 PM LMT. *Wynn's Your Future* states, "No one is sure of the time, except that it was about 9:00 AM." Biography *The Trail of Harry Thaw* by A. MacKenzie.

THOMAS, DYLAN October, 27, 1914 Swansea, Wales
Writer 7:00 PM GMT 3W57 51N38

☉ 03-♏-31 ☿ 22-♏-58R ♂ 19-♏-35 ♄ 02-♋-12R ♆ 00-♌-27 A 19-♊-46
☽ 25-♒-14 ♀ 10-♐-18 ♃ 13-♒-00 ♅ 07-♒-43 ♇ 02-♋-07R M 13-♒-52

Welch poet, who wrote some of the most stirring and passionate verse in contemporary literature. Besides poems, wrote short stories, motion picture scenarios, and radio scripts. His early death at 39 struck his readers as a literary tragedy.

DD: PC speculative. Old-file has 5:05 PM GMT. Date check *Americana*.

THOMAS, LOWELL April 6, 1892 Woodington, Ohio
Newsman 7:55 PM CST 84W38 40N06

☉ 17-♈-43 ☿ 04-♉-14 ♂ 14-♑-12 ♄ 25-♍-10R ♆ 06-♊-58 A 09-♏-34
☽ 20-♌-40 ♀ 01-♊-44 ♃ 05-♈-06 ♅ 04-♏-45R ♇ 07-♊-15 M 17-♌-28

Author, radio commentator, TV newsman, lecturer, and world traveler. Sent to Europe by President Wilson during World War I to prepare a historical record. Radio debut in 1930. First and most famous book, *With Lawrence in Arabia* (1924).

DD: CL quotes SS #898 (no time given). PC quotes SS and Drew for 7:30 PM CST. Old-file has 8:35 PM CST. CL also quotes *World Astrology*, June 1937, for "sunrise." (LMR computes sunrise at 5:38 AM).

THOMAS, RICHARD June 13, 1951 New York, N.Y.
Actor 5:00 AM EDT 73W57 40N45

☉ 21-♊-33 ☿ 07-♊-27 ♂ 15-♊-56 ♄ 25-♍-44 ♆ 16-♎-49R A 14-♊-11
☽ 28-♍-38 ♀ 06-♌-27 ♃ 10-♈-06 ♅ 08-♋-33 ♇ 17-♌-51 M 19-♒-30

On screen from 1969 in films that include *Last Summer, Cactus in the Snow,* and *Red Sky at Morning.* Played the role of John-boy in the TV series *The Waltons;* also in TV's *Roots Two.*

C: McEvers, unrecorded source. Same data in PC as "personal."

THURBER, JAMES   December 8, 1894   Columbus, Ohio
Writer   11:55 PM CST   83W00   39N38

| ☉ 17-♐-12 | ☿ 00-♐-19 | ♂ 23-♈-18 | ♄ 03-♏-35 | ♆ 14-♊-19R | A 24-♍-59 |
| ☽ 00-♉-23 | ♀ 19-♐-17 | ♃ 03-♋-06R | ♅ 17-♏-33 | ♇ 10-♊-39R | M 24-♊-14 |

American humorist, who illustrated his stories, fables and essays with caricatures, simplicity of art, and sophistication of humor. First a state clerk and a journalist; after 1926, a contributing editor to the *New Yorker* magazine. (1894-1961)

DD: PC quotes *Thurber* by B. Bernstein "which states he was born very late at night." That biography gives the date on p. 1, notes on p. 12, "Cesar Franck's symphony played Paris the night I was born," and on p. 14, "on a night of wild portend and high wind." Old-file has 00:15 AM CST.

TODD, MIKE   June 22, 1909   Minneapolis, Minn
Producer   6:06 PM CST   93W16   44N59

| ☉ 00-♋-52 | ☿ 19-♊-31R | ♂ 16-♓-36 | ♄ 21-♈-40 | ♆ 16-♋-13 | A 07-♐-20 |
| ☽ 00-♍-19 | ♀ 15-♋-43 | ♃ 08-♍-21 | ♅ 19-♑-51R | ♇ 25-♊-28 | M 28-♍-39 |

Most colorful producer of theatricals and movies since Ziegfeld; said to have had the soul of a carnival pitchman and the ambition of a Napoleon. Won the Oscar for *Around the World in Eighty Days.* Third marriage to Liz Taylor. Killed in a plane crash, March 23, 1958.

DD: CL from Nell Botterill, 1958. Same date in *Famous People* and *Current Biography* Obit; PC states same date in *Nine Lives of Mike Todd* by Art Cohn. Lyndoe in *Predictions,* June 1958, gives June 22, 1906, 3:28 AM CST. Tucker gives 1908.

TOLKIEN, J.R.R.   January 3, 1892   Bloemfontein, S.A.
Writer   9:00 PM LMT   26E13   29S08

| ☉ 12-♑-56 | ☿ 00-♑-07R | ♂ 16-♏-47 | ♄ 00-♎-07 | ♆ 06-♊-45R | A 16-♌-14 |
| ☽ 00-♓-11 | ♀ 09-♒-13 | ♃ 13-♓-57 | ♅ 05-♏-28 | ♇ 07-♊-15R | M 00-♊-04 |

Linguist, scholar, and author of the huge, best-selling trilogy, *The Lord of the Rings* (1954-56) — called a fantasy of the war between good and evil, although he denied it was allegorical. (1892-1973)

DD: PC quotes *Tolkien* by H. Carpenter, which quotes a letter by his father on p. 12, "... fetched the doctor about eight and then he stayed till 12:40 when we drank a whiskey." Dewey rectifies to 10:50 PM LMT. Old-file has 5:20 AM LMT.

TOLSTOY, LEO   September 9, 1828 NS   Tula, Russia
Writer   10:52 PM Zone #2   37E36   54N12

| ☉ 17-♍-05 | ☿ 20-♍-00 | ♂ 11-♑-04 | ♄ 00-♌-33 | ♆ 15-♑-42R | A 13-♋-49 |
| ☽ 22-♍-49 | ♀ 04-♌-41 | ♃ 11-♏-04 | ♅ 28-♑-42R | ♇ 06-♈-47R | M 07-♓-48 |

Russian novelist, moral philosopher, social reformer; renowned as the author of *War and Peace, Anna Karenina,* and more. Outstanding in reality of fiction and psychological insight. Married 1862; thirteen children. (1828-1910)

DD: Chart pictured in Adams' *One Hundred Horoscopes.* Same data in NN #719, stated speculative. PC quotes Adams for 10:30 PM LMT and NN for 10:52 PM. M.A., June 1912, gives August 28, 1828 OS, time unknown, speculative 7:20 AM.

TOWNSEND, PETER   November 22, 1914   Rangoon, Burma
Military   6:40 AM Zone 6.5   96E00   16N50

| ☉ 18-♏-46 | ☿ 09-♏-00R | ♂ 00-♐-25 | ♄ 01-♋-39R | ♆ 00-♌-26R | A 25-♏-08 |
| ☽ 01-♍-24 | ♀ 11-♐-48R | ♃ 14-♒-16 | ♅ 07-♒-57 | ♇ 01-♋-56R | M 26-♌-33 |

Military group commander; came into the public light for his romance with the young Princess Margaret of Great Britain; considered an unacceptable suitor with no claim to nobility.

C: Reynolds quotes Ebertin.

TRACY, SPENCER April 5, 1900 Milwaukee, Wis
Actor 1:57 AM CST 87W55 43N02

| ☉ 15-♈-05 | ☿ 26-♓-48R | ♂ 27-♓-48 | ♄ 04-♑-58 | ♆ 24-♊-28 | A 20-♑-50 |
| ☽ 27-♊-08 | ♀ 29-♉-04 | ♃ 10-♐-45R | ♅ 12-♐-20R | ♇ 14-♊-56 | M 16-♏-58 |

Leading star for thirty-seven years; Broadway in 1927; then motion pictures. Best actor awards for *Captains Courageous* (1937) and *Boy's Town* (1938). Films include *Boom Town, Inherit the Wind,* and *The Old Man and the Sea.* (1900-1967)

C: McEvers quotes D.C. Doane in Dell, February 1964. Same data in SS #906.

TREACHER, ARTHUR July 21, 1894 Brighton, England
Actor 6:00 PM GMT 0W10 50N50

| ☉ 28-♋-54 | ☿ 27-♋-33R | ♂ 16-♈-59 | ♄ 19-♎-10 | ♆ 14-♊-54 | A 27-♐-25 |
| ☽ 10-♓-59 | ♀ 25-♊-48 | ♃ 24-♊-29 | ♅ 11-♏-15 | ♇ 11-♊-20 | M 01-♏-28 |

Comedian character-actor; specialized in playing the butler, with no trouble in getting his laughs. Modest, witty, entertaining; also successful in radio.

C: *Wynn's Astrology,* January 1945.

TRUJILLO, RAFAEL October 24, 1891 San Cristobal, Dominican Republic
Statesman 7:35 AM LMT 70W07 18N24

| ☉ 00-♏-48 | ☿ 28-♎-26 | ♂ 01-♎-38 | ♄ 25-♍-22 | ♆ 08-♊-36R | A 22-♏-25 |
| ☽ 00-♌-00 | ♀ 10-♏-11 | ♃ 08-♓-18R | ♅ 01-♏-42 | ♇ 08-♊-30R | M 24-♌-03 |

President of the Dominican Republic, 1930-57; in power through control of the National Guard. Political harshness and unusual severity brought opposition plots and attempts to break his power, chiefly after World War II. Shot and killed in a revolution, May 30, 1961.

DD: Dewey quotes AFA, August 1965. PC quotes MMD for 7:30 AM LMT. *Tucker Research Quarterly,* January 1961, gives 7:53 AM EST.

TRUMAN, BESS February 13, 1885 Independence, Mo
First Lady 7:00 AM CST 94W25 39N06

| ☉ 25-♒-03 | ☿ 05-♒-05 | ♂ 24-♒-37 | ♄ 17-♊-18R | ♆ 20-♉-35 | A 19-♒-15 |
| ☽ 07-♒-20 | ♀ 04-♒-55 | ♃ 01-♍-39R | ♅ 02-♎-19R | ♇ 00-♊-11 | M 06-♐-11 |

Met Harry Truman at Sunday school when she was 6 and he a year older. Married, June 28, 1919, after he returned from World War I. One of her husband's assistants while he served in the Senate; edited his speeches.

DD: PC speculative. Old-file has 7:25 AM CST.

TRUMAN, HARRY S. May 8, 1884 Larmar, Mo
Statesman 3:43 PM LMT 94W16 37N30

| ☉ 18-♉-39 | ☿ 01-♊-16R | ♂ 17-♌-13 | ♄ 10-♊-17 | ♆ 20-♉-41 | A 10-♎-31 |
| ☽ 05-♏-00 | ♀ 03-♋-58 | ♃ 28-♋-05 | ♅ 24-♍-14R | ♇ 00-♊-24 | M 11-♋-51 |

U.S. president, 1945-52, during the end of World War II and beginning of the Korean conflict. Had a clothing store in Kansas; was a Captain in World War I; entered politics. As Vice-president, became president upon the death of Franklin Delano Roosevelt, 1945.

DD: *Horoscopes of U.S. Presidents* by D.C. Doane. *Constellations,* 1977, Lockhart quotes M. Meyer, 1936, "data from him, about 4:00 PM." Gleadow rectifies to 4:20 PM in AA, March 1952.

TUCKER, SOPHIE January 13, 1886 NS Minsk, Russia
Entertainer 12:00 Noon LMT 27E35 53N50

☉ 23-♑-13	☿ 00-♑-17	♂ 24-♍-19	♄ 03-♋-29R	♆ 22-♉-53R	A 22-♉-10
☽ 22-♈-07	♀ 03-♓-45	♃ 05-♎-56	♅ 07-♎-43R	♇ 01-♊-19R	M 21-♑-06

Star of the stage for sixty years; known for her big voice and flamboyant dress and jewels. Among her popular songs were "Some of These Days" and "I'm the Last of the Red Hot Mamas." (1886?-1966)

DD: PC quotes her autobiography *Some of These Days*. That biography, 1945, gives no date, place, or time. On p. 1 she states ". . . born on the road, somewhere from Russia across Poland to the Baltic, traveling in a covered wagon, . . . three months old when we reached Boston." *World Book* Obit gives 1884. *Famous People* gives January 13, 1888.

TUNISON, FANNIE W. September 17, 1866 Sag Harbor, N.Y.
Totally paralyzed 12:00 Noon LMT 72W18 41N00

☉ 24-♍-32	☿ 11-♍-49	♂ 04-♋-22	♄ 09-♏-20	♆ 11-♈-53R	A 07-♐-58
☽ 00-♑-41	♀ 10-♏-34	♃ 22-♑-25R	♅ 08-♋-04	♇ 14-♉-58R	M 26-♍-04

Born with a form of infantile paralysis; parents poor farmers. By age 30, the biggest wage earner in the family with the sale of paintings, sewing, embroidery, all done with her teeth and tongue; works at a specially designed chair and table. Good looking and bright; reads avidly. Neck muscles heavy, speech thick. Never idle.

C: M.A., July 1900, from *The Strand* magazine, May 1900.

TURNER, JOSEPH M. April 23, 1775 London, England
Artist 1:10 AM LMT 0W06 51N31

☉ 02-♉-40	☿ 05-♈-36	♂ 26-♌-51	♄ 03-♎-30R	♆ 20-♍-19R	A 15-♑-34
☽ 05-♒-22	♀ 28-♉-19	♃ 22-♉-30	♅ 00-♊-44	♇ 26-♑-31	M 20-♏-50

English landscape painter and etcher; worked with luminous light. A precocious success; exhibited from 1790. A miser; in later years became slovenly, solitary, and secretive; died wealthy and left his money to charity. (1775-1851)

DD: Chart pictured in Adams' *One Hundred Horoscopes*. PC quotes NN for 1:20 AM LMT.

TURPIN, RANDY June 7, 1928 Leamington, England
Boxer 5:45 PM BST 1W30 52N15

☉ 16-♊-42	☿ 09-♋-31	♂ 16-♈-23	♄ 15-♐-46R	♆ 26-♌-39	A 19-♏-04
☽ 04-♒-13	♀ 10-♊-10	♃ 00-♉-43	♅ 06-♈-54	♇ 15-♋-54	M 09-♍-01

First British Black boxer since 1891 to hold the World Heavyweight Championship by defeating Sugar Ray Robinson on July 10, 1951. Of the forty-five fights from 1946, had forty-three victories. (1928-1966)

C: Richard Adler from Addey in AQ, Spring 1952.

TWAIN, MARK November 30, 1835 Flordia, Mo
Writer 4:45 AM LMT 91W51 39N33

☉ 07-♐-34	☿ 18-♏-47	♂ 12-♐-58	♄ 00-♏-50	♆ 01-♒-38	A 09-♏-42
☽ 15-♈-37	♀ 21-♐-43	♃ 14-♋-44R	♅ 26-♒-52	♇ 12-♈-55R	M 17-♌-24

Samuel Longhorne Clemens, American writer who became famous as a humorist. Little formal education; a Mississippi River pilot; a miner in Nevada; a reporter in San Francisco. First book published in 1867. Works include *Tom Sawyer, Huckleberry Finn,* and *A Connecticut Yankee in King Arthur's Court.* (1835-1910)

C: Huggins in *The Astrology Magazine*, January 1970. Same data in SS #914.

ULM, CAPTAIN CHARLES October 18, 1897 Melbourne, Australia
Pilot Near sunset 144E58 37S47

☉ 24-♎-45	☿ 10-♎-45	♂ 05-♏-15	♄ 28-♏-56	♆ 22-♊-25R	A 17-♏-57
☽ 13-♋-25	♀ 25-♍-48	♃ 28-♍-03	♅ 27-♏-16	♇ 14-♊-32R	M 29-♋-27

An aviator, who left Oakland, California on December 3, 1934, and was lost at sea; the plane went down the following day East of Hawaii.

C: Holliday quotes Kraum in *Best of the NAJ*, 1979. (LMR computes sunset at 6:20 PM LMT).

UNG-YONG PARENTS May 23, 1934 Seoul, Korea
Notable 11:00 AM Zone #9 127E00 37N38

☉ 01-♊-16	☿ 12-♊-55	♂ 22-♉-24	♄ 27-♒-58	♆ 09-♍-36	A 17-♌-05
☽ 17-♍-32	♀ 18-♈-21	♃ 13-♎-47R	♅ 29-♈-18	♇ 22-♋-58	M 09-♉-24

Guinness Book of Records states that the parents were born on the same day at the same time. Father a teacher, mathematician. The place not stated, assumed as Seoul. Their son, Kim Ung-Yong, born March 7, 1963, at Seoul, no time recorded: an I.Q. estimated at 210; played chess before age 1; wrote poetry at 3; did integral calculus at 4.

C: Data quoted by Holliday.

VALENTINO, RUDOLPH May 6, 1895 Castalleneta, Italy
Actor 3:00 AM MET 17E14 40N53

☉ 15-♉-17	☿ 16-♉-33	♂ 08-♋-21	♄ 03-♏-04R	♆ 14-♊-22	A 01-♈-36
☽ 07-♎-16	♀ 21-♊-45	♃ 04-♋-07	♅ 18-♏-02R	♇ 10-♊-39	M 00-♑-50

Came to the U.S. in 1913; became a star after his role in *The Four Horsemen of the Apocalypse* (1921); fame for his romantic portrayals. Films included *The Shiek* (1921), *Blood and Sand* (1922), and *Monsieur Beaucaire* (1924). Idolized as a cult figure after his death at 31.

DD: *Constellations*, 1977, Bob Paige quotes *Valentino* by V. Tajari, "entry in family log." Same data from CL old file and in SS #919. BAJ, October 1926, states 3:30 AM MET, "from him directly to George McCormack." *Wynn's Astrology*, June 1935, gives 2:30 AM "from him."

VAN BUREN, ABIGAIL July 4, 1918 Sioux City, Iowa
Columnist 10:09 AM CWT 96W24 42N30

☉ 11-♋-48	☿ 20-♋-40	♂ 05-♎-15	♄ 13-♌-22	♆ 05-♌-53	A 01-♍-00
☽ 24-♉-50	♀ 06-♊-11	♃ 28-♊-04	♅ 27-♒-19R	♇ 05-♋-12	M 25-♉-01

Twin of Ann Landers (stated as born at 10:00 AM CWT). Together the girls wrote gossip columns from their high school and college days; married in a double ceremony in 1939; both became nationally syndicated advice columnists.

DD: PC quotes, "personal." LMR has a letter from "Dear Abby" in which she says, "Wrong data, do not include in *Profiles of Women*." *People* magazine, July 1976, notes "The twins were born 17 minutes apart." Date given by Ann Landers in a letter printed in *Celebrity Register*.

VAN DYCK, SIR ANTHONY March 22, 1599 Antwerp, Belgium
Artist 12:00 Noon LAT 4E25 51N15

☉ 01-♈-21	☿ 03-♓-34	♂ 06-♓-44	♄ 13-♎-55R	♆ 22-♌-56R	A 25-♋-59
☽ 05-♒-53	♀ 06-♈-05	♃ 10-♋-21	♅ 26-♈-31	♇ 20-♈-26	M 29-♓-22

Flemish painter, who gained fame for the many portraits he painted of the Flemish, Italian, and English society of his time. Also painted many religious and some mythological pictures. Son of a rich silk dealer; became an artist at 16; painter of the British court in 1632. (1599-1641)

DD: *Wynn's Astrology*, May 1944. PC speculates 12:45 PM LMT.

VELIKOVSKY, IMMANUEL June 10, 1895 Vitebsk, Russia
Writer 4:35 PM LMT 30E12 55N12

☉ 19-♊-25	☿ 12-♋-08	♂ 29-♋-58	♄ 00-♏-59R	♆ 15-♊-40	A 08-♏-20
☽ 26-♑-04	♀ 02-♌-20	♃ 11-♋-19	♅ 16-♏-39R	♇ 11-♊-27	M 25-♌-10

Physician in Palestine, 1923-38; psychotherapist and psychoanalyst in Europe, 1928-39; moved to U.S., 1929; writer and researcher. Controversial for thirty-seven years for his scientific theories. Books include *Worlds in Collision* (1950) and *Ages in Chaos* (1952).

DD: PC, speculative. Old-file has 4:00 PM LMT.

VESALIUS, ANDREAS	January 10, 1515 NS	Brussels, Belgium
Physician	5:45 AM LMT	4E22 50N52

☉ 19-♑-01	☿ 07-♒-09	♂ 14-♈-27	♄ 03-♐-29	♆ 16-♒-06	A 15-♐-10
☽ 13-♋-18	♀ 06-♓-02	♃ 06-♊-44R	♅ 23-♈-02	♇ 26-♐-58	M 16-♎-04

First great anatomist and most celebrated of all dissectionists. A master of knowledge of the body by age 20; a professor of anatomy at the University at 23. Published *De Humani Corporis Fabrica*. (1515-1564)

C: Holliday quotes Manly P. Hall in *Best of the NAJ*, 1979. Kraum in AFA, August 1961, quotes Garceus for 5:50 AM LMT, Cardan for 5:45 AM LMT.

VIDAL, GORE	October 3, 1925	West Point, N.Y.
Writer	11:00 AM EST	73E58 41N25

☉ 09-♎-55	☿ 07-♎-04	♂ 03-♎-10	♄ 12-♏-42	♆ 23-♌-59	A 08-♐-55
☽ 28-♈-40	♀ 20-♏-46	♃ 13-♑-37	♅ 22-♓-50R	♇ 14-♋-43	M 27-♍-41

Playwright, critic, novelist, essayist. Books include *Myra Breckenridge, Washington, D.C.,* and *Blood Kin*. Perceptive and inventive wit; an iconoclast in each of his professions. Unsuccessfully ran for Congress in 1960.

DD: CL quotes Drew. Old-file has 5:00 PM EST.

VILLA, PANCHO	October 4, 1877	Rio Grande, Texas
Bandit	4:19 AM LMT	98W49 26N23

☉ 11-♎-19	☿ 27-♍-57R	♂ 08-♓-31R	♄ 15-♓-08R	♆ 06-♉-49R	A 19-♍-14
☽ 07-♍-14	♀ 19-♏-47	♃ 26-♐-46	♅ 27-♌-50	♇ 25-♉-15R	M 18-♊-57

Mexican bandit chieftain, who sought to control Mexico in 1910 and again in 1914 during revolutionary upheavals. Attacked New Mexico in 1916. Reported as brutal and ambitious. Shot by enemies in an ambush, 1923.

DD: CL quotes Manly Hall for a biography that gives "sunrise," rectified by Hall. Same data in SS #936. PC gives June 5, 1878, Durango, Mexico, 9:00 AM LMT, "date verified, time speculative." Old-file has that same date, 6:00 PM LMT. *Americana* gives June 5, 1878.

VINSON, FREDERICK MOORE	January 22, 1890	Louisa, Ky
Jurist	10:50 AM CST	82W36 38N07

☉ 02-♒-41	☿ 16-♒-13R	♂ 11-♏-53	♄ 02-♍-34R	♆ 01-♊-52R	A 04-♉-40
☽ 26-♒-48	♀ 26-♑-14	♃ 22-♑-54	♅ 26-♎-41	♇ 05-♊-04R	M 20-♑-14

Law practice from 1911; member of the House of Representatives, 1923-38; associate justice, 1938-43; secretary of the treasury, 1945; chief justice of the U.S., 1946. (1890-1953)

C: Huggins in *The Astrology Magazine*, January 1970.

VISCONTI, LUCHINO	November 2, 1906	Milan, Italy
Movie director	Evening	9E10 45N27

☉ 09-♏-22	☿ 01-♐-09	♂ 02-♎-13	♄ 08-♓-23R	♆ 12-♋-34R	A 29-♉-06
☽ 26-♉-03	♀ 13-♐-50	♃ 11-♋-03R	♅ 05-♑-31	♇ 23-♊-30R	M 02-♒-56

A set designer, who made his first film, *Obsession*, in 1941; also a director of plays. One of the celebrated quartet of directors who've dominated Italian films since post-war. Of his historical and costume dramas, films include *Death in Venice, Boccaccio '70,* and *The Leopard*.

C: Penfield quotes *A Screen of Time* by Monica Stirling (1979); p. 7 states, "Milan on the evening of November 2, 1906." Ciro Discepolo gives 8:00 PM MET.

VONNEGUT, KURT   November 11, 1922   Indianapolis, Ind
Writer   8:00 AM CST   86W09 39N46

☉ 18-♏-24 ☿ 04-♏-04 ♂ 08-♒-19 ♄ 15-♎-10 ♆ 18-♌-09 A 06-♐-35
☽ 08-♌-57 ♀ 08-♐-52R ♃ 03-♏-25 ♅ 09-♓-42R ♇ 11-♋-03R M 23-♍-13

Master of science-fiction. Studied bio-chemistry for two years; anthropology for two years. In the Army, captured by Nazi, 1945. Post-war, wrote short stories for the "slicks" and sci-fi magazines. Novels include *Piano Player* (1952), *Sirens of Titan* (1959), and *Slaughterhouse Five,* (1969), made into a motion picture.

C: PC, "personal." (States from Walter Breen).

WADLOW, ROBERT   February 22, 1918   Alton, Ill
Giant   6:00 AM CST   90W10 38N53

☉ 03-♓-04 ☿ 18-♒-32 ♂ 00-♎-51R ♄ 09-♌-24R ♆ 05-♌-00R A 15-♒-22
☽ 25-♋-29 ♀ 14-♒-05R ♃ 02-♊-40 ♅ 24-♒-14 ♇ 03-♋-33R M 03-♐-26

At birth, weighed twelve pounds; was the size of 3-year-old at 6 months; grew to 8' 11", 491 pounds. Physicians said he had an overactive pituitary. On July 4, 1940, a brace chafed his left ankle; infection set in; he died July 15, 1940, at age 22.

C: Dewey quotes Garth Allen in AA, June 1973. PC gives the same data as B.C.

WAGNER, RICHARD   May 22, 1813   Leipsic, Germany
Musician   4:00 AM LMT   12E24 51N20

☉ 00-♊-35 ☿ 05-♉-35 ♂ 03-♒-54 ♄ 18-♑-55R ♆ 14-♐-34R A 28-♉-22
☽ 16-♒-05 ♀ 29-♉-42 ♃ 03-♌-41 ♅ 25-♏-45R ♇ 20-♓-26 M 27-♑-18

German composer and poet; a controversial and fascinating genius of the European artistic scene. Wrote dramatic operas with a revolutionary technique; first symphony at age 19. Tragic and sordid personal life with financial, moral, and marital difficulties. (1813-1883)

DD: Chart pictured in Adams' *One Hundred Horoscopes.* Same data in SS #939. BJA, October 1928, gives "sunrise, rectified to 4:11 AM LMT" by Bailey. Autobiography *My Life* (1911).

WALKER, JAMES   June 19, 1881   New York, N.Y.
Politician   3:30 PM LMT   73W57 40N45

☉ 28-♊-36 ☿ 23-♋-39 ♂ 28-♈-36 ♄ 08-♉-57 ♆ 15-♉-38 A 09-♏-56
☽ 10-♈-44 ♀ 15-♉-25 ♃ 15-♉-52 ♅ 10-♍-08 ♇ 28-♉-31 M 18-♌-15

Lawyer from 1912; became New York City's ninety-seventh mayor in 1925. Graft and corruption exposed in his administration; resigned on September 1, 1932. (1881-1946)

C: AA, October 1957, states, "published more than 20 years ago but unverified." Same data in SS #940. Biography *Beau James.*

WALLACE, MIKE   May 9, 1918   Brookline, Mass
TV personality   1:40 PM EST   71W07 42N20

☉ 18-♉-18 ☿ 00-♉-24R ♂ 15-♍-01 ♄ 08-♌-26 ♆ 04-♌-28 A 18-♍-48
☽ 07-♉-47 ♀ 03-♈-05 ♃ 15-♊-23 ♅ 27-♒-29 ♇ 03-♋-56 M 16-♊-47

Announcer and one-time MC of the quiz-show *Who Pays;* became known on *The Big Surprise* TV quiz show; reached fame with his *Mike Wallace Interviews.* Received the TV Emmy in 1970/71 and 1971/72 as correspondent for the *60 Minutes* series.

C: Scarsella from Baird.

WALLER, VEREL   April 6, 1911   No place given
Murderer   6:28 AM CST   97W00 35N00

☉ 15-♈-35 ☿ 01-♉-59 ♂ 17-♒-29 ♄ 06-♉-37 ♆ 18-♋-47 A 21-♈-06
☽ 19-♋-09 ♀ 16-♉-28 ♃ 12-♏-36R ♅ 29-♑-01 ♇ 26-♊-01 M 12-♑-35

Shot and killed his father, after father refused to give him $250 for treatment of the problems he had, which he thought to be sexual.

C: CL old data file.

WANAMAKER, JOHN July 11, 1838 Philadelphia, Pa
Entrepreneur 8:00 PM LMT 75W10 39N57

☉ 19-♋-11 ☿ 18-♋-01 ♂ 18-♊-07 ♄ 22-♏-21R ♆ 09-♒-34R A 29-♑-15
☽ 19-♓-11 ♀ 10-♊-34 ♃ 14-♍-49 ♅ 12-♓-13R ♇ 17-♈-53 M 21-♏-54

Merchant and philanthropist. In 1860, joined his brother-in-law in founding a clothing business in Philadelphia. This business grew into Wanamaker and Co, one of the largest department stores in the U.S. (1838-1922)

DD: PC from SS #946 (no time given). Old-file has 7:35 PM LMT.

WASHINGTON, BOOKER T. April 5, 1856 Franklin Co, Va
Educator 2:15 PM LMT 79W45 37N08

☉ 16-♈-12 ☿ 26-♓-30 ♂ 11-♎-43R ♄ 24-♊-42 ♆ 18-♓-56 A 25-♌-47
☽ 24-♈-14 ♀ 18-♓-27 ♃ 22-♓-49 ♅ 18-♉-52 ♇ 03-♉-43 M 20-♉-29

Born in slavery; became one of the great educational leaders; worked a lifetime to improve the life of the Black. Organized Tuskegee Institute, a school for Blacks in Alabama; served as its president from 1881 to 1915. (1856-1915)

DD: PC speculative. Old-file has 12:10 PM LMT.

WDOWINSKI, DR. DAVID May 26, 1896 NS Poland
Educator 9:00 AM LMT 16E00 50N00

☉ 05-♊-31 ☿ 24-♊-09 ♂ 03-♈-28 ♄ 14-♏-19R ♆ 17-♊-17 A 09-♌-33
☽ 27-♏-35 ♀ 23-♉-30 ♃ 04-♌-32 ♅ 21-♏-56R ♇ 12-♊-04 M 20-♈-59

Polish professor of psychology in the U.S. President of the Zionist-Revisionist organization of Poland, and hero of the revolt and last stand battle of the Warsaw Ghetto. Imprisoned in a Nazi concentration camp, April 19, 1943; sentenced to death; liberated 1945.

C: Skeetz quotes Lilyan Theodorff in AA, June 1949, "approximate time."

WEBB, BEATRICE January 22, 1858 Gloucester, England
Sociologist 10:20 AM LMT 2W15 51N52

☉ 02-♒-11 ☿ 17-♑-17R ♂ 07-♏-20 ♄ 24-♋-19R ♆ 20-♓-39 A 15-♈-36
☽ 28-♈-43 ♀ 23-♑-12 ♃ 06-♉-49 ♅ 25-♉-16R ♇ 04-♉-38 M 05-♑-57

English writer on economics and sociology. Worked as an associate of her father, a railway and industrial magnate; married in 1892. With her husband, Sidney Webb, wrote several masterly studies of economic conditions. (1858-1943)

DD: PC speculative. Old-file has 10:45 AM LMT.

WEBB, JACK April 2, 1920 Santa Monica, Ca
Actor 9:30 PM PST 118W29 34N01

☉ 13-♈-10 ☿ 21-♓-39 ♂ 06-♏-48R ♄ 05-♍-47R ♆ 08-♌-49R A 24-♏-18
☽ 10-♎-30 ♀ 19-♓-08 ♃ 08-♌-06R ♅ 03-♓-55 ♇ 05-♋-43 M 03-♍-20

On screen from 1948 in films that include *Sunset Boulevard*, *Dragnet*, and *Pete Kelly Blues*. Last film in 1961, *The Last Time I Saw Archie*, which he also directed and produced. Became primarily a producer of TV shows, including *Emergency!*

DD: PC, "personal." Old-file has 9:40 PM PST.

WERFEL, FRANZ September 10, 1890 Prague, Czechoslovakia
Writer 11:45 PM LMT 14E26 40N05

☉ 18-♍-08 ☿ 13-♎-39 ♂ 22-♐-10 ♄ 08-♍-42 ♆ 06-♊-49R A 06-♋-47
☽ 10-♌-59 ♀ 04-♏-06 ♃ 02-♒-50R ♅ 24-♎-43 ♇ 07-♊-53R M 14-♓-58

Austrian novelist, playwright, and poet; early works criticized the militaristic philosophy of the 1900s. Moved to the U.S. in 1940. Works include *The Pure in Heart* (1931) and *The Song of Bernadette* (1942). (1890-1945)

C: Reynolds quotes Ebertin.

WHISTLER, JAMES McNEILL July 10, 1934 Lowell, Mass
Artist 11:45 PM LMT 71W19 42N38

☉ 18-♋-11	☿ 18-♋-41R	♂ 26-♊-49	♄ 27-♒-21R	♆ 10-♍-16	A 25-♈-53
☽ 12-♋-28	♀ 15-♊-03	♃ 14-♎-38	♅ 01-♉-10	♇ 24-♋-08	M 13-♑-29

Often considered the most original American artist of the 1800s; best known for an oil painting of his mother. A master colorist, known for his etchings, pastels, and watercolors; almost 400 etchings and 150 lithographs. (1834-1903)

DD: PC, "recorded as just before midnight." Old-file has 11:40 PM.

WHITE, STANFORD November 9, 1853 New York, N.Y.
Architect 4:21 PM LMT 73W57 40N45

☉ 17-♏-26	☿ 09-♐-03	♂ 26-♌-40	♄ 29-♉-12R	♆ 10-♓-59R	A 09-♉-42
☽ 10-♓-35	♀ 01-♑-11	♃ 25-♐-17	♅ 10-♉-16R	♇ 01-♉-27R	M 22-♑-24

Millionaire. Kind and considerate with many friends; a fatherly manner and a penchant for young girls; seduced and kept the teenage Evelyn Nesbitt with erotic sex games. She later married Harry Thaw, who shot and killed White on June 25, 1906.

DD: CL from SS #964 (no time given). PC quotes SS for 4:00 PM. Adams pictures a chart for 4:15 PM LMT. Dewey states the data to be speculative.
The data for Evelyn Nesbitt are given in *Profiles of Women*.

WHITE, T.H. May 29, 1906 Bombay, India
Writer 3:30 PM JST 72E50 19N57

☉ 07-♊-06	☿ 24-♉-52	♂ 21-♊-02	♄ 14-♓-23	♆ 08-♋-53	A 17-♎-42
☽ 14-♌-57	♀ 03-♋-14	♃ 15-♊-59	♅ 07-♑-40R	♇ 21-♊-51	M 17-♋-24

English author, best known for his multi-volumed chronicles of King Arthur and his court, from *The Sword in the Stone* (1938) to *The Once and Future King* (1958). Taught at Cambridge until 1936. (1906-1964)

DD: PC speculative. Old-file has 10:00 AM LMT.

WHITE, WILLIAM ALLEN February 10, 1868 Emporia, Ks
Publisher 9:30 AM LMT 96W11 38N25

☉ 21-♒-15	☿ 04-♓-24	♂ 11-♒-50	♄ 04-♐-47	♆ 12-♈-56	A 20-♈-29
☽ 22-♍-34	♀ 24-♓-05	♃ 13-♓-27	♅ 09-♋-19R	♇ 14-♉-09	M 11-♑-31

World famous publisher and editor of the *Emporia Gazette* in Kansas; a novelist and biographer; awarded the Pulitzer prize for the best editorial, 1922. (1868-1944)

DD: PC, "from his autobiography." Old-file has 10:25 AM LMT. Drew pictures a chart for 1:25 PM LMT.

WHITNEY, JOHN August 17, 1904 Ellsworth, Maine
Heir 3:00 AM EST 68W25 44N33

☉ 23-♌-57	☿ 21-♍-09	♂ 01-♌-25	♄ 17-♒-10R	♆ 07-♋-22	A 04-♌-30
☽ 13-♏-13	♀ 05-♍-01	♃ 00-♉-12	♅ 26-♐-06R	♇ 21-♊-30	M 18-♈-16

Member of a prominent social family; inherited wealth. Spectacular polo player; interested in sports and gambling. Among his theatrical investments, co-producer and owner of *Gone with the Wind*.

C: *Wynn's Astrology*, March 1943.

WIENER, NORBERT November 26, 1894 Odessa, Mo
Prodigy 1:55 PM CST 93W57 39N00

☉ 04-♐-36   ☿ 14-♏-37   ♂ 21-♈-32   ♄ 02-♏-18   ♆ 14-♊-40R   A 00-♈-53
☽ 28-♏-15   ♀ 03-♐-40   ♃ 04-♋-32R   ♅ 16-♏-49   ♇ 10-♊-54R   M 00-♑-29

Son of a Harvard professor; knew his alphabet at 18 months; read at age 3. By 8, reading Darwin and Huxley; left high school in 1906 for college to study philosophy. Ready to go to Harvard at age 10; barred because of his age. Fond of sports; good swimmer.

C: M.A., July 1907, quotes Sarastro from *Occult Review*, rectified from a given time of 1:30 to 2:30 PM.

WILLARD, FRANCES September 28, 1839 Churchville, N.Y.
Social reformer 12:00 Noon LMT 77W53 43N06

☉ 04-♎-52   ☿ 21-♍-34   ♂ 27-♏-12   ♄ 05-♐-45   ♆ 10-♒-00R   A 15-♐-07
☽ 19-♊-26   ♀ 16-♎-24R   ♃ 23-♎-49   ♅ 13-♓-37R   ♇ 18-♈-08R   M 07-♎-24

American educator, who organized the temperance movement on the plan by which it attained national prohibition. President of the Woman's Christian Temperance Union from 1879 until her death in 1898.

DD: PC from SS #971 (no time given). Old-file has 11:35 AM LMT.

WILLIAMS, BEN AMES March 7, 1889 Macon, Miss
Writer 11:30 AM CST 88W34 33N07

☉ 17-♓-22   ☿ 20-♒-39   ♂ 14-♈-00   ♄ 14-♌-39R   ♆ 29-♉-44   A 26-♊-17
☽ 25-♉-26   ♀ 02-♉-42   ♃ 04-♑-51   ♅ 21-♎-16R   ♇ 04-♊-03   M 07-♓-53

Prolific writer of fiction; wrote and sold over 380 stories from 1916. His first book, *All the Brothers Were Violent*. Fifteen to twenty of his stories made into movies, including *Leave Her to Heaven* and *The Strange Woman*.

C: Ben Allen Fields in AA, March 1947; same data in SS #974.

WILLIAMS, TED August 30, 1918 San Diego, Ca
Baseball player 11:20 AM PDT 117W09 32N43

☉ 06-♍-33   ☿ 10-♍-57R   ♂ 08-♏-39   ♄ 20-♌-31   ♆ 07-♌-56   A 08-♏-50
☽ 00-♋-49   ♀ 14-♌-42   ♃ 09-♋-43   ♅ 25-♒-18R   ♇ 06-♋-23   M 13-♌-31

Began pro ball in 1937; career interrupted by five years combat as a Marine pilot. Voted the Most Valuable Player with the Boston Red Sox, 1946 and 1949. Manager of the Year of the Washington Senators, 1969; later became a fishing and game expert with Sears Roebuck.

C: CL from *Bulletin of Astro Science*, July 1958.

WINDELL, D.S. February 25, 1886 Zutphen, Holland
Swindler 12:00 Noon AMSTERDAM 6E12 52N07

☉ 06-♓-50   ☿ 07-♓-33   ♂ 19-♍-20R   ♄ 01-♋-28R   ♆ 22-♉-56   A 08-♋-00
☽ 04-♐-08   ♀ 26-♒-10R   ♃ 04-♎-01R   ♅ 06-♎-52R   ♇ 01-♊-10   M 03-♓-19

Successfully pulled off the biggest con stunt in banking history — a one-man coup of swindling several millions of pounds from several London banks in a single day. On April 22, 1909, cooly introduced himself to bank officers, negotiated his scheme, and fled.

C: *Astrological Bulletina*, 1951 Annual.

WINNER, N.G. July 16, 1869 Monticello, Iowa
Dwarf 8:30 PM LMT 91W02 42N15

☉ 24-♋-30   ☿ 04-♋-14   ♂ 28-♍-49   ♄ 11-♐-10R   ♆ 19-♈-34   A 14-♒-20
☽ 05-♏-15   ♀ 13-♌-07   ♃ 16-♉-30   ♅ 18-♋-05   ♇ 17-♉-48   M 04-♐-26

Traveled with the Ringling Brothers Circus as a sideshow attraction — 36" tall, 42 pounds. Brilliant conversationalist; first class entertainer. On February 3, 1896, married a woman eighteen years old — 40" tall, 65 pounds.

C: M.A., May 1896.

WOLF, HUGO　　　　March 13, 1860　　　　Blovenjgradec, Yugoslavia
Musician　　　　　　　3:00 AM LMT　　　　　15E05　46N30

☉ 22-♓-45　　☿ 10-♈-33　　♂ 24-♐-27　　♄ 20-♌-25R　　♆ 26-♓-41　　A 08-♑-21
☽ 07-♐-17　　♀ 01-♉-19　　♃ 15-♋-13　　♅ 04-♊-08　　♇ 07-♉-01　　M 08-♏-18

Austrian composer of approximately three hundred solo songs with piano accompaniment. Unhappy, irrascible, psychotic, and finally deranged: his mental instability brought on by venereal disease. Fame spread after 1889; but went into a sanitorium, September 20, 1897. (1860-1903)

DD: PC speculative. Old-file has 2:50 AM LMT.

WOLFE, THOMAS　　　October 3, 1900　　　　Asheville, N.D.
Writer　　　　　　　　11:30 AM EST　　　　　82W33　35N36

☉ 10-♎-00　　☿ 24-♎-25　　♂ 04-♌-03　　♄ 29-♐-12　　♆ 29-♊-16R　　A 11-♐-27
☽ 02-♒-34　　♀ 24-♌-43　　♃ 07-♐-06　　♅ 09-♐-22　　♇ 17-♊-39R　　M 26-♍-35

American novelist, who wrote *Look Homeward, Angel* (1929), *The Web and the Rock* (1939), and *You Can't Go Home Again* (1940). Though criticized for lack of discipline, eloquent and forceful in powerful prose. Taught at N.Y.U., 1924-30. When he caught pneumonia in 1938, died after surgery for brain infection.

C: PC quotes *Thomas Wolfe and his Family* by Mabel Wheaton as stating, "He was born after we left for school in the morning." That biography states on p. 46, "When we came home at lunch time Papa told us we had a brother."

WOLSELEY, GARNET J.　June 4, 1833　　　　Dublin, Ireland
Army commander　　　 11:55 PM LMT　　　　6W15　53N20

☉ 14-♊-03　　☿ 29-♉-25　　♂ 03-♌-30　　♄ 21-♍-22　　♆ 29-♑-06R　　A 17-♒-25
☽ 13-♑-30　　♀ 18-♉-05R　　♃ 26-♈-20　　♅ 22-♒-32R　　♇ 12-♈-29　　M 13-♐-21

Joined the army at 19; a gallant military career. Fought in the Burmese War at 20; severly wounded. Also fought in the Crimean War, the Indian Mutiny in 1857, and in China. Lost his right eye in battle. Chief of the Army, 1859-99. (1833-1913)

C: AFA, November 1942.

WONG, ANNA MAY　　January 13, 1905　　San Francisco, Ca
Actress　　　　　　　 8:56 AM PST　　　　　122W26　37N47

☉ 22-♑-53　　☿ 01-♑-14　　♂ 29-♎-57　　♄ 19-♒-55　　♆ 06-♋-20R　　A 19-♒-45
☽ 21-♈-24　　♀ 07-♓-05　　♃ 21-♈-39　　♅ 01-♑-26　　♇ 20-♊-08R　　M 05-♐-57

First Chinese actress to become a major box-office star in many silent films; sensational in Fairbank's *The Thief of Bagdad*. Films and stage abroad with a long string of hits in the 30s that gradually dwindled. Off screen a proud, aloof woman who never married.

C: CL quotes AFA, "Chart rectified from data given by her."

WOOODHULL, VICTORIA　September 23, 1838　　Homer, Ohio
Adventuress　　　　　　 5:45 AM LMT　　　　　82W31　40N15

☉ 29-♍-58　　☿ 22-♍-05R　　♂ 05-♌-45　　♄ 24-♏-47　　♆ 07-♒-49R　　A 28-♍-30
☽ 20-♏-07　　♀ 08-♍-29　　♃ 29-♍-21　　♅ 09-♓-42R　　♇ 17-♈-11R　　M 28-♊-16

Set up in a brokerage business by Cornelius Vanderbilt; with her sister made $700,000 in three years. They began a feminist periodical; she was a presidential candidate in 1872. Later moved to England to marry well. Continued writing and lecturing until the end of her 89 years.

DD: M.A., September 1921, "cast by Leo years ago." PC speculates 7:00 PM LMT. Old-file has 6:55 PM LMT.

WOOLF, VIRGINIA
Writer

January 25, 1882
8:45 PM GMT

London, England
0W06 51N31

☉ 05-♒-51	☿ 18-♒-40	♂ 27-♊-23R	♄ 05-♉-53	♆ 13-♉-46	A 20-♍-16
☽ 00-♉-09	♀ 29-♑-32	♃ 16-♉-37	♅ 18-♍-05R	♇ 27-♉-23R	M 17-♊-18

British novelist and essayist, with a superb use of language. In 1912 married Leonard Woolf, with whom she founded the Hogarth Press. Drowned herself in 1941, fearing the recurrence of a mental breakdown.

DD: PC speculative. Old-file has 3:30 AM GMT.

WRIGHT, FRANK LLOYD
Architect

June 8, 1867
8:00 PM LMT

Richland Center, Wis
90W23 43N21

☉ 17-♊-44	☿ 27-♊-43	♂ 22-♌-34	♄ 18-♏-50R	♆ 14-♈-39	A 23-♐-34
☽ 15-♍-23	♀ 19-♉-05	♃ 07-♓-01	♅ 07-♋-17	♇ 15-♉-21	M 18-♎-24

Innovative architect in office buildings and private dwellings; in 1900, started the "prairie style" rambling type house; in 1915 built the great Imperial Hotel of Tokyo. Author of *Experimenting with Human Lines* (1923) and *Modern Architecture* (1931). (1867-1959)

DD: PC, "per documents in Columbia University. Most other reference books give 1869 in error." Dewey adds: "The papers at Columbia include his mother's diary with the date. He himself said he was born in the evening in the middle of a storm." CL quotes Zeigler at 1869, 6:05 AM LMT. *World Book* and *Americana* give 1869.

WRIGHT, ORVILLE
Aviation pioneer

August 19, 1871
5:00 PM LMT

Dayton, Ohio
84W12 39N45

☉ 26-♌-27	☿ 23-♍-42	♂ 04-♏-32	♄ 03-♑-33R	♆ 23-♈-57R	A 21-♑-45
☽ 10-♎-56	♀ 06-♎-13	♃ 19-♋-20	♅ 28-♋-42	♇ 19-♉-52R	M 15-♏-18

With his brother Wilbur, invented and built the first successful airplane. On the toss of a coin, he piloted the first flight on December 17, 1903, of 120 feet in the air for twelve seconds. (1871-1948)

C: PC speculative. Old-file same data.

WRIGHT, WILBUR
Aviation pioneer

April 16, 1867
1:20 PM LMT

Millville, Ind
85W26 39N56

☉ 26-♈-19	☿ 00-♈-34	♂ 25-♋-52	♄ 22-♏-36R	♆ 13-♈-02	A 23-♌-48
☽ 00-♎-51	♀ 15-♓-55	♃ 00-♓-21	♅ 04-♋-50	♇ 14-♉-11	M 16-♉-55

With his brother Orville, invented and built the first successful airplane. In 1896 the men became interested in flight and began experiments in 1900. (1867-1912)

DD: PC speculative. Old-file has 12:55 PM LMT.

YOUNG, BRIGHAM
Mormon leader

June 1, 1801
11:00 AM LMT

Whitingham, Vt
72W52 42N47

☉ 10-♊-35	☿ 07-♊-56	♂ 28-♋-16	♄ 18-♌-45	♆ 17-♏-26R	A 02-♍-36
☽ 14-♒-58	♀ 01-♊-11R	♃ 01-♌-33	♅ 27-♍-47R	♇ 05-♓-42	M 26-♉-57

Joined the church in 1832; became an Apostle in 1835 and a missionary. When Joseph Smith was murdered, took charge and led his followers to Utah as settlers; became the second president. Known to have seventeen wives; fifty-six children. (1801-1877)

C: Chart pictured in Adams' *One Hundred Horoscopes*. Same data in NN #232 as speculative, founded on the "noon-point method," checked by the pre-natal epoch. Drew gives approximately 4:30 AM LMT.

YOUNG, ROBERT R.
Entrepreneur

February 14, 1897
4:53 PM CST

Canadian, Texas
100W23 35N55

☉ 26-♒-34	☿ 00-♒-14	♂ 16-♊-20	♄ 00-♐-19	♆ 17-♊-32R	A 09-♌-13
☽ 25-♋-19	♀ 13-♈-11	♃ 06-♍-24R	♅ 28-♏-55	♇ 11-♊-45R	M 00-♉-11

Self-made railroad baron; called "the boy-wonder of Wall Street"; made millions by selling short when he predicted the crash of '29. Assistant treasurer of G.M. in 1928; bought and sold stock to a fortune by 1933; lost heavily in 1938; recouped by 1954. Shot himself to death on January 25, 1958.

C: CL from Edwin Archer; speculative time in AA, 1958.

YEVTUSHENKO, YEVGENY July 18, 1933 Zima Junction, Russia
Writer 9:30 PM Zone #6 102E02 53N58

| ☉ 25-♋-31 | ☿ 13-♌-11R | ♂ 06-♎-30 | ♄ 14-♏-22R | ♆ 08-♍-20 | A 01-♈-24 |
| ☽ 11-♊-15 | ♀ 19-♌-00 | ♃ 19-♍-37 | ♅ 27-♈-19 | ♇ 23-♋-04 | M 00-♑-29 |

The most popular of contemporary Russian poets; the leading spokesman for the post-Stalin youth. Fully allegiant to national communism but undaunted in social criticism.

DD: PC speculative. Old-file has 10:00 PM.

ZEPPELIN, FERDINAND VON July 8, 1838 Constance, Switzerland
Engineer 10:30 AM LMT 9E20 47N38

| ☉ 15-♋-43 | ☿ 10-♋-12 | ♂ 15-♊-37 | ♄ 22-♏-27R | ♆ 09-♒-39R | A 25-♍-08 |
| ☽ 26-♑-35 | ♀ 06-♊-24 | ♃ 14-♍-14 | ♅ 12-♓-17R | ♇ 17-♈-52 | M 23-♊-57 |

Soldier from 1863-91. In 1900, constructed the first airship of a rigid type known as "Zeppelin." It crashed in landing, but he continued successfully in building and flying airships for the rest of his life. The most famous of derigible inventors. (1838-1917)

C: CL from a German astrological periodical.

ZIEGFELD, FLORENZ March 21, 1869 Chicago, Ill
Showman 10:20 AM LMT 87W39 41N52

| ☉ 01-♈-06 | ☿ 03-♓-40 | ♂ 15-♌-25R | ♄ 17-♐-09 | ♆ 16-♈-24 | A 27-♊-18 |
| ☽ 06-♋-26 | ♀ 18-♓-32 | ♃ 20-♈-55 | ♅ 13-♋-19 | ♇ 15-♉-32 | M 02-♓-13 |

With an excellent musical education from childhood, became a theatrical producer who introduced a new type of production, the Follies Revue in 1907, which became known as the Ziegfeld Follies. (1869-1932)

DD: Pat Crosley pictures a chart in AFA, November 1977, with MC 2 Pisces, Ascendant 16 Gemini. PC quotes the same source for 8:00 PM LMT, adding, "I personally prefer 8:00 AM." Old-file has 1:20 PM.

FOOTNOTES

[1] ADENAUR, KONRAD: Kimmel in AFA, May 1972, gives 10:02 AM.

[2] ALBERT, PRINCE: The profile and chart of Queen Victoria are given in *Profiles of Women*.

[3] ALBERT VICTOR: SS #16 gives 8:58 PM. Holliday quotes the biography *Clarence* for "nine o'clock," not specified AM or PM.

[4] ALDA, ALAN: Dewey states that MacKenzie quoted him in AA: "I think it was 5:06 AM. On the other hand, I think it was 6:05 AM. Seriously, I think it was 6:05 AM." However, Sedgewich writes, "The information came from a high school friend of his whose wife is an astrologer, and I'm sure she asked for the data directly as they have been together on numerous occasions."

[5] ALEXIS, CZARAVICH: Dewey quotes *Nicholas and Alexandra* by R. Massie, p. 112 for 1:00 PM LMT. Lyndoe in AA, July 1978, states that the chart was a copy of the one given to the Czarina at the time of her son's birth. Bailey in BJA, August 1915, gives 12:30 PM.

[6] ALLMAN, GREGG: The profile and chart of Cher Bono Allman are given in *Profiles of Women*.

[7] ALPERT, RICHARD: PC quotes M. Mayer for 9:20 AM EST.

[8] ANDREW, PRINCE: CL gives 3:30 PM GMT from newspaper on date.

[9] ASTAIRE, FRED: PC quotes Jansky for 9:30 PM CST.

[10] AUGUSTUS CAESAR: James Holden in AFA, September 1978, writes "No one knows for sure whether the date is September 21 or 22."

Gleadow in *Origin of the Zodiac* (1968) gives September 22, 63 B.C. Fagan writes: "According to the historian Suetonius, in his *Lives of a Dozen Caesars*, the future emperor was born just before sunrise on September 23, 63 B.C. OS at Rome. His coins show a sign of Capricorn, his Moon sign. As the Moon was in Capricorn on September 21 and 22, and went into Aquarius by sunrise of the 23rd, the date was probably the 22nd." LMR notes that in Fagan's calculations, the Gregorian proleptic calendar was not taken into consideration. The date conversion counts the year zero as one year; therefore the date 63 B.C. OS converts to 62 B.C. NS. Holden makes this correction; however, he states, "The Republican calendar was one day ahead of the Julian." In the *Explanatory Supplement to the Astronomical Ephemeris* (1961), the date conversion of March 2, 100 B.C., to February 29, 100 A.D. is minus two days. The proper conversion of September 23, 63 B.C., is therefore September 21, 62 B.C. NS, when the Moon is indeed in Capricorn. Since sunrise is 5:44 AM LMT, the quoted time of "just before sunrise" may be calculated at 5:35 AM LMT, give or take five minutes.

PC quotes *The Twelve Caesars* by Suetonius for September 22, 63 B.C. OS.

[11] BALLARD, GUY: The profile and chart of Edna Ballard, Guy's wife and Donald's mother, are given in *Profiles of Women*.

[12] BERLIOZ, HECTOR: Kraum in NAJ, April 1935, gives 5:23 PM LMT.

[13] BISMARCH, OTTO VON: Reynolds quotes Ebertin for 12:26 PM LMT. SS #99 gives 1:00 PM. PC states, "recorded between 1:00 to 2:00 PM."

[14] BLAKE, WILLIAM: PC quotes NN and Pagan for 7:15

[15] BOK, BART: PC gives 3:40 PM, "personal."

[16] BRADY, IAN: PC gives 12:40 PM GMT as B.C.

[17] BRAHE, TYCHO: *Constellations* 1977 quoted TYCHO BRAHE for 3:00 PM LAT. LMR finds no evidence of that time, since the biography, first published by Adam and Charles Black in 1890, states in a footnote on p. 12, "In several places in his writings Tycho alludes to the 13th of December as his birthday, but this is astronomically speaking, counting the days from noon, as he was born between nine and ten o'clock in the morning of the 14th." The time given of 9:30 AM is correct by this record, within a half hour one way or the other. Though not precise, the chart is worth including.

Eshelman has December 13, 1546 OS, 22:47 after Noon = December 14, 1546 NS, 10:47 AM, "according to the Sloane Ms 1638, now in the British Museum."

[18] BREMER, ARTHUR: Jansky H/N gives August 21, 1950 from AA.

[19] BROWN, EDMUND, JR.: The profile and chart of Linda Ronstadt are given in *Profiles of Women*.

[20] BRYAN, WILLIAM JENNINGS: The attending physician, Dr. Hill, stated the time as "a little after nine in the morning, about 9:15." SS#148 gives 9:04 AM. CL old file and Adams give 10:00 AM LMT.

[21] BURTON, SIR RICHARD: PC gives Torquay, England. Hertford verified in *World Book*.

[22] BURTON, ROBERT: February 8, 1576, OS. The year changes as New Year began March 1577.

[23] BYRD, RICHARD: SS#158 gives Noon.

[24] BYRON, LORD: Hypersentience Bulletin, June 1977, states "sundown." Huggins in *The Astrologers Magazine*, January 1970, gives 2:30 PM LMT. WEMYSS F/N #752 states that Varley gave 1:18 AM.

[25] CARREL, DR. ALEXIS: SS #174 gives 11:30 PM.

[26] CARSON, JOHNNY: PC gives 6:15 AM "personal." Gallo *Celebrity Horoscopes* gives 8:00 AM. CL quotes Lynne Palmer at 11:47 PM "from his mother." Elvins in AA, May 1967, rectifies to 7:19 AM "from a given time of 6:00 AM."

[27] CELLINI, BENVENUTO: PC gives 9:00 PM LMT, "from his autobiography which states he was born 4-5 hours into the night. As the Florentines counted from sunset, this would be 4-5 hours from sunset." Harmer in AQ, Fall 1957, gives 4:30 AM LMT.

[28] CHAMBERLAIN, RICHARD: Holliday has 6:37 PM from CL.

[29] CHEIRO: PC quotes NN at 11:30 AM LMT. Alan Leo in M.A., July 1928, states, "NN is in error, Cheiro himself corrected the data to that which Kraum quotes."

[30] CHURCHILL, SIR WINSTON: Prior data gave so many varied times that LMR kept no record until this recorded data was given. Davis rectifies the data to 1:19 AM LMT.

[31] CLIBURN, VAN: Gallo rectifies the data to 11:20 AM CST with information from his mother.

[32] COCTEAU, JEAN: Though the Gauquelin data comes from birth records, there is still doubt, since the autobiography states on p. 6, "3:50 AM," quoted accurately by PC.

[33] COOGAN, JACKIE: SS #220 gives 2:45 PM. Kraum in NAJ gives 2:00 PM.

[34] COSIMI, AGNOLO DI: The biography states, "born twelve hours after sunset of November 16, 1503 OS."

[35] CRANE, BOB: PC quotes CL at 4:00 AM EST.

[36] CUMMINGS, ROBERT: A client of Righter, as stated by him to LMR in 1967. PC gives 8:00 PM, "personal."

[37] DALADIER, EDOUARD: BJA, December 1938, gives 10:45 AM from *Raphael's Ephemeris* (1939). Same data in SS #242.

[38] D'ANNUNZIO, GABRIELE: WEMYSS F/N #187 gives 8:49 AM LMT, "according to Demain 1934."

[39] DA VINCI, LEONARDO: The biography quotes a diary: "A grandson of mine was born on April 15, Saturday, at 3:00 o'clock at night." Florentine days at that time were figured from sunset to sunset. Since the sunset time was 6:40 PM LMT, according to modern calculations the birth took place at 9:40 PM LMT of April 14, 1452 OS.

[40] DEAN, JAMES: PC gives 9:00 PM "from his father."

[41] DILLINGER, JOHN: A memo in George's personal notebook stated the data, "on a farm near Mooresville, Ind., data obtained from his father by V.D. Mansfield." In the biography *Dillinger, Dead or Alive?* by Jay Nash and Ron Offen, there is a newspaper ad quoted from June 22, 1934, which reads, "Birthday greetings to my brother, John Dillinger, on his 31st birthday." PC quotes *The Short and Violent Life* by Robert Cromie (1962) for "near midnight."

[42] DOOLEY, DR. TOM: McEvers quotes AFA for 2:30 AM CST, "from his mother."

[43] DOUGLAS, LORD ALFRED: PC gives 7:30 PM, "recorded." Old-file has 1:15 PM.

[44] EASTWOOD, CLINT: PC gives 6:30 PM PST as B.C. Old-file has 6:45 PM.

[45] EICHMANN, ADOLPH: Lyndoe in AA, January 1963, gives 8:17 AM as "the latest chart to come out of Germany."

[46] FERBER, EDNA: The publicly given date was 1887, as presented in *Information Please Almanac, Index to Women,* and Library of Congress. The autobiographies, *A Peculiar Treasure* (1939) and *A Kind of Magic* (1963), give no data.

[47] FERMI, ENRICO: McEvers quotes Jansky at 9:00 PM as B.C.

[48] FISHER, BOBBY: PC adds: "There is some question of whether the time was given in CST or CWT. Personally I prefer CST." *American Atlas* gives CWT.

[49] FITZGERALD, F. SCOTT: The profile and chart of Zelda Fitzgerald are given in *Profiles of Women.*

[50] FLAUBERT, GUSTAVE: PC quotes Guaquelin for December 12, 1821. Guaquelin #318 Vol 6 gives December 13, 1821. December 12 was given by Lyndoe in AA, with 9:15 AM LMT.

[51] FONDA, PETER: Since the year was questioned, the data was double-checked and validated by Tebbs in January 1979. The chart and profile of his sister Jane are given in *Profiles of Women.*

[52] FOSTER, STEPHEN: The place of birth is open to question, since *World Book* states, "on a family farm near Lawrenceville, Pa." Old-file gives a time of 12:50 PM.

[53] FRANCO, FRANCISCO: CL gives 4:30 AM Madrid time from AQ, Spring 1947; same data in SS #352. PC quotes SS for 4:00 AM, says 00:30 AM LMT "registered."

[54] FRAZIER, JOE: *Current Biography* gives EST. EWT taken from *American Atlas.*

[55] FREUD, SIGMUND: Same data on p. 1 of *The Life and Works of Sigmund Freud* by Ernest Jones (1953). Bruno Huber, "from research in Europe," gives 9:17 AM LMT. SS #359 gives 9:00 AM.

[56] GABOR, ZSA ZSA: For years the date has been concealed, usually given as 1923. For the time, March states: "Her mother was not that precise, she actually said the time of birth was 'dinnertime.' I would rectify the chart to Libra rising."

57 GACEY, JOHN W: The chart for CST is more graphic to progressed analysis. Since Illinois presents a time-zone problem, the CST is quite possible.

58 GAUGUIN, PAUL: PC quotes Gauquelin for June 7, 1848; this date is given in *Britannica*.

59 GELLER, URI: PC gives; 00:01 AM, "personal."

60 GLENN, JOHN: CSH gives CDT, as does the Research Dept. of AA, August 1972. *American Atlas* gives EDT. The location is apparently at a volatile border. PC quotes "his mother" at 4:30 PM EST.

61 GODFREY, ARTHUR: Holliday has Basgrouch Heights, N.J., 1:59 AM EST. CL gives August 30, 1903, 11:54 AM EST from AFA, May 1959. PC gives August 31, 1903, 2:30 AM, "personal," and quotes AFA for 11:45 AM.

62 GOEBBELS, PAUL JOSEPH: PC says 11:30 PM is a misprint, quotes Drew and NN for 10:30 PM.

63 GOERING, HERMANN: SS #399 gives 3:13 AM.

64 GORDON, CHARLES: SS #398 gives 9:30 AM.

65 GOUNOD, CHARLES: *Constellations*, 1977, Lockhart quotes his autobiography, published by Heinmann (1896) for 12:30 PM LMT. Although birth record is a preferred source, this data may be given serious consideration.

66 HAUPTMAN, BRUNO: There was prior confusion on the data, since the German police record gives November 26, 1897, and his driver's license reads a different date. CL quotes news clippings for 00:45 AM; SS #438 gives 1:10 PM. Davis rectifies the time of 1:00 PM from his mother, to 12:14 PM MET, using Koch tables.

67 HILTON, JAMES: PC states 2:30 AM, "recorded."

68 HOFFA, JAMES: Scarsella quotes Ziegler at 4:47 AM CST. Old-file has 6:35 AM CST.

69 HOFFMAN, DUSTIN: Jansky quotes Jason Goff for 5:25 PM PST from an article in *Kosmos*.

70 HUBBARD, ELBERT: SS #483 gives 1:03 PM. Old-file has 1:40 PM.

71 HUGO, VICTOR: Same data in SS #487. BAJ, June 1927, gives 10:30 AM.

72 HUNTER, BEN: Blanca Holmes in AA, October 1960, gives 11:46 PM PST, "from him." Because of her proclivity to rectify (as she herself has stated), the time from Omarr takes precedence.

73 JAGGER, MICK: PC gives 9:45 PM DBST, "personal."

74 JAPANESE EMPEROR, MUTSOHITO: Alan Leo in M.A., July 1910, gives "estimated 5:46 AM."

75 JOHN, ELTON: PC gives 4:00 PM BST, "personal."

76 KANT, IMMANUEL: *Chronical Nativities* gives April 22 as OS with May 3 NS. Since all of Germany was on the Gregorian calendar by 1700 that information is not applicable. However NN #972 prints the data for May 3, 1724.

77 KARAJAN, HERBERT VON: PC gives 10:00 PM, "recorded."

78 KEROUAC, JACK: PC quotes the biography for 5:10 PM. LMR verifies 5:00 PM.

79 KISSINGER, HENRY: Since the year was questioned, LMR verified the data with Kissinger's cousin, Margot Seitelman, whose profile and chart are given in *Profiles of Women*.

80 KNIEVEL, EVEL: Jansky H/N states 10:30 AM as B.C.

[81] KRAFFT, KARL ERNST: PC quotes *Unania's Children* by Ellic Howe for 12:50 PM.

[82] LAING, R.D.: PC gives 5:15 PM GMT, "personal."

[83] LAUDER, HARRY: Same data in SS #551. M.A., August 1909, quotes *Strand* magazine for 4:30 AM, rectified by Alan Leo to 3:18 AM. BJA, March 1931, Bailey states, "Time given as 2:30 and 2:45 AM, rectified to 2:29 AM."

[84] LEIGH, VIVIAN: Sunset time by courtesy of Los Angeles Library Science Department. PC gives sunset as 5:30 PM IST, adds that SS gives 3:00 AM. (SS #563, no time given.)

[85] LENIER, JULES: The profile and chart of his magician wife, Minnette, are given in *Profiles of Women*.

[86] LENNON, JOHN: *The Beatles* by H. Davis gives 7:00 AM BST. The profile and chart of his wife, Yoko Ono, are given in *Profiles of Women*.

[87] LIBERACE: David Hamblin in NAJ, Winter 1976, quotes *Astrology*, September 1960, at 7:25 AM.

[88] LINCOLN, ABRAHAM: *Horoscopes of U.S. Presidents* by D.C. Doane gives 2:10 AM LMT. WEMYSS F/N gives "between 7:00 and 11:00 AM."

[89] LODGE, HENRY CABOT: AQ, December 1961, quotes AA July 1961 for 4:00 AM.

[90] LUGOSI, BELA: Same data in SS #605. PC quotes SS for 1885. CL quotes Edward Doane for 1888. *Famous People* and *Notables in the American Theater* both give October 20, 1884.

[91] LUTHER, MARTIN: The letter states: "The three different horoscopes of Luther in 1001 NN are incorrect. October 22, 1483 is wrong. Tycho Brahe declared that Luther's mother recalled the hour and day but not the year. She stated that she was brought to bed on November 10th at 11:00 PM, Eisleben; rectified to 10:12 PM. The date is November 10, 1483 OS = November 19, 1483 NS." The editor confirms the date from *Baker's Biographical Dictionary*.

[92] LYNDE, PAUL: MacKenzie in AA, January 1975, gives 8:15 AM, "from him." Since he was a client of Gallo's, that quote is given as the preferred time.

[93] MACHIAVELLI, NICOLO: Blackwell found the data and sent it to Fagan: "Four hours after sunset, from *Vita De Nicolo Machiavelli*," which states, "The 3rd at 4 o'clock." Since the 3rd begins at sunset (of the 2nd by modern calculations), 4 o'clock is four hours after sunset, Florentine time. Sunset was 7:07 PM LMT = 11:07 PM LMT of May 2 OS = May 11, 1469 NS.

[94] MAETERLINCK, MAURICE: SS #634 gives 12:20 PM; same from Adams, *One Hundred Horoscopes*. PC adds, "Barbault gives 12:30 PM."

[95] MANN, THOMAS: *Current Biography*, 1942, states "exactly mid-day." Same data in SS #638. CL quotes AFA, January 1957, for 10:15 AM LMT.

[96] MARCONI, GUGLIELMO: SS #643 gives 9:00 AM. Bailey in BJA, August 1930, gives 9:00 AM MET, "from him."

[97] MARTIN, DEAN: McEvers quotes Jansky at 2:30 PM CST. PC gives 3:00 PM, "personal."

[98] MARX, KARL: Same data from Lyndoe, "official records." SS #654 gives 1:30 AM, Treves, Prussia. Rudhyar in AA, May 1938, gives "around 7:10 AM."

[99] MENUHIN, YEHUDI: PC gives the same data except for 1916, "personal." SS #673 gives January 22, 1917.

[100] MICHAELANGELO: The biography quotes his father's notebook: "A male child was born to me on Monday morning four or five hours before daybreak." Sunrise is 6:15 AM

LMT; therefore, 1:45 AM is approximate within one-half hour one way or the other. Though this is not precise data, it is well worth including.

[101] MOZART, WOLFGANG: Lyndoe specifies OS for January 27, 1756, but Austria was on the New Style calendar. WEMYSS F/N #180 gives the data for January 27, 1756, Gregorian.

[102] NEWMAN, PAUL: Dr. James Hayes in Leek's *Astrology*, February 1971, gives 6:12 PM. The profile and chart of his wife, Joanne Woodward, are given in *Profiles of Women*.

[103] NIETZSCHE, FRIEDRICH: Lyndoe in AA, July 1967, gives 10:07 AM as "accepted data."

[104] NOVARRO, RAMON: CL old file quotes Miss Whitney for February 6, 1900, 4:00 AM LMT. L.A. *Times* Obit and *World Book* Obit give 1899.

[105] ODETS, CLIFFORD: PC quotes SS #733 (no time given) for 1:33 PM EST.

[106] PATTON, GEORGE: *Ordeal and Triumph* by Ladislav Farago (1963) gives the same data on p. 41.

[107] PRESLEY, ELVIS: Despite the birth certificate, the debate continues as to the correct time. Dr. James Hayes reports that he was commissioned to do Elvis' chart a few years ago, with a time of 12:20 PM CST. Presley personally told Ruth Hale Oliver 3:25 AM in 1957, and he told Lynn Rodden (confirmed by his father at the time) 3:30 AM in 1972. (Lynn also relates that he gave her biblical quotes discounting astrology). Eugene Moore in AFA, April 1979, reports that a 4:35 AM birth time "was received by an astrologer who wrote the Mississippi bureau of records on April 17, 1958."

[108] RAFAEL: Fagan writes, "As Florentine time began at sunset of March 27, the painter must have been born, according to Vasari, who said "3 o'clock into the night on Good Friday, March 28 according to Florentine time," actually on Holy Thursday, March 27, 1483 OS, according to modern calculations.

[109] REMARQUE, ERICK MARIA: PC quotes Gauquelin at 8:00 AM MET. LMR cannot locate it in Gauquelin Vol 6. Old-file has 7:35 PM MET.

[110] REVENTLOW, LANCE: PC quotes Drew for 10:00 AM. LMR verifies that Drew stated 10:30 AM.

[111] REYNOLDS, BURT: PC gives 1:30 AM EST, Waycross, Ga, "personal." Dobyns quotes a colleague who stated that his mother gave Waycross, Ga.

[112] REZA, ZOOROSH ALI: Fagan in AA, April 1961, quotes the London *Evening News and Star*; "born at 8:20 AM GMT = 11:50 AM in Teheran." CL quotes Drew for 2:15 PM, Isfahan.

[113] RIBBENTROP, JOACHIM VON: SS #790 gives the same date, but 10:35 AM MET. AQ, Spring 1940, gives 1894, 10:35 AM.

[114] ROCKEFELLER, NELSON: CL quotes AFA, October 1959, for 12:00 Noon, "from him." Jansky H/N quotes AA, November 1968, at 11:59 AM EST, also notes the 12:10 PM time.

[115] ROONEY, MICKEY: *Constellations*, 1977, Donna Kaplan quotes *I.E. An Autobiography*, for 11:55 AM. SS #803 gives noon.

[116] RUSSELL, BERTRAND: Davis Hamblin in NAJ, Winter 1976, quotes NAJ, Spring 1970, for 5:45 AM LMT.

[117] SAINT-SAENS, CAMILLE: *Constellations*, 1977, Lockhart quotes data in Daulet's Diary of 6:45 AM LMT.

[118] SANDBURG, CARL: AFA, January 1963, gives the same data from his autobiography, *Always the Young Strangers*.

[119] SARTRE, JEAN PAUL: The profile and chart of his lifelong companion, Simone De Beauvoir, are given in *Profiles of Women*.

[120] SCHWEITZER, ALBERT: CL quotes Lyndoe at 11:55 PM LMT, and Rudhyar for "dawn."

[121] SEBRING, JAY: PC gives 1:05 AM EST, Detroit, Mich as B.C.

[122] SELLERS, PETER: AQ, Winter 1970, Revill gives September 6, 1925, Southsea, Hants.

[123] SHARIF, OMAR: Same data given in his autobiography, *The Eternal Male*.

[124] SHAW, GEORGE BERNARD: SS #843 gives 00:15 AM. CL old-file has 00:25 AM LMT.

[125] SHELLEY, PERCY BYSSHE: Craswell gives the same data from *Astrology* Vol 40 #3. PC adds that NN gives 5:00 PM. Old-file has 11:05 PM. Alan Leo in M.A., January 1897 gives 4:59 PM. The profile and chart of Mary Godwin Shelley are given in *Profiles of Women*.

[126] SHEPPARD, DR. SAM: *Karen Spahn quotes his autobiography Endure and Conquer* for 6:28 AM EST. PC gives 6:28 AM EST as B.C. The chart and profile of Marilyn Sheppard are given in *Profiles Of Women*.

[127] SINCLAIR, UPTON: Craswell quotes AFA, April 1962, for 2:48 AM LMT. Ralph Kraum's personal notebook has 9:15 AM.

[128] SLEZAK, WALTER: SS #848 gives 2:00 AM.

[129] SMOTHERS, TOM: PC gives 5:15 PM EST, "personal."

[130] SPAHN, WARREN: Storme in AFA, November 1962, gives 2:52:13 PM EST, from *Sports Magazine*, August 1961.

[131] STEVENSON, ADLAI: AA, March 1956, gives 3:36 PM PST, rectified by Wilmer. Pryor in AFA, October 1971, gives 7:40 PM PST. Scarsella quotes Baird for 9:20 AM.

[132] SWINEBURNE, ALGERNON: SS #884 same data; CL same data from AA, September 1961, quotes Jones in *Guide to Horoscope Interpretation at 10:47 AM LMT*.

[133] *TOSCANINI, ARTURO: Constellations*, 1977 gives the same data, but for 1868: "data from a letter giving the time and written by Toscanani's own hand, according to C.C. Zain. AFA data exchange, p. 303, confirms 1868 as the birth year," from Lockhart.
LMR copied 1867 directly from the CL files: same date in *World Book, Famous People*, from March and from Dewey quoting Ebertin; same in SS #905. Ebertin gives 3:00 AM from a 1930 German magazine, *Sterne Und Mench*. March states that Lyndoe rectified the time of 2:00 AM to 2:18 AM LMT.

[134] TRIKONIS, GUS: The profile and chart of his former wife, Goldie Hawn, are given in *Profiles of Women*.

[135] USTINOV, PETER: MacKenzie in AA, December 1977, states, "data reported by Davies" of 11:30 AM GMT.

[136] VERLAINE, PAUL: Same data from WEMYSS #61, from M.A. 1932, and in SS #927. PC quotes Wemyss, SS, and Gauquelin Vol 6 for Paris.

[137] WALLACE, GEORGE: Barbara Watters gives 5:40 PM CDT, stated in AFA, July 1972, as "alleged to be from the vital statistics records."

[138] WELLS, H.G.: CL quotes Walter Scott in AFA who says, "middle of the afternoon," rectified to 3:30 PM LMT.

[139] WILDE, OSCAR: Fagan quotes Robson for a stated 3:00 AM that Robson rectified to 2:39 AM LMT. SS #968 gives October 14, 1856; the same date is in *Americana*; however, biographers Arthur Ransome and T. Thurston give October 16, 1854.

[140] WILHELM, KAISER II: PC gives 2:45 PM, "recorded"; same data in AQ, November 1907. M.A., May 1902, states, "about 3:00 AM, announced in German papers."

[141] WINDSOR, DUKE OF: Reynolds quotes Ebertin for 10:00 PM GMT, London. The profile and chart of Wallis Simpson, the Duchess of Windsor, are given in *Profiles of Women*.

[142] WINGATE, ORDE: CL quotes the same source for 3:20 PM LMT. PC data verified by LMR.

[143] WINKLER, HENRY: Gene Steele states that Henry told him 9:56 AM. Since he was a client of Kelly's, that is the preferred time.

[144] YEATS, WILLIAM BUTLER: Although Fagan doesn't mention the source of the birth time, since he knew Yeats, the time probably came from Yeats personally.

'A' and 'B' DATA LISTING BY MONTH/DAY

GREGORY GODZIK	3	23	1959	PANCHO GONZALES	5	09	1928	V DE SICA	7	07	1901
ELTON JOHN	3	25	1947	GEORGE W LIPPERT	5	09	1849	RINGO STARR	7	07	1940
JAMES LOVELL	3	25	1928	FRED ASTAIRE	5	10	1899	JOHN CROW	7	08	1935
A TOSCANINI	3	25	1867	JEAN HOUSTON	5	10	1939	N ROCKEFELLER	7	08	1908
WILHELM BACKHAUS	3	26	1884	KARL E KRAFFT	5	10	1900	O RESPIGHI	7	09	1879
A E HOUSMAN	3	26	1859	D O SELZNICK	5	10	1902	O J SIMPSON	7	09	1947
BILLY CARTER	3	29	1937	N MACHIAVELLI	5	11	1469	NIKOLA TESLA	7	09	1856
WARREN BEATTY	3	30	1937	DONALD BALLARD	5	12	1918	ARTHUR ASHE	7	10	1943
V VAN GOGH	3	30	1895	HOMICIDE VICTIM	5	13	1949	ARLO GUTHRIE	7	10	1947
PAUL VERLAINE	3	30	1844	JIM JONES	5	13	1931	MARCEL PROUST	7	10	1871
HERB ALPERT	3	31	1935	RITCHIE VALENS	5	13	1941	VAN CLIBURN	7	12	1934
R CHAMBERLAIN	3	31	1934	GARTH ALLEN	5	16	1925	A MODIGLIANI	7	12	1884
OTTO V BISMARCK	4	01	1815	LIBERACE	5	16	1919	BOB CRANE	7	13	1928
EDMOND ROSTAND	4	01	1868	JOE SORRENTINO	5	16	1937	JERRY RUBIN	7	14	1938
HANS C ANDERSON	4	02	1805	ERIC SATIE	5	17	1866	JEAN-B COROT	7	16	1796
MARLON BRANDO	4	03	1924	B RUSSELL	5	18	1872	PHOEBE SNOW	7	17	1950
A DEGASPERI	4	03	1881	HONORE DE BALZAC	5	20	1799	D SUTHERLAND	7	17	1935
V GUS GRISSOM	4	03	1926	SIR L OLIVIER	5	22	1907	J H GLENN, JR	7	18	1921
W IRVING	4	03	1783	VANCE PACKARD	5	22	1914	CLIFFORD ODETS	7	18	1906
MISTINGUETTE	4	03	1875	RENNIE DAVIS	5	23	1940	EDGAR DEGAS	7	19	1834
KIRK O OAKES	4	04	1953	BOB DYLAN	5	24	1941	TOM MCLOUGHLIN	7	19	1950
RAFAEL	4	05	1483	JAMES ARNESS	5	26	1923	ERNEST HEMINGWAY	7	21	1899
H VON KARAJAN	4	05	1908	HENRY KISSINGER	5	27	1923	CAT STEVENS	7	21	1948
GREGORY PECK	4	05	1916	NARCOLEPTIC	5	27	1901	ALEX DUMAS	7	24	1802
A SWINBURNE	4	05	1837	VINCENT PRICE	5	27	1911	LEO GUILD	7	26	1911
MOSES B MAIMON	4	06	1135	CLINT EASTWOOD	5	31	1930	DOROTHY HAMILL	7	26	1956
RICHARD ALPERT	4	06	1931	DONALD KINMAN	5	31	1923	MICK JAGGER	7	26	1943
MERLE HAGGARD	4	06	1937	BROOKE SHIELDS	5	31	1965	ANDRE MAUROIS	7	26	1885
SIAMESE TWINS	4	06	1962	WALT WHITMAN	5	31	1819	GEO B SHAW	7	26	1856
EDMUND G BROWN	4	07	1938	LE PETOMANE	6	01	1857	TROY PERRY	7	27	1940
DAVID FROST	4	07	1939	J WEISMULLER	6	02	1904	GUY BALLARD	7	28	1878
ROBERTA COWELL	4	08	1918	MORGANA KING	6	04	1930	VIDA BLUE	7	28	1949
HOMICIDE	4	08	1948	DENNIS WEAVER	6	04	1925	ROBERT HORTON	7	29	1924
C BAUDELAIRE	4	09	1821	BILL MOYERS	6	05	1934	BENITO MUSSOLINI	7	29	1883
C STEINMETZ	4	09	1865	BEN HUNTER	6	06	1920	A SCHWARZENEGGER	7	30	1947
OMAR SHARIF	4	10	1932	THOMAS MANN	6	06	1875	HERMAN MELVILLE	8	01	1819
DAVID CASSIDY	4	12	1950	KIMI K MILLER	6	06	1965	IRA PROGOFF	8	02	1921
LEW ALCINDOR	4	16	1947	DAVID R SCOTT	6	06	1932	JAY W NORTH	8	03	1951
ANATOLE FRANCE	4	16	1844	PAUL GAUGUIN	6	08	1848	ERNIE PYLE	8	03	1900
HENRY MANCINI	4	16	1924	ROBERT CUMMINGS	6	09	1910	SIR LAUDER	8	04	1870
PETER USTINOV	4	16	1921	R S MCNAMERA	6	09	1916	PERCY B SHELLEY	8	04	1792
WILLIAM HOLDEN	4	17	1918	GUSTAVE COURBET	6	10	1819	G DEMAUPASSANT	8	05	1850
L STOKOWSKI	4	18	1882	J V COUSTEAU	6	11	1910	SIR A FLEMING	8	06	1881
CHARLIE TUNA	4	18	1944	RICHARD STRAUSS	6	11	1864	ALFRED TENNYSON	8	06	1809
KINMAN'S VICTIM	4	19	1915	LUCKY MALE	6	12	1952	ALAN LEO	8	07	1860
EDWIN LANEHART	4	19	1935	ALY KHAN	6	13	1911	BILLY JOE THOMAS	8	07	1942
RYAN O'NEAL	4	20	1941	PAUL LYNDE	6	13	1926	DUSTIN HOFFMAN	8	08	1937
RICHARD DEMONT	4	21	1956	W B YEATS	6	13	1865	LUCKEY FEMALE	8	10	1930
ROLLO MAY	4	21	1909	BURL IVES	6	14	1909	SIAMESE TWINS	8	10	1963
EDDIE ALBERT	4	22	1908	RALPH BELLAMY	6	17	1904	CZAR ALEXIS	8	12	1904
GLEN CAMPBELL	4	22	1936	SIR WM CROOKES	6	17	1832	JOHN DEREK	8	12	1926
IMMANUEL KANT	4	22	1724	CHARLES GOUNOD	6	17	1818	ROSS MCWHIRTER	8	12	1925
YEHUDI MENUHIN	4	22	1917	DEAN MARTIN	6	17	1917	JOHN L BAIRD	8	13	1888
JACK NICHOLSON	4	22	1937	E DALADIER	6	18	1884	STEVE BROWN	8	13	1938
LEONARDO DAVINCI	4	23	1452	LUCKEY FEMALE	6	18	1943	JOHN GALSWORTHY	8	14	1867
WARREN SPAHN	4	23	1921	F GAUQUELIN	6	19	1929	LOUIS DE BROGLIE	8	15	1892
LUCKEY FEMALE	4	24	1879	ELBERT HUBBARD	6	19	1856	EDNA FERBER	8	15	1885
HENRI P PETAIN	4	24	1856	ROCKWELL KENT	6	21	1882	DENNIS WHITNEY	8	15	1942
G MARCONI	4	25	1874	JOHN J O'NEILL	6	21	1889	ROBERT DE NIRO	8	17	1943
DR BART BOK	4	28	1906	JEAN P SARTRE	6	21	1905	ROBERT REDFORD	8	18	1936
JAPANESE EMPEROR	4	29	1901	JOHN DILLINGER	6	22	1903	NARCOLEPTIC FAM	8	20	1933
ZUBIN MEHTA	4	29	1936	ERICK M REMARQUE	6	22	1898	WILT CHAMBERLAIN	8	21	1936
J VON RIBBENTROP	4	30	1893	JEAN ANOUILH	6	23	1910	JOE CHAMBERS	8	22	1942
SCOTT CARPENTER	5	01	1925	DON EISELE	6	23	1930	CLAUDE DEBUSSY	8	22	1862
STEVE CAUTHEN	5	01	1960	DUKE-WINDSOR	6	23	1894	CHRIS CHUBBOCK	8	24	1944
JACK PAAR	5	01	1917	SIAMESE TWINS	6	24	1961	L BERNSTEIN	8	25	1918
P T DE CHARDIN	5	01	1881	DR A CARREL	6	28	1873	SEAN CONNERY	8	25	1930
DUKE-WELLINGTON	5	01	1769	A DE ST-EXUPERY	6	29	1900	GEORGE WALLACE	8	25	1919
WALTER SLEZAK	5	03	1902	AUTISTIC CHILD	7	01	1966	PRINCE ALBERT	8	26	1819
T H HUXLEY	5	04	1825	HERMANN HESSE	7	02	1877	CHRIS ISHERWOOD	8	26	1904
KARL MARX	5	05	1818	GEORGE SANDERS	7	03	1906	JOHANN V GOETHE	8	28	1749
SIGMUND FREUD	5	06	1856	C CARVALHO	7	04	1925	DON LOPER	8	29	1907
WILLIE MAYS	5	06	1931	STEPHEN FOSTER	7	04	1826	M MAETERLINCK	8	29	1862
ORSON WELLES	5	06	1915	JEAN COCTEAU	7	05	1889	J C KILLY	8	30	1943
FERNANDEL	5	08	1903	HENRY C LODGE	7	05	1902	ARTHUR BREMER	8	31	1950
DANIEL BERRIGAN	5	09	1921	MERV GRIFFIN	7	06	1925	ARTHUR GODFREY	8	31	1903

Name	Month	Day	Year
JAPANESE EMPEROR	8	31	1879
WILLIAM SAROYAN	8	31	1908
JOHN CAGE	9	05	1912
JOHN MITCHELL	9	05	1913
BILLY ROSE	9	06	1899
PETER SELLERS	9	08	1925
JAMES HILTON	9	09	1900
BEVERLY NICHOLS	9	09	1899
JOSE FELICIANO	9	10	1945
O'HENRY	9	11	1862
M CHEVALIER	9	12	1888
MAYFAIR BOY	9	13	1916
ROSSANO BRAZZI	9	18	1916
DR WALTER KOCH	9	18	1895
KING CHULALONGHO	9	20	1853
UPTON SINCLAIR	9	20	1878
AUGUSTUS CAESAR	9	21	- 62
HAMILTON JORDAN	9	21	1944
H G WELLS	9	21	1866
ALDO MORO	9	23	1916
MICKEY ROONEY	9	23	1920
F S FITZGERALD	9	24	1896
W PHILLIPS	9	25	1921
CHRIS REEVES	9	25	1952
G CLEMENCEAU	9	28	1841
MAX SCHMELING	9	28	1905
BOBBY STONE	9	28	1922
ENRICO FERMI	9	29	1901
JOANNE BURNELL	9	30	1977
MARC E JONES	10	01	1888
GEORGE PEPPARD	10	01	1928
ANOREXIA NERVOSA	10	02	1950
F FOCH	10	02	1851
BIRTH DEFECTS	10	04	1963
J F MILLET	10	04	1814
PHILIP BERRIGAN	10	05	1923
RICHARD GORDON	10	05	1929
HEINRICH HIMMLER	10	07	1900
R D LAING	10	07	1927
JOHN LENNON	10	09	1940
CAMILLE ST-SAENS	10	09	1835
JAY SEBRING	10	10	1933
GUISEPPE VERDI	10	10	1813
THIEF	10	12	1900
LENNY BRUCE	10	13	1925
SIAMESE TWINS	10	13	1974
JOHN DEAN	10	14	1938
F NIETZSCHE	10	15	1844
A SCHLESINGER	10	15	1917
SUZANNE SOMERS	10	16	1946
OSCAR WILDE	10	16	1854
MONTGOMERY CLIFT	10	17	1920
JOHN PAUL I	10	17	1912
EVEL KNIEVEL	10	17	1938
JACK ANDERSON	10	19	1922
KING MONGKUT	10	19	1904
ALBERT DYER	10	20	1904
BELA LUGOSI	10	20	1882
ARTHUR RIMBAUD	10	20	1854
DAVID ST CLAIR	10	21	1932
LORD A DOUGLAS	10	22	1870
DEREK JACOBI	10	22	1938
JOHNNY CARSON	10	23	1925
HARRY TRACY	10	23	1875
RICHARD E BYRD	10	25	1888
HELEN REDDY	10	25	1941
JACKIE COOGAN	10	26	1914
H R HALDEMAN	10	27	1926
P J GOEBBELS	10	29	1897
HENRY WINKLER	10	30	1945
ROBIN MOORE	10	31	1925
ZOOROSH A REZA	10	31	1960
CHEIRO	11	01	1866
STEPHEN CRANE	11	01	1871
LARRY FLYNT	11	01	1942
KEITH EMERSON	11	02	1944
WM C BRYANT	11	03	1794
JAPANESE EMPEROR	11	03	1852
ANDRE MALRAUX	11	03	1901
VIVIEN LEIGH	11	05	1913
ROY ROGERS	11	05	1911
ALBERT CAMUS	11	07	1913
SPIRO AGNEW	11	09	1918
GEORGE PATTON	11	11	1885
J WINTERS	11	11	1925
AUGUSTE RODIN	11	12	1840
B CELLINI	11	12	1500
M GAUQUELIN	11	13	1928
PRINCE CHARLES	11	14	1948
EDWARD WHITE, JR	11	14	1930
ERWIN ROMMEL	11	15	1891
ROBERT MATHIAS	11	17	1930
DR F REGARDE	11	17	1907
NATHAN LEOPOLD	11	19	1904
MARTIN LUTHER	11	19	1483
ANDRE GIDE	11	22	1869
MANUEL DE FALLA	11	23	1876
WM F BUCKLEY	11	24	1925
GEORGE MOSCONE	11	24	1929
H TOULOUSE-LATR	11	24	1864
BRUNO HAUPTMAN	11	26	1899
AGNOLO D COSIMI	11	26	1503
JIMI HENDRIX	11	27	1942
BRUCE LEE	11	27	1940
WILLIAM BLAKE	11	28	1757
NARCOLEPTIC FAM	11	28	1913
SIR W CHURCHILL	11	30	1874
JACK SHELDON	11	30	1931
LEE TREVINO	12	01	1939
GEORGES SEURAT	12	02	1859
CHARLES WATSON	12	02	1945
F FRANCO	12	04	1892
RICHARD SPECK	12	06	1941
ELLEN BURSTYN	12	07	1932
GREGG ALLMAN	12	08	1947
DAVID CARRADINE	12	08	1936
ADA BYRON	12	10	1815
MARARA JI	12	10	1957
HECTOR BERLIOZ	12	11	1803
ALFRED DE MUSSET	12	11	1810
ELBERT BENJAMINE	12	12	1882
ISABELLE PAGAN	12	12	1867
GUSTAVE FLAUBERT	12	13	1821
WILLY BRANDT	12	18	1913
URI GELLER	12	20	1946
DISRAELI	12	21	1804
MICHAEL T THOMAS	12	21	1944
GIACAMO PUCCINI	12	22	1858
JAPANESE ROYALTY	12	23	1933
TYCHO BRAHE	12	24	1546
LARRY CSONKA	12	25	1946
STEVE ALLEN	12	26	1921
HENRY MILLER	12	26	1891
OSCAR LEVANT	12	27	1906
LOUIS PASTEUR	12	27	1822
A VAILLANT	12	27	1861
LEW AYRES	12	28	1908
DR SAM SHEPPARD	12	29	1923
JON VOIGHT	12	29	1938
SANDY KOUFAX	12	30	1935
MICHAEL NESMITH	12	30	1942
LOTTE V STRAHL	12	30	1895
JOHN DENVER	12	31	1943
HENRI MATISSE	12	31	1869
NOEL TYL	12	31	1936
S WIESENTHAL	12	31	1908
J E HOOVER	1	01	1895
GUS TRIKONIS	1	01	1938
IAN BRADY	1	02	1938
KONRAD ADENAUER	1	05	1876
DIANA KEATON	1	05	1946
WALTER MONDALE	1	05	1928
P YOGANANDA	1	05	1893
GUSTAVE P DORE	1	06	1832
GARY MIDDLECOFF	1	06	1921
MURRAY I ROSE	1	06	1939
CARL SANDBURG	1	06	1878
ALAN WATTS	1	06	1915
JOHANNES KEPLER	1	07	1572
PR ALBERT VICTOR	1	08	1864
DAVID BOWIE	1	08	1947
ELVIS PRESLEY	1	08	1935
AUTISTIC CHILD	1	09	1962
RUDOLPH BING	1	09	1902
JIM BAILEY	1	10	1938
HERMANN GOERING	1	12	1893
JOSEPH JOEFFRE	1	12	1852
JACK LONDON	1	12	1876
KEN USTON	1	12	1935
ROBERT STACK	1	13	1919
BIRTH DEFECTS	1	14	1970
MARJOE GORTNER	1	14	1944
A SCHWEITZER	1	14	1875
MUHAMMAD ALI	1	17	1942
DR TOM DOOLEY	1	17	1927
JOE FRAZIER	1	17	1944
CONRAD MORICAND	1	17	1887
PAUL CEZANNE	1	19	1839
EDWIN ALDRIN	1	20	1930
JOHN C FREMONT	1	21	1813
JACK NICKLAUS	1	21	1940
UMBERTO NOBILE	1	21	1885
LORD BYRON	1	22	1788
DOUGLAS CORRIGAN	1	22	1907
EDOUARD MANET	1	23	1832
PAUL NEWMAN	1	26	1925
EDOUARD LALO	1	27	1823
WOLFGANG MOZART	1	27	1756
KAISER WILHELMI I	1	27	1859
ALAN ALDA	1	28	1936
CHARLES GORDON	1	28	1833
AUGUSTE PICCARD	1	28	1884
NARCOLEPTIC FAM	1	29	1952
DICK MARTIN	1	30	1922
MARIO LANZA	1	31	1921
NORMAN MAILER	1	31	1923
JACKIE ROBINSON	1	31	1919
FRANZ P SCHUBERT	1	31	1797
GRAHAM NASH	2	02	1940
TOM SMOTHERS	2	02	1937
ALICE COOPER	2	04	1948
FERNAND LEGER	2	04	1881
ADLAI STEVENSON	2	05	1900
ZSA ZSA GABOR	2	06	1915
LUCKY MALE	2	06	1926
RAMON NOVARRO	2	06	1899
RIP TORN	2	06	1931
STEPHEN CRANE	2	07	1917
JAMES DEAN	2	08	1931
JOHN RUSKIN	2	08	1819
JULES VERNE	2	08	1828
MARK SPITZ	2	10	1950
BURT REYNOLDS	2	11	1936
ABRAHAM LINCOLN	2	12	1809
HUGH DOWNS	2	14	1921
JAMES HOFFA	2	14	1913
ROGER B CHAFFEE	2	15	1935
JULES LENIER	2	15	1929
MAX BAER	2	16	1909
HAL HOLBROOK	2	17	1925
ROBERT BURTON	2	18	1577
JOHN TRAVOLTA	2	18	1954
WENDELL WILLKIE	2	18	1892
PRINCE ANDREW	2	19	1960
EDDIE ARCARO	2	19	1916
GEORGES BERNANOS	2	20	1888
SIDNEY POITIER	2	20	1927
SAM PECKINPAH	2	21	1925
PETER FONDA	2	23	1940
JAPANESE ROYALTY	2	23	1960
LANCE REVENTLOW	2	24	1936

GALILIE GALILEO	2	25	1564	A G BELL	3	03	1847	WATER SCHIRRA	3	12	1923
JIM BACKUS	2	25	1913	REX HARRISON	3	05	1908	A EINSTEIN	3	14	1879
HERB ELLIOT	2	25	1938	LEROY G COOPER	3	06	1927	MICHAELANGELO	3	15	1475
PIERRE A RENOIR	2	25	1841	EARLE BESSERER	3	07	1926	DR LOUIS BERMAN	3	15	1893
H DAUMIER	2	26	1808	ANTHONY A JONES	3	07	1930	MICHAEL LOVE	3	15	1941
C FLAMMARION	2	26	1842	PIET MONDRIAAN	3	07	1872	JOHN W GACEY	3	17	1942
VICTOR HUGO	2	26	1802	MAURICE RAVEL	3	07	1875	WM J BRYAN	3	19	1860
ORDE WINGATE	2	26	1903	BOBBY FISCHER	3	09	1943	SIR R BURTON	3	19	1821
HUGO BLACK	2	27	1886	HARRY BERTOIA	3	10	1915	A EICKMANN	3	19	1906
N COPERNICUS	2	28	1473	JAMES E RAY	3	10	1928	MARIA LA LAURIE	3	19	1787
ERNEST RENAN	2	28	1823	LAWRENCE WELK	3	11	1903	ALBERT SPEER	3	19	1905
HARRY BELAFONTE	3	01	1927	G D'ANNUNZIO	3	12	1863	EARL WARREN	3	19	1891
IVAR KRUEGAR	3	02	1880	JACK KEROUAC	3	12	1922	JERRY REED	3	20	1937

'A' and 'B' DATA LISTING BY YEAR

AUGUSTUS CAESAR	9 21 - 62
MOSES B MAIMON	4 06 1135
LEONARDO DAVINCI	4 23 1452
N MACHIAVELLI	5 11 1469
N COPERNICUS	2 28 1473
MICHAELANGELO	3 15 1475
RAFAEL	4 05 1483
MARTIN LUTHER	11 19 1483
B CELLINI	11 12 1500
AGNOLO D COSIMI	11 26 1503
TYCHO BRAHE	12 24 1546
GALILIE GALILEO	2 25 1564
JOHANNES KEPLER	1 07 1572
ROBERT BURTON	2 18 1577
IMMANUEL KANT	4 22 1724
JOHANN V GOETHE	8 28 1749
WOLFGANG MOZART	1 27 1756
WILLIAM BLAKE	11 28 1757
DUKE-WELLINGTON	5 01 1769
W IRVING	4 03 1783
MARIA LA LAURIE	3 19 1787
LORD BYRON	1 22 1788
PERCY B SHELLEY	8 04 1792
WM C BRYANT	11 03 1794
JEAN-B COROT	7 16 1796
FRANZ P SCHUBERT	1 31 1797
HONORE DE BALZAC	5 20 1799
VICTOR HUGO	2 26 1802
ALEX DUMAS	7 24 1802
HECTOR BERLIOZ	12 11 1803
DISRAELI	12 21 1804
HANS C ANDERSON	4 02 1805
H DAUMIER	2 26 1808
ABRAHAM LINCOLN	2 12 1809
ALFRED TENNYSON	8 06 1809
ALFRED DE MUSSET	12 11 1810
JOHN C FREMONT	1 21 1813
GUISEPPE VERDI	10 10 1813
J F MILLET	10 04 1814
OTTO V BISMARCK	4 01 1815
ADA BYRON	12 10 1815
KARL MARX	5 05 1818
CHARLES GOUNOD	6 17 1818
JOHN RUSKIN	2 08 1819
WALT WHITMAN	5 31 1819
GUSTAVE COURBET	6 10 1819
HERMAN MELVILLE	8 01 1819
PRINCE ALBERT	8 26 1819
SIR R BURTON	3 19 1821
C BAUDELAIRE	4 09 1821
GUSTAVE FLAUBERT	12 13 1821
LOUIS PASTEUR	12 27 1822
EDOUARD LALO	1 27 1823
ERNEST RENAN	2 28 1823
T H HUXLEY	5 04 1825
STEPHEN FOSTER	7 04 1826
JULES VERNE	2 08 1828
GUSTAVE P DORE	1 06 1832
EDOUARD MANET	1 23 1832
SIR WM CROOKES	6 17 1832
CHARLES GORDON	1 28 1833
EDGAR DEGAS	7 19 1834
CAMILLE ST-SAENS	10 09 1835
A SWINBURNE	4 05 1837
PAUL CEZANNE	1 19 1839
AUGUSTE RODIN	11 12 1840
PIERRE A RENOIR	2 25 1841
G CLEMENCEAU	9 28 1841
C FLAMMARION	2 26 1842
PAUL VERLAINE	3 30 1844
ANATOLE FRANCE	4 16 1844
F NIETZSCHE	10 15 1844
A G BELL	3 03 1847
PAUL GAUGUIN	6 08 1848
GEORGE W LIPPERT	5 09 1849
G DEMAUPASSANT	8 05 1850

F FOCH	10 02 1851
JOSEPH JOEFFRE	1 12 1852
JAPANESE EMPEROR	11 03 1852
KING CHULALONGHO	9 20 1853
OSCAR WILDE	10 16 1854
ARTHUR RIMBAUD	10 20 1854
HENRI P PETAIN	4 24 1856
SIGMUND FREUD	5 06 1856
ELBERT HUBBARD	6 19 1856
NIKOLA TESLA	7 09 1856
GEO B SHAW	7 26 1856
LE PETOMANE	6 01 1857
GIACAMO PUCCINI	12 22 1858
KAISER WILHELMII	1 27 1859
A E HOUSMAN	3 26 1859
GEORGES SEURAT	12 02 1859
WM J BRYAN	3 19 1860
ALAN LEO	8 07 1860
A VAILLANT	12 27 1861
CLAUDE DEBUSSY	8 22 1862
M MAETERLINCK	8 29 1862
O'HENRY	9 11 1862
G D'ANNUNZIO	3 12 1863
PR ALBERT VICTOR	1 08 1864
RICHARD STRAUSS	6 11 1864
H TOULOUSE-LATR	11 24 1864
C STEINMETZ	4 09 1865
W B YEATS	6 13 1865
ERIC SATIE	5 17 1866
H G WELLS	9 21 1866
CHEIRO	11 01 1866
A TOSCANINI	3 25 1867
JOHN GALSWORTHY	8 14 1867
ISABELLE PAGAN	12 12 1867
EDMOND ROSTAND	4 01 1868
ANDRE GIDE	11 22 1869
HENRI MATISSE	12 31 1869
SIR LAUDER	8 04 1870
LORD A DOUGLAS	10 22 1870
MARCEL PROUST	7 10 1871
STEPHEN CRANE	11 01 1871
PIET MONDRIAAN	3 07 1872
B RUSSELL	5 18 1872
DR A CARREL	6 28 1873
G MARCONI	4 25 1874
SIR W CHURCHILL	11 30 1874
A SCHWEITZER	1 14 1875
MAURICE RAVEL	3 07 1875
MISTINGUETTE	4 03 1875
THOMAS MANN	6 06 1875
HARRY TRACY	10 23 1875
KONRAD ADENAUER	1 05 1876
JACK LONDON	1 12 1876
MANUEL DE FALLA	11 23 1876
HERMANN HESSE	7 02 1877
CARL SANDBURG	1 06 1878
GUY BALLARD	7 28 1878
UPTON SINCLAIR	9 20 1878
A EINSTEIN	3 14 1879
LUCKEY FEMALE	4 24 1879
O RESPIGHI	7 09 1879
JAPANESE EMPEROR	8 31 1879
IVAR KRUEGAR	3 02 1880
FERNAND LEGER	2 04 1881
A DEGASPERI	4 03 1881
P T DE CHARDIN	5 01 1881
SIR A FLEMING	8 06 1881
L STOKOWSKI	4 18 1882
ROCKWELL KENT	6 21 1882
BELA LUGOSI	10 20 1882
ELBERT BENJAMINE	12 12 1882
BENITO MUSSOLINI	7 29 1883
AUGUSTE PICCARD	1 28 1884
WILHELM BACKHAUS	3 26 1884
E DALADIER	6 18 1884
A MODIGLIANI	7 12 1884

UMBERTO NOBILE	1 21 1885
ANDRE MAUROIS	7 26 1885
EDNA FERBER	8 15 1885
GEORGE PATTON	11 11 1885
HUGO BLACK	2 27 1886
CONRAD MORICAND	1 17 1887
GEORGES BERNANOS	2 20 1888
JOHN L BAIRD	8 13 1888
M CHEVALIER	9 12 1888
MARC E JONES	10 01 1888
RICHARD E BYRD	10 25 1888
JOHN J O'NEILL	6 21 1889
JEAN COCTEAU	7 05 1889
EARL WARREN	3 19 1891
ERWIN ROMMEL	11 15 1891
HENRY MILLER	12 26 1891
WENDELL WILLKIE	2 18 1892
LOUIS DE BROGLIE	8 15 1892
F FRANCO	12 04 1892
P YOGANANDA	1 05 1893
HERMANN GOERING	1 12 1893
DR LOUIS BERMAN	3 15 1893
J VON RIBBENTROP	4 30 1893
DUKE-WINDSOR	6 23 1894
J E HOOVER	1 01 1895
V VAN GOGH	3 30 1895
DR WALTER KOCH	9 18 1895
LOTTE V STRAHL	12 30 1895
F S FITZGERALD	9 24 1896
P J GOEBBELS	10 29 1897
ERICK M REMARQUE	6 22 1898
RAMON NOVARRO	2 06 1899
FRED ASTAIRE	5 10 1899
ERNEST HEMINGWAY	7 21 1899
BILLY ROSE	9 06 1899
BEVERLY NICHOLS	9 09 1899
BRUNO HAUPTMAN	11 26 1899
ADLAI STEVENSON	2 05 1900
KARL E KRAFFT	5 10 1900
A DE ST-EXUPERY	6 29 1900
ERNIE PYLE	8 03 1900
JAMES HILTON	9 09 1900
HEINRICH HIMMLER	10 07 1900
THIEF	10 12 1900
JAPANESE EMPEROR	4 29 1901
NARCOLEPTIC	5 27 1901
V DE SICA	7 07 1901
ENRICO FERMI	9 29 1901
ANDRE MALRAUX	11 03 1901
RUDOLPH BING	1 09 1902
WALTER SLEZAK	5 03 1902
D O SELZNICK	5 10 1902
HENRY C LODGE	7 05 1902
ORDE WINGATE	2 26 1903
LAWRENCE WELK	3 11 1903
FERNANDEL	5 08 1903
JOHN DILLINGER	6 22 1903
ARTHUR GODFREY	8 31 1903
J WEISMULLER	6 02 1904
RALPH BELLAMY	6 17 1904
CZAR ALEXIS	8 12 1904
CHRIS ISHERWOOD	8 26 1904
KING MONGKUT	10 19 1904
ALBERT DYER	10 20 1904
NATHAN LEOPOLD	11 19 1904
ALBERT SPEER	3 19 1905
JEAN P SARTRE	6 21 1905
MAX SCHMELING	9 28 1905
A EICKMANN	3 19 1906
DR BART BOK	4 28 1906
GEORGE SANDERS	7 03 1906
CLIFFORD ODETS	7 18 1906
OSCAR LEVANT	12 27 1906
DOUGLAS CORRIGAN	1 22 1907
SIR L OLIVIER	5 22 1907
DON LOPER	8 29 1907

Name	Mo	Dy	Year
DR F REGARDE	11	17	1907
REX HARRISON	3	05	1908
H VON KARAJAN	4	05	1908
EDDIE ALBERT	4	22	1908
N ROCKEFELLER	7	08	1908
WILLIAM SAROYAN	8	31	1908
LEW AYRES	12	28	1908
S WIESENTHAL	12	31	1908
MAX BAER	2	16	1909
ROLLO MAY	4	21	1909
BURL IVES	6	14	1909
ROBERT CUMMINGS	6	09	1910
J V COUSTEAU	6	11	1910
JEAN ANOUILH	6	23	1910
VINCENT PRICE	5	27	1911
ALY KHAN	6	13	1911
LEO GUILD	7	26	1911
ROY ROGERS	11	05	1911
JOHN CAGE	9	05	1912
JOHN PAUL I	10	17	1912
JAMES HOFFA	2	14	1913
JIM BACKUS	2	25	1913
JOHN MITCHELL	9	05	1913
VIVIEN LEIGH	11	05	1913
ALBERT CAMUS	11	07	1913
NARCOLEPTIC FAM	11	28	1913
WILLY BRANDT	12	18	1913
VANCE PACKARD	5	22	1914
JACKIE COOGAN	10	26	1914
ALAN WATTS	1	06	1915
ZSA ZSA GABOR	2	06	1915
HARRY BERTOIA	3	10	1915
KINMAN'S VICTIM	4	19	1915
ORSON WELLES	5	06	1915
EDDIE ARCARO	2	19	1916
GREGORY PECK	4	05	1916
R S MCNAMERA	6	09	1916
MAYFAIR BOY	9	13	1916
ROSSANO BRAZZI	9	18	1916
ALDO MORO	9	23	1916
STEPHEN CRANE	2	07	1917
YEHUDI MENUHIN	4	22	1917
JACK PAAR	5	01	1917
DEAN MARTIN	6	17	1917
A SCHLESINGER	10	15	1917
ROBERTA COWELL	4	08	1918
WILLIAM HOLDEN	4	17	1918
DONALD BALLARD	5	12	1918
L BERNSTEIN	8	25	1918
SPIRO AGNEW	11	09	1918
ROBERT STACK	1	13	1919
JACKIE ROBINSON	1	31	1919
LIBERACE	5	16	1919
GEORGE WALLACE	8	25	1919
BEN HUNTER	6	06	1920
MICKEY ROONEY	9	23	1920
MONTGOMERY CLIFT	10	17	1920
GARY MIDDLECOFF	1	06	1921
MARIO LANZA	1	31	1921
HUGH DOWNS	2	14	1921
PETER USTINOV	4	16	1921
WARREN SPAHN	4	23	1921
DANIEL BERRIGAN	5	09	1921
J H GLENN, JR	7	18	1921
IRA PROGOFF	8	02	1921
W PHILLIPS	9	25	1921
STEVE ALLEN	12	26	1921
DICK MARTIN	1	30	1922
JACK KEROUAC	3	12	1922
BOBBY STONE	9	28	1922
JACK ANDERSON	10	19	1922
NORMAN MAILER	1	31	1923
WATER SCHIRRA	3	12	1923
JAMES ARNESS	5	26	1923
HENRY KISSINGER	5	27	1923
DONALD KINMAN	5	31	1923
PHILIP BERRIGAN	10	05	1923
DR SAM SHEPPARD	12	29	1923
MARLON BRANDO	4	03	1924
HENRY MANCINI	4	16	1924
ROBERT HORTON	7	29	1924
PAUL NEWMAN	1	26	1925
HAL HOLBROOK	2	17	1925
SAM PECKINPAH	2	21	1925
SCOTT CARPENTER	5	01	1925
GARTH ALLEN	5	16	1925
DENNIS WEAVER	6	04	1925
C CARVALHO	7	04	1925
MERV GRIFFIN	7	06	1925
ROSS MCWHIRTER	8	12	1925
PETER SELLERS	9	08	1925
LENNY BRUCE	10	13	1925
JOHNNY CARSON	10	23	1925
ROBIN MOORE	10	31	1925
J WINTERS	11	11	1925
WM F BUCKLEY	11	24	1925
LUCKY MALE	2	06	1926
EARLE BESSERER	3	07	1926
V GUS GRISSOM	4	03	1926
PAUL LYNDE	6	13	1926
JOHN DEREK	8	12	1926
H R HALDEMAN	10	27	1926
DR TOM DOOLEY	1	17	1927
SIDNEY POITIER	2	20	1927
HARRY BELAFONTE	3	01	1927
LEROY G COOPER	3	06	1927
R D LAING	10	07	1927
WALTER MONDALE	1	05	1928
JAMES E RAY	3	10	1928
JAMES LOVELL	3	25	1928
PANCHO GONZALES	5	09	1928
BOB CRANE	7	13	1928
GEORGE PEPPARD	10	01	1928
M GAUQUELIN	11	13	1928
JULES LENIER	2	15	1929
F GAUQUELIN	6	19	1929
RICHARD GORDON	10	05	1929
GEORGE MOSCONE	11	24	1929
EDWIN ALDRIN	1	20	1930
ANTHONY A JONES	3	07	1930
CLINT EASTWOOD	5	31	1930
MORGANA KING	6	04	1930
DON EISELE	6	23	1930
LUCKEY FEMALE	8	10	1930
SEAN CONNERY	8	25	1930
EDWARD WHITE, JR	11	14	1930
ROBERT MATHIAS	11	17	1930
RIP TORN	2	06	1931
JAMES DEAN	2	08	1931
RICHARD ALPERT	4	06	1931
WILLIE MAYS	5	06	1931
JIM JONES	5	13	1931
JACK SHELDON	11	30	1931
OMAR SHARIF	4	10	1932
DAVID R SCOTT	6	06	1932
DAVID ST CLAIR	10	21	1932
ELLEN BURSTYN	12	07	1932
NARCOLEPTIC FAM	8	20	1933
JAY SEBRING	10	10	1933
JAPANESE ROYALTY	12	23	1933
R CHAMBERLAIN	3	31	1934
BILL MOYERS	6	05	1934
VAN CLIBURN	7	12	1934
ELVIS PRESLEY	1	08	1935
KEN USTON	1	12	1935
ROGER B CHAFFEE	2	15	1935
HERB ALPERT	3	31	1935
EDWIN LANEHART	4	19	1935
JOHN CROW	7	08	1935
D SUTHERLAND	7	17	1935
SANDY KOUFAX	12	30	1935
ALAN ALDA	1	28	1936
BURT REYNOLDS	2	11	1936
LANCE REVENTLOW	2	24	1936
GLEN CAMPBELL	4	22	1936
ZUBIN MEHTA	4	29	1936
ROBERT REDFORD	8	18	1936
WILT CHAMBERLAIN	8	21	1936
DAVID CARRADINE	12	08	1936
NOEL TYL	12	31	1936
TOM SMOTHERS	2	02	1937
JERRY REED	3	20	1937
BILLY CARTER	3	29	1937
WARREN BEATTY	3	30	1937
MERLE HAGGARD	4	06	1937
JACK NICHOLSON	4	22	1937
JOE SORRENTINO	5	16	1937
DUSTIN HOFFMAN	8	08	1937
GUS TRIKONIS	1	01	1938
IAN BRADY	1	02	1938
JIM BAILEY	1	10	1938
HERB ELLIOT	2	25	1938
EDMUND G BROWN	4	07	1938
JERRY RUBIN	7	14	1938
STEVE BROWN	8	13	1938
JOHN DEAN	10	14	1938
EVEL KNIEVEL	10	17	1938
DEREK JACOBI	10	22	1938
JON VOIGHT	12	29	1938
MURRAY I ROSE	1	06	1939
DAVID FROST	4	07	1939
JEAN HOUSTON	5	10	1939
LEE TREVINO	12	01	1939
JACK NICKLAUS	1	21	1940
GRAHAM NASH	2	02	1940
PETER FONDA	2	23	1940
RENNIE DAVIS	5	23	1940
RINGO STARR	7	07	1940
TROY PERRY	7	27	1940
JOHN LENNON	10	09	1940
BRUCE LEE	11	27	1940
MICHAEL LOVE	3	15	1941
RYAN O'NEAL	4	20	1941
RITCHIE VALENS	5	13	1941
BOB DYLAN	5	24	1941
HELEN REDDY	10	25	1941
RICHARD SPECK	12	06	1941
MUHAMMAD ALI	1	17	1942
JOHN W GACEY	3	17	1942
BILLY JOE THOMAS	8	07	1942
DENNIS WHITNEY	8	15	1942
JOE CHAMBERS	8	22	1942
LARRY FLYNT	11	01	1942
JIMI HENDRIX	11	27	1942
MICHAEL NESMITH	12	30	1942
BOBBY FISCHER	3	09	1943
LUCKEY FEMALE	6	18	1943
ARTHUR ASHE	7	10	1943
MICK JAGGER	7	26	1943
ROBERT DE NIRO	8	17	1943
J C KILLY	8	30	1943
JOHN DENVER	12	31	1943
MARJOE GORTNER	1	14	1944
JOE FRAZIER	1	17	1944
CHARLIE TUNA	4	18	1944
CHRIS CHUBBOCK	8	24	1944
HAMILTON JORDAN	9	21	1944
KEITH EMERSON	11	02	1944
MICHAEL T THOMAS	12	21	1944
JOSE FELICIANO	9	10	1945
HENRY WINKLER	10	30	1945
CHARLES WATSON	12	02	1945
DIANA KEATON	1	05	1946
SUZANNE SOMERS	10	16	1946
URI GELLER	12	20	1946
LARRY CSONKA	12	25	1946
DAVID BOWIE	1	08	1947
ELTON JOHN	3	25	1947
LEW ALCINDOR	4	16	1947
O J SIMPSON	7	09	1947
ARLO GUTHRIE	7	10	1947

A SCHWARZENEGGER	7	30	1947
GREGG ALLMAN	12	08	1947
ALICE COOPER	2	04	1948
HOMICIDE	4	08	1948
CAT STEVENS	7	21	1948
PRINCE CHARLES	11	14	1948
HOMICIDE VICTIM	5	13	1949
VIDA BLUE	7	28	1949
MARK SPITZ	2	10	1950
DAVID CASSIDY	4	12	1950
PHOEBE SNOW	7	17	1950
TOM MCLOUGHLIN	7	19	1950
ARTHUR BREMER	8	31	1950
ANOREXIA NERVOSA	10	02	1950
JAY W NORTH	8	03	1951
NARCOLEPTIC FAM	1	29	1952
LUCKY MALE	6	12	1952
CHRIS REEVES	9	25	1952
KIRK O OAKES	4	04	1953
JOHN TRAVOLTA	2	18	1954
RICHARD DEMONT	4	21	1956
DOROTHY HAMILL	7	26	1956
MARARA JI	12	10	1957
GREGORY GODZIK	3	23	1959
PRINCE ANDREW	2	19	1960
JAPANESE ROYALTY	2	23	1960
STEVE CAUTHEN	5	01	1960
ZOOROSH A REZA	10	31	1960
SIAMESE TWINS	6	24	1961
AUTISTIC CHILD	1	09	1962
SIAMESE TWINS	4	06	1962
SIAMESE TWINS	8	10	1963
BIRTH DEFECTS	10	04	1963
BROOKE SHIELDS	5	31	1965
KIMI K MILLER	6	06	1965
AUTISTIC CHILD	7	01	1966
BIRTH DEFECTS	1	14	1970
SIAMESE TWINS	10	13	1974
JOANNE BURNELL	9	30	1977

'C' and 'DD' DATA LISTING BY MONTH/DAY

Name	M	D	Year	Name	M	D	Year	Name	M	D	Year
M MUSSORGSKY	3	21	1839	HERBERT SPENCER	4	27	1820	BRIGHAM YOUNG	6	01	1801
FLORENZ ZIEGFELD	3	21	1869	LIONEL BARRYMORE	4	28	1878	A DI CAGLIOSTRO	6	02	1743
SIR A VANDYCK	3	22	1599	ODETTE SANSOM	4	28	1912	MARQUIS DE SADE	6	02	1740
HOMICIDE #5	3	23	1923	N KHRUSHCHEV	4	29	1894	SIR E ELGAR	6	02	1857
ROSCOE ARBUCKLE	3	24	1887	RICHARD HEADRICK	4	29	1917	SALLY KELLERMAN	6	02	1937
WILLIAM MORRIS	3	24	1834	CELESTE HOLM	4	29	1917	ALLEN GINSBURG	6	03	1926
JOHN W POWELL	3	24	1834	ROD MCKUEN	4	29	1933	DR L H SMITH	6	03	1921
BELA BARTOK	3	25	1881	B L OVERELL	4	30	1929	G J WOLSELEY	6	04	1833
GUTZON BORGLUM	3	25	1867	ROBERT SHAW	4	30	1916	SIR W PETTY	6	05	1623
PADRE PIO	3	25	1887	M VON RICHTHOFEN	5	02	1892	DR F TAYLOR	6	05	1923
JAMES CAAN	3	26	1940	BING CROSBY	5	02	1903	ALEXANDRA,CZARIN	6	06	1872
ROBERT FROST	3	26	1874	DR BENJ SPOCK	5	02	1903	CHE GUEVARRA	6	06	1928
LEONARD NIMOY	3	26	1931	MELL LAZARUS	5	03	1927	NATHAN HALE	6	06	1755
FERDE GROFE	3	27	1892	SUG RAY ROBINSON	5	03	1921	NEVILLE HEATH	6	06	1917
LUDWIG V MIES	3	27	1886	MANUEL BENITES	5	04	1936	PETER LORRE	6	06	1904
MAXIM GORKY	3	28	1868	ALICE FAYE	5	04	1912	AL JOLSON	6	07	1886
EDMUND MUSKIE	3	28	1914	OLIVER CROMWELL	5	05	1599	G B BRUMMELL	6	07	1778
KAREN A QUINLAN	3	29	1954	QUEEN EUGENIE	5	05	1826	RANDY TURPIN	6	07	1928
SEAN O'CASEY	3	30	1880	A P GIANNINI	5	06	1870	WILLIAM L CALLEY	6	08	1943
J S BACH	3	31	1685	ROBERT E PEARY	5	06	1856	FRANK L WRIGHT	6	08	1867
NIKOLAI GOGOL	3	31	1809	M ROBESPIERRE	5	06	1758	SANDRA V LEIKLE	6	09	1946
RENE DESCARTES	3	31	1596	R VALENTINO	5	06	1895	COLE PORTER	6	09	1891
WALLACE BEERY	4	01	1886	JOHANNES BRAHMS	5	07	1833	DUCHESS TATIANA	6	10	1897
LON CHANEY	4	01	1883	GARY COOPER	5	07	1901	F LEE BAILEY	6	10	1933
G CASANOVA	4	02	1725	EVA PERON	5	07	1908	SESSUE HAYAKAWA	6	10	1889
W P CHRYSLER	4	02	1875	R TAGORE	5	07	1861	PORTIA PORTER	6	10	1916
SIR A GUINNESS	4	02	1914	HARRY S TRUMAN	5	08	1884	I VELIKOVSKY	6	10	1895
HOMICIDE #12	4	02	1943	JAMES BARRIE	5	09	1860	JOHN CONSTABLE	6	11	1776
JACK WEBB	4	02	1920	JOHN BROWN	5	09	1800	RICHARD LEOB	6	11	1905
LESLIE HOWARD	4	03	1893	ANTON CERMAK	5	09	1873	JACKIE STEWART	6	11	1939
HENRY R LUCE	4	03	1898	HENRY KAISER	5	09	1882	GEORGE BUSH	6	12	1924
LUCKY #2	4	03	1897	MIKE WALLACE	5	09	1918	K HERRLIGKOFFER	6	13	1916
WAYNE NEWTON	4	03	1942	IRVING BERLIN	5	11	1888	BASIL RATHBONE	6	13	1892
ARTHUR MURRAY	4	04	1895	BURT BACHARACH	5	12	1929	RICHARD THOMAS	6	13	1951
PROSTITUTE #3	4	04	1903	F NIGHTINGALE	5	12	1820	HARRIET B STOWE	6	14	1811
JOSEPH LISTER	4	05	1827	DANTE G ROSETTI	5	12	1828	ANASTASIA	6	17	1901
SPENCER TRACY	4	05	1900	JOE LOUIS	5	13	1914	IGOR STRAVINSKY	6	17	1882
B T WASHINGTON	4	05	1856	SIR A SULLIVAN	5	13	1842	BIRTH DEFECTS	6	17	1939
POVL BANG/JENSEN	4	06	1909	BOBBY DARIN	5	14	1936	GRIGORI RASPUTIN	6	17	1872
D W DOUGLAS JR	4	06	1892	PIERRE CURIE	5	15	1859	HOMICIDE #9	6	18	1922
ANTHONY FOKKER	4	06	1890	RICHARD J DALEY	5	15	1902	PAUL MCCARTNEY	6	18	1942
HARRY HOUDINI	4	06	1874	YVES GAMONET	5	15	1933	GUY LOMBARDO	6	19	1902
LOWELL THOMAS	4	06	1892	HENRY FONDA	5	16	1905	BLAISE PASCAL	6	19	1623
VEREL WALLER	4	06	1911	DAME N MELBA	5	19	1860	JAMES WLAKER	6	19	1881
WILLIAM EYTHE	4	07	1918	JAMES STEWART	5	20	1908	J OFFENBACH	6	20	1819
J W FULBRIGHT	4	09	1905	PETER HURKOS	5	21	1911	BEN JONSON	6	21	1573
MARY PICKFORD	4	09	1892	R MONTGOMERY	5	21	1904	HOMICIDE #4	6	21	1901
GEORGE ARLISS	4	10	1868	ARTHUR C DOYLE	5	22	1859	CARL B STOKES	6	21	1927
WILLIAM BOOTH	4	10	1829	RICHARD WAGNER	5	22	1813	JACK DELINGER	6	22	1926
J PULITZER	4	10	1847	FRANZ MESMER	5	23	1733	MIKE TODD	6	22	1909
JOEL GREY	4	11	1932	UNG-YONG PARENTS	5	23	1934	S RUBINSTEIN	6	24	1908
LUCKY #3	4	11	1893	G W CARVER	5	24	1864	AMBROSE BIERCE	6	24	1842
TOMMY SMITH	4	12	1918	JAMES CRENSHAW	5	24	1908	JACK DEMPSY	6	24	1895
W Q JUDGE	4	13	1851	J C SMUTS	5	24	1870	LORD G KITCHENER	6	24	1850
JAMES B CABELL	4	14	1879	C MONTEVERDI	5	25	1567	GEORGE ORWELL	6	25	1903
F DUVALIER	4	14	1907	BENNETT CERF	5	25	1898	REV G VALE OWEN	6	26	1869
HOMICIDE #10	4	14	1920	DR D WDOWINSKI	5	26	1896	F BYWATERS	6	27	1902
HENRY JAMES	4	15	1843	PEGGY LEE	5	26	1920	EMMA GOLDMAN	6	27	1869
BEAUTY QUEEN	4	16	1945	S RZESHEWSKI	5	26	1912	NELSON EDDY	6	29	1901
CHARLES CHAPLIN	4	16	1889	RACHEL CARSON	5	27	1907	WILLIAM MAYO	6	29	1861
JOHN HODIAK	4	16	1914	JAY GOULD	5	27	1836	L TETRAZZINI	6	29	1871
WILBUR WRIGHT	4	16	1867	H H HUMPHREY	5	27	1911	CHARLES LAUGHTON	7	01	1899
J P MORGAN SR	4	17	1837	SAM SNEAD	5	27	1912	S S NIARCHOS	7	03	1909
CLARENCE DARROW	4	18	1857	IAN FLEMING	5	28	1908	LOUIS ARMSTRONG	7	04	1900
H HARTFORD	4	18	1911	DONALD D MACLEAN	5	28	1913	G LAWRENCE	7	04	1898
E G BROWN SR	4	21	1905	THOMAS MOORE	5	28	1779	ABIGAIL VANBUREN	7	04	1918
JOHN MUIR	4	21	1838	G K CHESTERTON	5	29	1874	WANDA LANDOWSKA	7	05	1879
NICOLAI LENIN	4	22	1870	BOB HOPE	5	29	1903	CECIL J RHODES	7	05	1853
J R OPPENHEIMER	4	22	1904	OSWALD SPENGLER	5	29	1880	W T STEAD	7	05	1849
SERGEI PROKOFIEV	4	23	1891	T H WHITE	5	29	1906	NICKY HILTON	7	06	1926
CHANCEY DEPEW	4	23	1834	ALBRECHT DURER	5	30	1474	MARC CHAGALL	7	07	1887
S A DOUGLAS	4	23	1813	JOE NAMATH	5	31	1943	KING HENRY VIII	7	07	1491
EDWIN MARKHAM	4	23	1852	N V PEALE	5	31	1898	FRITZ PERLS	7	08	1893
JOSEPH M TURNER	4	23	1775	PAT BOONE	6	01	1934	J ROCKEFELLER SR	7	08	1839
ANITA LOOS	4	26	1889	JOHN MASEFIELD	6	01	1878	F VONZEPPELIN	7	08	1838
SAMUEL F B MORSE	4	27	1791	TOM PARK	6	01	1924	LEGGS DIAMOND	7	10	1897

Name	Mo	Day	Year
FREDERICK FLICK	7	10	1883
JOHN GILBERT	7	10	1892
SUE LYON	7	10	1946
J M WHISTLER	7	10	1934
LEN HARVEY	7	11	1907
JOHN WANAMAKER	7	11	1838
LUCKY #6	7	12	1931
JOHN J ASTOR IV	7	13	1864
HELEN COULTHARD	7	13	1894
EDWARD FLANAGAN	7	13	1886
JOE SACRAMENTO	7	14	1874
TRYGVE H LIE	7	16	1896
N G WINNER	7	16	1869
ALEXANDER-GREAT	7	17	-354
JOHN J ASTOR	7	17	1763
JAMES CAGNEY	7	17	1899
ERLE S GARDNER	7	17	1887
ART LINKLETTER	7	17	1912
W M THACKERAY	7	18	1811
Y YEVTUSHENKO	7	18	1933
A J CRONIN	7	19	1896
CHARLES MAYO	7	19	1865
THEDA BARA	7	20	1890
ISAAC STERN	7	21	1920
ARTHUR TREACHER	7	21	1894
ROSE KENNEDY	7	22	1890
CR J GIBBONS	7	23	1834
MAX HEINDEL	7	23	1865
ROBERT GRAVES	7	24	1895
OMAR KHAYYAM	7	25	1050
DAVID BELASCO	7	25	1853
M PARRISH	7	25	1870
ALDOUS HUXLEY	7	26	1894
CARL G JUNG	7	26	1875
ESTES KEFAUVER	7	26	1903
MARY JO KOPECHNE	7	26	1940
SIR J REYNOLDS	7	27	1723
DONALD CRISP	7	27	1886
DAG HAMMARSKJOLD	7	29	1905
BOOTH TARKINGTON	7	29	1869
HENRY FORD	7	30	1863
CLAUDE BRAGDEN	8	01	1866
R H DANA	8	01	1815
FRANCIS S KEY	8	01	1779
F A BARTHOLDI	8	02	1834
HOMICIDE #11	8	02	1932
HENRY S OLCOTT	8	02	1832
ELY CULBERTSON	8	04	1891
RORY CALHOUN	8	08	1922
ARTHUR GOLDBERG	8	08	1908
H J BENNETT	8	09	1878
CHARLES FARRELL	8	09	1905
DR HUGO ECKNER	8	10	1868
NORMA SHEARER	8	10	1904
MIKE DOUGLAS	8	11	1925
R L STRACK	8	11	1932
CECIL B DEMILLE	8	12	1881
ALFRED VON KRUPP	8	13	1907
ANNIE OAKLEY	8	13	1860
JOE DUHEM	8	14	1931
AGA KHAN, SULTAN	8	15	1898
NAPOLEON I	8	15	1769
T E LAWRENCE	8	16	1888
DAVY CROCKETT	8	17	1786
JOHN WHITNEY	8	17	1904
MARSHALL FIELD	8	18	1834
RAFER JOHNSON	8	18	1935
MERIWETHER LEWIS	8	18	1774
BERNARD BARUCH	8	19	1870
OGDEN NASH	8	19	1902
WILLY SHOEMAKER	8	19	1931
ORVILLE WRIGHT	8	19	1871
BEAUTY QUEEN	8	20	1942
A RUDOLPH	8	21	1858
JEFF DAVIS	8	22	1883
DANIEL FROHMAN	8	22	1851
EDGAR L MASTERS	8	23	1869
BRETT HARTE	8	25	1839
SAMUEL GOLDWYN	8	27	1882
VINCENT AURIOL	8	27	1884
THEODORE DREISER	8	27	1871
C KETTERING	8	29	1876
TED WILLIAMS	8	30	1918
JOHN J ANTHONY	9	01	1902
E R BURROUGHS	9	01	1872
GENTLEMAN JIM	9	01	1866
ROCKY MARCIANO	9	01	1924
WALTER REUTHER	9	01	1907
HENRY GEORGE	9	02	1839
G R SIMMS	9	02	1847
ANTON BRUCKNER	9	04	1824
D H BURNHAM	9	04	1846
MICKEY COHEN	9	04	1913
THOMAS EAGLETON	9	04	1929
HENRY FORD II	9	04	1917
JESSE JAMES	9	04	1847
WERNER ERHARD	9	05	1935
J KENNEDY SR	9	06	1888
ANNE BANCROFT	9	07	1931
J P MORGAN JR	9	07	1867
ANTONIN DVORAK	9	08	1841
ROBERT TAFT	9	08	1889
LEO TOLSTOY	9	09	1828
HARRY S BRIDGES	9	09	1898
FRANZ WERFEL	9	10	1890
D H LAWRENCE	9	11	1885
LUCKY #5	9	11	1909
BIRTH DEFECTS	9	12	1950
HENRY L MENCKEN	9	12	1880
JESSE L LASKY	9	13	1880
JACKIE COOPER	9	15	1922
JAMES F COOPER	9	15	1789
KATHRYN MURRAY	9	15	1906
FRANCIS PARKMAN	9	16	1823
SEXTUPLETS	9	16	1973
FANNIE W TUNISON	9	17	1866
MASTER MARCUS	9	19	1955
KENNETH MORE	9	20	1914
LOUIS JOLLIET	9	21	1645
P DE RONSARD	9	21	1524
GUSTAVE HOLST	9	21	1874
A ONASSIS	9	21	1906
J INGEMAR	9	22	1932
PAUL MUNI	9	22	1897
MARK PHILIPS	9	22	1948
V WOODHULL	9	23	1838
D SHOSTAKOVICH	9	25	1906
WM FAULKNER	9	25	1897
T S ELIOT	9	26	1888
GEORGE GERSHWIN	9	26	1898
HOMICIDE #13	9	27	1955
LORRIANE LIELKE	9	27	1926
ED SULLIVAN	9	28	1902
FRANCES WILLARD	9	28	1839
TRUMAN CAPOTE	9	30	1924
ROBIN ROBERTS	9	30	1926
BIRTH DEFECTS	10	01	1926
MOHANDES GANDHI	10	02	1869
P V HINDENBURG	10	02	1847
WILLIE LEY	10	02	1906
GROUCHO MARX	10	02	1895
MARY CASE	10	03	1910
GORE VIDAL	10	03	1925
THOMAS WOLFE	10	03	1900
JUAN MARCH	10	04	1880
PANCHO VILLA	10	04	1877
HOMICIDE #1	10	05	1883
THOR HEYERDAHL	10	06	1914
LE CORBUSIER	10	06	1887
JENNY LIND	10	06	1820
LES RICHTER	10	06	1930
J W RILEY	10	07	1849
ED RICKENBACKER	10	08	1890
DAMON RUNYAN	10	08	1880
E W BOK	10	09	1863
RUTH ELLIS	10	09	1926
HOMICIDE #2	10	11	1919
ALEISTER CROWLEY	10	12	1875
L PAVAROTTI	10	12	1935
LILLIE LANGTRY	10	13	1853
EDWARD MATTHEWS	10	13	1931
PAUL SIMON	10	13	1941
E E CUMMINGS	10	14	1894
D D EISENHOWER	10	14	1890
LILLIAN GISH	10	14	1896
ROGER MOORE	10	14	1927
RICHARD CROMWELL	10	14	1626
DAVID BEN-GURION	10	16	1886
EUGENE O'NEILL	10	16	1888
PAUL ANDERSON	10	17	1932
ARTHUR MILLER	10	17	1915
M MASTROIANNI	10	18	1924
JUAN PERON	10	18	1895
GEORGE C SCOTT	10	18	1927
CPT CHARLES ULM	10	18	1897
GEORGE NADAR	10	19	1921
J STAMPONATO	10	19	1915
JOHN DEWEY	10	20	1859
TED SHAWN	10	21	1891
TIMOTHY LEARY	10	22	1920
BOBBY SEALE	10	22	1936
SARAH BERNHARDT	10	23	1844
DIANA DORS	10	23	1931
RAFAEL TRUJILLO	10	24	1891
PABLO PICASSO	10	25	1881
MOH R PAHLAVI	10	26	1919
EMILY POST	10	27	1872
THOMAS DYLAN	10	27	1914
JONAS SALK	10	28	1914
BILL MAULDIN	10	29	1921
CHARLES ATLAS	10	30	1893
EZRA POUND	10	30	1885
YVES MONTAND	10	31	1921
ALFRED NOBEL	10	31	1833
BILL PEARL	10	31	1930
GARY PLAYER	11	01	1935
AGA KHAN III	11	02	1877
L VISCONTI	11	02	1906
V BELLINI	11	03	1801
CHARLES BRONSON	11	03	1922
WILL ROGERS	11	04	1879
ART GARFUNKEL	11	05	1941
JOHN P SOUSA	11	06	1854
JAMES COOK	11	07	1728
BILLY GRAHAM	11	07	1918
C BARNARD	11	08	1922
LUCKY #1	11	08	1869
MARIE DRESSLER	11	09	1869
STANFORD WHITE	11	09	1853
RICHARD BURTON	11	10	1925
JOHN P MARQUAND	11	10	1893
LUCKY #7	11	11	1912
KURT VONNEGAUT	11	11	1922
F DOSTOEVSKY	11	11	1821
ALEX BORODIN	11	12	1833
PETER TOWNSEND	11	12	1914
R L STEVENSON	11	13	1850
MAMIE EISNEHOWER	11	14	1896
WILLIAM HEIRENS	11	15	1928
JAMES E GROPPI	11	16	1930
LOUIS DAGUERRE	11	18	1789
DOROTHY DIX	11	18	1861
A GALLI-CURCI	11	18	1889
PR R ORSINI	11	18	1931
I J PADEREWSKI	11	18	1860
ROY CAMPANELLA	11	19	1921
G R CLARK	11	19	1752
BILLY SUNDAY	11	19	1863
STAN MUSIAL	11	21	1920
H J O'LOUGHLIN	11	22	1908
WILLIAM BONNEY	11	23	1859
OTIS CHANDLER	11	23	1927
HOWARD DUFF	11	24	1917
JOHN V LINDSAY	11	24	1921
C LUCKY LUCIANO	11	24	1897
ANDREW CARNEGIE	11	25	1835
CARRY NATION	11	25	1846
ROBERT GOULET	11	26	1931
NORBERT WIENER	11	26	1894
FRIEDRICH ENGELS	11	28	1820

Name	M	D	Year
ERNST ROEHM	11	28	1887
A RUBINSTEIN	11	28	1829
PAUL PETTIT	11	29	1931
MARK TWAIN	11	30	1835
REX STOUT	12	01	1886
LUCIUS BEEBE	12	02	1902
JOSEPH CONRAD	12	03	1857
THOMAS CARLYLE	12	04	1795
RAINER M RILKE	12	04	1875
W HEISENBERG	12	05	1901
WILLIAM S HART	12	06	1870
RUDOLF FRIML	12	07	1879
B BJORNSON	12	08	1832
PERCY L CROSBY	12	08	1891
SAMMY DAVIS JR	12	08	1925
DIEGO RIVERA	12	08	1886
JAN SIBELIUS	12	08	1865
JAMES THURBER	12	08	1894
ROBERT KOCH	12	11	1843
F LAGUARDIA	12	11	1882
GENE MARKAY	12	11	1895
PROSTITUTE #2	12	11	1935
A SOLZHENITSYN	12	11	1918
E W DEMARA	12	12	1921
E G ROBINSON	12	12	1893
C H GILBERT	12	13	1874
HOMICIDE #3	12	13	1910
JAMES DOOLITTLE	12	14	1896
J PAUL GETTY	12	15	1892
L V BEETHOVAN	12	16	1770
RUSSEL BEITZEL	12	17	1900
ERSKINE CALDWELL	12	17	1903
ALLIGATOR MAN	12	18	1904
EARL C ANTHONY	12	18	1880
TYRUS R COBB	12	18	1886
DALAI-LAMA	12	18	1933
PAUL KLEE	12	18	1879
JOHN CANDIES	12	19	1919
JEAN GENET	12	19	1910
BRUCE CONNERS	12	20	1918
JEAN RACINE	12	21	1639
CLAUDIA JOHNSON	12	22	1912
GEORGE BRASNO	12	23	1911
JAMES B DUKE	12	23	1856
HELMUT SCHMIDT	12	23	1918
JOSEPH SMITH	12	23	1805
KIT CARSON	12	24	1809
HOWARD HUGHES	12	24	1905
M DE NOSTRADAMUS	12	24	1503
CARLOS CASTENEDA	12	25	1925
CONRAD HILTON	12	25	1887
ANWAR SADAT	12	25	1918
ROD SERLING	12	25	1924
H RUBINSTEIN	12	25	1870
MAO TSE TUNG	12	26	1893
ROBERT RIPLEY	12	26	1893
ROY BISSETT	12	27	1900
TITO SCHIPA	12	28	1889
PABLO CASALS	12	29	1876
WM GLADSTONE	12	29	1809
RUDYARD KIPLING	12	30	1865
BARRY GOLDWATER	1	01	1909
ROBERT KORNING	1	01	1901
JOSEPH STALIN	1	02	1880
CLEMENT R ATTLEE	1	03	1883
VICTOR BORGE	1	03	1909
FR J DAMIEN	1	03	1840
M VAN DERLUBBE	1	03	1909
POLA NEGRI	1	03	1897
J R R TOLKIEN	1	03	1892
JEANE DIXON	1	04	1904
LUCKY #4	1	05	1915
ALEX SCRIABIN	1	06	1872
DR B FINCH	1	07	1918
R D BANDARANAIKE	1	08	1899
DWARF	1	08	1909
R HALLIBURTON	1	09	1900
FINN MALMGREN	1	09	1895
ANDREAS VESALIUS	1	10	1515
ROBINSON JEFFERS	1	10	1887
WILLIAM JAMES	1	11	1842
HARRY K THAW	1	12	1871
HORATIO ALGER	1	13	1832
J J PERSHING	1	13	1860
SOPHIE TUCKER	1	13	1886
ANNA MAY WONG	1	13	1905
YUKIO MISHIMA	1	14	1925
MARTIN NIEMOLLER	1	14	1892
DR PETIOT	1	14	1897
DR M L KING	1	15	1929
ABDAL G NASSER	1	15	1918
F BATISTA	1	16	1901
ETHEL MERMAN	1	16	1908
GEORGE D LLOYD	1	17	1863
PROSTITUTE #4	1	17	1940
AL CAPONE	1	18	1899
MANUAL GARCIA	1	18	1866
CARY GRANT	1	18	1904
A P SINNETT	1	18	1840
CAPT JOHN SMITH	1	19	1580
EDGAR A POE	1	19	1809
F FELLINI	1	20	1920
C A LINDBURGH	1	20	1859
JOHN CARTEEK	1	22	1861
DAVID W GRIFFITH	1	22	1878
HJALMAR SCHACHT	1	22	1877
F MOORE VINSON	1	22	1890
BEATRICE WEBB	1	22	1858
HUMPHREY BOGART	1	23	1899
W F FALLON	1	23	1886
STENDHAL	1	23	1783
ORAL ROBERTS	1	24	1918
ROBERT BURNS	1	25	1759
W FURTWANGLER	1	25	1886
W S MAUGHAM	1	25	1874
VIRGINIA WOOLF	1	25	1882
D MACARTHUR	1	26	1880
LEWIS CARROLL	1	27	1832
ARTUR RUBINSTEIN	1	28	1886
ANTON CHEKHOV	1	29	1860
FREDERICK DELIUS	1	29	1862
HOMICIDE #6	1	30	1925
ANNA PAVLOVA	1	31	1882
T BANKHEAD	1	31	1903
EDDIE CANTOR	1	31	1892
SIR F BACON	2	01	1561
CLARK GABLE	2	01	1901
WILLIAM HICHMAN	2	01	1908
HAVELOCK ELLIS	2	02	1859
V G D'ESTAING	2	02	1926
JASCHA HEIFETZ	2	02	1901
JAMES JOYCE	2	02	1882
C LINDBERGH	2	04	1902
HANK AARON	2	05	1934
T DANIELSON	2	06	1922
FABIAN FORTE	2	06	1943
RONALD REAGAN	2	06	1911
BABE RUTH	2	06	1895
ALFRED ADLER	2	07	1870
CHARLES DICKENS	2	07	1812
SINCLAIR LEWIS	2	07	1885
ELMER A LIELKE	2	07	1924
E SWEDENBORG	2	08	1688
JACK LEMMON	2	08	1925
RONALD COLEMAN	2	09	1891
GYPSY ROSE LEE	2	09	1914
AMY LOWELL	2	09	1874
PROSTITUTE #1	2	09	1919
CAPT C SMITH	2	09	1897
BORIS PASTERNAK	2	10	1890
ALAN HALE SR	2	10	1892
HAROLD MACMILLAN	2	10	1894
ADELINA PATTI	2	10	1843
W A WHITE	2	10	1868
F RABELAIS	2	12	1494
JOSEPH ALIOTO	2	12	1916
LORD R CHURCHILL	2	12	1849
CHARLES DARWIN	2	12	1908
JOHN L LEWIS	2	12	1880
BESS TRUMAN	2	13	1885
JACK BENNY	2	14	1894
RONNIE KNOX	2	14	1935
JAMES PIKE	2	14	1913
CHRIS SHOLES	2	14	1819
ROBERT R YOUNG	2	14	1897
JOHN BARRYMORE	2	15	1882
JAMES FORRESTAL	2	15	1892
THOMAS MALTHUS	2	17	1766
O O MCINTYRE	2	18	1884
ADOLPH MENJOU	2	18	1890
RAMAKIRISHNA	2	18	1836
CHARLES M SCHWAB	2	18	1862
ANDRES SEGOVIA	2	18	1894
CHRIS EVANS	2	19	1847
SVEN HEDIN	2	19	1865
W FALCONER	2	21	1732
HOMICIDE #8	2	21	1925
JOHN H NEWMAN	2	21	1801
SIR R B-POWELL	2	22	1857
JAMES R LOWELL	2	22	1819
A SCHOPENHAUER	2	22	1788
ROBERT WADLOW	2	22	1918
SHELLEY BERMAN	2	23	1926
THOMAS GALLAGHER	2	23	1918
BARON ROTHSCHILD	2	23	1743
JOHN F DULLES	2	25	1888
SRI BABA MEHER	2	25	1894
D S WINDELL	2	25	1886
JOHNNY CASH	2	26	1932
BUFFALO B CODY	2	26	1846
EMILE COUE	2	26	1857
EMMA DESTINN	2	26	1878
DAVID SARNOFF	2	27	1891
RUDOLPH STEINER	2	27	1861
JOHN STEINBECK	2	27	1902
LINUS PAULING	2	28	1901
BUGSY SIEGAL	2	28	1906
MORARJEE DESAI	2	29	1896
BEDRICH SMETNA	3	02	1824
GILBERT ADRIAN	3	03	1903
CHILD MOLESTER	3	03	1933
RONALD SEARLE	3	03	1920
JIM CLARK	3	04	1936
MATT CVETIC	3	04	1909
JOHN GARFIELD	3	04	1913
CHARLES GOREN	3	04	1901
HOMICIDE #7	3	04	1926
KNUTE ROCKNE	3	04	1888
GEORGE DUMAURIER	3	06	1834
LUTHER BURBANK	3	07	1849
BEN A WILLIAMS	3	07	1889
BRAMWELL BOOTH	3	08	1856
O W HOLMES	3	08	1841
Y MOLOTOV	3	09	1890
YURI GAGARIN	3	09	1934
LELAND STANFORD	3	09	1824
ALEXANDER III	3	10	1845
VASLAV NIJINSKI	3	12	1890
FRITZ BUSCH	3	13	1890
H M HIRSCHBACH	3	13	1890
PERCIVAL LOWELL	3	13	1855
HUGO WOLF	3	13	1860
JERRY LEWIS	3	16	1926
PROSTITUTION	3	16	1904
RUDOLPH NUREYEV	3	17	1938
ROGER B TANEY	3	17	1777
N RIMS-KORSAKOV	3	18	1844
N CHAMBERLAIN	3	18	1869
RUDOLF DIESEL	3	18	1858
HENRIK IBSEN	3	20	1828
LAURITZ MELCHIOR	3	20	1890
B F SKINNER	3	20	1904

Name	Mo	Day	Year
ALEXANDER-GREAT	7	17	-354
OMAR KHAYYAM	7	25	1050
ALBRECHT DURER	5	30	1474
KING HENRY VIII	7	07	1491
F RABELAIS	2	12	1494
M DE NOSTRADAMUS	12	24	1503
ANDREAS VESALIUS	1	10	1515
P DE RONSARD	9	21	1524
SIR F BACON	2	01	1561
C MONTEVERDI	5	25	1567
BEN JONSON	6	21	1573
CAPT JOHN SMITH	1	19	1580
RENE DESCARTES	3	31	1596
SIR A VANDYCK	3	22	1599
OLIVER CROMWELL	5	05	1599
SIR W PETTY	6	05	1623
BLAISE PASCAL	6	19	1623
RICHARD CROMWELL	10	14	1626
JEAN RACINE	12	21	1639
LOUIS JOLLIET	9	21	1645
J S BACH	3	31	1685
E SWEDENBORG	2	08	1688
SIR J REYNOLDS	7	27	1723
G CASANOVA	4	02	1725
JAMES COOK	11	07	1728
W FALCONER	2	21	1732
FRANZ MESMER	5	23	1733
MARQUIS DE SADE	6	02	1740
BARON ROTHSCHILD	2	23	1743
A DI CAGLIOSTRO	6	02	1743
G R CLARK	11	19	1752
NATHAN HALE	6	06	1755
M ROBESPIERRE	5	06	1758
ROBERT BURNS	1	25	1759
JOHN J ASTOR	7	17	1763
THOMAS MALTHUS	2	17	1766
NAPOLEON I	8	15	1769
L V BEETHOVAN	12	16	1770
MERIWETHER LEWIS	8	18	1774
JOSEPH M TURNER	4	23	1775
JOHN CONSTABLE	6	11	1776
ROGER B TANEY	3	17	1777
G B BRUMMELL	6	07	1778
THOMAS MOORE	5	28	1779
FRANCIS S KEY	8	01	1779
STENDHAL	1	23	1783
DAVY CROCKETT	8	17	1786
A SCHOPENHAUER	2	22	1788
JAMES F COOPER	9	15	1789
LOUIS DAGUERRE	11	18	1789
SAMUEL F B MORSE	4	27	1791
THOMAS CARLYLE	12	04	1795
JOHN BROWN	5	09	1800
JOHN H NEWMAN	2	21	1801
BRIGHAM YOUNG	6	01	1801
V BELLINI	11	03	1801
JOSEPH SMITH	12	23	1805
EDGAR A POE	1	19	1809
NIKOLAI GOGOL	3	31	1809
KIT CARSON	12	24	1809
WM GLADSTONE	12	29	1809
HARRIET B STOWE	6	14	1811
W M THACKERAY	7	18	1811
CHARLES DICKENS	2	07	1812
S A DOUGLAS	4	23	1813
RICHARD WAGNER	5	22	1813
R H DANA	8	01	1815
CHRIS SHOLES	2	14	1819
JAMES R LOWELL	2	22	1819
J OFFENBACH	6	20	1819
HERBERT SPENCER	4	27	1820
F NIGHTINGALE	5	12	1820
JENNY LIND	10	06	1820
FRIEDRICH ENGELS	11	28	1820
F DOSTOEVSKY	11	11	1821
FRANCIS PARKMAN	9	16	1823
BEDRICH SMETNA	3	02	1824
LELAND STANFORD	3	09	1824
ANTON BRUCKNER	9	04	1824
QUEEN EUGENIE	5	05	1826
JOSEPH LISTER	4	05	1827
HENRIK IBSEN	3	20	1828
DANTE G ROSETTI	5	12	1828
LEO TOLSTOY	9	09	1828
WILLIAM BOOTH	4	10	1829
A RUBINSTEIN	11	28	1829
HORATIO ALGER	1	13	1832
LEWIS CARROLL	1	27	1832
HENRY S OLCOTT	8	02	1832
B BJORNSON	12	08	1832
JOHANNES BRAHMS	5	07	1833
G J WOLSELEY	6	04	1833
ALFRED NOBEL	10	31	1833
ALEX BORODIN	11	12	1833
GEORGE DUMAURIER	3	06	1834
WILLIAM MORRIS	3	24	1834
JOHN W POWELL	3	24	1834
CHANCEY DEPEW	4	23	1834
CR J GIBBONS	7	23	1834
F A BARTHOLDI	8	02	1834
MARSHALL FIELD	8	18	1834
ANDREW CARNEGIE	11	25	1835
MARK TWAIN	11	30	1835
RAMAKIRISHNA	2	18	1836
JAY GOULD	5	27	1836
J P MORGAN SR	4	17	1837
JOHN MUIR	4	21	1838
F VONZEPPELIN	7	08	1838
JOHN WANAMAKER	7	11	1838
V WOODHULL	9	23	1838
M MUSSORGSKY	3	21	1839
J ROCKEFELLER SR	7	08	1839
BRETT HARTE	8	25	1839
HENRY GEORGE	9	02	1839
FRANCES WILLARD	9	28	1839
FR J DAMIEN	1	03	1840
A P SINNETT	1	18	1840
O W HOLMES	3	08	1841
ANTONIN DVORAK	9	08	1841
WILLIAM JAMES	1	11	1842
SIR A SULLIVAN	5	13	1842
AMBROSE BIERCE	6	24	1842
ADELINA PATTI	2	10	1843
HENRY JAMES	4	15	1843
ROBERT KOCH	12	11	1843
N RIMS-KORSAKOV	3	18	1844
SARAH BERNHARDT	10	23	1844
ALEXANDER III	3	10	1845
BUFFALO B CODY	2	26	1846
D H BURNHAM	9	04	1846
CARRY NATION	11	25	1846
CHRIS EVANS	2	19	1847
J PULITZER	4	10	1847
G R SIMMS	9	02	1847
JESSE JAMES	9	04	1847
P V HINDENBURG	10	02	1847
LORD R CHURCHILL	2	12	1849
LUTHER BURBANK	3	07	1849
W T STEAD	7	05	1849
J W RILEY	10	07	1849
LORD G KITCHENER	6	24	1850
R L STEVENSON	11	13	1850
W Q JUDGE	4	13	1851
DANIEL FROHMAN	8	22	1851
EDWIN MARKHAM	4	23	1852
CECIL J RHODES	7	05	1853
DAVID BELASCO	7	25	1853
LILLIE LANGTRY	10	13	1853
STANFORD WHITE	11	09	1853
JOHN P SOUSA	11	06	1854
PERCIVAL LOWELL	3	13	1855
BRAMWELL BOOTH	3	08	1856
B T WASHINGTON	4	05	1856
ROBERT E PEARY	5	06	1856
JAMES B DUKE	12	23	1856
SIR R B-POWELL	2	22	1857
EMILE COUE	2	26	1857
CLARENCE DARROW	4	18	1857
SIR E ELGAR	6	02	1857
JOSEPH CONRAD	12	03	1857
BEATRICE WEBB	1	22	1858
RUDOLF DIESEL	3	18	1858
A RUDOLPH	8	21	1858
C A LINDBURGH	1	20	1859
HAVELOCK ELLIS	2	02	1859
PIERRE CURIE	5	15	1859
ARTHUR C DOYLE	5	22	1859
JOHN DEWEY	10	20	1859
WILLIAM BONNEY	11	23	1859
J J PERSHING	1	13	1860
ANTON CHEKHOV	1	29	1860
HUGO WOLF	3	13	1860
JAMES BARRIE	5	09	1860
DAME N MELBA	5	19	1860
ANNIE OAKLEY	8	13	1860
I J PADEREWSKI	11	18	1860
JOHN CARTEEK	1	22	1861
RUDOLPH STEINER	2	27	1861
R TACORE	5	07	1861
WILLIAM MAYO	6	29	1861
DOROTHY DIX	11	18	1861
FREDERICK DELIUS	1	29	1862
CHARLES M SCHWAB	2	18	1862
GEORGE D LLOYD	1	17	1863
HENRY FORD	7	30	1863
E W BOK	10	09	1863
BILLY SUNDAY	11	19	1863
G W CARVER	5	24	1864
JOHN J ASTOR IV	7	13	1864
SVEN HEDIN	2	19	1865
CHARLES MAYO	7	19	1865
MAX HEINDEL	7	23	1865
JAN SIBELIUS	12	08	1865
RUDYARD KIPLING	12	30	1865
MANUAL GARCIA	1	18	1866
CLAUDE BRAGDEN	8	01	1866
GENTLEMAN JIM	9	01	1866
FANNIE W TUNISON	9	17	1866
GUTZON BORGLUM	3	25	1867
WILBUR WRIGHT	4	16	1867
FRANK L WRIGHT	6	08	1867
J P MORGAN JR	9	07	1867
W A WHITE	2	10	1868
MAXIM GORKY	3	28	1868
GEORGE ARLISS	4	10	1868
DR HUGO ECKNER	8	10	1868
N CHAMBERLAIN	3	18	1869
FLORENZ ZIEGFELD	3	21	1869
REV G VALE OWEN	6	26	1869
EMMA GOLDMAN	6	27	1869
N C WINNER	7	16	1869
BOOTH TARKINGTON	7	29	1869
EDGAR L MASTERS	8	23	1869
MOHANDES GANDHI	10	02	1869
LUCKY #1	11	08	1869
MARIE DRESSLER	11	09	1869
ALFRED ADLER	2	07	1870
NICOLAI LENIN	4	22	1870
A P GIANNINI	5	06	1870
J C SMUTS	5	24	1870
M PARRISH	7	25	1870
BERNARD BARUCH	8	19	1870
WILLIAM S HART	12	06	1870
H RUBINSTEIN	12	25	1870
HARRY K THAW	1	12	1871
L TETRAZZINI	6	29	1871
ORVILLE WRIGHT	8	19	1871
THEODORE DREISER	8	27	1871

Name				Name				Name			
ALEX SCRIABIN	1	06	1872	TYRUS R COBB	12	18	1886	R VALENTINO	5	06	1895
ALEXANDRA, CZARIN	6	06	1872	ROBINSON JEFFERS	1	10	1887	I VELIKOVSKY	6	10	1895
GRIGORI RASPUTIN	6	17	1872	ROSCOE ARBUCKLE	3	24	1887	JACK DEMPSY	6	24	1895
E R BURROUGHS	9	01	1872	PADRE PIO	3	25	1887	ROBERT GRAVES	7	24	1895
EMILY POST	10	27	1872	MARC CHAGALL	7	07	1887	GROUCHO MARX	10	02	1895
ANTON CERMAK	5	09	1873	ERLE S GARDNER	7	17	1887	JUAN PERON	10	18	1895
W S MAUGHAM	1	25	1874	LE CORBUSIER	10	06	1887	GENE MARKAY	12	11	1895
AMY LOWELL	2	09	1874	ERNST ROEHM	11	28	1887	MORARJEE DESAI	2	29	1896
ROBERT FROST	3	26	1874	CONRAD HILTON	12	25	1887	DR D WDOWINSKI	5	26	1896
HARRY HOUDINI	4	06	1874	JOHN F DULLES	2	25	1888	TRYGVE H LIE	7	16	1896
G K CHESTERTON	5	29	1874	KNUTE ROCKNE	3	04	1888	A J CRONIN	7	19	1896
JOE SACRAMENTO	7	14	1874	IRVING BERLIN	5	11	1888	LILLIAN GISH	10	14	1896
GUSTAVE HOLST	9	21	1874	T E LAWRENCE	8	16	1888	MAMIE EISNEHOWER	11	14	1896
C H GILBERT	12	13	1874	J KENNEDY SR	9	06	1888	JAMES DOOLITTLE	12	14	1896
W P CHRYSLER	4	02	1875	T S ELIOT	9	26	1888	POLA NEGRI	1	03	1897
CARL G JUNG	7	26	1875	EUGENE O'NEILL	10	16	1888	DR PETIOT	1	14	1897
ALEISTER CROWLEY	10	12	1875	BEN A WILLIAMS	3	07	1889	CAPT C SMITH	2	09	1897
RAINER M RILKE	12	04	1875	CHARLES CHAPLIN	4	16	1889	ROBERT R YOUNG	2	14	1897
C KETTERING	8	29	1876	ANITA LOOS	4	26	1889	LUCKY #2	4	03	1897
PABLO CASALS	12	29	1876	SESSUE HAYAKAWA	6	10	1889	DUCHESS TATIANA	6	10	1897
HJALMAR SCHACHT	1	22	1877	ROBERT TAFT	9	08	1889	LEGGS DIAMOND	7	10	1897
PANCHO VILLA	10	04	1877	A GALLI-CURCI	11	18	1889	PAUL MUNI	9	22	1897
AGA KHAN III	11	02	1877	TITO SCHIPA	12	28	1889	WM FAULKNER	9	25	1897
DAVID W GRIFFITH	1	22	1878	F MOORE VINSON	1	22	1890	CPT CHARLES ULM	10	18	1897
EMMA DESTINN	2	26	1878	BORIS PASTERNAK	2	10	1890	C LUCKY LUCIANO	11	24	1897
LIONEL BARRYMORE	4	28	1878	ADOLPH MENJOU	2	18	1890	HENRY R LUCE	4	03	1898
JOHN MASEFIELD	6	01	1878	Y MOLOTOV	3	09	1890	BENNETT CERF	5	25	1898
H J BENNETT	8	09	1878	VASLAV NIJINSKI	3	12	1890	N V PEALE	5	31	1898
WANDA LANDOWSKA	7	05	1879	FRITZ BUSCH	3	13	1890	G LAWRENCE	7	04	1898
WILL ROGERS	11	04	1879	H M HIRSCHBACH	3	13	1890	AGA KHAN, SULTAN	8	15	1898
RUDOLF FRIML	12	07	1879	LAURITZ MELCHIOR	3	20	1890	HARRY S BRIDGES	9	09	1898
PAUL KLEE	12	18	1879	ANTHONY FOKKER	4	06	1890	GEORGE GERSHWIN	9	26	1898
JAMES B CABELL	4	14	1879	THEDA BARA	7	20	1890	R D BANDARANAIKE	1	08	1899
JOSEPH STALIN	1	02	1880	ROSE KENNEDY	7	22	1890	AL CAPONE	1	18	1899
D MACARTHUR	1	26	1880	FRANZ WERFEL	9	10	1890	HUMPHREY BOGART	1	23	1899
JOHN L LEWIS	2	12	1880	ED RICKENBACKER	10	08	1890	CHARLES LAUGHTON	7	01	1899
SEAN O'CASEY	3	30	1880	D D EISENHOWER	10	14	1890	JAMES CAGNEY	7	17	1899
OSWALD SPENGLER	5	29	1880	RONALD COLEMAN	2	09	1891	R HALLIBURTON	1	09	1900
HENRY L MENCKEN	9	12	1880	DAVID SARNOFF	2	27	1891	SPENCER TRACY	4	05	1900
JESSE L LASKY	9	13	1880	SERGEI PROKOFIEV	4	23	1891	LOUIS ARMSTRONG	7	04	1900
JUAN MARCH	10	04	1880	COLE PORTER	6	09	1891	THOMAS WOLFE	10	03	1900
DAMON RUNYAN	10	08	1880	ELY CULBERTSON	8	04	1891	RUSSEL BEITZEL	12	17	1900
EARL C ANTHONY	12	18	1880	TED SHAWN	10	21	1891	ROY BISSETT	12	27	1900
BELA BARTOK	3	25	1881	RAFAEL TRUJILLO	10	24	1891	ROBERT KORNING	1	01	1901
JAMES WLAKER	6	19	1881	PERCY L CROSBY	12	08	1891	F BATISTA	1	16	1901
CECIL B DEMILLE	8	12	1881	J R R TOLKIEN	1	03	1892	CLARK GABLE	2	01	1901
PABLO PICASSO	10	25	1881	MARTIN NIEMOLLER	1	14	1892	JASCHA HEIFETZ	2	02	1901
VIRGINIA WOOLF	1	25	1882	EDDIE CANTOR	1	31	1892	LINUS PAULING	2	28	1901
ANNA PAVLOVA	1	31	1882	ALAN HALE SR	2	10	1892	CHARLES GOREN	3	04	1901
JAMES JOYCE	2	02	1882	JAMES FORRESTAL	2	15	1892	GARY COOPER	5	07	1901
JOHN BARRYMORE	2	15	1882	FERDE GROFE	3	27	1892	ANASTASIA	6	17	1901
HENRY KAISER	5	09	1882	D W DOUGLAS JR	4	06	1892	HOMICIDE #4	6	21	1901
IGOR STRAVINSKY	6	17	1882	LOWELL THOMAS	4	06	1892	NELSON EDDY	6	29	1901
SAMUEL GOLDWYN	8	27	1882	MARY PICKFORD	4	09	1892	W HEISENBERG	12	05	1901
F LAGUARDIA	12	11	1882	M VON RICHTHOFEN	5	02	1892	C LINDBERGH	2	04	1902
CLEMENT R ATTLEE	1	03	1883	BASIL RATHBONE	6	13	1892	JOHN STEINBECK	2	27	1902
LON CHANEY	4	01	1883	JOHN GILBERT	7	10	1892	RICHARD J DALEY	5	15	1902
FREDERICK FLICK	7	10	1883	J PAUL GETTY	12	15	1892	GUY LOMBARDO	6	19	1902
JEFF DAVIS	8	22	1883	LESLIE HOWARD	4	03	1893	F BYWATERS	6	27	1902
HOMICIDE #1	10	05	1883	LUCKY #3	4	11	1893	OGDEN NASH	8	19	1902
O O MCINTYRE	2	18	1884	FRITZ PERLS	7	08	1893	JOHN J ANTHONY	9	01	1902
HARRY S TRUMAN	5	08	1884	CHARLES ATLAS	10	30	1893	ED SULLIVAN	9	28	1902
VINCENT AURIOL	8	27	1884	JOHN P MARQUAND	11	10	1893	LUCIUS BEEBE	12	02	1902
SINCLAIR LEWIS	2	07	1885	E G ROBINSON	12	12	1893	T BANKHEAD	1	31	1903
BESS TRUMAN	2	13	1885	MAO TSE TUNG	12	26	1893	GILBERT ADRIAN	3	03	1903
D H LAWRENCE	9	11	1885	ROBERT RIPLEY	12	26	1893	PROSTITUTE #3	4	04	1903
EZRA POUND	10	30	1885	HAROLD MACMILLAN	2	10	1894	BING CROSBY	5	02	1903
SOPHIE TUCKER	1	13	1886	JACK BENNY	2	14	1894	DR BENJ SPOCK	5	02	1903
W F FALLON	1	23	1886	ANDRES SEGOVIA	2	18	1894	BOB HOPE	5	29	1903
W FURTWANGLER	1	25	1886	SRI BABA MEHER	2	25	1894	GEORGE ORWELL	6	25	1903
ARTUR RUBINSTEIN	1	28	1886	N KHRUSHCHEV	4	29	1894	ESTES KEFAUVER	7	26	1903
D S WINDELL	2	25	1886	HELEN COULTHARD	7	13	1894	ERSKINE CALDWELL	12	17	1903
LUDWIG V MIES	3	27	1886	ARTHUR TREACHER	7	21	1894	JEANE DIXON	1	04	1904
WALLACE BEERY	4	01	1886	ALDOUS HUXLEY	7	26	1894	CARY GRANT	1	18	1904
AL JOLSON	6	07	1886	E E CUMMINGS	10	14	1894	PROSTITUTION	3	16	1904
EDWARD FLANAGAN	7	13	1886	NORBERT WIENER	11	26	1894	B F SKINNER	3	20	1904
DONALD CRISP	7	27	1886	JAMES THURBER	12	08	1894	J R OPPENHEIMER	4	22	1904
DAVID BEN-GURION	10	16	1886	FINN MALMGREN	1	09	1895	R MONTGOMERY	5	21	1904
REX STOUT	12	01	1886	BABE RUTH	2	06	1895	PETER LORRE	6	06	1904
DIEGO RIVERA	12	08	1886	ARTHUR MURRAY	4	04	1895	NORMA SHEARER	8	10	1904

Name	M	D	Year
JOHN WHITNEY	8	17	1904
ALLIGATOR MAN	12	18	1904
ANNA MAY WONG	1	13	1905
J W FULBRIGHT	4	09	1905
E G BROWN SR	4	21	1905
HENRY FONDA	5	16	1905
RICHARD LEOB	6	11	1905
DAG HAMMARSKJOLD	7	29	1905
CHARLES FARRELL	8	09	1905
HOWARD HUGHES	12	24	1905
BUGSY SIEGAL	2	28	1906
T H WHITE	5	29	1906
KATHRYN MURRAY	9	15	1906
A ONASSIS	9	21	1906
D SHOSTAKOVICH	9	25	1906
WILLIE LEY	10	02	1906
L VISCONTI	11	02	1906
F DUVALIER	4	14	1907
RACHEL CARSON	5	27	1907
LEN HARVEY	7	11	1907
ALFRED VON KRUPP	8	13	1907
WALTER REUTHER	9	01	1907
ETHEL MERMAN	1	16	1908
WILLIAM HICHMAN	2	01	1908
CHARLES DARWIN	2	12	1908
EVA PERON	5	07	1908
JAMES STEWART	5	20	1908
JAMES CRENSHAW	5	24	1908
IAN FLEMING	5	28	1908
S RUBINSTEIN	6	24	1908
ARTHUR GOLDBERG	8	08	1908
H J O'LOUGHLIN	11	22	1908
BARRY GOLDWATER	1	01	1909
VICTOR BORGE	1	03	1909
M VAN DERLUBBE	1	03	1909
DWARF	1	08	1909
MATT CVETIC	3	04	1909
POVL BANG/JENSEN	4	06	1909
MIKE TODD	6	22	1909
S S NIARCHOS	7	03	1909
LUCKY #5	9	11	1909
MARY CASE	10	03	1910
HOMICIDE #3	12	13	1910
JEAN GENET	12	19	1910
RONALD REAGAN	2	06	1911
VEREL WALLER	4	06	1911
H HARTFORD	4	18	1911
PETER HURKOS	5	21	1911
H H HUMPHREY	5	27	1911
GEORGE BRASNO	12	23	1911
ODETTE SANSOM	4	28	1912
ALICE FAYE	5	04	1912
S RZESHEWSKI	5	26	1912
SAM SNEAD	5	27	1912
ART LINKLETTER	7	17	1912
LUCKY #7	11	11	1912
CLAUDIA JOHNSON	12	22	1912
JAMES PIKE	2	14	1913
JOHN GARFIELD	3	04	1913
DONALD D MACLEAN	5	28	1913
MICKEY COHEN	9	04	1913
GYPSY ROSE LEE	2	09	1914
EDMUND MUSKIE	3	28	1914
SIR A GUINNESS	4	02	1914
JOHN HODIAK	4	16	1914
JOE LOUIS	5	13	1914
KENNETH MORE	9	20	1914
THOR HEYERDAHL	10	06	1914
THOMAS DYLAN	10	27	1914
JONAS SALK	10	28	1914
PETER TOWNSEND	11	12	1914
LUCKY #4	1	05	1915
ARTHUR MILLER	10	17	1915
J STAMPONATO	10	19	1915
JOSEPH ALIOTO	2	12	1916
ROBERT SHAW	4	30	1916
PORTIA PORTER	6	10	1916
K HERRLIGKOFFER	6	13	1916
RICHARD HEADRICK	4	29	1917
CELESTE HOLM	4	29	1917
NEVILLE HEATH	6	06	1917
HENRY FORD II	9	04	1917
HOWARD DUFF	11	24	1917
DR B FINCH	1	07	1918
ABDAL G NASSER	1	15	1918
ORAL ROBERTS	1	24	1918
ROBERT WADLOW	2	22	1918
THOMAS GALLAGHER	2	23	1918
WILLIAM EYTHE	4	07	1918
TOMMY SMITH	4	12	1918
MIKE WALLACE	5	09	1918
ABIGAIL VANBUREN	7	04	1918
TED WILLIAMS	8	30	1918
BILLY GRAHAM	11	07	1918
A SOLZHENITSYN	12	11	1918
BRUCE CONNERS	12	20	1918
HELMUT SCHMIDT	12	23	1918
ANWAR SADAT	12	25	1918
PROSTITUTE #1	2	09	1919
HOMICIDE #2	10	11	1919
MOH R PAHLAVI	10	26	1919
JOHN CANDIES	12	19	1919
F FELLINI	1	20	1920
RONALD SEARLE	3	03	1920
JACK WEBB	4	02	1920
HOMICIDE #10	4	14	1920
PEGGY LEE	5	26	1920
ISAAC STERN	7	21	1920
TIMOTHY LEARY	10	22	1920
STAN MUSIAL	11	21	1920
SUG RAY ROBINSON	5	03	1921
DR L H SMITH	6	03	1921
GEORGE NADAR	10	19	1921
BILL MAULDIN	10	29	1921
YVES MONTAND	10	31	1921
ROY CAMPANELLA	11	19	1921
JOHN V LINDSAY	11	24	1921
E W DEMARA	12	12	1921
T DANIELSON	2	06	1922
HOMICIDE #9	6	18	1922
RORY CALHOUN	8	08	1922
JACKIE COOPER	9	15	1922
CHARLES BRONSON	11	03	1922
C BARNARD	11	08	1922
KURT VONNEGAUT	11	11	1922
HOMICIDE #5	3	23	1923
DR F TAYLOR	6	05	1923
ELMER A LIELKE	2	07	1924
TOM PARK	6	01	1924
GEORGE BUSH	6	12	1924
ROCKY MARCIANO	9	01	1924
TRUMAN CAPOTE	9	30	1924
M MASTROIANNI	10	18	1924
ROD SERLING	12	25	1924
YUKIO MISHIMA	1	14	1925
HOMICIDE #6	1	30	1925
JACK LEMMON	2	08	1925
HOMICIDE #8	2	21	1925
MIKE DOUGLAS	8	11	1925
GORE VIDAL	10	03	1925
RICHARD BURTON	11	10	1925
SAMMY DAVIS JR	12	08	1925
CARLOS CASTENEDA	12	25	1925
V G D'ESTAING	2	02	1926
SHELLEY BERMAN	2	23	1926
HOMICIDE #7	3	04	1926
JERRY LEWIS	3	16	1926
ALLEN GINSBURG	6	03	1926
JACK DELINGER	6	22	1926
NICKY HILTON	7	06	1926
LORRIANE LIELKE	9	27	1926
ROBIN ROBERTS	9	30	1926
BIRTH DEFECTS	10	01	1926
RUTH ELLIS	10	09	1926
MELL LAZARUS	5	03	1927
CARL B STOKES	6	21	1927
ROGER MOORE	10	14	1927
GEORGE C SCOTT	10	18	1927
OTIS CHANDLER	11	23	1927
CHE GUEVARRA	6	06	1928
RANDY TURPIN	6	07	1928
WILLIAM HEIRENS	11	15	1928
DR M L KING	1	15	1929
B L OVERELL	4	30	1929
BURT BACHARACH	5	12	1929
THOMAS EAGLETON	9	04	1929
LES RICHTER	10	06	1930
BILL PEARL	10	31	1930
JAMES E GROPPI	11	16	1930
LEONARD NIMOY	3	26	1931
LUCKY #6	7	12	1931
JOE DUHEM	8	14	1931
WILLY SHOEMAKER	8	19	1931
ANNE BANCROFT	9	07	1931
EDWARD MATTHEWS	10	13	1931
DIANA DORS	10	23	1931
PR R ORSINI	11	18	1931
ROBERT GOULET	11	26	1931
PAUL PETTIT	11	29	1931
JOHNNY CASH	2	26	1932
JOEL GREY	4	11	1932
HOMICIDE #11	8	02	1932
R L STRACK	8	11	1932
J INGEMAR	9	22	1932
PAUL ANDERSON	10	17	1932
CHILD MOLESTER	3	03	1933
ROD MCKUEN	4	29	1933
YVES GAMONET	5	15	1933
F LEE BAILEY	6	10	1933
Y YEVTUSHENKO	7	18	1933
DALAI-LAMA	12	18	1933
HANK AARON	2	05	1934
YURI GAGARIN	3	09	1934
UNG-YONG PARENTS	5	23	1934
PAT BOONE	6	01	1934
J M WHISTLER	7	10	1934
RONNIE KNOX	2	14	1935
RAFER JOHNSON	8	18	1935
WERNER ERHARD	9	05	1935
L PAVAROTTI	10	12	1935
GARY PLAYER	11	01	1935
PROSTITUTE #2	12	11	1935
JIM CLARK	3	04	1936
MANUEL BENITES	5	04	1936
BOBBY DARIN	5	14	1936
BOBBY SEALE	10	22	1936
SALLY KELLERMAN	6	02	1937
RUDOLPH NUREYEV	3	17	1938
JACKIE STEWART	6	11	1939
BIRTH DEFECTS	6	17	1939
PROSTITUTE #4	1	17	1940
JAMES CAAN	3	26	1940
MARY JO KOPECHNE	7	26	1940
PAUL SIMON	10	13	1941
ART GARFUNKEL	11	05	1941
WAYNE NEWTON	4	03	1942
PAUL MCCARTNEY	6	18	1942
BEAUTY QUEEN	8	20	1942
FABIAN FORTE	2	06	1943
HOMICIDE #12	4	02	1943
JOE NAMATH	5	31	1943
WILLIAM L CALLEY	6	08	1943
BEAUTY QUEEN	4	16	1945
SANDRA V LEIKLE	6	09	1946
SUE LYON	7	10	1946
MARK PHILIPS	9	22	1948
BIRTH DEFECTS	9	12	1950
RICHARD THOMAS	6	13	1951
KAREN A QUINLAN	3	29	1954
MASTER MARCUS	9	19	1955
HOMICIDE #13	9	27	1955
SEXTUPLETS	9	16	1973

We calculate. . .You delineate!

CHART ANALYSIS

Natal Chart wheel with planet/sign glyphs. Choice of house system: Placidus (standard), Equal, Koch, Campanus, Meridian, Porphyry, or Regiomontanus. Choice of tropical (standard) or sidereal zodiac. Aspects, elements, planetary nodes, declinations, midpoints, etc.................2.00

Arabic Parts All traditional parts and more......1.00

Asteroids Ceres, Pallas, Juno and Vesta. Included in natal wheel + major planet aspects/midpoints.50

Astrodynes Power, harmony and discord with %'s for easy comparison.........................2.00

Chiron or Transpluto (not both) in wheel........N/C

Fixed Stars Robson's 110 fixed stars with aspects to natal chart.................................50

Graphic Midpoint Sort Proportional spacing highlights midpt. groupings. **Specify integer divisions of 360° (1 = 360°, 4 = 90°, etc.).**.........1.00

Harmonic Chart John Addey-type. Wheel format, harmonic asc eq. houses. **Specify harmonic number.**.................................1.00

Harmonic Positions 30 consecutive sets of positions. **Specify start harmonic number.**............1.00

Heliocentric Chart Sun-centered positions.....2.00

House Systems Comparison for 7 systems.......50

Midpoint Structures Midpoint aspects + midpoints in 45° and 90° sequence.....................50

Parans Meridian and horizon co-transits.......1.00

Rectification Assist 10 same-day charts **Specify starting time, time increment, i.e. 6 am, 20 minutes**................................10.00

Relocation Chart for current location **Specify original birth data and new location.**................2.00

Uranian Planets in wheel + half-sums...........50

Uranian Sensitive Points Pictures, A + B − C = personal points. 60' orb.....................3.00

HUMAN RELATIONSHIPS

Comparison Chart (Synastry) All aspects between the two sets of planets plus house positions of one in the other.............................1.50

Composite Chart Rob Hand-type. Created from midpoints between 2 charts. **Specify location.**....1.00

Relationship Chart Chart erected for space-time midpoint between two births..................2.00

CONCENTRIC WHEELS

Concentric Wheels Any 3 charts available in wheel format may be combined into concentric wheels, a traditional method of comparing charts. A typical example would be natal, progressed and solar return. Aspects of the 1st chart to the other two will be listed............................3.00 Deduct $1.00 for each chart ordered as a separate wheel.

PROGRESSIONS & DIRECTIONS

Progressed Chart secondary, in wheel format. **Specify progressed day, month and year.**.....2.00

Secondary Progressions Day-by-day progressed aspects to natal and progressed planets, ingresses and parallels by month, day and year. **Specify starting year, MC by solar arc (standard) or RA of mean Sun.**

5 years	3.00
10 years	5.00
85 years	15.00

Minor Progressions Minor based on lunar-month-for-a-year, tertiary on day-for-a-lunar-month. **Specify zodiacal (standard) or synodical lunar month, year, MC by solar arc (standard) or RA of mean Sun.**

Minor 1 year 2.00
Tertiary 1 year 2.00

Progressed Lifetime Lunation Cycles The 8 Moon phases a la Dane Rudhyar.................5.00

Primary Arc Directions Includes speculum. **Specify time measure: solar arc (standard), birthday arc, mean solar arc or degree/year. Specify starting year.**

1st 5 years 1.50
Each add'l 5 years .50

Solar Arc Directions Day-by-day solar arc directed aspects to the natal planets, house and sign ingresses by month, day and year. **Specify starting year. Specify time measure—same options as primary arcs.** Asc and vertex arc directions available for same prices.

1st 5 years 1.00
Each add'l 5 years .50

TRANSITS

Transits by all planets except Moon. Date and time of transiting aspects/ingresses to natal chart. **Specify starting month.** Moon-only transits available for same prices.

6 mos. 7.00
12 mos. 12.00

Outer Planet Transits Jupiter thru Pluto 12 mos..3.00

RETURNS

Returns in wheel format. Sun and Moon returns can be precession corrected. **Specify place, Sun-return year, Moon-return month, planet-return approximate date.**

Solar, Lunar or Planet....................2.00
13 Lunar...............................15.00

POTPOURRI

Biorhythm Chart The 23-day physical, 28-day emotional and 33-day intellectual cycles graphed for easy identification of high, low and critical days.
Per year...............................4.00
Per month.................................50

Custom House Cusps Table For each minute of sidereal time. **Specify latitude ° ' "**........10.00

Fertility Chart The Jonas method with Sun/Moon squares/oppositions to the planets, for 1 year. **Specify starting month.**....................3.00

Handling charge $1.00 per order
Ask for our free catalog
Same-day service

ASTRO COMPUTING SERVICES
P.O. BOX 16430
SAN DIEGO, CA 92116

NEIL F. MICHELSEN